EUROPEAN WRITERS
The Twentieth Century

EUROPEAN WRITERS

The Twentieth Century

GEORGE STADE

EDITOR IN CHIEF

Volume 10

YEVGENY ZAMYATIN

TO

PÄR LAGERKVIST

CHARLES SCRIBNER'S SONS / NEW YORK

Copyright © 1990 Charles Scribner's Sons

Library of Congress Cataloging-in-Publication Data
(Revised for volumes 10–11)

European writers.

 Vols. 5– . Jacques Barzun, editor, George Stade, editor in chief.
 Vols. 8– . George Stade, editor in chief.
 Includes bibliographies.
 Contents: v. 1–2. The Middle Ages and the Renaissance:
Prudentius to Medieval Drama. Petrarch to Renaissance
Short Fiction—v. 3–4. The Age of Reason and the
Enlightenment: René Descartes to Montesquieu.
Voltaire to André Chénier.—v. 5–7. The Romantic
Century: Goethe to Pushkin. Hugo to Fontane.
Baudelaire to the Well-Made Play—v. 8–9. The
Twentieth Century: Sigmund Freud to Paul Valéry.
Pío Baroja to Franz Kafka. v. 10–11. Yevgeny Zamyatin
to Pär Lagerkvist. Walter Benjamin to Yuri Olesha.
 1. European literature—History and criticism—
Addresses, essays, lectures. I. Jackson, W.T.H.
(William Thomas Hobdell), 1915–1983. II. Stade,
George. III. Barzun, Jacques.
PN501.E9 1983   809'.894   83–16333

ISBN 0–684–16594–5 (v. 1–2)   ISBN 0–684–18924–0 (v. 9)
ISBN 0–684–17914–8 (v. 3–4)   ISBN 0–684–17916–4 (v. 10)
ISBN 0–684–17915–6 (v. 5–7)   ISBN 0–684–18798–1 (v. 11)
ISBN 0–684–18923–2 (v. 8)

The following pamphlets in the Columbia University Press Series "Columbia
Essays on Modern Writers" have been reprinted in this volume by special
arrangement with Columbia University Press, the publisher:

Cambon, Glauco: *Giuseppe Ungaretti*. Copyright © 1967 Columbia University Press.
Ziolkowski, Theodore: *Hermann Broch*. Copyright © 1964 Columbia University Press.

The paper in this book meets the guidelines for permanence and durability of
the Committee on Production Guidelines for Book Longevity of the
Council on Library Resources

LIST OF SUBJECTS

Volume 10

LIST OF SUBJECTS
Volume 11

CONTRIBUTORS TO VOLUME 10

HENRYK BARAN
State University of
New York at Albany
VELIMIR KHLEBNIKOV

GLAUCO CAMBON †
University of Connecticut
GIUSEPPE UNGARETTI

GUY DE MALLAC
University of California at Irvine
BORIS PASTERNAK

SAM DRIVER
Brown University
ANNA AKHMATOVA

DORIS L. EDER
Hunter College
JEAN COCTEAU

INGA-STINA EWBANK
University of Leeds
ISAK DINESEN

ROBERT J. FRAIL
Centenary College, New Jersey
FRANÇOIS MAURIAC

EMERY E. GEORGE
University of Michigan
GYÖRGY LUKÁCS

DANIEL GEROULD
City University of New York
STANISŁAW IGNACY WITKIEWICZ

GEORGE G. GRABOWICZ
Harvard University
PAVLO TYCHYNA

HARVEY GROSS
State University of
New York at Stony Brook
GEORG TRAKL

WILLIAM E. HARKINS
Columbia University
KAREL ČAPEK

ALFRED MACADAM
Barnard College,
Columbia University
FERNANDO PESSOA

P. M. MITCHELL
Cornell University
GUNNAR GUNNARSSON

ERIKA OSTROVSKY
New York University
SAINT-JOHN PERSE

OMRY RONEN
University of Michigan
OSIP MANDELSHTAM

ALEX M. SHANE
State University of
New York at Albany
YEVGENY IVANOVICH ZAMYATIN

MIHÁLY SZEGEDY-MASZÁK
Indiana University
DEZSŐ KOSZTOLÁNYI

LARS G. WARME
University of Washington at Seattle
PÄR LAGERKVIST

HARRIETT WATTS
Herzog August Bibliothek,
Wolfenbüttel
JEAN ARP

THEODORE ZIOLKOWSKI
Princeton University
HERMANN BROCH

EUROPEAN WRITERS

The Twentieth Century

YEVGENY IVANOVICH ZAMYATIN

(1884–1937)

YEVGENY ZAMYATIN WAS a prominent figure in the development of Russian literature during the first decade after the Russian revolutions of 1917; he was a master prose stylist, engaging playwright, caustic literary critic, and inspiring teacher of writing techniques. His wit, imagination, verbal mastery, stylistic inventiveness, and close attention to compositional structure deeply influenced much of Soviet Russian literature in the 1920's. In the West he is best known for *My* (*We*, 1927), this century's first great anti-utopian novel, which anticipated and influenced the works of such varied writers as Aldous Huxley, George Orwell, and Anthony Burgess. Although *We*, with its prophetic vision, masterfully sustained imagery, telegraphic style, and skillfully developed and suspenseful action has justly earned Zamyatin a prominent place in world literature, other aspects of his art have had greater significance in the development of Russian literature. The literary merits of his exemplary stories still delight readers, while the finely honed caustic wit of his literary essays reveals a rare talent for sparkling, succinct, satiric criticism of the contemporary literary scene.

Zamyatin was born on 20 January 1884 in the small provincial town of Lebedian, in the heart of Russia's fertile region of black earth. It was an area renowned for peasants, monks, tavernkeepers, merchants, gypsies, horse fairs, ancient churches, apple orchards, rye fields, and a robust, vivid spoken Russian that Zamyatin mastered and later adapted with unparalleled virtuosity in his earthy works with their frank depiction of coarse, unsophisticated people. His father, Ivan Dmitrievich, was a Russian Orthodox parish priest who also taught at the local elementary school; his mother, Mariia Aleksandrovna, was a competent musician at whose piano young Zamyatin spent many childhood hours. His three brief autobiographies stress the significance of solitude and books for the young boy; they also reveal an analytic skepticism and a perverse stubbornness, both of which motivated his choice of career and grew more prominent in the mature writer: "In high school I received *A plus* on compositions, but was not always on good terms with mathematics. Perhaps that is why (out of stubborness) I chose the most mathematical of all careers—I enrolled in the Department of Naval Engineering at the St. Petersburg Polytechnic Institute."

Arriving in St. Petersburg in 1902, the young engineering student from the provinces was immediately caught up in the ferment of the city's life. This era of revolutionary fervor, demonstrations along the Nevsky Prospect, worker's strikes, galloping cossacks, and huge student meetings at the university and various institutes appeared to him in retrospect as a violent whirlwind. In 1905 he visited the Near East on an engineering assignment and on his return witnessed the famous Potemkin Mutiny in Odessa. Motivated more by a rebellious spirit and a desire for excitement than by concrete political considerations, Zamyatin joined the Bolshevik party, for "to be a Bolshevik in those years meant following the path of greatest resistance." He met his future wife, Liudmila Nikolaevna Usova, among the revolutionary cadres in 1905; in December of that year he was also imprisoned for subversive activities. During several months in solitary confinement he studied shorthand and English, languished in love, and wrote verse (which he considered an inevitable consequence of confinement). After his release in the spring of 1906, he traveled illegally to Helsinki, where he observed the Sunday Demonstrations of the workers' Red Guard and the outbreak of the Sveaborg Revolt.

On his return to St. Petersburg, Zamyatin completed his engineering studies in 1908 and was retained on the faculty of the Polytechnic Institute. His earliest, unpublished literary efforts date back to 1905, and his first three published stories are primarily of historical interest only. The story "Odin" (Alone, 1908) was completed concurrently with Zamyatin's degree project on a turreted warship; it was inspired by his prison experiences two years earlier. More the product of an unbridled, romantic imagination than real observation, "Odin" is unusually prolix for Zamyatin. It describes the suicide of a prisoner frustrated in love in the unmistakable style of Leonid Andreev at his worst, especially in the pseudo-symbolic abstract beginning and in the final tasteless paragraph describing the suicide's crushed skull. These were perhaps the very features that prompted the popular sensational novelist Mikhail Artsybashev, the literary editor of the journal *Obrazovanie* (Education), to publish the young author's work. Although Zamyatin claimed not to have published any other stories written before 1911, at least two did in fact appear in print. The sociopolitical satire entitled "Skazka o Gospodine Khoroshem i o miloi baryshne" (A Fable about Mr. Good and a Sweet Girl, 1909) indicates his abiding interest in colloquial folk stylization, while the story "De-vushka" (The Girl, 1910) centers on a woman driven by a primitive biological desire, providing a prototype for characters in later stories. The story is still couched, however, in the decadent style of the early 1900's, which Zamyatin happily soon overcame and eschewed in future works. None of the three pieces has ever been reprinted, and Zamyatin ruefully remarked in his "Avtobiografiia" (Autobiography, 1929) that when he met people who had read his first story, "I feel as embarrassed as I do when meeting an aunt of mine whose dress I once wet in public at the age of two."

In 1911 Zamyatin was again exiled from St. Petersburg, and then he began to write in earnest. He was aware of the shortcomings in his earliest stories, commenting that "in each I felt something that was 'not quite it.' " "It" came the following year when he completed his first short novel, *Uezdnoe* (*A Provincial Tale*), which was published in 1913 in the new literary journal *Zavety* (Behests) and brought him recognition throughout Russia.

Despite a thematic and stylistic variety that reflects the young writer's search for distinctive expression, Zamyatin's major theme in his prerevolutionary short novels is primitive philistinism in the form of provincial absurdity, bestiality, and ignorance. In *A Provincial Tale,* the keynote work of this period, the ignorant Anfim Baryba, conditioned by his environment, symbolizes the negative aspects of provincial life. Expelled from school for excessive stupidity, he steals, cheats, pimps, rapes, bullies, bears false witness, and finally becomes the town constable. Whatever human feelings he may have had at the beginning of his life are completely atrophied during the course of his career, and the final description of Baryba as "a resurrected idol from an ancient burial mound, an absurd Russian stone idol" endows him with symbolic significance; he represents a cruel, ossified, provincial Russia. The remainder of the characters resemble Baryba in their bestial, senseless existence, with perhaps the sole exception of the tailor Timosha, who, although Baryba's only friend, is capable of a decent impulse; he tries to save a thieving boy from being beaten to death by an irate tavern-keeper: "Devils, animals, isn't a man even worth a hundred rubles?" Zamyatin's reply is an ironic negative, for Timosha's humane impulse is rewarded by ostracism, a court conviction of aiding the robbers (in which Baryba's false testimony is instrumental), and finally execution.

The short novel *Na kulichkakh* (*A God-Forsaken Hole,* 1914) continues the same theme but shifts the setting to a remote Siberian garrison on the shore of the Pacific. Some of the characters—Shmit, Marusia, Polovets, Tikhmen—are endowed with qualities that raise them above the level of the surrounding bestial environment, yet the essential tragedy of human existence is made all the more poignant by their ultimate destruction. The protagonist, Polovets, possesses capabilities and aspirations but cannot carry anything through to completion. Seeking love and fame, he decides to begin life anew at the world's end, far away from his native Tambov. A dreamer and idealist, he resembles Lieutenant Romashov, the ill-fated hero of Aleksandr Kuprin's *Poedinok* (*The Duel*, 1905), to which *A God-Forsaken Hole* has frequently been compared. Both works give extremely negative pictures of garrison life and have similar plots: both heroes fall in love with married women and are forced into duels; in both instances, though for different reasons, the women request the heroes to play passive roles in the duels in order to ensure the husbands' safety. The two women, however, differ greatly: Marusia has integrity and loves her husband, not the hero; Kuprin's Shurochka is a schemer who does not love her husband but will sacrifice the hero Romashov's life for her own interests.

The outcomes of the two works are quite different: Romashov is shot in cold blood, a victim of Shurochka's seduction, but Polovets, in despair at Marusia's enmity after her husband Shmit's suicide, is later "swept up, whirled away by a drunken, hopeless revelry, by that same last revelry in which Russia revels, driven to the world's end." Here, as in *A Provincial Tale,* the finale takes on symbolic proportions; the frenzied, hopeless revelry engulfs not only Polovets but all of Russia. This apocalyptic vision of impending catastrophe, which anticipated World War I, the revolution, and the civil war, stresses the need for spiritual regeneration within Russia. Although both of Zamyatin's early novels depict negative aspects of provincial life, there is a shift in emphasis: in *A Provincial Tale* Zamyatin shows the successful rise to power of a provincial, animal-like inhabitant amidst others who are like him, while in *A God-Forsaken Hole* he describes the destruction of sensitive people endowed with some human feelings amidst animal-like inhabitants of a provincial garrison.

Zamyatin's second major theme, that of love, has a varied representation in his early tales of provincial Russia. Frequently love is represented as a biological function, although in a few instances Zamyatin focuses on a romantic, idealized, spiritual attachment between a man and a woman. For the characters of *A Provincial Tale* there can be no question of an idealized, spiritual love; in the case of Baryba and Aprosia, sex is simply an everyday physical function, an animal necessity that fails to relieve the tedium of provincial life. For Chebotarikha and Morgunov it functions only as a source of sensual gratification, one more component of a cruel animal existence devoid of human values. In *A God-Forsaken Hole* a similar automatic, instinctive behavior is exemplified by Katiushka, who sleeps with any man, begets children yearly, and represents the norm rather than the exception for garrison behavior. The theme of depraved sensuality is continued in the character of General Azancheev. By contrast, Polovets' love for Marusia is that of a romantic, idealistic, contemplative dreamer, primarily spiritual in nature; but it is unable to survive under the conditions of the garrison norm, and Polovets is remorselessly sucked into the universal drunken revelry at the novel's end.

1183

In Zamyatin's third short novel, *Alatyr'* (1915), the love theme assumes central importance, and it is developed with ironic humor and some affection. The women of the provincial town of Alatyr', once famed for its fertility, have come upon barren times, for there is a dearth of eligible bachelors. In particular, Glafira, the daughter of the district police chief, is likened to succulent rye, ripe for harvest. Her dreams of a lover-general on a white stallion manifest her biological need for fulfillment; and her ideal of ultimate happiness is exemplified by the police chief's cat, Milka, who contentedly suckles her four kittens. The positive, lyrical presentation of physical love contrasts sharply with the negative representation in *A Provincial Tale* and *A God-Forsaken Hole*. Glafira's chief rival, the archpriest's malicious daughter Varvara, is driven by the same biological urge but is depicted much less sympathetically.

The two male protagonists, contemplative dreamers who lack the biological urge, both view Glafira as a godly embodiment of an ideal. In the third novel, however, the dreamer is not isolated amidst a mass of unthinking beings, for most inhabitants of Alatyr' are striving for some particular dream or goal. Frequently their strivings appear ludicrous, and without exception their aspirations are completely frustrated. Kostia Edytkin, a self-made peasant poet who is tutored by Glafira in preparation for civil-service examinations, seeks literary fame and aspires to Glafira's hand. Shy and timid, his idolization of Glafira resembles Polovets' love for Marusia. A public reading of his major work, "Vnutrennii zhenskii dogmat bozhestva" (The Inner Feminine Tenet of Godliness), provokes the laughter of his entire audience, including Glafira, and his love is never reciprocated. Prince Vadbol'skii believes that all the problems of the world would be solved if everyone would speak one language. But his attempts to teach Esperanto to the provincial townspeople fail miserably. Instead of establishing universal brotherhood and world peace, his efforts precipitate a contest for his affection between his two best pupils, Glafira and Varvara. The police chief seeks to invent something beneficial to mankind, but all his attempts, including bread baked with bird droppings instead of yeast, are failures. Glafira's dreams of a general on a white stallion likewise remain unrealized. These dreams are needed to dispel the terrible daily tedium of Russian provincial life, but inevitably they are all frustrated. And in a moment of truth at the novel's end the poet Edytkin prophetically cries in anguish: "We are doomed! Doomed, doomed . . . ," a cry that recalls the symbolic finale of Zamyatin's first two novels and forces the reader to realize how pitiful and ludicrous are the inhabitants of Alatyr'.

First love is the theme of the charming story "Aprel'" (April, 1915), whose light and fresh tone distinguishes it from the rest of Zamyatin's early work. Told from a teenage girl's point of view, the story describes Nastia's first kiss and the budding of her first love. Threatened by the action of unsympathetic adults (the kiss was observed and reported to her mother) and by her boyfriend's feigned indifference, her love is reasserted with wonderful innocence and purity at the end of the story.

Since revolution became a central theme in Zamyatin's later work, it is surprising that the Revolution of 1905 does not figure more prominently in his early work. An exception is "Tri dnia" (Three Days, 1914), an impressionistic, first-person account of the Potemkin Mutiny, which he witnessed in Odessa. The revolution also serves as the background of the denouement of the story "Neputevyi" (The Ne'er-Do-Well, 1914), in which the hero, Senia, like Ivan Turgenev's Rudin, remains on the barricade after his comrades have wisely retreated—less because of his dedication to the revolution than as a tragic solution to the failures in his life. Of greater significance to the development of Zamyatin's art, however, is the rebellion of several characters, primarily dreamers, against their existing environment. Their rebellion, however, is not clearly defined; it is generally unsuccessful and often absurd.

Although all of these short novels and stories deal primarily with middle-class Russians—merchants, government officials, clergy, military officers—in provincial settings, among Zamyatin's other works written before the revolution there are several tales about peasant life. Their atmosphere is not, however, predominantly clean and healthy, nor do they suggest that Zamyatin "wanted to purify himself from the provincial town-life by a return to nature," as D. J. Richards contends. The story "Starshina" (The Elder, 1915) chronicles the chance rise of the huge, incredibly stupid peasant Tiurin to the post of village elder. Inspired by rumor, he appropriates the land of a local landowner and distributes it among the peasants of Lenivka (Lazyplace). He is arrested, tried, and then acquitted, for it is evident that his misdemeanor stemmed from ignorance rather than malicious intent. He does not, however, recognize his error and glows with self-satisfaction. Tiurin, in his extreme ignorance and bullying abuse of power, represents a peasant version of Baryba and of provincial inhuman obtuseness.

The grim story "Chrevo" (The Womb, 1915) is the most striking example of Zamyatin's biological primitivism. The robust peasant girl Afim'ia is given in marriage against her will to the old widower Petra. Unable to satisfy her ardent desire to bear a child by him, she takes a lover and suffers a miscarriage when Petra beats her mercilessly during a drunken rage. Murdering her husband with an axe satisfies her primal vengeance, but her guilt leads to hallucination and confession. The villagers see her off to prison with forgiveness, which indicates their understanding of and sympathy for the intolerable conditions of peasant life. The situation of a young peasant girl married against her will to an ugly widower recurs in "Pis'menno" (By Letter, 1916), and Dar'ia's prayers for salvation are answered when her hated husband, Eremei, is sent to a Siberian prison camp for murder and horse theft. However, his unexpected apologetic letter to Dar'ia describing the terrible conditions of his imprisonment evokes her pity, and, ironically, she leaves her lover to join her unfortunate husband in Siberia. The brutal subjugation of women, drunkenness, violence, and ignorance are the characteristics of peasant life, which provide the background for many of these stories. In "Kriazhi" (The Diehards, 1916), however, Zamyatin focuses on the strong physical attraction between two stalwart peasants, Ivan and Mar'ia, who, due to false pride, fail to realize their love for each other. Ivan's need to prove his worth before the proud Mar'ia results in his death, a loss she could have prevented by offering him some encouragement.

"Afrika" (Africa, 1916), the last of the peasant tales Zamyatin wrote before going to England, differs from the others in its arctic setting and in its peasant hero, Fedor Volkov, who resembles an Alatyr' dreamer. A boatman who ferries passengers from ships to shore, he sees a lovely gentry girl who speaks a foreign language with her parents. When the visitors jokingly respond to his inquiries that they are "from Africa," Africa becomes Volkov's cherished illusion, inexorably linked with the beautiful girl. He marries a local girl who resembles the girl of his dream, but the realities of everyday life drive the romantic idealist from his wife and hut. Volkov dies on the verge of gaining passage to his illusory Africa, probably happier while striving for his illusion than he would have been when he actually arrived at the real destination.

With the publication of *A Provincial Tale,* Zamyatin became friends with the modernist writer Aleksei Remizov, the naturalist Mikhail Prishvin, the critic Ivanov-Razumnik, and others of the *Zavety* group, whom the critic Marc Slonim and Zamyatin himself characterized as the nucleus of the Russian neorealist movement. A firm believer in the Hegelian dialectic, Zamyatin considered neorealism to be a synthesis of nineteenth-century realism (thesis) and twentieth-century symbolism (antithesis). He wrote: "The symbolists did their part in the development of literature, and to replace them in the second decade of the twentieth century came the neorealists, inheriting features of former realists as well as features of the symbolists." The realists attempted to depict a segment of life. The symbolists sought to describe man's complex feelings and to depict the essence of man's spiritual being; in doing so, they rejected the "real" world. The neorealists, like the realists, depicted the real world, but they found their truth by focusing on a few carefully chosen features, enlarging them to grotesque proportions. Zamyatin firmly believed that "apparent improbability—nightmarishness—reveals the true essence of a thing—its reality—more than probability does."

In accordance with his theories, Zamyatin developed a distinctive style, which is characterized by grotesque exaggeration, conciseness, structured and sustained imagery, and *skaz* narration (a stylized oral narration) and is determined by his firm belief in the primacy of the author's subjective impression. For Zamyatin, artistic truth could be best achieved through the creation of a synthetic image, by focusing on a few well-chosen features that convey the artist's impression and reveal the essence of the object depicted. The use of the grotesque, which is essentially an exaggeration of certain features at the expense of others, was more appropriate to Zamyatin's aims. The excessive, exaggerated obesity of Chebotarikha in *A Provincial Tale,* for example, is indicative of her unbridled appetites, both gastronomic and sexual, while Prince Vadbolsky's crafty nature is revealed by his lack of a chin. External description is minimal, there are no interior monologues, and the probing perambulations of an omniscient author are avoided. Emphasis is on *pokazyvanie* (demonstration), not on *rasskazyvanie* (narration). Rather than describe a person's character through third-person narration, Zamyatin preferred to reveal it through action or by means of one of three standard devices: metaphoric comparison (usually with an animal), a peculiar physical characteristic, or an epithet. In all three instances the device that is used delineates both a basic physical and a basic character trait.

The predominance of provincial settings in Zamyatin's early works was motivated to a great degree by stylistic considerations. On the one hand, it provided him with bright, new, concentrated images, and, on the other, it yielded rich linguistic material in the form of colloquial and regional expressions that could renovate the literary language. In all of his short novels Zamyatin makes use of *skaz*, a special mode of narrative prose in which a narrator, manipulated by the author but usually differing from him in language, social position, and outlook, is introduced, either explicitly or implicitly, as a stylistic device. Zamyatin's narrator speaks a Russian that is basically grammatically correct but contains numerous regional words as well as colloquial expressions that normally would be encountered only in conversation and were not a part of standard literary Russian. The peculiarities of the narrator's language are not only lexical but are also reflected in a highly stylized syntactical structure, characterized by numerous inversions. In addition to the use of *skaz*, traces of rhythmic and musical stylization began to appear in some of Zamyatin's works as early as 1914 and acquired much greater significance in later works.

In 1913 Zamyatin was granted amnesty due to the tercentenary of the Romanov dynasty, and he spent the next two years traveling throughout Russia on various engineering projects and publishing a series of technical papers in such journals as *Teplokhod* (The Ship), *Russkoe sudokhodstvo* (Russian Navigation), and *Izvestiia Politekhnicheskogo instituta* (Proceedings of the Polytechnic Institute). In March 1916 he was commissioned to supervise the construction of Russian icebreakers in England at Newcastle-on-Tyne, where he remained until the eve of the October Revolution. Zamyatin's sojourn in England resulted in a significant evolution in his worldview and in his fiction.

YEVGENY IVANOVICH ZAMYATIN

Upon returning to Russia in November 1917, Zamyatin renewed his acquaintance with Ivanov-Razumnik, a leader of the prewar *Zavety* group and the chief theoretician of the newly formed Scythians, and was drawn into a loosely organized circle of philosophers and writers that published two miscellanies under the title *Skify* (Scythians). Major aspects of Zamyatin's views were consonant with those prevalent among the Scythian group: his romantic conception of the revolution, his belief in an infinite series of revolutions in all spheres of human endeavor, his faith in intellectual heresy as the ferment of progress, and his vehement opposition to philistinism. His 1918 polemical article "Skify li?" ("Scythians?") represents the first public expression of the concepts that inspired his future critical essays and determined the direction of his prose fiction over the following decade. The essence of the spiritual revolutionary—concerned with spiritual and intellectual rather than political and economic revolution—is captured in Zamyatin's description of the galloping Scythian, who symbolizes freedom, unending movement, and solitariness: freedom to reject the present in the name of the distant future, unending movement as a guarantee of man's progress in the face of universal philistinism, and solitariness because the spiritual revolutionary and heretic is always an isolated figure who stands apart from the masses. The true Scythian invariably devotes his life to revolution, to an endless search that promises no attainment. Should the Scythian attain his idea, the idea would become philistinized; for him to retain the idea would prove that he is not a true Scythian.

Zamyatin welcomed the October Revolution as a positive elemental force but decried the brutal excesses of the Bolshevik dictatorship and the subsequent dogmatic glorification and canonization of "the victorious October Revolution." His political views were close to the Socialist Revolutionaries of the Left, and he criticized some Bolshevik policies in a series of political fables and articles published in Viktor Chernov's Socialist Revolutionary newspaper *Delo naroda* (The People's Concern) and Maxim Gorky's Social Democrat paper *Novaia zhizn'* (The New Life). Within a year after the October Revolution, however, all dissenting publications were closed, and Zamyatin ceased his political writing. Twenty fables, including four that spoofed Nikolai Lenin, were published under the title *Bol'shim detiam skazki* (Tales for Grown-Up Children, 1922).

Zamyatin had returned from England with two completed pieces: the short story "Pravda istinnaia" ("The Real Truth," 1917) and the short novel *Ostrovitiane* (*The Islanders*, 1918). Cast in the form of a servant girl's letter, which reveals her nostalgia for the country while eulogizing city life, "The Real Truth" is closely linked thematically and stylistically to Zamyatin's early stories. *The Islanders,* however, signals a new phase in his literary evolution characterized by synaesthetic stylistic innovation and a new treatment of his favorite themes of love, revolution, and philistinism. Zamyatin's former satiric depiction of the ignorance, bestiality, and spiritual bankruptcy of provincial Russians gives way to a concern with the smug egocentricity and materialism of the urban bourgeoisie. Although the setting, social class, narrative structure, and style are different from his earlier works, Zamyatin's basic concern with both the negation of the individual human personality and its unfettered development remain. The similarity of Zamyatin's considerations of provincial Russia and industrial England was astutely discussed by the Russian critic Iakov Braun, who saw provincial philistine absurdity and darkness on the one hand, and, on the other, an inert automation in the lifeless glitter of electric lamps.

Unlike Zamyatin's earlier short novels, *The Islanders* is a finely crafted work in which tightly structured action, impressionistic character depiction, and ironic satire are finely balanced. The plot centers on Kemble, the son of an impoverished noble family who falls in love with Didi, a dance-hall entertainer. On discovering that his betrothed has become his friend O'Kelly's mistress, he murders O'Kelly, is tried, and then executed. All of the characters are motivated by one of two forces—passionate love or philistine conformity. Both forces operate in Kemble, and his destruction occurs when his philistinism gains the upper hand. Likened to a lumbering tractor and truck, Kemble is characterized by squareness, a family trait that symbolizes the philistine need for order, respectability, and conformity:

> And now everything is as it should be: a rug and a fireplace, and above the fireplace a portrait of the late Sir Harold (that same square chin of the Kembles), and a mahogany table by the window, and a vase for Sunday carnations on the table. In all houses on the left side of the street can be seen green vases; on the right—blue ones. Lady Kemble lived on the right side, so she had a blue vase on her table.
>
> (*Sobranie sochinenii* 3.38–39)

To the product of such an environment, passionate love is a disrupting influence, an anarchical element symbolized by the disorderly growth of new foliage in the park and, ultimately, the hot, life-giving sun under which Didi first succumbs to O'Kelly. The dramatic conflict between the characters reflects a new thematic juxtaposition: dehumanized philistine conformity is opposed to and threatened by a personal rebellion fueled by a primal physical passion.

The same dramatic conflict between love and conformity underlies "Lovets chelovekov" ("The Fisher of Men," 1921), a story created from a discarded variant ending for *The Islanders* and set in London during the World War I bombing attacks by German zeppelins. Mr. Craggs, an apostle of The Society Against Sin and a monumental model of respectability, secretly earns a living by blackmailing lovers whom he hunts down in London's public parks. His wife, motivated by a desire for passionate love and for children, gradually rebels against her ordered, conventional existence and succumbs to her admiring neighbor, the church organist Bailey. As in *The Islanders,* nature (the sun, the parks, the fog) is the ally and symbol of the passionate rebellion against the confining conformity of the huge capital city.

The glorification of primitive, passionate love is also the subject of Zamyatin's fifth short novel, *Sever* (*The North,* 1922). The arctic setting and the protagonist Marei's naïveté echo the setting and the protagonist's simplicity in "Afrika," while Marei's futile attempt to construct a beacon that would dispel the winter darkness is reminiscent of Zamyatin's frustrated contemplative dreamers of the early provincial tales. Similarly, the rich, sensual merchant Kortoma extends the theme of negative sensuality and dehumanizing brutality established by Baryba, Morgunov, and General Azancheev. Despite such affinities with prerevolutionary works, the lyric treatment of the passionate love between the tempestuous Saami nomad Pel'ka and Marei endows the novel with a new Romantic admiration of the unspoiled primitive, which testifies to Zamyatin's appreciation of the northern stories of Jack London and Knut Hamsun.

The originality and stylistic mastery of Zamyatin's prose fiction has gained him recognition in the history of Russian literature, but his novel *We* has ensured him lasting fame in world literature and, more recently, has become an established classic in the burgeoning field of science-fiction criticism. Aptly characterized by George Woodcock as "the first novel of literary importance that presented a relatively complete vision of the negative results involved in the realization of Utopia," *We* anticipated Huxley's *Brave New World* (1932), deeply influenced Orwell's *1984* (1949), and set the pattern for contemporary anti-utopian fiction. *We,* which Zamyatin once described as the "most jocular and most serious thing" that he had written, represents the artistic summation of Zamyatin's philosophy, which had first been expressed in "Scythians?" It combines the Romantic Faustian legacy of infinite revolution, of always aspiring but never attaining, with a Rousseauesque predilection for the simple and primitive (as opposed to the complex and cultivated) and with a newly articulated juxtaposition of energy and entropy as the two elemental forces determining the physical universe and human society. The major literary antecedents, the Bible and Feodor Dostoevsky, are reflected in a world of the future too fantastic to be true, yet the philosophical problems that underlie its conflicts are universal and timeless. The moral and social problems are brilliantly cast in a first-person narrative sustained with the mathematical imagery and rational thought perfectly appropriate to the engineer who is building a glass spaceship in a rationally organized city of the future.

The central metaphor, as Richard Gregg has demonstrated, is the biblical legend of paradise, which Zamyatin expounds through his mouthpiece, the poet R-13, in Entry 11.

"You understand . . . the ancient legend about paradise. . . . It was about us, about today. Yes, think about it. Those two in paradise were given a choice: either happiness without freedom or freedom without happiness. There is no other choice. They, the blockheads, chose freedom, and what happened? Naturally, for ages thereafter they longed for shackles. For shackles, you understand. That's what the world has been yearning for. For ages! And only we have again guessed how to regain happiness. . . . No, listen, listen further! God of the ancients and we, side by side, at one table. Yes! We have helped God to defeat the Devil once and for all, for it was he who urged people to transgress the interdiction and to taste pernicious freedom, he was the cunning serpent. But we placed a boot on his head and crrunch! And we're all set: paradise again. And again we are simpleminded, innocent, like Adam and Eve. None of that jumble about good and evil: everything is very simple, paradisical, childishly simple. The Benefactor, the Machine, the Cube, the Gas Bell, the Guardians—all this is good, it's all majestic, beautiful, noble, exalted, crystalpure, for it guards our unfreedom, that is, our happiness."

(1972 ed., p. 55)

The incompatibility of freedom and happiness, as presented by R-13, represents a restatement of the philosophic kernel in Dostoevsky's "Legend of the Grand Inquisitor" in *Brat'ia Karamozovy* (*The Brothers Karamazov*, 1879–1880), and Zamyatin's Benefactor is a version of the Grand Inquisitor a millennium in the future. The satiric portrayal of a collectivist society stems from Dostoevsky's satiric treatment of the socialist Shigalev in *Besy* (*The Possessed*, 1871–1872) but undergoes a curious transformation in Zamyatin's novel through the equation of Christianity and communism as the origins of the rational, collectivist society of the glass city as opposed to the Rousseauesque and satanic rebels known as "Mefi" (from Mephistopheles) beyond the city. The strong anti-Christian overtones of the novel precluded its serialization in the émigré journal *Novyi zhurnal* (New Journal), edited by Mikhail Karpovich in the 1950's.

The influence of Dostoevsky's *The Possessed* and *Zapiski iz podpol'ia* (*Notes from Underground*, 1864) in Zamyatin's satiric portrayal of rationalist, utilitarian, utopian collectivist ideas and ideals was first pointed out by Braun and was subsequently discussed by numerous critics including Robert Jackson, who asserts that Zamyatin had sought "to show that man is essentially an irrational being." The essence of the Underground Man's rebellion, a desire to assert both himself as an individual and the supremacy of irrationality in human behavior, is symbolized by the equation $2 \times 2 = 5$, which is a renunciation of $2 \times 2 = 4$ and, consequently, of the entire real number system. The symbol of irrationality in Zamyatin's novel, $\sqrt{-1}$ (the square root of minus one), is an integral part of the imaginary number system, which does not reject but *includes* the equation $2 \times 2 = 4$ and the real number system. Zamyatin thus implies that irrationality is inherent in man and, rather than being eliminated by an operation as the Benefactor would like, should be integrated with rationality in the complete man. The implicit is made explicit in the words of D-503 to I-330 in Entry

28 when D-503 first learns from I-330 of the existence of other men beyond the Green Wall:

> "Aha! You won't leave yet! You won't leave until you have told me about them, for you love . . . them, and I don't even know who they are, where they come from. Who are they? The half that we have lost, H_2 and O, and in order to obtain H_2O, streams, seas, waterfalls, waves, storms—it is necessary that the halves unite."
>
> (1972 ed., p. 143)

Narrated in the first person like the *Notes from Underground,* Zamyatin's extended adaptation of the legend of Adam and Eve develops major themes expressed in his early fiction, particularly *The Islanders.* The seduction of the builder of the integral D-503 by the enigmatic I-330 and the revelation of the forbidden world beyond the city continues the passionate Rousseauesque rebellion against social conformity that has been reduced to the absurd in the depiction of the glass city. The philistine idea of salvation by force, which Zamyatin decries in "Scythians?" and satirizes through Vicar Dewley's "Testament of Compulsory Salvation" in *The Islanders,* becomes the rock on which the Single State has been built. Round, rosy O-90 is driven by the biological desire to bear a child—as many of Zamyatin's heroines are—and I-330 is another example of his passionate heroines, but with an unusual, enigmatic twist: is she motivated solely by sexual passion in a rebellion against conformity, as are Zamyatin's other heroines, or is her seduction of D-503 politically inspired by his position as builder of the spaceship? Some ten years after writing *We,* Zamyatin claimed that "the novel is a warning against the twofold danger which threatens humanity: the hypertrophic power of the machines and the hypertrophic power of the State." In successfully integrating significant philosophical questions with a penetrating psychological study of the protagonist, a satire of utopia, elements of adventure and love intrigue, and biblical and mathematical imagery, Zamyatin has created a literary work that has entered the pantheon of world literature.

Zamyatin's concern with the loss of human values at a time of deprivation and internecine struggle is reflected in his short stories about the revolution. In "Peshchera" ("The Cave," 1922) postrevolutionary St. Petersburg, besieged by famine, cold, and want, is likened to a wasteland of the glacial epochs when mammoths roamed the earth. Focusing on the inhabitants of one of Petersburg's cavelike apartments, Zamyatin describes how Martin Martinych and his sick wife, Masha, surrounded by the remnants of culture and civilization, retreat before the invading cold. The deprivation of warmth and proper nourishment saps Masha's strength, and she can no longer leave her bed. In order to provide her with warmth on her name day, Martin Martinych steals some logs. The fire momentarily restores some vitality in Masha, but soon it dies down. The theft is reported, and, unable to face the winter, Masha prepares to commit suicide, while Martin Martinych goes out into the wintry street so that she can be alone.

A tragedy about two ordinary human beings, "The Cave" was vehemently attacked by Communist critics for being hostile to the new regime. Accepting Zamyatin's depiction of conditions, they censured his "compassion for those disappearing people who were unfit for life" because they said the story had been intended to arouse malice against the Bolsheviks, who were responsible for those conditions (although the Bolsheviks are not mentioned in the story). The critics apparently ignored the main point, which is reflected in Martin Martinych's struggle with himself at the moment of the theft:

> And on a line delineated by his scarcely perceptible punctuated breathing, two Martin Martinyches grappled in a struggle to the death: the one, of old, of Scriabin, who knew he must not, and the new one, of the cave, who knew he must. He of the cave, with teeth grinding, trampled, strangled, the other . . . .

YEVGENY IVANOVICH ZAMYATIN

In his essay "Zavtra" ("Tomorrow," written *ca.* 1918, published in 1955), Zamyatin had written of the revolution and ensuing civil war: "Man was dying. The proud *homo erectus* was getting down on all fours and growing fangs and fur; the beast was conquering man." It was the writer's task to remind man that he was *homo erectus* and should stand on two feet. The same point is made in the allegorical story "Glaza" (Eyes, 1918), in which Zamyatin describes the subservience of a mangy dog that gives up its freedom to fill its belly with rotten meat. The human wisdom in the dog's eyes, however, leads Zamyatin to speculate that the dog was once perhaps a human and one day will again become a human. The dog's escape and return to subjugation may be an allegory for the revolution, but the central question is one of putting aside things of the flesh in order to consider human dignity and spirit.

In other words Zamyatin makes an obvious plea for man to rise above fratricide, to conquer primitive cruelty, for under certain circumstances any man is capable of killing. In "Mamai" ("Mamai," 1921) a meek, kindly bibliophile accumulates a cache of rubles to purchase rare books, only to discover that a mouse has eaten the money. Unable to bear the loss with equanimity, he seizes a letter opener and, like his Golden Horde namesake of the 1300's, skewers the guilty mouse. In Mamai's own little world the murder of the mouse bears the same symbolic weight as killing a fellow man. The same message is conveyed by contrasting descriptions in the vignette "Drakon" ("The Dragon," 1918), in which a Bolshevik dragon-soldier standing on the platform of a thundering streetcar coolly comments how in cold blood he has dispatched some intellectual to the heavenly kingdom and then bends over to pick up a frozen sparrow and warm it with his breath. The positive effect of human kindness and concern for others is reflected in the charming irony of the humorous story "Spodruchnitsa greshnykh" ("The Protectress of Sinners," 1922) in which would-be revolutionary marauders attempting to seize a convent's treasury are disarmed by the mother superior's kindly words and solicitous attention to their wounds. The satire of inhuman stupidity and bestiality in provincial Russia, which was so typical of Zamyatin's early prerevolutionary works, was replaced by a scathing attack on the automated philistinism of traditional societies in highly urban settings (London, St. Petersburg). Passionate love becomes a recurring central theme, symbolizing the rebellion of the individual against philistine conformity and social dogmatism.

The new thematic formulations and the new urban setting are accompanied by stylistic changes. Zamyatin retained the use of the grotesque, while deploying his three basic impressionistic devices—metaphoric comparison, physical characteristic, and epithet—more systematically and with much greater frequency. Often he applies all three devices to a single character. Comparisons, no longer restricted to the animal kingdom, become considerably richer in variety and originality, and the predominantly static images of the early period are at times replaced by what Viktor Shklovsky called "actional images," that is, images whose development in the course of the story represent changes within the character. Kemble's movements, for example, which are originally compared to those of a tractor, are later compared to those of a tractor mired in mud, then to a stalled tractor, and finally to a tractor with a broken steering mechanism. The intensification and systematization of Zamyatin's imagery devices culminate in the creation of an integrating image, or "mother metaphor," as Dmitri Mirsky has called it, which becomes the major unifying principle and relegates the plot to a position of secondary importance. The two most extreme examples in this respect are the stories "Mamai" and "The Cave," in which the integrating images of a cave and a ship, respectively, determine an entire system of derivative images.

An innovation in Zamyatin's fiction of this period is the introduction and sustained use of color symbolism, whereby specific colors become associated with and invariably accompany certain concepts. Flesh and human vivification are usually characterized by the colors pink or raspberry, while yellow and gold are attributes of the sun and frequently symbolize ardent passion, the life-giving force in man. Red, indicative of blood, flames, or revolution, and green, indicative of sprouting vegetation as another expression of the life force, complete the four-color complex, which is basic to the positive manifestation of the themes of love and revolution. Blue and blue-gray, at least in *We*, are used to symbolize rationality and order, while black and white, although lacking recurrent symbolic values, are also used systematically, primarily as fixed attributes and for vivid contrasts.

Zamyatin's narrative language underwent a significant change. He discarded the *skaz* narrative style of his early provincial tales as inappropriate to the urban setting of London, St. Petersburg, and the rational city of the future. Consequently, he also abandoned local, dialectal, and substandard words, and the presence of a narrator other than the author is not perceptible (with the exception of the first-person narrative of *We*). Instead, Zamyatin developed a condensed, staccato, elliptical style rich in rhythmic and phonic effects through which he sought to capture the extraordinary rush and dynamism of the revolutionary urban epoch.

The five years immediately following Zamyatin's return to St. Petersburg not only marked the apogee of his fictional writing but also represented a total commitment to the seething literary and cultural activity that was one of the astonishing by-products of the revolution. During the years of war communism (1918–1921) Gorky sought to alleviate the terrible privations of Russian intellectuals by the creation of numerous institutions and establishments that provided employment and housing for them. He was the chairman of virtually all such undertakings, and Zamyatin, who was elected to the boards of directors of three or four of them, met with Gorky frequently throughout this period. Gorky praised Zamyatin's mind and talent and considered him to be a connoisseur of the Russian language.

Zamyatin was charter member of the Union of Practitioners of Imaginative Literature, which was founded by the symbolist poet Fyodor Sologub and his wife Anastasiia Chebotarevskaia in March 1918, and in the following year he was elected to the Union's nine-man editorial board. Concurrently he served on the editorial board of the World Literature Publishing House, was actively involved in editing Russian translations of Wells, London, G. B. Shaw, O. Henry, and Romaine Rolland, and gave lectures in World Literature's studio for translators. He also served as editor of the journals *Dom iskusstv* (House of Arts, 1921), *Sovremennyi zapad* (The Contemporary West, 1922–1924), and *Russkii sovremennik* (Russian Contemporary, 1924), as well as several other would-be journals and literary newspapers, publication of which was denied by the Soviet government. When the Dom literatorov (House of Writers) and the Dom isskustv (House of Arts) opened their doors in 1918 and 1919, respectively, Zamyatin played a major role on their governing boards and was an active participant in their activities, which included literary readings, lectures, and various performances.

In addition to his lectures at World Literature's studio for translators, Zamyatin also gave a course on the writing techniques of imaginative prose in the new studio of the House of Arts in 1919 and another course on Russian literature at the Herzen Pedagogical Institute. His pupils included many talented young writers such as Veniamin Kaverin, Lev Lunts, Nikolai Nikitin, and Mikhail Zoshchenko. In February 1921 a group of young authors, including several of Zamyatin's pupils, formed a literary circle called the Serapion Brothers, and he frequently attended their meetings, where he spoke to them of plot, rhythm, and instrumentation. Some of the lectures on creative writing have been preserved and were published posthumously; these include "Sovremennaia russkaia literatura" ("Contemporary Russian Literature," 1956), "Psikhologiia tvorchestva" ("The Psychology of Creative Work," 1956), "O siuzhete i fabule" ("Theme and Plot," 1964), and "O iazyke" ("On Language," 1964).

Considering Zamyatin's prominence on the postrevolutionary literary scene, it was not surprising that he played an active role in the formation of the St. Petersburg section of the Vserossiiskii soiuz pisatelei (All-Russian Union of Writers, abbreviated VSP), which was organized in the spring of 1920 and became the leading writers' organization in the 1920's. The constituent meeting of the St. Petersburg section took place on 4 July, and Zamyatin was elected to the nine-member directorate empowered to organize the St. Petersburg section independently of the Moscow section and to widen considerably the criteria for admission. He was retained on the directorate throughout the 1920's and even served as chair of the St. Petersburg section in the mid 1920's.

It is perhaps ironic that Zamyatin's career as a playwright was inspired and subsidized by a government-sponsored organization. In late May 1919, at a meeting of the Bol'shoi khudozhestvennyi sovet Otdela teatrov i zrelishch v Petrograde (The Major Art Council of the Department of Theaters and Spectacles in Petrograd), Gorky presented his idea for the creation of a cycle of plays depicting the history of the world; its unifying theme would be man's intellectual development—the rise of superstition and religious cults on the one hand and the development of scientific thought on the other. A committee including Zamyatin was established, a detailed program was worked out, plays were assigned, and in 1920 Zamyatin wrote his first play, *Ogni sviatogo Dominika* (The Fires of St. Dominic, 1922).

Although set in sixteenth-century Spain, the play was contemporary in thought, for it focused on Zamyatin's favorite themes of heresy, humanism, and the fallibility of all monolithic truths. The play centers on the conflict between the two Santa Cruz brothers: Ruy, who has just returned to Seville after three years in a Dutch university and who reads books on the Index of Forbidden Books; and Baltasar, a dedicated supporter of the church who has sworn to root out heretics or, in twentieth-century terms, has become a zealous informer. Ruy clearly represents Zamyatin's philosophy that "heretics are the sole (bitter) medicine against the entropy of human thought," and he condemns the fawning sycophancy of those who do not protest their loss of freedom as well as the betrayal of truly Christian principles by the Inquisition. The most interesting figure in the play, however, is the enigmatic Baltasar, w̵ose denunciation of Ruy cannot be adequately explained in terms of his love for his brother's betrothed. His genuine horror at discovering a forbidden book in Ruy's possession and his persistent attempts to ensure the salvation of Ruy's soul through repentance testify to genuine belief that "murder, falsehood—everything in the name of the Church is more noble than the most noble of feats in the name of Satan and his servants, the heretics." If the play is perceived as a thinly veiled allegory of the Soviet regime—as it was viewed by several Soviet critics, including A. Efremin, who considered it to be a "lying and insulting degradation of the Soviet system of proletarian dictatorship"—then one could conclude that Zamyatin believed in communism, but not in perverted Bolshevism, just as Ruy believes in Christ, but not in the perverted church. Such a restrictive interpretation fails to grasp the universal significance of the play; no matter what the area of human endeavor, man must be free of all "coercive salvation," and whatever his own belief, he must respect and honor other men. If he does not, then he perverts his own goals and ceases being man.

Zamyatin wrote several more plays. Two of them are original works: *Atilla* (Attila, written between 1925 and 1927, published 1950) and *Afrikanskii gost'* (The African Guest, written between 1929 and 1930 and published in 1963). The remainder are stage adaptations of various prose works: *Blokha* (The Flea, 1926), from Nikolai Leskov's short story "Levsha" ("The Left-handed Craftsman," 1881); *Istoriia goroda Glupova* (The History of Sillytown), from N. Shchedrin's novel *Istoriia odnogo goroda* (*The History of a Town*, 1869–1870); and *Obshchestvo pochetnykh zvonarei* (The Society of Honorable Bell Ringers, 1926); and *Peshchera* (The Cave, written in 1927), from Zamyatin's own stories *The Islanders* and "The Cave." *Sensatsiia* (A Sensation) is a translated adaptation of Ben Hecht and Charles MacArthur's play *The Front Page* (1928). All eight plays were written within a single decade (1920–1930), but only *Ogni sviatogo Dominika, Blokha,* and *Obshchestvo pochetnykh zvonarei* have been published in the Soviet Union. *Blokha* was first performed by the Second Moscow Art Theater on 11 February 1925, *Obshchestvo pochetnykh zvonarei* by the Mikhailovsky Theater in Leningrad on 21 November 1925, and *Sensatsiia* by the Vakhtangov Theater in Moscow on 29 May 1930. The Vakhtangov Theater also premiered *Peshchera* during the 1927–1928 season, and *Istoriia goroda Glupova* was first staged by Vsevolod Meyerhold that same year.

Undoubtedly Zamyatin's increasing interest in the theater during the late 1920's was in part stimulated by the promise of lucrative royalties at a time when few of his works were being published. His skill at handling dialogue, his tendency toward showing rather than narrating, and his predilection for dynamic plots with a prominent love interest made the transition to writing plays both natural and easy. The same features augured his success as a scenarist in the fledgling Soviet movie industry, but he was deeply disappointed with the two films based on his fiction; he disliked *Northern Love* (1928, based on *The North*) because of a trite, middle-class happy ending, extensive cuts, and inappropriate captions, and *The House in the Snowdrifts* (1928, based on "The Cave"), because it was turned into a propaganda film about the "rotting ex-upper classes."

On completing *We* and concurrently with his playwriting, Zamyatin continued to explore new directions in prose fiction as well. A series of drawings by the artist Boris Kustodiev inspired the story "Rus'" ("In Old Russia," 1923), an eloquent eulogy to old provincial Russia, which is portrayed so negatively in *A Provincial Tale*. In this story Zamyatin also appears to extol the full range of human passions, including sex and even murder, for it is better to experience passion than to remain sinless in lukewarm, vegetative conformity. Dar'ia, ripe for marriage, selects the old merchant Vakhrameev for a husband, takes his young assistant as a lover, then poisons Vakhrameev and marries the assistant in a plot highly reminiscent of Leskov's "Ledi Makbet Mtsenskogo uezda" ("Lady Macbeth of Mtsensk District," 1865). As in "The Fisher of Men" and *The North*, Dar'ia's love is an expression of the essential life force, symbolized by a ripe, yellow apple, ready and waiting to be picked. The same style and tone prevail in "Kuny" (Midsummer Games, 1923), a brief descriptive sketch of traditional mating games in the far north on Midsummer's Eve.

Undoubtedly "Rasskaz o samom glavnom" ("A Story About the Most Important Thing," 1924) represents a unique attempt to create a new literary form on the basis of theoretical pronouncements expressed in his essays of that time. In "A Story About the Most Important Thing" three worlds are depicted: the world of a yellowish-pink caterpillar, Rhopalocera; the world of Kelbui and Orel peasants who are fighting on opposite sides in the Russian Revolution; and the world of a distant, dying star. The spatial intersection of the three worlds (Rhopalocera falls into the heroine's lap as she talks with the leader of the Kelbui rebellion, and the dying star finally collides with the earth) is at best artificial, and the unity of the story rests in the underlying philosophic conceptions and in the symbolic parallelism of events on earth and on the dying star. Although the fulfillment of sexual love is important, Zamyatin's message is much more comprehensive: life is truly life only when some basic function or purpose is being fulfilled. At such moments seconds become ages, and one moment of fulfillment is worth years of unfulfilled existence. Another factor contributing to the unity and philosophic import of the story is the unusual, unmasked intrusion in several crucial instances of the author himself through use of the first person singular, which equates the sensations of the author with those of all the characters. The effect is that of a fluid omniscient entity that is a part of each and every living thing, and this all-encompassing authorial spirit creates a trans-structural unity of the three plot lines.

"Iks" ("X," 1926), the longest and most successful of Zamyatin's stories that focus on the superficial adaptation to the Soviet revolution by ignorant and gullible philistines, combines a remarkably light, ironic humor and an eventful, anecdotal plot with literary parody. The story centers on ex-deacon Indikoplev, whose public recantation of the Orthodox faith is used ironically to highlight human gullibility: "Deacon Indikoplev, having publicly repented for having deceived the people for ten years, naturally now enjoyed the confidence of both the people and the authorities." The deacon, whose recantation is inspired by Marfism (when he observes the buxom Marfa bathing naked in the stream) rather than Marxism, is mistakenly taken for a Socialist Revolutionary fugitive and is apprehended after a comic chase by agents dressed in white straw hats, which prove to be the mysterious unknown special clothes that everyone has been anticipating since the story's beginning (hence the title "X"). Zamyatin skillfully parodies a variety of literary devices by having the narrator describe the action in literary terms such as thematic planes, catastrophe, discharge of emotion, false resolution, and ostranenie (estrangement).

In "Slovo predostavliaetsia tovarishchu Churyginu" ("Comrade Churygin Has the Floor," 1927), Zamyatin directs his irony at ignorant peasants who, upon hearing rumors of unrest in the capital, attack the local landowner in the name of Rasputin and Mars (instead of Marx). A tour de force of sustained skaz oratory, the story is a speech by a comrade for whom formal Russian syntax and Marxist terminology are new and unmastered skills. The pretentious distortion of forms and the misunderstanding of meaning, philosophical concepts, and moral values create the unique comic effect of the work.

The theme of human gullibility is the basis of the anecdotal parody "O chude proisshedshem v Pepel'nuiu Sredu" ("The Miracle of Ash Wednesday," 1926) in which a humble cloistered monk gives birth to a child. The presence of the authoritative Mephistophelian Dr. Voichek and Archbishop Benedict's caressing kindness to the dimpled, womanish canon Simplitsii (a playful hint at a homosexual relationship) lend some credibility to the canon's belief in the miracle of his giving birth to his son, Feliks. On the other hand, if one considers the smiles that continually crawl about Voichek's face, his laughter through tears as the dying Simplitsii reveals the secret of Feliks' miraculous birth to Feliks, and the death of a pregnant woman just prior to Feliks' birth, then a more earthly answer becomes apparent. In all probability a parody of some ribald medieval Czech tale about the evil powers of the Devil, the story has modern significance in that it mocks the gullibility of the simple, ignorant people who are all too ready to accept the improbable.

In Zhitie Blokhi (The Life of the Flea, 1929) Zamyatin uses the same impossible situation in writing a parodic history of the writing and staging of his play Blokha. After a visit from Aleksandr Dikii, the turbulent director of the Moscow Art Theater No. 2, the monk Zamutii begins to swell, just as Simplitsii does after his evening with the archbishop. He finally gives birth to a strange promiscuous creature called Blokha, and the rest of the story is a comic account of the trials and tribulations in staging Blokha in 1925 and 1926. Accompanied by

Kustodiev's drawings and couched in a pseudo-ecclesiastical style, the parody stands as a companion piece to *O tom, kak istselen byl inok Erazm* (The Healing of the Novice Erasmus, 1922).

Zamyatin's most significant contribution to prose fiction after *We* are two tragic stories: "Ela" (The Sloop, 1928) and "Navodnenie" ("The Flood," 1929). The protagonist of "Ela," a fisherman named Tsybin, is driven by one ambition: to own a fishing sloop. After three years of deprivation and saving, he purchases a sloop from a Norwegian widow with cold hands, who symbolizes death. As the newly purchased, unballasted sloop is towed home, a storm arises, and the sloop must be cut loose to save the towing ship. At the final moment Tsybin leaps into his sloop and perishes with it. Although Zamyatin was undoubtedly indebted to Gogol's "Shinel' " ("The Overcoat," 1842) for the story (deprivation through saving a meager income in order to purchase an inanimate object that will improve the hero's life; attainment of the object, with subsequent loss of both the object and the hero's life), the story represents the culmination of Zamyatin's northern cycle. For all three protagonists in these northern stories the dream for a better life is embodied in a concrete object: for Volkov, distant Africa; for Marei, a huge beacon; for Tsybin, a graceful sloop. Each of the dreamers meets with defeat: Volkov dies before attaining his goal and discovering it to be an illusion; Marei loses his wife, Pel'ka, while constructing the illusory beacon; and Tsybin loses his wife, Anna (her heart is broken), and ultimately his own life in quest of his sloop. In all three instances the hero rejects the present in the pursuit of future happiness and finds only death.

Zamyatin does not deny human aspiration to an ideal, but he does reject the naive hope that the attainment of a simple, material goal will automatically lead to a new and wonderful life. In espousing progress (unending movement forward) and in assailing all manifestations of philistinism, Zamyatin does not forget that man is mortal and that he should live to his fullest capacity. And a very important part of life for Zamyatin is, as we have seen, the consumation of a love rooted in strong physical desire. In this respect, the dreamers of Zamyatin's northern stories have failed: childless Anna's withered breasts, once filled to brimming, are mute testimony to a lack of love that cannot be set right by the purchase of a sloop; passionate Pel'ka's infidelity is a direct consequence of Marei's lack of interest in her; and Volkov's disillusionment with Iausta stems from her philistine attitude that a clean floor is of more immediate importance than warm love.

In "The Flood" Zamyatin returns to a theme he had earlier developed in "Chrevo"; motivated by the instinctual biological desire to conceive a child, both heroines commit unpremeditated axe murders and bury their victims in the earth. Neither heroine is able to find inner peace until she confesses her crime. In other respects the stories differ significantly. Afim'ia's infidelity in "Chrevo" is motivated by the impotence of her husband, and the murder is an act of revenge against her husband, whose drunken beatings caused her miscarriage. Sof'ia's thirteen-year infertility in "The Flood" is aggravated by the orphan girl Gan'ka's liaison with her husband. Motivated by a vague hope that Gan'ka's death will bring her husband back to her, Sof'ia murders her. The death and burial (symbolic planting of the seed in fertile earth) effect a psychological catharsis that enables Sof'ia to conceive a child with her husband. Both stories, but particularly many minute details of the murder scene in "The Flood," are indebted to Dostoevsky's *Prestuplenie i nakazanie* (*Crime and Punishment,* 1866) for all three works focus on the anguish that follows the crime. Like Raskolnikov, Afim'ia is cut off from humanity and beset by hallucinations. Her confession is complete, and her suffering is recognized and respected by the villagers and the author (who likens her face to a holy icon). Sof'ia's case is more complex because the murder enables her to achieve her biological fulfillment. She becomes estranged from her husband during pregnancy, and after giving birth she too suffers hallucinations, but the subsequent confession brings her spiritual relief. For both Afim'ia and Sof'ia, however, neither pride nor reason has marred the pacifying, cathartic confession, as is the case with Raskolnikov.

The legacy of Zamyatin the critic is no less significant than that of Zamyatin the writer. He began his career as a critic in 1914 with three reviews in Viktor Miroliubov's *Ezhemesiachnyi zhurnal* (Monthly Journal), and his first significant polemical essay "Scythians?" proved to be of paramount importance as the philosophic nucleus of future essays and of his philosophic masterpiece, the novel *We*. In "Tomorrow" Zamyatin reaffirms the heretic's role in effecting the cruel but wise law of never-ending dissatisfaction, onto which he grafts the Hegelian dialectic of thesis (yesterday), antithesis (today), and synthesis (tomorrow). He also asserts his faith in the written word as the sole means worthy of man in seeking to achieve human progress, an idea that found new form in Zamyatin's championing of satire as the antidote to philistinism in his lecture delivered at the celebration of the fortieth anniversary of Sologub's literary activity (hence the eulogistic tone, which is more reminiscent of Zamyatin's necrologies than of his critical articles).

The essay "Ia boius' " ("*I Am Afraid,*" 1921), in which Zamyatin attacks the growth of conformity spawned by nimble authors who slavishly followed changing political winds, provided Soviet critics and literary historians with several pithy quotations that they delighted in pointing to as examples of Zamyatin's aberrant "bourgeois individualism." They were especially incensed by such statements as "The Proletcult art is at present a step backward to the 1860's"; "Real literature can be created only by madmen, hermits, heretics, dreamers, rebels, and skeptics, not by diligent and trustworthy functionaries"; and Zamyatin's closing sentence, "And if this sickness [a new variety of Catholicism] is incurable, I am afraid that

the only future possible to Russian literature is its past." Similar ideas are developed in "Rai" ("Paradise," 1921) where Zamyatin ridicules the "majestic, monumental, and all-encompassing unanimity" of the proletarian poets, which results in gray, monophonic banality, and in "O segodniashnem i o sovremennom" ("The Day and the Age," 1924), where he distinguishes between the topical literature and nimble authors that live only for today and the truly contemporary literature that lives for an entire age.

A notable portion of Zamyatin's essays of the 1920's is devoted to the development of his conceptions of the energy-entropy dichotomy on a sociophilosophical level and of synthetism in contemporary Russian literature. While writing his fascinating biography of Julius Robert von Mayer, whom he considered to be the founding father of modern thermodynamic theory, Zamyatin was undoubtedly struck by the analogy between Mayer's thermodynamic concept of entropy ("the tendency of the universe's energy toward rest—toward death") and his own conception of human society as reflected in *The Islanders* and *The North,* where the universal tendency toward philistinism and spiritual death corresponds to entropy, while solar energy (Mayer's energy source corresponds to Zamyatin's symbolism) stimulates the ardent passions, spiritual or corporeal, that disrupt the tendency toward a lukewarm philistine equilibrium. The philosophic conception of energy and entropy became the central thesis in *We,* where the heroine I-330 states that "there are two powers in the world—entropy and energy. One leads to blissful rest, to a happy equilibrium; the other, to the destruction of equilibrium, to a tormentingly endless movement."

In October 1923, probably under the stimulus of an unusual essay on solar energy, "In the Beginning; an Interpretation of Sunlight Energy," published in the *Atlantic Monthly* (May 1923) by the British physicist and physiologist Frank C. Eve, Zamyatin summarized all his philosophical thinking in a brilliant essay entitled "O literature, revoliutsii, entropii i o prochem" ("On Literature, Revolution, Entropy, and Other Matters," 1924). Eve, in analyzing the basic motive power of life itself in physical terms of an energy flow to a lower potential, essentially removed the distinction between organic and inorganic chemistry. Entranced by the scientific extension of physical (thermodynamic) concepts to biology (life itself), Zamyatin went a step further and extended the concepts of energy and entropy to the social sciences and philosophy. Conversely, he extended sociophilosophic concepts, such as revolution, to the physical and biological sciences:

> Revolution is everywhere, in everything. It is infinite. There is no final revolution, no final number. The social revolution is only one of an infinite number of numbers: the law of revolution is not a social law, but an immeasurably greater one. It is a cosmic, universal law—like the laws of the conservation of energy and of the dissipation of energy (entropy). Someday, an exact formula for the law of revolution will be established. And in this formula, nations, classes, stars—and books—will be expressed as numerical quantities.
>
> (*Litsa*, p. 249)

But the essence of Zamyatin's philosophy, although cast in a new scientific form, had not changed appreciably from that expressed five years earlier in his essay on the Scythians.

Synthetism, a legacy of the Hegelian dialectic that Zamyatin used synonymously with neo-realism, received its greatest elaboration in his essay on the art and graphics of Iurii Annenkov, "O sintetizme" ("On Synthetism," 1922). Equally applicable to Zamyatin's own literary work, synthetism in literature signifies a compressed style, the union of fantasy and reality, impressionism, and a significant philosophic synthesis that looks to the future, for true realism consists in the distortion of "objective" reality. The same concepts underlie Zamyatin's extensive survey of contemporary fiction, "Novaia russkaia proza" ("The New Russian Prose," 1923), in which he rejects the proletarian return to prerevolutionary analytical realism in favor of formal experimentation and artistic synthesis. His final review of Russian literature of the 1920's, included in the essay "Moskva-Peterburg" ("Moscow-Petersburg," 1963), lacks the polemical verve of his earlier essays due to its retrospective character and foreign audience (it was written in France in 1933 and appeared then in Serbo-Croatian and German translations), but its calm tone in no way minimizes the sensitive perception of Zamyatin the critic and historian.

Unfortunately, the ideas espoused in Zamyatin's critical articles and in *We* were not acceptable to the Marxist critics who gained strength and sought hegemony in literature. From its inception in 1921, the New Economic Policy (NEP), with its relaxation of government controls in all areas of national life, had been recognized as a tactical retreat. After Lenin's death in 1924 factional differences among Communist leaders came to the surface, and the ensuing power struggle resulted in victory for Joseph Stalin and a retightening of government controls in all areas in 1929. Writers like Zamyatin who championed romantic individualism and literary independence and had been tolerated during the NEP now had to be converted or silenced, for Marxism demands that a writer be responsible to society for his actions and that his works be imbued with the proper Marxist ideology. Despite his romantic revolutionary ideology, Zamyatin had always been considered by the Communist critics to be an inner-émigré, bourgeois writer who exerted a negative influence on the so-called fellow-traveler writers (non-Communist writers sympathetic to the revolution). Communist party leaders under Voronskii's leadership rejected an attempt by the militant Communist *Na postu* (Onguardist) group to gain literary control in 1924, but the attempt was renewed by Communist and proletarian writers in 1929. The apolitical All-Russian Writers Union, the largest and most significant organization of talented authors in the Soviet Union at that time, had to be brought to heel by the party.

YEVGENY IVANOVICH ZAMYATIN

A frenzied campaign of vilification was launched by the Russian Association of Proletarian Writers against two of the most active and influential figures in the Moscow and Leningrad sections of the All-Russian Writers' Union, Boris Pil'niak and Zamyatin, ostensibly for the publication abroad of their respective novels *Krasnoe derevo* (*Mahogany,* 1929) and *We.* A man of courage and uncompromising principles, Zamyatin resigned from the Writers' Union, which had chosen to condemn him before investigating the allegations of his detractors. Zamyatin was dismissed from his editorial posts, his plays were withdrawn from production, journals and publishing houses ceased publishing his work, and his books were withdrawn from circulation and from library shelves. His illuminative essay on the writer's creative process, "Zakulisy" ("Backstage," 1930), which appeared in an independently published miscellany, was viciously denounced for its supposedly pernicious bourgeois theories of the writer's creative process. Realizing the hopelessness of his position as a writer in the Soviet Union, Zamyatin appealed directly to Stalin in June 1931 with an audacious letter transmitted by his friend Gorky:

> If I am not a criminal, I ask to be permitted to go abroad with my wife, temporarily, for at least a year with the right to return as soon as it becomes possible to serve great ideas in literature without fawning on small people, as soon as there is at least a partial change in the prevailing view of the literary artist . . . . I do not wish to conceal that the fundamental reason for my request for permission to go abroad together with my wife is my hopeless situation here as a writer, the death sentence which has been passed on me here as a writer.
>
> (*Litsa,* pp. 281–282)

In November 1931 Zamyatin left the Soviet Union with hopes of traveling to the United States, where he planned to stage several plays and to work in the film studios of Cecil B. De Mille, whom he had met in Moscow. He first stopped in Riga, where he visited the Theater of Russian Drama, which had staged his play *Blokha* for two seasons; then he went on to Berlin where he reworked *Blokha* with the help of German playwright Karl Zuckmayer and discussed staging it with the famous producer Max Reinhardt. After three weeks of lecturing in Prague, Zamyatin arrived in Paris, where he remained for the rest of his days with the exception of a few visits to his old friend, the artist Boris Grigor'ev, at Cagnes-sur-mer, a medieval town on the French Riviera. Originally, Zamyatin had planned to produce his plays, publish a series of new articles on the Soviet theater and literature, write a novel on Attila, and go to America on a lecture tour. Most of his plans did not come to fruition. All of his attempts to produce his plays abroad failed, with the exception of a 1933 production of *Blokha* in Brussels by Paul Oettly. He did, however, write a series of review articles that appeared in the French press and did publish several of his stories in French translation. The trip to America never happened.

He wrote a few short stories, which continued the new direction toward stylistic simplicity he had begun in the Soviet Union prior to his departure. His last six pieces can be characterized as short novellas with well-developed action and surprise endings that give them an ironic or parodic character. In "Desiatiminutnaia drama" (A Ten-Minute Drama), which was published in the Soviet Union in 1928, a drunken workman on a streetcar belligerently informs a young dandy of what the working class will do to the capitalists. Threatening words and gestures build a dramatic tension, which is unexpectedly discharged by a moist kiss from the drunk to the dandy, rather than a heavy blow. The longest of the novellas, "Mucheniki nauki" ("Another Turning of the Worm," 1962), written in the Soviet Union but published posthumously, has two surprises in the ending. The widow Varvara Stolpakova, who will do anything to ensure her only son's college education, goes to the civil registrar's office with her suitor, but unexpectedly marries her proletarian coachman Iakov instead. She is surprised, however, when upon returning home the hitherto silent and submissive Iakov demands complete subservience from his new wife. In "Videnie" (The Apparition, 1962) two drunken friends, haunted by an apparition of a white elephant, begin to fear for their sanity until they realize that the elephant is real. In "Chasy" ("The Watch," 1939) the meek Semion Zaitser is spurred by his love for Verochka to resist a man whom he believes to be stealing his precious watch, but his bravery backfires: his watch has not been stolen, and it is he who inadvertently has taken the watch of a passerby. In order to impress his girlfriend, Katia, the timid Petia Zherebiakin in the story "Lev" ("The Lion," 1939) becomes an extra in a ballet. In the role of a lion that is shot and falls from a cliff, Petia hesitates at the crucial moment and—to the merriment of Katia and the rest of the audience—fearfully makes the sign of the cross before plummeting downward. In "Vstrecha" (The Encounter, 1939) a prerevolutionary colonel encounters Popov, a political prisoner whose chessboard he once took. Remembering Popov's vow of vengeance, the colonel blanches with fear when he sees Popov recognize him and then reach into his pocket. The colonel closes his eyes in fright, but instead of a gun, Popov pulls out a pocket chess set and asks him to play.

The irony of the surprise ending is often supplemented by the parody of literary convention and the revelation of literary devices. It is likely that Zamyatin's turn to literary parody and to the composition of short action novellas had been inspired by Western influences in the early 1920's, particularly the work of O. Henry, which Zamyatin had admired and edited.

Zamyatin's major prose work in emigration, the unfinished novel *Bich Bozhii* (The Scourge of God, 1939), was conceived as a massive canvas depicting the struggle between dying Rome and the barbaric hordes of the East. The novel begins with a timeless description of a frenzied Europe in the wake of widespread natural disasters, thereby emphasizing the universality of the human response to a given situation and underscoring the importance of historical parallels, for in the struggle between Attila and Rome, Zamyatin saw a similarity to the twentieth-century conflict between Russia and the West. The natural tidal wave described at the opening of the novel presages the human tidal wave that is to flood from the East and engulf Rome. Shifting to the narrative proper, Zamyatin juxtaposes the decay of Rome and the strength and vigor of the barbarians and then describes the youth of Attila and his tutelage in Rome. Zamyatin completed only seven chapters of this work.

Zamyatin's last years were difficult. He received no author's honoraria from the Soviet Union, although he had been elected to the newly organized Writers' Union in 1934, and his failing health hindered his ability to make a living. In the fall of 1936 his doctor pronounced him incurably ill. His angina pectoris was compounded by a stomach ulcer, and on 10 March 1937 he died of a heart attack. A small group of friends, including Marc Slonim, Avgusta Damanskaia, Marina Tsvetaeva, and Roman Gul', followed his coffin to the cemetery of Thiais, where he was buried on the wet and dismal morning of 12 March. His death went unnoticed in the Soviet press.

Selected Bibliography

EDITIONS

INDIVIDUAL WORKS

FICTION
"Odin." *Obrazovanie* 11 (1908).
"Skazka o Gospodine Khoroshem i o miloi baryshne." *Novyi den'* 5 (17/30 August 1909).
"Devushka." *Novi zhurnal dlia vsekh* 25 (1910).
Uezdnoe. Zavety 5 (1913).
Na kulichkakh. Zavety 3 (1914).
"Neputevyi." *Ezhemesiachnyi zhurnal* 1 (1914).
"Tri dnia." *Ezhemesiachnyi zhurnal* 2 (1914).
"Aprel'." *Sovremennik* 4 (1915).
"Starshina." *Ezhemesiachnyi zhurnal* 1 (1915).

"Chrevo." *Russkie zapiski* 4 (1915).

Alatyr'. Russkaia mysl' 9 (1915).

"Kriazhi." In Zamyatin's *Uezdnoe.* Petrograd, 1916.

"Pis'menno." *Birzhevye vedomosti* 15,454 (21 March 1916).

"Afrika." *Severnye zapiski* 4/5 (April–May 1916).

"O sviatom grekhe Zenitsy-devy." *Delo naroda* 181 (15 October 1917).

"Pravda istinnaia." *Novaia zhizn'* 210 (24 December 1917).

Ostrovitiane. Skify II. St. Petersburg, 1918.

"Zemlemer." *Ezhemesiachnyi zhurnal* 1 (1918).

"Glaza." *Novaia zhizn'* 39 (10 March 1918).

"Drakon." *Delo naroda* 35 (4 May/21 April 1918).

"Znamenie." *Mysl'* I. St. Petersburg, 1918.

"Mamai." *Dom iskusstv* 1 (1921).

"Tulumbas: Poslanie smirennogo Zamutiia, episkopa obez'ianskogo." *Zapiski mechtatelei* 2/3 (1921).

"Lovets chelovekov." *Dom iskusstv* 2 (1921).

"Peshchera." *Zapiski mechtatelei* 5 (1922).

"Spodruchnitsa greshnykh." *Peresvet* II. Moscow, 1922.

Sever. Peterburgskii Al'manakh I. St. Petersburg, 1922.

"Detskaia." *Sovremennye zapiski* 12 (1922).

O tom, kak istselen byl inok Erazm. Berlin, 1922.

"Kuny." *Rossiia* 5 (1923).

"Rus'." St. Petersburg, 1923.

"V Zadonsk na bogomol'e." *Zhizn' iskusstva* 1 (1 January 1924).

"Rasskaz o samom glavnom." *Russkii sovremennik* 1 (1924).

Fonar'. Moscow-Leningrad, 1926.

"O chude proisshedshem v Pepel'nuiu Sredu." *Novaia Rossiia* 1 (1926).

"Iks." *Novaia Rossiia* 2 (1926).

My. Volia Rossii 2, 3, 4 (1927).

"Slovo predostavliaetsia tovarishchu Churyginu." *Al'manakh arteli pisatelei Krug* IV. Moscow, 1927.

"Ela." *Pisateli Krymu: Literaturnyi al'manakh.* Moscow, 1928.

"Desiatiminutnaia drama." *Dni* 1,459 (24 June 1928).

"Navodnenie." *Al'manakh Zemlia i fabrika* IV. Moscow, 1929.

Zhitie Blokhi. Leningrad, 1929.

Bich Bozhii. Paris, 1939.

"Chasy." In Zamyatin's *Bich Bozhii.* Paris, 1939.

"Lev." In Zamyatin's *Bich Bozhii.* Paris, 1939.

"Vstrecha." In Zamyatin's *Bich Bozhii.* Paris, 1939.

"Mucheniki nauki." *Novyi zhurnal* 67 (1962).

"Privetstvie ot Mestkoma pokoinykh pisatelei." *Grani* 51 (1962).

"Videnie." *Mosty* 9 (1962).

"Kratkaia istoriia Vsemirnoi literatury ot osnovaniia do sego dnia." *Pamiat'; istoricheski sbornik* 5 (1982).

PLAYS

Ogni sviatogo Dominika. Literaturnaia mysl'; al'-manakh I. St. Petersburg, 1922.

Blokha. Leningrad, 1926.

Obshchestvo pochetnykh zvonarei. Leningrad, 1926.

Atilla. Novyi zhurnal 24 (1950).

Afrikanskii gost'. Novyi zhurnal 73 (1963).

ESSAYS

"Skify li?" *Mysl'* I. St. Petersburg, 1918.

"Ia boyus'." *Dom iskusstv* I (1921).

Gerbert Uells. St. Petersburg, 1922.

"Serapionovy brat'ia." *Literaturnye zapiski* 1 (25 May 1922).

"L. Andreev." *Kniga o Leonide Andreeve.* Berlin, 1922.

Robert Mayer. Berlin, 1922.

"O sintetizme." In Iurii P. Annenkov. *Portrety.* St. Petersburg, 1922.

"Novaia russkaia proza." *Russkoe iskusstvo* 2/3 (1923).

"O literature, revoliutsii, entropii i o prochem." *Pisateli ob iskusstve i o sebe; sbornik statei* I. Moscow, 1924.

"Anatol' Frans." *Sovremennyi zapad* 2 (1924).

"O segodniashnem i o sovremennom." *Russkii sovremennik* 2 (1924).

"Vospominaniia o Bloke." *Russkii sovremennik* 3 (1924).

"Belaia liubov'." *Sovremennaia literatura; sbornik statei.* Leningrad, 1925.

"Zakulisy." *Kak my pishem; teoria literatury.* Leningrad, 1930.

"Zavtra." In Zamyatin's *Litsa.* New York, 1955.

"Sovremennaia russkaia literatura." *Grani* 32 (1956).

"Psikhologiia tvorchestva." *Grani* 32 (1956).

"O moikh zhenakh, o ledokolakh i o Rossii." *Mosty* 9 (1962).

"Moskva-Peterburg." *Novyi zhurnal* 72 (1963).

"O siuzhete i fabule." *Novyi zhurnal* 75 (1964).

"O iazyke." *Novyi zhurnal* 77 (1964).

COLLECTED WORKS

Uezdnoe; povesti i rasskazy. Moscow, 1916. First collection of short novels and stories.

Vereshki. Petrograd, 1918. Sole publication of four short vignettes: "Na divane" (On the Couch), "Zveriata" (Baby Animals); "Tramvai" (The Streetcar), "Sneg" (Snow).

Ostrovitiane; povesti i rasskazy. St. Petersburg, 1922.

Bol'shim detiam skazki. Berlin, 1922. Sole collection of twenty fables.

Na kulichkakh; povesti i rasskazy. St. Petersburg, 1923.

Nechestivye rasskazy Moscow, 1927.

Sobranie sochinenii. 4 vols. Moscow, 1929. Sole multivolume collection published while author was alive.

Bich Bozhii. Paris, 1939. Sole posthumous collection of previously unpublished prose fiction.

My. New York, 1952. First publication of uncorrupt text.

Litsa. New York, 1955. First collection of essays and articles.

Povesti i rasskazy. Munich, 1963.

Sochineniia. 3 vols. Edited by Evgenia Zhiglevich and Boris Filippov. Munich, 1970–. Sole posthumous multivolume collection.

AUTOBIOGRAPHY AND LETTERS

"Avtobiografiia." *Vestnik literatury* 2/3 (1922).

"Avtobiografiia." *Literaturnaia Rossia.* Edited by V. Lidin. Moscow, 1924.

"Avtobiografiia." In Zamyatin's *Sobranie sochinenii* 4. Moscow, 1929.

"Pis'mo Stalinu." In Zamyatin's *Litsa.* New York, 1955.

TRANSLATIONS

"The Cave." Translated by D. S. Mirsky. *The Slavonic Rievew* 4 (1923).

The Dragon: Fifteen Stories. Translated and edited by Mirra Ginsburg. New York, 1967.

"The Fisher of Men." Translated by Diana Matias. In *Modern Russian Short Stories.* Edited by C. G. Bearne. London, 1969.

A God-Forsaken Hole. Translated by Walker Foard. Ann Arbor, Mich., 1985.

The Islanders. Translated by T. S. Berczynski. Ann Arbor, Mich., 1978.

"Mamai." In *Soviet Literature: An Anthology.* Edited and translated by George Reavey and Marc Slonim. London, 1933.

A Soviet Heretic: Essays by Yevgeny Zamyatin. Edited and translated by Mirra Ginsburg. Chicago, 1970.

"The Turning of Another Worm." *Cosmopolitan* (March 1931).

"The Watch." Translated by Jacques Le Clercq. *Fiction Parade* 1 (May 1935).

We. Translated by Gregory Zilboorg. New York, 1924.

We. In *An Anthology of Russian Literature in the Soviet Period from Gorki to Pasternak.* Edited and translated by Bernard Guilbert Guerney. New York, 1960.

We. Translated by Mirra Ginsburg. New York, 1972.

We. Translated by Samuel Cioran. In *Russian Literature of the Twenties: An Anthology.* Edited by Carl R. Proffer, Ellendea Proffer, Ronald Meyer, and Mary Ann Szporluk. Ann Arbor, Mich., 1987.

BIOGRAPHICAL AND CRITICAL STUDIES

Braun, Yakov. "Vzyskuiushchii cheloveka; tvorchestvo Evgeniia Zamiatina." *Sibirskie ogni* 5/6: 225–240 (1923).

Brown, Edward J. *Brave New World, 1984, and We: An Essay on Anti-Utopia.* Ann Arbor, Mich., 1976.

Collins, Christopher. *Evgenij Zamjatin. An Interpretive Study.* The Hague, 1973.

Edwards, T. R. N. *Three Russian Writers and the Irrational: Zamyatin, Pilnyak, and Bulgakov.* Cambridge, 1982.

Efremin, A. "Evgenii Zamiatin." *Krasnaia nov'* 1: 228–235 (1930).

Franz, Norbert. *Groteske Strukturen in der Prosa Zamjatins: Syntaktische, semantische und pragmatische Aspekte.* Munich, 1980.

Gregg, Richard A. "Two Adams and Eve in a Crystal Palace: Dostoevsky, the Bible, and *We*." *Slavic Review* 24:680–687 (1965).

Jackson, Robert L. *Dostoevskij's Underground Man in Russian Literature.* The Hague, 1958.

Kern, Gary, ed. *Zamyatin's* We: *A Collection of Critical Essays.* Ann Arbor, Mich., 1988.

Leech-Anspach, Gabriele. *Evgenij Zamjatin; Häretiker im Namen des Menschen.* Wiesbaden, 1976.

Mihailovich, Vasa D. "Critics on Evgenii Zamiatin." *Papers on Language and Literature* 10:317–334 (1974).

Mirsky, Dmitry. *Contemporary Russian Literature, 1881–1925.* New York, 1926.

Rhodes, C. H. "Frederick Winslow Taylor's System of Scientific Management in Zamiatin's *We.*" *Journal of General Education* 28:31–42 (1976).

Richards, D. J. *Zamyatin; A Soviet Heretic.* London, 1962.

Scheffler, Leonore. *Evgenij Zamjatin; Sein Weltbild und seine literarische Thematik.* Böhlau, 1984.

Shane, Alex M. *The Life and Works of Evgenij Zamjatin.* Berkeley, 1968.

Shklovsky, Viktor. *Piat' chelovek znakomykh.* Tiflis, 1927.

Slonim, Marc. "Literaturnye otkliki: Evgenii Zamiatin." *Volia Rossii* 8/9:89–95 (1923).

Struve, Gleb. *Soviet Russian Literature, 1917–1950.* Norman, Okla., 1951.

Voronsky, A. "Evgeny Zamyatin." *Russian Literature Triquarterly* 2:153–175 (1972).

Woodcock, George. "Utopias in Negative." *The Sewanee Review* 64:81–97 (1956).

ALEX M. SHANE

STANISŁAW IGNACY WITKIEWICZ (WITKACY)

(1885–1939)

STANISŁAW IGNACY WITKIEWICZ is now accepted as Poland's outstanding modern dramatist and one of the most colorful figures in the history of the European avant-garde. Recognition, however, has come slowly, and the story of Witkiewicz's career over the past one hundred years—during his lifetime and posthumously—is as full of irony, paradox, and surprise as any of his plays. Witkiewicz reached maturity in a climate of fin de siècle symbolism and modernism; he did his principal work in the 1920's, when futurism, expressionism, dadaism, surrealism, and constructivism were the new currents; and he was discovered only in the late 1950's and early 1960's (twenty years after his tragic suicide) when Samuel Beckett and Eugène Ionesco, Max Frisch and Friedrich Dürrenmatt were foreign models for the Polish theater, recently liberated from the strictures of Soviet-imposed socialist realism. Previously dismissed by his contemporaries as a madman and practical joker, and forgotten during the German occupation and Stalinist era, Witkiewicz made a triumphant return, becoming an inspiration to a young generation of Polish theater artists and hailed abroad as a brilliant precursor of the theater of the absurd. Often the center of controversy and object of political censorship, Witkiewicz finally achieved success in the sort of totalitarian mass state that he had always warned would bring about the end of art and philosophy.

Along with Alfred Jarry, Vladimir Mayakovsky, and Antonin Artaud, Witkiewicz is a representative twentieth-century theatrical innovator who, through the force of an explosive artistic personality given to self-dramatization, attempted to impose his own avant-garde sensibility on the conservative theater establishment of the time. The works themselves, mixing contradictory currents in thought and strands of experience, are prophetic in feeling and attuned to future realities; they place the author outside his own time and nation and beyond normal categories of artistic genre and movement.

What the Polish playwright created was, most significantly, "Witkacy," the pen name and persona he devised (by telescoping his last and middle names) to distinguish himself from his artist father. It was as Witkacy that he was known to his friends and small circle of admirers, and I shall henceforth refer to the writer by this name because it best defines the unifying psyche behind all his works in the most diverse media and serves to evoke the character of the creator, who was always greater than the sum of his creations.

Multitalented by birth and by training, Witkacy was not only a playwright but also a painter, photographer, novelist, musician, aesthetician, philosopher, cultural critic, and expert on drugs, and he practiced and excelled in many fields of intellectual and artistic endeavor. But despite his hostility to its existing manifestations, it was theater to which Witkacy was most deeply attached, to which he constantly returned, and from which he expected the most—always to be disappointed. Considering the stage the measure of a nation's culture and drama the one form of art still capable of producing a brief, spectacular blaze, Witkacy worked tirelessly to create a new type of play that would put the theater on a par with painting and music, which had already undergone revolutionary changes.

Here lies Witkacy's special contribution to the twentieth-century avant-garde, and for this reason I shall stress his writings for and about the theater, as well as his projections of a theatricalized self and his depictions of a theatricalized society. In a real sense his works and life are all conceived as theater.

For Witkacy the central philosophical problem was that of unity in plurality, a problem that included both the existential issue of the individual confronting the outside world of otherness and the aesthetic dilemma of giving cohesive form to diversity. The multiplicity of selves playing roles as "Witkacy" battled with the need for firm definition and identity. Witkacy's preference for dramatic form, in which many voices and masks are assumed by a single author, is another expression of the dialectic of unity and plurality. The Witkacian mode of grappling with existence was a feverish conversation between the self, its doubles, and those threatening projections of a constraining world of otherness. In his letters and polemics, as well as in his plays, novels, and essays, Witkacy engaged in overheated disputation; his was a powerfully dialogic imagination.

Witkacy's aim was to create a total aesthetic and philosophical system, at the center of which stood the "I," the lonely uniqueness of the self. The personality of the creator, the richness of his experience and imagination, are in Witkacy's case the substance of his work, and a portrait of the artist and his life and times is therefore an indispensable introduction to his theory and practice of theater.

Witkacy is an author about whom it is difficult to make sound judgments. His output was bewilderingly vast; he left hundreds and hundreds of paintings, drawings, and portraits and over forty plays (of which twenty-two have survived in their entirety, others only in fragments). Important philosophical works have only recently been discovered and published, and more than a thousand letters to his wife still remain in manuscript. Specialists have begun to study Witkacy as a philosopher, as a painter, and as a photographer, but there is little agreement as to whether or not his oeuvre constitutes a coherent whole, and debate continues on the relation of his philosophy and aesthetics to his plays and novels. Although this once marginal figure has now been canonized as a classic of the avant-garde, much remains unresolved in our understanding of his career and interpretation of his works. Although a daunting amount has already been written about Witkacy, nothing definitive has yet been said.

The starting point for any investigation of the phenomenon "Witkacy" must be the writer's relationship to a remarkable father who was determined to make his son into an artist and who instilled in him from earliest childhood reverence for the creative powers of the individual. The dominant figure in the family drama, Stanisław Witkiewicz (1851–1915) was one of the creators of Polish cultural life at the end of the nineteenth century and something of a national hero at a time when Poland was partitioned by Russia, Prussia, and Austro-Hungary and the idea of nationhood was sustained by writers and intellectuals. As an occupied country, its language and cultural identity threatened, Poland looked to its poets for leadership. Rather than feeling at odds with society as in the bourgeois West, the artist in Poland was venerated as a seer who would serve as the conscience of the nation.

The Witkiewiczes were a large clan, upper-class although only from the lesser nobility, and were related to Józef Piłsudski, who became Poland's political strongman in the interwar years, and to the Gielguds, the family of the celebrated British actor Sir John. One of nine children, Stanisław Witkiewicz spent four years as an adolescent in Siberia, where his father had been exiled for his participation in the 1863 uprising against czarist oppression. Without funds, since the family lands had been confiscated by the Russian authorities, and never having completed high school, the handsome young Pole studied art in St. Petersburg and Munich before returning to Warsaw in 1871 to make his name as a painter and writer propagating the new schools of naturalism and impressionism. There he met and fell in love with the great actress Helena Modrzejewska (who in America became known as Modjeska) and would have followed her to California, where she went in 1876 to establish a community of artists, if he had not been too poor to pay his passage.

In 1883 Stanisław Witkiewicz married Maria Pietrzkiewicz, a thirty-year-old music teacher, and on 24 February 1885 his only son, Stanis-ław Ignacy, was born in Warsaw, part of the Russian sector of Poland. By 1890 a worsening case of tuberculosis, contracted during his impoverished student days in St. Petersburg, led the elder Witkiewicz to move to the small mountain town of Zakopane in the south of Austrian-occupied Poland, then considered to be a healthy spot for those with respiratory illnesses. At the height of his influence, Witkiewicz senior was able to popularize Zako-pane as a cultural center and fashionable resort for artists, creating a cult of the Tatra mountains and mountaineers and developing the Zakopane style of architecture based on the peasant log cabins. Inspired by the ideas of John Ruskin, William Morris, and Friedrich

Nietzsche, Stanisław Witkiewicz became the charismatic leader of a movement that sought spiritual renewal and preparation for national independence in the values of the Polish countryside and its local crafts, and he preached a rustic kind of socialism that opposed the mechanization of urban masses in huge, ugly cities. A "fighting man" committed to progressive social causes, the elder Witkiewicz, in contentious newspaper articles, attacked corruption and stagnation. But he was unable to support himself, even with his wife's earnings from music lessons, and had to accept financial help from other members of the family, particularly a younger brother.

The birth of his son gave Witkiewicz senior a creative opportunity to put into effect his most cherished pedagogic ideas about the development of artistic ability and the nurturance of free and independent spirits standing above the herd but dedicated to public service. Young Witkacy was, quite simply, to be a marvelous proof of the truth of his theories. "As for 'the system of instruction,' it consists of a total lack of any system," the elder Witkiewicz wrote on 8 November 1892 in one of his many letters to relatives detailing the educational program he had devised. The boy was allowed to pursue absolutely freely whatever interested him, and, tutored privately at home, he never attended school (although he did take the required examinations and receive the gymnasium diploma in 1903). Perhaps defending his own lack of formal schooling and justifying his snobbish refusal to send his son to study with the local peasant boys as much as he was attacking conformity, Witkiewicz senior declared, "Only a person who is truly self-educated thoroughly understands all the monstrous absurdity of today's system of education."

By the time he was seven, Witkacy was painting, playing the piano, reading Shakespeare in Polish translation, and starting to write and stage his own short comedies. The first of these, *Karaluchy* (*Cockroaches*, 1893), which deals with an ominous gray cloud of insects coming from America, he printed on his own press. Undoubtedly the theme of the play, the menace of mechanization (which recurred in his later dramas), reflects the discussions the boy heard at home about the Taylorization of work taking place in the United States. It was said that his fascination with everything in dialogue form was due to the influence of his godmother, the actress Modjeska.

Although his father was loving and seemingly permissive in urging his son to become whatever he wanted, the constant commands to be creative proved to be a terrible kind of cultural repression more insidious than philistine browbeating by a crass bourgeois father. Witkiewicz senior practiced coercion in the name of the highest moral and aesthetic ideals, and his constant supervision of his son's psychic development was an extension of his public role of teacher of the nation.

In more than five hundred letters of passionate instruction (collected under the title *Listy do syna* [Letters to His Son, 1969]), which sometimes sound like a blend of Zarathustra and Polonius, the elder Witkiewicz urges his son to be spiritually unfettered and to shun unworthy male and female companions. "We must go ever forward, my precious!" the father writes on 27 August 1903. "In intellectual concepts reach to infinity, in social ideas, go to the ultimate extremes of boundless universal love." Instead of pursuing selfish pleasures, the boy is told to rise above his lower nature and create a new "I." This Nietzschean concept of self-transcendence and perpetual renewal haunted Witkacy throughout his life and appears in all his mature works.

These attempts at self-construction inevitably failed because of the insurrection of suppressed desire, and, contrary to his father's intention of directing the boy's energies to outer goals, focused the young Witkacy's attention on an experimental study of his own personality that led to brooding self-absorption. As a child Witkacy had been free to play at art and life, finding both a great game, but upon reaching maturity the young man suffered persistent difficulty in achieving personal definition and a sense of vocation. Although he began exhibiting his paintings as early as 1901, the future writer found it impossible to commit himself to any career, due to inner uncertainty and a Nietzschean compulsion to live all the things that he had within him. Indeterminacy later became the affliction, or blessing, of the Witkacian hero.

At the beginning of the new century Witkiewicz senior moved to the seaside resort of Lovranno, on the Istrian peninsula (now in Yugoslavia) not far from Trieste, settling there permanently in 1908. The ostensible reason for the move was his declining health, but the great man was accompanied by a female admirer who paid most of the bills, and left behind in Zakopane a wife now compelled to keep a rooming house in order to support herself and her twenty-three-year-old son. Witkacy had already begun to oppose the imposition of his father's ideas, and in the growing estrangement between Stanisław Witkiewicz and his wife, took the side of his adored mother. Open hostilities between these two powerful individuals first broke out when Witkacy left home in 1905 to attend the Academy of Fine Arts in Cracow. Although he was an indifferent and undisciplined student and soon dropped out, the young man's decision to conform pained his father. In 1905, the elder Witkiewicz wrote:

What a peculiar mixture of contradictions life is and must each new generation unfailingly be the antithesis and reaction to the previous one? Did we really battle against the servitude of the school and herd mentality in art so that you and your peers could actually feel at home in the school system?

(*Listy do syna*, pp. 211–212)

In his artistic development Witkacy had moved away from an initial orientation to landscape, his father's preferred genre, and under the influence of Arnold Böcklin's fantastic canvases, such as *Island of the Dead* (1880), abandoned forever faithful reproductions of nature for the macabre and grotesque. In 1907 Witkacy spent almost three months in Paris touring the museums and galleries, where he became acquainted with the works of Vincent van Gogh, Paul Gauguin, Henri de Toulouse-Lautrec, and Paul Cézanne, already the classics of modernism, and discovered the latest trends in European art as represented by the nabis, fauves, and cubists. The following year the young artist began doing portraits and bizarre charcoal drawings, which were called *potwory* (monsters) by his father, with titles such as *Człowiek z wodną puchliną zaczaja się na kochanka swej żony* (A Man with Dropsy Lies in Wait for His Wife's Lover, 1905-1910) and *Książę ciemności kusi Św. Teresę przy pomocy kelnera z Budapesztu* (The Prince of Darkness Tempts Saint Theresa with the Aid of a Waiter from Budapest, 1913)—each a miniature cartoonlike drama.

Witkacy also began to create his own form of theater with the camera and produced a long series of photographic portraits of himself and his many alter egos, his family, friends, and surroundings. As a boy he had learned the value of photography for his creative work from his father, who had encouraged him to pose and play in front of the camera. He began his career as a photographer at the turn of the century, taking pictures of locomotives and the mountain scenery of Zakopane, but soon found his true subject in the human face, which often fills the entire picture and is both the foreground and the background. These psychic studies are revelations of the inner man behind the mask and of his terror in the face of existence. Witkacy kept photographing himself throughout his life, catching the look of incipient madness in his own haunted eyes as well as the social masks and camouflage of his role-playing persona.

Witkacy's close friends from his youth, whom he often drew and photographed, were the anthropologist Bronisław Malinowski; the mathematician, painter, and philosopher Leon Chwistek; and the composer Karol Szymanow-ski. Outstanding members of a talented generation of Polish artists and intellectuals, they had all embarked on successful careers in their early twenties, while Witkacy was still without any direction in life. Witkacy, Malinowski, and Chwistek read plays and poetry together, wrote bogus scientific treatises, and invented strange names for one another, inspired by Edgar Allan Poe, Oscar Wilde, and the decadents and dandies: Malinowski was Edgar, Duke of Nevermore, Chwistek was Baron Brummel de Buffadero de Bluff, and Witkacy was Dorian Fidious-Ugenta.

A stress on artifice and make-believe came with the setting. Zakopane in the early twentieth century was the stage for a highly theatricalized society, given to lofty tones and snobbish poses and teeming with quests for the absolute and with erotic intrigues, where conversations were sprinkled with citations from Nietzsche and Henri Bergson in the original and the "naked soul" was a frequent subject of discussion. Another of Witkacy's good friends, the pianist Arthur Rubinstein, commented at the time of his first visit in 1904 on the "hothouse atmosphere" he encountered in Zakopane, "with its intellectual overtones, and more often than not with its artificial gaiety, hiding so many dark and unhealthy passions."

Witkacy himself, in an essay written some years later, described the special spirit of the place, employing the hyperbolic style characteristic of its genius:

> For the weak, Zakopane is almost as fatal as meeting a truly demonic woman. For real Titans of the Spirit (to the extent that such beings exist anymore) it is a place in which their essence becomes concentrated, horizons open for them, and creativity—artistic, social, or scientific—produces new forms and builds new values.
>
> ("Demonizm Zakopanego"
> [Zakopane Demonism], 1919)

Although he traveled far and achieved a distanced point of view, Witkacy remained true to Zakopane and its mystique, returning to it and making it his lasting home. For him its mountains and demonism were associated with female sexuality, proliferation of forms, and creativity. "He derives such joy from contemplating nature," his father observed in a letter written to his sister Maria on 26 February 1901. "He cannot stand the city and enjoys each willow, each cloud, every curvature of the earth." Witkacy is emphatically a nonurban author, and his cities, like his masses, are faceless and all characterized by their absence of traits. All the trappings of Zakopane demonism—the perverse eroticism, artistic poses, and inflationary lying—appear in the writer's plays and novels, where they are subjected to distorting magnification.

In 1908 Witkacy met the modernist actress Irena Solska and became involved in a stormy love affair that lasted four years. A leading practitioner of demonism, Solska played the role of a devourer of men both on- and offstage and initiated the young Witkacy, seven years her junior, into what he later called "the metaphysical monstrosity of sexuality." However, in the process of contending with her histrionic world, he was able to define his attitude toward theater and acting and begin to shape his own creative method, working variations on the demonically theatrical by combining his own experiences and modernist literary models in the form of grotesque parody and self-conscious reductio ad absurdum. This technique finds its first expression in *622 upadki Bunga, czyli Demoniczna kobieta* (The 622 Downfalls of Bungo; or, The Demonic Woman), the autobiographical novel about his love affair that Witkacy wrote in 1910 and 1911, but that remained unpublished until 1972 (many of Witkacy's works were published posthumously). In this roman à clef Solska is the sexually insatiable, lying actress Acne (a passing but embarrassing ailment of youth) and Witkacy is the artist-in-embryo Bungo, an unfocused, introspective young man totally absorbed with his discovery and creation of himself, his artistic personality, and his theories of art.

In order to hold on to the perfidious Acne, who only values manipulated appearances, the young hero finds that he must master the actor's transformational abilities and abandon all attempts to be himself. Endowed with a protean nature and drawn to all forms of playing, Witkacy saw the actor as the very image of falsehood and alienation from self, dramatizing the modern crisis of personality. "A mask is a dangerous thing," a friend warns Bungo. "You can't be an actor in life. You won't succeed, because you won't be able to turn yourself entirely into a lie." By the end of the novel the young protagonist has joined in the "cabaret" that his degenerate circle of acquaintances has made of life. Due to this collective theatricalization, society itself and its institutions have become subject to endless metamorphosis that is only pseudo-change. The way in which the problem of disintegrating personal identity becomes extended into the social realm is a fundamental issue in Witkacy's later novels and plays.

In *Bunga* the inexperienced writer developed a complex self-irony by which he could stand outside his role as would-be artist even while playing the part and in fact becoming a true artist. His attitude is one of ambivalence toward himself and toward his calling. Witkacy puts into the mouth of one of Bungo's friends the warning, "I'm afraid that, although you might be an artist, you may become—and what is worse remain for your whole life—a little boy playing at art." Throughout his subsequent career he was judged by the world at large as an impudent prankster playing at art, and indeed the most Witkacian qualities of his mature work have their origin in his childish irresponsibility and refusal to be a serious artist according to the accepted Polish models of the time.

The moral stature of Witkiewicz senior as a lawgiver stemmed from his high-minded stance; art was something sacred, characterized by dedication to exalted ideals, lofty language, and solemnity of tone. Witkacy's revolt against his father's authority took the form of resistance to the prevailing high view of art. By his unusual educational system the elder Witkiewicz had deliberately made his son an outsider, beyond the norms of society, but then had expected the boy to conform to his preconceived notions of what such an independent individual should be. Witkacy rebelled against this subtle form of tyranny by an equally subtle form of subversion: through parody and playfulness he mocked himself as artist and called into question the grandiose mission of art. Leaving the elevated plane to his father, the son went down into the underground realm of unavowed antisocial impulses, secret desires, jokes, tricks, and games.

Witkiewicz senior, who was no prude, showed remarkable flexibility in appreciating his son's artistic originality, praising his "monsters," but tried to keep him out of unsuitable involvements with women, which might dissipate his creative energies, and cautioned him against publishing *Bunga* because of its unusually frank and vivid treatment of sexual matters, with the character of the protagonist's partner based on a highly respected actress. Most of all, the father worried about his son's troubled state of mind, warning him against dangerous habits such as smoking and playing with revolvers. Smoking was an addiction that Witkacy detested and wrestled with for many years, and revolvers played a significant role in both his art and his life. As a young man he made drawings of revolvers and had himself photographed brandishing a pistol, and he held his Browning pressed against his temple in more than one dramatic suicide attempt. Like the futurists and surrealists, Witkacy appreciated the value of a sudden, gratuitous pistol shot as a gesture of anarchic aggression. The heroes and heroines of his plays and novels always carry revolvers and are ready at any moment to shoot it out with themselves, their interlocutors, and the cosmos.

At the age of twenty-seven, without a profession or purpose in life and tormented by the enigma of his amorphous self, Witkacy was forced to live at the expense of his parents in his mother's boardinghouse—a fact that his father did not hesitate to call to his attention. Considering himself a useless parasite and feeling threatened by madness (a fear that haunted him all his life), the disturbed young man underwent psychoanalysis with a Polish psychiatrist then living in Zakopane, Dr. Karol Beaurain. The sessions, apparently terminated after several months, made Witkacy an enthusiastic follower of Sigmund Freud as a theorist and prober of the human psyche (although he admitted being too bored to finish reading Freud's *General Introduction to Psychoanalysis* [1917]), but on a practical level he only gained awareness that he suffered from an "embryo complex." Many years later he wrote a eulogy of Beaurain marked by characteristic Witkacian irony and nonchalance:

> Interested in my dreams, he suggested to me in 1912 a regular "practical course" in psychoanalysis, to which I joyfully agreed as a kind of "novelty"; but I entered into this experiment not without a critical attitude and some slight mistrust. . . . In a certain sense, Dr. de Beaurain [*sic*] wanted to save me from myself. Quite possibly it worked out well for me that he didn't succeed in doing so, since if I had "resolved" (as the psychoanalysts say) my complexes, I probably would have had to give up my work in my specialties, i.e., in literature, painting and philosophy, or at least change its nature radically—stop being myself to a certain degree.
> (*Niemyte dusze* [Unwashed Souls], pp.191–192)

Zakopane demonism and a sudden pistol shot brought to an end the embryonic phase of Witkacy's life on 21 February 1914 (four days before his twenty-ninth birthday), when his fiancée, Jadwiga Janczewska, whom he had decided he must marry in order to salvage his wasted life, committed suicide, shooting herself at the foot of a cliff after placing a bouquet of flowers nearby in a modernist gesture celebrating the beauty of death. The exact circumstances can never be known, but the handsome and elegant Szymanowski had recently arrived in Zakopane and was staying at the Witkiewicz pension, as was Janczewska, and some misunderstanding, jealous intrigue, or mystification led Witkacy to dash off into the mountains, and his fiancée—none too strong or healthy and perhaps overwhelmed by the strange and rarefied atmosphere among the elite of Zakopane—reacted hysterically.

Janczewska's death, for which he held himself responsible, was the most catastrophic event in the writer's life, plunging him into guilt-ridden despair and radically altering everything in his existence. Throughout the years he never forgot the event or failed to recall the place, the date, and the time. He became so obsessed with death and constantly talked of killing himself, convinced that sooner or later he would have to commit suicide. Now only concern for his mother kept him half alive. In his unrestrained grief Witkacy turned to his dearest friend, Malinowski, then studying anthropology at the London School of Economics, and in a series of anguished letters described himself as being finished, both as an artist and as a human being. Malinowski proved to be immensely supportive, but others of his friends, with whom he was frequently quarreling and breaking off relations, passed harsh judgments on his character. On learning of the tragedy, Chwistek, then in Paris, wrote to his sister about Witkacy: "He is a degenerate individual, equally removed from true art as from life, a perpetual embryo crazed by megalomania."

Malinowski had been invited to attend the Congress of the British Association for the Advancement of Science that was to be held in August in Adelaide and Sydney, Australia, and he suggested that Witkacy accompany him as a way of overcoming his sorrow and remorse. Afterward Witkacy would serve as the artist and photographer on the field expedition to New Guinea that Malinowski was already dreaming of. The two friends left England in early June and after changing ships in Colombo, Ceylon, where they spent two weeks sightseeing, they arrived in Fremantle on 21 July 1914, a week before Austria declared war on Serbia. In letters to his mother and father, mainly unsent, Witkacy recounted his sufferings during the trip, much of which he spent in his cabin reading Joseph Conrad's *Lord Jim* (1900) and thinking of ways to commit suicide. To his mother he wrote:

> The ocean voyage which forces me to reflect is the most hideous thing that could ever be devised to torment me. I don't know if I'll manage to make it to Colombo. It's only through an extreme effort of will that I resist an overwhelming death wish. I am worthless as a human being. . . . I am surely finished as an artist. . . . I am like a person covered with wounds who is bathed in sulfuric acid. Everything—the sea, people, the sky, every word is boundless torture. . . . Death is the only thing left. . . . such is my destiny. . . . Dearest Mother, forgive me.
>
> (Quoted in *Pamiętnik Teatralny* [1985], pp. 43–44)

The journey with Malinowski, which at first seemed so fatal, proved to be Witkacy's redemption both as a man and as an artist. Confrontation with the tropics opened his eyes to color, and his painting underwent a radical change, as glaring reds, yellows, and blues replaced the gloomy black and white. Discovery of exotic non-Western cultures gave him a new perspective for judging European civilization, much as it had for Gauguin and Conrad, and glimpses of rites and ceremonies in Ceylon and aboriginal dances in Australia helped him to envisage a ritual theater of metaphysical dimensions (the Balinese dancers had the same impact on Artaud in 1931). Witkacy came to admire the asymmetry and disproportion of the art of the East and dislike Renaissance perspective with rounded figure modeling.

The outbreak of World War I in August 1914, less than two weeks after his arrival in Australia, threw Witkacy into a new state of panic because of anxiety about his mother and his feeling that he should be home serving his country and seeking an honorable death on the battlefield as the only justification for a misspent life. Born in Warsaw and thus a Russian subject, Witkacy was exempt from military service as an only son, but he chose to volunteer for the Imperial Army, a decision impossible for his father to accept, since as a Polish patriot he was eagerly awaiting the approaching collapse of the Russian Empire. (Witkiewicz senior died in 1915 in his Adriatic retreat without ever seeing his son again, and received a hero's burial in Zakopane. Only his mother defended Witkacy's decision to fight for Russia.)

After endless bureaucratic difficulties because of his lack of the necessary papers, Witkacy left Australia in early September. Proceeding via Bombay, Aden, Port Said, Alexandria, and Salonika, he reached St. Petersburg by the middle of October and was accepted into the officers' training school by the end of November. Now the thirty-year-old ne'er-do-well succeeded for the first time in constructing for himself a new self and new life; he found the mask that had so long eluded him. An aunt in St. Petersburg wrote his mother:

> Before he was never the way he is now. Calm, almost joyful, he holds himself straight with his head raised high—he's completely shaken off the despairing state of apathy in which we saw him when he first came back. . . . He looks very nice in his uniform, neither the heavy boots, nor the thick coat, nor the sabre bothers him in the least.
>
> (*Listy do syna,* p. 641)

The four years that Witkacy spent in Russia are the least well documented of his life and the most subject to speculation and hearsay. We know only that he became a lieutenant in the elite Pavlovsky Regiment of the Life Guards, was wounded at the front in 1915, and was decorated with the order of Saint Ann Fourth Class for bravery and heroism. Sent back to St. Petersburg as a convalescent, Witkacy spent the rest of the war on limited service, with enough free time to visit the private Shchukin Gallery in Moscow and marvel at the many Picassos (he regarded Pablo Picasso as being on a par with the greatest of the old masters), paint a large number of fantastic compositions, and, always strapped for money, do commissioned portraits of fellow officers, embarking on what became his principal source of income. It was also in Russia that he first experimented with drugs and wrote most of his first long treatise on art, philosophy, and society, *Nowe formy w malarstwie i wynikające stąd nieporozumienia* (New Forms in Painting and Misunderstandings Resulting Therefrom, 1919), as well as a preliminary sketch for his *Pojęcia i twierdzenia implikowane przez pojęcie istnienia* (The Concepts and Principles Implied by the Concept of Existence, 1935), which he always referred to as his philosophical *Hauptwerk* (magnum opus).

At the time of the February Revolution, Witkacy was, according to his own account, elected political commissar by his regiment and witnessed at close quarters the overthrow of the Romanov Empire, the October Revolution, and the first seven months of Bolshevik rule. Characteristically the author described his experiences as an observer using the imagery of the stage:

> During the final days I had much food for thought in the spectacle of the Russian Revolution from February 1917 to June 1918. I can't call it anything but a spectacle since unfortunately I watched it as though from a box at the theater, not being able to take an active part in it due to my schizoid inhibitions.
>
> (*Niemyte Dusze,* p. 264)

These insights became the basis for his future plays and novels in which the most theatricalized societies are those in the throes of social upheaval and in which the classes who feel themselves on the margin of events, watching from outside as spectators or actors without parts, experience the theatrical quality of revolution.

Through his skills at transformation, impersonation, and trickery, Witkacy survived all the dangers of being a Pole and a former czarist officer in a new Communist regime gripped by paranoia about enemies. He reached Zakopane by 11 June 1918, somehow succeeding in bringing with him a sizable collection of portraits and compositions using astronomical motifs. (Many of these works were destroyed during the Warsaw Uprising in 1944.) The next six years were the most productive in his career; in an extraordinary outburst of creative energy, he painted hundreds of compositions and portraits, wrote over thirty plays (ten of which are lost), and published books and essays on aesthetics and philosophy. Finally, in his mid thirties, the ex-czarist officer achieved his goal and became an artist, or at least assumed the mask of an artist. For the first and only time in his life he was able to join forces with a group of like-minded painters, the formists, and exhibited with them until the movement disbanded in 1922, thus escaping briefly from the feeling of isolation that usually oppressed him.

The Polish formists were a loose association of artists with futurist and expressionist backgrounds, united in their opposition to naturalism and belief in the autonomy of art, but hardly very radical by western European standards. The political and cultural temper of newly independent Poland (reborn in 1919 at the Treaty of Versailles) was conservative and decidedly hostile to innovation in the arts. Censorship and government repression (formerly used to silence Polish nationalism) were now directed against anything suspected of being Bolshevik or anarchist, which included all forms of artistic experimentation. Writers were frequently harassed and arrested, magazines confiscated, and theaters raided.

As "Witkacy," the public stance that the painter-playwright now adopted was aggressive and flamboyant, a compound of the eccentricity and exhibitionism typical of the avant-garde personality. Adept at provoking scandal and always ready to quarrel with his many enemies, real and imagined, he attacked in a series of lectures and articles the provincialism, anti-intellectual tone, and lack of broad theoretical horizons in Polish cultural life, as well as the low level of its literacy and dramatic criticism. His outrageous behavior earned him notoriety but did nothing to further his acceptance by the public. But iconoclastic belligerence was only one of his masks. Another, more private "face," revealed in his letters, is that of a suffering martyr victimized by society and fate, who feels the approach of infirmity and old age while still in his thirties, constantly proclaiming, "The end is near for me," grubbing desperately for money to keep from going hungry, haunted by frightful dreams, and single-handedly battling an uncomprehending cultural establishment. "I'm expecting the worst," he wrote to a friend, "i.e., physical pain, blindness, fire, and imbecility."

Both dramatizations—swaggering assertion of self and horror in the face of existence—are opposing sides of the same perception of being, which finds expression in the playwright's view that art condenses our feeling of the unity and uniqueness of the individual confronting the mystery of existence. Performance aspects of life and art are the most deeply felt; every moment is a scene, whether recorded by the camera, played out in reality, or put on canvas or on the stage. Although most critics refused to see in Witkacy anything more than a prankster and buffoon, Tadeusz Boy-Żeleński was exceptional in recognizing that the "act" he was performing, no matter how absurd its outer form, had as its essence the nature of art. Boy wrote in 1921 that

> Witkacy is by birth, by race, to the very marrow of his bones an artist. He lives exclusively by art and for art. And his relationship to art is profoundly dramatic; he is one of those tormented spirits who in art seek the solution not to problems of success, but to the problem of their own being.
>
> (Quoted in *Pamiętnik Teatralny* [1985], p. 68)

The drama of Witkacy's relation to art became the subject of his dramas, and his creative work was devoted almost entirely to creativity and its twin, destructiveness. Ultimately Witkacy took art as seriously as his father had wanted him to, totally ignoring practical, material considerations in pursuit of creative freedom.

In the early and mid 1920's Witkacy devoted his greatest energies to the theory and practice of theater, feeling—as did many European avant-gardists of the period—that the stage was the chief bastion of artistic conservatism to be overthrown. His assault on the conventional theater of his day took place on many fronts. He wrote theoretical treatises and articles, gave lectures, engaged in polemics with critics while at the same time fighting to have his plays staged in the face of hostility, ridicule, and indifference; attending rehearsals; and eventually designing and directing productions himself.

All Witkacy's efforts to give drama the non-Euclidean coordinates of modern science and to bring the stage into the world of twentieth-century painting, which had already rejected realism, were based on his aesthetic theory of Pure Form. This crucial but difficult Witkacian concept follows from the author's ontological view of unity in plurality, which posits the directly given feeling of the unity of personality on the part of each Individual Being (the "I") confronting the plurality of all that lies outside (the "non-I"). From these existential premises there results a tragic sense of life, with feelings of frightful loneliness, consciousness of the accidental character of everything, recognition of the menace of nothingness, and bewilderment vis-à-vis an alien universe. Each individual is compelled to ask unanswerable questions, such as "Why am I precisely this being and not some other? In this place in infinite space and at this instant in infinite time? In precisely this group of beings, on this planet? And why do I exist? I could just as well not exist. Why does anything exist?"

Religion, philosophy, and art in varying ways attempt to ease the pain of existence. In *New Forms in Painting* Witkacy wrote:

> Artistic creation is an assertion of life in its metaphysical horror, and not a justification of this horror through the creation of a system of reassuring concepts, as is the case with religion, or a system of concepts rationally showing the necessity of this and not any other state of affairs for the Totality of Existence, as is the case with philosophy.

Art is to convey this metaphysical terror not by an imitation of reality or by the expression of ideas, but through the purely formal arrangement of elements, whatever they may be.

In this way the playwright-painter-philosopher hoped to recapture the metaphysical feeling of the mystery of existence that he felt was in danger of being lost forever in the mechanized routine of the perfect anthill society. This feeling is like something half remembered from a strange dream, or like the momentary gasp before a wonder of nature, in a sacred place, during a battle, or after a hard drinking bout, but only in art can it be given duration and be subject to production at will. In music, metaphysical feeling is produced by the formal construction of sounds, in painting of colors and shapes, in poetry of words. Freed of referentiality, drama becomes pure happening through time. The artistic essence of a play does not consist in the narratable content or in the lifelikeness of characters and actions, but rather in the dynamic tensions of its components.

Whereas the old masters were able, at least at times, to achieve Pure Form within the bounds of a normal representation of human feeling, character, or action, modern artists are driven to distortion and deformation in a quest for ever newer forms needed to arouse the viewer numbed by the feverish pace of life. Because the theater, which became detached from the religious mysteries in Greek times and then degenerated because of the Renaissance doctrine of imitation, had not yet passed through its modern period of formal exuberance, Witkacy felt that for a brief moment it might blaze up in a splendid final conflagration before the end.

Witkacy's theory of Pure Form in the theater and his continued attempts to explain it throughout his life created confusion among the critics, and even now there is no agreement as to how, if at all, his aesthetic views are embodied in his dramatic works. At least as they have been performed in his native land since 1956, when the bloodless October Revolution gave Poland greater independence from the Soviet Union and an autonomous cultural policy, his plays seem explosive in their political and social content, as witness their long history of troubles with censorship.

We can best understand Witkacy's Pure Form, and the seeming contradictions between his theory and practice, from two perspectives. The first is a historical one, in which we may place Witkacy's idea in the context of other theories propagated before and after him. The second is a biographical perspective, in which his theory may be viewed as an expression of the author's obsession with his own creativity. For the avant-gardist, art means the creation of new formal values. "The creating of forms means: living," wrote the German expressionist August Macke in 1912. For Witkacy, too, the play of forms was a deeply felt need, articulated in his oft-repeated phrase "insatiable craving for form."

In the early 1900's interest in new means of expression ran high, and artists were overwhelmed by a riotous proliferation of forms found in many hitherto overlooked sources. Paul Klee discovered new forms in childlike spontaneity, playfulness, and games, while Picasso and the cubists made formal revelations through their use of the tribal sculpture of Africa and Oceania. At the same time aestheticians studied the mysterious power that certain forms have to generate their own significance. In *Abstraction and Empathy* (1908) the German theorist Wilhelm Worringer contrasted the lesser realistic art of Greece and the western world with the higher art of abstraction of ancient Egypt, the Orient, and primitive art. The naturalistic tradition puts its faith in the cosmos and trusts reason and science; it is the child of a civilization that celebrates life and feels in harmony with nature. The geometric tradition of antinatural forms arises in cultures for whom the universe is threatening and the cause of metaphysical dread; an art of self-enclosed and necessary forms, it declares the priority of mind over the experience of nature. Witkacy's concern with the internal logic and autonomous life of forms coincides with the British critic Clive Bell's idea of "significant form," in which meaning resides in the relations and combinations of lines and colors, and bears resemblances to the Russian formalists' emphasis on art as technique and on the primacy of experiencing the artfulness of the creation. Witkacy shares with such theorists the belief that feeling does not give rise to form, but rather that form creates feeling.

In 1923 Witkacy published *Teatr* (Theater), a collection of essays in which he argues his nonmimetic view of poetry and theater, anticipating by a number of years later developments in literary and theatrical theory. For example, the New Criticism of the 1940's postulated a self-contained work of art whose constituent elements are in a state of reciprocal tension. In the 1950's Ionesco proposed a drama of pure movement arising from "a clashing of forms and lines, from abstract antagonisms, without psychological motivation." In the 1970's the British director Peter Brook spoke of the attempt, in times of crisis, to find new, purely theatrical forms free of didacticism and referentiality. Witkacy's major accomplishment in his theory of Pure Form was to have perceived early in the twentieth century that the theater as an art must have a special scenic language with its own lexicon and syntax, independent of real life.

Witkacy never claimed that Pure Form would eliminate reality from drama, do away with characters, plots, and ideas, or dispense with the author's experiences; rather, he argued that the traditional materials of drama, or content, should be subordinated to formal coherence. Pure Form is a boundary concept, a goal to be approached but never fully achieved. "The purest form," the author declared, "is always sullied by life." Realism and formism are end points in a nearly continuous series, with scarcely perceptible transitions ranging from make-believe in life to pure form in the theater: "We apparently cannot define where art begins and life ends."

Acknowledging the "mysterious nature of the gift of artistic creativity," Witkacy allowed that the work of art in Pure Form depended for its components on the talent, imagination, experience, feelings, and thoughts of the creator. Therefore, although his theory of art contained no ideological program about man and society (as did those of the futurists, expressionists, and surrealists), Witkacy's dramas, written as examples of Pure Form, do include his theories (philosophical, aesthetic, and cultural) as content or component elements, thereby devaluing these theories as authorial argument and, by formal structuring, transmuting them into aesthetic experience.

Transformation of life and reality into art was the central issue to which Witkacy constantly returned. Immersed from childhood in problems of creativity, the philosopher-playwright became the subject of his own creation: first, in making himself into an artist (according to his father's creative plan), and second, in making the process of creativity into the material of his art. Through the creative making of forms Witkacy joined art and life. The self-reflexivity of the artist's absorption in his own calling corresponds to the Spanish philosopher José Ortega y Gasset's notion of the "dehumanization of art," whereby the means of expression are converted into the substance of the work.

Witkacy goes one step further; he liberates the elements of drama—including his own ideas and theories used as content—and, relieved of traditional functions, they become part of a free play of forms. Although the theory of Pure Form in the theater seems serious and abstract, Witkacy's practice is quite the opposite; the stress on formal construction encourages play, not ideology, and mercurial transformations, not fixed positions. In making art out of theory (and not simply according to theory)

and in playing with many forms rather than choosing a single one, Witkacy joins early modernist exaltation of Art (with a capital *A*) to postmodernist eclecticism and frivolity.

The modern French theorist Patrice Parvis has suggested that "postmodern theater raises theory to the rank of a playful activity." In Witkacy's dramas, theory and practice interact, mutually consuming each other. The theory of Pure Form in the theater, far from being minimalist and exclusive, is voracious, swallowing other forms, recycling them, playing tricks with them, and spewing them out. For Witkacy, Pure Form is a new conception of theatrical art that can accommodate, in a way that no single "ism" ever could, a multiplicity of viewpoints, including modern scientific, philosophical, and aesthetic theory. The form of a Witkacian drama often becomes the subject of the play itself, as the characters discuss the theory of Pure Form. To understand what a radical leap forward the Polish playwright made into a new theatrical dimension, we need only imagine how unsettling it would be if in August Strindberg's *Miss Julie* (1888) the heroine began to discuss Strindberg's theoretical preface and its application to the drama in which she is appearing.

It is significant that Witkacy's attempt to transform the theater focused on the actor, not on stage design, theater architecture, or audience involvement. The theory of Pure Form opened the way for a new sensibility about performing and the performer. "For now," Witkacy wrote in 1922, "I'm interested in a new acting style." The Polish playwright shares Nietzsche's perception of the actor's art as a talent for lying and of the theater as lies. In Pure Form the actor-liar will be transformed into a technician who, rather than having simulated living experiences, will render his part in the total composition with mathematical precision. Instead of being an impersonator pretending to be someone real, displaying false emotions and engaged in the futile task of trying to compete with nature by copying it, the actor-technician can become a true creator, freed of the demands of truth to life and theatrical illusion; here Witkacy explicitly opposes the ideas of the influential Russian director Konstantin Stanislavsky and the psychological realism of the Moscow Art Theater.

In presenting the theatricalized self in a theatricalized society, the playwright, through extensive and precise stage directions, requires of the actor a conscious playing with forms emptied of their lying content. The actor's art of transformation, revealed as a series of tricks or stunts, becomes the substance of Witkacian drama, as performance replaces ideology.

For Witkacy the theater was a realm of freedom in which a man's sense of primeval wonder could be reinstated. Thus, although he denied that it should have any utilitarian function in promoting ethical or national goals, the playwright-philosopher argued that the stage as a social institution was able to oppose the mechanization of life, "the petrification of everything into one uniform, gray, undifferentiated pulp." By preserving metaphysical feelings, which are alike for all humans, the theater defends the values of the individual.

Witkacy maintained that the proportion of real-life and formal elements in drama would vary from work to work, because for every artist there were harrowing contradictions and clashes between the primordial formal impulse on the one hand and the content of feelings and ideas springing from the unconscious depths of the psyche on the other. "The development of an artist," the playwright confessed, "is a battle with life as raw material for the purpose of creating formal constructions in which form will dominate content."

In an appendix to his theoretical work Witkacy provided a list of the twenty-two plays he had written since 1918, indicating with a star the five that are closer to Pure Form and with a cross the seven nearer to the realistic; the remaining ten are not identified as to tendency. The playwright's attempts to make content subservient to form were always a matter of creative struggle, producing dramas of varying textures and giving rise to dynamic tensions as intense as those among the purely formal elements.

The best way to characterize Witkacy's dramas is to indicate briefly their collective materials and then to analyze aspects of formal construction, in particular techniques of discontinuity and disjunction, in selected plays. Summaries of plots cannot convey anything of the nature of works in which real-life actions and psychology are deformed and the laws of cause and effect and empirical logic have been suspended.

The dramatis personae of Witkacian drama belong to a degenerate band of stage characters playing roles from the modernist repertory: crazed artist, demonic woman, cosmopolitan playboy, rapacious tycoon, demented scientist, histrionic tyrant. These colorful types, who filtered down to the popular imagination in silent films, provide the playwright with an international dramatic idiom. When pushed to extremes of exaggeration, these modern commedia characters become self-consciously aware of their own theatricality and literary ancestry (upon which they may comment). Witkacy is not an avant-gardist who sweeps away the past to start from a tabula rasa; rather, his new forms are created out of old pieces, assembled and scrambled through eclectic parody, random borrowings, and associative montage. The Polish playwright cites himself and others, appropriates characters and episodes from his reading, and cultivates an aesthetic of surprise compounded of chance effects and the unforeseen.

Witkacy's first Pure Form play, *Pragmatyści* (*The Pragmatists*, 1920), written in 1919, enacts the confinement of consciousness and its baffled search for egress. Two seasoned performers, the pseudo-artist Plasfodor and his managerial friend Count Franz von Telek (who is scouting for cabaret talent) are trapped in a closed world of reciprocal exploitations in the company of Plasfodor's mute mistress and medium Mammalia (later revealed to be von Telek's sister, whom he seduced when she was eight), his sexually indeterminate maid Masculette, and a Chinese mummy from Saigon, where the two men had experimented with opium and vampirism. Witkacy borrowed von Telek from Jules Verne's science fiction novel *The Castle of the Carpathians* (1892), where he appears as an opera singer searching for the famous diva Stilla, who is actually dead but is made to seem alive in the castle through the use of voice recording and optical illusion. Attracted to the novel's setting in the Carpathian mountains (of which the Tatras in Zakopane were a part), Witkacy borrowed only the name of the character, but the trick apparition of the dead and the simulated performance are congenial devices, similar to those the playwright used.

The insatiable questers in *The Pragmatists*, seeking transformation into new forms of existence but falling back into old patterns of loneliness, boredom, and terror, observe their own thought processes and watch the others thinking and suffering until they are driven to despair, madness, and murder. The only two activities, which serve as existential time-killers, are orgy (drugs, sex, and endless conversation) and séance (calling up the dead).

In the early 1920's Witkacy avowed that he was "fighting with various ghosts," and several times he attended séances (then popular in Warsaw) conducted by celebrated mediums, at which he saw the ghost of his dead fiancée, Janczewska. The playwright even conducted his own séances until he was eventually caught pulling the strings that produced the spiritistic rappings. In these adventures we see the origin of one of Witkacy's striking devices for deformation, the living corpse. We also see his ambivalent attitude of belief and irony: endorsing the apparition yet (as manipulator of the strings) acknowledging the trick.

The Witkacian rising of the dead first occurs in *The Pragmatists*, when the corpse of Masculette, whose head has been smashed with a hammer by von Telek, gets up off the floor and walks out the door. Death is debased if killing does not have any lasting effect; murdered characters either continue as if nothing had happened or come back, not as otherworldly visions but as perfectly ordinary people resuming their daily lives. Denied the ability to die, Witkacy's "pragmatists"—those seeking ways to circumvent the tragic nature of life—are condemned to an eternal repetition of their existence.

Mister Price, czyli Bzik tropikalny (*Mister Price; or, Tropical Madness*, 1962), written in 1920, is an example of the contrasting mode designated by the playwright as more realistic. The fundamental difference of styles follows from two opposing dramaturgical premises. Whereas *The Pragmatists* takes place in synthetically constructed time and space, with unnatural groupings of disparate characters locked in inexplicable relationships, *Mister Price* has an identifiable geographic environment with recognizable customs and manners and real-life probabilities based on logically linked action and psychological motivation. Practical affairs—business and money—bring together like-minded characters in a sharp clash of wills. To give the illusion of reality according to the reigning dramatic conventions, Witkacy knew that he had to render all actions believable by offering detailed explanations of every step his characters take. Through subversive compliance, the theorist of Pure Form was able to play with the realistic conventions and expose their falsity by overinsisting on the authenticity of the proceedings.

A drama of British colonial life in Rangoon, *Mister Price* takes details of setting and elements of character and action from Conrad's *An Outcast of the Islands* (1896) and *Lord Jim* and then calls attention to the borrowing by having the Conradian characters cite Conrad's novels, thereby undermining the play's purportedly realistic premises. The device of the risen corpse, transferred into the context of more traditional dramaturgy where the law of cause and effect seems to hold sway, likewise proves subversive. The financial wizard Price, poisoned and shot by the demonic Elinor Golders, makes a miraculous return to life and triumphantly exits to begin a new career as a painter. After the fact, the audience, along with the other characters, learns of Price's Houdini-like skills as an escape artist, which have enabled him to substitute nail polish for the deadly Indian curare, deflect a bullet by moving his body, and play dead by temporarily stopping his heart from beating and suspending his pulse. Thus the artist-performer Price breaks out of his incarceration in the mad world of power and domination by a death-defying stunt that brings him freedom from the exploiters. The elaborate explanation of how the trick is done keeps *Mister Price* within realistic coordinates while at the same time ironically mocking them.

The first of Witkacy's plays to reach the stage was *Tumor Mózgowicz* (*Tumor Brainiowicz*, 1921), performed in 1921 at Cracow's respected Teatr Stary, where it provoked scandal and controversy. Unspecified as to formal or realistic tendency, *Tumor* is, in the words of its author, "a fantasy on the theme of the revolution in mathematics and physics." Its eponymous hero is a scientific genius and creator of a new system of transfinite numbers that he calls "tumors." Acts 1 and 3 take place in the children's nursery; act 2 is set on the tropical island of Timor (here the playwright draws upon Conrad's *Almayer's Folly* [1895], which he had been translating into Polish), where an erupting volcano and a thousand shrieking parrots provide a pseudo-naive backdrop in a pop-art style. The sources of modern creativity are to be found in the primitive and the child-like, used by the playwright to expose the oppressive authority of the European family and society. Witkacy's savages believe in absolutes but smell of raw meat; his young adolescents are weirdly precocious and prescient. (Among avant-garde playwrights Witkacy is almost alone in dealing extensively with childhood and creating complex children's roles—usually played by adults.)

It took almost a year to obtain permission from the censor to stage *Tumor*; the authorities found the play potentially subversive because it seemed unintelligible, and several higher censors in Lwów and Warsaw had to pass judgment before it could be approved. Even then unusual precautions had to be taken: it could be staged only after the official end of the season, as a private and experimental production; the number of performances was limited to two; and attendance was restricted to special invitation or written request.

The one-act *Nowe wyzwolenie* (*The New Deliverance*, 1922–1923), written in 1920, is formalist in orientation; radical temporal and spatial disjunction results in the unexpected joining of disparate components. The pivot for dynamic tensions is again the returning corpse, this time Shakespeare's Richard III, a figure at once historical and fictional, frequently mentioned in Witkacy's work as haunted by the ghosts of those he had murdered. The awesome hunchbacked tyrant, brandishing a two-handed sword, has wandered out of Shakespeare's play and fifteenth-century England into Witkacy's *New Deliverance*, where on one half of the stage two masked murderers keep him pinned against a pillar with huge daggers while on the other half, in a bourgeois salon, the aging demon Tatiana introduces suitors to her young protégée Amusetta. Finally, the rites of initiation turn sinister when the smug new dandy Florestan Snakesnout is revealed as a fraud and a group of thugs with pincers and blowtorch begin to torture him.

Accused by critics of failing to integrate dialogue and action and of giving his characters only digressions to speak, based on whatever came into his mind on the subjects of philosophy, culture, aesthetics, or mathematics, Witkacy replied, "I do not use the stage as a means for propagating my ideas, which I present in separate theoretical works in a purely conceptual, not symbolic, fashion. These ideas enter my plays involuntarily and never fully defined or exactly articulated." Yet the playwright does concede that the denouement of *The New Deliverance* can be seen as having ideological implications as well as formal coherence, suggesting "the triumph of the organized masses over the remnants of former individualism and self-devouring bourgeois civilization." Even if the characters voice his thoughts and quote his works, Witkacy argues that such conversations can be artistic links in the action, or even the action itself, and that physical movement is not necessary. The play of ideas as artistic forms thus takes the place of pragmatic talk "about emotional states, the market, and the price of textiles and the sewage system."

W małym dworku (In a Small Country House, 1948), a play of realistic tendency written in 1921, transposes the central Witkacian device of the risen dead to the familiar small world of the domestic triangle (usually avoided by the author). For that reason it has proved popular with Polish actors and audiences. The play takes its title and points of departure in setting, character, and situation from Tadeusz Rittner's *W małym domku* (In a Little House, 1904), a psychological study of a seduced wife and a jealous husband who shoots the unfaithful spouse and then himself. In 1920 the Polish actor's studio, Reduta, fiercely dedicated to Stanislavsky's realism, revived Rittner's play with great success. Witkacy's answer to this kind of drama consisted of undercutting its seriousness by reviving the dead wife at a séance conducted by her two adolescent daughters and letting her resume her former life, arguing with her husband and lovers about the true circumstances of her death.

The final act of *W małym dworku* pushes to paradoxical extremes the playful warping of life and death perimeters. First, the ghost—a kindhearted Medea—persuades her daughters to drink a mysterious dream-inducing liquid, actually a poison that transforms them into corpses. Then, in a wordless epilogue added in 1925, when the play was staged in Zakopane at the amateur Formist Theater (organized by the playwright and friends), the two children rise from their beds and follow their mother. To puzzled critics the playwright explained, "The mother as ghost—having seen the full horror of

life in that country house—prefers to take her daughters with her to the other world."

Witkacy created a grotesque theater of death dominated by the figure of the risen dead. Polish modernism had also been obsessed with thanatos, celebrated as a solemn rite of passage in the Eleusinian mysteries and in the Christian cycle of crucifixion and resurrection, as in the plays of Stanisław Wyspiański (1869–1907). While admiring the formal patterns in these works, which were the Polish avant-garde of his adolescence, Witkacy felt that the religious beliefs once animating the myths were long since dead. Transcendence gone, there is no heaven or nirvana, only the ultimate tedium of dying and being born. By a process of desacralization and acceleration, Witkacy rendered the patterns of death and rebirth nonchalantly brutal and ludicrous, creating what he called "comedies with corpses." No longer conclusive but instead repeatable, death is no more than a sarcastic spasm robbing man of any pretensions to greatness or heroism.

One of Witkacy's most complex realizations of Pure Form, *Kurka wodna* (*The Water Hen*, 1962), written in 1921, presents the spectator with pictures that constantly disintegrate, ever-shifting configurations of elements lacking any fixed viewpoint or single frame of perception. Characters do not inhabit the same space or move at the same tempo because time and place have grown various and variable and are in ceaseless motion. The displacements of setting, unnatural groupings, startling juxtapositions, equivocal presences, and enigmatic figures lost in a void are all aspects of what the critic Kenneth Burke in his *Dictionary of Pivotal Terms* (1937) calls "perspective by incongruity."

As the play opens, Edgar, in eighteenth-century costume, shoots the woman known as the Water Hen, who stands in a chemise under a gaslight before an open field by the seashore. Gradually this illimitable space becomes enclosed and peopled by an entire world of relationships that imprison the hero but fail to define him. Burdened with a father, wife, son, and several usurping doubles, Edgar can find no place in a world going increasingly awry. Finally, as revolution breaks out in the streets, the baffled antihero again kills the Water Hen, who has risen from the dead, and then blows out his own brains.

Where social and communal bonds have broken down, resulting in the creation of a theatricalized society, there remains only the adoption of poses and the making of gestures. Edgar is an actor trying out different ways of playing his part, but he is not sure for which role he has been cast or even what kind of play he is in. Uncertain of what they should feel or how they should behave, the Witkacian protagonists are in search of an acting style that will be convincing and justify their existence; Pure Form offers no single model, only a plurality of conflicting styles and modes. These roleless pretenders quote other authors and borrow lines and structural elements from other literary and dramatic works in a desperate attempt to sustain a performance that degenerates into parody.

In *The Water Hen* Witkacy develops the notion of culture as refuse, detritus from previous ages, a heterogeneous mass of shards and fragments that fails to coalesce. The ersatz concoctions and artifacts of modern pseudo-civilization lie everywhere in disarray. The stage of Edgar's life is littered with leftover costumes and ideas, old forms taken out of the theatrical storeroom, scraps of words already spoken, feelings already felt, which reduce him to the role of marionette. Since he cannot find himself, Edgar must perpetually change and become someone else. Such a provisional world cannot last long, and history is racing ahead out of control, no longer progressing in a straight line according to recognized laws. Revolution erupts suddenly as an act of spontaneous combustion, unplanned and unforeseen, revealing the unknown in all its violence and primordial destructiveness. Denied its identity, mankind plunges into the unpredictable.

At a time when the Italian and Russian futurists celebrated the machine and the German expressionists warned of the dehumanization of the masses through industrialization, Witkacy followed a different path in portraying the inner anxieties and afflictions brought about by the alliance of the technological and scientific revolutions with the superstate. The mechanization that the Polish playwright feared was psychological: the implanting of thought-control machines in men's minds, machines figuratively likened to clocks, seismographs, and self-monitoring mechanisms.

Oni (*They*, 1962), a drama "in two and a half acts" from 1920, undesignated as to tendency, is the first of a series of plays about society's tyranny over the individual. In an inauthentic world of lying, where ability to sway the masses is the ultimate measure of power, the tyrant-actor finds a stage on which to substitute bogus impersonation and mystification for the true feeling of the mystery of existence. Mankind is no longer sure who controls its fate and actually runs the world. The individual lives in constant dread of a masked power structure whose real identity and operation are unknowable given the manipulation of appearances. THEY—a ubiquitous and protean band of grotesque characters—are the secret government within the government who have usurped power and are determined to reform mankind by means of strict regimentation and the suppression of art.

The Chairman of the League of Absolute Automation, Seraskier Banga Tefuan is a creative artist turned authoritarian ideologue. He now writes avant-garde plays so absurd that they will help destroy that last refuge of decadent individualism, the theater, and he stages a masked ball at which THEY demolish the art collection of the aesthete Callisto Balandash, who goes to jail confessing to a crime he did not commit: the murder of his actress-mistress. Those who would do away with theater as art establish their own stage machinery in life. THEY, a bizarre mixture of extreme left- and right-wing fanaticism and paranoia, demonstrate the relativizing of political categories (as well as of life and death) in a dramatic universe freed by Pure Form from old-fashioned coordinates.

In *Gyubal Wahazar, czyli Na przełęczach bezsensu* (Gyubal Wahazar; or, Along the Cliffs of the Absurd, 1962) of 1921, which Witkacy called a "non-Euclidean drama" of formalist tendencies, the hero is absolute dictator of a sixth-dimensional political realm where Newtonian physics have been replaced by Albert Einstein's theory of relativity and Georg Cantor's theory of sets. Known as "His Onlyness," Wahazar is obsessed with the problem of the one and the many, seeing himself as a martyr to his people, whom he hopes to restore to the primal unity of the beehive, anthill, and hornet's nest. The dictator's subjects are only extensions of his thoughts, but by encompassing all those who are his instruments, he has become no more than the sum of these parts and is therefore replaceable. Morbidetto, head of the secret police, assassinates His Onlyness, whose glands are cut out by Dr. Rypmann, the scientist-technocrat managing reality behind the scenes, and are transplanted into the senile cult leader, Father Unguenty, who then, in a variant on the returning corpse, becomes Wahazar II.

In *Mątwa czyli Hyrkaniczny światopogląd* (*The Cuttlefish; or, The Hyrcanian World View*, 1923), written in 1922, Witkacy forecast the histrionics of totalitarianism in his dramatization of the performance aspects of the modern dictator who, by invented language and hyperbolic gesture, forges a new reality in the manner of a poet or mythmaker. Unspecified as to mode, *The Cuttlefish* aspires to Pure Form in its synthetic setting and disparate assemblage of figures. Against a black wall with a blood-red window that lights up occasionally, an animated statue, a Renaissance pope risen from the dead, and a contemporary artist, Paul Rockoffer, discuss worldviews with the Nietzschean strongman Hyrcan IV, creator of the imaginary kingdom of Hyrcania. For the hardier members of Witkacy's dramatis personae, performance and transformation are means of survival and freedom. They change masks and practice metamorphosis by flinging themselves into violent social upheaval; coup d'état becomes coup de théâtre. Thus the painter Rockoffer shoots the would-be superman and becomes Hyrcan V, a new breed of tyrant who hopes to unleash the creative powers of artistic revolution.

The last play listed in *Teatr* and the summation of Witkacy's accomplishment to this point, *Wariat i zakonnica* (*The Madman and the Nun*, 1925), written in 1923, deals with the tyranny of society over the individual in the form of psychiatric imprisonment. Equipped with a spectacular risen corpse that violates the laws of biology, the play is nonetheless realistic in tendency, as specified by the author, because the coherent setting and homogeneous cast of characters accord with traditional dramatic conventions.

Witkacy always felt threatened by insanity, which he regarded as an expression of rebellious individuality, and *The Madman and the Nun* (the title taken from an earlier painting exhibited in 1921) presents the creative personality as victim of cultural repression when science is used pragmatically to promote adjustment to the group. In *The Genealogy of Morals* (1887) Nietzsche refers to the social straitjacket by which man is made to conform and Witkacy's decadent poet and drug addict, Walpurg, exemplifies the destiny of exceptional beings who are locked in a padded cell and trapped in ever-widening circles of incarceration by body, family, society, state, cosmos.

The Freudian psychiatrist Grün hopes to cure Walpurg by rendering him normal and sending him back to society, lobotomized of the madness that constitutes his genius. Answering charges that the play was a caricature of Freud's theory, Witkacy explained that he admired its diagnostic techniques but doubted its therapeutic value. "If I had wanted to criticize psychoanalysis and satirize it, I would have written a monograph on the subject," he said. The fettered poet (whose consciousness alone is free) and the psychic healer prying into the recesses of his brain are a complementary pair. Grün is both the observing self, voyeuristically watching the instinctual behavior of his alter ego, and the controlling self attempting to curb the explosive creative energies of his double. The doctor alternately provides Walpurg with paper and pencil—tools of creation—and binds his arms in a straitjacket, encouraging his art and yet restricting it. Grün reduces psychoanalysis to a mechanistic system for fabricating puppets ready for the ant-hill society. As the only way out of these deadly constraints the mad poet hangs himself, and as his corpse lies on the floor the elegantly dressed dandy Walpurg, become his former self again, enters the cell and bids farewell to his keepers, who are now locked up as insane. Witkacy's best coup de théâtre and stage trick (effected by substituting a dummy for the body), Walpurg's feat of dissociation, whereby he splits in two and leaves behind his outer shell, is deeply ambiguous. Has the artist created a new form for himself or merely accepted society's valuation of a stereotype? Are his suicide and escape a triumph of mind over matter or a step back on the treadmill of what Nietzsche calls Eternal Recurrence, leading him to relive the same dreary story? Pure Form (the modality of the final act) can offer multiple endings and accommodate contradictory meanings.

After the publication of *Teatr* in 1923, the pace of Witkacy's writing for the theater slackened; only five complete plays have survived, and four of them were written in the next two years. *Matka* (*The Mother*, 1962), written in two weeks at the end of 1924, is Witkacy's most accomplished feat of legerdemain with forms that are taken as the discards of civilization. Playing fast and loose with the conventions and medium of drama, the author pits content against form in a daring challenge and almost brings off the triumph of the latter, as *The Mother* moves from the deformed naturalism à la Ibsen of the first act, through the drug orgy of the second act, to the Pure Form séance of the epilogue.

Leon, a would-be genius at social thought, hopes to combat regimentation and preserve individualism but must live off his alcoholic mother, who supports him by knitting. In order to pursue his ideas in leisure the young hero becomes a spy and pimp and turns his wife into a whore. After a wild cocaine party, during which his mother dies of an overdose, Leon suddenly finds himself in a black box without doors or windows by the side of his mother's corpse. From among many risen dead who fill the stage there appears a young woman who is his mother twenty-four years earlier; pregnant with Leon in her womb, she rips the dead mother to pieces, revealing the corpse to be a dummy made of straw and rags. Leon is annihilated by six workers who climb out of a tube that comes down from the ceiling.

In this play social criticism (soon to be one of Witkacy's major occupations) is itself a performance: Leon's lectures at the Illusion Theater provoke audiences to riot. Leon moves from role to role; spying is a form of theater involving disguise and the playing of parts. But the forms that Leon adopts are old and at odds with his search for new solutions. In the epilogue all borrowed structures are discarded and conventions abandoned; the mother's corpse is only a stage prop, the mountain landscape a theatrical set. When make-believe is stripped away, what remains is not reality but artifice—in other words, Pure Form, the triumph over content. And yet at the final moment the descent of the workers (paradoxically the revolution from below comes from above) is the reintroduction of substance, the revenge of content, devouring Leon and his elite views about the revolt of the masses and the approaching end of civilization—old forms that will not endure.

Witkacy's final surviving play from the 1920's, *Sonata Belzebuba, czyli Prawdziwe zdarzenie w Mordowarze* (The Beelzebub Sonata; or, What Really Happened in Mordovar, 1938), written in 1925, deals with the dilemma of the modern artist impelled to self-destruction by his own creativity. Like Thomas Mann in the writing of his novel *Doctor Faustus* (1947), the composer-hero of which makes a pact with the devil in order to create a new type of music, the Polish playwright has gone to the compositions of Arnold Schoenberg and the legend of Faust as sources for his ironic dramatization of the conflict between art and life. In the present age the lonely artist has become a buffoon, and selling one's soul to the devil is transformed into a cabaret act in hell, perceived as a tawdry Budapest nightclub. The composer is only a medium to whom the dark, destructive forces can dictate "The Beelzebub Sonata." Once the work of creation has been accomplished, the artist is no longer needed and can hang himself.

The year 1924 was a turning point for Witkacy; henceforth content gained the upper hand over form. Having spent six years attempting to provide models for Pure Form in painting and theater without achieving any positive impact on the artistic community, the author turned to impure genres and activities in which he could express his ideas and incorporate his experiences directly. His interests in character analysis, psychology, philosophy, cultural and social criticism, and national issues are no longer contained by the "insatiable craving for form," but spill out into a dialogue with reality. Witkacy claimed to have fulfilled his purely artistic program, which in no way depended upon public acceptance. His shift to the practical and utilitarian can also be explained by a desperate financial situation that forced him to earn a living by his pen and brush.

Thus, in 1924 Witkacy forever renounced painting as a pure art (formal constructions on plane surfaces) in favor of portraits, done in pastels, a mimetic applied art and commercial activity that he viewed with self-irony by establishing a mock-capitalist enterprise, the S. I. Witkiewicz Portrait Painting Firm, whose "Rules" were published in 1928; "Any kind of criticism on the part of the customer is *absolutely* ruled out," was a basic principle. Clientele fell into three groups: paying customers (primarily society ladies and children); women with striking, asymmetrical faces whom Witkacy called mediums and repeatedly sketched; and friends for whom the artist did distorted portraits gratis at all-night sessions called "orgies" and "séances," where he conducted controlled experiments with drugs, recording the dosage on the canvas and writing reports on the effects (the rational mind always supervising the excesses of the imagination). Metaphysical, antisocial drugs like peyote and mescaline result in psychedelic portraits filled with geometric shapes, reptiles, and monsters, capturing the strangeness of existence.

In 1923 Witkacy had married Jadwiga Unrug, a match not of passion but a beautifully artificial construction, in the opinion of the playwright; she continued to live in Warsaw while he remained most of the year in Zakopane with his mother, writing to his wife almost daily, with spontaneous abandon, about his frustrations and hardships, fears of inevitable penury, and obsession with suicide. Although he often exhibited his psychic portraits, which are among his best work in any media, the artist found it demeaning that he had to travel to provincial towns in search of customers and was humiliated by having to go to people's houses for sittings, referring to himself as "the old portrait prostitute." Even when his sight grew poor he was reluctant to wear glasses, which might frighten clients.

In 1927 Witkacy published a major novel, *Pożegnanie jesieni* (Farewell to Autumn), which he had begun two years earlier. Maintaining that the novel is "a bag into which you can cram everything without paying any attention to Pure Form," the author turned to the writing of fiction because the sort of philosophical novel that he wanted to read did not exist. *Pożegnanie jesieni* traces the impact of three revolutions, each more drastic than the preceding one, on an alienated group of artists, intellectuals, and pleasure-seekers. The hero, Athanasius Bazakbal, is a pseudo-Hamlet, constantly questioning his own identity and unable to choose among his many underdeveloped talents, "going from writing poetry and prestidigitation to improvising on the piano and making up new culinary dishes." Lack of spontaneous creative impetus keeps Athanasius from saying, "I am an artist," and his friend the Bolshevik poet and commissar accuses him of making art out of life and wanting "to watch the revolution from the best seat in the orchestra as though it were a play—better still, to have it all staged by those new, self-proclaimed social artists who try to make a pseudo-artistic performance out of everything."

Whereas in the plays Witkacy embodies similar characters and actions in external shapes and formally conceived structures, in the loosely constructed novel he provides fully articulated patterns of causation and motivation, offering as omnipotent narrator penetrating insight into the protagonists' thoughts and feelings. In fiction as in drama, the Polish author reveals himself to be a brilliant analyst of collective states of mind in periods of social disintegration (when problems of personal identity and class identity coincide) as well as a sardonic observer of the mechanisms of power and the rise of the totalitarian state.

Nienasycenie (*Insatiability*, 1930), written between 1927 and 1929, is Witkacy's most ambitious and original novel, a speculative dystopian fantasy grown to monstrous proportions and grotesque extremes of deformation. The narrative presents a bewildered young hero's sexual and social initiation and private pursuit of the mystery of existence, all of which is interrupted by leveling historical events: the appearance of the mind-lulling Murti-Bing pill and the arrival of the Chinese Communists, the mobile yellow wall, which first lays siege to Whiteguard Moscow and then threatens Poland and the West. These strata of the novel are all but buried by a torrent of philosophical reflections on the difficulty of conveying what actually happened, so chaotic and problematic is the reality, and these epistemological digressions shift emphasis from storytelling to problems of representation: the impossibility of saying anything new, the exhaustion of fictional forms, the inability of language to convey experience, and finally the absence of anything to convey. In *Insatiability* the form of the novel starts to break down as the narrator, Witkacy, wrestles with the hopeless task of recording the amorphous, hallucinatory experience of contemporary life in Poland, a country lacking in coherence and heading toward the void.

To deal with national issues, which had been rigorously excluded from his formalist plays, the author now developed a new type of work, mixing philosophy, sociology, and psychology with personal confessions and anecdotes, grotesque vignettes, and chatty advice on matters ranging from shaving to hemorrhoids. The first two examples of this idiosyncratic Witkacian hybrid, which moves beyond traditional genres by erasing the boundaries between fiction and life, the creator and his creation, are the unfinished philosophical novel *Jedyne wyjście* (The Only Way Out, 1968), written from 1931 to 1933, and *Nikotyna, alkohol, kokaina, peyotl, morfina, eter* (Nicotine, Alcohol, Cocaine, Peyote, Morphine, and Ether, 1932). *Jedyne wyjście* is an extended discussion, often in dialogue, between two of Witkacy's alter egos, a painter and a philosopher, about the relative merits of art and metaphysics as a defense against the impending mechanization of life under the totalitarian regime in which they live. In a form of suicide, the artist finally cuts the philosopher's throat. The book on drugs, written in haste in the hope of making money, warns of the dangers of addiction (cigarettes and vodka destroy the ability of the brain to function clearly; cocaine leads to deep depression and suicide). Such artificial means offer no escape from the problem of existence in all its metaphysical horror. Constantly battling his own dependence on nicotine and alcohol, Witkacy knew that for him art would always be the most powerful narcotic. He had once considered art the noblest of drugs, without harmful side effects or hangover, but he increasingly came to view it as counterfeit and falsified.

STANISŁAW IGNACY WITKIEWICZ

Drawing upon Ernst Kretschmer's theories of psycho-physical types as well as upon Freudian psychoanalysis, *Niemyte dusze* (Unwashed Souls) is the culmination of Witkacy's interest in collective psychology and a merciless dissection of Polish national character. Published only fragmentarily in journals in 1936, these "Studia obyczajowe i społeczne" (Studies of Social Manners and Morals) accuse the author's fellow countrymen of caring only about appearances, playing stage roles in life, living in a world of mythmaking and illusion, and refusing simply to be themselves—all traits that served to create the Witkacian mask and that give rise to the theatricalized societies of his dramas and novels.

Witkacy's last surviving play, which he worked on intermittently for seven years and completed in 1934, is *Szewcy* (*The Shoemakers*, 1948), a vast and complex work for the stage that reflects the author's growing preoccupation with social and historical issues affecting Poland. Like the unclassified prose works from the same period, *The Shoemakers* is wayward and unruly, appearing to burst the seams of its own dramatic form. Characters speak the stage directions, the audience is directly addressed and insulted, and signs are lowered bearing the inscriptions "Boredom" and "Boredom getting worse and worse." Here the playwright brings to perfection his techniques of aggressive digression and provocative tedium and frustration.

A microcosmic vision of the totalitarian ideologies and cataclysmic forces about to overrun Europe, the unseemly drama, interweaving the cerebral, political, and sexual, unfolds on the small stage of the master shoemaker's workshop, where Sajetan and his two apprentices discuss philosophy and the evils of capitalism while the bourgeois Prosecuting Attorney Scurvy and the demonic aristocrat Irina carry on a perverse flirtation. Social classes have lost their true functions and can only attempt to rape each other verbally and physically. After an abortive fascist coup d'état from above and a futile socialist rebellion from below, the final revolution, signaling an end to all ideology, is brought about by passionless technocrats who institute a gray reign of uniformity with no place left for individuals or creativity—only mechanized work and trivialized sex.

In the last troubled years of his life, failing health, personal unhappiness, and gloomy forebodings about the coming world catastrophe made Witkacy declare, "I live constantly on the edge of the abyss." Only philosophy was a great consolation, and in 1935 his major philosophical work, *Pojęcia i twierdzenia implikowane przez pojęcie istnienia* (The Concepts and Principles Implied by the Concept of Existence), a system of biological monadology attempting to reconcile positivism and metaphysics on which he had been working since 1917, was published in an edition of 650 copies, of which twelve were sold. The Polish phenomenologist Roman Ingarden said of Witkacy, "He was more of a philosopher than many of those who looked down on him. He was a philosopher because he dealt with issues with which he lived, in which he was personally interested and which deeply moved him."

During the 1930's Witkacy was deeply involved with Czesława Korzeniowska, seventeen years his junior and, in his words, the only woman he had ever loved other than his mother. Regarding Korzeniowska as "a beloved daughter" and his own "creation," the writer was driven to suicidal fits of depression whenever she left him because of his frequent infidelities. To his friend the German philosopher Hans Cornelius, whom he revered as a father and enlisted to help patch up quarrels with Korzeniowska, Witkacy wrote in 1937, "My nerves are already ruined and I feel old age approaching. I led too intense a life and I never spared myself. . . . I feel that I didn't take full advantage of my capabilities and use up everything I had in me."

Despite his deepening pessimism and declarations that the end was coming, Witkacy attempted to revive the Formist Theater in 1938, hoping to stage some of his works, and he even wrote a new three-act play (now lost), *Tak zwana ludzkość w obłędzie* (So-Called Humanity Gone Mad), containing Ida Volpone, a fascist, as one of the characters. He also published an essay, "O artystycznym teatrze" (On the Artistic Theater). In June 1939, feeling himself no longer an artist—the one justification for his existence—he wrote to a friend, "I'm choosing death. . . . An asphalt road in the sun with trees, ending in a yellow gate after which there is only total dimness and nothingness."

When the world disaster he had so often foreseen struck, and the Nazis invaded Poland, Witkacy and Korzeniowska fled to the East along with thousands of other refugees. With a bad heart and weak legs, the writer was forced to stop in the little village of Jeziory, unable to go on. When on 17 September the Soviets attacked from the East, Witkacy committed suicide that night in a wooded grove by cutting his throat.

On a striking dark-red portrait that he painted in 1931 the artist wrote above his signature, "For the posthumous exhibit in 1955." The prediction proved accurate. Like one of his own heroes Witkacy rose from the dead to enjoy a second life after 1956 as the dominant figure in modern Polish theater.

Selected Bibliography

EDITIONS

INDIVIDUAL WORKS
Because many of Witkacy's plays and novels appeared for the first time in the posthumously published collected works, they are listed here in the order in which they were written. Dates in parentheses indicate dates of composition; publication dates follow place of publication.

PLAYS
Karaluchy. Zakopane, 1893.
Pragmatyści (1919). Poznań, 1920.
Mister Price, czyli Bzik tropikalny (1920). Warsaw, 1962.
Oni (1920). Warsaw, 1962.
Nowe wyzwolenie (1920). Cracow, 1922–1923.
Tumor Mózgowicz. Cracow, 1921.
W małym dworku (1921). Cracow, 1948.
Kurka wodna (1921). Warsaw, 1962.
Gyubal Wahazar, czyli Na przeczach bezsensu (1921). Warsaw, 1962.
Mątwa czyli Hyrkaniczny światopogląd (1922). Poznań, 1923.
Wariat i zakonnica, czyli Nie ma złego, co by na jeszcze gorsze nie wyszło (1923). Cracow, 1925.
Matka (1924). Warsaw, 1962.
Sonata Belzebuba, czyli Prawdziwe zdarzenie w Mordowarze (1925). Warsaw, 1938.
Szewcy (1934). Cracow, 1948.

NOVELS
622 upadki Bunga, czyli Demoniczna kobieta (1910–1911). Warsaw, 1972.
Pożegnanie jesieni (1925–1927). Warsaw, 1927.
Nienasycenie (1927–1929). Warsaw, 1930.
Jedyne wyjście. Warsaw, 1968.

AESTHETICS, PHILOSOPHY, AND CRITICISM
Nowe formy w malarstwie i wynikające stąd nieporozumienia. Warsaw, 1919.
Teatr. Cracow, 1923.
Nikotyna, alkohol, kokaina, peyotl, morfina, eter. Warsaw, 1932.
Pojęcia i twierdzenia implikowane przez pojęcie istnienia. Warsaw, 1935.

MODERN EDITIONS

INDIVIDUAL WORKS
Bez kompromisu. Edited by Janusz Degler. Warsaw, 1976. Includes "Demonizm Zakopanego."
Czysta Forma w teatrze. Edited by Janusz Degler. Warsaw, 1977.
Jedyne wyjście. Edited by Tomasz Jodełka-Burzecki. Warsaw, 1980.
Narkotyki. Niemyte dusze. Edited by Anna Micińska. Warsaw, 1979.
"Panna Tutli-Putli." Edited by Juliusz Żuławski. *Dialog* 2:34–54 (1974).
Pożegnanie jesieni. Warsaw, 1983.
622 upadki Bunga, czyli Demoniczna kobieta. Edited by Anna Micińska. Warsaw, 1976.

STANISŁAW IGNACY WITKIEWICZ

COLLECTED WORKS

Dzieła wybrane. 5 vols. Warsaw, 1962; rev. ed., 1985.

Dramaty. Edited by Konstanty Puzyna. 2 vols. Warsaw, 1972.

Pisma filozoficzne i estetyczne. Edited by Jan Leszczyński and Bohdan Michalski. 4 vols. Warsaw, 1974–1978.

PAINTINGS, GRAPHICS, AND PHOTOGRAPHS

Franczak, Ewa and Stefan Okołowicz. *Nie-czysta Forma. Witkiewicz i Głogowski fotografie.* Cracow, 1985.

Hommage á Witkiewicz. Düsseldorf, 1980.

Jakimowicz, Irena. *Witkacy, malarz. Warsaw, 1985.*

Presences polonaises. Paris, 1983.

Sztaba, Wojciech. *Zaginione obrazy i rysunki.* Warsaw, 1985.

Witkacy. Wiersze i rysunki. Edited by Anna Micińska and Urszula Kenar, Cracow, 1977.

Witkiewicz. Essen, 1974.

CORRESPONDENCE

Listy do Bronisława Malinowskiego. Edited by Tomasz Jodełka-Burzecki. Introduction by Edward C. Martinek. Warsaw, 1981.

Witkiewicz, Stanisław. *Listy do syna.* Edited by Bożena Danek-Wojnowska and Anna Micińska. Warsaw, 1969.

TRANSLATIONS

The Anonymous Work. Translated by Daniel Gerould. In *Twentieth-Century Polish Avant-Garde Drama.* Ithaca, N.Y., 1977.

Beelzebub Sonata: Plays, Essays, Documents. Edited and translated by Daniel Gerould and Jadwiga Kosicka. New York, 1980. Includes *Beelzebub Sonata, Tumor Brainiowicz,* and *Dainty Shapes and Hairy Apes.*

"Childhood Plays." Translated by Daniel Gerould and Jadwiga Kosicka. *yale/theatre* 5: 10–58 (1974).

The Cuttlefish. Translated by Daniel and Eleanor Gerould. In *A Treasury of the Theatre.* Edited by John Gassner and Bernard F. Dukore. New York, 1970.

"A Few Words About the Role of the Actor in the Theatre of Pure Form." Translated by Daniel Gerould. In *Twentieth-Century Polish Avant-Garde Drama.* Ithaca, N.Y., 1977.

Insatiability. Edited and translated by Louis Iribarne. Urbana, Ill., 1977.

The Madman and the Nun and Other Plays. Edited and translated by Daniel Gerould and C. S. Durer. Seattle, 1968.

The New Deliverance. Translated by Daniel Gerould and Jadwiga Kosicka. In *New Directions 30.* Edited by James Laughlin. New York, 1975.

"On a New Type of Play." Translated by Daniel Gerould and C. S. Durer. In *The Madman and the Nun and Other Plays.* Edited and translated by Daniel Gerould and C. S. Durer. Seattle, 1966.

"On Pure Form." Translated by Catherine S. Leach. In *Aesthetics in Twentieth-Century Poland.* Edited by Jean G. Harrel and Alina Wierzbianska. Lewisburg, Pa., 1973.

Tropical Madness: Four Plays. Translated by Daniel and Eleanor Gerould. New York, 1972. Includes *The Pragmatists.*

"Witkacy. An Album of Photos, a Bundle of Letters." Translated by Daniel Gerould and Jadwiga Kosicka. *Performing Arts Journal* 7:59–75 (1983).

BIOGRAPHICAL AND CRITICAL STUDIES

Cahier Witkiewicz. Edited by Alain van Crugten. 5 vols. Lausanne, 1976–1984.

Conio, Gérard. "Witkacy et la Crise de la Culture Européenne." In Witkiewicz, *Les Narcotiques.* Lausanne, 1980.

Crugten, Alain van. *S. I. Witkiewicz: Aux sources d'un théâtre nouveau.* Lausanne, 1971.

Danek-Wojnowska, Bożena. *Stanisław Ignacy Witkiewicz a modernizm: Kształtowanie idei katastroficznych.* Wrocław, 1976.

Degler, Janusz. *Witkacy w teatrze międzywojennym.* Warsaw, 1973.

———, ed. *Spotkanie z Witkacym: Materiały sesji poświęconej twórczości Stanisława Ignacego Witkiewicza (Jelenia Góra, 2–5 marca 1978).* Jelenia Góra, 1979.

Dialectics and Humanism. The Polish Philosophical Quarterly 12 (1985). Special Witkiewicz issue.

Dziechcińska, Hanna, ed. *Literary Studies in Poland/Études Littéraires en Pologne, XVI: Stanisław Ignacy Witkiewicz.* Wrocław, 1986.

Gerould, Daniel. *Witkacy: A Study of Stanisław Ignacy Witkiewicz as an Imaginative Writer.* Seattle, 1981.

Kotarbiński, Tadeusz and Jerzy Eugeniusz Płomieński, eds. *Stanisław Ignacy Witkiewicz: Człowiek i twórca. Księga pamiątkowa.* Warsaw, 1957.

Michalski, Bohdan. *Polemiki filozoficzne Stanisława Ignacego Witkiewicza.* Warsaw, 1979.

Miłosz, Czesław. "S. I. Witkiewicz, a Polish Writer for Today," *Tri-Quarterly* 9:143–154 (Spring 1967)

Pamiętnik Teatralny 3 (1969), 3–4 (1971), 1–4 (1985). Special Witkiewicz issues.

Polish Review 18 (1973). Special Witkiewicz issue.

Pomian, Krzysztof. "Witkacy: Philosophy and Art." *Polish Perspectives,* 13:22–32 (1970).

Przegląd Humanistyczny 10 (1977). Special Witkiewicz issue.

Puzyna, Konstanty. "The Genius of Witkacy (Stanisław Ignacy Witkiewicz)," translated by Bolesław Taborski. *Gambit* 9:33–34 (1979).

Sokół, Lech. *Groteska w teatrze Stanisława Ignacego Witkiewicza.* Wrocław, 1973.

Speina, Jerzy. *Powieści Stanisława Ignacego Witkiewicza: Geneza i struktura.* Toruń, 1965.

Studia o Stanisławie Ignacym Witkiewiczu. Edited by Marian Głowiński and Janusz Sławiński. Wrocław, 1972.

Szpakowska, Małgorzata. *Światopogląd Stanisława Ignacego Witkiewicza.* Wrocław, 1976.

Sztaba, Wojciech. *Gra ze sztuką: O tworczości Stanisława Ignacego Witkiewicza.* Cracow, 1982.

Sztuka 2–3 (1985). Special Witkiewicz issue.

Teatr 6 (1985). Special Witkiewicz issue.

Le théâtre en Pologne/The Theatre in Poland 3 (1970), 6–7 (1978), 10–12 (1984). Special Witkiewicz issues.

Theatre Quarterly 5 (1975). Witkiewicz issue.

Witkiewicz. Génie multiple de Pologne. Festival Witkiewicz (Brussels, November 1981). Edited by Alain van Crugten. Lausanne, 1981.

DANIEL GEROULD

DEZSŐ KOSZTOLÁNYI

(1885–1936)

BORN IN SZABADKA, a small town in southern Hungary (today its name is Subotica, and it belongs to Yugoslavia), on 29 March 1885, Dezső Kosztolányi came from a family whose background reflected the new social mobility in Hungary at the close of the nineteenth century. His father, Árpád Kosztolányi, the headmaster of the grammar school in Szabadka, came from a family that could trace its origins back to the late ninth century, when Hungarians settled in the Danube basin; his mother, Eulália Brenner, was of German bourgeois origin.

When he was four and a half, the young Kosztolányi was taught to read and write by his grandfather, who soon afterward taught him English as well. This grandfather, Ágoston Kosztolányi, had fought as a captain in the army of Kossuth between 1848 and 1849, and after the suppression of the Hungarian revolution he went into exile, first in Turkey and later, having spent forty-two days on a stormy Atlantic Ocean, in North America.

The art of Kosztolányi is firmly rooted in his early experience. Fully convinced that man's character is developed in childhood and that the memories of the first years are the chief source of artistic inspiration, he made much of his double social allegiance. Taking the long tradition of his father's family as an example,

he tended to regard historical continuity as a precondition of culture, while his awareness of the rise of the bourgeoisie made him incline toward pragmatism.

In his late autobiographical work, *Bölcsőtől a koporsóig* (From the Cradle to the Grave, 1934), he puts special emphasis on those elements of his family legacy that had exerted considerable influence on his formative years. His great-great-grandfather had left the family estate surrounding the village of Nemoskosztlány, in the northwest of Hungary (a territory that today belongs to Czechoslovakia), and settled in the south. Whatever motives he may have had for this decision, the world he left behind was strongly feudal—the only landowners in the village were the Kosztolányis, who lived in three old castles—whereas the region where he settled down had virtually no nobility at all. Capitalism developed relatively early in Szabadka, and the Kosztolányis had to adapt themselves to the new conditions. A captain in Lajos' army during the Hungarian revolution of 1848–1849, Kosztolányi's grandfather, Ágoston Kosztolányi, was forced to earn his living in exile after the suppression of the revolution. He worked as a manual laborer in Philadelphia, New York, and Boston. When compromise between the Habsburgs and the Hungarians made it possible for him to return to his country, he opened a dry-goods store. A man of strong character, he made choices for his only son in the spirit of utilitarian positivism: he urged him to study science and made him marry the daughter of a prosperous drugstore owner.

As a result, Kosztolányi felt much more at ease with the bourgeois way of life than most Hungarian writers of his generation. Still, the underlying problems of Victorian pragmatism and the resistance to a utilitarian view of human existence known to readers of Charles Dickens' *Hard Times* (1854), Samuel Butler's *The Way of All Flesh* (1903), or Thomas Mann's *Buddenbrooks* (1901) were not quite absent from the small world that surrounded the young Kosztolányi. His father had neither the vitality nor the good humor of Ágoston Kosztolányi, who had taught his grandson how to read and write and to speak English, and the death of the grandfather brought melancholy into the family. It became obvious that the ardent follower of Kossuth had ignored the happiness of his son when making decisions for him. Although attracted to poetry, the son had been compelled to study science. A brilliant pupil of Hermann Helmholtz in Germany, he was asked to become the distinguished scientist's assistant there, but his patriotic father brought him back to Szabadka, where he could have none of the facilities for research; instead, he became headmaster of a local school. Depressed by the provincialism of intellectual life in a small town, he took to drinking. For the young Kosztolányi, it was a humiliating experience to go to a school where the drinking habits of the headmaster—his own father—were a subject of student gossip.

Depression is the mental state most frequently expressed in the earliest writings of Kosztolányi. The diary published posthumously as part of *Kosztolányi Dezső* (1938), a biography written by the author's widow, shows him to have been an avid reader of Blaise Pascal. Around 1900 he was struggling with the ideas of death and nothingness and with the dilemma of choosing between cre-

ative activity to which the artist is driven by some inner necessity as opposed to work forced upon him from the outside; when playing the piano, which he learned to enjoy at an early age, he was constantly reminded by his grandfather of the need to earn a living. At the age of fifteen he received some money for his shorthand writing, and up to the very end of his life he worked very hard as a journalist. Aware of the gap between the bourgeois and the artist, he developed a double identity, and his antinovel *Esti Kornél* (Cornelius Nightly, 1933–1936) is, among other things, an expression of his split personality. Obsessed by fear of poverty even though he could afford a much higher standard of living than most Hungarian writers of his generation, he became one of the leading journalists of his time, but he felt only contempt for money-making, topical news, and writing that claimed to be socially useful. He raised journalism to a higher level than anybody else in the language, and it is thus no surprise that his newspaper articles collected in twelve volumes after his death are widely read today, yet those familiar with his best poems and fiction cannot help regarding his work in journalism as a splendid waste of energy.

Very early in his life, Kosztolányi found his alter ego in his first cousin József Brenner, who later used the pen name Géza Csáth and who became one of the early followers of Sigmund Freud and published a scholarly work, *The Psychic Mechanism of Mental Illnesses* (1911), and wrote short stories, some of which were translated into English under the title *The Magician's Garden and Other Stories*. The two cousins had much in common; they shared an interest in psychology and in music. Their first translations were the result of a joint effort, and striking similarities can be found in their early short stories. After a few years, however, the differences between their characters became quite obvious: less committed to solid bourgeois values, Csáth endorsed an almost unqualified anarchism, whereas Kosztolányi was struggling with the problems caused by his split personality. Both took morphine, but

Kosztolányi never became an addict, while Csáth's career as a psychiatrist was destroyed by his drug habit.

Both were precocious children, but only Kosztolányi developed the self-control characterizing most major artists. He started very early; in 1901 *Budapesti Napló* (Budapest Daily), one of the best dailies of the period, published his poem "Egysír" (A Tomb). In 1903 and 1904 he studied German and Hungarian at Pázmány University, in Budapest. The cosmopolitan world of the second-largest city of the Austro-Hungarian monarchy made a great impact on him. His outlook and his conception of art underwent a radical change. In Szabadka he had viewed both history and art from the national perspective and had been harshly critical of the influence of Vienna, whereas his new experience in Budapest made him aware of the provincialism of Hungarian patriots and alienated him from a didactic conception of art. He became a close friend of Béla Zalai, Mihály Babits, and Gyula Juhász. These three people played a major role in Kosztolányi's formative years. Juhász and Babits aimed at revolutionizing Hungarian poetry as Kosztolányi did, while Zalai's field was philosophy. Among the three, only Zalai, who died in a Siberian prison camp in 1915, had no part in Kosztolányi's later life. Yet even he exerted a profound influence on Kosztolányi's career. The latter never quite got over the loss of his friend, whose *Allgemeine Theorie der System* (General System Theory, 1913–1914), a phenomenological investigation showing a keen interest in the philosophy of language, may have been a source of inspiration for Kosztolányi's later speculations about the nature of language. As for Babits, their friendship in later years developed into an artistic rivalry that was fruitful for both poets.

Unlike his three friends, Kosztolányi never finished his university studies. Having given up the idea of becoming a high-school teacher, he wrote articles for the provincial papers *Bácskai Hirlap* and *Szeged és Vidéke*, and in 1904 he went to Vienna to study philosophy. To his dismay, he found the university in Vienna hardly less conservative than the one he had left behind in Budapest, but he must have profited from his experience of the city. It was probably during this stay that he heard about Freud for the first time.

In 1906 the poet Endre Ady was sent to Paris by *Budapesti Napló*, and the same daily asked Kosztolányi to replace his colleague as permanent contributor. Poems by Ady and Kosztolányi appeared in the same paper on alternate Sundays, and a rivalry that divided both writers and readers developed between the two poets.

The correspondence of Babits and Kosztolányi indicates that the publication of Ady's *Új versek* (New Poems, 1906) came to them as a great surprise. In sharp contrast to Ady's two previous volumes, it revealed him to be an innovator, although his rhetoric and pathos seemed to be a belated form of the Romantics' egotistical sublime and as such unpalatable to the two younger poets. In any case, before the appearence of Ady's third collection of verse, Babits and Kosztolányi could view themselves as the chief architects of reform in Hungarian poetry, whereas after the success of *Új versek* they had to change their plans and define their aims in a somewhat altered context.

The tension between Ady and Kosztolányi became known to the public when the latter's first collection of poems, *Négy fal között* (Inside the Walls, 1907), was published. Ady reviewed it in a condescending tone for *Budapesti Napló*, comparing Kosztolányi to Károly Szász, an ambitious translator and mediocre versifier of the third quarter of the nineteenth century. Although there are some good points made in his article—the volume is undeniably eclectic and uneven—Ady's overall judgment was unjust, because Kosztolányi's early poetry suggests at least as many, if not more, starting points for later development than Ady's rather conventional first book of verse. It took the younger poet more than twenty years to answer the attack, which he did in a devastatingly cruel but witty reevaluation of Ady's poetry that was published ten years after the death of his opponent.

One of the remarkable observations made by Ady regards Kosztolányi's attachment to poetry written in German. While Ady himself was influenced by Charles Baudelaire and Paul Verlaine and while Babits became infatuated with Algernon Swinburne and the English writers of the turn of the century, Kosztolányi's chief source of inspiration came from the Viennese *Sezession* and Rainer Maria Rilke. In 1909 he published a long essay on the Moravian-born poet, and he included several poems by him in *Modern költők* (Modern Poets, 1913), a collection of translations. The guiding intention of *Nyugat* (West), a monthly periodical started by the generation of Ady, Babits, and Kosztolányi in 1908, was not only to bring innovation into Hungarian poetry but also to make Western literature available to Hungarian readers. Paradoxically enough, Kosztolányi, who was convinced of the impossibility of translating poetry, became probably the most important translator of his generation. Having mastered German, English, Latin, French, Italian, and Spanish in quick succession, he could cover a much wider range of styles than any of his contemporaries. His exceptionally sensitive ear made it possible for him to re-create the individual style of such Shakespearean plays as *Romeo and Juliet, King Lear,* and *The Winter's Tale*; it also helped him find hidden resources in the Hungarian language through which to render the highly idiosyncratic in the work of many poets, from François Villon to Rubén Dario, from John Donne to Giuseppe Ungaretti, from Friedrich Hölderlin to Antonio and Manuel Machado, from Li Po to Jorge Guillén, from William Blake to Karl Kraus, from the authors of medieval hymns or Japanese haiku to Walt Whitman, Friedrich Nietzsche, William Butler Yeats, Stefan George, Paul Claudel, Christian Morgenstern, Filippo Marinetti, Alexander Blok, and Amy Lowell.

Yet for all Kosztolányi's passionate interest in the possibilities of extending the sphere of Hungarian poetic diction, no other poet exerted such a deep influence on his early work as Rilke. This is especially obvious in his second book of verse.

A szegény kisgyermek panaszai (The Laments of a Small Child, 1910) is a masterpiece of the Hungarian Secession and one of the most highly organized volumes of poetry in the language. An example of that almost exaggeratedly stylized cult of childhood of which Gustav Mahler's *Kindertotenlieder* (1902) is another characteristic manifestation, it presents a small boy's world vision of plenitude, in contrast to adult life, which brings alienation and materialism. The child is more human because, not yet having learned how to conceal his defenselessness, he lives closer to the possibility of death. The very first words of the cycle, "As if he had fallen between the rails," take on a symbolic undertone, suggesting that man must live in constant fear of nothingness.

The whole volume is a kind of dramatic monologue in the sense that the poet speaks from behind the mask of a young boy. Romanticism is evoked with irony, and the double perspective is full of ambiguities. Seemingly innocent, the young child is possessed by violent emotions. His passionate love for his mother and his sadistic cruelty are portrayed in a way to suggest that Friedrich von Schiller's antithesis is no longer relevant: the naive is the sentimental—that is, the sophisticated.

A szegény kisgyermek panaszai immediately attracted the notice of both the critics and the general reader. The new parts added to it in the later editions did not spoil its unity, but testify to a stylistic development toward expressionism. The passage starting with the words "the sunflower, as a lunatic," for instance, presents the reader with the vision of a yellow flower seen from the window of a train so that it appears to be running fast and in passionate love with a frightening and drunken sun. The lyric self has become subordinated to an impersonal vision, and the decorative adjectives characteristic of the earlier passages are replaced by metaphoric verbs expressing violent emotions.

Since none of the parts in Kosztolányi's second volume has a title, montage plays an important role in its structure. The same device is dominant in *Őszi koncert* (Concert in Autumn, 1911), a semidramatic work. From the beginning of his career Kosztolányi had a strong inclination toward further experimentation with structural principles that seem to be of only secondary importance in his earlier works.

The war years, however, delayed his artistic development. From the moment his cousin Csáth and his younger brother enlisted, he lived in constant anxiety, and the death of his friend Zalai was a great blow to him. Being an advocate of bourgeois values and of the multiparty system, he could not sympathize with the first Hungarian Commune, which followed the war in 1919, or with the peace treaty of Trianon signed in the next year, by which Hungary lost more than two-thirds of its territory. These events brought disastrous consequences for him: Csáth committed suicide; Árpád Kosztolányi lost his job after forty years of service; and the younger Kosztolányi found himself cut off from both his sixty-three-year-old father and his native Szabadka, which from now on belonged to another country.

It hardly needs to be said that there may be some connection between these painful experiences and the sense of uncertainty that cuts so deep in the works Kosztolányi wrote during the war years. The short story *Káin* (Cain, 1916), an ironic parody of the biblical story, is the most explicitly anti-Christian work ever written by him and reflects the influence of Nietzsche's nihilistic critique of Christian morality formulated in *The Will to Power* (1901). No less strong is the irony in "Boldog, szomorú dal" (A Happy, Sad Tune, 1917), the first poem in the collection *Kenyér és bor* (Bread and Wine, 1920), although in this case there is a hint that the loss of transcendence may involve a devaluation of human existence.

Material progress goes hand in hand with spiritual impoverishment. Such is the idea underlying *A bús férfi panaszai* (The Laments of a Man of Sorrow, 1924), which its author intended to be a counterpart of his earlier cycle of poems. Although this volume as a whole is more uneven than its predecessor, there are parts in it that reveal the poet's consummate artistry in manipulating the relation between various textual segments. An extreme case is the passage starting with the words "I am thirty-two years old now." The first nineteen lines are in the present tense and give no more than a flat, complacent, uninteresting description of the speaker's happy state of mind, the result of what he has achieved in his life. After a single line, a brief remark still in the present tense although referring to the future, the first nineteen lines are repeated, but the present is replaced by the past tense. The slight changes result in a radical change of perspective: presence is transformed into absence.

Both cycles written by Kosztolányi have a strong narrative element. Their author had taken a serious interest in storytelling from the very beginning of his career, but it was not before the 1920's that he emerged as a major writer of fiction. Until the end of the war he did not aspire to become a novelist, and even *A rossz orvos* (The Bad Physician, 1921) is no more than a novella, somewhat resembling the narrative works of Csáth, whose principal abiding interest was case history. The anecdote about a couple who thoughtlessly call an incompetent doctor for their child because, although they cannot admit it to themselves, they want to get rid of the only fruit of their unhappy marriage, is indeed hardly more than an illustration of the workings of the unconscious.

Much more important is *A véres költő* (The Bloody Poet, 1922), the first of the four works that make Kosztolányi the best Hungarian novelist of the twentieth century. Written in a period when a strong reaction had set in against avant-garde experimentation and such traditional genres as the historical novel became fashionable, this novel may seem to be one of the works representing that vogue. But a less superficial reading reveals that its similarities with historical novels written after World War I are outweighed by Kosztolányi's attempt to examine the relationship between the spheres of the transcendental and the aesthetic.

True, the author made a close reading of Suetonius and Tacitus before he started writing his novel about Nero. Firmly convinced that history is a reinterpretation of the past in light of the present, he expresses his vision of the first Hungarian Commune in a chapter called "Revolution," which relates the events of a revolt against the Roman emperor. Though far from being a Marxist, he followed an idea similar to the one suggested at the very beginning of Marx's *The Eighteenth Brumaire of Louis Bonaparte* (1852): the revolution turns out to be a grotesque parody of an earlier event, the rebellion that led to the death of Julius Caesar. On that occasion, both the tyrant and his opponents had been of tragic magnitude, whereas the rebels with whom Nero fights are by no means superior to himself.

Kosztolányi goes out of his way to assert that circumstances turned Nero into a monster. To make his hero appear more human, he ignores several facts recorded by historians. In his novel the emperor does not force a homosexual relationship upon his opponent Britannicus, the son of the previous emperor, and he does not set Rome on fire. In the first chapters he is an innocent boy, horrified by the scene in which his mother, Agrippina, poisons her husband, the emperor Claudius. When put on the throne by his greedy and ambitious mother, he feels nothing but solitude; political institutions are alien to him. Little by little, however, he comes to realize that what seems to be mysterious is in fact nothing else than a manifestation of mean-mindedness. The chaos in his soul is presented as a reflection of the anarchy surrounding him. First manipulated by Agrippina, he later learns how to use her weapons. Agrippina, Britannicus, and Seneca must die one after another once the hero has lost his sense of any higher principle that might control human actions. Nero is shrewd enough to see that the leaders of the revolution can only bring about a new form of tyranny. It is a supreme irony that even Seneca is presented as

vulnerable to the destructive forces driving the emperor. As Nero's teacher, he is, after all, largely responsible for the formation of the emperor's character. The philosopher's life is at odds with his Stoic principles, a conflict that suggests that he cannot live up to his ideals, and Nero feels a kind of bitter satisfaction when Seneca calls Britannicus a traitor after having received the dead man's property as an imperial grant.

In this novel tyranny is treated as a crisis in public mentality and not susceptible to rational analysis. Nero's madness is the manifestation rather than the cause of the general state of things. If he is menacing, he is so because he seems to be one of us. The narrator does not show contempt for him and never suggests that his hero is inferior to himself or to the reader. There is only one character who apparently belongs to a superior level: Britannicus. While all the other figures have interior monologues, he is seen only from the outside, through the eyes of the others. He is the only being of whom the emperor is afraid. At the end of the novel, before his own death—which appears to be almost a mere accident in this chaotic world—Nero is still talking to the spirit of Britannicus. The barrier between them seems to be insurmountable to the emperor; that is why he has the impression he has not succeeded in destroying the son of Claudius.

The novel is partly about action and creation. Britannicus is a born poet and an entirely passive man, whereas Nero is a would-be artist who cannot understand that poetry cannot be written by a man of action. One of the funniest chapters is about a competition of actors in which the emperor is to win the first prize. Although the audience is given detailed instructions and is closely watched by members of the secret police, the emperor is paralyzed by stage fright and can hardly start his miserable performance. His naive cult of theatricality is a far cry from the highly sophisticated poetry of Britannicus, written in solitude. Yet it would be misleading to assume that the contrast made between the two characters is based solely upon an opposition between the contemplative and the active life. Kosztolányi certainly rejected any utilitarian approach to art. Believing that it was neither the poet's business nor within his competence to change society, he associated the utopia expressed in Ady's political poems with artistic flaws. When creating his Britannicus, he undoubtedly asserted his antididactic view of art, but he also raised a question about the possible relation of creation to a sense of the transcendental. There is a hint in the novel that the son of Claudius, the author of short, cryptic poems, may converse with a world that transcends the human sphere. If this is so, Kosztolányi's novel about imperial Rome may represent an early stage in its author's painful struggle with the implications of a post-Nietzschean world; it may ask whether man can live without the idea of a higher form of existence.

A similar problem is raised in *Pacsirta* (Skylark, 1924), a somewhat shorter novel. The title is a pet name given to a spinster by her parents, and the action takes place in the small town Sárszeg, a caricature of Kosztolányi's native Szabadka. On a certain Friday, in the last year of the nineteenth century, Skylark takes a train to visit some relatives, leaving her parents behind. Unhappy away from home, she is impatient to return after a week. For some reason or other, her train is late, and her father secretly hopes she has met with a fatal accident; but she arrives safely and is escorted home by her dear parents.

At issue here is not merely a portrayal of the unconscious. While it is true that Skylark's absence has a liberating effect on her father—it dawns upon the elderly Vajkay that the attachment to his daughter has made it impossible for him to have his own life, and thus he begins to hate her—the circular pattern suggests a more general meaning; it questions teleology.

On the one hand, the book is a psychological novel focused on Ákos Vajkay, whose lack of skill in verbal communication runs counter to the almost unfathomable depth of his inner life. At this stage of his career, Kosztolányi was a close friend of the psychoanalyst Sándor Ferenczi, and he criticized James Joyce's *Ulysses* (1922), as did Robert Musil in his *Tagebücher* (Diary, 1955), on the ground that interior monologue could only scratch the surface of psychic life because its deeper level was preverbal. While his daughter is away, Vajkay visits the local casino, where he is surrounded by people whose verbosity is in direct proportion to their superficiality. In the world of this novel communicativeness is opposed to depth of character.

On the other hand, the book has wider implications. The futility of the activity of the casino becomes symbolic of a mentality without any sense of purpose. This nihilism is presented in the novel as a feature characteristic of the Habsburg monarchy at the turn of the century. The members of the casino are old, not so much in a biological sense as in the sense that they have given up all expectations; they are in a psychological state that makes it impossible for them to seek meanings in events. Living in pure duration, which has neither end nor aim, they are attracted to an almost perverse denial of purposive behavior. Their hero is Werner, a Moravian lieutenant who has not learned a single word of Hungarian during his four-year stay in Sárszeg and who will be remembered chiefly for the incident in which he gets dead drunk, takes a steam bath in full uniform, and goes for a walk dripping wet.

An advocate of alternative readings, Kosztolányi often provides more than one key for interpreting his novels. Besides being a psychological novel and a satire on the Austro-Hungarian monarchy, *Pacsirta* is also a narrative about man's relation to the Christian heritage. Although brought up by a grandfather who had fought for the independence of Hungary and hated the Habsburgs, by the time he wrote his novels Kosztolányi had become fully aware of the ambiguities of the dual monarchy, of social backwardness and intellectual innovation. At first sight, the members of the casino are ridiculed; on second thought, however, their sense of futility may be a kind of wisdom.

If this is so, the monarchy on the eve of the nineteenth century may represent a stage in the history of human thought in which people cease to believe that mankind has a task to perform, that it is moving as a whole toward some goal. The Sárszeg of 1899 is presented as an epitome of the posthistorical state, of a loss of aims and purposes that the whole world must face sooner or later. (The name *Sárszeg* suggests muddled thinking.)

Having left her parents behind, Skylark bursts out crying in the train that is taking her to the relatives she is going to visit. A young, handsome boy is eager to help her in the belief that she is unwell or has come to grief recently. Skylark reacts with impatience and even anger, while she seems grateful to her other fellow traveler, an old and poor Catholic priest, who shows complete indifference to her suffering. The meaning of this short scene is fully ambiguous. The priest's behavior may suggest that salvation is to be sought in the next world, whereas the heroine's attitude might indicate that human existence as such is of tragic character: compassion is pointless, because suffering cannot be eliminated; we live in constant anxiety in the face of nothingness. We are not at home in this world and cannot hope to find retribution elsewhere.

Love conceals hatred; what seems to be provinciality is in fact wisdom. Values are ambiguous in the world of *Pacsirta*, and the same is true of *Aranysárkány* (*The Golden Kite*, 1925). Both novels are about Sárszeg, and both have been made into films (directed by Lászlo Ranődy). Antal Páger, possibly the greatest artist on the Hungarian stage in his time, was cited as best actor at the Cannes Film Festival in 1964 for his portrayal of Vajkay.

Some critics have argued that Kosztolányi's nihilism implies that the world is ruled by accidents and that the biological is the only authentic mode of existence. Even a rather superficial glance at *The Golden Kite* makes it possible to challenge these views. This work, the most complex if not the best of Kosztolányi's novels, clearly shows how strongly he reacted against the positivism of the late nineteenth century. The suicide of the hero, Antal Novák, a grammar-school teacher, is highly motivated: the humiliation he must undergo—he is beaten by his former students who could not pass their final examinations, and his only child, Hilda, escapes from the paternal home—makes it clear to him that his conception of the world has been unduly rationalistic. It is too late for him to change; he must die because he is unable to view himself as a teleological being rather than as a static essence. He is treated by the narrator as someone not aware that the subjectivity of time uncovers the reality of the world at its most real.

There are at least three kinds of time interrelated in this novel. Everyday life in Sárszeg follows the rhythms of natural cycles. Some teachers may have come to the grammar school with high expectations only to find that the routine of the small town knows neither development nor discontinuity; it has room only for uninterrupted duration. The narrator's focus on Novák is justified precisely because he differs from his colleagues in the sense that he is aware of another form of time. In chapter 12, shortly before his daughter's romantic escapade, he is looking at some stars through his telescope, lecturing her about a cosmic *longue durée* quite frightening because it is indifferent to man.

By contrast, the third mode of temporality is emphatically human. Teachers, students, and merchants all have such different conceptions of time in this novel that they can hardly communicate with one other. Psychological time seems to be autonomous, and this is reflected in the idioms spoken by the characters: they use different languages, dependent upon individual sensibility and social, professional, and generational factors. Chapter 14, for example, is about the last day spent in school by students in their final year. The headmaster makes a speech, taking it for granted that life begins at the end of one's school years. While listening to his words, Novák disagrees; his conviction is that the last day spent at school marks the end of human life. What this scene seems to underline is that although only the present exists, it has no dimensions; only expectation and memory can have duration. For the students, the future gives the illusion of freedom; for the adults, the past represents an intimacy they have lost.

Much impressed by Nietzsche's critique of traditional principles of evaluation, Kosztolányi was fully convinced that things have no values in themselves; all evaluation is made from a definite perspective. The very title of the novel suggests this perspectivism. It refers to an object, a kite used by the students, but as a name it is ambiguous. Kosztolányi believed that language was never innocent, and he exploited the fact that the Hungarian equivalents for *kite* and *dragon* are homonyms (*sárkány*). The gold-colored kite is flying high up in the sky when seen by the professors going to school early in the morning on a certain day. Some view it as a bad omen, while others see it as no more than a toy. To reassure a superstitious colleague of the harmlessness of the golden "dragon," Novák mentions that he will speak about kites when teaching Benjamin Franklin's experiments with electricity, but the very word he employs—*istennyila,* a metaphor for *kite* literally meaning "God's arrow"—suggests menacing forces behind everyday reality, forces Novák fails to recognize.

Novák's fatal mistake is his ignorance of the role irrationality plays in life. His favorite composer is Robert Schumann, but he is quite unaware of the German composer's madness, as he is unaware of the chaos within himself. He is an excellent teacher of physics and mathematics, a first-rate chess player, and a man famous for his accurate weather forecasts, but he has neither a sense of humor nor a feeling for history. Viewing all younger people as pupils and regarding pupils as objects, he is unable to understand stupidity or passion. After his daughter has escaped with one of his favorite students and he has been beaten by those who could not pass their final examinations, all he can do is admit failure. The continuity he

has cherished all his life has no more relevance. Patriarchal authority, the basis for family life, has been undermined, as has tradition, the principle underlying education. He must realize that he has made a serious mistake when assuming the right to give purposes to other people.

When writing *The Golden Kite,* Kosztolányi turned his back on one of the most influential traditions of nineteenth-century novels, that of the bildungsroman or *Erziehungsroman* (novel of education). Kosztolányi's hero is viewed with tragic irony by the narrator, and the novel as a whole is a devastating critique of the positivism on which the writer had been brought up. The concept of time expressed in the book may have been influenced by Saint Augustine's treatment of present, past, and future in his *Confessions* (397–401), and it certainly shows analogies with Martin Heidegger's analysis in *Sein und Zeit* (*Being and Time,* 1927). Within-timeness is interpreted in terms of care, concern, and anticipation; durations have no length in the sense of a quantitative stretch; and world-time is treated as more objective than any possible object and also more subjective than any possible subject. In other words, the world created by Kosztolányi is governed not by the rules of biological life, as some critics have argued, but by those of *Dasein.* The ontological interest manifest in this novel contests the premises on which nineteenth-century ideas of character are based.

Just as Kosztolányi's poetry reveals an interest in the potential relations among different textual formations, so does his narrative prose. Antal Novák's fate is summed up when he remembers the words "Quem dii odere," the first part of a maxim that ends with "paedagogum fecere" (The gods hated him, so they made him a teacher). In *Pacsirta* a fictitious document creates intertextual relations: the heroine's letter to her parents is quoted in the text, and it gives an all-around, albeit indirect characterization of the miserable spinster. *The Bloody Poet* is headed by a few words from Tacitus and Suetonius, and a similar technique is followed in *Édes Anna* (translated as *Wonder Maid,* 1926); in this case the text is preceded by a Latin prayer, which gives a parabolic character to the story that follows.

The first chapter of Kosztolányi's fourth novel contains no more than a short anecdote about Béla Kun, the leader of the first Hungarian Commune. His regime has just fallen, and he is leaving Hungary in an airplane. A piece of jewelry slips out of his hand, drops, and is found by someone in a park in Buda. The last sentence of the chapter is full of irony, suggesting that the story may be pure fabrication.

To a certain extent *Wonder Maid* could be called a social, perhaps even a political novel. The story begins on 31 July 1919. Ficsor, the concierge in the house of Kornél Vizy, a civil servant, is eager to make his landlord forget about his behavior during the Commune. From March 21, when the Communists took over, through the end of July he had been a spokesman of the proletariat vis-à-vis the traditional middle class, but now he wants to do a service for Vizy to give the impression that he has never supported the Communists. Mrs. Vizy, a middle-aged woman who has turned bitter since the loss of her only child, is about to fire her maid, so Ficsor will bring her a new girl.

There may be something symbolic in the fact that Anna, the new maid, was born in 1900. In any case, her fate seems to suggest that the twentieth century is radically different from the previous century. The intimacy of domestic life and the optimism based on a belief in the victory of science and technology have been replaced by unresolved tensions. The peasant girl who seems to be a perfect maid murders Kornél Vizy and his wife after having been humiliated by Jancsi Patikárius, Mrs. Vizy's irresponsible nephew.

At the trial only one witness, Miklós Moviszter, an old and ailing physician, tries to defend Anna Édes. His arguments are those of a Christian liberal. He believes in God's mercy, a principle that also underlies the Latin prayer serving as a motto for the novel, and he blames the murdered couple for having used their maid as

if she were a machine. In the name of individual self-determination, he argues that she has not been allowed to marry or to quit.

Far from suggesting the possibility of any political solution, the novel portrays the relation between the oppressor and the oppressed as damaging for both sides. Anna is viewed from the inside as an inarticulate person who cannot understand her situation. The novel is a remarkable attempt to present a character who is hardly accountable because she is almost entirely unable to communicate. The crisis is delayed in a way that makes the tension almost unbearable, and Kosztolányi makes a powerful case for the idea that Anna is cornered by other human beings. She finds herself in a situation with no way out, and her defenselessness becomes symbolic of man's state in the world. Still, despite all its superb artistic qualities, *Wonder Maid* may be somewhat less complex than *The Golden Kite.*

Having finished *Wonder Maid,* Kosztolányi set about writing *Mostoha* (Stepmother, 1965), a novel about a young wife who does everything she can in order not to become the malignant stepmother known from fairy tales. But the traditional role is forced upon her by her husband's children as well as inadvertently by herself. For a while the author had weighed the possibility of developing a minor character for this novel whose name, Esti, meaning "someone belonging to or living in the evening," could suggest that his thoughts and emotions are those of someone advanced in years. Later on, however, he realized that Esti was not in conception a character in a traditional sense but rather an epitome of the ideas Kosztolányi developed on language in the previous few years. He left *Mostoha* unfinished and eventually started working on a new book (*Esti Kornél*) in which Esti is the main character.

During the 1920's linguistics gradually replaced psychology as Kosztolányi's chief interest. He developed an aversion to the use of foreign words and organized a purist movement. "It is possible to know a foreign language, but it is quite impossible to know it well. . . . My mother tongue is the only serious language for me," he wrote in 1922 in *Nyelv és lélek* (Language and Soul, 1971). In 1930 he sent a long letter to the eminent linguist Antoine Meillet, then professor at the Collège de France, and took issue with Meillet's complaints about the linguistic division of Europe made in his influential book *Les langues dans l'Europe nouvelle* (Languages in Contemporary Europe, 1928). Kosztolányi accused Meillet of considering thought prior to and separate from language. He regarded the French scholar as a belated exponent of the rationalism inherited from some seventeenth- and eighteenth-century thinkers who envisaged a universal language modeled on mathematics. In his essay "A tudomány nyelve" (The Language of Science, 1933), he insists on the interdependence of linguistic relativity and the aesthetic principle of organic form, and in a series of articles entitled *Túlvilági séták* (Walls Taken in the Next World, 1931) he goes as far as to claim that thinking is done only through language.

Undoubtedly it was his impatience with the view that style is of secondary importance in narrative fiction that led Kosztolányi to the assumption that language operated at the deepest level of human consciousness, and thus his speculations must be viewed as by-products of his artistic development. To justify his meticulous care for his prose style, he resorted to a linguistic reinterpretation of the Romantic concept of national character. In *Pár szó a nyelvújításhoz* (A Few Words on Language Reform, 1932) he not only calls language a social product but also maintains that each language must be regarded as a convention belonging to one particular community. In a longer essay on purism published in the same year ("Nyelvtisztítók és nyelvpiszkítók" [Purism and Abuse in Language]), he develops a conventional theory of meaning, and in an article that has the untranslatable title "Lge" (meaning both "word" and "verb," 1933) he takes pains to emphasize the contextual nature of connotations, defining context as a situation. In *A lélek beszede* (The

Language of the Soul, 1933) he goes even further, arguing that connotations are always historical phenomena and thus serve as a basis for the changing interpretations of any "given" text.

By the later 1920's Kosztolányi became fully convinced that different languages create divisions in the world and impose different value systems. Having posited correlations between linguistic structure and nonlinguistic behavior, he suggested that each language embodies or at least implies a highly specific metaphysics. His hypothesis that speech communities select, classify, organize, abstract, and evaluate experience differently somewhat echoes Wilhelm von Humboldt's ideas, which may have been known to him; it also resembles Benjamin Lee Whorf's assumption that thinking is a use of materials already patterned by one's mother tongue.

Politically, Kosztolányi's language-oriented cultural relativism involved an unlimited tolerance of all minorities. Aesthetically, it meant a radical historicism that in some degree anticipated Hans-Georg Gadamer's hermeneutics. The thesis that the worldview of each community differs from that of any other community because the specific internal structure of their respective languages conditions customs and beliefs led him to the formulation of a radically historical view of interpretation. In his confessional autobiography *Bölcsőtől a koporsóig* he takes African and American black music as examples of his claim that any convention seems to be natural for the members of the community in which it has evolved.

His theoretical insights and creative writing are clearly interrelated. "A holló" (The Raven, 1913) is his earliest essay containing a hint that the world picture may shift from tongue to tongue. It is a defense of his own translation of Edgar Allan Poe's poem. Twenty years later he formulated a more general justification of his practice as translator. In the essay *A tíz legszebb szó* (The Ten Most Beautiful Words, 1933) he distinguishes between translators working on the plane of the signified and those working on that of the signifier, indicating that he himself preferred to concentrate on the latter. As an essayist, he aimed at a kind of verbal analysis that anticipated the Hungarian structuralists of the 1960's. At a time when the Russian formalists developed methods of close reading, he was the only critic in Hungary to practice a similar approach to literature. Many of his essays on individual authors, foreign and Hungarian, early and contemporary, are textual analyses of individual works. In one of the earliest of these, "Tanulmány egy versről" (The Close Reading of a Poem, 1920), a full-scale examination of Wolfgang von Goethe's short lyric "Über allen Gipfeln," he sums up some of the principles underlying his organicist view of literature, ideas that closely resemble those of Stéphane Mallarmé, Paul Valéry, and Joyce. Comparing the literary artifact to a new word that is radically different from preexistent language, he speaks of the disappearance of the creator in his work and insists on the importance of all structural elements perceptible to the reader. In 1928, in the essay "Káté az irásról" (ABC of Writing), he ascribes similar characteristics to the novel:

> The truly creative writer presents things and disappears behind them. He never gives explanations. He can be influential only if he produces something sensible for us. He resembles creative nature. Neither argues or preaches. They simply exist. A brook can do without footnotes. The wood needs no epithets. A good narrator hides the depth of life and presents only surfaces. He knows everything but remains silent.
>
> (*Nyelv és lélek,* p. 455)

Whatever originality Kosztolányi may have had as a translator and as an essayist, the ultimate test of his insights into the relation between language and thought is in *Esti Kornél,* a work of narrative fiction based upon the assumption that language is not a means of communication but a mode of human consciousness. Written between 1925 and 1936, the year of the author's death, it represents a major shift

in emphasis: psychological authenticity is replaced by the ideal of a text that creates rather than reflects meaning. The first of the thirty-five disjointed chapters of this antinovel presents the title hero as the best friend of the anonymous narrator. Together they plan to compose a book that will have none of the conventional continuity of novels and will be based on the hypothesis that language speaks for us.

To some extent Esti can be called a second self of the narrator, a relation that suggests the psychological implications so obvious in Kosztolányi's earlier works. In her biography of her husband, the writer's wife suggested that the idea of writing *Esti Kornél* might have originated in the game Kosztolányi played with his own son. He pretended to have another child, "Kornélka," who was wicked, lived in the chimney, and ate lion flesh. Since Esti is portrayed as an anarchist and a bohemian, whereas his anonymous counterpart seems to be a bourgeois of good manners, it is also possible that Kosztolányi drew inspiration from his memories of his friendship with Csáth, who questioned bourgeois values with more daring than he himself ever did.

Interesting as the autobiographical and psychological implications may be, they can only help us explain the creative process rather than the finished work. Interpretation is made difficult by the fact that there is no close-knit structure. The chapters are loosely tied together, and the relation between the only constant elements, Esti and his anonymous friend, becomes problematical at the point when Esti becomes the narrator in approximately one-half of the chapters. Should his friend be regarded as a primary storyteller throughout the work? That question cannot be answered, because the concept of the stable ego is rejected by Kosztolányi. While the opposition between Esti's anarchist and his friend's conventional behavior seems to be clear at the beginning of the work, soon the distinction becomes blurred. On the one hand, Esti himself becomes a successful writer, respected by the society he wished to undermine in his youth; on the other hand, his avant-garde conception of narrating is realized not only in the stories related by himself, but also in those told by his friend. He openly rejects the ideal of a well-made plot and does not once pretend to tell what actually happened. He has no claim to traditional credibility; in one case, for instance, he tells us only what kind of an experience a certain person could have had, had he not died earlier.

Most chapters are retrospective and inward-oriented. At the outset Esti warns his friend that only a fragment can be worthy of a poet, and the work of which he is an alleged co-author certainly fails to meet the traditional criteria of continuity. Yet there are hints that the order of the chapters may suggest some kind of a pattern. Apart from the introduction, both *Esti Kornél*, published as a separate volume in 1933, and *Esti Kornél kalandjai* (The Adventures of Cornelius Nightly), printed as one of the five subtitled sections of *Tengerszem* (Tarn, 1936), Kosztolányi's last prose collection, contain seventeen chapters. This in itself raises the question of possible correlations between the two halves of the work. In the first half, the chapters are numbered, whereas in the second half they have subtitles, but the same metaphors are used throughout the whole work. In the eighth chapter of the first half, Pali Mogyoróssy, a journalist, turns mad and is taken to a lunatic asylum. The chapter ends with a scene in which Mogyoróssy finds himself in a building with endless corridors and no exit. Man's futile attempt to find a way out of a labyrinth seems to symbolize the act of dying. The mirror, a surface giving the impression of the infinite, a supreme value Esti misses in the world, is a metaphor for art. In the final chapter, "Az utolsó fölolvasás" (The Last Reading), the two key metaphors are combined. Having become a writer, Esti is about to read from his works for a distinguished audience, but he cannot find his way to the room where people are waiting for him. Lost in a building that seems to have no way out, he has a stroke and falls. His dead body is found fac-

ing a mirror as if he were still looking at himself.

This chapter has a counterpart in the last section of the first half of *Esti Kornél,* a chapter relating a seemingly very common incident. The hero takes a streetcar, but it is rush hour, and there is hardly any room for him to stand on the step. Little by little he can move inward, but by the time he can find a seat, the car arrives at the terminal. The very slow rhythm of the narrative, together with a system of connotations, suggests that the story can also be read as an allegory of life, with "getting off" as a metaphoric allusion to death.

There are many such correlations between the two halves of the work, and these suggest that artistic reasons prompted Kosztolányi not to publish the stories in the order in which they had been written. In the introduction the anonymous narrator recalls the first words of Dante's *Divine Comedy* (1321), and the sequence of the stories reveals that Esti's relation to his friend is somewhat similar to Vergil's relation to Dante. Esti is an interpreter of human fate; for him events are not more than a pretext for some generalization. Sometimes there is, in fact, hardly any story: in the long twelfth chapter the hero, Wilhelm Eduard von Wüstenfeld, a German baron who is president of all sorts of societies, is asleep from the beginning to the end of the session described, and in "Kézirat" (Manuscript) Esti discusses a novel he has not read at all. This work comes very close to the ideal of a plotless narrative, about which several writers, from Gustave Flaubert to Virginia Woolf, have dreamed.

As for the values underlying Esti's interpretations, first and foremost he respects the integrity of the human individual. At the age of eighteen, on his first trip abroad, when he is kissed by an insane girl with whom he is traveling in the same compartment, he is filled with the same compassion for the girl's mother that he later feels for whores or for his journalist colleague Mogyoróssy, who has gone mad and must be taken to a lunatic asylum.

As a born interpreter, Esti is a man of words

rather than of deeds. He can feel sympathy for different kinds of people because he has learned many languages and has seen many parts of the world. His perception is that mankind is characterized by diversity rather than by uniformity, that the limits of one's language are identical with the limits of one's world, and that the different languages represent different modes of behavior and ways of life. His relativism is also supported by his awareness of history as a process in which new values are created and old values destroyed and by his sense of humor, which makes it possible for him to see things in constantly changing perspectives.

In his view truth is dependent on belief systems, and the word *natural* has no meaning in the context of spatial and temporal relativism. Still, it would be misleading to call him a nihilist, because he does have a great respect for native cultures. He is a traveler whose life is sharply divided into two halves. As a young man, he delights in speaking many languages, thus always changing his perspective. As he grows older, he gradually becomes aware that unlimited freedom is an illusion and that not all values are accessible to him because the barrier between the alien and the familiar is insurmountable. In a somewhat paradoxical way, Kosztolányi's experimental work, which set an example for the generation of postmodern writers of the 1970's who broke out of the existing traditions of Hungarian prose, has a deep structure, one that may remind the reader of a very old tradition: the allegory of life as pilgrimage. Esti is a kind of prodigal son who has learned the lesson that it is futile to escape from home.

While working on *Esti Kornél,* Kosztolányi also tried to find new modes of expression for lyric poetry. The origins of his experimentation can be traced back to the longest section of *A bús férfi panaszai* (1924), composed in 1920, that is a kind of diary in unrhymed iambic feet about his son's diphtheria. Four years later, he started writing in free verse. Although *Meztele-nül* (Naked, 1928), the next volume of verse he published, is not great poetry, its historical significance and its role in Kosztolányi's artistic development cannot be questioned. Free verse liberated his diction from the sentimentality of some of his earlier poems and thus paved the way for his more objective late style.

In 1929 *A Toll* (The Pen), a left-wing periodical, sent a circular to prominent Hungarian writers, asking them to say how they would define the significance of Ady's work ten years after the poet's death. Kosztolányi's long pamphlet *Az irástudatlanok árulása* (The Treason of the Illiterate) was hotly debated from the very day it was published. What is more, it has continued to excite controversy ever since.

Few would deny that Kosztolányi was right to dismiss misinterpretations of Ady based upon the idea that literature is no more than an instrument of nationalistic propaganda. Besides, most of the poems he criticizes are undoubtedly inferior, so his pamphlet represents a healthy reaction in the sense that it warns readers against an indiscriminate praise of all the poems written by Ady. Still, it would be misleading to deny that Kosztolányi's aim was not only to criticize specific poems but also to effect a radical devaluation of Ady's poetry as a whole. His conclusion that Ady is a minor artist whose importance is limited to some first-rate poems is far-fetched; but Kosztolányi's implicit intention was to emphasize the distance between Ady's work and his own. In this sense, his attack on the older poet was justified, especially since it was made at a time when Kosztolányi was trying to create an idiom radically different from Ady's.

Számadás (A Summing Up, 1935), Kosztolányi's last collection of verse, was published as the final selection in his *Kosztolányi Dezső összegyűjtött költeményei* (Desző Kosztolányi's Collected Poems, 1935). It contains ninety-six poems and is certainly one of the great volumes of poetry in Hungarian. As in the case of *Esti Kornél,* or *A szegény kisgyermek panaszai* for that matter, Kosztolányi made an elaborate design when he rearranged the poems, which were written over a period of time. The sequence of seven self-addressing sonnets, which gives its title to the volume as a whole, recalls the world of *Esti Kornél* insofar as it expresses compassion for those who have been humiliated and questions the identity of the speaker. The interrelations between Kosztolányi's antinovel and his last collection of verse are further emphasized by the poem "Esti Kornél éneke" (The Song of Cornelius Nightly). If *Az irástudatlanok árulása* is a kind of negative ars poetica, the same can be said about this poem. In this case, the poet whose work is treated with reserve is not mentioned by name, but both external and internal evidence suggests that "Esti Kornél éneke" is an attempt to take issue with the highly moral conception of poetry put forward by Babits.

When *Esti Kornél* was published, Babits wrote a fairly unfavorable review of the book in *Nyugat,* the periodical with which both poets had been associated for twenty-five years. While Babits was a highly serious poet and critic, he had an imperfect sense of humor and a rather conservative taste in narrative fiction. The main charge he brought against the work being that it was not a novel, he appeared to have failed to understand its guiding intention. His criticism may have aroused the indignation of the author, who had been his close friend in the past. In response to the review, Kosztolányi defined his ideal of the good work of art. Comparing the poem to a riddle, he insisted that its surface should be sophisticated and resistant to superficial approaches. Style must be governed by economy, "a semblance of depths," as Esti puts it in the poem named after him.

Economy is indeed a characteristic feature of Kosztolányi's late poetry. An extreme case is "Októberi táj" (October Landscape), a three-line text. Having translated many Japanese poems, he wished to create something so terse that it would remind the reader of the haiku form. Like its models, his poem contains a vision of a season and sentences that are joined without any apparent causality. What makes his poem unique is the way he hints at the interrelations between the human and the natural world. In the first line, the adjective "véres" (bleeding) suggests the intrusion of the human element, whereas in the other two lines synaesthesia, as in "sárga csöndbe" (in a yellow silence) and "lángoló igék" (flaming verbs) warns the reader that the vision presented is seen through human eyes blurred by passionate emotions.

A similar tension can be felt in the fifteen-line poem "Vörös hervadás" (Red Withering). The title itself, an oxymoron suggestive of both life and death, contains in embryo the paradox elaborated in the poem: existence is made meaningful by the nothingness that follows it. Autumn may suddenly be transformed from a symbol of plenitude to one of alienation, as "Őszi reggeli" (Breakfast at Fall), the ten-line poem immediately following "Vörös hervadás," further suggests. (These poems can be found in *Számadás.*)

Tragedy is treated as a source of the creation of supreme values in Kosztolányi's last collection of verse. The twelve-line poem "A vad kovács" (The Wild Blacksmith) presents suffering as the only way toward knowledge, and a similarly stern interpretation of human existence is expressed in other poems. In 1933 Kosztolányi discovered a tumor in his mouth, which he immediately associated with cancer. (He had cancer of the gum.) This may have strengthened his preoccupation with death and with Stoicism, although both had been permanent characteristics of his work from the beginning of his career.

If there is a difference between his earlier and later Stoicism, it must be ascribed to a shift in emphasis: while in the early 1920's he had been an avid reader of Seneca, by the second half of that decade he developed an interest in the ideas of Marcus Aurelius, the Roman emperor whose *Meditations* were composed between A.D. 170 and 180 in Pannonia, a territory that later became part of Hungary. One of the four pieces in *Latin arcélek* (Roman Profiles), a section in *Tengerszem*, Kosztolányi's last prose collection, is about Aurelius, who maintained that principles could never be realized in practice, that injustice could thus never be eliminated, and that it was futile to seek vengeance. The poem "Marcus Aurelius," one of the earliest pieces in the volume *Számadás*—it was written four years before Kosztolányi discovered his illness—is about the man who was both an artist and a moral thinker. The point Kosztolányi makes here is that the emperor was fully aware of the moral ambiguities inherent in civilization, yet he was ready to fight against virtuous barbarians because they were ignorant. Marcus Aurelius is praised in the poem for his inquiring mind and his strong intellect, which makes him aware that he must be prepared to come to grips with death.

He is called a "beggar emperor," and man's position in existence is summed up in this oxymoron. It suggests that life must be viewed from the perspective of death, in which all human beings are equal. All individuals take on true moral significance at the moment of death because the disappearance of any human being from this world involves the loss of an autonomous world. This idea underlies "Halotti beszéd" (Funeral Oration), written in imitation of the style of a piece of twelfth-century Hungarian prose.

"Hajnali részegség" (Daybreak Drunkenness), the penultimate poem in *Számadás,* is a long meditation on transcending the limits of a post-Christian sense of being. At the outset the lyric self is speaking to the reader as to a fellow traveler about the monotony and pointlessness of everyday existence. Unable to sleep, he looks out the window and watches people lying in their beds, closed up in flats that resemble boxes or cages. The lack of any telos is further emphasized by a vision of the speaker's home as it might be after a hundred years, in ruins with weeds growing in the cracks, when "no one can tell whether it had been a home or a pigsty." Still, as the speaker looks up at the starlit sky, he suddenly becomes aware of a world that is radically different from the waste-land of living from day to day. The suggestion that the awareness of this superior form of existence has been lost since childhood could be taken as a proof of this poem's indebtedness to the Romantics, but the lines following the vision blame man for his lack of courage to face the fundamental questions of existence, the futility of any kind of teleological view of life (religious or historical), the irreparable loss of human values, and the possible end of civilization in a self-torturing, self-destructive way that goes beyond the heritage of the early nineteenth century because it has none of the pathos of the Romantics. At a pivotal point in the monologue there is a shift in tone: the speaker himself becomes the addressee, whereas the closure brings a return to the initial speech situation. The last two lines—"Still, I may have been the guest of a grand and unknown Lord"—express a vague admission of some distant transcendental power.

With supreme irony the last poem, "Ének a semmiről" (A Song upon Nothing), denies any kind of certainty. In sharp contrast to the free conversational tone of "Hajnali részegség," this much shorter text has six fairly regular stanzas with an *a a a b a* rhyme scheme. Nothing comes closer to an existential interpretation of human fate in Kosztolányi's work than this poem, which presents the soul as a stranger in this world and argues that man is more familiar with nothingness than with being.

At the time *Kosztolányi Dezső összegyűjtött költeményi* (including the new volume of verse entitled *Számadás*) was published, Kosztolányi was gravely ill. Three times he visited specialists in Stockholm; eleven times he had blood transfusions; and he survived nine operations. While his condition rapidly deteriorated, he took to morphine to ease his pain, and in a desperate attempt to escape from the boredom of his marriage, he started a love affair with a married woman whose maiden name was Mária Radákovics. "Szeptemberi áhítat" (September Ecstasy), a poem published in the October 1935 issue of *Nyugat,* is a love poem written for this woman, although she is not even mentioned in the text. A pantheistic meditation on nature, it has fine lines, but as a whole cannot be compared with the close-knit structure and perfect self-control that characterize "Ének a semmiről" and thus it is no more than a kind of supplement to its author's poetic achievement.

Tengerszem, the last book published during Kosztolányi's lifetime, on the other hand, not only is the largest collection of prose he ever published but also contains very fine stories. Besides *Esti Kornél kalandjai,* it has four other sections. *Végzet és veszély* (Danger and Destiny) is a sequence of narratives, varied in tone and written at different times, whereas *Toll-rajzok* (Sketches) consists of short pieces, witty by-products of a first-rate journalist. More unified is the brief section called *Egy asszony beszál* (A Woman Is Talking), in which a middle-class wife tells an unnamed woman about the way her slow rise in the world has gone together with a gradual exhaustion that has led to a complete loss of both strength and desire.

Even more interesting is the sequence entitled *Latin arcélek.* Two of the stories examine the possibilities of human behavior in a state of defenselessness. The slave described in "Silus" seeks a rational explanation for his suffering but is found ridiculous even by those who feel compassion for him, and he is bitten by the most miserable of dogs. Common sense must fail in the face of suffering, which can bring nothing but humiliation. More appropriate seems to be the reaction of a poor girl treated violently by the soldiers of the emperor in "Paulina." Crying in anger, she breaks into a torrent of abuse against all who have power, including the emperor himself. Her passion is a manifestation of the individual's integrity; her desperate curse is interpreted as the voice of truth by the poet who happens to listen to her.

Kosztolányi viewed power as a destructive force. The emperor portrayed in "Aurelius" is human precisely because he is reluctant to use force. Still, the emperor's position sets strict limits to his wisdom: his common sense is purely defensive, and in any case, it is quite inefficient in any situation in which violent emotions are at work.

Irrationality cannot be abolished because it is an inalienable characteristic of existence. Such seems to be the message of "Caligula," the last of the Latin profiles. Albert Camus could not possibly have known about this highly dramatic work, yet it certainly anticipates the French writer's play. Kosztolányi's Caligula is possessed with the idea of absolute freedom. He is fully convinced of the absurdity of existence, and his ambition is to turn violence into an art.

Nineteen-thirty-six, the year when *Tengerszem* was published, brought much suffering for Kosztolányi. One of the many operations he underwent robbed him of his voice, and he had to communicate in writing thenceforth. He died in Saint John's Hospital in Budapest on 3 November 1936.

At the time of his death Kosztolányi was generally regarded as one of the best Hungarian writers of the early twentieth century. His reputation continued to rise in the next decades. Babits, in an important essay, revised his earlier estimate of Kosztolányi's achievement. From the poets Attila József and Sándor Weöres to the novelists Sándor Márai and Géza Ottlik, prominent representatives of the next generations drew inspiration from his works. There was only one period when his influence declined: from the late 1940's through 1956 his works were not published at all. Some populists who were convinced that art had to rely on peasant culture found his insistence upon bourgeois values unpalatable, whereas György Lukács and his followers criticized his work for lacking political commitment.

After 1956 Kosztolányi's books began to appear at fairly regular intervals. Once again, a new generation turned to his work for inspiration. Furthermore, some works written in the 1950's testified to a continued interest in his art: for example, János Pilinszky, a fine religious poet, modelled his "Négysoros" (Quatrain;

published in his collection *Harmadnapon* [On the Third Day, 1959]) on Kosztolányi's "Octóberi táj." The postmodern generation that emerged in the 1970's viewed him as a precursor: the poet Dezső Tandori continued his experiments with montage, and the novelists Péter Esterházy and Lajos Grendel took *Esti Kornél* as a starting point for their deconstructions of narrative continuity. More and more of his works have been translated into other languages, despite the fact that his great emphasis on the distinguishing features of the Hungarian language makes his works less translatable than those by any other major Hungarian writer. He seems to have been especially successful in France: in recent years two different translations of *Esti Kornél* have been published there.

His essays have given an impetus to Hungarian literary scholarship, and 1985, when the hundredth anniversary of his birth was celebrated, brought many new publications. He is one of the most widely read and discussed writers in his native country. By general consent, his position is unique in Hungarian literature: he is the only author in the language who has succeeded in writing first-rate works in both lyric verse and narrative prose.

Selected Bibliography

EDITIONS

INDIVIDUAL WORKS

POETRY
Négy fal között. Budapest, 1907.
A szegény kisgyermek panaszai. Budapest, 1910.
Őszi koncert. Kártya. Budapest, 1911.
Mágia. Békéscsaba, 1912.
Lánc, lánc, eszterlánc . . . Békéscsaba, 1914.
Mák. Békéscsaba, 1916.
Kenyér és bor. Békéscsaba, 1920.
A bús férfi panaszai. Budapest, 1924.
Meztelenül. Budapest, 1928.

FICTION
Boszorkányos esték. Budapest, 1908.
Bolondok. Budapest, n.d. (1911).

A vonat megáll. Budapest, n.d. (1911?).
Beteg lelkek. Budapest, n.d. (1912).
Bűbájosok. Budapest, 1916.
Káin. Budapest, 1918.
Páva. Budapest, n.d. (1919).
Béla, a buta. Budapest, 1920.
A rossz orvos. Budapest, 1921.
A véres költő. Budapest, 1922.
Pacsirta. Budapest, 1924.
Aranysárkány. Budapest, 1925.
Édes Anna. Budapest, 1926.
Esti Kornél. Budapest, n.d. (1933).
Tengerszem. Budapest, 1936.

PLAYS
Lótoszevők. Budapest, 1910.

MISCELLANEOUS PROSE
Mécs. Békéscsaba, 1913.
Katina-arcok. Budapest, n.d. (1917).
Tintaleves papírgaluskával. Budapest, n.d. (1927).
Alakok. Budapest, 1929.
Bölcsőtől a koporsóig. Budapest, 1934.

POETRY AND PROSE
Öcsém. Békéscsaba, 1915.
Tinta. Gyoma, 1916.
Zsivajgó természet. Budapest, 1930.

POSTHUMOUS EDITIONS
Idegen költők anthológiája. 2 vols. Budapest, 1937.
Próza. Budapest, 1937.
Szeptemberi áhitat. Budapest, 1939.
A bábjátékos. Gyoma, 1940.
Hátrahagyott művei. 11 vols. Budapest, n.d. (1940–1948).
Babits-Juhász-Kosztolányi levelezése. Budapest, 1959.
Mostoha és egyéb kiadatlan művek. Novi Sad, 1965.
Álom és ólom. Budapest, 1969.
Füst. Budapest, 1970.
Nyelv és lélek. Budapest, 1971.
Hattyú. Budapest, 1972.
Negyvennégy levél. Szabadka, 1972.
Én, te, ő. Budapest, 1973.
Sötét bújócska. Budapest, 1974.
Ércnél maradandóbb. Budapest, 1975.
Patália. Budapest, 1976.
Látjátok, feleim. Budapest, 1976.
Egy ég alatt. Budapest, 1977.
Színházi esték. 2 vols. Budapest, 1978.

DEZSŐ KOSZTOLÁNYI

Európai kepeskönyv. Budapest, 1979.
Napló. Budapest, 1985.

COLLECTED WORKS
Kosztolányi Dezső összegyűjtött költeményei. Budapest, 1935. Contains *Számadás.*
Összes novellái. 3 vols. Budapest, 1981.
Összes versei. 2 vols. Budapest, 1984.

TRANSLATIONS BY KOSZTOLÁNYI

Guy de Maupassant összes versei. Budapest, 1908.
Oscar Wilde: A páduai hercegnő. Budapest, 1908.
Molière: A szeleburdi. (Budapest?) 1911.
Calderón: Úrnő és komorna. (Budapest?) 1912.
Georges Courteline: Négy kis bolondság. Budapest, 1912.
Thomas Mann: Tristan. Budapest, 1912.
Jules Renard: A smokk. Budapest, 1913.
Modern költők. Budapest, n.d. (1913).
Rostand: A két Pierrot. (Budapest?) 1913.
Tristan Bernard: A csendes férj. Békéscsaba, 1913.
Heinrich Mann: Ronda tanár úr. Békéscsaba, 1914.
Byron: Mazeppa. Gyoma, 1917.
Henri Barbusse: A pokol. (Budapest?) 1918.
Henri Bernstein: Tisztitótűz. (Budapest?) 1918.
Balzac: Két elbeszélés. Budapest, 1919.
Lord Alfred Douglas: Wilde Oscar és én. (Budapest?) 1919.
Byron: Beppo. Békéscsaba, 1920.
Huysmans: A különc. Budapest, 1921.
Oscar Wilde: Salome. Budapest, 1921.
Marcel Prévost: Don Juan őnagyságák. Budapest, 1923.
Wilde: Dorian Gray arcképe. Budapest, 1923.
Wilde: Firenzei tragédiák. A szent parázna. Budapest, 1923.
Guy de Maupassant versei: És első elbeszélései. Budapest, 1924.
Paul Bourget: A négyek regénye. Budapest, 1924.
Goethe: A napló. Budapest, 1925.
Mauriac: A szerelem sivataga. Budapest, 1925.
Shakespeare: Téli rege. Budapest, 1925.
Oscar Wilde költeményei. Budapest, 1928.
Paul Géraldy: Te meg én. Budapest, 1928.
Thornton Wilder: Szent Lajos király hídja. Budapest, 1928.
Szent Imre himnuszok. Budapest, 1930.

Shakespeare: Romeo és Júlia. Budapest, 1930.
Kínai és japán versek. Budapest, 1931.
"William Faulkner: Akkor este." In László Cs. Szabó, ed., *Mai amerikai dekameron.* Budapest, 1935.
Lewis Carroll: Évike Tündérországban. Budapest, 1936.

TRANSLATIONS

The Bloody Poet: A Novel About Nero. Translated from the German translation by Clifton P. Fadiman with a prefatory letter by Thomas Mann. New York, 1927.
The Golden Kite. Translated by Anny Reitzer. Vienna, 192–.
Wonder Maid. Translated by Adam de Hegedűs. London, 1947.
Nero. Translated by Adam de Hegedűs. London, 1947.
The Golden Dragon (fragment). Translated by Godfrey Turton. Budapest, 1948.

BIOGRAPHICAL AND CRITICAL STUDIES

Ady, Endre. *Az irodalomról.* Budapest, 1961.
Babits, Mihály. *Irók két háboru közt.* Budapest, n.d. (1941).
Bori, Imre. *Kosztolányi Dezső.* Novi Sad, 1986.
Brunauer Dalma, Hunyadi, and Stephen Brunauer. *Dezső Kosztolányi.* Munich, 1983.
Karátson, André. *Le symbolisme en Hongrie.* Paris, 1969.
Király, István. *Kosztolányi. Vita és vallomás.* Budapest, 1986.
Kiss, Ferenc. *Az érett Kosztolányi.* Budapest, 1979.
Kosztolányi, Dezsőné. *Kosztolányi Dezső.* Budapest, 1938.
Mész, Lászlóné, ed. *A rejtőzködő Kosztolányi.* Budapest, 1987.
Rába, György. *A szép hűtlenek. Babits, Kosztolányi, Tóth Árpád versfordításai.* Budapest, 1969.
Rónay, László. *Kosztolányi Dezső.* Budapest, 1977.
Szegedy-Maszák, Mihály. "A regény, amint írja önmagát". Budapest, 1980.
———. "Organic Form and Linguistic Relativity." In *Proceedings of the Tenth Congress of the International Comparative Literature Association. New York, 1982.* New York, 1985. Vol. 2, pp. 142–146.

MIHÁLY SZEGEDY-MASZÁK

GYÖRGY LUKÁCS

(1885–1971)

TO AMERICAN READERS the premier Marxist aesthete, thinker, and public figure, the Hungarian György (Georg) Lukács, may well appear to be one of the most surprising and interesting figures in twentieth-century literary criticism and philosophy. The scion of a culture whose language is inaccessible to most Western readers, Lukács wrote his first two books in his native tongue and then went on to establish a European reputation in German. In Europe, where his work has been translated into almost every language from Spanish to Russian, he has been known for much longer than he has been known here; but the unexpected lies not only in the somewhat belated gift to us of an excellent writer and critic. Pointedly surprising, from our cold-war point of view, is the phenomenon of a profound Marxist thinker, one whose life and work belie much of what the young have here been taught about that competing system as a view of history and as a mode of being. Marxism, if we are to believe our schoolteachers and platoon sergeants, is evil, antireligious, and threatening to the integrity and continuity of culture as we know it. Reading major work by and about Lukács, we become acquainted with a man of a broad and passionate European outlook, a nondogmatic thinker and teacher, and one committed to the idea of preserving a sense of the totality of cultural tradition. Here is a political radical who is at the same time a cultural conservative and a thinker who does not by any means proscribe religious experience.

Surprising, too, may seem the fact that Lukács was a man of genuine humility. He was always willing, indeed eager, to subject his thinking to self-examination, self-critique, and, if need be, rejection of prior stages of his thought and writing. It is well known, for example, that in later years he repudiated his early writings as belonging to a stage of no longer valid subjective idealism. Not everyone has shared in this dour view, of course. Thomas Mann, who first became acquainted with Lukács's work through the German edition of the 1910 collection of essays *A lélek és a formák* (*Soul and Form*) wrote, in the 1955 *Festschrift* (celebration text) for the seventy-year-old Lukács: "Ever since then, I have been following his critical work with attention, respect, and very much to my profit. What arouses my sympathy with it first of all is the sense for continuity and tradition by which it is guided, and to which for the most part it owes its existence." If critics, as they so often do, ignore key works by Lukács the university student, they do so much to their detriment, for it is frequently here that seeds of the later harvest in critical insight and systematic thought are planted.

One vital aspect of Lukács's commitment to tradition is the special predilection with which he addresses himself to works of the eighteenth and nineteenth centuries; discussion, often in fine detail, of novels by Johann Wolfgang von Goethe, Honoré de Balzac, Leo Tolstoy, and Feodor Dostoevsky, for example, is one of his specialties. He tended to distrust the modern, and despite revisions of his thought on moderns such as Franz Kafka, prominent critics have held this to be a serious shortcoming in Lukács's view of art. Susan Sontag holds that this is precisely what we can expect of Marxist critics. Whether we agree that this blind spot in Lukács's vision does damage to his work may well depend on our overall assessment of the man and of his contribution. We are invited, in other words, to give Lukács and his oeuvre equal time before making up our minds. But that his "road to Marx" does not lead the Hungarian thinker down the road of socialist realism in the worst sense—namely, of attention to tenth-rate Stalinist fiction—comes as perhaps the biggest surprise of all. In Lukács's development the personal and the existential take their positions side by side with the professional, and this may provide us with a key to the man's intellectual integrity. As he writes in the opening chapter of *Die Theorie des Romans* (*The Theory of the Novel,* 1920), philosophy, "both as a form of existence and as that which determines the form and content of imaginative writing, is always a symptom of the rift between inner and outer, a sign . . . of the noncongruence between soul and action." It is not too much to suggest that Lukács's career was devoted to efforts to make the rift heal.

EARLY YEARS: 1885–1911

György Bernát Lőwinger was born on 13 April 1885, the second son of a wealthy upper-middle-class Budapest Jewish family. His father, József Lőwinger, was a successful banker (in 1906 he became director of the Hungarian General Credit Bank in Budapest) and, as a man of broad cultural interests, a generous patron to Hungarian artists of rank (Béla Bartók,

for example). By the son's later account, as well as from the voluminous correspondence between father and son, the elder Lukács became his son's patron as well. Of his mother (*née* Adél Wertheimer), who stood on ceremony and set great store by social status, young Lukács was far less fond. The family name changed to Lukács in 1890. Nine years later, the father bought a patent of nobility; early writings by the son (through 1916) are signed "von Lukács." The "von" he dropped, to be sure, on his entry into the Hungarian Communist Party in December of 1918, but he clearly detested class, privilege, and protocol from an early age. Even wealth, by his own later admission, never meant much to him. As Lukács came to resent his father's constant preaching on success as a means to social advancement, the seeds of rebellion were planted in the home; this is truly where the younger Lukács took his first step on his road to Karl Marx. Yet, by old-fashioned standards, home also had a nourishing ambience. Among his sister Mici's music teachers figured none other than the young Bartók, and Mann was a regular guest in the Lukács household. To be sure, Lukács and the novelist did not meet at this early stage; later meetings were, of course, to prove legendary.

If there is one word that characterizes Lukács's development, it is consistency. Consistent with his rejection of his father's snobbish conception of making one's way in the world, themes of defeat, lack of success, and tragedy interested Lukács from early on. As a child he read Edmondo De Amicis, James Fenimore Cooper, Charles Lamb's *Tales from Shakespeare* (1807), and the *Iliad,* and according to his own account he sympathized with the victims rather than with the heroes. An excellent student, but with little taste for Latin and Greek, Lukács gravitated toward modern languages and literature instead. English, French, and German (the last-named spoken at home) came to him easily, and at school he took a particular interest in such authors as Charles Baudelaire, Goethe, Gerhart Hauptmann,

Gottfried Keller, and Algernon Swinburne. Lukács regarded Friedrich Hebbel as the founder of modern tragedy (a belief shared by very few critics in our time) as well as an immediate precursor of Henrik Ibsen, and in Lukács's lifelong preoccupation with drama the achievements of Hebbel and Ibsen loom large.

In the fall of 1902—also the year of his earliest publications—Lukács enrolled in the University of Budapest and embarked on a course of study in economics and law (the latter at his father's wish). Not much later he switched fields, to literature and sociology, only to find, unusual as this may seem to us, that his previous courses enriched and deepened his nascent interest in art and literature, which he studied in the larger contexts of human society and history. The impulse to relate the small to the large, the particular to the universal, eventually defined the method of all of Lukács's mature work in criticism, as well as in the philosophy of art. Already here Lukács shows affinity with the concept of totality, one of his major categories in philosophy. Affinity, elective or not, as much as style, defines the man. Long before *The Theory of the Novel* Lukács was convinced—to use a saying of Johann Fichte that Lukács himself quoted—that "this is the age of absolute sinfulness," and a primitive version of dialectical vision was already all-important for him during his so-called aestheticist period. Art for art's sake is a topic Lukács himself treated, yet at the same time he saw that art and literature do make valid truth claims and that the social ills they depict are real. In the Hungary of Lukács's student days more was wrong in the public sphere than met the eye: provincialism, rising anti-Semitism (since about 1900), and rising unemployment were compounded by callous indifference on the part of those in power. The individual seemed powerless. Lukács and his fellow students felt that some aspects of their lives simply could not be changed, except—possibly, in the future—by radical means. The sense of tragedy, in theory as in practice, was in the air.

Man, they felt, is essentially alone; he has no hope of communing with his fellow humans. (One rare glimmer of hope is revealed in Lukács's 1907 essay on Paul Gauguin.)

Alienation in its several senses probably best suggests the mood of those years, but Lukács's reading at this time shows lively engagement. At the university he studied the social criticism of Georg Simmel (*Die Philosophie des Geldes* [The Philosophy of Money, 1900]) as well as *Geistesgeschichte* (intellectual history) as written by Wilhelm Dilthey in his seminal study *Das Erlebnis und die Dichtung* (*Poetry and Experience,* 1905); in 1909 he attended Dilthey's and Simmel's lectures in Berlin. He also worked his way, for the first time, through volume 1 of Marx's *Das Kapital* (1867). That the student should have read Marx before his absorption in G. W. F. Hegel (which did not come until 1914) only bespeaks his precocity, as does the fact that he took his doctorate twice: in 1906 in law at the University of Kolozsvár (now Cluj-Napoca, Romania), and in 1909 in philosophy at Budapest. His thesis, "A tragédia metafizikája" ("The Metaphysics of Tragedy," 1911) derived from what eventually became his prize-winning two-volume study *A modern dráma fejlődésének története* (History of the Development of the Modern Drama, 1911).

Even before that landmark work of his youth, Lukács was a prolific essayist. Besides being engrossed in the plays of Hebbel and of Ibsen and the thought of Søren Kierkegaard, by 1909 he had also written on Novalis, Rudolph Kassner, Arthur Schnitzler, Richard Beer-Hofmann, and August Strindberg. Lukács quickly gained status as a respected collaborator in two of the era's leading Hungarian periodicals: *Huszadik Század* (Twentieth Century, 1900–1919) and *Nyugat* (Occident, 1908–1941). A number of the essays were versions preliminary to those he later included in *Soul and Form.*

The suggestion by Mary Gluck that we think of Lukács not as a literary critic but as a "philosopher of literary forms" validates itself in his earliest work. Lukács's medium of expression was the essay, but he was also interested in the practical work of the drama, the first genre that tied him down. At home he read every play that he could, and in 1904, after a stint as reviewer for the newspaper *Magyar Szalon* (Hungarian Salon) and after some bureaucratic difficulties, Lukács and two friends, Sándor Hevesi and László Bánóczy, founded the Thália Társaság (Thália Company). Their aim was to stage little-performed, mostly avant-garde works. Lukács and his friends and classmates, the young Béla Balázs and Zoltán Kodály among them, had long been dissatisfied with the lack of an avant-garde stage in Hungary comparable with such a European enterprise as Otto Brahm's Freie Bühne (Free Stage) in Berlin. Unlike their Western European models, however, the Hungarians were eager to avoid identification with any one period label or movement, such as realism or naturalism. So it came about that, after some heterogeneous evenings, during which even Goethe had the boards (with his early Weimar one-act play *Die Geschwister* [Brother and Sister, 1776]), the company concentrated on the then avant-garde playwrights Hebbel, Hauptmann, Ibsen, Anton Chekhov, and Maxim Gorky. The Thália Company always labored under financial difficulties, as it had a tiny, select audience, but by 1908, when it finally had to close its doors, it had brought to interested Hungarian audiences dramas that no one else in the Hungary of those days thought of performing, which in itself seems to be a lasting achievement. Equally significant were the stimulations that the Thália experience lent Lukács and the friendships that it and similar involvements helped him form. It was Bánóczy who, in a letter dated 5 August 1906, wrote to Lukács in Berlin about the Kisfaludy Society essay competition in the modern drama and encouraged his friend to enter with what became Lukács's history of the subject.

All of Lukács's friendships from this point on were seminal, and in time the names came to belong to scholars and artists of world rank.

The literary historian Marcell Benedek was a Thália associate; for a brief time in 1911 Lukács coedited the periodical *A Szellem* (Spirit), with the art historian and critic Lajos Fülep; and through Balázs, Lukács met Kodály and became acquainted with the music of Bartók, as well as with the revolutionary poetry of Endre Ady, whom he met in 1906. The reading of Ady's *Új versek* (New Poems, 1906) constituted a turning point in Lukács's spiritual career.

Lukács's entire world of feeling and thought grew out of personal experience. The aesthetician and art historian Leó Popper, son of the distinguished cellist Dávid Popper (who himself married Lukács's sister, Mici), was probably Lukács's closest friend at this time; from him Lukács learned to distrust studies of influence and to concentrate on the perception of quality in art. The painter Irma Seidler, whom Lukács met in Budapest in December of 1907 and who designed the cover for the German edition of *Soul and Form,* was also a good friend. Together, the three of them made a pilgrimage to Florence and to Ravenna in May of 1908, and for Lukács the trip was an eyeopener. In *A modern dráma fejlődésének története* he claims that Marxism, in order to prove itself as a system comparable in power to medieval Christianity, would in time have to bring forth art similar in quality to work by Dante Alighieri and Giotto. For Lukács the streets of Florence "sang." But tragedy followed soon thereafter. A close relationship developed between Lukács and Seidler, but because of his work, Lukács could not commit himself to a liaison. He wished, rather, to translate into his life the condition of "eternal longing" about which he was learning from the broken-off engagement of Kierkegaard to Regine Olsen. Seidler broke with Lukács in November of 1908 and married Károly Réthy. The marriage was an unhappy one; after an unfortunate affair with Balázs, and with her ambitions as a painter frustrated, Seidler committed suicide by leaping into the Danube on 18 May 1911. Not long afterward Lukács received word that Popper, who had for a long time been suffering from tuberculosis, had succumbed to his illness in Italy in October of the same year.

With the passing of these two friends an era came to an end for Lukács, both emotionally and intellectually—the era of subjective idealism, aestheticism, Platonism. He saw no future outside the community of like spirits he envisioned, and that community, by his lights, clearly did not exist yet. For a time Lukács contemplated committing suicide, but then, in an effort to overcome this morbid impulse and, as it were, in honor of Seidler, he wrote "A lelki szegénységről" (On Poverty of Spirit, 1911), a strange hybrid of epistle, dialogue, and lyrically attuned philosophical meditation. A young man accuses himself of having caused the death of a woman friend. He bares his soul to the sister of the dead girl (who records their dialogue in the form of a letter to the young man's father); they argue in depth, elaborating on the subjects of mysticism and practical ethics; he will not be dissuaded from his guilt, both legal and metaphysical. Two days following the interview with the sister, the young man shoots himself. On his desk lies the Bible, open at a pertinent passage from Revelation (3:15–16). Lee Congdon speaks of the young Lukács's creating the role of Mann's character Tonio Kröger, and up to a point he is right. But the experience with Seidler and Lukács's particular way of finding a way out of his quandary—overcoming a suicidal impulse by depicting suicide in a work of literature—bespeaks no affinity more eloquent at this point than with the Goethe of *Die Lieden des jungen Werthers* (*The Sorrows of Young Werther,* 1774, 1787) Like Goethe, Lukács went on living and creating—to high old age.

The two principal works of Lukács's early period are a literary history and a volume of essays. *A modern dráma fejlődésének története* was written in 1907; in 1908 it won the Krisztina Lukács Prize of the Kisfaludy Society. Skimmed over by most critics of Lukács, *A modern dráma* is an unjustly neglected work. If

it is still of frankly aestheticist orientation, some nascent Marxist insights already shine through. One such is evident in the very subject of the book, an investigation of bourgeois cultural values.

Chapters 5, "Hebbel und die Grundlagen der modernen Tragödie" (Hebbel and the Foundations of Modern Tragedy), and 6, "Henrik Ibsen, Versuch, eine bürgerliche Tragödie zu schaffen" (Henrik Ibsen: An Attempt to Create a Middle-Class Tragedy), are the core of the study. In examining the ways in which modern European drama peaks in the work of these two giants, Lukács is concerned with the theater as a public medium rather than with plays published and made available for private reading and study.

Tellingly, his estimate of the drama's development is somewhat negative—drama, Lukács argues, has moved away from sensuous presentation toward what he calls "intellectualism," which "as a form of spiritual processes shows the strongest tendency to sunder that community, to isolate people from one another, and to stress their differences" (the German term is *Unvergleichbarkeit,* "incomparability"). Quite apart from this tendency, serious drama, which according to Lukács seems to have ceased in Europe with Victor Hugo and Percy Bysshe Shelley, was not possible on the German stage until Hebbel's time. Gotthold Lessing had no background to create what he was working hardest to achieve: a truly German middle-class drama with its own characteristic problematic. Lukács speaks of Lessing's cold mathematicity and similarly judges such later dramatists as Heinrich von Kleist, Franz Grillparzer, and Friedrich von Schiller (wrongly, perhaps, with respect to such works as *König Ottokar* [*King Ottocar,* 1825] and *Don Carlos* [1787]). In such an atmosphere of calculation no tragedy can come about. By tragedy Lukács means a genre that tells us about our separateness and of the necessarily problematic nature of this condition. In his search for such a genre Lukács goes back to the ancients and to Shakespeare; both give, in his estimation, "fresco-like monumentality and naturalistic detail." Only Goethe's *Götz von Berlichingen* (1773) and Schiller's *Wallenstein* (1798–1799) bring adumbrations of such a healthy tendency (possibly one could add to this list Goethe's mature dramas *Iphigenia in Tauris* [1787] and *Torquato Tasso* [1790]).

If calculation and intellectualism are one extreme at which no tragedy is possible, then, Lukács argues in volume 2, excessive devotion to detail is surely the other. In chapter 10, "Möglichkeiten und Grenzen des Naturalismus" (Possibilities and Limitations of Naturalism), he gives a foretaste of what he later says about this movement, and in particular about Émile Zola, in his later, major work on the European novel. Lukács does not consider naturalism as a fit medium for the portrayal of social ills: "The dramas of German naturalism are dramas of the goallessness of middle-class ideals." Naturalism is the complete means for the expression of fruitless longings; it portrays the politics of passive suffering, of keeping still, of the absence of action: "These dramas portray no battles." The result is tendentiousness as opposed to active and fruitful engagement, and Lukács will not stand for tendentiousness as an aesthetic principle, any more than he will for preaching in early and middle Ibsen. In chapter 11 Lukács is equally negative on impressionism; its presentation of fleeting impressions runs counter to concern with the category of totality. On Maurice Maeterlinck, Lukács is a bit more positive: "His dramas are . . . filled with great moments of beauty"; Maeterlinck is a strong symbolist.

According to Lukács, Hebbel is the most genuinely tragically attuned of all modern playwrights, perhaps of all dramatists of any period. "With Hebbel, the dialectic and the deepest dissonances of modern life became tragic vision; his form proceeded from the substances of contemporary existence." With Goethe, Schiller, and later dramatic poets, tragedy and philosophy did not grow from the same root. This, however, is the case for Hebbel's oeuvre; it satisfies the formulation "Trag-

edy is modern if it grows organically from the life of our day." And modern life and worldview must be attuned in perfect harmony. Inner necessity governs the sense of tragedy, of choice, in *Judith* (1841), the protagonist of which accepts the burden of guilt that God lays on her. In Hebbel's great women characters, Lukács perceives compelling unity of purpose, action, and suffering; besides *Judith,* he discusses *Genoveva* (1843) and, centrally, *Maria Magdalena* (1844). In this last-named work, played (as the others are not) in bourgeois German dress, the clash of old and new is realized in a finely tuned tragedy of feelings. Lukács perceives the German tragedian's struggle for his vision of the Absolute; in *Agnes Bernauer* (1852), we might add, Hegel's principle of tragedy as the confrontation of right with right is clearly invoked. In chapter 3 of *A modern dráma* Lukács quotes Hegel's *Vorlesungen über die Aesthetik* (*Aesthetics,* 1835–1838) on just this point. Hegelian, too, is Lukács's understanding of Hebbel's effort to locate the given struggle within the passing historic moment.

Hebbel's work, to Lukács, is all of a piece. His discussion of Ibsen is far more developmental. Senses of irresolvability and relativity, the power of sight—these are basic forces in Ibsen's unfolding sense of the tragic. Lukács traces the Norwegian dramatist's career from the early *Catiline* (1850), through "comedies" like *Brand* (1866) and *Peer Gynt* (1867) and the dramas of "fighting romanticism" *Et dukkehjem* (*A Doll's House,* 1879) and *En folkefiende* (*An Enemy of the People,* 1882). These last two plays are Ibsen's exemplary pieces of social message, of preachment, and as such cannot as yet be taken seriously. In *Gengangere* (*Ghosts,* 1881) there is a fully matured dramatic art for perhaps the first time—we are offered a tragedy of fate, of unalterable character—and in *Hedda Gabler* (1890), for all its brutality and grotesqueness, there is a deep pathos.

Lukács devotes a great deal of space to Ibsen's dramatic technique, especially to aspects of symbolism (as in *Bygmester Solness* [*The Master Builder*, 1892]), and to other means for putting middle-class guilt feelings on the stage, means that, Lukács argues, Ibsen borrowed from the French. Irony and pathos are the governing components of the tone of Ibsen's mature plays. The highest point is reached with *Hedda Gabler* and *Vildanden* (*The Wild Duck*, 1884; this had been a favorite of Lukács's since Thália days). In *Rosmersholm* (1886), *Fruen fra havet* (*The Lady from the Sea*, 1888), and *John Gabriel Borkman* (1896) we have the master. Ibsen's mature work arises "totally from the soul of the stage."

A modern dráma shows traces of Marxism carefully thought through; so, by implication, does the delicate *Soul and Form*. The personal element in this collection of essays is Marxian and dialectical, while the lyrical, nuance-filled tone and above all the theme of the soul's search for acceptable forms of consciousness and creative self-fulfillment are Platonic and Kantian, not to mention secessionist. In the introductory essay the stress is on the Platonic: "There are . . . two kinds of spiritual reality: life is one and living the other." Further, there are two poles of writing, the critical and the poetic. In the essay on Kassner the problem is pursued: the poet, who lives and writes in form, is serene and secure; the critic, whose unchangeable attitude is *Sehnen* (longing), lives in a world of relativity. In essays further on in the volume, there are handsome tributes to Novalis, Theodor Storm, and Stefan George as being embodiments of the romantic, the bourgeois poetic, and the symbolist-impressionist temperaments, respectively. There is a lively dialogue on Laurence Sterne and, among writers now largely forgotten but dear to Lukács, Beer-Hofmann, Charles-Louis Philippe, and Paul Ernst come in for affectionate and often sensitive treatment (essays on the latter two were added to the German edition, published in 1911).

Emotionally and existentially, the central piece of the little book is the second essay, about Kierkegaard and Regine Olsen; this is Lukács's lyrical tribute to Seidler, with whom he could not unite. The principle of the essay is Kierkegaard's own choreographic experience: pure gesture, transparency of being. After breaking off his engagement to Regine, the philosopher writes in his diary: "No husband could be more faithful to his wife than I am to her." Gesture and form are basic for the early Lukács. Mann thought *Soul and Form* a beautiful book; he also plagiarized from it a passage for *Der Tod in Venedig* (*Death in Venice*, 1913).

If *A modern dráma* and *Soul and Form* have one red thread running through them, it is the theme of loneliness and of the soul's categorical need to break through to a sense of common humanity. As Lukács wrote not much later in *Esztétikai kultúra* (Aesthetic Culture, 1913): "That which is individual to the depths of the soul far transcends the merely individual." It was time to test that proposition.

HEGEL AND COMMUNITY: 1912–1917

Lukács spent the years 1912 to 1917 primarily in Heidelberg. He always traveled a great deal, and it would not be practical to trace his journeys in detail here, but between September 1911 and May 1912 he was once again in Florence, and Berlin, Budapest, and locations in France and Italy were frequent destinations during these active years. In 1911 *Soul and Form* appeared in Berlin, and this was also the year during which Lukács attempted to obtain his *Habilitation* (postdoctoral qualification for university teaching) at the University of Budapest. His efforts met with failure; he had not waited out the required three years following the doctorate, and he was also criticized for "dilettantism" (his other doctorate was in law). After an attempt to qualify in philosophy at the University of Pozsony (now Bratislava, Slovakia), Lukács informed his ever-solicitous father that he had decided to relocate abroad.

In terms of concrete results, the decision was a happy one; efforts to meet with a community of like-minded individuals were beginning to be successful. These are the years of encounter with the thought of Martin Buber and the excitement about Jewish mysticism; of Lukács's interest in the fairy tale; of studies in the cinema (which Lukács finds a totally distinctive art form); of further preoccupations with Dilthey; and of interest in Benedetto Croce. His most important association of these months, however, was with the German Jewish philosopher Ernst Bloch, a close contemporary. Bloch and Lukács had already met in Berlin in 1910 in Simmel's seminars and were reintroduced in Budapest the following year. Bloch, whom the critic Jürgen Habermas has somewhat ironically called "a Marxist Schelling," is today best remembered for his monumental three-volume *Das Prinzip Hoffnung* (*The Principle of Hope*, 1954-1959) and for his youthful *Geist der Utopie* (The Spirit of Utopia, 1918). Ideas worked out in the latter, along with Lukács's qualified rejections of these ideas, were probably the substance of their conversations, a virtual two-man laboratory of philosophy, during those seminal days in both Germany and Hungary. At the bottom of their friendly disagreement, according to the Lukács scholar and critic Sándor Radnóti, lay "the problem of the 'world abandoned by God,' the identical term used by Bloch and Lukács but not with the same meaning." The disagreement may be summarized as follows: Lukács held that although man, in his search for freedom, must find his redemption in God, this necessity, in the known world of activity and achievement, must remain unspoken. Man is attached to and dependent on God, but his imperative is to act, in this wicked world, in his consciousness and historical present, on his own. Bloch's position was that man does not and cannot act apart from experiencing the divine presence within himself and that this presence of an obscure demiurge both presupposes and expresses itself in an impossible search for utopia, the community that cannot be.

In part the disagreement revolved around the old ethical and metaphysical polarity of immanence versus transcendence, but, as Radnóti rightly points out, awareness of man's need for religion was present in the thinking of both men. What they disagreed on—the bottom line of their disagreement, in fact—is the question of whether change in a utopian, messianic dimension is possible in a practical sphere. The difference, we might suggest, lay no less in the two philosophers' respective capacities to articulate their chiliastic expectations. From this point of view it is interesting to observe that even in Lukács's mature aesthetics, the great blind spot is music. In *Geist der Utopie* Bloch devotes considerable space to the philosophy and theory of that most mental and least articulate of arts. What interests Lukács, by sharp contrast, is tragedy—tragedy as art and as an ethical category. In moving from "The Metaphysics of Tragedy" to *The Theory of the Novel*, Lukács moves, by paradoxical leap, from a vision of unattainable practical tragic being over to the category of totality. Totality, in its full paradoxical implications, came to interest Lukács as a wholeness of being in which ethics and aesthetics form part of the world of consciousness, though as categories of the mind ethics and aesthetics must be kept strictly separate. Lukács's interest at this time in Jewish mysticism and in the question of the free interpretation of biblical texts is another indication of this vision of the essential unity of the great wealth of nature, history, and intellect; in this last-named, twofold enthusiasm Lukács acknowledged the Jew in himself for the first and the last time.

At Heidelberg Lukács was warmly received by Max Weber and his Sunday afternoon circle and deeply impressed the great master of sociological thought with his brilliant conversational ability and the force of his personality. To Weber and his friends and disciples Lukács was already known, of course, as the author of *Soul and Form* (in its German version), and people of the stature of the neo-Kantian Emil Lask and Friedrich Gundolf, the eminent disciple of Stefan George, sought his company and counsel. Caution is recommended, however, in attempts to write the history of Lukács's contacts at this time; in a statement dating from April 1966, the aging philosopher himself corrects the misconception that he had connections with the circle of George. Nor did he ever study under Weber; he had gone to Heidelberg to work primarily on his *Habilitationsschrift* (qualifying essay for a university appointment). The essay—or rather, projected book—was to have as its subject the nexus between ethics and philosophy of history as exemplified in the thought and work of Dostoevsky. The project had to be abandoned (Lukács found that it exceeded his powers at the time), but on the basis of recently deciphered notes for the book found in Heidelberg in 1972, Congdon gives us a very helpful summary of the contents. From this summary we glimpse the full range of Lukács's preoccupation with Dostoevsky during his utopian years, a preoccupation that his association with Weber—an intense devotee of Dostoevsky and of all aspects of Russian culture—helped foster without a doubt.

Weber, who learned Russian in order to follow events of the 1905 revolution in the Russian press, was certainly one source of Lukács's enthusiasm for Russia and things Russian at this time. The other of two main sources was his acquaintance with and subsequent marriage to a fascinating Russian woman, Yelena Andreevna Grabenko. She and Lukács met through the kind offices of Balázs at the seaside resort town of Bellaria, near Rimini, in August 1913. Grabenko was connected with terrorist groups in Russia, and she had served a prison sentence for her activities. At the time she met Lukács, her nerves and health were a ruin, and she had come to western Europe to study painting and to begin a new life. She was anything but physically attractive, but Lukács admired the keenness of her mind and felt attracted to ways in which she reminded him of heroines in Dostoevsky's novels. Lukács, whose interest in Russia had by then also been nurtured by Mann (at least by the Russian and Slavophile elements in *Tonio Kröger* [1903]),

fell in love with Grabenko, and they were married, much to the chagrin of Lukács's family, probably in late May 1914. The wedding was in Heidelberg, which is also where they settled down. The neurotic pianist Bruno Steinbach, with whom Grabenko shortly became infatuated, joined them; István Hermann, Lukács's Hungarian biographer, tells how this ménage à trois was responsible for the mildly infernal conditions under which Lukács was compelled to work—he wrote *The Theory of the Novel* in one room while in the other Steinbach was suffering his nervous fits and Grabenko was attempting to soothe him. Karl Jaspers seems to have played a helpful role here, in that Lukács actually took Steinbach to the great psychiatrist for treatment. Grabenko and Lukács also traveled to Hungary together; in Budapest, she met Béla Kun (who, she said, reminded her of Vautrin, the arch-criminal in Balzac) and frequented the company of the sculptor Béni Ferenczy and other artists. In 1917, when Lukács returned to Budapest for good, she remained behind with Steinbach and later returned to Russia and was not heard from again. Some Lukács scholars believe she may have fallen victim to Stalin's purges. The marriage was annulled late in 1919.

Little wonder if, under such conditions, Lukács could produce only incomplete work. In somewhat grotesque contrast with the fullness of his work during the century's opening decade—with the two-volume *A modern dráma* and the twice-published *Soul and Form*—the Heidelberg period was essentially a time of fragments. The *Heidelberger Philosophie der Kunst* (Heidelberg Philosophy of Art, 1912–1914) and the *Heidelberger Ästhetik* (Heidelberg Aesthetics, 1916–1918) are both manuscripts left as torsos, edited well after the philosopher's death (included in *Werke*, vols. 16 and 17). *The Theory of the Novel* was intended as an introductory essay to the unwritten Dostoevsky book. Still, at least *The Theory of the Novel* is a major accomplishment, a virtual prolegomenon to Lukács's numerous mature studies in the criticism of the European novel. Dedicated to Grabenko, it may be said to be Lukács's expression of thanks both to her and to Weber. There can be no question that the unsung hero of *The Theory of the Novel* is Dostoevsky, the novelist who, according to Lukács, did not write novels. That statement, made with such conviction at the very end of the book, is the work's moment of Hegelian triumph and, as such, reminds us of Lukács's renewed interest in Hegel at this time. There is another reminder of this in the July 1962 preface to the new Luchterhand edition (in the paperback series), in which Lukács names as his philosophical points of departure Hegel, Goethe, and Romanticism. This triunal configuration of interests alone implies that we have a period piece (despite Lukács's protestation in that same preface that *The Theory of the Novel* is of an explosive rather than a preservative character) as well as suggesting that Lukács's wealth of interests at this time included genre theory and the bildungsroman. Nevertheless, among these allied interests it is Hegel's thought that determines structure and method in this treatise.

In dissent from John Locke's model of the mind as a passive receptor of impressions, Immanuel Kant held that the intellect actively forms its own categories and modalities (such as quality and relation) by means of which it organizes data and makes sense of reality. In addition to and behind the perceivable world, however, Kant posited another, indeterminate reality, the so-called *Ding-an-sich* (thing-in-itself), accessible only to intellection and contemplation. This, Hegel contends, renders Kant's way of knowing a static and ultimately unproductive theory. For the thing-in-itself Hegel substitutes the concept of history; for intuition, direct knowledge; for contemplation, planning and action. What Hegel is interested in is a philosophy of labor and of the ultimately triumphant (if somewhat mystically formulated) Absolute Mind. He contributes a vision of an arena where men do have the power to improve their lot—an arena of movement, of

change. The concept of dynamism and change became basic, of course, for both Marx and Friedrich Engels, as well as for Lukács's mature philosophic position.

The Theory of the Novel should not, then, be thought of as just another theory of literature; we will look there in vain for a stylistics, or for rhetorical, mythical, or other models for analysis. What this beautifully, clearly written theory is concerned with instead is the great epic forms; it is, as its subtitle states, a "historico-philosophical essay," that is, an essay in the philosophy of history as applicable to these forms of the great epic: epic poetry, the novel, transitional and synthesizing forms. In the first of its two parts, "The Forms of the Great Epic in Their Relation to the Closed or Problematic Nature of the Totality of Culture," we find a detailed meditation in historical dialectics. By "totality of culture" Lukács means historical totality; manifestations of the epic and the novel are subsumed, in his system, under questions asked about the absence versus presence of "transcendental homelessness." The world of Greek life and creativity, Lukács argues, was free of such a sense of homelessness. It was a closed culture; within it, there was as yet no chasm between the inner and the outer worlds, no self-conscious questioning of the human condition and consequently no anxiety-ridden search for appropriate creative responses to what we may perceive as aspects of the insufficiency of that condition:

> . . . the Greek knows only answers, but no questions; only solutions (even if puzzling ones), but no enigmas; only forms, but no chaos. He still draws the shaping circle of forms this side of paradox; and all that, since the time of the actualization of paradox, would have to lead to flatness, leads him to creative fulfillment.
>
> (1971 ed., p. 23)

Lukács perceives such creative fulfillment first of all in the Greek epic, in the works of Homer (for his epics are the only true ones). The epic, the means of poetic realization of the world of Homer's living man, had only one question: How can life become essence? But the world of the questions posed by art is also that of philosophy's problems. This seems to be what Lukács means when he says that "the Greek has his answers earlier than he asks his questions." In Greek culture, then, totality may be defined as the realm within which "beauty makes the world's meaning visible." A typology is possible within this closed system as well. The reason for this is that in history the Greeks traverse all stages of consciousness as well as of their realizations, which are constituted by the "great, timelessly paradigmatic forms of shaping the world: epic, tragedy, and philosophy." Epic poses the question of life's essence, to which answers are available only from perspective, from distance. Here is where we have the horizons of tragedy, the vivifying power of forms offered in a public medium. Finally, it is in philosophy that essence, having separated itself from its realization in life, rises to the status of problem, of transcendent reality. If this does not constitute a Hegelian triad, it is because the "thesis" of epic essence and the "antithesis" of tragic vivification are not cancelled, or raised to a higher reality, in the "synthesis" of philosophy. Each holds its own within an integral totality. Lukács, it seems, would agree that looking here for an instance of Hegelian *Aufhebung* (sublation) would reflect our cultural quandary. Our world is much larger than the Greeks'; we cannot possibly place ourselves within their unbroken circle.

Following instructive observations on the medieval epic (in chapter 1 of part 1) and on Dante, whom he perceives to be a representative of synthesis between the epic and the novel (chapter 3), Lukács settles down to the business of defining the inner form of the novel (chapter 4) and what he calls its limitations and significance within the horizon of the philosophy of history (chapter 5). Placed within the realm of historic totality in the modern world, the genre of the novel is the medium for self-conscious questioning, reflection, ago-

nized re-searching, and irony. Considerable time is spent, in chapter 5, with the demonic: "The novel is the epic of a God-forsaken world; the psychology of the protagonist of the novel is that of the demonic." One further point in typology: the hero of a drama knows no inwardliness; the hero of a novel knows only a world of total interiorized adventure. Whether he will succeed in his quest is not a settled matter (whereas to the protagonist of an epic, success is a foregone conclusion). In the novel, irony is a needed and powerful instrument: it is the "freedom of the poet vis-à-vis God," the means whereby in a God-forsaken world God can still be found.

Part 2 of *The Theory of the Novel* is an "attempt to arrive at a typology of the forms of the novel." In four chapters, Lukács examines key examples of the genre by Miguel de Cervantes, Balzac, and Henrik Pontoppidan (chapter 1); by Gustave Flaubert (2); by Goethe (3); and by Tolstoy and Dostoevsky (4). As Lukács perceives Homer's epics to be the only true ones in Greek culture and Dante's to be a sole example of its genre, so he predicates of *Don Quixote* (1605, 1615) that "it had to remain, as is incidentally almost every truly great novel, the sole significant objectification of its type." In this mixture of poetry and irony and of elements of the grotesque and the sublime, Lukács glimpses the most truly meaningful example of what he calls the novel of abstract idealism. Arising from and reacting to a literature of bad novels of chivalry, Cervantes' work is in part exposed to the very dangers to which these predecessors succumbed: "With the increasingly prosaic state of the world, with the withdrawal of the active demons, . . . there arises the dilemma of the demonic narrowing of the soul." With *Don Quixote* we do not as yet have a realistic novel in the ordinary sense; the hero's quest is a subjective one. Here Cervantes himself comes deftly to explore the possibilities of self-conscious fiction. In Balzac the stakes are very different, and here is where Lukács thinks to glimpse a successful example of abstract-idealist narrative: the hero's attempts to measure his progress in the world are pitted against a plethora of similar attempts by figures similarly obsessed demonically, characters who constitute, in effect, the central figure's sociohistorical background. Don Quixote's unceasing struggle with sorcerers and enchanters is replaced, in Balzac's *La comédie humaine* (*The Human Comedy*, 1842–1848) by a vision of society that is at cross-purposes with the hero, thereby defining itself as well as the individual.

With Flaubert and the novel of romantic disillusionment Balzac's vision of overwhelming yet fragmented historical totality is replaced by the vision of another fragmentation: the dimension of the hero's self-centered meditations upon the past. Here the sense of continuity, of narrative and of the epic quest, is saved by square confrontation with the problem of time in the novel. Comment on *L'Éducation sentimentale* (*Sentimental Education*, 1869) is then followed by an attempted synthesis through analyses of Goethe's *Wilhelm Meisters Lehrjahre* (*Wilhelm Meister's Apprenticeship*, 1795–1796), to Lukács the exemplary pedagogical novel, and of Tolstoy's *Voina i mir* (*War and Peace*, 1864–1869). In the *Apprenticeship* Lukács perceives recovery of that wholeness of vision that earlier novels of epic ambition lack: "Humanity, the fundamental frame of mind underlying this kind of creative shaping, demands an equilibrium between activity and contemplation, between wishing to influence the world and receptivity toward it." With Tolstoy Lukács is disillusioned; he refers to the "nursery mood" of the epilogue to *War and Peace*, "in which all search has come to an end"; this is "of a deeper disconsolateness than the ending of the most problematic novel of disillusionment." With Dostoevsky, we move beyond the novel's confrontation of the dialectic of history and society; "Dostoevsky wrote no novels. . . . He belongs to the new world." How much this "new world" is Lukács's vision of a utopia and how much the author of *The Theory*

of the Novel wanted the novel to recover the sociohistorical integrity of the epic is visible from this one statement alone.

Lukács's deep interest in a systematic aesthetics (as opposed to genre theory) is attested to in two monumental fragments dating from this time: the *Heidelberger Philosophie der Kunst* and the *Heidelberger Ästhetik*. Despite the two-year interval in their composition, the two manuscripts are interconnected. Both grapple with problems that are worked out later in *Die Eigenart des Ästhetischen* (The Characteristic Nature of the Aesthetic, 1963), Lukács's definitive statement in the field. *Soul and Form* is dedicated to the memory of Seidler; the Heidelberg manuscripts do not, but perhaps should, bear an inscription to Popper, as it is in part his heritage that they make an effort to preserve. The philosophy half addresses itself to problems of art as expression and communication, to the phenomenology of creative versus receptive behavior, and to historicity and timelessness in the work of art. Added to these concerns, in the second half, are chapters on the laws and on subject-object relations of aesthetic thought as well as on the transcendental dialectics of the idea of beauty. At the end of the second volume there is an added section, a lecture with two sketches, entitled "Das Formproblem der Malerei" (The Problem of Form in Painting).

In their external particulars and fates, the three works here touched on reflect, of course, more than their author's personal circumstances. The outbreak of war in August 1914 interrupted many lives and labors; at least Lukács was fortunate in that he could see *The Theory of the Novel* published (completed in the winter of 1914–1915, it appeared in book form in 1920). The war itself, supported by some of Europe's foremost intellectuals, Guillaume Apollinaire and Mann among them, was passionately rejected by Lukács, Bloch, and others of their generation. To the specter of the possibility that Germany might win the war, Lukács could respond only by asking the desperate question: "Who will save us from Western civilization?"

ON THE ROAD TO MARX: 1917–1929

The answer to that not wholly rhetorical question seemed not long in coming, but to this day Lukács's road to Marx is not fully mapped. It was, first and foremost, an inner road, not free of stumbling blocks and of great leaps of the imagination. *The Theory of the Novel* ends with the statement, "The novel is the form of the age of absolute sinfulness, in Fichte's words, and must remain the dominant form as long as the world is ruled by these stars." Absorbed once again in the study of Marx, Lukács encountered Marx's Eleventh Thesis on Feuerbach: "The philosophers have only *interpreted* the world, in various ways; the point, however, is to *change* it." Reading that sentence, Lukács himself must have felt chided, to say the least. But how was society to be transformed? How was the individual to reconcile the soul's aspirations with the insufficiencies, entrenched reactionary ways, and—with war in progress—failures of culture in the public sphere? That capitalism was one of the archvillains seemed clearer to Lukács than ever. But as there was not just one problem, there could not be any single way to a solution. The history of Lukács's transition "from romanticism to bolshevism," as the title of Michael Löwy's study so well puts it, is in effect a history of the questions he asked and the partial answers he found between, roughly, the summer of 1914 and the fall of 1918.

Recent literature on Lukács has suggested that clear traces of proto-revolutionary questioning may already be found in the 1911 dialogue "A lelki szegénységről." There, the young man is convinced that he is legally blameless in the death of the young woman and arrives at the conclusion that only divine laws are fit to judge us. His answer to his dilemma is his proposal of goodness: "Goodness is grace."

Saint Francis of Assisi and the medieval mystics whom Lukács studied and admired are invoked. From here, it seems but a step to the radical mysticism and violent, self-sacrificing religiosity of the Dostoevskian terrorist figure. Indeed, at this time Lukács was not only planning a book on the Russian novelist, but also was fascinated with Yelena Grabenko because of her resemblance to Sonia in *Crime and Punishment*. His own early moments of feeling that he himself possessed Dostoevskian potential Lukács kept private for a time, but only in part; in a letter to Ernst written as early as May 1915, Lukács spells out the problem, which is "to find the paths that lead from soul to soul. And all else is *but instrument*." The letter contains the same quotation from act 3 of Hebbel's *Judith* on which Lukács's 1919 essay "Taktika és etika" ("Tactics and Ethics") ends: "If you [God] place a sin between me and my deed, who am I to quarrel with you about it, and to escape from what you impose!"

The recurrence of this quotation in Lukács's writings from this period suggests his sense both of proportion between specific personal ambitions and of the opportunities that may already in 1914 have seemed to lie ahead. Weber's grave doubts concerning the Dostoevsky book were indeed followed by the collapse of Lukács's hopes at Heidelberg. To Balázs he clarified his need to publish *The Theory of the Novel* without delay, as he felt that his days for sustained effort in scholarship were drawing, temporarily at least, to a close. But while his personal academic plans foundered, his sense of community, the goal toward which he was always striving, lived on in Lukács as it did in his many friends and admirers. Not long after the outbreak of the war, Lukács made a number of trips back to Budapest. Very unwillingly, he did a tour of military duty (in stark contrast to Balázs, who cheerfully enlisted), serving for a time with the postal censorship and obtaining a disability discharge in the summer of 1916. His friend's almost mystical embrace of war and frontline duty constituted one of the very few moments of disagreement between Balázs and Lukács; Lukács's volume of essays in defense of his friend, *Balázs Béla és akiknek nem kell* (Béla Balázs and Those Who Have No Use for Him, 1918), is also one of his very few literary studies dating from this period.

Overriding personal disagreements was a great constellation of agreements, in principle as in practice, among Lukács and a number of young people seriously interested in cultural renewal. In the fall of 1915 Lukács and close friends in Budapest founded the Sunday Circle (also known as the Lukács Circle); cofounders were Balázs (in whose Budapest apartment many of the early meetings took place), Fülep (to whose periodical *A Szellem* Lukács had contributed both "The Metaphysics of Tragedy" and "A lelki szegénységről") and such figures of later distinction as the art historian Arnold Hauser and the sociologist Karl Mannheim. Charles de Tolnay, the renowned Michelangelo scholar, joined the group somewhat later. Early in 1917 the founding members of the Sunday Circle initiated a series of lectures under the designation of the Free School for the Humanities. Lectures were delivered by, among others, Balázs (dramaturgy), Béla Fogarasi (philosophical thought), Fülep (post-Kantian aesthetics), Lukács (ethics), and Bartók and Kodály (folk and contemporary music). These lectures and seminars enjoyed marked success; Gluck points out that they were also carefully structured. Radical cultural politics, active efforts to change the status quo—first in the cultural sector and, later, in Hungarian public life—were beginning to be on the weekly agenda of leading intellectuals. If the above lectures seem innocent enough, we must remember that they were not innocent to the extent that they encouraged leading members of the group, certainly Fogarasi and Lukács, to make a number of imaginative leaps between theoretical metaphysics and ethics on the one hand and practical ethics and politics on the other. As Congdon writes: "In concert with Fogarasi, Lukács made a sharp distinc-

tion between ethics and politics"; in an ethical dimension, we perceive a strongly Kantian Lukács taking, during the spring of 1918, a personal position that shies clear of an ethical idealism placed in the service of political action. Over political involvement, an activity that perpetuates institutions and thus, at least ultimately, tyrannical control over mankind, Lukács favored what has been referred to as "ethical 'direct action.'"

Insistence on change by such peaceful means may seem strange in a time of war, and perhaps stranger still, considering that the great October Revolution had been initiated almost four months to the day before Fogarasi's lecture on Kant (on 5 March 1918). To Lukács, a solid admirer of Russian culture and letters, the revolution seemed the embodiment of the promised utopia. For a time he could forget what Georges Sorel, whose syndicalist thought and influence on Ervin Szabó he admired, had said about the deleterious effects of the French Revolution on Western society—namely, that the latter was worse off, rather than better, as a result. Lukács came to admire Nikolai Lenin and came to examine especially the Hegelian bases of Marxist philosophical and politico-economic thought. He also began to take a more active interest in political developments in the wake of defeats for the Central Powers and the virtually unresisting collapse of the monarchy in October of 1918. Already the year before, he and Balázs had joined an antiwar organization whose dream was a United States of Europe and, consequently, an end to all further wars. The least that can and should be said of Count Mihály Károlyi's nonviolent achievement in establishing a Hungarian republic is that it put an end forever to the decadent and widely despised Austro-Hungarian hegemony, but, for all that, his efforts met with no favor from the Entente, Russia, or Lukács himself. The Hungarian Communist Party, organized in November of 1918, turned out to be the most powerful oppositional factor to this short-lived regime, and Lukács, Balázs, and Fogarasi joined the party in December of that year. As an intellectual Lukács met with some opposition from the top cadre of the party (he needed the support of Béla Kun, the Hungarian Soviet leader, with whom he was then on good terms). Although not appointed to membership in the Central Committee, Lukács was made people's vice-commissar on education.

The transformation of the doctor of philosophy and aspirant to a *Habilitation* at Heidelberg into Comrade Lukács, people's commissar in charge of workers' education, may indeed seem to be a strange assumption of a new identity, and not only to us. The poet Anna Lesznai, one of Lukács's best friends, has often been quoted as saying that Lukács's "conversion took place in the interval between two Sundays: Saul became Paul." To the "religious" conversion was added a great secular event: in the spring of 1917 he met Gertrúd Bortstieber, who became his second wife and his faithful companion for over forty years. They had actually first met in the home of Lukács's parents when he was quite young; then later, in Thália days, in 1906 they met again, when she wrote to him to express her admiration for his essay on Ibsen; now, in 1917, she was attending his lectures at the Free School. She was married, to the mathematician Imre Jánossy (who died soon afterward), with two sons; she and Lukács also had a daughter. She was an economist and a warm and sensible woman with a positive and cheerful outlook and a personality that reminded Lukács of the "plebeian" heroines of the Swiss writer Gottfried Keller. This may sound like a replay of his reaction to Grabenko, but the relationship with Gertrúd was a lasting one. In his new politico-cultural ambitions she gave him solid support, and she was as ardent a disciple of Hegel as Lukács himself. Following the collapse of Kun's Soviet Republic, they emigrated to Vienna, where they lived together and were married in 1920.

In his capacity as party functionary and (in effect) undersecretary of education, Lukács threw himself into his work, theoretical as well as practical. He attended endless meetings in the House of Soviets, participating in some-times bitter debates over fine points of doctrine; visited workers' education centers; canceled and made university appointments; and, most important for us here, wrote a great number of essays. Among these, "Tactics and Ethics" stands out, and not only because it is the earliest of the essays that are now regularly classed among his political writings. Others in a class with "Tactics and Ethics" are: "Was ist orthodoxer Marxismus?" ("What Is Orthodox Marxism?" 1919); "Die moralische Sendung der kommunistischen Partei" ("The Moral Mission of the Communist Party," 1920); "Zur Frage der Bildungsarbeit" ("The Question of Educational Work," 1921); *Moses Hess und die Probleme der idealistischen Dialektik* (*Moses Hess and the Problems of Idealist Dialectics,* 1926); and the "Blum-Thesen" ("Blum Theses," 1928). His biggest and most important essay—a book within a book—from the Budapest-Vienna period is "Die Verdinglichung und das Bewusstsein des Proletariats" ("Reification and the Consciousness of the Proletariat"); it was included along with "What Is Orthodox Marxism?" in his collection of 1923, *Geschichte und Klassenbewusstsein* (*History and Class Consciousness*). Of these pieces, "Tactics and Ethics" and "What Is Orthodox Marxism?" will interest us for their practical and theoretical content, while "Reification and the Consciousness of the Proletariat" is important both for its attempts to clarify Lukács's understanding of the concepts of alienation and reification and for the clues that it provides to Lukács's later approach to problems in Hegelian-Marxian literary criticism and aesthetics.

"Tactics and Ethics" is clearly a transitional piece; Lukács wrote it from a fervently and self-consciously ethical point of view. Lukács here distinguishes between immediate and long-range social goals and describes the means that may legitimately be used to attain goals of either category. There is the mere *fact* of class struggle and the sense that that class struggle makes: "Transcending mere fact, it [the sense of the struggle] . . . sees to it that there comes about a social order different in quality from all that has existed hitherto, one that no longer knows oppressor and oppressed, one in which the age of economic dependence, degrading to human dignity, shall cease." This is an almost utopian vision of what Marx himself called for. And now comes the rub: a theoretically and unconditionally ethics-based system does not underlie the Marxist vision: "Hegel's system has no ethics; with him ethics is replaced by that system of material, intellectual, and societal goods in which his social philosophy culminates." In the sphere of practical imperatives Lukács is even more outspoken and comes as close to the basic questions posed by Jean-Paul Sartre as he ever does:

> . . . ethical self-consciousness points to the fact that there are situations—tragic situations—in which it is impossible to act in such a way as not to commit a crime; but at the same time it also teaches us that even if we have to choose between two crimes, there does exist a criterion for correct versus incorrect action. This criterion is: sacrifice.
>
> (*Utam Marxhoz* [My Road to Marx, 1971], 1.196)

The individual, faced with his choice, has to sacrifice his lower being to his higher. Examples are given from Dostoevsky and from Hebbel. High on the list of the unspoken suggestions made here is that of a truly dialectical use of literature—art, with its implicitly accepted truth claims, illumines life.

"What Is Orthodox Marxism?" also dates from 1919, but intellectually and above all emotionally it is a later piece than "Tactics and Ethics." Most important, even in its earlier version (the one examined here) it is an effective prolegomenon to the three-part "Reification and the Consciousness of the Proletariat."

Dialectic materialism, as advanced in the Marx-Engels *Herrn Eugen Dührings Umwälzung der Wissenschaft* (*Herr Eugen Dühring's Revolution in Science*, 1878) and in Engels' *Ludwig Feuerbach und der Ausgang der klassischen deutschen Philosophie* (*Ludwig Feuerbach and the Outcome* [*sic*; Demise] *of*

Classical German Philosophy, 1888) and as summarized by G. H. R. Parkinson, consists mainly in the following: dialectics is "the highest form of thinking. This thinking has two main features. First, it grasps things and . . . thoughts, . . . not in isolation but in their interconnection. . . . Second, it views things as moving rather than as fixed." In his *Dialektik der Natur* (*Dialectics of Nature,* 1873–1882), Engels himself says,

> It is, in other words, the history of nature as of human society out of which the laws of dialectics are abstracted. They are not anything but the most general laws of these two phases of historical development, as of thought itself. And as a matter of fact they are reducible in the main to three such:
> the law of the shift from quantity into quality, and vice versa;
> the law of the interpenetration of opposites,
> the law of the negation of negation.
>
> (*Marx-Engels Gesamtausgabe* [46 vols., Berlin, 1975–], 1.26.175)

Dialectics, in opposition to Hegel, also involves study of the constitution of reality; for Marxists, reality is something material, not purely mental. (And we might observe that since Engels contends that rationality arises out of inanimate matter, mental activity ultimately partakes of material reality by dint of its origins.)

What, then, to the Lukács of 1919, is orthodox Marxism? Marxism, he says, is first and foremost a method. It does not mean subscribing to the substance of Marx's theories or findings. (It is possible, of course, to question this latter statement.) It is a method both for undertaking study and for effecting change. It is the dialectical method. Lukács also speaks of the sudden changeover of quantity into quality and of the negation of negation. Marx borrowed the dialectical method from Hegel and with it the mechanism of change according to the thesis-antithesis-synthesis cycle, a process whereby two polar opposites are cancelled and at the same time preserved (German *aufheben* implies both cancellation and preservation) in the higher union arrived at by synthesis. For Lukács, dialectics brings historical method into the chaos of facts; isolated facts can always be evaluated in a hundred ways. This is why, from Hegel's standpoint, it is important that we understand the parts from the whole, and not the whole from the parts. Just as theory is at one with practice, so the movement is at one with the final goal, and that final goal is revolution. Orthodox Marxism is, then, following the method of revolutionary dialectics; the decision to act precedes the facts. Facts there will always be, and we cannot wait for them to tell us whether the time to act has come.

Who should act to effect change, and why, is the subject of the investigation undertaken in the three essays making up "Reification and the Consciousness of the Proletariat." In the first, "Das Phänomen der Verdinglichung" ("The Phenomenon of Reification"), Lukács argues that in primitive societies, where barter constitutes the basis of commerce and members of the community enjoy its goods directly and unselfconsciously, there is a simple one-to-one relation among producers, goods, and consumers, whereas in a capitalistic society these relationships are complicated by means of what Marx has called "commodity fetishism." That is, not only is it true that money constitutes a means for separating humans from goods; it is also the case that a self-conscious relation between product and producer comes about. That part of the producer capable of production becomes itself a commodity, which he sells; it comes to be separated from him, becomes a thing—is reified, from Latin *res* (thing, matter, affair). This means further that the worker, who is the seller of skills and energies he does not in fact own (for these are owned by his employer), becomes separated from a part of himself. He has, as a consequence, an opportunity to become aware that he is both the subject engaged in the production of historical change (both by means of the commodities he produces and by dint of his own transformation into a commod-

ity) and the object worked by the change, the result of the change, himself. This sounds as paradoxical as true dialectical thinking should sound, and we may compare it with John Milton's paradox of the fortunate fall. That is, the question arises (as it does not, generally, in the minds of Lukács's critics): *should* the worker feel alienated thereby? Is reification synonymous with alienation? On the one hand, reification, like the fall, may seem a negative event; on the other, it is positive in that it makes its subject-object aware of his responsibility vis-à-vis his unique historical position and thus invites action.

How philosophy since Kant accounts for the implications and consequences of reification is the subject of the second essay, "Die Antinomien des bürgerlichen Denkens" ("The Antinomies of Bourgeois Thought"). Lukács argues that history is a concrete totality and that this concrete totality is first of all a subject and only then an object of contemplation; modern philosophy has arisen, Lukács states, out of the reified structure of consciousness. His first way station is Kant, in whom the antinomies of middle-class philosophical thought are most pronounced—so much so, in fact, that the thing-in-itself, seen as residing side by side with the moral imperatives of practical reason, the juxtaposition of necessity with freedom, is a characteristic of the way ordinary, decent citizens think. As Kant, in effect, fragmented reality between his first two critiques, so his followers are incapable of grasping reality as a whole. Here Lukács turns to Hegel, who succeeded in resolving some of the most important of the Kantian antinomies of reason. Hegel, to be sure, grasped the importance of the principle of history. For him historic becoming is what sublates (cancels and yet preserves) the opposition between body and soul, as well as the antinomies of the thing-in-itself:

> With this [new] focus, in which the two principal counterweights of thing-in-itself irrationality—concreteness of individual content and totality now positively viewed—appear in their

unity, the relation of theory and practice at the same time undergoes change, and with it, that of freedom and necessity. Here, the element of reality made by us loses its more or less fictional nature; we have—in the . . . prophetic words of Vico—made our history ourselves, and once we are capable of viewing the whole of reality as history, . . . then we have truly elevated ourselves to the position where reality can be grasped as our "active engagement."

(*Werke*, 2.327)

But Hegel was still not able to grasp the true identity of the locus of this *Tathandlung* (active engagement); it was left to Marx to see that the arena as well as the actor together are constituted not by abstract Absolute Mind, but by a social class. This social class, by virtue of its unique historical position, is the proletariat. The body of the third essay, "Der Standpunkt des Proletariats" ("The Position of the Proletariat"), clarifies Lukács's reasons as to why this should be the case.

History and Class Consciousness is central in Lukács's oeuvre and has justly been called one of the most brilliant works of political philosophy of our time. It influenced such thinkers as Theodor Adorno, Bloch, Lucien Goldmann, Herbert Marcuse, and Sartre, and among its distinguished attackers were Karl Kautsky, Nikolai Bukharin, Kun, and (indirectly) Lenin. Lukács himself became his own severest critic; in 1934 he equated the idealism of the book outright with fascism (although, Löwy feels, this was understandable in view of the victory of the Nazis just the year before). In 1967, toward the end of Lukács's life, came a calmer and more constructive critique, in which the attempt of 1923 to find the "identical subject-object of history" stands essentially defended. It is the book's practical politics that the aging Lukács felt still deserve censure. From other postmortems it seems equally clear that this messianic utopian had in the 1920's essentially spent his political energies, in the sense of party work, at least. His various recantations of *History and Class Consciousness* are, in any event, very different in spirit from that of the "Blum Theses." The "Blum Theses," which bear Lukács's party name, the pseudonym Blum, were a point-by-point outline for action directed at achieving the revolution in Hungary. Written in 1928 and 1929, at a time of bitter controversy within party ranks as to why the Hungarian Soviet experiment of 1919 had failed, the "Blum Theses" recommended bourgeois-democratic revolution for Hungary instead of the dictatorship of the proletariat favored by Kun and his party faction. The Comintern, at its Sixth Congress, opposed the theses as a "rightist threat," and subsequently the Hungarian Communist Party, at its Second Congress in February and March 1930, rejected them outright as a "false and opportunistic document." These extreme reactions caused Lukács to leave Vienna in 1929 and to withdraw from active politics for the next quarter century.

SOCIALISM AND REALISM: 1929–1945

The evolution of Lukács's thought, both political and aesthetic, may in part be traced by certain subtle shifts he makes in his ideological positions in the course of an extended discussion. Just as in *The Theory of the Novel* he shifts his ground almost unnoticeably between history and society (in the course of his discussion of the vision of Flaubert versus that of Goethe), so there are subtle equivocations throughout *History and Class Consciousness* on a distinction now considered important, namely, between dialectical and historical materialism. More important, there is at least an added emphasis, in the 1926 essay on Moses Hess, on Hegel's element of reconciliation and realism, an element that Lukács's thinking of three years before lacks. Political constructions that may be placed on Lukács's writings from the later Vienna period should in no way obscure the significance they hold for his need to accommodate himself, from 1929 on, to the ascendancy of Stalin, and with that event, to the demands of a new literary and critical policy. Socialist realism was declared the official party line as early as August 1934, and some sources have dated its origins from two years earlier.

After leaving Vienna, Lukács still undertook several trips for the purpose of doing political work. For several months during 1929 he was in Horthy's Hungary, illegally directing party activity; in 1931 he moved to Germany and engaged in underground political work there until Hitler came to power. In 1933 Lukács published his famous essay "Mein Weg zu Marx" ("My Road to Marx") in the journal *Internationale Literatur*. Between 1929 and 1931 he resided in Moscow, working at the Marx-Engels-Lenin Institute under the directorship of David Riazanov; he settled in the Soviet capital in 1933, living and working there continuously until the summer of 1945.

Once there, Lukács became a research associate at the Institute of Philosophy of the Soviet Academy of Sciences and did systematic work on Marxist aesthetics and literary criticism, establishing, in the process, what became a life-long friendship with Mikhail Lifchitz. Lifchitz compiled several volumes of excerpts from Marx and Engels on literary criticism, and together he and Lukács elaborated a loyal and at the same time independent view of Marxist literary theory, above all on the issue of realism. At the first Congress of the newly established Union of Soviet Writers, held in August 1934, Andrei Zhdanov echoed the views of Marx and Lenin in exhorting writers to reflect in their novels and other works the transformation of society by means of revolution, to educate the workers in the new reality within the framework of the dialectics of history, and to make the best, in the process, of the classical (that is, bourgeois) literary heritage. For Lukács this last directive meant preservation of the German classical heritage first of all. In part independently he then adopted the position of "Great Realism." Zhdanov had called for a writer who would be an "engineer of souls"; in indirect response Lukács held that the artist's first responsibility is to create art, that is, a rich but indirect reflection of reality. A realist is an artist; being a card-carrying party member is not enough. Here too we can see how methodically Lukács ignores, in his criticism, most of the fiction produced by the Stalinist "engineers of souls" and turns for his examination of literary values to the classical tradition instead. Lukács's culture heroes in European fiction are Goethe, Sir Walter Scott, Balzac, Stendhal, German writers of the second half of the nineteenth century, Tolstoy, Dostoevsky, Gorky, Mann, and—necessarily belatedly—Alexander Solzhenitsyn.

The Moscow period is a generous decade and a half of sustained effort in the fields of literary aesthetics and criticism. Lukács wrote and published numerous essays in journals such as *Internationale Literatur* (Berlin) and *Literaturny kritik* (Moscow), both of which he helped edit for a time, and in the Hungarian-language *Új Hang* (New Voice, Moscow). He also published, partly as the fruit of work done mostly in the Soviet Union, as many as ten volumes of literary criticism, from the slender *Gottfried Keller* (1940) to *Wider den missverstandenen Realismus* (*The Meaning of Contemporary Realism*, 1958). Of interest here are the most important five: *Goethe és kora* (*Goethe and His Age*, 1946), *Balzac und der französische Realismus* (Balzac and French Realism, 1952), *Der historische Roman* (*The Historical Novel*, 1955), *Der russische Realismus in der Weltliteratur* (Russian Realism in World Literature, 1949), and *Thomas Mann* (*Essays on Thomas Mann*, 1949).

In their narratives all the major writers Lukács evaluates make a series of significant choices (not least in the process of revising their work), thus evolving their views of the rich totality of reality that their narratives depict. For Goethe, whom Lukács considers to be a transitional figure with stages of work coming both before and after the French Revolution, what matters in *Wilhelm Meister's Apprenticeship* is the harmonious development of the personality of his hero, as well as the development according to disposition and talent of the many other characters of the novel. In this work revision was extremely important to Goethe; Lukács observes that the *Apprenticeship* goes significantly beyond the preoccupation with a career in the theater that takes up most of the early draft, *Wilhelm Meisters theatralische Sendung* (*Wilhelm Meister's Theatrical Mission,* written from 1777 to 1785, published in 1911). In the final version the performance of *Hamlet* as a symbol for fulfillment of Wilhelm's professional ambitions is retained, but the novel itself develops along realistic lines in portraying a rich array of Enlightenment society, taking its character types from both the nobility and the rising bourgeoisie. With the Tower (a secret society formed by Wilhelm's friends to keep track of his movements, to help him) there is also an element of the utopian. The emphasis throughout the work is on humanist social criticism and, ultimately, on the education of the central character and of those around him. In revising and expanding his conception, Goethe also shows himself to be a master of narrative structure: there is a tightening of scenes and an increase in dramatic concentration.

The two versions of the *Apprenticeship* certainly fall on either side of the French Revolution, and one wonders whether Lukács consciously evaluates the Goethe of *The Sorrows of Young Werther* compared with the Goethe of the *Apprenticeship* in the light of that major political event. Without giving a satisfactory answer, Lukács discusses the traditional split, in bourgeois views of the eighteenth century, between the Enlightenment and *Sturm und Drang* (storm and stress) and observes, rightly, that the two are not antagonistic to each other and that *Werther* is deeply indebted to both. Lukács is convincing in his evaluation of the portrayal of the conflict between the individual and society in *Werther;* he is less so in stating that in the work Goethe "shows, in the portrayal of passionate love, the irresolvable contradiction between personality development and middle-class society." The difficulties in

such an evaluation are perhaps nowhere better attested than in Goethe's play *Torquato Tasso,* which the French critic Jean-Jacques Ampère is said to have called "an intensified *Werther.*" Lukács, who comments on this insight, knows that *Tasso* already represents withdrawal as well as emotional and political defeat (see his article "Nathan und Tasso" ["Lessing's Nathan and Goethe's Tasso," 1922] in *Die Rote Fahne* [The Red Flag] and Löwy's comment on it).

Perhaps nowhere is our need to look at dialectics as a background for choices by the critic rather than by the author more clearly demonstrated than in Lukács's discussion of Lessing's *Minna von Barnhelm* (1767), read and contrasted with his analysis of Hölderlin's *Hyperion* (1797–1799). In the discussion of *Minna,* too, the social background and the socioeconomic clockwork action of the plot are touched on. But by far the greater counterweight to the argument rests in Lukács's comparison of the language of the dialogues in Lessing's play to the music of Wolfgang Mozart. "The hovering weightlessness which in a dance tempo conquers all murky perils, . . . this is the . . . basis of the Mozartean spirit in this comedy." No such "comparative arts" approach is possible in attempts to understand postrevolutionary Hölderlin. The atmosphere of victory and yet despair in *Hyperion,* the moment of Pyrrhic victory in the novel, takes us back to the agonized ideology of Lukács's essay "Tactics and Ethics," only with the divine injunction to commit sin removed. As Lukács writes in the Hölderlin essay: "What [Hölderlin] hopes for . . . is precisely a complete revolution of his world. . . . His recoiling refers to revolutionary methods, which, quite in the style of idealistic ideologues of the Revolution, he fears would perpetuate the evils of the status quo in another form." That not merely the mood but the very method of analysis differs—that, in a deeper sense, Lukács the dialectician is in each instance in harmony with the demands of his subject—seems incisively clear.

Lukács the historically and socially oriented critic is again undividedly himself when he turns from the age of Goethe to the age of the nineteenth-century French novel. Here, his great subjects are the realist Balzac (already discussed in *The Theory of the Novel*), such major but intermediary figures as Stendhal and Flaubert, and the naturalist Zola; Lukács's views on naturalism as a movement and a technique had already found their expression in *A modern dráma*. In these comparative analyses the great historical watershed, for Lukács, is the revolutionary year 1848, which preceded Balzac's death by just two years. For Lukács, Balzac—whose most productive years came well before that key date—is the prototype of the great French critical realist (that is, a narrative artist who, while he has not had the benefits of instruction in the demands of socialist realism, has the talent to depict society and the individual dialectically and with a keen critical eye). Balzac is interested in the turmoil of life and society in a great transitional age, when, in the midst of the rise of the lesser fortunes of the peasantry and the greater ones of the bourgeoisie, motivation and character are shaped by the desire to acquire new wealth. Balzac, Lukács contends, understood in depth the human implications and consequences of the development of French capitalism. What most impresses Lukács, however, is that, despite Balzac's having been a legitimist—an admirer of the nobility and of royalty—he had the objectivity to depict the complexity of social change that went against the interests of the class with which he sided personally: "His greatness consists precisely in the fact that—despite his political and philosophical prejudices—he observes and portrays all arising contradictions with eyes of great integrity." This, in brief, also lies at the heart of Lukács's great admiration for the narrative art of Sir Walter Scott and for the historical novel as the comparable manifestation of a legitimate fictional genre. In "Georg Lukács and His Devil's Pact," George

Steiner suggests that if we do not take Scott seriously today that is most probably unjust; Lukács also suggests that it is our loss. The author of *Quentin Durward* (1823) and *The Heart of Midlothian* (1818) is a great narrative artist and every bit as honest as Balzac in depicting political change.

The decline of French bourgeois fiction comes, in Lukács's evaluation, after 1848. This year, as Lukács sees it, lies between Balzac and Zola and helps explain the strange turns that Zola's art took toward a naturalism hostile alike to man, society, and art. Zola, whose social sympathies and courage in the stand he took in the Dreyfus affair are famous, nevertheless had a fatal critical flaw in his artistic makeup, which allowed him repeatedly to criticize both Balzac and Stendhal. The latter two, Zola contended, suffered from a wrongheaded romanticism; their descriptions (note the terminological shift, here, from earlier *depiction*) of life are flawed by their insistence on constructing unbelievable situations and, above all, characters. Zola was unhappy with the gross ending of *Le rouge et le noir* (*The Red and the Black*, 1830), and we may grant him his point. In contrast, Lukács points to the crude and self-defeating naturalism in Zola's own practice, a tendency that shows the fatal cleft not in his ideology (as is the case with Balzac) but in his art.

> Zola's "scientific" method aims at the average and at the gray, statistical median. The point, however, where all inner contradictions are blunted one against the other, where the great and the small, the noble and the mean, the beautiful and the disgraceful appear equally as mediocre "products," is the death of every great literature.
>
> (*Werke*, 6.516–517)

But Zola's road as an artist did not lead him into a blind alley of defeat; he was able to escape into the school of the unadulterated romanticism of Victor Hugo. Lukács was appreciably more positive toward other examples of the European novel after 1848, and here is where his interest in such German novelists as Keller, Wilhelm Raabe, and the late Theodor Fontane becomes important. Equally interesting is the fact that Lukács does not neglect any major European figure. His essay "Die Tragödie Heinrich von Kleists" (The Tragedy of Heinrich von Kleist), included in his 1951 volume *Deutsche Realisten des 19. Jahrhunderts* (German Realists of the Nineteenth Century), shows particularly well how willing Lukács was to revise earlier critical estimates of individual writers (in this instance, since his view in *A modern dráma*).

Least of all, perhaps, does he neglect the great Russians of the golden age of realist fiction; he sees two of its leading representatives, Dostoevsky and Tolstoy, as standing solidly in the tradition of Balzac. It is small wonder that Dostoevsky, who translated *Eugénie Grandet* (1833), should have modeled one of his central characters on one in a work by Balzac: "Raskolnikov is the Rastignac of the second half of the nineteenth century." Dostoevsky's principal characters, Raskolnikov among them if not at their helm, are on field campaigns of self-discovery; they commit (or at the very least discuss or advocate) crimes, not in order to improve society, but in order to become better acquainted with themselves. Here is where Raskolnikov's Napoleon theme acquires fatal significance. Lukács's view of Tostoy, if this is possible, is more Balzacian yet: Tolstoy was not merely on the side of the nobles; he was a nobleman—turned revolutionary peasant. This, at least, as Lukács saw it, was Lenin's estimate of him. Among Tolstoy's great themes is the development of the peasantry between the freeing of the serfs in 1861 and the revolution of 1905. With the other two revolutionary years 1789 and 1848, 1905 completes a triad of the great historical watersheds before 1917. Tolstoy's major novels, *Anna Karenina* (1873–1876) and *War and Peace,* pursue sensitive and yet universal critical realism within the bounds of the single, all-embracing narrative structure: "Tolstoy further develops the traditions of Fielding and

Defoe, Balzac and Stendhal, yet in a period in which the flowering of realism in Europe had itself long since come to an end." Indeed, Lukács did not have much sympathy with such contemporary developments in the novel as James Joyce's *Ulysses* (1922), which he considered a surrealist work. Even with Bertolt Brecht, whose early plays show the tendentiousness Lukács abhors, there was only a later reconciliation.

The one major novelist of the first half of the twentieth century for whose work Lukács maintains unalloyed affection and respect is Mann. Beyond meeting in Vienna in 1922— the encounter that resulted in the telling Leo Naphta portrait in Mann's *Der Zauberberg* (*The Magic Mountain,* 1924)—and in Weimar in 1955, the two men—distantly, to be sure— remained each other's warm admirers. The volume *Essays on Thomas Mann* unites three major essays on Mann and also contains Lukács's 1909 review of *Königliche Hoheit* (*Royal Highness,* 1909), in addition to some minor writings on the great bourgeois novelist. Especially incisive, as we might expect, is Lukács's commentary on *The Magic Mountain,* particularly on the effect that the great arguments between Settembrini and Naphta have on Hans Castorp and on the treatment of time in the novel. Lukács's tribute to Mann's one great historical novel, *Lotte in Weimar* (1939), is at the same time the Marxist critic's tribute to the "giant Goethe, [this] Gulliver in the Lilliput of Weimar, in his constantly endangered, yet uninterruptedly self-rescued intellectual, artistic, and moral perfection." Moreover, the novel itself takes its material from the past in order to show realistically a way to an enlightened future. With this, we are reminded of Lukács's interest in thinking that brings Goethe and Mann together elsewhere as well, preeminently in the area of studies in the late novel *Doctor Faustus* (1947). The development of Mann shows an important parallel to and at the same time a telling contrast with that of Goethe. Both are artists who lived and transmuted into art the tragedies of their times; in the words of a late pronouncement by Lukács, Mann is the last great critical realist.

THE PHILOSOPHER: 1945–1971

The innocent pursuit of literary criticism seems to have helped Lukács avoid arrest during the purges; he was finally arrested on 29 June 1941, one week to the day after Germany attacked the Soviet Union. Although the arrest was not of a political nature but was made in the framework of the extreme xenophobia that followed the attack, there was an attempt to obtain from Lukács a confession that during the years of his Soviet emigration he had worked as a Trotskyite agent. Naturally, he would confess to no such thing. He was released on 26 August, partly through the intervention of Mátyás Rákosi (who became Stalinist premier of Hungary between 1952 and 1956). The Lukácses stayed in the Soviet Union until the end of the war, and in 1945, when given the option either to remain or to settle permanently in Germany or in Hungary, Lukács and his wife chose Hungary. They arrived in Budapest, all but on the tracks of the victorious Red Army, on 1 August 1945. Lukács was immediately made a member of Parliament and of the presidium of the Hungarian Academy of Sciences and later accepted the chair of aesthetics and of philosophy of culture at the University of Budapest.

Four major philosophical works of this period are *Der junge Hegel* (*The Young Hegel*, 1948), *Die Zerstörung der Vernunft* (*The Destruction of Reason*, 1954), *Die Eigenart des Ästhetischen*, and *Zur Ontologie des gesellschaftlichen Seins* (Toward an Ontology of Social Being, 1976). Of these, only *The Young Hegel* still dates from Lukács's years in Moscow; dedicated to Lifchitz, the substantial book served as a dissertation that helped Lukács obtain a doctorate from the Soviet Academy of Sciences in 1938. The two-volume *Die Eigenart des Ästhetischen* was begun in 1955; two major events in the philosopher's life punctuating its progress were the 1956 uprisings and the death of his wife on 28 April 1963 (the work is dedicated to her memory). With qualifications, then, all four of these works can be said to belong to what, if only for convenience, might be called Lukács's third and last Budapest period.

As one of Lukács's major attempts to write a history of modern philosophy, *The Young Hegel* is, of course, a study of the development of a specific philosopher. This is the sense in which the book is of some use, for example, to the Hegel scholar Walter Kaufmann. At the same time there is no going past the fact that it is also a careful presentation of Lukács's own views, especially in its closing chapters. In four substantial parts, Lukács traces Hegel's development through four stages of his career, the periods at Berne (1793–1796), Frankfurt (1797–1800), and Jena (1801–1803 and 1803–1807). The last is, of course, the period of *Phänomenologie des Geistes* (*The Phenomenology of Spirit*, 1807), the crowning work of his youth. The most interesting parts of each book concern, respectively, Hegel's perspectives on ancient and medieval history, his first studies in economics, his ideas on labor and teleology (a chapter that prefigures central ideas of the *Ontologie* of Lukács), and the center of gravity of the *Phenomenology*. Of exclusive interest to Hegel scholars might be, for example, the Frankfurt period, and within it, Hegel's friendship with Hölderlin (who obtained a position for him there), and the discussion of the *Systemprogramm* (*Fragment of a System*, 1796), thought to be a collaboration among Hegel, Hölderlin, and Schelling. Referring to the break with Schelling, Lukács observes that Schelling's *System des transcendentalen Idealismus* (*System of Transcendental Idealism*, 1800) and the *Phenomenology* have nothing in common, since Schelling's thinking stops where Hegel's begins, "with the philosophy of praxis." Hegel's third understanding of history, which took the form of enthusiasm concerning Napoleon's victory at Jena in 1806 (an attitude Hegel shared, significantly, with Goethe), strengthened rather than weakened the philosophical outlook and powers of the author of *Phenomenology.*

It is in chapter 4 of part 4—"Die 'Entäusserung' als philosophischer Zentralbegriff der 'Phänomenologie des Geistes' " (" 'Alienation' as the Central Philosophical Concept of *The Phenomenology of Spirit")*—that we see a trenchant presentation of Lukács's views in conjunction with those of Hegel. The chapter is also a central example of Lukács's practice of going back to an earlier position and rethinking it. In *History and Class Consciousness,* Lukács's one previous attempt to write a history of bourgeois philosophy, he identifies *Verdinglichung* (reification) as the source of alienation in the proletariat, an experience that, in turn, leads to increased class consciousness. There, alienation from oneself and from the social milieu is the point; Lukács's ideas on reification came largely from Simmel. In Moscow Lukács could study Marx's *Economic and Philosophical Manuscripts of 1844,* which were discovered and deciphered only after 1923, and it is from this study that the distinctions he draws in *The Young Hegel* benefit. In Hegel's thinking on economics and labor Lukács discerns three senses of Hegel's use of *Entäusserung* (alienation): "the complicated subject-object relationship connected with every economic and social activity of man"; "the specifically capitalistic form of 'alienation,' what Marx is later to call fetishism"; and "a broad philosophic generalization of this concept: 'alienation' means . . . the same as thinghood or objectivity; it is the form in which the genesis of objectivity, objectivity as dialectical moment, is represented, on its way as subject-object, over 'alienation,' back to itself." This last, according to Lukács, forms a central concept in Hegel's dialectical model and, reading Lukács's *Die Eigenart des Ästhetischen,* we see that it plays a central role there as well.

The typology of alienation that Lukács offers in *The Young Hegel* indeed suggests that Lukács does not consider alienation in its worst aspects to be a permanent condition of man

and society; as we would expect, his view of that society, as of Hegel's model for socioeconomic relations within it, emerges as an essentially optimistic one. To come to grips with Lukács's view of pessimistic and irrational currents in later European philosophy, we must turn to *The Destruction of Reason.* In tackling this highly controversial work, which has had perhaps more than its share of hostile critical reaction, we must remind ourselves that, later as earlier, Lukács stands squarely in the camp of the Enlightenment and of rationalism. Obscurantism in its various forms he condemns outright. Schelling, Schopenhauer, Kierkegaard, and Nietzsche are, by Lukács's lights, four leading representatives of philosophic irrationalism, but his rogues' gallery extends all the way to the representatives of race theory and thus to the preparers of the way for Hitler. Indeed, the strong title of the book suggests that Lukács is discussing not merely decline in the quality of European thought but its total disintegration. The fact that he even adds an appendix to the volume, entitled "Über den Irrationalismus der Nachkriegszeit" ("On Irrationalism in the Postwar Era"), clearly indicates that this cantankerous speaker and thinker means to carry on the fight to the threshold of his very own day.

What, then, are the hallmarks of irrationalist thought? First, in Schelling, comes the concept of *intellektuelle Anschauung* (intuition), allied with his Romantic philosophy of nature, which leads to a kind of pantheism shared to an extent by Goethe, Friedrich Jacobi, and other German writers and thinkers of the eighteenth century. In Goethe, however, these ideas do not anywhere receive the theological coloring that they do especially in the later Schelling. In Schopenhauer, whose *Die Welt als Wille und Vorstellung (The World as Will and Representation,* 1819) actually predates an important phase of Schelling's development, Lukács glimpses a more sophisticated irrationalist, one who knows how to capitalize on such notions as pessimism, despair, and the futility of political endeavors. Lukács identifies

Schopenhauer's entire ideological position as a function of conditions in Germany during the Wilhelminian era. Kierkegaard, albeit of a different locale and background, is a kindred spirit. Both attack Hegel's dialectical model and dismiss Hegel's philosophy of history as pure nonsense. Because—Kierkegaard's professed Christianity notwithstanding—Lukács considers them to believe in nothing, he designates both Schopenhauer and Kierkegaard as religious atheists. (In fact, in later existentialism, of which Kierkegaard is a harbinger, theological and atheistic models exist side by side.) But it is in Nietzsche that irrationalism as a real forerunner of fascism first raises its head, from the overall superficiality of his training and knowledge to his interest in biologically underpinned sociology and all the way to his notions about eternal recurrence and the Superman. It has been said that *The Destruction of Reason* is grossly unfair to thinkers like Nietzsche and that, generally, it is a polemical work of little merit. It does, for all that, contain statements granting positive traits to some of the philosophers it devalues. And a look at the desperate postwar situation sketched in the appendix should convince us that the polemic itself does, to a significant extent, carry its point.

Taking up, in its turn, the hefty two-volume *Die Eigenart des Ästhetischen,* we come to a very different landscape of feeling, as of thought. Although the work is only a part of a much larger projected whole, it is itself encyclopedic in scope, comprising some 1,700 printed pages in the Luchterhand edition. At its core lies the inquiry concerning what makes the aesthetic experience aesthetic rather than something else. This, which Lukács identifies as *Eigenart* (particularity; the term has also been translated as "specificity" or "characteristic nature"), necessarily lies at the center of the energies of man, who makes, appreciates, and theorizes about art. The world of art is the world of human beings:

. . . the central construction of the aesthetic sphere, of the work of art, can be grasped as such only to the extent that in it a maximum of unfolded subjectivity, cleansed of all mere particularity, is realized together with a maximal objectivity, every time with the maximal approximation to objective reality, through the mirroring of said reality.

(*Werke*, 12.227)

The work of art, then, is an instance of mirroring, of the reflection of reality. In discussing the category of reflection, Lukács stresses that it is closely akin to mimesis, or representation; he refers, of course, to Aristotle, but the term *Wiederspiegelung* (reflection) suggests Plotinus, whom Lukács is known to have read and admired.

As in earlier works, Lukács once again stresses that knowledge is itself a reflection of reality, and in introductory chapters of *Die Eigenart des Ästhetischen* he inquires into different categories of knowledge and into how they differ as acts of reflection. Magic, religion, and science are discussed, and what Lukács says about the difference between science and art is highly suggestive. Science, for him, de-anthropomorphizes experience; that is, it presents aspects of reality independent of us in origin, shape, or character (this lies, we may suggest, at the bases of science's refusal to entertain its questions in a teleological way). Art, by contrast, is humanly oriented; it is a quite closely anthropomorphic reflection of reality, leading us, in Hegel's sense, back to ourselves. To the question of what makes art art—what, that is, raises an instance of reflection to the level of art—Lukács answers that it is the ability of the work to make us experience a world, an expanded sense of ourselves, our environment, and our history. *Die Eigenart des Ästhetischen* then goes on to discuss in great detail such topics as the abstract forms of reflection (for example, rhythm, symmetry, proportion) and a number of arts, both major and minor. Here many of the ideas first broached in the *Heidelberger Ästhetik* are worked out in their final form; here too is where Lukács pays final homage to the aesthetics of his friend Popper, in the discussion of the art of Pieter Brueghel in chapters 15 and 16 of volume 1. It also seems that the later Lukács tends to devalue religious experience and hence art with religious subjects. To such art, as to ornament, he would assign the category of "worldlessness" insofar as they do not constitute great art in a secular sense.

Lukács's final work, the *Ontologie,* is available complete both in a Hungarian translation and in the German original (*Werke,* vols. 13 and 14). Of the three volumes of the Hungarian edition, the first consists of a history of modern ontology, reviewing the achievements of the neopositivists and of Nicolai Hartmann, Hegel, and Marx; the second consists of "systematic chapters"; and the third is a "prolegomenon." What has so far been seen as the central portion of this giant work, the discussion of the ontology of labor, comprises chapter 1 of volume 2. To understand it more clearly, however, we must go back to volume 1, chapter 3, to Lukács's discussion of ontology as understood by Hegel. The first and last ontological problem seems to be that of a proper view of the relation between nature and society. On the one hand, since Galileo and Sir Isaac Newton, nature has been understood in terms of its objectivity and laws—its "unshakably solid ontological base"; on the other, nature does not lend itself to the deduction, from this base, of any social ontology whatever. Lukács and Hegel agree that the categories of society, history, and teleology must be kept discrete from questions of natural causality. Thus Lukács's central concern with the ontology of labor, and with teleology within the human sphere of self-definition, clarifies itself as a philosophy of purpose, of projection, and of making. We have come full circle; the argument is strongly reminiscent of a neglected work of Lukács's youth, *Esztétikai kultúra,* in which he counterposes mere aesthetic enjoyment with the making of the work of art and writes, "Form is the maximum expenditure of energy among the given possibilities of a given situation. . . . Outwardly, form imposes limitations; inwardly, it creates infinity everywhere." In his end is Lukács's beginning. Both the work by the twenty-eight-year-old and the one by the octogenarian are motivated by strongly ethical positions. Lukács had planned to write an *Ethics,* but he did not live to do so; he died, at the age of eighty-six, on 4 June 1971. He was buried next to his wife at Kerepesi Cemetery, Budapest, in a special section reserved for leading personalities of the socialist movement.

At the conclusion of his discussion of Lukács in *Marx, Engels und die Dichter* (*Marx, Engels, and the Poets,* 1959), Peter Demetz writes: "We will do well to read Lukács's oeuvre, in which there unfolds one of the extreme possibilities of modern literary theory, as a palimpsest, behind whose red script there shine forth, repeatedly and indelibly, the golden letters of German philosophical idealism." This seems to be an excellent way to understand the significance of the contribution of Lukács for our cultural sphere. Red and gold in combination are, in the German cultural tradition, a symbol of wealth, and it is on the wealth, and on the rich totality of the Lukácsian legacy, that the stress should be laid. If it does not seem too heretical to say, Marxism as Lukács gives it to us has as much to teach us as does the German-idealist half of his thought; we should cherish and strive to preserve the two together. There is, to be truthful in another direction, also something to criticize about a man and writer who lived as long as Lukács did and whose activities and achievements challenge comparison with those of Goethe. It has been said many times that Lukács's ideas are heavily indebted to thinkers who immediately precede him; that in his estimation of cultural phenomena contemporaneous with himself he has serious blind spots; that in his polemicizing he can be one-sided and downright unfair. A comment is also in order on the count of language. Interviewers have at times had difficulty editing his torrent of unpunctuated speech, and his writing, in the later works especially, has been rambling and repetitious; too often it seems that he will never say in twenty words what he can say in two thousand. Yet once we are beyond the faults, we recognize that they take their origins in the humane energies of a cultivated and, ultimately, generous mind. Lukács will be remembered for his lifelong eagerness to communicate exciting insights and to construct theories and offer applications that are as innovative as they are wholesomely provocative. His following in both East and West has indeed been considerable. In a time when we are once again stringently redefining the modern, it will be profitable to listen to one who, while he works within the limitations of a given system, is yet able to tell us that a modern work of art is one that remains modern regardless of the age that produced it.

Selected Bibliography

EDITIONS

INDIVIDUAL WORKS

A lélek és a formák (Kísérletek). Budapest, 1910.

A modern dráma fejlődésének története. 2 vols. Budapest, 1911.

Die Seele und die Formen. Essays. Berlin, 1911.

Esztétikai kultúra (Tanulmányok). Budapest, 1913.

Balázs Béla és akiknek nem kell. Gyoma, 1918.

Taktika és etika. Budapest, 1919.

Die Theorie des Romans. Ein geschichtsphilosophischer Versuch über die Formen der grossen Epik. Berlin, 1920.

"Nathan und Tasso." *Die Rote Fahne.* 13 August 1922, p. 4.

Geschichte und Klassenbewusstsein. Studien über marxistische Dialektik. Berlin, 1923.

Lenin. Studie über den Zusammenhang seiner Gedanken. Vienna and Berlin, 1924.

Moses Hess und die Probleme der idealistischen Dialektik. Leipzig, 1926.

Gottfried Keller. Kiev, 1940.

Írástudók felelőssége. Moscow, 1944.

Balzac, Stendhal, Zola. Budapest, 1945.

Goethe és kora. Budapest, 1946.

Goethe und seine Zeit. Berne, 1947.

A polgári filozófia válsága. Budapest, 1947.

Essays über Realismus. Berlin, 1948.

Der junge Hegel. Über die Beziehungen von Dialektik und Ökonomie. Zurich, 1948.

Der russische Realismus in der Weltliteratur. Berlin, 1949.

Thomas Mann. Berlin, 1949.

Deutsche Realisten des 19. Jahrhunderts. Berlin, 1951.

Balzac und der französische Realismus. Berlin, 1952.

Beiträge zur Geschichte der Ästhetik. Berlin, 1954.

Die Zerstörung der Vernunft. Berlin, 1954. Also published in Hungarian as *Az ész trónfosztása. Az irracionalista filózófia kritikája.* Budapest, 1954.

Der historische Roman. Berlin, 1955.

A különösség mint esztétikai kategória. Budapest, 1957.

Wider den missverstandenen Realismus. Hamburg, 1958.

Die Eigenart des Ästhetischen. Vols. 11 and 12. In *Werke.* Neuwied and Berlin, 1963.

COLLECTED WORKS

Werke. Edited by Frank Benseler. Vols. 2, 4–17. Neuwied and Berlin, 1962–. Vols. 1 and 3 are forthcoming.

Utam Marxhoz. Válogatott filozófiai tanulmányok. Edited by György Márkus. 2 vols. Budapest, 1971.

Ifjúkori művek (1902–1918). Lukács György Összes művei. Edited by Árpád Tímár. Budapest, 1977.

MODERN EDITIONS

Die Seele und die Formen. Essays. Sammlung Luchterhand, no. 21. Neuwied and Berlin, 1971.

Die Theorie des Romans. Ein geschichtsphilosophischer Versuch über die Formen der grossen Epik. Sammlung Luchterhand, no. 36. Neuwied and Berlin, 1971.

A társadalmi lét ontológiájáról. Translated from the manuscript of *Zur Ontologie des gesellschaftlichen Seins* by István Eörsi and Gábor Révai. 3 vols. Budapest, 1976.

LETTERS AND MEMOIRS

Briefwechsel 1902–1917. Edited by Éva Karádi and Éva Fekete. Stuttgart, 1982.

Record of a Life: An Autobiographical Sketch. Edited by István Eörsi. Translated by Rodney Livingstone. London, 1983. Includes four-part taped interview with Lukács, Lukács's "*Gelebtes Denken:* Notes Towards an Autobiography," and his interview with *New Left Review.*

TRANSLATIONS

The Destruction of Reason. Translated by Peter Palmer. Atlantic Highlands, N.J., 1981.

Essays on Thomas Mann. Translated by Stanley Mitchell. London, 1964.

Goethe and His Age. Translated by Robert Anchor. New York, 1969.

The Historical Novel. Translated by Stanley and Hannah Mitchell. Introduction by Fredric Jameson. Lincoln, Nebr., 1983.

History and Class Consciousness: Studies in Marxist Dialectics. Translated by Rodney Livingstone. Cambridge, Mass., 1971.

"In Search of the Bourgeois." In *The Stature of Thomas Mann.* Edited by Charles Neider. New York, 1947. Pp. 469–473.

The Meaning of Contemporary Realism. Translated by John and Necke Mander. London, 1963.

Reviews and Articles from "Die Rote Fahne." Translated by Peter Palmer. London, 1983. Includes "Lessing's Nathan and Goethe's Tasso."

Solzhenitsyn. Translated by William David Graf. London, 1969.

Soul and Form. Translated by Anna Bostock. Cambridge, Mass., 1974.

Studies in European Realism. Translated by Edith Bone. Introduced by Alfred Kazin. New York, 1964.

Tactics and Ethics: Political Essays, 1919–1929. Translated by Michael McColgan. Edited, with an introduction, by Rodney Livingstone. New York, 1972.

The Theory of the Novel: A Historico-Philosophical Essay on the Forms of Great Epic Literature. Translated by Anna Bostock. Cambridge, Mass., 1971.

The Young Hegel: Studies in the Relations Between Dialectics and Economics. Translated by Rodney Livingstone. Cambridge, Mass., 1976.

BIOGRAPHICAL AND CRITICAL STUDIES

Almási, Miklós. "Lukács—The Moral Philosopher: A Contribution to His 'Invisible' Portrait." *The New Hungarian Quarterly* 99:26–35 (1985).

Arato, Andrew, and Paul Breines. *The Young Lukács and the Origins of Western Marxism.* New York, 1979.

Bahr, Ehrhard, and Ruth Goldschmidt Kunzer. *Georg Lukács.* New York, 1972.

Ban, Sung-Wan. *Das Verhältnis der Ästhetik Georg Lukács' zur deutschen Klassik und zu Thomas Mann.* Frankfurt and Berne, 1977.

Congdon, Lee. *The Young Lukács.* Chapel Hill, N.C., 1983.

Demetz, Peter. *Marx, Engels, and the Poets: Origins of Marxist Literary Criticism.* Translated by Jeffrey L. Sammons. Chicago, 1959 and 1967.

Eörsi, István. "*His Master's Voice:* Absurd Documentary Play in Two Parts." Translated by Emery George. *Cross Currents* 4:209–275 (1985). A play on the life and work of Georg Lukács, based on Lukács's *Record of a Life: An Autobiographical Sketch* (see above).

Feenberg, Andrew. *Lukács, Marx and the Sources of Critical Theory.* New York and Oxford, England, 1986.

Fehervary, Helen. "Georg Lukács: The Tragedy of the Jacobin." In *Hölderlin and the Left: The Search for a Dialectic of Art and Life.* Heidelberg, 1977.

Fekete, Éva, and Éva Karádi, comps. and eds. *György Lukács: His Life in Pictures and Documents.* Budapest, 1981.

Georg Lukács zum siebzigsten Geburtstag. [Festschrift.] Anonymously edited. Berlin, 1955.

George, Emery. "The Tape Recorder as Tragic Hero: Observations on István Eörsi's Play *His Master's Voice.*" *Cross Currents* 4:191–207 (1985).

Gluck, Mary. *Georg Lukács and His Generation, 1900–1918.* Cambridge, Mass., 1985.

Goldmann, Lucien. *Lukács and Heidegger: Towards a New Philosophy.* Translated by William Q. Boelhower. London, 1977.

Grunenberg, Antonia. *Bürger und Revolutionär. Georg Lukács, 1918–1928.* Foreword by Frank Benseler. Cologne and Frankfurt, 1976.

Hanak, Tibor. *Lukács war anders.* Meisenheim am Glan, 1973.

Heller, Ágnes. "Lukács's Aesthetics." *The New Hungarian Quarterly* 24:84–94 (1966).

———, ed. *Lukács Reappraised.* New York, 1983. Includes essay by Sándor Radnóti.

Hermann, István. *Lukács György élete.* Budapest, 1985.

Jameson, Fredric. *Marxism and Form.* Princeton, N.J., 1971.

Keller, Ernst. *Der junge Lukács, Antibürger und wesentliches Leben: Literatur- und Kulturkritik, 1902–1915.* Foreword by Frank Benseler. Frankfurt am Main, 1984.

Királyfalvi, Béla. *The Aesthetics of György Lukács.* Princeton, N.J., 1975.

Köpeczi, Béla. "Lukács in 1919." *The New Hungarian Quarterly* 75:65–76 (1979).

Kurrik, Maire. "The Novel's Subjectivity: Georg Lukács's *Theory of the Novel.*" *Salmagundi* 28:104–124 (1975).

Kutzbach, Karl August, ed. *Paul Ernst und Georg Lukács. Dokumente einer Freundschaft.* Emsdetten, Westphalia, 1974.

Lichtheim, George. *George Lukács.* New York, 1970.

Löwy, Michael. *Georg Lukács: From Romanticism to Bolshevism.* Translated by Patrick Camiller. London, 1979.

Lunn, Eugene. "Marxism and Art in the Era of Stalin and Hitler: A Comparison of Brecht and Lukács." *New German Critique* 3:12–44 (1974).

———. *Marxism and Modernism: An Historical Study of Lukács, Brecht, Benjamin, and Adorno.* Berkeley and Los Angeles, 1982.

Marcus-Tar, Judith. *Thomas Mann und Georg Lukács. Beziehung, Einfluss und "repräsentative Gegensätzlichkeit."* Foreword by István Hermann. Cologne and Vienna, 1982.

Matzner, Jutta, ed. *Lehrstück Lukács.* Frankfurt am Main, 1974.

Mészáros, István. *Lukács's Concept of Dialectic.* London, 1972.

Parkinson, G. H. R. *Georg Lukács.* London, 1977.

———, ed. *Georg Lukács: The Man, His Work, and His Ideas.* London, 1970.

Pasternack, Gerhard. *Georg Lukács: Späte Ästhetik und Literaturtheorie.* Königstein im Taunus, 1985.

Pinkus, Theo, ed. *Conversations with Lukács: Hans Heinz Holz, Leo Kofler, Wolfgang Abendroth.* Anonymous translation. Cambridge, Mass., 1975.

Raddatz, Fritz J. *Georg Lukács in Selbstzeugnissen und Bilddokumenten.* Reinbek bei Hamburg, 1972.

Reis, Thomas. *Das Bild des klassischen Schriftstellers bei Georg Lukács. Eine Untersuchung zur Wirkungsgeschichte literarischer Topoi in seiner Literaturtheorie und Ästhetik.* Frankfurt am Main, 1984.

Sontag, Susan. "The Literary Criticism of Georg Lukács." In *Against Interpretation and Other Essays.* New York, 1966.

Steiner, George. "Georg Lukács and His Devil's Pact." *The Kenyon Review* 22:1–18 (1960). Reprinted in *Language and Silence: Essays on Language, Literature, and the Inhuman.* New York, 1967.

———. "An Aesthetic Manifesto: Georg Lukács' System." In *Language and Silence.* Pp. 340–347.

Urban, George. "A Conversation with Lukács." *Encounter* 37:30–36 (October 1971).

Wellek, René. *Four Critics: Croce, Valéry, Lukács, and Ingarden.* Seattle, 1981.

Witschel, Günter. *Ethische Probleme der Philosophie von Georg Lukács. Elemente einer nichtgeschriebenen Ethik.* Bonn, 1981.

Witte, Bernd. "Benjamin and Lukács: Historical Notes on the Relationship Between Their Political and Aesthetic Theories." *New German Critique* 5:3–26 (1975).

SPECIAL ISSUES OF PERIODICALS

"Georg Lukács: A Symposium." *Cambridge Review* 93:85–100 (1972).

In Memoriam György Lukács (1885–1971). The New Hungarian Quarterly 47 (1972).

Special Lukács Issue (parts 1 and 2). *Telos* 10 (1971) and 11 (1972).

Georg Lukács. Text + Kritik 39, 40 (1973). Edited by Frank Benseler.

Weimarer Beiträge 31:533–601 (1985).

BIBLIOGRAPHIES

Hartmann, Jürgen, comp. "Chronologische Bibliographie der Werke von Georg Lukács." In *Festschrift zum achtzigsten Geburtstag von Georg Lukács,* edited by Frank Benseler. Neuwied and Berlin, 1965. Pp. 625–696.

Gábor, Andor, comp. "Biobibliographie von Georg Lukács." *Text + Kritik* 39, 40:79–88 (1973).

Lapointe, François H. *Georg Lukács and His Critics: An International Bibliography with Annotations (1910–1982).* Westport, Conn., and London, 1983.

EMERY GEORGE

ISAK DINESEN

(1885–1962)

ISAK DINESEN WAS the name under which the Danish baroness Karen Blixen made her unique, and uniquely international, contribution to the literature of the twentieth century. She wrote all her major works first in English and then in Danish, producing—as it were—two originals; and, though her subjects were, on the one hand, twentieth-century Africa and, on the other, Europe of a hundred and more years ago, her first literary success was in the United States, with the publication of *Seven Gothic Tales* in 1934.

It is necessary to appreciate that Isak Dinesen is not so much a pseudonym for Karen Blixen as a symbolic definition of her persona as a storyteller. Dinesen, her father's family name, defines her roots; Isak, Hebrew for "laughter," points to her aims as a kind of divine joker. For Isaac was the son whom the Lord made Sarah conceive and bear to Abraham when she was ninety and he a hundred; a victory of the imagination over impossibility. Not only was Isaac late-born, as were Isak Dinesen's tales—she was forty-nine when *Seven Gothic Tales* appeared—but he was also the token of a divine comic plan, for "Sarah said, God hath made me to laugh, so that all that hear will laugh with me" (Genesis 21:6). Sarah's laughter is at that end of the range where the comic meets the marvelous, as in Shakespeare's late romances. Similarly Isak Dinesen, who felt a deep affinity with the creator of those plays and even borrowed from one

of them the title for her second collection of stories, *Winter's Tales* (1942), wanted her readers to laugh with her at the human condition—a laughter similarly provoked by a compound of wit, irony, and awe.

Nor, therefore, was the original intention behind her half-pseudonym (the anonymity of which was in any case soon exploded) to hide her feminine identity as much as to create imaginative space for herself. Toward the end of her life she could claim that she had never concerned herself with feminism, that "competition between man and woman is a sterile and disagreeable phenomenon," and that woman's function is "to expand her own being" ("En baaltale," 1953; English translation, "Oration at a Bonfire," in *Daguerrotypes and Other Essays* [1979]). Unlike Currer Bell (pseudonym of Charlotte Brontë) or George Eliot (pseudonym of Mary Ann Evans) in the nineteenth century, she was not aiming for a male author's freedom but rather for a detached, godlike freedom from her ordinary self. She had chosen to write under a pen name, she told an interviewer in 1934, for the same reason that her father had done so: in order to "express himself freely, give his imagination free rein" (*Politiken,* 1 May 1934).

There are, then, at least three classes of reasons why Isak Dinesen is important to the student of literature, and those three will structure this essay. She is important as a brave and gallant person who wrung serene and elegant art out of an often harrowed life. She is important as a Danish talent, yet also as an utterly individual one, in a European literary tradition of which she was always conscious. And above all, she is important as a supreme teller of stories. Like Scheherazade in the *Thousand and One Nights,* to whom she so often compares herself, and like the other storytellers who appear within her own stories, she exercises her imaginative powers to hold the reader spellbound. She was defiantly aware that such powers might well be out of tune with modern society and modern literature. Interviewed by Daniel Gillès for Belgian television shortly before her death, in the summer of 1962, she voiced this defiance:

> I am periodically accused of being "decadent." That is no doubt true, as I am not interested in social questions, nor in Freudian psychology. But the narrator of the *Thousand and One Nights* also neglected social questions. . . . As for me I have one ambition only: to invent stories, very beautiful stories.
>
> (Svendsen, ed., pp. 177–178)

The very fact that the Baroness Blixen is here obviously playing up to the interviewer's expectations of her persona helps to make these statements characteristic of Isak Dinesen. Her life and her art have merged, and for the moment she has become a character out of one of her own stories—like the ancient aristocratic Miss Malin Nat-og-Dag in "The Deluge at Norderney" (in *Seven Gothic Tales*), who scorns the idea that "the Lord wants the truth from us." "Why," she says, "he knows it already, and may even have found it a little bit dull. Truth is for tailors and shoemakers, my lord. I, on the contrary, have always held that the Lord has a penchant for masquerades." The same old lady, as the ineluctably rising floodwaters spell imminent death, transforms that dull factual truth into the vicarious fiction of the closing lines of the story: " 'À ce moment de sa narration,' she said, 'Scheherazade vit paraître le matin, et,

discrète, se tut' " ("At this moment in her story," she said, "Scheherazade saw the morning dawn and fell discreetly silent").

LIFE INTO ART

The French word *discrète* can be translated by several English adjectives, all hovering around the notion of the effortlessly decorous, the consciously simple, the art which—in the words of Shakespeare's *A Winter's Tale*—"itself is nature." Isak Dinesen, with the feeling for the exactly right word that characterizes all her writing, does *not* translate it—handing us thereby a word that denotes not only the decorousness of Scheherazade and the self-consciousness of Miss Malin Nat-og-Dag, but also the manner in which, in her published work, Dinesen transmutes her own life into art. Two of her works are ostensibly autobiographical: *Out of Africa* (1937) and its after-vibration nearly twenty-five years later, *Shadows on the Grass* (1961). But the relation between these accounts of African experience and the facts of her life in Africa—marriage, syphilis, divorce, love affair, business failure, death of her lover—is nothing if not *discrète*. She left it for the "tailors and shoemakers" to deliver the "dull" truth. Not that it *is* dull, nor that biographers as sensitive and scholarly as Clara Svendsen and Frank Lasson in Denmark or Judith Thurman in the United States could ever be called shoemakers. Thanks to them, and to others who knew Dinesen well, not least her own brother, Thomas Dinesen, her life history has been very fully documented.

But the voice that opens *Out of Africa*—"I had a farm in Africa, at the foot of the Ngong Hills"—is that of a storyteller rather than that of a personal historian. It is the voice of Scheherazade as much as of Karen Blixen. Of course there is a factual background to the book, but what matters is not whether the events she relates *really* happened. For example, toward the end, in the section entitled "Farewell to the

Farm," she tells us about trying to find "some central principle" in the series of disasters that were befalling her: the loss of the farm, the death in an airplane crash of her beloved Denys Finch-Hatton, and so on. She goes out looking for a "sign" that will make clear to her "the coherence of things," and what she sees is a big white cock confronting a small gray chameleon:

> He was frightened, but he was at the same time very brave, he planted his feet in the ground, opened his mouth as wide as he possibly could, and, to scare his enemy, in a flash he shot out his club-shaped tongue at the cock. The cock stood for a second as if taken aback, then swiftly and determinately he struck down his beak like a hammer and plucked out the Chameleon's tongue.
>
> (p. 369)

She kills the chameleon, as he could not live without his tongue, and then she sits there, unable to move; "such a dangerous place did the world seem to me." But gradually, over the next few days, it dawns on her that she has been "in a strange manner honoured and distinguished" by this answer to her call for a sign:

> The powers to which I had cried had stood on my dignity more than I had done myself, and what other answer could they then give? . . . Great powers had laughed to me, with an echo from the hills to follow the laughter, they had said among the trumpets, among the cocks and the Chameleons, Ha ha!
>
> (pp. 369–370)

The question whether this really happened is irrelevant. The pressure of the writing and the significance given to the event show that, if the chameleon had not existed, it would have been necessary—as Voltaire says of God—to invent him. For this little tale of two African animals makes the point so often reiterated in Dine-

sen's more obviously fictive stories: tragedy, pity, and self-pity are for human beings, but the vision of the gods is comic. To be granted that vision is the gift of the artist, and of the aristocrat. As the old lord says in what is probably the most Danish of all Dinesen's tales, "Sorrow-Acre" (in *Winter's Tales*): "The very same fatality which, in striking the burgher or peasant will become tragedy, with the aristocrat is exalted to the comic. By the grace and wit of our acceptance hereof our aristocracy is known."

Another example of the unimportance of fact in Dinesen's accounts of African life is the story of the king's letter that forms the second part of *Shadows on the Grass*, "Barua a Soldani" (Letter from a King). She tells how she had presented the King of Denmark with the skin of a lion she had shot; and how, coming across a native with a broken leg and having no morphine to relieve his pain, she placed the king's letter of thanks on his chest, telling him that, as a "barua a soldani," it would be efficacious. It was, and thenceforth the letter became a kind of talisman on the farm, asked for by the natives as a magic cure of very serious illness. Now, the letter exists in the Dinesen archives, well-preserved and spotless, to contradict the "truth" of the story; it cannot possibly have passed from hand to hand, as the story has it. But the story exists, to assert a different kind of truth: the bond between two races, or cultures, which consists of a common belief in the magic of kingship. The letter of the story is, in her own words, a sign of "a covenant . . . between the Europeans and the Africans."

This, then, is how autobiography turns into art in Dinesen's two books about Africa. She writes, not about her life and surroundings as such, but about the patterns and meanings she sees in them. No doubt similar processes of transmutation lie behind the more obviously invented stories of *Seven Gothic Tales, Winter's Tales,* and her later collections of tales. Readers of Judith Thurman's fascinating biography *Isak Dinesen: The Life of a Storyteller* will be guided to see the author as an adolescent in "Peter and Rosa" and her childhood sense of otherness in "Alkmene" (both in *Winter's Tales*); and they will see the figures of her aunts in "Supper at Elsinore" (in *Seven Gothic Tales*) and "The Pearls" (in *Winter's Tales*), to mention only a few convincing echoes of her life in her tales. What links all these—her African works and her fiction, her life and her art—is that sense of pattern and meaning that she articulated in a letter to her sister, written to convey the experience of flying "over the African plains and the Ngong Hills with Denys." It is the happiness of seeing not only Africa, but also all life from above: "Here I must say with Father Daniel (?) in 'Jacques,' that God has far more imagination than we have, something I don't consider he shows a great deal of in everyday life. Because by myself I could have discovered neither Africa nor Denys" (Anne Born, trans.). (At this distance in time, she obviously could not be sure of the name of the father confessor, who articulates the moral of the story.) This letter was written in October 1930; and the story she refers to as "Jacques" is one which she had written before leaving for Africa in 1913. (It was published only posthumously, as "Uncle Théodore," in *Carnival: Entertainments and Posthumous Tales,* 1977.) But the idea that "God has far more imagination than we have" is one that, early and late, informs both her life and her work.

She herself certainly felt that God had exercised his imagination in making her the product of a meeting of two opposed traditions in Danish social and cultural life. Born on 17 April 1885, Karen Christentze Dinesen ("Tanne" to her family) was the daughter of Wilhelm Dinesen and his wife, Ingeborg, née Westenholz. The Dinesens were a family of landed gentry, not titled but related to one of the leading families of the nobility, the Frijses. The Westenholzes were wealthy businessmen with their own kind of prominence in Danish affairs: Ingeborg Westenholz' father, Regnar, had been minister of finance and her maternal grandfather a councillor of state. Dinesen un-

doubtedly exaggerated the polarity in her ancestry, which she defined as aristocracy versus bourgeoisie. But there is no doubt that the two families embodied different, if not antithetical, life-styles. The Dinesens' was basically feudal, self-confident, hedonistic—a latter-day (and, as the twentieth century wore on, somewhat anachronistic) version of the life-style caught so wonderfully in Dinesen's story "Copenhagen Season," published in *Last Tales* (1957). The Westenholzes were self-made, hard-working, and earnest; they had strongly developed consciences, were nonconformists —Unitarians—by confession, and espoused liberal causes—such as feminism—by conviction. Dinesen always claimed that she was like her father's family and that her mother's family disliked her. She seems to have had a particular bond with her father, whose life story could well have come out of one of her own tales. Indeed, biographers suggest that he was the model for Ib Angel in "Copenhagen Season."

True to the military traditions of the family, Wilhelm Dinesen had fought as an officer on the losing side in two wars, the Dano-Prussian War of 1864 and the Franco-Prussian War of 1870–1871. His experience of the Paris Commune left him disillusioned and sick at heart, and he left Europe for America, where he lived for some time as a hunter among the Indians in Wisconsin. He admired their intuitive wisdom and their sense of honor and integrity; they responded with affection and named him "Boganis" (hazelnut)—a name under which he was later to publish several books. Recalled to Denmark in 1874, he spent a few unsettled years in touring Europe, vainly attempting to join the Russo-Turkish War (1877–1878) on the Turkish side. By 1879 he was back in Denmark to settle down for the rest of his life as a landowner and, from 1892, a member of Parliament. As a younger son, he was not to inherit the family estate of Katholm in Jutland; he bought instead a tract of land on the Sealand coast, between Copenhagen and Elsinore. On it were several major houses: one, Folehave, was to become the home of the Westenholz matriarchy, Isak Dinesen's grandmother, known as "Mama," and Aunt Bess, who dominated much of her early life. Another, Rungstedlund, became the home of Wilhelm Dinesen's family: the home in which Isak Dinesen grew up and to which she returned from Africa, in 1931, to spend the rest of her days. It was a romantically historical building, established as a village inn in the sixteenth century and famous for having housed the great Danish poet Johannes Ewald for a couple of years in the 1770's. In 1958 Dinesen was instrumental in establishing the Rungstedlund Foundation which now owns the historic building, keeps the garden and surrounding woodland as a bird reserve, and has the rights of her literary works.

The decisive event of Dinesen's childhood was the death of her father by suicide in 1895, shortly before her tenth birthday. It left her bereaved of not just a father figure but her closest mental and temperamental ally; she felt an alien and a rebel in the household at Rungstedlund where Ingeborg Dinesen was left to bring up five young children with the vigorous support—not to say supervision—of the Westenholz ladies at Folehave. There followed years of being taught by a governess and of attempting to develop a definite but undirected artistic talent. Dinesen went to art school and later (1903–1906) attended the Royal Academy of Fine Art in Copenhagen; in 1907 she made her debut as an author with an uncanny story, "Eneboerne" (The Hermits, reprinted in *Osceola*, 1962). It was published in the Copenhagen monthly *Tilskueren* under the pseudonym of Osceola, the name of a half-caste Indian who had led the Seminoles against American troops in the 1830's and whom her father—significantly—had admired. Under the same pseudonym in the same year but in a different magazine, *Gads danske Magasin,* she published a wildly romantic story, "Pløjeren" (The Ploughman, reprinted in *Osceola*), and in 1909, again in *Tilskueren,* appeared the first story to suggest her mature control and her powers of satire, "Familien de Cats," reprinted in *Osceola* and included as "The de Cats Family" in *Carnival.* If she had hoped to follow in her father's footsteps as an author—his *Jagtbreve* (Letters from the Hunt) in 1889 had been very successful, though a second volume, *Nye Jagtbreve* (New Letters from the Hunt), in 1892 proved less so—she was disappointed. Little note was taken of her tales, and the impulse to write was lost. These last few years before World War I were lacking in aim; a brief period at an art college in Paris in 1910 came to nothing, and her main stimulus seems to have been in the social life of the young aristocratic set centered on the Frijs family.

It was, however, this circle that Dinesen's God decided to step into to exercise his imagination. Among the Frijs relatives there were two young Swedish noblemen, the barons Hans and Bror von Blixen-Finecke, second cousins of Karen Dinesen and twin sons of Baron Frederik of Näsbyholm in the southernmost province of Sweden. Karen fell in love with Hans, who did not return her feelings. At Christmas 1912 she announced her engagement to Bror, and just over a year later, on 14 January 1914, she was married to him, on the very same day that she first set foot on African soil. To ordinary mortals this may seem a strange pattern of events; to Isak Dinesen it had, in retrospect, the self-evidence of an imaginative pattern. In a letter which she wrote to her brother Thomas in April 1931, a few months before leaving Africa for good, a letter that crystallizes all her fears of returning to Rungstedlund and her feelings that "death is preferable to a bourgeois existence," she stated clearly and simply "the fact that the atmosphere at home has never suited me and that I got married and put all my efforts into emigrating in order to get away" (Anne Born, trans.).

Bror Blixen was, as the horrified Westenholzes did not hesitate to point out, an extraordinarily unsuitable marriage partner: pleasure loving, promiscuous, amoral, unintellectual. His main distinction seems to have been an incredible physical stamina; allegedly he is the original of the great white hunter Robert Wilson in Ernest Hemingway's story "The

Short, Happy Life of Francis Macomber" (1938). By the time he died in a car crash in 1946, he had hunted on three continents—Africa, North America, and Europe—and been three times married and divorced, but his greatest glory had been in taking European royalty on safaris in the African highlands. In marrying the wrong twin—insofar as he was not the one she loved—Dinesen married the right man to take her away from "a bourgeois existence" to a world that was, much like the one sought by her father, at once more primitive and more aristocratic.

British East Africa—from 1920 the Crown Colony of Kenya—was in the early decades of the twentieth century not only a hunters' paradise but also a land of peculiar opportunity. The English historian A. J. P. Taylor identifies its settlers as "Englishmen [who] escaped democracy and high taxation by establishing themselves in Kenya as territorial aristocrats on the old model." Other nationalities were attracted, too; and, after toying with the idea of a rubber plantation in Malaya (which might have made of Dinesen a female Joseph Conrad), the engaged couple turned their thoughts to a farm in East Africa. The impetus was in a sense aristocratic; their mutual uncle, Count Mogens Frijs, came back to Denmark from a Kenyan safari and extolled the beauties of the country and its economic potential. The finance, on the other hand, was bourgeois: a family-limited company was set up, its capital almost entirely Westenholz money, its chairman Dinesen's maternal uncle Aage Westenholz, and its purpose to acquire arable land in East Africa to be managed by Bror Blixen. Bror went out to Africa in 1913 and, with a typically highhanded gesture, promptly sold the seven hundred acres that he had come to farm and instead bought the Swedo-African Coffee Company, 4,500 acres, waiting to be turned into a coffee plantation, near Nairobi. This was to be the Ngong Farm of *Out of Africa*. In real life it was also the Karen Coffee Company, whose fortunes were to become part of Karen Blixen's life—as, indeed, of the destiny of Isak Dinesen. It was an ill-

fated venture from the start; the land was too high and the soil too acid for securely profitable coffee-growing, and Bror had neither the experience nor the application to be a successful manager. The true story of Karen Coffee is one of continual struggle against droughts, failed or too small crops, falling coffee prices, and pressure from dissatisfied shareholders at home in Denmark. In 1921 the Westenholz family insisted on the dismissal of Bror as manager; thereafter Karen Blixen ran the farm. By the late 1920's it was clear to everyone but herself, stumbling from one financial crisis to another, that the end was inevitable. In December 1930 the company forced the sale of the farm to a property developer who turned the land into residential lots and, ironically, gave this new bourgeois suburb of Nairobi the name Karen. The Baroness Blixen herself stayed on the farm to see the last coffee harvest and the resettlement of her black workers; this done, she returned to Denmark, knowing—as she was later to put it in a letter—that "half of me was lying in the Ngong Hills."

That half is a qualitative rather than quantitative measure; it refers to the quality of life left behind rather than the quantity of experience contained between her landing in Mombasa in January 1914 and her sailing from there at the end of July 1931. The quality of her life in Africa was to be distilled into *Out of Africa* where, because no dates are given and because the material has been so carefully selected, the reader is presented with a timeless and homogeneous past. From that book no reader could guess that, of the seventeen years between her first arrival in Africa and her last departure, three and a half were spent in visits to Europe. These were mainly to see her family in Denmark and to receive painful and often prolonged treatment of the syphilis she had contracted from her husband soon after marriage. Bror Blixen does not figure in *Out of Africa*, nor therefore does the gradual collapse of the marriage, that, despite Karen Blixen's illness, had known a few happy years of shared excitement about African life. It had weathered the problems of the early years of World War I when the Swedes in East Africa were suspected of German sympathies and hence ostracized—a suspicion finally allayed, in the case of the Blixens, when Thomas Dinesen was awarded the Victoria Cross for heroism while fighting with the British army on the French front. Against odds, Karen Blixen retained affection for her husband, just as he in his way remained fond of her; but his promiscuity and general irresponsibility drove their life from crisis to crisis. In 1921 she had reluctantly to agree to a separation, and in 1925 the divorce was made absolute—enabling Bror to marry again and leaving Karen to wonder whether she could still be called Baroness Blixen.

The importance to her of this question must seem strange from a contemporary democratic point of view. But it must be understood in order to appreciate how Isak Dinesen grew out of Karen Dinesen via Karen Blixen. "If it did not sound so beastly," she wrote to her brother Thomas in September 1926, "I might say that, the world being as it is, it was worth having syphilis in order to become a 'Baroness'; but I certainly do not think this is applicable to everyone" (Anne Born, trans.). To most of us, her bargain must seem as unacceptable as that of Faust selling his soul to the devil. But writers—Christopher Marlowe, Johann Wolfgang von Goethe, Thomas Mann—have made great art out of the Faust story, not, obviously, by *being* latter-day Fausts but by exploring the myth. Similarly, what we see in this letter is the writer in the process of turning her own life into myth. To be a baroness was not a simple status question, much as Karen Blixen enjoyed the social position that her title conferred in the colony's hierarchy. The real significance of the title was symbolic, an embodiment of the European aristocratic and heroic past and of the African feudal and heroic present. Her pride in the title is of a different dimension from social snobbishness; it is a proud acceptance of the bargain—however unrecognized as such at the time—by which she had acquired the title. Pride in this sense is defined in the section of *Out of Africa* called "From an Immigrant's Notebook":

> Pride is faith in the idea that God had, when he made us. A proud man is conscious of the idea, and aspires to realize it. He does not strive towards a happiness, or comfort, which may be irrelevant to God's idea of him. His success is the idea of God successfully carried through, and he is in love with his destiny. As the good citizen finds his happiness in the fulfilment of his duty to the community, so does the proud man find his happiness in the fulfilment of his fate.
>
> (p. 261)

To find it worth having syphilis in order to become a baroness is, in the words of this paragraph, to be in love with one's destiny. This idea—of salvation through proud fulfillment of one's own nature or "faith in the idea that God had when he made us"—is fundamental to Dinesen's life *and* art. That is, Karen Blixen evolved the idea in her life as an "immigrant," and Isak Dinesen informed the characters in her stories with it.

In *Out of Africa* such faith informs not only a few selected European aristocrats but also the natives themselves. "The Negro," she writes, "is on friendly terms with destiny, having been in her hands all this time." Destiny informs the animal creation, too: the gazelle, Lulu, who is the subject of part of the first section of the book, "Kamante and Lulu," and the lions against which the white hunters match themselves. On a euphoric New Year's morning, she tells us in the section called "Visitors to the Farm," Denys Finch-Hatton and she came upon and shot first a lioness and then her mate; and as they sat there drinking their breakfast claret and looking at the magnificent bodies of the dead lions, "they were, all through, what they ought to be."

Of all creatures in *Out of Africa*, Denys Finch-Hatton is, all through, what he ought to be. To make him so, Dinesen was particularly *discrète*, writing as a storyteller and not as a biographer. In the book he seems to appear from nowhere; he listens to her stories; he shares some epiphanic moments, like the vision of the lions just mentioned; he takes her up in his airplane, thus enabling her to get an overview of Africa that is more metaphysical than geographical: " 'I see,' I have thought, 'This was the idea. And now I understand everything.' " His death, when that same airplane crashes, and his burial in the Ngong Hills—in a grave that later becomes a haunt for lions at sunrise and sunset—are part of the extraordinary movement through disaster toward "understanding everything" that forms the last section of *Out of Africa,* "Farewell to the Farm." In real life Finch-Hatton first met Karen Blixen in 1918 and soon became the great love of her life. Their relationship lasted until a rupture that occurred within the last year or so before she left Africa when, it would appear, her distraught state caused her to place too great demands on him. For making no demands, in the worldly sense, had been the keynote of this relationship (so unauthentically romanticized in the Meryl Streep and Robert Redford affair in Sydney Pollack's film of *Out of Africa* [1985]). An aristocratic nomad with a military and adventurous career reminiscent of her father's, Finch-Hatton would turn up at Karen Blixen's farm, bringing wine and books and records, and would vanish again when the next safari called. At various times he owned a great deal of land and property in Africa, but for a period the farm was his only home between safaris. Twice she mistakenly thought herself pregnant by him; at no time was there any question of his standing by her, in the sense of offering marriage or financial security. But none of this comes through in *Out of Africa,* where what matters is not what the "real" Denys has done or not done, but what he *was.*

In many ways the "biographical" Finch-Hatton relates to his namesake in *Out of Africa* as myth does to reality. The younger son of the thirteenth Earl of Winchilsea, educated at Eton and Oxford, he becomes in the book the quintessential, timeless aristocrat:

He could have walked arm in arm . . . with Sir Philip [Sidney], or Francis Drake. And the people of Elizabeth's time might have held him dear because to them he would have suggested that Antiquity, the Athens, of which they dreamed and wrote. Denys could indeed have been placed harmoniously in any period of our civilization, *tout comme chez soi,* all up till the opening of the nineteenth century. He would have cut a figure in any age, for he was an athlete, a musician, a lover of art and a fine sportsman. He did cut a figure in his own age, but it did not quite fit in anywhere.

(p. 215)

Sociologically Finch-Hatton was one of these "territorial aristocrats on the old model" referred to by A. J. P. Taylor. In the myth of the book he is the romantic wanderer who does not "fit in" with industrialized and bourgeois Europe and so is drawn to the both more primitive and more aristocratic world of Africa. "Africa was keeping him," she wrote when first introducing him in the chapter "Visitors to the Farm," and so there is a peculiar rightness—a completion of a pattern, a destiny—in his death and burial: "It was fit and decorous that the lions should come to Denys's grave and make him an African monument. 'And renowned be thy grave.' Lord Nelson himself, I have reflected, in Trafalgar Square, has his lions made only out of stone." The life and death of Denys thus fit into the heroic and tragicomic pattern of the book, as no ordinary extramarital love story would have done. Her love for him is diffused throughout *Out of Africa* but is most movingly transmuted into art in the passage in which she both celebrates his being wholly what he ought to be and describes the way this quality brings out the rightness of everything around him. In this exquisite simplicity of its language, it becomes a twentieth-century Song of Songs:

When he came back to the farm, it gave out what was in it; it spoke,—as the coffee-plantations speak, when with the first showers of the rainy season they flower, dripping wet, a cloud of chalk. When I was expecting Denys back, and heard his car coming up the drive, I heard, at the same time, the things of the farm all telling what they really were. He was happy on the farm; he came there only when he wanted to come, and it knew, in him, a quality of which the world besides was not aware, a humility. He never did but what he wanted to do, neither was guile found in his mouth.

(p. 225)

If, then, *Out of Africa* shows Dinesen transmuting her life into art, we are fortunate to have a gloss on that process in the letters she wrote to members of her family in Denmark between 1914 and 1931. These were edited by Frans Lasson and published as *Breve fra Afrika: 1914–1931* in 1978. (An English translation by Anne Born, *Letters from Africa,* was published in 1981.) They provide, on the one hand, documentary evidence of her life in this period, and they are in a very literal sense a source of *Out of Africa;* for, as Frans Lasson points out in his introduction to the *Letters,* Dinesen used her letters to her mother as memoranda while writing her work on Africa. On the other hand, they also provide a portrait of the artist in that they show, in Lasson's words, "a ceaselessly unresting struggle to reach clarification and understanding of herself." In that respect they are as important to an understanding of her artistic nature as are John Keats's letters to students of his poetic genius. They show her feeling her way toward a style as well as toward a philosophy of life.

Not all of the letters are of the same nature. Those to her maternal aunt, Mary Bess Westenholz of Folehave, tend to be part of a continuing debate between the two of them on issues such as religion, the liberation of women, and sexual morality. Here we see the Isak Dinesen who in 1923–1924 labored on a long essay on love and marriage in the modern world. (The essay was published posthumously as "Moderne Ægteskab og andre Betragtninger" in *Blixeniana 1977;* an English translation, *On Modern Marriage,* was published in 1986.) This is the socially conscious woman who wrote to Aunt Bess in 1926 that "feminism should probably

be regarded as the most significant movement of the nineteenth century" and whose essay explores what she sees as the basic nineteenth-century error of confusing love—which is an experience between free individuals—and marriage—which is a public, dynastic commitment. (Clearly there is also much autobiography behind this essay.) The letters to her mother are full of domestic details and accounts of social life in the colony and safaris on the plains. They also reveal her deep affection for her family, her plain bourgeois interest in their affairs. But through all this, and rising to a crescendo as the agony of leaving Africa and returning to a bourgeois existence approaches, runs a note of self-analysis and self-assertion. Thus, in one of the last letters she wrote to her mother, in March 1931, she felt prompted to sum up her life, which at this moment meant her African life:

Of all the idiots I have met in my life—and the Lord knows that they have not been few or little—I think that I have been the biggest. But a certain love of greatness, which could not be quelled, has kept a hold on me, has been "my daimon". . . . A great world of poetry has revealed itself to me and taken me to itself here, and I have loved it. I have looked into the eyes of lions and slept under the Southern Cross, I have seen the grass of the great plains ablaze and covered with delicate green after the rains. I have been the friend of Somali, Kikuyu, and Masai, I have flown over the Ngong Hills,—"I plucked the best rose of life, and Freja be praised."

(*Letters from Africa: 1914–1931,*
Anne Born, trans., p. 416)

We hardly need that last self-conscious quotation, from the skald's song in Act IV of the Danish poet-dramatist Adam Gottlob Oehlenschläger's tragedy *Hagbarth and Signe* (1814), to see that here personal misery is translating itself into literature—into the images, patterns, and rhythms of a kind of prose poetry. The step from here to *Out of Africa* is a short one.

It is in her letters to her brother, Thomas

Dinesen, that she is most openly self-revealing. He was her confidant, both before and after his stay on her African farm between 1920 and 1923. Thomas Dinesen's position involved considerable demands on emotional (and sometimes also financial) capital, never more so than when receiving the letter of 10 April 1931 in which his sister, for all her assertion that she is *not* saying "help me and sustain me, or I will die" (Anne Born, trans.), is in fact saying exactly that. (The circumstances surrounding a probable suicide attempt by her at about this time are not clear.) Yet this same letter also mentions her having started to write a book in English and having been told by an English publisher, to whom she had sent a section for comment on her command of the language, that "the leisurely style and language are exceedingly attractive." The seesaw movement between despair and resolution that the letter communicates is no doubt genuinely felt, but it is felt with the partial detachment of the artist who, even as she feels, watches herself feel. Dinesen was aware of this quality in herself, and it is again in a letter to Thomas that she identifies it most clearly. It is a very long letter, written on 5 September 1926, containing among other things her insight that "loving one's destiny unconditionally" is "the condition for real happiness"; from this follows her defiant statement that "it was worth having syphilis in order to become a 'Baroness' "; and then, to show why that statement is not "applicable to everyone," she proceeds to define her own uniqueness:

> I myself feel that a certain kind of shape and color in my surroundings, a certain amount of "showing off" . . . is the expression of my personality, is what is called a natural necessity for me; without these things I am . . . an actor without a stage, a violinist without hands or at least without a violin.
>
> (*Letters from Africa: 1914–1931,*
> Anne Born, trans., p. 284)

In the letter to her mother quoted earlier we saw how the person named Karen Blixen wrote herself into a persona, soon to be called Isak Dinesen. In this letter to Thomas she insists upon the "natural necessity" to her of such a process with a fierce honesty that refuses to compromise with objections—call them moral or puritanical or bourgeois—to "showing off." Life to her must be an act, a performance. When she wrote the letter, her stage was Africa; some years later it was to be the printed word. That this, too, was a "natural necessity" is foreshadowed in the closing paragraphs of the letter, where she explains to Thomas that writing to him has been a necessity before settling to write fiction: "I was feeling so uncertain and could not do anything about it until I had heard my own voice, seen myself in that mirror that is the person to whom one is speaking,—taken stock of myself." Dinesen's life after Africa can be briefly told, for even though it was only then that she became officially an author, all that really made her the author she is happened before. She did, of course, survive the return to Denmark, where she took up residence with her mother at Rungstedlund. She was ruined, financially, physically, and emotionally, but willpower—the sense that to realize her destiny now was to become a writer—saw her through to the publication of *Seven Gothic Tales,* the manuscript of which was ready by the spring of 1933, not much more than eighteen months after her return. An American publisher, Robert Haas (whose firm subsequently merged with Random House), recognized the merit of her stories, and when he published them in January 1934, the reading public did so too. Chosen as Book of the Month in February, the book was a commercial success as well as a critical one.

Willpower, fed by public acclaim, also saw Dinesen through the rest of her life to her death at Rungstedlund, at the age of seventy-seven, on 7 September 1962. It made her persist through long spells of illness: her syphilis, though brought under control to the point of not being infectious by her early medical treatment, had not been arrested; symptoms of tabes dorsalis—degeneration of the spine—

had begun to appear as early as 1921, and in the last three decades of her life she was to suffer long periods of excruciating pain, despite operations performed to sever spinal nerves. In the end her body literally wasted away, but her spirit remained strong and gallant. "A certain amount of 'showing off,' " as she had put it to her brother, was more than ever "a natural necessity" for her. Its superficial signs were heavy eye makeup (long before such cosmetics were in common use), spectacular clothes, and a penchant for a diet of champagne, oysters, and asparagus. Its fundamental drive was to remain a Scheherazade despite personal suffering and national crisis. (Denmark was under German occupation from 1940 to 1945, and Dinesen was sympathetic to the gathering resistance movement, the position of Rungstedlund enabling her to assist, in the autumn of 1943, the action to help Danish Jews to escape to neutral Sweden.) Again in the words of her 1926 letter to her brother, she remained an actor *with* a stage, refusing to play the part of the invalid.

This was never more true than on her one and only visit to the United States, from January to April 1959, when, emaciated and living largely on stamina and amphetamines, she carried out an amazingly heavy program of talks and readings and kept up a hectic pace of social engagements—including a luncheon party given by Carson McCullers, where the other two guests were Arthur Miller and Marilyn Monroe. For Isak Dinesen those three months in New York, even though she had to spend a few weeks of them in the hospital recharging her energy, were truly a period of being lionized—a term particularly appropriate in her case, as she always prided herself on having been known as "the Lioness" in the Kenya colony. Her American biographer Thurman speaks of the extraordinary rapport that Dinesen established with her New York audiences; the contrast, she notes, between, on the one hand, the physical frailty of the seventy-four-year-old woman, who seemed to them "incalculably old," and, on the other, her sheer presence and personality, whether she delivered an address or retold one of her stories verbatim from memory, made them feel that "this was the wise, noble and heroic survivor of the past—the master—they had been expecting." The talk she gave to the American Academy of Arts and Letters, "On Mottoes of My Life" (reprinted in *Daguerrotypes and Other Essays*), forms the best brief introduction to the life and art of Isak Dinesen, if only because what she describes as "the first real motto of my youth"—the paradoxical order given by Pompey to his crew of timid sailors, "Navigare necesse est, vivere non necesse" (It is necessary to sail; it is not necessary to live)—is so clearly the fundamental principle of her whole life.

In Denmark, where after her mother's death in 1939 she was mistress of Rungstedlund, her audience had more ambivalent feelings. *Seven Gothic Tales,* which she did not so much translate as rewrite into Danish (having been dismayed by the attempts of professional translators), was published as *Syv fantastiske Fortaellinger* (1935) in the middle of the depression in a Europe torn by social and political unrest. True to the Scandinavian tradition of looking for contemporary relevance in works of literature, her countrymen were less able than her American and British readers to see her tales as works of art; to them she seemed at best escapist, at worst reactionary and even perverse. (This last judgment was made in a review by Frederick Schyberg in the leading newspaper *Berlingske Tidende,* 25 September 1935, which Dinesen kept and begrudged till the end of her days.) *Den afrikanske Farm* (1937), the Danish version of *Out of Africa*, did much to reassure her Danish readers of her humanity and sense of reality, and when *Vinter Eventyr* (1942), the Danish edition of *Winter's Tales,* was published in the middle of the Nazi occupation, the Danishness of this book—its feeling for the landscape, the life, and the history of Denmark—had a very special appeal. So, in the 1940's Dinesen began to be recognized as a major author in her own country and as a patriot. Oppressed and bored by the Occupation, she wrote as a light relief her only novel, *Gengaeldelsens Veje* (*The Angelic Avengers,* originally written in Danish and published in 1944 under the pseudonym of Pierre Andrézel and with the smoke screen of "translated into Danish by Clara Svendsen"; English and American editions published in, respectively, 1946 and 1947). The critics, having dismantled the pseudonym, were ready to credit this Victorian Gothic crime story with being an anti-Nazi political allegory. By the early 1950's she was something of a cult figure for a group of young literati, but she was also reaching a wide Danish audience through a series of popular radio talks. Now nationally and internationally famous, she joined the distinguished band of writers *not* to be awarded the Nobel Prize for Literature; in his speech when accepting the prize in 1954, Hemingway referred to her as a writer more deserving of it than himself, and in 1957 she was widely—and, as it turned out, wrongly—regarded as the leading candidate.

The same year—1957—saw the publication of her *Last Tales* (Danish version, *Sidste Fortaellinger,* also 1957), followed the next year by *Anecdotes of Destiny* (Danish version, *Skaebne Anekdoter,* also 1958). Of the five *Anecdotes,* four had already appeared as magazine stories, three of them in the *Ladies' Home Journal,* which published a number of her stories between 1950 and 1962. The table of contents of *Last Tales* is a compendium of her literary plans in the last decade of her life. There are three groups of stories, "New Gothic Tales," "New Winter's Tales," and—the first and largest group—"Tales from *Albondocani.*" Dinesen did not live to complete any of the volumes for which the stories in *Last Tales* had been ultimately intended. The most ambitious of these was *Albondocani,* which she had been planning since 1950. It was to be her own *Thousand and One Nights,* an immense novel of interlocking stories, each self-contained and yet also connected through shared characters with the others, and all set in the kingdom of

Naples in the 1830's. She wrote as long as there was any strength left, aided by her faithful secretary, amanuensis, and companion (and, in the end, literary executor) Clara Svendsen. As late as 1961 she was revising old stories and working on new ones. But much of her strength went, at the end of the 1950's, into a final evocation of the Africa that she had left nearly thirty years earlier, *Shadows on the Grass,* which was written in English but first appeared in Danish as *Skygger paa Graesset* in 1960 before being published in English in 1961.

Isak Dinesen never did return to the real Africa, as against that world of memory where "half of me was lying in the Ngong Hills." Twice she had planned to—in 1935 she tried to be appointed war correspondent in the Italo-Ethiopian war, and just before World War II she hoped to make a pilgrimage to Mecca with her old Somali servant Farah—but each time the plans fell through. In 1960 *Life* wanted to send her to report on the struggle for independence in Kenya—an offer that points to the ironic gap between the perceived image of the writer and the actual condition of the woman, who (as she had to accept) would not have survived the journey, and who in any case (as she realized) would not have wanted that kind of a homecoming.

Nor did she ever set any of her tales on African soil. Africa was autobiography, though—as we have seen—when she wrote about her life in Africa, it translated itself into art. Africa made her as an artist, not merely because her *Gothic Tales* was conceived and partly written there, but also because there she learned to see the pattern of things, to recognize aristocracy, whether in animals or men, white or black. Above all, there she learned to treasure the quality that produces such insights: the imagination. It was, according to *Out of Africa,* the natives on her farm that were her best teachers:

The Negro is on friendly terms with destiny, . . . Amongst the qualities that he will be looking for in a master or a doctor or in God, imagination, I believe, comes high up in the list. . . . When the Africans speak of the personality of God they speak like the Arabian Nights or like the last chapters of the book of Job; it is the same quality, the infinite power of imagination, with which they are impressed.

(p. 23)

So of course she puts her own life into her tales, insofar as, whatever their setting and ostensible subject, they trace the patterns of extraordinary destinies and extraordinary greatness of mind. Above all, they both celebrate and exercise "the infinite power of imagination." Rarely do the *facts* of her life enter in even as surreptitious a form as they do in "The Cardinal's Third Tale," one of the *Albondocani* stories included in *Last Tales*. Lady Flora Gordon, a Scottish noblewoman of immense size, beauty, wit, and wealth, whose spiritual arrogance involves both a denial of the love of God and a Swiftian disgust with mankind, is transformed, mysteriously, into someone who experiences "a mirthful forbearance with and benevolence towards the frailty of humanity." The agency of the mystery is partly an old friar and partly the glorious immensity of St. Peter's in Rome, where she spends hours in contemplation of the bronze statue of the apostle. But the crucial part of the pattern is autobiography transmuted into a demonstration of God's imagination. Lady Flora kisses the foot of the statue, still moist and warm from the lips of a young Roman workman; four weeks later she discovers a syphilitic sore on her own lip—and welcomes it as a symbol, a covenant with humanity.

More often autobiography enters the tales as artistic self-reflectiveness. Two of the stories in *Winter's Tales* are about an English writer, Charles Despard, whose experiences mirror her own. In the first, "The Young Man with the Carnation," he is in despair, having written one great book and feeling that he could never write another, until the tragicomic coincidences of one night prove to him the infinite potential of God's, and hence the artist's, imagination. In the second, "A Consolatory Tale," he is older,

successful, and bitterly aware of the professional writer's commandments:

Thou shalt love thy art with all thy heart and with all thy soul, and with all thy mind. And thou shalt love thy public as thyself. . . . All human relationships have in them something monstrous and cruel. But the relation of the artist to the public is amongst the most monstrous. Yes, it is as terrible as marriage.

(p. 291)

Even more radically, Dinesen explores in some tales the wonder of the artist's gift *and* the sacrifice of ordinary human happiness that it demands. Perhaps this is done most poignantly in "Tempests" (in *Anecdotes of Destiny*), which is also one of the very few stories she wrote originally in Danish.

The plot weaves a traveling production of Shakespeare's *The Tempest* together with a real shipwreck off the Norwegian coast, so as to lead the heroine, a wonderfully inspired actress in the part of Ariel, to realize the danger of confusing life and art and the necessity of giving up the idea of marrying the man she loves. The artist's lot is sacrifice, and she is told by her director/Prospero: "In return we get the world's distrust—and our dire loneliness. And nothing else." Yet, for the many storytellers within Dinesen's often Chinese-box–like stories there *is* something else: the story itself. Thus in "The Dreamers" (in *Seven Gothic Tales*) there is "the much-renowned storyteller Mira Jama himself, the inventions of whose mind have been loved by a hundred tribes." Mira has outlived his own talent. He is bored with life; the world no longer cares for him; nor does he much care whether he lives or dies. "But," he says, "the tales which I made—they shall last."

TRADITION AND THE INDIVIDUAL TALENT

That Isak Dinesen's tales have lasted, and are likely to last, is partly because she speaks with a voice that her finest critic, Robert Lang-baum, has called "the voice of European civilization." Her readers are bound to sense that she writes with a keen awareness of European literary traditions. She herself, though she was an avid reader, liked to disclaim any erudition; she would refer to the erratic education she had received, and above all she would stress that she belonged, like her own Mira Jama, to the oral tradition of storytelling:

> Denys, who lived much by the ear, preferred hearing a story told, to reading it; when he came to the farm he would ask: "Have you got a story?" I had been making up many while he had been away. In the evenings he made himself comfortable, spreading cushions like a couch in front of the fire, and with me sitting on the floor, cross-legged like Scheherazade herself, he would listen, clear-eyed, to a long tale, from when it began until it ended.
>
> (*Out of Africa*, p. 226)

But she also admitted that the stories she thus told Finch-Hatton were never the entire tales that she eventually published, only the shorter stories-within-stories of which her fiction is so full. She liked to have each story completely worked out in her head—to have told it at least to herself—before she wrote it down; but in writing she would take infinite pains, rewriting a whole page to change a single word. Her written stories are not only rich in incident and detail and polished in style, they are also highly complex literary organizations which demand the reader's attention to allusions and symbols, to echoes and parallels. From "The Roads Round Pisa," which (in the Danish and British—but not the American—editions) opens *Seven Gothic Tales*, to *Ehrengard*, which was the last story she completed (it appeared posthumously in 1963 in both Danish and English), the reader has to be prepared to find himself in a labyrinth, requiring him to retrace his steps and reassess events and characters as new turns in the story change the meaning of what has gone before. If we trust the tale rather than the teller, then her storytelling combines a primitive appeal to everyone's love of hearing a story told with a highly sophisticated literary art.

An obvious aspect of that sophistication is an undertow of reference to major European writers. At the climax of "The Roads Round Pisa" Giovanni and Agnese speak to each other in quotation (in Italian) from Dante's *Divine Comedy*. These two young, noble, and beautiful people have met just once before, a year earlier when, in a tragicomic version of the substitute bride story, he deflowered her, thinking she was someone else. There is no language for them now except Dante's poetry of repentance and forgiveness, but unless the reader recognizes the lines, he will miss the meaning of a crucial episode in the story. This is an extreme example, but less extreme ones abound.

The plays of Shakespeare are so much present beneath many of the stories that they form a kind of background mythology. The use of the Ariel figure and of *The Tempest* as a whole in "Tempests" is only the most outstanding example. The character of Lady Flora in "The Cardinal's Third Tale" needs to be understood in relation to Jonathan Swift's work, as does Councillor Mathiesen in "The Poet" (in *Seven Gothic Tales*) in relation to Goethe's. Indeed, as the Councillor's most treasured and formative memory is of two years spent in Weimar, "in the atmosphere of the great Geheimrat Goethe," the German poet figures both as a theme and as an actual person in the story. So does Lord Byron in the late and not fully revised "Second Meeting" (in *Carnival*), while Henrik Ibsen makes an appearance as a collector of folktales and songs—"our old national treasures,—pearls, if you like"—in "The Pearls." Other Scandinavian writers appear, too, notably the great Danish poet Johannes Ewald, whose connection with Rungstedlund made him particularly alive to Dinesen. He and the wayward young king Christian VII are the principal characters of "Converse at Night in Copenhagen" (in *Last Tales*). These historical figures can appear in person because nearly all

Dinesen's stories are set in the past. But, significantly, in one of her two stories that take place in the modern age, "Carnival" (in *Carnival*)—the story she wrote in 1926 after her therapeutic letter to her brother—one of the young ladies at the masquerade party is dressed as "the young Soren Kierkegaard—that brilliant, deep, and desperate Danish philosopher of the forties."

This does not mean that, to enjoy Dinesen's tales, one must be fully versed in European literary history, but it does mean that part of that enjoyment is a sense of listening to a dialogue between the storyteller and the poets and thinkers of the past. And this in turn is part of a wider experience of being in touch, through the narrator's voice, with the past. In *Seven Gothic Tales* several of the stories open as pieces of cultural history, though without appearing to strain for historical effect. Take, for example, "The Deluge at Norderney":

> During the first quarter of the last century, seaside resorts became the fashion, even in those countries of northern Europe within the minds of whose people the sea had hitherto held the role of the devil, the cold and voracious hereditary foe of humanity. The romantic spirit of the age, which delighted in ruins, ghosts, and lunatics, and counted a stormy night on the heath and a deep conflict of the passions a finer treat for the connoisseur than the ease of the salon and the harmony of a philosophic system, reconciled even the most refined individuals to the eternal wildness of the coast scenery and the open seas.
>
> (p. 121)

By the time of her last completed story, *Ehrengard,* the sense of long ago has entered into the tone of the voice itself, and the story opens with exquisite simplicity:

> An old lady told this story.
>
> A hundred and twenty years ago, she began, my story told itself, at greater length of time than you or I can give to it, and with a throng of details and particulars which we can never hope to know. The men and women who then gradually built it up, and to whom it was a matter of life and death, are all long gone.
>
> (pp. 3–4)

And yet even here, the past is not a general long ago but a specific stage in European history:

> The very country in which it began, developed and came to an end, may be said to have faded out of existence. For it was, in those good days, a fair, free and flourishing small principality of old Germany, and its sovereign was responsible to no one but God in Heaven. But later on, when times and men grew harder, it was silently and sadly swallowed up into the great new German Empire.
>
> (p. 4)

Here we have a key to the settings of Dinesen's stories. Whatever European (and very occasionally Asian) country and whatever decade of the nineteenth century (excepting the tale set in the Danish thirteenth century, "The Fish," in *Winter's Tales*) she chooses for each tale, the choice is of a place and time *before* "times and men grew harder." That is, place and time in her fiction matter less as geography and history as such, and more as conditions for a quality of life, an attitude of mind. The virginal Ehrengard von Schreckenstein in an idyllic German principality in the 1840's, the old Prince Potenziani who fights a duel but dies from love on the roads around Pisa in 1823, the von Galens and Angels of the 1870 Copenhagen winter season—all share, and share with the culture that has produced them, that "faith in the idea that God had, when he made us" that Dinesen found in the natives on her African farm. But to the reader—though not to the characters—these separate worlds also share that sense that is so strong in the last section of *Shadows on the Grass,* "Echoes from the Hills," of a world nearing its end and having, as the narrator in "Copenhagen Season" puts it, "one foot in the grave." They are aristocratic, heroic, and doomed worlds.

From Dinesen's biographers we learn that, when asked about the meaning of "gothic" in the title of her first collection of tales, she explained it as referring to the gothic revival in art and literature and defined her period as beginning with the death of the poet Ewald in 1781 and ending with the fall of the Second Empire in France in 1871, "the last great phase of aristocratic culture." More specifically she would point to her kinship with the English Gothic tradition and the age of Byron. There is no horror in her tales, and little of the supernatural. "The Supper at Elsinore" with its ghost is exceptional, and "The Sailor-boy's Tale" (in *Winter's Tales*) could be seen as a happy inversion of Samuel Taylor Coleridge's "The Rime of the Ancient Mariner" (1798, 1817), in that the sailor boy saves the life of a peregrine falcon that then becomes an old Lapp woman who in turn saves his life. But "The Monkey" (in *Seven Gothic Tales*) is more truly representative of Dinesen's version of the gothic; the way that the Virgin Prioress of Cloister Seven and her pet monkey metamorphose in and out of each other is not seen as supernatural but rather as a natural manifestation of the closeness of the very refined and the brutal or barbaric. What Dinesen most fundamentally shares with the early English Romantics, notably Coleridge, is the ability to make the most fantastic events seem most natural. In her Danish translation of the title of her first book, "gothic" indeed becomes "fantastisk." She also shares with the Gothic movement in late- eighteenth- and early- nineteenth-century English literature the fundamental impulse to provide her readers with an emotional outlet in a rational and mechanistic age. Hence the appeal of, and the sometimes half-guilty response to, her extravagant fiction in the realistic and socially conscious 1930's.

If Dinesen's admiration of aristocratic culture and her regret at its disappearance determined her choice of settings for her tales, there are also clearly more purely aesthetic reasons for her devotion to the past. In an interview in the Danish newspaper *Politiken* on 1 May 1934, when the author of *Seven Gothic Tales* had been revealed as Karen Blixen, she explained that she had set her tales in the past

"because . . . only in that way did I become perfectly free." Freedom in this sense is also what her pseudonym aimed at, freedom to create her own fictive world, freedom from the expectations of real life. In the interview with Daniel Gilles for Belgian television shortly before her death she developed the formal implications of such freedom: "With the past I find myself before a finished world, complete in all its elements, and I can thus more easily recompound it in my imagination. Here, no temptation for me to fall back into realism, nor for my readers to look for it." The ultimate attraction of the past, then, is not so much its pastness, or romantic evocativeness, as its completeness. Seeing at once the beginning and the end of a period or a phase in culture is like seeing Africa from Denys' airplane over the Ngong Hills; it gives the artist that godlike detachment which Dinesen saw as so essential to the storyteller. "Recompounding" the past, so that beginnings and ends are seen to be woven together into astounding patterns, is the essence of her narrative art. For a single, compact illustration of this, the reader might turn to her late, never finally revised story "Second Meeting." Within it, the owner of a marionette theater—himself Byron's alter ego, waiting on this "second meeting" to turn the life of the poet into a story—tells Byron of "a very great story" that he has not yet had the courage to make into a play. It is the story of the day of Pentecost, but its focus is not on the apostles, tumbling to the floor as the Holy Spirit descends on them and makes them speak in tongues, but on "one slim and graceful figure only, Milord, [who] in this hour of the hurricane remains serene":

The Virgin stands unmoving, her face turned upwards, her hands crossed upon her breast. As you will know from the paintings, upon Good Friday all blood had sunk from her face. Now once more it mounts to her cheeks in one sweet roseate wave, and she again looks like a maiden of fifteen. In a low voice—and for this I shall have to use my loveliest soprano—she cries out: "Oh, is it you, sir? After these thirty-four years, is it you?" Between the distant first meeting of those two and the present meeting lies the story.

(*Carnival,* pp. 336–337)

Turning the Pentecost into a love story between Mary and the Holy Ghost is bound to seem, to many, in poor taste, at best bizarre, at worst decadently iconoclastic. All those adjectives can be applied to Dinesen's art, but they all need to be tempered by an awareness of how, as here, an extraordinary aesthetic detachment controls the impact of her narration. Through the statuelike beauty of the Virgin as the still center of a tumultuous scene—reminiscent of the miraculous ending of Shakespeare's *The Winter's Tale*—the main impulse communicated is not erotic; it is an aesthetic satisfaction at a destiny fulfilled, a pattern completed. Between the Annunciation thirty-four years ago and the descent of the Holy Spirit in the present "lies the story"; and it lies in the minds of the narrator and the reader rather than on the page.

The "perfect freedom" which Dinesen spoke of as a precondition for her art also meant a freedom both to draw on and to detach herself from the various movements and "-isms" of European literature. Her relationship with the gothic strain in the Romantic movement has already been touched on. Her sense of landscape and of its interaction with man—be it in Africa or Europe—has much in common with the nature romanticism of William Wordsworth. At the same time, in her almost obsessive use of the image of the mask, and of life as a marionette play, she owes something to the more complex, ironic romanticism of the Germans—to Ludwig Tieck and Heinrich Heine—even as she also shares this obsession with more modern poets, such as William Butler Yeats. As early as 1904 she had written a marionette comedy, "Sandhedens Haevn" ("The Revenge of Truth"), for the family; she revised it in Africa, and its publication in *Tilskueren* in May 1926 gave her the stimulus to draft her first gothic tales. (An English translation of "The Revenge of Truth" is included in Donald Hannah's critical study.) But perhaps the most timeless aspect of Romanticism in her work is its central myth: that of a paradise lost.

Out of Africa, as Robert Langbaum was the first to show, is one of the great pastorals in European literature; in writing about the feudal society on her farm, the natural aristocracy of the natives, and the wild grace of the animals, she is, Langbaum writes, "reconstructing that organic life of the European past projected by the romantic mythology." And when she loses the farm, he continues, "we see reenacted in miniature the crisis of modern Europe, the breakup of social organization based on love and mutual obligation."

These are large terms, but no larger than those used by Dinesen herself. As late as her American Academy talk, "On Mottoes of My Life," she could describe her meeting with the animals of Africa as "a return to those happy days when Adam gave names to the beasts of Eden" and speak of the understanding and love she felt for the natives as "as strong a passion as I have ever known." In *Out of Africa* she voices the fear that the industrial revolution has cut European civilization off from its roots in nature:

Perhaps the white men of the past, indeed of any past, would have been in better understanding and sympathy with the coloured races than we, of our Industrial Age, shall ever be. When the first steam engine was constructed, the roads of the races of the world parted, and we have never found one another since.

(pp. 215–216)

She is not writing here about race relations as such, but about what the modern world has lost. In pointing to "the particular, instinctive attachment which all Natives of Africa felt" toward Denys Finch-Hatton and a few other people of his kind, she is both lamenting the state of modern technological and bourgeois civilization and celebrating the few heroic survivors from an older civilization. Primitive instinct and aristocratic refinement meet and merge in all her heroes, whether they come from life, like her father and Denys; from history, like Lord Byron; from folktales, like the old lord in "Sorrow-Acre"; or purely from her own invention, like Prince Potenziani in "The Roads Round Pisa." They are unfit for "real" life; they dream, wander, hunt, and pursue sexual adventures; their love affairs with their own destinies tend to lead to death. In celebrating the beauty and wholeness of their lives, as against the dreariness and fragmentation of modern civilization, Dinesen had much in common with the French symbolist poets whom she and Denys had read and admired together.

Indeed the story in *Winter's Tales* called "The Invincible Slave-Owners," which is about two young German girls' absurdly heroic attempt to keep up their aristocratic life-style though they are penniless, ends with a couple of lines from Charles Baudelaire's poem "Le beau navire" ("The Beautiful Ship")—thus summing up the apparently pathetic life of the heroine, Mizzi, as *triomphant* (triumphant) and *majestueux* (majestic or magnificent). In her admiration of style above morality, of the heroically destructive and self-destructive life above a sympathetic concern for fellow lives, Dinesen could well be seen—and often has been seen—as a decadent in the sense that some French and English writers of the 1890's are termed decadent. The moribund syphilitic baroness who in 1961 wrote of the Virgin's blush when she reencountered the Holy Ghost at Pentecost would seem a classic example of latter-day decadence. But if we use this term, we must also realize that her version of decadence is a peculiarly robust one, as preoccupied with the glorious processes of life as with degeneration and death. In a letter to her mother in 1923 she wrote of having reread Oscar Wilde and found that he had not worn well: "It is all so thin and feeble that one feels like spitting it out again" (Anne Born, trans.). Instead, she writes, she has turned to the great Danish Romantic writers, notably Oehlenschläger, in whom she finds "profundity and

nobility." Her own art of storytelling may represent "art for art's sake" in that it disclaims any social and moral purpose and often glorifies the amoral or even immoral. But it is saved from being "thin and feeble" by its profound exploration of how life itself becomes art.

It is perhaps not coincidental that the robustness and the profundity are both most evident in her Danish stories. Take "Peter and Rosa," which is set in the neighborhood of Rungstedlund and in an unsurpassed way renders the arrival of spring after a long Scandinavian winter. The sky over the "dead" landscape "dissolved into streaming life"; the snow melts, and the ice that has covered the sound from the Danish to the Swedish coast begins to break up. The eponymous hero and heroine, who are cousins and both fifteen, have been brought up in a pious and otherworldly parsonage: "Death was zealously kept in view and lectured upon." Peter, held to his books by his uncle who wants him too to become a parson, dreams of becoming a sailor. Rosa, a Cinderella in an old frock and botched shoes, has her own dream, in which she is "the loveliest, mightiest and most dangerous person on earth," but she also believes that "some time, something horrible would happen to her." Both young people are full of contradictions and of potentials; the pattern of the story resolves all these in one glorious catastrophe. The coming of spring stirs Peter to the decision to run away to sea, even as it also stirs both of them into a still unrecognized erotic love for each other. He confides his plan to Rosa, who gives it away to her father, the parson, and then immediately feels like a Judas and so agrees to go with Peter down to the sound to watch the ice breaking up. Caught up in the ecstasy of the "infinite, swaying wet world" of the melting ice, they realize too late that the floe on which they stand has separated from the land ice and is drifting out to sea. Calmly accepting death as their destiny, they are swept down by the current, clasped in each other's arms. Among much that is remarkable in this story, on both the naturalistic and the symbolic levels, there is the fact that as readers we do not in the end focus on the death by drowning, nor on the grief of those left behind. The *Liebestod* becomes a fulfillment, a freezing of two young lives at the moment of their greatest perfection into the kind of immortality that Keats celebrates in his "Ode on a Grecian Urn" (1820). It is not so much art for art's sake as a dialogue between life and art.

The Danishness of this story, like that of "Sorrow-Acre," is partly a matter of the feel of a place and a season; in "Sorrow-Acre" it is the brief high summer, "that week wherein the lime-trees flower" that "seems to unite the fields of Denmark with those of Elysium." Partly it is a matter of style and thought. The Danish literature that she read and absorbed from childhood on has left traces throughout Dinesen's work. Two of its most famous names should be mentioned. Hans Christian Andersen, the nineteenth-century storyteller, is her forerunner in terms of narrative tone, the combination of the deadpan and the fantastic, as in the tale of the figurehead which Peter tells Rosa within the story. Søren Kierkegaard, the writer and philosopher whose influence outside Scandinavia has probably been greater in the twentieth century than it was in the nineteenth, helped to shape the intellectual and moral climate into which Karen Dinesen was born. The writer Isak Dinesen had an ambivalent relationship with him; it is as the author of "A Seducer's Diary" (the famous last section of volume 1 of *Enten-Eller* [translated as *Either/Or,* 1843]) that he is impersonated in "Carnival," and she would associate his insistence on ethical choice—the imperative either/or—with the Westenholz seriousness from which she had to escape. But in the intensity with which her characters embrace their destiny as a calling—Peter thinks "the sight of me will make God sad" because in not becoming a sailor, "I have crossed his plans"—there is a commitment to self-realization that is as strenuous in its way as any Kierkegaardian imperative, or as any Ibsenite hero's or heroine's urge to follow his or her vocation.

Dinesen can write both from inside and from outside a Scandinavian consciousness. In "The Roads Round Pisa," the central intelligence, "a young Danish nobleman of a melancholy disposition," voices the Northerner's customary inferiority complex before southern European civilization. He thinks

> how plainly one must realize, in meeting the people of this country, that they had been living in marble palaces and writing about philosophy while his own ancestors in the large forests had been making themselves weapons of stone and had dressed in the furs of the bears whose warm blood they drank. To form a hand and wrist like these must surely take a thousand years, he reflected. In Denmark everybody has thick ankles and wrists, and the higher up you go, the thicker they are.
>
> (p. 20)

But Count August von Schimmelmann, as the whole story shows, is limited by excessive self-doubt and is not a reliable judge of the two cultures. When the judge is the story itself, the verdict can be more subtle. It is most beautifully so in "Babette's Feast," first published in the *Ladies' Home Journal* in 1950 and later included in *Anecdotes of Destiny*. In a yellow wooden house in a small Norwegian fjord town live two elderly sisters, daughters of a dean who had christened them Martine and Philippa, "after Martin Luther and his friend Philip Melanchthon." He had also founded a particularly pious and pleasure-renouncing sect. Into this home and community comes Babette, a wild-eyed refugee from the fighting on the Paris barricades in 1871, and also (we learn at the end) a superb cook at the Café Anglais. Pity and faith in "the example of a good Lutheran life" persuade the sisters to keep this Papist under their roof; fearing her ability to cook—"in France, they knew, people ate frogs"—they show her how to prepare a split cod and an ale-and-bread soup. Babette watches the demonstration with a face "absolutely expressionless" and proceeds to become a model cook and maid-of-all-work in the puritanical household. After some years she wins ten thousand

1299

francs in a French lottery and, as a favor, asks to be allowed to prepare "a real French dinner" for the celebration of the hundredth anniversary of the dean's birth. Mysterious ingredients arrive from Paris, and on the birthday the brothers and sisters sit down to turtle soup, *blinis demidoff,* and *cailles en sarcophage,* which they serenely consume "as if they had been doing so every day for thirty years." They drink the Veuve Cliquot, 1860, which they know cannot be wine, as it sparkles, and this "lemonade," they find, "lift[s] them off the ground, into a higher and purer sphere." When the feast is over, and the brothers and sisters have tumbled home through the snow in a state of bliss, Martine and Philippe seek out Babette, exhausted in a kitchen full of greasy pots and pans, to thank her for "quite a nice dinner." To their amazement they find, first, that she has spent all of her ten thousand francs on this dinner worthy of the Café Anglais and, second, that she insists she has done it for her own sake, or rather for the sake of her art: " 'I am a great artist!' she said."

No thumbnail sketch of this story can do justice to the genial irony with which Dinesen has rendered the meeting of the northern, puritanical and the southern, sensuous consciousness. In the innocent bliss of the brothers and sisters, which they perceive as an exalted spiritual state, lies a tongue-in-cheek answer to a good deal of morally strenuous northern literature. But this is not all. The genuine goodness of the two sisters, their physical as well as spiritual purity and sweetness, is as fully realized and as attractive as the more sophisticated, more "European," attitude of Babette. Hence, there is more than irony in Philippa's speech that ends the story. Holding Babette in an unpuritanical embrace, she finds words of consolation for the artist faced with a future of "second best"; her words bridge the gap between the two cultures: " 'Yet this is not the end! I feel, Babette, that this is not the end. In Paradise you will be the great artist that God meant you to be! Ah!' she added, the tears streaming down her cheeks. 'Ah, how you will enchant the angels!' "

It would be wrong to overemphasize the national aspect of Dinesen's themes; even here the dichotomy is not so much French versus Norwegian as one Kierkegaardian "stage"—the "aesthetic"—versus another—the "ethical." (Possibly Philippa, in her last words, rises to the third, the "religious.") Her characters are on the whole not much determined by their nationalities; they are simply larger than life—sometimes quite literally so, as in the case of the huge Lady Flora Gordon or the Amazonian Athena in "The Monkey." Even then they are, like nearly all the women in the stories, incredibly beautiful. Defying Count August von Schimmelman's notion of thick Danish ankles, the body of one of the masqueraders in "Carnival" is of such perfection that "at whatever place—throat, arm, waist, or knee—you cut her slim body through with a sharp knife, you would have got a perfectly circular transverse incision." In "The Roads Round Pisa" we hear of a girl so lovely that the statue of St. Joseph at the basilica turns his head to look at her, "remembering the appearance of the Virgin at the time they were betrothed"; her daughter in turn "was so fair that it was said in Pisa that when she drank red wine you could follow its course as it ran down her throat and chest." Nationality, in her men and women, is mainly important as giving local habitation and a name to typical qualities, as with the young Danish sailor in "The Immortal Story" (in *Anecdotes of Destiny*) who comes to represent all innocent, virginal youth. He is the Paul of Bernardin de Saint-Pierre's *Paul et Virginie* (1788).

It is in this area—her characterizations—that we most clearly see Dinesen as belonging with her own generation of European writers: the post-Freudians who, in Langbaum's words, "effect a transition from the individual to the archetypal character." Langbaum places her with the "more massive" writers of that generation—Rainer Maria Rilke, Franz Kafka, Thomas

Mann, James Joyce, and T. S. Eliot—and finds a particular kinship between Dinesen and Mann, whose fiction moved from the psychological and naturalistic (as in *Buddenbrooks,* 1901) to the mythical (as in the Joseph novels, 1933–1943, or *Doctor Faustus,* 1947). Clearly this is not a question of following fashion; we have seen in an earlier section how naturally, in writing of Africa, she translates life into myth. Yet part of the excitement of reading her is being, naturally and effortlessly, in contact with European literary history from romanticism to modernism.

The European quality of her writing, finally, is also a matter of language. Dinesen is one of the few remarkable writers—Conrad and Vladimir Nabokov are two others—who, though their mother tongue was not English, have written great literature in English. She is all the more remarkable for being one of those who—like Samuel Beckett—seem to work in two languages with equal ease. As we have seen, for all but some of her late works she did her own "translations" into Danish. She is virtually unique for having continued to write in English while living in Denmark, and while the African experience of using English as a daily language receded further and further into the past.

Initially, she told her brother Thomas in a letter of 10 April 1931, she decided to write in English "because I thought it would be more profitable" (Anne Born, trans.). But the desire for a larger audience and higher sales cannot have been, then or later, the main motive. English would have had a particular emotive connotation in that—though her letters home were written, of course, in Danish—much of her African life was lived within that language. Above all, it was her lover's language, and the language in which, Scheherazade-like, she told him stories. But in the end, what probably matters most is the very fact that it was *not* the language of Karen Dinesen; like her pseudonym and like her preference for the past, the foreign language gave her the freedom to ma-

nipulate her material. Anyone operating in a language not his or her own does so with an amount of self-consciousness. In reading Dinesen one is aware of this self-consciousness as a profound aesthetic pleasure, an enjoyment of the sheer craft of handling English and making it—like the lions she shot in Africa—"all through what [it] ought to be." As the many passages quoted will have shown, the English she wrote was in the deepest sense her own, a clear, uncluttered, precise style, able to range from the ecstatic to the wryly comic and to achieve intricate effects by pellucid understatements. By her unerring choice of words and cadences she made her language seem the exact tool for the "very beautiful stories" that she declared it was her ambition to invent.

"VERY BEAUTIFUL STORIES"

We must conclude by asking what Isak Dinesen meant when, in the interview for Belgian television, she spoke of her only ambition as being "to invent stories, very beautiful stories." This can be done briefly, for several reasons. One is that most of the answer should already have emerged in the previous section of this essay. Another is that each reader will obtain the whole answer only by going and reading Isak Dinesen for him- or herself. Yet another is that, in doing so, the reader will find that many of her stories—and especially the stories within her stories, for her characters are forever explaining things to each other by means of telling a story—expound the philosophy and aesthetics (and the two are to her the same) of her storytelling. Thus, in a story such as "The Cardinal's First Tale," one of the *Albondocani* stories in *Last Tales,* we have what is virtually Dinesen's poetics. "The divine art," says the Cardinal, "is the story. In the beginning was the story. At the end we shall be privileged to view, and review, it—and that is what is named the day of judgment." He is lamenting the rise of the novel, a new art form (for this story is set in the 1820's) that is "ready to sacrifice the story itself" for the sake of "individual characters," and that aims to bring the reader into such close sympathy with its characters that, as a consequence, the story "evaporates, like the bouquet of a noble wine, the bottle of which has been left uncorked." In his mannered fashion he reminds us that, while Dinesen's art feeds on many European traditions, it does *not* want to be seen in the tradition of the great English and American nineteenth-century novel. It does *not* direct itself to creating sympathy, "a wide fellow-feeling with all that is human," as George Eliot puts it in *The Mill on the Floss* (1860), nor does it ask for pity for those caught in the web of fate, as do the novels of Thomas Hardy. Dinesen glories in tracing that web and, as we have seen, the divinely *comic* vision it reveals. Nor do her characters struggle with a sense of sin, as do Nathaniel Hawthorne's—one could imagine her rewriting *The Scarlet Letter* (1850) to a very different purpose—or with the problem of making fine moral discriminations, as do Henry James's. From the depths of this tradition it would be natural to exclaim, as Dinesen—cleverly spiking our critical guns—makes the lady listening to the cardinal exclaim: " 'O God,' said the lady. 'What you call the divine art to me seems a hard and cruel game, which maltreats and mocks its human beings.' " For it is clear that in her pursuit of "the divine art," in which the artist imitates God the creator because God has the greatest imagination, Dinesen sees the key to that art in plot and pattern, not in character. And the God of this conception is not one of mercy and love but one who has, above all, what the valet in "The Deluge at Norderney" defines as "the tremendous courage of the Creator of this world." Hence, to appreciate the beauty of her stories, we may need to divest ourselves of some of our Anglo-Saxon preconceptions about fiction and be open to the sheer courage of her plots and the balanced intricacies of her patterns.

By now it will be obvious that to give an account of an Isak Dinesen story is a long-winded business; you cannot simply describe a mood or outline a situation. You have to tell the plot because, in its arabesques, it is the essence of the story; it reveals the presence of the divine storyteller. Of all the stories, none shows this more clearly than "The Roads Round Pisa"—indeed the title itself suggests that the truth lies in the patterns made by the characters' movements *round* Pisa. To slice right through those patterns, the story shows all the characters, in various ways, as schemers and plotters. What they do not understand until the end is what the Witch says at the end of the marionette comedy that two of the characters go to see in the course of the story (the comedy is Dinesen's own "The Revenge of Truth" mentioned above): "The truth, my children, is that we are, all of us, acting in a marionette comedy. What is more important than anything else in a marionette comedy, is keeping the ideas of the author clear." In the end, old Prince Potenziani dies in (if not of) the insight that he has been "too small for the ways of God"; and the old countess in a key speech sums up both the philosophy and the narrative technique (for, again, the two are one) of the story:

Life is a mosaic work of the Lord's, which he keeps filling in bit by bit. If I had seen this little bit of bright colour [a baby born to Prince Potenziani's ex-wife and the man for whom she abandoned the prince] as the centerpiece, I would have understood the pattern, and would not have shaken it all to pieces so many times, and given the good Lord so much trouble in putting it together again.

(p. 49)

As it happens, even the old countess does not see the whole pattern; and herein lies another aspect of the beauty of Dinesen's stories, that which keeps them from merely being stories about stories, patterns about patterns. "It is not a bad thing in a tale that you understand only half of it," says Lincoln in "The Dreamers."

In the best tales, there is a mystery at the heart of the story. It may be one of identity: even the cardinal in his first story cannot answer the universal question "Who am I?" as he cannot know which of two identical twins (only one of whom was rescued from a fire) he really is: the one destined for the priesthood or the one meant to be an artist. It may be human psychology—despite the cardinal's and Dinesen's tenets—breaking through the pattern; the study of adolescence in "Peter and Rosa" fascinates quite apart from any divine plan. Or it may be a symbol that hints wordlessly at the unspeakable and the unpatternable, like the seashell left by the sailor boy in "The Immortal Story" for his love of one night, or the unstained wedding sheet in "The Blank Page" (in *Last Tales*).

For in the end, while Dinesen's art is immensely self-conscious and self-reflective and draws much of its strength and polish from being so, what humanizes it and leaves the poetics of the Cardinal behind is the awareness that life will forever refuse to be fitted into stories. Four stories, at least, deal directly with the danger of trying to play God with human beings. In "Echoes," one of the "New Gothic Tales" in *Last Tales,* the story of the great singer Pellegrina Leoni, who has lost her voice, is taken up from "The Dreamers." In the earlier story we saw her die; here she is living in a remote Italian village and is trying to write a young boy into her own story by teaching him to sing with the voice she used to have. Ultimately he rejects her, and she realizes that she has been "too bold, venturing to play with human hands on an Aeolian harp." She also understands that "one can take many liberties with God which one cannot take with men." "The Poet," in an ambitious context of historical and cultural reference that has made Langbaum call it "a miniature history of Europe," centers on the old councillor's godlike scheme to turn a young man, Anders, into the kind of poet he, the councillor, thinks he should be. It involves writing a plot for him: an unhappy love story, using the lovely young dancer, Fransine, whom the councillor is about to marry. But the plot misfires; he is shot by Anders and, mortally wounded, given his deathblow by Fransine. "You!" she cries at him, as she lifts and flings a heavy stone at him, "You poet!" And the symbolism, as he crawls at her feet, suggests that, instead of being the creator in an earthly paradise, he has been the serpent. There is something diabolical about trying to usurp God's role, and the same suggestion hovers around Herr Cazotte, the great painter, seducer, and arch plotter of *Ehrengard,* who with wonderfully comic irony is defeated in his elaborate scheme to seduce the eponymous heroine. Life, in the form of the young womanhood and fierce integrity of Ehrengard, defies the artist.

Perhaps the most remarkable of these four stories, at once most bizarre, moving, and haunting in its implications, is "The Immortal Story" (in *Anecdotes of Destiny*). Mr. Clay, an immensely rich tea-trader in Canton—"a tall, dry and close old man"—is unable and unwilling to accept that there is such a thing as fiction, and so, when he hears of a story that "never has happened, and . . . never will happen, and that is why it is told," he insists on making it happen. The story is that of a sailor who is paid five guineas to spend the night with the wife of a rich old gentleman, so as to beget an heir for him. With the aid of his clerk, Elishama—a Wandering Jew figure—Mr. Clay stages this story, using the once beautiful but now blowsy daughter of his onetime trading partner (for whose bankruptcy and suicide he is responsible) as the wife and a fresh young Danish sailor, "little more than a boy," as the stud. But the story refuses to come true. The young man falls deeply in love with the woman, whom he perceives as unutterably young and beautiful, and when, after a night of love, he is told by the clerk of the role he is supposed to have played in the story, he can only say: "But that story is not in the least like what happened to me." He goes off to his ship, leaving behind his greatest treasure, a big shining pink shell, for his beloved Virginie, and leaving Elishama with the shell at his ear:

> There was a deep, low surge in it, like the distant roar of great breakers. Elishama's face took on exactly the same expression as the sailor's face a few moments ago. He had a strange, gentle, profound shock, from the sound of a new voice in the house, and in the story. "I have heard it before," he thought, "long ago. Long, long ago. But where?"
>
> (p. 231)

Here, in one configuration, we may see and hear the answer to the question why Isak Dinesen is a beautiful storyteller. With forms as labyrinthine, as polished, and as beautiful as the seashell, she will please us and tease us until, perhaps, we feel we have had enough of pattern and wish for more of rough, real humanity. And just then she will haunt us with "a new voice," with unanswerable questions and a hint of things heard "long ago. . . . But where?" Only a great writer can do that.

Selected Bibliography

EDITIONS

ENGLISH EDITIONS
Seven Gothic Tales. New York and London, 1934.
Out of Africa. London, 1937; New York, 1938.
Winter's Tales. New York and London, 1942.
The Angelic Avengers [by Pierre Andrézel, pseud.]. London, 1946; New York, 1947.
Last Tales. New York and London, 1957.
Anecdotes of Destiny. New York and London, 1958.
Shadows on the Grass. New York and London, 1961.

POSTHUMOUS ENGLISH EDITIONS
Ehrengard. New York and London, 1963.
Essays. Copenhagen, 1965.
Carnival: Entertainments and Posthumous Tales. Chicago, 1977.

POSTHUMOUS EDITIONS IN ENGLISH TRANSLATION
"The Revenge of Truth." In Donald Hannah, *Isak Dinesen and Karen Blixen: The Mask and the Reality.* London, 1971.
Daguerrotypes and Other Essays. Translated by P. M. Mitchell and W. D. Paden. Chicago, 1979.
Letters from Africa: 1914–1931. Edited by Frans Lasson, translated by Anne Born. Chicago, 1981.
On Modern Marriage, and Other Observations. Translated by Anne Born. New York, 1986.

DANISH EDITIONS
Syv fantastiske Fortaellinger. Copenhagen, 1935.
Den afrikanske Farm. Copenhagen, 1937.
Vinter Eventyr. Copenhagen, 1942.
Gengaeldelsens Veje [by Pierre Andrézel]. Copenhagen, 1944.
Daguerrotypier. Copenhagen, 1951. Two radio talks.
Sidste Fortaellinger. Copenhagen, 1957.
Skaebne Anekdoter. Copenhagen, 1958.
Skygger paa Graesset. Copenhagen, 1960.
Sandhedens Haevn: En Marionetkomedie. Copenhagen, 1960. First published in *Tilskueren* (May 1926).

POSTHUMOUS DANISH EDITIONS
Osceola. Edited by Clara Svendsen. Copenhagen, 1962. Collection of her early Danish stories and poems.
Karen Blixens Tegninger: Med to Essays af Karen Blixen. Edited by Frans Lasson. Copenhagen, 1969. Drawings and two essays.
Efterladte Fortaellinger. Edited by Frans Lasson. Copenhagen, 1975. Posthumous tales.
"Moderne Ægteskab og andre Betragtninger." In *Blixeniana 1977* (the yearbook of the Karen Blixen Society, edited by Hans Andersen and Frans Lasson). Copenhagen, 1977.
Breve fra Afrika: 1914–1931. 2 vols. Edited by Frans Lasson. Copenhagen, 1978. Letters.
Blixeniana 1983. Copenhagen, 1983. A selection of juvenilia.

POSTHUMOUS EDITIONS IN DANISH TRANSLATION
Ehrengard. Translated into Danish by Clara Svendsen. Copenhagen, 1963.

ISAK DINESEN

BIOGRAPHICAL AND CRITICAL STUDIES

Arendt, Hannah. "Isak Dinesen, 1885–1962." In *Men in Dark Times*. New York, 1968.

Bjørnvig, Thorkild. *The Pact: My Friendship with Isak Dinesen*. Baton Rouge, La., 1983.

Blixen-Finecke, Bror von. *The African Hunter*. Translated from the Swedish by F. H. Lyon. London, 1937; New York, 1938.

Bogan, Louise. "Isak Dinesen." In *Selected Criticism*. New York, 1955.

Brandes, Georg. "Wilhelm Dinesen." In *Samlede Skrifter* 3:189–196 (119)

Cate, Curtis. "Isak Dinesen: The Scheherazade of Our Times." *Cornhill Magazine* 171:120–137 (Winter 1959–1960).

———. "Isak Dinesen." *Atlantic Monthly* 204: 151–155 (December 1959).

Claudi, Jørgen. *Contemporary Danish Authors*. Translated by Jörgen Andersen and Aubrey Rush. Copenhagen, 1952.

Davenport, John. "A Noble Pride: The Art of Karen Blixen." *The Twentieth Century* 159: 261–274 (March 1956).

Dinesen, Thomas. *My Sister, Isak Dinesen*. Translated by Joan Tate. London, 1975.

Gillés, Daniel. "La pharoanne de Rungstedlund." *Isak Dinesen: A Memorial*. Edited by Clara Svendsen. New York, 1965.

Hannah, Donald. *Isak Dinesen and Karen Blixen: The Mask and the Reality*. New York, 1971. Includes a translation of "The Revenge of Truth."

Henriksen, Aage. *Det Guddomelige Barn og Andre Essays om Karen Blixen*. Copenhagen, 1965.

Henriksen, Liselotte. *Isak Dinesen: A Bibliography*. Chicago, 1977.

Johannesson, Eric O. *The World of Isak Dinesen*. Seattle, Wash., 1961.

Langbaum, Robert. *The Gayety of Vision: A Study of Isak Dinesen's Art*. London, 1964; New York, 1965.

Lasson, Frans and Clara Svendsen, eds. *The Life and Destiny of Isak Dinesen*. London, 1970.

Migel, Parmenia. *Titania: The Biography of Isak Dinesen*. New York, 1967.

Stafford, Jean. "Isak Dinesen: Master Teller of Tales." *Horizon* 111–112 (September, 1959). Interview.

Svendsen, Clara, ed. *Isak Dinesen: A Memorial*. New York, 1965. Memorial anthology of essays on Isak Dinesen.

Thurman, Judith. *Isak Dinesen: The Life of a Storyteller*. New York, 1982.

Trzebenski, Errol. *Silence Will Speak*. London, 1977. Biography of Denys Finch-Hatton.

Vowles, Richard B. "Boganis, Father of Osceola; or Wilhelm Dinesen in America, 1872–1874." *Scandinavian Studies* 48:369–383 (1976).

Walter, Eugene. "The Art of Fiction: Isak Dinesen." *Paris Review* 43–59 (Autumn 1956). Interview.

Wescott, Glenway. "Isak Dinesen, the Storyteller." In *Images of Truth*. New York, 1962.

Whissen, Thomas R. *Isak Dinesen's Aesthetics*. Port Washington, N.Y., 1973.

INGA-STINA EWBANK

FRANÇOIS MAURIAC

(1885–1970)

FRANÇOIS MAURIAC CAME from a family that had lived in the Gironde region for three hundred years. His immediate ancestors did not belong to what is often called "the aristocracy of the grape," although they owned vineyards at Malagar and Sainte-Croix-du-Mont. There were a number of doctors, lawyers, magistrates, and priests in the family, and Mauriac always felt alienated from the oligarchy of commerce whose private houses lined the Pavé des Chartrons in Bordeaux.

Mauriac was born on 11 October 1885. Less than two years after Mauriac was christened in honor of Saint François de Sales, his father died from a cerebral abscess. His paternal grandparents died soon after, and he was raised in a feminine milieu dominated by Madame Coiffard, his maternal grandmother. His father's brother—never a professed believer—was an intermittent visitor to the household. This habitué of Bordeaux's café society added a ribald touch to an otherwise stolid environment of scrupulous piety. Mauriac was content with these limited horizons because they provided him with everything he wanted as a child and all he needed as a writer. Time did not turn him into a traveler. The abbé Péquignot, imbued with Blaise Pascal and refreshingly cosmopolitan, made a powerful impression on Mauriac when he was a student at Grand-Lebrun, the Marianite school in Bordeaux.

On 3 June 1913 Mauriac married Jeanne Lafont at Talence, her father's estate outside Bordeaux. They settled in the sixteenth arrondissement in Paris, where Claude, their first son, was born. The crowning achievement of Mauriac's career was the awarding of the Nobel Prize in literature (1952). This confirmed his reputation as a quintessential man of letters. His novel *Le désert de l'amour* (*The Desert of Love,* 1925) was awarded the Grand Prix du Roman by the Académie Française in 1925. In 1933 he became one of "the forty immortals" who comprise the Académie. The previous year he was elected to preside over the prestigious Société des Gens de Lettres.

Throughout his life he was an active critic and journalist. As early as 1912 he founded a literary review called *Les cahiers.* After World War II he exerted a powerful influence over the literary journals *Figaro* and *Figaro littéraire.* In the early 1950's Mauriac served as the head of the editorial board of *La table ronde.* In 1953 he broke with his "bien-pensant" (self-righteous) colleagues and transferred his loyalties to *L'Express.* Nevertheless, the publishers of *La table ronde* continued to importune him for novels.

During the occupation of France, Mauriac was an outspoken critic of the Vichy regime, and he contributed articles to the *Cahier noir,* under the pseudonym of "Forez." This newspaper was an influential organ of the French Resistance, published by the clandestine press Les Editions de Minuit. In 1943 articles written by Mauriac appeared in the Swiss, Portuguese, and Balkan press; one of them was cited by Charles de Gaulle in a radio talk to the French before the liberation. Mauriac spent most of the war in hiding, and he narrowly escaped capture several times. Yet, after the war he refused to take part in the purges directed against the collaborators.

Mauriac's work represents a skillful attempt to fuse the personal and the collective by locating and coordinating the richness of childhood within the parameters of social, political, and religious forces. As he said in his Nobel lecture, "all landscapes of the world are revealed in the horizons we have known as children."

In 1969, some fifteen years after the appearance of his last work of fiction, Mauriac published a short novel entitled *Un adolescent d'autrefois* (An Adolescent from Bygone Days; translated in English as *Maltaverne*). The words *adolescent* and *autrefois* evoke images of a young man's enchanted world in southwestern France at the turn of the century. Mauriac was born in 1885, the year of Victor Hugo's death. Inasmuch as Hugo symbolizes the triumphant voice of epic ideals, in conjunction with the creation of a new Christian spirit, Mauriac represents man after the Fall—sullied and guilt-ridden. Hugo was a visionary; the land he longed for did not exist on any map. For Mauriac, however, the landscape of his youth—the summer and winter kingdoms of paradise and exile—was a place fashioned from his memories and desires, containing all the elements of his sorrow and joy.

One is reminded of Friedrich von Schiller's remark in *Über naive und sentimentalische Dichtung* (*On Naive and Sentimental Poetry*, 1795–1796) that "all nations have . . . an age of innocence. Every man has . . . his golden age, which he remembers with more or less enthusiasm as he is more or less poetical." Mauriac has long been identified as a "poet-novelist." Like many other members of the generation of

1885, he was influenced by the symbolist poets Arthur Rimbaud, Charles Baudelaire, and Stéphane Mallarmé, and by his own personal favorite, Francis Jammes. The influence of the gentle and bucolic strain in the poetry of Jammes, which vividly portrays the Provençal legacy of the Languedoc region, is evident in Mauriac's first volume of verse, *Les mains jointes* (Joined Hands, 1909). However, it is important to note that in his fiction, where sin is constantly struggling with Divine Grace, Mauriac displays his kinship with the distraught and divided personality reflected in Baudelaire's *Les fleurs du mal* (*The Flowers of Evil*, 1857).

In Mauriac's fictional universe the word *autrefois* reconstructs, in the labyrinth of memory, the lives of young people "all disorganized and dislocated," as Alain-Fournier referred to the period of adolescence. Alain-Fournier's novel *Le grand meaulnes* (*The Wanderer*, 1913) was one of many works that contributed to a modern French cult of adolescence. As Mauriac in his old age revived the idealism of his youth, he strove to recapture the plaintive and tremulous passions of a young man.

One of the constant themes in his fiction is that young people possess the haunting conviction that an all-consuming happiness is within reach and that it will fulfill them. Rayner Heppenstall voiced the opinion of many critics when he observed that "Mauriac's vision of the world stopped in 1910 and remained there." Mauriac himself proclaims this view: "At the end of youth, everything that is going to grow to full fruition has already taken root within us. As we prepare to step across the threshold of our adolescence, 'les jeux sont faits, rien ne va plus' [the die is cast, nothing more can happen]."

This is not to say that Mauriac's writing suffers from any kind of atrophy. If anything, this closure makes his novels impervious to outside influence, and hence they seem more self-contained and forbidding. Two atmospheres blanket everything: summer and winter solstices, scorching vineyards and shuttered houses set against the nocturnal accompaniment of murmuring pines.

In a retrospective account of his youth entitled "Bordeaux ou l'adolescence" (Bordeaux or Adolescence, 1926) that was later included in his autobiography, *Commencements d'une vie* (Beginnings, 1932), Mauriac describes in flowing, lyrical prose the lifelong intoxication (some would say obsession) he felt for the region of La Guyenne with its "implacable summers"—a countryside, he writes, from which he had "never emerged." Bordeaux, he explains, represents the entire history of his body and soul. The streets and houses of the city are the events of his life. Although he remained in Paris from the time of his arrival there at the age of twenty to attend the university, he visited his family estate at Malagar every summer and during the Easter season. His affinity for the region is evoked in the following scene:

> When the train slows on the bridge over the Garonne and I see in the twilight the entire length of the city wedded to the bend of the river, I look for the place, marked by some bell tower or church steeple, of a moment of happiness, some suffering, sin, or dream.
>
> (ch. 8)

Mauriac claims that a "Wall of China" separated this region from the rest of the universe. However, inside this wall there exist "numerous different climates," each one having its particular sky, flowers, animal life, and atmosphere. He also laments various aspects of his Catholic upbringing that repressed him and made him a prisoner. He refers to himself as "un fils ingrat" (an ungrateful son), who always fears a confrontation with the past with each return to Bordeaux. Indeed, it would be impossible, he confesses, to live again in that "city of stone" where the streets are obstructed by his childhood sorrows. This internalized and mystical city became for him the "funeral museum of his aborted existence." In contrast to the stark materiality of the town, Mauriac also remembers the sand dunes of the Landes and the verdant arbors and vine-clad hills of the Garonne plain—a land where he never stopped living and from which he was never detached:

> The man that I became still lives as a child sitting at the end of a lane and listening to the wind in the pines—the wind of the autumn equinox that confronts the warm fragrance of the immense forest, revealing itself in swaying treetops, rolling clouds, and the sound of the sea embedded in the sky.
>
> (ch. 9)

Maltaverne contains all the salient features of Mauriac's oeuvre. Similar in theme and content to his major texts, this charming novella conveys the anguish and energy of Mauriac's childhood and his incipient search for a consistent identity as a writer. Some of the remarkable traits of this autobiographical work are the consummate fervor and analytical intensity of the narrative, the economy of phrase, and the correlation of the landscape with the mood of the characters. The creation of atmosphere has often been cited as one of the hallmarks of Mauriac's style.

In many ways this work completes the trajectory initiated by the early novels. Most critics contend that Mauriac's career reached its apex with the publication of *La Pharisienne* (*A Woman of the Pharisees*, 1941) and that his postwar novels are not of the same caliber. Nevertheless, we see in the later novels a revision of his early writing in which the innocence of youth and, consequently, its exposure to contamination are refracted through the prism of experience. This indicates that even after many years of creative silence, Mauriac's interest in what can be regarded as the "hermeneutics of purity" was still keenly alive.

In a work that resembles a religious manifesto entitled *Ce que je crois* (*What I Believe*), written in 1962, Mauriac extols this notion of the purity of youth:

> I really should not address this topic: firstly, because of my old age. When one has weathered the storm and arrived in port, one is in no posi-

FRANÇOIS MAURIAC

tion to lecture those who are still at sea, or those who have not yet been aboard ship. However, I am just as much the Christian now as I have ever been, and the infirmity of my condition should not deprive me of the right to advise young people that it is necessary for them to remain pure.

(ch. 4)

Mauriac states that he was born into a world without Sigmund Freud, a world "at the antipodes" from contemporary views of sexuality. Furthermore, unlike comparatively modern youths who seem rapidly to outgrow childhood, he has always remained "the child that he was." He regards purity as a prerequisite for clarity (*la lumière*), which in its highest form is the greatest of all possessions—"the possession of God."

Through a series of flashbacks *Maltaverne* recounts the coming of age of a narcissistic and somewhat morose young man named Alain Gajac. The younger son of a wealthy landowner, he enters into a secret pact with Simon Duberc, a son of the custodian of the Gajac estate at Maltaverne. Simon, without revealing his intentions to either his mentor (the village priest) or to his parents, has decided to renounce his vows and run away to Paris. Alain disagrees with Simon but commiserates with his feelings of helplessness, and the two young men pledge themselves to an authentic search for the true meaning of Christian revelation.

For Simon the quest quickly degenerates into a decadent, aimless life. Nevertheless, it is only after collaborating with Alain in an unsuccessful plot to challenge Madame Gajac's influence that he rejects the secular world and reforms, with the hope of reentering the seminary. Alain's fortunes take a sudden turn when his older brother dies and he finds himself vying with his domineering mother for hereditary privileges, his father having died some time before. He rejects the marriage of convenience arranged for him and finds himself enthralled by an older woman named Marie who works in a Bordeaux book shop. She admits that she was once involved in a scandalous

affair with an older man. After overcoming his initial shock, Alain decides to draw Marie and Simon into his confidence. He hopes to persuade her to marry him in order to subvert his mother's intentions.

While Madame Gajac is away on business, the three young people spend a night at Maltaverne, Alain and Marie in each other's arms. On this basis the lovers try to assume a permanent and mutual bonding. Nevertheless, Madame Gajac is appalled by their insolence and is resolved to force Alain into the marriage she has planned. In one of the most unusual and macabre series of events in any of Mauriac's novels, Alain admires an attractive girl bathing near Maltaverne. He follows her at a respectful distance, but she hears his footsteps and runs into the woods. Alain later learns that the girl was Jeannette Séris, his prearranged fiancée, who has now grown to an age of comeliness that inspires his love. Unfortunately she is raped and murdered in the forest. The perpetrator is caught, and Alain gives evidence of what he had seen of her last moments alive. He also discovers that his mother's intentions were motivated by sincere affection for Jeannette.

Although Marie is momentarily captivated by the charms of the mysterious countryside, she eventually abandons the group and declares herself unfit for marriage with Alain. Simon withdraws, and the protagonist decides to pursue his studies in Paris. There he becomes completely "indifferent to the suffering of others" as his nihilism deepens: "I was lying to myself when I proclaimed that there is nothing to life; the fact that I do not possess the key to this absurd world is not proof that it doesn't really exist" (ch. 11). At the end of the novel he confirms that he has never been anything more than a provincial bourgeois, clinging to the memory of his much vilified Bordeaux and to the security of his ancestral estate. He calls this the "phenomenon of latent resemblance."

We observe in this work many of the motifs that Mauriac embellished in his major novels: the invisible or ineffectual father; the tyrannical mother (an Agrippine, an Athalie); the bashful or deformed protagonist; the fallen woman; a profound religious crisis; a Pascalian sense of reverence for the kingdom of God within each person; a criticism, but not rejection, of the accoutrements of a well-to-do household; and, last, on a stylistic level, metaphors used to amplify certain inexpressible emotions. We may also note a reliance on verbs beginning with the prefix *dé-* that underscore the psychological density of the essential conflicts (*déraciner, déchiffrer, délivrer, décharger, dérober, dévisager, démasquer,* and *démunir*).

As in many of his novels, there appears to be a rather ambiguous relation between character and plot, as if the plot were merely an extension of the protagonist or an emanation that takes the form of outward circumstances. We witness a suffering Promethean hero chained to his rock of sin (*le péché*) while vultures of guilt peck at his insides.

In the sequel to *Maltaverne,* published posthumously in 1972 from fragmented notes, Mauriac seems to be unable or unwilling to prevent his own voice from conspicuously entering the narrative. The structure of the work, entitled *Maltaverne* (like the English translation of *Un adolescent d'autrefois*), is desultory, and one comes away feeling that the attempt to tie up loose ends is inextricably clumsy and perhaps unwarranted. In the most haunting and compelling part of the work, the narrator looks back over some eighty years of suffering as an alienated person and sees in the destruction of the Landes "a ruin within himself, a desolation." Most of the older properties have been sold to paper manufacturers, and without this backdrop for his ruminations, the narrator becomes a victim of his own self-effacement. It is ironic that Alain conjures up an image of himself as an octogenarian, reflecting on his life in the year 1970—the year of Mauriac's death. In another place Mauriac speaks through the narrator and observes: "The diary of adolescence—what madness to play out one's life holding this one card!"

The year 1952 was something of an annus mirabilis for Mauriac. In May he was received as a member of the Académie des Sciences, Belles Lettres et Arts de Bordeaux. He said on this occasion that Paris had done nothing for him but bring forth the riches accumulated during the years he had lived in Bordeaux. In that same year he was awarded the Nobel Prize in literature. Mauriac greeted the news with some astonishment. He had no false modesty about his work, yet he believed that it belonged to a past that was no longer of topical interest. Furthermore, he politely suggested in an interview that the selection committee had done an injustice to Georges Duhamel, Jules Romains, André Malraux, André Maurois, and Paul Claudel—all literary giants in their day.

Mauriac was credited for "the deep spiritual insight and the artistic intensity with which he has in his novels penetrated the drama of human life." His acceptance speech in Stockholm may be compared to the one delivered by Albert Camus five years later. Beginning modestly with an expression of surprise that the world of his childhood should have interested foreign readers, Mauriac nevertheless admits that the same phenomenon was true for Charles Dickens, George Eliot, and Leo Tolstoy. Then he concedes that many readers have found a bleakness of vision in his novels:

> The works that have remained alive in the memory of men are those that have traced the entire human drama and those that have not tried to evade the irremediable solitude in the midst of which each and every one of us must confront our personal destiny.

However, Mauriac regrets that critics had not observed the important role that children play in his fiction:

> Here you will find the first kisses and the first loneliness—everything I have cherished in the music of Mozart. People see the vipers in my works, but not the doves that nestle there; childhood is a lost paradise because it inevitably leads to the mystery of evil.

Endearing portraits of innocent children are found in *Le sagouin* (*The Little Misery*, 1951), *Le noeud de vipères* (*Vipers' Tangle*, 1932), and *A Woman of the Pharisees*, yet it must be noted that the bulk of Mauriac's fiction concerns the concupiscence of rather appealing young adults. However, one senses throughout his work the impulse to reprimand the cold indifference of many adults toward children.

Mauriac is often associated with a group of writers who were influential in fomenting a Catholic revival in French letters during the first forty years of the twentieth century. In this group we find the paleontologist and religious thinker Pierre Teilhard de Chardin (1881–1955), who is often mentioned in Mauriac's later journals; Étienne Gilson (1884–1978), a philosopher who studied the history of humanism; Gabriel Marcel (1889–1973), a phenomenologist and Christian existentialist; Georges Bernanos (1888–1948), a Catholic polemicist who wrote powerful, melodramatic novels in which grace, corruption, and evil are fused with human psychology; and Jacques Maritain (1882–1973), a convert to the Catholic church who was a Thomist philosopher and an eloquent champion of liberal and socially concerned Catholicism. Mauriac's commitment to the ideals offered by these men varied at different periods of his life. Under the influence of Maurice Barrès, he leaned toward the Catholic Right and its standard bearer, the activist group Action Française. Later in life he was compelled to reexamine the principles of this movement and, indirectly as a result of the rise of fascism in Italy and Spain, which he publicly denounced, developed what is generally considered a progressive spirit in modern Catholic thinking, a form of liberation theology.

Mauriac's literary influences were markedly diverse. As a schoolboy he delighted in the writings of Dickens, and he brooded over Emily Brontë's *Wuthering Heights* (1847)—a novel that "told so little and hinted so much." Honoré de Balzac was an early favorite, and the idea of incorporating characters from a novel into later works and depicting them at different stages of growth or attrition seems to have been inspired by the author of *La comédie humaine* (first series published 1842). Mauriac was impressed by the coherence and unity of Balzac's technique, yet, in an essay entitled *Le roman* (The Novel, 1928), he acknowledged his debt to Dostoevsky:

> In the midst of the nineteenth century a novelist appeared whose prodigious genius was applied against the grain. He did not attempt to unravel this skein that is the human psyche. He was careful not to introduce a preconceived order or logic into the psychology of his characters, nor did he express in advance any judgment about their intellectual and moral value . . . these are not rational beings, so inexplicably mingled in them are the base and the sublime, the lowest impulses and the highest inspirations . . . these creatures are loaded with inherited burdens and stains, subject to malaise, capable of almost anything, and of whom one can expect everything, fear everything, hope everything.
>
> (pp. 49–50)

Mauriac learned from Dostoevsky that ambitious writers could no longer limit themselves to the formula of the French psychological novel, as practiced by the masters Stendhal or Gustave Flaubert or an innovator like Paul Bourget, in whose works the characters are carefully shaped in the rigorous, ornate fashion of the gardens at Versailles. In this context we note the influence of André Gide, who initiated a series of lectures on Feodor Dostoevsky in the 1920's. Mauriac noted in his *Mémoires intérieurs* (1959): "There is nothing random in my readings. All my sources touch one another: Pascal, Racine, Gide" (ch. 12). From a purely literary point of view, Mauriac considered the satanic majesty of Gide's presence as both novelist and critic one of the significant factors in his development as a writer. He cites the feverish anticipation he experienced as a young man when he first read *Les nourritures terrestres* (*Fruits of the Earth*, 1897) *L'Immoraliste* (*The Immoralist*, 1902), and *La porte étroite* (*Strait Is the Gate*, 1909).

Mauriac was also influenced by *le culte de la mémoire* enshrined by Marcel Proust in *À la recherche du temps perdu* (*Remembrance of Things Past*, 1913–1927). The notion of describing an epoch "from the inside" was fortified and legitimized by Proust's legacy. Furthermore, the profound influence of Proust on the generation of writers that succeeded him is marked by Mauriac in the following passage:

> Regarding the knowledge of man—in spite of Maritain's warning against sophism—nothing can deter us from moving forward. We have masters to imitate who have preceded us on this route, and the magic spell that used to forbid the approach of certain subjects has been broken. Those sensuous mysteries from which Maritain warns us to avert our gaze are the means, Proust teaches us, by which we shall reach the whole of man. Beyond the social, family life of man there exists a more secret life, and the key that ultimately delivers man to us is often found beneath the layer of mud which hides him from our eyes.
>
> (*Le roman*, pp. 42–44)

Proust and Mauriac invite comparison for similar reasons—their infallible selective memory and their alchemy with words.

In an essay entitled *Mes grands hommes* (*Men I Hold Great*, 1949), Mauriac reveals his familiarity with the writings of Molière, Voltaire, and Jean-Jacques Rousseau. In a collection of prefaces published in 1966 under the title *D'Autres et moi* (Other Writers and Myself), Mauriac includes an homage to Joris-Karl Huysmans, whose novel *À rebours* (*Against the Grain*, 1884) has become a classic of late-nineteenth-century decadence. Along with Barrès, Huysmans refined the Dostoevskian strain of the narcissistic protagonist, known as the *culte du moi* theme of the modern novel.

The contemporary French Catholic novel was initiated by Léon Bloy, among others. His writing is often regarded as a forerunner of the achievement of Mauriac's early novels, in which narrative and dramatic elements supersede ideological content. Nevertheless, Mauriac's greatest affinity is reserved for Jean Racine and Pascal, the seventeenth-century dramatist and philosopher, respectively, in whose works Jansenist overtones create a twilight mood of somber passion and human solitude. Mauriac's fiction has often been called Racinian. We witness the same intensity as well as a clarity and polish that give his work a classical resonance. Apropos of Racine, Mauriac wrote a perceptive summary of his genius, all the more striking because it applies with almost equal felicity to his own work:

> What belongs to Racine alone is the rigorous continuity of passion and reflection, expressed by a few ordinary words that somehow compose music . . . a music that forbids reverie, bound, as it is, to a ferocious reality. There is no escape, no glance at a star, never the least respite to meditate calmly on the destiny of others. We are enclosed in a cage, confronting naked passions that describe our innermost selves. Our story is told with a lucidity that the fury of these passions neither limits nor alters.
>
> (*Mémoires intérieurs*, pp. 162–163)

Even more preeminent than the influence of Racine, however, is that of Pascal—his spiritual mentor from adolescence to old age. Alain Gajac, in *Maltaverne*, carries with him the Brunschvicg edition of Pascal's works, which he opens on certain evenings as an "effervescent spring to quench the thirst of his soul." There are more references to Pascal than to any other author in Mauriac's writings: a glance at an index reveals over thirty citations in the two volumes of *Mémoires*, and about the same number in the *Bloc-notes* (Notebooks, 1958).

As a French *moraliste*, Pascal is a true descendant of Michel de Montaigne in his delight in the study of human nature:

> Pascal casts a tragic light on the valleys and mountaintops of the same heart and nature that attracted Montaigne's observation. His lightning thoughts clash against a brasslike sky, and resound throughout the human landscape where

the author of the *Essais* walked without fear. What was merely a hollow became an abyss, and what was only a mountain now touches the sky.

(*Oeuvres complètes*, vol. 8)

Mauriac contends that Pascal summarized Proust's complex delineation of love when he wrote: "In the presence of a lover, we merely experience the temporary cessation of dread." Many writers attribute Mauriac's fascination with Pascal to the pervasiveness of the Jansenist milieu among the bourgeoisie of the Gironde region at the turn of the century. They were either anticlerical or pious to the point of absurdity. Frequent confession was not encouraged, and many *dévots* approached a priest only before the Holy Days in order to discharge their endless scruples. Mauriac writes about "the lie wrapped up in the truth" that deforms the conscience of a child in that narrow world of the provinces.

Mauriac's youth, like that of Pascal, had been studious and withdrawn. At about the age of thirty, he yielded to the same seduction of society that tempted Pascal, but neither man was ever really dazzled by success. Like Pascal, Mauriac saw the doctrine of predestination for the monstrous aberration that it was. However, this did not prevent him from recognizing in his family's attachment to property a holy and venerable trait, not at all disagreeable to God. There is an element of paradox in Mauriac's life in that he retained, along with a vigorous and refreshing sensuality, a need for the sensible consolations of a religion that, in G. K. Chesterton's words, was often "found wanting."

Since Mauriac's reputation derives primarily from the popularity of his fictional works, they are generally the focal point of essays devoted to him. They will be examined in light of the following themes, underscored in most critical accounts of his work: (1) tension between worldliness (a pagan love of nature) and religious faith; in *Dieu et Mammon* (*God and Mammon,* 1929) Mauriac refers to this conflict as Cybele versus God; (2) the will to dominate; this will to power is an aspect of the character of the pharisee—a self-righteousness that is intimidating to weaker personalities—and is also bound up with the privileges of inheritance and ownership of land; (3) provincial boredom that touches on a certain loneliness in the cosmos—an obvious debt to Pascal; and (4) bourgeois complacency, social conformity, and avarice contrasted with authentic Christian piety and compassion.

Mauriac's productive imagination enabled him to create characters who embody certain human motives and emotions. It is no coincidence that his major works represent a gallery of portraits drawn in such a convincing manner that they seem to live autonomously outside the texts that enclose them. Mauriac stated his own intentions as a novelist: to reveal the element in human nature that holds out against God—the innermost evils and dissimulations—and to illuminate the hidden source of sanctity in people who, in the eyes of the world, seem to have failed. In twenty novels written during a period of over forty years, Mauriac was able to revise his memory of Bordeaux, that rich storehouse of his youth, to modify and distend it by means of acute introspection, to allow it to permeate his consciousness as a writer, and to immortalize it in his art.

NOSTALGIA FOR NATURE: THE EARLY NOVELS

When World War I broke out in August 1914, Mauriac was still weak from a bout of pleurisy that had afflicted him some years before. Unfit for military service, he enlisted in the Red Cross. He was stationed in France until December 1916, when he was transferred to Salonika, on the eastern front. He remained there for a few months, ill with fever, until he was discharged and returned to France in 1918. He was in Paris by June, physically restored but spiritually sick. His diary for that year is a chronicle of distress—perplexing, it would seem, for someone who had every reason to be satisfied with marriage (he had wed Jeanne Lafont on 3 June 1913), fatherhood (in April 1914 his first son, Claude, was born), and a widely acclaimed book of poetry. This period insinuates the crisis that came to a head some ten years later.

By the end of World War I Mauriac had seen enough of Paris to juxtapose it with the provinces. He summarized his thoughts in an essay entitled *La province* (Province), published in 1926. This cosmopolitan city was a "thickly populated solitude," compared with Bordeaux, where a person could not be alone. Paris was a city of individuals, while in a provincial town, the "family grew where it stood." He notes that "in a large city the world was watching you, but in the country you were only looking at yourself." Even though life in the provinces often disguises some rather bitter feuding, Mauriac could never wholly detach himself from its prosaic good sense, its unchanging rhythm, and the occasional glimpses of sanctity that hypocrisy could not conceal.

No subtleties of psychological analysis are required to direct us to the persistent influence on Mauriac of the people of the Landes, whose roots go deep into the soil; hence the frequent identification of human beings with certain aspects of nature. This phenomenon gives his work a characteristic stamp, and one could easily single out the abundance of metaphors taken from nature that are not superimposed as artificial adornment but always fused in conformity with the actions of his characters. In his introduction to Mauriac's *God and Mammon*, Ramon Fernandez refers to "a very precise memory of landscapes . . . the odor and the contact of beings and dwellings."

Nostalgia became one of Mauriac's predominant emotions, to such an extent that it could be described as his raison d'être. A deep current of regionalism runs through his novels, most of which are set in the Gironde region. Many of the characters in these works savor, with varying degrees of pleasure and disgust, the Paris of La Belle Époque, but they almost always end up kneeling in a Bordeaux confessional. In his autobiography, *Commencements d'une vie*, he reinforces this contrast:

> However much we may play the Parisian . . . when it is necessary to descend into ourselves as writers, to seek landscapes and characters, it is not the Champs Elysées or the Boulevards that we find within us, nor our comrades and friends from La Rive Gauche—but the family estates, the lusterless moors, the most somber suburbs of Bordeaux, seen through the misty windows of a school bus. Our characters are born here . . . resembling our grandparents and cousins—all that provincial fauna I used to spy upon as a frail child.
>
> (ch. 10)

In a passage from *Le mal* (*The Enemy*, 1926), Mauriac describes the Landes (tree-topped dunes along the Atlantic coast) as "arid, featureless, and uniform," but like the human heart, "informed by grace and trained to seek austerity."

It is precisely in this concept of place that we discern the difference in temperament between Mauriac and a nationalist, reactionary writer like Charles Maurras. However, in the works of many other Catholic authors of the period, attachment to family, nation, and religion is often accompanied by attachment to a particular locality. This association was elevated to a patriotic ideal in the writings of Barrès. Early enthusiasts of Barrès accused him of betrayal when his writing became authoritarian. Others maintain that Barrès did not reverse his position so much as develop it. In the trilogy entitled *Les déracinés* (The Uprooted, 1897), the concept of nationalism is soundly debunked. But in his later fiction a defense of community, more nuanced than that of Maurras, was offered as a guide through which the individual could grow spiritually and culturally beyond his own limits. Nevertheless, his detractors saw this as an ideology that opposed individualism. Mauriac's work resembles the second phase of Barrès in that landscape emerges as a civilizing force, teaching the individual to admire tradition and to beware of qualities that have only personal relevance.

On the other hand, Mauriac's concept of geographical locality differs from that of Barrès and other traditionalists in a fundamental way. The keynote of Barrès's Lorraine is its harmony. It projects an image of values greater than the self; in this way potential anarchy is subdued. Mauriac's Bordeaux is a symbol of conflict. Memories of childhood innocence clash with the first encounters of adolescent temptation. The boats anchored in the Garonne port evoke dreams of faraway places. Even in the countryside rival voices call out—that of Pan and that of Christ. One of the reasons why the world of Mauriac's novels is so spatially limited is that Bordeaux had already provided him with an adequate image of dilemma. As a Christian writer Mauriac saw the marks of a dual nature in every human habitation. Due primarily to the influence of Barrès and Maurras, any writer who favored the rights of the individual against those of the community was viewed as blatantly encouraging the decomposition of society. This idea was very much in the air when Mauriac was preparing his first novels, all of which are melancholy studies of young people at various stages of religious difficulty.

L'Enfant chargé de chaînes (*Young Man in Chains*) was written between 1909 and 1912, when it was serialized in the *Mercure de France*. It was published in book form by Grasset in 1913. The chains in question are the temperament, heredity, and milieu of the protagonist, Jean-Paul Johanet. One of Mauriac's most subjective novels, it portrays the initial enthusiasm and eventual disillusionment of the protagonist when he becomes involved in the Catholic social movement and tries to put theory into practice.

The first few pages of the novel serve to introduce the characters who act as guides for Jean-Paul during his formative years. We encounter Marthe Balzon, a distant relation whose love for him is at first unrequited. In Paris Vincent Hiéron introduces Jean-Paul to the Christian democratic group Amour et Foi (Love and Faith). During summer vacation Jean-Paul attends meetings at Bordeaux and then makes a pilgrimage to Lourdes. Later, in an ungainly and self-conscious way, he befriends another group member, named Georges Elie. The experiment fails because, among other reasons, this carpenter's son cannot discuss poetry. Jean-Paul forces himself to ignore the fact that the incompatibility of their characters and backgrounds makes a mockery of the friendship.

Jean-Paul strives to retain some sense of vocation as an apostle, but he cannot stifle his feelings of superiority. Eventually, he adopts the patriarchal tone of the group's leader, Jérôme Servet. Many readers have seen in Jean-Paul a composite of Mauriac's own youth. He goes to Paris to pursue studies in which he is only halfheartedly interested (Mauriac had enrolled at the École des Chartes, a division of the Sorbonne, in order to study paleography). He inclines toward romantic wish fulfillment and hopes to locate an echo of his emotions in literature. His failure to accept the movement's values and ideals leads him to seek gratification in the dissolute atmosphere of Montmartre. The portrait of Jean-Paul is hardly of heroic dimensions, and yet Mauriac may have been unduly harsh when he wrote in the preface to the 1929 edition that the protagonist was "ridiculous."

This novel does not analyze the introverted atmosphere of the family that dominates much of Mauriac's later fiction. Although somewhat conventional in its description of "les vieux dégouts et les écoeurements quotidiens" (the time-worn disgust and pernicious nausea) of Paris, we observe flashes of poetic insight when the author depicts the bracken and marshland of the Landes. More than anything else, Mauriac drew on his brief encounter with Marc Sangnier's Catholic movement, the Sillon, and offers in *Young Man in Chains* a retrospective assessment of this crusade. The inclination of Jean-Paul toward modernism and his refutation of neo-Thomism disposed him to look favorably on the Amour et Foi group. However, one of the principal reasons for his disenchantment is the increasing tendency of the leader to enunciate political, as opposed to religious, objectives. Mauriac has Vincent Hiéron express a longing for the past when the group was free from factionalism. He also regrets the imperious temporal ambitions of Jérôme Servet, who has virtually replaced Christ in the hearts and minds of his followers.

It would be infelicitious, however, to accept this work as an unconditional indicator of Mauriac's opinion of the Sillon. It is not a document but a novel, and an accomplished one at that, in which the Catholic democratic group is satirized by transforming the leader into a caricature. In the same way the main character is exaggerated to the point of censure. Thus the novel explores Jean-Paul's unsuitability for collectivist action. Furthermore, he is incapacitated by his bourgeois refinement. Contact with working-class people gives him the urge to "se désencanailler" (disinfect himself) by wearing exotically tinted pajamas (a reference to Colette, suggesting the hero's attempt to go to the other extreme).

Mauriac seems to imply that Jean-Paul was typical of the majority of Servet's followers. Nevertheless, the faults lay not so much with the party as with the individuals concerned. Mauriac offers no constructive suggestions in order to improve on what the Sillon group stood for. The novel ends in a whimsical fashion with Jean-Paul's redemption through Marthe. This first love affair and the prospects of a happy marriage, however, do not seem to erase the "mornes tristesses" (dismal melancholy) from Jean-Paul's life, and he confirms his restless desire to "probe into the intricacies of human souls." The closing words of the novel are inscribed in a letter written by Jean-Paul:

> At this very hour you, Marthe, are sitting on your bed in a large room in the country. . . . My last letters rest on the mantelpiece, in the light of a lamp. Their passionate words awakened in you a joy that, perhaps, you had no longer anticipated. . . . You are smiling bravely, Marthe, at all my possible deceptions. You absolve them in advance. Your meticulous love foresees, as its future revenge, an increase in tenderness—and the serenity of silent acts of forgiveness.

We are left wondering what Jean-Paul has done to merit such unwavering devotion.

In June 1914 *La robe prétexte* (*The Stuff of Youth*) was published by Grasset. The novel is cast in an autobiographical form and covers Mauriac's adolescence preceding his move to Paris. Whereas *Young Man in Chains* reveals the influence of Barrès in its cynical, detached style, *The Stuff of Youth* is warm, discursive, and filled with gentle humor, and there is an air of intimacy and simplicity about it that is disarming. The opening lines resemble the dreamlike atmosphere of Proust's magic world of reminiscence:

> Grandma kissed the top of my head, as she always did when she came to say good-night, and took away the lamp. The luminous circle that it made upon the ceiling followed her and disappeared. It seemed as though the walls of my room drew apart. . . . My little bed was now adrift upon a sea of shadows.

The boy sleeps with a sense of brooding mystery and awakes on Easter Sunday morning. His cousin Camille rushes into the room, and Jacques responds to her presence with a mixture of embarrassment and pleasure. The children are eleven years old when the story begins, and the plot more or less recounts Jacques's infatuation for Camille as they assume predetermined roles in their respective families (Jacques with some consternation, and Camille dutifully).

An explanation of the title is found in the book itself: "Just as a young Roman, having attained the age of manhood, discards the 'robe prétexte' (*praetexta*), the white purple-edged tunic that was the insignia of adolescence, I said farewell to my sixteenth year" (ch. 31). The setting of the novel is Château-Lange, the matriarchal estate of Jacques's grandmother (the country home of Mauriac's grandmother was Ousillane). The narrator's mother dies from tuberculosis soon after her husband, a painter, leaves the family in order to capture "the unknown blue of Tahitian nights." Before dying in Tahiti he sends his son an apologetic farewell letter. (It is interesting to note that Mauriac perceived his father as a sensitive man who was something of an outcast among the *bordelais* landowners.) Later, while in Paris, Jacques attends an exhibition where he overhears a critic praise his father's achievement as an artist: "He combines Ingres' drawing with Delacroix's use of light, and synthesizes the styles of his age. . . . In him we witness the totality of art, just as the Bible, Aeschylus and Claudel make all other literature superfluous" (ch. 27).

We observe in this passage a glimpse of Mauriac's mastery of overstatement, which he uses for satirical effect. In this work we also encounter certain character types that reappear in later novels: the devout bourgeoise, her nun-companion ("eyelids habitually lowered, like a cautious hen"), the profligate uncle ("drifting in from the casinos of Aix-les-Bains"), the faithful servant and spinster, Octavie, who, ever fearful of masculine advances, keeps a man's stovepipe hat in her vestibule to discourage overzealous gallants (Octavie was the name of the maid of Mauriac's grandmother), the repulsive Alsatian schoolteacher, the scheming interloper, and the diplomatic, tea-drinking abbé (inspired by the abbé Péquignot).

Nonetheless, our main concern in the novel is with the protagonist who is suspended between the security of a Catholic ambiance and his awakening sensuality: "At school I was one of those scrupulous young people for whom the ignorance of evil saved one from evil. I did not think there was a higher ambition than to renounce all kinds of impurity, and to pass over the world like some great archangel" (ch. 27). *The Stuff of Youth* has been compared to Colette's *La maison de Claudine* (1922) because

of its pastel coloring and vivid detail. Jacques emerges into an adult world, but this transition requires pain and sacrifice. José Ximenès, his mystical Spanish classmate (who is recast as Augustin in *Préséances*), tries to preserve the mystery of youth, but the task is beyond his powers, and he becomes disconsolate and dies. Camille evolves into a woman who is "indifférente" and "affairée" (phlegmatic and practical), and Jacques's only consolation derives from his faith.

Taken together, Mauriac's first two novels show many similarities in style and composition: both rely on the causality of external events to shape the narrative, and in both of them the plot is reinforced by the inclusion of impressionistic tableaux and memorable vignettes. These features are also found in Mauriac's next two novels, *La chair et le sang* (*Flesh and Blood*)—begun in 1914 but not published until six years later—and *Préséances* (*Questions of Precedence*), which appeared in 1921.

Flesh and Blood marks a decisive step in Mauriac's development. The narration is clear and concise, and the themes are more diverse: comparison of Catholic and Protestant attitudes, satirical depiction of bourgeois smugness, contrast of the hothouse environment of the Parisian salons with the healthy simplicity of rural life, and the keen perception of class distinction. We note that Mauriac's ability to incorporate theological concerns into imaginative writing is far more effective here than in earlier attempts. We also witness, in Édouard's demise, the first of many deathbed redemptions that occur in Mauriac's novels. Édouard, the morbid son of the landowner, Dupont-Gunther, shoots himself in a hotel room at Châlons-sur-Marne (his suicide was probably inspired by that of Charles Demange, a nephew of Maurice Barrès).

The story traces the movements of a former seminarian, Claude Favereau, as his life intersects with the people who live on the estate where he has assumed his father's occupation as groundskeeper. Claude undergoes a spiritual crisis, brought on, in part, by his ardent, sensual nature. However, he reaches out to Édouard, who is depicted as a would-be aesthete, capricious and bored with existence, and this action satisfies his anguished craving for purity.

Flesh and Blood is basically a collection of subplots, yet its chief attraction is the exquisite representation of nature. The novel was written at Mauriac's country estate of Malagar, and the rustic setting is carefully intertwined with the significant events of the novel that, at times, seem to be induced by subtleties of landscape and climate.

In 1928 Mauriac wrote that his novel *Questions of Precedence* satirized bourgeois society "in an unnecessarily exaggerated fashion." As in the case of Alphonse Daudet's Tartarin novels, this mordant caricature of the wine merchants of Bordeaux is, nevertheless, an admirable critique of vanity. The principal character in the book, Augustin, is an amalgam of Rimbaud and Alain-Fournier's Augustin Meaulnes. Florence, a woman who is fascinated by Augustin but who marries one of the heirs of the commercial aristocracy, is a prototype of Gisèle de Plailly in *Le fleuve de feu* (*The River of Fire,* 1923)—an equally distraught and tarnished heroine.

Augustin, the illegitimate son of an apostate priest who eventually withdraws to a Trappist monastery, despises the *banalité* of social privileges. He disappears to Africa, and even after the disillusioning effect of seeing him at the end of the novel considerably older and less appealing, he retains his aura as a representative of mysticism, idealism, and romantic rebellion, against which social pretensions and superficiality are to be weighed.

The alliance of *sensibilité* and satire in this novel attracted the attention of Proust. He wrote that Mauriac captured the echo of "an interior life that I am not sure I understand, but that I wish, more than anything else, I could come to love."

The River of Fire is written with economy of phrase and detail. Its five chapters are dramatic situations condensed into narrative. It owes something to the influence of Jacques Rivière, a friend of Mauriac's who had been converted to Catholicism by Claudel when they were prisoners of war. Rivière claimed that this work was a religious catharsis of deep and abiding persuasiveness. Mauriac was, at that time, collaborating with Rivière as editor of *La nouvelle revue française,* which published *The River of Fire* in three installments.

The protagonist of the novel is Daniel Trasis, a blasé young businessman who, with his partner, Raymond Courrèges (he appears again in *The Desert of Love*), deals in automobiles, tinned food, and American uniforms. In an obscure hotel in the Pyrenees he admires and pursues Gisèle de Plailly, a character of haunting ambiguity. The night before she intends to leave with her guardian, Lucille de Villeron, Gisèle goes to Daniel's room, and the two young people consummate their passion. The following day they go their separate ways. Information pertaining to Gisèle's past is offered by means of flashback techniques. In the final scene we see Gisèle, who assumes that Daniel has lost interest in her, transfigured into an angel of mercy, caring for children in a half-ruined village church. Daniel sees her kneeling alone, "her mind centered upon some inner truth, imploring with joined hands that darkness in which the faithful can see and hear their Savior." Daniel immediately perceives the futility of his aimless life, blesses himself with holy water, and leaves the church in order to follow his obscure destiny.

This theatrical ending is offset by the character of Madame de Villeron. Here is a woman dedicated to good works, but who is nevertheless responsible for a great deal of harm in doing them; Gisèle, in fact, accuses her of spiritual blackmail. Mauriac refers to Lucille's life as "hidden behind a smiling mask," and he writes that her vocation is to "open a passage through the thickets of the world." In order to do this, she places herself "at the very rim of that river of fire, that fatal gulf . . . of poisoned memory." In this pointedly psychological study

Mauriac articulates the dual nature of the human psyche—the "genius" at variance with "moral instruments." In his major novels he attempts to demonstrate, on a wider canvas, the conditions implicit in this work: that the human heart is a labyrinth of cross purposes and the mind is a network of contradictions; that self-examination and humility will inevitably invoke Grace, through which redemption is attained.

Mauriac's novella *Génitrix* (1923), with its powerful analysis of obsessive maternal love, and *The River of Fire,* with its scenes of passion, provoked inflammatory critical reactions from the Catholic Right. In his memoirs Mauriac cites the remark of General Castelnau to the effect that he would not want to see Mauriac's books in the hands of his children. The abbé Bethléem, in his *Revue des lectures,* warned Catholic readers about this dangerous, if not pornographic, writer. Although *The River of Fire* was a success, Mauriac was troubled by the public's image of himself as a morbid, disconsolate Catholic. From a literary point of view it seems that the novels *Le baiser au lépreux* (*A Kiss for the Leper,* 1922), *The Enemy,* and *The Desert of Love,* represent a shift in emphasis on Mauriac's part, in that he provides an indirect apology for Christianity by objectively revealing the emptiness of life without authentic piety.

A Kiss for the Leper was the first of Mauriac's novels to enjoy wide popularity. The book is somewhat restricted in scope but flawless in execution, and it invites comparison with some of Ivan Turgenev's novellas. The characters are drawn with an unfailing sureness of touch. Charles Du Bos wrote that the book virtually abolished everything Mauriac had written before. It was the first of a series of novels that established his reputation as a critically acclaimed novelist.

The story derives its intensity from the physical setting of the Landes, around which "poplars, planes and oak trees shook their plaintive leaves against the rainy sky," and "the sunsets of years gone by reddened the wild ferns and heather." Jean Péloueyre is the idealistic and sensitive, but physically repulsive, son of a widowed landowner. The reading of Friedrich Nietzsche has persuaded him that if people are divided into masters and slaves, he need only look into the mirror in order to confirm that he belongs to the second category. Jean's father, in order to keep his inheritance from passing to his sister, Félicité de Cazenave, and her bachelor son, Fernand (the principal characters in *Génitrix*), conspires with the village priest to arrange a marriage for his son with an attractive peasant, Noémi, whose parents are dazzled by the prospect of sudden wealth.

Noémi's desperate effort to hide her repulsion for her husband undermines her health and serenity, until Jean goes to Paris for a few months, ostensibly to do research work in La Bibliothèque Nationale. Here he leads a pitifully lonesome existence. When he returns home he observes the healthy bloom that Noémi has acquired during his absence. He resigns himself to self-sacrifice and contracts tuberculosis from a sick friend. Noémi fills his last days with ardent ministration, kissing him from time to time "as saints once bestowed their blessing on lepers." Noémi is condemned to permanent widowhood because of a clause in her marriage contract forbidding her to remarry. She chooses not to violate it, although a young doctor is attracted to her. Nevertheless, this unpolished and unintelligent woman perceives the grandeur of her renunciation, looks after her property with competence, and is charitable to those around her.

Mauriac wrote an epilogue to the novel, which was published separately in his collected works. Noémi describes what it is like to care for Jean's father, Jérôme, who resembles Molière's *malade imaginaire* in his egotism and vanity. *A Kiss for the Leper* was the first of Mauriac's works to be translated into English. The success of the novel derives from his use of understatement and his genius for poetic suggestion, and it is by means of these techniques that so much beauty is distilled from disgust and exasperation. For this reason *A Kiss for the Leper* marks a turning point in Mauriac's career. From this point on, pity, repulsion, and shame are exceeded and transcended, and only the stern joy of abnegation remains.

To these early works we should add *The Enemy*, composed as an autobiographical novel between 1921 and 1923. After it was serialized in the magazine *Demain* (1924), Mauriac was unhappy with the results and refused to allow it to be published in book form until it came out in a limited edition in 1935 (the first part was published as *Fabien* by Les Amis du Sans Pareil in 1926). This novel portrays the childhood and rite of passage into manhood of Fabien Dézaymeries. The title is taken from one of his observations as he returns to Paris after the Easter holidays:

> The old stones of palaces and bridges lay basking in the soft radiance of a misty sun. The city was full of young bodies responsive to the call of spring. . . . It was the time of year when the enemy within finds a ready ally in the outward scene. . . . when parted lips and seeking eyes disregard the dangerous abyss.
>
> (ch. 2)

Both *The Enemy* and *Génitrix* reflect the austere surveillance under which Mauriac passed his early years. These works contain, in embryo, the mastery of craft that Mauriac demonstrates, while adding more intricate patterns, in *The Desert of Love* and in all subsequent works. Furthermore, Mauriac begins to examine human relationships in terms of animal instincts. Such behavior is vigorously explored in *Les anges noirs* (*The Dark Angels*, 1936) and *Thérèse Desqueyroux* (1927), in which particular attention is given to female characters who respond to frustration and claustrophobia. The principal interest in *The Desert of Love*, however, lies in Raymond Courrèges's brief encounter with Maria Cross and in the effect her rejection has on him. At first he is depicted as "a young forest, gray and suffering." When he becomes a furtive and accomplished rake, he is described as a young animal, a wild bird, a young dog, and a goat. In this novel Mauriac achieves, on a larger scale, the synthesis found in *Génitrix*.

In comparison with Mauriac's more substantial novels, we recognize in these apprentice works the development of characters who, as they become less directly autobiographical, become more imposing and memorable. In the novels written at the height of his career, Mauriac constructs the series of prisons that house his characters in unified narratives sustained by implicit metaphors. Awareness of sin has become a liability, and the background of family intrigue, evident in the early works, is given a more sinister effect, resulting in an allegorical representation of human motivation, in which vice and virtue are interlocking parts.

THE TRANSPARENT NIGHT: THE PRINCIPAL ACHIEVEMENTS OF MAURIAC'S CAREER

We would not gain a complete idea of Mauriac as a novelist by limiting our discussion to the half-dozen masterpieces that seem destined to endure as cultural artifacts. For this reason the early novels have been reviewed; they represent the formative stage of his imaginative writings, in which the mystique of the family and religious elements form integral parts of the action and structure.

Just as Stendhal's masterpiece *Le rouge et le noir* (*The Red and the Black*, 1830) had for its inception the account of a murder trial, the origin of *Thérèse Desqueyroux* can be traced to the Canaby trial, which took place at Bordeaux in 1906. In a journal entry Mauriac recalled his vivid impression of a woman accused of attempting to poison her husband. Thérèse Desqueyroux is a creature of excruciating sophistication, and her struggle is in part determined by her own confusion as to why she commited the crime.

The story unfolds retrospectively in Thérèse's mind as she takes the train from Bordeaux to Saint-Clair. She reconstructs the events leading to the trial (the case is dismissed when the La Trave family withholds evidence, in order to preserve her father's political ambitions) and is determined to confess to her husband, Bernard. However, his family conspires against her to the extent that she is confined to her room. When Bernard leaves on a two-month trip, Thérèse refuses exercise or solid food, but she drinks coffee in order to counteract the nausea induced by habitual cigarette smoking. When Bernard returns he agrees to set her free in Paris with a small inheritance. She strives to regain her health and lucidity, but it is clear that liberation from her husband's household has not purged her of unresolved tensions stemming from her own troubled nature.

This novel was scandalous. Some critics labeled it horrifying and immoral. Catholic commentators rejected Mauriac's contention that it was meant to serve as an "indirect apology" for Christianity. On the other hand, many critics saw the work as "Mauriac's *Phèdre*," and it was often compared to Flaubert's *Madame Bovary* (1856). It is generally acknowledged that the work has a poetic quality unsurpassed in Mauriac's fiction. Furthermore, Thérèse personifies Mauriac's own frustrations and spiritual dilemma. This conflict was intensified by the hostility of critics who viewed his work as incompatible with Catholic doctrine. In an interview Mauriac confessed: "*Thérèse Desqueyroux* was indeed a novel of revolt. Thérèse's story was my drama, my cry of protest."

Mauriac's crisis of conscience is related to the view he expressed in an essay entitled *Le jeune homme* (The Ardor of Youth), written in 1926. He criticizes the moral subversion of individuals who deny universal values to which all people can aspire. To marvel at the uniqueness of each person's incoherent network of desires and emotions is to invite human beings to become admiring spectators of their own labyrinth, instead of urging them to cultivate what is ethical and noble in themselves.

In the postwar generation of the 1920's,

Mauriac was aware of the tendency to worship impulse and to indulge in every fancy. The originators of these troubled waters, he writes, are Rimbaud, Dostoevsky, Freud, Gide, and Proust. To the artist in Mauriac, resistance to the imposition of constraints on fictional characters was necessary and constructive; to the moralist in him, the same revolt must have been disconcerting. His essay "*Le roman*" seems designed to discipline the overarching products of the imagination and, in a sense, to announce a restriction on his own inventiveness. Thus, we see that with the writing of *Thérèse Desqueyroux* Mauriac had reached a stage in his development at which the complexity of the individual was so profound that it could not be circumscribed within any a priori morality, including the Catholic moral code. This crisis, which was alleviated by the intervention of Charles Du Bos, who introduced Mauriac to the abbé Jean-Pierre Altermann, turned him into a writer who began to use his critical and journalistic work in order to defend the Christian faith. Nevertheless, his novels continue to reveal a preoccupation with the fatality of evil. Those written after *Thérèse Desqueyroux* belong to what is often called "the literature of sanctity," in that they explore a subject of endless fascination—what happens when the divine intrudes on the mundane.

During this painful transition Mauriac was composing his *Vie de Jean Racine* (The Life of Racine, 1928). Referring to *Phèdre*, he writes that in this play there are two protagonists: a woman in love and God. He points out that Racine's greatest insight was to perceive that "carnal love is not only evil, but fatal to human happiness; yet it is an evil we cannot help committing."

The mercurial Gide was quick to discredit the ambivalence of this position. In a letter to Mauriac, later published in 1928 in *La nouvelle revue française*, Gide seems to enjoy playing the role of devil's advocate:

In this work you show a greater advance in your knowledge of human behavior than in any of your novels. But for all the involutions of your specious thought, Racine's point of view as an aging Catholic and your own differ to such an extent as to be positively opposed. . . . What you seek is the permission to remain a Christian without having to burn your books; and it is this that makes you write them in such a way that you will not have to disown them, even though you claim to be a Christian. . . . Yet, you are not sufficiently Christian to cease being a writer. Your particular artifice is to make accomplices of your readers. . . . If I were more of a Christian I would be less your disciple.

Mauriac defended himself against this half-taunting, half-eulogistic critique by writing *God and Mammon,* a work in which he analyzes his own conscience. He is reluctant to conform to Jacques Maritain's opinion that a novelist must portray characters in an objective manner, without manipulation. Mauriac admits that his own personality was fused into his creations, and he announces his decision to improve the moral effect on his novels by "purifying the source."

In 1931 Mauriac added *Le bonheur du chrétien* (The Joy of the Christian Life) to *Les souffrances du pécheur* (The Anguish of the Sinner, 1928) and published them together under the title *Souffrances et bonheur du chrétien* (*Anguish and Joy of the Christian Life,* 1931). Only in the former did he recognize the man he had become—still a cripple but now walking with crutches. He wrote to Gide that he had been "inoculated" by Christianity; he had not chosen it: "I shake the bars all the more violently because I know they are indestructible."

This new orientation can be noticed in Mauriac's next novel, *Ce qui était perdu* (*That Which Was Lost*), written in 1929 and published the following year. Unlike *Destins* (*Lines of Life,* 1928)—often compared to Colette's 1920 novel *Chéri*—which is unsympathetic toward Bob Lagave, a spoiled, handsome youth, too much loved and too easily debauched, *That Which Was Lost* attempts to vindicate religion by depicting innocent victims unable to counteract the effect of one diabolical character. As in other works, religion is offered as the only solace for ravaged souls. Although the novel explores with great delicacy the almost incestuous bond between Alain Forcas and his sister Tota, Mauriac reserves his unqualified compassion for the saintly Irène de Blénauge, whose death from a drug overdose is described in the following manner:

> Sinking, drowning, she could not regain the surface, nor the air. . . . She was in a frenzy—her nails broken, her elbows torn and bleeding. . . . She must pass through this darkness, into which she had so madly plunged, to the final moment. But as she languished, she sought love, and she cried out the name that is above all other names.
>
> (ch. 15)

In every novel written after the examination of conscience in the late 1920's (except for *Le mystère Frontenac* [*The Frontenac Mystery,* 1933], which is a hymn to family life), suffering is the preeminent motif of Mauriac's fiction. As he writes in the essay *Le romancier et ses personnages* (The Novelist and His Characters, 1933), the task of the "romancier édifiant" (the novelist concerned with moral and spiritual improvement) is to shed light on that aspect of saintliness that endures in the "miserably human." Characters like Elisabeth Gornac in *Lines of Life* and Alain Forcas in *That Which Was Lost* prove themselves worthy of grace. Through a process of metaphysical reduction, we are allowed to penetrate the inscrutable mask of a Brigitte Pian (*A Woman of the Pharisees*) or any of the so-called whited sepulchers of her kind, and we understand that even the most debased and criminal life can be redeemed. Mauriac's principal theme derives from St. Augustine's maxim "Etiam peccata serviunt" (God makes use of our worst inclinations), and his final message seems to be "Thou shalt not judge."

The execution of this belief is evident in *Vipers' Tangle* and *The Dark Angels,* novels that suggest there is indeed a hierarchy of evil.

In these novels Divine Grace does not appear in any supernatural form to regulate events, but it nevertheless shapes the destinies of Louis in *Vipers' Tangle* and Gabriel Gradère in *The Dark Angels*. Grace is not providential, but rather an aspect of profound insight, gained from experience and therefore circumstantial. In this way Mauriac has placed a spiritual matter in what is essentially a secular context. His traditional themes appear even more somber and despairing than before, yet his intentions as a novelist are expressed through variations of attitude and circumstance. It is as though the underlying pattern of these novels becomes a massive symbol that must be interpreted before the essential message of the books can be grasped. This is certainly the case for the three short novels written in the 1950's that reveal the same inner cohesion and direction.

Critics have seen implausible coercions and artificial moral situations in these earlier novels "informed by Grace." For example, *The Dark Angels* resembles a detective story inasmuch as it is a study of a murderer redeemed, but this is not to say that Mauriac has altered his focus or been less incisive in probing the innermost recesses of the human mind. This is what makes *Vipers' Tangle* so engaging. The interior monologue of the protagonist (Louis's family name is not disclosed) is a reflection of the plots and counterplots that have beset him all his life. Yet in the end, his solitude within a family whose members for the most part look eagerly ahead to his death enables him to break the knot and to reveal his true Christian understanding. In a novel written by Roger Martin du Gard, *Jean Barois* (1913), we witness the same dilemma produced in *Vipers' Tangle*: should a vow taken by a freethinker to refuse the ministrations of a priest at the moment of death be obviated when evidence of a genuine conversion occurs? The inclusion of such difficult questions in his novels suggests that Mauriac had no intention of sidestepping sensitive issues, and this can be seen as one aspect of his theological disposition.

Les chemins de la mer (*The Unknown Sea*, 1939) is one of Mauriac's longest and most intricate novels. The story revolves around two families, their respective destinies, and their complex interrelationships. Like other French writings of the period around 1939, it seems to reflect the Stavisky affair, and hence deals with the bankruptcy and decline of a once wealthy family. The title refers to the movement of the heroine, Rose Révolou, toward the obscure presence of God. The significance of the novel's title is suggested by her thoughts as she leaves her ancestral home and settles in Bordeaux as a devout Christian:

> The life of most people is a dead-end street and leads nowhere. Others know, from childhood, that they are headed toward an unknown sea. Already the sharpness of the wind surprises them, and they can taste the salt on their lips. As they cross the last dune the boundless waves buffet them with sand and spray. They have only to immerse themselves in the surrounding waters.
>
> (ch. 20)

We perceive in these various rituals of purification and exaltation a movement toward stasis, or cessation of conflict. We should keep in mind that the tensions of the post-Dreyfus years in France and the failure of the Third Republic in the 1930's helped to create novels that sought to impose one particular view of the world. This genre is often referred to as the *roman à thèse*, or ideological novel.

This is the context in which to examine Jean-Paul Sartre's stringent criticism of *La fin de la nuit* (*The End of the Night*, 1936), in *La nouvelle revue française* of February 1939. Sartre reproached Mauriac for his lack of objectivity, for predetermining his heroine's salvation, and for judging her conduct; in short, for violating the neutrality of the artist's stance. Sartre was not yet the social prophet he was to become, and in a climate of literary opinion exacerbated by the threat of war, he sounded a sharp discord amid the plaudits of the Académie Française. Mauriac viewed this critique as undermining his entire artistic practice. His ultimate response appeared in an essay entitled "Vue sur mes romans":

> The fact that a novelist knows the minds of his characters is a convention no one can escape. I have been reproached for judging my heroes and heroines and for playing God with them. Let me remind you that, on the contrary, they are free at every moment and resist all judgment. In fact, they assume their own identities, and for all eternity they study the outlines of their figures with every gesture that they make.
>
> (*Figaro littéraire,* 15 November 1952)

Perhaps as a result of Sartre's comments, Mauriac composed *A Woman of the Pharisees* with great care and discipline, and the author's presence is excluded by a series of conventional devices. Sartre was perhaps unfair in singling out Mauriac for a problem that accosts every novelist. Furthermore, the strategy that Mauriac evinced throughout his career with respect to the ambiguity of the third-person discourse is far more subtle and effective than other forms of participatory narrative.

The intrusion of gratuitous information in *The End of the Night* is an attempt on Mauriac's part to reaffirm the traditional bond between author and reader that was gradually disappearing from the literature of his time. Like many of his contemporaries Mauriac was a direct descendent of romanticism in that he considered the intensity of an experience to be the measure of its worth. Thus Thérèse, who is jilted by a lover and comforted by Alain Forcas in *That Which Was Lost,* who visits a psychologist in "Thérèse chez le docteur" (Thérèse at the Doctor's, one of the short stories collected in *Plongées* [Studies, 1938]), who writes her confession in "Conscience, instinct divin" (Conscience: Intuition Through God, 1927), and who in *The End of the Night* disrupts her daughter's marriage plans by allowing the fiancé, Georges Filhot, to enter into a compromising relationship with her, is placed outside of any sanctimonious interpretation. By offering ambiguous judgments in *The End of the Night,* Mauriac allows Thérèse to function metaphorically as an erotic, moral, psychological, and aesthetic cipher. As the author he maintains and controls the heroine's anxieties, and in this way our curiosity is continually gratified.

It is paradoxical that *A Woman of the Pharisees,* which is one of Mauriac's most widely recognized artistic achievements, is also his most derivative. The description of the narrator, Louis Pian, with his hermetic smile, his inquisitiveness, and his aloof but gentle disposition, reveals many autobiographical traces. Louis and his sister Michèle display the emotions of children, but they speak the language of adults. Jean de Mirbel, an *enfant terrible* who is placed under the protection of the *curé de Baluzac,* bears a strong resemblance to the hero of Alain-Fournier's *The Wanderer.* The abbé Ernest Calou is modeled after the *curé de campagne* of Georges Bernanos' novel *Journal d'un curé de campagne* (*The Diary of a Country Priest,* 1936). As a young priest he is vigorous and unshakable in his faith, but Madame Pian disparages him, and he is virtually immobilized by his superiors and reduced to abnegation. He says in one of his letters to Louis: "Now I stand before my God, denounced and stripped of merit—more disarmed than anyone in the world. Perhaps this is a state of affairs deserving of men who claim, if I dare say it, to have led a virtuous life" (ch. 14).

The characters of Léonce Puybaraud and his wife, Octavie Tronche, who are dependent on Brigitte Pian's financial support, evoke the piety and humility of Léopold and Clotilde in Léon Bloy's novel *La femme pauvre* (*The Woman Who Was Poor,* 1897). Madame Pian is not unlike many of Bloy's miserly and treacherous literary patrons. In this novel Mauriac reveals inherited features of the practitioners of the saga genre, exemplified in the work of Georges Duhamel, Roger Martin du Gard, and Jules Romain. Their novels depict a vanishing society based on the old bourgeois values.

There is the same valedictory element in *A Woman of the Pharisees,* and it is widely regarded as an eloquent testimony to the fact that the old order was coming to an end.

By the time Sartre had written his essay, Mauriac's first play, *Asmodée (Asmodée, or, The Intruder,* 1938), was being performed, and its success was noteworthy. The play takes its title from the name of the lame devil in Alain René Lesage's novel *Le diable boiteaux (The Devil on Two Sticks,* 1707). Mauriac attempts to depict the domestic turmoil behind the serene facade of provincial mores. The dramatic energy with which the characters probe each other's conscience accounts for the effectiveness of the play. As in his novels, he isolates the protagonists to an unnatural degree. This results in a claustrophobic condition that has the disturbing continuity of a nightmare. Sartre understood that the theater suited Mauriac's manner of thinking as well as the classicism of his method. However, opposition to the artificiality of neoclassical models was in full swing. Mauriac did not sympathize with this reaction, and he defended his aesthetic standards in many critical essays.

Mauriac wrote three other plays. Chief among them is *Les mal aimés* (The Unfortunate Lovers, 1945), which has an affinity with Anton Chekhov's work. At about the age of fifty, perhaps because he was beginning to recapitulate convenient patterns in his novels, he started a second career as a political commentator. For the next three decades he was one of the most widely read and controversial political journalists. A claim can be made for identifying him as an important exponent of French nationalist writing. However, Mauriac's career is one in which literary, moral, and religious issues are constantly interwoven with political ones. When he began to write novels again in the 1950's, he claimed that he was not so much "disgusted with all the politics" but "sick of the exhibitionism" in contemporary literature.

The novels from this period are allegories of Christian life, and it is evident that he never lost his touch for the reproduction of local color. *The Little Misery, Galigaï (The Loved and the Unloved,* 1952), and *L'Agneau (The Lamb,* 1954) are temperaments viewed through fiction, just as Mauriac's political writing represents history viewed through temperament. In this way politics provided him with a counterweight for the religion of memory.

It is interesting to note that Brigitte Pian makes an appearance in *The Loved and the Unloved,* and we observe that the pharisee in her is not entirely dead, as was suggested in *A Woman of the Pharisees.* The marriage of Jean de Mirbel and Michèle Pian is not without its problems, as Brigitte predicted, and she allows arrogance and pride to overshadow the lucidity with which she had previously condemned her Machiavellian tendencies. It is as if Mauriac had resurrected Madame Pian in order to circumvent orthodox interpretations of her character and to enable his readers to accept his fictional world on more complex terms.

Mauriac admired the pragmatism of de Gaulle, and after World War II he regarded France's mission as a moral leader—particularly with respect to the former colonies of Morocco and Algeria—as emblematic of the country's efficiency and stability. Nevertheless, he continued to observe world affairs from a Christian vantage point. The primacy of faith in his life is apparent from the numerous essays, journal entries, and devotional writings that amplify his religious beliefs.

Mauriac's novels have been widely translated, adapted for the stage, serialized for television, and made into films. Many writers, imitative of D. H. Lawrence, have regarded sensuality as an aspect of the spiritual. On the other hand, Mauriac's characters seem the most substantial when their spirituality is portrayed in graphic, sensual terms. Much of his work is the reclamation of a secret place, with its own laws and language. Paris is an alien city, at once attractive and sinister— a vanity fair with the Père-Lachaise cemetery hovering in the background. The "pure" Mauriac cannot be found there; we must journey to the Landes and witness the meridional twilight.

During his long lifetime many honors, unsolicited though not unwelcome, were bestowed on François Mauriac. On 5 September 1970, three days after his death, his body lay in state at the Institut de France. The eulogies were punctuated by the distant rumble of thunder. Throughout the evening thousands of mourners paid their respects to a man who, despite his convictions, had always tried to reconcile his differences with other people without being either didactic or evangelical. One is reminded of Mauriac's description of the pilgrim from Emmaus: "Christ, who now walks beside you, has left the others behind so that you can know him better."

Selected Bibliography

EDITIONS

FICTION

L'Enfant chargé de chaînes. Paris, 1913.
La robe prétexte. Paris, 1914.
La chair et le sang. Paris, 1920.
Préséances. Paris, 1921.
Le baiser au lépreux. Paris, 1922.
Le fleuve de feu. Paris, 1923.
Génitrix. Paris, 1923.
Le désert de l'amour. Paris, 1925.
Coups de couteau. Paris, 1926.
Un homme de lettres. Paris, 1926.
Thérèse Desqueyroux. Paris, 1927.
Le démon de la connaissance. Paris, 1928.
Destins. Paris, 1928.
Ce qui était perdu. Paris, 1930.
Le noeud de vipères. Paris, 1932.
Pèlerins. Paris, 1932.
Le drôle. Paris, 1933.
Le mystère Frontenac. Paris, 1933.
Le mal. Paris, 1935. (First part published as *Fabien.* Paris, 1926.)
Les anges noirs. Paris, 1936.
La fin de la nuit. Paris, 1936.
Plongées. Paris, 1938. Includes: "Thérèse chez le docteur," "Thérèse à l'hôtel," "Le rang," "Conte de Noël," and "Insomnie" (first published as "La nuit du bourreau de soi-même"; Paris, 1929).
Les chemins de la mer. Paris, 1939.
La Pharisienne. Paris, 1941.

Le sagouin. Paris, 1951.
Galigaï. Paris, 1952.
L'Agneau. Paris, 1954.
Un adolescent d'autrefois. Paris, 1969.
Maltaverne. Paris, 1972.

POETRY

Les mains jointes. Paris, 1909.
L'adieu à l'adolescence. Paris, 1911.
Le disparu. Mercure de France. Paris, 1918.
"Huit poèmes." In *Anthologie de la nouvelle poésie française.* Paris, 1924. Pp. 341–346.
Orages. Paris, 1925.
Le sang d'Atys. Paris, 1940.

PLAYS

Asmodée. Paris, 1938.
Les mal aimés. Paris, 1945.
Passage du malin. Paris, 1948.
Le feu sur la terre. Paris, 1951.
Le pain vivant. Screenplay. Paris, 1955.
Le feu sur la terre. Edited by R. J. North. London, 1962.

BIOGRAPHIES

La vie de Jean Racine. Paris, 1928.
Blaise Pascal et sa soeur Jacqueline. Paris, 1931.
La vie de Jésus. Paris, 1936.
Sainte Marguerite de Cortone. Paris, 1945.
Les pages immortelles de Pascal. Paris, 1947.
De Gaulle. Paris, 1964.

ESSAYS

Petits essais de psychologie religieuse. Paris, 1920.
Bordeaux. Paris, 1926.
La province. Paris, 1926.
La recontre avec Pascal and *L'Isolement de Barrès.* Paris, 1926.
Le jeune homme. Paris, 1926.
Le tourment de Jacques Rivière. Paris, 1926.
Divigations sur Saint-Sulpice. Paris, 1928.
Dramaturges. Paris, 1928.
Le roman. Paris, 1928.
Supplément au 'Traité de la concupiscence' de Bossuet. Paris, 1928.
Dieu et Mammon. Paris, 1929.
Mes plus lointains souvenirs. Paris, 1929.
Voltaire contre Pascal. Paris, 1929.
Paroles en Espagne. Paris, 1930.
Trois grand hommes devant Dieu. Paris, 1930.
L'Affair Favre-Bulle. Paris, 1931.
Le Jeudi-Saint. Paris, 1931.
René Bazin. Paris, 1931.

Souffrances et bonheur du chrétien. Paris, 1931.

Commencements d'une vie. Paris, 1932.

Le romancier et ses personnages and *L'Education des filles.* Paris, 1933.

Discours de réception à l'Académie Française. Paris, 1934.

Journal. 5 vols. Paris, 1934–1965.

Les maisons fugitives. Paris, 1939.

Le cahier noir. Paris, 1943.

Ne pas se renier. Paris, 1944.

Le baillon dénoué. Paris, 1945.

Le recontre avec Barrès. Paris, 1945.

Du côté de chez Proust. Paris, 1947.

Journal d'un homme de trente ans. Paris, 1948.

Mes grands hommes. Monaco, 1949.

Terres franciscaines. Paris, 1950.

La pierre d'achoppement. Monaco, 1951.

La mort d'André Gide. Paris, 1952.

Écrits intimes. Geneva and Paris, 1953.

Paroles catholiques. Paris, 1954.

Bloc-notes, 1952–1957. Paris, 1958.

Le fils de l'homme. Paris, 1958.

Mémoires intérieurs. Paris, 1959.

Le nouveau bloc-notes, 1958–1960, 1961–1964, 1965–1967. Paris, 1961–1970.

Ce que je crois. Paris, 1962.

Nouveaux mémoires intérieures. Paris, 1965.

D'Autres et moi. Edited by Keith Goesch. Paris, 1966.

Le dernier bloc-notes, 1968–1970. Paris, 1971.

COLLECTED WORKS

Oeuvres complètes de François Mauriac. 12 vols. Paris, 1950–1956.

The Collected Edition of the Novels of François Mauriac. Translated by Gerard Hopkins. 17 vols. London, 1946–1961.

Oeuvres romanesques. 2 vols. Paris, 1970.

Oeuvres romanesques et théâtrales complètes. Edited by Jacques Petit. 2 vols. Paris, 1979.

SELECTED TEXTS

Mauriac par lui-même. Edited by Pierre-Henri Simon. Paris, 1953.

Pages choisies. Edited by Roger Pons. Paris, 1955.

François Mauriac, une étude et un choix de textes. Edited by Marc Alyn. Poetes d'aujourd'hui, no. 77. Paris, 1960.

Mauriac avec Mauriac. Edited by Jean Touzot. Paris, 1977.

TRANSLATIONS

FICTION

The Dark Angels. Translated by Gerard Hopkins. London, 1951.

The Desert of Love. Translated by Gerard Hopkins. London, 1949. New York, 1951.

The End of the Night. Translated by Gerard Hopkins. London, 1947.

The Enemy. Translated by Gerard Hopkins. London, 1949.

Flesh and Blood. Translated by Gerard Hopkins. London, 1961. New York, 1963.

The Frontenacs. Translated by Gerard Hopkins. New York, 1961.

The Frontenac Mystery. Translated by Gerard Hopkins. London, 1952.

Génitrix. Translated by Gerard Hopkins. London, 1950.

A Kiss for the Leper. Translated by Gerard Hopkins. London, 1950.

The Knot of Vipers. Translated by Gerard Hopkins. London, 1951.

The Lamb. Translated by Gerard Hopkins. London, 1955.

Lines of Life. Translated by Gerard Hopkins. London and New York, 1957.

The Little Misery. Translated by Gerard Hopkins. London, 1952.

The Loved and the Unloved. Translated by Gerard Hopkins. New York, 1952.

Maltaverne. Translated by Jean Stewart. New York, 1970.

The Mask of Innocence. Translated by Gerard Hopkins. New York, 1953.

Questions of Precedence. Translated by Gerard Hopkins. London, 1958. New York, 1959.

The River of Fire. Translated by Gerard Hopkins. London, 1954.

The Stuff of Youth. Translated by Gerard Hopkins. London, 1960.

That Which Was Lost. Translated by J. H. W. McEwen. London, 1951.

Thérèse. Translated by Gerard Hopkins. London and New York, 1947.

The Unknown Sea. Translated by Gerard Hopkins. London and New York, 1948.

Vipers' Tangle. Translated by W. B. Wells. London, 1933.

A Woman of the Pharisees. Translated by Gerard Hopkins. London, 1946.

Young Man in Chains. Translated by Gerard Hopkins. London, 1961. New York, 1963.

PLAYS

Asmodée; or, The Intruder. Translated by Basil Bartlett. London and Toronto, 1939.

BIOGRAPHIES

De Gaulle. Translated by Richard Howard. Garden City, N.Y., 1966.

Life of Jesus. Translated by Julie Kernan. New York, 1951.

Margaret of Cortona. Translated by Barbara Wall. London, 1948.

Saint Margaret of Cortona. Translated by Bernard Frechtman. New York, 1948.

ESSAYS

Anguish and Joy of the Christian Life. Translated by Harold Evans. Wilkes-Barre, Pa., 1964.

The Black Notebook. London, 1944.

The Eucharist, The Mystery of Holy Thursday. Translated by Marie-Louise Dufrenoy. New York, 1961.

God and Mammon. Translated by Bernard and Barbara Wall. London, 1936.

The Inner Presence: Recollections of My Spiritual Life. Translated by Hirma Briffaut. Indianapolis, 1968.

Mémoires Intérieures. Translated by Gerard Hopkins. London, 1960. New York, 1961.

Men I Hold Great. Translated by Elsie Pell. London, 1952.

Proust's Way. Translated by Elsie Pell. New York, 1950.

The Son of Man. Translated by Bernard Murchland. Cleveland, 1960.

What I Believe. Translated by Wallace Fowlie. New York, 1963.

Words of Faith. Translated by Edward H. Flannery. New York, 1955.

CORRESPONDENCE

Correspondence André Gide–François Mauriac. 1912–1950. Paris, 1971.

Correspondence 1916–1942 François Mauriac, Jacques-Émile Blanche. Edited by Georges-Paul Collet. Paris, 1976.

BIOGRAPHICAL AND CRITICAL STUDIES

Alyn, Marc. *François Mauriac.* Paris, 1960.

Begley, Ann M. "The Quest of the Infinite in the Fiction of François Mauriac and Georges Bernanos." Ph.D. diss., Columbia University, 1981.

Bendz, Ernst. *François Mauriac, Ebauche d'une figure.* Paris, 1946.

Boerbach, B.-M. "Introduction à une étude psychologique et philosophique de l'oeuvre de François Mauriac." *Neophilologus.* 1942. Pp. 241–275.

Brée, Germaine, and Margaret Guiton. *The French Novel from Gide to Camus.* New York, 1962.

Cormeau, Nelly. *L'Art de François Mauriac.* Paris, 1951.

Du Bos, Charles. *François Mauriac et le problème du romancier catholique.* Paris, 1933.

Fabrègues, Jean de. *Mauriac.* Paris, 1971.

Flower, John Ernest. *Intention and Achievement: An Essay on the Novels of François Mauriac.* Oxford, 1969.

Garaudy, Roger. *Literature of the Graveyard.* Translated by Joseph M. Bernstein. New York, 1948.

Glénisson, Émile. *L'Amour dans les romans de François Mauriac: Essai de critique psychologique.* Paris, 1970.

Grall, Xavier. *François Mauriac, journaliste.* Paris, 1960.

Heppenstall, Rayner. *The Double Image: Mutations of Christian Mythology in the Work of Four French Catholic Writers of Today and Yesterday.* London, 1947.

Hourdin, Georges. *Mauriac, romancier chrétien.* Paris, 1945.

Jarrett-Kerr, Martin. *François Mauriac.* New Haven, Conn., 1954.

Jenkins, Cecil. *Mauriac.* New York, 1965.

Kushner, Eva. *Mauriac. Les Écrivains devant Dieu Collection.* Paris, 1972.

Landry, Anne Gertrude. *Represented Discourse in the Novels of François Mauriac.* Washington, D.C., 1953.

Laurent, Jacques. *Mauriac sous de Gaulle.* Paris, 1964.

Majault, Joseph. *Mauriac et l'art du roman.* Paris, 1946.

Moloney, Michael. *François Mauriac: A Critical Study.* Denver, 1958.

North, Robert J. *Le catholicisme dans l'oeuvre de François Mauriac.* Paris, 1950.

O'Brien, Conor Cruise (O'Donnell, Donat). *Maria Cross.* London, 1954.

Paine, Ruth Benson. *Thematic Analysis of François Mauriac's "Génitrix," "Le Désert de l'amour," and "Le Noeud de vipères."* University, Miss., 1976.

Palante, Alain. *Mauriac, le roman et la vie.* Paris, 1946.

Peyre, Henri. *French Novelists of Today.* New York, 1967.

Rideau, Émile. *Comment lire François Mauriac.* Paris, 1945.

Robichon, Jacques. *François Mauriac.* Paris, 1953.

Roussel, Bernard. *Mauriac: Le péché et la grâce.* Paris, 1964.

Scott, Malcolm. *Mauriac, the Politics of the Novelist.* Edinburgh, 1980.

Séailles, André. *Mauriac.* Paris, 1972.

Smith, Maxwell A. *François Mauriac.* New York, 1970.

———. "The Theater of François Mauriac." *American Society Legion of Honor Magazine* (Spring 1966).

Sonnenfeld, Albert. "The Catholic Novelist and the Supernatural." *French Studies* (October 1968).

Speaight, Robert. *François Mauriac: A Study of the Writer and the Man.* London, 1976.

Stratford, Philip. *Faith and Fiction: Creative Process in Greene and Mauriac.* South Bend, Ind., 1963.

Turnell, Martin. *The Art of French Fiction.* Norfolk, Conn., 1959.

Vandromme, Pol. *La politique littéraire de François Mauriac.* Paris, 1957.

BIBLIOGRAPHY

Goesch, Keith. *François Mauriac: Essai de bibliographie chronologique, 1908–1960.* Paris, 1965.

ROBERT J. FRAIL

VELIMIR KHLEBNIKOV

(1885–1922)

VIKTOR VLADIMIROVICH KHLEBNIKOV (his literary pseudonym was Velimir, often misspelled Velemir), a leading figure in Russian cubo-futurism, was both lauded and derided during his lifetime, and his heritage has continued to attract divergent critical responses decades after his death. Some, like the great linguist and Slavist Roman Jakobson, proclaimed him an unmatched master of verbal art, while others, such as Joseph Brodsky, the best contemporary Russian poet, have described his work as "a phenomenon of towering incoherence." The response to Khlebnikov has depended in good measure on how critics have viewed several major aspects of his literary career: the publicity with which Khlebnikov and the other cubo-futurists arrived on the literary scene of the 1910's; his life, which has given him an aura of a poetic *iurodivyi* (fool in Christ); the boldness of his verbal experiments, which render many of his texts very difficult; his singleminded intellectual preoccupation with theories of history, which set him apart from most of his contemporaries; and the unpredictability of his literary output, where lines of genius may appear next to near doggerel.

Attitudes toward Khlebnikov have evolved with the course of Soviet history. His works enjoyed a growing reputation in the 1920's and early 1930's (leading to the publication of a five-volume edition in the years 1928–1933), and such major poets and writers as Vladimir Mayakovsky, Nikolay Zabolotsky, Yury Olesha, and Vsevolod Ivanov acknowledged their indebtedness to his oeuvre. However, even though he had "accepted" the October Revolution, Khlebnikov's writings were too iconoclastic for official spokesmen for Soviet culture during the Stalin years. Occasional publications on him and small editions of his works continued to appear, but Khlebnikov increasingly fell into disfavor.

In 1951, at the height of Stalinist obscurantism, the poet Vissarion Saianov could proclaim: "In Soviet poetry, there is no place for Khlebnikov." Since the late 1960's, however, increasing attention has been paid to Khlebnikov's writings and life in both the Soviet Union and the West, with the centenary of his birth in 1985 bringing the publication of several important editions and collections of scholarly studies.

Although Khlebnikov's life was difficult, it was not made tragic by a personal encounter with history, such as has been common for modern Russian authors. Here he differs from such major figures as Nikolay Gumilev, Osip Mandelshtam, Marina Tsvetaeva, Boris Pasternak, and Anna Akhmatova. Ironically, this absence of conflict with the Soviet state deprives Khlebnikov of a crucial element in the eyes of many Russian intellectuals: his life and work appear to lack that depth of commitment, existential choice, and authenticity that is seen by many as central to being a poet in Russia. This view, coupled with Khlebnikov's belonging to a line of linguistic experimentation and cultural revolt, rather than to the acmeist-centered trend of reassertion of cultural traditions and moral values, has limited his significance for some readers.

Khlebnikov is considered a difficult poet—one of the most complex in Russian literature. Those who would study him face many obstacles, inherent in both his biography and oeuvre. Documentation on Khlebnikov's life is sparse, a result not only of the dislocations caused by the revolution and civil war, but also of his many journeys through Russia, which were not conducive to the accumulation of a personal archive. What we presently know of Khlebnikov essentially amounts to an outline of his life, and it is doubtful that scholars will ever have at their disposal material sufficient in quantity and quality to fill out a full-fledged, detailed biography. Much of what we do know comes to us through the medium of memoirs—a suspect genre, perhaps most useful for conveying popular, almost mythological, conceptions of Khlebnikov, but of limited use in revealing the poet's inner self.

That inner self is movingly conveyed by Khlebnikov's texts, but here readers and researchers face problems that go beyond the usual questions about the relationship of art to outside reality. Khlebnikov's death at age thirty-seven left him without an opportunity to establish "definitive" versions of many of his works. As a result, in many cases there is uncertainty that we are dealing with correct texts. Since Khlebnikov's writings are often complex, replete with layered meanings, including autobiographical allusions, these textual problems are an important obstacle to researchers and readers.

Why read or study Khlebnikov? In part, for the sake of the historical record. Khlebnikov stood in the front rank of a broad avant-garde movement in Russian literature and the arts during the 1910's and the 1920's. His heritage continues to attract poets and writers to this day; such contemporary figures as the poet An-drey Voznesensky and the late writer and dissident Andrey Amalrik are indebted to him, and we may expect him to have an impact on Russian literature for a long time to come.

The other reason for examining Khlebnikov is the sheer beauty of so much of his language, the boldness of his imagination, and the sense of wonder that permeates so many of his texts. There is the pleasure of his made-up words (coinages), which challenge the reader's sense of language. There are the meanings layered on meanings, sometimes within an extraordinarily small passage; uncovering these leads the reader to marvel at Khlebnikov's skill as a gnomic poet. There are the utopian ideas, in which science mixes with fairy tale and which anticipate so much in modern science and science fiction. Finally, there is the mythological strain—at times overt, at other times an undercurrent—that gives more than a few of Khlebnikov's works the power to disturb and fascinate. Such writing simply cannot be ignored.

LIFE

The fourth of five children of a minor government official, Khlebnikov was born on 9 November 1885 (28 October, according to the old calendar) in a steppe encampment in the Chernoiarsk district of Astrakhan province (a location now known as the village of Malye Derbety in the Kalmyk Autonomous Republic). On his father's side the family had deep roots in the merchant class in the old trading city of Astrakhan. His mother's family included ancestors among the Cossacks of the Zaporozh'e region of the Ukraine. Both sides of this lineage were a matter of pride for Khlebnikov.

The family moved around during his childhood, in the process giving Khlebnikov exposure to many of the nationalities within the Russian empire. The family's most permanent place of residence was Astrakhan, a city that for centuries had played the role of a crossroads of East and West and that assumed an important role in their son's writings.

VELIMIR KHLEBNIKOV

Khlebnikov's parents shared with their children their varied interests and talents. His father was an ornithologist and forestry specialist, an associate of prominent figures in biology, and himself the author of a number of scientific publications. The father's love for the study of nature was shared by both Khlebnikov and his brother Alexander. Their mother, Ekaterina, a graduate of the exclusive Smolny Institute, had a strong background in history and passed her interest in this subject to her son. The Khlebnikov children showed their aptitude for painting and drawing, which they were taught at home. Khlebnikov's sister Vera became a professional artist, and he himself could draw very well, as shown by a number of surviving sketches.

Khlebnikov was regarded by his teachers as a promising naturalist and mathematician. In line with these interests, in the summer of 1903 he took part in a geological expedition to the Dagestan region. Two years later, he and Alexander went on a student naturalist expedition into the Ural Mountains. One result of his expeditions and other work in ornithology was the publication of a few articles. Another was the infusion into Khlebnikov's art of a whole layer of imagery and language from nature.

Khlebnikov's formal education was somewhat checkered. After secondary school he enrolled in 1903 in Kazan University, which prided itself on its mathematical traditions, and where he briefly studied mathematics and the natural sciences. In the fall of 1908 Khlebnikov transferred to St. Petersburg University, where he initially continued to study the natural sciences. In the fall of 1909 he enrolled in the philological division. Here, he first studied Slavic philology and even had plans to transfer into the division of Oriental languages. But by 1910 Khlebnikov's attendance record had become spotty, and in June 1911 he was dismissed from the university for not paying tuition. By then he had devoted himself fully to literature and had embarked on life within the circles of St. Petersburg bohemia.

The literary milieu of Russia during the first decades of the twentieth century saw a flowering of individual talents combined with increasing fragmentation and struggle among groups. Poetry was the dominant sphere of literature during this time, and preeminent within it were the symbolists, who numbered in their ranks such figures as Dmitry Merezhkovsky, Zinaida Gippius, Valery Bryusov, Fedor Sologub, Andrey Bely, Alexander Blok, Innokenty Annensky, and Vyacheslav Ivanov. The symbolists had come on the scene in the mid 1890's and within a few years had succeeded in moving the center of gravity within literature away from realism, with its focus on the didactic and utilitarian functions of art (particularly prose), and toward a new appreciation of cultural traditions, an exploration of the technical side of poetry, and a renewal of the Romantic emphasis of the poet's individuality. They proclaimed the attractions of the aesthetic, of the darker aspects of the human psyche, and of the mystical realms that they saw underlying the surface of the world. Their achievement is a major component of what has come to be known as the Silver Age of Russian literature.

By the time Khlebnikov arrived in St. Petersburg, the symbolists were in a period of self-questioning. Although at the height of their influence, with their own publishing houses, journals, and an attentive readership, they were on the verge of the internal polemics that by 1910 brought about their dissolution as a movement. A succession of organizations, publications, and changing group loyalties and alliances followed. Khlebnikov, the young man from the provinces, found himself squarely in the midst of this exciting cultural chaos.

Like other aspiring writers of the time, Khlebnikov had felt the influence of symbolism. He read selections of French and Belgian poets (Charles Baudelaire, Paul Verlaine, and others) and acknowledged the impact of major novels by Sologub and Bely. Personal contacts also played a role in his development. Khlebnikov had corresponded with and had met the classicist and poet Vyacheslav Ivanov, whom he greatly admired and to whom in 1909 he dedicated a Whitmanesque poem in prose, "Zverinets" ("The Menagerie"). In turn, Ivanov regarded the young man as a promising talent. Once in the capital, Khlebnikov frequented the famous "Tower" gatherings hosted by the symbolist *maître,* where leading figures from all spheres of culture and education exchanged ideas and read and criticized each other's works. He was befriended by the prose writer Alexey Remizov and the poet Mikhail Kuzmin, and there was talk of publishing one of his works in the newly formed magazine *Apollon* (Apollo). But this came to naught, and by early 1910 Khlebnikov's path in literature had diverged from that of the symbolists and the emerging acmeist movement.

Through the efforts of the minor poet and jack-of-all-trades Vasily Kamensky, who in October 1908 published an experimental work of Khlebnikov's, "Iskushenie greshnika" (A Sinner's Temptation; his first appearance in print), Khlebnikov became associated with a group of impressionist artists and writers that included Dr. Nikolai Kulbin, an eclectic theoretician and successful sponsor of avant-garde causes; the reclusive, talented poet and artist Elena Guro; her husband, the composer and artist Mikhail Matiushin; and the three Burlyuk brothers, particularly David, an artist of some talent and an organizer-entrepreneur par excellence. With them Khlebnikov participated in two important 1910 miscellanies that are regarded as a preface to futurism in Russia: *Studiiya impressionistov* (Impressionists' Studio), organized by Kulbin, and *Sadok sudei* (A Trap for Judges), in which David Burlyuk played a major role. The former featured what is still Khlebnikov's best-known work: the short poem "Zakliatie smekhom" ("Incantation by Laughter," 1910), composed of neologisms derived from the Russian root *smekh-* (laugh). In late 1910 Matiushin, impressed by Khlebnikov, came up with a plan to publish a collection of his works; the idea did not work out, and new initiatives came to the fore.

David Burlyuk, the "father of Russian futurism," had a major impact on Khlebnikov's life. During the summer of 1910 and again during the summer of 1912 Khlebnikov stayed with the Burlyuk family in Chernyanka near Kherson (Crimean Peninsula), where the Burlyuks' father was the manager of a huge estate. The enormous property, filled with archaeological remnants from the time of the Scythians, impressed Khlebnikov, who was going through a period of fascination with the Slavic past. Not surprisingly, Scythian elements make an appearance in his works during this period. Chernyanka was a meeting place for other poets who became allied with the Burlyuks, and its atmosphere helped shape the initial aesthetic platform of the newly formed Hylaea group, with which Khlebnikov became associated.

As related in the memoirs of the poet Benedikt Livshits (*Polutoraglazy strelets* [*The One-and-a-Half-Eyed Archer*, 1933]), Hylaea was formed in late 1911 and early 1912. Its members—Khlebnikov, the Burlyuks, Guro, Livshits, Mayakovsky, and Aleksei Kruchenykh—were influenced by the latest developments in the visual arts (cubism and the primitivism of Mikhail Larionov and Natalia Goncharova), as well as by the archaeological and historical traditions of Scythia. During 1912 some members of this group participated in the lively polemics on modern art taking place in the capitals and published a number of new works. In December, after intense discussions, the Hylaeans came out with their programmatic collection *Poshchechina obshchestvennomu vkusu* (A Slap in the Face of Public Taste), which includes a manifesto by the same name (signed by Khlebnikov, although he did not subscribe to all its points), and samples of works by members of the group. Khlebnikov's writings—including "Bobeobi pelis'guby" ("Bo-be-o-bee sang the mouth," 1908–1909, a short experimental poem in which sounds are correlated with colors—are the centerpiece of the miscellany.

1334

The appearance of the miscellany succeeded in attracting the public's attention to the new movement, though most of the critical comments were unfavorable. The Hylaeans continued their assault on the literary establishment with, among others, the publication in February 1913 of the miscellany *Sadok sudei, II* (*A Trap for Judges, II*); participation in March 1913 in an issue of a magazine put out by the avant-garde art group Soiuz molodezhi (The Union of Youth); and in the same month publication of an excellent collection, *Trebnik troikh* (The Missal of the Three). All of these feature works by Khlebnikov. Numerous other Khlebnikov texts were published in the collection *Troe* (The Three) in September 1913.

Sometime during 1913 the Hylaeans became known as the futurists or cubo-futurists and became reconciled to a name they initially opposed. By the autumn of 1913 they had managed to capture the public's attention, perhaps not so much with their writings as with public actions designed to create a sensation. For example, their major public recital in Moscow in October was preceded by a publicity stunt: for several days, members of the group paraded around the main street of Moscow reciting their poetry aloud, wearing painted faces and costumes that deliberately broke the dress code in polite society. The recital itself, at which members of the group made outrageous statements and insulted the audience, was a "happening." It, and like appearances, generated all the publicity David Burlyuk and his friends could have wished for.

Cubo-futurism flowered during this brief period. An extended tour of provincial cities by several of the poets won them even greater notoriety. The group continued to attract the disdain and opprobrium of most newspapers. However, it also won a kind of semi-acceptance from some major figures in literature. Publications continued apace during 1914, and Khlebnikov's work continued to be featured prominently. He also published three collections of his texts, *Ryav! Perchatki: 1908–1914* (Roar! The Gauntlets: 1908–1914, 1913) *Izbornik stikhov* (Selected Poems, 1914), and *Tvoreniia 1906–1908* (Creations 1906–1908, 1914), although others were responsible for the editing and actual appearance of the volumes. Although he protested against the poor quality of the editing, having his works printed had considerable significance for Khlebnikov.

During the period 1912–1914, Khlebnikov played an active role in the cubo-futurist group. His poetry was pointed to by the Hylaeans as proof of their claims to priority over the Italian futurism of Filippo Marinetti. For Mayakovsky, Kamensky, and others it was a treasure-house of inspiration in both subject matter and technique. Khlebnikov was treated as the group's leader—as someone whose art was the embodiment of futurist aesthetics and poetics. If Burlyuk served as Hylaea's brains and Mayakovsky as its voice, Khlebnikov was its soul.

Participation in cubo-futurism, and the literary notoriety he gained through it, came at the price of family conflicts. Khlebnikov's father, deeply upset over his son's interruption of his studies, opposed his literary activities. Thus, the elder Khlebnikov wrote in mid January 1909 to his daughter Ekaterina: "From Sviatoshino he again sent off something for publication in Petersburg. He would have let me read the manuscript, but I didn't care to discuss these matters." And again, toward the end of January: "He cannot send you his works. He does not have them with him. I read them— three short pieces. One of them is ill with new words, another is pretentious, the third is quite insignificant." The young poet had disappointed family expectations that he would pursue a scientific career. Moreover, he made monetary demands, was unwilling to plan for the future, and seemed incapable of holding a steady job or providing for his own needs. Exasperated, Khlebnikov's father wrote in 1914 to Alexander: "He and I have, at least in word, diametrically opposed conceptions of what life is about and, in general, of anything at all."

1335

For his part Khlebnikov often declared his dissatisfaction with his family. In a letter from mid 1912 the poet ironically assured his father that the family honor would not suffer from his publications. And in the summer of 1914, Khlebnikov described his feelings while in Astrakhan in a letter to Matyushin: "As for me, I am dying spiritually. Some kind of change, disappointment; a loss of faith, dryness, callousness. I know only, that I shall meet my death calmly."

Already during this period Khlebnikov's personality and incidents from his idiosyncratic life-style began to coalesce into a biographical legend. In 1914, Kamensky wrote in a brief essay, "O Khlebnikove: slavozhd'" ("On Khlebnikov: Gloryleader"): "Khlebnikov is a most noteworthy individual, who in his modest, somehow unearthly isolation, approaches legendary sainthood. . . ." Khlebnikov's shyness, absorption in his ideas and visions, and lack of drive to "conquer" made him stand out in the artistic-literary milieu of loudly conflicting groups and individuals and rendered him ill-suited for the role of artistic and intellectual leader of the cubo-futurists.

Engrossed in his writings, disinterested in money or a career, without a steady job or source of income, the poet had no permanent residence and often depended on others for survival. In the spring of 1909 he wrote to his mother: "I am becoming a son of the street," although he added in the same sentence the ambiguous "by the way, don't search for the semblance of truth in what I write." To the credit of his friends, particularly David Burlyuk, it must be said that if they sometimes exploited Khlebnikov and treated his works unceremoniously by publishing them carelessly, they also recognized his distinctiveness and were very supportive of his literary endeavors. Helping Khlebnikov was not easy, especially since he developed a passion for travel and would shuttle between Petersburg, Moscow, and his family's home in Astrakhan. His few possessions, mostly his manuscripts and notebooks, went with him. This nomadic existence was the antithesis of the organized, stable life enjoyed by most other writers of the time, whatever their aesthetic orientation.

Khlebnikov's own diary fragments, as well as memoirs by others, suggest that he was capable of an unusual degree of indifference to the requirements of ordinary social discourse. Not surprisingly, his relationships with women were not very successful. Although he fell in love a number of times, he seems to have usually played the role of the spurned suitor. His most serious involvement was with the artist Nadezhda Nikolaeva, known in artistic-literary circles as the "Chinese Madonna." Her image, as well as the images of some other women Khlebnikov knew (particularly the aristocratic Vera Budberg, whom he met in September 1915), is found in a number of his works.

An important aspect of Khlebnikov's prewar biography is his activities on behalf of Slavic nationalist causes. The young man arrived in St. Petersburg from the provinces, where such strains, often translating into right-wing politics, were quite strong. Khlebnikov felt keenly the humiliation of Russia's defeat in the Russo-Japanese War; his poem "Pamiatnik" (The Monument, 1910?) prophecies revenge in the future. At a time when some of the Slavic peoples—particularly those within the Austro-Hungarian Dual Monarchy—lacked political independence, Khlebnikov eagerly espoused their various causes. In October 1908 following the annexation by Austria of Bosnia and Herzegovina (an act that prompted a wave of protests in Slavic countries), he put up an anti-Austrian and anti-German proclamation at the university. The document, reprinted by a newspaper, appealed for military conflict: "War for the unity of the Slavs, from wherever it should come, from Poznan or from Bosnia, I welcome you!" Although several weeks later Khlebnikov acknowledged that the atmosphere of Petersburg had caused the "freezing" of his "Slavic feelings," this cooling off was apparently temporary, and pan-Slavic ideas continued to preoccupy Khlebnikov, who studied the history and the ethnography of various Slavic peoples and sought to recreate an imaginary Slavic "Golden Age." At the end of 1909 he considered taking a trip to Montenegro. Later, in 1913, he became an occasional contributor to the short-lived newspaper *Slavianin* (The Slav), where he published a short story and some ideological articles—very anti-German—on the situation of the Slavs.

During the same period Khlebnikov apparently had some links with the right-wing Black Hundreds movement. The extent of his sympathies and activities, if any, for this monarchist, anti-Semitic political cause may never be known, but there are curious echoes in some of Khlebnikov's works, and there is the evidence of a quarrel in late November 1913, at the cafe-cabaret The Stray Dog, with Mandelshtam. The cause of the quarrel was the recent verdict by a Kiev jury exonerating Mendel Beylis, a Jew accused of the crime of ritual murder of a Christian boy. Presumably Khlebnikov, like others on the extreme right, disagreed with the outcome of the sensational case, and he was undoubtedly challenged on this score by Mandelshtam, himself a Jew.

Khlebnikov's nationalism expressed itself in the sphere of culture as well as politics. It was a factor in his hostile reaction to the January–February 1914 visit to Russia by Marinetti. Some of the artists and poets close to Khlebnikov, such as Kulbin, received Marinetti with honors. Khlebnikov and Livshits, outraged by what they saw as servility to a foreigner, issued a leaflet protesting this reception, and Khlebnikov angrily declared his separation from Hylaea.

The outbreak of World War I caused a change in the activities of the futurists, as it did for other movements in Russian literature and culture. The country's attention turned toward the front. Group polemics became blurred, permitting, in 1915, a previously unimaginable joint publication by futurists and symbolists, the miscellany *Strelets* (The Archer). The futurists, mostly young men, were subject to the draft, and the group suffered from the call up of many of its members, who found themselves scattered throughout Russia and only to a limited degree able to participate in joint publications.

The war and its aftermath of political upheavals rendered Khlebnikov's existence far more precarious. The network of his supportive friends and family gradually unravelled. A life that had been unsettled by choice increasingly became so by necessity. For a time Khlebnikov continued his peregrinations between Astrakhan and the two capitals. He spent much of the summer of 1915 with David Burlyuk near Moscow. In the autumn he was a visitor at the vacation houses in Kuokkala of Petrograd cultural figures. He also became a friend of the three Siniakov sisters, whom he visited at the estate of Krasnaia Poliana near Kharkov and to whom he devoted several works.

Khlebnikov's life took a dramatic turn on 8 April 1916 when, during a visit to his family in Astrakhan, he was drafted and sent as a private to a reserve regiment. Army life stunned the poet, who was unprepared for its casual brutality, which sometimes led to the death of the draftees. He launched appeals to his family and friends, asking either to be exempted on medical grounds or at least given responsibilities more appropriate to his background. The once militantly anti-German Khlebnikov, who in his 1908 proclamation had called for "sacred war . . . for the rights of the Slavs," now wrote to his friend and quasi-disciple, the poet Grigorii Petnikov: "I am in a very dark mood. Three weeks among the insane, and again a medical review board in my future, and nothing that would indicate that I will be freed. I am in tight hands." And he appealed from a military hospital to his old friend, the highly placed Kulbin (a professor in the Military-Naval Academy):

I can only become a punished soldier whose future lies in a punishment detail. Steps, orders, the killing of my rhythm drive me mad by the end of evening drill, and I can't tell my right leg from the left. . . . What shall I do with the oath of military service, I, who have already sworn an oath to

Poetry? . . . Because of the cursing, monotonous and heavy, the feeling for language is dying within me. . . . I am a dervish, a yogi, a Martian, anything one wishes but a private of a reserve regiment.

(*Sobranie proizvedenii* 5.309–310)

The appeals had only a limited effect. Following tests in a hospital in Astrakhan, Khlebnikov was sent in December 1916 to the 90th infantry regiment near Saratov. The atmosphere was sufficiently oppressive that in Feburary 1917 Khlebnikov requested a transfer to the front lines—a request denied on the grounds of his total lack of military polish.

The poet remained stationed in Saratov until the spring, when he was freed from the army by the February Revolution. In April 1917 he traveled to Kharkov to visit Petnikov, where he suddenly again faced the danger of active duty. He was saved through the help of a friend of Petnikov, who had him sent for psychiatric examination. The fact that he wrote futurist verse helped win him leave for five months.

Throughout the war years Khlebnikov continued to write and to refine his ideas concerning history and language. At the end of 1914 he put together a brochure with some results of his historical theorizing, *Bitvy 1915–1917: Novoe uchenie o voine* (Battles of 1915–1917: A New Teaching about War, 1914). In April 1916 his best prose work, the tale "Ka," appeared in the collection *Moskovskie mastera* (Moscow Masters). His friendship with the Kharkov-based Petnikov, head of a new futurist group, Liren' (Lyroon) (it also included Nikolai Aseev and the three Siniakov sisters), proved particularly beneficial. Liren' arose toward the end of 1914, lasted until 1922, and during its existence published many of Khlebnikov's works. The younger poets regarded Khlebnikov as their leader, and fell in with his various projects. In spite of his army service, Khlebnikov was actively in touch with them, particularly Petnikov, during this entire period.

The realities of wartime not only dispelled Khlebnikov's earlier martial sentiments but led him toward visions of a human brotherhood that transcended borders. He also attempted to bring into being some of these ideas. At the end of December 1915 he was chosen "the king of time" by his friends and took this designation partly seriously. In 1916, assisted by Petnikov, he fulfilled an idea he already mentioned in 1914 by forming the Obshchestvo Predsedatelei Zemnogo Shara (Society of the Presidents of Planet Earth; alternatively known as the Society of the 317). Modeled on the Platonic conception of philosopher-kings, this organization was to include international figures from the sciences and the arts, such as H. G. Wells and Rabindranath Tagore, and was to unite mankind in opposition to existing governments. Khlebnikov was quite serious about the society, which for him represented a new stage in the development of futurism; he issued documents on its behalf until the end of his life.

The nature of Khlebnikov's utopian ideas during this period is well-illustrated by the manifesto *Truba marsian* ("The Trumpet of the Martians"), published in 1916 in Kharkov and signed by members of Liren', but written by Khlebnikov himself. Its title and central metaphor are derived from Wells's *War of the Worlds* (1898). On behalf of his friends, Khlebnikov declares that they are different from "men of the past," who were only able to construct states in space, whereas they, armed with new ideas, will begin the building of a new union along the axis of time.

Another idea of the declaration, reiterated in other works, is that of a split between generations, the older and younger, necessary because the elders have sent the young to their death in the war and because their concerns differ radically from those of youth:

We call into a land where trees speak, where there are scientific unions similar to waves, where there are spring armies of love, where time flowers like the cherry tree and moves like an engine piston, where a trans-man [*zachelovek*] in a carpenter's apron saws times into boards and handles his own future like a lathe operator.

(Tvoreniia, p. 603)

The manifesto lays out another antithesis central to Khlebnikov's thinking of the war period, that of *priobretateli* (the acquirers) versus *izobretateli* (the inventors). After listing the historical "sins" of the former, the document ends with this assertion:

> This is why the inventors, fully conscious of their special nature, of their different customs, and of their special mission, separate themselves from the acquirers into an independent state of time (lacking space) and place between themselves and *the others* bars of iron. The future will decide who shall wind up in a zoo, the inventors or the acquirers, and who will gnaw on an iron poker with his teeth.

(Tvoreniia, p. 603)

A kind of summary of Khlebnikov's ideas is found in the "Vozzvanie predsedatelei zemnogo shara" ("An Appeal by the Presidents of Planet Earth") dated 21 April 1917. He proclaims in verse form the "establishment" of the *Pravitel'stvo Zemnogo Shara* (Government of Planet Earth) and draws visions of what will happen to "states of space"—existing governments—in the future. They have caused the universal slaughter of the world war and, Khlebnikov asserts, are being deprived of the power to do so again. In the future governments will have the status of voluntary associations, like societies of Dante lovers or of rabbit breeders. Toward the end of the poem-manifesto Khlebnikov speaks of the

> Blue banner of anarchy,
> The banner of giddy dawns, of morning suns
> Is raised and is waving above the earth.

(Tvoreniia, p. 613)

The mention of anarchy suggests that the notion of Government of Planet Earth had specific political underpinnings in the anarchist camp.

After his release from the army Khlebnikov initially experienced a need to move about. As he wrote about the summer of 1917 in his memoir "Oktiabr' na Neve" ("October on the Neva"): "I felt a real hunger for space and on trains, bursting with people who had betrayed War and were glorifying Peace, and Spring with its gifts, I travelled twice, there and back, the route Kharkov—Kiev—Petrograd. Why? I myself don't know."

The one-time quasi-monarchist Khlebnikov had welcomed the February Revolution and the downfall of the Romanov dynasty. By then, of course, his own ideas were much bolder than the political promises of the Provisional Government. When the Bolshevik coup d'état took place in October (November, new style) 1917, Khlebnikov was in Petrograd with Petnikov. "October on the Neva," written for the first anniversary of the October Revolution, reveals his disdain toward the Kerensky government. Works by Khlebnikov from the civil war period generally show him siding with the Reds (for example, the image of Lenin in the poem "Noch' v okope" ["A Night in a Trench," 1920]), whom he sees as ushering in a new period of freedom. However, he is very conscious of the suffering caused by both sides in the civil war, and he records the horrors to which he was a witness. His deeply rooted yearning for freedom, transcending all political structures, is shown by a brief ironic poem from early 1922:

> A police station is a great thing!
> It is a place for the meeting
> Between me and the state.
> The state reminds me
> That it still exists!

(Tvoreniia, p. 177)

Nineteenth-century Russia gave birth to the term *khozhdenie v narod* (going to the people), which refers to attempts by members of the gentry and intelligentsia to share the lot of the peasantry. During the civil war Khlebnikov followed this scenario by necessity. With conditions in the country growing increasingly worse, his wanderings became a search for survival. On trains overflowing with soldiers and refugees Khlebnikov traveled from city to city and, where possible, worked at odd jobs. Together with the masses of the people he suffered frequent privation. He saw the events of the civil war through their eyes and heard their assessments of what transpired—all this to an extent matched by few of his contemporaries. Throughout this time he continued to create. The master record of this period is the *Grossbuch,* a ledger book filled with writings, some still unpublished (apparently for political reasons).

A brief period of respite from Khlebnikov's wanderings came from late 1918 through January 1919, when, on returning to Astrakhan, he worked for a Red Army newspaper, *Krasnyi voin* (Red Warrior), to which he contributed a number of pieces. In the spring of 1919 Khlebnikov came back to Moscow to work on a project to publish a major edition of his works. This was a matter of great concern to the poet, who had seen so little of his work in print. The initiative for this endeavor came from Mayakovsky. Khlebnikov was helped in organizing the materials by the young linguist, literary scholar, and futurist poet Jakobson, the author of the first scholarly study of Khlebnikov. Sadly, the publication plans fell through. Later that spring Khlebnikov left for Kharkov, where he spent the next several months, fell seriously ill with typhus, and, in a great burst of creative energy, wrote a number of major poems. Kharkov came under the control of the White forces for half a year, and Khlebnikov once again found himself in danger of being drafted, this time into the Volunteer Army of General Anton Denikin. He saved himself by being admitted into a mental hospital for psychiatric observation. While in the clinic, at the request of psychiatrist Vladimir Anfimov, he wrote several poems on subjects suggested to him by the physician.

A contemporary, the philologist and poet Moisei Al'tman, has left this portrait of Khlebnikov in 1920:

Shaggy-haired, dishevelled, with long uncombed hair, with a tangled beard, he immediately appeared as someone special. There was in him something childlike, something touching; among all those around him who thrust themselves forward Khlebnikov alone was the incarnation of complete oblivion of the self. By comparison with him Tolstoy's Platon Karataev might appear pretentious. . . .

Sometimes Khlebnikov completely forgot his verses; it would happen that a poem would be read in his presence, and he would praise a line and ask, Who wrote this? And then it would turn out that this was Khlebnikov's own poem, and he had completely forgotten about it. I have never since met someone in whom the feeling of property, of any kind of "I-ness," was absent to such a degree.

A. Parnis, publ. " 'Ulozhitsia li v strochku slovo?' " *Literaturnaia gazeta,* 13 November 1985.

In the late fall of 1920 Khlebnikov moved to Baku. Initially, he worked for the local branch of the Russian Telegraphic Agency (ROSTA, an information and propaganda arm of the Soviet government). Later, he obtained a job in the education and propaganda section of the Caspian Fleet, and was housed in a dormitory with sailors.

In April 1921 Khlebnikov realized a long-standing fascination with the Orient by sailing to the town of Enzeli in northern Iran with a small Bolshevik force in support of a local revolutionary movement. The expedition was unsuccessful, but the experience enchanted Khlebnikov and provided him with material for a number of works. His position was that of a lecturer for the troops. Although he did in fact give some talks, he had a good deal of flexibility, and he would wander off on prolonged journeys away from the Russian forces. Remarkably, he emerged unscathed from his journeys: the Persians regarded him as a Russian dervish (*urus-dervish*), listened to him and treated him with kindness. On one of his trips he ended up in the household of an Iranian nobleman in the village of Khalkhal, Zorgam Os-

Sultan, where for a month he served as the tutor of the khan's children. He returned to Russia with the Red Army at the end of July.

Between September and November of 1921 Khlebnikov lived in the mountain resort of Pyatigorsk in the Caucasus, where he was being treated for malnutrition. He supported himself by working as a night watchman in the office of the local ROSTA and continued to write intensively. At the end of the year, Khlebnikov returned to Moscow. He lived there for several months, preoccupied with preparing the publication of a number of his major works. He also performed at two evenings devoted to his art.

The effects of the civil war, particularly the lack of food, were still felt in Moscow—a desperate situation for Khlebnikov, who had repeated bouts with illness. He was helped materially by Mayakovsky and others, but soon became estranged from his old futurist comrades because of a growing, desperate fear that they had appropriated his manuscripts. These suspicions were completely unjustified, but they preyed on Khlebnikov's mind. Embittered, he voiced his paranoia (without naming names) in the finale to his last great work, *Zangezi* (1922).

In mid May 1922, fleeing starvation and very ill, Khlebnikov traveled to the village of Santalovo, near the northern city of Novgorod, in the company of the artist Petr Miturich (a new disciple, and later the husband of Khlebnikov's sister Vera). After attempts to get necessary medical assistance had failed, he died there some weeks later, on 28 June 1922. Khlebnikov was bured in a local cemetery; in 1960 his remains were reburied in Moscow.

A VISION OF HISTORY

Although he was not the only poet of the Silver Age to have a background in the sciences, Khlebnikov was most unusual in what he did with his knowledge of scientific subject matter and method. His broad, if somewhat shallow, knowledge of various fields and his experience with the gathering and analysis of data were fused with a commitment to a utopian vision. Already in 1904, in an untitled essay "Pust' na mogil'noi plite prochtut . . ." ("Let them read on my gravestone . . ."), where he speaks of his imagined future achievements in the third person, Khlebnikov outlines his visions of a "distant future" and claims that his "dreams were inspired." These ideas mixed science with transspecies ethics: "He found the true classification of the sciences, he linked time with space, he created a geometry of numbers"; "He raised high the banner of Galilean love, and the banner's shadow fell on many noble animal species." Throughout his life Khlebnikov pursued some of these early challenges.

Khlebnikov's scientific speculations were an attempt, in Yeats's terms, to regain a "center" that would "hold." This activity was founded on paradox, since the futurist poet sought to apply the product of nineteenth-century civilization, the scientific method, to a problem that originated in that same civilization—the disintegration of a rationalistic world view. In essence, he applied mathematics to the human experience in history: initially to make sense of Russia's fate, and subsequently to offer hope to humanity as a whole. From such strivings he produced a body of speculation and writings on the nature of time.

A fuller understanding of Khlebnikov's theories provides a good foundation for comprehending much of his literary heritage. It also helps to clarify his conception of futurism, which went beyond the assault on contemporary poetic and artistic practice, as launched by the futurists as a group. For Khlebnikov futurism (*budetlianstvo*) was an attempt to transform drastically the human condition, and he saw his investigations and proposals as the tools to create a new, better situation for mankind.

In his late work *Otryvok iz dosok sud'by* (A Fragment from the Boards of Fate, 1922–1923) Khlebnikov explains why he studied the nature of time: "The first decision to search for the laws of time appeared a day after Tsushima, when the news of the Tsushima battle reached the Yaroslav region, where I lived in the village of Burmakino, at Kuznetsov's house. I wanted to discover a justification for the deaths." Thus, a commitment that lasted throughout Khlebnikov's life stemmed from his desire to make sense of the celebrated disaster that befell the Russian fleet at the hands of the Japanese in May 1905. (Actually, it is likely that an earlier naval defeat, rather than Tsushima, prompted Khlebnikov's promise to himself.)

Within a few years the poet's quest for answers led him to develop a general theory of temporal cycles, according to which particular events and figures are repetitions of earlier ones. The first major exposition of this conception came in the philosophical dialogue *Uchitel' i uchenik* (*Teacher and Student,* 1912). All peoples, Khlebnikov notes, experience such events as the creation and downfall of a state, victory and defeat in war, and so on. If a sufficiently large number of such events is surveyed systematically, the data falls into cyclical patterns. The poet suggests that a fixed number of years separates analogous moments in time.

Thus, for example, Khlebnikov finds that a state falls every 1,383 years; every 951 years a military campaign ends in victory for the side that defends itself against the attack; a state is founded every 413 years or a multiple thereof. Khlebnikov further contends that these and similar results reflect a more fundamental periodicity, which may be expressed in terms of an indeterminate equation in 3 variables. The Pupil, Khlebnikov's alter ego in the dialogue, claims to have found that "time z separates like events, where $z = (365 + 48y)x$, and where the values of y may be positive and negative." As is made clear in the other examples in the pamphlet, different solutions may be obtained for z. Three of these—365, 317, and 48—are given particular emphasis by the poet, who builds around them many of his speculations about cycles.

In the essay Khlebnikov reveals a key source of his own thought by linking it to the world view of the Near Eastern city-states. He also draws a parallel between his discovery about the periodicity of time and Prometheus' gift of fire to mankind—thereby simultaneously aggrandizing himself and presenting himself as a potential martyr. This action is characteristic of Khlebnikov's tendency to project himself into cultural heroes and various historical figures.

The war gave Khlebnikov a new stimulus to delve into the patterns of history. *Bitvy 1915–1917: Novoe uchenie o voine,* written in the second half of 1914, extends his theorizing. Here Khlebnikov attempts to predict the occurrence of sea battles in the then-current conflict, based on analogies with battles between Islam and the West during the crusades. In the last section of the booklet Khlebnikov goes on to claim a cyclicity in the births of prominent individuals. He argues that the successive appearance in Russian culture of figures with opposing ideological and cultural orientations revolves around the number 28.

Khlebnikov's letters from this period offer some rare, moving glimpses of his historical work. He collects and analyzes historical data in the manner of an experimental scientist. He makes occasional predictions, sometimes unsuccessfully. Waiting in Astrakhan to verify his claim that a major naval battle will occur at the end of 1914, Khlebnikov declares himself ready to abandon his calculations if he is proved wrong. When the naval engagement fails to materialize, Khlebnikov analyzes his calculations, claims to have found the cause of the error, devotes a separate poem to the mistake, and admits that, "the path chosen by me is erroneous, and I don't advise anyone to follow it."

The war period produced another important pamphlet, *Vremia mera mira* (Time—The Measure of the World, 1916). Here, Khlebnikov continues the basic approach of his earlier writings, although his argument is enriched by analogies with physics. He carries further the twin themes of recurrences in the fates of nations and individuals, claiming that the laws governing these two spheres of cyclicity are the same, the only difference being that the basic unit of measurement for the former is a year, while in the latter case the unit of measure is the day.

Toward the end of his life Khlebnikov reformulated his ideas. On 17 December 1920, while in Baku, he "discovered" the "fundamental law of time"; after a lecture on this subject he wrote to his sister Vera depicting his achievement as a reenactment of the battle of Saint George and the dragon. He presented portions of his theory in several works. The most important is a treatise Khlebnikov worked on in his last two years, portions of which were published as three small pamphlets during 1922–1923. This work bears the overall title *Doski sud'by* (The Boards of Fate). The remaining portions of the larger text, as well as a variety of preparatory materials, have survived, and are kept in the State Archive of Literature and Art in Moscow.

In the new version of Khlebnikov's theory the "movement" of history revolves around the numbers 2 and 3:

> I understood that time is built on the powers of two and three, the smallest even and odd numbers. I understood that the repetitive multiplication by themselves of twos and threes is the true nature of time, and when I recalled the ancient Slavic belief in "even and odd" I decided that wisdom is a tree that grows from a seed. Superstitions in quotes. After discovering the significance of even and odd in time, I had the sensation of having a mousetrap in my hands, and within it ancient fate like a trembling little animal.
>
> (*Sobranie sochinenii* 3.473)

According to the poet, a period of 2^m separates analogous historical events, while 3^n days separate an event from its antithesis or "counterevent." In one of Khlebnikov's many statements of these principles he explains: "Deed and punishment, action and retribution. If in the first point the victim dies, in 3^5 [days] the killer shall die."

In his treatise Khlebnikov ranges over human history, linking pairs of events—from battles in ancient times to developments in the civil war in Russia—through a variety of arithmetical calculations. Stretches of statements such as "The government of Miliukov-Kerensky 10/III 1917 was established 3^5 days before the government of Lenin-Trotsky-10/XI 1917" are supplemented by elaborate tables displaying different types of like and unlike historical parallels. Such factual material is punctuated by Khlebnikov's musings on time, on the significance for mankind of his discovery, and on his own fate. Khlebnikov often constructs elaborate analogies, drawn from nature, from mythology, and other spheres of experience, to characterize the structure of time, and particularly the seesaw-like experience of humanity in history—from high to low, from triumph to disaster. With the experience of World War I and the internal struggle in Russia fresh in his mind Khlebnikov looks to his discovery to help guide mankind, to provide a way of peering into the future and thus "taming fate." He sees in his last, most important theory yet another triumph of the Presidents of Planet Earth, of his fellow futurists. As he states in the poetic preliminary to *Doski sud'by*:

> I shall flood with the strength of my thought
> The buildings of existing governments
> The city of Kitezh will grow magically
> $\cdot$ $\cdot$ $\cdot$ $\cdot$ $\cdot$ $\cdot$
> Oh, watch of mankind, ticking,
> Move the arrow of my thought!

Such passages give Khlebnikov's treatise a certain poignancy and grandeur.

Despite his claims Khlebnikov was filled with doubt that his work would be accepted by war-ravaged humanity and thus relieve its sufferings. With irony he wrote to a friend that "If people do not want to learn my art of foretelling the future. . . . I shall teach it to horses. Perhaps the state of horses will turn out to be a more capable pupil than the state of humans." In *Zangezi* he expresses even sharper doubts about his fate as an unrecognized prophet.

How is one to evaluate this component of Khlebnikov's heritage? The essentially mythological notions of cyclicity, of historical retribution, provide the intellectual foundation for such major works as the poems "Gibel' Atlantidy" (The Fall of Atlantis, 1912) and "Nochnoi obysk" ("The Night Search," 1921). There are also various works, particularly in the later period, where Khlebnikov's calculations are integral to his poetry and prose (*Zangezi* is the best example of this), resulting in an original, often effective fusion of the word and number. Clearly, our picture of both the man and his work would have been very different without his commitment to the realm of time.

KHLEBNIKOV AND FUTURISM

Today it is generally acknowledged that Khlebnikov's poetic theory and practice coincided only partially with the widely publicized tenets of cubo-futurism. At times, he disagreed with points in the group's platform; in fact, his thinking was frequently far bolder than that of his comrades. Still, the ideas put forward by Hylaea as a collective entity were a major factor in how Khlebnikov has been read and viewed. They provide an important perspective on his literary heritage and particularly on his approach to the problem of language.

Hylaea, more broadly cubo-futurism, was created by individuals with different ambitions, varying levels of education and culture, divergent tastes in literature and art, and very different literary gifts. Mostly provincials, outsiders in the salons of Petersburg and Moscow, they were united as much by being against the dominant tendencies in culture as by a coherent program that accurately reflected their own literary practice. In this, they were characteristic of the many avant-garde movements in twentieth-century Europe.

A major factor in the formation of cubo-futurism was its proximity to and participation in the revolution in the visual arts. Members of Hylaea, especially David Burlyuk, played a role in bringing to Russia the new postimpressionist trends in painting that were sweeping through western Europe. At the same time, artists who are now recognized as major twentieth century figures, such as Larionov, Goncharova, Kazimir Malevich, and Vladimir Tatlin, contributed to the futurist endeavor and helped shape the group's thinking on many matters. This interaction between the visual and verbal arts was reflected in the program advanced by the futurists.

"A Slap in the Face of Public Taste," Hylaea's opening salvo in its struggle to gain recognition, proclaims its hostility to the existing order in literature and to both contemporary and nineteenth-century writers: "The past is crowded. The Academy and Pushkin are more incomprehensible than hieroglyphics. Throw Pushkin, Dostoevsky, Tolstoy, etc., etc., overboard from the Ship of Modernity." The group proclaimed its own superiority and relevance: "Only *we are the face of our Time.* The horn of time trumpets through us in the art of the word." Still, though these attacks and self-praise were effective as public relations vehicles, the manifesto was limited on the specifics of Hylaea's poetics: it affirmed a rejection of existing poetic language and called for the expansion of the boundaries of poetic vocabulary through the free creation of new words.

The emphasis on the need for a new lexicon proved lasting and, indeed, was reflected in the writings of most of the Hylaeans. By contrast the rejection of Russia's classics was largely a rhetorical device. Whether through imitation or parody, literary traditions—Russian and foreign—are an important factor in the creations of the futurists and certainly in Khlebnikov's writings.

A major document of Hylaea was the unsigned manifesto in *Sadok sudei, II* (1913). Although rather eclectic, it lists a number of ways in which, it claims, the Hylaeans were transforming poetic language. These include a willingness to disregard the ordinary rules of syntax and morphology, to underscore the graphic and phonic side of words used in poetic works, and to introduce rhythms that violated the usual expectations for Russian verse. The manifesto emphasizes the role of chance in the creative process, particularly in the sphere of orthography. It also stresses the richness of a poet's vocabulary as the justification of his activity.

There is much here that applied to Khlebnikov. His work features frequent *sdvigi* (shifts) in meter. To the dismay of many—and the delight of some—he sometimes uses constructions that are not possible in normative Russian, although they are more frequent in conversational language or in the language of children. Khlebnikov is vitally concerned with sound and with using such devices as homonymy and paronomasia (punning, sound play) to suggest new meanings for words in his works. And throughout, by various means, he is committed to the expansion of his poetic lexicon.

Perhaps the single most important futurist document is the joint Khlebnikov and Kruchenykh pamphlet *Slovo kak takovoe* (The Word as Such, 1913), which includes theoretical formulations and illustrations of their use by the futurists. The influence of cubist aesthetics can be seen in such statements as: "Painters-Futurists like to use parts, cross-sections of bodies, while Futurist-Poets [like to use] cut up words, half-words, and their whimsical, sly combinations (transrational language [*zaumnyi iazyk*]). This produces the greatest degree of expressiveness." The title of the pamphlet is explained in a statement that poets who preceded the futurists were too concerned with the human soul, not realizing that it is an artificial creation. The futurists, the pamphlet asserts, have been more concerned about the word than some bedraggled "psyche," and their disregard has led to "her" death. Should the

new poets create a new one? "No! Better that they live for a while on the word as such *and not on themselves.*" This statement recalls Vladimir Markov's view of the thrust of Hylaea: for its practitioners "the word itself becomes the primary fact and hero of poetry."

For many critics the concepts of "the word as such," and especially of "transrational language," *zaum'*, were synonymous with futurism as a whole. There was a special danger in this identification, because it was often accompanied by reducing *zaum'* to the way it was handled by Kruchenykh, who was extremist, even simplistic, in his approach to the task of verbal creation. Kruchenykh's use of transrational language often involved verbal creations that appear to be pure sound, with a semantic core that is either tenuous or altogether missing. Unfortunately, readers and critics who dismissed such "meaningless" poetry—and this term is questionable even in application to Kruchenykh—extended their indictment of him to the other futurists, including Khlebnikov.

In fact, as both a theoretician—the creator of what the Soviet linguist Viktor Grigor'ev has called an "imaginary philology"—and as a verbal experimentor of genius, Khlebnikov handled these problems rather differently from most of his futurist colleagues. However wide-ranging his ideas, which at one point included consideration of a poetic language of numbers, Khlebnikov's approach had *meaning* at its very core. It is this fundamental basis of Khlebnikov's language theory and poetic practice that really defines his distinctive position, not only within futurism but Russian literature as a whole.

THEORIES OF LANGUAGE AND VERBAL EXPERIMENTS

In the 1919 essay "Svoiasi" ("Self-Statement") intended as an introduction for a planned edition of his works, Khlebnikov casts a retrospective glance at his own linguistic practice. In so doing, he differentiates between two approaches:

> To find, without breaking the circle of roots, the philosopher's stone for transmuting all Slavic words, one into another, to freely melt down Slavic words—that was my first approach to the word. This was the self-sufficient word [*samovitoe slovo*] outside of daily life and utilitarian benefits.
>
> Seeing that roots are merely phantoms, behind which stand the strings of the alphabet, to find the overall unity of the world's languages, built from the units of the alphabet—that was my second approach to the word. The path towards a world transrational language.
>
> (*Tvoreniia,* p. 37)

Behind these passages stands a spectrum of linguistic theory and poetic creation, which began early in Khlebnikov's career. The 1908 essay "Kurgan Sviatogora" (Sviatogor's Mound) contains this important statement:

> And if language, living and existing on the lips of the people, can be likened to Euclid's geometry, then cannot the Russian people allow itself a luxury, inaccessible to other peoples, to create language in the likeness of Lobachevsky's geometry, of that shadow of other worlds? Does not the Russian people have a right to that luxury? Shall the Russian wisdomry [*umnechestvo,* the intellectuals], always thirsting for rights, refuse the one which is handed to it by the very will of the people: the right of verbal creation?
>
> He who knows the Russian village, knows about words formed for a moment, and with the life span of a butterfly.
>
> (*Neizdannye proizvedeniia,* p. 323)

Khlebnikov's comments on noneuclidean geometry and on the short-lived verbal creations of the village offer two models for the formation and use of lexical coinages, which by then were common in his oeuvre. Khlebnikov continued to create a wealth of such forms throughout his life and thus accumulated a special lexicon of unparalleled richness. Many of his coinages are relatively easy to understand; others, as has been shown by Grigor'ev and Ronald Vroon, defy any unambiguous interpretation.

Behind the twin approaches to verbal creation outlined in "Self-Statement" lies a set of ideas about language in general which are at odds with much in linguistic science, but which proved particularly productive for Khlebnikov. Broadly speaking, the poet placed a special value on the past of language, for in it he saw possibilities for the future. Primeval language, he writes in *Teacher and Student,* resonated with higher forces that we no longer comprehend: "Only the growth of science will allow us to discover the entire wisdom of language, which is wise because it itself was a part of nature." Several years later, in the article "Khudozhniki mira!" ("Artists of the World!" 1919), Khlebnikov claims that languages have betrayed their "glorious past," when they served as means of mutual understanding, of overcoming man's condition since Babel, and now are a tool of division and war.

Khlebnikov felt that the poet need not confine himself to using language in its contemporary state but is free to range and bring into his purview elements from earlier stages of the language or elements that are potential but unrealized. One way to do this is by borrowing from other Slavic languages, which may contain forms, lost in Russian, that reflect a prior Slavic linguistic and cultural unity. Another involves the inclusion of forms from regional dialects, particularly attractive for their frequent revelation of nonstandard morphological and grammatical combinations. But the primary method relies on deliberate manipulation by the poet of existing verbal material and on the formation of coinages.

In his articles Khlebnikov outlines different methods of lexical creation. One, which he terms "internal declension of words," led him to postulate an etymological analogue to the case system of Russian (and other inflected languages). Certain words, he says in *Teacher and Student,* are differentiated only by a vowel within their root morpheme, and the relationship between such vowels is similar to that prevailing between case endings of a given word. Thus, the words *bobr* (beaver) and *babr* (Siberian tiger) may be seen as deriving from the "internal declension" of their common stem *bo-*, the former representing the "accusative" and the latter the "genitive" case. The meaning of these "cases" is opposite to what is found in the normal case system, and so a beaver may be hunted, treated by man as prey, while a tiger should be feared, for man himself might be hunted by the beast.

Although this, and similar examples, have no validity in linguistics, they have great potential in poetry. Their use in verse, frequently in the same line or adjacent lines, offers opportunities for the interplay of sound and meaning, since they are sufficiently close in form to create the effect of poetic etymology, of paronomasia.

"Internal declension" is representative of Khlebnikov's use of morphological units (prefixes, suffixes, roots) to form coinages. But early on he also focussed on another approach, which led him in the direction of working with individual sounds (sometimes Khlebnikov uses the term *letters*). In "Razgovor Olega i Kazimira" ("Oleg and Kazimir. A Conversation") he notes the significance of the first sound of a word: "It is important to note, that the fate of sounds over the length of a word is not the same, and the initial sound has a special nature, different from the nature of its companion sounds." The initial sound serves as a kind of skeleton for the word and may contain its meaning—frequently, Khlebnikov asserts, an underlying, rational core that does not change over time. As an illustration, Khlebnikov cites here the fact that in Russian two names for Spain begin with an *I* (*Iberiia, Ispaniia*), and for England with an *A* (*Angliia, Albion*), while the names of many German thinkers start with a *Sh* (Schopenhauer, Schlegel, Schiller) or a *G* (used as the equivalent in Russian of both *G* and *H* in German, hence Goethe, Heine, Hegel, etc.).

This theory too is linguistically incorrect; again, however, it served as the foundation for a wealth of creative explorations and poetic orchestration. It led Khlebnikov to such devices as forming new words by replacing an initial letter. Thus, from *dvorianin* (nobleman, gentleman) comes *tvorianin* (creator), from *lebed'* (swan) comes *nebed'* (sky-bird). Such coinages are used with great effect by the poet.

A focus on the potential of individual sounds, particularly consonants, led Khlebnikov fairly early on into a more ambitious project: the development of an *azbuka uma* (alphabet of the intellect), a *zvezdnyi iazyk* (language of the stars). Analysis of collections of words beginning with the same letter allowed him to isolate what he regarded as its fundamental, invariant meaning. To take one example: "*Ch* means a shell. A surface, internally empty, filled or embracing another volume. Skull (*cherep*), cup (*chasha*), goblet (*chara*), stocking (*chulok*), . . ." At their core the meanings of the consonants are spatial and transcend the differences of individual languages. As Khlebnikov notes in "Khudozhniki mira!": "The alphabet, common to many peoples, is a short lexicon of the spatial world, so close to your art, oh painters, and to your paintbrush."

The creation of the "language of the stars" was a major element of what Khlebnikov saw as his "second approach to the word"—the development of a universal transrational language (there were other varieties of Khlebnikov's *zaum'*, including, for example, the languages of birds and gods). It had both a poetic and a utopian component. Some of Khlebnikov's poems, such as "Slovo o El' " (The Song of L), are poetic proofs of the validity of his etymologies; this is increasingly frequent in works from the final period. At the same time the promise of a "language of the stars" lay in its being able to re-create the original unity of mankind: it could serve as another tool in the hand of the futurist, on par with his discoveries in the realm of time. As Khlebnikov wrote about transrational language in the article "Nasha osnova" ("Our Fundamentals," 1919):

"Only it can unite people. Rational languages already divide them."

WORKS

The corpus of Khlebnikov's artistic works is usually divided by editors and critics into several broad categories: short poems (*stikhotvoreniia*), long poems (*poemy*), prose tales, plays, and the so-called "supertales" (*sverkhpovesti*).

At its core, Khlebnikov's work deals with his major concerns, history and language, but he presents these matters through an extraordinarily diverse array of settings, characters, and situations. This thematic heterogeneity is part of a deliberate program. His patriotism and his concern for Russian culture led him to explore its past and to try to use the cultural heritage of other peoples within the Russian empire and on the Eurasian continent as a whole. As he writes in the programmatic essay "O rasshirenii predelov russkoi slovesnosti" ("Expanding the Boundaries of Russian Literature," 1913): "The brain of the earth cannot only be Great Russian. Better, if it were continental."

A letter to Kruchenykh from early 1913 includes a catalog of challenges for the futurists:

> 1) To compile a book of ballads (participants—many or one). What?—Russia in the past, the Sulims, Ermaks, Sviatoslavs, Minins etc. . . . Vishnevetskii. 2) To sing of Russia beyond the Danube. The Balkans. 3) To take a trip to India, where men and gods are together. 4) To look into the Mongol world. 5) Into Poland. 6) To sing of plants. These are all steps forward. 7) Japanese versification . . . 8) To look into the dictionaries of the Slavs, Montenegrins, and others—the gathering of the Russian language is still not completed—and to select many beautiful words, precisely those that are beautiful.
>
> (*Sobranie proizvedenii* 5.298)

Khlebnikov's oeuvre contains many examples of how he himself carried out these tasks, most of which are linked to the past rather than the future. Yet his wide-ranging cultural interests went beyond this list and the lengthier one found in "O rasshirenii predelov." Thus, Khlebnikov also sought to assimilate into Russian literature material from such diverse areas as Egyptian history and religion, Greek and Roman literature, and the prose of Giacomo Leopardi, to name but a few.

This spectrum of goals and themes is one of the reasons why Khlebnikov is considered a difficult poet. Many of the personal names and historical, cultural, and literary motifs that crowd his writings are outside the purview of even a well-educated reader. They require delving into dictionaries and encyclopedias in a search for answers. Since Khlebnikov frequently takes liberties with his material, including the transcription of names, such pursuits are sometimes unsuccessful; in fact, a number of key allusions in Khlebnikov's works remain a puzzle to scholars.

Although Khlebnikov's works show some influence of the nineteenth-century heritage, particularly in poetry (Alexander Pushkin, Feodor Tyutchev, Mikhail Lermontov), he is closer to the genre categories and stylistic practices of eighteenth-century Russian classicism. At times Khlebnikov reaches much further into the past, as he resuscitates genres largely absent in contemporary literature (for example, his use of the Platonic dialogue and of the genre of "dialogues of the dead"). But he also sometimes draws on the achievements of symbolist drama (Maurice Maeterlinck, Feodor Sologub).

A notable feature of Khlebnikov's art is his experimentation with various aspects of the literary work. As discussed earlier, language is a major aspect of this endeavor. Khlebnikov also plays with other elements of a text, including plot organization and the dramatis personae. Such explorations led Jakobson to emphasize Khlebnikov's *obnazhenie priema* (baring of the device). However, it must be emphasized that Khlebnikov's undermining of literary conventions is almost always motivated: its roots lie in the meaning he seeks to communicate.

VELIMIR KHLEBNIKOV

In studying Khlebnikov questions of how he wrote and handled his manuscripts are particularly important. Burlyuk and others who published him have recorded Khlebnikov's difficulties with finalizing a work. He had a marvelous gift for poetic creation, which functioned as a kind of imaginative engine. In the words of Mayakovsky, Khlebnikov could "not only on request immediately write a poem (his mind worked round the clock only on poetry), but could give this work the most unusual form." This verbal facility made it dangerous, according to some memoirs, to have Khlebnikov proofread his own work, because he might either rework a text or use it to write something entirely new. It has also led to questions about his intention in a number of texts, where there may not be a fair copy and where there are several different drafts. Some have even questioned whether the notion of a definitive text is applicable to Khlebnikov's poetics.

Khlebnikov often did not have control over his texts. Since a number of his autographs have been lost, particularly those from before the war, this situation is a serious one for researchers. In the past, typographical errors have been treated as Khlebnikov's own neologisms, in the process distorting his meaning. More recently, an unresolved controversy about the arrangement of major sections in a long poem, "Noch v okope" (A Night in a Trench, 1921), suggests the potential dimensions of the textual problems—and hence about the degree of experimentation with narrative flow.

SHORT POEMS

This category is very diverse: it includes experimental verse fragments, lyrics, and texts in which lyric, epic, and dramatic elements are mixed together. Basically, we group here anything that does not clearly fit into the category of longer poem.

Khlebnikov's earliest known work, the poem "Ptichka v kletke" (Little Bird in a Cage) dates back to April 1897, when he was eleven years old. This text anticipates his mature writings in its focus on a topic drawn from nature and in the precision of its attempt to penetrate into the world of the bird. The directness of diction and detailed re-creation of the bird's current and past existence foreshadow the startling departures from the conventions of literary representation that are so characteristic of Khlebnikov's poetics and that Yury Tynyanov, in his introduction to *Sobranie proizvedenii,* called "new eyesight."

Approximately a decade separates this poem from a group of fairly short texts in which Khlebnikov's linguistic experiments are in full swing and the power of the "self-sufficient word" is demonstrated. The dating of some of these is tentative, but they are generally considered to have been written between 1908 and 1911, and so belong to Khlebnikov's "Pan-Slavic" phase.

Many of the short poems, particularly the earlier ones, are miniature nature scenes. The lyric "I" is often presented as a witnessing to something in the world around him. Khlebnikov's use of neologisms makes these scenes particularly striking (although very difficult to translate). Typically, the neologisms make up only a small fraction of the vocabulary in one of these works, but their presence creates an aesthetic challenge. The reader is forced to try to approximate the meaning of the coinages from their constituent parts, from analogues in existing language, and from the poem as a whole.

The following quatrain is a characteristic example of how this works. It is first given in transliteration (to convey some degree of its linguistic virtuosity) and then in translation:

Negol' sladko nezhnoi skazki,
Mlennik divnykh dev'ikh nog,
Ia v setiakh zlatoi poviazki,
Ia umru v tvoikh rukakh.

Langour-bird of a sweetly tender fairy tale,
From joy swooning captive of wondrous maiden's
 limbs,

I am in the nets of a golden headdress
I shall die in your hands.
(*Neizdannye proizvedeniia*, p. 103)

The challenge of these four lines is to assimilate the coinages at the start of the first two lines. *Negol'* has been shown by Vroon and Grigor'ev to be modeled on the Russian word *shchegol'* (sandpiper)—which is not immediately obvious even to a native reader. The word *mlennik* is simpler: it results from the substitution of the initial consonant in the word *plennik* (captive). In both cases, real root and suffix morphemes of Russian are used to create combinations not normally present but still possible in the language and understandable to a greater or lesser degree.

Another short poem from this period goes as follows:

Zhilets-byvun ne v etom mire,
Ia blizko vechnost' mog uznat'.
Ona zhivet s druz'iami v mire,
Ona slyvet bezdum'ia mat'.

Lodger-inhabitant not in this world,
I was able to know eternity up close.
She lives with her friends in peace,
She is known as the mother of mindlessness.
(*Neizdannye proizvedeniia*, p. 97)

Besides the coinages (*byvun, bezdum'ia* [genitive sing.]), easily comprehended and embedded within a framework of two grammatically correct sentences, this quatrain illustrates another aspect of Khlebnikov's art: its connection to myth. The imagery of eternity, startling in its immediacy and unconventionality, hints at the cosmic, at reality outside our three-dimensional universe. The poem is devoid of allusions to specific myths, but through a kind of spontaneous mythologization the imagery generated gives the reader a feeling that the quatrain offers a glimpse into a realm of the sacred.

Following his "Pan-Slavic" period, Khlebnikov's short poems become much more varied in both method and subject matter. Of course,

there are cases where verbal coinages, of whatever variety, are the dominant device in the text. The famous "Incantation by Laughter" falls into this category, as does "Bo-be-o-bee sang the mouth," in which different parts of a face in a portrait are correlated with what Khlebnikov termed "sound painting"—the use of pure sound to convey colors. Most of the time, however, Khlebnikov uses coinages and other types of neologisms to enrich his lexical options in a given work, without necessarily thrusting them into the foreground.

In general, Khlebnikov's later works, particularly those from the civil war period, are written in a simpler language than is the case with his prewar poems. This is related to Khlebnikov's reaction to the tragedies of war and civil conflict, his increasing preoccupation with his theories of history, and his hopes and doubts about his own role in transforming society.

A superb example of such a work, and Khlebnikov's ability to be crystal clear in both his language and his message is the poem "Otkaz" ("Refusal") from the civil war period. The English version is by Paul Schmidt:

I would rather
Watch stars
Than sign a death warrant.
I would rather
Hear flowers murmur
("It's him")
When I'm out in the garden
Than see a gun
Shoot down a man
Who wants to shoot me down.
Which is why I would never
Be a governor.
Ever.
(*The King of Time: Selected Writings of the Russian Futurian*, p. 34)

Like any lyric poet, Khlebnikov frequently writes of nature. He often assumes the role of a witness to what is found in the world around him, and the poem becomes a terse record of the observations and responses of the poetic "I." This situational framework results in many striking pieces, due largely to Khlebnikov's profound knowledge of the plant and animal kingdoms. He is always specific: the lyric "I" never speaks of a "flower," "bird," or "animal," but uses the name, sometimes drawn from folk nomenclature, of the particular type of flower, bird, or animal. He provides details about the natural world that an unprepared reader may regard as a flight of pure fancy, as an exercise in figurative language, as evidence of "transrational contents." When examined more closely, such details almost invariably turn out to be extraordinarily accurate.

This is not to suggest that Khlebnikov's short poems are merely an assembly of verbal photographs. On the contrary, he is extremely bold in his use of simile and metaphor, often creating problems for the unprepared reader when he ranges far from the immediate scene. The freedom with which he draws on the resources of culture and nature to convey his meaning are often reminiscent of the English metaphysical poets, while his extended tropes, often piled on each other, recall the poetics of the baroque.

Both the precision and the freedom of Khlebnikov as lyric poet are well represented in two relatively late, charming works, connected through some of their imagery:

> The sayings and sallies of spring
> Poke through the pages of winter's volumes,
> And somebody blue-eyed reads
> The scribblings of frost-frazzled nature.

> A little gold ball flies through the net
> Of a budding poplar's branches.
> These days the golden coltsfoot moves
> Like a huddle of golden turtles.

> Alive with glad tidings,
> A spring-green Koran,
> My poplar up early expects
> Emissaries of dawn.
> Out to snare the sun-fish
> In the blue pond overhead,

> It tosses its meshes
> And neatly nets the bellow of bulls,
> A lazy-pacing thunderhead
> And the bright fragrance of a summer storm.
> My poplar-angler,
> Natural tower,
> You cast your green meshes
> High and wide from your trunk
> And there! the god of springtime
> Gapes, a sun-fish astonished
> In the boat-bottom
> Of every glittering leaf.
> Green mouth greets high heaven,
> Eats it up! Snare for sun-gods,
> My high-flying Poplar
> With horn-roar and wind-bellow
> Unleashes a wallop
> That washes the meadow
> In a wave of blue vodka.

> (*The King of Time: selected Writings of the Russian Futurian*, pp. 25–26)

Some of Khlebnikov's short poems demonstrate an aspect of his creative method that has been explored fruitfully by scholars in recent years: his tendency to create hidden meanings, resulting in dense, semantically complex works. The poet's linguistic virtuosity led him to place special value on *dvuumnaia rech'* (doubly rational discourse, one with built-in multiple meanings) and he utilizes a variety of devices to bring this type of discourse into being (homonyms, palindromes, anagrams). To achieve this purpose, he also introduces verbal material from folk proverbs and sayings, charms, and omens. With their meanings within meanings, certain of Khlebnikov's texts come to resemble a rebus, or a Russian *matreshka* doll. Although such constructions occur in various genres, they are particularly striking when found within the bounds of a short, highly condensed work.

Finally, it is important to note that many of Khlebnikov's short poems gravitate toward the epic, rather than the lyric. They seem to be fragments of an epic narrative, and in fact, as noted by Jakobson and others after him, Khlebnikov often combined them into larger wholes.

We find numerous examples of this in both his long poems and his *sverkhpovesti* (super-tales).

LONGER POEMS

Khlebnikov left behind more than thirty works that belong to the category of the *poema*. They are significant within his own oeuvre and form an important episode in the rebirth of the genre as a whole in twentieth-century Russian literature.

The *poemy* display Khlebnikov's versatility in questions of genre, in subject matter, and in diction. In some cases he resurrects traditions of eighteenth-century classicism and unabashedly draws on archaic usages; in others he creates verse of Pushkinian lightness; elsewhere his neologisms are given free reign. Many of the poems show evidence of Khlebnikov's orientation toward the theater: they are either wholly or partly structured as dramatic dialogues, and rudimentary stage directions are occasionally included. In a number of works, the composition is very loose: the term *nanizyvanie* (stringing together) has been used to describe what appears to be a free succession of scenes and motifs. Some of the long poems serve as vehicles for his theories; in other cases Khlebnikov plays with folkloric or mythological themes, often treating them with considerable humor. By and large, the *poemy* are the most accessible of Khlebnikov's works and provide a ready opening into the world of his imagination.

Khlebnikov's first full-size *poema* is "Vnuchka Malushi" (Malusha's Granddaughter), which was completed in the summer of 1909. The story begins in pagan Kiev and involves a daughter of Prince Vladimir, Lyudmila. Bored with her life and threatened by marriage to an old man, she complains to a water goblin. A friendly werewolf, who turns into a lynx, takes her on a trip through time and space and deposits her in twentieth-century St. Petersburg. There, she meets women university students and leads them into a rebellion against their studies: the girls enthusiastically burn their textbooks, as their teachers run away.

There are clear echoes of literary traditions in this work. Most important, the easy mixture of the real and the fantastic in the story recalls the tongue-in-cheek plot of Pushkin's Slavic *poema* "Ruslan and Lyudmila" (1820), as do some of the details of the plot. Nikolay Gogol's "Noch' pered Rozhdestvom" ("The Night Before Christmas," 1832), which also contains a supernatural flight to St. Petersburg, is another major source for Khlebnikov.

The poem, filled with details of the Slavic pagan pantheon and of medieval Kiev, reflects Khlebnikov's early preoccupation with Slavdom. Although his concerns had a special ideological undercurrent, we should note that interest in Slavic themes was widespread in early twentieth-century culture, finding expression in literature, art, and music (Igor Stravinsky's *Rite of Spring* [1913]). The burning of the textbooks expresses an important theme in Khlebnikov's prewar writings: the rejection of nineteenth-century rationalism and an affirmation of an instinctual core in life. Also characteristic for Khlebnikov is the use of a narrative anachronism.

One of the most striking early poems is "Zhuravl'" ("The Crane," 1909), which presents an apocalyptic, surrealist scenario of *vosstanie veshchei* (the revolt of things). Set in St. Petersburg, the poem describes how inanimate objects—bridges, buildings—come to life and gather themselves (together with reanimated corpses) around a giant building crane to form a colossal bird—a crane—which begins to bring doom to humanity (the homonymic pun is deliberately used by Khlebnikov). The horrific vision, in which, among other details, babies are offered to the new senseless god, ends abruptly, as the crane unexpectedly departs, but the slaughter envisaged in the poem stands as the poet's warning to mankind.

The apocalyptic theme of "The Crane," repeated elsewhere in Khlebnikov, has been related to similar warnings in such symbolist works as Valery Bryusov's "Kon' bled" (Pale Horse, 1904). At the same time the fear of "the revolt of things" fit in well with futurist concerns and was treated by Mayakovsky in several of his works.

The primitivist orientation of Hylaea is notably reflected in the long poems "Lesnaia deva" (The Forest Maiden, 1911), "I i E. Povest' kamennogo veka" (I and E. A Tale of the Stone Age, 1911–1912), and "Vila i leshii" (The Vila and the Wood-Goblin, 1912).

The first of these, originally entitled "Pan," is set in a kind of Slavic Stone Age. It is a rather bare-bones story of love and murder and involves a prehistoric poet, an unnamed rival, and the girl they both desire. Much of the work's primitivist quality derives from its naive, swift-moving narration and from its use of language to create an atmosphere of unconventionality, of the unexpected. Although the story ends tragically, with the killing of the poet, the presentation makes it hard to take this seriously.

"I i E," perhaps the best of this group of poems, is very different in its approach. It is set in the Paleolithic proper; the single-vowel names given the protagonists, a young man and his beloved, reflect this early stage in the development of mankind; the rhythms, based largely on short lines (iambic dimeter), create the impression of a primitive's dynamic brevity. The plot involves love and triumph through self-sacrifice. After the girl "I" disappears in the forest, following a vision, she is found by "E." The two unwittingly commit sacrilege in a place sacred to another tribe, are condemned to be burned, but are saved by a divine being during the execution and are chosen to rule that tribe.

The work is both serious and charming, although its import for Khlebnikov is somewhat unclear, in spite of the explanatory note he attaches to the text. The poem's real strength lies in its fresh language and fast rhythms, which effectively combine to give an atmosphere of prehistoric man's vision of the world.

Khlebnikov returns to the Slavic primitive in "Vila i leshii." The plot is particularly thin, and centers on the attraction of an aging *leshii* (wood goblin) for a *vila* (a South Slavic nymph). Its earlier drafts show a narrative progression, with an ending; however, the version that was published (unpolished) is mainly a description of the *vila's* teasing of her would-be lover and of the forest landscape that surrounds them. There are some unexpected interludes in the plot: their presence is matched by the mixing of disparate elements in the language. The poem has been described as an idyll; this is appropriate to its lazy, peaceful atmosphere.

"Shaman i Venera" (The Shaman and Venus, 1912) partly shares in the primitivist orientation, although this is supplemented by a specific ideological message. The poem involves another pair of protagonists (a frequent occurrence in Khlebnikov), a Siberian shaman and Venus, who has fled the modern world that no longer appreciates passion. Much of the work charmingly and lightly describes the interplay between them, as the goddess' coquetry meets with her host's brusque but kind response. At the end Venus returns to a mankind that has realized its error.

The antithesis between a life ruled by emotions and a life ruled by logic, resolved with a kind of happy end in this poem, leads to a very different conclusion in "Gibel' Atlantidy" (The Fall of Atlantis, 1912). Here Khlebnikov transforms the familiar myth into a story of retribution. Atlantis is destroyed in punishment for the murder of a slave girl, who is a symbol of passion, by a priest, who embodies reason and who does not heed her warning that both of these principles are necessary in life. As the slave girl's severed head rises Gorgon-like above the city, Khlebnikov describes a flood in terms reminiscent of Pushkin's *Mednyi Vsadnik* (*The Bronze Horseman*, 1833). The scene of disaster is a clear warning to modern man.

Among Khlebnikov's other prewar long poems, the splendid "Khadzhi-Tarkhan" (1913) deserves special mention. It is a kind of panegyric to the city of Astrakhan, very much in the tradition of eighteenth-century verse. Appropriately, it is filled with shifting images of the city and its environs, episodes from its colorful past, and allusions to Khlebnikov's own family history. This diverse material allows Khlebnikov to meditate on some broader themes related to his concerns about the nature of Russian culture in relation to Asia and the West, to the longer-term direction of Russian history, and to the possible role of the futurists in shaping that development.

A gap of several years separates the early long poems and Khlebnikov's return to the genre. During and after his "Kharkov period," he produced a new body of *poemy,* startling in their power. By and large, these works deal with contemporary themes and with Khlebnikov's own visions of humanity's future.

The most important of the Kharkov long poems is "Poet" ("The Poet," 1919, 1921), one of the works that Khlebnikov wrote on a topic set by Dr. Anfimov. In this case the subject is "carnival," and, indeed, "Carnival" is an alternate title for the work.

The poem describes a procession that takes place during a spring carnival. Khlebnikov blends details from Russian folklore with images of nature into a brilliant, although at times hard to follow, sequence of episodes. The carnival serves as a setting for a conversation between a trio of characters: a *rusalka* (water nymph), the Virgin Mary, and the poet. Their interchange deals with the nature of human life, and the water nymph, who may be seen as an embodiment of poetry, condemns the poet (Khlebnikov's double) for betraying the world of imagination for a world of rationalistic, scientific calculations. At the end the poet sends the Virgin and the water nymph, representatives of the world of the past, into exile for a period and chooses to join them.

The conflict expressed in the text, both explicitly and through a chain of associations, can be related to Khlebnikov's own dilemma at being pulled in different directions by his art and by his theories of time. The poet's decision to join the two "sisters in misfortune" is an affirmation of Khlebnikov's own commitment to poetry.

The stay in Kharkov also produced an important work dealing with the civil war, "A Night in a Trench" (1920). The poem describes a battle between White and Red forces in a spot where stone statues from antiquity are standing. The ferocity of the struggle is conveyed very effectively, while the civil conflict as a whole is seen as a manifestation of a higher-level opposition within nature itself, between Russia's northern and southern regions. Although a positive description of Lenin appears, Khlebnikov's gloomy assessment of the country's self-torments is conveyed by the ending, when the stone statue exclaims, in response to the narrator's query, that the war will be followed by typhus.

In the autumn of 1921 Khlebnikov wrote a series of works that can be termed poems of retribution. The best of these is "The Night Search," which is linked by theme and certain elements of style with Blok's *Dvenadtsat'* (*The Twelve,* 1918). Set in Petrograd after the Bolshevik takeover, it deals with a group of sailors who search an apartment of a family with White connections. They discover a young man, Vladimir, and execute him in the presence of his old mother. After killing another White officer, the sailors have a wild drinking party, during which their leader, an older man, recalls Vladimir's courage. He feels tormented and challenged by an icon of Christ, grows maudlin and thinks of Christ as a girl he may court, and conducts a conversation about death with God. His ramblings are interrupted by a realization that the apartment is on fire, deliberately set by Vladimir's mother, who has also barred the exit. The old sailor emulates Vladimir's courage in death, while his companions are unsure whether to choke to death or shoot themselves. The old woman utters the poem's final line, "Whatever you wish!"

"The Night Search" is very interesting in terms of Khlebnikov's own development. The action embodies the idea of event and counter-event, central in his theories about time. Also, although the outcome of the plot is rather unrealistic, the characterizations of the sailors, and particularly the old sailor's psychological reactions to the events, are handled extremely well, with a fine interweaving of reality and symbolism.

Notable among the late poems is "Truba Gul'-Mully" ("Gul-mullah's Trumpet," 1921–1922), the product of Khlebnikov's visit to Iran. It is essentially a diary of his journeys—a record of his personal encounter with Asia, a continent that figured so prominently in his thought. To the Persians Khlebnikov is the "priest of flowers," and both men and nature are shown as welcoming him. The poem is filled with details of Persian life intermixed with anthropomorphic images of nature, resulting in a charming, optimistic atmosphere, indicative of Khlebnikov's attitude toward the entire experience.

The poem also contains another level, involving an analogy Khlebnikov draws between himself and Sten'ka Razin, a symbol of social revolt that appears in many of his works (two long poems are devoted to him). Here, Khlebnikov opposes his own actions and ideas to the famous rebel of the seventeenth century. As told in song and story, Razin had drowned a Persian princess he had captured. Khlebnikov wants to be an "anti-Razin," to save the girl—an act that would be emblematic of his role as a President of Planet Earth, a prophet of peace.

Perhaps the most unusual of Khlebnikov's late poems is "Ladomir" ("Goodworld," 1920, 1922). The title is a coinage, one that literally means "harmonious world"; it is related to the expression *mirovoi lad* (world order, harmony). As indicated by the implications of this title, the poem unfolds a vision of mankind in the next era, but there are intermingled with this descriptions of miseries endured by the Russian people in the past, and of the revolutionary violence that swept away the old order. Although the poem suffers from being repetitious, it contains many striking passages and, as his fullest vision of the future, is important in terms of Khlebnikov's development. Indeed,

the text is a catalogue of his ideas, a kind of index to late Khlebnikov. Conceptions discussed in detail in his articles and utopian prose are here condensed into a few lines; by the same token, anyone who approaches Khlebnikov through "Goodworld" will need to delve into his other writings in order to understand much of it.

The world described in the poem, particularly in its last part, is one of universal harmony, one that places science at the service of mankind, one that encompasses nature as a whole. More than a few poets since Khlebnikov found appealing such prophecies as "I see the freedoms of horses / And the equality of cows." Naturally, within this universe the futurists will take their proper place:

> Those youths, who swore an oath
> To tear down languages,—
> You have guessed their names—
> Walk crowned with wreaths.
> (*Tvoreniia*, p. 291)

PLAYS

Khlebnikov is the author of a small number of plays. All of these are very short; for the most part, they are intended only to be read. The plays are in prose, verse, or a mixture of both. In general, they are similar in their unconventionality—in the way that Khlebnikov plays with space and time, plot, and character development.

The majority of Khlebnikov's plays date from before the war. His "Slavic" phase produced three important works. The first, "Snezhimochka" (Snowchild Baby, 1908), is modeled after Alexander Ostrovsky's nineteenth-century theatrical fairy tale *Snegurochka* (*The Snow Maiden*, 1873), and this dependence is explicitly acknowledged within the play. In both works a fairy-tale being leaves the safety of the forest and mingles with human beings. Khlebnikov's heroine experiences the ironies of contemporary Russia: she witnesses a political assassination and is arrested by the police. Like her prototype, she melts, but Khlebnikov turns her disappearance into a cultural triumph. In the last act, where a number of young people participate in a kind of festival devoted to reawakening traditional "Slavic virtues," her sacrifice is hailed as a mystery and a pledge for the future.

In spite of this ideological ballast, "Snezhimochka" is quite charming. Its effect is enhanced by differentiation of the characters' discourse. The forest scenes are filled with wondrous creatures, whose language contains a number of neologisms, while the city dwellers speak in appropriate varieties of modern Russian.

"Devii bog" (The Virgins' God, 1911) is quite complex in its plot and obscure in its meaning. It is a kind of mystery play set in medieval Kiev. An unknown man, the Virgins' God, arrives and is welcomed by girls who surround him in ecstatic dance. Conflict arises when some in the town seek to attack the newcomer and when his female worshipers take up arms in his defense. After various episodes, which include tests of the man's supposed divinity, he and his companions are exiled for the sake of the community's harmony.

In "Self-Statement" Khlebnikov claims that "Devii bog" arose "unexpectedly and spontaneously like a wave," that it was written without a single change being made, and that it can be used "to study a madman's thought." If this is true, then the play represents a remarkable fusion of Greek and Roman myths (of Artemis and Actaeon, for example) with the conventions of symbolist theater (especially Sologub's "Liturgiia mne" [Liturgy to Me], 1907). At the same time Khlebnikov repeatedly emphasizes in the play the artifice of what is taking place, thus undermining the very model he apparently imitates.

The simplest of the "Slavic" plays is "Asparukh" (1911), which is a reworking of an anecdote from the *History* of Herodotus. In book 4, as part of his discussion of the Scythians, the great historian tells of the fate of the Scythian king Scyles, whose love of things Hellenic led to his condemnation by his own people, his flight into exile, and his eventual death. Khlebnikov takes over this narrative, changing it slightly to have the protagonist die following the discovery that he embraced Greek culture. In the process Khlebnikov commits a deliberate anachronism by giving the protagonist the name of a seventh-century Bulgar khan. The change appears to be motivated by potential etymological punning (*Asparukh* means "tamer of horses," from the Turkic *asp*, "horse"). The play may be regarded as an allegorical warning to those of Khlebnikov's contemporaries who, in his eyes, had betrayed their native culture to the attractions of the West.

Two of Khlebnikov's plays, "Chertik" (The Little Devil, 1909) and "Markiza Dezes" (The Marquis Desaix, 1909, 1911), originate in his early experiences in the literary and artistic circles of Petersburg. They are both witty satires aimed specifically at the new *Apollon* (where Khlebnikov was to have been published), but the older symbolist poets are also made fun of. Anachronisms reign supreme in the two works. "Chertik" features the little devil of the title, the Slavic god Perun, the statue of Hercules, a mammoth, and two sphinxes. "Markiza Dezes" presents a portrait leaving its frame and the appearance of the painter Raphael.

Both texts are deeply indebted to literary and theatrical traditions: in the one case to Johann Wolfgang von Goethe (the second part of *Faust* [1832]) and Blok (the plays *Balaganchik* [*The Puppet Show*, 1905] and *Neznakomka* [*The Stranger*, 1906]), in the other to Pushkin (*Povesti Belkina* [*The Tales of Belkin*, 1830], "Pir vo vremia chumy" ["A Feast During the Plague," 1830]) and Alexander Griboedov (the comedy *Gore ot uma* [*Woe from Wit*, 1822–1824]). In fact, we have the personal testimony of Jakobson that the conversational language and rhythms of "Markiza Dezes" are a product of Khlebnikov's study of Griboedov's perennially quotable lines.

In addition to its role as literary satire, "Markiza Dezes" has a serious side, for it develops the same theme of "the revolt of things" as in the poem "Zhuravl'." The principal difference is that the action takes place at an art exhibition, rather than in the whole of St. Petersburg. However, the warning of danger to humanity, depicted by having furs and skins used in clothing come to life while people turn to stone, is very much the same.

Khlebnikov's interest in experimenting with theatrical and narrative conventions is manifested in two short works. One, "Gospozha Lenin" ("Mrs. Laneen," 1909), develops a key device used by Maeterlinck in his play *Les Aveugles* (*The Blind,* 1891): the dramatis personae are the "voices" of different senses of a woman, and what transpires is presented through the words of the Voice of Sight, Voice of Hearing, and so forth. This experiment is well founded, since the woman turns out to be a psychiatric patient. The other play is "Mirskontsa" ("The World in Reverse," 1912). Here, the experiment involves a reversal of the normal time flow: a series of five amusingly handled scenes takes the main characters from death and old age into their baby carriages.

In 1915 Khlebnikov wrote what is probably his best play, *Oshibka smerti* (*Death's Mistake*). This charming work, staged in 1920 with Khlebnikov's participation features Miss Death, hostess of a tavern with twelve dead guests. The Thirteenth Guest arrives and, after some exchanges, tricks Miss Death with a pun, leads her to kill herself, and frees the others. At the conclusion Miss Death also comes to life and joins the celebration.

Once again, Khlebnikov plays with theatrical conventions and engages in literary-theatrical polemics. The unexpected inversion of the plot and the use of language as a device to make it come about owes much to Blok's theater. At the same time a deeply pessimistic play by Sologub, *Pobeda smerti* (The Triumph of Death, 1908), is challenged by Khlebnikov's terse plot and its ironic finale.

Death's Mistake also reflects other types of influence. The figure of Miss Death is derived from Russian folk theater, which also provides a model for Khlebnikov's extensive use of various language jokes (homonymy, play with names). At the same time, the idea for the central setting of the play, a party with corpses, and for some of the details in the proceedings was very likely reinforced by Pushkin's celebration of "life on the edge of death" in his "Feast During the Plague."

Khlebnikov wrote only two plays in his final years. One of these is "Bogi" (The Gods, 1921), in which divinities from various mythologies communicate in one of the varieties of transrational language. The other is "Pruzhina chakhotki" (The Mainspring of Consumptive Disease, 1922), subtitled "Shekspir pod stekliannoi chechevitsei" ("Shakespeare Under a Glass Lens"); its action occurs within the bloodstream of a writer. While interesting, these minor experiments are of lesser importance than those Khlebnikov had done in the past. By then, however, his orientation towards drama found a more important vehicle for self-expression, the supertale *Zangezi.*

PROSE TALES

Khlebnikov's heritage in prose is small, but it includes several superbly crafted works. He was a master of the short text and used it as a vehicle for thematic, compositional, and stylistic experimentation.

Two early works, "Pesn' miriazia" (The Song of the Peaceful One, 1907) and "Iskushenie greshnika" (A Sinner's Temptation, 1908), are virtuoso performances in the use of coinages to create fantastic scenes in which nature and mythology are interwoven. These are, in effect, prose equivalents of similar experiments in the "Slavic" short poems from this time.

Writing coinage-laden prose had certain limitations, and Khlebnikov explored other approaches. One was to follow in the footsteps of other writers. The most obvious case of this is a brief text from 1911, "Velik-Den'" (Easter Day), which is subtitled "Podrazhanie Gogoliu" ("Imitation of Gogol"). The story has a minimal plot, which revolves around a young man from the city who visits a Ukrainian village, is overwhelmed by the peasants' authentic Slavic clothing and customs, and wonders why people throughout Russia don't imitate the local folk. He is fascinated by a village girl and pledges allegiance to her and to her dream to defend Russia and the rights of its people.

This tendentious expression of Khlebnikov's nationalistic ideas is largely interesting because of its model. From the early Gogol, and especially from his *Taras Bulba* (1835), Khlebnikov borrows the Ukrainian setting and the patriotic theme as well as the great prose writer's use of extended similes and metaphors to enrich a narrative.

Slavic thematics reappear in the stories "Smert' Palivody" (Palivoda's Death, 1911), "Zhiteli gor" (Mountain Folk, 1912, 1913), and "Zakalennoe serdtse. Iz chernogorskoi zhizni" (The Tempered Heart. From Montenegrin Life, 1913). The first of these, included in the supertale "Deti Vydry" (The Otter's Children), is very close to Gogol's *Taras Bulba* and "Strashnaia mest' " ("A Terrible Vengeance," 1831) in both its rich style and its theme (Ukrainian Cossack struggles against their foreign enemies). Gogolian tropes likewise enrich the second tale, which features a brief anecdote from the life of the inhabitants of the Carpathian mountains. Like Gogol, Khlebnikov uses figurative language to bring into his text diverse motifs, often far removed from the immediate setting. In this case, he introduces numerous references to Slavic history and culture. The third is also an ethnographic excursus, this time into the life of a people whose traditions of independence and cultural integrity held a special significance for Khlebnikov. Again, a minor anecdote forms the core of the plot. However, the story is enriched by details drawn from a scholarly study of the Montenegrins and by linguistic borrowings, not only of words but also phrases, sayings, and proverbs.

In contrast to these examples of ornamental prose stand two stories from 1913, "Okhotnik Usa-Gali" ("Usa-Gali") and "Nikolai." Intended as parts of a cycle, each depicts a notable hunter and portrays his exploits, his proud independence, and his relationships to both men and nature. The model for these works is likely Pushkin's short story "Kirdzhali" (1834). The language used is simple and precise; the descriptions are realistic; the ability to depict animals and birds "from within" is uniquely Khlebnikov's.

The period of World War I and the civil war brings Khlebnikov's principal achievements in prose. The first of these is a 1915 text, "Ka," which may be classified as a novella, although it has also been termed a "short novel." This is one of Khlebnikov's strangest, most challenging, and most fascinating works.

The title refers to the Egyptian concept of the *ka*—a man's active double, his personal "genius." The narrative relates some of the "deeds" of the autobiographical hero and his double, who is endowed with the ability to travel in time and space and to pass from dream to dream. This power is used to motivate the text's most prominent feature: its constant narrative "shifts," thanks to which the "I" and the Ka visit a variety of real and imaginary worlds. These include, among others, society in the year 2222, Russia during World War I, paradise as imagined by Muslims, and Egypt during the reign of the "heretic" Pharaoh Akhnaten (Amenhotep IV).

Although the language of "Ka" is precise and clear, the work itself is very difficult. The text is filled with historical references and literary allusions, and is studded with exotic names. Some of this material still needs to be clarified by scholars. Even more difficult are integrating into a single whole this kaleidoscope of themes and motifs, which has been compared to Arthur Rimbaud's *Les illuminations* (*Illuminations,* 1886) and relating the varied historical and cultural reminiscences to the work's autobiographical level. Khlebnikov draws parallels between the autobiographical narrator and the religious reformer Akhnaten (repeated in some of his essays). Also, a major part of the text is devoted to a reworking of a celebrated Oriental narrative, the story of Layla and Majnun, best known through a twelfth-century poem by Nizami. Khlebnikov weaves himself and his *ka* into a reworking of this tale of fated, hopeless love. The personal import for the author of these and other aspects of "Ka" remains to be determined.

Another major work from Khlebnikov's later years is "Esir" (The Slave, 1918–1919). This is a narrative about the adventures of Istoma, a Russian fisherman from seventeenth-century Astrakhan. Captured and sold into slavery by Kalmyk Tatars, he escapes and travels for years in India, seeing its many wonders before returning home. The tale is reminiscent of a noted medieval travelogue by the merchant Afanasy Nikitin, who also journeyed to India.

Istoma's journey is not only physical but also intellectual and spiritual. Khlebnikov carefully though tersely shows how the young fisherman's mental horizons are startlingly broadened by his exposure to the cultures and religions of the subcontinent. The tale reflects Khlebnikov's preoccupation with the Orient, and particularly with Indian religious and philosophical thought.

By placing Istoma in the time of a famous seventeenth-century revolt, that of the Cossack leader Sten'ka Razin, and by referring to different movements in India and China, Khlebnikov is able to suggest an analogy to the revolutionary situation of his own time. It is noteworthy, therefore, that his protagonist is launched on a path of spiritual rather than political liberation and is brought to understand the Indian concept of the external world as *maya* (illusion).

Deserving of note among Khlebnikov's late prose works is the story "Malinovaia shashka" (The Crimson Saber, 1921). It is devoted to an episode from the biography of a minor poet, Dmitrii Petrovskii, who was a friend of Khlebnikov and who himself left a memoir about their relationship. The story is set in the time of the civil war, and is notable for its ironic treatment of the protagonist, its powerful imagery of the ravages of the period, and its return to the ornamental style in the tradition of Gogol.

Khlebnikov's prose also includes a number of works usually termed "utopias," in which he sketches out his visions of humanity's future. One of the most interesting is the 1918 "Lebediia budushchego" ("Swanland in the Future"). It is composed of short sections, each describing different aspects of Khlebnikov's vision of the future. In science-fiction style he describes how newscasts from around the planet are projected on walls or even on clouds; how the clouds become fields in which aerial farmers raise crops; and how individual settlements are linked with the world by airships and by television. In the future world, Khlebnikov asserts, not a single animal species is allowed to disappear; it is found that the eyes of animals emit special rays which help cure human illness; and mankind, having taken to the skies, moves toward a universal community of all living creatures.

It will be recalled that Khlebnikov wanted to enroll Wells in the Society of Presidents of Planet Earth. The "utopias" earn the poet his own place in early 20th century science-fiction of the Wellsian variety.

SUPERTALES

Khlebnikov's major experiments in genres involve his attempts to create an altogether new literary kind, what he called the *sverkhpovest'* (supertale) or *zapovest'* (transtale). Although he wrote the first of these before the world war, it was not until the end of his life that he provided a kind of definition of such texts. This is found in the introduction to *Zangezi,* the last of the supertales:

> A tale is made of words, as the construction unit of a building. The construction unit is the small stone of equivalent words. A supertale, or transtale, is constructed out of independent fragments, each with its special god, its special faith, and its special rule. To the Muscovite question: "How dost thou believe?"—each answers independently from its neighbor. The building block,

the stone of the supertale, is the first-order tale. The supertale resembles a statue made from different kinds of stone of different colors—the body of white stone, the cloak and garments of blue stone, the eyes of black stone. It is carved from differently colored blocks of the Word, each constructed differently. Thus we find a new kind of work in the realm of verbal art. A story is architecture composed of words. An architecture composed of "stories" is a supertale. For the artist, the block is not a word, but a first-order story.

(*Tvoreniia*, p. 473)

The description focuses on the fact of including different independent texts within the framework of a larger work. This is, in fact, what is found in Khlebnikov's practice. However, the passage begs the question of how these units relate to each other, both in terms of their arrangement and in terms of meaning. Also, critics have differed in the application of this label to certain of Khlebnikov's texts: in some collections, "Voina v myshelovke" ("War in a Mousetrap") is included in this group, while in others it is numbered among the longer poems.

The first of the new genre is "Deti Vydry." Published in 1914, it consists of works written between 1911 and 1913. It is made up of six sections, each of which is termed a *parus* ("lacunar," though usually translated as "sail"). The sections vary widely in genre and include prose tales, a theatrical sketch, a narrative poem, a philosophical disquisition in verse, and a poetic "dialogue of the dead."

The title of the work refers to its two protagonists, the so-called Children of the Otter (brother and sister). In the course of the work they travel through time and visit a number of different historical scenes filled with diverse characters. The work opens in the days of the world's creation, as imagined by a minor Siberian people, the Orochi; it ends within the soul of Khlebnikov, identified with the Son of the Otter. In the process Khlebnikov has an opportunity to describe his early ideas on historical cycles, to polemicize with economic and biological determinism (Karl Marx and Charles Darwin), and to present such scenes as a Paleolithic mammoth hunt, an Arab caravan traveling through the Volga River region in medieval times, and the destruction of the *Titanic.*

The diversity of genre and content is matched by the absence of a sustained point of view within the work as a whole. The principal element of cohesion within "Deti Vydry" is provided by the Son of the Otter, who, starting with his role as a culture hero in the beginning of the work, serves as a model of heroic behavior emulated by the many other dramatis personae. Given his identification with Khlebnikov in the last section, the underlying theme of "Deti Vydry" may be a glorification of heroism—found throughout history and most recently among the futurists themselves. This message is not very profound, but it is consistent with the self-images propagated by the Hylaeans.

Unlike "Deti Vydry," "War in a Mousetrap" is much more uniform in both the genre of its component parts and in its subject matter. The work is made up of poems published during the period 1915–1918; Khlebnikov worked on putting these together into a larger whole from 1919 on. Khlebnikov himself called "War in a Mousetrap" a *poema.* However, his compositional method provides grounds for including the work among the supertales.

As its title indicates, war is the primary theme of "War in a Mousetrap," which contains some of Khlebnikov's most moving condemnations of World War I. The poet asks ironically:

Is it true, that young men have gone down in price? That they are cheaper than land, a barrel of water, or a wagonload of coal?

(*Tvoreniia*, p. 457)

There are striking, grotesque images of death and mass human slaughter, such as

Death was combing itself
Its mighty hair
And the midges of unneeded lives
Vainly tried to bite it.

(*Tvoreniia*, p. 458)

But Khlebnikov not only laments the reality of war but attempts to fight it. The "mousetrap" referred to in the title is wielded by the futurist. Armed with a mathematical understanding of history, he confronts nightmarish figures from folklore who become symbols of the destruction of humanity. Still, even he is not always successful. In an early section Khlebnikov laments that he is now a prisoner of "malicious old men"—that is, he is in the army. And, in the next to last section, he despairs of humanity's ability to come to its senses and warns of the arrival of new judges. These are, courtesy of Jonathan Swift, horses, a wiser species than human beings have proved to be, claims Khlebnikov.

Interwoven among the sections of "War in a Mousetrap" devoted to the theme of war are several love poems, among Khlebnikov's best. Their intimacy strikingly contrasts with the pathos and frequent cosmic imagery of the other portions of the supertale and humanizes and enriches its autobiographical and lyrical "I."

A very interesting example of a supertale is "Sestry-molnii" (Sisters-Lightning Flashes). Portions of it date back to 1915–1916; the last section was written in October 1921 in Pyatigorsk. Unfortunately, the work is not finalized. Khlebnikov apparently did not have his earlier manuscripts when he returned to it in 1921, and this led to the duplication of certain passages in the different sections.

"Sestry-molnii" is made up of three parts. The first is the "Razgovor molnii" ("Conversation of the Lignting Flashes"), who enumerate their many incarnations, not only within human beings but also within parts of nature. This theme of rebirth returns in the third and last section. In between, we have a dramatic sketch in verse. Entitled "Strastnaia ploshchad' " ("Passion Square"), it features a monk in a monastery cell (like Pimen in Pushkin's *Boris Godunov* [1825]) reading an account of the Crucifixion. What is striking here is that this is a soliloquy by one of the executioners, who has a kind of class-based perspective on events (he refers to himself as a "gloomy son of labor"). The scene of the Passion acquires a very contemporary significance through a sign—attached to the cross, or simply put up in the square?—with the slogan "He who does not work, does not eat!"

Two supertales have their origin in Khlebnikov's Kharkov period. The puzzlingly titled "Azy iz uzy" (possible translation: I's [Liberated] from Chains) is another instance of a work which may also be treated as a long poem. It is made up of poems dealing with the Asian continent: the varieties of its cultures and faiths, its bloody, colorful past, and its revolutionary present. As in "War in a Mousetrap," a love subtheme is present, expressed in part through a projection of the poet and his beloved into the figures of the Titan Prometheus and Asia (cf. Percy Bysshe Shelley). The other supertale, "Tsarapina po nebu" (A Scratch Across the Sky), was completed in 1921. It is an exposition of Khlebnikov's historical and linguistic theories: portions of it are written in different "languages" developed by the poet, including the "Language of the Stars." Unfortunately, it lacks the personal component found in other examples of the genre, and this weakens it considerably.

Khlebnikov's final and most successful supertale, *Zangezi*, is divided into twenty separate sections, termed *ploskosti* (levels, or planes). Most of these were written between 1920 and 1922 and assembled into a single text in early 1922. As in "Deti Vydry" the content of the individual sections varies greatly, from a transcription of birds' songs in level 1 to the "Gore i Smekh" ("Sorrow and Laughter") episode in what may be regarded as level 20. Once again, as in Khlebnikov's first "supertale," the principal element of cohesion is provided by the presence of a central figure in most of the levels—the poet-prophet Zangezi, who declaims his "songs" each morning from a stone platform in the mountains. Typically, each of Zangezi's songs occupies a separate section. He has a diverse audience, one which encompasses both people and nature. The human listeners include disciples, who exclaim: "We the believers, we await. Our eyes, our souls—a floor for your steps, oh unknown one!" It also includes some far less respectful passers-by, who comment, "Fool! The sermon of a forest fool!"

The noted literary historian Tynyanov linked *Zangezi* with the tradition of German Romantic drama, particularly the plays of Ludwig Tieck. Indeed, Khlebnikov's text has a clear theatrical framework and was staged within a year of Khlebnikov's death. The work lacks any real dramatic qualities, but it is rich in sound, its ideas are presented in very palpable form, and its protagonist draws an audience's attention.

Zangezi, modeled on Khlebnikov himself, serves as his spokesman for his final ideas about the nature of time and language. The name, a combination of the names of two rivers, Zambezi (Africa) and the Ganges (Asia), is emblematic of human unity. He is also called *changara* by his disciples. This is a neologism, derived from the Sanskrit Śaṅkara, which is the name of the celebrated ninth-century exponent of Vedanta. The neologism suggests that Zangezi may be regarded as a teacher in the Indian tradition—as someone whose words help strip away from the listener the veil of *maya.* The figure of Zangezi, as well as his goal of teaching his listeners about his ideas, also recalls Friedrich Nietzsche's Zarathustra.

In his role as Khlebnikov's double, Zangezi is handed his creator's most cherished discoveries in the realm of language and time. Thus, in level 4 he reads from the *Boards of Fate;* in levels 7, 8, and 12 he uses the "Language of the Stars" to explain the revolution; and in level 18 he unrolls an account of history in terms of his "basic law of time." Elsewhere, he sings songs composed by means of the "self-sufficient word" (level 13), of sound-painting (level 15), and of transrational language (level 9).

Like his creator Zangezi oscillates between hope and doubts about the future, between assertions of his power as an enchanter ("Forward, terrestrial globes") to denials of newspaper stories that he has cut his throat in despair over the loss of his manuscripts. And, in level 6 he grows elegiac about his own existence, uttering his own and Khlebnikov's best epitaph:

I have come like a butterfly
Into the hall of human life,
And must spatter my dusty coat
As signature across its bleak windows,
As a prisoner scratches his name
On fate's unyielding windowpane.
Human life is paper thick
With grayness and boredom!
The transparent NO of its windows!
Already I have worn away
My bright blue glow, my pointillated patterns,
My wing's blue windstorm. The bright motes
Of my first freshness are gone, my wings waver,
Colorless and stiff. I droop despairing
At the windows of the human world.
Numbers, eternal numbers, sound in the beyond;
I hear their distant conversation. Number
Calls to number; number calls me home.

Selected Bibliography

EDITIONS

INDIVIDUAL EDITIONS

Uchitel' i uchenik. Kherson, 1912.
Igra v adu. Moscow, 1912. (With A. Kruchenykh.)
Igra v adu. 2nd ed. Moscow, 1913. (With A. Kruchenykh.)
Riav! Perchatki: 1908–1914. St. Petersburg, 1913.
Izbornik stikhov: 1907–1914. Edited by A. Kruchenykh. St. Petersburg, 1914.
Tvoreniia: 1906–1908. Moscow, 1914.
Bitvy 1915–1917: Novoe uchenie o voine. Petrograd, 1914.
Vremia mera mira. Petrograd, 1916.
Truba marsian. Khar'kov, 1916.
Oshibka smerti. Moscow, 1917.
Ladomir. Khar'kov, 1920.
Noch' v okope. Moscow, 1921.
Vestnik Velimira Khlebnikova, 1–2. Moscow, 1922.
Zangezi. Moscow, 1922.
Otryvok iz dosok sud'by, 1–3. Moscow, 1922–1923.
Stikhi. Moscow, 1923.

Zapisnaia knizhka Velimira Khlebnikova. Edited by A. E. Kruchenykh. Moscow, 1925.

Nastoiashchee. Moscow, 1926.

Vsem. Nochnoi bal. Moscow, 1927.

Neizdannyi Khlebnikov, no. 1–30. Edited by A. E. Kruchenykh et al. Moscow, 1928–1934.

Zverinets. Edited by A. Kruchenykh. Moscow, 1930.

COLLECTED WORKS

Sobranie proizvedenii Velimira Khlebnikova. Edited by N. Stepanov. Introduction by Yu. Tynianov. 5 vols. Leningrad, 1928–1933.

Izbrannye stikhotvoreniia. Edited by N. Stepanov. Moscow, 1936.

Stikhotvoreniia. Edited by N. Stepanov. Leningrad, 1940.

Neizdannye proizvedeniia. Edited by N. Khardzhiev and T. Grits. Moscow, 1940.

Stikhotvoreniia i poemy. Edited by N. Stepanov. Leningrad, 1960.

Sobranie sochinenii. Edited by Vladimir Markov. 4 vols. Munich, 1968–1972.

Ladomir. Poemy. Edited by B. Romanov. Moscow, 1985.

Stikhotvoreniia, poemy, dramy, proza. Edited by R. V. Duganov. Moscow, 1986.

Stikhi. Poemy. Proza. Edited by Serafima Blokh and Vladimir Roitman. New York, 1986.

Stikhi. Poemy. Proza. Edited by Serafima Blokh and Vladimir Roitman. New York, 1986.

Tvoreniia. Edited by V. P. Grigor'ev and A. E. Parnis. Moscow, 1986.

TRANSLATIONS

Collected Works of Velimir Khlebnikov. Volume I. Letters and Theoretical Writings. Translated by Paul Schmidt. Edited by Charlotte Douglas. Cambridge, Mass., 1987.

The King of Time: Selected Writings of the Russian Futurian. Translated by Paul Schmidt. Edited by Charlotte Douglas. Cambridge, Mass., 1985.

Snake Train: Poetry and Prose. Edited by Gary Kern. Introduction by Edward J. Brown. Translated by Gary Kern et al. Ann Arbor, 1976.

BIOGRAPHICAL AND CRITICAL STUDIES

Baran, Henryk. "Xlebnikov and the Mythology of the Oroches." In *Slavic Poetics: Essays in Honor of Kiril Taranovsky.* Edited by Roman Jakobsen et al. The Hague, 1973. Pp. 33–39.

——— . "Chlebnikov's Poem 'Bech.'" *Russian Literature* 6:5–19 (1974).

——— . "On the Poetics of a Khlebnikov Tale: Problems and Patterns in 'Ka'." In *The Structural Analysis of Narrative Texts.* Edited by A. Kodjak et al. Columbus, 1980. Pp. 112–131.

——— . "On Xlebnikov's Love Lyrics: I. Analysis of 'O, červi zemljanye.'" In *Russian Poetics: Proceedings of the International Symposium at UCLA, September 22–23, 1975.* Edited by Th. Eekman and D. S. Worth. Columbus, 1983. Pp. 29–44.

——— . "Temporal Myths in Xlebnikov: From 'Deti Vydry' to 'Zangezi.'" In *Myth in Literature.* Edited by A. Kodjak et al. Columbus, 1985. Pp. 63–88.

Cooke, Raymond. *Velimir Khlebnikov: A Critical Study.* Cambridge Studies in Russian Literature. Cambridge, 1987.

Duganov, R. V. "Problema epicheskogo v estetike i poetike Khlebnikova." *Izvestiia Akademii Nauk. Seriia literatury i iazyka* 35:426–439 (1976).

Grigor'ev, Viktor Petrovich. *Grammatika idiostilia. V. Khlebnikov.* Moscow, 1983.

——— . *Slovotvorchestvo i smezhnye problemy iazyka poeta.* Moscow, 1986.

Jakobson, Roman. *Noveishaiia russkaia poeziia. Nabrosok pervyi: Viktor Khlebnikov.* Prague, 1921.

Kamensky, V. "O Khlebnikove: slavozhd'." In V. V. Khlebnikov, *Tvoreniia: 1906–1908.* Moscow, 1914 [no page numbers].

Lanne, Jean-Claude. *Velimir Khlebnikov. Poete futurien.* 2 vols. Paris, 1983.

Lönnqvist, Barbara. *Xlebnikov and Carnival: An Analysis of the Poem "Poet."* Stockholm, 1979.

Markov, Vladimir. *The Longer Poems of Velimir Khlebnikov.* Berkeley and Los Angeles, 1962.

Mayakovsky, Vladimir. "V. V. Khlebnikov." In *Major Soviet Writers: Essays in Criticism.* Edited by Edward J. Brown. New York, 1973. Pp. 83–88.

Mirsky, Salomon. *Der Orient im Werk Velimir Chlebnikovs.* Munich, 1975.

Nilsson, Nils Ake, ed. *Velimir Chlebnikov: A Stockholm Symposium.* Stockholm, 1985.

Parnis, A. E. "Iuzhnoslavianskaia tema Velimira Khlebnikova. Novye materialy k tvorcheskoi biografii poeta." In *Zarubezhnye slaviane i russkaia kul'tura.* Edited by M. P. Alekseev. Leningrad, 1978. Pp. 223–251.

Petrovsky, D. "A Tale about Khlebnikov: Memoirs of Velimir Khlebnikov." Trans. by Lily Feiler. In V.

Khlebnikov, *Snake Train: Poetry and Prose.* Edited by Gary Kern. Ann Arbor, 1976. Pp. 273–313.

The Russian Avant-Garde III. Velimir Khlebnikov. Special issue of *Russian Literature* (January 1981).

Stepanov, Nikolai. *Velimir Khlebnikov: zhizn' i tvorchestvo.* Moscow, 1975.

Vroon, Ronald. *Velimir Khlebnikov's Shorter Poems: A Key to the Coinages.* Ann Arbor, Mich., 1983.

———. "Velimir Khlebnikov's 'Razin: Two Trinities.'" *Slavic Review* 39:70–84 (1980).

———. "Velimir Khlebnikov's 'I esli v "Khar'kovskie ptitsy" . . .': Manuscript Sources and Subtexts." *The Russian Review* 42: 249–271 (1983).

Weststeijn, Willem G. *Velimir Chlebnikov and the Development of Poetical Language in Russian Symbolism and Futurism.* Amsterdam, 1983.

———, ed. *Velimir Chlebnikov (1885–1922): Myth and Reality.* Amsterdam, 1986.

HENRYK BARAN

JEAN ARP
(1886–1966)

I N 1954, AT the age of sixty-eight, Jean Arp received one of the most prestigious awards that can be given to a sculptor, the International Sculpture Prize at the Bienniale Exhibition of Venice. When asked later, however, what he would have done had he ever been forced to choose between sculpture or poetry, Arp replied that he would have chosen to be a poet. Questioned in another interview about the relation of his collages to his poetry, Arp maintained that the collages were "poetry made with plastic means." He could have given a similar response had the question been about his drawings: that they were script, written with pictorial means. On occasion, Arp gave titles such as "calligraphy" and "écriture" to his india ink drawings, and he produced a number of drawings that resemble Chinese written characters, or ideograms.

Although better known to the general public as a painter and sculptor, Arp was an innovative and influential poet, and his poetry in German and French has ultimately been held in the highest esteem by fellow poets. This poet's poet was also a poet's illustrator; throughout his life he enthusiastically collaborated with friends, producing prints to accompany volumes of poetry, theirs and his own, and illustrations for the reviews published by the different avant-garde movements with which he was associated. The written word and the visual image were closely linked in Arp's own perception of his creative output, and words, both

spoken and written, were as important a stimulus to his artistic imagination as contour, space, form, and color. His visual impulse was often carried over into his perception of language, and he characterized the sense of sculptural volume that he ascribed to words: "For me words have always kept their newness, their mystery. I handle them like a child playing with blocks. I feel them, I mold them—like sculptures. I attribute to them a plastic volume independent of their meaning." Possibilities for verbal interpretations of Arp's sculptures and reliefs are generated in turn by the suggestive and often ambiguous titles he gave to his later plastic works once they were finished. Composition of these titles, he explained, sometimes became more important to him than the works themselves.

The illustrations and poems Arp contributed to publications of the various groups with which he was involved document his participation in almost all the important European avant-garde movements from 1912 up to the beginning of World War II. His association with Blaue Reiter expressionism in Munich, with the expressionist Sturm Gallery in Berlin, with Dada in Zurich, Paris, and Cologne, with Kurt Schwitters' Merz movement in Hannover, with surrealism in Paris, and with a series of European constructivist movements in the 1920's and 1930's frequently led him to the collaborative production of manifestos and reviews, to which he contributed poems and graphic illustrations. Arp is represented in the *Blaue Reiter Almanach* of 1912, in the expressionist journal *Der Sturm* (The Storm), in the Zurich publications *Dada* and the *Zeltweg* (The Tentpath), in the *Dadameter Schammade* published together with his friend Max Ernst in Cologne, in the Paris reviews *Cahiers d'art* (Journals of Art) and *La révolution surréaliste* (The Surrealist Revolution), in the Dutch *De Stijl* (The Style) publications and Schwitters' Hannover *Merz,* in the Paris constructivist journals *G* and *Circle et carré* (Circle and Square), and in the important Paris-based American literary review *transition.* Despite his participation in a broader spectrum of avant-garde movements than that attributable to almost any poet or artist in the first half of the twentieth century, Arp was able to develop and maintain his own distinctive style in his visual and his verbal art. He pursued his lifelong explorations of language and plastic form independent of whatever movement he was affiliated with at any particular moment, and this artistic independence made it possible for him to contribute to such a variety of movements without assuming the dogmatic stances often taken by particular groups. The only programmatic designation Arp insisted on for his work was that of "concrete art," and an investigation of what he meant by this term will lead us through decisive moments of stylistic development in his own artistic and poetic career.

It is no surprise to find Arp at home in both French and German contexts. Born 16 September 1886 of a German father and an Alsatian mother in the city of Strassburg, he grew up trilingual, speaking German, French, and the Alsatian dialect spoken in his home. The two names by which he is known as a poet and artist, Hans Arp and Jean Arp, attest to his birth into two different cultures and poetic traditions. An indifferent student, he spent his hours in the classroom drawing and composing poems. By age fifteen, he had been admitted to a circle of Alsatian poets and artists led by the expressionist writer and editor René Schickele and by Arp's instructor of drawing,

the young Strassburg painter Georg Ritleng. In 1903 two texts by Arp, one in German and one in dialect, were published in reviews put out by his circle of acquaintances in Alsace. By 1904 Arp had assembled a collection of poems in German into a volume entitled the *Logbuch* (Log), which he sent to a Berlin publisher. The publishing house lost this manuscript, a collection which would otherwise have provided us with evidence of Arp's poetic beginnings. As a child, he had immersed himself in works by German Romantic poets such as Novalis, Clemens Brentano, and Achim von Arnim as well as in the philosophical texts of the seventeenth century German mystic Jakob Böhme. The vocabulary and themes of the few early poems that have survived reflect the neo-Romantic mannerism of German poetry at the turn of the century, and the poems are populated by figures from German fairy tales and folk poetry. Arp's literary interests as a youth in Strassburg included the French texts of Arthur Rimbaud, Lautréamont, and the Belgian symbolist poet and playwright Maurice Maeterlinck.

In 1900 Arp persuaded his parents to let him leave his high school in order to enroll in the Strassburg Academy of Art as a student of painting. Dissatisfied with the instruction at the academy, Arp studied on his own for the next three years with painters in Strassburg. In 1904 he traveled for the first time to Berlin and to Paris. After this initial exposure to Paris, he begged his father for permission to continue his studies there at the Académie Julien. Instead, his father sent him to the Academy of Fine Arts in Weimar, where Arp became a close friend of Igo Hauptmann, son of the famous German playwright Gerhart Hauptmann. In 1907 Arp's work was exhibited in Paris for the first time, along with paintings by Henri Matisse and Paul Signac, and in 1908 he finally entered the Académie Julien. While profiting from his contact with other painters in Paris, Arp was frustrated by the instruction he received at the academy and complained bitterly that students were forced by their teachers to do nothing but imitate when they painted. Arp left Paris for Weggis in Switzerland, where his family had moved two years before, and spent a considerable part of the next six years alone in the mountains, reading intensively and trying to develop a style in which he could paint and write without having to copy or to describe what already existed in the world for all to see.

During these years he made occasional trips to Paris, where he witnessed the initial experiments of the cubists and became friends with Robert and Sonia Delaunay, who soon launched a postcubist movement labeled "Orphism" by the French poet Guillaume Apollinaire. Together with friends in Switzerland, including the painter Paul Klee, Arp founded a movement in Lucerne called the *Moderner Bund* (The Modern Association). This group mounted the first exhibition shown in Switzerland of contemporary painting from Paris, including works by Pablo Picasso, Paul Gauguin, and Matisse in addition to works by Arp himself and other association members. By 1912 Arp was also in active contact with the Blaue Reiter expressionists in Munich, where he was especially attuned to the painting and poetry of the Russian Wassily Kandinsky. Kandinsky had just made a decisive breakthrough as painter to a nonrepresentational style and early in 1912 had published the German version of his essay "Über das Geistige in der Kunst" ("Concerning the Spiritual in Art"), the most important philosophical justification of abstract art written by any artist in the early twentieth century. Kandinsky's theoretical arguments, as well as his work, were significant to Arp in his own search for a nonrepresentational style. In effect, Kandinsky functioned as Arp's ideal mentor, the teacher who was finally offering the kind of direction and encouragement that the young painter had tried in vain to find in the various academies he had attended and abandoned.

In the same year, 1912, Arp was writing poems considerably more radical in style than his visual work at the time. Many of these texts were later included in volumes of poetry associated with his Dada years in Zurich, *der vogel selbdritt* (Bird with Two Others) and *die wolkenpumpe* (The Cloud-pump), both published in 1920. Although the Romantic themes and vocabulary characteristic of his earliest poems were still present in the poems written between 1912 and 1915, they now appeared in combinations and variations that were highly original and distinctive in style. In an early poem from *der vogel selbdritt,* the apocalyptic atmosphere to be found in much of German prewar expressionist writing was transformed by Arp into a topsy-turvy fairy-tale world in which black winds descend from the stars, queens fall from milking stools, and houses spin like tops:

Black winds hang like chains from the stars.
Grappling irons attack black lacquered walls.
The maps of the cities glow.
The houses run on seven rubies or spin like tops on
    diamonds.
Thunderclaps roll through the vast courtyards and
    the queens are toppling from milking stools.
From the necks of the earth climb the tenants and
    subtenants with their galvanized spiders.
Out of the glue come little glass skeletons tolling
    like chaos.
Who will bear up our little coffin beneath the cool
    morning star?

(1.32)[1]

Although the atmosphere of these poems is not always expressly apocalyptic, it is almost invariably elegiac, with fairy-tale figures transplanted into a landscape resembling, at one moment, the Hades of Greek antiquity into which dead souls are transported and, at the next, a celestial realm of interstellar space populated by angels and pilgrim fish:

The nightbirds carry burning lanterns in the beams
    of their eyes.
They steer delicate ghosts and ride on wagons with
    delicate veins.
The black wagon is harnessed to the mountain.
The black bell is harnessed to the mountain.
The black rocking horse is harnessed to the moun-
    tain.

[1] All page references in the text are to the 3-volume *Gesammelte Gedichte* (1963–1984), unless otherwise noted.

The dead bring saws and tree trunks along to the
  pier.
The harvest falls from the maws of birds onto the
  iron threshing floors.
The angels land in baskets of air.
The fish take up their walking sticks and roll in the
  stars toward the exit.

                           (1.34)

In another poem from this collection galaxies
are transformed into cosmic hourglasses, up-
ended so that time runs out in a trickle of stars:

Immense hourglasses filled with stars are reversed.
In subterranean corridors there are throngs of black
  flowers and crystalline coffins.
Heraldic beasts race at a gallop for the horizon.
Great white hares drink from white lava streams.
He also sees the seas hanging perpendicular like
  mirrors in mountains but does not flee with the
  amateur rabble into the arches.
He reaps the snow harvest.
He weighs the snow anchor and from the giant
  bird's blood he fells crystals of flesh and of blood.

                           (1.39)

Apocalyptic themes, obliquely rendered,
also play an important role in Kandinsky's poetry and visual work from 1910 to 1914, and
Kandinsky was an inspiration to Arp as a poet
as well as an artist. Arp valued the poems published in 1912 in the volume *Klänge* (Sounds)
as highly as he valued Kandinsky's paintings
and woodcuts; later, in *Jours effeuillés* (Days
with Leaves, 1966), he cites Kandinsky as the
first poet to produce what Arp called "concrete
poetry," as well as one of the first painters to
produce "concrete art":

> In 1912 I visited Kandinsky in Munich. He re-
> ceived me with greath warmth and generosity. It
> was the moment at which abstract art was begin-
> ning to transform itself into concrete art, that is to
> say, that avant-garde painters were no longer in-
> stalling themselves before an apple, a guitar, a
> person, or a landscape in order to convert or re-
> solve these things into colored circles, triangles,
> and rectangles. To the contrary, they were now
> creating lines, planes, forms, colors, autonomous

compositions directly from their most intimate
joy, their most personal suffering.

                           (p. 369)

Arp considered Kandinsky to be producing direct, autonomous compositions with words as
well as with lines, planes, forms, and colors.
He praised Kandinsky for employing language
so that words are called upon to engender an
organic cycle, as in nature, of birth, growth,
metamorphosis, and death. In his later essays
on concrete art Arp maintains that the concrete
artist must produce directly like a plant growing its fruit rather than indirectly by copying
what nature or man has already produced.
Natural processes of generation must manifest
themselves in the work of art, and the concrete
work of art is above all to be experienced as
process rather than end product, as an organic
work on its way to becoming. In *Jours effeuillés*
Arp explains how he believed that Kandinsky
achieved this effect in his early poems:

> Through the progression of words and the pro-
> gression of phrases in these poems, the reader is
> reminded of the constant flow, of the perpetual
> becoming of things, more likely than not in a tone
> of black humor, but that is what is special about
> concrete poetry: it is neither sententious nor di-
> dactic. Kandinsky places the reader before an
> image of words that die and become, before a
> dream that dies and becomes. Through Kan-
> dinsky's poems, we are present at the eternal
> cycle of becoming and of disappearing, at the
> transformation of this world.

                           (p. 370)

Many of Arp's poems, such as the ones above,
from 1912 throughout the Dada years can be
characterized in the same terms that Arp uses
to describe Kandinsky's poems in *Sounds.*
Through the progression of words and images,
micro- and macrocosmic landscapes are
brought into being, transformed, and then allowed to dissipate, all colored by Arp's own
playful, disarming black humor. In this sense,
Arp himself was producing concrete poems by

1912, although his stylistic breakthrough in the visual sphere did not come until 1917.

In 1913 Arp's family left Weggis for Zurich, and Arp traveled to Berlin, invited there by Herwarth Walden to take over direction of the Sturm gallery, the most important art and literary center of Berlin expressionism. Arp organized exhibitions, wrote for Walden's journal *Der Sturm*, and coproduced a monograph on modern French painting, the first study of its kind to be published in Germany. In 1914, before the outbreak of World War I, Arp met the young German painter Max Ernst in Cologne, and the two became friends for life. On 3 August 1914, when Germany declared war on France, Arp left Cologne on the last train allowed to cross the border and arrived safely in Paris. There he took up residence in the Bateau Lavoire of Montmartre, where he began to associate with Picasso, Amedeo Modigliani, and the French poets Max Jacob, Apollinaire, and Arthur Cravan. Arp was commissioned by old friends from Strassburg to decorate the offices and temple of the Paris Theosophical Society, a project that proved to be his last in France until his return in the 1920's. Arp and his younger brother François, also in Paris, were still in as much danger of being drafted, this time by the French army, as they had been in Germany, and both left Paris to join their parents in Zurich. In 1915 Arp made two of his most important acquaintances in Zurich: first, the artist and dancer Sophie Taueber, who became his wife in 1922; and second, the German poet Hugo Ball, who opened the Cabaret Voltaire in Zurich on 5 February 1916.

Arp and Sophie Taueber were undoubtedly among the quieter participants in the Dada evenings at the Cabaret Voltaire. Nevertheless, Sophie prepared puppets for Dada stage productions and joined dancers such as Mary Wigham from the Laban modern dance troupe in presenting avant-garde dance programs for Dada soirées. Arp was involved on all fronts of the Zurich Dada scene. He was in intense contact with the four other original Zurich dadaists: Hugo Ball, Tristan Tzara, Marcel Janco,

and Richard Huelsenbeck. He designed and painted sets for the stage and participated in poetry experiments such as the composition and performance of simultaneous poems delivered in three languages at once and in the group composition of aleatory texts. These automatic poems were part of an all-out Dada assault on reason and were precursors to the practice of automatic writing soon to be championed by the French surrealists. In one of his accounts of Dada activities in Zurich—*Unsern täglichen Traum* (Our Daily Dream, 1955)— Arp described the automatic poetry that he was writing together with Tzara and their Viennese fellow Dadaist Walter Serner:

> Automatic poetry arises directly from the poet's intestines or other organs that have stored up useful reserves. . . . The poet crows, curses, sighs, stutters, yodels, whatever seems right at the moment. His poems are like nature, they laugh, rhyme, stink like nature. Insignificant nothings, or what men call nothings, are as precious to him as the most elevated rhetoric: because in nature, every particle is as beautiful and important as a star, and only men take it upon themselves to determine what is beautiful and what is ugly.
>
> (p. 54)

At the same time that Arp was contributing to the often raucous evenings at the Cabaret Voltaire, he was absorbed by day in the texts of Böhme and Lao Tse, studying the structural means by which both philosophers were able to incorporate duality into a metaphysical model of unity. The principle of sustaining tension engendered by bipolar oppositions within a unifying structure or image was already fundamental to Arp's own work and thought. Although he had not yet discovered his own visual means by which to express it, such tension manifested itself consistently in his poetry, in particular at the level of German compound words, which he often used to embody contraries within one composite word. Arp was involved with Ball in an intensive philosophical and aesthetic dialogue on questions of Renaissance mysticism and German Romantic *Na-*

turphilosophie, discussions which Ball recorded in his diary *Die Flucht aus der Zeit* (*The Flight out of Time,* 1946). For two years Arp had also been producing duo-collages with Sophie Taueber in a subdued rectilinear cubist format. These austere duo-productions he characterized as a joint attempt to create mandalas and anonymous signposts for mystical contemplation.

Arp persevered in his search for a nonrepresentational visual style in the midst of Dada cacaphony in the Speigelgasse. The breakthrough finally came in 1917, in the village of Ascona by the Lago Maggiori in Swiss Ticino. After the strict bilateral symmetry characteristic of his 1916 Dada woodcuts, Arp suddenly shifted to the production of biomorphic forms based on a structural principle he had deduced from studying the organic debris cast up on the shores of the lake. This underlying structure, which he considered to be fundamental to natural growth and metamorphosis, Arp designated as the "fluid oval."

The fluid oval could embody processes of natural metamorphosis that the geometric figures of the perfect circle or parallelogram could not depict, and the closed elliptical curve became Arp's lifelong structural emblem for organic flux and growth. The geometrical figure of the oval, in contrast to the perfect circle, is an ellipse, a closed curve with two foci rather than one central point. Thus the fluid oval provided a visual structure that Arp could use to incorporate the bipolar tensions and energies he was already able to embrace in the language of his poems. Having arrived at his principle of the fluid oval, Arp established a style that was later adopted by the surrealists under the designation of biomorphic abstraction. It was a principle that he himself elaborated—in words, on paper, in plaster, wood, bronze, and stone—to the end of his days. The oval also evolved into Arp's most important multivalent sign; it functions, according to its context, as navel, egg, head, eyes, and as the seed in plants and in animal life. Rather than reproducing the products of nature, Arp saw

himself as creating according to natural organic laws, producing what he later designated "concrete art," natural life forms in the process of materializing out of the artist's imagination into the world. In 1917 one of the reliefs based on the structural principle of the fluid oval was given the name "Earthly Forms" by its maker. Arp soon began to use this title as a generic designation for all the biomorphic drawings, prints, and reliefs he had produced from 1917 to 1920. The organic inspiration and the irrationality of his Dada poetry and art, Arp characterized as a form of natural reason that goes beyond reason, a "without sense" that is not nonsense, a mode expressive of nature's operations, which can never be comprehended within the narrow limits of human logic. He writes in *Unsern täglichen Traum:*

> Dada is for nonsense, which does not mean without any sense. Dada is as senseless as nature and life. Dada is for nature and against art. Dada is direct like nature and like nature wants to give its essential place to each thing. Dada is moral the way nature is. Dada represents an infinite sense and finite means. For the dadaists, the meaning of art is life.
>
> (p. 50)

Arp's total output as a Dada poet actually encompasses three styles: the expressionist evocations of apocalypse, world upheaval, and ironic disjuncture in the poems we have already considered from *der vogel selbdritt,* published in 1920; the highly associative, experimental Dada texts of *die wolkenpumpe,* also published in 1920; and the more rigorously structured, rhymed "nonsense" verse that was eventually published in 1924 in the volume *Der Pyramidenrock* (The Pyramid Skirt), with certain poems that can be dated back to 1917. One element common to all these styles is the exuberant humor and playfulness that pervades the language and images of the poems, regardless of their thematic content. Arp was also working in three distinct visual styles during the immediate pre-Dada years and the Dada years: his own collages with a rectilinear cubist grid and the duo-collages he produced with Sophie Taueber; the heraldic, symmetrical woodcuts that constituted his earlier Dada illustrations; and the "earthly forms" of the later Dada years. Poems in the volume containing the most aggressively irrational Dada verse, *die wolkenpumpe,* approximate Arp's biomorphic drawings and woodcuts in their suggestiveness and in their reliance on the process of free association by artist and reader. Similarly, the strict bilateral symmetry of his patterns of verbal symmetry—that is, the succession of rhymed couplets and the pairing of lines into sets of synonyms or polar oppositions—give coherent form to Arp's "nonsense" poems of the Dada period and the early 1920's.

When the war ended in 1919, Zurich Dada had also come to its natural conclusion, with its founders dispersed throughout Europe. Ball had already left the movement in 1917; Tzara now left for Paris, Huelsenbeck for Berlin, and Arp, also for Berlin, and then for Cologne, where he met up again with his prewar friend Ernst. Arp maintained active contact with the next wave of Dada movements that emerged in Germany, Holland, and France. He was no longer, however, an official "member" of any group and was particularly distanced from the politically activist side of Berlin Dada. Nevertheless, he did continue to collaborate extensively with his friends, in particular with Ernst in Cologne and with Schwitters and his Merz movement in Hannover. Ernst left Cologne in 1922 for Paris, where he, along with Tzara, became an important figure in the emergence of French surrealism. Arp was also frequently in Paris and in close contact with Ernst, Tzara, André Breton, and Paul Eluard.

Throughout the 1920's he maintained his associations with both the surrealists and the constructivists, while exploring for himself new thematic material and compositional approaches. In 1922 Arp was in attendance at what is usually designated as the final demise of Dada, the Constructivist Congress in Weimar. Other artists present in Weimar included Tzara as well as Theo van Doesberg, the Dutch artist and architect associated with the De Stijl movement. In 1924 Arp began a close association with the Dutch abstract painter Piet Mondrian in Paris and at the same time was intimately involved in activities of the surrealists. In 1925 he participated in the first group exhibition mounted by the surrealists, and in the same year, having been refused Swiss citizenship by officials in Zurich because of the "mental derangement" attested by his poetry, he officially moved to France, where he was granted citizenship in 1926. Arp continued to write poetry in German, and his poems were then translated by one or the other of his surrealist friends into French. He himself did not compose poems directly in French until 1936. Between 1926 and 1928 he was involved, together with Sophie Taueber and Theo van Doesberg, in a large-scale constructivist project, the design and decoration of a café and dance hall, La Aubette, in Strassburg.

In 1927 his surrealist friends organized Arp's first one-man show in Paris for which Breton prepared an introduction and the catalogue for the exhibition. Arp, for his part, collaborated in publication of the review *La révolution surréaliste.* In 1927 Eugene Jolas included poems by Arp for the first time in his review *transition. Transition,* the most important English-language avant-garde publication of the 1920's and 1930's, was already committed to publishing all of James Joyce's as-yet-unnamed *Finnegans Wake* (1939) in serial form under the title "Work in Progress," and Jolas was the first editor and translator to make generally available to an English-speaking readership texts by German expressionists and dadaists as well by the French surrealists. In 1928 the constructivist Aubette opened its doors to an uncomprehending Strassburg public, and in the same year Arp exhibited in important surrealist shows in Brussels and Paris, along with Ernst, René Magritte, Joan Miró, André Masson, Man Ray, and Klee. In 1931 Arp and Taueber were among the founding members of the Paris abstract movement associated with the journal *Circle et carré* organized by their friend, the poet and painter Michel Seuphor. They remained important contributors to this group until 1934, and in 1933 Arp was influential in convincing wealthy modern art collectors in Switzerland to buy paintings by the abstract Dutch painters Mondrian and Georg Vantongerloo.

In 1934 Arp became an important liaison between the surrealists and his old friend Kandinsky, who had left what remained of the Bauhaus in Germany after Hitler's rise to power and arrived in Paris to spend the last ten years of his life in exile there. There is little doubt that Arp provided an important stimulus to Kandinsky in Kandinsky's shift in 1934 from the geometrical painting of his Bauhaus years to a biomorphic abstract style that was based on the observation of protozoa, embryonic form, and primitive, invertebrate organisms. By 1938 Kandinsky himself was no longer talking of abstract or nonrepresentational art but had taken over for his own use Arp's terminology and was writing essays on "concrete art." In 1937 Arp became a participant in a group of Swiss artists, the Allianz, which was dedicated to the cause of concrete art. Throughout the 1920's and the 1930's, what is striking about Arp's activity on the European avant-garde scene is his unusual eclecticism and his capacity to define and work in a style that embraced surrealism as well as abstract constructivism, movements that were frequently at loggerheads with one another and, on occasions, declared themselves to be diametrically opposed.

At the beginning of the 1920's Arp began to reduce his poetic and visual idiom into what he characterized as an "object language." His subject matter was no longer drawn primarily from nature; instead, it consisted of familiar, mundane human objects—plates, forks, knives, clocks, bow ties, shirtfronts, hats, buttons, and bottles—and of highly stylized parts of the human body—eyes, navels, lips, mustaches, breasts, and torsos. Arp's technique of juxtaposing these objects in unexpected combinations in his poems, drawings, and reliefs reflect in part his poetic involvement with the surrealists. Like all the surrealists, Arp was an avid reader of the nineteenth-century French poet Lautréamont and an admirer of Lautréamont's definition of the poetic metaphor: a juxtaposition of images to create a shock effect equivalent to that provoked by the fortuitous encounter of an umbrella and a sewing machine on a dissecting table. Arp's surprising combinations and amalgamations of objects in his collages and poems corresponded as well to Ernst's surrealist variation on Lautréamont's formula. Ernst's arrival in Paris had been announced with great anticipation by Breton, who admired the unpredictable, dreamlike juxtaposition of elements that Ernst achieved in his collages. Once in Paris, Ernst defined the principle of collage in terms that were received enthusiastically by the nascent surrealist movement: the collage must provide a site for the unexpected encounter of two unrelated elements on a plane alien to both. Ernst compared the desired effect of his collages to the chance meeting between a canoe and a vacuum cleaner in a forest, with the result that the canoe and the vacuum cleaner make love.

Arp's object language lent itself to such surrealist encounters and pairings, and in the first group exhibition mounted by the surrealists he announced the marriage between elements of his object language in works with titles such as "Navel-Bottle," "Bird-Mask," "Rhymed Stones," and "Mountain, Navel, Anchor, Table." The object language also made its way into the seven "Arpaden" that Arp produced for Schwitters in the fifth issue of *Merz* in 1923. The "Arpaden," a term that Arp had also used for poems published in *die wolkenpumpe*, appeared in *Merz* 5 as a suite of black-and-white woodcuts that embodied Arp's object combinations such as the "navel-bottle," the "mustache-hat," and the "mustache-clock." Schwitters' *Merz* publications in the 1920's were representative of the constructivist style that had evolved from Dada in Germany and Holland at the same time surrealism had developed out of Dada in Paris.

Arp, as we have emphasized, was one of the few artists to remain in close contact with both movements, and his object language could accommodate itself to either style, visually and verbally.

The object language appeared throughout the 1920's in poems that are more concentrated and laconic than Arp's freewheeling verse from the Dada years. Yet the reduced objects themselves are still polysemic and capable of all the radical and unexpected interactions that took place between words and images in the Dada and pre-Dada texts. In the group of poems "Vier Knöpfe zwei Löcher vier Besen (Four Buttons Two Holes Four Brooms, 1924), seven knives, four holes, four buttons, and four brooms are swept up in a mock heroic apocalypse comparable to the upheavals enacted by words in *der vogel selbdritt*:

> From the seven knives, two plunge themselves
> into the light.
> Greedily they cut two circular holes into the heart
> of light.
> Out of the two holes fall four buttons, two holes,
> and four brooms.
> When holes fall out of holes
> the buttons spring from the mountains.
> The table drawers can no longer be opened.
> The trains come to a standstill.
> Ditto the clocks, the windmill wings, the walking
> sticks.
>
> (1.176)

Arp's poem oscillates radically from the mundane and concrete to the purely abstract: from two kitchen knives to holes falling out of holes, from household utensils to an assault on the heart of light. The same oscillation prevails between commonplace annoyance and tragedy on a grand scale: from the banality of a button popping off to suicide leaps from mountain peaks; from the everyday frustration experienced at a stuck drawer to national disasters in which trains and clocks are stopped. The seemingly innocuous, absurd image of unbuttoned mountains can be read in the poem's context of catastrophe as an earthquake or erupting volcano. In terms of Arp's own poetic iconography, real catastrophe has struck when the windmills—and, by implication, the winds—and the walking sticks—which in earlier poems are able to wander on their own to the outermost limits of the universe—are brought to a standstill. This disaster depicted in Arp's object language of the 1920's is ironic, comic, banal, abstract, and cosmic all at once, and each of the object words he deploys is called upon to manifest in itself the entire emotional register of the poem and its radical shifts in perspective.

Bipolar, generative energies are brought to the fore and exhibited in the structuring of many of Arp's poems from the 1920's. The title of one of his most important collections of poems, *weisst du schwarzt du,* written in 1922 and published in 1930 with illustrations by Ernst, plays with the primary opposition of white to black. Arp puns on the German verb *wissen* (to know), which in the second person singular present tense becomes *du weisst,* in order to create two new verbs *weissen* and *schwarzen,* derived from the German adjectives for white and black, *weiss* and *schwarz.* A literal translation of Arp's neologisms would be "if you white, you black." Poems from this collection often evolve dialectically in terms of one word or phrase evoking its opposite, for example, in the first half of the first poem:

> They walk a square
> a circle
> a point
> and rotate on the point
> punctually halfway round
> and continue
> and don't want to rat out
> on the rat-round mat
> at the twelfth-most flat
> and shorten the short
> and lengthen the long
> and thin down the thin
> and fatten the fat
> and always remain face-to-face.
>
> (1.126)

1373

Here Arp reconciles the square to the circle and reduces the two mutually exclusive geometrical figures to a point, which then divides and develops anew through a progression of contraries. Each half-rotation around the point is met by the complementary and opposite 180-degree rotation. The point itself is transformed into a clock when Arp introduces it as the adverb "punctually." The rotation of the hand around the clock from six o'clock to twelve o'clock is balanced by a mirror image of rotation in the opposite direction, throughout which the elements remain "face-to-face," in generative opposition.

In the 1930's Arp introduced a number of new compositional approaches to his visual art as well as to his poetry. The death of his mother in 1929 left a profound impression on Arp and his attitude toward artistic creation. On the one hand, it seems to have triggered in him a longing for permanence, for assurance against the inevitable decomposition of all organic life forms; on the other, it awakened a need to integrate actual death and destruction into the act of composing the work of art. Arp's response to this psychological crisis was a return to his earlier observation of processes of growth and metamorphosis in nature, but his focus now widened to emphasize more than ever the complete natural cycle of birth, growth, decline, and death. Arp's yearning for permanence found expression in a new medium, that of sculpture. "Concrétion humaine" ("Human Concretion") was the title he gave to many of the initial sculptures he produced in the early 1930's, the term *concretion* he defined as the "natural process of condensation, hardening, coagulation, thickening, growing together." As he branched out into the production of sculptural concretions, Arp began to experiment with two other compositional techniques that he felt also embodied processes of nature: torn-paper collages and the permutation of a limited number of elements in reliefs, in collages, and in his poems. The first papers Arp tore up for recombination into new works were some of his own Dada drawings and prints that he had discovered mildewed and disintegrating because of inadequate storage conditions in his attic. Soon he also began tearing up coarsely grained black paper and pasting the torn fragments on white paper. One result of this technique was to expose the individual fibers of each torn edge, giving his pasted collage elements the impression of having received an electric shock that had left their hair standing on end. This tearing of papers and drawings for collages and the breaking up of one combination of elements so that those elements might be reconstituted into another configuration Arp regarded as an enactment of the organic cycle of combination, separation, and recombination of basic elements in nature. To his own varied arrangements and combinations of such elements, he gave the collective title "constellations."

Arp referred to the natural law that expresses itself in the perpetual reordering and constellating of given elements as the "law of chance." There is considerable evidence that Arp's concept of the law of chance grew out of his lifelong interest in the texts of Lao Tse and in the constellations cast with yarrow sticks and interpreted in the Chinese Book of Changes, the *I Ching.* Although Arp evoked the law of chance most often in dicussions of his torn-paper collages, in *Unsern täglichen Traum* he also cites the principle in retrospect to describe the work he and Sophie Taueber had been producing in 1915, even before Zurich Dada:

> I continued to develop the collage by allowing the order of elements to be determined automatically, without any interference from my own volition. I called this approach working in accord with the law of chance. This law of chance, which contains within it all laws and is as incomprehensible to us as the primal ground from which all life arises, can only be experienced by total surrender to processes of the unconscious. I maintained that whoever follows this law will create pure life.
>
> (p. 74)

Works that he and Taueber produced in accordance with the law of chance Arp designates as concrete art. Again in *Unsern täglichen Traum,* he writes:

> In 1915, Sophie Taueber and I painted, embroidered, and pasted together works that were probably the first examples of concrete art. These works are self-contained, independent realities. They have no logical meaning; they are not products of a reality that can be conceptualized. We discarded everything that had to do with imitation or description so as to give free play to the elementary, the spontaneous in us. Because the distribution of the planes, their interrelationship and their color could not be rationalized, I declared these works to be ordered by the law of chance. For me, chance is but an aspect of the inexplicable reason, the incomprehensible order that governs nature.
>
> (p. 51)

The principle of constellating and reconstellating a limited number of elements is one that Arp also applied to words. A moving example of this poetic technique, written soon after the death of his mother, is a series of variations that Arp called "Träume vom Tod und Leben" (Dreams of Life and Death, 1930). Jolas published one set of these variations under the title of "The Skeleton of the Day" (Das Tagesgerippe in German) in 1930 in a special section of *transition* titled "The Laboratory of the Word." Each stanza of "The Skeleton of the Day" presents a new constellation of a basic series of elements, including leaves, wings, bells, words, hands, eyes, lips, fire, light, and earth. Normally, these elements are signs of fecundity and the propagation of formal energies in Arp's work, but this poem constellates dreams of death as well as life. The first two stanzas introduce Arp's object-words as signs of life, even though a shadow of impending formlessness and the loss of identity is cast over the eyes and the flames:

> The eyes converse like flames on waves.
> The eyes would like to withdraw from the days.
> The flames have no name.

> Each flame has five fingers.
> The hands caress the wings in the sky.

> Out of the words the lips emerge
> like beauty from the waves of the day.
> Beauty is embraced by light
> like the bell by kisses.

In the third stanza, the constellation is already one of death, in which names will perish and the graves are brighter than the light of day:

> But what has come in its place?
> The wings fall from the peak of the table
> like earthen leaves
> before the lips.
> Night is entrenched in the wings.
> The skeleton of light empties the fruits.
> The body of kisses will never awaken.
> It was never real.
> The sea of the wings rocks these tears.
> The bell speaks with the head
> and the fingers lead us through the fields of air
> to the nests of the eyes
> Where the names perish.
> But what has come in its place?
> In the height of the sky
> neither sleep nor wakefulness
> for the graves are brighter than the days.

By the seventh stanza, the elements have constellated themselves into an elegiac lament at the death not only of an individual but potentially of the earth itself:

> Where are the leaves?
> The bells have withered.
> It no longer rings upon earth
> where once we walked.
> The light is in shreds.
> The tracks of the wings lead into emptiness.
> Where are the lips?
> Where are the eyes?
> Hideous their heart shattered between the heads.
> The last breath drops like a stone from the bodies.
> Where once we spoke blood now runs from the fire
> and the formless wreath turns over in the black
>   ground.
> Forever invisible the beautiful earth.
> The wings no longer hover over us.
>
> (1.228–232)

1375

Not until the poems written after the death of his wife, Sophie Taueber, in 1943 does Arp approach the elegiac intensity that he reaches via the word-constellations in "The Skeleton of the Day." The constellation poems, however, can also be poems celebrating birth and the renewal of life, as announced in a series of elements presented in the first stanza of "Davos Configuration II" (1930):

The egg of fire. The egg of water. The egg of
    in a silken sack. The egg of air.
The standing man and the standing woman. The
    Sitting man and the sitting woman. The lying
    man and the lying woman.
The ladder of bone leans against the trunk of flesh.
The man has a staff of bone. The woman has a staff
    of flesh.
The standing egg. The sitting egg. The lying egg.

This constellation poem progresses through a series of dismemberings and recombinations that ultimately lead to a stanza of sexual union between man and woman and to an image of profound reintegration of mankind into nature:

If a stone falls from its stem, a woman comes
    with her apron of water and leans the ladder
    of bone against the egg of fire.
The woman's hat of flesh greets the man's staff
    of bone.
The landscape of air fills up with men and women
    who tear off their leaves, break in their hats,
    hurl all the letters of the alphabet at the
    flying eggs.
The stem of fire. The stem of earth.
The leaves of man. The leaves of woman.

                 (1.200–204)

The result of Arp's constellations in "Davos Configuration II" is his own variation on the German Romantic *Urpflanze,* or primal plant, as it was originally envisioned by the poet Johann Wolfgang von Goethe. By the end of the constellation series, destruction, separation, and recombination have resulted in an integrated expression of growth that incorporates the four primal elements and transcends the division of organic forms into animal and vege-

table life and the separation of the sexes. Human beings find themselves reintegrated into a natural rhythm of genesis as leaves, receiving and generating life forces and transmitting these energies through stems of fire and air. The power of words to initiate such transformations was defined by Arp in the 1933 article "Transition's Revolution-of-the-Word Dictionary." Arp gave all his constellation poems the generic title "configuration"; Jolas explains in his dictionary what Arp meant by the term: "Configuration (Hans Arp) . . . creative production that combines the images and the sounds of the unconscious without the intervention of reason." Arp's lifelong interest in the Romantics and his affinity with the poetics of surrealism combine to produce this definition of the configuration, an alternative designation for his compositional principle of "constellation." With Arp's final image in the "Davos Configuration II," a theme is announced that reappears as the title of his collected works in French: *Jours effeuillés.* Arp played on countless occasions with the dual significance of the most common French and German nouns for "page": *feuille* and *Blatt.* The leaf of the page is the same word as that for the leaf of a plant. Integral components in the life of plants, leaves—as well as flowers and fruits—are immediate demonstrations of the plant's productivity and growth. The title of Arp's collected volume of his poetry, *Jours effeuillés,* seems to imply that pages of poetry must grow daily from the poet's pen. Words on pages can convey life-giving forces to and from the natural environment, just as leaves, growing from the plant, convert sunlight into organic nourishment, and return oxygen to the atmosphere. In his essay "L'art concret" ("Concrete Art") in *Jours effeuillés,* Arp specified that the work of art must grow and mature like a fruit on the tree, but the leaves of plants and paper seem to offer an equally appropriate metaphor for artistic creation, especially in light of Arp's twentieth-century variation on the Romantic aesthetic, which demanded that the artist attempt to restore mankind's ruptured relationship with nature and reintegrate human production into the generative processes of nature.

The years 1940 to 1942 Arp and Sophie Taueber spent in semi-exile with fellow artists in Grasse, an extremely productive period for all involved. Arp's activities in Grasse, a temporary refuge from German occupation forces in World War II, paralleled many aspects of his artistic life in Dada Zurich, a similar situation in which he worked closely with other artists in exile during World War I. In Grasse he and Sophie now participated with Sonia Delaunay and Alberto Magnelli in the collaborative production of lithographs. In his own drawings Arp returned to the india ink biomorphic abstraction of the Dada years, and these works frequently recapture the immediacy and vitality of his Dada drawings. Often he had no access to paintbrushes, so he began to dip his fingers into black tempera and paint directly with his hand onto the page. Because of the wartime scarcity of paper, Arp invented yet another compositional procedure dictated by the necessity to draw on wrinkled paper that had been used to wrap parcels when no other paper was available. He was soon re-creating the effect of these *papiers froissés* (wrinkled papers) by crumpling unused sheets of paper for his work, in particular for the finger paintings.

The poetry from the years in Grasse, for the most part in French, makes highly sophisticated and original use of the hermetic themes and images that had so fascinated Arp's fellow surrealists in Paris and had played a role in Arp's poems even before his Dada days. These poems present in surprising new combinations the iconography of alchemy depicting the unification of opposites in terms of the sexual union between man and woman. These "alchemical" texts, dedicated to Robert Delaunay, who had died at the beginning of the Arps' stay in Grasse, were published privately in 1941 in the collection *Poèmes sans prénoms* (Poems without First Names) with illustrations by Sophie Taueber. Arp's hermetic Renaissance and Baroque sources reveal themselves unmistak-

ably in the imagery of "Je suis un point" ("I am a point") from this collection. With his period/point, Arp reactivates a Renaissance emblem of center point and circle, the micro/macrocosmic structure in which the microcosmic point contains all the potential actualized in the macrocosmic whole. Arp was intimately acquainted with Renaissance, Pythagorean, and medieval geometrical mysticism. The image of the center projecting the circle was all but an intuitive element of his formal vocabulary. He modifies the image, however, as did Böhme, and renders the center in terms of its implicit duality. The center is bifocated to engender an elliptical curve, or oval, and the bifocal point develops in the sense of Böhme's *aufgetahner Punkt* (exfoliating point).

The initial figure of this poem—included in *Jours effeuillés*—is that of the circle squared, a geometrical representation of the alchemical unification of opposites, in this case male and female. The poet as point projects himself into a complementary point in his visionary dream charged with the imagery of alchemical sublimation, coagulation, and crystallization. The microcosmic point, projected into its dream double, dilates to embrace the macrocosm, eternity reaching to the four corners of terrestrial space:

> I am a point
> and dream of a point
> four-cornered eternity.
> I lance my lance into the eye of the heart.
> My feet balance the air.

The point exfoliates as contraries begin to interact, engendering one another in the dream projection. Heights produce depths, and sublimation is accompanied by coagulation into organic life:

> I lick the high and the low.
> The soul of the heart takes flight
> and plants an animal.
> The animal swells up
> and laughs
> and fans out across the air.

The point is spun into a rotating wheel, the result of interaction between the opposing forces of centrifugal and centripetal motion. The wheel of contraries spins through a series of images which are preceded by all shades of red—in alchemy the color that announces the successful marriage of contraries:

> I turn the wheels of reds.
> I turn my key
> like this.
> I close the door.
> I close the circle.
> Finally the water wells up between you and me
> and carries the us
> this way
> that way
> like this
> like that.
> A bell sings within my mouth
> like this
> like that.
> It is the hour of the minute.
> It is the hour of the air.
>
> (p. 171)

The hermetic circle closed, the process of transmutation commences within the vessel of the heart, or the alchemical retort. The initial "I" of the poem is divided into a "you" and a "me," whereby a new synthesis is reached, the "us." A new set of contraries now engenders itself, contraries reduced to the most simple clichés of direction and manner: "This way / That way," "Like this / Like that." A resonance at the cores of Arp's bipolar structures is struck, and a bell sings within the vessel of the poet's mouth, resounding throughout the chamber of the head. Time itself is simultaneously crystallized into the point of a minute and sublimated into an endless expanse of the air, diffused from an initial point in time to the four corners of eternity.

Arp and Sophie finally left Grasse at the end of 1942; all their attempts to emigrate to the United States via Marseilles, port of departure for most of the surrealists who managed to es-

cape from France, had come to naught. The surge of productivity and renewed artistic experimentation in the Grasse years was cut brutally short by Sophie Taueber's accidental death on 12 January 1943 in Zurich. Devastated by shock and remorse, Arp's initial response as an artist was complete paralysis. Gradually, however, simple elegiac lines for Taueber began to emerge, and from these fragments Arp began to build up poems:

> I speak little, everyday phrases
> softly to myself.
> To give myself courage
> to distract myself
> to forget the great sorrow,
> the great helplessness in which we live.
> I speak little, simple phrases.
> The seas are flowers.
> The clouds are flowers.
> The stars are flowers
> that bloom in the sky.
> The moon is a flower.
> But the moon is also a giant teardrop.
>
> (2.49)

A series of highly unstructured, profoundly disturbing gray-on-gray watercolors titled "La vie de pinceau" (Life of the Brush) provided the transition from Arp's artistic paralysis to resumption of his work as painter, even though he did not sculpt again for another four years. The faint traces of black-and-white figuration that emerge out of the gray depths of "La vie de pinceau" constitute Arp's first tentative steps back to full-scale production of his visual configurations, constellations, and concretions.

The poetry throughout the 1940's, however, rarely departed from the haunting, tragic evocation of Taueber's absence and of Arp's most traumatic and personal confrontation with death and irreconcilable human loss. Indeed, this elegiac tone never ceased to overshadow the old inventive playfulness that still resurfaced from time to time in his late writing. Nonetheless, out of his helpless despair at

Taueber's death, Arp managed to create some of his most remarkable texts, such as the poem "Die Ebene" ("The Plain," 1945) in which an endless undifferentiated blue begins to approximate the gray-on-gray monochromatic void characteristic of almost all "La vie de pinceau." A chair is all that is left of discernible form on earth in this startling and vivid evocation of entropy—the irreversible negation of all formative energy and all potential for differentiation—rendered here as a vast, unbroken expanse of asphalt:

I found myself alone with a chair on a plain
  that lost itself in an empty horizon.
The plain was flawlessly covered with asphalt.
Nothing, but absolutely nothing, could be
  distinguished on it besides myself and the chair.
The sky was interminably blue.
There was no sun to bring it to life.
An inexplicable, rational light illuminated the
  endless plain.
This eternal day seemed to me artificially projected
  out of some other sphere.
I was never sleepy nor hungry nor thirsty nor hot
  nor cold.
Since nothing happened or changed on this plain
Time was but a far-removed ghost.
Time still lived a little in me
and primarily because of the chair.
Because of activities I undertook with the chair
I did not wholly lose my sense of the past.
Off and on I hitched myself before the chair
like a horse
And trotted with it, first in a circle and then
straight ahead.
That this procedure was successful I can assume.
If it were indeed a success I cannot determine.
There was nothing present in space
against which I could measure my movement.
Whenever I sat on the chair I pondered in sorrow
but without despair
why the center of the earth should emit such a
black light.

(2.47–48)

In the mid 1940's Arp began to make new use of the torn-paper collage—the technique developed in response to his mother's death—to prepare illustrations for new publications by old Dada friends. For example, all the woodcuts in Tzara's *Vingt cinq et un poèmes* (1946) (Twenty-five Poems Plus One) Arp composed by tearing up and recombining prints from the volumes he had illustrated for Tzara during the Dada years. Meanwhile, Arp's own writing was becoming better known and the first anthology of his verse in French, *Le siège de l'air* (The Seat of Air) appeared in 1946. It was followed in 1948 by an anthology of writings in English translation, *On My Way*, published in New York, and in 1953 by an anthology of his poetry in German, *worttraüme und schwarze sterne* (Word-Dreams and Black Stars), published in Wiesbaden.

Although Arp was writing much of his poetry in French in the 1940's and 1950's, his thematic material and images still reflect his early interest in the German Romantic *Naturphilosophie* and in the texts of Böhme. One example is the poem "Pousses" ("Sprouts"), written in 1953 and included in *Jours effeuillés:*

The light strews pearls throughout a garden.
Beautiful sprouts started on their way
play of pearls.
Long live the pearls!
Living columns, svelte
cadence of the stalks.
Shadow and stalk seem to merge
and now they leave the dream
and grow up like blades into the blue.
A life of infinite instants.
From every sprout springs forth a hand
and five sprouts from every hand.
Memories of sighs cause their mouths to open
enveloped in veils of vegetative stars.
The articulating cavities begin to foam and
  whistle
lace of veins
Adamic perfume.
The furious stalks disperse themselves
like lightning in an immense depth of flesh.
The superior members raise themselves and extend
  beyond the trunk

Masses of filaments, taut, delirious.
At last the fine consonants
emerge from their sheaths of embalmed moon.
The tortoiseshell fan of a lovely surrounding
is poised not far from the play of pearls.

(p. 395)

This poem was designated by Arp to accompany a mongraph on the sculpture of François Stahly, a young friend of Arp's in Meudon whose work embodies a sense of organic growth similar to that in Arp's own sculpture.

Arp frequently uses the point, or the period, not as a punctuation sign to mark the end of a sentence but as a sign of beginning, representing an initial moment of organic genesis. Here he transforms the point into the double image of pearl and dewdrop, signaling the plethora of growth announced in the title "Sprouts." With the reflections of the morning sunrise in the dewdrops, the germinating interplay of pearls, points, light, and sprouts begins, and the cry "Vive les perles" (Long live the pearls) launches new life into its next phase of the growth, differentiation, and development of stems. Each dewdrop/pearl/point/sprout is a microcosmic expression of infinite potential for universal growth, growth that must be initiated in each discrete instance of germination. Life in the garden is one of the infinite instants and instant infinities, the extreme of contraries and contradiction compacted into every germinative point. Man and plant become one expression of growth, as each sprout ramifies into a hand and every hand produces, in turn, five-finger sprouts. Stems, stars, and bones become one in a cosmic weave, in a veil of plant-stars. Breath is introduced to the poem, and articulation can begin. The articulation is that of what Böhme called the Adamic tongue, in which the act of naming is one with that of creating. The web of differentiating life is sublimated into the diffuse perfume of man before the fall, and the stems and veins separate and structure a cosmic body of flesh that echoes Böhme's concept of the materialized cosmos as divine corporeality. In Böhme's texts every instance in which the divinity begins to materialize itself into a corporeal universe is initiated by a spark, or what Böhme often calls a lightning flash, struck between contraries. From the cadence of stems, growth in Arp's poem culminates in the actual power of speech. This is the last seed to germinate—the word as logos, which man himself may pronounce in order to create life. The primal generative point of the poem "Sprouts" is not to be understood as one single starting point from which all life develops. Rather, the germinating point repeats itself in each individual instance of growth. Every moment of germination is an instant infinity, life itself the cadence of such instants. The play of pearls in the first and final image is effervescent; dewdrops alight in the sun before they evaporate. There is no suggestion that the pearls are strung together in a continuous chain. Instead, they are strewn at random like seeds, glittering from the tips of freshly germinated sprouts, sparkling in momentary configurations, each point a potential expression of the infinite.

Böhme also combined the image of the pearl with that of the germinating sprout. A trembling *Perlenzweig* (pearl branch) is born at the moment of shock, the confrontation of opposites. The pearl branch itself embodies the conjunction of opposites as it grows into glorious life that is born out of angst and death. An example of how Böhme uses this image is to be found in the second volume of his *Von der Menschen Werdung Jesu Christi* (*Concerning the Incarnation of Christ,* 1620):

So when his angst tastes of freedom, realizing that it is such a quiet and gentle source, at that moment the angst source recoils and in this shock, the bitter inimical death is shattered, because the shock is one of greatest joy and the ignition of divine love. And thus the pearl branch is born, it stands now in trembling joy, but also in great danger, for death and the source of angst are its root and its surroundings, just as a lovely green branch grows up out of stinking manure and receives another essence, smell, being and source than that of its mother from which it is born: the source of nature is characterized in the same way, that out of evil, out of angst, glorious life is born.

(Jakob Böhme, *Sämmtlichte Schriften*, ed. by Peuckert, Stuttgart, 1957, vol. 4, p. 172)

Arp and Böhme develop their images of sprouts or the pearl branch with identical dynamics and with the same final goal. Arp's germinative process culminates, as does Böhme's, in glorious life accompanied by sublimation of earth into another smell, the "Adamic perfume." Arp's lightning flashes, like Böhme's moment of shock and ignition, play in the cosmic depths of materialized flesh. There is no way to prove that Arp had actually read this very passage, but the compacted image of the pearl, the shock, and the igniting lightning flash occurs again and again in Böhme's texts. "Sprouts" is an interesting demonstration of how Arp, through the use of certain key images, incorporated into his poems Böhme's dialectical interpretation of organic growth as the manifestation of divine corporeality in the process of becoming.

Arp continued to illustrate books for friends throughout the 1950's, including collections by Ivan Goll and Alexander Frey. The illustrations for these volumes are examples of a new style Arp adopted, drawings and prints with nervous, irregular lines that his second wife, Marguerite Hagenbach—referring to their similarity with the lines produced by seismographs—designated as "earthquake-lines." In the 1950's Arp also undertook the production of a number of major graphic folios published in limited editions to accompany his own texts and the texts of others. The most important of these series was *Dreams and Projects* (1952), a folio of twenty-eight woodcuts with Arp's prose and poems in French, German, and English translation, commissioned and published by his friend, the New York art dealer Kurt Valentine.

Two other important folios appeared in the 1960's, *Vers le blanc infini* (Towards White Infinity, 1960) and *Le soleil recerclé* (The Recircled Sun, 1966). The eight etchings and eight poems of *Vers le blanc infini* comprise Arp's most eloquent, sustained homage to Sophie Taueber. *Le soleil recerclé*, with sixteen woodcuts, contains seventeen poems in French, most of them previously unpublished.

In the final decade of his life, from 1955 to 1966, Arp, at long last financially independent as a world-famous sculptor, was able to travel extensively, making trips to the United States, Mexico, Greece, Israel, and Egypt. His health, however, became more and more fragile, and he suffered a series of heart attacks that kept him bedridden for considerable periods of time. Arp's sense of his own impending death, in addition to the loss of Taueber, played a more and more obvious role in his poetry of the late 1950's and 1960's. Many of the poems became overtly religious, oscillating between despair at man's desperate lot on earth and appeals to angels for some sign of the "sacred infinity," of "the great eternal feast." Yet Arp's lyric imagination continued to transport him beyond the obvious in many of his poems. The earlier magical figures from romantic fairy tales even resurface on occasion in poems such as "Ein Stag fährt Gondel" (Gondola Travel) of 1956:

> A stag is rowing his gondola.
> Legendarily he shakes his antler crown
> overgrown like a Christmas tree
> with rosy-red cheeks
> sceptres of glass
> rhymed objects.
> Before him in the gondola
> in a large wicker basket
> lies a long black beard
> filled with will-o'-the-wisps
> tractable lightning flashes
> sundial petals
> tiny spoons that stick out their tongues.
> Unfortunately the stag is not able
> to mount all his pretty things

in his antler crown.
But the antlers might still grow
and then each thing
could find its place there.
The stag asks nothing more
than the right to row on undisturbed
and legendarily to shake
his whispering antler crown.

(1.231)

Although Arp's creative energies as a visual artist were in decline in the 1960's, words were still able to lead him down paths as yet unmarked on his earlier pages. The 1961 extended homage to the life of words, "Worte" (Words), contains one of the most appropriate characterizations of Arp's own indebtedness to words throughout his lifelong imaginative exploration of man's precarious existence on this earth:

Words from mouth to abyss.
Words for fishing in cloudy waters.
Appropriate wordplays
for devilishly dark depths.

(3.132)

But words, in turn, are indebted to Arp, the poet, and to the pages on which he printed and illustrated them. The intent was always the same; again, it is best expressed in "Worte":

Words that are the dream light
of a shadow existence.
A word-bouquet
that lets all its flowers
speak up at once.

(3.130)

The poet's word, black on white, leaves an imprint of meaning, of demarcation on the page. Like so many of the black lines drawn on paper by his brush, however, the contours of Arp's words are invariably ambivalent, suggesting much more than that which they literally spell out across the page. Diverse images and levels of reference within words and visual forms must be activated and brought to light within the context and organization of the page. It is up to the artist or poet to create the page as an environment in which chosen words or forms can unfold to reveal their multiplicity of meanings. The multivalence of words is at the crux of the poet's imaginative use of language, and Arp's insistence on multivalent readings for all his works bears witness to the poetic impulse underlying his artistic production, be it visual or verbal.

Arp's fundamental approach to all questions of form is documented in a penciled note found in his papers after his death in 1966 and now in the archives of the Fondation Jean Arp et Sophie Taueber-Arp in Clamart, France:

Seed-forms
Logi spermatiroi [sic]
Rationes seminales
The radience [sic] of forms

Forms that give birth to new forms, words that engender new words are the means by which the artist may produce "radient form," form that is open-ended, generating perpetual new energies, interpretations, and life. For Arp valid formal expression was seminal, never final. Unable to declare any of his own works to be irreversibly finished, he initiated ever-new variations on what already existed, and many of these variations were then chosen to stand on their own alongside the originals. Arp also produced variation after variation on his poems, making any definitive dating of the poetry a bibliographer's nightmare. With all his variations, Arp sought to uncover new layers of meaning and unexpected correspondences in language. Through his elaboration of puns, in the verbal arabesques that grew out of an initial sound, word, or image, with the permutation of a limited set of verbal elements, Arp invited, coaxed, and cajoled words to expose themselves, to recombine and propagate themselves in ever-new configurations on ever-new pages. For this reason Arp's encounters with words were a stimulus to all the creative personalities with whom he was involved throughout his life. And for this reason he continues to intrigue and inspire poets today in search of new ways to release the endless generative energies that Arp demonstrated, poem by poem, to be present in the written and the spoken word.

Selected Bibliography

GERMAN EDITIONS

INDIVIDUAL WORKS

der vogel selbdritt. Berlin, 1920.
die wolkenpumpe. Hannover, 1920.
Der Pyramidenrock. Zurich and Munich, 1924.
Konfiguration. Paris, 1930.
weisst du schwarzt du. Zurich, 1930.
Muscheln und Schirme. Meudon, 1939.
Auch das ist nur eine Wolke. Basel, 1951.
wortträume und schwarze sterne. Wiesbaden, 1953.
Behaarte Herzen, Könige vor der Sintflut. Frankfurt am Main, 1955.
Auf einem Bein. Wiesbaden, 1955.
Unsern täglichen Traum, Errinerungen, Dichtungen und Betrachtungen aus den Jahren 1914–1954. Zurich, 1955.
Worte mit und ohne Anker. Wiesbaden, 1959.
Mondsand. Pfüllingen, 1960.
Zweiklang: Sophie Taueber Arp–Hans Arp. Zurich, 1960.
Sinnende Flammen. Zurich, 1961.
Logbuch des Traumkapitäns. Zurich, 1965.

COLLECTED WORKS

Gesammelte Gedichte. Vol. 1, 1903–1939. Wiesbaden and Zurich, 1963. Vol. 2, 1939–1965. Wiesbaden and Zurich, 1974. Vol. 3, 1957–1966. Wiesbaden and Zurich, 1984.

FRENCH EDITIONS

INDIVIDUAL WORKS

Des taches dans le vide. Paris, 1937.
Sciure de gammes. Paris, 1938.
Poèmes sans prénoms. Grasse, 1941.
Rire de coquille. Amsterdam, 1944.
Le blanc aux pieds de nègre. Paris, 1945.
Le siège de l'air. Poèmes 1915–1945. Paris, 1946.

Le voilier dans la forêt: Poèmes. Paris, 1957.
Vers le blanc infini. Lausanne, Paris, 1960.
L'ange et la rose. Forcalquier, 1965.

COLLECTED WORKS

Le Soleil recerclé. 1966.
Jours effeuillés: Poèmes, essais, souvenirs 1920–1965. Paris, 1966.

TRANSLATIONS

Arp on Arp. Edited by Marcel Jean. Translated by Joachim Neugroschel. New York, 1972.
The Dada Painters and Poets. Edited by Robert Motherwell. New York, 1951. Includes selected translations of Arp's poems.
Dreams and Projects. Translated by Ralph Manheim. New York, 1951–1952.
On My Way: Poetry and Essays, 1912–1947. Translated by Ralph Manheim. New York, 1948.
Read, Herbert. The Art of Jean Arp. New York, 1968. Includes selected translations of Arp's poems.
Three Painter/Poets: Arp, Schwitters, Klee. Edited and translated by Harriett Watts. Harmondsworth, England, 1974. Includes selected translations of Arp's poetry.

BIOGRAPHICAL AND CRITICAL STUDIES

Ades, Dawn. Dada and Surrealism. London, 1974.
Bleikaston, Aimée. "Jean Hans Arp: The Voice of the Poet," Arp: 1886–1966. Stuttgart, 1986.
Döhl, Reinhold. Das literarische Werk Hans Arps. 1903–1930. Stuttgart, 1967.
Forster, Stephen and Rudolf, Kuenzli eds. Dada Spectrum: Dialectics of Revolt. Iowa City, Iowa 1979. Includes Alistair Grieve, "Arp in Zurich" and Richard Sheppard, "Dada and Mysticism: Influences and Affinities."
Forster, Stephen, ed. Dada Dimensions. Ann Arbor, Mich., 1985. See Jane Hancock, "Arp's Chance Collages" and Harriett Watts, "Periods and Commas: Arp's Seminal Punctuation."
Giedion-Welcker, Carola. Hans Arp. Stuttgart, 1957.
Grieve, Alistair. "Arp in Zurich." In Dada Spectrum: Dialectics of Revolt. Edited by Stephen Forster and Rudolf Kuenzli. Iowa City, Iowa, 1979.
Hancock, Jane. "Arp's Chance Collages." In Dada Dimensions. Edited by Stephen Forster. Ann Arbor, Mich., 1985.

———. "Die Philosophie in Arps Former sprache—Versudi einer Deutung." *Arp: 1886–1966.* Stuttgart, 1986.

Last, R. W. *Hans Arp: The Poet of Dadaism.* London, 1969.

———. *German Dadaist Literature: Kurt Schwitters, Hugo Ball, Hans Arp.* New York, 1973.

Liede, Alfred. "Hans Arp und der Tod." In *Dichtung als Spiel.* Vol. I. Berlin, 1965.

Marchiori, Giuseppe. *Arp, Fifty Years of Activity.* London, 1964.

Michand, Eric. "Hans Arp zwischen Himmel und Hölle': Die Ethik in der Sprache der Kunst." *Arp: 1886–1966.* Stuttgart, 1986.

Poley, Stephanie. *Hans Arp: Die Formensprache im plastischen Werk.* Stuttgart, 1978.

Read, Herbert. *The Art of Jean Arp.* London, New York, 1968.

Richter, Hans. *Dada, Art and Anti-Art.* London, 1965.

Rubin, William. *Dada, Surrealism and Their Heritage.* New York, 1968.

Seuphor, Michel. *Mission spirituelle de l'art.* Paris, 1953.

———. *Les sources litteraires chez Arp et Mondrian.* Geneva, 1974.

Sheppard, Richard. "Dada and Mysticism: Influences and Affinities." In *Dada Spectrum: Dialectics of Revolt.* Edited by Stephen Forster and Rudolf Kuenzli. Iowa City, Iowa. 1979.

Soby, James Thrall, ed. *Arp.* Garden City, N. Y., 1958.

Trier, Eduard, intro. and ed. *Jean Arp, Sculptures: His Last Ten Years.* Translated by Karen Philippson. New York, 1968.

Usinger, Fritz. *Hüldigung für Hans Arp.* Merzhausen, 1981.

Watts, Harriett. "Periods and Commas: Arp's Seminal Punctuation." In *Dada Dimensions.* Edited by Stephen Forster. Ann Arbor, Mich., 1985.

———. "Arp, Kandinsky and the Legacy of Jakob Boehme." *The Spiritual in Art: Abstract Painting. 1890–1985.* New York, 1986.

———. "Hans Arp als Dichter." *Hans Arp zum 100 Geburtstag i ein Lese- und Bilderbuch.* Zurich, 1986.

———. "Hans Arp and the Principle of Constellations." *Hans Arp: 1886–1966.* Stuttgart, 1986.

BIBLIOGRAPHY:

Bleikasten, Aimée. *Hans Arp.* 2 vols. London, 1981.

HARRIETT WATTS

HERMANN BROCH
(1886–1951)

INDUSTRIALIST AND POET, mathematician and mystic, rationalist and irrationalist—these are the points of Hermann Broch's emotional compass. His attempt to chart them successively in philosophy, literature, and political action constitutes the basic impulse of his life. Distinguishing between the main trends of contemporary thought, he referred to the position of the positivists as *cogito ergo sum,* and that of more existentially oriented thinkers as *sum ergo cogito.* For himself, he concluded, the most satisfactory formulation was *cogito et sum,* with the emphasis on the synthesizing conjunction.

Broch longed for totality and simultaneity—two words that occur with overwhelming frequency in his writing. He wanted to encompass all of life—and all at once. This accounts for his literary gigantism, that Gargantuan touch inflating everything he undertook to elephantine proportions. It explains a novel like *Die Schlafwandler* (*The Sleepwalkers,* 1931–1932), which sprawls over a period of thirty years and ranges in style from pure lyricism to the abstraction of the essay. It produced the monstrous sentences, textured with "but," "nevertheless," "yet," and "so," that soar—or lumber, as the case may be—over pages on end. Broch not only wanted to get everything in; it was his aim to achieve a stylistic synthesis of the most disparate elements of being and thought. At his worst, Broch is ponderous, humorless, pedantic, and presumptuous. At his best, he

opens up unplumbed areas of literary experience in a manner worthy of his literary idols, James Joyce and Franz Kafka.

Broch never romanticized the details of his life. He said that he had at least one thing in common with Kafka and Robert Musil: "We all three have no real biography. We lived and wrote, and that's all." This is not much of an exaggeration. Apart from a few symbolic turning points in his career, Broch's life was one of the mind—a fact highlighted by the impoverished, almost ascetic existence that he led during his last twenty years. At the age of sixty-two he welcomed a ten-month stay in the hospital because it gave him more time to devote to his intellectual work. Yet Broch was no escapist. "The ivory tower is immoral," he said. During his lifetime he saw his share of reality: industrial life in Europe and America before World War I; labor disputes and unemployment in the 1920's; Hitler's prisons in the 1930's; and the impoverished immigrant's-eye view of New York in the 1940's.

Born in Vienna on 1 November 1886, Broch belonged to the brilliant constellation of apocalyptic poets and writers who chronicled the decline of European civilization as it manifested itself in the Austro-Hungarian Empire at the end of the nineteenth century: Kafka, Musil, Rainer Maria Rilke, Georg Trakl, and other stars of a lesser order. Although he was twelve years younger than Hugo von Hofmannsthal, Broch came to realize that they emerged from similar backgrounds, and his study *Hofmannsthal und seine Zeit* (*Hugo von Hofmannsthal and His Time,* 1955) assumed the proportions of a symbolic autobiography. This generation of writers devoted themselves to the analysis of a society grown sick and to the search for new values to replace the old. The vision of Broch's dying Vergil is related to the revelations of Rilke's *Duineser Elegien* (*Duino Elegies,* 1923). His *Die Schuldlosen* (*The Guiltless,* 1950) are first cousins of Musil's *Der Mann ohne Eigenschaften* (*The Man Without Qualities,* 3 vols., 1930–1942). And the characters in *The Sleepwalkers* wander through an often Kafkaesque landscape.

Unlike the others, however, Broch was not first and foremost a professional writer. When his first novel appeared in 1931, Hofmannsthal, Rilke, Trakl, and Kafka were dead; Musil had been writing for more than twenty-five years. Meanwhile, Broch had become, as he later said cynically, a captain of industry. As the older son of a tyrannical Jewish textile merchant, Broch was expected to enter the family business. After secondary school, where one of his classmates was the future composer Alban Berg, he audited lectures on philosophy and mathematics at the University of Vienna, but as a dutiful son his first obligation from 1904 to 1906 was to his training at the Institute for Textile Industry. He then received his engineering diploma at the Textile School in Mülhausen (Alsace-Lorraine) and in 1907 undertook a business trip to the United States, where he observed cotton-growing and milling procedures in the South.

In 1908, after military service as a volunteer officer's candidate in Zagreb, Broch settled down to work as an assistant director in the Teesdorf Mills outside Vienna, which his father had recently acquired. As early as 1907 he had taken out patents for a new cotton-mixing appliance and process. By 1915, when his father retired, he was ready to assume the management of the family concern. For the next ten years he could indeed be called a captain of industry. In addition to supervising the mills, he directed a local military hospital (an experience that provided background for his first novel), served on government advisory councils, and acquired the reputation of a skillful mediator in labor disputes.

During this entire period, however, Broch was engaged in what he called a "double profession." A young man of his intellectual passion could not be satisfied with a business career. Pursuing an autodidactic course of philosophical readings ranging from Immanuel Kant and Arthur Schopenhauer to Friedrich Nietzsche and Otto Weininger, Broch prepared for a critical scrutiny of modern culture, as revealed in his unpublished notes headed "Kultur 1908–1909" (Culture 1908–1909). The immediate result was a series of essays and philosophically oriented literary reviews published between 1913 and 1922 in the liberal Catholic journals *Der Brenner* and *Summa.* Even before his marriage to Franziska von Rothermann in 1909, Broch had become a convert, but the Catholic element in his work is not pronounced; toward the end of his life he made a conscious effort to "expurgate the remnants of Catholicism" from his thinking. He was attracted to these journals, rather, because *Der Brenner* (in which Trakl's poetry originally appeared) featured the brilliant satirical moralist Karl Kraus, whose work Broch greatly admired, and because *Summa* followed a stated policy of ethical reconstruction on a cosmopolitan level. In these articles and in a series of unpublished studies written from 1922 to 1927, Broch developed the theory of values and philosophy of history upon which his literary works depend—indeed, from which the novels directly emerged.

Broch asked himself the question that has concerned historians for generations: How is it possible to determine the essential reality of a given historical period? He begins by reducing the epistemological problem to one of ethics. Any phenomenon, he maintains, can be explained ultimately by the values of a given epoch. In periods of cultural unity, as at the height of the Middle Ages, this is a simple matter. All human activity can be judged as good or bad, right or wrong, by reference to the Christian values handed down by God and interpreted by the church. The individual is confronted with no ethical decisions and suffers no moral crises because life is regulated by one central authority. But Broch sees history as a dialectic process of bimillennial cycles. Our present cycle—the Christian Era—emerged two thousand years ago from the ruins of the declining pagan era. Developing organically, it reached its apogee in the Middle Ages and then, at the beginning of modern times, became hypertrophied. He recapitulates his theory in the "Historical Digression" of *The Sleepwalkers*: "That criminal and rebellious time called the Renaissance, that time in which the Christian system of values was split into a Catholic and a Protestant half" brought about "the process of the five-hundred-year dissolution of values." In place of the former total system there emerged gradually many partial systems of value. To illustrate this pluralism Broch cites such commonplaces as "business is business," "war is war," and "l'art pour l'art."

Contemporary man, living at the end of a historical cycle, is caught between an old system of values that is no longer adequate and a future one that has not yet crystallized. The dilemma of "no longer and not yet"—a key phrase in Broch's rhetoric—is the object of his interest. At this point Broch's speculations begin to merge with those of other contemporary thinkers, for modern man is faced with an essentially existential problem. The "partial systems" are secular ones: the man who lives according to the maxim "business is business" has no recourse to a supreme authority if he encounters a situation that does not fit into his narrow framework. If he is not committed to any single partial system, his dilemma is complicated by the necessity of making empirical choices between systems often in conflict. The result of this pluralism, when the fragile security of the partial system has collapsed, is chaos and despair. Broch sees two possibilities of behavior. A man can attempt to escape the anguish of the present by forgetting himself in the delirium of erotic love or by clinging to the mystical tenets of religious sectarianism. This first possibility leads to ethical guilt because it is a flight from reality and responsibility. Or he can take upon himself the burden of freedom by disavowing the facile solutions of partial systems and attempting to make "realistic" decisions. This involves alienation and loneliness since freedom is a road chosen by few, but it prepares the way for the future and a new system of values by sweeping away the residue of the past.

Broch's dialectic process pushes God right out of the picture. He is concerned, like Kant, with finding what he calls "the Earthly Absolute"—ethical values postulated solely on the fact of man's existence. He never denies the existence of the transcendental. As a matter of fact, it plays a major role in his thought, for part of the total synthesis of opposites that Broch hopes to achieve in his *unio mystica* is the reconciliation of life and death, the here and the beyond, the present and the future. For this reason symbols have an important function. We cannot know what is transcendental; but things and actions on earth can "echo" or "mirror" the divine. In this, as in many other respects, Broch is close to Romantic poets like Novalis, who regarded natural phenomena as hieroglyphs, or *chiffres,* of the transcendental. And precisely this "Romantic" aspect of his work links him with German contemporaries like Hermann Hesse and Thomas Mann while distinguishing him from other existential authors with whom he has much else in common. However, man must create his ethical values as though there were nothing outside this world. Here Broch reaches a solution that is close to Albert Camus's concept of human dignity and solidarity. Later, in his theoretical essay "Trotzdem: Humane Politik" (Nevertheless: A Humane Politics, 1950), Broch developed this idea into a more elaborate system. But at this point his ethical postulate is summed up best by the biblical quotation that closes *The Sleepwalkers*: "Do thyself no harm: for we are all here" (Acts 16:28).

One might well ask why Broch found it necessary to put all of this into fictional form. The decision—indeed, the necessity—can be explained by the intellectual crisis of the forty-year-old. Broch's marriage broke up in 1923, a victim in part of his growing associations with the artists and intellectuals he had met in the World War I literary cafés of Vienna. In 1925 Broch resumed his study of philosophy, mathematics, and physics at the University of Vienna. And in 1927 he shocked his family by selling the textile mills in order to devote himself fully to his studies. To be sure, there were certain practical motivations. Broch sensed that an economic crisis was approaching and felt that his move was financially sound. But it would be cheap to doubt the sincerity of his motives. As a man whose whole life was devoted to "cognition," he had reached a point in his philosophical work from which he could not go on without further study and total commitment. Fortunately for literature, Broch went back to the university just at a time when absolutes were becoming unfashionable. In philosophy the logical positivists had discarded metaphysical speculation in favor of problems that could be solved by mathematical demonstration. As Broch wrote, Ludwig Wittgenstein and his followers regarded ethics as "unscientific" and "mystical." (Broch himself had studied with Rudolf Carnap, Hans Hahn, Karl Menger, Moritz Schlick, and others.) For Broch this realization was unsettling; he wrote in a letter of 5 December 1948:

> I discovered something else: those areas of philosophy that are inaccessible to mathematical treatment—primarily ethics or metaphysics—become "objective" only in the realm of theology. Otherwise they become relativistic and, ultimately, "subjective." It was this subjectivity that

forced me into the area where it is radically legitimate, namely into literature.
>
> (*Kommentierte Werkausgabe,* vol. 13/3, p. 288)

Broch's language is ponderous, but the meaning is clear. Ethical absolutes are possible only within a theological system. But our theological system—Christianity—has disintegrated, as Broch had concluded in his philosophy of history. If ethical postulates outside of theology are by definition relative or subjective, then one should deal with them in a form that is frankly subjective—in literature.

After nine semesters, consequently, Broch gave up his plans for an academic career and undertook his first novel. This pattern repeated itself several times during his life when he found it necessary to turn to literature in order to express ideas that are not the legitimate concern of philosophy. For this reason—and with some justification—Broch has been called "a writer *malgré lui.*" He certainly never wrote a novel simply to satisfy an aesthetic impulse. He even coined the expression "epistemological novel" to designate his works. But even if he reached literature by the back door, Broch was a born writer. When he allowed himself to succumb to what he called "the temptation to tell stories," he was capable of writing with a creative surge matched by few of his contemporaries. When his works sag, it is because he has tried to load them with too heavy a burden of unassimilated speculation.

For Broch, then, literature is an epistemological shortcut—what he sometimes called "an impatience for cognition." In a "methodological prospectus" of his first novel that he wrote in 1929 for his publisher he explains:

> This novel is based on the assumption that literature must concern itself with those human problems that are rejected by science because they are not open to rational treatment . . . and with those problems whose solution science, in its slower and more precise progress, has not yet reached. The area of literature between the "no longer" and

"not yet" of science has thus become more limited, but also more secure; it encompasses the whole realm of irrational experience, specifically in the border area where the irrational manifests itself as deed, thus becoming expressible and representable.

(*Kommentierte Werkausgabe*, vol. 1, p. 719)

This conception of the proper realm of literature supplied the title for his novel. "Sleepwalkers" are individuals existing in a state of suspension between two ethical systems or two cycles of reality—just as the sleepwalker lives between sleeping and waking, partaking of both. Broch's sleepwalkers are no longer satisfied by the ethical codes of the past, yet they cannot free themselves completely. In his novels Broch is always concerned with the critical *Grenzsituationen* (border situations) in which a man's accepted standards are shown to be deficient by the intrusion of something irrational—what Broch calls the "irruption from below." Because the behavior of the characters is no longer rational but motivated by vague irrational impulses, the novels take on the dreamlike quality often associated with Kafka's fiction.

The Sleepwalkers belongs to a group of major German novels that analyze the disintegration of society culminating in the catastrophe of World War I: Musil's *The Man Without Qualities,* Mann's *Der Zauberberg* (*The Magic Mountain,* 1924), Hesse's *Demian* (1919), and Joseph Roth's *Radetzkymarsch* (*The Radetzky March,* 1932). In structure and style, however, it is far more radically experimental than the others. Broch was never a man to shrink from the consequences of consistency; his unwillingness to compromise led him to give up first his business career and then his academic pursuits. During the four years he was working on his novel, he read widely and eagerly exploited any techniques that seemed expedient for his own purposes. The result is a work that shows the clear influence of such diverse authors as John Dos Passos, André Gide, Joyce, Kafka,

and Aldous Huxley and yet manages to attain an astonishing degree of artistic integration.

"The age of the polyhistorical novel has dawned," he announced to his publisher in a characteristic letter of 5 August 1931. (For his faith, patience, and advice Dr. Daniel Brody of the Rhein-Verlag should take his place in the annals of publishing beside Thomas Wolfe's editor, Maxwell Perkins.) Broch had noted the polymath tendencies of Mann, Musil, Huxley, and other contemporaries. Most writers, he observed, regarded their erudition as "a block of crystal" from which they chipped off scintillating bits to insert into their stories in the form of "cultivated" conversations. Like them, Broch hoped to achieve "polyhistorical" totality, but he did not want to slacken the tension of the narrative. Nor did he want, at the other extreme, to interrupt the action for the subjective ruminations of the author. Why not be absolutely consistent? He came up with the idea of separating these functions of the rational and the irrational completely—by including seventeen chapters of pure lyricism as a vehicle for the subjective voice of the narrator and ten chapters of an essay entitled "Zerfall der Werte" ("The Disintegration of Values"), which comprises roughly the ideas on theory of values and philosophy of history developed during the 1920's. Between these two extremes the action is suspended.

The novel is a trilogy. *Pasenow oder die Romantik* (*Pasenow, or Romanticism*) takes place in the year 1888 in Berlin and the province of Brandenburg and centers on members of the Prussian nobility. *Esch oder die Anarchie* (*Esch, or Anarchism*) shifts to the urban working class of Cologne and Mannheim in 1903. *Huguenau oder die Sachlichkeit* (*Huguenau, or Objectivism*), finally, is localized in the bourgeois society of a small village on the Mosel in the months preceding the November Revolution of 1918. Even this external organization reveals the symbolic structure. Just as the sequence in time traces the emergence of a new "objective" man from the romanticism and anarchy of the past, so too the movement from east to west signifies a progression from Eastern mysticism toward Western rationalism—a geographical symbolism that would not have been lost on Mann, who was fond of playing with similar conceits.

This development is reflected in the style of the parts. *Pasenow* is written in such a subtle parody of late-nineteenth-century realism that the incautious reader might take the novel to be a period piece from the pen of Theodor Fontane—a comparison that several contemporary critics made. Only careful attention to Broch's use of point of view reveals that the narrator has carefully excluded himself from the story; every incident is consistently related in its filtration through various shifting focuses. "Reality" turns out to be anything but the stable world of traditional realism, and its breakdown is anticipated stylistically. In *Esch* this collapse is overt. There is no longer even the exterior semblance of order, and this chaos is reflected in the hectic expressionistic prose that can rise, on demand, to a high pitch of lyricism. In *Huguenau* the structure corresponds to the complete disintegration of reality. There is no homogeneity of style: lyric, dramatic, narrative, expository, and reportorial elements occur independently in separate chapters. The analytic disintegration of style mirrors the objective attitude of the hero toward reality.

Within this framework Broch tells the story of four representative individuals. Joachim von Pasenow is a "romantic" because he clings desperately to values that virtually everyone else regards as outmoded. His *Trägheit des Gefühls* (emotional lethargy) lends to his character a certain old-fashioned quaintness, but it renders him almost totally unfit to deal with any situation that does not fit into his narrow code, whose romantic values are symbolized by his lieutenant's uniform. Whenever he is confronted by a perplexing situation, he anxiously fingers the buttons to make sure that he is properly enclosed and insulated against outside forces. To be "dragged down" into civilian life, where his military code is not valid, where he is not protected by his uniform, represents the gravest threat to his existence. The threat of irrationalism, the "irruption from below," comes in the form of love. Pasenow's code has no place for a purely human relationship; in his mind, love is either degraded to pure eros, as in his affair with the barmaid Ruzena, or it is sublimated into a quasi-religious experience. His complete incompetence in dealing with the reality of love is the point of the novel. The story ends on his wedding night, when Joachim is rendered temporarily impotent by his inability to treat Elisabeth as a woman instead of as a symbol of the divine. Our last glimpse shows Joachim lying fully dressed beside his new bride, nervously straightening his jacket when it falls open to reveal his black trousers. (In the symbol-laden book black stands for the dark recesses of erotic desire.)

Pasenow sets the pattern for the following volumes. In all three we are shown a thirty-year-old man whose system of values is threatened for the first time by irrationality. (This is, by the way, the pattern in Kafka's *Der Prozess* [*The Trial,* 1925] as well as in Jean-Paul Sartre's *La nausée* [*Nausea,* 1938], Camus's *L'Étranger* [*The Stranger,* 1942], and several other major novels of the twentieth century.) While Pasenow's reaction to the "irruption from below" is a desperate, "romantic" clinging to the past, August Esch, at loose in the "anarchic" pluralism of the present, lives by the down-to-earth motto "business is business." As an accountant he views the whole world in terms of bookkeeping. Until his thirtieth year this conception was quite adequate; nothing made him question the debits and credits of life. Then, without warning, he is fired from his job. Esch knows that he has made no mistake in his books. Dismissed in order to cover up the embezzlement of a superior, he has been punished for another man's crime. This realization upsets Esch's cosmic account book. Instead of going to the police, Esch makes the mistake of blackmailing the embezzler for a good recommendation for another position. By trying not to become involved, he complicates the situation. The debit of guilt must be offset by the credit of expiation in order to keep the accounts straight. If the perpetrator is not punished, then someone else must suffer. The whole novel, one of Broch's strongest narratives, is moved along by Esch's attempts to reestablish the cosmic harmony. He interprets everything that happens in terms of the initial debt. Thus when he meets Ilona, the partner of a knife-thrower in a burlesque show, he sees her in his confused mind as a symbol of the divine who must suffer crucifixion every night because of the unexpiated guilt in the world: "Without order in the accounts there was also no order in the world, and as long as there was no order, Ilona would continue to be exposed to the knives, Nentwig would continue, insolent and hypocritical, to escape his penance." Esch, like Pasenow, is caught between two women, but can accept neither of them as a person. While Ilona represents the spiritualization of love, Mother Hentjen, whom he eventually marries, offers simple forgetfulness in erotic union. In view of the elaborate parallelism of the two volumes it is significant that Pasenow, the "romantic," chooses the solution of spiritualization in his marriage to Elisabeth, while Esch, in the face of a chaotic world, seeks oblivion in the arms of Mother Hentjen. Both incur guilt by fleeing ethical responsibility.

Eduard von Bertrand is the only figure who connects volumes 1 and 2. In the first he is Pasenow's acquaintance, a former officer who had done the unheard of—given up his uniform for the world of business. In the second he has become owner of the shipping company that employs Esch. Bertrand represents still a third ethical position: the aesthetic one. Conscious, like Pasenow and Esch, of the existence of various sets of values, he tries to stand above them—not bound, but also not yet completely free. He advises Pasenow to rid himself of outworn values and to live freely. Unable to accept the consequences of his own advice, he commits suicide in volume 2, a true victim of the dilemma of "no longer and not yet." He

never actually appears in volume 2; we encounter him only in the context of Esch's thoughts and visions.

In all of Broch's novels sex functions as a key symbol of man's response to reality. Pasenow is rendered impotent because he is unable to come to terms with love. Esch hurls himself into sexual intercourse with complete abandon in an attempt to forget reality. The sterility of Bertrand's aesthetic position is emphasized by his homosexuality. The only figure who masters sex and thus triumphs over reality is Huguenau, the "hero" of volume 3. No repressions, self-abandonment, or deviation for him. He goes to the brothel once a week for "hygienic" reasons, and when it seems like an expedient thing to do, he rapes Mother Hentjen, Esch's wife.

In this final volume Esch and Pasenow have both ended up in the little Mosel village: Pasenow as commandant of the town and Esch as owner and editor of the local newspaper. Their inability to come to grips with reality brings the two men together in a religious sect, but it is precisely this longing for a vague mystical escape that constitutes their ethical guilt. This spurious harmony is disrupted when Huguenau arrives on the scene. Huguenau's objectivism, his complete break with the past, is symbolized by his desertion from the army. During the six months before the November Revolution he is a totally free, or "valueless," man, bound in no way to any standards of the past. (It is a position that he is unable to sustain: at the end of the novel he slips back into the conventional system of values as soon as the "holiday mood" of the war is over.) Broch does not imply that Huguenau is an admirable man—far from it; many of his actions are contemptible. Yet in a letter to his translator Willa Muir, Broch calls him "my portrait or at least (to use Freud's language) my superego" because he represents, during this six-month "vacation," the objective approach to reality that is necessary in order to overcome the useless ideals of the past and take vengeance on Pasenow and Esch for their ethical evasions. His freewheeling attitude makes it possible for Huguenau to arrive in town, a penniless deserter, and within a short time become one of the leading citizens. He swindles Esch out of his newspaper and bullies Pasenow into submission so that the commandant will not report him as a deserter. During the revolution he murders Esch, and as a final gesture of contempt for those who adhere to mystical ideals, rapes Esch's wife. When the revolution is over, Pasenow and Esch are dead; the forces of objectivism have won out over the romanticism and anarchy of the past.

Although the three volumes can be read separately, they constitute a trilogy in which the strongest links of continuity are leitmotifs and symbols. Pasenow is characterized repeatedly by his "emotional lethargy"; Esch is identified by the "impetuosity" with which he responds to the anarchic world about him; and Bertrand's disengagement is signified by his "deprecatory gesture," which is picked up by Pasenow and Esch and thus occurs in all three volumes. The symbol of the uniform, which is central in volume 1, figures in the other parts, but in a degraded, "de-romanticized" form. The customs inspector Korn, unperturbed by the reality that Esch finds so disturbing, struts about in the authority of his uniform. The members of the Salvation Army, who find the illusion of stability in their sectarianism, wear a uniform. Conversely, the shattering of reality is signified by the loss of uniform, as in the case of the troubled patients of the military hospital in volume 3. In all three volumes travel is a symbol of escape to freedom. Bertrand's business takes him all over the world, but since he never frees himself completely from the past, he returns to Germany and dies there. In volume 2 Esch dreams of going to America. When his dream cannot be fulfilled, he buys himself a reproduction of the Statue of Liberty as a symbol of his longing, and in volume 3 Huguenau notices it, with contempt, on Esch's desk. These, as well as many of the other leitmotifs and symbols that recur through all three volumes, give the trilogy as a whole a consistent

texture and contribute to the effect of simultaneity and totality that Broch was eager to achieve.

In volume 3 the focus is expanded to embrace more than the Huguenau-Esch-Pasenow plot. To represent the themes of disintegration and alienation, Broch constructs a series of parallel plots connected, in the manner of Dos Passos, by occasional nodal chapters. At the same time, the various parallel plots are sustained in an inner tension by a counterpoint technique derived from Huxley. In these narrative strands Broch depicts disintegration, for instance, in the person of the shell-shocked veteran Gödicke, who must laboriously reconstruct his personality from the disparate elements that he finds in his consciousness when he comes out of his coma. The spiritual imbalance of the age is personified by the wounded Lieutenant Jaretzki, an architect by profession (that is, an exemplum of proportion), who has lost an arm and must now get used to an artificial limb. And the progressive stages of loneliness are shown in the story of Hanna Wendling, who is gradually alienated from her husband while he is at the eastern front. These subplots, only tenuously connected with the main action, are all part of Broch's attempt to attain symbolic totality.

At either extreme of these graded narrative sections, the lyrical portions and the discursive essay "The Disintegration of Values" are built into the novel in a delicate counterpoint to the other chapters. At first glance the tale told in the ballad seems even more incongruous than the essay. While the essay at least deals overtly with the problems suggested by the narrative, the lyrical passages tell an apparently unrelated story: the love between a girl from the Salvation Army in Berlin and the Jew Nuchem—a love doomed to failure because of irreconcilable religious differences. We gradually realize, however, that the narrator of the ballad, Dr. Bertrand Müller—perhaps a spiritual heir of Eduard von Bertrand but certainly not physically identical with him—is at the same time the author of "The Disintegration of Values." Since the essay, in turn, embraces the various plots, he is by extension the author of the entire novel.

Now we begin to understand the implications of Broch's decision to give up philosophy in order to write fiction. He found modern philosophy inadequate because it neglected vast areas of human experience: the irrational, the ethical, the metaphysical. Hence, the "irrational" implications of the essay had to be dealt with as plots or stories showing the actual confrontation of human beings with irrational or ethical decisions; the essay produces the fiction. At the same time, Broch had learned from his study of modern science that even in the so-called pure sciences cognition is not absolute, but relative. Just as in the physics of Albert Einstein or Werner Heisenberg the phenomenon observed is affected by the position and nature of the observer, so too in the philosophical disciplines every idea is conditioned by the character of the person who thinks it. In order to present an idea, one must at the same time present the personality of the thinker. The subject of observation, as Broch put it, must be projected into the field of observation as an *object* of observation. This was a notion that fascinated Broch, and—notably in his 1936 essay on Joyce—he discussed its applicability to the works of writers like Joyce and Gide. (The technique that he finally evolved is indebted in no small measure to Gide's *Les faux-monnayeurs* [*The Counterfeiters*, 1926], which he greatly admired.) The subjective personality of the writer had to be defined in the lyrical passages in order to justify, as it were, the theoretical essay of the same writer. In the essay and the plots Bertrand Müller is the observing subject; in the ballad he exposes himself as an *object* of observation. What we have, then, amounts to an absolute or totally self-contained novel that represents the full extent of Bertrand's consciousness from the rational down to the depths of the irrational. The ballad is ultimately the only "subjective" strand of the entire book; as such, it is properly written in the "subjective" mode, namely in lyrical form.

Years later, in connection with *The Guiltless,* which has a similar lyrical "supervoice," Broch explained: "The only thing that can possibly match the enormous volume of our time is the volume of the I or the Self; and it, in turn, is so large that it cannot be expressed purely in fictional form, but requires purely lyrical forms." It is this emphasis on the lyrical nature of the subject that distinguishes Broch's work from, say, Mann's *Doktor Faustus* (*Doctor Faustus,* 1947), where the personality of the narrative subject is clearly defined—but in the narrative mode and for purposes of irony rather than in the lyrical mode for reasons of cognition.

Broch had great hopes for his novel. Although it was begun as an epistemological exercise, he was not unaware of its literary merits. Designating it frequently as "a *novum* in the form of the novel," he hoped for wide publicity. He was eager for the work to be selected by the Book-of-the-Month Club in the United States and even discussed the possibility of filming it with Warner Brothers. (These were hopelessly unrealistic dreams, but it should be pointed out in Broch's defense that his common sense was outweighed at this time by financial distress.) Broch, having become keenly aware of his position in the world of literature, compared his work with assurance to the novels of Joyce, Mann, Gide, and others. He was particularly pleased when Edwin and Willa Muir undertook the English translation of *The Sleepwalkers,* because they had translated Kafka. And Broch was initially attracted to the Rhein-Verlag, which published his works, because in 1927 it had brought out the German translation of *Ulysses* (1922).

The complicated relationship of Broch to Joyce can barely be sketched here, but it is exceedingly important. As soon as Broch read *Ulysses*—while he was working on the third draft of his own novel—he was struck by the similarity of intention. "If I had read *Ulysses* before I wrote *The Sleepwalkers,*" he confessed to Willa Muir, "my novel would have remained unwritten." He urged his publisher to stress the connection between his book and *Ulysses:* "I agree to any propaganda that couples me with Joyce." In a letter to his friend Frank Thiess he called Joyce "my literary superego." Yet this adulation must not obscure the true relationship. Joyce's impact on *The Sleepwalkers* is much less specific than that of Dos Passos, Huxley, or Gide. The only explicit alteration that Broch undertook after he read *Ulysses* was to remove the Odysseus framework that originally introduced and concluded the third volume as an archetypal analogy. Otherwise *The Sleepwalkers* is organized according to entirely different structural principles. Broch often contrasted his own "additive" technique—the separation of the rational and the irrational into various parallel strands—with the "synthetic" method of Joyce. He was most impressed by Joyce's awareness of "the mission of literature [to create] a cognition that embraces totality" and by the "inner simultaneity" of *Ulysses.* He felt that Joyce came closer than any other contemporary to fulfilling the requirements of the polyhistorical novel, which he saw foreshadowed in Goethe's late novel, *Wilhelm Meisters Wanderjahre* (*Wilhelm Meister's Travels,* 1829). The essay that Broch wrote in honor of Joyce's fiftieth birthday is a brilliant interpretation of Joyce's work, but at the same time it is a statement of Broch's own position. He never accepted Joyce's method wholeheartedly. In his letters and essays Joyce's name appears dozens of times, but it is always obvious that Broch regards Joyce as a challenge and uses him as a foil for his own thoughts. Although *Der Tod des Vergil* (*The Death of Vergil,* 1945) is much closer to Joyce than is *The Sleepwalkers,* he employed in it a technique that he explicitly contrasted with Joyce's "psychoanalytic pointillism." It is impossible to think of Broch without the impact of Joyce. Yet in his approach to literature, as in everything else, Broch vacillated between two poles.

At the other pole stood Kafka. "Art which does not render the totality of the world is not art," Broch stated again and again—and most elaborately in the essay "The Style of the Mythical Age," which he wrote in English on commission as an introduction to Rachel Bespaloff's *On the Iliad* (1947). But there are two ways to achieve totality: the complicated way of the "polyhistorical" novel and the simple way of myth. In the former, Broch felt, Joyce was unexcelled. But mythic literature is of a higher order altogether, and here Kafka was master. "Myth is the archetype of philosophy," Broch claimed. "Either poetry is able to proceed to myth or it goes bankrupt." In myth the irrational and rational elements of being are united in one grand vision; there is no need for the analytic methods of the polyhistorical novel and the intellectual gymnastics of the *poeta doctus.* In primitive myth we see a stage of intuitive knowledge of unity before cultural disintegration has set in. And literature, if it is to be worthwhile, must go forward until it succeeds in establishing a new myth. Kafka, Broch felt, intuitively attained with simple means such mythical validity that he had no need of the "complicated" techniques of Joyce. Broch hoped to achieve something like a synthesis of Joyce and Kafka in what he called the "metanovel." In an important letter to the critic Friedrich Torberg (10 April 1943) he formulated "three imperative, yet unrealizable requirements" for the new novel: it must employ total radicality of means; it must strive to attain cognition of death; and it must achieve radicality of myth. These three imperatives are subsumed, Broch concluded, in a fourth and most important one: the *Totalitätsgewicht* (totality-gravity) of the work of art.

While *The Sleepwalkers* enjoyed a considerable critical success, it earned very little in royalties. Broch, virtually penniless since the sale of the textile mill, had to scramble to make ends meet. From 1932 to 1934 he tried his hand at virtually every literary form that promised an income, from lectures to film scripts and radio talks. In addition to writing literary and philosophical essays he devoted a great deal of energy to his projected "Filsmann" novel, an autobiographically based study of the conflict between labor and management in the industrial society of the Weimar Republic. The only fruit of this activity, beside some fragments, was his play *Die Entsühnung* (*The Atonement*, 1961), performed in 1934 in Zurich. In letters to his publisher Broch also blocked out elaborate plans for a series of stories revolving around the signs of the zodiac:

> The zodiac stories are an experiment. They attempt to make the reader "experience" certain primal symbols of the human soul, such as the lion, the bull, the fish, but also the triangle; that is, to produce an emotional situation from which it becomes self-evident that these images assumed that metaphysical symbolic character that bestows upon a concrete and often trivial object the power of representing a great supersensory realm.
>
> ("Bemerkungen zu den 'Tierkreis-Erzählungen'" [Notes on the "Zodiac Tales"], *Gesammelte Werke*, vol. 10, p. 187)

Although Broch never completed this project, five stories subsequently found a place in *The Guiltless*. The plan itself is of interest because it reveals Broch's growing curiosity about the nature of symbols. (The triangle, for instance, is an important symbol in *The Guiltless* for the emptiness of a hermetically isolated existence.) This fascination with symbols ties in with Broch's theory of the novel as it developed in connection with Joyce and Kafka. "If there is any meaning in art, then it lies principally in being able to express totality with a limited number of motives."

The only longer work completed during these two years was the novel *Die unbekannte Größe* (*The Unknown Quantity*), which Broch wrote in six weeks in 1933. Although unquestionably inferior to the four major novels, it is a symptomatic effort, resulting from a grandiose scheme that Broch outlined in a lengthy correspondence with Warner Brothers. Broch liked to regard himself as a mediator between two cultures. He envisaged a series of six motion pictures that would familiarize the general public with the mind of the scientist in order to combat the anti-intellectualism of the times. (It was one of his pet ideas that film is the only adequate art form for modern society since it is the legitimate product of an industrialized collective society. For similar publicist reasons he had the novel printed as a newspaper serial.) The project—like most of Broch's ambitious enterprises—got no further than this first novel, which was to be the basis for the scenario. The book is not unlike C. P. Snow's *The Search*, which appeared the following year and also traced the disenchantment of a scientist with his work. The basic pattern is again the "irruption from below" in the life of a young mathematician. The "unknown quantity" of the title, which does not fit into his hyperrational system, appears in the forms of a love affair and the death of his brother. Broch was interested in demonstrating that the scientist's reaction to the problems of existence is not different from that of the politician, the businessman, or the technologist. The novel is far too hastily and schematically executed to claim any literary merit; it is little more than a variation on the theme of *The Sleepwalkers*. But one important ingredient has been added: death as a manifestation of the irrational. Broch's earlier protagonists had to come to terms with love. Richard Hieck learns that life alone does not embrace all experience: "Death and life together constitute the totality of being."

In 1935 Broch left Vienna to live in the Tyrolese village of Mösern near Seefeld. Here, and later in the Styrian Alps around Alt-Aussee, he worked on his "mountain novel," known variously as *Der Versucher* (The Tempter, 1953) and *Die Verzauberung* (The Bewitchment, 1969). Like Mann's novel, *Die Verzauberung* depicts a "magic mountain"—but instead of rendering in hermetic isolation a model of contemporary civilization, it goes to the other extreme and portrays the mythic origins of human society. Like *The Sleepwalkers*, this novel deals with a critical year in which traditional values are threatened by the intrusion of irrational forces. But Broch is concerned here not with an individual or group of individuals but with a village as a collective society. It is a study in mass hysteria. The novel relates how the isolated village of Kuppron comes under the spell of the stranger Marius Ratti, who arrives with promises to relieve the destitution of the people. He proposes to open up the ancient gold mines in the nearby mountains and preaches a return to the values of the primitive Celts who originally inhabited the area, persuading the villagers that their troubles stem from the meretricious effects of modern industrialization. He works the villagers up to such a pitch that they actually render a human sacrifice to the powers of the mountain before their hysteria subsides.

As sheer narrative this is the most impressive of Broch's novels. There is virtually no intrusion of speculative thought; all the meaning has been assimilated into the action. Yet the work has several important levels of meaning beyond the plot itself: political, psychological, and mythical. In the first place the novel constitutes an analysis of the rise of Nazism. Marius Ratti has personal characteristics borrowed from Adolf Hitler: his physical appearance as well as his perverse chastity fit the popular image of the Führer. He exerts an almost irresistible magnetism on those who listen to him, and he gathers about him a group of young enthusiasts resembling storm troopers. His political technique depends on the resuscitation of primitive myth as well as the creation of a scapegoat in the person of the Protestant Wetchy, who is both an "outsider" and, as a machine salesman, the representative of industrialization. The corruption of Kuppron corresponds almost step by step to the seduction of Germany in the 1920's and 1930's.

The specific points that Broch borrowed from contemporary politics anticipate the proposals for a study on mass hysteria that he submitted in 1942 and 1943 to various American foundations. Broch's *Massenwahntheorie* (Theory of Mass Psychology, 1979), which shares with Sartre's *Réflexions sur la question juive* (*Portrait of an Anti-Semite*, 1946) the ef-

fort to understand the psychological basis and effects of prejudice, emerged as a consistent extension of his theory of values and philosophy of history. The protagonists of his first novel exist in an intermediate "sleepwalker" state between systems of value; their consciousness is one that Broch defines as a "twilight condition" in his mass psychology: "While an isolated individual is prone to accept his being confronted with inexplicable phenomena, the human mind within the 'prepanicky' mass seeks an 'explicable' cause for the phenomenon, primarily a human one. The alien bearing all marks of the non-ego becomes its very symbol." A fearmonger like Marius exploits these inchoate anxieties, for the mass eagerly follows any leader who promises to relieve its uncertainty. *The Sleepwalkers* ends with man's longing for "a leader to take him tenderly and lightly by the hand, to set things in order and show him the way." In his theory of mass psychology Broch warns that often a false prophet comes in the guise of the true leader. Superficially resembling the leader, he promises instead of a new reality merely a return to an old system of values. Humankind, as T. S. Eliot observed, "cannot bear very much reality." This is how Broch explains the almost mystical appeal of Hitler; and this justifies the function of Marius Ratti in the novel. The escape has a temporary appeal, but its satisfaction cannot last, for the old system ignores too much present reality; in order to support the system, it is necessary to do violence to any inexplicable phenomenon. But eventually reality, asserting itself, ousts the false leader and inaugurates a new era.

On this level the novel presents the paradigm of an eternal mythic process. Following the theories of Johann Jacob Bachofen, Broch depicts a society just emerging from the state of matriarchy. The good forces of the village, eventually overcome by Marius and his gang, are represented by Mother Gisson, a modern hypostasis of the *magna mater*, whose very name suggests an anagram of the word *gnosis*. She has found what Broch calls the "knowledge of the heart"—an *unio mystica* of spirit and body, life and death, present and future. Her warnings go unheeded as the villagers respond ever more blindly to the inducements of Marius. Yet she realizes that this hysteria is part of the inevitable historical process, for an antichrist like Marius is needed to sweep away the old order so that a new order can emerge: "My time is up, but it is without end . . . the stranger will wander on and pass away . . . then you will no longer believe in hatred." When the villagers sacrifice a girl to the mountain in order to gain access to the gold, they symbolically reenact a primitive Celtic rite. They do not realize that their sacrifice is a travesty and not redemption, for it is a step back into the strictures of the past rather than an advance into the freedom of the future.

In an English synopsis of the novel that he submitted to the Guggenheim Foundation in 1940 Broch wrote the following justification:

> It is quite within the realm of possibility to give "objective descriptions" of events involving mass psychology. A procession of medieval flagellants, the roar of a football game, the crowds in front of the Berlin Reich Chancellery listening to Hitler's strange inflections from the balcony, the horrors of a pogrom—all these can be vividly brought to life. But all such depictions—even though they have historical validity—remain empty words. They merely state the facts of certain mass movements, failing to say anything about their true function and effectiveness. For enlightenment on these points one must turn to the mind of the individual; one must ask why and in which manner the individual participates in that incomprehensible mass behavior. How is it possible that man, when under that spell, is prepared to accept the crudest lies as gospel truth; how can a person otherwise prudent and capable of self-criticism, become involved in the most fantastic adventures; why do archaic tendencies believed long buried come to the fore; why do supernatural trends suddenly appear within rational minds? Only the individual who has fallen under the spell can explain.

(unpublished manuscript,
Yale University Library)

Here Broch implicitly refers to the political, psychological, and mythical dimensions of the novel. But the last sentence opens our eyes to still another aspect. This novel also emerged as the answer to a methodological dilemma. In his studies of mass hysteria Broch had gone as far as he could. For the ultimate answers he had to turn to the subjective element, the mind of the individual. The novel is a first-person narrative by the village doctor, who came to Kuppron some ten years earlier in order to escape the chaos of the city and find peace in a union with nature. He witnesses, even participates in, the events of the terrible six months in the village. Then, in the nine months immediately following, he sets down his memories of all that has happened. Ostensibly it is the calm record of an objective observer—one who is "otherwise prudent and capable of self-criticism." What makes the novel a frightening indictment of mass hysteria is the fact that the narrator himself changes without realizing it. At the end he reports that everything has returned to normal. Mother Gisson is dead; Marius Ratti has been absorbed into the village council; life goes on. The doctor himself has been so much caught up in the web of complicity that he does not realize how radically the village has actually changed. The narrator is not trustworthy. Again Broch is playing tricks of relativism on the reader. The narrative subject turns out to be, at the same time, a narrative object. When we reach the end of the novel, we gradually realize that we must reevaluate everything we have read in the light of the shifting character of the doctor himself. Things have returned to "normal" in the village only because he himself has come to regard the new situation as normal. In reality a whole cultural epoch has died away and been replaced by a new one.

Although *Die Verzauberung* was originally planned as part of a "religious trilogy," Broch never finished even this first volume. Between 1934 and 1936 he wrote two drafts, and in 1950 and 1951 he worked on a third revision. (All three versions, none of which has been translated into English, have been published in German.) He called it variously his "mountain novel," "Demeter; or, The Bewitchment," "The Stranger," and "The Wanderer," as in his mind the emphasis shifted from the symbolism of the mountain to the figure of Mother Gisson and to the character of Marius. Yet even in its unfinished form the novel represents, next to Mann's *Doctor Faustus,* the most profound fictional portrayal of the rise of irrationalism in Germany during the Hitler era. The three versions differ generally only in style, acquiring progressively more symbolic density. It was another intellectual crisis that caused Broch, in 1936, to give up a major novel that was so near completion. He wrote in a letter to Friedrich Torberg on 10 April 1943:

> While I was writing my mountain novel, I noticed the tendency toward myth—discovered it successively, so to speak—and discovered at the same time the inadequacy of my beginning, so that I simply left the book as it was—especially since it had simply become unbearable for me to disguise this inadequacy in fictional form.
>
> (*Kommentierte Werkausgabe,* vol. 13/2, p. 320)

This sentence marks the culmination of an attitude that had been growing in Broch's mind for some time. As early as 1933 we find him asking, in a spirit of inquiry, whether literature is a legitimate pursuit. Although he is skeptical enough to pose the question, he finds that there are at least two good answers. First, literature is a shortcut to knowledge—what he calls "cognition through form"—because it arrives intuitively at results that science and philosophy can reach only through a sequence of tedious preliminary steps. Second, it serves, in our secular age, as a surrogate for religion. Gradually, however, his doubts grew stronger. Is not literature, he muses uneasily, an aesthetic escape from reality? Is the writer not simply trying to create in his mind an artificially ordered universe in which it is easier to live than in the world of reality? Ultimately Broch reaches the conclusion that art is immoral, for in its search for beauty it flees ethical responsibility by effacing distinctions between good and evil. If our everyday reality, according to his theory of history, is not in itself real—if we are living in a state of "no longer and not yet" between true cultural epochs—then our literature is not actually a reflection of reality (which would be legitimate), but a reflection of a mere *reflection* of reality. In the era of gas chambers, when the ethical imperative is reduced to the simplest mandate of love for one's fellow man, it is "a sacrilege" to seek escape through art. And any attempt to beautify the horror of existence through art amounts to "perjury."

Rejecting both literature and "pure" philosophy, Broch returned to the studies of political theory that he had interrupted after World War I and, specifically, to the elaboration of a set of antifascist "Resolutions" that he intended to submit to the League of Nations. Then in 1937 he was invited by a friend at Radio Vienna to read a story for a broadcast and, "not least for financial reasons," accepted the assignment. With an irony increasingly characteristic of his life, Broch was forced to resort to literature in order to express his skepticism about literature. Although his education contained no background in classics and his knowledge of Latin was rudimentary, Broch had become interested in Vergil as a consequence of the publicity surrounding the Roman poet's bimillennial celebrations in 1930. In particular, he was impressed by a work entitled *Vergil: Vater des Abendlands* (Vergil: Father of the Occident, 1931) by the popular cultural critic Theodor Haecker, in which he became acquainted with the legend according to which the dying poet wanted to burn his *Aeneid.* Because of his belief in the two-thousand-year cycle of history Broch was able to regard Vergil, who came between the pagan and Christian eras, as a prototype of the modern man of "no longer and not yet." And the legend implied that Vergil, too, must have entertained similar doubts regarding the legitimacy of literature if he wanted to destroy his lifework. The result was an eighteen-page story entitled

"Die Heimkehr des Vergil" ("Vergil's Home-coming," written in 1937 and published in 1976), in a nutshell the plot of the entire *Death of Vergil.* Immediately realizing that he had not done justice to the potentialities of the subject, Broch began writing a longer version, but he still thought that it could be mastered within the framework of an eighty-page novella—just as Mann, only a short time before, had originally conceived of his massive *Joseph* tetralogy (1933–1943) as a brief narrative.

At this point a second impetus was added. On 13 May 1938, on the day after the *Anschluss,* Broch was arrested in Alt-Aussee as the result of a denunciation by the village mailman, who suspected him of Communist leanings. During his three weeks in jail he came face to face with the imminence of death. He had hitherto been concerned theoretically with the problem of death; now he was confronted with its existential actuality. Whereas he had previously considered Vergil primarily as a prototype of the artist in a valueless society, he now devoted his attention to the *death* of Vergil: "*Vergil* was not written as a 'book,' but (under Hitler's threat) as my private discussion with death."

Toward the end of July Broch managed with the aid of various friends abroad (including Joyce, who was pleased with Broch's essay on his work) to get out of Austria. He made his way via London to Scotland, where he spent two months with his translators Willa and Edwin Muir. Having received a U. S. visa with the assistance of Mann and Einstein, Broch came to the United States, where he arrived practically penniless in October of 1938. For several years and despite his own hand-to-mouth existence Broch devoted himself selflessly to relief work for the American Guild for German Cultural Freedom, living in Princeton, Cleveland, Connecticut, and New York City, where he found many friends among the refugee intellectuals. By 1940 and with the support of a grant from the Guggenheim Foundation the bulk of *Vergil* was finished. But Broch spent three more years—especially after 1942,

when he moved into the house of his friend the cultural historian Erich Kahler—in Princeton publishing the German manuscript and collaborating on the English translation being done by Jean Starr Untermeyer, whom Broch had met during a sojourn at the artists' colony at Yaddo. In 1945 the book was published simultaneously in English and German by the Pantheon Press in New York—to considerable critical acclaim in this country and to benign neglect abroad. The composition of the work is completely different from that of *The Sleepwalkers,* which was a pronounced case of additive composition and architectonic structuring. *The Death of Vergil* grew organically from within, by accretion and enrichment, from a story of eighteen typed sheets to a printed work of more than five hundred pages.

The book depicts the last eighteen hours of Vergil's life—an obvious parallel to Joyce's work. Vergil arrives at the harbor of Brundisium on a September evening. He is borne through the reeking streets of the slums up to the palace of Augustus (part 1). After a fitful night (part 2) in which he is beset by visions of self-recrimination at the waste of his own life, he spends his last morning (part 3) talking with various friends. Just before he dies he gives in to Augustus' wish not to burn his manuscripts, but he elicits from the emperor, in return, the right to free his slaves. Then, in a final vision (part 4) he glides gently into death.

Many readers have been perplexed, even dismayed, by the work. Huxley, in a letter to Broch (10 April 1945), criticized the use of extensive philosophical lyricism with no contrasting passages of narrative:

My own feeling is that quantity destroys quality and that though, intrinsically, the sentences of which these sections are composed are rich with beauty and meaning, the very number of them—because of their intensity and their stylistic strangeness—imposes a strain upon the reader's mind and makes him, in the long run, incapable of reacting adequately to them.

(*Kommentierte Werkausgabe,* vol. 13/2, p. 457)

Many readers, even the most sympathetic, would probably agree with Huxley. The effect of the work is akin to reading a five-hundred-page psalm: there is the same mixture of rhapsodic fervor, erotic imagery, and hymnic effusion. Only the third section is frankly narrative: it consists largely of conversations between Vergil and various visitors, including the dramatic high point of the work: the confrontation with Emperor Augustus. The long second section, on the other hand, is totally lyrical, unrelieved by any narrative, with disembodied imagery that remains frustratingly intangible.

Part of the difficulty in dealing with this work lies in the fact that Broch was consciously striving to create a new genre; to treat it as a novel is to criticize it unfairly. Alone among Broch's major prose works, it does not bear the designation "novel." In his letters and essays Broch consistently referred to it as a lyrical work. He insists in his "Bemerkungen zum 'Tod des Vergil'" (Comments on *The Death of Vergil,* written in 1944 and published in 1955) that the book is "a poem, though not in the sense of a single lyrical outburst and also not in the sense of a poem cycle on a central theme; yet a poem and, moreover, one that extends in a single breath over more than five hundred pages." The book is thus a novel only in the broad sense of German Romantic writers like Friedrich Schlegel, for whom the novel was "progressive" and "universal," embracing all poetic forms. To understand this is not to accept the method uncritically. Broch forgets that lyric poetry is effective precisely because it concentrates into a highly compressed distillate the emotion that evaporates when spread out over hundreds of pages. Few readers, if any, are capable of reading through the second part without being bogged down and thus losing the intended lyrical impact.

Despite this central problem, the book is one of the major literary works of the century; the conception alone is a daring step forward in the realm of poetry. Broch is concerned again with the resolution of the antinomies of life. From the very first page we are struck by a barrage of contrasts: above and below, within and without, here and beyond, past and present, motion and rest, I and all. Especially in the first half of the novel, life is presented as completely fragmented; nothing is whole. Vergil becomes increasingly aware of the dissonances of life and of the necessity to resolve them in order to attain any semblance of harmony. In *The Sleepwalkers* Broch presents this breakdown through disintegration of style, descending from the lyricism of the narrative poem to the rationality of the essay. Here he wishes to do more than depict fragmented reality; he wants to show the resolution of it all—in Vergil's mind as well as in style. Resolution is possible only when all aspects of reality can be brought together in a simultaneous vision: past, present, and future as well as life and death. A resolution of this sort can be accomplished only in sentences of a grand scope, and so Broch conceived as the underlying pattern of his book the idea "one thought, one moment, one sentence." This almost monomaniacal consistency produced some of the longest sentences ever written in the German language—sentences beside which even the more adventurous efforts of Mann pale. "One can probably claim," Broch asserted proudly in his comments on the novel, "that the sentences in the adagio of the second part belong to the longest in world literature." Broch justified this by his assumption that only a poetic form is "capable of producing unity of the disparate and making it plausible, for in a poem the utterance does not fulfill itself in the rational expression, but in the irrational tension between the words, between the lines, in short: in the 'architecture of meaning.'"

Broch buttressed this "architecture of meaning" in various ways. Each of the four sections has a central image (water, fire, earth, and ether) as well as a basic mood, which Broch conceives in such musical terms as *andante, adagio, maestoso.* The repetition and development of the various motives is treated consciously as musical variation. Broch's "Bemerkungen zum 'Tod des Vergil'" indicates to what an incredible extent even the slightest details of the work have been plotted to intensify the "architecture of meaning." In German literature there is no other prose work besides Rilke's *Die Aufzeichnungen des Malte Laurids Brigge* (*The Notebooks of Malte Laurids Brigge*, 1910) that demands the same degree of sustained attention, as though one were reading a poem.

Within this "symphonic" framework the book displays a distinct rhythm of development. In "The Arrival" Vergil is shocked into an awareness of the disjointedness of life. In his feverish state he is keenly aware of polarities: the leisure above deck on board the ship and the agonies of the slaves groaning over their oars in the galley; the blue sky above and the dark waters below; the stench and poverty of the slums and the luxury of Augustus' lofty palace. That night, as these impressions unite with memory in his feverish vision ("The Descent"), he comes to the frightful realization that his life as well as his work have excluded an entire half of existence; he has willfully shut out grief and ugliness for the sake of beauty alone. What the first part presents in visual contrasts and the second part in lyrical inner vision, the third part ("The Expectation") recapitulates in dialectical arguments between Vergil and his friends. In "The Homecoming," finally, all of these conflicting elements are resolved in a grand vision of unity as Vergil dies.

Vergil arrives at three important turning points during these last hours. The first comes during the night when he decides, as a gesture of expiation, to burn the *Aeneid*. In Vergil's mind his masterpiece has become a symbol of his own imperfection. For just as he had carefully filtered all disturbances out of his own life, so too had he distilled the reality of his poem until there was nothing left but beauty. The *Aeneid* is thus a living memorial to his "perjury" of reality, and he feels that he can atone for his guilt only by consigning his work to destruction.

The second turning point comes at the end of his audience with Emperor Augustus, a brilliant exercise in dialectics between the representatives of two cultural epochs. Augustus is an idealized totalitarian; for him all life revolves around the state, and the individual finds meaning only through service to the state. Vergil, on the other hand, is what Broch called a pre-Christian—he has his foot all but on the threshold of a new system of Christian values in which a concern for the individual will outweigh the totalitarian concept of imperial Rome. Because neither of these strong-willed men can understand the other, the dialogue does not become real communication but merely a statement of position in which they talk past each other. It illustrates the dilemma of "no longer and not yet," for Augustus represents an age that is virtually past while Vergil speaks with the voice of an era that has not yet come. (Actually the theme of "no longer and not yet" is subtly altered in this novel to "no longer and yet already" because Vergil has such strong premonitions of the future.) Vergil tries to explain his decision to destroy the *Aeneid,* but Augustus objects that the poet has fulfilled his ethical responsibility by creating an epic of the state in all its glory. He is of course offended when Vergil insists that the present Roman state is in itself no longer real, but merely the symbol of a human reality that still lies in the future: the Christian world. At this point the story takes an unexpected twist that betrays the novella origin of the plot. The two men have grown increasingly heated in the defense of their respective positions and the argument becomes intensely personal. Suddenly Vergil, relenting almost without motivation, agrees to give Augustus the manuscript. He has perceived, Broch implies, that it calls for an even greater sacrifice to forgo his desire to burn the manuscript. By destroying his poetry he would merely have gained a passing satisfaction; it would be a gesture of defiance. But by renouncing this wish he is able to commit an act of human love, thus anticipating in his own way the era of human commitment that is to come.

The third turning point comes at the end.

Vergil's death, though lyrical in tone, is not abstract, disembodied, or intangible. It is related at each step to a great mystical vision that derives its imagery from the story of the creation—but a creation experienced in reverse. Step by step, as he sinks out of life, Vergil feels himself moving progressively back through earlier stages of being: back through Paradise; back through the stages of animal, plant, and mineral life; back through the original separation of light and dark to the source of all being. And at that point—two pages from the end of the book—reunited with God, he turns around and, in one final vision, surveys all of life and reality. From this new position of reunification with the All he can now see the pattern of wholeness in life. All the polarities have disappeared. In death all opposites are reconciled. Life and death become one and the same. It is a conjuration of the *coincidentia oppositorum* unmatched in literature, perhaps, since the ecstatic visions of such fourteenth-century mystics as Meister Eckhart. (Certainly its closest modern counterpart is to be found in Novalis' lovely and mysterious *Hymnen an die Nacht* [*Hymns to the Night,* 1800].) In the hymnic prose of the finale this ending is plausible and stirring. Where the second part of the book fails in its cerebral and spiritualized lyricism, this section captures the imagination through its tactile vividness and carries the reader along with Vergil into the final vision of unity. Here, where the contradictions outlined in the first part are recapitulated and resolved, the reader feels that the long road has been worthwhile. The effect is that of an intense lyric poem, but a poem escalated into cosmic dimensions. This final section, which represents the *terminus ad quem* of the preceding five hundred pages, is one of the most powerful passages in modern literature.

The representation of death and dying in which the work culminates is more than a gesture of literary virtuosity. It fulfills an important function in Broch's development, paving the way for future thought. If we live in fear of death, then we cannot free our minds for the ethical problems of life. Broch wanted, by bringing death into his life and work, to annul its threat and thus open the way to an ethical system based not upon fear of death but purely upon the demands of life. In *The Unknown Quantity* death functions as no more than the manifestation of the irrational "irruption from below." Mother Gisson, in *Die Verzauberung,* achieves a "knowledge of the heart" in which life and death are one; but Broch portrays her from the outside, as an ideal, through the not-unbiased eyes of the doctor, and the reader must accept her spiritual harmony as an article of faith. In *Vergil* Broch wanted actually to render the experience of death—and to allow the reader to share in it—as an extension of life rather than as chaos and nothingness. This is the meaning of the fourth part, in which Vergil moves toward death through a series of transformations revealing that death is the source and complement of life—that it is merely another form of life. In this way death constitutes a resolution of the introductory opposites, for grief and agony, sickness and misery are elongations of death protruding into life, just as death is an extension of life into another realm—another typically Romantic attitude that Broch shares with contemporaries like Rilke and Hermann Hesse. When Vergil comes to terms with death, he likewise resolves the dissonant elements of the earlier passages by accepting them as an inevitable complement to life. Now that death—and its various extensions—no longer constitutes a threat, Broch can devote himself to a purely existential analysis of life in this world.

Broch considered that he had "finished [his] literary career once and for all" with *The Death of Vergil.* During the last ten years of his life he regarded his occasional literary work as a distinct and unpleasant intrusion on more important undertakings. Throughout Broch's life an absolute consistency of thought and action is apparent. In *The Death of Vergil* he reached the conclusion that ethical action was the responsibility of the individual. Since he saw a possibility for "concretization of ethics" only in poli-

HERMANN BROCH

tics, he devoted most of his energies to political theory and practical service. As a matter of fact, his literary work is almost totally confined to the brief period from 1928 to 1940; even his last novel, completed in 1949 and 1950, is based largely on stories written during the 1930's. During and after the war Broch was indefatigable in his efforts to help Jewish refugees and, from his meager resources, to send CARE packages to needy friends in Europe. In the early 1940's he worked actively with other prominent intellectuals for the project "The City of Man: A Declaration on World Democracy," and in the late 1940's he drafted ambitious plans for an international university and publicized his "Bill of Duties." His "absolute incapacity to hurt anyone" prompted him to spend hours answering letters—sometimes as many as two hundred and fifty a month. During the last five years of his life he frequently spoke almost mystically of the "seven projects" that he had in hand, and he was fond of comparing himself to Kafka's "Country Doctor," who, drive as hard as he may, can never reach the next village.

Broch was a dynamo of energy, capable of working intensively for eighteen hours a day. As he felt himself growing older this natural energy was intensified by what he called his "panic of not finishing." This "panic" was surely not lessened by the fact that he had no steady means of support. He was particularly anxious to complete his three-volume study of mass psychology because he hoped, on its merits, to obtain a professorship at Princeton's Institute for Advanced Studies that would afford him some measure of financial security. (He turned down a position at the East German University of Jena.) Meanwhile he lived at the expense of various foundations—Guggenheim, Rockefeller, Bollingen, Oberlaender, the American Academy of Arts and Letters—and from the income of occasional commissioned "literary" projects. Thus in 1947 he accepted a commission from the Bollingen Press to write an introduction to a translation of Hofmannsthal's prose. Although Broch began with a sense of contempt for a poet he regarded as a

fin de siècle dandy, he gradually overcame his repulsion "as a homosexual relationship develops slowly between the chambermaid and the lady." The result, published only posthumously as *Hugo von Hofmannsthal and His Time,* is one of the great cultural analyses of that fascinating epoch.

In 1949 Broch married for a second time, to Anne Marie Meier-Graefe, and moved from Princeton to New Haven, where efforts were in progress to obtain for him an honorary professorship in the German department at Yale University. He was on the point of returning to Europe for the first time since his emigration when a heart attack abruptly ended his life on 31 May 1951. At the time of his death various groups in the United States and Austria were proposing him for the Nobel Prize, an honor he might well have received had he lived a few years longer. Broch is buried in Killingworth, Connecticut—a strange resting place for a man whose intense sincerity alone prevented him from becoming a caricature of the European intellectual.

Broch's last novel, prompted by financial urgency, grew from humble beginnings to significant proportions—a pattern we have repeatedly observed. In 1949 Broch received the proofs of five early stories that his publisher wished to reprint as a book in order to profit from the critical acclaim that Broch had won with *The Death of Vergil.* As Broch read through the stories, he became aware both of their inadequacies and of the common theme that seemed to run through them all. He decided to supplement the old stories with a few new ones, put them into a framework, and publish them as a "novel in eleven stories"—*The Guiltless.* The result, an indictment of the political indifference that led to the rise of National Socialism, is a direct offshoot of Broch's political theories. He explains his intentions in an epilogue:

The novel portrays German conditions and types of the pre-Hitler period. The figures chosen for this purpose are completely "unpolitical"; inasmuch as they have any political ideas at all, they hover in a vague and foggy realm. None of them is directly "guilty" for the Hitler catastrophe. For that reason the book is called "The Guiltless." Yet precisely this is the intellectual and emotional atmosphere from which . . . Nazism won its real powers. Political indifference is ethical indifference and hence, in the last analysis, closely related to ethical perversion. In short, the politically "innocent" are already situated rather deep in the realm of ethical guilt.

(*Gesammelte Werke,* vol. 5, p. 361)

Like *The Sleepwalkers* the novel is architectonically structured, spanning the full gamut of styles from lyricism to essayism. It is introduced by a parable after the fashion of Martin Buber's Hasidic tales—a fact not without interest since the theme of engagement between the I and the Thou is reminiscent of Buber's philosophy. The narrative consists of three groups of stories that take place in 1913, 1923, and 1933; each cycle is introduced by a "Canto" (not unlike Bertolt Brecht's ballads in their style) that represents the "voice" of the era.

The central figure is the young Dutch merchant Andreas, a man who has spent his life fleeing every sort of commitment. Because of his "fear of exams," he originally left school and home, emigrating to South Africa. This "fear of exams" is the symbolic motive of his existence. Whenever a situation arises in which he is compelled to make a decision, he simply moves on. As a result of his ready adaptability—like Huguenau's—he accumulates a fortune in diamonds. A man neither good nor bad, he remains completely without attachments in life. When we first catch a glimpse of him in a Paris café in 1913 he has just lost his mother. Ten years later, in Germany, Andreas is seeking the comforts of home and love without being willing to commit himself in return. He rents a room in the home of an elderly baroness and gradually manages to insinuate his way into her affections as the son of the house. At the same time he engages in a love affair with a young girl, Melitta. Hilde-

gard, the baroness' daughter, regards the two acts as irreconcilable. If Andreas has forced his way into two different sets of lives, then he must face the consequences and commit himself to one or the other. He has won the confidence of the baroness as well as Melitta. One or the other must be hurt, ultimately, when he breaks off the relationship. Hildegard urges Andreas to make up his mind; finally she takes action herself. She tells Melitta that Andreas is going to marry her, Hildegard; Melitta commits suicide. That same night Hildegard invites Andreas into her bedroom and, in one of the weirdest love scenes in literature, deliberately renders him impotent so that he will never again be tempted to desert her mother or make another girl unhappy. Ten years later, when Andreas is comfortably established with the baroness, Melitta's grandfather finds him. In their conversation Andreas becomes aware of his great guilt. Until now he had regarded Hildegard as Melitta's murderess; now he sees that it was his own lack of moral responsibility that really caused her death, and he commits suicide. This is the skeletal plot of the stories.

As usual Broch has filled out the very slight plot with symbolic elements that bear the burden of meaning. Among them is the triangle, which occurs unobtrusively in many of the stories as an image of the artificially isolated existence that tries to shield itself from commitment to reality. Then, the entire novel is based loosely on the legend of Don Juan. Various of the names are borrowed from the legend (Andreas buys a house from a certain Herr von Juna) and many of the episodes correspond to the archetypal structure of the legend (the avenging grandfather comes to Andreas as a reincarnation of the stone guest). Further, the Andreas plot is paralleled by the contrasting story of the schoolmaster Zacharias. The two men represent the gamut of human nature from A to Z; Broch hopes to achieve symbolic totality by implying that their attitudes embrace the whole range of human behavior. Whereas Andreas represents ethical guilt out of total lack of commitment, Zacharias is the born follower, who commits himself blindly to a false system of values (Nazism). Their failure to respond to the actualities of existence is revealed, again, in sexual symbolism. Andreas' incompetence is signified by his ultimate impotence and suicide while Zacharias, an ideological tyrant in public, is beaten by his wife when he gets home at night. The only integrated figure of the novel is the grandfather. An authority on beekeeping, he is closely linked to the powers of nature. Structurally his spirit permeates the entire novel, since the "Cantos" at the beginning of each section are ostensibly the songs that he sings as the conscience of his age.

On the one occasion when Andreas and Zacharias meet, they discuss Einstein's theory of relativity. Zacharias, the adherent of the closed system, rebels against the idea that reality is not hard and fast. As a teacher of mathematics he believes that he is justified, for pedagogic reasons, in ignoring new theories because they would confuse his pupils. In other words, he closes his eyes to any new conception of reality and follows a false prophet who promises to uphold the old order. Andreas, on the other hand, finds in the theory of relativity a perfect justification of his emotional liability and reluctance to take a stand. He allows himself to avoid the necessity of making decisions by saying that in a relativistic world all values are equally valid. It is only in his great confession, when the grandfather has convinced him of his guilt, that he admits, "I thought that I was fleeing irresponsibility, and in truth it was responsibility that I was fleeing. That is my guilt." In a world without absolutes, Andreas concludes, the proper human attitude cannot be attained "by a turn toward good, but only through a turning away from what is evil on earth." Because of his relativism he had failed to react against evil and thus had become guilty.

This last is not merely a piece of logical sophistry, but rather the result of Broch's most vital concern during his last years: his humane politics. He had concluded that political absolutes, as expressed in the Bill of Rights, are just as invalid in our time as religious absolutes because they too are founded on the notion of inalienable transcendental rights of mankind. Broch pleaded instead for a supplement, which he called the "Bill of Duties" and which he submitted for consideration to the United Nations and other world organizations. We do not need to assume the existence of transcendental rights, Broch argued. An entire system of ethics can be established upon the "earthly absolute" of total enslavement—the one act this side of death that deprives humanity of all dignity. Assuming that total enslavement is the absolute evil, it is the responsibility of the individual—in fact, his duty—to rebel against any act that threatens to lead to enslavement of humanity in any form. In other words, since absolute good is unknown, we do not always know what we should act *for*; entire totalitarian systems have been justified by the claim that they are acting on behalf of the good of the people. But since we do know what is absolutely *evil* here on earth, it is our duty at any time to reject any threat to human freedom and dignity.

Broch has come a long way since *The Sleepwalkers,* for *The Guiltless* is actually an indictment of purely "objective" men like Huguenau and passive followers like the villagers of Kuppron. *The Sleepwalkers* ends with the exhortation to brotherly love: "Do thyself no harm: for we are all here." In his theory of humane politics Broch concluded that a positive affirmation of solidarity is not enough. It is man's duty to rebel "negatively" (his own term) against absolute evil on earth. This is the position of a man who has witnessed the horrors of totalitarianism and the concentration camp, which he came to regard as the modern manifestation of absolute evil. This new ethical attitude explains his efforts to reshape the political thought of the postwar world by supplementing the conception of human "rights" with a bill of human "duties."

It is one of life's ironies that Broch, who struggled against "literature" most of his life, will always be known primarily as a novelist. The work he most prided himself on—his theory of values, epistemology, philosophy of history, mass psychology, and political theory— either remained virtually unknown or found no more than indirect expression in his novels. Attempts to present Broch as a systematic philosopher are probably futile. His own "impatience for cognition" prevented him from evolving any real system, and his total commitment to life engendered a dynamic development rather than any static and formalized attitude. His "philosophy" is to be found as much in his life, letters, and fiction as in his philosophical essays and theoretical fragments. In the last analysis, moreover, his ideas are not so original as he thought. To be sure, he formulated his own unique syntheses and coined brilliant phrases that appeal to the mind. But the elements of his thought, if not derivative of Kant's critical idealism and G. W. F. Hegel's dialectics, often parallel the existential analysis of thinkers like Karl Jaspers or Camus. This is not to denigrate the substance of Broch's thought. There is nobility in his conception of man's freedom and responsibility, just as there is dignity in the pattern of his life. But his real contribution is literary. Whereas one of his ideas often summons up associations with many other thinkers of the past and present, a page of his prose is instantly recognizable as his alone.

Broch never made his works easy for the reader. He once wrote that Joyce's weakness was his uncompromising attitude, but the second part of The Death of Vergil is just as thorny as Finnegans Wake (1939), without the compensation of Joyce's wit and sense of realism. On the other hand, Broch never made life or writing easy for himself. He was conscious of a mission in life, to which he devoted himself with absolute consistency and an almost messianic zeal. Yet the reader who is willing to follow Broch into the mazes of his works— whether the analytic landscape of The Sleepwalkers or the luxuriant jungle of The Death of Vergil—and to succumb to the curious synthesis of rationalism and mysticism will come away enriched. Broch's vision of the immanence of death will probably be regarded as his most original contribution to human experience. His evocation of the totality and simultaneity of life is his greatest achievement in literature.

Selected Bibliography

EDITIONS

INDIVIDUAL WORKS

Die Schlafwandler. 3 vols. Munich and Zurich, 1931–1932.

Die unbekannte Größe. Berlin, 1933.

James Joyce und die Gegenwart. Rede zu Joyce's 50. Geburtstag. Vienna, Leipzig, and Zurich, 1936.

Der Tod des Vergil. New York, 1945.

Die Schuldlosen: Roman in 11 Erzählungen. Munich and Zurich, 1950.

"Trotzdem: Humane Politik." Neue Rundschau 61: 1–31 (1950).

Die Entsühnung. Zurich, 1961.

COLLECTED WORKS

Die Gesammelten Werke. 10 vols. Zurich, 1952– 1961. Many of Broch's works were first published posthumously in this edition: Vol. 1. Gedichte. Edited by Erich Kahler. 1953. Vol. 2. Die Schlafwandler: Eine Romantrilogie. 1952. Vol. 3. Der Tod des Vergil. 1952. Vol. 4. Der Versucher: Roman. Edited by Felix Stössinger. 1953. Vol. 5. Die Schuldlosen: Roman in elf Erzählungen. Edited by Hermann Weigand. 1954. Vol. 6. Dichten und Erkennen. Edited by Hannah Arendt. 1955. Vol. 7. Erkennen und Handeln. Edited by Hannah Arendt. 1955. Vol. 8. Briefe: Von 1929 bis 1951. Edited by Robert Pick. 1957. Vol. 9. Massenpsychologie. Schriften aus dem Nachlass. Edited by Wolfgang Rothe. 1959. Vol. 10. Die unbekannte Größe und frühe Schriften. Edited by Ernst Schönwiese. 1961.

Kommentierte Werkausgabe. Edited by Paul Michael Lützeler. 13 vols. Frankfurt am Main, 1974– 1981. This edition, now the most complete one, contains notes as well as bibliographical references. Vol. 1. Die Schlafwandler. Vol. 2. Die unbekannte Größe. Vol. 3. Die Verzauberung. Vol. 4. Der Tod des Vergil. Vol. 5. Die Schuldlosen. Vol. 6. Novellen. Prosa. Fragmente. Vol. 7. Dramen.

Vol. 8. *Gedichte*. Vol. 9/1. *Schriften zur Literatur (Kritik)*. Vol. 9/2. *Schriften zur Literatur (Theorie)*. Vol. 10/1. *Philosophische Schriften (Kritik)*. Vol. 10/2. *Philosophische Schriften (Theorie)*. Vol. 11. *Politische Schriften*. Vol. 12. *Massenwahntheorie*. Vol. 13/1. *Briefe 1913–1938*. Vol. 13/2. *Briefe 1938–1945*. Vol. 13/3. *Briefe 1945–1951*.

SUPPLEMENTARY EDITIONS

Hermann Broch–Daniel Brody. *Briefwechsel 1930–1951*. Edited by Bertold Hack and Marietta Kleiß. Frankfurt am Main, 1971.

Hermann Broch. *Bergroman*. Kritische Ausgabe in vier Bänden. Edited by Frank Kress and Hans Albert Maier. Frankfurt am Main, 1969.

TRANSLATIONS

The Death of Vergil. Translated by Jean Starr Untermeyer. New York, 1945.

The Guiltless. Translated by Ralph Manheim. Boston, 1974.

Hugo von Hofmannsthal and His Time: The European Imagination, 1860–1920. Translated, edited, and with an introduction by Michael P. Steinberg. Chicago, 1984.

Short Stories. Edited by Eric Herd. London, 1966.

The Sleepwalkers: A Trilogy. Translated by Willa and Edwin Muir. London and Boston, 1932.

The Unknown Quantity. Translated by Willa and Edwin Muir. London and New York, 1935.

BIOGRAPHICAL AND CRITICAL STUDIES

Arendt, Hannah. "The Achievement of Hermann Broch." *Kenyon Review* 11:476–483 (1949).

Bier, Jean-Paul. *Hermann Broch et "La Mort de Virgile."* Paris, 1974.

Brinkmann, Richard. "Romanform und Werttheorie bei Hermann Broch: Strukturprobleme moderner Dichtung." *Deutsche Vierteljahrsschrift für Literaturwissenschaft und Geistesgeschichte* 31:169–197 (1957).

Brude-Firnau, Gisela, ed. *Materialien zu Hermann Brochs "Die Schlafwandler."* Frankfurt am Main, 1972.

Cohn, Dorrit Claire. *The Sleepwalkers: Elucidations of Hermann Broch's Trilogy*. The Hague, 1966.

Durzak, Manfred. *Hermann Broch in Selbstzeugnissen und Bilddokumenten*. Reinbek bei Hamburg, 1966.

———. *Hermann Broch*. Stuttgart, 1967.

———. *Hermann Broch: Der Dichter und seine Zeit*. Stuttgart, 1968.

———. *Hermann Broch: Perspektiven der Forschung*. Münich, 1972.

Freese, Wolfgang, and Karl Menges. *Broch-Forschung: Überlegungen zur Methode und Problematik eines literarischen Rezeptionsvorgangs*. Munich and Salzburg, 1977.

Kahler, Erich. *Die Philosophie von Hermann Broch*. Tübingen, 1962.

———, ed. *Dichter wider Willen: Einführung in das Werk von Hermann Broch*. Zurich, 1958.

Kessler, Michael, and P. M. Lützeler, eds. *Hermann Broch: Das dichterische Werk. Interpretationen, Aspekte, Kontexte*. Tübingen, 1987.

Koebner, Thomas. *Hermann Broch: Leben und Werk*. Bern, 1965.

Koopmann, Helmut. *Der klassische-moderne Roman in Deutschland: Thomas Mann, Alfred Döblin, Hermann Broch*. Stuttgart, 1983.

Kreutzer, Leo. *Erkenntnistheorie und Prophetie: Hermann Brochs Romantrilogie "Die Schlafwandler."* Tübingen, 1966.

Loos, Beate. *Zeit und Tod: Der Bergroman Hermann Brochs und seine dichtungstheoretischen Voraussetzungen*. Frankfurt am Main, 1971.

Lützeler, Paul Michael. *Hermann Broch: Ethik und Politik. Studien zum Frühwerk und zur Romantrilogie "Die Schlafwandler."* Munich, 1973.

———. *Hermann Broch: Eine Biographie*. Frankfurt am Main, 1985.

———, ed. *Materialien zu Hermann Broch "Der Tod des Vergil."* Frankfurt am Main, 1976.

———, ed. *Brochs "Verzauberung."* Frankfurt am Main, 1983.

Mandelkow, Karl Robert. *Hermann Brochs Romantrilogie "Die Schlafwandler."* Heidelberg, 1962.

Martini, Fritz. "*Der Tod des Vergil*." In *Das Wagnis der Sprache*. Stuttgart, 1954.

Menges, Karl. *Kritische Studien zur Wertphilosophie Hermann Brochs*. Tübingen, 1970.

Mitchell, Breon. *James Joyce and the German Novel, 1922–1933*. Athens, Ohio, 1976.

Modern Austrian Literature. Special Hermann Broch Issue. 13/4 (1980).

Schlant, Ernestine. *Die Philosophie Hermann Brochs*. Bern, 1971.

———. *Hermann Broch*. Boston, 1978.

Simpson, Malcolm R. *The Novels of Hermann Broch.* Bern, 1977.

Steinecke, Hartmut. "Hermann Broch." In *Deutsche Dichter der Moderne.* Edited by Benno von Wiese. Berlin, 1965.

——. *Hermann Broch und der polyhistorische Roman. Studien zur Theorie und Technik eines Romantyps der Moderne.* Bonn, 1968.

Strelka, Joseph. *Kafka, Musil, Broch und die Entwicklung des modernen Romans.* Vienna, 1959.

——, ed. *Broch heute.* Frankfurt am Main, 1978.

Thieberger, Richard, ed. *Hermann Broch und seine Zeit. Akten des Internationalen Broch-Symposiums.* Nice, 1979. Bern, 1980.

Untermeyer, Jean Starr. "Midwife to a Masterpiece." In *Private Collection.* New York, 1965.

Weigand, Hermann J. "Broch's *Death of Vergil*: Program Notes." *Publications of the Modern Language Association* 62:525–554 (1947).

——. "Hermann Broch's *Die Schuldlosen*: An Approach." *Publications of the Modern Language Association* 68:323–334 (1953).

Ziolkowski, Theodore. "Zur Entstehung und Struktur von Hermann Brochs *Schlafwandler.*" *Deutsche Vierteljahrsschrift für Literaturwissenschaft und Geistesgeschichte* 38:40–69 (1964).

——. "Hermann Broch and Relativity in Fiction." *Wisconsin Studies in Comparative Literature* 3:365–376 (1967).

——. "Hermann Broch's *The Sleepwalkers.*" *Dimensions of the Modern Novel.* Princeton, N.J., 1969.

——. "Broch's Image of Vergil and Its Context." *Modern Austrian Literature* 13:1–30 (1980).

BIBLIOGRAPHIES

Jonas, Klaus W., and Herta Schwarz. "Bibliographie Hermann Broch." In Hermann Broch–Daniel Brody, *Briefwechsel 1930–1951.* Frankfurt am Main, 1971.

Sammons, Christa. "Hermann Broch Archive—Yale University Library." *Modern Austrian Literature* 5/3–4:18–69 (1972).

Additional bibliographical information may be found in the individual volumes of the *Kommentierte Werkausgabe.*

THEODORE ZIOLKOWSKI

GEORG TRAKL

(1887–1914)

LIFE, MILIEU, CONTACTS

GEORG TRAKL WAS born on 3 February 1887 in Salzburg, Austria; he died on 3 or 4 November 1914 in the psychiatric ward of a military hospital in Cracow, Poland. He lived his brief, troubled life in a time and place marked by radical cultural innovation and incipient social and political disaster. The time was the *Jahrhundertwende* (turn of the century), which, in spirit, extended from 1900 to the outbreak of World War I. The place was Austria under the Habsburg monarchy in the era of its greatest cultural achievements; Trakl's immediate contemporaries included— among a host of others—Sigmund Freud, Ludwig Wittgenstein, Gustav Mahler, Arnold Schoenberg, Oscar Kokoschka, and Gustav Klimt. It was also the era of the monarchy's corruption and decay, conditions fully recognized by such writers and critics as Arthur Schnitzler and Karl Kraus, but denied by traditional Austrian (especially Viennese) insouciance. Hermann Broch named the Habsburg monarchy in its long period of decline and dissolution—the sixty-eight year reign of Emperor Franz Joseph (1848–1916)—*die fröhliche Apokalypse* (the gay apocalypse).

Broch's witty and apposite oxymoron characterizes a brilliant, affluent, and creative society, but a society whose artists and intellectuals were engaged in sending out the message that the situation was both serious and possibly hopeless. We can hear it in the valedictory aura of Mahler's two greatest works, *Das Lied von der Erde* (*Song of the Earth,* 1908–1909) and his Ninth Symphony (1908–1909). (When Mahler attempts the mode of high affirmation, as in the Eighth Symphony [1906], his music loses authenticity.) The unpopularity of Freud's work in Austria was more than a matter of the prophet being without honor in his own country; what Freud had to tell his fellow citizens was (rightly or wrongly) understood as a critique of a profoundly sick and decayed civilization.

There were other symptoms, social and political, of impending troubles. Newly emergent Austrian liberalism, distinguished for its easy tolerance and faith in historical progress, was challenged in the last two decades of the nineteenth century by an abrasive, violent style of right-wing political behavior. Among the new men of the Right was Georg von Schönerer, who, according to Carl Schorske, "elevated anti-Semitism into a major disruptive force in Austrian political life." It was Schönerer whom Adolf Hitler acknowledged as his "teacher," a political activist who exploited the vicious possibilities of programmatic anti-Semitism.

Politics was one barometer of the moral and cultural climate; the private testimony of contemporary witnesses was another. The great pianist and teacher Artur Schnabel, who studied in Vienna from 1888 to 1898, comments in his memoirs on the generalized sense of malaise prevalent at that time:

> The upper classes in Vienna seemed to know they were doomed. It was a last escape into sweet superficiality, into an aesthetically pleasant defeatism. . . . Life in such an atmosphere was not enjoyable for everyone. I, for one, did not feel entirely happy there. The spirit of defeatism gradually permeating the air hemmed in creative impulses and the healthy development of higher gifts, both not yet rare among the Viennese. . . . The feeling of decadence was so strong that the best intellects began to distrust the honesty of their own impulses and validity of the values they believed in.
>
> (*My Life and Music,* pp. 13–14, 32)

The career and work of Trakl are in complete harmony with the apocalyptic mood of his age. He is perhaps the most doom-haunted artist of the *Jahrhundertwende*; if we survey the titles of his poems, we discover the range and variety of an obsessive concern with a world dissolving in corruption and decay. We have these ominous legends at the head of Trakl's poems: "Verfall" ("Ruin," 1913), "Untergang" ("Downfall," 1914), "Vorhölle" ("Limbo," 1914), "Die Ratten" ("The Rats," 1913), "Trübsinn" ("Melancholy," 1913). In 1914, four years before Oswald Spengler began publishing *Der Untergang des Abendlandes* (*The Decline of the West*, 1918–1922), Trakl wrote his own somber meditation on historical pessimism, the poem called "Abendland" ("The Occident"). Dedicated to the poet Else Lasker-Schüler—whom Trakl had briefly met in March 1914—the last stanza of "The Occident" projects a stunning vision of an urban apocalypse:

> *Ihr grossen Städte*
> *Steinern aufgebaut*
> *In der Ebene!*
> *So sprachlos folgt*
> *Der Heimatlose*
> *Mit dunkler Stirne dem Wind,*
> *Kahlen Bäumen am Hügel.*
> *Ihr weithin dämmernden Ströme!*
> *Gewaltig ängstet*

> *Schaurige Abendröte*
> *Im Sturmgewölk.*
> *Ihr sterbende Völker!*
> *Bleiche Woge*
> *Zerschellend am Strande der Nacht,*
> *Fallende Sterne.*

> You mighty cities
> Built up of stone
> In the plain!
> So the silent outcast
> With darkened forehead
> Follows the wind,
> Leafless trees on the hill.
> You far-off, fading streams!
> The fearsome red glow of sunset
> Strikes terror
> In the thunderclouds.
> You dying peoples!
> Pale wave
> Shattering on the shore of night
> Falling stars.
>
> (1.140)[1]

We note some of the more compelling biblical images: the stone cities of the plain (Sodom and Gomorrah), the fleeing outcast with the mark of Cain on his forehead, and the terrifying flow of the Occident's last sunset. Trakl juxtaposes his sequence of apocalyptic imagery without providing syntactical connecting structures; this "suppression of 'links in the chain'"—as T. S. Eliot called the figure of rhetoric known as parataxis—allows Trakl a vividness and intensity that might otherwise be attenuated in conventional narrative arrangement.

The English and American reader will recognize a similarity, both of content and method, between Trakl's "The Occident" and the phantasmagoric landscape of "What the Thunder Said," the last movement of Eliot's *The Waste Land* (1922):

Who are those hooded hordes swarming
Over endless plains, stumbling in cracked earth

---

[1] All citations from Trakl's poetry are taken from the two-volume critical edition, *Dichtungen und Briefe,* edited by Walther Killy and Hans Szklenar. Salzburg, 1969.

Ringed by the flat horizon only
What is the city over the mountains
Cracks and reforms and bursts in the violet air
Falling towers
Jerusalem Athens Alexandria
Vienna London
Unreal

Both Trakl and Eliot are visionary poets, prophets making their "eschatological threat." They share the inheritance of symbolism and its radical techniques of composition. Their depictions of historical catastrophe were partly in response to cultural conditions; early interpretations of *The Waste Land* read it as a critique of the 1920's and its mood of fashionable despair. But Eliot denied that *The Waste Land* was a diagnosis of the ills of society; it was written out of intense personal suffering, and had, he remarked, cost him dearly in experience. For poets like Eliot and Trakl, "the imagination is always at the end of an era"; the apocalypse—the recurrent myth of the end of the world—becomes a trope for personal anxiety and disorder in the psyche.

The bare facts of Trakl's life tell an astonishing and dismaying story of pathological behavior. When he was fifteen he began experimenting with chloroform, and by the time he had finished his studies at the gymnasium he was a confirmed drug addict. At one time or another, Trakl took veronal, morphine, opium, and cocaine. It was a self-administered overdose of cocaine that killed Trakl in November 1914. In addition to the drug-taking, Trakl was known as a heavy consumer of alcohol and on occasion drank himself into insensibility. This grotesquely self-destructive behavior has convinced psychiatrically oriented critics that Trakl, from his fifteenth year on, suffered from schizophrenia, the well-documented but mysterious disease that has its origins in the physical and psychic changes associated with adolescence and that often eventually leads to incurable dementia. The alienist who made the final diagnosis of Trakl's mental condition noted that he suffered from dementia praecox, a nineteenth-century term of nearly worthless heuristic value.

Although we have no precise clinical picture of Trakl's illness, it is clear he belonged to that large and hardly exclusive band of modern *poètes maudits* whose sickness, it is frequently alleged, was also the source of their creative powers. A short list of twentieth-century poets who were confined for mental illness, suffered recurring psychotic episodes, or committed suicide while of unsound mind, includes Ezra Pound, Hart Crane, Robert Lowell, Paul Celan, Dylan Thomas, John Berryman, Theodore Roethke, Sylvia Plath, and Anne Sexton. It sometimes seems that in our times madness has been a precondition for the practice of poetry and that the poet pays dearly for his gifts. The Devil raves in Thomas Mann's *Doctor Faustus* (1947):

Do you believe in anything that possesses *ingenium* [genius] that does not partake of hell? *Non datur* [it is not given]. The artist is the brother of the criminal and the madman. Do you think that any fully living work ever came into being without its maker having learned to understand the nature of the criminal and madman?

Trakl was the fourth of six children born to Tobias and Maria Trakl. Tobias was a successful hardware dealer in Salzburg, and the family lived in prosperous middle-class circumstances. There was a large, elegantly furnished house, many servants, a governess, and piano lessons for the children. Otto Basil records that Georg's younger brother Fritz reports: "Things went very well for us; we had a large home and lived in that comfortable and complacent ease which no one today can anymore imagine." If, however, the family's outward behavior seemed normal, there was a network of inner tensions that exerted their effect on the developing child. Neither father nor mother enjoyed a close relationship with the children. Tobias Trakl was fifteen years older than his wife, and over fifty when Georg was born. Maria was an aloof, neurotic woman who took opium and

1411

suffered from periods of depression. She had been raised as a Catholic, but Georg and his siblings were baptized in the Protestant faith of their father. When young Georg was five, he was enrolled in a Catholic day school; on two afternoons a week, however, he took Protestant religious instruction from Parson Aumüller, an experience that could only have been confusing to the sensitive child.

In 1892 Margarethe (Grete) Trakl, the poet's beloved younger sister, was born. Grete doubtless was the single human being closest to him; the exact nature of their intimacy, however, is a matter of disagreement among Trakl scholars. On the basis of certain thematic insistencies in early work—most dramatically in the unpublished "Blutschuld" ("Incest")—some exegetes, including Theodor Spoerri, have argued that actual sexual relations existed between brother and sister. All Trakl scholars, however, have remarked on the persistent image of *die Schwester* (the sister) that haunts Trakl's verse, early and late. Michael Hamburger, in his fine essay on Trakl, urges caution in using poetic texts to draw biographical conclusions:

> . . . neither the references to incest in Trakl's early work nor the personage of the sister in the later poems permits any biographical deductions. Incest is one of many forms of evil that occurs in Trakl's work; and the personage of the sister is a kind of spiritual alter ego, an anima figure so that in certain poems a brother-sister relationship symbolizes an integration of self. Trakl used many other legendary or archetypal personages in his poetry, not to write his autobiography, but to compose visionary poems of an unprecedented kind.
>
> (*Contraries: Studies in German Literature,*
> p. 295)

It may cast some light on this dark matter to recall how Lord Byron transmuted the scandalous actuality of his liaison with his half sister Augusta Leigh into poetic fiction. She appears in *Manfred* (1817) as Astarte, an anima figure who is not only Manfred's spiritual semblance but his exact physical counterpart:

> She was like me in lineaments—her eyes,
> Her hair, her features, all, to the very tone
> Even of her voice, they said were like to mine;
> But softened all, and tempered into beauty.
> (2.2. 105–108)

Obviously the poet who gazes into the mirror of the self encounters his own image, and, from the Freudian point of view, reveals his overwhelming preoccupation to direct his sexual energy inward. The love of Byron and Trakl for their sisters is a thinly veiled narcissism, a primitive stage in human sexual development. But we might note—as Robert Graves tells us—that Astarte was one of the many names for the White Goddess, the muse who represents the ultimate source of the poet's creative energy.

It should also be mentioned that incest as a literary subject was in the air of the decadent *Jahrhundertwende.* Ulrich, the hero of Robert Musil's *Der Mann ohne Eigenschaften* (*The Man Without Qualities*, 1930–1942) is deeply involved with his sister Agathe; the third volume of Musil's unfinished novel of life in the kingdom of Kakania—Musil's scatological name for the Habsburg monarchy—offers a minutely analyzed account of their complex sexual relationship. Ulrich and Agathe represent, in Ulrich's words,

> . . . this desire for a doppelgänger of the opposite sex, this craving for the love of a being that will be entirely the same as oneself and yet another, distinct from oneself, a magical figure that is oneself. . . . This old, old dream of the essence of love meeting, unhampered by the limitations of the corporeal world, in two identical-distinct figures.
>
> (3.282)

In the same year that Grete was born, 1892, Trakl began his formal schooling. He spent five years in the Catholic elementary school, and when he was ten he entered the *humanistisches Staatsgymnasium,* the state-run secondary school. From September 1897 to July 1905 he attended the gymnasium; he was a poor student, and because of unsatisfactory grades in Greek, Latin, and mathematics he was required to repeat the fourth form. He continued to make poor grades, and in the seventh form (September 1905), he officially withdrew from the gymnasium. From his thirteenth year on Trakl had piano lessons with the composer August Brunetti-Pisano, and displayed particular enthusiasm for the Romantic composers Frédéric Chopin, Franz Liszt, and later Richard Wagner. The interest in Wagner was evidently stimulated by the literary example of Charles Baudelaire and the symbolist understanding of music as the nonreferential art of pure form. Basil writes that "friends of his youth also report that he gave unambiguous approval to Wagner's glorification of incest in *Die Walküre.*

Under the influence of the French symbolist poets, especially Baudelaire and Paul Verlaine and their German counterparts Stefan George and Hugo von Hofmannsthal, Trakl wrote his earliest poems in 1904. At this time he also joined a *Dichterverein* (poet's club) which first called itself "Apollo," then "Minerva." This circle of congenial and like-minded young poets was united in its veneration of those two prophets of modernism, Friedrich Nietzsche and Feodor Dostoevsky; their spiritual presence was felt everywhere in the German-speaking world of the *Jahrhundertwende.* The characteristic aura of Trakl's early poetry is generated by the tension between Nietzschean frenzy and Dostoevskian despair.

Trakl's forced withdrawal from the gymnasium provoked a vocational crisis; it was decided (a most fateful decision as it turned out) that he should become a pharmacist. In the fall of 1905 he entered on a three-year apprenticeship in the Salzburg pharmacy, at the White Angel. His profession gave him unlimited access to a great variety of drugs. From the time of

his adolescence to the year of his death in 1914, he was a consistent, heavy user of narcotics. The pervading sensory dislocation and the deliberate use of synaesthesia found in all of his poetry are the results of taking narcotics.

In 1906 Trakl wrote two one-act verse tragedies, *Totentag* (All Souls Day) and *Fata Morgana.* Both plays were produced by the Salzburg city theater. *Totentag* was well received by the local newspaper, *Der Salzburger Volksblatt* (The Salzburg People's Press) but the *Fata Morgana* was judged a flop. Disappointment over the failure temporarily crippled his creative impulses and led him to experimenting with stronger narcotics, especially morphine and veronal. However, toward the end of 1907, he started work on a three-act tragedy, *Don Juans Tod* (Don Juan's Death). The manuscript of this work was evidently destroyed in 1912.

Early in 1908 Trakl successfully sat for the preliminary examination in pharmacology that qualified him for university study. He moved from Salzburg to Vienna in September 1908 and enrolled in the university for the four-semester course in pharmacology. He sat for his oral examinations in June and July 1910 and was awarded the master's degree in pharmacy. It was in 1910 that his work revealed a definitive breakthrough toward formal mastery. He wrote "Verfall" ("Decline"), "Die Schöne Stadt" ("The Beautiful City") and "Der Gewitterabend" ("The Stormy Evening," 1913). These poems combine technical brilliance in manipulating traditional elements of form, especially meter, rhyme, and stanza, with Trakl's unique handling of Romantic and symbolist imagery.

From 1 October 1910 to 30 September 1911, Trakl was on active duty as a one-year volunteer with the medical service of the Austro-Hungarian army. He was stationed in Vienna; after the completion of his enlistment, he was transferred to inactive status to serve in the army reserve district of Innsbruck. He returned to Salzburg for a brief period to work as a pharmacist at the White Angel, but he found the work so uncongenial that he asked to be returned to active duty in the army. Accordingly, he was assigned to serve in the pharmacy of a garrison hospital at Innsbruck for a six-month probationary period beginning in April 1912. It was in Innsbruck that he was introduced to Ludwig von Ficker, the editor of *Der Brenner*, and his coworkers Carl Dallago, Karl Borromäus Heinrich, and Karl Röck. *Der Brenner*, named after the nearby mountain pass, was a bimonthly journal that maintained the highest aesthetic and ethical standards. Among the Viennese avant-garde it had an especially high reputation, and earned from the acerbic and fastidious Kraus the following encomium, reported by Basil: "One knows that the only honest Austrian review appears in Innsbruck—and one should also know, when one is in Germany rather than Austria, that the only honest review likewise appears in Innsbruck."

Der Brenner, its editor Ficker, and Innsbruck itself became the steady center around which Trakl's increasingly disordered and mentally alienated existence turned. From 1912 to his death in November 1914, Trakl published at least one poem in every issue of *Der Brenner*. Ficker played a multiple role in Trakl's life as editor, critic, and spiritual advisor and comforter. After Trakl suffered a particularly severe bout of depression and mental anguish in March 1913, Ficker offered him refuge in his own home in Innsbruck and with his brother at Schloss Hohenburg near Igls. In April, Franz Werfel, then a reader for the Leipzig publisher Kurt Wolff, was impressed with the poems by Trakl he had read in *Der Brenner*. He suggested that Trakl put together a volume; after some negotiations involving format and the number of poems, Wolff published in July 1913 Trakl's first book of poems called simply *Gedichte* (Poems).

Trakl's last year of life, 1914, was crowded with personal incident and apocalyptic event. Despite recurrent attacks of depression and severe mental confusion, he remained steadily prolific and continued to publish in *Der Bren-*

ner. Toward the end of May he corrected the proofs of his second collection *Sebastian im Traum* (Sebastian Dreaming), which Wolff published posthumously in 1915. With the exception of the trip to Berlin in March, he remained in Innsbruck until he left in August for the eastern front.

Between 15 and 25 March Trakl was in Berlin comforting his sister Grete, who was severely ill from the aftereffects of a miscarriage. Grete, a gifted pianist, had taken up residence in Berlin to study with the eminent pianist and composer Ernst von Dohnányi. There she had married the book dealer Arthur Langen, a man considerably older than herself. In Berlin Trakl also had several meetings with the poet Lasker-Schüler; she recorded her impressions of the poet in a poem:

Seine Augen standen ganz fern.
Er war als Knabe einmal schon im Himmel.

Darum kamen seine Worte hervor
Auf blauen und auf weissen Wolken.

Wir stritten über Religion,
Aber immer wie zwei Spielgefährten,

Und bereiteten Gott von Mund zu Mund.
Im Anfang war das Wort.

Des Dichters Herz, eine feste Burg,
Seine Gedichte: Singende Thesen.

Er war wohl Martin Luther.

Seine dreifaltige Seele trug er in der Hand,
Als er in den heiligen Krieg zog.

—Dann wusste ich, er war gestorben—

Sein Schatten weilte unbegreiflich
Auf dem Abend meines Zimmers.

His eyes were those of an outsider.
Like a boy he was once more in heaven.

Thus his words poured forth

On blue and white clouds.

We quarreled about religion,
But always as two playfellows,

We prepared God's way from mouth to mouth
In the beginning was the Word.

The poet's heart, a mighty fortress,
His poems: singing theses.

He was indeed Martin Luther.

He held in his hand his three-personed soul,
As he marched in the holy war.

—Then I knew, he had died—

Ungraspable, his shadow lingers
On the evening of my room.

In July 1914, just a few weeks before Austria-Hungary declared war on Serbia and Russia, an event of singular generosity briefly eased Trakl's always desperate financial circumstances. Ficker received, from an unknown donor, the sum of 100,000 Austrian crowns with instructions that he divide the money among needy Austrian artists. Accordingly, Ficker allotted 20,000 crowns each to Trakl and Rainer Maria Rilke. The mysterious Maecenas turned out to be the philosopher Ludwig Wittgenstein, who wished to divest himself of a considerable patrimony. Poet and philosopher came close to an actual meeting. Trakl, confined in the psychiatric ward of the Cracow military hospital, learned from Ficker that Wittgenstein was attached to the Cracow command. Trakl sent Wittgenstein a postcard urging that he visit him in the hospital. Unfortunately, Wittgenstein was away on a reconnaissance mission; when he returned to his Cracow post, he learned that Trakl had died three days earlier and had already been buried. Later, as recorded by Basil, Wittgenstein was said to have remarked of Trakl's poems: "I do not understand them; but their tone pleases me. It is the tone of true genius."

At first Trakl seemed to have welcomed the outbreak of the war; he came from a patriotic, middle-class family loyal to the emperor Franz Joseph. The war also offered an immediate solution to the problems of vocation; on 24 August he joined, with his old rank of dispensing pharmacist, a medical detachment in Innsbruck. The detachment was sent to Galicia in Austrian Poland, where it first saw combat. Under the command of thoroughly incompetent generals, the Austrian Second and Third Armies suffered a series of major defeats. Trakl's medical detachment took part in the bloody action at Grodek. Without the help of physicians or medical supplies, Trakl was left in charge of nearly ninety severely wounded men who occupied a barn. For two days and two nights he listened to the cries and groans of the tormented soldiers, but he was helpless to do anything for them. He rushed out of the barn only to witness a scene of ghastly horror; from a row of leafless trees swung a group of hanged men, Ruthenians whom the Austrians had executed because they were suspected of being spies or Russian sympathizers.

This proved too much for Trakl, and on the general retreat from Grodek he suffered a major psychotic episode. At the evening meal he announced to his fellow officers that he intended to shoot himself; however, he was restrained and disarmed. In the middle of October he was ordered to the hospital at Cracow for observation of his mental condition. Ficker hastened to Cracow and visited with Trakl on 25 and 26 October. Ficker vainly tried to secure his friend's release from close confinement in the hospital's mental ward; he feared (quite correctly) that the lack of freedom and the depressing atmosphere could only worsen Trakl's condition. During the visit Trakl read to Ficker two poems, "Klage" ("Lament") and "Grodek." These were the last poems Trakl wrote; "Grodek" is arguably Trakl's greatest sustained lyric.

When Ficker returned to Innsbruck, he received the following letter from Trakl, dated 27 October 1914:

GEORG TRAKL

Dear, honored friend!
I send enclosed copies of the two poems I promised you. Since your visit to the hospital, my despair has doubled. I feel I am already beyond this world. Finally, I want to add, that in case of my demise, it is my wish and will that my beloved sister Grete should own all the money and other goods I possess. I embrace you deeply, dear friend.

Your
George Trakl

(Ludwig von Ficker, "Der Abschied" in *Errinnerung an George Trakl: Zeugnisse und Briefe,* Salzburg, 1959, p. 210)

This letter was, in effect, a suicide note. A week later, in the evening of 3 November, Trakl died of an overdose of cocaine. He was buried in a local cemetery in Cracow; in 1925 his remains were removed to the Tyrol and reburied in Mühlau near Innsbruck. His sister Grete survived him three years; on 21 November 1917, she shot herself while attending a party.

SHORTER POEMS

"Sommer" ("Summer," 1915), from Trakl's second published collection, *Sebastian im Traum,* exemplifies the technical mastery of his mature style:

> *Am Abend schweigt die Klage*
> *Des Kuckucks im Wald.*
> *Tiefer neigt sich das Korn*
> *Der rote Mohn.*
>
> *Schwarzes Gewitter droht*
> *Über dem Hügel.*
> *Das alte Lied der Grille*
> *Erstirbt im Feld.*
>
> *Nimmer regt sich das Laub*
> *Der Kastanie.*
> *Auf der wendeltreppe*
> *Rauscht dein Kleid.*
>
> *Stille leuchtet die Kerze*
> *Im dunklen Zimmer;*
>
> *Eine silberne Hand*
> *Löschet sie aus;[2]*
>
> *Windstille, sternlose Nacht.*

At evening the cuckoo's clamor
Grows still in the wood.
Deeper bends the grain,
The red poppy.

Over the hill
A black thunderstorm threatens.
The ancient song of the cricket
Fades in the field.

The chestnut leaves
Do not stir.
Your dress rustles
On the winding stair.

Quietly the candle gleams
In the dark room;
A silver hand
Quenches it;

Windless, starless night.

(1.136)

What immediately strikes the reader is the rich progression of images. Normal connectives are repressed; there is not a single "and" or "but" in the entire poem. Images are related to each other not by syntax but through tonal progression—a method we would identify as more musical than grammatical. Trakl's image includes not only visual experience but also what the ear hears—the cuckoo's clamor and the cricket's song—and what pressures—the bending of the grain and poppies—are recorded by the poet's kinaesthetic sense. A loosely metrical arrangement that alternates two- and three-stress lines moves the poem gently from daylight to darkness. In the introduction to the translation, *Twenty Poems of George Trakl,* the poet Robert Bly speaks of "the magnificent silences" in Trakl's poetry. There are expressive pauses be-

---

[2] The critical edition edited by Killy and Szklenar gives *löschte* and *löschet* as a variant. I feel *löschet* to be correct.

tween images, between stanzas, and a long fermata separating the silver hand from final darkness. The rustling of a dress quietly signifies the entrance of a woman whom the poet's voice addresses with the intimate *dein*. She enters the poem almost unnoticed; it is not certain that it is her silver hand that puts out the candle. We have no clue to the woman's identity; her shadowy presence is the last of summer's images before the darkness drops. Trakl's paratactic sequence of images weaves a texture of felt experiences; it is a method that recalls such vivid evocations of the world of sense as John Keats's "The Eve of St. Agnes" (1820) and the great odes.

The frequently anthologized and discussed "Ein Winterabend" ("A Winter Evening," 1915) exemplifies this method:

> *Wenn der Schnee ans Fenster fällt,*
> *Lang die Abendglocke läutet,*
> *Vielen ist der Tisch bereitet*
> *Und das Haus ist wohlbestellt.*
>
> *Mancher auf der Wanderschaft*
> *Kommt ans Tor auf dunklen Pfaden.*
> *Golden blüht der Baum der Gnaden*
> *Aus der Erde kühlem Saft.*
>
> *Wanderer tritt still herein;*
> *Schmerz versteinerte die Schwelle.*
> *Da erglänzt in reiner Helle*
> *Auf dem Tische Brot und Wein.*

> When snow drifts down against the window,
> Long tolls the evening bell,
> The table is prepared for many
> And the house is well appointed.
>
> Many on their wanderings come
> On dark paths to the gate.
> Golden blooms the tree of grace
> From the earth's cool sap.
>
> Wanderer steps silently inside;
> Pain has turned the doorsill to stone.
> There gleam in clearest radiance
> On the table bread and wine.
>
> (1.102)

The structure of "A Winter Evening" is based on the familiar conventions of the German folk song as it was imitated by such Romantic practitioners as Heinrich Heine in his most celebrated poem, "Die Lorelei" (1823–1824):

> *Ich weiss nicht, was soll es bedeuten,*
> *Dass ich so traurig bin;*
> *Ein Märchen aus alten Zeiten,*
> *Das kommt mir nicht aus dem Sinn.*

Trakl follows the form of the ballad stanza with its alternating lines of four and three stresses; however, he uses the rhyme scheme *abba* rather than *abab* and establishes a falling (trochaic) rather than a rising (iambic) meter. The movement of trochees helps to maintain the prevailing elegiac tone as well as to support the strongly linked sequence of images. Linkage is also provided by grammatical subordination ("Wenn der Schnee . . . "), by the conjunction "Und" in line 4, and by the semantic resonances of each pair of lines. In stanzas 1 and 2 the first two lines direct our attention to the outside world of darkness and falling snow; the second pair of lines brings us inside the house, into a world of warmth and light. The imagery carries a weight of allegorical intent that is not present in the more purely descriptive "Summer"; "the tree of grace" (the Cross) and the "bread and wine" (the Eucharist) strongly suggest that we interpret the poem within a Christian context.

"An den Knaben Elis" ("To the Boy Elis"), written in the spring of 1913, makes use of free verse lines organized in triplets and concludes with a pregnant silence followed by a gnomic single line. This technique of spatial rhythm— a mannerism in Trakl—may have been suggested by Rilke:

> *Elis, wenn die Amsel im schwarzen Wald ruft,*
> *Dieses ist dein Untergang.*
> *Deine Lippen trinken die Kühle des blauen*
> *   Felsenquells.*

GEORG TRAKL

Lass, wenn deine Stirne leise blutet
Uralte Legenden
Und dunkle Deutung des Vogelflugs.

Du aber gehst mit weichen Schritten in die Nacht,
Die voll purpurner Trauben hängt,
Und du regst die Arme schöner im Blau.

Ein Dornenbusch tönt,
Wo deine mondenen Augen sind.
O, wie lange bist, Elis, du verstorben.

Dein Leib ist eine Hyazinthe,
In die ein Mönch die wächsernen Finger taucht.
Eine schwarze Höhle ist unser Schweigen,

Daraus bisweilen ein sanftes Tier tritt
Und langsam die schweren Lider senkt.
Auf deine Schläfen tropft schwarzer Tau,

Das lezte Gold verfallener Sterne.

Elis, when the blackbird calls in the dark wood,
This is your downfall.
Your lips drink in the coolness of the blue rock
   stream.

Stop! When your forehead softly bleeds
Primeval legends
And the dark omen of the flight of birds.

But you walk with quiet steps into the night,
Richly hung with purple grapes,
And move your arms more beautifully in the blue.

A thorn bush sings,
Where your moon-haunted eyes are.
O Elis, how long have you been dead.

Your body is a hyacinth,
In which a monk dips
His waxen fingers.
Our silence is a black cave,

From which at times a gentle animal steps forth
And slowly closes its heavy eyelids.
On your temples black dew drips.

The final gold of fallen stars.

(1.84)

Our first question might very well be, who is the boy Elis? A number of critics have identified a "historical" Elis, who lived in Sweden; others, including Herbert Lindenberger, see him as a figure in Trakl's private mythology. However, such knowledge does not help very much. All symbolist and postsymbolist mythologies are "private"; euhemerism—the belief that the gods of mythology had their origin in historical kings and heroes—is a long-discredited theory. Better questions to ask are: What *kind* of a poem *is* it? What is its literary *genre*? The imagery offers a powerful clue: the beautiful youth Hyacinthus was loved by Apollo but also by the West Wind. As Robert Graves retells the myth in *The Greek Myths*, one day Apollo was teaching the boy how to hurl the discus "when the West Wind caught it in midair, dashed it against Hyacinthus' skull, and killed him. From his blood sprang the hyacinthus flower." Trakl's "Elis" is a lament for a slain god—or in more formal terms a pastoral elegy. The slain god is also the Christ with his crown of thorns and his wounded body open to the probings of a sinister doubting Thomas.

Like that of the traditional pastoral elegy, the world of "Elis" is situated in an enclosed space, sealed off from the real world. But its version of pastoral is disquieting, a place of displacement and decline. Unlike what Northrop Frye has called in his *Anatomy of Criticism* "the green world" of Andrew Marvell's "The Garden" (1681) or Shakespeare's Arcadian comedies, "Elis" is a tainted pastoral and its color is blue. (The color blue and blueness are thematic throughout Trakl's work. Novalis' *blaue Blume*, as Herbert Lindenberger notes, seems an obvious source of the image.) There is consistent use of synaesthetic imagery: we experience a deliberate confusion between things seen and things heard. "[A] forehead . . . bleeds / Primeval legends . . . A thorn bush sings . . . / . . . silence is a black cave . . . " Synaesthesia, the crossing of the circuits of perception, may be attributed to the deracinating effects of the narcotics Trakl consistently used. However, the use of synaesthetic imagery held a central position in symbolist poetics; both Baudelaire and Arthur Rimbaud made mention of its aesthetic importance. Rimbaud's impassioned remarks in *Une saison en enfer* (*A Season in Hell,* 1873) constitute a celebrated theory of the *dérèglement des sens:*

> I invented the color of vowels! *A* black, *E* white, *I* red, *O* blue, *U* green.—I regulated the form and movement of every consonant, and, with instinctive rhythms, I was proud to have invented a poetic speech open some day to all the senses. I reserve the right of translation.

The last poem Trakl wrote is the very great "Grodek." The poem succeeds in every possible way: in its congruence of technical means and expression, and in its careful control of feeling with its mounting tension and final apocalyptic outburst. For reasons of euphony and rhythm I have departed slightly in my translation from a strictly literal rendering. In this kind of poetry the music is as important as the meaning:

Am Abend tönen die herbstlichen Wälder
Von tödlichen Waffen, die goldnen Ebenen
Und blauen Seen, darüber die Sonne
Düstrer hinrollt; umfängt die Nacht
Sterbende Krieger, die wilde Klage
Ihrer zerbrochenen Münder.
Doch stille sammelt im Weidengrund
Rotes Gewölk, darin ein zürnender Gott wohnt
Das vergossne Blut sich, mondne Kühle;
Alle Strassen münden in schwarze Verwesung.
Unter goldnem Gezweig der Nacht und Sternen
Es schwankt der Schwester Schatten durch den
*   schweigenden Hain,*
Zu grüssen die Geister der Helden, die blutenden
*   Häupter;*
Und leise tönen im Rohr die dunkeln Flöten des
*   Herbstes.*
O stolzere Trauer! ihr ehernen Altäre
Die heisse Flamme des Geistes Nährt heute ein
*   gewaltiger Schmerz,*
Die ungebornen Enkel.

At evening the autumn woods echo
With murderous weapons, echo the golden plains,
The blue lakes, and over all the sun
Descends to darkness; the night embraces
Warriors dying, the savage cries
Of their broken mouths.
And quietly gathering in the meadowland
A crimson cloud: within lives an angry god,
The spilt blood—cold as the moon;
All streets dissolve in black corruption.
Beneath the branches of night and stars
The sister's shadow stirs through the silent grove
To greet the ghosts of heroes, the bleeding heads;
And softly the dark flutes of autumn resound in the
    reeds.
O stiff-necked grief! You brazen altars
The spirit's blazing flame this day is fed by brutal
    pain,
Our children's children yet unborn.

(1.167)

To the reader who has previously entered Trakl's haunted world, the structure and imagery of "Grodek" are familiar. The poem falls into two strophes (lines 1–9, lines 11–17) separated by line 10: "Alle Strassen münden in schwarze Verwesung." This line has neither syntactic nor strictly lexical connection with what precedes it and what follows it. However, it serves as a pivot, as a kind of expressive irrelevancy on which the poet moves the reader from the descriptive to the hortatory. As is frequently the case with Trakl, the season is autumn and the time of day is evening, which with the rising of the stars deepens into night. The stream of images from Trakl's personal vocabulary includes the golden plains, the blue lakes, the dreadful coldness of the moon, and the black streets of corruption. The recurrent figure of *die Schwester* makes her final appearance with a greeting which is also "a kind of valediction." These images all occur in previous poems, and their sequence in "Grodek," rendered in a rising crescendo, culminates in anguished apostrophe: a convulsive and ambiguous prophecy.

"Grodek" might be compared with Wilfred Owen's "Strange Meeting" (1920). There are obvious similarities of subject matter; both poems originated in a personal response to the

1419

horror and pity of war. Owen's subtext is Dante's downward journey into Hell:

> It seemed that out of battle I escaped
> Down some profound dull tunnel, long since
>   scooped
> Through granites which titanic wars had groined.
> Yet also there encumbered sleepers groaned,
> Too fast in thought or death to be bestirred.
> Then, as I probed them, one sprang up and stared
> With piteous recognition in fixed eyes,
> Lifting distressful hands as if to bless.
> And by his smile, I knew that sullen hall;
> By his dead smile I knew we stood in Hell.
>
> (ll. 1–10)

Our immediate sense of this poem is the close articulation of its parts affected by the heavy iambic meter (with its slant rhymes) and by the grammatically precise narrative syntax. The poet is everywhere present in his poem; his encounter with his other is in the epic tradition of Odysseus' meeting with Elpenor or Dante's with Brunetto Latini. There is no explicit use of metaphor or allegory, except, of course, that the downward journey is an archetype for the spiritual quest. Meter and syntax serve a direct mimetic function, shaping the movement of thought and feeling. Thus Owen's poem is both representational and classical, and, although it was written in the twentieth century, stands outside the tradition of modernism.

In contrast, "Grodek" can stand as paradigmatic for the modernist poetic; every feature of its style represents a break with the mimetic tradition and its structures of articulation. Whereas "Strange Meeting" is written in first-person discourse, the poet of "Grodek" is nearly absent from his poem—at least until the dissonant prophecy of the final three lines. The metric of "Grodek" is "free" but richly modulated by alliteration:

> *Es schwankt der Schwester Schatten durch den*
>   *schweigenden Hain . . .*

Most important for the theory of the modernist lyric is Trakl's characteristic handling of syntax, his paratactic sequence of images. It is precisely Trakl's attitude toward syntax that identifies him as a postsymbolist poet, that is, a modernist poet. In a statement of great theoretical interest, Donald Davie hazards a definition of modern poetry that is formulated on the problem of syntax:

> . . . the break with the past is at bottom a change of attitude towards poetic syntax. It is from that point of view, in respect of syntax, that modern poetry, so diverse in all other ways, is seen as one. And we can define it thus: *What is common to all modern poetry is the assertion or the assumption (most often the latter) that syntax in poetry is wholly different from syntax as understood by logicians and grammarians.*
>
> (*Articulate Energy,* p. 148)

Davie points out that the modernist poet tends to handle "syntax like music," as Trakl consistently does.

LONGER POEMS: MUSIC AND ASSOCIATION

"Grodek" stands as a near perfect example of Trakl's mastery of the short lyric. He also composed a group of longer free-verse poems and experimented with that mixed genre, the prose poem favored by the French symbolist poet, Rimbaud. Trakl's discovery of Rimbaud's work was a shaping event in his development as a poet; Lindenberger remarks, "It was above all Rimbaud's mediation which made Trakl the characteristically modern poet that he is." Under the influence of Rimbaud, Trakl composed "Helian" (1913) a free-verse poem of some ninety lines, and two long prose poems, "Traum und Umnachtung" ("Dream and Madness," 1914) and "Offenbarung und Untergang" ("Revelation and Downfall," 1914–1915).

"Helian" is a crucial work in the Trakl canon. Lindenberger notes that " 'Helian,' together with those of Rilke's *Duineser Elegien* [usually known as the *Duino Elegies*] that date back to 1912, is probably the first major poem in German written in an uncompromisingly symbolist style. From beginning to end one senses the vitality that accompanies the discovery of a new way of expression." "Helian" is a difficult work; I refer the reader to Lindenberger's detailed and meticulous interpretation. Most important, Lindenberger points out that the poem cannot be understood either as allegory or disguised autobiography. It is a poem whose meaning develops through the interplay of contrasting groups of images. Briefly, these images illuminate a world before the Fall—and a world in which forces of evil have entered and corrupted. First, the images of prelapsarian happiness in the second and third stanzas:

> Abends auf der Terrasse betranken wir uns mit
>   braunem Wein.
> Rötlich glüht der Pfirsich im Laub;
> Sanfte Sonate, frohes Lachen.
>
> Schön ist die Stille der Nacht.
> Auf dunklem Plan
> Begegnen wir uns mit Hirten und weissen Sternen.
>
> Evenings on the terrace we got drunk on brown
>   wine.
> The peach gleams red in the leaves;
> Gentle sonata, happy laughter.
>
> Lovely is the stillness of the night.
> On a dark plain
> We meet shepherds and white stars.
>
> (1.69)

In contrast, we have such archetypal images of the Fall as the "ravaged garden," a city square fallen into ruins, and the disinherited son entering "the empty house of his fathers."

"Helian" raises the vexing question about the structural suitability of using symbolist method for a long or longer poem. Although "Helian" is less than one hundred lines long, well within the limits set by Edgar Allan Poe for the length of an effective poem, we may sense that the wholesale use of parataxis places a strain on the reader's imaginative ability to make the connections the poet programmatically neglects to make. The skeptical reader may also feel that Trakl is employing an extreme mode of free association: the "word salad" that is a symptom of schizophrenia. The terms of our understanding and appreciation necessarily are compromised, or at least rendered hermeneutically unreliable. The critic Gustav Kars comments:

> The symptoms which point to schizophrenia are so unsettling that one could ask whether an attempt to interpret Trakl was really worth the effort, whether a literary or intellectual confrontation with him was really possible, since it would naturally be hopeless to claim to interpret the products of an insane imagination.
>
> (quoted in Sharp, p. 192)

It is in the longest of Trakl's prose poems, "Dream and Madness," that we confront a text whose total substance seems to have been derived from a psychotic episode—or, more precisely, from four related episodes. The poem's title, "Dream and Madness," offers a caveat: we enter a region inhabited by all the terrors of the night. The poem's dramatis personae includes a young boy (the protagonist), the stony-faced mother, and the violated sister. We follow this benighted family group in a series of hallucinated episodes set against the remembered landscape and architecture of Salzburg. There is no plot as such; the poem moves by a process of continual metamorphosis as the human figures merge into each other and their positions shift and change. The following passage is from the second part of the poem:

> Hunted by bats, he lurched into the darkness. Breathless, he entered the ruined house. In the courtyard he, a wild deer, drank from the blue waters of the spring until he grew cold. Feverish, he sat on the icy stairs, raging against God that he might die. O, the gray face of horror, as he raised his round eyes over a dove's mutilated throat. Scurrying over strange stairways, he met a whore and grabbed at her hair and seized her mouth. Fiendish creatures followed him through dark streets, and an iron clatter tore his ear. An altar boy, he quietly followed the silent priest along autumnal walls; under withered trees he

drunkenly inhaled the scarlet of the priest's sacred cassock. O the ruined disc of the sun. Sweet torments devoured his flesh. In a desolate passageway his own bleeding shape appeared before him, stiff with excrement. He more profoundly loved the sublime works of stone: the tower which with hellish grimaces nightly storms the blue sky of stars; the cool grave wherein man's flaming heart is preserved. Woe to the unspeakable guilt which [the heart] makes known. But when, all his mind ablaze, he walked down the autumnal river under leafless trees, there appeared to him a flaming demon in a coat of hair, . . . [his] sister. Upon awakening, the stars at her head were extinguished.

(1.148–149)

The texture of discordant images linked by sudden transitions again suggests a technique of extreme free association. But a full and sympathetic reading of "Dream and Madness" reveals, beneath the torrential flow of Trakl's imagination, what Theodor Adorno calls its "moments of logicality." In his unfinished *Ästhetische Theorie* (*Aesthetic Theory*, 1970) Adorno gives a brilliant, characteristically aphoristic account of the orders that lurk beneath the apparently disorderly surface of Trakl's poems:

> On the face of it, his poems seem to progress by association; but when we look more closely we see logical categories come into play indirectly and in a dimly discernible way, categories such as the musiclike ascendence and descendence of individual moments, the distribution of values, the relations between beginning, continuation and conclusion. The image components are part of these formal categories, but their real legitimacy derives from those relations which organize the poems, lifting them above the contingency of the poet's inventiveness. Thus, even association represents rational aesthetic form. In the phenomenon of association where one instant summons another there is the same cogency as in inferences of logic and music.
>
> (p. 405)

Adorno's appeal to the "inferences of logic and

music" has particular resonance; music, in its many forms, is importantly present in Trakl's poetry. (For a systematic musical analysis of Trakl's poetry, see Albert Hellmich's *Klang und Erlösung.*) We recall his early musical training and the fact that his sister Grete was a talented concert pianist. Most likely, it is Grete who is playing the "chords and sonatas" in this line from "Psalm": "Es sind Zimmer, erfüllt von Akkorden und Sonaten . . . " (There are rooms, filled with chords and sonatas . . .). There is a realm of explicit musical reference in both the titles and texts of other poems, as in "Musik im Mirabell" ("Music at Mirabell"): "Das Ohr hört nachts Sonatenklänge . . . " (The ear hears at night sonatas sounding . . .). Adorno points out that the word "sonata" accumulates a special meaning: " 'Sonata' . . . has an absolutely unique ring in the poems by Georg Trakl, giving rise to diffuse associations, none of which suggests any reference to an actually existing sonata." Thus, "sonata" becomes metonymic for music, and for the kind of poetry Trakl composes: a poetry rich in structural complexity but without much semantic depth.

Adorno proposes a method of analysis that might take into account openings and closures, moments of "ascendence and descendence," repetitions of motifs and other formal structures. These elements can be subsumed under the larger category of rhythm; any interpretation of Trakl's poems must recognize their extraordinary handling of both the traditional metrical forms and the subtler rhythms of free verse. Unlike the Anglo-American tradition, where the dominance of the iambic pentameter was unchallenged until Walt Whitman and Gerard Manley Hopkins, German poets, at least since Friedrich Klopstock in the eighteenth century, wrote unmetered and unrhymed verse. Among the metrical innovators whose work influenced Trakl was the poet Friedrich Hölderlin. To show what Trakl derived from Hölderlin, we cite the opening strophe of Hölderlin's apocalyptic hymn "Patmos" (1802) and follow with the opening strophe of Trakl's "Das Gewitter" ("The Thunderstorm"):

GEORG TRAKL

Nah ist
Und schwer zu fassen der Gott
Wo aber Gefahr ist, wächst
Das Rettende auch.
Im Finstern wohnen
Die Adler und furchtlos gehn
Die Söhne der Alpen über den Abgrund weg
Auf leichtgebaueten Brüken.
Drum, da gehäuft sind rings
Die Gipfel der Zeit, und die Liebsten
Nah wohnen, ermattend auf
Getrenntesten Bergen,
So gieb unschuldig Wasser,
O Fittige gieb uns, treuesten Sinns
Hinüberzugehn und wiederzukehren.

Near is
The God, and hard to grasp.
But where danger looms, there also
grows salvation.
In darkness dwell
The eagles and fearless walk
The sons of the Alps over
The abyss on lightly built bridges.
Therefore, since round about
Are heaped the peaks of time
And the most beloved live near,
Grow weary on most isolated mountains,
Give us innocent water,
O give us wings, with truest minds
To go over and to return.

Ihr wilden Gebirge, der Adler
Erhabene Trauer.
Goldnes Gewölk
Raucht uber steinerner Öde.
Geduldige Stille odmen die Föhren,
Die schwarzen Lämmer am Abgrund,
Wo plötzlich die Bläue
Seltsam verstummt,
Das sanfte Summen der Hummeln.
O grüne Blume—
O Schweigen.

You savage mountains, the eagles'
Sublime sorrow.
A golden cloud
Smokes over the stony waste.
The pines breathe a patient stillness,
The black lambs at the abyss,
Where suddenly the blueness

Strangely grows silent,
The soft humming of the bumblebee.
O green flower—
O silence.

(1.157)

Hölderlin uses a short line that carries two to four strong stresses but maintains a norm of three. This prosody generates an intense, varied movement that closely follows the God-intoxicated rhetoric of Saint John the Divine. Imprisoned on the island of Patmos, he invokes the inscrutable God who dwells with his eagles in an allegorized mountain landscape. Turning to Trakl's "The Thunderstorm," we find that he has borrowed Hölderlin's mountains, eagles, and *Abgrund* (abyss), as well as his strongly stressed rhythms. In the last three lines of the quoted strophe, we note a musical diminuendo; the number of stresses goes from three to two to one:

> *Das sánfte Súmmen der Húmmeln.*
> *O grüńe Blúme—*
> *O Schwéigen.*

A similarly stressed prosody governs the prophetic cadences of "The Occident." Earlier we quoted the concluding strophe of this vision of the end of the world seen in "the fearsome red glow of sunset." The opening strophe depicts a nocturnal landscape:

> *Mond, als träte ein Totes*
> *Aus blauer Höhle,*
> *Und es fallen der Blüten*
> *Viele über den Felsenpfad.*
> *Silbern weint ein Krankes*
> *Am Abendweiher,*
> *Auf schwarzem Kahn*
> *Hinüberstarben Liebende.*

> *Oder es läuten die Schritte*
> *Elis' durch den Hain*
> *Den hyazinthenen*
> *Wieder verhallend unter Eichen.*
> *O des Knaben Gestalt*

Geformt aus kristallenen Tränen,
Nächtigen Schatten.
Zackige Blitze erhellen die Schläfe
Die Immerkühle,
Wenn am grünenden Hügel
Frühlingsgewitter ertönt.

Moon, as if a dead thing walked
Out of a blue cave,
And many blossoms fall
Across the rocky path.
Silver, a sick thing weeps
By the evening pond
In a black boat
Lovers crossed over to death.

Or that Elis' footsteps
Ring out through the grove
The hyacinth one
Again, dying away under oaks.
O the shape of that boy
Formed from crystal tears,
Shadows of the night.
Jagged lightning illuminates his temples
Ever cool.
When on the verdant hill
A spring thunderstorm resounds.

(1.139)

The strophe divides into two; after the eighth line we have the fermata or hold which marks a significant silence. In the first eight lines the moon, like "a dead thing," exerts its power seemingly to cause and reveal an inner landscape peopled by a "sick thing," dead lovers, and Elis, the mythic hyacinth boy. These images are leitmotivs from Trakl's musical vocabulary; they are either self-referential—that is, their meaning is closely contextual, defined by the other images and structures of the poem—or they operate as symbols and are open to interpretation. In "The Occident" Trakl uses both kinds of images, and the private vision of the first strophe modulates to an evocation of an urban apocalypse. Elis is first seen walking through the grove, his temples illuminated by jagged flashes of lightning; in the third strophe he changes to a Cain-like outcast, a wanderer in the cities of the plain, and

With darkened forehead
Follows the wind,
Leafless trees on the hill.

Trakl formulated no theories about his handling of image and symbol; however, his poetic practice moved toward the symbolist doctrine, articulated by Frank Kermode, "that poetry might be written with something other than words." Both his images that are self-referential and his images that are explicit symbols serve to mitigate the stubbornly discursive nature of language—so much so that it is perhaps more than metaphoric to say that his poems approach the condition of music. When Wittgenstein said that he didn't understand Trakl's poems, but that he admired their tone, he was not only paying Trakl a polite and pretty compliment but he was also saying, as Eliot has said on many occasions, that poetry can communicate before it is understood.

IMAGE AND ISOLATION

We are accustomed to experience difficulty in reading and construing modern poetry; it is the task of criticism to bring into the clear the message encoded in lines such as these from Eliot's "Gerontion" (1920):

Think at last
I have not made this show purposelessly
And it is not by concitation
Of the backward devils.

The Oxford English Dictionary tells us that "concitation" is an obsolete word meaning "stirring up" and that it went out of the language in 1656. "The backward devils" allude to the legendary false prophets whom Dante encounters in *Inferno* 20. Their heads are twisted to the rear; their appropriate punishment is to gaze eternally behind them. A little homework illuminates the apparent obscurity of these lines. The notorious difficulties of Pound's *Cantos* (1919–1959) are generated by the wholesale use of allusions, quotations, and a private shorthand.

Trakl's poems are difficult in ways that do not yield to merely looking things up. Here is the text of "Im Osten" ("On the Eastern Front"):

Den wilden Orgeln des Wintersturms
Gleicht des Volkes finstrer Zorn,
Die purpurne Woge der Schlacht,
Entlaubter Sterne.

Mit zerbrochnen Brauen, silbernen Armen
Winkt sterbenden Soldaten die Nacht.
Im Schatten der herbstlichen Esche
Seufzen die Geister der Erschlagenen.

Dornige Wildnis umgürtet die Stadt.
Von blutenden Stufen jagt der Mond
Die erschrockenen Frauen.
Wilde Wölfe brachen durchs Tor.

Like the wild organ of a winter storm
The black wrath of groaning troops,
The crimson surge of slaughter,
Defoliate stars.

Night beckons dying soldiers, shattered heads,
And silver glint of arms.
The ash-tree of autumn shadows
Sighing ghosts.

Thorny wasteland strangles the city.
From bloody steps
The moon hunts terrified women.
Wild wolves broke through the door.

(1.165; trans. quoted from Gross, *Plans for an Orderly Apocalypse and Other Poems,* p. 36)

Trakl's poem bristles with problems for the translator, who must answer the question that always arises: To what extent can sense be sacrificed to sound? In Trakl's case the orchestration of rhythm and tonal color often overwhelms propositional sense; it seems more important to find the proper English equivalents for alliteration and accent than to insist on lexical precision. Thus I am careful to follow Trakl's distribution of four- and three-stress

lines in "Dornige Wildnis umgürtet die Stadt . . ." (Thorny wasteland strangles the city . . .) and "Die purpurne woge der Schlacht . . ." (The crimson surge of slaughter . . .). Another kind of difficulty offers the translator an extraordinary imaginative challenge: how to handle the radical image in the fourth line, "Entlaubter Sterne"? Like similar images in Trakl's poems, it has no syntactical anchoring but apparently floats free of what precedes it. The literal meaning of *entlaubt* is "stripped of its leaves," and we wonder what kinds of stars have leaves. Only the stars in Trakl's magical and sinister universe. I translate "Entlaubter Sterne" as defoliate stars because I wish to maintain the iambic rhythm and to underline the strangeness of the image; the Latinate adjective followed by the simple "star" creates a harsh semantic dissonance.

Translation, it has often been said, is also interpretation. In effect, I have offered two readings of the Trakl poems considered here: first, the versions reconstructed by my translations; second, the actual, detailed explications. I have, where I felt it is appropriate, made the connections between the sad facts of Trakl's life and the perplexities of his texts. But, in general, I have adhered to the New Critical doctrine that the proper thrust of criticism must be directed toward the poem rather than the poet. The defect of the psychiatrically oriented studies of Trakl is that the scandal of his life overwhelms the interest of his poetry. Consequently, such studies tend to overlook considerations of genre, technique, and literary tradition. Trakl is a modern master of the sonnet and its rigorous formal requirements, but this has generally escaped emphasis.

My approach has been to locate Trakl in the mainstream of European modernist poetry. At almost the very moment that Trakl entered the period of his greatest productivity, Pound and his friends published the imagist "manifesto" in 1913. Pound defines the image as "that which presents an intellectual and emotional complex in an instant of time." Trakl and Pound were mutually unaware of each other's work and theories, but their practice and advocacy of composing in images have their common origins in the poetics of symbolism. For the symbolist, poetry had achieved the "immense future" of which Matthew Arnold spoke; it had acquired special powers of revelation and transcendence. But the poet who might wish to assume these powers paid the price of isolation, or, as we now say, alienation. The reciprocal tensions between image and isolation are brilliantly charted by Kermode in his *Romantic Image.* Kermode tells us that postsymbolist poetry is informed by two controlling assumptions:

> . . . that the image is, in Wyndham Lewis's phrase, the 'primary pigment of poetry'; and that the poet who uses it is by that very fact differentiated from other men, and seriously at odds with the society in which he has to live. . . . These two beliefs — in the image as a radiant truth out of space and time, and in the necessary isolation or estrangement of men who can perceive it — are inextricably associated.
>
> (pp. vii, 2)

Kermode's insights are uncannily appropriate to the image-haunted, half-mad — or wholly mad, depending on which psychiatrist you read — Trakl. If we read "image" to stand for creative energy and its works and "isolation" to stand for the modern poet's struggle to work out a modus vivendi between himself and society, we recognize the larger relevance of Kermode's insights. No poet of our age has escaped the necessity of making the choice, as William Butler Yeats put it, between "perfection of the life or of the work." Some have made better adjustments than others. Others could not (or would not) avoid a direct encounter with the terrible angels, and learned, as Rilke tells us in the *Duino Elegies* that "beauty is nothing/ but the beginning of terror" (*Duineser Elegien, Erste Elegie,* Stephen Mitchell, trans., p. 151). No modern poet knew this better than George Trakl.

Selected Bibliography

EDITIONS

Gedichte. Leipzig, 1913.
Sebastian im Traum. Leipzig, 1915.
Die Dichtungen. Salzburg, 1938.
Aus Goldenem Kelch: Die Jugenddichtungen. Salzburg, 1939. Juvenilia.
Dichtungen und Briefe. 2 vols. Edited by Walther Killy and Hans Szklenar. Salzburg, 1969.

TRANSLATIONS

Georg Trakl: Poems. Translated by Lucia Getsi. Athens, Ohio, 1973.
"On the Eastern Front" and "Grodek." In Harvey Gross, *Plans for an Orderly Apocalypse and Other Poems.* Ann Arbor, Mich., 1968.
Selected Poems: George Trakl. Edited by Christopher Middleton. Translated by Robert Grenier, Michael Hamburger, David Luke, and Christopher Middleton. London, 1968.
Twenty Poems of Georg Trakl. Translated by James Wright and Robert Bly. Madison, Minn., 1961.

BIOGRAPHICAL AND CRITICAL STUDIES

STUDIES OF TRAKL

Basil, Otto. *Georg Trakl in Selbstzeugnissen und Bilddokumenten.* Reinbeck bei Hamburg, 1965.
Detsch, Richard. *George Trakl's Poetry: Toward a Union of Opposites.* University Park, Pa., 1983.
Errinnerung an Georg Trakl. Darmstadt, 1959. Includes Trakl's letter to Ludwig von Ficker.
Goldmann, Heinrich. *Katabasis.* Salzburg, 1957.
Graziano, Frank. *Georg Trakl: A Profile.* Durango, Colo., 1983.
Hamburger, Michael. "Georg Trakl." In his *Contraries: Studies in German Literature.* New York, 1970.
Heidegger, Martin. "Georg Trakl: Eine Erörterung seines Gedichtes." In *Merkur* 7:226–258 (1953).
———. *Poetry, Language, Thought.* Translated by Albert Hofstadter. New York, 1971.
Hellmich, Albert. *Klang und Erlösung: Das Problem musikalischer Strukturen in der Lyrik Georg Trakls.* Salzburg, 1971.
Killy, Walther. *Über Georg Trakl.* Göttingen, 1960.

Klein, Johannes. "Georg Trakl." In *Expressionismus als Literatur.* Edited by Wolfgang Rothe. Bern and Munich, 1969.

Lindenberger, Herbert. *Georg Trakl.* New York, 1971.

Methlagi, Walter and William E. Yuill, eds. *Londoner Trakl-Symposion.* Salzburg, 1981.

Ritzer, Walter. *Neue-Trakl Bibliographie.* Salzburg, 1983.

Sharp, Francis Michael. *The Poet's Madness: A Reading of Georg Trakl.* Ithaca, N.Y., 1981.

Spoerri, Theodor. *Georg Trakl: Strukturen in Persönlichkeit und Werk.* Bern, 1954.

Weiss, Walter and Hans Weichselbawn, eds. *Salzburger Trakl-Symposion.* Salzburg, 1978.

GENERAL WORKS
OF THEORY AND CRITICISM

Adorno, Theodor W. *Aesthetic Theory.* Translated by C. Lenhardt. London, 1984.

Blackmur, Richard P. *Form and Value in Modern Poetry.* Garden City. N.Y., 1957.

Broch, Hermann. *Hugo von Hofmannstahl and His Time: The European Imagination, 1860–1920.* Translated by Michael P. Steinberg. Chicago, 1984.

Davie, Donald. *Articulate Energy.* London, 1955; New York, 1958.

Fowlie, Wallace. *Rimbaud.* Chicago, 1965.

Kermode, Frank. *Romantic Image.* New York, 1957.

Schnabel, Artur. *My Life and Music.* London, 1961.

Schorske, Carl. *Fin-de-Siècle Vienna.* New York, 1980.

Sokel, Walter H. *The Writer in Extremis: Expressionism in Twentieth-Century German Literature.* Stanford, Calif., 1959.

Trilling, Lionel. "Art and Neurosis." In his *The Liberal Imagination.* New York, 1950.

Willett, John. *Expressionism.* New York, 1970.

HARVEY GROSS

SAINT-JOHN PERSE

(1887–1975)

A MAN WELL versed in a variety of literatures (who shall remain unnamed) once met Saint-John Perse on the way to a gathering of international celebrities. Thinking that it would interest Perse, he mentioned that another famous Frenchman would be present: a diplomat named Alexis Leger. Perse simply smiled in response. It was not until later, when introductions were made, that his informant learned that Perse and Leger were one and the same. Of course, the man's embarrassment was great. Yet his error was quite natural, for few people knew of the double life that the poet/statesman led. As Perse himself said, he always practiced the art of "splitting [his] image," masking or denying his identity in one realm while he devoted himself to the other (in contrast to other French writer/diplomats such as Paul Claudel, Jean Giraudoux, or André Malraux). Under both names, however, he made history in his century: as Perse, a Nobel Prize winner, he is considered by many critics the greatest modern French poet; as Leger, he was probably the most important political figure in France in the years prior to World War II. Aside from this intriguing duality, the complexity of his life and work, in both the literary and diplomatic domains, is so great that he can be considered one of the most fascinating figures of our time—puzzling, paradoxical, an enigma to be explored.

Almost equally paradoxical is the fact that Perse, the poet, is relatively little known to American audiences (except through *Anabase* [*Anabasis,* 1924] in T. S. Eliot's 1930 translation), although all his finest poems were written and first published in the United States and although he had the good fortune to be translated into English by distinguished poets such as Denis Devlin, Robert Fitzgerald, and Richard Howard. There are of course many reasons why Perse is thus far appreciated mainly by those whom Stendhal had called "the happy few," but the fact remains that even fewer of these are Americans. No less interesting than the literary figure Perse is the statesman Leger. Yet readers in this country tend to know just as little about him, despite the exceptional importance of his dealings with major political figures in America (such as Francis Biddle, John F. Kennedy, and Franklin Delano Roosevelt) and of his role in shaping history before World War II.

Perhaps this rather limited knowledge and appreciation is due to the lofty images usually presented of both the poet and the diplomat, which make him appear inaccessible, unapproachable, a member of an elite who functions in realms far above ordinary men. Yet nothing could be farther from the truth. Anyone well acquainted with the life and work of Perse/Leger realizes that although both were extremely complex, they were not only accessible but were always motivated by a desire for contact with and by concern for those whom the poet/statesman held in the highest esteem:

human beings of all races, nations, persuasions, occupations, and ages. This desire and this concern, moreover, were not the outgrowths of a theory, an abstract literary or political idea, but were the results of a series of lived experiences and personal convictions that took an entire lifetime to be expressed yet were based primarily on the unusual circumstances that marked every stage in the life of Perse/Leger.

Actually, he was born with neither of these names. (The first is the best known of his pseudonyms—there were also others; the second is a shortened form of his full given name, which evolved as he did and reached its final and most famous version at the time of his entry into diplomatic service.) The child whose birth took place on 31 May 1887, on a small island located off the coast of Pointe-à-Pitre (Guadeloupe) named Saint-Leger-les-Feuilles and owned by his family, was christened Marie-René Alexis Saint-Leger Leger. He was the only son of wealthy colonialists with an ancient and noble lineage who had ruled in the "Isles of Winds" (French West Indies) for centuries and had the habit of calling themselves "Men of the Atlantic," as though the sea were their true homeland.

His childhood on the private isle of his family and on the plantations they owned resembled a season in paradise. He was surrounded by exotic animals imported from all parts of the globe to further enhance the richness and variety that nature lavished on this part of the world, and nursemaids and servants doted on him and anticipated his every wish. Young Alexis (or Allan, as his mother liked to call him) had every advantage one could dream of for the growth of body and mind: he swam in the limpid waters of the Caribbean, sailed from an early age, rode horses on the endless beaches, explored the fabulous sites of his birthplace, and learned about botany, the classics, mathematics, and physics from private tutors and of the cult of Shiva from a beautiful Hindu woman who was a family servant. He even enjoyed the cataclysms of nature—the mighty storms, the rumbling of La Soufrière (Guadeloupe's volcano), and the tales of earthquakes.

A life of such ease and splendor might have turned another boy of his age into a spoiled, rather smug creature. But young Alexis already showed inclinations quite different from what one might expect in someone of his background and upbringing: he craved solitude, spent long hours in the company of animals, explored the flora and fauna of the region with intense interest, enjoyed the company of the natives, and, as soon as he was a little older and attended school in Pointe-à-Pitre, spent most of his free time among ships and sailors. He also began to write.

His earliest attempt at literature, at the age of ten, took the form of a chronicle published in his school's newspaper and was entitled "Mouvement du port" (Movement in the Port). There is also some evidence that he tried his hand at writing poetry at this time.

He might have continued this idyllic existence had not a natural disaster literally rent the world in which he had lived, uprooted his family, and resulted in the first of a number of exiles he experienced in his life: in 1897 a major earthquake shook Guadeloupe, partially destroying Pointe-à-Pitre, devastating a great deal of his family's property, and spelling financial ruin for several of its members. It seemed the end of an epoch, for grave economic crises were anticipated. Alexis' father decided that they must seek another place to live and a different way of life. Quite naturally, he thought of France, the place from which his ancestors had come long ago. After an exploratory journey there, he returned and announced that Saint-Leger-les-Feuilles would be sold, the great house emptied of its furnishings, and their birthplace abandoned. In 1899 Alexis and his family boarded a transatlantic liner in Pointe-à-Pitre that took them to Pau in the south of France.

Life in Pau was quite different from that in the West Indies. Although it was a cosmopolitan city, comparable in the variety of its occupants and visitors to the international ambiance of Guadeloupe, its climate, the attitude of its people, and its language (which had none of the lilting charm of Creole) at first struck Alexis as a form of estrangement, even of exile. And the European education that his father wished him to have and that he now pursued at the Pau school felt somewhat restrictive to this adolescent who had been so accustomed to an equilibrium between the life of the mind and that of the body. Although he excelled in his studies, completing his two baccalaureates with distinction, receiving the Grand Prize in rhetoric, and brilliantly passing his examination in philosophy, he would surely have felt surrounded by prison walls had he not spent his summers in the wild countryside of the Basque region and the northern parts of Spain and indulged his passion for mountain climbing in the Pyrenees.

It was during one of these expeditions that he met Francis Jammes, a poet who became his first real friend and someone with whom he could share his ideas on poetry. For at this time Alexis had begun to write his first important poetic work, "Images à Crusoé" ("Pictures for Crusoe," 1909). It was a striking poem, especially considering that its author was barely eighteen. In it many autobiographical themes (the sense of exile, the loss of a former paradise, the hatred of cities, and the artificiality of "civilized" life) are expressed in the persona of the arch-islander Robinson Crusoe. Just as important as the writing of this poem, however, was the meeting with the great poet Claudel, arranged by Jammes in 1905. Claudel was a mature writer and a scholar with extensive culture, who had just returned from a stay in China and who presented the young man with a copy of "Les Muses" ("The Muses"), probably the most magnificent of his *Cinq grandes odes* (*Five Great Odes*, 1910), and he must have seemed an overwhelming presence. Yet the two might have become friends at that time, for they shared many experiences and convictions, had not Claudel's orthodox Catholicism, verg-

ing on fanaticism, almost destroyed the possibility of future encounters. Claudel, who had a passion for converting people, decided to try his hand with Alexis. The attempt was a total failure since the latter considered himself a pagan or, as he put it, unable to "feel completely Christian [since] like all true children of the islands [he was] *saved from the moment of birth.*"

Life continued in France. Alexis enjoyed his studies at the University of Bordeaux. Everything might have gone quite smoothly for the young man had not a tragic event occurred that once again changed the entire course of his life: in 1907 (when he was just twenty) his father died suddenly, leaving Alexis—as the only son—to assume the entire responsibility for four bereaved and helpless women (his mother and three sisters). There was no longer any question of literary pursuits or studies purely for pleasure. He had to choose a profession that could assure his family's livelihood. It was decided that as the head of the household he should follow his father and embark on a career in law. Since he undertook his legal studies at the University of Bordeaux, he remained within easy reach of his relatives.

Secretly (and characteristically), however, at the height of the period of mourning for his father (whom he had loved deeply), in the summer of 1907 Alexis wrote the first of the luminous poems in the group entitled "Pour fêter une enfance" ("Celebration of a Childhood"). This was followed, in the course of the next year, by another group of poems, "Eloges," which, together with "Pictures for Crusoe" and an early poem, "Écrit sur la porte" ("Written on the Door"), appeared in the 1911 volume *Éloges* (*Éloges and Other Poems*, 1944), the first important work published by the young poet. The title itself, he said, seemed to him to be "so beautiful" that he "would never want another, even if [he] published several volumes of poetry."

What is so striking about "Celebration of a Childhood" and "Éloges" is not only the fact that they constitute the key to the entire work of the poet—for they announce the leading themes, the prevalent tone, and the fundamental purpose of poetry as he saw it—but also that they were written during a period filled with grief yet spoke primarily of praise, of celebration, of joy. While this might at first appear contradictory the poet provides clues to an important attitude that he maintained during his entire life: this attitude is revealed in the equation "Mourning-capacity," which can be found in a letter to a friend at this time, and in another affirmation, "To grieve is to grow emotionally." To Claudel, Alexis wrote during this period that he had "learned to suffer without sadness" and even "to feel joy," thus admitting that polar opposites could—and even must—coexist, as light balances darkness, and death life. The two groups of poems, taken together, affirm a number of penchants already present in the young man's first great creation: the celebration, praise, and eulogy of universal experiences (in this instance, of childhood) which never cease to predominate in his subsequent poetry (extending even to the singular celebration of "great age" in his last long poem, *Chronique* [*Chronique,* 1960]; the aura of fable or legend; the sense of timelessness; and the presence of a place that is impossible to define but that here suggests a world of energy and harmony where the vegetable, the animal, and the human are linked by mutual respect and profound understanding. Praise functions as an act here, an instinctive, almost physiological response to the world in all its immediacy, and it is a total response that acquiesces to everything—tenderness and violence, continuity and schism, beauty and ugliness, living and dying—creating a union of experiences usually considered diametrically opposed.

In technical terms these poems already show the exceptional gifts of the young poet. One notes his use of the verset (a line of free verse, unequal in length, found most frequently in the Bible), which moves with slow and serene splendor; complex metrical structures (Alexandrines, octosyllables, decasyllables, hexasyllables) that, however, are so skillfully used they pass almost unnoticed in the majestic flow of poems that do not seem to be concerned with technical prowess; interjections where syntax is ignored, verbs disappear, and ellipsis reigns (or where language tends toward silence); a vocabulary that is evocative or suggestive of dreams and at the same time has all the rigor and exactitude of such disciplines as natural history and various other domains of knowledge; poetry that neither recounts nor translates experience, that does not explain but expresses or rather imposes itself on the reader, and whose major function is to make the marvelous spring from the banal.

Moreover, they contain thematic elements and a network of images that establish the base for the poet's entire oeuvre: a profound sense of vitality that sometimes approaches ferocity; vigor, fecundity, intensity that never becomes frenetic; the exuberance of everything; the joy of emotions and sensations; paradise, but also paradise lost (i.e., the evocation of the past but also a movement away from and beyond the past, announced by the persona of the nomad, the voyager, who is present in almost all of the poet's works). Among the most prevalent images are those of water, wind, trees, horses, ships, fabulous or mythological figures, dreamers, storytellers, and various types of cataclysms, the unleashing of natural forces (prefiguring some of the later poems, such as *Pluies* [*Rains,* 1944], *Neiges* [*Snows,* 1944], and *Vents* [*Winds,* 1946]). Quite striking also in these early poems is the exuberant eroticism (totally unabashed and devoid of any puritanical elements) and the insistence on a joining of dream and action (which is continually affirmed in the long line of poetic creations that stretches over nearly seventy years).

In the period that followed the writing of these poems, Alexis pursued his studies at the University of Bordeaux. He did not, however, limit himself only to law but expanded into political science and sociology, ethnology, and anthropology, besides exploring such philosophers as Friedrich Nietzsche, Baruch Spinoza, and G. W. F. Hegel (at a time when Henri Bergson was most in fashion). He was equally active in areas that were not intellectual, developing for example a passion for aviation and eagerly following all the exploits of the Wright brothers. He also probed the domain of poetry ever more deeply and made Pindar, Claudel, Léon-Paul Fargue, Arthur Rimbaud, and Jules Laforgue his guides or companions in this venture, thus clarifying many of his own ideas in the process. However, exploration of other poets' work, no matter how stimulating or enlightening, could not suffice. He had to undertake his own struggle with creation.

The poetry that emerged then revealed quite different preoccupations than those of *Éloges*. Transposing current thoughts and feelings and far less idyllic than the former poems (although retaining the note of celebration, the sense of nobility, and the forceful imagery), the new works show, by their very titles, the direction his imagination was taking: "Récitation à la gloire d'une Reine" ("Recitation to the Glory of a Queen"), "Amitié du Prince" ("Friendship of the Prince"), "Histoire du Régent" ("Story of the Regent"), collected under the title *La Gloire des Rois* (The Glory of Kings, 1924). The poems had nothing to do with royalty in the historical sense, nor did they depict regal figures of a known variety. Instead, they spoke of legendary creatures and of incarnating drives and ideals that dominated the poet's life at this time. If one considers the two most important poems of the group, "Recitation to the Glory of a Queen" and "Friendship of the Prince," one finds that the first centers on woman as an object of intense sexual desire but also as a mythic figure resembling fertility goddesses of the most ancient kind: voluminous and gravid (yet, paradoxically, sterile), the Queen of this poem seems one of the telluric divinities, if not the Earth Mother herself, surrounded by a group of youths aspiring to be her consorts, whose chants express the violent yearning underlying this work, which is essentially a hymn in honor of the Queen of Desire. The second centers on the figure of the Prince (sometimes also called the King, and thus the consort of the Queen of the first poem). His portrait emphasizes traits diametrically opposed—or complementary—to those of the central figure in "Recitation to the Glory of a Queen" and suggests that he is the male counterpart of the female divinity who appears there. But his predominant traits (leanness, acuity, secretiveness) and his epithets ("Enchanter," "Dissident," "Taciturn Prince") also seem to reveal ideals toward which, one suspects, the young poet himself aspired.

Indeed, the tendency toward secrecy, harshness, silence, and lack of inner peace—attributed to the Prince—manifested itself in the life of Alexis and reached the proportions of a crisis in the year 1909. This was a period of grave self-doubt, of the refutation and even the destruction of past work and of attacks upon art itself. "Art was a head like Ubu," Alexis exclaimed, considering art as grotesque as Alfred Jarry's famous figure that was the sum of all of man's vices. He even summed up his distaste in the equation, "Art-onanism." The only thing even more revolting than to write poetry, according to him, was to be published. Both seemed to him to be linked to putrefaction, impotence, or decrepitude, and to be feared as much as any symptom of decline, "like the threat of dentures." And yet, in a typically paradoxical move, he permitted some of his early poems to be published at this time.

The year was not only a time of crises, however. It also brought the start of new friendships. Most important among them was that of Jacques Rivière, an accomplished essayist and critic associated with *La nouvelle revue française,* one of the most prestigious literary magazines in the country. After becoming secretary of this review (then under the aegis of André Gide) in 1911, Rivière was instrumental in the publication of *Éloges* there.

The young poet's initial contact with Gide was highly problematic. Strangely enough, the problems that arose had as their source Alexis' handwriting. For Gide, aside from appreciating their contents, found the manuscript pages of *Éloges* so beautiful that he would not part with them. The secretary charged with making a copy for the printer (at a time when Xerox machines had not yet been invented) made many errors in the process of transcription because Alexis' handwriting was so difficult to read. Thus when the poems appeared on 1 June 1911 in *La nouvelle revue française,* Gide, and even more so Alexis (or Saintleger Leger, as he had signed his work) were outraged by the misprints that disfigured the poems. To make amends, Gide immediately reprinted *Éloges* correctly and also proposed publication of the work in book form by the Editions Gallimard. Alexis, on the other hand, decided to chastise the guilty handwriting in a manner characteristic of his unusual personality: he submitted it to harsh discipline and forced it to undergo a complete transformation until it finally assumed a new form, still beautiful but obviously the result of rigorous training.

At the time of the publication of *Éloges* in book form, Alexis had some hesitations about the name he wanted to use. It seemed to him that the pseudonym he had chosen when the poems appeared in *La nouvelle revue française* did not sufficiently disguise him. To ensure at least partial anonymity, other ways had to be found. He remembered a strategy that Claudel had once used and requested Gide to print only the title of the work on the cover, thus leaving it "free of the author's name" (which only appeared on the flyleaf inside). He explained his wish by saying that "poetry should always preserve something approaching anonymity" (thus voicing a lifelong predilection, expressed in the use of various pseudonyms).

The appearance of *Éloges,* a major event for the young poet, also brought him the friendship of Valery Larbaud, a writer, translator, and man of letters who took as much pleasure in promoting the literary careers of others as in his own work. It was he who wrote the first critical article on *Éloges,* evoking comparisons with Homer, Vergil, the best of Walt Whitman and Victor Hugo, José Maria de Heredia and François de Malherbe. This was high praise indeed. Yet despite such critical acclaim Alexis decided to undertake nothing more in France than the preparation of a career that would permit him to "go far away, one day."

The career he had begun to think of was the diplomatic service, which seemed to combine his past training with the lure of travel. He decided to explore the possibilities in this domain before plunging into the demanding task of preparing for the examinations required for entry into the field. For this purpose he visited various friends of his father in Paris, but it was Philippe Berthelot, a diplomat in the Ministry of Foreign Affairs, who convinced him to enter diplomacy. The affinities between the two men were great, and it is even possible that Berthelot served as a model for the young man or at least profoundly influenced the choice of paths he followed. At any rate, after their meeting Alexis set out to study for the necessary examinations.

However, to make his work less abstract and more interesting, he took several trips outside of France for "educational" purposes. One of these was especially important not only for diplomatic but also for literary reasons: he went to England to study its industries, mining centers, and labor unions, but there he also met Joseph Conrad (who later became a close friend), William H. Hudson, William Butler Yeats, and others. Perhaps most meaningful, though, was his encounter in London with the great Indian poet, Rabindranath Tagore, whose *Gitanjali* appeared to Alexis a work of genius. He decided that it must be brought to France, and he interested Gide in translating it. The work appeared there in 1914, thanks to his discovery.

Back in France, while studying for his examinations, Alexis continued to meet various poets, formed a friendship with Paul Valéry, who was very different from Alexis in his literary penchants, and saw Claudel again on various occasions. On one of these he spoke to the latter of a plan he hoped to carry out one day "to conduct a work like an *anabasis* under the leadership of its chieftains," adding: "The word itself seems so beautiful to me that I would like to encounter the work that could carry such a title. It haunts me."

The year 1914, though one of world disaster, brought personal triumph to Alexis Leger (as he now called himself). He succeeded in passing his examinations and entered diplomatic service. Although his beginnings were rather humble—he occupied a modest post in the Press Service at the Quai d'Orsay, then was sent out of Paris to Bordeaux and was subsequently assigned to work at the Maison de Presse—he finally succeeded, in 1916, in being selected for a mission to China. This was what he had been waiting for: a chance to leave France, where he had long felt like a stranger, to abandon the past and start a new life full of risk and adventure, and to slake his thirst for travel, space, the unknown. It seemed to him that he stood at a major crossroad in his life.

A trip from Europe to China, in those days, took months. He found that the crossing of so many seas, the succession of numerous ports of call, and the passing of various meridians created a sense of strangeness, alienation, loneliness. All this was intensified when he first landed in Peking, which seemed to him a place "out of space, out of time." As he wandered through the labyrinth of foreign streets, he saw only a kingdom of shades where nothingness reigned. And the immensity of the country, its aura of agelessness, the purity of the air, and the intense cold made everything appear unreal, spectral to the newcomer. Yet he was also oddly drawn to this landscape and the people of this country. For as he began to observe them at a closer proximity, he saw their vitality, their sense of adventure, their gaiety, and the process of change they were undergoing at this time.

He began acquainting himself with the Chinese (in contrast to the old-time French officials who shut themselves up in the confines of the diplomatic quarter) and spent time with native politicians, writers, and scholars. He even acquired a Chinese name: Lei Hi-gnai, or Thunder Beneath the Snow. Although he was forced to move in diplomatic circles and among many colleagues of whom he was quite critical because of their narrow outlook and preconceptions regarding China, he found ways to escape, mostly by riding at dawn in the outskirts of Peking. He now owned an extraordinary Mongolian horse that soon became one of his closest companions. He called his horse Allan (the childhood name his mother had given him) and developed such an uncanny sense of communion with him that they sometimes seemed "of one body." The natives called it magic or a form of "animal magnetism."

Soon, however, the world of politics claimed his attention. In the summer of 1917, a revolution broke out in the provinces, followed by a coup d'état and a fierce battle in Peking. Leger was sent on a mission that quenched his old thirst for risk and excitement but that he also found greatly amusing: he had to lead the president of the Chinese Republic, his wife, concubines, children, and a whole retinue of servants to a refuge in the inviolate diplomatic quarter. So colorful was the exploit that he sent a highly entertaining account—told in a pastiche of official language and filled with tongue-in-cheek humor—of the adventure to his minister, Alexandre Conty, also in China. Unfortunately, it reached Paris by mistake and seriously threatened his reputation at the Quai d'Orsay. Had he not had the high patronage of Berthelot to protect him, Leger's nonconformist attitude might have harmed him considerably.

His superiors would probably have been even more shocked had they known of another (secret) activity that absorbed him so much that he spent every free moment in a hiding place among the hills above Peking in a Taoist temple, writing. It was there, in a landscape of timelessness and endless vistas, where dreams and visionary states prevailed, that after years of abstinence from poetry *Anabasis* was created. It was a work of far greater scope than anything he had written before, a kind of epic that went beyond those "brief indulgences of the past," and that corresponded to the poem of which he had spoken to Claudel years ago, yet also reflected the vastness he had encountered in China.

Not set in any particular location but rather in a mythic place impossible to situate in time but as if existing since time immemorial, the poem is dominated by a figure named "the Stranger," "the Voyager," "the Teller of Tales," who emerges as the chieftain of a vast people of nomadic tribes, as the celebrant in strange archaic rituals, as the brother of the poet (or his double). He is far more than a projection of personal glory or a self-portrait of the poet, but is rather a hero of epic, even cosmic, proportions. Yet the work, with all its endless perspectives and visionary dimensions, is full of details from that "whole world of things" that the poet always honored (and with images that only Leger's life in China could have produced). Constructed in ten "Chants," beginning and ending with a "Song," the work in its very structure emphasizes movement as well as the cyclical nature of existence. Marked by a thematic alternation between motion and arrest of motion, arrival and departure, possession and freedom from possession, conquest and exile, attachment and detachment, eroticism (harsher and more explicit than formerly) that is both encounter and a form of loneliness, the poem, as Perse later said, is essentially an expression of "solitude in action." And its central figure emerges as a prince without a kingdom, a prophet without religion, a conqueror without victory engaged in a quest without beginning, without end, without a moral. New images arose in this work that were of major importance: the desert (and its opposite or parallel, the sea), birds, the West, and lightning (a symbol of revelation, both illuminating and destructive).

Anabasis was not published until many years later (in 1924, after its author's return from China), but its form and content, the greatness of its scope and the sureness of its execution, made it the first of the long line of major works that established him as one of the finest of contemporary poets.

At the time of its creation, however, he was as deeply involved in the world of action as in that of the dream. His diplomatic work and rapid rise in that sphere allowed him more freedom and involvement with all aspects of China, including discussions with specialists of renown and close friendships with Chinese political leaders and famous writers (such as Lou Tseng-tsiang and Liang Ki-chao). At this time he felt totally removed from the European literary scene. When letters came from Claudel, Gide, or Rivière, he reacted with indifference. The only European writer with whom he felt he could share his thoughts and feelings was Conrad. To him he wrote some of the most significant letters of this period, speaking of his obsession with the sea in the interior of China (a landlocked place) and of his realization that "the sea is within us"—thus providing the key to a vast poem, one of his most magnificent, written almost forty years later, *Amers* (*Seamarks*, 1957)

So fascinated was Leger with China that he probably would have remained there for many more years, especially since the president of the Chinese Republic had asked him to become his political adviser in 1920, had not China's treatment at the Paris Peace Conference led its delegates to leave without signing the peace treaty. Obviously this made it impossible for Leger to accept the offer of a post in the Chinese government and even forced him to admit that it was time to leave China.

Before doing so, however, he carried out a dream he had had ever since his arrival in China: an expedition into Central Asia. He intended to go first to Kalgan and from there begin his journey into Outer Mongolia; he would then cross the Gobi Desert and go as far as Ourga and the seat of the "Living Buddha." His companions were two friends who were experienced in such expeditions and his Mongolian horse, Allan. They set out on 9 May

1920. Strange events began to occur as soon as they penetrated into the desert: at one point, for example, horse and horseman stopped and, at the same instant, turned their faces (inexplicably) in the direction of the sea. The travelers also encountered camel drivers whose "gaze resembled that of seafarers," and they discovered that the wagons used by the nomads of the deserts were rigged with sails and that the Mongol lamaseries used coral and mother-of-pearl to decorate their altars and conch-shells in their religious services. On the high plains, the scenery became "extraplanetary," resembling lunar craters or the "Seas of the Moon" (as the ancient astronomers had called them).

It was on Alexis' thirty-third birthday that the three companions reached the goal of their long journey: the "Tolgoït of Ourga," fabled capital of the land of nomads and seat of the "Living Buddha." They had crossed the frontiers into the unknown and gazed at what seemed the other side of life. It was an experience that Alexis never forgot. And, as if to ensure the indelible memory of this revelation, a sacred object appeared on his path at the final stage of the voyage: a shaman's "thunder stone" that, in an uncanny encounter of symbols, coincided with the Chinese transcription of his name: Thunder Beneath the Snow.

He knew then that he had arrived at the end of his quest. It was time to leave Asia. At the moment of parting, all the material possessions acquired during his stay in the Orient seemed insignificant. The only mementos of his stay on the other side of the world that he took with him were three objects: a stele with his Chinese name, a horse's skull found in the desert, and the shaman's thunder stone—the symbolic sum of his profoundest experiences.

A new stage in his life began in 1921. He returned to France for a short time, saw his family and some of his friends, and was astonished to learn that during (and despite) his long years of absence from the European literary scene, his renown as a poet had grown: *Éloges* still elicited great interest; Darius

Milhaud had set some of its poems to music; Guillaume Apollinaire had spoken of him in a lecture; and Marcel Proust had expressed admiration for his work in a passage of *À la recherche du temps perdu* (*Remembrance of Things Past,* 1912–1927). A number of his literary friends (especially Fargue and Larbaud) insisted on seeing what he had written during his years in the Far East. He had brought back a trunk filled with manuscripts but was quite secretive about his work. They continued to pursue the matter. Finally, to have done with their pleas, he dipped into the sea chest and pulled out a large sheaf of paper. The title it bore was, of course, "Anabase."

This incident made him wish to leave France again to ensure his predilection for distance and privacy. He was thus delighted when, only a few months after his return, he was requested to join the French delegation to the International Conference on Limitation of Armaments in Washington, D.C., as a political expert in Asian affairs. On the ship that carried the group across the Atlantic he found himself in the company of such luminaries as Berthelot and Aristide Briand. The latter, head of government and minister of foreign affairs, often referred to as the "Apostle of Peace" because he had put all his skills at the service of the League of Nations to put his dream of peace into action, intrigued Leger especially. He noticed that his interest was reciprocated, and several times, when they were the only ones on deck during the stormy autumn sea voyage, Briand spoke about possible posts that Leger might occupy in his government. But the latter felt divided between the lure of travel, the independence that distance from Paris provided, and the equally alluring prospect of working with Briand, with whom he had many affinities. Legend has it that a pronouncement made by Leger launched him on the path to political fame, but it is just as likely that Briand's reaction to the remark, which confirmed the latter's nature of dreamer and man of action, tipped the scales and convinced Leger that this was a man with whom he could work.

It happened during an official cruise along the Potomac River when someone suggested to Briand that he write his memoirs. At this Leger is reputed to have murmured, "A book is the death of a tree." Briand, upon hearing these words, began to muse, his gaze lingering on the magnificent oaks along the shore as if he had been deeply touched by Leger's remark. At any rate, at the last moment, when the ship taking the French delegation back to Europe was ready to cast off and Briand once more beckoned Leger to his side, the latter acquiesced to the position he had been offered. Briand ordered that his passage be instantly arranged, not even giving Leger time to pack "a pyjama or a toothbrush." And that is how Leger's career as one of France's most important statesmen began.

From this moment on it was Alexis Leger the diplomat who occupied center stage. His other self, the poet, existed only as a masked figure standing in the wings. The former's rise to fame was rapid, beginning as soon as he returned to Paris. He became part of the central administration at the Quai d'Orsay as director of political and commercial affairs and was second in command in matters concerning Asia and Oceania. Only a few years later, Briand made him the director of his cabinet.

And yet the poet was not exactly dormant. He had secretly returned to the world of literature and resumed contact with writer friends. They spoke to him of the continued interest in his work in avant-garde circles of music and literature and among members of a new movement called surrealism. Two of its most famous members, André Breton and Louis Aragon, were so deeply affected by his poetry that they spoke of it as one speaks of a first love. Of course he wore his mask well in political circles and only among artists, as fellow conspirators, did he reveal his other face. Even there, though, he proceeded with caution, allowing only portions of *Anabasis* to be published and without a signature (in *La nouvelle revue française* and a review called *Intentions*). When he founded a new magazine with

the Princess Caetani, Larbaud, Fargue, and Valéry (named *Commerce* from a line in *Anabase*), he only agreed to do so anonymously. His behavior may have been motivated by his innate sense of secrecy, his belief that art should be essentially anonymous, and his love of duality—but it could also have been founded on caution and a realistic concern for his new career. He decided to adopt a pseudonym further removed from "Leger" than the "Saintleger Leger" he had used in the past for the publication of *Anabasis* in book form by the Editions Gallimard.

He toyed with various possibilities. For a while "Archibald Perse" pleased him, perhaps because it was so different from his real name (or because it had a humorous sound). But then one day another name appeared mysteriously and imposed itself by its rhythms and sonorities: "Saint-John Perse." A secret self was born and duly named. He delighted in the idea that almost no one suspected him of such ambiguity. At the Quai he was the suave, promising young statesman whose entire life seemed centered on political activities; among writers, he was the poet of "Images of Crusoe" and *Éloges,* already the idol of some and the peer of others whom he considered men of genius.

Among the latter was James Joyce, whose *Ulysses* (1922) had recently been published. They shared many predilections and often met at the Princess Caetani's house in Versailles where luminaries from the world of literature and music assembled. Another writer of great stature was Rainer Maria Rilke, who had decided to undertake the German translation of "Images of Crusoe" and with whom Perse also had many profound affinities. As flattering as this project was, Perse hesitated in permitting it since he did not really wish to have an early work brought to light through publication. Rilke ultimately abandoned the translation, finding it too difficult.

At this time, however, Perse published *Anabasis,* a work that launched his career as a poet of world renown. The work appeared in

January of 1924, first in *La nouvelle revue française* and shortly afterward in two different editions by Gallimard, all signed with his new (though somewhat shortened) pseudonym: "St.-J. Perse." A Russian translation followed and then that of Eliot. The ascent of the poet was both swift and sure. But that of the diplomat was equally astonishing, an "anabasis" just as glorious. For the year 1925 was a milestone in Leger's political career: Briand nominated him head of his government, and Berthelot (the secretary general of foreign affairs) became his immediate superior. Thus the two men with whom he was linked by both affinities and friendship were now his close associates. He was well on his way to traveling the highroads of politics.

The project of major import in which he was involved that year was the preparation and negotiation of the Locarno agreement, one of the most important political issues at that time. It was meant to improve the system of collective security for France, which was deprived of territorial safeguards and exposed to danger because of the insufficient power of the League of Nations and the lack of British guarantees of solidarity against Germany. The aim of the meeting at Locarno was to arrive at a pact that would ensure the safety of the Rhine region by an agreement with Germany and an alliance with Britain. Leger worked closely with Briand on every step of this enterprise, the first meeting of its kind between French and German heads of state. So great was Briand's confidence in Leger that he was the only person allowed to be present at this historic encounter.

Almost immediately afterwards, Leger had to turn his attention to the other side of the world, for the Chinese Nationalist crisis of 1925 and 1926 demanded his expertise. He was designated to decide the direction of French diplomatic action in the Far East.

If the demands made on Leger were great, those that involved St.-J. Perse were no less so. A new edition of *Éloges* was brought out by Gallimard in 1925 and a deluxe edition of *Anabasis* followed in the same year. Various foreign translations were also under way. Decidedly, the poet was threatening to come to the forefront. It suddenly seemed to Leger that despite his new pseudonym the literary half of his self was in danger of being discovered. He therefore decided to take more drastic measures than before. He forbade any further publication of his work in France and from then on allowed only foreign translations of *Anabasis* to appear in print. To all appearances, the poet St.-J. Perse had fallen silent.

He immersed himself totally in his work at the Ministry of Foreign Affairs. After the crisis in China, other matters in Europe occupied both Briand and Leger. They had begun to work on a pact designed to result in an international renunciation of war as an instrument of national politics. Conceived and carried out by Leger, it resulted in the Briand-Kellog Pact, an audacious document that paved the way for an even more audacious project: a federal union of Europe. He worked passionately on the preliminary plans, wrote the text of the pact as well as the speech that Briand read on the day of its signature, and had the profound gratification of hearing his words pronounced before the representatives of fifteen nations who met in Paris to sign the agreement that combined dream and action, a far-reaching vision and realistic measures (an equation to which Perse always subscribed).

After a while, however, despite the exhilaration of the political arena, he inwardly yearned for the other side of his being. Secretly, at night and during his infrequent leaves, he turned to poetry once more. Sometimes he also gave in to the desire to see some of his former writer friends and meet others who interested him. He began to frequent Adrienne Monnier's bookstore, La Maison des Amis des Livres, and the establishment across the street, Sylvia Beach's Shakespeare and Company. In the former, he always found Fargue and Larbaud; in the latter, he met Archibald MacLeish, Allen Tate, Ezra Pound, e. e. cummings, Eliot, and Joyce.

Yet, as stimulating as this world of artists

was, as welcome a contrast as it provided to the Quai d'Orsay, he needed other forms of escape that could bring him silence, distance, and the renewal of his creative powers. Thus he began to take his vacations at sea, exploring the Atlantic by sailboat. He usually traveled alone, for he valued the solitude that was so rarely his. During these voyages he wrote. When he returned, he had a faraway look in his eyes and a contraband treasure—both of which he had to dissemble or hide, for he could let nothing of his other face show in the world of politics. Only later (at the age of retirement) did he plan to let it come to light.

At this time, however, he had other concerns. The project that he and Briand were involved in was the organization of a federal union of Europe, an enterprise of unusual initiative and courage in those days of economic crisis and one typical of Briand's constructive bent of thought, to which Leger fully subscribed. He studied the procedures necessary for the project's realization and was also solely responsible for drawing up the memorandum outlining all the aspects of this new and audacious plan, to be presented to the twenty-seven European members of the League of Nations at a meeting in Geneva on 9 September 1929. The memorandum showing the advantages of a federal bond between European nations that would establish continual solidarity between them and the possibility of solving problems of common interest to them received a unanimously favorable response. All the representatives promised to submit the plan to their governments for further study and asked Leger to gather and record the various nations' reactions, to draw conclusions from this survey, and to prepare a report to be submitted at the next meeting of the League of Nations.

The memorandum he presented (as the representative of the French government) before the League of Nations contained a number of interesting points: the need for a pact establishing a united Europe and consecrating the solidarity of European nations; the necessity for creating a mechanism that would ensure the means necessary to accomplish this task; and the need to establish the essential direction and the general conceptions of a European committee in order to guide its work for organizing Europe. Leger concluded with an appeal to the nations of Europe that emphasized the responsibility of governments to work collectively for the benefit of the European community and of all humanity.

The project of a united Europe was, unfortunately, never realized. The forces of destruction were already gathering. When Leger tried one last time, in 1935, to take up the thread of a collective organization of Europe, the odds against him were already far too great. As far as Briand was concerned, this dream would have taken more than a lifetime to carry out—and his life was about to end. In 1932, just as peace in Europe was ending, Briand was on the point of dying.

Leger assisted him in his last hours and heard him, in his delirium, speak of Europe in tones of anguish, as if he had a tragic vision of its fate. It seemed an ominous portent for the future. When Briand was buried, the hope of peace went with him to the grave. His death marked the end of an era, the demise of plans for international harmony. For Leger it was the termination of a long period of companionship in dream and action. With Berthelot also gone from the political scene due to retirement, Leger now stood alone, obliged to carry on a heritage that appeared increasingly fragile in those times of violence. As he crossed the threshold of another epoch, he had the premonition that after the glorious ascent, a descent was about to begin.

However, the next seven years were ushered in by a personal victory that seemed to belie such predictions: Leger was promoted to ambassador and, most important of all, became secretary general of foreign affairs (inheriting Berthelot's post). It was the key position in the French government, making him in actuality more powerful than the minister of foreign affairs. Given the times, constant vigilance was required of him. In Germany the Nazi party had begun its rise to power. He was convinced that the French and British must unite to face this menace and must make no more concessions to that government. But despite his insight and vast power, it soon became evident that Leger was doomed to become the defender of lost causes. The Locarno Treaty had been written at a time when there was still hope that the conflict between France and Germany could be settled. Now there was no longer any chance of agreement. All one could do was to work for containment. That at least was how Leger saw it. Unfortunately, however, he had to serve under a variety of foreign ministers with whom he was not in agreement (and who would not accept his resignation when offered). Despite his high ideals and his fundamental liberalism, as a servant of the state he would have to do many things that went against his convictions.

Thus, in April 1935 he had to accompany Pierre Laval to the Conference of Stresa (where the latter met with Benito Mussolini) although the two men disagreed on the objectives of that meeting. Only a short while later, they both encountered Joseph Stalin in Moscow. This time Leger succeeded in obtaining the Franco-Russian Pact, a treaty of mutual assistance between the two countries that turned Russia away from the old notion of a military alliance with Germany. The third dictator Leger met (making him one of the few diplomats to have encountered all three personally) was Adolf Hitler. This time he traveled once again in unwelcome company—with Edouard Daladier (who, like Laval, favored appeasement of Hitler) to Munich in September 1938. Leger sat at Daladier's side, prompting him to ask questions and to object to the demands Hitler was making. At certain points Leger himself shot questions at Hitler, probed, attacked, used all his skill to achieve his aims—principally, to prevent the invasion of the Sudetenland. But to no avail. The disastrous outcome of the Munich Conference is well known.

These were dark days. Crisis followed crisis.

On 1 September 1939 World War II broke out. It was the end of all dreams of peace. The edifice that Briand and Leger had attempted to build was now in ruins. A manmade cataclysm threatened to dehumanize the world. In the midst of such vast destruction, his own personal misfortune seemed small matter indeed. It happened at the end of May 1940, shortly after the threat of a German invasion put Paris in a state of panic. The government was full of upheaval. Daladier had to resign in favor of Paul Reynaud, and the latter was put under pressure by Leger's enemies to unseat him. But in order to accomplish this, another post had to be found for him (preferably one that would discredit him by assigning him an impossible task). The best plan seemed to be to send him as ambassador to Washington with the mission of convincing the United States to enter the war—which was sure to be a failure. Reynaud signed the decree of Leger's replacement and left to Daladier the unpleasant task of informing Leger. On 19 May Leger learned of his "disgrace." His response was characteristic of his innate nobility and concern for France's welfare: he refrained from attacking those who had betrayed him, since doing so might add to the chaos of a country already wracked by the upsets in its government, but he refused to accept the post of ambassador to Washington and insisted on being "taken off active duty." Only his final words to Daladier were as full of rage as of dignity: "I have a right to the full extent of injustice."

It was the end of the man known as Alexis Leger, that powerful figure who had reigned in French foreign affairs during the most crucial years between world wars. As he stood ready to leave French soil on 16 June 1940, he was a man divested of every glory he had accumulated since his return from China. The past was gone, the future a complete unknown. After having ascended to such great heights, he had reached the lowest point in his life. Exile in its harshest form was now his.

New York, where he landed on 14 July,

seemed hostile and violent in the summer heat. He lived in a large, impersonal hotel in Manhattan, which added to his feeling of alienation and solitude. Now and then news reached him from Europe, but it took on the form of repeated blows: he learned that the Vichy government had divested him of his nationality, confiscated his possessions, and eradicated his Legion of Honor; that a press campaign raged against him; and that the Germans had ransacked his apartment and pillaged all his papers—including his unpublished manuscripts, which meant that his entire poetic output of over two decades was lost, apparently irremediably. He himself had sunk into an abyss of isolation, muteness, and immobility.

Only slowly did he begin to recover and seek human contact once more. Among the first persons he agreed to see was Katherine Biddle, the sister of Princess Caetani and the wife of the attorney general of the United States, who came from Washington to welcome him. Another friendly move came from that city, this time from a fellow poet, MacLeish, who offered him the post of literary consultant at the Library of Congress, of which he was the director. Perse hesitated somewhat at first but finally accepted and moved to Washington at the beginning of 1941. He found a small lodging, established a spartan mode of life, and always kept his suitcases half packed as a reminder of his nomadic existence. The more sedentary side of his life took place at the Library of Congress, where he began to research and compile a reference book (never published) entitled "A Selection of Works for an Understanding of World Affairs Since 1914." Aside from this activity, the part of him that had been a diplomat seemed dead and forgotten. Yet the poet had still not come to the fore. When MacLeish suggested that he begin writing again, he almost rudely insisted that this would never happen.

Paradoxically, however, when his new friends the Biddles loaned him their country house on Long Beach Island, New Jersey, that summer, a poem formed within him and de-manded expression. He sensed that it would be more powerful than anything he had written before. Perhaps he also knew that it would mark a turning point in his life. And indeed this was the case, for once *Exil* (*Exile,* 1942), the poem he then wrote, had seen the light, others followed at the rate of one a year: "Poème à l'étrangère" ("Poem to a Foreign Lady," 1942), *Rains* (1943), *Snows* (1944), and *Winds* (1945).

The title *Exile* is as harsh, as naked as the state it describes. Neither plaintive nor personal, as one might at first be led to think, the poem speaks of exile as an eternal and universal state, as a beginning not an end, as a descent into nothingness as the necessary prelude for ascent. Everything must first be reduced to essentials (as is the imagery, which is limited to sand, bone, stone, skulls—all that is arid, nil, void). Only when the threshold that leads to "nothing" has been crossed can there be a turning and a return. The same images then reveal their other side: sand becomes the essence of nakedness (and thus of purity), bone reveals its incorruptible nature and stone its irreducible quality, the void becomes the symbol of plenitude and exile both an exit and an entry. Other major images that reveal a basic duality are also present: lightning (both destruction and creation), the desert (a place of sterility but also of revelation), the Stranger or Wanderer (an outcast but also a Prince of Exile), wind (a force that both annihilates and inspires), and the Poet (whose very nakedness ensures his freedom and who, having abandoned the past, assumes his birthright and his heritage).

The poem's structure is in itself revealing: consisting of seven parts and thus based on a number that is a universal symbol of creation, of change after a cycle has run full course, it traces the path that leads from non-being to being, from detachment to engagement, from void to plenitude, and from despair to affirmation. The language of the poem is also particularly interesting and shows a further development when compared to past works: it combines a vocabulary that is as stripped down, as spare as the subject it treats, yet it is also extremely complex, full of rare, at times archaic, words or erudite terms that come from a wide variety of fields (botany, geology, history, zoology, geography, astronomy, navigation).

There is no question that *Exile* marked a new phase in the life of its creator. As he wrote the last words of the poem, "And the hour has come, o Poet, to state your name, your birth, and your race," he knew that Alexis Leger was gone and Saint-John Perse had come to life.

The years of his greatest creativity followed. Saint-John Perse (as he now signed his work) emerged from the shadows. *Exile* appeared almost instantly in French in *Poetry* magazine and was then reproduced in Marseille, Buenos Aires, Neuchâtel, and, finally, in a clandestine edition in France—all within the space of a year. But another work was already in progress: "Poem to a Foreign Lady," dedicated to a mysterious woman (not identified) also in exile and thus linked to Perse by emotional ties but also by their joint status as "aliens." The poem is a dialogue between the "foreign lady" and "the man from France" who attempts to console this woman in mourning by evoking the charms of animals and the marvels of nature. Suddenly however, as if arrested in the midst of his exhortations by the magnitude of her suffering, the poet, seeing the true face of tragedy, bows before her pain and joins her in sorrow. Instantly though, after having "sung of yesterday, of the far away, of pain at its origin," he adds, "but also the splendor of living." And, having paid tribute to the profound paradox of existence, the equilibrium between pain and joy, mourning and celebration, the Stranger/ Poet begins his wanderings anew. The path on which he embarks is both a forward thrust and a return, freedom from memory and memory reclaimed. Toward the end of the poem, his chant is one that goes beyond the human but is also most poignantly human, invoking the remote and grandiose as well as the familiar and humble:

I go forth, o memory, with the stride of a free man
. . . amidst the song of the hourglass trees and,
my brow bare, wreathed with phosphorescent
    bees . . .
whistling for my tribe of Sybils, whistling for my
    people of non-believers,
I still caress, as in a dream . . . among so many
    invisible beings,
my dog from Europe who was white and, more
    than I,
a poet.

The year that had elapsed since *Exile* was written had led the "alien" back to the world of the human once more. And even the bitterness of the exiled diplomat gave way to humanistic concerns: Alexis Leger expressed his solidarity with the French resistance, aided the representatives of La France Libre (despite his refusal of the invitation made by Charles de Gaulle to join him in London), wrote to Churchill analyzing the workings of the French underground, and gave a speech in memory of Briand. Evidently, a flow of feeling now developed in Perse. It began to inundate his poetry, for it can be no accident that after the harsh and solitary splendor of *Exile,* the work he undertook next celebrates a force of nature whose fructifying role has been known since the beginning of time: rain.

Rains is reputed to have been composed during a trip to the American South that evoked memories of his childhood days. Its beginnings are said to have taken place during a thunderstorm in Savannah, Georgia, a torrential downpour that lasted all night. The poem, however, instantly exceeds any such personal experience, for its opening and penultimate sequence frame it with a striking image, "the banyan tree of rain," which links past and present, the near and the far, memory and the purgation of memory. The nine sections of the work (a number highly significant in the oeuvre of

Perse, symbolizing gestation, fruitful search, the crowning of efforts, the accomplishment of creation) to trace the purification and liberation effected by Rains, which appear in the guise of female dancers and warriors as well as of lightning that vivifies desire and provokes laughter of Olympian proportions. The great tasks accomplished by the Rains are manifold: ablution, purification, purgation of everything in the world—the living and the dead, the strong and the violent, the doubting and the prudent, culture, knowledge, and even poetry itself. But the work goes even further to recognize that purification verges on the Void, that language cannot render the ineffable, and that the true celebration of the Rains must take place not only through ellipsis but in silence, in an unwritten poem by an awed and mute poet who remains standing at the threshold of creation.

Conrad Aiken, in speaking of *Rains,* called it a "litany of litanies" that produced a metamorphosis in its readers and led them to a true knowledge of being. Another poet, Allen Tate, who edited the *Sewanee Review,* offered to publish *Rains* there, taking infinite care to have the work appear in a perfect rendition. In many respects a "poet's poem," it seems quite fitting that its earliest and most ardent admirers were poets.

The next work was quite different from *Rains. Snows* was written during the following winter in New York at a time of anguish concerning his mother (who had remained in France), about whom he had recently received distressing news. Aged and far from her son, her difficulties were in part caused by his name, since it associated her with his former life as a statesman who was now very much out of favor. There was no way he could help her, and he deeply regretted their many separations. All his longing, sorrow, and tenderness culminated in this poem, dedicated to her. It was an intimate offering, as gentle, subtle, and secret as snow, filled with familial details (which had not appeared in his work since "Celebration of a Childhood" and *Éloges*). She

is evoked, bent with sorrow and great age, in a pose of silent waiting, full of grace and wordless understanding, among images arising from snow—mysterious, fragile, dreamlike. Their tender, almost mute dialogue crosses a vast expanse, seas agitated by strife; it mingles regret with smiles, yearning with communion, until language itself reaches its most ancient form and moves, finally, into a realm where pure silence reigns. "Let them leave the two of us to that language without words that you know so well, o you who are all presence, o you who are all patience!" he chants. And after dawn has risen in a transformed land of grace and mercy where all the snows form a vast, white rose-window and yield dreamlike perspectives, the poem ends as if covered by snow—in ellipsis, whiteness, silence: "From hence, this page where nothing is inscribed."

A year later, on Seven Hundred Acre Island, a retreat near Dark Harbor, Maine, that belonged to a friend, Perse undertook a strange and paradoxical task. He wrote to a friend that in the solitude of this place he hoped to achieve the destruction of the poet within him, to "strangle the only being which was basic to [him]." And yet he had also come here to complete his greatest poem to date. He sensed that it would outstrip all his past achievements as a poet—that it would be a work grand in scope and vision, filled with his own (and the universe's) vastest powers, infused with a gigantic breath (of human and cosmic nature) and thus diametrically opposed to the attempt at silencing the poet within him by strangulation.

Winds is indeed not only the lengthiest of his works thus far, but also the most intricate in design. Eight pages long, divided into four sections and twenty-six parts, the poem celebrates winds both as forces of nature and as divinities that triumph over "straw men in a straw year"—over all that is dry and sterile—as they liberate "desire that sings." The poem itself is shaken by their gusts, the "great tree of language" is caused to murmur anew, and the narrator's words are freshened by the Winds, his companions. He proclaims the advent of new life, urging haste in seizing the moment: "To hasten! to hasten! Words of the living man!" As the winds increase in force, the divinity of the storm appears, full of license and erotic power, awakening everything in his path until seed and sap swell and rise: vanquishing all that was formerly withered and hollow: scattering barriers, dead bodies, rigid monuments, and works now meaningless; awakening new writings of the future. "Everything to be done anew! Everything to be said anew! And the scythe of the gaze sweeping over all that has been acquired!" the poet exclaims and proceeds to mow down the "Basilica of Books," altars that have lost all meaning, dryness and dust of archives, all that is parched, fetid, or rotting. His cry resounds in the wind: "To leave! to leave! Words of the living man!" Having paid homage to the god, he moves beyond the narrow world of men, free, drunk on new wine, "as if pierced by lightning," his face in the wind, going beyond all limits, singing the glory of the typhoon with laughter and desire.

His movement is ever westward. The Poet-Voyager, led by his "Master of song," the Wind, travels toward the splendors of the West, place of death and rebirth, the "true homeland of all men of desire" (as Claudel says). New lands, new waters, new women, new years, new texts appear. And a new being is formed—hard, emaciated, reduced to skeletal purity (as is the shaman)—who reaches summits never attained before. He is the Poet, now speaking as an oracle in a double tongue. However, having reached the highest point, illuminated by a vision, and having performed extrahuman exploits, he must turn back. For the cry of the human must be heeded by the Poet. Returning to the world of men, he affirms that the Poet must "bear witness" to the human and must incite man to live. Yet the Poet must never forget his revelation and in his works must reflect "the other shore," the "black Sun of the nether regions," while at the same time celebrating the human world and becoming an integral part of it. But lest a life among men, with its calm and prudence, softness, and redundancy,

cause the Poet to forget his vision, the Winds will ever serve as a goad, an irritant, to remind him of his encounter with the divine. Renewing him and his works by their force they will continually strip off the old leaves of the tree of language and incite new poetic growth.

It seems certain that *Winds* was a turn of the tide for the poet who had gone to the solitary island in order to destroy the deepest part of himself but who instead emerged with the conviction that his true place was among poets. For Perse came to the fore at this time: he terminated his functions at the Library of Congress and signed a contract with the Bollingen Foundation that would allow him to devote himself exclusively to poetry.

Yet no new work of poetry by Perse appeared for over ten years. It seemed as though he had exhausted his breath in *Winds* and had to undergo a period of waiting, a "literary fast" as he said, until his forces welled up once more and resulted in another creation. In the interim, he traveled, gathered impressions, stored up information, collected the raw materials for a poem that he knew would be "the most ambitious" of his works but that he refused to begin while preoccupied by worries and sadness (such as that caused by the death of his mother in 1948) for he had sworn to himself "to bring to it only joy, free and freely given." He would wait, no matter how long it took, for he recognized "no other object in poetic creation than the liberation of joy, or more exactly, 'pleasure' in its very essence—the most mysterious, the most useless, and thus the most sacred."

It is not unlikely that the "'pleasure' in its very essence" of which he had spoken came to him in the form of a woman. True, women had always been a vital part of his life (although he was very secretive about his various liaisons and had only one "official" mistress, a French countess), but this woman seemed the companion he had long sought. She was an American from an old and distinguished family, had traveled widely in Europe, had spoken French since childhood, and felt a particular attachment to France; besides, she had the physical attractions he always responded to, shared many of his interests, and also understood his need for solitude and independence. Her name, although for a long time he only referred to her as "D." in letters to friends, was Dorothy Diana Russell (née Milburn). Despite his reserve, it was quite evident that from around 1950 onward she had become an important part of his life. It is also probable that his next poem was influenced by this source of joy.

The creation of the work stretched over a number of years, quite fittingly since it was vaster than anything he had written so far and dealt primarily with the love of an entire lifetime: the sea. Yet at its very center another great love is celebrated: that of woman. Everything he had experienced and was experiencing flowed into this poem, which seems like the culmination of his whole life: *Seamarks*. Its very title announces the many levels on which the poem can and should be read (in the French original, *Amers*, it can be given a triple interpretation: marks on the coastline to guide ships, thus linking shore and sea; the plural of the adjective *amer*, i.e., bitter or salty, which, in the work of Perse, is associated with acuity and vitality; and "à mers," a dedication to the seas). Its great length (over one hundred and eighty pages) attests not only to the vastness of its scope (befitting the subject) but also to the singular achievement of its author in sustaining poetic intensity throughout such an enormous work.

From the very outset *Seamarks* speaks of the profound meaning of the poem for its creator and the long maturation (over forty years) it required until it could come into existence at a time when

the javelins of Noon
vibrate at the portals of joy [and] the drums of the
    void
give way to the fifes of light.

The poet rejoices in his task and asks a jubilant force to lead him in his great enterprise. The grandeur of the work is also underlined by its structure, which is a variation on the ancient Greek drama and befits the antiquity or eternity of its subject. Built on a design of concentric circles (which echoes ritual and theatrical processions around an altar), at its very center stands the ninth (and therefore most significant) sequence of the "Strophe," entitled "Étroits sont les vaisseaux" ("Narrow Are the Vessels"). It has been compared to the *Song of Songs* and is without a doubt the greatest erotic poem in the French language.

Everything converges on this portion of the vast poem, for here, more than anywhere else in the work, the Sea and the love act are inextricably linked. Miming, or rather incarnating, the rise and fall of the waves (of the sea and of desire), "Narrow Are the Vessels" expresses the union of the lovers ("the man from the sea" and "the woman of the shore"), from its inception to their love play and final consummation. At the moment of orgasm the lovers transcend the human and participate in a mythic rite. Conducted on two levels, "Narrow Are the Vessels" traces the sex act both in concrete, explicit, singularly direct fashion (devoid of all inhibition or prudery) and in mythological images of a universal nature. It celebrates the human and that which exceeds the human, the temporal and the eternal, the mortal and the immortal, the profane and the sacred, and it is thus the most complete celebration of the human act of creation as the mirror of divine creation.

One can hardly imagine a greater tribute to the beloved or to the poet's greatest loves, woman and the sea, joined in one surpassing whole. When *Seamarks* reached completion in 1956, the summit of all its creator had felt during a lifetime seems to have been reached, for in the final litany of the vast poem, the sea is revealed as the sum of all ambiguities, the union of all opposites, the ultimate great paradox:

Sea of Baal, Sea of Mammon; Sea of all ages and
    names,

Uterine Sea of our dreams, Sea haunted by the true
    dream,
. . . .

O you, offense and splendor! furor and calm,
O you, both love and hate, Inexorable and Exorable,
O you, who know and know not, who speak and
    speak not,
. . . .

O blood relative and distant kin, incest and
    ancestress,
O you, immensely compassionate to all perishable
    things,
Sea forever irrefutable, Sea at last inseparable!

And at the end of *Seamarks,* the voice of the poet exclaims jubilantly: "High noon . . . man free of his shadow, at the limit / of his riches." Surely, this affirmation echoes Perse's feelings at that time. The man who had arrived empty-handed, a shadowy figure in an alien land, had reached his zenith. It only remained for him now to end his exile. This happened in 1957, the same year as the publication of *Seamarks* by Gallimard, when a group of friends and admirers presented him with a property on the southern coast of France, allowing him to return after an absence of seventeen years.

Strangely enough, he felt quite alienated when he arrived in France. Even his house and land on the edge of the Mediterranean could not dispel the sensation. As he surveyed the vast expanse of water that surrounded the Giens peninsula, the cliffs that led down to the sea, the brilliant light of the Midi, he exclaimed "But how far I am from the Atlantic!"—the ocean of his youth and birthplace of his ancestors. Besides, the landscape seemed to him unsuited to his temperament. He who loved trees but disliked flowers saw only the latter in overbearing profusion. Then too, this was a place of immense loneliness, and his house, although it was all simplicity and pure outlines, seemed empty and still foreign.

It was only when he finally turned to the sea and plunged bodily into it that he began to recover somewhat. He still felt some hesitation about beginning to write again. Not until autumn did he reach a decision that suited his dualistic lifestyle: he would live half the year in France, the other in America, thus being both nomad and landowner, a man of the Atlantic and the Mediterranean, who balanced East and West, winter and summer, companionship and solitude, and living like a migratory bird, following the seasons. Another major decision followed in the spring: he married Dorothy Russell in April 1958, thus entering matrimony for the first time at the age of nearly seventy-one.

When they both returned to "Les Vigneaux," as his property was called, it seemed indeed as if "a new era" had begun. Everything was certainly changed: he was now a husband, no longer an exile or a nomad but a man "of one place," something resembling a solid citizen. This might have spelled confinement for someone of his temperament had he not found a highly original solution to this unequivocal state: he decided that he was doubly married (or married to two women) by the simple and amusing expedient of using his wife's first name (Dorothy) in America and the gallicized version of her middle name (Diane) in France, besides dividing their life between the house they owned in Georgetown and the property on the Giens peninsula in France.

In the summer of 1959 he began to write once more, working on a great poem whose subject matter is both unusual and characteristic of its creator: *Chronique,* a celebration of old age. "Its title," he explained, "should be taken in its etymological sense, i.e., a poem to the earth, to man, and to time—all three combined in the same timeless notion of eternity." No longer in the epic mode but rather a hymn or an ode, the work is relatively short and much more intimate than the grand creations of the previous decades. It is also striking in its simplicity—a quality that can only be attained after numerous anabases and exiles, when winds have grown still, rains have abated, and the sea's waves have grown calmer. In some sense a return to the early poems of *Éloges,* *Chronique* speaks with the voice of a solitary man seated in the serene and silent splendor of "great age." Arranged in eight chants (eight being a universal symbol of cosmic equilibrium), the poem's very first utterance, "Great age, here we are," immediately establishes both the universality of the experience and the double meaning of "great" age as both "grand" and "old." Old age is depicted not as a state of decrepitude or a cause for sorrow but as "a route of embers, not ashes," full of fire and fever, illuminated by an admittedly setting sun but one that is full of splendor. Evening and "the man of evening" who appear here are celebrated as having completed a cycle yet being filled with a vision even vaster than before. Roads without limit stretch beyond death; voyages, discoveries, and conquests are of even greater magnitude, and great age is the summit of an entire lifetime. Speaking for all of humanity now, for the living and the dead of all time, by giving a résumé of all his past works the poet voices their legacy as well as his own. But he also still sings of women who, their lips red with the juice of the pomegranate, render death's grip vain, and of knowledge that can only come with great age. Finally, he turns his gaze earthward (the place from which all life arises and to which it must return) and celebrates the earth, "last to come in our praises . . . O memory, in the heart / of man, of the lost kingdom!" Once having recognized this lost/found kingdom, the poet's tone changes, for his steps are now oriented toward the egress and his song becomes one of leave-taking. At the end of the poem there stands the striking image of the celebrant, his arms raised in a ritual gesture to present an offering of all that his life has been—the ardor, yearning, and untold love of all his years. The final words are overwhelming in their simplicity and grandeur: "Great age, here we are. Take measure of the heart / of man."

It seemed like a last work, a poetic testament. But this was not the case. Paradoxically, what followed was one of the most intense periods in Perse's life. Honors followed honors; prize upon prize was bestowed upon him. It all culminated in the Nobel Prize, which he was awarded in the winter of 1960, crowning his achievements in poetry. His acceptance speech was, characteristically, a celebration of poetry rather than an acknowledgement by a poet laureate. Its very first sentence expressed this humility with utter simplicity: "I accept, for poetry, the homage it has been rendered here, and which I hasten to return to it."

It was also a time of great activity, extensive travel by ship and on horseback, jet plane, and yacht to South America, the American Northwest, the Caribbean, the Mediterranean. His poetry traveled as far and wide as he. Translations appeared in almost every country in the world and in every imaginable language. But it was not only the works of the past that marked these years. In 1962 he undertook a fascinating project in collaboration with Georges Braque. It was an encounter between the poet and the painter in which each independently pursued a subject of intense interest to them both: birds.

For Perse it was an opportunity to celebrate a figure that had haunted him since the start of his life. *Oiseaux* (*Birds,* 1963), the poetic text that is part of the joint venture with Bracque, instantly establishes the fact that the central bird image of the poem goes beyond (but does not deny) the characteristic traits of birds. From the very start, "the Bird" is defined as one of man's "blood brothers," whose "ardor," "avidity," and "duality" relate him not only to man in general but specifically to the poet— this poet. The Bird's evolution in air and on earth, as well as his resemblance to a ship in his configuration, makes him a denizen of three elements of his creator's predilection and a juncture or unification of all these. He is also seen as combining the natural and the supernatural and, finally, as poetry itself. His flight becomes "a poetry of action" by means of which he consumes himself but also undergoes rebirth as does the phoenix. The Bird is also comparable to the word, "magically charged: a center of force and action, the heart of lightning," which "loses all meaning at the outermost limits of felicity." More than even poetry itself, the Bird reaches the summit of experience, becomes the "Master of the Dream" as he thrusts on to ever greater heights, toward the mystic center where all opposites are unified, to the very source of the cosmic cycle. And yet the poem, for all its transfiguration of the Bird into a figure of visionary splendor, is a precise study of his anatomy and his extraordinary physical performance, so detailed and scientific that it might have been written by a skilled ornithologist. Perse here shows his enduring mastery in combining the loftiest flights of the imagination and the ability to glimpse the marvelous in the most concrete things.

Despite the fact that this poem was completed close to Perse's seventy-fifth birthday and could in many ways be considered a fitting conclusion to his work, it is not his last. Six years of silence followed the appearance of *Birds,* due not so much to a "literary fast" or a long period of preparation but rather to the fact that the tides of inspiration were ebbing because the end of life was approaching. Perse had reached the "great age" of eighty-one. But other works followed in the next seven years that were both a farewell and a moving expression of his final visions, battles, and continuing greatness. They form a slim volume (hardly more than twenty pages long), *Chant pour un équinoxe* (*Song for an Equinox,* 1975), but one so intense and complex that it contains the entire range of human emotions and the poet's most profound revelations.

The first poem of this final group was written in 1968: "Chanté par celle qui fut là" ("Sung by One Who Was There"). The voice speaking is that of a woman who will soon be bereaved: it is a grave and yearning voice that sings of love, loss, and remembrance to the accompaniment of images that indicate that everything is about to end. She addresses her beloved, already moving into the shadow of death, attempting to comfort him by evoking animals and the beauties of nature (as the man had done for the woman in "Poem to a Foreign Lady," written decades earlier); Ceres, the Earth Mother of the gentle hands; and life, which takes everything under its wing. Solace is coupled, however, with a passionate desire to bring the last spark to the embers, to infuse the glow of life into the beloved by means of memories—even though it be but for a moment—as she chants: "I am yours, o my love, among all the feasts of / remembrance. Listen, listen, o my love, / to the clamor of a great love at the ebb of life." And although neither turns away from the sight of Death approaching, she transforms the last journey into an expedition to the region of the setting sun—the place of ultimate adventure and revelation—a voyage "toward the great Indies of the West." At the end of the poem the sum of all that has been (which is offered up by the celebrant of *Chronique*) is placed on the lips of the woman "who was there," so that she inherits and becomes the living repository of remembrance.

Three more years passed before Perse wrote his next poem. He had begun to ail. Surely he recognized the signs that time was running out. He and his wife remained in France on the edge of the sea to which he had become reconciled, among the trees he had planted and the animals that had become their companions. Friends came from all parts of the globe. He had erected a mast on his property (as though it were a ship), where he raised a flag with his visitors' initials. Beside it another small flag always flew, called "Blue Peter" in nautical terminology, which signals a ship "ready to cast off." Everything seemed a prelude to the final departure. Each work written might well be the last.

The one that emerged next was "Chant pour un équinoxe" ("Song for an Equinox," 1971). As brief as his first poem published over sixty years previously, it condensed into less than two pages all the major themes of his entire life's work and was evidence of his still awesome artistry.

The title of the poem reveals the fundamental nature of poetry as song. And this song celebrates the equinox, the moment when the two halves of the year, day and night, fecundity and sterility (and, by extension, creation and destruction) are in perfect balance, in total equilibrium. As the work opens, thunder resounds—as if to signal a revelation—rain begins to fall, and with its power to purify and rejuvenate, causes love to rise and "life to flow upstream toward its origins." The poet, speaking in the accents of the seer, proclaims that everything is returning to its wellsprings so that all might begin again, anew. Suddenly, mysteriously, snow appears—as pure and tender as in the poem written for his mother. The sky seems full of stillness, the earth liberated from all its burdens. It is a mute, motionless instant, an awesome pause before a vision of rebirth appears:

And somewhere in the world . . .
a child is born into the world whose race
nor rank nobody knows,
and genius strikes with sure blows that pure brow.

In this revelation of cyclical movement where death rejoins birth the dying poet makes a legacy of his art to an unknown, newborn child. And at the end of the poem, he addresses the Earth that he celebrated in "Chronique" and chants, "O Earth, our Mother / . . . life takes its course," thus acquiescing to the vast flow of existence that goes beyond a single life. The final lines affirm not only the renewal of life but of poetry itself:

A song which did not know its origin rises in us,
a song which will not have its estuary in death:
equinox of this hour between Earth and man.

Only a year later Perse wrote a poem very different from "Song for an Equinox," entitled "Nocturne," which is not a song but a piercing cry. As its title suggests, it is a night poem, full of dread and bitterness. This brief, anguished outcry (barely a page long) is the sole utterance of despair found in the entire work of the poet. It rails against fate and its harsh, impersonal,

unyielding dictates. Everything that the poet had celebrated in the past now seems null and void. Even the blazing noonday sun that in *Seamarks* makes man appear immortal is now denounced as a betrayer. Despair colors everything. The transitory nature of human existence is felt in all its pathos, for nothing seems to remain of a mortal's passing on this earth. He cries out: "Our works are scattered, our tasks without honor, and our grain without harvest." And the poem ends upon the image of a female grim reaper who gathers a life devoid of all meaning, sterile and vain, with total indifference, impervious to loss or gain, chaff or grain, as she moves inexorably onward.

The poem, singular in that all of Perse's other work is one vast affirmation, is so strikingly human that it adds meaning to all the rest. At the same time it is also a turning point. For only this journey to the end of night can bring about a metamorphosis by which symbols are reversed and destruction is revealed as creation. As such it lends insight into the last poem of Perse, written only a year before his death: "Sécheresse" ("Drought"). Initially the title evokes aridity, sterility, a wasteland. And indeed, the images at the start of the poem suggest just that. Yet shortly, the meaning of "drought" changes and reveals its true function: the world, in order to be re-created, must first be annihilated. The lowest point of existence must be reached (as we have seen in *Exile*) before the upward turn of the cycle can occur. In that sense drought is the necessary dessication of life, the purification by heat and fire, so that all that is corrupt and corruptible can be stripped away, and a higher reality can be brought about. From an initially negative symbol, drought becomes the sign that identifies the Chosen one or the poet/shaman. He becomes the agent of destruction who, from a fiery apocalypse, can proclaim the advent of a new beginning, imminent rebirth:

The time will come again which shall restore the rhythm of the seasons; the nights will bring back the

living waters to the earth's teats;
. . . life shall rise once more from its subterranean
hiding places.

And love also (or the creative, reproductive energy of the universe) will renew everything: the seared wasteland will be revitalized by rain. Even time will acquire a new meaning: chronological, mortal time will give way to eternal, sacred Time (to which the poet/seer addresses himself). As he moves toward the point of epiphany, where opposites are unified, he proclaims the ultimate paradox: "Blind noon illuminates us." At the end of his quest, the Chosen one, face to face with the sacred, pronounces his final incantation where he voices the belief that union with the divine follows annihilation and that the destruction of the mortal state precedes resurrection on a higher plane. Although in no way a negation of his lifelong adherence to no particular religion, but rather an affirmation of the divine, the dream of the poet here attains the dimension of a sacred vision, limitless and everlasting.

In the remaining months of his life Perse arranged the poems he had written during the previous seven years in the order he wished them to take in the final volume of his work (which appeared one month after his death), *Chant pour un équinoxe.*

And, as if the title had been a prophecy, Saint-John Perse/Alexis Leger died at the time of the autumnal equinox: 20 September 1975. He was buried on the edge of the Mediterranean, thus closing the circle of his life that had led from sea to sea.

Selected Bibliography

EDITIONS

INDIVIDUAL WORKS
Éloges. Paris, 1911.
Anabase. Paris, 1924.
La Gloire des Rois. Paris, 1924.
Exil. Marseille, 1942.
Poème à l'etrangère. New York, 1943.
Neiges. Buenos Aires, 1944.
Pluies. Buenos Aires, 1944.
Vents. Paris, 1946.
Amers. Paris, 1957.
Chronique. Paris, 1960.
Oiseaux. Paris, 1963.
Chant pour un équinoxe. Paris, 1971.

COLLECTED WORKS
Chant pour un équinoxe. Paris, 1975. Contains "Sécheresse," "Chant pour un équinoxe," "Nocturne," "Chanté par celle qui fut là."
Oeuvres complètes. Paris, 1972. This volume contains all of Perse's poetry, with the exception of "Nocturne" and "Sécheresse," an extensive correspondence, literary speeches, homages, notes and a chronology.
Quatre poèmes, 1941–1944. Buenos Aires, 1944. Contains "Exil," "Poème à l'étrangère," "Pluies," "Neiges."

TRANSLATIONS
Anabasis. Translated by T. S. Eliot. London, 1930.
Birds. Translated by Robert Fitzgerald. New York, 1966.
Chronique. Translated by Robert Fitzgerald. New York, 1949.
Éloges and Other Poems. Translated by Louise Varèse. New York, 1944.
Exile and Other Poems. Translated by Denis Devlin. New York, 1949.
Saint-John Perse: Collected Poems. Translated by W. H. Auden, et al. Princeton, N.J., 1971.
Seamarks. Translated by Wallace Fowlie. New York, 1958.
Song for an Equinox. Translated by Richard Howard. Princeton, N.J., 1977.
Winds. Translated by Hugh Chisholm. New York, 1953.

CORRESPONDENCE
Letters of Saint-John Perse. Edited and translated by Arthur Knodel. Princeton, N.J., 1979.

BIOGRAPHICAL AND CRITICAL STUDIES

Bosquet, Alain. *Saint-John Perse.* Paris, 1977.

Caillois, Roger. *Poétique de Saint-John Perse.* Paris, 1954.

Charpier, Jacques. *Saint-John Perse.* Paris, 1962.

Emmanuel, Pierre. *Saint-John Perse: Praise and Presence.* Washington, D.C., 1971.

Galand, René. *Saint-John Perse.* New York, 1972.

Knodel, Arthur. *Saint-John Perse: A Study of His Poetry.* Edinburgh, 1966.

Little, Roger. *Saint-John Perse.* London, 1973.

Loranquin, Albert. *Saint-John Perse.* Paris, 1963.

Murciaux, Christian. *Saint-John Perse.* Paris, 1960.

Ostrovsky, Erika. *Under the Sign of Ambiguity: Saint-John Perse/Alexis Leger.* New York, 1985.

ERIKA OSTROVSKY

GIUSEPPE UNGARETTI
(1888–1970)

THE EGYPTIAN CITY of Alexandria enjoys the unique distinction of having given Europe two of its finest modern poets: Giuseppe Ungaretti and Constantine Cavafy. It was not so strange for the Greek Cavafy to be born in the city that had been for centuries the center of Hellenistic culture and was still harboring a thriving Greek colony. But it was incongruous for Ungaretti, patriarch of modern Italian poetry, to be born in Alexandria and to spend there the first twenty years of his life. On that stormy night of 10 February 1888, when he came into the world, his working-class parents—Tuscan immigrants—could hardly have dreamed of the exceptional literary future that was in store for their newborn son. Obviously, the wind of poetry "bloweth where it listeth," and any reader of Ungaretti's autobiographical pages in the collected travel memoirs *Il deserto e dopo* (The Desert and After, 1961), can see for himself how providential this peculiar destiny turned out to be for the poet.

The pattern that emerges from Ungaretti's life is one with the unfolding of his literary career. The element of chance marking his improbable beginnings was converted into spiritual necessity at the end, so that nobody now could imagine modern Italian poetry without Ungaretti or Ungaretti himself without his remote African birth. What might have been a hopeless handicap—his coming into the world and growing up in a place so utterly alien to Italian culture and not even on the periphery of the Italian linguistic area—became a unique asset. It impelled him to seek, on many levels, the "promised land" of his fathers. *La terra promessa* (The Promised Land) is, in fact, the title of a volume of his verse published in 1950, but above all it is a myth pervading his poetry from the very start. In poems like "Popolo" ("People," 1916), "1914–1915" (1933), "Terra" ("Earth-Motherland," 1947), the Promised Land appears as Italy, which "finally spoke / to the son of emigrants / . . . with the fatal grace of millennia." On a more symbolic level in the 1950 *Terra promessa* sequence, the myth takes the shape of the never-never land that has lured Aeneas away from forsaken Dido and that Aeneas' pilot, Palinurus, will never reach. Throughout Ungaretti's work, the inner quest for "an innocent country" persists beyond any geographic reference. Finally, it was the Italian tradition as embodied in the smooth verse of Petrarch, Ugo Foscolo, and Giacomo Leopardi that relentlessly attracted foreign-born Ungaretti. The promised land of a poet is the timeless poetry that sustains and liberates him, a tradition rediscovered.

Thus the myth of a Promised Land shaped Ungaretti's poetry as a quest for roots, fulfillment, innocence, and form; and he owed the poignancy of that quest to the accident of birth that had placed him in the predicament of a prodigal son of Italian culture. This is, so to speak, his "negative" debt to Egypt and Alexandria, while a specifically positive one must be seen in the colorful Arabic folklore, in the voluptuous fantasy and biblical desert vision that haunt his verse as a counterpoint to the Promised Land myth. Time and again Alexandria rises in the horizon of a poem as the fairyland city that is both native and foreign:

> I saw you, Alexandria,
> Friable on your ghostly foundations
> Become sheer memory to me
> In a suspended embrace of lights
> . . . .
> I am of another blood and never lost you,
> But in that loneliness of a ship
> Sadder than usual there came back
> The regret that you, foreign, should be
> My native city.

These lines are from "1914–1915," a poem written in 1932 and included in *Sentimento del tempo* (Sentiment of Time, 1933). Elsewhere the poet remembers Alexandria's minarets "garlanded with lights," or the ceremonies of its labyrinthine Jewish quarter, or the whole white city in the consuming embrace of the sun, vanishing aft:

> From the white-painted
> ship
> I saw my city
> disappear,

and a Thousand-and-One-Nights spell will be cast on him:

> In the eye
> of Thousand-and-one-nights
> I have rested
>
> In the abandoned gardens
> she was alighting
> like a dove

Both quotations are from Ungaretti's first book, *Il porto sepolto* (The Submerged Seaport, 1916). In a later poem, written in 1924 and called "Ricordo d'Affrica" ("Memory of Africa"), the desert-born mirage is Diana, goddess of light, suddenly appearing in the palm clumps "between the endless plain / and the wide sea . . ."

But the 1916 poem, "In memoria" (Memorial), penned at a village on the Italian front during World War I, embodies Ungaretti's African background as an excruciating experience of exile, not as delectable mirage. Mohammed Sheab, his Egyptian fellow student who killed himself in Paris because he could no longer be an Arab and had no homeland left, haunts Ungaretti as a reminder of what it means to lose one's roots. For Ungaretti too sees himself as a nomad. In poem after poem he envisages the lure and the curse of a wandering life:

> In no part
> of the earth
> can I
> make my home

Thus "Girovago" ("Wanderer") of 1918. It is this autobiographical persona that links in one imaginative experience the two poles of Ungaretti's world: the Desert and the Promised Land, memory and hope, loss and fulfillment. As late as 1960 he wrote:

> One roams the desert with remains
> Of an earlier image in one's mind,
> Of the Promised Land
> Nothing else is known to the living.

His work therefore develops through the several stages of an ever-renewed quest that is as personal as any confession can be and yet transcends the merely personal. The poet himself said of his early volume later retitled *L'Allegria* (The Joy, 1931) that

> This old book is a diary. The author has no other ambition, and he believes that even the great poets had no other, than to leave a fine autobiography . . . form worries him only because he wants it attuned to the variations of his spirit, and, if he has any progress to show as artist, he

would like it to point also to some perfection he has attained as man.

(from the foreword to the 1931 edition of *L'Allegria*)

And he clinched the point by naming the entire sequence of his published verse *Vita d'un uomo* (Life of a Man). Yet in the introductory note to the 1960 book called *Il taccuino del vecchio* (The Notebook of an Old Man), he says that, though most of the verse therein took its cue from very personal events, these "motifs . . . should no longer count as the author's own in the work, if he has managed to give it the life of poetry."

If so, poetry was to Ungaretti neither what it was for T. S. Eliot (an "escape from personality") nor what it had been, in Eliot's opinion, for generations of Romantics (an effusive "expression of personality"), but a search for the archetypal meaning of personal experience. This makes his essential biography directly relevant to his work, where he neither hides nor imposes his own self, but questions it to look for revelations that will outstrip the merely private sphere. (The significance of his poetical "diary" is further enhanced by the involvement with crucial experiences of modern history, including two world wars.) We have already seen what it meant for Ungaretti to be born in Egypt to parents of peasant origin from Tuscan Lucca (his father was drawn to Egypt by the demand for foreign workers created by Ismail Pasha's government with its great public-works projects). Along with the exotic Muslim elements described in the initial chapters of *Il deserto e dopo,* the growing Italian boy absorbed from Alexandria the suggestions of remotest history and certain vital contacts with modern French culture, which had made itself felt in Egypt ever since Napoleon's time. Two French brothers with important positions, Henri and Jean Thuile, befriended the young Ungaretti and opened their rare library to him.

French was a second language to him almost from the start—he attended a French school in Alexandria—while Italian remained his mother tongue, the language of the home, also heard in the diaspora of workers about town, with the languid melody of Arabic impinging from the background. For the rest of his wandering life Ungaretti carried this in his memory—Alexandria and its chorus of tongues, its gardens on the edge of desert and sea, and its submerged Pharaonic seaport which provided a symbolic title for his earliest booklet, *Il porto sepolto.* Since French culture, so germane to Italian and so blessed with prestige, had always been close to bilingual Ungaretti, it was logical for him to sail for France in 1912 and spend the next three years in Paris, attending the courses of Henri Bergson and other luminaries at the Collège de France.

But his Parisian education, to be sure, was not confined to university classrooms. Those were the years in which the artistic revolution stirring all over Europe found its main focus in the French capital, which afforded a haven to restless talents of every nationality. Here were the fauvists headed by Henri Matisse, Maurice de Vlaminck, and Edouard Vuillard; the cubists Pablo Picasso, Fernand Léger, Georges Braque, and Juan Gris; the futurists loudly advertised by Filippo Tommaso Marinetti, also born in Alexandria; here André Gide developed his omnivorous consciousness; and here gravitated expressionism from beyond the Rhine, imagism from beyond the Channel. In such a thrilling atmosphere Ungaretti found all the stimulation he needed. He met practically every major figure in the artistic world of the cosmopolitan capital and struck up a friendship with Guillaume Apollinaire, the Italian-born French poet of Polish extraction who was superseding the cultist heritage of *symbolisme* with his Whitmanesque poetics of directness, modernism, and free analogy. Listening to Ungaretti talk of his long-dead friend in the 1960's, one hardly realized that almost half a century had elapsed since Apollinaire's death in 1918. They had respectively enlisted in the French and in the Italian army, and if the author of *Alcools* (1913) and *Calligrammes* (1918) did not physically survive the war, it was lucky that Ungaretti at least should be spared, for unlike Apollinaire he was just at the beginning of his literary career.

Apollinaire too was a restless exile in search of a homeland (he obtained French citizenship while serving in the army), and in him Ungaretti could sense a brother. The parallel between Ungaretti's early experiments in verse and Apollinaire's ventures is certainly a marked one. Both poets modernized diction, simplified syntax, and abolished punctuation, all of which gave a sense of suspended flow to their free rhythm, and gave further emphasis to their already vivid imagery. One recalls the analogous attempts of their contemporary William Carlos Williams, also a visitor to Paris before and after World War I. But Ungaretti's debt to his colorful fellow poet, amply acknowledged by himself and documented by Luciano Rebay and G. Sempoux, is no passive borrowing. Beyond the technical affinities one can always hear each poet's unmistakable voice.

One of Apollinaire's war poems, "A l'Italie" ("To Italy," 1915), is a passionate plea for Italy's joining the struggle on the French side in the name of a common Latin culture, and it is dedicated to Ardengo Soffici, the futurist writer and painter from Florence who had been doing so much to foster the vogue of avant-garde French art in his native country. Around the café tables of Montparnasse, Soffici, Giovanni Papini (another Florentine iconoclast), Apollinaire, and Ungaretti had a chance to discuss their dreams of creative revolt. And it was Papini and Soffici's magazine *Lacerba* that published Ungaretti's first poems in February 1915. *Lacerba* was competing with Giuseppe Prezzolini's *La Voce* (The Voice) for the role of Italian rallying center for new writers and revolutionary thinkers; *La Voce* had introduced Ungaretti to modern Italian culture during his Egyptian days. Paris and Apollinaire's friendship in particular were for Ungaretti an integral phase of his cultural formation, yet at the

same time a way station to his Italian motherland.

Italy's entry in the war on the Allied side in May 1915 induced Ungaretti to volunteer for the Italian front against the Habsburg Empire. It was there, in the stony Carso region of the eastern Alps, that he jotted down several of his best poems, in which flashes of insight burst through established prosodic convention to capture the immediacy of inner experience. Wireless imagination, he called it, in the wake of his fellow Alexandrian Marinetti. Meanwhile, he strove to keep in touch with the war-shattered republic of letters. As chance had it, help came in an unforeseen way from Lieutenant Ettore Serra, who one day recognized in a withdrawn buck private the author of certain promising pieces he had read in a Florentine avant-garde magazine. Ettore Serra promptly saw to it that Ungaretti's new sheaf of poems, the harvest of the trenches, would be collected in book form. In this way *Il porto sepolto* was privately printed at Udine in the neighborhood of the front lines. Somehow the limited edition (eighty copies) found its way to a number of responsive readers, thereby obtaining for the young soldier-poet important recommendations that made it possible in 1919 for him to secure an influential publisher (Vallecchi of Florence) and a larger audience. A new edition, enriched by an additional section that gave its title to the whole book, *Allegria di naufragi* (Mirth of Shipwrecks, 1919), led to Ungaretti's recognition as the foremost poet of the new generation.

Along with the radically innovative style, another powerful reason for this early success was the unrhetorical approach to the formidable theme of the moment: mass war. In contrast to Gabriele d'Annunzio's heroic myth, in which war affords a chance for superhuman gestures, Ungaretti's poetical persona embodies the intense awareness of man's existential precariousness in the face of impending death; and he interprets the military predicament as the shared burden of countless men whose anonymity is acknowledged in his own:

Eccovi un uomo
uniforme
Eccovi un'anima
deserta
uno specchio impassibile . . .

Here is a uniform
man
Here is a desert
soul
an impassable mirror . . .

This is the beginning of a poem appropriately called "Distacco" ("Detachment"), in which the opening line may ironically echo the *Ecce Homo* of Christian liturgy. But anonymity is redeemed in brotherhood, as the poem "Fratelli" ("Brothers") emphasizes with its simple question—a question ideally addressed to any of the forgotten myriads that marched to their deaths in whatever drab uniforms on those trench-furrowed, shell-scarred battlefields of Europe: "What is your regiment/brothers?" Then again in "Peso" ("Weight") the poet opposes his own "lonely" and "bare" soul "without mirages" to the "peasant" soldier who "entrusts himself to the medal/of Saint Anthony/ and goes in lightness"; the poet carries the weight of a disabused modern consciousness, one that sets him apart from his simpler fellow soldiers. Yet fellow men they are, and in a haikulike poem like "Soldati" ("Soldiers") he expresses this common bond by comparing their (and his) lot to that of leaves clinging to their trees in fall.

Or he may, as in "In dormiveglia" ("Half Awake"), compound the sense of violence and animal fear in the image of men "huddled/in the trenches/like snails in their shells," until by a sudden reversal of the imagination the insistent rattle of rifle fire will bring back to him the familiar noise of (Lucchese) stonecutters feverishly hammering away at the lava cobblestones of his streets, while he listens to them "unseeing/half asleep." And to the "cold," "hard," "dry," "refractory," "totally soulless" stone of a war-beaten mountain he compares his own "unseen" suffering as a creature ("Sono una creatura" ["I Am a Creature"]). If the closeness of death makes him feel close to so many unknown men in the hour of danger, it also immerses him in an alternately dehumanizing and regenerating involvement with the elements:

Lurking in ambush
in these entrails
of rubble
for hours on end
have I dragged
my carcass
worn out by mud
like a shoe sole
or like a seed
of hawthorn . . .

That is the first part of "Pellegrinaggio" ("Pilgrimage"), which climaxes in the return to the sense of menaced, separate consciousness. Elsewhere the self is effused in the fleeting phenomena of the cosmos ("Annientamento" ["Annihilation"]) or takes stock of its own history in a communion with the sanctifying elements ("I fiumi" ["The Rivers"]), or grasps the analogy between outer destruction and inner grief in the shell-torn village of San Martino del Carso. In the poem of that name the poet's own heart is "the most tortured village" where "no cross is missing."

As a war poet, Ungaretti joins the company of Apollinaire, Charles Péguy, Wilfred Owen, Ernst Stadler, and August Stramm, blown to the four winds by the wasteful fury of the conflict whose horror and pity they evoked in their several tongues.

Unlike them, he survived, and thus had a chance to develop beyond his dramatic literary initiation, but even if he hadn't, there is no doubt that both as a whole and in the sampled excellence of pieces like "The Rivers," Ungaretti's first contribution to Italian poetry would have sufficed to recommend his name to future generations. He would have been the Owen of Italian letters, a voice cut short too soon but not to be forgotten. As it happened, he found himself confronting the responsibility of his great promise in the changing climate of the postwar years. The excitement of war was subsiding into an uneasy peace fraught with unsolved problems; war-weary Italy, like other countries that had been weakened by the awful effort, teetered for a few years between communist revolution and the old parliamentary system, then settled into the compulsory order of Benito Mussolini's fascist regime. Art outgrew the turbulence of Umberto Boccioni's prewar futurism to freeze into the magic of Carlo Carrà's and Giorgio De Chirico's "metaphysical" painting, where manikins populated abstract spaces or empty piazzas yawned. Then it passed to the "Novecento" style—a kind of classicist modernism with academic overtones. Literature lost the buoyant revolutionary temper of the old *La Voce* and *Lacerba* days; while Marinetti's impresario-like vociferousness became a harmless institution, the magazine *La Ronda* spread the word of a new classical style, in the austere name of Leopardi. By and large, despite the iconoclastic experiments of Pirandello on the stage, the prevalent tone was now one of introspective restraint. Ungaretti's growth as a writer after *Allegria di naufragi* can be partly understood within this context of restoration.

There is no reason, however, to subordinate his personal literary development to the quasi-official Italian aesthetics of the time or to the political vicissitudes that fostered it. After all, he did not passively register a cultural climate, but rather contributed to it signally, and while the neosymbolist movement of "hermetic" poetry took shape around his work (and Eugenio Montale's) in the 1920's, he also aroused sharp dissent in some quarters. Benedetto Croce, the most authoritative figure of modern Italian culture, rejected his poetry as artificial; Antonio Gramsci, the radical thinker, slighted him along with the whole of hermeticism as irrelevant to the cultural needs of the time; the critic Francesco Flora, three years after the publication of Ungaretti's *Sentimento del tempo,* attacked his elliptical diction as too mannered; the charge of obscurity was often echoed. Now

that Ungaretti's poetry has long ceased to be controversial, we can look back on the polemics of those two decades between the world wars as part of the new ordeal through which his art had to assert itself.

After a few years in Paris (following the transfer of his regiment to the French front in 1918) he settled in Rome with his French wife in 1921. Before returning to Italy, he had published in Paris a French edition of his selected verse, partly self-translated and partly written directly in French: *La guerre* (The War, 1919). He never lost touch with the world of French letters and art, where he could count on the support of such friends as Jean Paulhan. We have seen what a powerful stimulus had come to his early work from the liberating example of his friend Apollinaire. But Arthur Rimbaud, along with Charles Baudelaire, had also acted as a catalyst from the start, and now Stéphane Mallarmé, the very Mallarmé against whose esoteric abstraction Apollinaire had reacted for the sake of an open utterance, came to be increasingly felt in Ungaretti's poetics. To a large extent, however, Mallarmé's influence (to use a discredited word) blends into that of Petrarch and Leopardi. Ungaretti had reached Italy by way of France. And if it was on the Italian battlefields that he fully "recognized" himself as creature (to quote from "The Rivers"), the parallel self-recognition as poet had to come, in due time, from the ancestral master of stylistic perfection: melodious, inward-looking Petrarch, the fountainhead of a European lyrical tradition that had lasted for centuries.

Ungaretti, the initial outsider, was in the ideal situation of being able to come to the Italian tradition on his own. What others, raised on native soil, could take for granted, he never did, with the consequence that his growing attraction to the Petrarchan model of self-contained melody was no less a personal discovery than the metric freedom of his beginning phase had been. The freely repossessed tradition, while exquisitely Italian, was also broadly European, and Ungaretti remained immune from whatever complacent provincialism the nationalistic age might have encouraged. He discovered Petrarch through Mallarmé, and working with the great tradition for him was ceaseless experiment. *Poésie pure,* fin-de-siècle *symbolisme,* led him all the way back to a remote poetry of timeless purity. Thus we see, once again, the providential pattern: his circuitous itinerary was a cultural homecoming, and the homeland's literature in turn needed him, the foreign born, to restore on a new basis the continuity it had lost.

One way for Ungaretti to root himself more firmly in his Italian homeland was to contribute actively to literary journals and literary sections of the daily press. His literary journalism includes essays on Petrarch and Leopardi or on versification. It took a broader shape between 1931 and 1934, when he sent articles as a foreign correspondent to the Turin daily, *La gazzetta del Popolo,* from his revisited native Egypt, from Corsica, from Holland, and from several parts of Italy, especially the southern and central areas. These articles, collected in book form as *Il deserto e dopo,* clearly transcend journalism; they approach autobiographical prose of a mythic range. The poet speaks at every turn; essential phases of his inner development are recapitulated (with the exception of the French one), and motifs like the myth of Italy as Promised Land, to be later developed in books of verse in the 1950's and 1960's, make themselves clearly heard. In other words, these trips to sundry countries and regions are part of Ungaretti's "self-recognition."

The last part of *Il deserto e dopo,* which consists of translations from the folk poetry and art verse of Brazil, reflects his experience in that country, where he held the chair of Italian literature at the University of São Paulo from 1936 to 1942. The poetical fruits of those years —years marked by sorrow (the loss of his little son Antonietto) as well as by a renewed contact with the exotic nature Ungaretti's nomadic instinct seemed recurrently to need—appeared in 1947 in a book titled *Il dolore* (Grief), which couples private bereavement with the shared grief of the Italian people and of mankind at large in the bewildering predicament of World War II. In 1942 the Italian government invited Ungaretti to occupy a chair of Italian literature at Rome University. The offer was motivated by the poet's *chiara fama* (bright fame); he accepted it and held the post until his retirement in 1962. If the circumstances of the appointment were exceptional, there were no political strings attached to it, as was recognized by the postwar Italian governments, which never revoked it. Nor did Ungaretti take it as a sinecure. A number of students have attested to the effectiveness of his eloquence from the chair, and those who heard his course on Leopardi at Columbia University in the spring semester of 1964 likewise remember his passionate delivery. The poet put all of himself into his teaching. Meanwhile, outside the classroom another audience had begun to respond to Ungaretti's voice in America, particularly since Allen Mandelbaum made a representative choice of his verse available to American readers in 1958. Poets like Robert Lowell, Galway Kinnell, and Anthony Hecht translated some of Ungaretti's work as part of their own poetical experience, proving once again that the energy of significant poetry can be contagious.

Ungaretti's vitality was indeed exceptional, and it showed in his conversation as well as in the unrelenting rhythm of his work. During the twenty-five years that elapsed from the end of World War II, *Il dolore* was followed by several more volumes of verse or prose and by a number of rich verse translations—from William Shakespeare, Luis de Góngora, Jean Racine, and finally William Blake. Some of these volumes, which since 1942 had been appearing as part of the *Life of a Man* series, were the result of long work begun in the 1930's, and, needless to say, the translations are integral to Ungaretti's original poetry as part of his stylistic experience; they are all self-recognitions, like the landscapes of three continents that were so poignantly assembled in *Il deserto e dopo.*

The nomad persona and the myth of a Promised Land are two basic constants of Ungaretti's imagination; they mirror a uniquely mobile personal history and broaden its scope to more than personal significance. But the constancy to be expected of poetical images is not a matter of hard-and-fast identity. Such images are mythic projections of experience and they partake of experience's own protean richness; they could hardly do justice to it if they were to constrain it into stiff abstractions. Thus we find that Ungaretti's correlated mythical images, the nomad figure and the Promised Land, reappear from beginning to end in ever-changing shapes of vision and meaning, and even their correlation shifts as the emphasis alternately falls on the individual, communal, terrene, or ultramundane nature of the Promised Land, on its historical availability or transcendence, on the fulfillment, finality, or hopelessness of the wanderer's quest, whatever historical garb he may don. Much in the same way, a leitmotiv changes yet remains recognizably the same through its manifold appearances in the course of a musical score. As the constancy of a theme through its musical metamorphoses is stressed by the cyclical recurrence it may have, in a human existence or in a civilization there can be cycles of historical recurrence, and these in turn find expression in the world of art and thought. Ungaretti's existential situation—the longing of an uprooted man for valid roots—had undergone its cycles as he found and lost and found his home again; in keeping with this cyclical pattern, the theme of a Promised Land unfolded through several metamorphoses in the course of his poetry, which parallels the stages of personal, as well as cultural, experience. In a way, Ungaretti had reached his Promised Land already in 1916, when during a brief lull in the fighting on the Italian front he could say of that rocky terrain and of the Isonzo water that kept washing away so much blood,

> Questo è l'Isonzo
> e qui meglio
> mi sono riconosciuto
> una docile fibra
> dell'universo

> This is the Isonzo
> and here better
> have I recognized myself
> a responsive fiber
> of the universe

The meaning is both geographic, the Isonzo being Italy's Jordan, and spiritual, a matter of harmony with the living universe in the enhancing presence of death. What man desecrates with his wars, the elements later reconsecrate.

But the Promised Land is periodically lost and reattained, and each time in a different way. In the decades between the two wars, as chiefly represented by *Sentimento del tempo*, Africa itself often becomes, in the wizardry of memory, something like a Promised Land, though with the uncertainty of mirage—a lost country. Another aspect of the Promised Land is, throughout *L'Allegria* and *Sentimento,* the lost Eden of childhood ("I seek an innocent / country"). It reappears personified in the fleeting, doomed grace of the poet's child in the strongest poem in *Il dolore,* "Tu ti spezzasti" ("You Shattered"). In the same collection "Defunti su montagne" ("The Dead on Mountains") seems to indicate a haven of hope in Masaccio's religious art. Art, tradition, and memory each appear as a refuge, a Promised Land, especially in Rome occupied by the German troops and harrowed by the signs of an internecine war. But memory, as "Caino" ("Cain") forcefully states in *Sentimento del tempo,* is also guilt and torment. Death can then be a release, thus a final haven, a Promised Land (see "Inno alla morte" ["Hymn to Death"] and "La morte meditata" ["Meditations on Death"] in *Sentimento*). Yet "Motherland—Mother Earth" in *Il dolore* anchors us to its undying promise, which is that of a life-giving civilization.

The cycle repeated itself for Ungaretti with the return to Italy in 1942. Another war was waiting for him there, a much more cruel one to witness than the 1914–1918 one in which he had taken part as a young soldier on both Italian and French soil. *Allegria,* the paradoxical "mirth of shipwrecks," had been possible then, but now only grief, *Il dolore,* could speak. The two titles complement each other; the "feeling of time" has intervened to age the persona, now tried by manifold bereavements. One does "go home again," to one's people, to one's memories, to begin all over. It is and it is not the same. The new cycle is not so much a repetition of as a variation on the theme.

Yet there is a recurrence after all; the voice has redescended from the rarefactions of the first part of *Sentimento del tempo* to a directness already obvious in that book's "Inni" ("Hymns"), especially "La Pietà," which, unlike so much earlier and later Ungaretti, hearkens back to the knotty cadences of Jacopone da Todi, the medieval religious poet, rather than to Petrarch's distilled elegance. That much is certainly true of most of *Il dolore,* despite the unavoidable traces of Petrarchan-Mallarméan obliquity; for it is as if the poet here touches earth again, to find once more the immediacy of *L'Allegria,* though in another key. There is more explicitness than in the first book and a louder tone. After that phase of self-renewal the trajectory from immediacy to stylistic abstraction resumes, to come to a head in the consummate Petrarchism of *La terra promessa,* in which the poet ties himself to the most exacting of closed prosodic forms, the canzone and the sestina. Nothing so formal had developed yet in *Sentimento del tempo;* the *Terra promessa* is Petrarch with a vengeance. When partial overlappings of composition are taken into account (since the first cue for *La terra promessa* came from the early 1930's), the cyclical pattern still emerges unmistakably. It is re-echoed in the stylistic oscillations to follow, from the narrative explicitness of *Un grido e paesaggi* (A Cry and Landscapes, 1952) (especially the introductory biographical recapitulation called "Monologhetto" ["Little Monologue"]) to the *Terra promessa*–like manner of *Il taccuino del vecchio.* Concomitantly, the persona renews its arrivals and departures, the last glimpse of the Promised Land being of Mount Sinai, through a desert the living cannot hope to negotiate in their ceaseless wandering. As the persona says in "Il capitano" ("The Captain," from *Sentimento del tempo*), this poet is still "ready for all departures."

Ungaretti ripened without stagnating. The kind of Petrarchan classicism into which he increasingly tended to reshape his style was the conquest of a tireless experimenter and not a matter of acquiescence to the literary past. This will be even clearer if we bear in mind that the peculiarly Petrarchan stylization of absence and memory alternated in Ungaretti with a Jacoponic (and very modern) convulsiveness, to the point where, at times, smooth melodic rhythm and stressed syncopation enhance each other contrapuntally in the same poem. Chorus 14 of *La terra promessa* may be one salient illustration, with its staccato lines working as a foil to the more regularly fluent ones. Also, Petrarch himself was often seen by Ungaretti through the baroque reflector of Góngora, while Shakespeare's sonnets and Racine's tragedy appealed to him avowedly in the same way—as examples of baroque style in the Petrarchan tradition. Certainly one aspect of Ungaretti's approach to Petrarch is comparable to Sergei Prokofiev's treatment of eighteenth-century music in the *Classical Symphony* (1917); one would use the term "parody" in this connection if the word could be stripped of its deflating implications.

Ungaretti's modernity is cogently expressed by the relationship between the "individual talent" to "tradition," in Eliot's terms. The significance of his long search for a disciplining form that could both condense and release his riotous imagination emerges by contrast from the groping quality of his first known attempts, which date from the early Paris days and are collected (along with the many variants to poems of his first two books) in *Poesie disperse* (Uncollected Poems, 1945), with an important preface by the former *La Voce* critic Giuseppe De Robertis. The earliest of these poems are Ungaretti's prehistory, and they show him posturing as an imp à la Aldo

Palazzeschi, the genial Tuscan futurist who, before maturing into one of the considerable authors of Italian fiction, long amused himself by venting alternately his comically perverse and his sentimental moods in free verse. In his sentimental vignettes Palazzeschi is much more the *crepuscolare* (one of the so-called twilight poets, who wrote in a muted, quotidian, nostalgic vein and formed a school of some importance in those years) than the tough futurist to whom, according to Marinetti's Paris *Manifesto* of 1909, all such delicate attitudes should be alien. While in the course of his subsequent development Ungaretti dropped the defiant comicality to be seen in some of his apprentice work, Palazzeschian sentimentality proved harder to shed. The process of strengthening and compression many of his lyrics underwent through assiduous revisions leads precisely from that kind of "crepuscular" abandon to a terser diction.

A case in point is "Noia" ("Ennui"), whose final version in *L'Allegria* consists of seven lines strategically lopped off from the twenty that composed the original draft, now given as an independent poem of the same title in *Poesie disperse*. In the longer version the persona gesticulates sentimentally and comments freely on the scene ("To whom can I donate / a drop of tears / of sluggish humanity / At the mercy of life . . . "). The clipped version looks like a casual notebook entry; actually, it has reached its proper form by being pruned of excess comment and of all emotional references to the speaker:

> *Anche questa notte passerà*
>
> *Questa solitudine in giro*
> *titubante ombra dei fili tranviari*
> *sull'umido asfalto*
>
> *Guardo le teste dei brumisti*
> *nel mezzo sonno*
> *tentennare*
>
> This night too will pass away

> This loneliness around
> hesitant shadow of the streetcar wires
> on the wet asphalt
>
> I look at the heads of the coachmen
> in their half sleep
> nodding

The speaking "I" is now present only once, as a contemplative function ("I look at the heads of coachmen / . . . nodding"), and everything is sharply focused on the few objects (the streetcar wires projecting their swaying shadows on the wet asphalt) that suffice to evoke a melancholy urban night. The drama of the self has been objectified, and all comment, impersonally yet very poignantly, has shrunk to the resigned initial statement: "This night too will pass away." But that in turn is echoed and prolonged, as time concretely felt in Bergsonian fashion, in the final verb that concludes the poem without a period: *tentennare* (to nod), predicated of the drowsy coachmen. This nodding, likewise, parallels the swaying of streetcar wires in the previous three lines. The poem thus composes itself in two informal tercets, preceded by the meditative gesture that encompasses the whole, and its parallel structure is reinforced by paratactic syntax, utterly conformable to the unliterary vocabulary and simplified grammar Ungaretti, stimulated by Apollinaire's example, favors in this phase. Other traits that contribute to the success of the poem were there from the start, especially the network of alliterative sounds gathering the seven lines into a hidden harmony; but in extracting his pearl from the mother shell, Ungaretti has also polished it. He has changed the comically descriptive *faccioni dei brumisti* (big ruddy faces of the coachmen) into the sober and more distant *teste* (heads); on the other hand, he has retained the Milanese dialectal colloquialism *brumisti* for "coachmen" to particularize his scene; and he has eliminated the three lines that followed the coachmen stanza in the original version, both because they brought the obtrusive "I" back and because they obstructed the free flow of felt duration in which the infinitive verb *tentennare* resolves the final version. The lines are unmetrical, yet the third one is an effortless hendecasyllable with a swaying effect. This approach is typical of the *Allegria* phase, which does away with traditional prosody and with punctuation as a whole to achieve an effect of slow, transfixed speech, but without getting totally rid of the hendecasyllable because, as Ungaretti later discovered, it constitutes the natural cadence of the Italian language. It thus can quite unobtrusively emerge in the midst of shorter, uncadenced, sometimes extremely short lines.

The technical procedure described here applies to many other poems and may well typify Ungaretti's quest for essentialness, sometimes manifested in the extreme concision of certain poems—which aroused no end of both hostile and approving response. In some poems the process of structural and stylistic purification went so far as to split off one initial poem into two different ones; thus, "Chiaroscuro" is a chip off the original block of "In memoria" (which heads the section *Il porto sepolto* of *L'Allegria*). "Chiaroscuro" is centered on the impressions of the contemplating self through a night of intense memory, while the pruned version of "In memoria" is focused on the dramatis persona Sheab; and if one takes the trouble of checking it with the initial draft, one will find that much sentimental affectation has been dropped to the advantage of the epitaph-like poem. Likewise, the poem "Levante" ("Near East"), whose original draft appears under the title "Nebbia" ("Fog") in *Poesie disperse*, underwent several transformations to attain the arabesquelike agility of its final form, in which Ungaretti experiments with onomatopoeia and imagery in such a way as to suggest the piercing sinuosities of Arab music and the voluptuousness of Oriental poetry. What was a disorderly accumulation of subjective imagery has become a winding gracefulness, without impoverishment. The persona no longer imposes with his redundant confessions; he simply objectifies himself as "a young man" standing "towards the stem, alone" to contrast the noisy merriment of dancing Syrian emigrants astern. Their "shrill arabesques" of clarinet music, clapping of hands, and tapping of feet evoke in him the contrapuntal vision of Jewish funerals in his hometown of Alexandria, which he is now leaving behind: on Saturday nights they wind silently with their lights after the hearse through the maze of alleys. The sea, "ashen," "quivers sweet restless / like a pigeon." At the end the persona identifies himself as the observer by introducing the verb *odo* ("I hear"), with the whole previous scene as its object, while his consciousness is on the verge of "sleep." He is thus both inside and outside the poem, actor as well as spectator. Comparison with the initial version will show that again, as in "Noia," the poet cut with faultless surgery.

So Ungaretti purged in his own development the various rhetoric (whether of the obstreperous or of the languid kind) which was in the air. Yet attentive perusal of *L'Allegria* indicates that some of d'Annunzio's sensualism, for instance, filtered into the leaner diction of Ungaretti, while the futurist plea for unconventional imagery, free utterance, and modernist topics found in his controlled energy a truer fulfillment than was possible with Marinetti's centrifugal pyrotechnics of *parole in libertà* (words at liberty). Who can deny the stark modernism of the following image in "Perché?" ("Why?"), a typical war poem:

> *Si è appiattito*
> *come una rotaia*
> *il mio cuore in ascoltazione*

> It has flattened itself out
> like a railroad track
> my listening heart

It would be equally hard to miss the d'Annunzian note in "Transfigurazione" ("Transfiguration"), where the persona, resting from trench warfare, feels himself reborn, feels himself to be "in the children's faces / like a pink fruit / glowing / among the stripped trees"; or in "Giugno" ("June"), where the Oriental beauty he dreams of in his night of distress as a "panther" is fondled by his imagination and appeals to him with all the sweetness of her "tar black" eyes and "gold-brown skin." But these are assimilated elements of his own experience, not literary echoes. He makes generally good use of the freedom that Marinetti noisily wastes and that d'Annunzio, for all his lavish genius, often squanders. Both the mechanical and the erotic imagery are sharply focused and correlated to the pensive existential self. This is why, as the critic Luciano Anceschi has remarked, Ungaretti's poetry relies so heavily on elliptical analogy.

This is not to say that he always succeeds. There are, even in the revised edition of *L'Allegria*, instances of overstrained baroque analogy. Then the "fuse of the imagination" (as Emily Dickinson would have called it) misfires and the poem sounds utterly contrived, "Attrito" ("Attrition") being an example. There are also cases of cloying mannerism, like the whole first part of "Annihilation," a poem that, after some unnecessary talk of plucked daisies, chirping crickets, and "modulated" heart, does redeem its incongruous beginning on a powerful note of cosmic effusion shading into death. These are the faults the critic Flora resented and unduly magnified in 1936 at the expense of Ungaretti's very substantial accomplishment—an accomplishment made possible precisely by that process of elliptical reduction, which, despite its occasional byproduct of shrilly telescoped images, resulted on the whole in exciting discoveries of vision and sound. Like Dickinson, whose imagistic epiphanies often strikingly anticipate his experiments, Ungaretti's real talent is centripetal, to the point of occasionally compressing a whole world of vision to one or two ecstatic lines, like the much discussed

> *M'illumino*
> *d'immenso*
>
> I am illumined
> with immensity

or the equally famous "D'altri diluvi una colomba ascolto" ("I Listen to a Dove from Other Deluges," from *Sentimento del tempo*).

These are thresholds from which the poet is about to leave vision and poetry itself for a mystical silence that yawns within and around his utterance, so strongly dependent is it on resonant pauses; but thresholds they are, rather than normative examples, even if we want to emphasize the haiku-like tendencies of Ungaretti. At the other end of his range we have the controlled effusion of nondiscursive narratives, as in "The Rivers," where the autobiographical "I" recapitulates the formative stages of his own history as identified with the Egyptian Nile, scene of his birth and adolescence, the Parisian Seine, the place of his tumultuous initiation to art and virility, the Tuscan Serchio, "from which two millennia perhaps / of [his] farming ancestors drew water," and the Alpine Isonzo, marking his present initiation to fullest awareness of life and death in a homecoming to the ancestral land and to the elements themselves:

> *Questi sono i miei fiumi*
> *contati nell'Isonzo*
>
> These are my rivers
> counted in the Isonzo

The last river, in the ordeal of war, is the locus of "self-recognition," which culminates the previous stations of the persona's existential pilgrimage: the prenatal memories, the "burning unconsciousness" of adolescence in Africa, the "self-knowledge" out of first manhood's chaotic experiences in the Seine's "turbid" waters. The river image becomes the archetypal pattern of the whole poem, in Bergsonian key, as often happens with Ungaretti, whose most characteristic poems tend to be experiential processes involving the self in the dimension of inner time rather than sheer timeless moments of insight. The climate of the poem is sacramental, and the persona paradoxically celebrates his *allegria* (mirth) in the presence of probable death through an act of communion with the elements; he is a "Bedouin" who huddles near his "war-soiled clothes" to "receive / the sun," after walking on water "like an acrobat" (of the Christlike variety) and resting "like a relic" in the same water, while "the Isonzo / flowing / smoothed [him] / as a stone of its own." A baptismal ceremony is enacted, with clear implications of death and resurrection.

The work of stylistic sharpening mirrors the purification of the existential self these poems celebrate, and we can read them as a "diary," a comprehensive book, while dwelling more eagerly on those pages that best express the author's singular powers, whether these be the arresting imagery, often synaesthetically hovering among the visual, auditory, and tactile-kinetic fields, or the searching use of vowel patterns in poems that renounce ostensible rhyme, or a certain candor of utterance that tends to focus on individual words. War is both felt in its tragic cruelty and transcended in a kind of Franciscan *perfetta letizia* (perfect mirth, therefore *allegria* in a way).

The postwar volume *Sentimento del tempo* resumes and develops certain main features of the wartime poetry. The Bergsonian title coherently expresses the theme and inner form of most of the poems, which often revolve around the experience of time as an inner cycle: day and night encompassing the arc of a whole life ("O Notte" ["O Night"]), the four phases of day ("Paesaggio" ["Landscape"]), the four seasons as phases of earth and of the soul ("Stagioni" ["Seasons"]), the climactic season of summer, the elusive magic of dawn or evening or autumn. This informing thematics was implicit in the structure of *L'Allegria*'s verse, which emphasized temporal process as an inward devel-

opment resulting not infrequently in a sense of mythic time. Enhanced inwardness, however, now makes for more abstract language, and while the individual word is still fruitfully stressed, it no longer tends to stand by itself in the isolating emphasis typical of so many minimal length lines from the previous phase. Punctuation reappears. The lines now gravitate toward traditional metric shape. The vocabulary includes those literary words Ungaretti had deliberately rejected in *L'Allegria* in his effort to break with the academic convention, and the style moves from the earlier syntactic simplicity toward complex structures of clause subordination. Petrarch looms on the horizon, absence involves the persona who is so expressively "present" in the wartime book, and the mythical perceptions achieved there without erudite reference now seek embodiment in classical mythology: Juno, Cronos, Apollo, Diana, Penelope, Olympus.

To be sure, these are no hoary clichés; but they are evocations. Diana "clothed in light" springs from the remembered Egyptian oasis; Juno is woman in her carnal power; Apollo is the diffuse presence of light in the open skies; Aphrodite emerges unnamed from the Ligurian Sea, a metamorphosis of the elements which the poem captures in the fleeting play of color and light. The "Fine di Crono" ("End of Cronos") is an intangible event having to do with the abolition of measured time in the spellbound consciousness:

> Innumerable Penelopes, stars,
>
> The Lord embraces you again!
>
> (Ah, blindness!
> Avalanche of nights . . .)
>
> And offers Olympus again,
> Eternal flower of sleep.

This mood of rapturous contemplation between memory and dream engenders its own myths, like those of "Alla noia" ("To Ennui") and "Isola" ("Island"), which verge on hallucination, yet owe their success to the crystalline quality of diction. Here evocative magic reaches a threshold. The language itself is stylized to an extent beyond which only the volumes of the 1950's go. While the play on "phonic values," as Alfredo Gargiulo calls them in his pioneering preface to the 1933 edition of *Sentimento del tempo,* continues along the lines set forth in *L'Allegria,* rhetorical stylization on the whole has gone a long way from that book, indeed has reversed its central direction.

At this point the poet breaks through the cocoon of his own cherished mirages to reattain, beyond what threatened to become a mere manner, dramatic utterance. We thus have the second part of *Sentimento del tempo,* called "Hymns," which neatly offsets the first. The simplest way to describe the transition is to call it a passage from evocation to invocation. It is as if "pure poetry" were no longer enough, and the poet were accordingly reverting to the naked existential self of the wartime poems. The persona that savors the exquisite poisons of ennui ("To Ennui") or caresses the mirage of Aphrodite ("Silenzio in Liguria"), or descends into the bewitched maze of his own dream ("Island"), now desperately confronts existence with ultimate questions ("La pietà"). The pleasures of imagination are shattered; what is wanted is an assurance of meaning, and if the poet was king in his own realm of evanescent artifacts, now he asks whether he has "torn apart heart and mind / to fall a slave to words," and he acknowledges that he "reigns over phantoms." The crisis of poetry is also the crisis of mankind at large: the persona speaks out of his own wounded isolation, but speaks also for his fellow men, whose choragus he becomes, in the course of the poem, before God— the persistently silent addressee of the impassionated utterance. God might be only a dream, yet men refuse to surrender it. His silence makes him inaccessible. He is embodied in the blank spaces between the reiterated questions. If God is absence, prayer is despair; in the con-clusive part of the poem, this mood is sealed by the discarding of the choral address in favor of a third-person statement that weighs all of man's works, his prideful creations, to find them wanting. Man thinks he can "broaden his possessions" while "from his feverish hands / Boundaries only issue, endlessly." Man

> clinging on the void
> To his own cobweb,
> Fears nothing, seduces nothing
> But his own cry.

And man

> repairs the waste by raising tombs,
> And to conceive you, O Eternal,
> He has but blasphemies.

"La pietà" is one of the crucial statements in twentieth-century poetry, a religious probing of our culture, though in no merely devotional key. The biblical eloquence is sustained by much dazzling imagery and even more by the solemn cadence which the alternation of agonizing questions with silence engenders. The language is blunt, rugged, reminiscent of Jacopone da Todi's medieval asperity. The rest of the "Hymns" stick to this keynote, with "Cain," "La preghiera" ("The Prayer"), and "Dannazione" ("Damnation") playing memorable variations and a further sequence titled "La morte meditata" ("Meditations on Death") providing the logical conclusion. Man stands in judgment on himself; the Bible, not pagan mythology, is now his text; prayer and anguish supersede the earlier sorcery. Cain is the inner self of us all. Radical questions arise, to remain unanswered:

> *Come il sasso aspro del vulcano,*
> *Come il logoro sasso del torrente,*
> *Come la notte sola e nuda,*
> *Anima da fionda e da terrori*
> *Perché non ti raccatta*
> *La mano ferma del Signore?*

> Like the sharp boulder of volcanoes,

Like the gnawed pebble of the torrent,
Like night itself alone and bare,
O soul fit for the slingshot and for terrors
Why aren't you picked up
By the firm hand of the Lord?

These lines are from "Damnation." In "The Rivers," when war was all around but not within him, the poet had envisaged his own elemental self as a stone gently polished by the Isonzo's friendly waters into harmonious form: time was no enemy, nor were the elements. Here, the same key image recurs, with inverted value. The world of time and of the elements is infernally threatening; the soul is at their mercy and can hope for safety only from the unresponsive Transcendent. War is within, not without: a worse predicament by far for the poet who had said "My torture / is when / I don't believe myself / in harmony." There is no question, now, of finding peace as "a docile fiber / of the universe."

As happens, this malaise was prophetic of the new apocalyptic conflict that went on smouldering for some time in men's troubled souls during the uneasy lull between the two wars, and the very imagery and tone of "Damnation" may supply a cue to the most impressive poem of *Il dolore,* the fruit of bereavement in Brazil and of return to war-tortured Italy. This work, "You Shattered," commemorates the poet's son, struck down by premature death overseas, in a savage cosmic setting where chaos still lurks:

> I molti, immani, sparsi, grigi sassi
> Frementi ancora alle segrete fionde
> di originarie fiamme soffocate
> Od ai terrori di fiumane vergini
> Ruinanti in implacabili carezze,
> —Sopra l'abbaglio della sabbia rigidi
> In un vuoto orizzonte, non rammenti?

> The many, immense, sparse, gray boulders
> Still quivering from the secret slingshots
> Of original suffocated fires
> Or at the terrors of virgin torrents
> Rushing down with implacable caresses,

> —Stiffly standing over the dazzle of the sand
> In an empty horizon, don't you remember?

The human disorder of war did not manage to taint the cosmic elements in *L'Allegria.* Here instead, the universe itself, far from being a peaceful haven, is the creation of demonic violence: nature is desert and jungle juxtaposed, and the very intricacy of syntax in the rush of clauses that makes up most of the massive first section of the poem mirrors a choking pain. Then, at the end of section 1, the elflike child nimbly appears, an incongruous manifestation of grace in the midst of all this barbarous terror. Section 2 shows him as an angelic creature who "raised" his "arms like wings," always dancing. The voice has now moved from the initial exasperation to a serene register, and the convolutions of section 1 have relaxed into the simple, short utterance that of itself suggests the momentary presence of peace. But nature is cursed, and section 3, in compressed form, renews the strain of the outset: the child was a "happy grace" foreign to this savage world, and therefore doomed to succumb to its "hardened blindness"; he was a

> troppo umano lampo per l'empio,
> Selvoso, accanito, ronzante
> Ruggito del sole ignudo.

> too human gleam of light for the impious,
> Shaggy, relentless, whirring
> Roar of the naked sun.

The powerful images, climaxing at the end in paroxysmal synaesthesia, come in supporting pulses of panting rhythm, which in turn echoes the staccato effect of the very first line. Unlike the preceding sequence ("Giorno per giorno" ["Day by Day"]), which tells the sorrow of personal loss on the level of private memory, this visionary outburst, spiraling through a musical alternation of andante mosso and largo, crescendo and diminuendo, takes on mythic proportions to depict a satanic world to which love, innocence, and grace are fleeting visitors at best. Our understanding of the poem will deepen further if we read it against the background of Leopardi's "A Silvia" ("To Sylvia," 1828), on whose rhetorical structure it is freely patterned, for Leopardi too begins by asking a beloved young dead one if she remembers her short happy days on earth, and he likewise concludes on a note of despairing accusation of Nature, after envisaging in Silvia the grace and promise of which young life is capable.

Nothing else in *Il dolore* equals this peak of measured energy, yet the ensuing poems, written in the shadow of the German occupation ("*Roma occupata*," a section of *Il dolore*), are far from anticlimactic. They complement the masterpiece by balancing personal grief with communal grief, the tragedy of one man with the tragedy of a whole people, and once again the collection of verse coheres in a book that demands to be read as such and not just for the sake of whatever isolated successes may be culled from its pages. Prayer and lament set the tone; Rome comes to life as a city, indeed as the scene and epitome of civilization itself, which is now in danger, and the poet in the threatened city shares the pain of his people. Though the rhetoric may occasionally become overly explicit, one consistently feels that Rome, and by the same token everything Italy is and stands for, has never been so much the poet's home. Now he really inhabits the city, and it is *his* city, as the land is his—in suffering, *dolore*. Thus the last piece, "Terra," aptly seals the book, no matter what objections can be raised against the stylistic involution that mars it when considered as an independent poem. Like *Sentimento del tempo* the volume has a binary structure in which the second part thematically balances the first and represents a progression of experience beyond the climax reached there. Part 1 is exile and the memory of exile, part 2 the return to the Promised Land.

But the Promised Land is more than just a city or an ancestral country; it is civilization itself, and as such it provides an antiphon to the devastations unleashed by tropical Nature. "The Dead on Mountains" implicitly answers the stoic resignation of "You Shattered." In the "Brazilian" piece savage Nature inexorably destroys innocent grace (personified in the poet's child), but in the "Roman" piece a hope glimmers in the very midst of despair. This hope rises for the poet from a contemplation of Masaccio's *Crucifixion* in the church of San Clemente, where he reads the story of so many crucifixions brutally re-enacted by contemporary man, yet by the same token the power of art and form over barbarism, and the message of human redemption all this sorrow will yield. Here, in war-torn Europe, the barbarism elsewhere displayed by a ravenous Nature has found an even more dreadful expression in human violence; but chaos will not prevail in the end. This assurance answers also the excruciating doubts of "La pietà," for art no longer seems utter vanity, incarnating as it does man's saving will to form in the face of destruction. If the second part of *Sentimento del tempo* sounds like a rejection of all human endeavor, after the stern fashion of the Book of Ecclesiastes, here instead the religious appeal is in a humanistic vein, and God is addressed as "Genitrice mente" (Engendering Mind), in the style of Neoplatonic Renaissance thinkers who saw in God an inspiring source of creativity rather than an inaccessible judge.

After *Il dolore, La terra promessa* (1950) embarks on a further consummation of experience and sets the tone for most of the poetry to come in Ungaretti's second postwar phase. The title, as we saw, brings to fruition his central myth, but the Promised Land, the place of fulfillment, is only glimpsed in imitations or loss. Aeneas' "choruses," which would have been part of the title sequence had the author followed the *Aeneid*'s cue more closely, were still in inchoate form at the time of publication and therefore left out. This omission matters, for Aeneas, of the personae introduced into the sequence, is the only one to set foot on his Promised Land of Italy after the various wanderings Vergil recounts. The others—forsaken Dido and ill-starred Palinurus—are left behind by Aeneas, the former through an act of his will, the latter through accident, a further toll the gods imposed on the Trojan rovers. Thus the theme is one of utter loss, as if to make ironic the title itself. Dido sings in nineteen "choruses" her story of love attained and lost; memory rehearses the moments of irrevocable happiness, then the cruel disappearance and the ravages thereby inflicted on her soul, until she sees her moral image in the blighted landscape of No. 18, and, with the desolate resignation of laconic No. 19, she seals her fate. The loss of love being to her one and the same thing with the loss of youth, her vicissitudes reflect the torment of aging, and the poet himself obliquely looms behind his articulate persona who, on the other hand, owes some of her traits to Racine's *Phèdre* (*Phaedra*, 1677) one of the works that occupied Ungaretti as a translator after World War II. He tells us in the foreword that Dido's autumnal figure represents also the decline of a civilization. Whether the reader is or is not inclined to follow these allegorical pointers, the fact remains that Dido's voice lives through the many modulations of bitter or enchanted recall, present distraction, wistful contemplation, and final renunciation, as one of the valid expressions of the experience of personal decline. It is a voice skillfully passing from the immediacy of "cry of love, cry of shame" (No. 3) to the involved Petrarchan elaborateness of much more oblique utterances, both mobility and elegance of style fitting the poetical mask very different from Vergil's Dido yet no less passionately dignified, even to the point where she drinks her bitter cup to the dregs of inner degradation.

In the two very formal compositions that encase Dido's sequence, Ungaretti brings his Petrarchan experience to a complete consummation. Their stately style, marked by abstract vocabulary, complexity of construction, and closed meter, fits their respective themes; it also acts as a foil to the more animated ejaculations and meditations of Dido. In the first piece, which precedes Dido's sequence, the poet sings his own descent into the inner abyss of oblivion and nothingness (the death of the senses) and his subsequent rise to another sphere of being at the call of the Platonic "first image" that still glimmers, in Promised Land fashion, through the world of inconstancy. Thus he offsets by dedication to vision and form the inevitable loss whose degrading impact Dido can only stop by dying. This introductory "canzone" ties in with the symmetrical sestina of Palinurus, who symbolizes questing man overtaken by the twin delusions of dream and feverish action, and by them doomed. He has become stone, nothing else is left of his struggle with the untrustworthy waters: "Thus I became non-mortal fury." He personifies the fate of our Faustian civilization as well as the process whereby art immobilizes life into a perennial form. Both he and the poet keep striving for the Promised Land to the very last; Palinurus is the defeated man of action, the poet is the man of contemplation (the only one with a chance left), and Dido, the defeated creature of passion. Together, they make up man's sundered inner trinity.

Il taccuino del vecchio, appearing ten years after, prolongs *La terra promessa* in theme and form, even to the extent of incorporating some of the "choruses" originally assigned to Aeneas (they are collectively designated as "Last Choruses for the Promised Land"). In between, *Un grido e paesaggi* came in 1952 as a throwback to the less elaborate stages of Ungaretti's career. Its mainstay is a long narrative piece called "Little Monologue" which stems from the vivid prose of *Il deserto e dopo.* It seems somehow a new version of "The Rivers": a retelling of the writer's pilgrimages in the light of the meaning they can yield in retrospect. Yet the recapitulating voice has a very different tone; it unwinds from the spool of memory with an unremitting urgency that the 1916 poem, with its suspended images and unpunctuated free stanzas, never attains. "The Rivers" is a poem of wonder flowing in mythic time; "Little Monologue" is closer to historical time and narrative prose and contains a critique of experience the ecstatic earlier poem does not envisage. "The Rivers" is essentially a celebration of

GIUSEPPE UNGARETTI

fulfillment, a finding of the self in a reliable universe, while "Little Monologue" is an ironic facing of disenchantment: "Poets, O poets, we have donned / All the masks; / But one is only one's own self . . . "

This mask motif, oddly reminiscent of Ezra Pound's gesture toward the end of *Pisan Cantos* (1948) ("Pull down thy vanity . . . "), thematically springs from the occasion of the poem, which has to do with the author's birthday in February and thus with the Carnival season. Carnival in Corsica, carnival in Brazil, and in a way, carnival in Egypt (the Shi'ite Muslim festival of moon amulets) form a set of recurrent celebrations of the equivocal through the several places the poet has visited in the course of a long life, until the eerie meaning of all masquerades comes home to him, the seeker of truth. Toward the end of the reminiscence the nightmarish prophecies of a hallucinated Arab woman are deflated by the peasant common-sense wisdom of the poet's mother; masks, dreams, irrational visions are all equivocations man should learn to discard, as the autobiographical persona has done. Better face the emptiness of winter, of old age, of disenchantment, and mind the biblical warning "Thou art dust. . . ." Dreams are for children; yet, the poem asks, why does childhood so suddenly become a fading memory? The conclusion is

> Nothing, nothing else is there on this earth
> But a glimmer of truth
> And the nothingness of dust,
> Even if, in incorrigible madness,
> Toward the lightning splendor of mirages
> Living man, deep down and in his gestures
> Forever seems to tend.

Experience is the progressive exorcism of illusion, yet will bare truth be enough? The Leopardian dilemma runs through this poetical monologue just as it does through Ungaretti's entire career, an ever-resumed journey toward the ever-changing Promised Land. For, if a man's choice is between the desert and a mirage, as some of the *Il taccuino del vecchio* intimates, there is no hope. Ungaretti's undeniable religious inspiration is of the stern, not of the facile consolatory, variety. From his loss he draws his sustenance, and thus, as he writes in *Il taccuino del vecchio*, rather than give up, he pursues his quest:

> We flee toward a goal:
> Who will ever know it?
>
> Not of Ithaca do we dream
> Lost in sea wanderings,
> But our aim goes to Sinai over sands . . .

"Non d'Itaca si sogna," for you can't go home again, yet even Sinai is not a definitive goal, for

> if [our life on earth] is cut short on top of Sinai,
> The law is renewed for those who are left,
> Illusion will rage again.

Poet, seer, thinker are one and the same thing, priests of truth, but this hard-won truth must be shared, or else life will have been in vain. Here Ungaretti seems to echo that passage of Plato's *Republic* where the philosopher liberated from the shadow-knowledge of the cave is admonished not to turn his back forever on his former fellow inmates.

And Ungaretti kept faith with this generous asceticism. As a poet, he did (to say it with Pound's Propertius) "keep his erasers in order," but emulating Mallarmé's, Petrarch's, or Leopardi's purity never meant for him what it would have meant for the lord of Axel's castle; on the contrary, he insisted on sharing his message and his love of form with other people, contact being provided by "joy," by "sorrow," and by the very uncertainties of the human condition. Consequently, he is one of very few modern writers who pursued a goal of "absolute poetry" and achieved a breakthrough to dramatic immediacy and historical relevance. This nonsolipsist openness to experience made him ceaselessly question himself, prodding him toward the kind of Platonic perfection that the "canzone" from *La terra promessa* had hermetically adumbrated, while showing him the impossibility of retaining it beyond the glimpsed moment. The "first image," like Wallace Stevens' "first idea," dawns on the mind's horizon only fleetingly, for it is a lost wholeness, a lost purity. For Ungaretti, however, it alone made the difference between being and nothingness, and the failure to capture it only rekindled to the very end the twin challenge of life and art.

Youth, the ordeal of war, the commitment to poetry, and the regaining of an ancestral homeland in time of trouble had been enough of a challenge; now old age had come, with its attendant losses to be weathered in the shadow of approaching death. There was still the relentless task of art. After the exemplary formal achievement of *La terra promessa* and the confessional utterances of "Little Monologues" and *Il taccuino del vecchio* Ungaretti's work seemed to have come full circle; but we saw him repeatedly break the circle, in competition with his own glorious past. A fierce energy surged in the poet who denied old age in the very act of acknowledging it. As one of his "Proverbi" of 1966 has it, "he who was born to sing / sings also in dying"; and thus arose, after the translations from Blake (1965), the surprising love poems of *Dialogo* (Dialogue, composed from 1966–1968) and of *Nuove* (New Poems, 1968–1969), which are enriched by one remarkable piece, "L'impietrito e il velluto" (Petrifaction and Velvet), in the 1970 edition of the collected poems (*Tutte le poesie,* first published in 1969), which he worked on with Leone Piccioni and Mario Diacono, adding explanatory notes to his poetical texts. He died in the late spring of 1970 after a last trip to the United States, where he was honored with the International Books Abroad Prize at the University of Oklahoma.

The "dialogue" of 1966–1968 is with a young woman, Bruna Bianco, whose lyrical responses are included in part 2 of the short cycle; whether intentionally or not, the poetical exchange recalls Johann Wolfgang von Goethe's

famous one with Marianne von Willemer in *Westöstlicher Divan* (*The West-Eastern Divan,* 1819). Style runs the gamut from the convoluted (if vibrant) sophistication of "La conchiglia" (The Shell) to the stark directness of "E' ora famelica" (It Is a Hungry Hour). *Nuove,* in turn, offers the climactic utterance of an unabated lyrical voice that can evoke, on the eve of its final silence, the remote beginnings of Ungaretti's imaginative existence through ecstatic surrender to a stirring womanly presence, Dunja the young Croatian beauty: she suddenly reminds him of the old Croatian nurse who had initiated him to fairytales in faraway Egypt. To the very last, the child lived on in the venerable old man, providing him with the deep faith that could survive any amount of natural shocks and doubts. The result was a language repossessed, a word spoken in time, but for all time. Nomad Ungaretti had found his home in the ancestral Italian language, though he kept looking through the sands of time for the Promised Land that could not be finally granted to the living.

Selected Bibliography

EDITIONS

INDIVIDUAL WORKS

Il porto sepolto. Udine, 1916.– With critical apparatus and commentary by Carlo Ossola. Milan, 1981.

La guerre: Une poésie de Giuseppe Ungaretti. Paris, 1919.

Allegria di naufragi. Florence, 1919. *L'Allegria.* Milan, 1931. *Vita d'un uomo. L'Allegria.* Milan, 1942.

Sentimento del tempo. Introduction by Alfredo Gargiulo. Florence, 1933.

Vita d'un uomo. Poesie disperse. Introduction by Giuseppe De Robertis. Milan, 1945.

Derniers jours. 1919. Milan, 1947.

Vita d'un uomo. Il dolore (1937–1946). Milan, 1947.

Il povero nella città. Milan, 1949.

Vita d'un uomo. La terra promessa. Frammenti. Milan, 1950.

Vita d'un uomo. Un grido e paesaggi. Milan, 1952.

Vita d'un uomo. Il taccuino del vecchio. Foreword by Jean Paulhan and other testimonials. Milan, 1961.

Vita d'un uomo. Il deserto e dopo. Milan, 1961.

Apocalissi e Sedici traduzioni. Ancona, 1965.

Il Carso non è più un inferno. Milan, 1966.

Dialogo. By Giuseppe Ungaretti and Bruna Bianco. Turin, 1968.

"Idee del Leopardi sulla crisi del linguaggio e sulla lingua." *Civiltà delle Macchine* (3 April 1971), 19–26.

Lettere a un fenomenologo. With an essay by Enzo Paci. Milan, 1972.

Invenzione della poesia moderna. Lezioni brasiliane di letteratura (1937–1942). Naples, 1984.

Gli scritti egiziani. Edited by Luciano Rebay. Milan, 1988.

COLLECTED WORKS

Vita d'un uomo. Tutte le poesie. Edited by Leone Piccioni, with critical studies by the editor, Giuseppe De Robertis, Alfredo Gargiulo, and Piero Bigongiari and self-analytical essays and notes by the author and Ariodante Marianni. Milan, 1969–1970.

Per conoscere Ungaretti. Edited by Leone Piccioni. Milan, 1971.

Vita d'un uomo. Saggi e interventi. Edited by Mario Diacono and Luciano Rebay. Milan, 1974.

TRANSLATIONS BY UNGARETTI

Traduzioni: St. John Perse, William Blake, Góngora, Essenin, Jean Paulhan. Rome, 1936.

Vita d'un uomo. 40 sonetti di Shakespeare tradotti. Milan, 1946.

Vita d'un uomo. Da Góngora e da Mallarmé. Milan, 1948.

Vita d'un uomo. Fedra di Jean Racine. Milan, 1950.

Andromaca di Jean Racine, Atto III. Turin, 1958.

Vita d'un uomo. Visioni di William Blake. Milan, 1965.

Saint-John Perse: Anabase. Contains also T. S. Eliot's translation with the poem's French text. Verona, 1967.

Frammenti dall'Odissea di Omero. Turin, 1968.

Ezra Pound tradotto da Giuseppe Ungaretti. Milan, 1969.

CORRESPONDENCE

Jean Paulhan–Giuseppe Ungaretti, Correspondence 1919–1968. Edited by Luciano Rebay and Jean-Charles Vegliante. Paris, 1988.

TRANSLATIONS

Agenda. Giuseppe Ungaretti Special Issue. Edited by Andrew Wylie. 8/2 (Spring 1970). Multilingual translations.

Imitations. Translated by Robert Lowell. New York, 1961.

Life of a Man. Translated and introduced by Allen Mandelbaum. London, Milan, and New York, 1958. Rev. ed., Ithaca, N.Y., 1975.

The Promised Land and Other Poems. Translated by Sergio Pacifici. New York, 1957.

Selected Poems by Giuseppe Ungaretti. Translated by Patrick Creagh. Harmondsworth, England, 1969.

BIBLIOGRAPHICAL AND CRITICAL WORKS

Anceschi, Luciano. *Le poetiche del Novecento.* Milan, 1962.

Bigongiari, Piero. *Poesia italiana del Novecento.* Milan, 1960.

Bo, Carlo. *Otto studi.* Florence, 1939.

Buxó, José Pascual. *Ungaretti traductor de Góngora.* Maracaibo, 1968.

Cambon, Glauco. "Ungaretti, Montale and Lady Entropy." *Italica* 37:231–238 (1960).

——— . *Giuseppe Ungaretti.* New York, 1967.

——— . *La poesia di Ungaretti.* Turin, 1976.

Cary, Joseph. *Three Modern Italian Poets: Saba, Ungaretti, Montale.* New York, 1969.

Cavalli, Gigi. *Ungaretti.* Milan, 1958.

Cecchetti, Giovanni. "Giuseppe Ungaretti." *Italica* 26:269–279 (1949).

Crémieux, Benjamin. *Panorama de la littérature italienne contemporaine.* Paris, 1928.

Croce, Benedetto. *Letture di poeti.* Bari, 1950.

Contini, Gianfranco. *Esercizi di lettura sopra autori contemporanei.* Florence, 1947.

De Campos, Haroldo. "Ungaretti e a poética do fragmento." *Correio da Manhã* (28 May 1967).

——— . "Ungaretti e a vanguarda." *Suplemento Literário di "O Estado de São Paulo"* 494 (10 August 1966).

De Nardis, Luigi. *Mallarmé in Italia.* Milan, 1957.

De Robertis, Giuseppe. *Scrittori del Novecento.* Florence, 1946.

Flora, Francesco. *La poesia ermetica.* Bari, 1936.

Friedrich, Hugo. *Die Struktur der modernen Lyrik.* Hamburg, 1956.

Gargiulo, Alfredo. *Letteratura italiana del Novecento.* Florence, 1943.

Genot, Gérard. *Sémantique du discontinu dans "L'Allegria" d'Ungaretti.* Paris, 1972.

Giuseppe Ungaretti, Atti del Convegno internazionale di studio. Various authors. Urbino, 1979.

Gútia, Joan. *Linguaggio di Ungaretti.* Florence, 1959.

Hanne, Michael. "Ungaretti's 'La Terra Promessa' and the 'Aeneid.' " *Italica* 50:3–25 (1973).

Hinterhauser, Hans. *Moderne italienische Lyrik.* Goettingen, 1964.

Jones, F. J. *Giuseppe Ungaretti.* Edinburgh, 1977.

——— . *The Modern Italian Lyric.* Cardiff, 1986.

Mariani, Gaetano. *Tecnica e poesia nella lirica del Novecento.* Padua, 1958.

Mezzacappa, Carmine. *Noia e inquietudine nella "Vita d'un uomo" di Giuseppe Ungaretti.* Padua, 1970.

Ossola, Carlo. *Giuseppe Ungaretti.* Milan, 1975.

Papini, Giovanni. Review of *Il porto sepolto. Il Resto del Carlino* (4 February 1917).

Pento, Bortolo. *Poesia contemporanea.* Milan, 1964.

Petrucciani, Mario. *La poetica dell'ermetismo italiano.* Turin, 1955.

Piccioni, Leone. *Vita di un poeta: Giuseppe Ungaretti.* Milan, 1970.

Poggioli, Renato. "Contemporary Italian Poetry." *Voices* 128 (Winter 1947).

Pozzi, Gianni. *La poesia italiana del Novecento.* Turin, 1965.

Prezzolini, Giuseppe. Review of *Il Porto Sepolto. Il Popolo d'Italia.* (28 May 1918).

Ramat, Silvio. *L'ermetismo.* Florence, 1969.

——— . *Storia della poesia italiana del Novecento.* Florence, 1976.

Rebay, Luciano. *Le origini della poesia di Ungaretti.* Rome, 1962.

——— . "Ungaretti fra *Le Trio des Damnés* e *L'Eudémoniste* di Jean-Léon Thuile." *Forum Italicum* 20:44–82 (1986).

Sempoux, André. "Le premier Ungaretti et la France." *Revue de Littérature Comparée* 37: 360–367 (1963).

Spezzani, Pietro. "Per una storia del linguaggio di Ungaretti fino al *Sentimento del tempo.*" In *Ricerche sulla lingua poetica contemporanea.* Edited by Gianfranco Folena. Padua, 1966.

Vallone, Aldo. *Aspetti della poesia italiana contemporanea.* Pisa, 1960.

SPECIAL ISSUES OF PERIODICALS

Letteratura 35–36 (1958). Edited by Alessandro Bonsanti.

L'Herne. Edited by Piero Sanavio. Paris, 1969.

Books Abroad. 44 (1970). Edited by Ivar Ivask.

L'Approdo letterario 57/18 (March 1972). Edited by Mario Luzi.

Forum Italicum 6/2 (June 1972). Edited by Michael Ricciardelli.

GLAUCO CAMBON

FERNANDO PESSOA

(1888–1935)

HISTORICAL CONTEXT

To INCLUDE A Portuguese author, even one as great as Fernando Pessoa, in a series dedicated to major European writers is to raise unanswerable questions, all of which turn on the definition of the European tradition. How is it, for example, that Renaissance Italian literature is a model for the rest of Europe, while eighteenth-century Italian literature is of secondary interest? Is there something we can actually define as the European tradition, or does that idea vary with the fluctuations of European political or economic power? Is there a mainstream European tradition to which peripheral cultures are attached like so many tributaries? And if so, what is the fate of artists from these secondary cultures? Are they always to be considered as second thoughts when lists of the "great artists" are compiled? Is it possible for a nation of reduced political and economic power to produce art of primary importance? To some extent, this essay attempts to address this last question with an eye toward vindicating at least one figure in Portuguese literature: Fernando Pessoa.

History has not been kind to Portugal, a small, poor nation perched on the Atlantic edge of Europe, just slightly larger than the state of Maine or the Irish Republic. At no time was Portugal, like Italy, a center of European culture, and yet, for all its limitations, Portugal achieved great things. Its explorers reached India by sailing around the tip of Africa in 1498, and its navigators (many of whom, like Sebastian Cabot and Ferdinand Magellan, were employed by foreign monarchs) opened the Americas and sailed around the world. Portugal was never a military power, yet it once possessed an empire that at its height included territories in China, India, and Africa. That empire no longer exists. Portugal today is an impoverished, politically immature nation, struggling to enter the twentieth century before the century ends.

An artist in such a society finds himself in an ironic situation. The artist must depend as much, or more, on foreign art than he does on what is produced at home—which means that for Pessoa the European tradition of his own day was something he read about in books, something he absorbed by reading instead of experiencing it at first hand. Having to stand both inside and outside a society that in comparison with more developed countries is almost by definition backward inevitably places the artist in the role of both cultural and artistic critic. Thus an artist like Fernando Pessoa wrote in two contexts, one in which he expressed his social concerns and another in which he expressed his aesthetics. It is true that any writer divides himself between his social and aesthetic concerns, but artists from peripheral or secondary societies have greater responsibilities within their societies than do their more cosmopolitan counterparts. This is especially true because the intellectual community in these societies tends to be small and therefore more prominent than it is in mainstream nations. Artists are less able to remain aloof from social and political issues and are much more apt to be required to comment on virtually every matter of concern to society.

Fernando Pessoa was profoundly engaged with the plight of Portugal. At the same time he was a poet and man of letters whose writings put him among the great authors of the twentieth century. He is separated from a wider readership, first and obviously, because he wrote in Portuguese, and second, because even within the narrow confines of Portuguese literary history, he was an enigma. Pessoa published few books during his lifetime, choosing to print poems and articles in magazines, and until fairly recently, the bulk of his published works have remained dispersed. An even greater editorial problem is that at his death he left behind a huge number of unpublished manuscripts that are only now, one by one, beginning to appear. It is as if Pessoa continues, fifty years after his death, to write new books.

To understand Fernando Pessoa we must first locate him in his Portuguese context and consider how Portuguese history shaped his sensibility. If there is a single element that unifies the Portuguese people throughout their history, it is their language. Unlike the Spaniards, whose religion spurred their political unification—Spanish medieval history is the struggle not of Spaniards against Moors but of Christians against Moors, just as Spanish history in the sixteenth and seventeenth centuries is the struggle of Catholic orthodoxy against Protestant heterodoxy—the Portuguese have found community through their native tongue. An outstanding example of this identification of nation with language is the Portuguese national epic, *Os Lusíadas* (*The Lusiads*, 1572), by Luiz Vaz de Camões (1524–1580). This great Renaissance epic, which influenced Milton and was praised by Voltaire, differs from other epics, ancient and modern, in that it deals with an actual historic accomplishment carried out by real men: Vasco da Gama's voyage around Africa to India in 1497 and 1498.

While Camões's poem contains the usual epic machinery—invocations of the muses, pagan gods and goddesses—it is really a song of praise dedicated to all that is great in Portuguese history: deeds of valor, great loves, voyages of discovery. What links these events is the Portuguese language. Indeed, the goddess Venus protects Vasco da Gama and his men on their voyage because their Portuguese is so much like her Latin. For Camões and for Fernando Pessoa, the Portuguese national spirit is one with the Portuguese language. Pessoa remarks in his diary, *Livro do desassossego* (Book of Disquiet, 1982), which he wrote under the name Bernardo Soares: "I have no political or social feelings. I have, nevertheless, in one sense a deep patriotic feeling. My country is the Portuguese language" (frag. 15, vol. 1, p. 17). This sense of national linguistic unity does not exist among the Spaniards. The sharp differences between Castilians and Catalonians or Castilians and Basques derive from linguistic differences and from the kind of hatred that has arisen as a result of the linguistic hegemony of Castile, a linguistic hegemony that is merely one more manifestation of political domination.

Certainly language is the enduring factor that enabled the Portuguese to differentiate themselves from the Spaniards. When Philip II of Spain (himself half Portuguese) annexed Portugal to the Spanish crown in 1580, he assuaged outraged Portuguese patriotism by declaring that he would not impose Castilian on the people. The Spanish occupation lasted until 1640, a reminder then and always of the fragility of Portuguese institutions and of the weakness of Portuguese military power. The only national institution not subject to outside intervention was language, the repository of great national historic events—events that might be commemorated in marble or bronze, but that found a more lasting monument in words.

Language as a symbol of national unity became important in the rest of Europe during the Romantic period, but in Portugal it has been a constant. This is one reason why the Portuguese have always been depicted—especially by Spanish poets of the sixteenth and seventeenth centuries—as melancholy and homesick, suffering from *saudades,* the Portuguese variety of homesickness, or the German *Heimweh;* this affliction is typical of the Romantic era, abounding in exiles forced to leave their homeland (and language) because of politics, war, and economic upheavals. The Portuguese invented it, and their popular culture is filled with songs of nostalgic recollection.

The identification of country and language compensates to some extent for the weakness of Portuguese institutions other than the monarchy and the church. Even the monarchy took a long time to transform itself from a mere ruling house in the feudal sense to the symbol of the nation. Religion, too, in Portugal seems more a matter of traditional faith than an arm of national policy as it was in Spain—hence the weakness of the Inquisition in Portugal. Only in the bizarre case of King Sebastian, who ruled from 1557 until 1578, can it be said that there existed a Portuguese institution involving all social classes. But even that institution was ephemeral.

Sebastian succeeded to the throne at the age of three and spent his childhood and early youth largely in isolation, under the tutelage of the Jesuits. These ascetic tutors instilled in the young king a military religious fervor blended with the self-analytic spiritual exercises of their order. Large doses of exercise and practice with arms, along with spiritual rigor, imbued Sebastian with a crusading zeal that made him fanatically devoted to the idea of being a soldier for Christ against the Moors. In 1568, at fourteen, he attained his majority, and with virtually no one to control him, the boy king grew increasingly willful and arrogant.

His hope to be the first king among his European contemporaries to lead a successful crusade were dashed in 1571, when the combined Spanish and Italian fleets destroyed the Turkish flotilla at Lepanto. Sebastian's own fleet was scattered by a storm in 1572. Failure at sea obliged him to turn to a land campaign. Accordingly, in June 1578 he landed an army of some twenty thousand troops at Tangier. In late July he marched south to Alcácer-Quivir (Ksar el Kebir), which he reached in early August—his army without food and out of communication with the fleet. A Moroccan army attacked the next day, and despite a heroic defense, Sebastian's army was wiped out: at least eight thousand were killed, including the king himself.

Immediately after this disaster, legends that would form the core of *sebastianismo,* or Sebastianism, began to circulate. The king's body was never recovered, and rumor declared that he was still alive. A number of fraudulent Sebastians appeared in Portugal and elsewhere, but the Spaniards quickly proved them false when Philip II claimed the Portuguese throne. Still, a foolish, probably deranged, king whose folly had caused the death of thousands was turned into a myth, a symbol of the Portuguese nation in captivity, a royal Quixote who had failed in a noble cause but who might return someday to lead Portugal to greatness. This national savior, a combination of Richard the Lionhearted and Jesus Christ, became the messiah of a secular religion. Sebastianism, which reappeared in the Brazilian northeast in the late nineteenth century as an antirepublican doctrine, also appealed to Fernando Pessoa, who took on Sebastian's voice in one of the poems in his book *Mensagem* (Message, 1934), a mystical meditation on Portuguese history:

> Mad, yes, mad because I desired greatness
> Such as Fortune does not grant
>
> (5.42)[1]

---

[1]All quotations, unless otherwise indicated, are taken from the eleven-volume edition of *Obras completas* (Lisbon, 1974–1984).

Was Pessoa mad to idealize Sebastian? Perhaps, but no more than William Butler Yeats was mad to seek the sources of Irish nationalism in the myths and prehistory of Ireland.

Portugal managed to survive as a nation independent of the Spanish only through linguistic community. In all other senses—economically, politically, institutionally—even after securing her independence from Spain in the seventeenth century, Portugal was a kind of phantom nation. During the eighteenth and nineteenth centuries, she was beset by dynastic and social upheavals that were settled by foreign intervention rather than by the Portuguese themselves. Abroad, Portugal found herself the pawn of two great powers: England, with its expanding mercantile-industrial empire, and France, whose imperialistic policies swept away all continental opposition. Portugal is the prototype of the twentieth-century "third world," or underdeveloped, nation, a producer of agricultural products and an importer of manufactured goods. Paradoxically, Portugal was herself an imperial power with overseas possessions.

The Napoleonic years brought Portugal to the brink of disaster and stripped Brazil from its possession. At the same time, the example of the French Revolution and the presence of the French on the Iberian Peninsula planted the seeds of political liberalism, which manifested itself first in the Freemasons, who represented anti-absolutist energies throughout the Ibero-American world. In Portugal, however, these new forces could not manage to organize themselves into political parties, and although there were sporadic uprisings during the first half of the nineteenth century (1837, 1838, and several times during the 1840's) no radical transformation of political life took place.

In the nineteenth century, Portugal seemed headed for some sort of constitutionalism, but just what sort was not clear. The active political groups relied too much on charismatic leadership and too little on ideology, and as a result, political parties as such remained extensions of their leaders instead of expressions of policy. Portuguese politics came to resemble a tennis match, with the monarch acting as referee. Some recovery from the devastation of the Napoleonic years took place under King Pedro V, who ruled from 1853 until 1861: roads improved, a rail line was opened between Lisbon and Oporto, and modern telegraphic communications were planned from Lisbon to the Azores and ultimately across the Atlantic. But even these signs of life were pitiful examples of just how backward Portugal was even midway through the century. Lisbon was a small city of fewer than two hundred thousand inhabitants. It was unhealthy, had an inadequate water supply, and was ravaged by epidemics: cholera and yellow fever broke out in 1856 and 1857, and in 1865 bubonic plague appeared.

The Portuguese economy could be restored only by reducing the public debt (most of it owed to foreign banks) and by bringing expenditures under control. These measures were finally undertaken in the 1870's. The politicians continued to form and break alliances; the Spaniards, under General Prim, began to talk in pan-Iberian terms not heard since Philip II; but in 1888, the year of Pessoa's birth, the nation was, in fact, at peace and actually stirring out of its lethargy. Education reforms were bringing literacy to more people, writers of quality—the great novelist Eça de Queiroz among them—began to publish, and the Portuguese began to look toward their African colonies, Mozambique in East Africa and Angola in Southwest Africa, as sources of economic growth.

Here Portugal ran afoul of two other imperial powers active in Africa, England, and Germany. These countries ultimately determined Portugal's future simply by pursuing their own interests. England and Portugal had maintained friendly relations for centuries, and since the Napoleonic wars the English stood behind the Braganças, the Portuguese ruling house. On 11 January 1890 the British foreign minister, Lord Salisbury, demanded that the Portuguese withdraw from certain African territories or the British would recall their ambassador from Lisbon, which obviously meant war. Salisbury was trying to limit both Portuguese and German territorial control in Africa, but his threat (known as the Ultimatum in Portugal) sent a shock wave through the nation. Antimonarchist forces immediately took heart, and soldiers in Oporto even staged an abortive republican revolt. The Brazilian Braganças had themselves fallen to a military coup in 1889, so the occasion seemed propitious to many.

Economic prosperity vanished because of a series of international financial disasters that began in 1890, when the Argentine economy, in which both the Spanish and the Portuguese had heavily invested, collapsed. Portugal was once again on the brink of bankruptcy. She lurched unsteadily toward the twentieth century, with both England (eager to isolate the Boers) and Germany (seeking to increase its African holdings) trying to carve up Portuguese Africa. King Carlos I sought to alleviate Portugal's diplomatic and economic situation by practicing a kind of shuttle diplomacy, visiting each of the powers to negotiate in turn, but it was clear that war, with Africa as its first theater, was imminent. The Boer War broke out on 11 October 1899 and Portugal was obliged to side with the British in order to keep her colonies. At the same time, an irreversible process had begun in Portuguese politics.

On 1 February 1908, the Portuguese royal family was ambushed in Lisbon. King Carlos was killed, as was the heir apparent, Prince Luís Felipe. The republicans not only refused to denounce this violence, but also went so far as to solicit money to help the families of the regicides. The monarchy fell on 4 October 1910. The last Portuguese king, Manuel II, fled Portugal and settled in England, where he died in 1932. On 5 October a provisional government was formed with Teófilo Braga, a literary historian imbued with the same positivist fervor that had animated the Brazilian republicans, as its president. The monarchy, the church, and the aristocracy were the principal targets of these idealists, who were really bour-

geois (and in some cases aristocratic) reformers rather than social revolutionaries.

Very soon, however, Portugal was once more in turmoil because of events abroad. When World War I broke out, Portugal feigned neutrality while giving passive support to the Allies. The ruling Democrats believed that active support would help Portugal retain her African colonies, so in 1916 they seized some German ships in Portuguese waters. Germany declared war, and soon the Portuguese had thousands of troops fighting in France. The strain on the economy produced domestic hardship on such a scale that on 5 December 1917 violence broke out. Disaster followed disaster: the new government, led by Major Sidónio Pais, could stabilize neither the economy nor the political system; by 1918, the Portuguese escudo was virtually worthless; on 14 December 1918, Sidónio Pais was assassinated, and the Democrats returned to power. In 1920 Fernando Pessoa dedicated a poem to the memory of Sidónio Pais, "A memória do Presidente-Rei Sidónio Pais" (In Memory of President-King Sidónio Pais), idealizing him as the momentary incarnation of King Sebastian.

For seven more years Portugal was on the brink of anarchy. Ultimately the army was the only body left with enough cohesion and discipline to take charge of what would soon be chaos. There were three abortive military coups in 1925, and on 28 May 1926 General Gomes da Costa, a veteran of World War I, seized power in a relatively mild coup. He was soon deposed and replaced by General Carmona. The military men found they were governing nothing more than a vast foreign debt, so, in 1928, they turned to an economics professor at the University of Coimbra, Dr. António de Oliveira Salazar, to restore the economy.

Salazar cut expenses, raised taxes, and put the nation on an even financial keel. In 1932 he became prime minister and continued to rule Portugal almost until his death in 1970. His formula for Portuguese prosperity was simple: a balanced budget and tight control over national politics. To many Portuguese this must have seemed a sensible program, since economic instability had been the curse of the nation for centuries and the only concrete political accomplishment the Portuguese could point to in modern times was the destruction of the monarchy. Accepting Salazar meant accepting political repression, especially of the Left. While accommodation to dictatorship brought the advantage of neutrality in the Spanish Civil War (1936–1939) and World War II, it has meant that Portuguese politics in the waning decades of the twentieth century have not advanced. The nation is still politically stunted and unsure of its role in modern Europe.

Fernando Pessoa, who seems not to have left Lisbon between 1905 and 1935, the year of his death, witnessed the process of modern Portuguese history from the fall of the monarchy to the rise of Salazar. He remained a mystical monarchist until his death and even openly espoused Sebastianism. But in politics, as in every other aspect of his life, Pessoa was a poet, and, like so many poets of his age, he viewed the turmoil of the century with horror, preferring to idealize the past rather than working to perfect the present. Like so many other modern poets—Yeats, Ezra Pound, T. S. Eliot, Wallace Stevens—he became a reactionary more out of disdain for present ineptitude than out of a desire to turn back the clock. The final poem of *Mensagem,* his mystical vision of Portugal, summarizes his paradoxically pessimistic and optimistic view of twentieth-century Portugal:

Fog

Neither king, nor law, nor peace, nor war
Defines with its outline and being
This dark fulmination of the earth
Which is Portugal in its saddening—
Glow without light or heat
Like the glow of the will-o'-the-wisp.

No one knows what thing he desires.
No one knows what soul he has,
Nor what is evil nor what is good

(What distant anguish weeps nearby?)
All is uncertain and in the past.
All is scattered, nothing is whole.
Oh Portugal, today you are fog . . .

Now is the time!

LIFE AND WORKS

We are perhaps rather too inclined to think that individuals are not totally responsible for their actions, that people behave as they do because of genes, childhood, or environment. We find it difficult to talk about the individual personality because we have been taught, especially by psychoanalysis, to think of personality in abstract terms. However, if we wish to understand Pessoa, we must restrain our tendency to treat him as a case history and deal with him as a unique individual, a genius who managed to transcend the limitations and ravages of the first ten years of his life. This first decade affected Pessoa's personality to such an extent that his having become an artist is something of a miracle, a triumph of the individual will over personal adversity. At the same time it is also true that if he had not suffered psychological disasters, Pessoa might not have become a great artist. His life, as terrible as it was, was the crucible in which the artist was created.

Fernando Antonio Nogueira Pessoa was born in Lisbon on 13 June 1888. His father, Joaquim de Seabra Pessoa, was a music critic for the Lisbon newspaper *Diario de noticias.* His mother was Maria Madalena Pinheiro, whose family came originally from the Azores. There was nothing unconventional in the family except that Pessoa's father was of new-Christian origin; that is, he was a descendant of Jews who at some point in the remote past had converted to Christianity.

That such a fact is recorded at all is a sad reminder that anti-Semitism is a plague Western civilization cannot seem to cure. It is also a testimony to the attachment of all the Iberian peoples, Spaniards and Portuguese alike, to the notion of "purity of blood." There was some stigma attached to being of "mixed blood" (although the notion is totally unscientific and is quite properly a matter of folklore), and in 1925, Pessoa found himself (and several of his friends) attacked by one Mario Saa in his *A invasão dos judeus* (The Invasion of the Jews) for being of Jewish origin. Thus, anti-Jewish sentiment, older than the Inquisition on the Iberian Peninsula, came to blend with Portuguese politics in the early decades of the twentieth century, much as it did in France during the Dreyfus Affair. Perhaps Pessoa was secretly gratified by this attack, because the figure of the Wandering Jew had been associated with that of the artist in the modern world since the Renaissance, especially during the Romantic period. Being branded an outsider was nothing more than an acknowledgment of the central issue of Pessoa's life.

When Pessoa was five years old, his father, only forty-three, died. That death was followed in the next year, 1894, by that of Pessoa's brother. Small wonder then that the boy invented an imaginary playmate, the Chevalier de Pas, in whose name he wrote letters to himself. Unlike real people, Pessoa's imaginary playmate could not die, but what makes the Chevalier unique is that he wrote letters to Pessoa and was not just a mute interlocutor in the boy's games. At the age of six, Pessoa had already seen that written words can endure and might contain or define a personality. The Chevalier was not just the boy's alter ego or a literary character come to life; he was a person, a style, created by the boy but possessed of his own personality and existing on his own. In time, Fernando Pessoa created a world of heteronyms, "other names," who emanated from him, but who wrote and thought in ways quite different from those of Pessoa.

In 1895 Pessoa's mother decided to remarry. Her new husband was the Portuguese consul in Durban, South Africa, João Miguel Rosa. Mrs. Pessoa agreed to marry by proxy, and the marriage was thus held in Lisbon while Rosa awaited his bride in Durban. If at first he was beseiged by death, now the boy was involved in a fairy tale complete with an invisible stepfather. The Gothic atmosphere thickened in 1896, when Pessoa's grandmother was institutionalized for insanity. How did the boy feel as he saw one adult after another disappear from his immediate family? We do not know how he survived these repeated blows, but we do know that in 1895, at the age of seven, Pessoa wrote his first poem—which he dedicated to his mother.

In 1896 Pessoa and his mother moved to Durban to live with João Miguel Rosa. Again Pessoa's sense of estrangement was probably immense: an eight-year-old Portuguese boy was set down in a subtropical city facing the Indian Ocean in which English, Afrikaans, and indigenous languages were spoken by a heterogeneous population that included a considerable number of people of Indian and Pakistani descent. He was sent to an Irish Catholic school, where he immediately dedicated himself to the English language, to "speaking and writing the most academic English possible" (Seabra, p. 181). The language he sought to learn was not the language ordinary people would speak but the language of literature. Pessoa was clearly trying to use language as a mask, an invisible hiding place. He turned speech into something as close as possible to written language, that is, to art.

For Pessoa life itself was fast becoming art, a peculiar form of theater with one actor playing all the parts. At the same time he must have realized that he could never fully integrate himself into South African society, that although he was obliged to speak and write English at school and in daily life, he was also expected to speak Portuguese at home with his mother, stepfather, half-sister, and half-brothers. Thus he did not react against his native language in the way so many immigrants do, rejecting it in favor of the language of the new society.

The great literary experience of Pessoa's childhood, one he never tired of repeating throughout his life, was reading Charles Dickens' *Pickwick Papers.* When asked about early readings later in life, Pessoa replied: "In my childhood and early adolescence there was for me—I lived and was educated in English territory—one supreme and all-inclusive book, Dickens' *Pickwick Papers.* Even today . . . I read and reread it" (Seabra, p. 181). In *Livro do desassossego* he remarks, "Already having read the *Pickwick Papers* is one of the great tragedies of my life" (frag. 218, vol. 1, p. 245). Later in the same book he returns to Dickens and makes an observation that may help us to understand just what he saw in the novel:

> There are people who really suffer because they haven't been able to live in real life with Mr. Pickwick and shaken hands with Mr. Wardle. I am one of them. I have shed real tears over that novel because I wasn't able to live in those times, with those people, real people.
>
> (frag. 510, vol. 2, p. 254)

Pessoa may have seen that Dickens partly derives his characters from language, that from one point of view the book is a gallery of English speech types. This certainly must have been of interest to a boy who had been acutely conscious of linguistic differences since a very early age. Here we have a book in which the narrator—Dickens' literary mask—pretends, as Cervantes pretends centuries earlier, to be "the editor of these papers," not the inventor, but merely the purveyor of already written documents. The author-narrator hides behind a mask; that is, Dickens writes the text, then pretends to have found it, and comments on it as an amused editor. It would have been possible for Pessoa to imagine Dickens composing his text as if he were creating a mental theater, where he could be each of his characters while being himself at the same time.

Pessoa may also have identified with the situation of Sam Weller, a boy of the streets, with a father whom he loves and who loves him in turn, but who exercises little control over him. Mr. Pickwick is Sam's second father, a step up on the moral, social, and economic hi-erarchy, but lacking the street wisdom of the elder Weller. Sam must combine the better elements of both fathers in order to rise above his origins and to survive.

Viewed in another way, Sam is the union of the spirits of his two fathers, a boy born of men without female intervention. Indeed, Weller senior is a widower constantly running afoul of widows interested in matrimony, while Mr. Pickwick is resolutely celibate. The ambiguity of Pickwick's character with regard to women is a source of humor: when he attempts to broach the subject of taking on a valet (Sam) with his landlady, Mrs. Wardle, she thinks he is proposing marriage. Thus the relationship between Sam and Mr. Pickwick suggests the union of an older man and a young girl—Sam is Mrs. Wardle's rival. Pessoa himself was sexually ambiguous, a misogynist at times, at others (ca. 1920) mawkishly in love with an office girl named (significantly) Ofelia de Queiros. He may have found consolation in the notion that the author is both father and mother to his creations.

By 1899 Pessoa had adapted well enough to the English-speaking world of Durban to matriculate in the Durban high school, and, at least as far as English composition was concerned, Pessoa was a success: he won the Form Prize. At eleven, Pessoa seemed well on the way to becoming an English writer, even having invented an English-writing replacement for the Chevalier de Pas in an imaginary pen pal named Alexander Search. But still the family was harassed by death. In 1901 Pessoa's half-sister died and the whole family went to Lisbon for the burial. There Pessoa renewed his contact with Portugal and his family, in particular an aunt who wrote sonnets in what Pessoa called the "absolute style of the eighteenth century" (Seabra, p. 181).

In 1902 Pessoa returned to Durban, where he entered commercial school and learned business English and bookkeeping, skills that enabled him to eke out a modest living as a commercial correspondent and translator throughout his adult life. We do not know the reason for this training, unless it was that his family insisted on it as a means to secure employment for a son without fixed ambitions. In 1904 Pessoa returned to high school, where in December he published a critical essay on the English historian Thomas Babington Macaulay in the student magazine. He then took the university entrance examinations and performed so well that he won the Queen Victoria Memorial Prize. The following year, 1905, he took additional examinations for entry into the arts and letters division, which required him to read John Milton, Lord Byron, Percy Bysshe Shelley, John Keats, Alfred Tennyson, Thomas Carlyle, and Edgar Allan Poe. At the same time, he was writing poetry in English, although he wrote one poem in Portuguese on the death of his half-sister.

The year 1905, then, is clearly a year of crisis in Pessoa's life. On the surface, he appeared to be a success, completely assimilated into the English-speaking world. And perhaps he was aware that another writer born outside this world, Joseph Conrad, had managed to find a place in English literature. Thus the seventeen-year-old Pessoa was faced with choices that determined the rest of his life: the adolescent was to define the adult. With his knowledge of English, together with his skill as a writer, he could have gone to England to seek a literary career; or he could have stayed in South Africa, soon to become a battleground. There were many possibilities for Pessoa in the English-speaking world, but he abandoned all of them, unlike his half-brothers, who continued their education in England, where they eventually settled.

In 1905 Pessoa returned to Lisbon with his family, intending to begin a university program there. This seems odd since Pessoa's education had been entirely English until then; he had attended no Portuguese schools since he was eight and had received no training in composition and style, the areas that probably mattered most to him. Why did he decide to return to Lisbon, a city more foreign to him than Durban by this time? There are no clear answers to

this question, although it is possible that the young Pessoa thought he could have a greater impact on Portuguese language and literature than he could on English literary life. If this was his reason for choosing Lisbon, he was correct. In English, Pessoa wrote competent late-Victorian verse (or, in his sonnets, mock-Elizabethan verse), but his English poetry is interesting only as a digression from his writing in Portuguese. The English poems are quaint period pieces; the Portuguese poems renovate a national literature.

Pessoa, perhaps, felt patriotic longings, not for politics, but for language, sensing that part of him remained in the Portuguese language. If his latter works provide any insights into his thinking in 1905, then this must be the case: Pessoa must have learned his English and assimilated his English culture much in the way an actor learns his part, and when the time came for a choice, he returned to his original identity, the Portuguese language.

In Lisbon, Pessoa was under the tutelage of his uncle General Henrique Rosa, a poet, who set about orienting his nephew with regard to Portuguese letters. Through his uncle Pessoa became familiar with the work of two poets whose influence on him, in his early phase, was decisive: Cesário Verde (1855–1886) and Camilo Pessanha (1867–1926). At this time Pessoa also began to read French poetry, especially Charles Baudelaire, who was a major influence on both Verde and Pessanha, and he also read German philosophy, especially Arthur Schopenhauer and Friedrich Nietzsche. Nor did he abandon English literature, continuing to read Shakespeare and William Wordsworth. Given his literary vocation, Pessoa probably needed university instruction only as a framework, learning on his own what he would need as a writer.

In 1906 Pessoa matriculated in the Curso Superior de Letras, but abandoned the program almost immediately. Pessoa could not accept the political reality of Portugal, and participated (although to what extent it is difficult to say) in the student strike against the dictatorship of João Franco. But he was so alienated by the experience that he left the university. Pessoa never took any Portuguese degrees, and his idea of entering the Curso Superior seems like a flight of patriotic fancy, given the low standards of that institution compared to those of Durban. But he did not leave Portugal to pursue studies elsewhere. In fact, he did not leave Lisbon for the rest of his life.

What lessons did Pessoa learn from his readings in Portuguese literature? What did the poetry of Verde or Pessanha mean to his literary formation? He learned first that Portuguese literature, like Portugal itself, was an underdeveloped literature and that the work of these two poets was an assimilation of the literary devices of the French symbolist movement, from Baudelaire through Stéphane Mallarmé. From about 1880 to 1920 Portuguese poetry was in a phase of imitation, much like the phase that Spanish-American poetry was passing through then. The poetic movement called modernism in Spanish America, which contains figures such as Rubén Darío, José Martí, Julián del Casal, and Manuel Gutiérrez Nájera, is a collective attempt to bring Spanish poetry up to date, to assimilate the lessons of European poetry from romanticism to symbolism. The result was a literary revolution that revitalized poetry in Spanish and paved the way for the avant-garde writers of the 1920's and 1930's.

Literature in Portugal was intimately connected with politics, to a much greater extent than in Spanish America. This had been true especially since 1871, when Antero de Quental organized a series of lectures known now as the "Casino Lectures," which were a cause célèbre in Portuguese intellectual life because the government of the marquis of Avila canceled them. These controversial lectures were revolutionary because they sought to introduce new ideas into Portugal, and new ideas in the late nineteenth century meant republicanism in politics. The ideas the intellectuals were importing (from France primarily, but also from England and Germany) were related to positivism (Auguste Comte and Herbert Spencer), to Darwinian evolution, and to the nineteenth-century fascination with determinism that manifests itself in the writings of Émile Zola. Even in literary criticism, in the person of Hippolyte Taine, we find determinism: Taine declared he could virtually map a writer's career by isolating the effects on him of his race (his biological heritage), his milieu (his environment), and the literary climate in which he was nurtured—his tradition, and the influences he was likely to receive.

The second half of the nineteenth century was the great age of literary realism, concerned with the minute details of ordinary life in relation to the process of history. The notion that history is a linear, developmental process, derived from thinkers like G. W. F. Hegel in philosophy and Charles Darwin in the natural sciences, was complemented by the nineteenth century's awareness that industrial progress had totally transformed the way people understood human history: history could be measured by a society's technology. An "advanced" society had steam engines; a "primitive" society did not. The inevitable conclusion people drew from technological progress was that the inventors of machines were inherently superior to the rest. At this time the idea of modernity began to take hold in the western mind, especially in places such as Portugal that seemed to be excluded from progress. Like beings excluded from Paradise but suddenly given a glimpse of it, the Portuguese intellectuals demanded modernization at any cost. The past was to be discarded. Pessoa, probably more "modern" than any of his contemporaries, could never accept this doctrine.

The lessons Pessoa gleaned from Verde and Pessanha were invaluable. That these poets belonged to the assimilative phase of modern Portuguese poetry does not mean that they were mere imitators. On the contrary, to these poets (and to others) fell the hard task of bringing the literary lessons of contemporary European lyric poetry into Portuguese. To say that they simply translated or copied Baudelaire or others is to forget that "translation" required a reshaping of the native literary language—no minor job, especially in a provincial literary environment with a minuscule readership.

Verde's contribution to Portuguese literature was paradoxical: first, he was a cosmopolite, projecting a Baudelairian image through clothes and public manner. He was the poet as dandy, the living work of art, who expressed his rejection of bourgeois society by affecting an aristocratic pose. But Verde balanced this sophisticated style with a rediscovery of rural Portugal and country life. He did not idealize nature, as did the Romantics of the early nineteenth century or depict pastoral Portugal as a repository of genuine national values, as did so many figures in the late nineteenth century. Instead, Verde, in a way similar to Thoreau, envisioned the land as a place where it was possible to work hard, enjoy good health, and experience community with one's fellow man. He denounced the city as a source of corruption and alienation, much as many urban dwellers in the United States did in the 1970's.

Verde reflects the realist strain in the century—materialist, bourgeois, determinist, fascinated by the minutiae of everyday life—while Pessanha reflects the idealist, symbolist side of the age. The ultimate source for both of these contrary tendencies is Baudelaire: Pessanha's work springs from Baudelaire's intimate, self-analyzing side, while Verde derives from Baudelaire's anti-Romantic, dandy side. In Pessanha we see the alienated, neurotic poet of the nineteenth century, the kind of poet we associate with Edgar Allan Poe, while Verde was the bold, self-confident nineteenth century poet we see in Walt Whitman. He was also something of an exotic, a traveler who lived many years in the Portuguese colony at Macão, where he cultivated the "artificial paradise" of opium. Although he never mastered literary Chinese, he introduced a touch of Chinese culture into his poetry. His main contribution to Portuguese poetry and to Pessoa was his rigor as a poet, his constant refining of his poetry and his searching for lucidity over musicality.

His participation in the controversial literary magazine *Orpheu* (Orpheus, 1915), to which Pessoa also contributed, linked him to Pessoa's literary generation.

Pessoa thus found himself living in a Portugal that was trying to modernize itself politically without going through a bloody social revolution. This meant that Portuguese radicals were actually republicans and not social revolutionaries. In literature as well the younger generation of writers was trying to discard sentimental romanticism in order to copy the lessons of the French symbolists. Pessoa would prove to be more radical than his contemporaries in both politics and literature.

In 1907 Pessoa's mother and stepfather had returned to Durban, and, at nineteen, he was alone in Lisbon. With some money inherited from a great-aunt, he founded a publishing company he called Ibis, a nickname his family used for him. Pessoa was not the first young author to think that he could both write and publish books, and he was not the first to go bankrupt. The Ibis company failed, and Pessoa's fortunes hit bottom: he was alone, without friends, unloved, and politically alienated from the majority of Portuguese intellectuals.

In the following year King Carlos and the crown prince were assassinated, a prelude to the republican revolution of 1910. Pessoa, though still a young man, in no way sympathized with the republicans. He detected the essentially middle-class nature of a revolution that eradicated a government consecrated by tradition and replaced it with a government mired in self-interest, a government whose right to exist was based on principle instead of tradition and was in that sense "foreign" and not "naturally" Portuguese. Pessoa's attitude toward the republicans and his almost mystical monarchism brought him under suspicion for years to come.

At the same time the opening decade of the twentieth century brought about a real revolution in the plastic arts and in literature. The first radical changes in European art and literature to reach Pessoa and his generation were the experiments of the cubists and the Futurist Manifesto of 1909—but Pessoa needed time to assimilate their lessons. In any case their initial impact was visual, not verbal. It is hard to imagine just how strange the experiments of the cubists were to the Portuguese, especially to Pessoa, a man brought up in the provincial, Victorian environment of late-nineteenth-century Durban. We can only suppose that he and his contemporaries must have thought they were seeing art through a kaleidoscope. Their sense of cultural belatedness must have been immense and no doubt imbued them with mixed feelings of eagerness to experience the new and fear that they would never be able to understand it—acceptance and rejection at the same time.

Cubism and futurism are antithetical approaches to aesthetic perception. They both depart from the impressionists' analysis of vision, a kind of phenomenology of perception, and move that analysis away from science into the realm of imagination. The cubists depicted a static world, often the same still lifes of objects on a table that had been part of the European tradition since the Renaissance, seen simultaneously from many sides. This method transcends the impressionist technique of representing the play of light over surfaces because it renders the object depicted more as a function of imagination than as an object of intellectual analysis. Painting thus began to detach itself from representation in order to explore its own possibilities in what would ultimately be called nonrepresentational or abstract art.

The futurists were much more programmatic than the cubists because they sought to create more than a new style. Their movement combined aesthetics and politics. They aspired—and that they published their manifesto in industrial Milan and in Paris, the cultural capital of Europe, supports this—to galvanize industrial Italy into a totally modern state. They viewed all the institutions of the past with open scorn: they wanted to destroy museums, cathedrals, and even governments that linked present-day Italy to the preindustrial world. Their doctrine called for destroying the past and extolling the new world of machines. Unlike the cubists they loved motion and sought to interpolate it in all their works of art, literary or plastic. A typical futurist poem included the sounds of factories and was printed so that its typography would reflect the multifarious, clamorous world of the twentieth-century city; a typical futurist painting depicted people or machines in motion, often violent motion. The futurists loved violence and war and idealized strength, and they became forerunners of Italian fascism, supporters of Benito Mussolini.

The repercussions of futurism were felt far and wide. While we tend to think that cubism was the more important movement because of the stature of painters like Picasso and Braque, we find that futurism attracted huge numbers of advocates all over Europe, from Russia, where Vladimir Mayakovsky urged Russians to be barbarous Scythians, to England, where Percy Wyndham Lewis published the significantly named review *Blast,* intended to shock England out of aesthetic and political complacency. Europe in the first decade of the new century was in an aesthetic, political, social, and moral crisis, and the futurist fascination with war machines and violence prefigured what was to come.

The futurists' delight in simultaneous phenomena broke open the arts by destroying the barriers between forms of expression. Poetry became a visual as well as an aural art; painting and sculpture were no longer limited to the static. Like so many avant-garde groups of the early twentieth century, they wanted to make art and artists relevant to their society, to eradicate the estrangement between art and society that had appeared among the Romantic poets and that had reappeared with the symbolists. They sought to find a social niche for the artist so that he would no longer be alienated. Unfortunately, they were utopian in that desire and became the tools of politicians rather than their associates.

By 1912 Fernando Pessoa—now twenty-four

years old—had begun to react to the new literary and artistic currents sweeping Europe. While he collaborated in the symbolist magazine *Aguia* (Eagle), edited by republicans in Oporto, he maintained his scornful attitude toward the republic. But his attitude toward literary symbolism had definitely changed: he read and took seriously the German Zionist Max Nordau's *Degeneration* (1892–1893), in which Nordau applied the theory of physical degeneration to western art, literature, and society and concluded that Europe was in a state of decadence and hysteria; because of urbanization, morality and taste were on the wane. This book probably made Pessoa see that symbolism was simply one more style, not an end in itself. However, he did not reject symbolism out of hand, as many avant-garde poets did in Europe and the Americas.

Instead, Pessoa began to write in several styles, revealing to himself the myriad possibilities within his own personality. He also began a long friendship with Mário Sá-Carneiro, a poet who lived in Paris and who shared Pessoa's literary interests. It was as though Pessoa began to take on personalities that would oppose given tendencies in Portuguese society: republicanism was in vogue, so he became a mystical monarchist; elements of sentimental romanticism were present in Portuguese literature, so he became a symbolist; the symbolists were ascendant, so he became a futurist; the futurists were bent on destroying the past, so he became a pagan neoclassicist.

After 1912 Pessoa can be seen to embody what Keats calls "the chameleon poet," an idea Keats defines in a letter to Richard Woodhouse:

> As to the poetical Character itself (I mean that sort of which, if I am anything I am a Member; that sort distinguished from the wordsworthian or egotistical sublime; which is a thing per se and stands alone) it is not itself—it has no self—it is every thing and nothing—It has no character—it enjoys light and shade; it lives in gusto, be it foul or fair, high or low, rich or poor, mean or elevated—It has as much delight in conceiving an Iago as an Imogen. What shocks the virtuous philosopher, delights the camelion Poet. It does no harm from its relish of the dark side of things any more than from its taste for the bright one; because they both end in speculation. A Poet is the most unpoetical of any thing in existence because he has no Identity—he is continually in for—and filling some other Body—The Sun, the Moon, the Sea and Men and Women who are creatures of impulse are poetical and have about them an unchangeable attribute—the poet has none; no identity—he is certainly the most unpoetical of all God's Creatures.
>
> (28 October 1818)

Keats meant that he was able to turn himself into someone or something else. He could transform his ego, the "I" of lyric poetry, into another "I." He could write from disparate points of view. While outwardly similar ideas can be found in Robert Browning, Yeats, the early Pound, and Eliot, these poets remained linked to the dramatic: they projected characters in order to use them as masks, but they did not turn themselves into something different. Walt Whitman, taking the character he invented as a combination of dramatic persona and alternate self, bridged the invention of dramatic characters and the projection of alternate identities. Whitman's character Walt is simultaneously a hero and a bard, a heroic poet-persona who records his own visions of American realities. He is concerned with preserving his present sensations rather than with attempting to make the past live again. He is immersed in the flow of everyday life, in the unfolding of history. It is no wonder that Pessoa could blend the lessons of the futurists and the example of Whitman (whom he had begun to read in this period) and that the result would be a series of poetic personalities.

When World War I began in 1914, Pessoa embarked on the literary project that would make him into an entire poetic generation. The proliferation of personalities actually began in 1912, when it occurred to Pessoa to write some poems in a "pagan mode," in semi-irregular verse. Thus the poet Ricardo Reis was born, although at the time he was only a style and a literary point of view. In fact, two other heteronyms, two other poets, took shape before Ricardo Reis received a name and an identity: Alberto Caeiro and Álvaro de Campos. Alberto Caeiro appeared full-grown on either 8 March or 13 March 1913, as Pessoa himself says:

> I went up to a high commode and, taking a piece of paper, began to write, standing, as I write whenever I can. And I wrote some thirty-odd poems all at once, in a kind of ecstasy the nature of which I will never be able to define. It was the triumphal day of my life and I will never be able to have another like it. I began with a title, *The Keeper of Herds.* And what followed was the appearance of someone in me, to whom I quickly gave the name Alberto Caeiro.
>
> (Seabra, p. 185)

The imaginary correspondents, the Chevalier de Pas and Alexander Search, now move onto a higher plane of being. These playmates become facets of a poetic generation that never existed, alternative possibilities within a single individual. It is fascinating to see how Pessoa visualizes the poets to whom he gives metaphoric birth:

> Álvaro de Campos was born in Tavira, on the fifteenth of October, 1890 (at 1:30 P.M., according to Ferreira Gomes; it's true because I've worked out his horoscope based on that hour and it's accurate). As you know, he is a naval engineer (by way of Glasgow), but now he is here in Lisbon, in retirement. Caeiro was of average height, and even though he was really fragile (he died of tuberculosis), he didn't seem as weak as he was. Ricardo Reis is just slightly shorter, but stronger, and standoffish. Álvaro de Campos is tall (1.75 meters; two centimeters taller than I), thin, and, with a tendency to slump. They are all clean-shaven—Caeiro blond, pale, with blue eyes; Reis dark-skinned; Campos somewhere between fair and dark, a vaguely Portuguese-Jewish type, with straight hair parted on the side, uses a monocle.
>
> Caeiro, as I said, had barely any formal education—he only went to primary school. He was orphaned at an early age, and stayed at home living off some modest rents. He lived with an old aunt, a great-aunt. Ricardo Reis, educated in a Jesuit school is, as I said, a doctor. He has lived in Brazil since 1919: He exiled himself from Portugal because he is a monarchist. He is a Latinist by education and a semi-Hellenist by self-education. Álvaro de Campos had a vulgar secondary-school education; later he was sent to Scotland to study engineering, first mechanical then naval. On vacation once, he went to the Orient: The result was the poem "Opiario." An uncle from Beira, a priest, taught him Latin.
>
> How can I write in the name of these three? . . .
>
> Caeiro, out of pure and unexpected inspiration without knowing or even planning that I would write. Ricardo Reis, after an abstract deliberation that quickly coalesced in an ode. Campos, when I feel a sudden impulse to write and I don't know what about. (My semi-heteronym Bernardo Soares [the name Pessoa used to write *Livro do desassossego*], who by the way resembles Álvaro de Campos in many ways, always appears when I am tired or sleepy, when my ratiocination faculties and my inhibitions are a bit suspended; that prose is a constant fantasy. Soares is a semi-heteronym because while his personality is not mine, it is not different from mine, rather a simple mutilation of mine. Me minus ratiocination and pretense. His prose, except when ratiocination contributes its "tenue," to mine, is the same as what I'm writing here, the same Portuguese.) While Caeiro wrote Portuguese badly, de Campos wrote it reasonably well, but with lapses. . . . Reis writes better Portuguese than I, but with a purism I consider exaggerated.
>
> What's hard for me is to write Reis's prose—as yet unpublished—or de Campos'. Simulation is easier, perhaps because it is more spontaneous, in verse.
>
> (2.13–14)

Pessoa's mind, as we see, was teeming with poetic activity in the World War I era. Curiously, while he published isolated poems and prose pieces in magazines, he published few books: four collections of English poems and *Mensagem.* This also explains why the publication of Pessoa's complete works has been an editorial nightmare: editors have had to gather the works he published in magazines and collate them with the myriad unpublished manuscripts he left at his death. Knowing when a given text was written, by which heteronym, and for what occasion are minor problems; in some cases Pessoa's handwriting is illegible, and in others there are variants that make a "definitive text" an ironic goal.

After 1915 Pessoa went through a long crisis regarding adherence to the doctrines of any school or movement. As in so many other things (his acceptance of symbolism, his acceptance of futurism) he was contradictory in this. The idea of dedicating himself totally to any one style was impossible. The chameleon poet was condemned to a life of metamorphosis. But the metamorphosis caused him to repeat the developmental process of twentieth-century poetry itself: he began in the lyrical, objective style of the late symbolists, moved into the strident iconoclasm of the avant-garde, and then achieved a kind of autonomy in the multifaceted mode of the heteronyms.

This would seem the opportune moment to examine some poems by Pessoa "himself" and the heteronyms, such as the first sonnet in his 1918 collection, *35 Sonnets,* written in English:

I

Whether we write or speak or do but look
We are ever unapparent. What we are
Cannot be transfused into word or book.
Our soul from us is infinitely far.
However much we give our thoughts the will
To be our soul and gesture it abroad,
Our hearts are incommunicable still.
In what we show ourselves we are ignored.
The abyss from soul to soul cannot be bridged
By any skill of thought or trick of seeming.
Unto our very selves we are abridged
When we would utter to our thought our being.
We are our dreams of ourselves, souls by gleams
And each to each other dreams of others' dreams.

(11.156)

The archaism of Pessoa's English is immediately striking. He writes in the style of a Michael Drayton or a John Donne, masking his identity behind it. The method mirrors the message of the poem itself, a meditation on the impassable gulf between the human word (the signifier) and the thing represented by the word (the signified). Because language, Pessoa seems to say, is the vehicle of thought itself, we are alienated from ourselves by the very mechanism through which we attempt to understand ourselves. Communication between individuals is impossible because it is impossible for the individual to communicate with himself. We are locked in Nietzsche's "prison-house of language," and there seems to be no way out. Pessoa abandoned this meditation and took up other themes with his various heteronyms, but this poem summarizes his relationship with himself, his society, and his heteronyms. He was an isolated individual, capable of expression, but incapable or unsure of communication.

Pessoa's first heteronym, Alberto Caeiro, is strikingly different from Pessoa himself. Caeiro is a sensationalist and believes that the individual is nothing more than a perceiving machine, a conduit through which sensory data pass. He disdains metaphysics or any nonempirical way of looking at the world as a mystification, a way of using words to generate false realities that cannot be perceived. In this, Caeiro is very much like the Argentine writer Jorge Luis Borges, who, inspired by David Hume and George Berkeley, espoused very similar theories during the 1920's. Borges sought to reduce the human ego to nothingness and to dismiss memory as a fiction derived from repetition. Here we see Caeiro defining himself and his point of view:

IX

I am a keeper of herds.
The herd is my thoughts
And my thoughts are all sensations.

I think with my eyes and my ears
And with my hands and feet
And with my nose and mouth.
To think a flower is to see it and smell it
And to eat a piece of fruit is to know its meaning.
That's why when on a hot day
I feel sad for having enjoyed it so much,
I stretch out on the grass,
And I close my hot eyes,
I feel my whole body sprawled on reality,
I know the truth and I am happy.

(3.37–38)

This is a poem in which the speaker rejoices in the sensorial flux of the world without care for the future. Caeiro, unlike Christian poets who feel set free when they sense the possibility of salvation, exults in his own mortality. His only world is the here and now; his only reality is the one he perceives. This intimate vision of the self contemplating itself in the act of perception reappears in the following poem:

XX

The Tagus is more beautiful than the river that
  flows through my village.
But the Tagus is not more beautiful than the river
  that flows through my village
Because the Tagus is not the river that flows
  through my village,
The Tagus holds great ships
And still sailing along it,
For those who see in all things what is not there
Is the memory of the galleons

The Tagus flows down from Spain
And the Tagus enters the sea in Portugal.
Everybody knows that.
But few people know which is the river of my village
And where it goes
And where it comes from.
And for that reason, because it belongs to fewer
  people,
The river of my village is freer and greater.

People go down the Tagus to get to the World.
Beyond the Tagus there is America
And the fortune of those that find it.
No one ever thought about what's beyond
The river of my village.

The river of my village doesn't make you think of
  anything.
He who stands on its banks is only standing on its
  banks.

(3.44–45)

There is a mixture of joy and irony in these poems: joy at the mere fact of being alive, and irony concerning the false claims of those imbued with metaphysics. There is also an echo of Verde in this poem, his celebration of country life, here symbolized by the river that flows by Caeiro's village. The village river is superior to the Tagus because fewer people are involved in its perception. The possibility of confusing one's vision or becoming alienated is therefore lessened. To have clarity of vision it is necessary to contemplate in solitude, a solitude much like that of the reader alone with a text. The purpose of this poetry is to provide the reader with a verbal landscape that he may contemplate alone in order to purge his mind of other verbal realities. Similarly, the poet is able to attain something the exercise of his senses does not in itself allow him, an escape from time. He will live as long as readers make his voice come alive. The work of art achieves the immortality the body never possesses.

There is also a hint here of the happiness to be derived from Horace's golden mean. Others may take the high road to adventure or wealth, but for Caeiro true happiness does not come from being a Faustian overreacher. It comes instead from achieving unity with his world through the only possible means for such communication: the senses. And having grasped that he is part of the flux of phenomena, Caeiro longs to be able to accept not being part of it, to accept the inevitability of death. In poem 43 of *O guardador de rebanhos* (The Keeper of Herds, translated as *The Keeper of Sheep*), Caeiro apostrophizes a passing bird, "Pass, bird, pass, and teach me to pass!" (*Obras completas* 3.64).

Álvaro de Campos, the next heteronym, is also a sensationalist, but he does not imitate Alberto Caeiro's almost Buddhist quietude. De

1490

Campos is charged with futurist energy and revels in simultaneity. He also aspires to epic grandiloquence, as we see in these fragments from his long homage to Whitman, "Saudação a Walt Whitman" ("Salute to Walt Whitman"):

Infinite-Portugal, June eleven, nineteen hundred
    fifteen . . .
Yeaaaah!
From here from Portugal, with all epochs in my
    brain,
I salute you, Walt, I salute you, my brother in
    Universe,
I, with my monocle and my exaggeratedly tight coat,
I am not unworthy of you, and you know it, Walt,
I am not unworthy of you, it's enough just to salute
    you not to be . . .
I so close to inertia, so easily full of tedium,
I am one of yours, and you know it, and I understand
    you and love you,
And even though I never met you, having been born
    around the year in which you died,
I know that you loved me too, that you met me, and
    I am happy.
I know that you knew me, that you contemplated me
    and explained me,
I know what I am, be it on the Brooklyn Ferry ten
    years before I was born,
Be it uptown on the Rua do Ouro thinking about all
    that is not the Rua do Ouro.
And just as you felt all, I feel all, and here we
    are hand in hand,
Hand in hand, Walt, hand in hand, dancing the
    universe in our soul.
. . . .
Look at me: You know that I, Álvaro de Campos,
    engineer,
Sensationalist poet,
I am not your disciple, I am not your friend, I am
    not your bard,
You know I am YOU and that makes you happy!
. . . .
Now that I am almost dead I see it all clearly.
Great Liberator, I return submissively to you.
. . . .
Hail and farewell, long live the great bastard of
    Apollo,
Impotent and fiery lover of the nine muses and the
    graces,

Cable car from Olympus to us and from us to
    Olympus.

                    (2.204–214)

The poetic voice of Álvaro de Campos expends its energy in apostrophe, speaking directly to Whitman much in the way the priest speaks directly to God in the mass. Instead of saying "Domine, non sum dignus," de Campos tells Walt explicitly that he (de Campos) is worthy of him. The purpose of apostrophe is as much to call attention to the speaker as it is to invoke the spirit of the deceased Whitman. Images of consubstantiation run through the poem, to the point that de Campos informs Whitman that they are one and the same person. Walt, the heteronym of Mr. Whitman, finds his double in Álvaro de Campos. Fictions imitate fictions. Álvaro de Campos is no more real than Whitman's persona Walt, and each exists only in the subsistent reality of the printed word. The paradox of the sensationalism of Caeiro and de Campos is that its proponents are both imaginary beings.

Less frenetic, imbued with the calm that derives from stoic resignation, the poetry of Ricardo Reis, Pessoa's classicist, monarchist heteronym, is like an oasis of tranquillity compared to that of Álvaro de Campos. Perhaps less attractive to modern taste, especially if we think of the poetic fashions of 1914, the year the following poem was written, Reis's verses nevertheless echo a European classical tradition that was far from dead:

Only this freedom do
The gods allow us: to submit
To their will voluntarily.
And this is only right
Because only in the illusion of freedom
Does freedom exist.

So the gods themselves
On whom weighs eternal fate
Practice to achieve their calm and deep
Ancient belief
That their lives are divine and free.

We, imitating the gods,
As little free as they on Olympus,
Like one who on the beach
Builds castles to fill his eyes,
Let us build our lives
And the gods will know how to thank us
For being so like them.

(4.40–41)

The gods delude themselves into thinking they are free—even though they know they are also bound by the iron laws of fate—and we should imitate them. Self-delusion, the imitation of the gods, will make us all happy; in fact, says Reis, this is the only way to live. Here again we see Pessoa's existentialist dilemma, the one we find in Pessoa's English sonnet, namely, the isolation of the individual soul. Reis acknowledges the abyss, the meaninglessness of life, and advocates self-delusion as a means to survive.

This embracing of fictions is also an apologia for writing because to write is to create an aritificial reality, for both the writer and the reader. Pessoa's contribution to western literature is precisely this: he shows that poetry is a way of experiencing other realities, other identities, and that the imagination, despite human frailty and mortality, knows no limits. This vindication of the human imagination links him strongly to most of the avant-garde movements of the early twentieth century, especially to surrealism, and constitutes a noble defense of human dignity in a century of human degradation and slaughter.

The defense of art as the last bastion of human dignity is also the central theme of Pessoa's greatest prose work, *Livro do desassossego* which he began to write in (approximately) 1914 and continued to compose until his death in 1935. Because Pessoa published so little in the course of his life, it may be argued that this book constitutes the nucleus of all his writing. There can be no doubt that it summarizes his thought on all subjects and reflects the peculiar reality of Pessoa as a writer. That is, Fernando Pessoa was a *writer* but not a *publishing writer.* The distinction is critical. It explains why, on the one hand, we can point to no "major works" by Pessoa (he carefully avoided gathering his works into volumes), and, on the other, why we can see in him the crisis of the writer in our century. He writes, and here we inevitably think of Franz Kafka's "Hunger Artist" or any of Samuel Beckett's crippled narrators, because he cannot refrain from writing, because writing, like breathing, is a way of affirming existence. Publishing is just the opposite of writing: it turns the flow of verbal imagination into the dead letters on the printed page. To write is to live; to publish is to die.

Livro do desassossego is another bibliographic and textual dilemma. It did not appear in Portuguese as a "totality" (the word is inaccurate since the volume is composed of numerous fragments, of which there may, conceivably, be more) until 1982—rather a late date for a masterpiece to be turning up written by a man dead for forty-seven years. Pessoa had published bits of the text in various magazines but had never managed to meld all the pieces into a finished whole. What we have are scattered pieces from different periods compiled and edited by Pessoa's literary editors. The order may not reflect Pessoa's final intentions, if in fact he had any.

We do know that Pessoa wrote the fragments under the "semi-heteronym" Bernardo Soares (a banal, utterly common name, like John Smith) and used them to record his fluctuating states of mind. Superficially, the book chronicles Bernardo Soares' anguish over two decades, but that anguish is most fruitful because Pessoa transforms it into a text that challenges the very frailty and mortality it pretends to chronicle. *Livro do desassossego* is one of the great poetic autobiographies of the twentieth century, not because it is a "soul laid bare," but because it is the act of writing as a challenge to existential collapse. It is a heap of verbal fragments, yet it accomplishes in one volume what

Pessoa sought to do with all his heteronyms, to demonstrate the infinite possibilities latent in the human imagination.

Its point of departure is a revised vision of the prison imagery that has played so central a role in western thought from the time of William Godwin's *Caleb Williams* (1794) until the very recent writings of Alexander Solzhenitsyn: life as imprisonment, the world as a jail. Pessoa's variation on this theme is to unite it with the notion of the world as a stage. That is, he (or his alter ego, Soares) understands the world as a prison without cells, a place where each individual is incarcerated in his epidermis, where profound communication is impossible. In Pessoa's world, human interaction depends on language, but since the linguistic code is collective and not individual, the individual must adapt his personal message to the collective code. In doing so he becomes an actor mouthing a part rather than a person communicating with his fellow man. All communication is deferred, subject to error, and incomplete. We are all actors, all speaking through personae, the masks that both identify us for others and lock us within ourselves.

It is not by chance that we find all these ideas constantly recurring in a book that is simultaneously a mirror and a mask, not the writing of Fernando Pessoa but the jottings of Bernardo Soares, a man who never existed. Fragment 212 contains the complete panorama of Pessoa-Soares:

I have attended, anonymously, the gradual death of my life, the gradual collapse of all I have wanted to be. I can say, with that truth that needs no flowers to make its death known, that there is nothing that I have desired, or of which I have even for a moment dreamed, which has not disintegrated below my window like some dust that looks like solid rock which falls from a vase on a high floor. It seems, even, that Destiny has always sought to make me love or want that which it arranged to show me the next day I never had or would have.

Ironic spectator of myself, I have, nevertheless, never lost my desire to attend life. . . .

I am, to a great extent, the very prose I write. I develop in periods and paragraphs, I punctuate myself, and in the chaotic flow of images, I dress up, like a child, as a king with a newspaper crown or in the way I make a rhythm out of a series of words, I wreath my head, the way crazy people do, with dry flowers that remain alive in my dreams. . . . I have become a character in a book, a read life. What I feel is (without my wanting it to be) felt just so that what has been felt can be written down. Whatever I think turns into words mixed with images that destroy it, opened into rhythms that are something else completely. From rewriting myself so often I have destroyed myself. From thinking myself so much I am by now my thoughts but not myself. . . .

I am a kind of playing card, an ancient and unknown card, the only one left from a lost deck. I have no meaning, I know nothing of my worth, I have nothing to compare myself to to find it, I have nothing to use to find out who I am. And in this way, in the successive images in which I describe myself—not without truth, but with lies—I remain more in the images than in myself, speaking myself until I no longer exist, writing with my soul as ink, a soul useful for nothing else but writing. But the reaction passes and I resign myself again. I regain consciousness of what I am, although that may be nothing. And something like a tear without weeping burns in my immobile eyes, something like an anguish I've never had harshly irritates my dry throat. But, oh, I don't know what I wept for, if indeed I wept, nor why I didn't weep. Fiction accompanies me like my shadow. And what I want is to sleep.

(*Livro do desassossego*, vol. 2, pp. 238–241)

This fragment is dated 9 February 1931. Many of those that follow it are of an earlier date. We read the *Livro do desassossego* in the way we read all great works, first struggling through a consecutive reading, then returning to specific fragments, and then reading in the way the book was composed, pell-mell, with no beginning and no end. We are locked, with Pessoa, in the prison-house of language.

The final twenty years of Pessoa's life were the logical coda to the explosive period between 1913 and 1915 when the heteronyms made their debut. However, it is worth noting how two of his interests acquired greater prominence in this life during these two decades: spiritualism and politics. He was so taken with spiritualism that in 1916 he actually considered setting himself up in Lisbon as a professional astrologer. And even as late as 1930, he was involved in pranks and hijinks with the English magus Aleister Crowley (helping Crowley stage a bogus suicide), although, as with so many things in his life, it is difficult to judge exactly how seriously he took the ideas he expressed with such passion. The spiritualism spilled over into his poetic life in that he cast horoscopes for his heteronyms, thus attributing to them a destiny as real or fictitious as any other.

When Pessoa and his friends launched an avant-garde literary magazine, *Orpheu*, in 1915, they were branded as monarchists and Jews. While Pessoa never defended himself against the latter charge, he certainly made no attempt to mask his monarchist sympathies. He presented his Sebastianist views on many occasions and even defended in print the military dictatorship in Portugal. Whatever Pessoa's reasons may have been for adopting this political stance, they were never of any use to him in forwarding his career or bettering his economic position. He was regarded as a misfit, even failing in 1932 to win a sinecure at the Museu Bibliografico in Cascais as a curator. His failure as ideologue is certainly comparable to Ezra Pound's long flirtation with Musolini, and we must balance, in both cases, the worth of the writings against the folly of the politics.

The only public recognition Fernando Pessoa ever received for his poetry was the Antero de Quental Prize, Category B (it seems Pessoa's book *Mensagem* had too few pages for Category A), which he won in 1934. Increasingly alienated from society, with the bulk of his writing still in manuscript, he died on 30 November 1935 of cirrhosis of the liver brought about by prolonged abuse of alcohol. His last writing? An article protesting the new laws against secret societies, especially the Masons. Yet one more lost cause.

Selected Bibliography

POETRY

English Poems. 3 vols. Lisbon, 1921. Vol. 1: *Antinous.* Vol. 2: *35 Sonnets.* Vol. 3: *Epithalamium.*
Mensagem. Lisbon, 1934.
Obra poética. Rio de Janeiro, 1960.
Obras completas. Colecção "Poesia." 11 vols. Edited by João Gasper Simoes, Luis de Montalvor, et al. Lisbon, 1974–1984.

PROSE

Páginas íntimas e de auto-interpretação. Edited by Georg Rudolf Lind and Jacinto do Prado Coelho. Lisbon, 1966.
Páginas de estética e de teoria e crítica literárias. Edited by Georg Rudolf Lind and Jacinto do Prado Coelho. Lisbon, n.d. (1968).
Textos filosóficos. 2 vols. Edited by Antonio de Pina Coelho. Lisbon, n.d. (1968).
Da república (1910–1935). Edited by Maria Isabel Rocheta, Maria Paula Morão, and Joel Serrão. Lisbon, 1979.
Sobre Portugal: Introducção ao problema nacional. Edited by Maria Isabel Rocheta, Maria Paula Morão, and Joel Serrão. Lisbon, 1979.
Ultimatum e páginas de sociologia política. Edited by Maria Isabel Rocheta, Maria Paula Morão, and Joel Serrão. Lisbon, n.d. (1979).
O banqueiro anarquista. Lisbon, 1981.
Livro do desassossego. 2 vols. Edited by Maria Aliete Galhoz, Teresa Sobral Cunha, and Jacinto do Prado Coelho. Lisbon, 1982.

LETTERS

Cartas de amor. Edited by David Mourão-Ferreira and Maria da Graça Queiroz. Lisbon, 1978. Pessoa's love letters to Ofelia de Queiros.

FERNANDO PESSOA

TRANSLATIONS

Fernando Pessoa: Sixty Portuguese Poems. Edited and translated by F. E. G. Quintanilha. Cardiff, 1971.

The Keeper of Sheep. Translated by Edwin Honig and Susan M. Brown. Riverdale-on-Hudson, N.Y., 1986.

Poems of Fernando Pessoa. Edited and translated by Edwin Honig and Susan M. Brown. New York, 1986. Includes "Salute to Walt Whitman" (extracts).

Selected Poems: Fernando Pessoa. Edited and translated by Peter Rickard. Austin, Tex., 1971.

Selected Poems. Translated by Edwin Honig. Introduction by Octavio Paz (see Paz below). Chicago, 1971.

Selected Poems. Translated by Jonathan Griffin. Harmondsworth, Eng., 1974. 2d ed., 1982.

"Towards Heteronymy." In *The Poet's Work: 29 Masters of 20th Century Poetry on the Origin and Practice of Their Art.* Edited by Reginald Gibbons. Boston, 1979.

BIOGRAPHICAL AND CRITICAL STUDIES

Gaspar Simões, João. *Vida e obra de Fernando Pessoa: História de uma Geração.* 2 vols. Lisbon, 1938.

Güntert, Georges. *Das fremde Ich: Fernando Pessoa.* Berlin, 1971.

Guyer, Leland Robert. *Spatial Imagery of Enclosure in the Poetry of Fernando Pessoa.* Ph. D. diss., University of California, Santa Barbara, 1980.

Jakobson, Roman. *Lingüística e comunicação.* São Paulo, 1969.

———. "Os oxímoros dialéticos de Fernando Pessoa." In his *Lingüística, Poética, Cinema.* São Paulo, 1970.

Monteiro, George, ed. *The Man Who Never Was: Essays on Fernando Pessoa.* Providence, 1982.

Paz, Octavio. "Fernando Pessoa, el desconocido de sí mismo." *Cuadrivio.* Mexico City, 1965. This essay appears as an introduction to Edwin Honig's translation, *Selected Poems,* listed above.

Prado Coelho, Jacinto do. *Diversidade e unidade em Fernando Pessoa.* 4th ed. Lisbon, 1973.

Roberts, William H. "The Figure of King Sebastian in Fernando Pessoa." *Hispanic Review* 34:307–316 (1966).

Seabra, Jose Augusto. *Fernando pessoa ou o poeto-drama.* São Paulo, 1974.

Sena, Jorge de. *O poeta é um fingidor.* Lisbon, 1961.

Severino, Alexandrino. *Fernando Pessoa na Africa do Sul.* São Paulo, 1969.

Silva, Agostinho da. *Um Fernando Pessoa.* Porto Alegre, 1959.

SPECIALIZED JOURNAL

Persona, published by the Centro de Estudos Pessoanos of the Faculdade de Letras at Porto, is a magazine dedicated to the study of Fernando Pessoa.

PORTUGUESE HISTORY

Livermore, Harold Victor. *A New History of Portugal.* 2nd ed. Cambridge, 1976.

ALFRED MAC ADAM

GUNNAR GUNNARSSON

(1889–1975)

UP TO THE beginning of World War II, Copenhagen was the capital city that most attracted young Icelanders who wanted to acquaint themselves with the larger world. Iceland had been a part of Denmark for centuries, and the Icelanders were in many ways culturally dependent on Denmark. Until 1911 Iceland did not have its own university, and Icelanders seeking advanced education normally went to Denmark, although some studied in other countries. In 1918 Iceland won its independence but was joined in personal union with Denmark and then gained independence in 1944. Danish was, and is, the first foreign language of Icelanders, and until the 1940's not a few Icelandic authors wrote in Danish, no doubt, to appeal to a larger audience than they could reach in their homeland.

The most successful of the Icelandic writers who have written in Danish is Gunnar Gunnarsson, who lived in Denmark for over thirty years, returning to Iceland after he had achieved international fame second only to that of his younger countryman, Halldór Laxness. Unlike other renowned authors who have elected to write in second languages, Gunnarsson never ceased using Icelandic entirely. Early poems in Icelandic appeared in 1906, and after his return to Iceland in 1939 he again took up writing in his native language.

The books that are written in Danish do, however, constitute Gunnarsson's major literary contribution, notably the two series of novels *Borgslægtens Historie* (The History of the Family at Borg, 1912–1914) and *Kirken paa Bjerget* (The Church on the Hill, 1923–1928, also known as *Af Uggi Greipssons Optegnelser,* From U. G.'s Notebook), and the historical novel *Jón Arason* (1930). Although Gunnarsson wrote in Danish, the places and people he depicts are Icelandic, so that he can be said to be a major Icelandic writer. Although Gunnarsson and Laxness have different attitudes and points of view, parallels can nevertheless be drawn between the two. Their political and philosophical differences can be explained chiefly by the difference in their ages—some thirteen years—although Laxness is more of a searching soul, whereas Gunnarsson was more historically and retrospectively oriented.

There is little to tell of Gunnar Gunnarsson's life that has not been transmuted into narrative in his semiautobiographical novels. Like the protagonist of "The Church on the Hill," he was born on a farm (at Valpjoófastaður in Iceland on 18 May 1889). Again, as did Uggi, he lost his mother at an early age and cultivated her memory. Similarly, he published his first verse when but seventeen years old and, like all Icelanders, he read assiduously. That he should become a writer was a decision made after he (like Uggi) had spent two terms at a Danish folk high school (Askov)—after which time he held various jobs to keep body and soul together. More than he indicates in the novels, however, he read widely while at Askov and familiarized himself with works by Dickens,

Hall Caine, and other foreign as well as Danish authors, presumably including Thomas Hardy. The parallelism that presents itself between some of his work and that of John Galsworthy is, however, apparently accidental.

When only seventeen years old, Gunnarsson published two volumes of poetry in Icelandic, *Vorljóð* (Spring Poems, 1906) and *Moðurminning* (Remembering Mother, 1906). The early verse is evidence of a strong poetic vein in the young author and of his ability to work within the confines of traditional alliterative Icelandic prosody. The poems are lyrical and sensitive and quite as admirable as the verse of many other, older contemporary Icelandic poets. Here and there we are reminded by metrical similarities of the popular nineteenth-century poet Páll Olafsson (1827–1905), to whom Gunnarsson was related and whose poetry he later edited in 1944.

Despite this promising beginning as an Icelandic poet, once he was in Denmark Gunnarsson turned all his energies to writing in Danish. Trying his hand at Danish poetry, in 1911 he published a thin volume of verse, *Digte* (Poems), but his Danish poetry did not have the appeal or strength of his Icelandic poetry. Here, and in his autobiographical work *Den uerfarne Reisende* (The Inexperienced Traveler, 1927), the frequency with which trees and woods are mentioned is striking; Gunnarsson came from a country that had practically no trees. The discovery of nature in Denmark is the major theme of the Danish poems, although there are others, notably feelings of solitude and longing, memories of childhood, and the emotions of a young man in love. Only the last two poems have Icelandic motifs. One of these was occasioned by Gunnarsson's having watched a ship being loaded that was to sail to Iceland. He asks himself, "Why have I become a stranger at home? and why a stranger here?"—and provides a curious answer that it is because he always was and always remains himself.

A year after the publication of his Danish poems, Gunnarsson issued the first volume of the tetralogy *Borgslægtens Historie*, which immediately marked him as an author to be reckoned with on the Danish literary scene. The fourth and final volume was published only two years later; and a complete edition of the tetralogy appeared in 1915 and went through twelve printings in almost as many years.

For all its success, *Borgslægtens Historie* is not without its weaknesses, especially the first volume, *Ormarr Ørlygsson*, which must be looked on as a kind of novelistic apprenticeship. Gunnarsson's skill in developing a story and in describing people and places markedly improves through successive volumes. While all four novels are sentimental, the story is gripping and grows more convincing as it develops.

Characteristic of all the volumes is Gunnarsson's use of the interior monologue, the detailed presentation of what goes on in the minds of his characters. This is noticeable early in the story, particularly in the case of the merchant Bjarni, whose demise as a businessman is rapid after an ill-advised effort to disregard the most powerful man in the district, Ørlygur, about whom we learn at the start of the narrative that he is always generous to those who are really in need, but also that under no circumstances will he be crossed. When Bjarni foolishly refuses to give precedence in the weighing in of wool to Ørlygur's son, Ormarr, his fate is sealed. Gunnarsson is careful to tell the reader exactly "what passed through the merchant's mind."

The somewhat clumsy beginning provides a background for subsequent action, makes clear Ørlygur's influential position in the district, and suggests the stock from which the title figure springs. A few pages later it becomes apparent that the novel is concerned principally with Ormarr's development. When Ormarr shows musical talent he is sent to Copenhagen, the gateway to a larger world. His artistic quest is astonishingly successful, although ten years of training are passed over with little comment. Gunnarsson's technique here seems to be one of jumping from high point to high point in the narrative, while delaying action through long reflections or descriptions that keep the reader waiting expectantly for the new high point.

Dissatisfied because success comes so easily, Ormarr creates a scandal during his debut by shifting suddenly from Beethoven to the French composer Émile Waldteufel—with the result that his violin teacher collapses and dies on the spot. In another sudden shift Ormarr is overcome by a longing to return to Iceland: he gives up a promising career as a concert violinist only to become an equally successful shipping magnate. With the aid of his father, he gradually takes over a shipping line, but for the second time many years are passed over without explanation. We next find Ormarr as the full-fledged millionaire director of a shipping line who has been decorated by the king of Denmark. Once more he is uncertain when faced with good fortune, and once more he retreats from the scene of his success. He is uncomfortable in the absence of obstacles.

Ormarr, who is hounded by success, is the antithesis of his brother, Ketill, the villain of part 2 of the tetralogy, who, although a clergyman, lacks both his father's and his brother's sense of duty. In the first volume Ketill, who is to marry the wealthy Alma, makes his foster sister, Rúna, pregnant during a visit to Iceland. On his return to Iceland, Ormarr feels obligated to marry Rúna for the sake of both her honor and the honor of the family. The last part of the first volume makes extensive use of the interior monologue so that we have a full realization of the motives that make the characters act as they do. There is a noticeable lack of dialogue through which the same purpose might be achieved dramatically.

In the second volume of the tetralogy, *Den danske Frue paa Hof* (The Danish Mistress of Hof, 1913), Ketill's wife, Alma, is the central character. Changes in attitudes and in the characters of various persons involved are described in detail. Alma is a pure, unsoiled soul misused by an unloving husband; Ketill shows himself to be a clever hypocrite and a master of duplicity. The second volume also devotes considerable space to descriptions of farm life and weather conditions, especially of winter in Iceland. Such descriptions explain some of the international appeal of much writing by Icelanders and especially by Gunnarsson. Iceland is distant enough from the rest of Europe and geographically unusual enough to exercise a certain esoteric attraction on foreign readers, not least on Danish readers who, if only for political reasons, had a vested interest in the distant island in the north Atlantic.

In *Den danske Frue paa Hof* Ketill the schemer wants to obtain his father's farm for himself as had originally been planned, although now the farm is to be given to Ormarr because of Ketill's affair with Rúna—a matter that remains unknown outside the immediate family. Through his sermons, Ketill eventually turns his parishioners against his father, once the most powerful man in the district, and he is gradually abandoned by all those who had previously worked for him and whom he had previously helped. Ormarr returns at the crucial moment, when from the pulpit Ketill has declared his father to be the father of Rúna's child. Shocked, Ørlygur dies, but not before revealing to the congregation that Ketill himself is the guilty party.

Not only does Orlygur die at this juncture but Ketill's wife suddenly loses her reason: Gunnarsson resorts to an overly dramatic plot element for which the reader is scarcely prepared, although he includes occasional omens (a technique reminiscent of Icelandic sagas). The turn of events crushes Ketill, who now seeks the Lord's mercy and forgiveness through a life of penitence, assuming another identity—that of the one-eyed beggar Gæst. The other characters assume Ketill to have drowned himself after his villainy has been revealed. He is not recognized until just before his death, although it has been clear to the reader that Gæst indeed must be Ketill.

The course of events that moves rapidly in the first volume and slows down in the second, goes at a snail's pace in the third, *Gæst den*

Enøjede (*Guest the One-Eyed,* 1913). Here the action takes place some twenty years after Ørlygur's death and Ketill's disappearance. The novel is concerned with the events of only a few days, specifically the last days of Gæst's life. Gæst has spent his later life wandering throughout Iceland and doing good deeds—he has lost an eye rescuing a child from a burning building—and he lives on alms. Hitherto he has never gone back to his native district, but just prior to his death, he returns to Borgarfjorður district and meets young Ørlygur, who is his son by Rúna. The novel ends sentimentally with the touching death of the now self-sacrificing Ketill, while a continuation of the narrative with a new generation is anticipated.

The short final volume of the series, *Den unge Ørn* (The Young Eagle) is a somewhat irrational and psychologically depressing tale of the third-generation Ørlygur of Borg, son of Ketill/Gæst the One-Eyed and namesake of old Ørlygur. Much affected by the death of Ketill and his Danish wife, young Ørlygur wavers between a desire to lead a life that would be a kind of penance and his love for a simple but admirable country lass—a union to which Ketill had given his blessing on his deathbed. Driven by an urge to accomplish the impossible, Ørlygur clambers up a mountain peak that only an eagle is supposed to be able to reach in order to build a (useless) cairn that might be seen from afar, and then to descend, scarcely escaping with his life, but having achieved the peace of mind that would permit him to lead a satisfying and strenuous life with his beloved. A new generation of the family at Borg imbues a mixed heritage of strength and resourcefulness with faith and promise.

The idea of presenting the history of a family in novel form is not unusual, but Gunnarsson's work is very different from the best-known examples of such novels: Thomas Mann's *Buddenbrooks* (1901) and John Galsworthy's *Forsyte Saga* (1906–1922). It is noteworthy that Galsworthy chooses the word "saga" to identify his series of novels about the Forsyte family,

for some of the Icelandic sagas are family sagas and Gunnarsson's "The History of the Family at Borg" may be viewed as an attempt at a modern family saga. We must, however, beware of overstressing the parallels between the Old Icelandic saga—a kind of historical novel—and the twentieth-century sociopsychological novel.

After completing "The History of the Family at Borg" in 1914, Gunnarsson published another novel, *Livets Strand* (The Shore of Life), the next year. On the one hand, the new novel describes in detail the life of an isolated community on the Icelandic coast and provides extensive description of the area and its natural phenomena; on the other, it makes extensive use of the interior monologue rather than stressing outward action. Throughout the book we are aware of the intimate thoughts of the several characters and are thus in a position both to judge them and to predict what their actions must be, although the characters themselves seem to be guided by forces beyond their control. The novel consists of numerous short, interdependent chapters that tend to close with unanswered questions about the fates of certain characters, while the following chapters are concerned with different characters in the community—although to be sure the fates of the many individuals are interconnected. There is no effort made to deal with more than a small part of the Icelandic shore. Even Reykjavik, the capital of Iceland, is distant. Denmark and Danish trade are sensed as a presence in the small community without being introduced into the foreground. While the novel is entitled "The Shore of Life," it might be said to depict but "a shore of life," for it is only life along a certain stretch of the Icelandic shore that is examined. Aside from the fishermen and their families who make up the community, there is a clergyman, Sturla, a physician, Páll, and a merchant, Thorður. In this small, closed society there are two continuing interdependent struggles, one political, the other economic: the clergyman has represented the district in the Icelandic parliament for many years (and shown himself to be one of the more enlightened members of that body); the merchant is overcome by a desire for power and wants to replace the clergyman as the representative in parliament—a position for which he is quite unqualified.

On the whole the narrative is tragic; readers of older novels generally expect difficulties to be overcome, right to triumph, and heroes of a story to achieve their goals, but such expectations are by no means met in *Livets Strand.* Everything goes wrong that can go wrong. The clergyman's early and penetrating faith in the Lord and His goodness seems to be unfounded and his prayers go unanswered. His wife dies in childbirth; his first child drowns together with her playmate, the son of Finnur, who has had to give up his family farm in order to meet his debts to the merchant. The beginnings of a new cooperative movement are destroyed by arson, although this fact is known only to the reader through an interior monologue of the arsonist who not only goes undiscovered but is given recognition for having saved papers from the office of the cooperative. Ultimately, the narrative supports the clergyman's loss of faith in the divine order of the universe and his conclusion that only the greatest arbitrariness rules human affairs.

At the end of the narrative the clergyman provides a metaphorical explanation of the title of the book, having just buried his drowned daughter:

> Life is but a shore upon which we are all washed up and suffer shipwreck—everyone in his own way! Life plays with us like a dangerous wave, smiles to us only to make our fall and despair the greater. We are all but bodies washed ashore . . . bodies on the shore of life.

Several metaphors and motifs repeat themselves, and various motifs and threads from the earlier part of the narrative are developed or explained toward the end. Thus, in the first chapter, Blid, the older daughter of the clergyman, plays with colored stones on the beach as a child; in the last paragraph of the last chapter her father, who has now lost his mind, is likewise sitting on the beach playing with colored stones.

The touching and sentimental end of the story is somewhat reminiscent of "The History of the Family at Borg." That the two novels also share plot devices may be considered a flaw in the construction of the second book if we are already familiar with the tetralogy. In both works the mind of a major character snaps at a critical juncture, and that individual is doomed to a meaningless existence. Similarly, a highly respected character is unjustly suspected of an illicit relationship with a woman for whom he is responsible. The idyllic note struck at the beginning of *Livets Strand,* rather than presaging the conclusion, furnishes a contrast to the long chain of unhappy events that constitute life along a particular stretch of the Icelandic shore.

Varg i veum (Wolf in Sacred Places, 1916) is unlike Gunnarsson's earlier novels. Its title, Icelandic rather than Danish, immediately sets it off from his other works. While a Dane might recognize the older word *varg* (wolf), he would scarcely know that *í véum* means "in a sacred place" or recognize the religious conceit. As in *Livets Strand* we must wait until the very end of the story before an explanation of the title is provided. In the last chapter the protagonist, Ulv—whose name means "wolf"—acquires insight into the nature of his character. When the title is translated, the Danish reader probably senses an echo from Henrik Pontoppidan's famous short story "Ørneflust" ("Flight of the Eagle") about an eagle which, having been brought up in a barnyard, cannot fly free into the heavens that otherwise would have been its destiny.

From the beginning there is a suggestion that life is meaningless. While the main characters, a young man and a young woman, might have created a compatible and happy existence through self-recognition and mutual understanding, they achieve understanding of one another too late to do so. The young man Ulv's life is wasted despite his having been born into a family whose connections can assure him success as a government official or politician. Unlike Gunnarsson's earlier and but one of his later works, *Varg i veum* takes place in Reykjavik and to a large extent revolves about discussions of personalities and party politics in the capital. Ulv is a complex—but in the context of daily experience scarcely credible—character who on the one hand wants to champion Icelandic culture and nationality but on the other is carried away by self-indulgence and a propensity to wrath—he is the center of one scandal after another. Only when he has rejected his disorderly way of life, married his long misunderstood love (the daughter of the minister of justice), and begun a new career as a fisherman, is a resolution apparently imminent. But on his first fishing voyage, Ulv meets his death at sea. Immediately before drowning he feels a sense of victory over himself. The direction and intent of the narrative seem at first unclear, but the final message must be interpreted as nihilistic. While many a tragic note is struck in Gunnarsson's earlier novels set in rural and coastal areas, there is always present a sense of some substance to human existence. Society in the Icelandic capital, however, is shown to be both highly politicized and degenerate.

In retrospect the first part of the novel *Drengen* (The Boy, 1917) seems to be a preliminary sketch for the later autobiographical volume, *Skibe paa Himlen* (*Ships in the Sky*, 1925), since in both Gunnarsson describes childhood experiences as seen through the eyes of a child and relates the superstitions of an old woman who works for the child's parents. But the development of the narrative is at variance with that of the later novel. The title "The Boy" is apt, for the central character never really grows up. His deportment is naive and his relation to nature innocent and childlike. The external chronology is difficult to ascertain. As in Gunnarsson's first novel, there are jumps in time, at first merely between the ages of eight and ten, but later between the ages of ten or twelve and eighteen, when the boy acquires erotic aware-ness and when people begin to look down on him because he lacks ambition and owns nothing, although he enjoys peace of mind and is happy. The narrative is developed primarily in the form of interior monologues, so that we are never at a loss to know what the boy, Skuli, is thinking.

Skuli has a poetic nature. He senses the sound of a silver string, as it were, resounding within him, and he composes—or seems to hear—poetry at various crucial moments, including the moment of death. Without seeking it, he goes willingly to his death on an ice floe, an event that tends to round out the narrative, since we are told at the beginning that a river near his home had spared the child's life. That the ocean now takes his life is something to which he can acquiesce fully.

The novel can scarcely be viewed as realistic, for Gunnar Gunnarsson treats the boy's experiences as removed from the ordinary course of a human life, the several stages of a normal existence. The main character is spared the cares, responsibilities, and worries that ordinarily beset every member of society. He makes no effort to create a place for himself in society, nor is he a God-seeker. While the landscape is Icelandic, Skuli is sufficiently removed from the problems of everyday life to make the place of action inconsequential.

One of the most popular of Gunnarsson's works is *Edbrødrene* (*The Sworn Brothers*, 1918), a historical novel that incorporates many characteristics of the adventure story. Its multinational appeal probably derives more from its historical elements (life in Norway in the ninth century and the settlement of Iceland in its last quarter) than from the many narrow escapes and colorful adventures of the two sworn brothers Leif and Ingolf. The novel was translated into Swedish the year after its publication and two years later the English translation came out in London, to be followed by an issue in New York in 1921. A Dutch translation also appeared in 1921 and a Finnish in 1925. The German translation did not appear until 1933, but was reprinted several times, including a special edition intended for German soldiers in 1943. The Czech translation appeared in 1946. A note to the eighth edition of the Danish original (1932) states that *The Sworn Brothers* is to be considered the first in a series of historical novels of which the novel *Jón Arason* (which appeared in 1930) is the seventh volume. The plan was not, however, carried out. There is a substantial difference between the products of the years 1918 and 1930. *The Sworn Brothers,* despite its intention to depict life authentically in the Viking age and give insight into the pagan customs of the time, is more imaginative and lighter reading than *Jón Arason,* which is in part a documentary history of the last Catholic bishop of Iceland, who lived in the sixteenth century.

The two sworn brothers are radically contrasting characters. Leif has the more independent mind and is the more daring of the two, while Ingolf champions older values and is considerably less choleric than his foster brother. At the start of the story, young Leif, aged twelve, makes fun of the pagan gods in whom Ingolf believes. Leif also meets up briefly with a Christian hermit and is momentarily both puzzled by and attracted to the tenets of Christianity. Although the language at the beginning of the novel is something of a literary pastiche based on the old sagas, the descriptions of nature and expository accounts of religious activities connected with pagan belief and usage are not amenable to this style and it soon loses the quality of a pastiche. Gunnarsson takes considerable pains to describe the active life of the Vikings and draws on both historical and archaeological evidence to support his narrative. Concentrating on the lives of only a few Norwegians of the mid- and late-ninth century, he interweaves in his fictive narrative some of the extant factual evidence about the earliest history of Iceland: its discovery, rediscovery, and settlement. And the situations and motivations he develops are entirely plausible.

Because of the psychological differences between the two sworn brothers, there is an un-dercurrent of tension that serves to generate action and pathos, ensuring a series of crises and dramatic incidents. Leif is really the *primus motor* of the story, and when he meets death through the sword that he has stolen from a Christian hermit (and thus fulfills the hermit's prophecy that he who lives by the sword will die by the sword), the novel reaches its conclusion.

Different in substance and construction, as well as in language, is the next novel, *Salige er de Enfoldige* (*Seven Days' Darkness,* literally Blessed Are the Pure of Heart, 1920). It shows the interplay of multiple psychic tensions during an influenza epidemic in the Icelandic capital—the so-called Spanish influenza—in 1917. Just as the title contains a biblical allusion, so too the structure of the novel has a biblical association, for it is divided into the activities of seven days. The narrative opens with the tragic conclusion to six days of mounting pressures against the leading character, a physician named Grim Ellidagrim, who loses his mind at the beginning of the seventh day. He is indeed pure of heart, but he is overcome by the forces of injustice, hatred, and evil that are embodied in another physician, Páll Einarsson, with whom he is forced to work during the critical week of the epidemic. The narrator of the tale, which is told in the first person, is Jón Oddsson, an admirer and co-worker of Grim.

The account of the first two days is devoted to lengthy descriptions of accidental or planned meetings involving several characters and to protracted and repetitious conversations about personal relationships—conversations that seem at first to lead nowhere. Intertwined with the small talk about personal matters is a discussion about spiritualism, to which occasional reference is made in the course of the week's events. Not until the third day are we aware of what Jón Oddsson calls the hidden forces that seem to concentrate on Grim and his wife, Vigdís, in order to destroy them. During the third and later days there are many references to quickly shifting emotions, changing facial expressions, feelings of weakness and hopelessness, fears and premonitions. Curiously enough, there is on the whole relatively little treatment of the epidemic itself; the novel concentrates more on arguments about abstractions and on the relations among the main characters in the story.

A discussion about *Weltanschauung* between Grim and his antagonist, Páll, leads to mention of the "pure of heart" and the provocative declaration by Páll, "Blessed are the pure in heart." Grim experiences sudden changes of mood in a series of moving and emotional scenes that relate to death, love, marriage, friendship, and his calling as a physician, while he continues to do his utmost to help others who are suffering and dying from the epidemic disease. The precipitating cause of his psychic demise is trivial: when he returns home at night he finds Páll in the same room with his wife. It is as if Grim's gradual mental breakdown has been carefully prepared and cultivated by Páll, although the motivation for such deliberate wickedness is not apparent. The novel ends with a moral reflection by the author's persona, who declares that the only divine force is composed of goodness and love, and that the conclusion to be drawn from what has happened is simply that human beings must be charitable to one another.

The novel's outward action is severely limited. What is important are the emotional tensions and crises experienced by several characters and notably by the physician, Grim. While the narrative, particularly from the third day on, holds our attention, the continuous concern with emotional problems makes it somewhat wearing and identification with the characters can be difficult. As a psychological portrayal, it is one-sided and not commensurate with the psychological finesse of various other writers of the twentieth century. The reader does not have the sensation that Gunnarsson himself could have been a party to the experiences and emotional distress that pervade the novel. Nevertheless, it was a commercial success, and in the 1920's and 1930's it

was translated into Czech, Dutch, English, Estonian, Finnish, German, Hungarian, Polish, and Swedish; so we must conclude that it had an appeal associated with life in those decades.

During the early years in Denmark, while Gunnarsson was attempting to establish himself as a writer and while he was working on his first major novel, he also wrote many short stories. The first collection of the stories was not published, however, until after "The History of the Family at Borg" had appeared between 1912 and 1915.

Most of the short stories contained in the two volumes *Smaa Historier* (Short Stories, 1916) and *Smaa Historier, Ny Samling* (Short Stories, New Collection, 1918), give the impression of having been written with a light hand for publication in newspapers, to no small degree as pot boilers. Many are humorous, all are sentimental, but a few strike a more serious note. Recurrent is the motif of impending death—most strikingly exemplified in "Sandheden" (Truth), which consists of an old man's monologue before a judge justifying the murder of a child for unclear motives of revenge. Grotesque is the tale of an Icelandic-American in "Den sidste Rus" (The Final Ecstasy) who dreams of experiencing death as a thrill: he tempts fate by walking at night by the harbor only to be stabbed from behind and to die without a sound—that is, without having experienced a thrill. The most amusing of the stories, "Da Lykken gik J. J. Snóksdal forbi" ("Fortune Passes By," literally When Good Fortune Passed J. J. Snóksdal By) is from the second collection. In this anecdotal tale a young man is shown to lack faith in his own good fortune: when given the opportunity to borrow a large sum of money from a wealthy investor, he lets the opportunity slip away from him by fearing to ask first for a thousand crowns, then for five hundred crowns, and finally asking for a mere fifty crowns, which the investor simply pulls out of his wallet and gives to him.

The themes of several of the other stories are unoriginal, although they are well enough put together to be momentarily engaging. A note of sentimentality runs through all these stories, some of which employ the overworked topos of a heart-rending situation on Christmas Eve.

The stories making up the later collections *Ringen* (The Ring, 1921) and *Den glade Gaard og andre Historier* (The Happy Farm and Other Stories, 1923) likewise have no claim to the status of great literature, but they are entertaining and represent the better kind of sketch or short story that is still published in leading Copenhagen newspapers. "The Ring" is a miscellany of seven stories without unity that differ in both content and length. Two of the stories are about individuals who can be called originals and are amusing. Two others take place in medieval Norway and give insight into the class differences of the period. The short tale "Trællen" (The Thrall) is a shockingly tragic story of the noble-born thrall, or slave, who is attracted to his queen and meets his death proudly as a result of his infatuation. Another story, "Kongesøn" (A King's Son), which is long enough to have been published separately in both Dutch and German translations, relates the birth and childhood of the young king Haakon Haakonsson of Norway—a subject that has attracted varied imaginative treatment, notably by Henrik Ibsen in his play *The Pretenders* (1864). Gunnarsson attempts a pastiche of Old Norse saga style through recurrent use of the very brief answers in dialogue. While this technique is not without effect, it verges on affectation. Several stories deal with eccentrics, while others are entirely descriptive and tend to create a mood. With few exceptions—notably "Regnbuen" (The Rainbow)—the location of the stories and sketches is Iceland.

In the second later collection, one sketch stands out: "Den gyldne Nu" (The Golden Present). By chance, a traveler finds himself at a farm where his grandfather's brother had visited some fifty years earlier. The idyllic simplicity of life on this isolated farm extends to a realization of the artificiality of telling the time. Here only the present is of importance, and the measure of time is left to a sundial. The farm has not kept up with the times but is the embodiment of a happy and philosophically sound existence. Helpfulness and kindness are exhibited by the farmer-host who as a matter of course does what he can to help his guest. The latter finds that his horses have been taken care of and his saddle repaired before he rises the next morning. For the visitor the location of the farm becomes a magic valley where "undisturbed [one] can still enjoy life's greatest gift: the golden present."

Another collection of short stories, *En Dag tilovers og andre Historier* (An Extra Day and Other Stories), was issued in 1929 between the concluding volume of the autobiographical series "The Church on the Hill" and the historical novel *Jón Arason*. It is a grab bag of sketches and stories partly humorous and partly sentimental; only the first and the last are of particular note. The first, the title story, is an adjunct to an important aspect of the autobiographical hero's life in the fourth volume of "The Church on the Hill." In this anecdotal tale related in the first person, the Uggi Greipsson/ Gunnar Gunnarsson character, under a different name, meets his former fiancée, "Annemarie" of *Den uerfarne Reisende*, twenty years after they have parted. The last story, "I Staalgusen ved Stiklastad" (A Fog of Steel at Stiklastad), is a pastiche that draws on the story of Thormod the Skald in the saga of Ólaf Haraldsson from Snorri Sturluson's poetic chronicle, *Heimskringla*. In several of his sketches Gunnarsson shows himself to be more humorous than in his novels, but they generally lack the real substance that would recommend them to an international audience today.

Viewed from the standpoint of the literary historian, Gunnarsson's attempts to gain a foothold in the theater are evidence that he is not a compelling dramatist. His first two plays, issued in 1917 under the title *Smaa Skuespil* (Short Plays) are slight, melodramatic, and sentimental. The first, *Brødrene* (The Brothers), depicts the love-hate relationship of two brothers, an editor and a university professor. The second, *Ramt* (Struck), concerns a clergyman who after five years of happy married life suddenly discovers that he is suffering from leprosy. He becomes a skeptic and threatens God: if the clergyman ever meets Him, God will have to justify this blow.

The play that follows, *Dyret med Glorien* (The Animal with a Halo, 1922), is quite different, being written in verse with a strong tendency to alliteration in imitation of Old Norse poetry. The plot is diffuse, and the significance of the title is not apparent until the very end, when even here the statement by the doctor in the play about the "halo of insanity, our pact with God" is a metaphor capable of more than a single interpretation. The characters are complexly interrelated, and suggest various tensions within the society they represent. The son of the man and wife, who speak harshly to one another and early in the play are shown arguing about him, meets his death by a drowning that is not accidental. At one point the boy is identified by Halli, a skald, or Old Norse poet, as "the son of God." The language of the dialogue is highly sophisticated and employs a large vocabulary coupled with syntactical acrobatics that make it difficult to follow. There are lengthy monologues as the action develops, and there is a strong suggestion of Old Norse verse. At the beginning of the play, an analogue with Henrik Ibsen's *Brand* in the speech of a clergyman is implied, but its overall tenor nevertheless suggests expressionistic drama of the early twentieth century. The dramatist's intent is not so much to depict realistic action but rather to engage the imagination of the reader or the viewer without any clearly definable didactic purpose.

With the publication of *Leg med Straa* (Playing with Straw, 1923), which was to become the first novel in the "The Church on the Hill" series, Gunnarsson showed that he had achieved a higher level of artistic accomplishment. The five volumes constituting the series are unmistakably autobiographical in nature. The author describes events from his childhood—and in such detail that one feels the narrative cannot have been evoked entirely from memory but must have been re-created on the basis of his adult observation of children and their activities. Gunnarsson follows the behavior of a child and that of other persons as seen through his eyes with such veracity and sensitivity that we nod in recognition of scenes and experiences that are common denominators of early youth. The novel has no single strand of development beyond that of the central character. Gunnarsson is never in a rush to get on with his narrative, allowing himself the leisurely use of much detail, and because of the charming simplicity and mimetic quality of the account, the reader never tires. The narrative is convincingly true to life in developing a casual sequence of happenings that are not methodically linked. The many threads of childhood are woven into an overall pattern, but there is no obtrusive woof or warp. All the incidents seem credible and realistic. While the story is basically supranational, the details of daily existence and of the landscape are unmistakably Icelandic. Non-Icelandic as well as Icelandic readers can easily identify with the little boy who, "now grown, is the narrator." Incorporated into the novel is considerable description of life in Iceland around 1890, so that for all its psychological substance it can also serve as a cultural document—just as an outright autobiography by the author might have done.

Many incidents attest keenness of observation on the part of Gunnarsson—for example, the lengthy imaginary ride on horseback when Uggi, the little boy, seats himself on a visitor's saddle after it has been removed from the horse; or the imaginary farms that the children create by using stones to outline property and buildings. The importance of poetry and the printed word for the Icelanders has not been forgotten: Uggi's uncle writes poetry on the occasion of Uggi's first birthday, for example. Uggi learns to read by carrying around a copy of an old newspaper that he deciphers by asking people first about single letters and then about words. Nor is the role of superstition in daily life overlooked. Old Begga, a hired woman on the farm, is an unending source of superstition and weird tales with which she entertains the little boy when she is in the mood to do so. Time and again there are references and allusions to Old Icelandic literature. Old Begga tels Uggi that he is a direct descendant of the great tenth-century Icelandic poet Egill Skallagrimsson and has some undefinable relationship to the "rabble at Borg." The allusion is, amusingly enough, to some of the prominent figures in the admirable classical literature preserved in Old Icelandic. We are provided with a series of pictures of days, situations, and happenings that, taken together and modulated by the child's relations to a large number of individuals, convincingly sum up the experiences of early childhood.

The second volume in the series, *Skibe paa Himlen* (*Ships in the Sky*) (which gives the title to the combined translation of the first two volumes in English), takes the story of Uggi through his sixth year, to the death of his mother in childbirth. Although the years covered in these first two volumes are few, there is the sense of an evolving technique at work in the narration. Age differences in the child are noticeable as are the differences in the child's perceptions and reactions. Even the vocabulary is progressively enlarged. There are in particular many proverbial phrases that the boy notices, some of which he understands and others of which he misinterprets or simply fails to comprehend.

Here again there is no conventional line of narration, but rather a sequence of events and impressions drawn from Uggi's life. The particular charm of the story lies in the interpretation of many statements by adults or the statements by adults as transmitted by other children—words that are either incomprehensible to Uggi or that are mysterious. To Uggi, as to all children, much that happens seems to have no explanation and therefore evokes absurd theories that can only be supported by the child's faulty logic.

Each of the many persons who has an impact on Uggi is clearly delineated. The various characters' idiosyncrasies are not simply a matter of invention on Gunnarsson's part but are generated by combined reflection and observation. To be sure, the author must have been gifted with a remarkable memory, but he was capable of an unusual and possibly unique penetration of the psyche of the child and the way in which the child reacts to the people and situations that confront him. Everything seems true to life and, as in the preceding volume, can be labeled naturalistic. One should bear in mind the novel is very nearly an autobiographical document.

While the setting is late-nineteenth-century Iceland and the social conditions are those with which most readers outside of Iceland are not familiar, the narrative contains so much that is common to all human experience that the non-Icelandic reader of today is able to find in Uggi's childhood reflections of his own, whether at sixty, forty, or only ten years' remove. In this, Gunnarsson's novel is unmistakably a classic.

Family scenes that suggest domestic tension are especially poignant. There are enough indications for the reader to understand what goes over Uggi's head, and he is able to envisage a much larger, more synthetic picture than the child, for whom many images and experiences are kaleidoscopic. The attention span of the child is naturally limited, with the consequence that many themes that are introduced are intentionally not developed. Gunnarsson simply moves in a new direction as a result of a shift in the outward scene or a sudden recollection by the child, or by the intrusion of an adult into his semi-mythical world. This extends to sad and even tragic events, the impact of which is not fully grasped by Uggi, although they cause him temporary anguish.

The title *Ships in the Sky* refers to the child's belief that if he watches the sky intently enough he will see ships pass by—but the ships usually pass at the very moment his glance is elsewhere. *Playing with Straw*, the title of the preceding volume, is as literally down-to-earth and matter-of-fact as *Ships in the Sky* is mythical and imaginary. Thus the two novels represent two stages in the child's development and the psychological transition is made from the tangible world to the world of the imagination, or at least the amalgam of the actual with the imagined.

Continuing the development of the boy Uggi chronologically, the lengthy third volume of the series, *Natten og Drømmen* (*The Night and the Dream,* 1926) begins on his eighth birthday which, like many other days, brings reminiscences of his deceased mother. "Everything was now much changed from what it had been before; the days, the people, the animals, I myself, all the things in the world and even God in heaven." Life has assumed a different cast now that he can no longer turn to his mother for whom the new housekeeper, Soffia, is no adequate substitute—although on this very birthday she is to marry his father and become the children's stepmother. Uggi attempts to explain events much in terms of the supernatural and of rewards and punishments meted out by God. He shares an attitude of piety with most of the other characters of the novel. Their belief is not merely superficial; it permeates their concept of the world and informs their decision-making. The careless and thoughtless world of early childhood is past, and the realities of everyday life, coupled with the inscrutability of God's will, are ever in Uggi's consciousness. His mother's death and the painful experiences he has had subsequently have had a deleterious effect on his faith, so he feels that he no longer loves God with a full and confident heart. His relationship to the divine he now identifies as turbid and sinister.

Now that Uggi is older, adults tend to speak to him in their own language but in a manner that he sometimes fails to grasp. For example, when Soffia explains to him that she and his father are to marry he understands the words but does not understand how they hang together or the implications of her rambling dialogue. He is a child, but he no longer lives merely for the moment without an awareness of what has happened in the past or without some trepidation regarding future events and God's will. The many situations and the flow of joy and sorrow, disappointments and successes, that characterize every childhood are woven into a fluid narrative that seems to constitute a whole rather than a random sequence of events and impressions. Uggi's shifting attitude toward the nature about him and his increased use of imagery and metaphors when he describes what he sees and feels reveal Gunnarsson's consummate skill. Writing in the first person, he gives the impression that what he describes belongs to the present and is not being brought to light out of the past by an older man remembering his childhood. The slight changes in the function of language suggest Uggi's growing older and give new insights into contemporary Icelandic culture.

Uggi is eager to attend school, in particular to acquire foreign languages. When he does attend his first school in a neighboring trading center, he is impressed by another boy who can speak Danish because his mother is a Dane and whose home is furnished in Danish rather than Icelandic style. Little by little poetry is brought into the realm of the everyday, most frequently in the form of songs. Uggi reads everything he can lay his hands on—prose and poetry—and even undertakes to teach himself some Danish by reading a Danish book with the aid of a dictionary. Although it cannot have been so to Uggi, the reader finds it amusing that this book is a textbook on astronomy. For all his childish emotions and his desire to demonstrate his virility when performing tasks on the home farm, it is apparent that he is intellectually a cut above most of his playmates and that he is a prospective candidate for higher education. He is nevertheless frustrated in his efforts to pursue a course of study. There are brief patches of schooling, but the economic needs of the family prevent him from following the requisite academic path that would lead to the Latin school in Reykjavik.

Whereas in the first two volumes time moves

very slowly, *The Night and the Dream* covers a considerable span of years without, however, accounting for them all. At one place a hiatus is indicated by the phrase "the years passed." Uggi has slipped into early manhood, and his way of thinking has become correspondingly more mature. He falls in love and writes poetry. The chosen, a girl on a neighboring farm, politely but firmly declines his attentions. Many of his emotions are translated into verse, and just as Gunnarsson did at seventeen, young Uggi sends a poetry manuscript to a printer in Akureyri. After some months he is taken aback to receive a package that contains many copies of a pamphlet containing his verses. After some hesitation, he distributes the pamphlets to everyone on the farm, without, however, receiving any acknowledgment or comment. He is aware of the debt he owes to other writers whose works have fallen into his hands, particularly to the nineteenth-century poet of the Jutland heath, Steen Steensen Blicher, and, in Danish translation, to Maxim Gorky.

Whereas in the earlier volumes the dominant note has been one of a joyous and carefree life, as the narrative progresses the practical problems of daily life and a sequence of unhappy events strike a darker chord. Life is more soberly viewed as the young man grows aware of its complexities and the burdens of responsibility.

The description of a shipwreck and its aftermath, especially of the flotsam that the farmers, hard hit by a long and severe winter, are able to recover from the shore, suggests an actual event that made a lasting impression on the author when young.

On the night of the dream of the title, Uggi walks along a well-trod path beside which he sees a row of books—book upon book, large and small, thick and thin. He stops, and a fearful joy makes his heart beat faster: "I knew at once that I had written all these books. I also knew that it was a dream, and I thought to myself, you must read the titles and try to remember them when you wake." In great haste he opens book after book, reads and reads so

that he can remember the contents, but when he awakes he can remember neither titles nor a single line from a single book. He asks himself, "How can you manage to write all those books?" By 1926, when *The Night and the Dream* appeared, Gunnarsson's dream had already become a reality.

Possibly to emphasize that Uggi has grown into manhood, Gunnarsson incorporates into the narrative certain incidents of a somewhat melodramatic nature, including getting lost in a snowstorm. Two brief infatuations with neighboring young women are standard fare for a young man growing up, and lead nowhere. Although Uggi's ambition is to become a writer, he feels he cannot reveal his intentions to anyone. It is no longer a matter of waiting for ships in the sky. "All my life I had, so to speak, slept and dreamed. Now it was time to awaken, time to get to work." Like the young men in the Icelandic sagas, he must leave his small island to see the world, to acquire knowledge, experience, and understanding. When he reads an article in an Icelandic periodical about Danish folk high schools, he makes a crucial decision to go to Denmark. Danish is the one foreign language he knows and in which he should be able to make rapid progress. In the so-called folk high school—a kind of one-year liberal arts college—he will be able to choose his subjects. Financial help from his family and from friends and neighbors makes it possible for him to attend the winter semester of a folk high school in Denmark. These details are presented in such a matter-of-fact, realistic manner that they clearly derive from the author's experience; in point of fact, Gunnarsson went to Denmark under identical circumstances in order to attend the best known of the Danish folk high schools at Askov.

The fourth and fifth volumes of "The Church on the Hill" have not been translated into English. The reason is apparent. These volumes, thinly disguised autobiographical accounts of Gunnarsson's early years in Denmark, have left the charm and appeal of insight into the mind of the child and the adolescent behind, while at the same time replacing the exotic quality of an Icelandic setting with familiar western European surroundings. Volume four, *Den uerfarne Reisende* (1927), begins where volume three leaves off, on shipboard between Iceland and Denmark. A new approach is evident from the first page. The naiveté of the early narrative is replaced by a mature and more sophisticated imagery that, not without considerable originality, conveys scenes familiar to many non-Icelandic and notably Danish readers. But because Gunnarsson is an Icelander, his descriptions of the Norwegian coast and especially of its many trees, and later of the flat and fruitful island of Zealand, are full of wonder and admiration; most readers will be astonished to find an appreciation of such a commonplace phenomenon as trees, about which Gunnarsson writes: "One doesn't understand a tree until one knows it during all seasons of the year and in all kinds of weather. On the whole trees are difficult; one can get to know a tree at night and by sensing its contour discover that one has never seen it before." The sight of trees in Norway in September moved him to say: "I was so glad and happy that it hurt. I had not known this aspect of the loveliness of the earth, of the power of creation." The coast of the island of Zealand is found to be enchanting: "Is there anything more gentle, more intangible, more impossible to describe?" Gunnarsson even mentions falling in love with Denmark, at least temporarily—a kind of early infatuation.

While the sea journey had been moderately rough, its significance is inward and psychological, not external. The transition from provincial Reykjavik to the sophisticated capital of Copenhagen—one of the cathedrals of mankind, to use Gunnarsson's metaphor—is not seamless. Uggi is immediately struck by the interplay between the water of the sound and the many towers of the Danish capital, which give it, in his words, its singing profile.

The folk high school Uggi attends is named Kolind in the novel, but the description of the school corresponds precisely to Askov in central Jutland. Having arrived before the beginning of the term, Uggi spends a month working on a farm, a situation that permits him to fall in love and thus to interweave in the narrative a love story that is carried through until the end of the volume. He is skeptical of both the religious cast and the patriotic coloring of the school's program—aspects of the folk high school that are recognizable three quarters of a century later. But he does not underestimate the possibilities that the school holds for him, and he is intent on his studies and his books.

By now it is apparent that Gunnarsson is no longer writing autobiographical fiction but rather thinly veiled autobiography in which only names and place-names have been altered. The protagonist begins to judge people whom he meets without establishing their characters in some definitive fashion as had been the case in the earlier volumes. His likes and dislikes are subject to change as in real life. He is more mature in his actions, but he makes numerous errors in judgment. Since Gunnarsson's book is so demonstrably autobiographical, the reader is not surprised to find the author writing in a confessional mood from time to time. He indicates occasions on which he has been silent when he should have spoken and on which he has spoken when he should have been silent; he fails to appreciate the good intentions of people he has met along the way; he lets pride and ambition spoil his relationship with the fiancée he has left in the countryside when he goes to Aarhus—Denmark's second-largest city—in order to seek his fortune as a writer.

Prior to going to Aarhus he has worked for a time as a common laborer and worked in a cooperative store. The account of his activities and thoughts at this time supply a kind of documentary record in contrast to the interpretive re-creation of his childhood in the first three volumes of the series. Despite some minor difficulties he admits having had with the Danish language, he shows himself to be a born writer, so that the reader can now identify with the adult author.

Uggi's stay in Aarhus is the nadir of his existence; it brings him closer to utter despair and finds him contemplating suicide. An analogy may be drawn with Knut Hamsun's novel *Sult* (*Hunger*, 1899): Like Hamsun's autobiographical protagonist, Uggi is a penniless writer in a large city who is unable to pay his rent, who grows weak from hunger, and whose salvation lies only in the occasional fee he is able to earn through his pen. He has even been forced to divest himself of some of his beloved books and, as he says earlier in the story, he really lives only in "invented worlds." At the end of the volume there are signs that he will be able to subsist on his writing, but there is a cruel bitterness that has affected his relationship with his fiancée: when she comes to Aarhus and locates him, he is unable to explain himself or even to accept the blame for the deterioration of their relationship, and the couple part in silence.

Hugleik den Haardtsejlende (Hugleik the Fearless Seafarer, 1928), the final volume of the series "The Church on the Hill," chronicles Gunnarsson's first years in Copenhagen—in particular his financial difficulties and his slow acceptance as a writer. The title of the volume is a name that the narrator used for himself as a child; it is almost the only link that connects the last with the first volume of the series. Having left the "withered leaves of hope" behind him Aarhus, he is thrown into a whirlpool of unrelated experiences in the Danish capital. What hitherto has been an example of the novel of development (*Entwicklungsroman*) becomes an autobiographical document recording the trivia of daily life in Copenhagen's proletarian cafés and garrets, to a large extent in the company of other Icelanders. The attractive unity of Icelandic cultural life recedes, but there is no corresponding replacement by Danish cultural life. The protagonist meets a large number of people by chance; they are briefly described without their playing any role in the development of the narrative or having any demonstrable impact on Uggi.

Uggi grows more sophisticated in his literary taste. He reads contemporary literature, including the criticism of Georg Brandes, and goes to hear the Danish novelist and elocutionist Herman Bang, an interjection of literary actuality into purported fiction. He meets and has long discussions with persons, chiefly men, of various philosophical and political persuasions. One of his friends is a theosophist and a follower of Rudolf Steiner; another is a socialist. Uggi is himself not attracted to any particular political doctrine. As far as religion is concerned, he declares himself a materialist. It is unexpected therefore, that he falls in love with a Roman Catholic Danish girl, whom he marries toward the conclusion of the narrative.

Most important to his development as a writer is the early vision of Iceland that is to provide the background of his novels:

> As I lay there that evening and could not sleep, a new and unexpected Iceland burst into my consciousness. Landscapes, people, seasons, and a certain cosmic quality, a tone in the light, a taste of the earth, the rhythm of life, the peculiar expanse of my insular years . . . I now saw my task and perceived a nucleus within my vain childish dreams, behind all my youthful fumbling.

Will he, he asks himself, ever be able to realize these visions from within him without their splintering into a thousand pieces?

The novel is overburdened with descriptions of Uggi's pecuniary difficulties and everyday experiences that, as often as not, are indicative of his poor judgment. When at last a novel is accepted by Denmark's leading publisher and many months of frustration and hunger are past, Uggi has time to dream—to "sail with the ships in the sky." "Now things begin gradually to mature within him and to bloom at the proper time." While he and his bride are visiting Iceland, a telegram arrives with news that his novel is a great success. The young couple subsequently move to a pleasant suburb of

Copenhagen, where their first child is born. These events take place about the time that World War I begins.

Having related a story close to his own world, Gunnarsson was now released to be more inventive and objective. Thus the next novel, *Svartfugl* (*The Black Cliffs*, literally The Black Bird), from 1929, has nothing in common with earlier work. It is a murder mystery set in the beginning of the nineteenth century in rural Iceland and consists chiefly of extensive legal hearings that end with the confession and conviction of the guilty parties. The narrative is written by the chaplain in whose parish the crimes have been committed; he is moved to put pen to paper to relate the long and tragic tale the very day he loses his own son by drowning, in November 1817. This frame seems arbitrary, having no direct bearing on the events or persons whose misdeeds give rise to the legal case, although formal ecclesiastical functions provide occasions when there is direct contact between the chaplain and the murderer, Bjarni Bjarnason. The title refers to a black bird viewed as an omen of death, and is twice mentioned. Because Gunnarsson maintains a high level of suspense in his story—despite the lengthy hearings—and because the place of action—rural Iceland—is unusual, the book attracted many readers. Besides going through several editions in Danish, it has been translated into Dutch, English, Estonian, French, German, Italian, Polish, and Swedish.

Continuing his efforts to re-create the Icelandic past in a series of imaginative historical works and also to imbue Old Icelandic literature with new life, Gunnarsson wrote one play and four novels in the 1930's that make free use of historical evidence as well as persons and situations from the saga literature.

Rævepelsene (The Sly Foxes, literally Fox Skins, 1930) is a comedy based on the Icelandic Bandamanna saga. Although this saga contains a great deal of dialogue, the finesse

and subtely of the story are in part lost in Gunnarsson's dramatic version. The action drags at the beginning of the play; the author demonstrates once more that his forte is not the stage.

In contrast, one has but to read the first few pages of *Jón Arason* to realize that it is a narrative masterpiece in striking contrast to the novel that immediately preceded it, *The Black Cliffs,* and to many of the short stories that Gunnarsson produced from economic necessity around this time. Although the established church of Iceland is Lutheran, Jón Arason, the country's last Catholic bishop, is, curiously enough, a national hero even today. From the very start, Gunnarsson makes it apparent that Arason was an honorable, gifted, and able man of great energies, strong in his faith and ever intent on performing God's will and helping other human beings spiritually and materially.

The novel begins with a familiar medieval topos: dreams by Jón's mother when she is pregnant with him, especially a dream about an eagle losing its head that is a premonition of Jón's fate. From childhood onward, he is an individual of great promise, eager to learn and desirous of serving the Lord. At the age of fourteen, when he commends himself to the Lord, it is clear that the path he is to follow is ecclesiastical. It is an act of love and charity that Jón, as soon as he has been consecrated a priest, marries a young woman met by chance who has been abandoned after having been made pregnant by another priest (marriage in the priesthood was still allowed by the church in Iceland of the sixteenth century). Later in the novel, the sons of Jón play an important role, as they did historically. Because Jón had a large family it is possible today for many Icelanders to claim him as a direct forebear.

To begin with, Jón is a lucky man. He succeeds in everything he undertakes and is looked on by everyone as a leader. In whatever he does, he feels that he is following God's will. His abilities are recognized early by his ecclesiastical superiors, and he advances quickly within the church, despite some minor opposition to his appointment as bishop of Hólar. But a third of the way through the novel the reader is forewarned that difficulties will ensue in the wake of Martin Luther's new ideas, although more immediate political unrest and personal animosity engender the conflict that is ultimately to be Bishop Arason's bane. Jón himself reads premonitions of misfortunes to come in his mother's dreams, in the sand in the hourglass (often an ominous symbol) that is his prized heirloom, and in the restlessness of his blood.

Some two-thirds of the novel chronicles the rise of Jón Arason and his children. The last third documents ecclesiastical politics in Iceland coupled with the new royal regime in Denmark that exploited Luther's reformation in order to enrich itself at the expense of the church.

As the storm clouds gather after the accession of King Christian III of Denmark and Norway, considerably more pathos enters the narrative. Descriptions and dialogues based part on fact and part on plausible hypothesis convey the conflict between crown and cross and the internal dissension that is to rend Iceland's tiny population—divided from the beginning between the two bishops of Hólar and Skálholt, for reasons of ecclesiastical administration and because of the vast size of the country and the difficulties of rapid communication and travel. This mere physical division would exacerbate the tension between conflicting confessional persuasions.

Jón Arason bases the defense of his authority on the intricacies of the Icelandic law code. While he remains true to God and king, he refuses to buckle under to his enemies, who are likely to use force and break the peace, partly because of their misinterpretation of royal decrees that emanate from the Lutheranism that the Danish church now embraced and partly because they no longer fear interdicts of the Roman church that Jón represents. Jón and his sons lose a legal suit when his antagonists disregard Icelandic legal tradition and fail to keep their word. When Jón and his followers are made captive while he is saying Mass in the cathedral at Skálholt, his fate is sealed. He has remained such a popular figure that he is felt by the king's representative to be a danger to those Icelanders who have worked themselves into positions of power. The clash has resulted from the collision of two nominally valid but contradictory legal positions both based on the same source: the Danish crown. Jón represents the older order that has sworn to uphold an ecclesiastical system that has been—arbitrarily and extralegally—superseded, while his antagonists accept the new order of a national church that can be used to their personal advantage—although it means a flaunting of earlier oaths and the established law of the country. Since Jón was ordained, even his enemies could not deny him the right to say Mass. The only certain way of preventing Jón's party from fomenting a reaction to his mistreatment is to take his life. A long series of unsubstantiated charges are leveled against him, and a judgment for capital punishment is given in an outrageous abuse of the judicial system. On 7 November 1550, Jón Arason and two of his sons were beheaded. Although he has lost his life and the Roman church its authority, Jón's good name is not besmirched. When, the next spring, the corpses of Jón and his sons are dug up by men from the Hólar district, the bells of each church that the cortege passes are rung in honor of a martyred hero who exemplifies strong Christian faith and national pride.

Gunnarsson draws on all available historical evidence, which is fleshed out through lengthy dialogues that may reasonably approximate what happened in Jón Arason's last days and last hours. Nevertheless the reader may become impatient toward the end of the narrative, since its conclusion is foregone and the lack of historicity to the closing dialogue is apparent. One note that might be overlooked by non-Icelandic readers is the political position Jón Arason takes—an attitude that doubtless represents Gunnarsson's as well—that Iceland even in the late Middle Ages and early modern times was a sovereign state ruled by the king of Denmark, not a mere appendage to Denmark. A

GUNNAR GUNNARSSON

major flaw in Jón Arason's tactics was his belief that the Danish crown would respect the jurisdiction of Icelandic law and govern within its restrictions and limitations. In point of fact, this position is more representative of late-nineteenth and early-twentieth-century opinion, prior to the legal independence granted Iceland in 1918, than of any widespread conviction of earlier centuries.

Moving backward in time, Gunnarsson's novel *Jord* (Earth, 1933), is a broad canvas depicting in great detail the life of the early settlers of Iceland, starting with the founder of Reykjavik, Ingólfur Arnarson, at the end of the ninth century. The narrative deals with the life histories of three generations: Ingólfur, his son Thorsteinn, and his grandson Thorkell Moon. While in many ways Gunnarsson's descriptions of events are highly speculative, he nevertheless takes pains to exploit the historical evidence as preserved in the Icelandic documents *Landnámabók* and *Íslendingabók*—the Book of Early Settlements and the Book of the Icelanders, respectively. Sympathetically and understandingly, he endeavors to penetrate the metaphysical world of the pagan religion that predominated in Iceland until the year 1000. The reader is impressed with the apparent reality of the heathen mythology, which contains many elements that can be viewed as a primitive understanding of natural phenomena as well as certain parallels with Christian belief. The novel is based on extensive ethnographic study and historical reflection and is in its way an attempt to fill a lacuna in early Icelandic history. The conclusion provides a bridge to Gunnarsson's next novel, *Hvide-Krist* (White Christ, 1934), for Ingólfur Arnarson's great-grandson marries a young Christian woman and we learn that during the life of the great-grandson, himself a local chieftain, Christianity is officially adopted in Iceland.

Jord is one of several novels that Gunnarsson meant to subsume under the general title of "Landnám," that is, the "taking of land" or the early history of Iceland. A note at the end states that it is meant as one of a projected series of twelve novels about the history of Iceland, of which *The Sworn Brothers* is to be looked on as volume 1, *Jord* as volume 2, and *Jón Arason* as Volume 7. As elsewhere in his historical imaginative writing, Gunnarsson's language in *Jord* is partly a pastiche based on the Old Icelandic sagas. At times it seems stilted and willfully archaic, but at other times Gunnarsson uses the modern technique of the interior monologue, unknown to classical Old Icelandic literature.

Hvide-Krist deals with the introduction of Christianity into Iceland around the year 1000. The basic historical facts about this period are to be found in the same sources Gunnarsson drew on for *Jord,* but he attempts to animate history by interrelating actual events with the lives and fates of individuals. Moreover, he uses an oral style of narration that is suggested by the Icelandic saga. Most of the novel consists of lengthy oral messages between a son, Svertingur Runolfsson, and his father, Runolfur Ulfsson. The length and detail of these oral reports strain credulity even more than comparable matter from the Old Icelandic sagas. What we know from historical sources to have been a great change—the acceptance of Christianity under pressure from King Olaf Tryggvason of Norway—is made the more dramatic and immediate by showing how individual lives are affected by the struggle between paganism and Christianity, and by the ominous power of the Norwegian king in the background, even though Iceland at the time was an independent country not politically subject to Norway. Gunnarsson cleverly interweaves into the narrative an element not mentioned in the historical sources: the economic importance to Iceland of commerce with Norway. To be sure, the nominal Christianization of Norway adopted by the Althing (the Icelandic parliament of the thirty-nine rulers of the several districts in Iceland and their followers) in the year 1000 was an effort to avoid severe damage to the Icelandic legal tradition and possibly even civil war, but

1514

Gunnarsson shows the additional, tacit motivation of economic forces. While this may seem to be a superimposition of modern thought on the past, the possibility can scarcely be denied.

There is but a suggestion of the Icelandic style in this novel. It is not a pastiche and therefore does not seem distanced from reality. Gunnarsson has had to deal once more with the intricacies of Icelandic law, a necessity that doubtless discouraged him from attempting to emulate the oral saga style otherwise.

Continuing the series of novels dealing with the early history of Iceland, Gunnarsson next wrote *Graamand* (Gray Man, 1936), a highly inventive literary renewal of the short saga of Thorgil and Haflithi that is a part of the collection from the thirteenth century entitled *Sturlunga Saga*. While the nucleus of the story is taken from the saga, Gunnarsson does not follow the sequence of events, the method of narration, or the style of the older work. Nor does he indicate that the story is set in the early twelfth century. The reader gathers the impression at the beginning of the book that the six-year-old beggar lad Olaf Hildisson will be the central character because he is at the center of the action. But as in the Icelandic saga many fates are intertwined, and Olaf meets a violent death long before the struggle between two Icelandic chieftains comes to a close. As in the saga, there are so many characters that the reader occasionally has difficulty remembering their intricate relationships. But the modern story is told with considerably more pathos than the original and is much longer. Details, motivations, and dialogue lacking in the original are additionally supplied. The novel was very well received in the Danish press, but an awareness of its origin seemed to be lacking on the part of contemporary critics.

Whereas Gunnarsson had hitherto produced realistic or historical narratives, the novel *Vikivaki* (a folk dance, subtitled "Jake Sonarson's Posthumous Papers") from the year 1932—it was written between two of the historical novels—is a long ghost story. The device of a story within a story serves to protect the author from charges of exaggerated fantasy. The beginning and the end as well as two intervals in the telling are supplied by the nominal editor of the posthumous papers, a close friend of the deceased.

According to the papers, the widower Jake Sonarson is visited on New Year's Eve by a dozen of the dead after Jake has unwittingly set the table in his modern farm house for a festive evening. One of the ghastly visitors is a head and another is a body without a head. They come from various eras of the past. The head, it turns out, belongs to Grettir, the hero of *Grettirs Saga*. At first the ghosts think they have entered paradise and look on Jake as God the Father but subsequently and for many months Jake and his guests merely live an agreeable if grotesque existence on the farm, cut off from the world except by radio and telephone. But eventually disagreement and dissension arise and Jake ages rapidly. Salvation would seem to lie in being able to climb a golden ladder to heaven; but when Jake cannot produce enough gold, he builds a wooden stairway that can be gilded, which indeed suffices to allow the ghosts to ascend. Soon after, Jake's corpse is found on the ground beside the wooden staircase he has constructed.

The weakness of the novel lies in its length. What might have been a clever short story in the hands of another writer, perhaps Karen Blixen, takes 300 pages to tell. The title refers to an Icelandic dance with complicated movements. The dance is accompanied by poetry of which there are many lengthy examples. The head of Grettir speaks in alliterative verse that is a pastiche of much skaldic verse in the Old Icelandic sagas. Curiously enough, there is also an awareness of modern English literature, for both Mark Twain and Joseph Conrad are mentioned in the course of the narrative.

Gunnarsson's next novel, *De Blindes Hus* (The House of the Blind, 1933), is a strangely empty tale with some parallels to *Vikivaki* since events are self-contained and divorced from daily life. Much dialogue and reflection by the blind men, Sigurbjörn and Hjört, fill the narrative, but there is little outward action. The story, without real substance, is presumably meant to suggest the uneventful life of the blind through trivial events that assume exaggerated importance, an intention implied by the excessive use of italics. The novella—and it is no more than that judged from standpoint of length as well as content—can only be looked on as an experiment that was not very successful.

Gunnarsson's single most successful work is the novella *Advent*, published in Copenhagen in 1937. *Advent* is the sentimental tale of Benedikt, who makes a pilgrimage of sorts into the mountains on the first Advent Sunday of every year in order to locate straggling sheep overlooked when the flocks have been gathered and driven home in the autumn. The novella describes Benedikt's twenty-seventh venture of this kind; he is accompanied by his dog, Leo, and by a bellwether. Only by heroic effort do they survive a severe snow storm that lasts many days and causes them to spend Christmas Eve in an underground shelter buried by snow. Despite the storm, Benedikt's efforts meet with success: he locates a number of lost sheep before he returns to society as a sort of mythical figure.

After returning to Iceland, Gunnarsson wrote his first novel in Icelandic, *Heiðaharmur* (Sorrow on the Heath, 1940), and then rewrote it for publication in Danish as *Brandur paa Bjarg* (Brandur on the Bjarg Farm, 1942). While Brandur and his daughter, Bjargföst, are central figures, the work can be described as a collective novel in that it gives a picture of the times before 1900 in rural Iceland. Gunnarsson's long, slow-moving narrative is in substance reminiscent of Laxness' novel *Sjálfstætt folk* (Independent People, 1934–1935). The association is not accidental, for Gunnarsson had translated Laxness' other best-known novel, *Salka Valka,* into Danish in 1934. The atmosphere of *Brandur paa Bjarg* is set

in the first sentence: "Bjargföst was born in a time of need and of death." Various kinds of catastrophes plague the Icelanders, and especially those farmers who are living inland in the district Gunnarsson describes. Integral to the story are the natural misfortunes—bad weather and subsequent crop failure coupled with inadequate fish catches—that befell Iceland at the end of the nineteenth century and the concomitant "America fever," the drive that sent many Icelanders to seek their fortunes in the New World. Brandur upholds traditional values and opposes the rush to emigrate. He is ever ready to help distant neighbors less fortunate than he, but most of the odds are against him, as they are likewise against continuing the farming activity that has characterized the district for several hundred years. Many of the activities that constitute communal life are described, including various social gatherings. It is not a little surprising to find one of the characters, a physician, himself a native Icelander (but who has had his training in Denmark) reflecting at one of these gatherings that "in everything that may be called culture and civilization, these people were far behind."

The mood that permeates the narrative can be sensed from the beginning paragraph of chapter 6:

> A farm out in the country, indeed but a small hut among the mountains, lives its own life and has its own fate, a life and a fate that only to a limited degree is dependent on the individuals who come and go in the houses. Who comes and who goes—or dies—there has no particular influence on the existence of the land. The currents of life that are in motion there day and night are altered only immaterially when individuals are exchanged one for the other or someone dies.

As in any farming community, the weather and its influence are especially important. Weather conditions and the landscape are described metaphorically and in detail in a vocabulary that seems larger than in Gunnarsson's earlier books. This aspect of *Brandur paa Bjarg* is even more pronounced in the sequel to the novel,

Sálumessa (Requiem, 1952), and in its Danish version, *Sjælemesse* (1953), about which a Danish critic stated that the language was "un-Danish." The sequel has the daughter, Bjargföst, as a central character. It is also a picture of the times, in this case the early years of the twentieth century. We sense that the advent of modern technology is inescapable and will ultimately alter the lives of even those Icelanders far removed from its port of entry, Reykjavik.

In Gunnarsson's final bit of imaginative narrative, in the Danish version of *Brimheiði* (Surf Heath, 1954), entitled *Sonate ved Havet* (Sonata by the Sea, 1955) the idiosyncrasy of language is more pronounced. An analogy can be drawn with the earlier *Advent,* for the central character, Sesar, is, like Benedikt, a kind of mythical character, a man who is devoted to good works—although Sesar meets a tragic end. There is, however, no comparison between the accessibility of the two novellas. *Advent* is a simply told tale with a clear line of development, whereas Gunnarsson's last work is demanding if not tortuous reading, without plot or traditional chronological progression.

In retrospect one may again contrast Gunnarsson with his younger countryman Laxness, for they are the two modern Icelandic writers who have unquestioned international stature and have been translated most widely. Whereas Laxness, who writes in his native Icelandic, is oriented to the world at large, Gunnarsson is oriented to Scandinavia. Both writers nevertheless depict their homeland—Laxness critically and progressively, Gunnarsson affectionately and conservatively. Both transcend the limitations of national boundaries and overcome the strictures of writing in lesser-known languages. That both writers are Icelandic has presumably enhanced them with an esoteric quality that has attracted translators in many parts of the world. On the Scandinavian literary scene they complement one another, as is emphasized by the fact that Gunnarsson translated some of Laxness into Danish, and Laxness some of Gunnarsson into Icelandic.

Gunnarsson was neither a chauvinistic nor xenophobic nationalist; he was rather a proponent of Scandinavian cultural and political unity. In practice he was a mediator between Iceland and Denmark. In theory he championed the pan-Scandinavian ideal, as is evident in the collection of speeches entitled *Det nordiske Rige* (The Nordic Realm, 1927). Between February 1925 and the summer of 1927 Gunnarsson made several addresses, chiefly to Scandinavian students, exhorting them to work for a pan-Scandinavian union. When one compares the local concern of Gunnarsson's imaginative writing with the vehemence of his concern for the Scandinavian idea, one is surprised by the apparent discrepancy. His novels and short stories draw on Icelandic material and are without intimation of the pan-Scandinavian spirit that informs his speeches. He advocated not merely cultural unity but united political action of a kind that would clearly delimit Scandinavia vis-à-vis the rest of the world. As he asserted in an address to the student union in Copenhagen on February 1927,

> The Nordic spirit spreads out far. And just as it is the tautness of a bow that determines the force of the arrow, it is the complex nature of the Nordic spirit within the whole that reveals its wealth and strength. Hans Christian Andersen, Strindberg, Ibsen, Runeberg, Snorre—if only to choose one name from each country—they are the North, the Nordic spirit, complex but nevertheless one.

In this same speech he urges the Danes to become more oriented toward the other Scandinavian countries and less toward foreign neighbors: "Denmark has become England's vassal; we live by the grace of England and will in the future more and more develop into a kind of Gibraltar here at the entrance of the Baltic." One notes unexpectedly a slight anti-English bias (that may not have served Gunnarsson well in the next decade).

Gunnarsson agitated for a stepped-up exchange of Scandinavian youth in the several

Nordic nations and urged Scandinavian students to travel in the other Scandinavian countries. In a speech given to students on a journey to the North Cape in the summer of 1927, he spoke up with vigor for a Scandinavian peoples' state, what one supposes to be a republic rather than a federated kingdom. He had already warned students that they were being governed by maiden aunts of both sexes who imparted to them narrow ethical and national points of view. He nevertheless believed that the Scandinavians were possibly the only true democrats in the world and concluded in favor of a union of independent republics, a peoples' state: "A peoples' Nordic state, that is our goal, it should be every Scandinavian's goal; it should at least be the goal of all Scandinavian youth" (*Det nordiske Rige*, p. 106). "One people—one people: that is what we are" (p. 11) is the leitmotiv of his first address on 14 February 1925, also to the student union in Copenhagen. He realized that his point of view would be characterized as utopian, but noted also that we are surrounded by utopian ideas and direction since become reality. He felt driven to speak since, he says, one assumes responsibility by not speaking as well as by speaking. Unwittingly, Gunnarsson here expressed views about "the Nordic" that would later tend to ingratiate him with German National Socialism and its admiration for the Nordic ideal—and possibly account for the great popularity that several of his books enjoyed in Germany, not only before but also during World War II, although there is no trace of a National Socialist point of view in any of his works.

While some of Gunnarsson's works—novels or short stories—have appeared in twenty-six languages in addition to Danish and Icelandic, he is only moderately well known and somewhat arbitrarily represented in English translation: a one-volume abridgment of "The History of the Family at Borg;" three-fifths of the autobiographical work "The Church on the Hill"; the three novels *The Sworn Brothers, The Black Cliffs,* and *Seven Days' Darkness;* the novella *Advent;* and a scattering of short stories printed in various periodicals. To be sure, there is enough in English so that one can pass a fair judgment on Gunnarsson as a narrator, a keen observer of people and places, a master of the description of nature, and the creator of distinctive characters; but his penetrating understanding of Icelandic rural life, his aptitude for reworking historical material, and his culturally determined patriotism are inadequately represented.

Selected Bibliography

POETRY

Móðurminning. (Remembering Mother.) Akureyri, 1906.
Vorljóð. (Spring Poems.) Akureyri, 1906.
Digte. (Poems.) Copenhagen, 1911.

NOVELS

Ormarr Ørlyggson. Af Borgslægtens Historie. (The History of the Family at Borg.) Vol. I. Copenhagen, 1912.
Den danske Frue paa Hof. Af Borgslægtens Historie. (The Danish Mistress at Hof.) Vol. II. Copenhagen, 1913.
Gæst den enøjede. Af Borgslægtens Historie. (*Guest the One-Eyed.*) Vol. III. Copenhagen, 1913.
Den unge Ørn. Af Borgslægtens Historie. (The Young Eagle.) Vol. IV. Copenhagen, 1914.
Livets Strand. (The Shore of Life.) Copenhagen, 1915.
Varg i Veum. (The Wolf in Sacred Places.) Copenhagen, 1916.
Drengen. (The Boy.) Copenhagen, 1917.
Edbrødre. (*The Sworn Brothers.*) Copenhagen, 1918.
Salige er de Enfoldige. (*Seven Days' Darkness.*) Copenhagen, 1920.
Leg med Straa. Af Uggi Greipssons Optegnelser. (*Playing with Straw: Compiled from Uggi Greipsson's Notes.*) Vol. I. Copenhagen, 1923.
Skibe paa Himlen. Af Uggi Greipssons Optegnelser. (*Ships in the Sky.*) Vol. II. Copenhagen, 1925.
Natten og Drømmen. Af Uggi Greipssons Op-

tegnelser. (*The Night and the Dream.*) Vol. III. Copenhagen, 1926.

Den uerfarne Reisende. Af Uggi Greipssons Optegnelser. (The Inexperienced Traveler.) Vol. IV. Copenhagen, 1927.

Hugleik den Haardtsejlende. Af Uggi Greipssons Optegnelser. (Hugleik the Fearless Seafarer.) Vol. V. Copenhagen, 1928.

Svartfugl. (*The Black Cliffs.*) Copenhagen, 1929.

Jón Arason. Copenhagen. 1930.

Vikivaki. Jake Sonarsons efterladte Papirer. (Folk Dance.) Copenhagen, 1932.

De Blindes Hus. (The House of the Blind.) Copenhagen, 1933.

Jord. (Earth.) Copenhagen, 1933.

Hvide-Krist. (White Christ.) Copenhagen, 1934.

Graamand. (Gray Man.) Copenhagen, 1936.

Advent. Copenhagen, 1937.

Heiðaharmur. (Sorrow on the Heath.) Reykjavik, 1940. Danish version: *Brandur paa Bjarg.* (Brandur of the Bjarg Farm.) Copenhagen, 1942.

Sálumessa. (Requiem.) Reykjavik, 1952. Danish version: *Sjælemesse.* (Requiem.) Copenhagen, 1953.

Brimheiði. (Surf Heath.) Reykjavik, 1954. Danish version: *Sonate ved Havet.* (Sonata by the Sea.) Copenhagen, 1955.

SHORT STORIES

Smaa Historier. (Short Stories.) Copenhagen, 1916.

Smaa Historier, Ny Samling. (Short Stories, New Collection.) Copenhagen, 1918.

Ringen. Syv Historier. (The Ring. Seven Stories.) Copenhagen, 1921.

Den glade Gaard og andre Historier. (The Happy Farm and Other Stories.) Copenhagen, 1923.

En Dag tilovers og andre Historier. (An Extra Day and Other Stories.) Copenhagen, 1929.

Verdens Glæder. En Tylvt Historier. (Wordly Pleasures. A Dozen Stories.) Copenhagen, 1931.

Trylle og andet Smaakram. (Trylle and Other Small Fry.) Copenhagen, 1939.

PLAYS

Smaa Skuespil. (Short Dramas.) Copenhagen, 1917.

Dyret med Glorien. (The Animal with a Halo.) Copenhagen, 1922.

Rævepelsene eller Ærlighed varer Længst. (The Sly Foxes or Honesty Lasts Longest.) Copenhagen, 1930.

ESSAYS AND ADDRESSES

Det nordiske Rige. (The Nordic Realm.) Copenhagen, 1927.

Sagaøen. (The Saga Island.) Copenhagen, 1935.

TRANSLATIONS

Advent. Translated by Kenneth C. Kaufman. London, 1939. (Republished as *The Good Shepherd.* New York and Indianapolis, Toronto, 1940.)

The Black Cliffs: Svartfugl. Translated by Cecil Wood. Madison, Wisc., 1967.

"Fortune Passes By." Translated by W. W. Worster. *American-Scandinavian Review* 12:475–483 (1924).

Guest the One-Eyed. Translated by W. W. Worster. (Abridged translation of *Borgslægtens Historie.*) New York, 1922.

The Night and the Dream. Translated by Evelyn Ramsden. New York, Toronto, and London, 1938.

Seven Days' Darkness. Translated by Roberts Tapley. New York, 1930; London, 1931.

Ships in the Sky: Compiled from Uggi Greipsson's Notes. Translated by Evelyn Ramsden. (Translation of *Leg med Straa* and *Skibe paa Himlen.*) New York, London, and Toronto, 1938.

The Sworn Brothers: A Tale of the Early Days of Iceland. Translated by C. Field and W. Emmé. London, 1920; New York, 1921.

CRITICAL STUDIES

Arvidsson, Stellan. *Gunnar Gunnarsson islanningen.* Stockholm, 1960.

Elfelt, Kjeld. *Gunnar Gunnarsson. Et Essay.* Copenhagen, 1927.

Gelsted, Otto. *Gunnar Gunnarsson.* Copenhagen, 1926.

Höskuldsson, Sveinn Skorri. "Gunnar Gunnarsons förste år i Danmark." *Gardar* 8: 5–28, 1977.

P. M. MITCHELL

ANNA AKHMATOVA

(1889–1966)

PART OF THE remarkable generation of major Russian poets who came to maturity in the decades before World War I, Anna Akhmatova is one of the most arresting. Her time is now recognized as a great age of Russian poetry, although for its poets it was a fearsome one. Among poets of the first rank, Akhmatova alone managed somehow to live though the era of great trial and to make a quiet end at the last, free from persecution and honored in her own land. In the 1920's Alexander Blok died in despair, suffering from illness and accesses of madness; shortly after, Akhmatova's first husband, Nikolai Gumilyov, was executed by the state as a counterrevolutionary; the "peasant-poet" Sergey Yesenin died by his own hand, as did the leading futurist Vladimir Mayakovsky in 1930. One of Akhmatova's closest friends and also one of Russia's greatest poets, Osip Mandelshtam, was arrested and died in a prison camp in 1938; Marina Tsvetaeva, another major poet of the era, hanged herself in 1941. In his declining years Boris Pasternak was bitterly reviled in the Soviet Union and was very close to being expelled from it; he died in 1960, tormented by the danger under which his loved ones lived for his sake.

Akhmatova was convinced that she had managed to survive the years of being hounded and threatened simply through the capriciousness of fate. But as the last relatively peaceful decades of her life drew to a close and more

and more of her recent poetry once again became available to the public, gradually it became clear that Akhmatova was not only the last remaining poet of that extraordinary time but also one of its finest. The unpretentious, intimate love lyrics on which her first reputation was built had given way to themes of great breadth and high seriousness. To the perfected "Akhmatova style" of the early period, she added extraordinary experiments in the long narrative form. Among them are *Rekviem,* written in the late 1930's, an epic cry for the people of Russia in the grip of the Stalinist terror, and *Poema bez geroia* (*Poem Without a Hero,* 1940–1962), Akhmatova's masterwork. It is a kind of parable with commentary on art and the age—a recollection, a philosophical reflection, and a calling to account.

With these works, as well as shorter pieces and fragments that found their way into print posthumously, Akhmatova's position became not just that of another writer who was rehabilitated after Stalin's death, but that of chronicler and spokeswoman for her era, the very symbol of uncompromising artistic integrity in the face of repression and literary regimentation.

For more than thirty years, between 1922 and 1956, Akhmatova's poetry was denied publication in the Soviet Union; by the mid 1950's most people there and abroad were not aware that she was still living. She was thought to have been swept away in one of the cataclysms

1521

that had followed one upon the other since the revolution. But as her name slowly came into prominence again, it was broadly associated with great personal dignity and moral rectitude, and her work became the ultimate justification for the long decades of official persecution.

Anna Andreevna Gorenko was born on 23 June 1889 near Odessa. Akhmatova was a family name, her grandmother's, and like many Russian names, it is of Tartar origin. It prompted Tsvetaeva to write in 1916: "That name is an immense sigh / And it falls into a depth which is nameless." Tsvetaeva probably had in mind the predominantly sad tenor of Akhmatova's love poems, but the Tatar sound of Akhmatova's pseudonym also evokes a host of other associations in the context of her poetry: something of Russia's early history, something of Old Russia, medieval Muscovy, the old patriarchal way of life.

Soon after her birth Akhmatova's family resettled near St. Petersburg at Tsarskoe Selo, which had its own rich associations with Russian history and culture. Here was the Summer Palace, the Versailles of Catherine the Great, with its immense park, memorials of national victories, as well as memories of Alexander Pushkin, who had spent his school years at the lycée there. Pushkin and poetry, along with the cultural history of Russia, became Akhmatova's two major motifs besides the dominant love theme in the carefully circumscribed themes of the early works.

Akhmatova spent her young years at Tsarskoe Selo "in the patterned stillness, in the cool nursery of the young century." She was educated mostly there, although she later did advanced literary studies in St. Petersburg. While still a schoolgirl, she met and formed a close attachment to the fledgling poet Gumilyov. Both young people came under the influence of Gumilyov's erudite mentor, the accomplished poet Innokentii Annenskii. Later the young couple became part of the intellectual excitement in the bohemian-artistic circles of Peters-

burg before the wars. They traveled twice to Paris around this time; the first trip was their wedding trip in 1910, and in 1911 they went there again. It was a time of great creative ferment in both capitals, and one of rapid intellectual cross-fertilization. Paris had just "discovered" Russian literature through the essays of Melchior de Vogüé, and Sergei Diaghilev's Ballets Russes had just burst upon western Europe.

When they returned to St. Petersburg, the two aspiring poets formed a nucleus of a group of more or less like-minded writers who enjoyed being together for nights on the town, but who also thought and talked seriously about poetry. Whatever their differences, they agreed on one point: that the reigning poetic "school," Russian symbolism, had had its day. They felt that its metaphysical yearnings for "other worlds" had led too far away from the real world, that the symbolists had lost the possibilities of the real world's richness for poetry. The group first identified itself as the Poet's Guild, the name stressing the craft of poetry rather than inspiration or mystical revelation; later the name accepted and still applied to the movement was acmeism. Gumilyov and the theoreticians claimed that his not very descriptive term signified, beyond craftsmanship, a "return to the planet earth," a renewed perception of things "like Adam's at the dawn of creation."

Similar ideas were current at that time in France and among writers in English. In Paris Jules Romains and his group and also Ezra Pound were saying much the same thing; it was not long before T. S. Eliot formulated his ideas on the evocative powers of the object in poetry. In Russia, futurists and other groups as well as the acmeists had been rethinking the relationship among word and thing and metaphor. They responded with original, varied, and often very productive approaches—at least until the growing literary regimentation of the late twenties put an end to speculation and experimentation in poetry.

In their heated polemics both post-symbolist movements tended to reject or at least to obscure their connections with their symbolist predecessors. Still, the new movements did contain much that was new and that resonated with the spirit of the time. Acmeism was thus able to attract from the very beginning one of the greatest modern Russian poets, Mandelshtam. It was Akhmatova's poetry, however, that was first identified as exemplary of acmeist principles. Her first book, *Vecher* (Evening, 1912), had been written before the acmeist "manifestos" (one of them composed by Gumilyov) were even published. Akhmatova's volume seemed to strike exactly the right note in illustrating the new approach to lyric poetry. With its later companion work, *Chetki* (Rosary, 1914), it achieved enormous popular and critical success; together, the two small and unpretentious volumes accounted in large part for the early success of acmeism.

Because of the inordinate amount of attention allotted to Mayakovsky and the futurists now, it is rather difficult to recall that in the early 1920's poetic opinion in Russia was almost equally divided between the partisans of Akhmatova and those of Mayakovsky. Both factions, however, shared the conviction that, in Romains' words, "poetry over the last twenty years has too often lost contact with and even the feeling of the real." Moreover, the fondness of the older generation for arcane philosophies, their almost aggressive erudition and fascination with recherché sciences, resulted in a poetry that was often difficult to comprehend even for the initiated, and sometimes it was entirely opaque.

Like Annenskii, the acmeists did not deny the existence of "other worlds"; they merely found them unsuitable for contemporary poetry. Thus, when Akhmatova's deceptively simple love lyrics appeared, they were enthusiastically welcomed not only by readers but also by scholars and critics who sought an illustration of the "new currents" they sensed in Russian poetry. "Pesnia poslednei vstrechi" (Song of the Last Meeting), which appeared in *Vecher*, is probably one of her best-known poems, and

it exemplifies Akhmatova's early work in the context of the "new currents."

So helplessly my breast grew cold,
Although my steps were light.
I drew onto my right hand
My left-hand glove.

It seemed there were a lot of steps,
Though I knew there were only three.
Among the maples, an autumn whisper
Begged: "Die with me!

I'm deceived by my despairing,
Inconstant, cruel fate."
I answered, "Dear one!
So have I. I'll die with you . . ."

This is the song of the last meeting.
I glanced up at the dark house.
Only in the bedroom candles burned
With an uncaring yellow light.

Tsarskoe Selo
29 September 1911
(*Stikhotvoreniia i poemy*, p. 30)

Translations of this kind, which attempt to render merely the primary sense of the words themselves, cannot give the least suggestion of Akhmatova's mastery of and innovations in the techniques of versification. Much of the stir caused by little poems like this one derived precisely from the tension between the very ordinariness of the settings and diction on the one hand and the sophistication in rhythms and sound patterning on the other. In an age when poets consciously sought, as Gumilyov observed, "to break the bonds of meter," Akhmatova was one of the few who did so successfully. She even established what was generally accepted as "the Akhmatova line," which, in one description, is called "a combination of iambs and anapests." (The original of the above poem is written in this meter.)

During a period when the established canons of versification were being questioned, Akhmatova preferred to work close to the outside edge of what the canon permitted, making full use of available licenses. When she varied the accepted standards, she did so by modifying some readily recognizable form rather than by rejecting those standards totally as many of her contemporaries did.

Akhmatova also helped to establish broader limits in rhyme, bringing into final acceptance what had earlier been perceived as notably "experimental" or even "punning" rhymes. Her sound-patterning was recognized as extraordinary and even served scholars as raw material for weighty linguistic studies in versification theory. The original of the poem at hand, for example, shows an interesting relationship on a high to low scale between the stressed vowel sounds and the semantic meaning of the lines in which they occur. By far the highest tonality occurs in the line "Although my steps were light," while the lowest corresponds with the lines from the last verse, "I glanced at the dark house," and "with an uncaring yellow light." By similar, though often much more complex, means, Akhmatova increases the affective quality of the semantic sense of her words.

It is the words themselves, however—words as *words,* an entirely unexpected kind of poetic diction—that intrigued Akhmatova's first critics. Gone were the muddy abstractions and grandiloquent verbiage of the older generation of symbolists: in their place was ordinary language, words suggestive of weight, mass, and texture—words suggestive of the acmeists' world.

Around the turn of the century, linguists like Aleksandr Potebnia in Russia had been rethinking the relationship between words and poetry; their perceptions were echoed by poets like Mandelshtam and later restated by formalist critics. In effect, the age had come upon an entirely new way of looking at poetry. Potebnia's famous assertion that "poetry and prose are linguistic phenomena" was not some

sort of exercise in circular reasoning: it was rather a rejection of the age-old idea of *ut pictura poesis* and the more recent dictum that poetry is "thinking in images" or in general that imagery is the specificum of poetry. The intuition of the age was that the word itself was valuable *in* itself, not just as a vehicle for metaphor. From this locus there was a conscious attempt by poets to restore value to the word and "thingness" to the thing. Akhmatova's *oveshchestvlenie* (reification) and Mayakovsky's "realization of metaphor" (or for that matter, Velimir Khlebnikov's "trans-sense language") are merely different approaches to that same end.

Contemporary critics singled out poems of this sort as representing a renewed perception of the world. The humble, concrete details— the glove, a flight of steps, a bedroom window—suggest not metaphors for something else but the things themselves, which, in their juxtaposition in the given context, have their own powers of evocative association.

The critics also commented on the acmeists' general tendency to render even abstracts concrete: "breast" here, for example, instead of "soul," "spirit," or even the near-abstract "heart." Similarly, the idea of motion (and the related emotion) is expressed in the physicality of action. A coldness growing at the breast expresses the realization of rejection. Feigning indifference to the blow is transmitted by the lightness of the footsteps; grief, wounded pride, and confusion are conveyed by the drawing of a glove onto the wrong hand. This last blurred perception is reinforced by the person's mistaking the number of steps (there is besides a likely suggestion of tears and a possible hint at stumbling).

The actions themselves are given a further degree of concreteness by another characteristic device of Akhmatova's: they are incorporated into a brief dramatic scene. The everyday vocabulary is complemented by the syntax and conversational cadences of ordinary speech, which occurs frequently in a kind of attenuated dialogue. Even though most of the lyric poems are of four or less stanzas of four lines each, the poet usually manages to indicate a setting and often even time of day or year—all contributing to the general impression of a certain, if not precisely solid, reality.

As is the case here, the setting most often chosen takes the form of a house (a facade, or an interior) or its surroundings (garden, orangery, croquet court, etc.). Usually, the setting is merely suggested by some detail of architecture or furnishing (here, the steps; elsewhere stair-rail, balusters, gate, hammock, cornice, embroidery frame, and the like). The device occurs so frequently that it evolved quite early into a kind of simple but effective symbolic system that uses the details of the house. In this system, an empty house stands for great loss; an inaccessible one, rejection; an abandoned one, loneliness. Doors can be an access to the loved one or desired object; more often they are barred or locked. Windows can act as the eyes of a house and, as in the example at hand, can carry the emotional weight. In this poem the steps down from the entrance to the house suggest not only departure but the confusion after parting (presumably the final one). The house is darkened—that is, no longer welcoming (in poems with a lighter mood, the lighted house stands for welcome). Only the bedroom window shows a light, but it is "uncaring," indifferent.

Akhmatova's poetry depends not on traditional devices or figures based either on comparison (simile, metaphor, etc.) or contiguity (synecdoche and the like) but on juxtaposition of things in a context, and this juxtaposition somehow transmits the lyrical force of the poem. Note that the above work contains hardly any traditional rhetorical figures at all. One may argue that the candlelight at the end is an example of the pathetic fallacy, a special case of personification, or make the same claim for the rustling leaves, but the "personification" of the candlelight is so minimal as to make one hesitate even to use the term,

and the pathetic fallacy of the autumn leaves is the most clichéd one in the repertory and can scarcely be said to pack a metaphorical punch. The effect of the poem depends not on such tired figures but on something similar to what has been called "psychological parallelism." This is a statement or description of some external phenomenon that is placed in juxtaposition to the persona of the poem, with the result that, based on neither comparison nor any logically explainable contiguity, one perceives an emotional connection. A good example occurs in the second stanza above: there is no really logical explanation of a connection between the three steps and the words in the autumn rustling; yet it is somehow understood that death would not be unwelcome.

Compare "Ia i plakala i kaialas'" (1911), which opens with a more readily discernible example of the same device. The oppression of remorse is present in the heavy atmosphere preceding the storm:

> I both wept and I repented,
> If only the skies would thunder!
> My dark heart was drained
> In your unlivable house.
> The pain I know is unendurable,
> The shame of the road back . . .
> How awful to go in to one unloved,
> The unloved one who is quiet and humble.
> I will bend to him in my finery,
> My necklaces tinkling:
> He will ask only: "My beauty!
> Where have you been praying for me?"
> (*Stikhotvoreniia i poemy*, p. 53)

Besides the peculiar instances of "psychological parallelism," there is a recurrence of the other devices discussed above. In regard to the system of house images, for example, the Russian word *nezhiloi*, translated here as "unlivable," means both "uninhabited" and "uninhabitable": a house without love.

Although the first half of the poem is an uncharacteristically direct expression of emotion, the substitution of the body for the spirit is again apparent here, and the concreteness of action serves to convey the abstract emotional state. In the second half of the poem, we observe again the brief dramatic scene in a suggested interior as well as the crucial function of simple concrete detail. Here, it is the frequently employed detail of feminine attire, in this case the tinkling beads.

The emotional force of the poem derives not so much from the initial statement of strong emotion, but from the imagined charade at the end. It is the last lines that establish the lyrical moment as remorse after betrayal. There is a clear suggestion that the deception was calculated, that the occasion for finery was given as going to church, although the real reason was an assignation. The pain of the continuing deception becomes acute as the persona pictures the return home, the forced hypocrisy of the greeting, and the innocent question of "the quiet one" that recalls the full enormity of the deception.

In later poems of this type the lyrical "I" becomes even more distant, often through the much greater use of impersonal expressions and similar grammatical means that are available in Russian but not in English. And in general, there is an increasing tendency for the lyrical persona to separate herself from the persona of the poem, almost as though she is observing herself in a mirror or addressing herself as a second person. This is indeed what happens in the poem just cited and even more clearly in the one following, "Proterty si kovrik pod ikonoi." This distancing is one characteristic that prevents the treatment of the distinctly dominant theme of tragic love, rejection, and abandonment from ever becoming mawkish or overly sentimental:

Under the icon, a frayed rug,
It is dark in the cool room
And the thick, dark-green ivy,
Winding, has covered over the wide window.

A sweet scent streams from the roses,
The icon light crackles, barely burning.

The linen chests have been painted brightly
By the loving hand of a village artisan.

And at the window, an embroidery frame
    shines white . . .
Your profile is delicate and severe.
You hide your kissed fingers squeamishly
Underneath your kerchief.

And it's frightful for your heart to beat;
There is such regret and longing in it now . . .
And in your rumpled braids is hidden
The scarcely sensed smell of tobacco smoke.

(*Stikhotvoreniia i poemy*, pp. 79–80)

Here, there is a succession of already familiar images (the house, the setting—an interior complete with shaded-over window—plus the concrete details of decor, dress, and coiffure). There follows the peculiar shift from the lyrical persona to a direct address, almost as if the persona of the poem were observing herself in a mirror. This odd distancing later expands to become an important feature of Akhmatova's mature poetry.

Together with the general tone of restrained emotion, the preference for impersonal grammatical expressions, and the careful economy in words, such distancing can convey heightened emotion without sentimentality. The same stance allows for Akhmatova's often striking juxtaposition of the sacred and the profane, as we see here, without shock to religious sensibilities or offense to good taste. (Akhmatova's epigones were especially fond of the juxtaposition, without understanding her method; in the 1920's and 1930's they produced some especially bad results, like the one satirized in Vladimir Nabokov's novel *Pnin* [1957]).

The juxtaposition of the sacred and the profane is related to a deeper level of ethics and morality, of conscience, of sin and retribution, guilt and expiation. These themes are implicit in the early poetry but come to the fore only in the later period. For the moment, then, we can consider the matrix of themes simply in the form of a highly developed religious imagery, one that lends extraordinary richness and color to a lyricism that is typically spare and laconic. The vocabulary itself is studded with biblical and liturgical words: chausuble, icon, crucifix, archangels, censers, monk's cell, Lot's wife, Herodias' daughter, a panoply of saints—George, Eudoxia, Paraskeva, John the Baptist, and so on. The persona of the poem is often cast as homeless, destitute, a wanderer meekly resigned to her fate—an image that is understandable much more as a part of Old Russian Orthodoxy than in Western Protestant or Roman Catholic terms. In this context, resignation in trial is a sign of Christian strength, and acceptance of suffering is a means of identification with the suffering of Christ. Rejection of the world, of home and its comforts and possessions could lead to the monastery but also to the pilgrimage or just to a seemingly aimless wandering over the land. Since renunciation of worldly things is assumed to have followed some great personal tragedy, these wanderers were considered close to God, and their prophecies were carefully heeded.

The presence of religious references, Orthodox assumptions, and ecclesiastical imagery in poetry where the theme of earthly love is dominant creates an admittedly striking juxtaposition. This feature of Akhmatova's poetry in the hands of a less sensitive writer could—and did—lead to embarrassing examples of bad taste. Worse still, it was later misconstrued, either by ignorance or by design, and used as a basis for attacking Akhmatova's poetry on moral grounds as "pernicious" to Soviet youth.

Of course the attitudes and imagery drawn from Russian Orthodoxy are part of a matrix of themes that might be called the Russian cultural heritage. The broader, more inclusive thematics can take many forms besides the Orthodox: for example, Russia's great, ancient cities, its historical sites, the old patriarchal way of life, the old estates and village life, folk art and tradition. The religious themes are not autonomous, but rather an organic part of a system of cultural associations.

Thus it is perfectly acceptable and natural for a poetic persona who in one poem is a St. Petersburg sophisticate and habitué of bohemian *caves* to turn in the poem—"Pesenka" (Folk Song, 1911)—into a woman on her knees weeding in a kitchen garden, listening to a peasant girl who weeps near the fence for her lost love.

> At sunrise,
> I sing of love;
> On my knees in the garden
> I'm pulling pigweed.
>
> I tear it out and throw it away—
> May it forgive me.
> I see a barefoot girl
> Weeping at the wattle fence.
>
> Terrible to me are the ringing wails
> Of the voice of woe;
> Stronger and stronger is the warm smell
> Of the dead pigweed.
>
> A stone instead of bread
> Will be my reward.
> There is only the sky over me,
> And with me your voice.
>
> Tsarskoe Selo

In the Russian folk tradition the lyric song is the woman's genre, and its subject is typically unhappy love: love lost, abandonment, betrayal. It is therefore not surprising that Akhmatova should make use of the genre. She does not, however, attempt to write in the folk manner but instead prefers merely to suggest the frame of reference, as in the poem above. Sometimes she employs highly stylized versions of the form, as in "So dnia Kupal'nitsy-Agrafeny":

> Since the Feast of Saint Agrafena
> He's kept my raspberry kerchief.
> He is silent, and exults like King David.
> In his frosty cell the walls are white,
> And no one talks with him.
> I shall go and stand on the threshold,
> I shall say: "Give me back my kerchief."
>
> (*Stikhotvoreniia i poemy*, p. 75)

Interpretation of the poem depends on details of Old Russian culture, the peasant folk tradition, Russian Orthodoxy, and the patriarchal way of life. The dating by church calendar helps to set the frame of reference. Saint Agrafena is the Russian version of Saint Agrippina, whose feast day precedes that of Saint John the Baptist (Ivan Kupalo), or Midsummer. The kerchief here displaces the red ribbon, symbol of maidenhood. The raspberry symbolizes maidenhood also, so that the raspberry-colored kerchief compounds the image. Thus, the naive persona of the poem has been seduced on Midsummer's Eve, then abandoned by a lover now grown haughty, cold, and distant—like a monk, sufficient to himself. It is worth noting here the architectural imagery, where the room or house with a barred door becomes a cell with a threshold that one is forbidden to cross.

While one must be careful not to exaggerate the especially Russian cultural aspect of Akhmatova's poetry illustrated here, it is an important one. Akhmatova herself spoke of this aspect metaphorically in a poem of 1916, "Pridu tuda, i otletit tomlen'e." The reference to the ancient northern cathedral city of Novgorod carries the suggestion of pre-Muscovite Rus and a stern and demanding Orthodoxy: "In me there flows a drop of Novgorod blood / Like a piece of ice in frothy wine."

Critics have tended to be carried away by the "Russianness" of the poet and their own ideas of "the Russian soul." The fact is, of course, that the "Old Russian" persona in the last poem referred to is only one among a number of different—and not always very compatible—personae. The abandoned peasant maid of "Folk Song" is someone quite other, and the same is true for the naive country miss dreaming in a brightly woven hammock on a summer's day ("Zharko veet veter dushnyi" [The Oppressive Wind Blows Hot]). Neither persona has much in common with the woman rejected by her lover in "Song of the Last Meeting," or the unfaithful, elegant wife in the poem cited just after it ("I Both Wept and I Repented"). There is moreover the rather daunting intellectual poet of the literary soirees and the grande dame in a feathered hat on a carriage ride in the Bois de Boulogne as well as a beggar-woman, a wanderer, a pilgrim. While the personae may vary widely, the subject remains very nearly constant: a woman's tragic love. Very few poems, less than a tenth of the whole, have no real connection with the dominant theme. These have mostly to do with the nature of poetry, and as events crowded one upon the other after 1914, the subject became increasingly Russia itself. The restriction of theme was not, as some less thoughtful critics felt, a morbidly single-minded preoccupation but a matter of conscious stylistic choice. Akhmatova never said so directly; much as she loved to talk about poetry and poetic theory, she avoided writing about the practice of her art. The one article she did write in the early period, however, has something revealing to say on the question here. It is a short review printed in 1913 on the death of the young poet Nadezhda L'vova and the posthumous appearance of her first volume. "How strange it is," Akhmatova observes, "that when women—who in real life are so strong and so sensitive to all of love's enchantments—begin to write, all that they know is a love that is tormenting, morbidly perceptive, and despairing." In a poetic restatement of the idea, she is explicit about her position:

> Never think that in delirium
> And tormented by longing
> I cry my misfortune loudly:
> Such is my trade.

The remarkable thing is that the limited subject matter points to Akhmatova's ingenuity rather than to some tiresome repetitiveness. The variety in treatment of the single motif is in itself a technical tour de force.

Her first six volumes of poetry, published between 1912 and 1922, not only share the common thematic material but also demonstrate a notable stylistic consistency. Apart from an increasing restraint in emotional expression and a greater resignation before the events that overtook Akhmatova in this momentous decade, it is difficult to speak of any marked change throughout this period. As the Soviet critic E. Dobin very properly observes, "There is no early Akhmatova." She emerged as a mature poet with her very first volume; it is hard to find poems in it that one could comfortably label "juvenilia" or "apprentice work." Similarly, it is difficult to find anything of the poet's mature years that is not in some way prefigured in the first six books. These represent what we call "the early period" simply because it was followed by a hiatus of over thirty years when Akhmatova was, for political reasons, forbidden to publish. The early volumes are *Vecher, Chetki, Belaia staia* (The White Flock, 1917), *Podorozhnik* (The Plantain, 1921), *U samogo moria* (At the Very Edge of the Sea, 1921), and *Anno Domini MXMXXI* (1921).

In the ten years between *Vecher* and *Anno Domini,* Akhmatova's whole world crumbled. Catapulted to fame with the publication of *Chetki,* much courted in the poetic and intellectual circles of the heady period before the wars, Akhmatova had early reached the pinnacle of success. Her marriage to Gumilyov was, by all accounts, tempestuous, and their son Lev, Akhmatova's only child, was born in 1912. With the onset of the war came the end of the idyll: the night life of the capital, with its poetry readings and carousing, the suburban respectability of life in Tsarskoe Selo, the old patriarchal way of life on the estate deep in the countryside of Tver' province. Gumilyov enlisted in the cavalry on the outbreak of hostilities (he was twice decorated for bravery in the field). The poets and friends in Akhmatova's circle were scattered by the dislocations of the time. The hardships of the war years increased as the war passed into revolution. Gumilyov, who had been posted to London, returned to Russia immediately after the revolution broke out, but the marriage did not survive the long separation, and Akhmatova and Gumilyov were divorced. She lived alone and in penury, her room furnished with lawn furniture dragged in from someone's garden. She took what stultifying jobs she could get: for a while she was a clerk in the Agronomy Institute; once she was seen on the Obvodnyi Canal, selling herring from one of the packets distributed to writers when they would otherwise have gone hungry.

By 1921 Gumilyov was convicted as a counterrevolutionary and shot. Akhmatova had already withdrawn from public life, but she was sought out and hounded because of her class and her earlier association with an enemy of the people. After 1922, no editor dared accept her work for publication and, like so many others at the time, she continued writing but "into her desk drawer."

Akhmatova's position was increasingly difficult but bearable until 1934, the beginning of the Stalinist Terror. Her son Lev had just reached his majority and was arrested on trumped-up charges. In that year the party secretary of Leningrad, Sergei Kirov, had been murdered. There followed a chain reaction of political arrests, interrogations, and executions, which climaxed in the Great Purge (1935–1938). The show trials and liquidation of the "enemies of the people" began. The population of the prison camps grew to unbelievable proportions—from six million in 1937 to ten million by 1940–1942.

The mindless Terror came to an end only because of World War II and the need to concentrate all the national efforts in the battle against the invading armies. Lev, who had been released after his first arrest in 1935, was imprisoned again in 1938 and sent to the camps; he was freed early in the war to serve in the military. Akhmatova was "rehabilitated," and her poems written on the theme of Russia at war had an immense success. Survivors of the terrible seige of Leningrad remember her verses being repeated in the bomb shelters, and veterans recall that her poem "Muzhestvo" ("Courage") was recited on the battlefield.

By the end of the war, a complete edition of

Akhmatova's works was in progress, and her rehabilitation seemed at last secure. (In 1940 the collection *Iz shesti knig* [From Six Books] had appeared, but it was premature: the book was recalled from bookstores and library shelves shortly after its publication and was destroyed. Most of the 1940 poems were published in later collections, in the late 1950's and early 1960's.)

In 1946 the war was over, and the Central Committee of the Communist party decided that it was time for "fresh ideological developments"—meaning that the relative literary freedom of the war years had to be drastically curtailed—for "the further flowering of Soviet culture." The vehicle for the attack was Andrei Zhdanov's report on two Leningrad journals which had published stories of Mikhail Zoshchenko and some of Akhmatova's poems. The whole weight of the party machinery was brought to bear on the light satire of Zoshchenko and the totally apolitical poetry of Akhmatova. Absurd charges of all sorts were brought against the two, but among the most absurd was that "they saw war primarily as pain and suffering" (that is, not as Joseph Stalin saw it, as a "school to test the fiber of the Soviet people"). The following poem, "Shcheli v Sadu vyryty," about the siege and bombardment of Leningrad, was singled out for its *bezideinaya antinarodnost'*, an untranslatable monument of party cant meaning literally "idea-less anti-peopleness":

> Trenches are dug in the garden
> And the lights are out.
> Petersburg orphans,
> Children mine!
>
> Underground, it's hard to breathe;
> Pain drills into the temples;
> Through the bombing is heard
> A child's thin voice . . .
> (*Stikhotvoreniia i poemy,* p. 212)

Akhmatova was expelled from the Writers' Union, thus deprived not only of the possibility of publishing her work, but also of income and the indispensable social benefits. She again went into seclusion, living in great hardship, and was persecuted through the late 1940's by various party "organs," as the official agencies are called. In 1949 her son, who had been living quietly as an established scholar and Orientalist, was once again arrested and sentenced to fifteen years of exile and hard labor (there were no real charges cited, and even official accounts assume his arrest was part of the campaign against Akhmatova). It is not surprising that at this time there appeared an odd little cycle of poems called "In Praise of Peace," which, except for a certain technical accomplishment and a scattering of Akhmatova's most usual images, could have been written by any party hack ("Where a tank rumbled, / There is now a peaceful tractor . . ."). One can only hope that the publication of this drab little cycle had the effect of improving in some degree her son's position.

Like many of her colleagues who were out of favor, Akhmatova found some measure of refuge and means of support in taking on literary translation as a kind of piecework. After Stalin's death and the "thaw," she was able once again to publish original poems ("Petrograd 1916" and "Asia"), and to her great joy, her son was released from the camps. She was rumored to be well on the way to complete rehabilitation. Then the Hungarian revolt broke out, and in the consequent tightening-up, nothing came of the rumors. Akhmatova was this time spared the brunt of the attack, perhaps because no one wished to repeat the awful Zhdanov era. Of such times in her life, Akhmatova wrote "Posledniaia roza" (The Last Rose, 1962). The Princess Morozova here is a noblewoman exiled to Siberia by the Tsar for holding—and defending—beliefs contrary to officially accepted ones:

> I've had to bow down with Morozova,
> To dance with the stepdaughter of Herod,
> To fly away with the smoke from Dido's pyre
> So I can go again to the stake with Joan.
> Oh Lord! You see how tired I am

Of resurrection, of dying, of living.
Take everything away, only let me feel
Once again the freshness of this bright red rose.

By 1958, however, the process of rehabilitation was begun again in earnest, and later that year, the first appreciable edition of Akhmatova's poetry since 1922 was published, *Posledniaia roza* (The Last Rose). Akhmatova never dared trust her rehabilitation, but this time it lasted through the remainder of her life.

Now that Akhmatova has been for so long fixed among the premier poets of Russia, it is difficult to recall that in the middle to late 1950's she was very nearly forgotten in the West and that in the Soviet Union she was considered to be an obscure figure, certainly not one who was very "relevant." Older readers typically remembered "the left-hand glove drawn onto the right" and often a good deal more, but most were surprised that Akhmatova was still among the living. As individual poems found their way into print both in the Soviet Union and abroad, it became clear that Akhmatova not only had retained both a high level of creativity and a consistency of style throughout the decades of enforced silence but had also undergone a remarkable development in her worldview. Her themes and images once carefully restricted to the worlds familiar to her from personal experience, now open out to encompass the whole world, and draw deeply on the European cultural tradition as well as the Russian.

This is partially illustrated by the rather spare total of representative poems from the 1920's and 1930's. At critical times during those years Akhmatova had to burn her archive, and much was lost simply in the vicissitudes of those years. Around 1939–1940, however, there was an extraordinary burst of creative activity. Along with a large number of poems in the usual short format, Akhmatova wrote the better part of two long narrative poems. She brought to completion *Requiem* and composed the "Petersburg Tale," which served as the narrative line for the lengthy and complex *Poem Without a Hero.* If the latter was a markedly new departure for Akhmatova, *Requiem* was a natural development from her earlier work, a kind of culmination.

It is clear from Akhmatova's comments on Blok's *Vozmezdie (Retribution,* 1939) that she thought narrative poems could be successful only if they did not repeat forms already used (like Pushkin's, for example). Akhmatova worked out an original form for *Requiem,* a combination of the epic and the lyric. In one sense, it is an epic lament for Russia caught in the Terror, but it is made up of short lyrical poems and incidental pieces (introductions, dedication, epilogues). The means of expression in the lyric poems is essentially the one worked out in the six books up to 1922. Her techniques and versification, her idiosyncratic symbolic system, her diction and tone are all immediately recognizable here. The central poem of the work is an excellent example. It is entitled "Prigovor" ("The Sentence"), and while its simplicity and understatement suggest an epic calm in the face of tragedy, the intensity of the moment is increased many times by the pathetic effort of the will to overcome a grief that borders on madness:

And the stone word fell
On my still living breast.
Never mind, I was ready after all,
I'll manage somehow or other.

I have lots to do today:
I have to kill my memory completely,
I've got to turn my soul to stone,
I've got to learn to live again—

And if not . . . The hot rustle of summer
Is like a holiday outside my window.
For a long time, I've had a presentiment of this
Bright day and empty house.
                                        Summer 1939

The quiet conversational tone, the simple, workaday words contrast with the high seriousness of the content. The transformation of abstracts into concretes, the special meaning given the interior through the image of the window, and finally the image of the abandoned house all have—just because they fall within the context of Akhmatova's poetry—an immeasurably greater impact than they would in isolation.

According to the short prose introduction, Requiem had its genesis in Akhmatova's experience of the long lines of women outside the Leningrad prisons, where they waited for news of their loved ones imprisoned there. It was a time when "only the dead smiled, glad to be at peace, and Leningrad flapped like a useless appendage around its prisons."

The body of the work itself opens with a lyric poem about someone beloved who was swept up in the Terror, someone who might stand for Lev, for Mandelshtam, for Akhmatova's third husband Nikolai Punin, or for all those arrested in the night and taken away in those frightful years. Note once again how the images and devices already characteristic of Akhmatova in the first period transmit the import of the poem. There are rich lexical borrowings from an earlier Russian culture with its Orthodox foundations. (The word for chamber, gornitsa, is almost obsolete; bozhnitsa, here translated literally as "shrine," could be an icon corner or icon stand; an icon itself figures in one image.) Further, there is the familiar image of an interior setting and the symbolic doorway. And again, the Russia of history, of medieval Muscovy, is evoked—this time through the reference to the Kremlin walls—in "Uvodili tebia na rassvete" (They Led You Away at Dawn):

They led you away at dawn;
I went after, as if following your coffin.
Children wept in the darkened chamber
The candle at the shrine spilled over.
The cold of an icon on your lips,
A deathly sweat on your brow . . . Can't be
    forgotten!

And I, like the wives of the Streltsy
Shall howl under the Kremlin's towers.
                    (Sochineniia 1. 355)

The Streltsy were a standing infantry at the time of Peter the Great who sided against him in a palace plot. Many were beheaded on the square in front of the Kremlin, others hanged before its wall—in full sight of their wives and families. In this context, then, Peter figures as cruel despot (and in the eyes of the Orthodox common folk of his time, the Antichrist). The relationship is clear enough between the "poor little wives of the Streltsy"—the tender diminutive is used—and the women of Requiem standing in lines at the prison walls.

The breathless hesitancy that marks so many of the early lyrics is also here. There is a rapid build-up to a breaking point; the melted wax on the votive candle spills over. Control is gone, and the lyric persona "howls like the wives of the Streltsy."

But it is restraint of emotion, rather than release, that we have come to expect in Akhmatova's poetry, or at least a return to a kind of resignation after the breaking point. In Requiem this indeed follows; in the next lyric, the contrast is complete. There is a certain calm, but it is a calm that is not quite sane, for the persona of the poem is divorced from her suffering self. A jingly meter jars with the content, and madness hovers:

Quietly flows the quiet Don,
Into the house comes the yellow moon,

Comes in with his hat cocked jauntily,
The yellow moon sees a shadow.

This woman is sick,
This woman is alone,

Husband in the grave, son in prison,
Pray for me a little.

In the following brief lyric, "Net, eto ne ia" (No, That Is Not I, 1940), the separation becomes complete, and before the halting rhythms quite resolve themselves, the poem comes to a full stop: ". . . what happened, let black cloths cover over / And let the lamps be carried out . . . Night."

There follows a jumble of impressions: a memory of happier days, before the revolution in Tsarskoe Selo, contrasted with the lines of disheartened women outside the prisons in the bitter winter cold; the utter horrors of the time, and of men of the time; the poet's grief for her son and for her people.

And only dusty flowers,
And the clinking of the censer chain, and footprints
Going nowhere.

This leads to the central poem, "The Sentence." The extraordinary effect of this poem and those preceding it depends in large part on recognition of the style of the early Akhmatova, and on the irony engendered as a result of the discrepancy between her younger self and the present person—between "the gay little sinner of Tsarskoe Selo," as she is called here, and the shabby, gray-faced woman standing in the prison lines, just another among a nation of suffering women.

From "The Sentence," the *Requiem* moves on again through changes of atmosphere and diction until it reaches the end in two final, moving quatrains. Here, Akhmatova generalizes the properly lyrical cry of the passages just preceding into the universality of the Mother suffering for the Son.

The Magdalene struck her breast and sobbed,
The beloved disciple turned to stone,
But there, where the Mother stood silent,
No one even dared to look.
　　　　　　　(*Stikhotvoreniia i poemy*, p. 192)

The two epilogues that follow take up the themes, progressing once again from lyric to epic in stance. Here, the poet becomes not only witness and chronicler, but ultimately judge.

The epilogues close with a reference to the great rivers of Russia, echoing the first lines of the dedication: "Before such grief, mountains bend, / The great river cannot flow. . . ." There are reprises in the body of the poem—the quietly flowing Don, the swirling Yenisei—resolving at the end in the river of Petersburg /Leningrad: "And ships go quietly along the Neva."

Requiem was an apogee, in some sense a capstone for Akhmatova's oeuvre up to its time of composition. After 1922, when the last volume of the early series was published, only a few of a great many poems written in the intervening years remained. These survived almost by accident, among them those memorized by the author or her close friends, some that had escaped burning by the author herself in the worst days of the Terror, and random pieces tucked away in some forgotten place and turned up later. The surviving poems were gathered first into a cycle called "Iva" ("The Willow") and later incorporated into one entitled "Trostnik" ("The Reed"), whose stylistic and thematic consistency with respect to earlier volumes is marked.

There is no suggestion in the poems of "The Reed" of the burst of creativity that led to the composition of *Requiem* at the end of the 1930's or of the astounding creative leap around 1940, which inspired the composition of central parts of *Poem Without a Hero*. This, her masterwork, haunted her until its completion in 1962, that is, to within three years of her death. The introduction begins:

From the year 1940
As from a tower, I look upon everything.
As though I were bidding farewell again
To that which I'd long since bid farewell,
As though I had crossed myself
And walk off under dark vaults.

When *Poem Without a Hero* first reached the reading public, it was puzzling, difficult to understand, quite unlike the pieces Akhmatova's readership had come to expect. Even today, well over a quarter-century later, we are still far from a complete or definitive reading. Although in style and technique there is scarcely any passage in the *Poem* that is not prefigured somewhere in Akhmatova's earlier work, the expansion of theme and the broadening of the cultural fund from which the images are drawn are so great that it is difficult to reconcile the work with the author of *Belaia Staia* and *Podorozhnik.* Akhmatova herself openly referred to it as a "private poem," accessible only "to those who knew the Petersburg circumstances" of the time, those who knew the Petersburg world of Russian art and letters before World War I. The vaunted acmeist clarity is something far distant from the *Poem;* it has more in common with symbolist works (indeed, Akhmatova once referred to it as "a polemics with Blok").

The poem is built around a "Petersburg Tale" of 1913, that is, the year before the cataclysm. The tale itself is one of foolish young love: a young cornet in the dragoons falls hopelessly in love with a dancer from the Suvorinsky Theater and, despairing, puts a pistol to his temple. Instead of the story, there is the event itself—only one among others, scarcely important on any grand scale, scarcely even symbolic in any direct sense. And yet there is in this purely personal tragedy something that might be generalized: the hopelessness, helplessness, and even foolishness of the act must have seemed characteristic of Akhmatova's class and time. These are evoked in a "hellish Harlequinade," a masque of shades—a symbolist's, not an acmeist's, Petersburg.

If the "Petersburg Tale" is an allegory for its time, it is also a laying to rest of old ghosts for Akhmatova, a catharsis. The second part, however, is an undisguised parallel with Pushkin's "Razgovor knigoprodavtsa s Poetom" ("Conversation Between a Bookseller and a Poet," 1825). Both works have to do with freedom of expression and censorship, belleslettres and philistinism, creativity and repression.

An epilogue departs in attitude, content, and tone from both parts preceding. It was written in the darkest days of World War II, in the summer of 1942. Akhmatova had endured part of the siege of Leningrad and the terrible bombardment, and, apparently by some caprice of the bureaucracy, she was among those flown out in the evacuation to the rear. She was sent eventually to Tashkent, where she completed the epilogue.

The epilogue is set in the appalling present. With thoughts of Tashkent, of Tobruk, of New York, there is the ever-present awareness of Akhmatova's beloved city on the Neva; it is the theme of Petersburg that runs through all three parts and provides the most obvious surface link among them.

On one level *Poem Without a Hero* deals with the history of Russia in the modern age. It looks back, from a vantage point on the eve of a second great national trauma (the German invasion of Russia during World War II) to 1913, the "last year" before World War I, the revolution, and civil strife. Implicit are the years between, years of dislocation, hardship, and suffering, and, unmentioned here but allpervasive, the Terror.

On another level, a more personal one, are lyrical reminiscences, an idiosyncratic recollection of the earlier time, and, in the present, a kind of apologia pro vita sua. On a deeper level, however, the *Poem* is about poetry—and poets. This theme ultimately unites the several and sometimes disparate other themes: the city, the nation, the time, the cataclysms, the persona of the poem, and her memories. The matrix of themes concerning poetry and poets can appear openly on the surface, but most often it is submerged or obscured through literary mystification, or literally "masks" ("My workbox has a triple bottom"). By indirect hints and allusions, by encodings and even literal encipherment, Akhmatova refers to the great poets—and not so great—who had lived in this perilous time and who all came to a tragic end. But Akhmatova is not only a preserver of memory, a chronicler: the Author, the only one among all those shades who is still alive, is also an accuser, a judge, and, in this sense, an avenger.

Like *Requiem, Poem Without a Hero* begins with a complex accumulation of prefatory pieces: a few prose paragraphs called "In Place of a Preface" as well as what is presented as an excerpt from one of Akhmatova's private letters. There are three dedications in verse, followed by the six-line "Introduction."

"In Place of a Preface" seems to be merely a statement of times and circumstances of composition; as a matter of fact, it provides keys for decoding the deliberate mystifications of the text. If the foreword dedicates the work to its first hearers—friends and compatriots who perished in the awful blockade of Leningrad— a variant notes that this dedication does not displace the original ones "which continue to live out their own lives in the Poem." Indeed, an odd thing about the poem is that the variants— rejected passages, passages written but not included, passages definitely related but never intended for inclusion—are in a sense very much a part of the poem. It seems clear that Akhmatova felt this to be so, and it is sure that interpretation would be very nearly impossible without them.

The first "Dedication" is to a poet ("It is on your rough draft that I'm writing"). The poet is what will be called here The Poet, that is, the generalized figure of the true poet—who is the hero of this *Poem Without a Hero*. In the course of the poem, recognizable, individual poets fade into and out of the generalized figure. Here, and in important passages later, it is Mandelshtam; the date specified, and internal references (e.g., to "lashes like Antinous") make the identification reasonably sure. The "Second Dedication" is not in question: it is to Ol'ga Afanas'evna Glebova-Sudeikina, the actress-dancer of the Suvorinsky Theater, and heroine of the "Petersburg Tale" described above. The "Third and Last Dedication" is to a person removed from the "Petersburg Tale" of 1913. It was Sir Isaiah Berlin, who chanced upon an opportunity, while serving in 1946 as a British Embassy official in Russia, to meet Akhmatova at her flat in the House on the Fontanka. Akhmatova seemed to need assurance of her reputation in the "other world" (that is, in the West). Despite the extreme danger of meeting privately with Westerners in the increasingly repressive Stalinist postwar years, she agreed to the meeting.

The innocent literary interview precipitated a nightmare of consequences that haunted her for years to come. Sir Isaiah had barely begun his conversation with Akhmatova when he heard his name being shouted in the courtyard. Incredibly, the voice was that of Randolph Churchill, Winston Churchill's son, who was looking for an interpreter and had tracked Sir Isaiah down. Entirely unaware of the gravity of his mindless indiscretion, Churchill persisted until Berlin took him away. Akhmatova, with real bravery, consented to receive the English critic again, and the dreadful consequences in those years of Stalin's extreme paranoia followed inevitably. The connection with Churchill, however tenuous, was too much to be borne. The Leningrad journals that had printed Akhmatova's poems (and Zoshchenko's satires) were taken to task, and the poet herself was viciously attacked. She was expelled from the Writers' Union and again deprived of the right to publish.

The first part of the poem, the "Petersburg Tale," is also entitled "Nineteen Thirteen." It is the year Akhmatova elsewhere calls "the last year": that is, the last year of the old world, before 1914, before 1917, before the beginning of the end. The tale opens with epigraphs from Wolfgang Amadeus Mozart's *Don Giovanni* (1787), from Pushkin, and from Akhmatova's own poetry from before World War I: the associations are with music, the stage, tragic love, retribution and remorse, New Year's celebration, innocence and sorcery, Pushkin and poetry—themes worked out in ingenious ways within the text following. Before the opening lines there are what appear to be stage directions for a setting in an old palace on the Fontanka, now divided into living spaces, where Akhmatova had a room during these years. The author waits for a New Year's guest, but ghosts from the past come uninvited in fancy dress.

The opening lines are recognizably Akhmatova's—one of them is a direct quotation from a poem of the early years—but very quickly it becomes clear that we are dealing with a very different kind of poetry or, perhaps, with a very different kind of cultural fund from which the images are drawn. The earlier, limited categories of images suddenly widen to encompass all of Western culture. The persona of the poem, who calls herself "the Author," speaks to the masked shades who come to her door:

And, as though remembering something,
  Turning halfway round,
    I say quietly:
"You must have made a mistake: The Venice of the
      Doges
  Is next door . . . But you'll have to leave
    Your masks and capes and staffs and laurels
In the hallway today.
  I have an idea to celebrate you now,
    New Year's revellers!"
This one as Faust, that as Don Juan,
  Dappertutto, Jochanaan,
    The least forward—as a northern Glan,
      Or the murderer Dorian,
        All whispering to their Dianas
          The lines they learned by heart.

What a remarkable difference in tone, in lexicon, in point of reference. (Akhmatova had, it is true, experimented in the early days with "decadent" poetry—the Edwardian *goût du XVIII*, for example—but she excluded such poems from her published collections.)

Something akin to the initial "stage directions" occurs at this point in the narrative, and the "play" goes forward:

The walls fell back for [the masks];
  The light flared up and sirens wailed.
    And the ceiling bowed upward like a dome.

I don't care what people will say . . .

What do I care about Hamlet's garters,
  What's the whirlwind of Salome's dance to me,
    What do I care about the Iron Mask's foot-
      steps,
    I am more iron than they . . .
And now whose turn is it to be frightened,
  Turn away, draw back, give in.
    And beg mercy for ancient sins?
It's all clear:
  If not to me, then to whom [should they come]?
    Not for them have I prepared supper;
      The path I've taken is not for them.
He's hidden his tail under his coattails . . .
  How lame he is, and elegant! . . .
    I hope you didn't dare to bring here
      The Prince of Darkness?
This mask, is it skull or face—
  This expression of malicious hurt
    That only a Goya could paint.

Everyone's pet and joker—
  Beside him even the foulest sinner
    Is blessing incarnate . . .

As the *Poem Without a Hero* appeared, first in small fragments, then later as connectable narrative pieces, Akhmatova's readers were amazed at the artistic shift, at the remarkable growth and development, at a poetry so unlike what they had come to expect from Akhmatova. It was not long however before the extraordinary consistency of the Akhmatova style was noted, despite the unexpected images and obscurity of references. Scholarship since that time has concentrated on unravelling the relationship of those images to the sense of the text and on tracking down and illuminating those references. The job is now sufficiently complete to permit reading with a greater degree of confidence than was possible when the poem first reached the public. The excerpt above, for example, which is roughly the first fifty lines of the poem, seemed altogether puzzling at the time it appeared; the lines are now fairly understandable, and the ideas they contain are recognized as central to the content as it is developed in the poem. The references to Russian and world literature, to the arts in general, are not merely an evocation of the cultural history of the West but have specific relationships to the dramatis personae of the "Petersburg Tale." The images help to elaborate the story that played itself out in 1913 between a smitten dragoon and a pretty actress. For example, the subtitle "Petersburg Tale" is also the subtitle of Pushkin's *Mednyi Vsadnik* (*The Bronze Horseman,* 1833), another tale of unfortunate love and sad death in the phantasmagorical city on the Neva. The epigraph to the whole is from Mozart's *Don Giovanni,* which has its own connections with Pushkin, and with Pushkin's Don Juan tale, "The Stone Guest." Furthermore, the very close connection with Pushkin (there is an enormous number of such connections throughout the poem) is also, for Akhmatova, a connection with poetry in general.

The masquerade scene is a kind of allegory of Petersburg society, the bohemian-artistic world of "le tout Pétersburg" in the years just before the cataclysm. The dragoon's story is representative of the madness, the delirium, the perceived decadence of that society in that time. The mummers act out the role, but they are also people of the time, the Don Juan masking Blok, one of the great poets of the age, and Dappertutto representing not only E. T. A. Hoffman's doctor, but the famous theater director Vsevolod Meyerhold, and so on. The work is not simply a *poème à cléf:* by evoking real figures of the era, and with them those of the world of art, the poem is able to say something not only about the society of the time, but also about the artist in it.

The Author compares herself to the mummers and finds herself "more iron than they," than even "the man in the Iron Mask." Not only has she survived to this New Year's eve of 1940, not only is she able to recall that "hellish Harlequinade," she can recall—and also judge. "Whose turn is it now to be afraid . . . to beg mercy for long past sin?" It was not these sinners she had intended to entertain this night. One of them, "lame and elegant," a Mephistopheles figure, is identified as the poet Mikhail Kuzmin. The sin is not yet clear, but the sinfulness is characterized in the strongest possible terms.

There then follows a brief lyrical passage in which the Author observes that she alone of all these is still alive, that when she awakens in the morning, no one will judge *her.* But she fears that tonight she may meet herself as she was back then, in 1913—a meeting she does not want "this side of the valley of Jehoshaphat," that is, this side of the Last Judgment. She muses further on the nature of time ("As in the past the future ripens / So in the future the past rots"), and interpolates in a short passage, a "Guest from the Future," not a ghost but a living person. It is none other than Sir Isaiah Berlin, "who does not waft the coldness of Lethe / And in whose hand there is warmth."

The narrative returns to the midnight revel, and the Author happens upon a mask who "does not figure in the lists" of charlatans, frauds, and corruptors ("Cagliostros, *mages,* Messalinas"). This central figure's disguise is a milepost, and represents Akhmatova's friend Mandelshtam. Whatever the identification of this mask (and it is accepted that individual identities in the poem can change, fade from one to another, replace each other in a constantly shifting reality), he represents the True Poet. He is "contemporary of the terebinth in the Plain of Mamre, the eternal interlocutor of the Moon." It is he who writes "laws of iron"; from him the "Hammurabis, Lycurguses and Solons should take lessons." He does not wait for "fame and gout" to plant him in chairs with official honors; rather he "carries his triumph through the flowering heather in the wilderness."

And as a True Poet, he is innocent, guiltless: in general, "sins don't stick to Poets." The Poet must serve his art whatever the cost; he must "dance before the Ark or perish." (In point of fact, Mandelshtam's poetry led to his arrest and exile to a Siberian camp, where he died in the winter of 1938.)

In this chapter, the guiltless True Poet is clearly opposed to the sinful, false one. But the Author interrupts her own narrative here: "Let their own poetry tell the story." The night wears on, "we only dream a cock's cry; the Neva steams beyond the window—and the *Teufelstanz* of Petersburg stretches into the bottomless night."

Once again, the images of the mummers pass before the Author, then again the poets, then The Poet once more—and the Author at last ends the chapter: "For one minute of peace alone / I would give up peace eternal."

Before the next chapter there is an "Intermezzo": visions of Petersburg evenings in 1913, snatches of lovers' conversations, whispers of assignations, nightlife in the artistic cabarets. Figures emerge not unlike those in the masque—and above them, more elegant, higher than them all, is the head of Madame de Lamballe.

Then, in the depths of the hall, "or the stage, or Hell, or the top of Goethe's Broken," the heroine of the tale is introduced, and appears in Chapter 2 as the "Columbine of the 1910's." Following her, in uniform and casque, comes the lovesick dragoon, a trickle of blood down his cheek. The stage is set for the second act, and the melodrama plays itself out against the background of a Petersburg prima's boudoir: the nightmare of the world outside wafts in on the mists of the Neva; poets appear and meld into others. The Pierrot in a dragoon's jacket comes closer to his end; as to the heroine's horoscope, it has long since been cast.

The third chapter opens with reminiscences of poets and Petersburg in 1913 ("That was the last year . . ." is the epigraph from Akhmatova's fellow acmeist Mikhail Lozinskii; it follows a quotation from Mandelshtam).

> And accursed by Tsaritsa Avdot'ia
> Dostoevskyan and run amok,
> The city went off into its fog.
> . . . .
> And along the legendary embankment
> There came near not the calendar
> But the real Twentieth Century.

The "Fourth and Last Chapter" picks up earlier themes from the narrative and weaves them together. It is not the Author who speaks, but Silence itself who points to the body of the dragoon stretched across the actress' doorway—Silence who calls herself Conscience, who finally places the finished tale on the windowsill and walks off on tiptoe. The Tale is over—but the Poem is not complete. An "Afterword" follows:

> All is in order: the Poem lies there,
> And, in character, keeps silent.
> But what if suddenly a theme tears loose,
> Knocks at the window with its fist—
> And from afar is there a response
> To this call, a frightful sound—
> A boiling up, a moaning, a bubbling
> And a vision of crossed arms? . . .

Part 2 of the poem is called "Reshka," which means "odd," as in "odd and even," the other side of the coin. It is written in entirely different form from the first, in short numbered stanzas. Despite its own mystifications, it serves as a kind of clarification or key for the mysteries in part 1.

An editor (who sounds like the publisher in Pushkin's "Conversation Between a Bookseller and a Poet") complains in the tones of a philistine and bureaucrat that he cannot understand the poem, nor "why we need all these thoughts on the Poet, and this swarm of some sort of phantoms or other." The Author responds with her characteristic indirection: "My workbox has a triple bottom"; "I write in mirror writing and there is no other way for me." But even so, the Author's intent in her assertions about the Poet and his opposite become much clearer in the repetition here. Whatever the identity of the historical persons behind the masks of the Milepost or the Demon, they represent the True Poet, whose poetry assures immortality.

The third hero, who "lived barely twenty years," is of course the fledgling poet and suicide of the narrative, Vsevolod Kniazev.

The composite Poet is juxtaposed to the false one, here in the guise of Cagliostro:

Old Cagliostro appears,
Himself a most elegant Satan,
Who does not weep with me over the dead,
Who does not know what conscience means,
And what it is for.

The hellish Harlequinade whirls to a full stop: "Only mirror dreams mirror, / Silence guards silence."

Omitted stanzas are indicated at this point; one may assume they refer to Akhmatova's darkest years of fear and repression. The Poem then resumes with indirect hints of the Terror, the Author's own feeble and ultimately ineffective protestations of innocence, and just after that, her reflections on secret drawers and "mirror writing." There is a brief vision of some future time when an unknown person will honor the Author's departed shade, "a time when this [present] storm will have passed away."

At this point, *Poem Without a Hero* itself takes on its own reality as a person, one who seems to be in part a masked lady from Pushkin's time, in part the Muse, in part, perhaps, an alter ego of the Author. At the end she speaks once again of and to the Poet, to whom she promises retribution and reward.

There is a brief epilogue written in the summer of 1942, the most despairing days of the war, with Leningrad in ruins and Akhmatova herself evacuated to Tashkent. The nightmare of the past merges with the nightmare of the present: "And wringing its hands, / Russia marched before me to the East." Like the end of the poem itself, the epilogue is not an ending: the poem does not come to rest in the last line.

The deliberately simple reading of the poem given here still leaves many—and essential—questions unanswered. It seems clear enough that the masquerade is a kind of allegory, a Feast During the Plague; at the same time it evokes as players in the masque the artistic and literary world of Petersburg. The little drama of the poet-dragoon and the doll-like actress seems an appropriate parable for that world, for that era, for that special class. Certainly, Petersburg itself is the obvious symbol for Russia before the revolution, and the references to the awful dislocations that followed the revolution are certainly accessible. Even knowing this, however, we feel far from understanding the poem and can complain with the editor-bureaucrat in part 2, "You've got three themes at once in there . . . you can't tell who's in love with whom . . . or who the hero is." What is the relationship between the "Petersburg Tale" of the lovesick dragoon and the masques in the midnight Hoffmaniana? If the poet-dragoon is the "third" hero, how are we to understand "the main hero," or what we have called here the True Poet? And what are we to understand by the False Poet "before whom the foulest sinner is blessing incarnate"? What message does this central, repeated juxtaposition carry?

Insofar as the poem is a vehicle for a moral-philosophical view, the opposition here is one of crucial importance. It is worth noting in this regard that from the earliest days, the acmeists claimed to represent a specifically strong moral position. It is perhaps not surprising that little was made of this claim in critical circles—the mores of the time and the personal conduct of the young acmeists did not immediately suggest moral rigor. Nevertheless, the acmeists consciously felt that their rebellion against the symbolist poets was in part a rebellion against the ambiguities of the older generation's moral position.

In simplest terms the symbolists had come to accept broadly current fin-de-siècle assumptions about decadence and decline, which made blame for the lack of individual morality and responsibility somehow irrelevant. It is clear that for Akhmatova and Mandelshtam one of the things that significantly distinguished the acmeists from the symbolists was moral concern. Even before the revolution, they rejected the old decadent idea that the concept of *dégénérescence* included a kind of inevitability that put individual transgression and guilt outside the frame of reference. No one was to be blamed, no one was guilty, "all is permitted to the one who dares," no one is responsible for his own actions—or for his fellow man. It is at this point that the argument reaches the complete inversion of the Judeo-Christian ethic: it is, in the poem's terms, the "blackest sin." To save, to help, at the very least to pity one's fellow man in his plight is an essentially biblical injunction. But how much fuller a meaning is attached to it by those who lived through the repressions of Stalin's time, when often even the barest offer of help or the slightest expression of pity was tantamount to sealing one's own fate. Akhmatova, who had for so long and so often been afflicted and at the same time shunned by others, braved exile or worse not only by refusing to compromise her own artistic integrity but also by offering such help as she could give to those even less fortunate. It is in no way surprising that she should adopt a moral stance in *Poem Without a Hero,* and judge not only by the measure of the poet's responsibility to his or her art but also by the measure of man's responsibility to man.

How is all this worked into the "Petersburg Tale," which is about a thoughtless actress and a foolish dragoon? What did Akhmatova mean when she called the work a "private poem" that could be understood only by those who knew "the Petersburg circumstances" of the time? She may well have been referring specifically to the question above, that is, the relationship between the story of a lovestruck young officer and the "blackest sin," the refusal or inability to love one's brother, to be responsible to one's neighbor, to feel human sympathy for one's fellow man. The question can be answered only by reference to two bits of biographical information, inconsequential in themselves, but absolutely essential here.

The mask representing "the foulest sinner" has been identified conclusively by R. D. Timenchik and associated Soviet scholars as Akhmatova's contemporary, the talented poet Kuzmin. The dragoon officer Kniazev appears to have been an object of Kuzmin's affection. Nevertheless, when Kniazev died, it was said that Kuzmin was unable to grieve for him. Moreover, Kuzmin gave the impression that he cared for no one and felt no responsibility for anyone (Kuzmin's porte-parole in his novel *Kartonnyi domik* [*House of Cards*] says as much). Whatever the case, Akhmatova, according to biographical sources, came to view Kuzmin as one

> Who wept not with me over the dead,
> Who doesn't know the meaning of conscience
> And what it's for.

The image of the poet unable or unwilling to mourn for his dead friend becomes generalized to those who honored neither humanity nor poetry in their refusal to reach out in sympathy to their suffering brothers.

One may observe that in such a view of things, the moral judgment ultimately overwhelms the aesthetic one; and this seems to have been the case, insofar as we can infer from the memoirs about Akhmatova. One might further expect this to be an artistic fault, and yet somehow it seems not at all to reduce the force and effectiveness of the work.

Thus the strong sense of moral values, of sin and retribution, of conscience and vindication that is firmly if quietly rooted in the old acmeist tradition becomes a dominant theme in *Poem Without a Hero.* The theme affirms both the innocence of the true poet and his right to be. It condemns equally the merely indifferent and the most zealous persecutors. The *Poem* is a judgment, but in the very act of remembering and recording, the Author also exacts retribution.

Akhmatova kept working on *Poem Without a Hero* well into the final decade of her life. It was, however, in no sense her last major work. Despite illness and advanced years, she wrote right up to the end. In the early 1960's there was even another of those astonishing bursts of creative originality that mark the earlier points in her career.

By 1964 Akhmatova was seventy-five. She was fully rehabilitated at last, and the larger part of her work had been accepted in the Soviet Union. Her final decade was more peaceful than any she had known since before World War I. In December 1964 she was permitted to travel to Catania in Italy to accept the Taormina Prize for poetry. From Italy, Akhmatova traveled to England to receive an honorary degree at Oxford.

Honored abroad and acclaimed at home, Akhmatova did not rest on her laurels: she had not only continued to be productive but found time to help and encourage young poets of talent—and even stood bravely in their defense when necessary. Although almost pathologically fearful that the campaign of persecution against her might resume at any time, Akhmatova did not hesitate to risk the safety of her own position when the cause was just. In 1964 she openly came to the assistance of Joseph Brodsky. He was then an unknown, unpublished poet whose talent Akhmatova much admired. She wrote of young poets like Brodsky,

> I no longer weep for me or mine,
> But if only I did not have to see on this earth
> The golden brand of failure
> Stamped on a still-unwrinkled brow.

In a society used to aesopic language, this quatrain, printed in a major Soviet literary journal, was an astonishingly direct plea for the artistic freedom of young poets and clearly placed Akhmatova herself in jeopardy. Moreover, when Brodsky was sentenced in a "show trial" recalling the Stalin era, she immediately circulated a petition for his release. At that time in the Soviet Union, this gesture on Akhmatova's part was one of supreme courage and humanity.

To Russians of Akhmatova's generation, this kind of bravery was the highest virtue. Reaching out to help one's fellow in pain or need, the simplest of Christian virtues, had often meant to that benighted generation inviting their own destruction. For them, cowardice—not reaching out to one's fellow, *not caring* about his fate—was the greatest sin: this is the moral argued in *Poem Without a Hero*. The true poet must reach out to and speak for his fellow; the poet is innocent, but he must suffer.

> Let it be so. Without executioner and block,
> There's no place on this earth for the poet.
> It's for us to wear the penitent's shift,
> To walk with a candle and howl.
>
> 1935
> (*Sochineniia* 3.47)

In autumn 1965 Akhmatova had a heart attack and never fully regained her strength. She died in March 1966 and, according to her wishes, was laid to rest with the ancient rites of the Orthodox Church.

Selected Bibliography

EDITIONS

INDIVIDUAL WORKS
Vecher. St. Petersburg, 1912.
Chetki. St. Petersburg, 1914.
Belaia staia. Petrograd, 1917.
Anno Domini MCMXXI. Petrograd, 1921.
Podorozhnik. Petrograd, 1921.
U samogo moria. Petersburg, 1921.
A number of collections drawing on the above and adding new original verse appeared between 1940 and 1965. Poems from 1922 to 1940 were collected under the title *Trostnik* (The Reed), and those up to 1964 under *Sed'maia Kniga* (The Seventh Book). Neither of these last two books was ever printed as a separate volume, but both appeared in collections.

COLLECTED WORKS
Beg vremeni. Moscow and Leningrad, 1965.
Sochineniia. Edited by G. Struve and B. Filippov. 3 vols. Munich and Paris, 1967–1983.
Stikhotvoreniia i poemy. Edited by V. M. Zhirmunskii. Leningrad, 1976. Contains variants of *Poem Without a Hero*.
Pamiati Anny Akmatovoi: Stikhi, Pis'ma, Vospominaniia. Paris, 1974.

ANNA AKHMATOVA

TRANSLATIONS

Poems of Akhmatova. Translated and introduced by Stanley Kunitz with Max Hayward. Boston, 1973.

Poems of Akhmatova. Translated by Lyn Coffin. New York, 1983.

Requiem and *Poem Without a Hero.* Translated by D. M. Thomas. Athens, Ohio, 1976.

Selected Poems. Translated by Richard McKane. London, 1969.

Selected Poems. Edited by Walter Arndt. Translated by Walter Arndt, Robin Kemball, Carl Proffer, Assya Humessky. Ann Arbor, Mich., 1976.

Way of All the Earth. Translated by D. M. Thomas. Athens, Ohio, 1979.

BIOGRAPHICAL AND CRITICAL STUDIES

Chechelnitsky, Inna. "Anna Akhmatova's Poem Without a Hero." Ph.D. diss. Brown University, 1982.

Chukovskaia, L. *Zapiski ob Anne Akhmatovoi.* 2 vols. Paris, 1976–1980.

Chukovskii, K. "Akhmatova i Maiakovskii." *Dom Iskusstv* 1: 23–42 (1921).

Dobin, E. *Poeziia Anny Akhmatovoi.* Leningrad, 1968.

Driver, Sam. *Anna Akhmatova.* New York, 1972.

Eikhenbaum, Boris. *Anna Akhmatova.* Petrograd, 1923.

Haight, Amanda. *Anna Akhmatova: A Poetic Pilgrimage.* New York and London, 1976.

Leiter, Sharon. *Akhmatova's Petersburg.* Philadelphia, 1983.

Nedobrovo, N. "Anna Akhmatova." *Russkaya mysl'* *VII* 1915, Part II, 50–68.

Pavlovskii, A. *Anna Akhmatova.* Leningrad, 1966.

Timenchik, R. "Akhmatova i Pushkin: Uchenye zapiski Latviiskogo gosudarstvennogo Universiteta (Riga)," vol. 215, *Pushkinskii sbornik,* ser. 2 (1974), 32–55.

Toporov, V. *Akhmatova i Blok.* Berkeley, 1981.

Verheul, L. *The Theme of Time in the Poetry of Akhmatova.* The Hague and Paris, 1971.

Vinogradov, V. *O poezii Anny Akhmatovoi.* Leningrad, 1925.

Zhirmunskii, V. *Tvorchestvo Anny Akhmatovoi.* Leningrad, 1973.

SAM DRIVER

JEAN COCTEAU
(1889–1963)

JEAN COCTEAU IS an extraordinary phenomenon. Surely the most versatile and one of the most lively and prolific of twentieth-century artists, he worked in and left his mark on nearly all media of artistic expression. Cocteau's creative career spans fifty years, from 1909 through the early 1960's. It comprises the production of over twenty volumes of poetry, half a dozen novels, more than a dozen plays and spectacles, several ballets, a host of critical and journalistic works, and half a dozen memorable films—not to mention innumerable drawings, paintings, and murals. As W. H. Auden said, to mount a retrospective on Jean Cocteau would require a warehouse to accommodate all his works. Cocteau looked upon his life as a series of phases, moltings, or *mues*. The impression one receives of him is that, having achieved distinction in one medium, he promptly abandoned it for another. In fact, however, despite the dazzling versatility of his oeuvre, there is a consistency, a continuity of vision and style underlying its variety and seeming discontinuity.

Cocteau's personality was as brilliant and multifaceted as his artistic career. Born on 5 July 1889 in Maisons-Laffitte, an elegant Parisian summer resort celebrated for horse racing, Cocteau regarded himself as quintessentially Parisian. He sprang from the *grande-bourgeoisie* that engendered Proust and Gide. His family was made up of stockbrokers, diplomats, and naval officers who were kindly disposed to the arts; indeed, several members of the family were artistic. Cocteau early contracted what he called "the red-and-gold disease"—a passion for the theater, including the circus. He thought of his relatives as dilettantes, and it was not until he was in his twenties that he realized how demanding an artistic vocation would be. From believing that the muses had been kindly fairies surrounding his cradle, he came to see them as praying mantises "who devour whomever they marry."

Socially and economically favored, Cocteau knew everyone worth knowing across the spectrum of the arts. He was a consummate publicist who lived most of his life in the limelight. However, he argued that though he was among the most celebrated, he was the least known of poets, for he believed that the true poet is the most invisible of creatures. It was part of his code that elegance is a virtue and that true elegance is unobtrusive, indeed invisible. Cocteau thought, as did William Butler Yeats, that the poet must possess a *sprezzatura* such that certain often darned and cobbled passages appear to have been tossed off complete and perfect on the first assay. He recognized, as Jean-Philippe Rameau observed, "Il est difficile d'avoir l'air facile" (it is difficult to cultivate an easy air). Although he was a brilliant and inexhaustible conversationalist and polemicist, Cocteau enjoyed silence and solitude, and indeed sought them out from time to time. The glittering, mercurial surface personality, essentially Gallic and best described as quicksilver (*vif-argent*), was the obverse or mirror side of a more somber self explored in works that embody Cocteau's myth of the poet, notably in *Orphée* (*Orpheus,* both the play [1927] and the film [1950]).

When Cocteau was nine, his father committed suicide after a financial failure. The elder Cocteau never had to work, and his death did not plunge his family into straitened circumstances, for the Lecomtes, Cocteau's well-to-do maternal grandparents, came to his mother's aid. His father's early death, and the manner of it, however, appear to have contributed to his youngest son's obsession with death and suicide and possibly also to his homosexuality. Cocteau early discovered a strong and abiding attraction to his own sex, along with a fatal attraction to "le sexe surnaturel de la beauté" (the supernatural sex of beauty). The legend of Narcissus suffuses all his work.

Despite his many talents, Cocteau was a poor scholar, failing in his studies at one school after another. He attended the Petit and Grand Condorcet and then the École Fénélon. A former tutor of Gide's helped him study for the *bachot,* but he did not gain a baccalaureate and never attended a university; all his degrees were honorary. At the age of fourteen or fifteen, Jean ran away from home and spent a year in the red-light district of Marseille, living with bohemians, tramps, pimps, and prostitutes. He found this a liberating experience, sexually and socially; when he returned to Paris and his family, further efforts to tame him were few.

The figure of Dargelos, the brutally handsome school vamp who lords it over Paul and the other boys in *Les enfants terribles* (*The Holy Terrors,* 1929), is based on a real-life personality from his school years who may have bested the young Cocteau in a snowball fight. The erotically charged memory was indelible, and Dargelos (who appears also in the film *Le sang d'un poète* [*1930, The Blood of a Poet,* 1948]) became the prototype for a series of *hommes fatales,* men whom Cocteau idolized, who became for him either sons or lovers, and

many of whom died young. The list includes Roland Garros, the flying ace to whom Cocteau dedicated the poems of *Le Cap de Bonne-Espérance* (The Cape of Good Hope, 1919); Jean Leroy; the writer Raymond Radiguet, who, though half Cocteau's age when they met, exerted a profound influence upon him; Jean Bourgoint (together with Cocteau himself the model for Paul in *The Holy Terrors*); Maurice Sachs; Jean Desbordes; Marcel Khill, with whom he traveled "around the world in eighty days" in 1936; the actor Jean Marais, who declared he owed everything to Jean Cocteau; and finally Edouard Dermit, who was his gardener, became his legal heir, and could, with honesty, echo Marais. There were also several tentative, abortive alliances with women, among whom were the actress Madeleine Carlier, the model for Germaine in *Le grand écart* (The Great Split, translated as *The Grand Écart,* 1923), and Valentine Hugo, the artist who married Victor Hugo's grandson and later became mistress to Cocteau's archenemy, André Breton. Cocteau remained very close to his mother all his life and continued to live with her until he was forty. For a short while in his early twenties, unknown to her, he frequented his own picturesque *garçonnière* in the magnificent and ramshackle Hôtel Biron in the Faubourg Saint-Germain, also occupied by, among others, Auguste Rodin and his secretary, Rainer Maria Rilke, Henri Matisse, Isadora Duncan, and Edouard de Max.

Cocteau was launched as a salon poet of *la belle epoque* in April 1908, when the actor Edouard de Max organized a reading for him at the Théâtre Femina. Cocteau's early poems were read to instant acclaim. He was then under the influence of Oscar Wilde, Aubrey Beardsley, and Countess Anna de Noailles, and continued thus for several years. With hindsight, Cocteau later condemned his first three volumes of verse: *La lampe d'Aladin* (Aladdin's Lamp, 1909), *Le prince frivole* (The Frivolous Prince, 1910), and *La danse de Sophocle* (Sophocles' Dance, 1912). They were also coolly reviewed in Gide's *Nouvelle revue française.* They are not included in Cocteau's *Oeuvres complètes* (1946–1951), which are, in any case, incomplete. Although "poet" was the proudest title to which Cocteau laid claim, he came to despise his apprentice work as derivative and insipid. These early poems reflect a poetic world blown to pieces by World War I.

Cocteau was exempted from military service on medical grounds and did not have to serve in World War I. He nevertheless volunteered for active service, but was rejected. He accompanied the aviator Roland Garros on reconnaissance flights from Villacoublay until Garros was shot down behind enemy lines. Cocteau wished to be a war correspondent, but instead served as a Red Cross ambulance driver in Champagne and Flanders. In the course of bringing aid to the wounded as part of the extraordinary convoy organized by Misia Sert, he saw the devastation of Rheims. Later, he joined Étienne de Beaumont's ambulance convoy on the Belgian front and spent some time in the trenches with the marines at Coxyde and Nieuport. This marine battalion was wiped out after he left. He saw action at the Battle of the Somme, was granted a leave in 1915, and did not return to the war. Out of Cocteau's war experiences he wrote two volumes of poems, *Le Cap de Bonne-Espérance* and *Discours du grand sommeil* (Discourse of the Great Sleep, 1916–1918) and the novel *Thomas l'imposteur* (*Thomas the Imposter,* 1923).

Once the war was over, Cocteau found himself one of a scintillating galaxy of stars of study, studio, stage, screen, salon, and society. Among those with whom he collaborated in artistic efforts were Colette, Lucien Daudet, Marcel Proust, André Gide, Guillaume Apollinaire, Alain Fournier, François Mauriac, Paul Claudel, Francis Jammes, Max Jacob, Blaise Cendrars, T. S. Eliot, W. H. Auden, Jean Genet, Edouard de Max, Sarah Bernhardt, Edmond Rostand, Mistinguett, Edith Piaf, Sacha Guitry, Jean Marais, Charlie Chaplin, Sergei Diaghilev, Vaslav Nijinsky, Tamara Karsavina, Léonide Massine, Michel Fokine, Léon Bakst, Isadora Duncan, Pablo Picasso, Amedeo Modigliani, Georges Braque, Juan Gris, Igor Stravinsky, Erik Satie, Georges Auric, Louis Durey, Arthur Honegger, Darius Milhaud, François Poulenc, and Germaine Tailleferre.

In addition to his young men, or *gosses,* Cocteau also habitually attached himself to certain master artists—or *monstres sacrés,* as he regarded them—from whom he drew inspiration and whose genius, in whatever medium, seemed to fertilize his own. Such were Diaghilev, Stravinsky, and Picasso, and to a lesser extent, Satie. The only one of his young men from whom he drew inspiration and instruction was Raymond Radiguet. It has been observed that Cocteau appears to have needed an external stimulus to set his own creative powers in motion. Thus, it was Diaghilev's injunction in 1912, "Étonne-moi!" (Astonish me!) that launched Cocteau upon his career in ballet, which culminated in the ballet spectacle *Parade* (first performed in 1917). He conceived the idea and wrote the scenario, then engaged Diaghilev as producer, Picasso as set and costume designer, and Satie as score writer. Diaghilev and his Ballets Russes inspired Cocteau to become first a draughtsman and painter, then an impresario in his own right. Cocteau worked on several ballets besides *Parade* in conjunction with the Ballets Russes: *Le dieu bleu* (The Blue God), *Roméo et Juliette* (Romeo and Juliet), and *Le train bleu* (The Blue Train). He met Stravinsky in 1910. Three years later, impressed by the experience of attending the premiere of *Le sacre du printemps* (*The Rite of Spring*), Cocteau apprenticed himself to this new master. The savage rhythms of *The Rite of Spring* inspired him to write his first original work of literature, *Le Potomak* (The Potomac), conceived in 1913 but not published until six years later. It is dedicated to Stravinsky.

Cocteau's encounter with Picasso was even more important and fruitful, for Picasso as well as for Cocteau. When Cocteau introduced the painter to Diaghilev, Picasso recognized the possibilities of designing for the stage. By bringing Picasso's art out of the atelier and onto the boards, Cocteau helped revolutionize and galvanize stage design and, at the same time, helped Picasso gain recognition as the foremost visual artist of the time. Further, this move inspired many other French artists to work for the theater and ballet. Cocteau also discovered and publicized the new music of "les Six": Auric, Honegger, Milhaud, Poulenc, Tailleferre, and Durey.

In tracing and assessing a career as protean as Cocteau's, it may sometimes seem helpful, if difficult, to divide it into certain phases or periods. During the second decade of this century, Cocteau was in his twenties; although poetry was his first and abiding preoccupation, he devoted this early period principally to the production of ballets and spectacles. Yet because of his eclectic talents, it is difficult to describe, classify, or categorize Cocteau's works. Cocteau himself used a single word to describe all he did. Thus his poetry is *poésie,* his novels are *poésie de roman,* his plays are *poésie de théâtre,* his criticism is *poésie critique,* his films are *poésie cinématographique,* and his drawing and painting, *poésie graphique.* For Cocteau, poetry held immense power and fascination. It was his primary medium; he wrote poetry all his life. Poetry was for him an exalting spirit akin to, but outside, religion. This spirit was to evoke in Cocteau's works an angelic quality that shows a striking affinity with that of Rilke. The figure of the angel first appears in the poems of *Le Cap de Bonne-Espérance,* having been naturally suggested by metaphysical flights inspired by Cocteau's actual flights with Roland Garros. The angel assumes increasing significance in succeeding volumes: *Discours du grand sommeil,* a requiem for those slaughtered in the trenches, and more personal significance in *L'Ange Heurtebise* (The Angel Heurtebise), the central poem of *Opéra: Oeuvre poétique* (1927), in which he is a surrogate for the dead Raymond Radiguet. The angel is a winged messenger or muse who epitomizes or embodies the powers of poetry.

Although in the period just before and after World War I Cocteau devoted himself chiefly to the production of ballets and spectacles, he also wrote and published three novels, one of which—*Le Potomak*—may well be the most curious novel ever written. Cocteau regarded it as the "preface" to the rest of his work. It is a stream-of-consciousness potpourri of poetry, prose, letters, dialogues, confessions, and drawings centering on "the potomak," a strange creature like a winged jellyfish. The drawings are extraordinary, Thurber-like cartoons depicting the warfare between two clans, the Eugènes and the Mortimers. The Mortimers are a solid bourgeois couple; the Eugènes are mysteriously hostile and bent on frightening and persecuting the Mortimers. Cocteau commented that both the writing and drawing of *Le Potomak* had been automatic. At this time he was submitting himself to the kind of "dérèglement de tous les sens" (disorientation of the senses) that Rimbaud had advocated; in particular, he tried to sleep and dream as much as possible and, believing that the consumption of sugar promoted dreams, he swallowed large amounts of sugar daily. *Le Potomak* is virtually untranslatable; only excerpts from it have been published in English.

In the program notes to *Parade,* which Francis Steegmuller has called the first modern ballet, the poet Guillaume Apollinaire used the word *surrealist* for the first time. Apollinaire hailed Cocteau for having brought about "the alliance of painting and dance, of music and the plastic arts, which is the sign of a more complete art. From this new alliance has resulted something beyond realism . . . surrealism." The question arises: was Cocteau actually a surrealist? The answer is yes and no. He was surrealist in all but name and allegiance. He held and practiced many of the tenets of surrealism, professed by the movement of that name founded in the early 1920's by André Breton as successor to Tristan Tzara's dadaism. Surrealism, as expounded by Breton, held that art should portray thought without the intervention of reason, and, as he writes in *Qu'est ce que le surréalisme?* (*What Is Surrealism?,* 1934), should transmute "those two seemingly contradictory states, dream and reality, into a sort of absolute reality, of surreality, so to speak." Cocteau, too, blends dream and reality and believes in bringing the night into full daylight. Yet Cocteau was never a member of the surrealist movement, for he and Breton were inveterate enemies. Cocteau was too much of an individualist to belong to any movement. Further, he was habitually less willing than Breton to surrender conscious control in expressing what he found in the subconscious. While Breton and many of the surrealists espoused the far left or communism, they considered Cocteau to belong to the right. This was not the case, for Cocteau was strictly apolitical and on friendly terms with many leftists and Communists among Montmartre and Montparnasse artists. The surrealists, however, cordially loathed Cocteau for having been born with a silver spoon in his mouth, for his Rive Droite antecedents and manners, and for the publicity and success that attended his every move. For them he never lived down his initial success as a salon poet.

The period between 1919 and 1923 was particularly productive for Cocteau. In June 1919, at a memorial reading for Apollinaire, who had recently died, Cocteau was introduced by Max Jacob to the young writer Raymond Radiguet. Radiguet at this time was seventeen, Cocteau thirty. Cocteau was immediately captivated by this brilliant, unruly young man. During the following four years they spent much time together, traveling to the Riviera, to Arcachon, and even to England. Their relationship has been compared with that of Paul Verlaine and Arthur Rimbaud, Radiguet being a prodigy who showed signs of youthful genius, although in his case for prose rather than poetry. Radiguet came from a large, working-class family; his parents were bitterly opposed to Cocteau's influence upon him and did their best to separate them. In fact, Cocteau acted as a surrogate father as well as a lover to his young protégé, who was as turbulent as Rimbaud and much given to alcohol and prostitutes. In his turn, Radiguet, who held ideals of

classic simplicity, exerted a beneficial artistic influence upon Cocteau. It was during their association that Cocteau wrote his two most limpid novels, *The Grand Écart* and *Thomas the Impostor,* two of his most death-haunted and impressive volumes of poems, *Discours du grand sommeil* and *Plain-chant* (Plainchant, 1923), and the critical work *Le secret professionnel* (*Professional Secrets,* 1922). Radiguet imbued Cocteau with his own aim of returning to the classics and emulating masterpieces. They worked together at the same table—Radiguet on his first novel, *Le diable au corps* (Devil in the Flesh, 1923, influenced by Choderlos de Laclos's *Les liaisons dangéreuses* [*Dangerous Liaisons,* 1782]) and then on *Le bal du Comte Orgel* (Count Orgel, 1924), Cocteau on *The Grand Écart* and later on *Thomas the Impostor,* which he declared owed something to Stendhal's *La chartreuse de Parme* (*The Charterhouse of Parma,* 1839).

The intensely creative relationship with Radiguet was cut short by the latter's tragic death from typhoid poisoning in December 1923; he was not yet twenty-one. Cocteau was devastated, though he observed that he had always had the presentiment that Radiguet was only "on loan." Cocteau saw himself as left behind "amid the rubble of what was once a workshop for cutting crystal." Shortly after the death of his "marvelous boy," Cocteau took to his bed, saying he would never write again. Invited to Monte Carlo by Diaghilev to recuperate, he was introduced to opium by the musicologist Louis Laloy. Cocteau was to smoke opium for many years and to undertake several cures before finally ridding himself of his addiction. *Opium* (1930) is the record of the protracted disintoxication Cocteau underwent in the winter and spring of 1928–1929.

Like much of Cocteau's work, *The Grand Écart* is autobiographical and, like *Thomas the Imposter,* it explores the dividing line separating childhood or adolescence from manhood or maturity. The protagonists of both novels are of the "pure in heart," who must grow up—or die. Jacques Forestier of *The Grand Écart* grows up after a tragic love affair and a failed suicide attempt. Guillaume Thomas de Fontenoy, hero of *Thomas the Imposter,* sees action in the theaters of war best known to his author, and dies. The receptions accorded these two novels were quite different: *The Grand Écart* was popular, almost a cult novel (like the even more successful work *The Holy Terrors*), while the better crafted war novel was poorly received because it was wholly without heroics or patriotic rodomontade.

Because Cocteau's work—as Neal Oxenhandler points out in *Scandal and Parade* (1957)—is so subjective, poetic, and mythic and so lacking in socioeconomic or psychological dimensions and context, his plots must often strike readers as particularly weird or grotesque. Plot summaries of his novels and plays run the risk of sounding crazed; for this reason they are subordinated here as much as possible to discussion of the latent significance of the works.

The style of these two novels is aphoristic and sometimes dazzling; in its confusion of objects and persons, the animate and the inanimate, it is decadent. Here, for instance, is Cocteau's evocation of the city of Venice (from *The Grand Écart*, in *Oeuvres complètes*, vol. I, p. 17): "Venice by day is a country fair shooting gallery full of crumbs. At night . . . a negress in love, dead in her bath with her paste jewels." Or here is his view of the two enemy armies mired cheek by jowl in the trenches of World War I (from *Thomas the Imposter*, in *Oeuvres complètes*, vol. I, p. 114): "Soon hunter and prey became rooted plants, face to face, Siamese twins united by a membrane of mud and despair." On his final tour of duty through the trenches, Thomas passes the sector occupied by Zouave troops: "In a thousand cellars the Zouaves slept in rows like bottles. They were broken on days of orgy" (p.157). Thomas is struck by the wind stirring "an ember of a plaint in the little glass insulators atop the telegraph poles, like the bells of lily of the valley" (p. 176). Naturally, such passages are more striking in Cocteau's French, which is simultaneously remarkable for its clear surface and turbulent depths. In this regard it reminds one of and is as epigrammatic and telling as Kafka's German. Cocteau declared that while for many style is a complicated way of saying simple things, for him it is a simple way of saying complicated things.

Jacques Forestier shares many characteristics of Jean Cocteau. He is a sensualist yet a naïf, witty but sympathetic, and it is his destiny, like a Petrarchan lover, to be forever wounded by beauty. The objects of his interest and affection are of indeterminate sex and sexual orientation, male and female, homosexual and bisexual. Forestier cherishes "memories of human beauty, which were so many wounds." As Bettina Knapp points out in *Jean Cocteau* (1970), "Not only is Jacques's character splintered, but so are all the other beings portrayed in this novel who are, in effect, projections of the central character." In a curious passage, the author observes that human beings, like planets, have a lit and a shadowed side:

> Half shadow, half light: that is the illumination of the planets. Half the world rests, the other works. But a mysterious force emanates from that half that dreams. And with man it happens that the sleeping half contradicts the active half. True nature speaks through it. If man learns from it to put his light side in order, the shadow side may become dangerous. Its role will change. It will send up miasmas. We will see Jacques caught in the grip of this night of the human body.
>
> (1.20)[1]

Jacques spends much of his time plunged in the "night of the human body," struggling toward the light, his subconscious shadow self alternately aiding and leading him astray.

Jacques Forestier is a poor scholar. He is studying for the *bachot* in the Touraine, but is

---

[1] All citations, unless otherwise noted, are from the eleven-volume edition of *Oeuvres complètes* (Lausanne, 1946–1951).

expending much more time and energy being initiated into the mysteries of sex. A school-fellow introduces him to his mistress, Louise, who in turn introduces Jacques to Germaine, with whom he falls in love. Peter Stopwell, an English version of Dargelos, makes overtures to him, is rebuffed, and eventually steals Germaine from him. Germaine and Louise are demimondaines who earn fifty francs in the theater for fifty thousand in bed. Germaine is Jacques's first woman. Before falling in love with her, Jacques "felt the desire to be of those whom he thought to be beautiful . . . not to be loved by them." Now he believes himself cured of such narcissistic yearnings, for he wants to possess Germaine, not to *be* her: "For the first time he experienced desire that was not a malaise. For the first time he did not hate his own image." However, the author's attitude to his character's love is ambivalent; he writes that Jacques's "abnormal love grew slowly, normally," and, whereas his attitude to Forestier is always sympathetic, his attitude to Germaine is consistently scathing. His purity of heart enables Jacques to continue loving Germaine in spite of her slatternly manners, her seamy surroundings, and his knowledge that she is kept by the wealthy Nestor Osiris. Osiris never suspects Forestier as one of Germaine's lovers, even when Germaine openly avows him. Jacques continues to love Germaine even after he surprises her in bed with Louise. However, when Germaine transfers her affections to Stopwell, Jacques realizes it is all over and tries to kill himself. He is discovered and restored to life, though certain Coctelian reflections on destiny and determinism do not hold out much hope for his future. The author observes that "our life's map is folded in such a way that we do not discern the main road that traverses it, but, little by little, as it is unfolded, see always a new route branching off. We think we can choose, but have no choice" (*The Grand Écart*, in *Oeuvres complètes*, vol. I, p. 20). And this novel contains Cocteau's famous metaphor, rendered more powerful by its evocation of the Holocaust: "Despite the difference in classes, life is transporting us all together at great speed in a single train toward death" (p. 88).

Lewis Galantière, who translated *Thomas the Imposter* into English, called that work both a war book and a fairy tale. Like *The Grand Écart*, it is more *récit* than novel. It centers upon two luminous personalities, Thomas and the Princess de Bormes, and a third, paler one, Henriette, the princess's daughter; these three play out their destinies against the dark theater of war. The princess is modeled on Misia Sert, beloved of Henri de Toulouse-Lautrec, Auguste Renoir, Paul Verlaine, Stéphane Mallarmé, and Claude Debussy, and Diaghilev's only female confidante. Misia Sert was a patron of the arts who, during World War I, obtained permission from General Gallieni to form a convoy of ambulances to bring aid to the wounded and carry them back from the front. She used her own limousine and couturiers' vans for this purpose. Cocteau enrolled in Sert's service in 1914. Her extraordinary personality and adventurousness are well captured in Cocteau's Princess de Bormes. Compared with the noble and disinterested princess, Mme Valiche, the nurse, is a greedy, vulgar scavenger of war, a vulture. Sixteen-year-old Guillaume Thomas de Fontenoy poses as nephew to a famous general. He is a poet of action, a born liar whose lies tell the truth, and who is, as Cocteau puts it, "artificial . . . without artifice." The princess takes him under her wing. Imbued with the same ardent spirit of adventure, they travel to the front together in the same carriage, like the poet and his muse entering the underworld in *Orpheus*.

Although Cocteau drew upon his own fantastic war adventures in this novel, he told his mother that he had Stendhal's Fabrice and his marginal view of the Battle of Waterloo in mind as he presented Thomas's experiences.

The princess and her protégé are two innocents for whom war is a game, a play. In an image that verges on the awkward, even the repellent, Cocteau shows them both confronting war with the eagerness of children gazing into a *pâtissier's* window. As is usual, there is a disparity between the levity of Cocteau's style and the gravity of his subject, but the novel's ironies are usually effective. Each of the protagonists longs for "the great moment": what the novel reveals is that the great moment is death. Never has war been looked at through such ingenuous eyes, nor so vividly. The wounded and dying are described as El Greco monks, elongated, greenish specters. The city of Rheims has been set ablaze; to Thomas it recalls the pyre of Joan of Arc, while "the cathedral was a mountain of old lace."

Sexually awakened by Henriette's mother (although, unlike other mothers in Cocteau, the princess never oversteps her maternal role), Guillaume Thomas falls in love with the pallid Henriette. As is usual in Cocteau, however, this love has incestuous undertones. Guillaume Thomas and Henriette view themselves as brother and sister. Before he fully realizes his love, Thomas gets himself posted to the Belgian front with the help of Pesquel-Duport, the princess's journalist lover, who is only too happy to get rid of the young man because he believes he is a rival for the princess's love. Thomas transfers his love for Henriette to the battalion. After being cold-shouldered initially, he becomes its mascot. Because of his zeal and imperviousness to danger, he is selected for particularly risky missions. Carrying a message for his commander to the enemy lines, Thomas is struck by a bullet: "'A bullet,' he said to himself. 'I am lost if I don't pretend to be dead.'" The author comments on this final ruse: "But in him, fiction and reality were one. Guillaume Thomas was dead." Henriette, on hearing of his death from the grisly nurse, Mme Valiche, poisons herself, her mother growing instantly old when she learns of her daughter's death.

Cocteau devoted the 1920's and 1930's largely to drama; however, before he pioneered the modernization of Greek tragedy for the contemporary French stage, he produced two wildly surreal and eclectic vaudeville pieces in the early 1920's: *Le boeuf sur le toit* (*The Do-Nothing Bar*, 1920) and *Les mariés de la Tour Eiffel* (*The Eiffel Tower Wedding Party,* 1923). Both are farces, the first a mime with music by Milhaud and set by Raoul Dufy, the second with music by "les Six" and costumes by Jean Hugo.

Before discussing Cocteau's considerable contribution to modern French drama, it would be well to define what he intended by *poésie de théâtre.* He meant a poetry of the theater, of the boards, a theater of spectacle, rather than poetry applied to drama. With his immense interest in production and in all the resources of the drama—sets, properties, lighting, costumes—he wrote plays that make the most of stage effects and mixed media to bring the resources of dance, spectacle, and music into the theater. This is already apparent in Cocteau's ballets and spectacles of the 1910's and 1920's and continues to be one of the trademarks of his dramas of the 1920's and 1930's. He disliked the "poetic" theater and purplish dialogue of such dramatists as Edmond Rostand and Maurice Maeterlinck; by contrast, the language Cocteau writes for the stage is often, particularly in his adaptations of Greek drama, bare and stripped.

Cocteau's *Antigone* (1927), his first excursion into reviving the classics, is perhaps the most striking example of this bareness. It is a very bleak, contemporary version of Sophocles' play, which Cocteau termed "an aerial view of Greece." Produced in Paris in 1922 with scenery by Picasso, music by Honegger, and costumes by Coco Chanel, its cast included Cocteau himself in the role of the Chorus, which has been modernized and streamlined into a voice issuing from a hole at center stage, like that of a news commentator. The young Antonin Artaud played Tiresias; Charles Dullin, Creon; and a beautiful Greek actress who spoke not a word of French, Genrin Athanasion, was Antigone. Cocteau was the first to adapt Greek drama to the contemporary French stage; he was followed by Gide, Jean Giraudoux, Jean-Paul Sartre, and Jean Anouilh. Cocteau followed *Antigone* with a pared-down version of Shakespeare's *Romeo and Juliet,* in which he played Mercutio. Cocteau was still suffering intensely from the loss of Radiguet, opium was undermining his health, and he had chronic insomnia. He spent the summer in Villefranche-sur-Mer, staring into the mirror, drawing self-portrait after self-portrait.

It was in December 1924 that Cocteau, seeking solace for his grief, returned to Catholicism. Jacques Maritain was the instrument of his conversion, along with Père Charles Henrion, a Saharan missionary. Cocteau received communion in Maritain's private chapel on the Feast of the Sacred Heart in June 1925. Cocteau had said he found it agony to be a believer without a faith, but his reversion to Catholicism did not last long. Although he also introduced two of his young men, Maurice Sachs and Jean Bourgoint, to the church, he soon abandoned it again. Not so opium. The poems of *Opéra: Oeuvre poetique* are opium-filled fantasies. The poem at their center, *L'ange Heurtebise* (1926), was, Cocteau claimed, virtually automatic writing. Going to see Picasso in his studio on the rue la Boétie one day, in the elevator he hallucinated he heard a voice saying, "My name is on the plate." On the plate he read the name "Ascenseur Heurtebise." So the figure of the angel Heurtebise entered Cocteau's work. Prior to this he had felt himself constantly accompanied by the ghost of the dead Radiguet. With the automatic writing of the intensely spiritual and erotic poem *L'ange Heurtebise,* a poem about his personal muse or guardian angel, the poet temporarily laid the ghost to rest, although Heurtebise reappears in *Orpheus.*

It was *Orpheus,* written at Villefranche in 1925, that declared Jean Cocteau a force to be reckoned with in the literary world. It is an extraordinary play from which, a generation later, he made an even more haunting film. Cocteau was obsessed by the figures of Orpheus and of Oedipus; he wrote dramas about each of these mythic beings who transgressed human limits, one by entering the underworld, the other by violating the strongest human taboo in killing his father and marrying his mother. Orpheus, the archetypal poet, fascinated Cocteau because united within this figure are such oppositions as solar and lunar, Apollonian and Dionysian, male and female, reason and unreason. Cocteau said that *Orpheus* was the first work to bring night into full daylight. He also acknowledged the play to be autobiographical, saying, "Twelve dramatic years are projected, hidden, in it."

Orpheus comprises a single act composed of thirteen scenes; it produces the effect of a painting by Giorgio de Chirico or Salvador Dali. The characters are doubled. Orpheus and Eurydice together seem to constitute a single androgynous figure, but Orpheus is also doubled by his horse and by Death, as Eurydice is doubled by the figure of Heurtebise, a glazier who assumes the role of guardian angel. The characters pass through mirrors into the after-life; Heurtebise flies; Death, as often in Cocteau's work, is a beautiful woman; she has two attendants and plenty of technical support. The play was first produced by the Pitoëffs in June 1926, with Georges Pitoëff playing Orpheus and his wife in the role of Eurydice; in a later production Cocteau played the role of Heurtebise.

The play contains parodic as well as autobiographical elements. Thus the horse, a kind of circus animal with the legs of a man, satirizes Dada and surrealism and their worshipful reliance on the unconscious. In the legend, Orpheus' poetic powers enthrall the beasts; in Cocteau's play, Orpheus is bewitched by his horse, representing his subconscious. Orpheus deciphers messages the horse transmits through hoofbeats. One of these messages, "Madame Eurydice reviendra d'enfer" spells "merde," recalling the opening words of Alfred Jarry's *Ubu Roi* (1896). Eurydice keeps breaking windows to attract the glazier, Heurtebise, who is her confidant while Orpheus neglects her. Jealous of the horse who claims all Orpheus' attention, Eurydice kills it, but is herself poisoned through Aglaonice's treachery. Aglaonice is the leader of the bacchantes, to whom Eurydice formerly belonged, and from whom Orpheus rescued her.

As in the legend, Orpheus follows Eurydice to hell and brings her back, but looks at her and loses her. He is then torn apart and decapitated by a mob of howling bacchantes. However, Cocteau stages a cheerful comic epilogue in heaven to provide an uncharacteristically upbeat ending. Orpheus, Eurydice, and Heurtebise are together. Orpheus recognizes Heurtebise as his wife's guardian angel and his horse as the devil Eurydice killed, which is why she had to lose her own life. Orpheus gives thanks to God: "We thank thee for having saved me because I adored poetry, and thou art poetry." Possibly Cocteau is poking fun at himself for his recent "reconversion" to Catholicism, as well as at surrealism, through the parodic Pegasus to which Orpheus listens spellbound in the opening scenes. Perhaps the ending is designed to comment on the epigraph to the play, taken from the poem *L'ange Heurtebise:* "Qu'il est laid le bonheur qu'on veut. / Qu'il est beau le malheur qu'on a" (How ugly is the happiness one desires. / How beautiful is the unhappiness one has).

The most striking scenes in *Orpheus* are those in which Death enters Orpheus' household and Orpheus, with the aid of the gloves Death leaves behind, pierces the mirror and enters the underworld in search of his wife. Here Cocteau uses his favorite symbol, the mirror, to great effect. Appearing to reflect an identical world to the one we live in, it is in fact the doorway to a realm that is its obverse, a world through the looking glass. "Mirrors are the doors through which Death comes and goes. . . . You have only to watch yourself all your life in a mirror, and you'll see Death at work like bees in a glass hive."

The film of *Orpheus,* which Cocteau made in 1950, is longer, more complex, and better unified than the play. Cocteau described it as "an immortal thriller." The circus horse has disappeared and is replaced by Death's funereal Rolls-Royce; mysterious radio messages received and emitted by this vehicle replace the morse code tapped out by the horse. Death's attendants, Azrael and Raphael, have become two sinister motorcyclists, who cause the deaths of Eurydice and Cégeste. The device of doubling has increased, for now Orpheus is doubled by the younger, more popular poet, Cégeste. Death has become a more central, an even more commanding figure. She is Cocteau's muse. It is clear that she loves Orpheus and that he loves her. When Heurtebise asks Orpheus whether it is Death or Eurydice that he wishes to rejoin, Orpheus replies, both. Like the Sphinx in *La machine infernale* (*The Infernal Machine,* 1934), Death is tried and condemned for overstepping the boundaries of her assigned role. She is not Death itself, but one of the supernumeraries of the ultimate Death. Cocteau's view of the universe is Kafkaesque. The film's atmosphere is ominous; much of it was filmed in the destroyed barracks of St. Cyr. Jean Marais plays Orpheus; Edouard Dermit, Cégeste; Marie Déa, Eurydice; and Maria Casarès, Death.

While undergoing another opium cure, this time in a clinic at St. Cloud, Cocteau heard and was riveted by the story of someone he knew, Jean Bourgoint, which caused him to write his novel *The Holy Terrors.* Jean Bourgoint was a tall, blond, handsome young man who had recently entered Cocteau's life and who lived in bohemian disorder with his sister, Jeanne, and a widowed mother. Jeanne, too, was extremely beautiful and worked as a model. Brother and sister, though not actually twins (Jeanne had a twin brother who shunned them both), shared the same room and the same bed, though now in their twenties. Jeanne, somewhat crazed, had been briefly married to a businessman whom brother and sister ultimately ostracized and expelled, as it were, from the family. Cocteau fashioned Jean and Jeanne Bourgoint into Paul and Elisabeth of *The Holy Terrors.* (The author said that another model for Elisabeth was furnished by Greta Garbo; he imagined her as she had been at the age of eighteen.) Cocteau wrote the book in about three weeks, at the rate of seven to seventeen pages a day, while at St. Cloud, in a creative fever that resembled the "automatic" transmission of the poem *L'ange Heurtebise,* though in a more sustained fashion. Perhaps the best introduction to his work for someone who does not know Cocteau, *The Holy Terrors* is also his most typical or essential work. Haunted by the themes of death and incest, the book has a hallucinatory, oneiric, and mythic quality. On publication it was an instant success and became a cult novel for the young.

Again, Cocteau's protagonists are children who cannot grow up and who inhabit an enchanted childhood realm. Their mother, who dies, and the kind doctor who takes care of them in sickness and, implausibly, in health too, are of no importance. Dargelos, Paul, and Elisabeth loom larger than life and fill the whole canvas. Paul and Elisabeth are twin halves of a single being. They are inseparable; they "adored, devoured each other," and "no one could foresee the moment when these two sundered portions of a single being would cease from strife and become one again." This dual androgynous being attracts into its orbit, to be electrocuted by its alternating current, a young boy and girl, Gérard and Agathe. Gérard, a classmate of Paul's, first adores Paul, then transfers his love, through Paul, to Elisabeth. Agathe, a fellow model of Elisabeth's, is first attracted to her and then, through her, to Paul. Paul is slow to realize his attraction to Agathe; he does so when he realizes she is the mirror image of Dargelos, his boyhood idol.

The Holy Terrors is a tautly constructed novel; nearly everything in it is doubled. It opens with a snowball fight in which the bully Dargelos (who reappears in *The Blood of a Poet*) fells Paul, who is left bleeding in the snow. Gérard rushes to his aid and transports him back to his room. Their transit through snow and darkness resembles those journeys into the afterlife (compare that in *Orpheus*) that are essential to Cocteau. Elisabeth and Paul double each other, as do Paul and Gérard, Elisabeth and Agathe, and, finally, Agathe and Dargelos. Paul loves Dargelos, who is expelled from school for injuring him. Paul then must stay at home, where Elisabeth will brook no rival for his love. Gérard, through loving Paul, comes to love his sister, but love makes him clairvoyant: he realizes Elisabeth is a vestal virgin, whom "none might violate, save at the price of life itself." Elisabeth is wooed and won by Michael, a worldly young man with a fortune, but her husband-to-be is killed in an automobile accident (in the same manner as Isadora Duncan) on his wedding night. When Agathe is introduced into his life, Paul does not realize he loves her until he recognizes her as Dargelos in female shape. But when Agathe makes the fatal avowal of her love for Paul, Elisabeth determines to thwart them. Her brother writes a letter declaring his love; significantly, he feels incapable of expressing his feelings directly, and, even more significantly, his love letter is directed, by mistake, to himself. Elisabeth purloins and destroys this letter. She then informs her brother that Agathe loves Gérard, and works on Gérard, whom she knows to be in love with herself, to propose to Agathe. Gérard and Agathe marry. Dargelos reappears to bring about the fateful ending. A world traveler, he is also a collector of poisons and commends himself to "Snowball" (Paul) with a lump of a dark, noxious-smelling substance, which Paul duly ingests— not, however, before he has written a suicide note to Agathe, which this time she receives. As Paul lies on his deathbed, she learns that he loved her but that Elisabeth betrayed them both. Elisabeth then shoots herself; her *Liebestod* is simultaneous with her brother's:

> She saw . . . knew that the knot that bound them still held fast. . . . Courage, one little moment longer and they will be where flesh dissolves, where souls embrace, where incest lurks no

more. . . . Still, by a single thread of light the Maiden Goddess holds him out of darkness; his stone body is still penetrated by one last all-pervading thought of life. . . . Still, her finger on the trigger, like one clasped with her lover in the act of love, Elisabeth watched and waited on his pleasure, cried out to him to hasten his mortal spasm, to accompany her into the final moment of mutual rapture and possession, mutual death. (*The Holy Terrors,* trans. Rosamund Lehmann, pp. 190–192)

The Holy Terrors, like *Orpheus, The Blood of a Poet, The Infernal Machine,* and *Les parents terribles* (translated as *Intimate Relations,* 1938) is one of the works that embodies Cocteau's personal myth, which centers on the Oedipus complex.

In 1930, Cocteau enjoyed his first popular theatrical success with his tour de force, *La voix humaine (The Human Voice).* This work, with its sardonic title, is a monologue for a single actress. The instrument or means is that almost banal accessory of stage comedy, the telephone. We hear a monologue, half of a jilted woman's dialogue with her lover. She knows that when she rings off, this man who has been her raison d'être for five years, will be lost to her forever. In the course of their conversation, it is revealed he is about to marry. The woman's life sputters on the edge of extinction, for she has lost both the desire and the courage to go on living. This is a skillfully crafted and moving play, and some fine actresses have performed it with great success, among them Berthe Bovy, Anna Magnani, Ingrid Bergman, and Lillabil Ibsen. Later, in 1940, Cocteau wrote for Edith Piaf another single-character play, *Le bel indifférent (The Indifferent Beau).*

The masterpiece among Cocteau's dramas, certainly his finest adaptation of Greek tragedy, is *The Infernal Machine,* which was produced in 1932. It was directed by Louis Jouvet, with sets and costumes by Christian Bérard. Cocteau condenses the tragedy of Oedipus—of which he had already treated the final episode in *Oedipe-roi (Oedipus Rex)* in 1928 as an opera with score by Stravinsky—into four acts. The title *The Infernal Machine* is explained by the initial words of the Voice or Chorus: "Watch, spectator, unwind before you a tightly wound spring that will slowly uncoil the length of a human life; it is one of the most perfect machines devised by the infernal gods for the mathematical annihilation of a mortal." This play is a powerful expression of Cocteau's fatalism. In it, he posits that our desires, as well as our acts, are predetermined. Free will and free action are "thinkable" only; in fact, they do not exist. The story of Oedipus exemplifies such a creed, while the swallowing up of free will in determinism is integrally linked to Cocteau's theory of the relationship of time to eternity. Anubis demonstrates to the Sphinx that time is merely a fold in the continuum of eternity: "Le temps des hommes est de l'éternité pliée." If we fold a piece of cloth, pierce and hold it together with a brooch, then unfold it, who would believe that all those little holes reappearing at intervals had been made by the same instrument? It is a graphic analogy.

Cocteau adds to the Oedipus legend the mythical figures of the Sphinx and Anubis, who appear in the second act. The encounter between Oedipus and the Sphinx, who is in a sense Anubis' double, is the real center of the play. The triangle between Oedipus, the Sphinx as young girl, and Anubis as avenging nemesis, is, as Frederick Brown observes in *An Impersonation of Angels* (1968), reminiscent of the Orpheus-Eurydice-Death triangle. And the Sphinx, while trying to save Oedipus from death, merely preserves him for marriage with his mother. In a sense she prefigures Jocasta.

The opening act of *The Infernal Machine* is indebted to *Hamlet.* The ghost of Laius, Oedipus' father, appears on the ramparts of Thebes to warn the sentinels of an untoward event. When those he wishes to warn most urgently, namely Tiresias and Jocasta, appear, he cannot communicate with them but remains silent and invisible, reminding one of the appearance of the ghost of Hamlet's father before Gertrude in the fourth act of *Hamlet.* Invisible gods haul

Laius away; like the Sphinx, who is rebuked and held in check by Anubis, he has transgressed divine laws in vainly seeking to save mortals from their destiny.

In the second act, while the ghost of Laius tries to warn Jocasta, Oedipus goes to encounter the Sphinx. He finds this scourge has manifested itself as a young girl in white with a jackal's head in her lap (Anubis). The dialogue between Oedipus and the Sphinx is Cocteau at his sparkling best; this is a scene full of wit and élan, like George Bernard Shaw's depiction of the encounter between Caesar and Cleopatra. In a role parallel to that of Death in *Orpheus,* the Sphinx falls in love with Oedipus and, desiring that he triumph over her so that she may be delivered from her fate of killing mortals, tells him the answer to the riddle with which he may confound and kill her. Thereupon Oedipus, a brash young hero, slings her over his shoulder and advances in triumph upon Thebes to marry Queen Jocasta. All Oedipus' attempts to evade the destiny prophesied for him, like the Sphinx's intervention in his fate, are foiled, however. As Anubis says to the Sphinx, who is now weary of and rebellious against her fate: "We must obey. Mystery has its mysteries. The gods possess their gods. We have ours; they have theirs. That is what is called infinity." The third act presents the wedding night of Oedipus and Jocasta in the womblike palace of Thebes. Oedipus has first to endure a tedious interview with the blind prophet Tiresias, who seems to share some of the characteristics of Shakespeare's Polonius, ever spying on others and serving as the prologue to bad news. Looking into his eyes, Oedipus is momentarily blinded in anticipation of his own self-punishment.

In none of his plays does Cocteau's ability to endow objects with life and to make them seem disquieting witnesses and accomplices in the actions of his characters appear more tellingly than in *The Infernal Machine.* We see how Jocasta's scarf conspires, from her initial appearance, to strangle her, how her gold brooch holds a special fascination for Oedipus. Beside the nuptial bed stands the cradle of the son whom Jocasta all but admits to Oedipus she abandoned because of a dreadful prophecy. Jocasta almost recognizes Oedipus when he takes off his sandals and reveals his wounded feet. While they lie side by side, dozing and wracked by nightmares, the rug at the foot of the bed appears to metamorphose into Anubis. Worst of all is Jocasta's nightmare presaging incest. Jocasta dreams she is nursing a child, but the child melts into a sticky paste or fluid that overspreads her body, clinging to her lips and thighs. At the end of the act, Jocasta stares into the indispensable Coctelian mirror.

The fourth and final act presents Oedipus' tragic enlightenment and self-blinding, the subject of the Cocteau-Stravinsky opera. After seventeen prosperous years, a plague has descended on Thebes, and a scapegoat is sought. A messenger arrives to deliver the news that Oedipus' supposed father, Polybus, has died and that, on his deathbed, he revealed that Oedipus was only his adopted son. Oedipus recalls the stranger he met and killed at the crossroads between Delphi and Daulia. Jocasta now recognizes in this stranger her husband, Laius, and in Polybus' foster child, now her husband, her own son. She hangs herself with her scarf. Then Oedipus blinds himself with her brooch. The enlightened and blinded Oedipus is led away between his daughter, Antigone, and the spirit of his mother, Jocasta, who is no longer his wife, having been purified of incest by death.

During the 1930's journalism and criticism were also taking up their fair share of Cocteau's time. At the beginning of the 1920's *Paris-Midi* had offered Cocteau a column in which to write about contemporary art; appropriately, he called this series "Carte Blanche." In 1935 *Le Figaro* offered him a weekly column in its Saturday edition, for which Cocteau wrote a series of reminiscences of his life and acquaintances between 1900 and 1914. These were later published as *Portraits-souvenirs* in 1935. In the spring and early summer of 1936, at the invitation of *Paris Soir,* Cocteau set out on a "journey round the world" in the steps of Phineas Fogg; the magazine financed the trip and he in turn produced a series of articles. He took along his male companion of the time, Marcel Khill, kept a detailed journal of his travels, and greatly enjoyed the trip.

In 1937 Cocteau met Jean Marais, the handsome young actor who was to exert a beneficent influence on Cocteau and who was partly responsible for turning his interest from drama to film. Theirs was a very creative partnership. Marais entered Cocteau's life while playing the Chorus in *Oedipus Rex;* he then won a role he greatly coveted, when Jean-Pierre Aumont was prevented from playing it because of a film commitment, that of Galahad in Cocteau's *Les chevaliers de la table ronde (The Knights of the Round Table,* 1937).

In the late 1930's and throughout the 1940's Cocteau was to write many more plays; however, none so original or so successful as *Orpheus* and *The Infernal Machine,* unless we include the scandalous *Intimate Relations* of 1938, which was banned when produced in Vichy France in 1941. Here once again, Cocteau's subject is incest, but this time it is not distanced or lent the dignifying mantle of Greek myth. Instead, Cocteau brings incest up to date. His play is a well-made Parisian boulevard drama enacted by recognizable contemporary types: the smothering mother, Yvonne; the henpecked father, George, who is trying to rejuvenate himself through an affair; his young son, Michael, who loves Madeleine and is trying to liberate himself; and Aunt Leo, who, through her sympathetic machinations, saves Michael from the destiny of Oedipus.

The play, inspired by Cocteau's relations with his mother as well as by what Jean Marais had confided to Cocteau of his own situation, was written as a stage vehicle for Jean Marais and Yvonne de Bray. The plot is dominated by a mother who is in love with her son till death do them part, and who does everything to demonstrate this but copulate with him onstage. She refuses to let him marry the girl he loves. The three acts unfold through a series of carefully prepared discoveries and peripeties. Yvonne, a diabetic, almost kills herself by mistake in the first act by taking an overdose of insulin. She is devastated to learn that her son has a lover. The girl, Madeleine, returns his love but has an older lover for whom she feels pity; his name is George. When, with trepidation, the son brings his parents face to face with his intended, his father is appalled to discover his son and he both love the same woman. He confesses to his wife, but the parents then decide to withhold from Michael the knowledge that his father is Madeleine's former lover. They also conspire to prevent Michael from marrying the girl by persuading him that Madeleine does not really love him, but simply wishes to improve her social position. This is a flaw in the play, for as the family is presented, such a marriage could hardly be advantageous to Madeleine; also Michael is much too easily duped into doubting her love for him. The play is further flawed by the theme of order (as embodied particularly in Aunt Leo) versus disorder (as represented by Yvonne) because this theme of bourgeois versus bohemian is not properly integrated with Cocteau's extremely orderly plot; indeed, it seems like an unintegrated vestige of *The Holy Terrors.*

The parental lie almost succeeds until Aunt Leo, identifying with Madeleine and determined that the girl shall not make the kind of sacrifice of her beloved that Leo once made for her voracious sister, intervenes to restore the young lovers to each other. This is too much for Yvonne; recognizing that she is no longer the center of her son's life, she kills herself, as she almost did at the play's beginning. *Intimate Relations* was translated to the screen in 1948 in a faithful, airless version of the play; Cocteau wrote the script and Jean-Pierre Melville directed what many consider to be Cocteau's film masterpiece.

Cocteau had become a popular playwright at the beginning of the 1930's, but was no longer writing *poésie de théâtre* or theater of spectacle. Toward the end of the 1930's he began to write boulevard plays, alternating historical dramas or fairy tales with contemporary ones. *The Knights of the Round Table* (1937) is a dramatic recasting of the Arthurian legend, more specifically of the struggle between Arthur and Merlin. Cocteau claimed the idea for the play originated in a dream. It is a play that, like *Intimate Relations,* is about the struggle between order and disorder. Several subplots are interwoven: the secret love of Lancelot and Guinevere; Galahad's search for the Grail; the revolt of Merlin's servant, Ginifer; and the conflict between Merlin and Arthur. Here we have doubling with a vengeance, for *The Knights of the Round Table* stars a true and a false Guinevere, a true and a false Gawain, and so on, each doubled pair being played by the same actor or actress. False selves betray themselves through tricky, artificial diction and behavior, but, as may be imagined, this play is quite a challenge to its actors. It was not well received.

After this excursion into the early Middle Ages, Cocteau returned to contemporary Paris for his play *Les monstres sacrés* (also translated as *The Holy Terrors,* 1940). As in *The Knights of the Round Table,* an obsessive theme of this drama is the conflict between reality and illusion. It centers upon a triangle of actors: a famous acting couple, Esther and Florent, and the young soubrette Liane, who, first worshiping Esther and then transferring her attentions to Florent, temporarily disrupts their successful twenty-five-year-old marriage. For Esther and Florent, actors on the grand scale, illusion is reality; acting is their life. Their marriage may be a pale simulacrum of the life they live when the curtain goes up, but it is a haven and provides equilibrium for them both. Liane is an ambitious, cunning little vixen who attaches herself to them both largely out of a self-serving desire to advance her own career; she is the reality principle invading their unreal world. She is finally expelled—to Hollywood, to become a film star—when the two of them unite against her.

The play *The Holy Terrors* was followed by a less successful play that Cocteau found very

difficult to write—*La machine à écrire* (*The Typewriter,* 1941). Written in Perpignan, to which Cocteau escaped in 1940, it is his sole effort to portray small-town provincial France. Like *Intimate Relations* it was pronounced immoral and banned by the Vichy government. Cocteau next tried to revive an ancient form, the "verbal opera" popular at Versailles in the time of Louis XIV, in *Renaud et Armide* (1943). Written in courtly alexandrines, it treats the famous story of Renaud and Armide and enables Cocteau to handle one of his favorite themes, broached already in the Lancelot-Guinevere story in *The Knights of the Round Table* and again in *L'Aigle à deux têtes* (*The Eagle with Two Heads,* 1946), of an impossibly ideal love. Renaud is mortal and Armide immortal, so that their love can be consummated only in death. Armide sacrifices her immortality to her love for Renaud. This play is poetic theater in the traditional sense of the term.

The Eagle with Two Heads dates from Cocteau's stay in Brittany during the last days of the German occupation. It was produced after the war. This historical costume drama, set in a Ruritanian castle, relates the fateful and fatal encounter of one of Cocteau's regal muse figures with a poet-assassin. The doomed couple themselves constitute the double-headed eagle, a symbol of conflict within unity. The tragic, romantic, sequestered queen is based on the figure of Elisabeth of Austria, who was assassinated at the turn of the century. In the play the queen has lost her husband, the king, in a hunting accident. She has subsequently consigned herself to a living death, moving about aimlessly from castle to castle, leaving the rule of her subjects in others' hands. When Stanislaus enters her window, bent on killing her, she is struck by his extraordinary resemblance to her dead husband; she falls in love with him. She shelters her assassin, knowing that he will kill her, although he reciprocates her love. Their double murder-suicide is as spectacular as one could wish. Jean Marais had asked Cocteau to write a play for him in which, during the first act he would remain silent, in the second "cry with joy," and in the third, fall backward down the stairs. The result was *The Eagle with Two Heads.*

Bacchus (1952), produced in 1951, is yet another costume drama. It is based on the myth of Bacchus, which Cocteau was intrigued to learn survived in Vevey, Switzerland, where, at harvest, a Bacchus was elected to rule the town for a week, after which he was symbolically murdered. The central character in Cocteau's play is the peasant Hans, a figure who, like Luigi Pirandello's Henry IV of 1922, has been so mistreated that he has feigned madness in order to survive. As Bacchus, he is in a position to exact vengeance; however, he is one of Cocteau's pure anarchist poets and his vocation as such is self-immolation. He is flanked by one of Cocteau's most attractive strong women, Christine, and by her idealistic and insipid brother, Lothar. Like *The Eagle with Two Heads, Bacchus* has a political subplot, which is considerably more intricate than that in the earlier play but which, as there, does not really amount to anything, the focus of both plays being impossible love, impossible purity, and impossible heroism. Nevertheless, what the play has to say about religion caused a furor; Cocteau was accused by François Mauriac of sacrilege.

Like many others, Cocteau's many-branched career suffered an eclipse during World War II. The puritanical regime of Vichy France banned two of his plays: *Intimate Relations* and *The Typewriter.* He and Jean Marais were vilified by the press for their homosexuality; Cocteau, in addition, was censured for promoting the German sculptor Arno Breker and for expressing antiracist views. Cocteau was deprived of Marais's company for some time when Marais was called up; on one occasion, refusing to salute the flag brandished by French Vichy youth dressed in German uniforms, Cocteau was roughed up. One of the few good effects of the war for Cocteau was that it made it difficult to procure opium; this and Marais's influence finally persuaded him to kick the habit. In 1943 Mme Cocteau died. Her son wrote movingly of her death, using a characteristic image of life and death as two sides of the same coin. At his dead mother's bedside, Cocteau said: "Je nous sentais bien proches comme les deux faces d'une pièce de monnaie qui ne peuvent se connaître mais ne sont séparées l'une de l'autre que par l'épaisseur du métal" (I felt we were as close as the two sides of a coin, which cannot know one another yet are separated one from the other only by the thickness of the metal).

The period of the 1940's and 1950's was one of a new career for Cocteau as a filmmaker. A poet-cinematographer, rather than a *cinéaste,* Cocteau loved cinema for its ability to fuse reality with fantasy, to transform *Dichtung* into *Wahrheit.* He hailed cinema as the tenth muse possessing the mysterious power of rendering the unreal real. Cocteau's first venture in this new medium had been *The Blood of a Poet,* made as early as 1930. In making this film, Cocteau worked without a script. It is divided into four parts, "The Wounded Hand; or, The Scars of the Poet" and "Do the Walls Have Ears?" followed by "The Snowball Fight" and "The Profanation of the Host." To create this expression of the upwelling of mythic autobiography Cocteau said he had delved as deeply into himself as a deep-sea diver exploring the ocean bed. His desire was to reveal poetry's very genesis. The film is full of characteristically obsessive Coctelian images of the wounded poet, mirrors, statues, an angel, Dargelos, and the snowball fight at the Cité Monthiers. The film was financed by the Vicomte Charles de Noailles, who gave Cocteau a million francs to make it. (De Noailles also subsidized Luis Buñuel and Dali's surrealistic *L'âge d'or.*)

Not until the 1940's did Cocteau return to filmmaking. In addition to his own delight in film, Jean Marais's desire to be a film star as well as a stage actor was another strong inducement. In 1943 Cocteau worked on the dialogue for *Le baron fantôme* (The Phantom Baron, 1943) and *L'Éternel retour* (The Eternal Return, 1943), and in 1947 he wrote the dialogue for *Ruy Blas. L'Éternel retour* is a modernized version of the Tristan-Isolde myth, in the mood of the Lancelot-Guinevere story of *The Knights of the Round Table*.

Cocteau's first important postwar excursion into cinema was *La belle et la bête (Beauty and the Beast,* 1945). In adapting this fairy tale by Mme Leprince de Beaumont, Cocteau cast Marais as the Beast and Josette Day as Beauty. The music, as in most of Cocteau's films, was composed by Georges Auric; the sumptuous costumes (modeled on Gustave Doré) and settings are by Christian Bérard. The film was shot in the Touraine in the summer and fall under very difficult circumstances. Quite aside from the financial difficulties attending the realization of such a lavish conception during a period of postwar austerity in France, Cocteau was so disfigured by eczema that he had to direct through a paper mask pinned to his hat, with slits cut out for his eyes and mouth. To apply the gum and hair necessary for Marais's makeup took five hours a day and caused the actor to break out in boils. Cocteau then contracted jaundice. Nevertheless, he rose to meet each challenge, surmounted innumerable obstacles, and found the making of this film a great satisfaction.

In 1947 Cocteau bought the house at Milly-la-Fôret, near Fontainebleau, with Jean Marais; he was to live there for the next fifteen years. During this year, too, Edouard Dermit (nicknamed Doudou) entered his life, becoming a rival to Marais (nicknamed Jeannot) and eventually supplanting him. Dermit was a Yugoslav and came of a mining family, although he had aspirations to be a painter. He became Cocteau's chauffeur, then his gardener at Milly, then his companion, and finally was adopted by him as his son and heir. The rivalry portrayed in *Orpheus* between Orpheus (played by Marais) and Cégeste (played by Dermit) derived from real life, but although Dermit supplanted Marais as Cocteau's companion, Cocteau and Marais remained good friends until the end of the writer's life. Dermit acted in several of Cocteau's plays and films—notably in *Les enfants terribles, Orpheus,* and

Le testament d'Orphée (The Testament of Orpheus, 1959).

In 1947, Cocteau also published one of his most considerable critical works, *La difficulté d'être (The Difficulty of Being).* This is a collection of essays modeled on Montaigne's *Essais,* although Cocteau's style is closer to the succinct, aphoristic style of Pascal's *Pensées* than to Montaigne's flexible, diverse, and ebullient style. Here Cocteau explains why he has had to try his hand at so many media:

> Why do you write plays, the novelist asks. Why do you write novels, the dramatist asks. Why make films, asks the poet. Why do you draw, asks the critic. Why write, the designer asks. Yes, why, I ask myself. So that my grain may fly everywhere. The breath that lives in me . . . impels me everywhere. It is not inspiration, it is expiration. . . . This spirit emanates from a zone man cannot plumb. . . . I am not my own master. I am made for obedience.
>
> (*La difficulté d'être,* Paris, 1947, p. 66)

In an essay on reading, Cocteau points out that books are mirrors that reflect us. The better we read, the more we are reading ourselves. As for writing, Cocteau saw it as lovemaking and a duel with death. In good writing a transfusion of the spirit takes place between the writer and the reader.

Several other essays concern suffering and death. Cocteau's unforgettable portrait of the dead writer Proust is best read in the original French:

> *Couché raide et de travers, non parmi les coquilles d'huîtres de la séquestrée, mais dans un sarcophage de détritus d'âmes, de paysages, de tout ce qui ne put lui servir dans Balbec, Combray, Méséglise . . . bref tel que nous admirâmes plus tard, pour la dernière fois, sa dépouille auprès de la pile des cahiers de son oeuvre qui continuait, elle, à vivre à sa gauche comme le bracelet montre des soldats morts, Marcel Proust nous lisait, chaque nuit, "Du côté de chez Swann."*
>
> (*La difficulté d'être,* p. 105)

Cocteau contradicts Descartes: it is not existence that causes us to think, but suffering. Further, Cocteau observes that God thinks us, but without thinking of us, or being aware of our suffering. The title of the collection comes from a remark attributed to the French writer Bernard le Bovier de Fontenelle. When in 1757, at the age of one hundred, Fontenelle lay dying, his doctor asked him how he felt. Fontenelle replied, "I feel the difficulty of being." Cocteau says he has felt this all his life, having arrived on earth with an ill-sorted and ill-disposed cargo of gifts and sensibilities.

The Difficulty of Being is an impressive critical work, probably Cocteau's most notable achievement in the genre of criticism. In 1952 he published *Journal d'un inconnu* (translated as *The Hand of a Stranger*); ten years later he brought out *Le cordon ombilical.* When he was about sixty he began keeping a journal, posthumously published as *Le passé défini* (*Past Tense,* 1983–1985).

The film of *Orpheus* has already been discussed in connection with the play, although it was not made until 1949–1950. It won the first prize at the International Film Festival in Venice. Cocteau adapted some of his plays and novels for the screen. Thus, Cocteau filmed his play *Intimate Relations* in 1948, with Jean Marais as Michel, Yvonne de Bray as Yvonne, Gabrielle Dorziat as Aunt Léo, Josette Day as Madeleine, and Marcel André as Georges.

The film of *The Holy Terrors* is based on Cocteau's adaptation of the script, but was directed by Jean-Pierre Melville. The movie recaptures the atmosphere of the novel; however, Cocteau regretted the director's decision to have an actress play both Dargelos and his double, Agathe (the actress was Renée Cosima), for Cocteau could find no actress plausible in the essentially male role of Dargelos.

Cocteau's final film is the extraordinary work *The Testament of Orpheus,* of which he is author, star, and director. Filmed at Les Baux de Provence in 1959 and first screened in 1960, this is a compendium or retrospective of Cocteau's artistic career, which is filled with real-life companions, friends, and fellow artists. Cocteau himself appears in the role of the poet-protagonist, with Jean Marais as Oedipus and Edouard Dermit as Cégeste, and there are appearances by Picasso, Charles Aznavour, Maria Casarès, and Yul Brynner, among others. This film, which François Truffaut helped finance with the prize money from his own *Les quatre cents coups* (*The 400 Blows,* 1959), was never commercially released; indeed, it is more contrived and superficial than *Orpheus,* more like a personal album of snapshots than an unfolding myth. Yet Cocteau was clearly a pioneer in film, although he came to it late in life. The American film critic Pauline Kael is no doubt justified in describing Cocteau as a true progenitor of the New Wave.

In 1950 Cocteau and Dermit were guests of Francine Weisweiller at her villa, Santo Sospir, in Saint-Jean-Cap-Ferrat, near Villefranche. Mme Weisweiller was the wife of a wealthy banker and was interested in the arts. During the 1950's she became Cocteau's patron, offering him a permanent haven in his favorite part of the Riviera; each summer he occupied the studio at Santo Sospir and painted murals on its walls. He, Edouard Dermit, and Mme Weisweiller became an inseparable trio.

In the Midi, Cocteau was known preeminently as a graphic artist rather than as a writer. He had drawn and painted all his life, made wire sculptures on a small scale, and designed tapestries and costume jewelry, but in late middle age he took to painting murals and frescoes and making ceramics. Cocteau's drawings—he illustrated many of his own books—are unmistakably his; as a draughtsman, he has a very clear, clean line; many of his drawings are cartoonlike and humorous. However, his work as a graphic artist is generally judged to be more derivative than his poetry, fiction, or films. He decorated several chapels and churches—St. Pierre at Villefranche, Notre Dame de France in London, and Saint-Blaise-des-Simples near Milly-la-Forêt.

He also painted the *salle des mariages* of the Menton Mairie city hall.

Honors began to be heaped upon Cocteau when he was in his sixties. In 1949 he became a Chevalier de la Légion d'Honneur. In the fall of 1955 he was elected first to Colette's empty seat in the Royal Academy of Language and Literature of Belgium and then to the Académie Française. Many were amazed that this *enfant terrible* of the 1920's should be acknowledged by and received into that most august body of French *littérateurs.* The University of Oxford also awarded Cocteau an honorary doctorate in June 1956.

Cocteau had relatively frail health, but he possessed a tough will and temperament. He drove himself relentlessly, even during times of illness. In June 1954, shortly after visiting Spain, he returned to Paris and was temporarily immobilized by chest pains, diagnosed as myocarditis. In December 1958 he suffered a severe internal hemorrhage and was forbidden to move or to work for some months. While immobilized in bed he began work on the long poem that is his last, *Le requiem,* composed over a period of three years (1959–1961) and published in 1962. It constitutes a kind of Dantesque journey through what Cocteau had called the night of the human body. This is a piercing record of physical pain, as *La crucifixion* (1946) is an account of the poet's psychological anguish, modeled on Christ's passion. In the 1950's Cocteau also published the volumes of poetry *Clair-obscur* (1954) and *Paraprosodies* (1958). In April 1963 Cocteau suffered a second heart attack while in Paris. Jean Marais took him to his home at Marnes-la-Coquette and, on 5 July, his seventy-fourth birthday, the still ailing poet returned by ambulance to his own home at Milly-la-Forêt. On 11 October Edith Piaf died. Cocteau, as a friend and admirer of the chanteuse, was called for an interview. Sinking fast himself, Cocteau was shocked and saddened by her death. After the interview he announced: "The boat is sinking." Cocteau died the same day. He was buried in the chapel of Saint-Blaise-les-Simples, which he himself had decorated and which had originally served as a sanctuary for lepers, beneath his own inscription, "Je reste avec vous."

Cocteau's most notable achievements during a long, crowded, diverse, and glittering career were in theater and film. His poetry is little read or understood and, like some of his fiction, it is virtually impossible to translate. Bettina Knapp is right in seeing his most important contribution to this century as rallying and bringing into the theater the resources of all the arts. He mixed media in a truly creative way. Cocteau's surface brilliance and diversity play over a rather limited stock of dark and irreducible themes, of which the most pervasive is his lifelong love affair with death. The Orpheus works show how the poet must die and be reborn innumerable times until his final death, which is immortality. It is questionable how long or well Cocteau's work will last. He was a consummate technician and innovator, but his work is littered with modern contraptions and devices that may soon be dated and become mere detritus. Even the best of Cocteau often verges on the camp. Nevertheless, the popular notion of Cocteau as a dabbler and dilettante is certainly wrong; he was a master craftsman, thoroughly engaged in all he did, doing little with the left hand. Francis Steegmuller, his biographer (1970), aptly epitomizes Jean Cocteau with this quotation from Oscar Wilde: "I put my talent into my works and my genius into my life."

Selected Bibliography

EDITIONS

INDIVIDUAL WORKS

POETRY
La lampe d'Aladin. Paris, 1909.
Le prince frivole. Paris, 1910.
La danse de Sophocle. Paris, 1912.

Le Cap de Bonne-Espérance. Paris, 1919.
Plain-chant. Paris, 1923.
Poésie 1916-23. Paris, 1925.
L'ange Heurtebise. Paris, 1926.
Opéra: Oeuvre poétique, 1925-27. Paris, 1927.
Allégories. Paris, 1941.
La crucifixion. Paris, 1946.
Poèmes. Paris, 1948.
Appogiatures. Monaco, 1953.
Clair-obscur. Monaco, 1954.
Paraprosodies. Monaco, 1958.
Le requiem. Paris, 1962.

FICTION
Le Potomak. Paris, 1919; def. ed., Paris, 1924.
Le grand écart. Paris, 1923.
Thomas l'imposteur. Paris, 1923.
Le livre blanc. Paris, 1928.
Les enfants terribles. Paris, 1929.
La fin du Potomak. Paris, 1940.

DRAMA/BALLET/SPECTACLE
Parade. Paris, 1919.
Le boeuf sur la toit. Paris, 1920.
Les mariés de la Tour Eiffel. Paris, 1923.
Antigone. Paris, 1927.
Orphée. Paris, 1927.
Oedipe-roi. Paris, 1928.
La voix humaine. Paris, 1930.
La machine infernale. Paris, 1934.
Les chevaliers de la table ronde. Paris, 1937.
Les parents terribles. Paris, 1938.
Les monstres sacrés. Paris, 1940.
La machine à écrire. Paris, 1941.
Renaud et Armide. Paris, 1943.
L'Aigle à deux têtes. Paris, 1946.
Bacchus. Paris, 1952.

FILMS
Le sang d'un poète. Paris, 1930.
L'Éternel retour. Paris, 1943.
La belle et la bête. Paris, 1945.
La voix humaine. Paris, 1947.
Ruy Blas. Paris, 1947.
L'Aigle à deux têtes. Paris, 1947.
Les parents terribles. Paris, 1948.
Les enfants terribles. Paris, 1950.
Orphée. Paris, 1950.
Le bel indifférent. Paris, 1957.
Le testament d'Orphée. Monaco, 1959.

ESSAYS
Le coq et l'arlequin. Paris, 1918.
Carte blanche. Paris, 1920.
Le secret professionnel. Paris, 1922.
Picasso. Paris, 1923.
Lettre à Jacques Maritain. Paris, 1926.
Le rappel à l'ordre. Paris, 1926.
Opium: Journal d'un désintoxication. Paris, 1930.
Essai de critique indirecte. Paris, 1932.
Portraits-souvenirs, 1900-1914. Paris, 1935.
Mon premier voyage. Paris, 1937.
Le Greco. Paris, 1943.
La difficulté d'être. Paris, 1947.
Lettre aux Americains. Paris, 1949.
Jean Marais. Paris, 1951.
Gide vivant. Paris, 1952.
Journal d'un inconnu. Paris, 1952.
Erik Satie. Liége, 1957.
Le cordon ombilical. Paris, 1962.
Le passé défini. Vol. 1, 1951–52. Edited by Pierre Chanel. Paris, 1983.
Le passé défini. Vol. 2, 1953. Edited by Pierre Chanel. Paris, 1985.

COLLECTED WORKS
Oeuvres complètes. 11 vols. Lausanne, 1946–1951.

TRANSLATIONS

Antigone. Translated by Carl Wildman. London, 1962.
Bacchus. Translated by Mary Hoeck. New York, 1963.
The Blood of a Poet. Translated by Lily Pons. New York, 1949.
——— . Translated by Carol Martin-Sperry. New York, 1985.
A Call to Order. Translated by Rollo H. Myers. London, 1926.
Cock and Harlequin. Translated by Rollo H. Myers. London, 1921 and New York, 1927.
Cocteau's World: An Anthology of Writings by Jean Cocteau. Translated and edited by Margaret Crosland. New York, 1973.
The Devil and the Good Lord. Translated by Kitty Black. New York, 1962.
Diary of a Film. La belle et la bête. Translated by Ronald Duncan. London and New York, 1950.
Diary of an Unknown. Translated by Jesse Browner. New York, 1988. Also translated as *The Hand of a Stranger* by Alec Brown. London, 1956.

The Difficulty of Being. Translated by Elizabeth Sprigge. London, 1966 and New York, 1967.

The Eagle Has Two Heads. Translated by Ronald Duncan. London, 1948. Also translated as *The Eagle with Two Heads* by Carl Wildman. London, 1961.

The Eiffel Tower Wedding Party. Translated by Dudley Fitts. New York, 1963.

The Grand Écart. Translated by Lewis Galantière. New York and London, 1925. Also translated as *The Miscreant* by Dorothy Williams, London, 1958.

The Holy Terrors. Translated by Rosamund Lehmann. New York, 1957. Also translated as *Enfants terribles* by Samuel Putnam, New York, 1930; and as *The Children of the Game* by Rosamund Lehmann, London, 1955. Translations of *Les enfants terribles.*

The Holy Terrors. Translated by Edward O. Marsh. London, 1963. Translation of *Les monstres sacrés.*

The Human Voice. Translated by Carl Wildman. London, 1951.

The Infernal Machine. Translated by Carl Wildman. New York, 1936.

———. Translated by Albert Bermal. New York, 1963.

Intimate Relations. Translated by Charles Frank. London, 1963.

Journals of Jean Cocteau. Translated and edited by Wallace Fowlie. New York, 1956.

The Knights of the Round Table. Translated by W. H. Auden. New York, 1963.

My Journey Round the World. Translated by Peter Strachan. London, 1958.

Oedipus Rex. Translated by e. e. cummings. New York, 1963.

Opium: Diary of a Cure. Translated by Margaret Crosland and Sinclair Road. London, 1957.

———. Translated by Ernest Boyd. New York, 1932 and London, 1933.

Orpheus. Translated by Carl Wildman. New York, 1933.

———. Translated by John Savacool. In *The Infernal Machine & Other Plays.* New York, 1963.

Paris Album: 1900-14. Translated by Margaret Crosland. London, 1956.

Past Tense: The Cocteau Diaries. 2 vols. Translated by Richard Howard. New York, London, and San Diego, 1987–1988.

Professional Secrets. Translated by Richard Howard. New York, 1970.

Round the World Again in Eighty Days. Translated by Gilbert Stuart. London, 1937.

Thomas the Imposter. Translated by Lewis Galantière. New York, 1925. Also translated as *The Imposter* by Dorothy Williams. London, 1957 and New York, 1960.

The Typewriter. Translated by Ronald Duncan. London, 1947.

The White Paper. Paris, 1957.

BIOGRAPHICAL AND CRITICAL STUDIES

Brown, Frederick. *An Impersonation of Angels: A Biography of Jean Cocteau.* New York, 1968.

Crosland, Margaret. *Jean Cocteau.* London, 1955.

———. *Cocteau's World: An Anthology of Writings.* New York, 1973.

Fifield, William. *Jean Cocteau.* New York, 1974.

Fowlie, Wallace. *Jean Cocteau: The History of a Poet's Age.* Bloomington, Ind., 1966.

Fraigneau, André. *Jean Cocteau par lui-même.* Paris, 1957.

Gilson, René. *Jean Cocteau: An Investigation into his Films and Philosophy.* Translated by Ciba Vaughan. New York, 1969.

Kihm, Jean-Jacques. *Cocteau.* Paris, 1960.

Knapp, Bettina L. *Jean Cocteau.* New York, 1970.

Oxenhandler, Neal. *Scandal and Parade: The Theater of Jean Cocteau.* New Brunswick, N.J., 1957.

Peters, Arthur King. *Jean Cocteau and the French Scene.* New York, 1984.

Sprigge, Elizabeth, and Jean-Jacques Kihm. *Jean Cocteau: The Man and the Mirror.* London, 1968.

Steegmuller, Francis. *Cocteau: A Biography.* Boston, 1970.

DORIS L. EDER

KAREL ČAPEK

(1890–1938)

LIFE

KAREL ČAPEK WAS born on 9 January 1890 in the village of Malé Svatoňovice in northeastern Bohemia, a land noteworthy for mountain scenery, coal mining, and the disproportionately large number of writers it has given to the Czech nation and to the world. His father, Antonín Čapek, was a country doctor and provincial intellectual who managed local amateur theatricals. His mother, Božena, also an intellectual, recorded local folklore. The family was not far removed from peasant stock, and Karel's maternal grandmother commanded a rich repertoire of rhymed proverbs.

Karel's elder brother, Josef, was also destined for fame as a painter and writer. Three years older than Karel, he looked after his younger brother and played with him; the two brothers remained close for most of their lives. They made their literary debut jointly as "the brothers Čapek," and a number of their later works were written together. Josef also illustrated many of the published editions of Karel's works. A third child, Helena, born in 1886, became a minor writer who left reminiscences of her more famous brothers.

Karel was weak and sickly and was plagued by ill health for much of his life. Malé Svatoňovice was celebrated as a mountain place of pilgrimage, and his mother took him to the local shrine to pray that he might have stronger lungs.

Karel finished school in Brno in Moravia, after which he rejoined his family, then living in Prague. In 1909 he enrolled as a student of philosophy in Charles University. Meanwhile the brothers had made their literary debut with a philosophical parable, "Návrat věštce Hermotina" (The Return of the Prophet Hermotinos), which appeared in the newspaper *Lidové noviny* on 18 January 1908. This was followed by a stream of stories, causeries, feuilletons (a form similar to an American newspaper column with some characteristics of the essay), aphorisms, and reviews of books and art exhibitions, published in various Prague papers and journals.

In 1910 Josef went to Paris to continue his art studies, while Karel went to Berlin briefly and enrolled in the university there. He joined Josef in Paris in the summer of 1911, and the two returned to Prague that autumn. There they did much with their reviews to introduce cubism to Czech art, and Josef subsequently painted in the cubist style. The brothers' early writing even featured a kind of literary "cubism," as Czech critics called it, based in part on refractions of multiple points of view.

Karel enrolled again in Charles University, obtaining his doctor's degree in 1915 with a dissertation on objective methods in aesthetics. A volume of the brothers' collected writings appeared the following year under the title of *Zářivé hlubiny* (The Luminous Depths).

Calcification of several spinal vertebrae exempted Čapek from military service during World War I. Extraordinarily painful, the illness remained with him throughout the 1920's, making it difficult for him to turn his head and forcing him to walk with a cane. A medical student at the university once surprised him with the news that his condition was a rare one and that at the faculty of medicine they called it "Čapek's disease."

During the war years he took the position of tutor to the son of Count Vladimír Lažanský on the count's estate in western Bohemia. Although he scarcely spoke Czech, the count was a Czech patriot and openly expressed his hope for the victory of the Allies. During this time Čapek wrote most of his collection *Boží muka* (Wayside Crosses), a volume of metaphysical tales he published on his return to Prague in 1917.

The next year saw the appearance of a popular treatise on American pragmatist philosophy, *Pragmatismus čili Filosofie practického života*, which Čapek published as a postwar pro-American gesture. The pragmatism of William James and the philosophy of Henri-Louis Bergson were the two strongest intellectual influences of his life. But Čapek was a poet and avant-garde writer as well as a thinker at this period, and in 1920 he brought out a volume of translations of modern French poetry, *Francouzská poezie nové doby*, which includes selections ranging from Charles Baudelaire to Guillaume Apollinaire. Although Čapek wrote poetry for only a short time in his youth, this volume became a crucial influence on Czech avant-garde poetry of the 1920's. It is especially noteworthy for its natural syntax, a quality that was virtually new in Czech verse of the period, which was dominated by the ponderous and contrived syntax of the Czech Parnassians and symbolists. In the same year Čapek's play *Loupežník* (The Outlaw) was published and staged at the National Theater in Prague.

At this time Čapek made the acquaintance of the young actress Olga Scheinpflugová. Their lifelong friendship culminated in marriage, but only years later, in 1935, since Karel's ill health frustrated plans for an earlier union. Although Čapek's influence helped launch Olga's career, and although she appeared as a star in a number of his plays, her career remained relatively independent of his. Later she became a novelist and produced a semifictionalized account of their married life, *Český román* (A Czech Novel, or Romance, 1946).

Čapek's next play, *R.U.R.,* opened at the National Theater on 25 January 1921. His greatest popular success, though by no means his outstanding artistic achievement, the play introduced the figure of the robot to the stage. Translated into many languages and performed all over the world, it brought Čapek world fame—a fame unprecedented for a Czech writer—as well as the envy of many of his contemporaries.

The success of *R.U.R.* was repeated with *Ze života hmyzu* (published in English as *The World We Live In* and *And So Ad Infinitum,* 1921). *The World We Live In* was coauthored by his brother Josef, who was largely responsible for the striking theatricality of the piece. An allegory with elements taken from the theatrical revue and ballet, this work also achieved worldwide recognition.

Čapek's theatrical successes led to a brief period in which he attempted stage direction at the Prague Municipal Theater, where he directed some thirteen plays during the years 1921 through 1923. He was remembered for a production of Percy Bysshe Shelley's *The Cenci,* perhaps the first ever undertaken on the Continent.

Since his return to Prague in 1917, Čapek had been an active contributor to the newspaper, writing feuilletons and causeries and publishing stories. He and his brother contributed to *Národní listy*, the organ of the National Socialists, but in March 1921 they went over to *Lidové noviny*, a middle-of-the-road paper edited by Eduard Bass. *Lidové noviny* supported the new president of Czechoslovakia, T. G. Masaryk; thus Čapek moved to a more conservative position of support for Masaryk and his program for "building" the young republic; this political shift, combined with Čapek's newly gained fame, brought him the envy and hatred of the leftists, who at this time were extremely influential in Czech letters. In particular, they dominated the avant-garde that Čapek had deserted. He retained his earlier aestheticism, but from this time on it was associated with the intimate, the familiar, and the "homey"; Čapek never repeated the kind of success with the avant-garde that he had achieved with his translations of French poetry.

During the 1920's Čapek concentrated on newspaper work, and his journalistic writings were of great significance for his literary development. The feuilleton, which in his treatment approaches the essay form, is one of his principal genres, and he even wrote several feuilleton novels (serialized novels), such as *Továrna na Absolutno* (*The Absolute at Large,* 1922). Newspaper work no doubt kept him in closer touch with the world around him and helped to curb his aestheticism; it also laid a base for his final period of the 1930's, in which his anti-Hitler stance was dominant.

But Čapek remained fundamentally an aesthete; this quality, added to the middle-class life-style he cultivated as a successful author, led him to pursue a variety of hobbies and collection manias. He and his brother gardened at the villa they shared in a Prague suburb (each occupied half), and Karel raised dogs and cats and took photographs. He collected oriental carpets as well as exotic phonograph records from all over the world. Travel was another pastime, both in Czechoslovakia and abroad, to Italy, England, Holland, Spain, and Scandinavia. All these occupations inspired journalistic pieces, sometimes whole series of them or separate books.

These interests, however, did not prevent Čapek's involvement in public and political life. In 1924 he founded the society of Pátečníci, the "Friday Circle," a group of writers, artists, academicians, and politicians, many of whom supported Masaryk. They met weekly at Čapek's home, and occasionally Masaryk himself attended. Čapek's friendship with Masaryk led him to publish the three volumes of *Hovory s T. G. Masarykem* (*President Masaryk Tells His Story,* 1928–1935) and, after Masaryk's death, an essay entitled "Mlčení s T. G. M." (Silence with T. G. M., 1935). Friendship with Masaryk also occasioned many attacks on Čapek.

At this time Čapek and his brother took part in an attempt to found a National Labor Party modeled on the British Labour Party. But their efforts, largely confined to intellectuals, produced a poor showing in the 1925 elections and subsequently came to nothing. Čapek was elected president of the Czech P.E.N. Club in 1925 and helped to found a P.E.N. Club in Slovakia.

Although Čapek had published a number of plays, novels, and collections of stories in the years 1917 to 1924, he devoted the late 1920's almost entirely to journalistic activity. He aligned himself with Masaryk's "building" posture to such a degree that he even asserted to his friends, "Now I must help to educate the nation." Only with the publication of two volumes of detective tales, *Povídky z jedné kapsy* (Tales from One Pocket, 1929) and *Povídky z druhé kapsy* (Tales from the Other Pocket, 1929), did he come out of his "hibernation" and return to literature in the stricter sense. His last years were devoted less to journalistic activity than to artistic production.

Čapek's writings in the mid-1930's constitute his finest achievement, though they are less well known than plays such as *R.U.R.* and *The World We Live In.* His trilogy, *Hordubal* (1933), *Povětroň* (*Meteor,* 1934), and *Obyčejný život* (*An Ordinary Life,* 1934), is undoubtedly his masterpiece; it is a cycle of philosophical novels in some ways unique in modern fiction. Although not as famous as *R.U.R.,* his novel *Válka s mloky* (*The War with the Newts,* 1936) is probably more successful artistically as a work of science fiction, and the novel form probably better serves the writer's scientific imagination.

This penultimate period was followed by a final period of less successful antifascist writing. The rise of Hitler in Germany made obvious the need to develop a Czech resistance, but Čapek's talents fitted him better to treat philosophic and scientific matters than to indulge in the sort of heavy-handed allegory he then attempted. The Munich settlement of September 1938 brought Čapek to a crisis. The new regime in Czechoslovakia was pro-Hitler, and many of his friends strenuously encouraged him to emigrate. But he refused to go. He sought to lose himself in creation and took up work on the novel *Život a dílo skladatele Foltýna* (*The Cheat,* 1939), the savage unmasking of a vain, egoistic artistic poseur and hack. He never completed the novel.

Depressed and spiritually exhausted, Čapek's health declined after the Munich settlement. His lungs were inflamed, and on 25 December 1938 he died. Since the new regime was hostile, there was no question of a public funeral, and he was buried privately.

The Nazis invaded and occupied what was left of Czechoslovakia on 15 March 1939. Curiously, the Gestapo knew nothing of Čapek's death and came to his house to arrest him; they took away his brother, Josef, who died at Bergen-Belsen only a few weeks before the end of World War II. Čapek's widow destroyed his extensive correspondence.

EARLY WORK

Much of Čapek's early writing was done with his brother, Josef. Indeed, the Čapeks represent a relatively unique case of successful joint authorship. To be sure, the first literary forms in which they worked were extremely slight, and much of this work can be considered decadent in the formal as well as the moral and aesthetic sense. (Literary decadence implies excessive aestheticism and a tendency to produce elegant, polished trifles.) Their joint authorship was in part a mystification designed to intrigue the public, and presumably one brother or the other was usually the primary author of any given piece.

Their early writings were later collected under the title of *Krakonošova zahrada* (The Garden of Krakonoš, 1918), which refers to a fairy-tale giant from the brothers' homeland. These early pieces, feuilletons and causeries, are fruits of a Czech postsymbolist movement that arose around 1910. A major impulse in shaping these works was the desire to challenge middle-class values and vested interests and to flirt with a new avant-gardism, one not very deeply digested. As members of this postsymbolist generation, the brothers retained much of the metaphorical and allusive manner of the symbolists, while abjuring their positive mystical vision. In retrospect, "postsymbolism" proved to be a purely transitional movement, a time of searching for a new way, and its influence on the brothers' work did not last; within several years, it gave way to expressionism in the work of both brothers. Czech literary critics have named this transitional generation the "Čapek generation" (after both brothers) or the "pragmatist generation." The deep influence of American pragmatism on these postsymbolist writers could hardly be demonstrated literally (though Karel did, of course, publish a popular tract on pragmatism), but the name is perhaps meaningful in that it suggests a fresh literary attempt to deal with reality, albeit on conditional philosophical terms. Bergson's influence was probably greater and more widespread, and the term "vitalism" is also applied to this period in Czech literature. A narrower (and perhaps retrogressive) influence was the German writer Paul Ernst's neoclassicism, an attempt to impose strong classic form on otherwise decadent material deriving from symbolism.

A major subject of the Čapeks' work is eroticism, which the adolescent and possibly still virginal brothers approach in a largely tongue-in-cheek manner: they can neither take it quite seriously nor transcend it. A sketch entitled

"Olga Desmond" depicts the nudity of a Berlin cabaret dancer, a nudity that serves to remind the spectator that we are all "temples of God and that the Holy Spirit abides in us." Yet that nudity falls short of the ideal, for Olga has but two breasts; a more authentic erotic goddess would be the Phrygian Diana, with her sixteen mammary glands. Equally brash are pieces commenting on the politics and economics of the times. However, there are a few pieces that augur a brighter literary future. "Systém" (The System) looks forward to the utopian themes in the later writing of both brothers. Prohibitions against sexual contact among the workers of an American factory lead the workers to revolt and murder; the story's paradox is an inverse transmutation of lofty ideals into savagery. This theme of man's dehumanization as the price paid for civilization pervades the brothers' utopian pieces of the early 1920's.

Zářivé hlubiny (The Luminous Depths, 1916) contains later—and longer—pieces, and was actually the first of the two collections to be published, in 1916. The image expressed in the title story is memorable, though it fails to express quite as much as the authors must have intended: the vision of a radiant young girl on the liner *Titanic* haunts a survivor of the shipwreck; without her he is spiritually dead. In the middle of these lyrical images (presumably Josef's) a piece of philosophical ratiocination (probably Karel's) is inserted: man's ability to control nature becomes ever more perfect, but the perfection of technology serves only to hurl him more swiftly toward his fated doom.

Included in "The Luminous Depths" is an earlier verse play by the two brothers, *Lásky hra osudná* (The Fateful Game of Love), written in 1910. Ernst's neoclassicism advocated the strong influence of Renaissance forms, in this case that of the commedia del l'arte, and by 1910 there were other models reflecting its influence on the theater. The brothers used the commedia to mock the cult of illusionism in symbolism, as well as to poke fun at eroticism. In spite of the play's vigorous wit and parody, the Czech public was too little acquainted with symbolist theater to comprehend it, and the play went unperformed until 1930.

The influences of postsymbolism and neoclassicism were transitory in the work of both brothers, and separation from Josef left Karel free to go his own way. *Boží muka* (Wayside Crosses, 1917), was the first result. The tales in this book are infused with a deep pessimism, partly due to World War I, but partly innate in Čapek; elsewhere he tries desperately to mask this pessimism with a superficial optimism, but here, liberated by the insights of the war, it is pervasive. The title of the volume contains an ambiguity: *Boží muka* means literally "God's torment," but the term is applied to crucifixes and wayside shrines. The phrase refers to God and man's mutual torment as they seek to find one another, as well as to the miracle that they will do so. Čapek later denied that he had meant the collection to have a religious character and added that it referred instead to the waiting out of the war years and to the hope that a miracle would come. But it is difficult to put the religious dimension of the book aside entirely; Čapek does not reject religion here, but rather he confines it to a dimension in which it exists but has no force.

A number of the stories in "Wayside Crosses" concern miracles and their epistemological status. The opening tale, "Šlépěj" ("The Imprint"), is inspired by David Hume's speculations concerning an isolated footprint in the sand. Two men find a mysterious footprint in fresh snow. It is a miracle, but a miracle that changes nothing. Miracles cannot help man, for they come from the Absolute, whereas man's existence is relative.

The same idea is expressed more originally in the tale "Ztracená cesta" (The Lost Way). Two men walking in the dark stumble and lose their way in an open field, where one of them suddenly apprehends the whole truth of his life. But upon returning to the road, he loses this insight forever. The field is the Absolute, the road the world of the relative, a world conditioning and limiting thought and at the same time making it possible.

A long story entitled "Hora" (The Mountain) borrows its symbols from the genre of the detective story and from G. K. Chesterton's novel *The Man Who Was Thursday*. A murderer escapes to climb a mountain, pursued by the police. His crime puts him outside man's relative world, and in his association with the mountain he apparently takes on the qualities of God. People even fear that he may be God. This absolute, existential quality of the criminal act places Čapek's murderer close to the criminals of Fyodor Dostoevsky, while the man's enormous size recalls Chesterton's Thursday. But in the end God fails to reveal Himself, and even in the criminal act man fails to come to know Him.

The final story of the collection, "Pomoc!" ("Help!"), makes a kind of transition from the agonized, tortured world of Čapek's metaphysics to the concrete pragmatic world at the end of World War I, a world longing and waiting to be remade. A man is awakened by a woman's cry for help, but after investigating he finds no one. In the end he decides that the cry must be his own. The story ends on a surprising note of ambiguity: after the painful waiting of night a new day dawns, but whether this is a new start or merely another day of tormented waiting, the author does not say.

Between 1918 and 1920 Čapek published a number of short stories that were subsequently reissued under the title of *Trapné povídky* (*Money and Other Stories*, 1921). These stories are unlike most of Čapek's literary works in that they lack a philosophical or science-fiction dimension, but rather have conventional plots, characters, and themes, largely without any element of the fantastic. Their rather melancholy mood and subdued endings recall the stories of Anton Chekhov, and their deeply unhappy protagonists are trapped in dilemmas they cannot resolve. "Košile" ("The Shirts") is the story of a widower who suspects that his housekeeper has been stealing from him. He searches her cupboards and finds

many of his possessions. But his righteous anger offends rather than shames her and, though he begs her to remain, she leaves him. Sadly he realizes that he is now completely alone.

In 1920 Čapek published a volume of collected causeries on language and style, *Kritika slov* (A Critique of Words). Philosophical influences on the collection include those of Bergson and the American pragmatists, but the specific literary inspiration was the work of the Viennese journalist and writer Karl Kraus. The subjects of these short pieces range from journalistic clichés (Foreign Influences, Ardent, Task) to metaphysical abstractions that involve reification (-ism, Nature, Politics, God). Among Čapek's finest journalistic works, these causeries remained largely unknown abroad, perhaps because they were published several years before he had made his world reputation.

Finally, Čapek's first full-length play, *Loupežník* (The Outlaw) had its premiere at the National Theater in Prague on 2 March 1920. It represents a new beginning in Čapek's work, but one that subsequently led nowhere, and hence it can conveniently be placed at the end of this section on Čapek's early writing. "The Outlaw" mixes realist and symbolist styles and reveals the marked influence of Henrik Ibsen, August Strindberg, and Frank Wedekind, and very likely the philosophical influence of Friedrich Nietzsche. The hero, a nameless outlaw, comes from nowhere and goes nowhere and is a law unto himself; he is emblematic of youth's heedless will and reckless yearning. He lays siege to a country villa where the heroine, Mimi, is kept prisoner by her staid, conservative parents. He quickly wins her love, and she prepares to elope with him. The parents are powerless to fight him, since their weapons are those of age and convention, while he fights with the strength of youth and love. He is defeated only by the aged servant Fanka, a folk character who draws her strength not from love (her own love was unrequited), but from her very being and from her spiritual relation to the soil. She outwits the outlaw and drives him away, and Mimi, who will never love again so deeply, is saved by her.

The play is a powerful one and has remained in the repertoire of the Czech National Theater. Certainly it deserves a better fate than it has received over the decades in which it failed to win a place among Čapek's better-known works. Particularly strong is the play's stage conception, for which Josef Čapek was probably responsible. The scene is the outside of a country villa, converted into a real fortress by the parents and symbolic of their conventional values. This fortress is placed at the edge of a forest, the world of nature and love belonging to the outlaw. The brothers even made provision for an outdoor staging of the play, one that greatly reinforces its symbolic and poetic qualities.

The essential weakness of "The Outlaw" is hardly the mixture of realistic and symbolic styles, a mixture we find in the plays of Ibsen, Wedekind, and Chekhov (though in Čapek's work these styles do at times alternate with disconcerting speed). It is rather in the conflict between two conceptions of love. The outlaw loves spontaneously and naturally; he stands for the right to love without restraint. But such love would deny to Mimi the permanent self-definition her own love implies and indeed demands. Mimi's elder sister, seduced and abandoned, has been destroyed by this conflict, and her parents have taken refuge in their conventions in a vain attempt to deny it.

It is clear that this conflict between views of love is tragic and that the play is rightly a tragedy. Thus, Čapek was wrong to end the drama with a comic resolution deriving from the comic nature of the earthy servant Fanka. He did so as a concession to his new philosophy of pragmatic relativism: all human points of view must somehow contain something of the truth, and Mimi's "truth" of eternal love can hardly be more significant than her father's "truth" of the fortress that stands as a defense against love. Čapek carried this philosophy of ethical relativism, a by-product of his pragmatism, from

this early period into the mature period of the 1920's.

The variety of styles found in these early works is remarkable (though it is true that some are to be partly associated with Josef Čapek): they include symbolism, decadence, psychological realism, neoclassicism. We can posit a general artistic development from symbolism to expressionism, in which the latter term denotes an extreme form of subjectivism as the artist distorts reality in his need to express and objectify his deepest inner feelings. Expressionism constituted the dominant style in Čapek's next period. Also, in this early period Čapek established a habit that was to become characteristic: his works appear in successively alternating styles as he develops. Thus, *Money and Other Stories* opposes psychological realism to the metaphysical symbolism and allegories of "Wayside Crosses," while the two conflicting styles are combined in "The Outlaw."

UTOPIAN WRITING AND WORKS OF SCIENCE FICTION

The next period of Čapek's development emerged with the birth of a new symbol, one that was completely expressionistic—the robot. The term, destined to enter most of the languages of the world, was introduced by Čapek in his next play, though it had actually been coined by Josef Čapek for a story the year before. *Robot* derives from the Czech word *robota,* "toil" or "servitude."

Čapek's *R.U.R.* (which stands for "Rossum's Universal Robots"—the title is the English name of a cartel manufacturing the robots and was thus designed to suggest the international character of a giant enterprise) was published in 1920 and premiered at the National Theater in Prague on 25 January 1921. In spite of the English title, the names of the characters suggest a mixture of nationalities, and there is no implication that the author meant to blame only England or the United States for the plight in which the world finds itself.

Although Čapek's play contains many dramatic weaknesses, the conception of the robot as a stage character was an act of artistic inspiration, and the robot, marching up and down the stage stiffly and mechanically, was a brilliant piece of theatrical invention. Far more than any of the German expressionistic playwrights who were his contemporaries, Čapek conceived an eloquent symbol of the modern world and its contradictions.

Čapek's robot does not lack a literary pedigree, however. The Jewish legend of the golem of Prague, who is to be given life in times of danger to his people, is a local source obviously known to him. Mary Shelley's novel *Frankenstein* suggests certain details of Old Rossum's attempts to discover the secrets of human life, as does H. G. Wells's *Island of Dr. Moreau.* And Wells's *Food of the Gods* (1904) inspired the factory director Domin's observation that larger-than-life-size robots are unfeasible to manufacture because they only fall apart.

Although they have their antecedents in older literature, Čapek's robots have a peculiarly insistent significance for modern times. They represent the machine and its power to liberate man from toil, but at the same time they symbolize mankind's dehumanization by his own technology. Man is an inefficient instrument from a purely technical point of view, and hence the implication that he must either become a machine or be destroyed by machines. Something of this multiple, expressionistic complex of meanings is found in the plays of the early German expressionists, particularly in Georg Kaiser's *Gas, Part 1* (1918), in which the workers grow enormous legs or arms according to which member is employed in factory work. Both plays also take technology to its irrational limit: in Kaiser's play the gas explodes, although the engineers had calculated its formula correctly; in Čapek's play, the formula manufactures robots, but those robots ultimately turn into human beings—that is, into the irrational beings they were supposed to supplant.

Unfortunately, Čapek found it necessary to mediate his expressionistic symbol of the robot with a more conventional, realistic depiction of the human world. This was clearly essential for artistic contrast: the robot represents a concept that is generalized and abstract whereas human beings are real and concrete; they suffer and experience happiness. To have given an expressionistic treatment of human beings would have been to render them equally abstract and deprive them of their humanity; the proof of this is that Kaiser's *Gas,* in which the expressionistic line is more consistent, today seems lifeless and boring.

The construction of *R.U.R.* caused the author difficulty, probably because there were few models for a drama of this sort, as opposed to the more familiar literary patterns of utopian science fiction. The concept almost necessarily contained elements of both comedy and melodrama, and this, combined with the mixture of expressionistic and realistic styles, posed problems the author could not resolve.

The play opens with a "comedy prologue." Helen Glory, daughter of the president of the R.U.R. trust, comes to visit the island where the robots are manufactured. Her apparent motive is curiosity, but in fact she intends to incite the robots to rebel and assert their equality with human beings. Her efforts at provocation are rendered ineffectual and ludicrous because she cannot tell robots from human beings. This piece of comedy is by no means gratuitous, however, for it suggests that human beings are already partly dehumanized. In the end Helen abandons her crusade, comes to terms with the directors of the factory, and marries their leader, Domin.

Act 1 is the crucial act of the play from the point of view of dramatic structure, and the two acts that follow are in a sense anticlimactic. In the course of the first act we learn that robots all over the world are rising against their human masters and that human beings have lost their power to reproduce. Horrified by this news, Helen burns the manuscript containing the essential secret of the robot's manufacture. With this manuscript Domin had hoped to buy the directors' freedom when the world becomes ruled by robots.

In spite of the rapid melodramatic course of events, Čapek made time for philosophical discussion: to reflect what mankind's passing from the world might mean. He introduces an electrified grill that the robots cannot cross until they have taken the factory power plant. This delay also buys time for the play; without it the drama would presumably have been over at the end of Act 1. The delay is also essential to establish why the robots have revolted against and gained independence from their human masters. Dr. Gall, the scientist, suggests that he had introduced a certain "nervous irritability" in the robots to please Helen, who wanted them to possess a soul. But this is far from certain, and it seems more likely that nature permits the robots, who have already taken over man's work and responsibilities, to occupy his place in life.

Act 2 ends with the robots crossing the electric grill and with the death of all the human beings on the island save one: the engineer Alquist, who is spared because he still works with his hands. The robots order him to reconstruct the secret of their manufacture, now lost with the destroyed manuscript. To do so he must dissect live robots. Alquist is unable to do this, but as he laments his weakness he notices that his two robot servants, Primus and Helen, have fallen in love. Now the robots themselves will reproduce, he concludes.

Thus the play turns in a circle ideologically, denying the very thesis it had asserted for dramatic purposes: that modern civilization threatens to destroy humanity by removing the elements of struggle from human life. This thesis is contradicted by the implication that life and love will not perish. The fact that the two robots fall in love reasserts this contradiction expressionistically.

The play also serves as a "comedy of truth," in which the author's relativist philosophical point of view again prevails in that he does not reconcile opposing viewpoints. Helen Glory represents pure sentiment unchecked by reason. Her initial sympathy for the robots, who do not precisely deserve it, sets the action of the drama going, and when it appears that they are dangerous, her mindless act of burning the manuscript dooms man by depriving him of his bargaining chip. Countering Helen's view is Domin's vision of man as master of the universe (his name implies this) and of humanity freed from toil and servitude. Opposed to him is Nána, Helen's nurse, for whom all inventions are "against the Lord God." Alquist the engineer, on the other hand, holds a Tolstoyan faith in work and its ability to ennoble humanity. These viewpoints rarely mesh. The creativity and free spirit celebrated by Alquist are not the toil and drudgery from which Domin would liberate the world.

Kenneth Burke observes that *R.U.R.* fails primarily because it lacks eloquence; the intensity of Čapek's ideas is never matched by a comparable intensity of language. In fact, Domin and Alquist do achieve a certain eloquence of philosophical statement. But Helen, who ought to be the most eloquent personage in the drama, fails pitifully, probably because her views do not correspond to any given philosophic creed. As one critic has observed, the spectator might conclude from the way the play is constructed that humanity disappears from the earth because Helen cannot mind her own business.

Other faults mar the dramaturgy: the existence of only one copy of Old Rossum's manuscript, and the fact that Helen is the only woman on the island (except her nurse), while the men who work there are well paid. The latter fault suggests a symbolic flaw in the conception of the play: the island symbolizes sterility, while the robots, like certain earlier puppet figures in Čapek's work, suggest the author's own fear of sterility. Čapek was aware of flaws, no doubt, and is said to have liked *R.U.R.* the least of all his plays. But in spite of the work's faults, probably no other play on the dangers of modern technology has so captured the public's imagination.

Elements of the theme of industrialized civilization and its dangers return in Čapek's later science-fiction novel *The Absolute at Large* and in his play *Věc Makropulos* (*The Macropulos Secret,* 1922). But the real successor to *R.U.R.*—a work that satisfactorily resolves the contradictions in the earlier drama—is Čapek's science-fiction novel *The War with the Newts*.

The greater success of *The War with the Newts* may well be due to its genre: it is a novel, the typical form for science fiction, rather than a theatrical melodrama. The major literary influences are those of Wells and, in particular, Jonathan Swift, whose precedent accounts for the dominant role of satire in the novel. (*R.U.R.* totally lacks satire.) A *roman feuilleton,* or serialized novel, *The War with the Newts* appeared in *Lidové noviny.* The looser form of the novel and the satiric tone permitted the author to introduce the most diverse kinds of writings in brilliant parodic fashion: newspaper articles, memoirs, scholarly works, manifestos. Every conceivable typographic device available in a newspaper font was employed for parodic effect, and there is even an obscure historical note printed in an older "Gothic" Czech type, as well as an extremely blurred tiny photo of a giant newt.

The science-fiction novel makes no attempt at literal realism, and even the introduction of details does not necessarily suggest realism; in this respect, the novel is unlike the drama or the film. In *The War with the Newts* the unreality of the novel's particular treatment of technological danger to civilization never disturbs the reader. There is, however, a certain disturbing inconsistency in the point of view. The author poses as an historian who tells of mankind's destruction, but he sometimes intrudes to comment on the details he narrates. He says that he cannot know whether the human race will survive the attack of the newts or not, although the "historian" who studies the sources must already know the answer to this question.

Like the robots of *R.U.R.,* the giant newts are a complex symbol and not only represent technology's capacity to free human beings from toil but also symbolize mankind debased by its own civilization. In the epilogue to the first book edition of the novel Čapek protests against the word *utopian* as applied by critics of the novel, but he would have accepted the more precise literary label of *dystopian.* (A dystopia is a utopia turned inside out, one with negative features.) Like Swift, Čapek employs the image of another world to show us the faults of our own, and the world of the newts is an allegory of the contemporary world.

The novel's action develops from the discovery of a species of giant newt off the coast of Sumatra. The newts are readily tamed. Soon they are trained to perform all sorts of human tasks, so long as they can work in or near the water, and they exchange pearls for knives with which they can defend themselves against sharks. An enormous slave trade in newts flourishes. But deep under the ocean they create their own empire, and from it they eventually launch an attack on humanity. Multiplying rapidly, they demand the right to lengthen the coastline so that they will have more territory in which to breed. Terrified, the great powers offer to sacrifice parts of China to them, but this compromise is not enough, and soon the newts inundate half of Europe. At this point Čapek cuts off the narrative without conclusion. Will mankind survive? he asks. Certainly the newts can leave some strips of land on which human beings will live, if only as slaves to the newts. But perhaps the newts will attack one another; there is no reason their political order should be more cohesive than mankind's.

Published in 1936, the novel makes a number of anti-Nazi gibes. Chief Salamander, the newt dictator, is actually a human being, a German sergeant from World War I. But, although there are jokes at the expense of both Nazism and Communist totalitarianism, capitalism is the central target of Čapek's satire; in 1936 he hardly foresaw that the rise of Hitler would constitute a unique danger to civilization, and the blind, rapacious greed of the democratic powers seemed to him an adequate cause for their mutual destruction. As in *R.U.R.*, it is civilization that will bring mankind's fall. Unlike the earlier work, however, this satirical allegory of man's fate contains no silvery ray of vitalist optimism, perhaps because time's passage had only weighted the balance against the individual for Čapek. *The War with the Newts* is Čapek's masterpiece in the science-fiction genre. True, the newt was perhaps not so incisive a symbol of technological civilization as the robot had been, but as Čapek observes in the novel's epilogue, there was a reason for his choice: it was necessary to remind human beings that they are not masters of the universe, that life and nature are greater than man and do not need him for their purposes.

All of Čapek's science-fiction creations oppose an absolute ideal in the name of relativism; absolutism for Čapek is equated with humanity as a whole, with society and civilization, whereas relativism characterizes the fate and happiness of individual persons. This point is made most strikingly in the satirical novel *The Absolute at Large.* The work appeared in weekly installments in the newspaper *Lidové noviny*; it was deliberately planned as a serial, and as a result is rather episodic.

The Absolute at Large continues the dystopian tradition of *R.U.R.* but in a less serious vein. While the earlier work takes as its point of departure the idea of a robot, an artificial person who performs work, this novel's imaginative source is the concept of atomic energy and its liberation through nuclear fission. The subject is a reflection of the contemporary efforts of Lord Rutherford to split the atom.

In the novel an engineer invents a process for the industrial utilization of atomic energy, but the process has one great drawback: the annihilation of matter releases the spiritual energy of the Absolute, and those who are in its vicinity undergo religious conversions and perform miracles; there are even mass conversions and large-scale religious crusades and wars. Another drawback becomes apparent once the process is put into large-scale use: it creates such an abundance of goods that the economic system breaks down, and there are no means to distribute goods that are now valueless because there are so many of them. Factories are surrounded by oceans of products that cannot be moved, even though scarcities exist a few miles away. The novel thus appears to have two disparate themes—technological utopia and religious mania—but in fact these two themes are one. Self-sacrificing idealism and unlimited production are two classic prerequisites for utopia, and the novel shows the futility of the utopian ideal.

The Absolute at Large is uneven in its execution and did not please Čapek's critics. The opening twelve chapters, with their imaginative description of the creation of a utopia, are brilliant and exemplify Čapek's best satire in the manner of Swift. But they are followed by a rather labored chronicle of world history and its endless wars and crusades. A lengthy and somewhat tedious Napoleonic episode reminds us of the main literary source of this part of the novel: Anatole France's *Penguin Island.* The novel ends with a curiously bathetic resolution: the madness finally passes and life returns to normal. A few of the novel's characters meet at a Prague tavern to eat sausages, drink beer, and comment on what has happened. Rather than faith in an absolute, they agree, man needs to have faith in his fellow human beings, for they are all basically good.

No doubt this ending is unsatisfactory, and it gave fuel to the fires of Čapek's critics. And no doubt its optimism barely conceals the writer's deeper pessimism. Still, it does represent a first sign that Čapek was turning away from nihilism toward a philosophy of democracy based on faith in the little man, and in this it anticipates his writing of the 1930's.

The play *The World We Live In* was coauthored by Josef Čapek, and received its premiere at the National Theater in Prague on 8 March 1922. The play was almost as successful as *R.U.R.* had been. *The World We Live In* grew out of the brothers' reading of the French entomologist Jean Fabre. The fable and beast epos are genres that use the world of animals to create an allegory of human morality, and the brothers conceived their satirical play, which they also compared to the medieval miracle dramas, in this spirit. Such a conception was virtually new to the modern stage, and they made its execution even more original by incorporating techniques taken from the ballet, revue, film, and pantomime. In general the theatrical qualities of the work predominate over its dramatic ones, and the play is relatively static; with a good production, however, the loss is slight.

The play's raisonneur is Man, a tramp who observes insects and comments on their behavior. The three acts introduce the themes of love, family life, and war, all enacted within insect society. The first act, with its frivolous and flirtatious butterflies, who are doomed to an early death, recalls the erotic parody of the brothers' early verse play, *Lásky hra osudná* (The Fateful Game of Love, 1922), and imparts a sense of the futility of life and its eternal cycle of falling in and out of love. The second act focuses on beetles and emphasizes the insularity of their family life, with its hard facade of coldness turned toward the world. The tramp reflects that the failures of their society must be due to its anarchic individualism and that the authority of the state is the answer. Thus we pass to the world of the ants, to war and a totalitarian order in which two colonies of ants destroy each other senselessly.

Throughout the play a chrysalis is struggling to be born. She declares that with her birth something new, "some great message," will come into the world. But no sooner is she born than she perishes, which seems to imply a parodic attack on literary symbolism. In the play's epilogue the tramp, initially the play's raisonneur, becomes its protagonist as he himself struggles with death.

In the play's original ending the tramp dies. In reply to their critics the brothers protested that they had not intended to be pessimistic and that a criticism of social evils (or even the fact of death) is not necessarily pessimistic. Still, they supplied an alternative ending, leaving it to the director of the production to decide which one to employ. In the second ending the tramp awakens from a bad dream of death and then takes a job that a woodcutter offers him. This new ending may make the brothers seem oblivious to the tragedy of individual death, but their view is presumably a biological one, rooted in nature.

In 1922 Čapek published a new play, *The Macropulos Secret,* which premiered at the National Theater in Prague on 21 November of that year. The play attacks the concept of eternal life as yet another false dream of utopian absolutism; eternal life would benefit neither man as an individual nor the human race. The theme is hardly new, of course, as the well-known legends of the Wandering Jew and the Flying Dutchman illustrate.

Critics have customarily taken Čapek's play as a reply to George Bernard Shaw's *Back to Methuselah* (also 1922), in which Shaw voices the opinion that a greatly increased life span would benefit man. Čapek protested that he had not even read Shaw's play, which had just appeared, but this did not lay the critics' opinion to rest. What is more likely is that *The Macropulos Secret* is a reply, not to Shaw, but to H. G. Wells's *Food of the Gods*, in which Wells argues that a greater physical stature would be advantageous to man. Čapek's earlier *R.U.R.* contains a specific remark that suggests Čapek knew Wells's romance and was opposed to its central concept: in Čapek's play Domin tells Helen that efforts had been made to develop robots larger than normal human beings, but that these giants soon fell apart. (Čapek's view was, apparently, biologically more sound than Wells's.)

The Macropulos Secret is a melodrama with a complicated plot involving an old manuscript and an inheritance. The heroine, Emilia Marty, a celebrated singer, offers testimony that will clear up a long-standing legal suit and the inheritance of an enormous fortune; in return for her assistance she wishes only to receive an old manuscript preserved among the belongings of the disputed estate. This manuscript was the work of her father, the Greek physician Macropulos, who served at the court of the emperor Rudolph II. The manuscript contains the secret of immortality, a secret that the daughter has used in order to survive more than three hundred years. She has lived five different lives under different names, but always employing the initials E. M. for Elena Macropulos. She needs now to recover the manuscript in order to reacquire the complicated formula for prolonging life, so that she may live another sixty years. However, her long life has left her spiritually empty and profoundly bored and so, when she again comes into possession of the secret, she renounces it and offers it to the other characters of the drama. They argue about its best use, but finally a young girl takes the paper and burns it in the flame of a candle.

The play's melodramatic character has often led critics and spectators to underestimate its strength. Its comic aspects are quite sophisticated, and the heroine is one of Čapek's most successful stage characters. In general, Čapek had great difficulty in creating successful dramatic or fictional characters, and it may be that his propensity for nonhuman personages—puppets, robots, newts—was a reaction to this professional weakness, perhaps one that cloaked a deeper psychological sterility or fear of sterility. *The Macropulos Secret* has survived on the stage, especially in its celebrated operatic setting by Leoš Janáček.

In 1924 Čapek published a second dystopian novel, *Krakatit*. Like his first novel, *The Absolute at Large, Krakatit* was inspired by the possibility of atomic fission and by Lord Rutherford's experiments in atom splitting. But while *The Absolute at Large* is a satire based on the "useful" applications of atomic energy, *Krakatit* focuses on the violent ones and thus anticipates the atomic bomb. Written at a time when Čapek's spinal disease caused him acute pain, the novel has an intense, dreamy, almost feverish quality.

A complex allegory, the novel fails, probably because its allegorical burden is too heavy. A young inventor discovers the secret of liberating nuclear energy and develops an explosive substance, krakatit, named for the volcano Krakatoa. He falls in love and has all sorts of adventures, during which the allegory informs the reader that his basic fault is the destructive spirit he brings to the world, a spirit expressive of his own inner turmoil and sensuality. Finally he meets a figure who represents God, an old man who tells him that he can be saved only if he uses his discovery to develop a cheap source of energy to aid human beings in their work.

Outside this third period but belonging to it, apparently as a kind of afterthought, is the play *Adam Stvořitel* (*Adam the Creator*), the joint work of the two brothers. It was first produced at the National Theater in Prague in 1927 but was largely unsuccessful.

Adam the Creator continues the tradition of *R.U.R.* and *The Macropulos Secret;* it is a comedy on a utopian theme. The play recalls an earlier dystopian fantasy by Josef Čapek, the play *Země mnoha jmen* (*The Land of Many Names,* 1924), in which a new continent emerges over the surface of the waters, bringing hope of a new life, but only serving with time as a pretext for fresh struggles and wars. Another influence, no doubt, is Shaw's *Back to Methuselah,* here definitely and finally rejected for its conception of the role of human will in evolution.

Dissatisfied with God's world, Adam destroys it with the Cannon of Negation, an expressionist symbol of his anarchic, nihilistic will. But Adam himself continues to exist, since he has forgotten to deny himself as well. The Voice of God then commands him to recreate the world; a heap of earth is to serve as the Clay of Creation. Adam's first attempts turn out disastrously. He finally has the idea of creating his own double, Alter Ego, to assist him, forgetting that his double will treat him as he treats others. In fact, Alter Ego turns out to be quarrelsome, suspicious, and opinionated. The world is divided between the two, each taking half of the Clay of Creation.

Adam creates individuals of genius, while Alter Ego uses molds to produce people en masse. The two parties engage in an endless series of wars, finally deposing their leaders. Adam and Alter Ego take refuge on the very heap of clay they had once used for creation. There is too little clay left to create a man, and in response to Adam's disgusted kicks, a misshapen dwarf, Zmetek, arises from the pile. Then Adam and Alter Ego decide to destroy the world again with the Cannon of Negation. But Zmetek will not permit this; he hopes to stay alive and see better things. So the world, with all its faults, is permitted to endure.

The play illustrates the contradictions and inadequacies of Čapek's philosophy of vitalism: Adam criticizes God's creation as defective, but he is part of it himself; and if Adam creates badly in the play so does life, which has, after all, created Adam himself. Only Zmetek, the cripple and beggar, can be taken as a successful example of life's spontaneous creation, and he is shown to be generous and hopeful for a better future. He is reminiscent of the eponymous hero of Jaroslav Hašek's *The Good Soldier Schweik* (1921–1923) who, in his earthy realism, remains free from posing and self-deception. In spite of the play's failure, the figure Zmetek is a bridge to Čapek's democratic world of the 1930's.

Thus Čapek's dystopian period came to an end. Its success was mixed, more because of the limitations of his ideas and the inadequacy of the relativist philosophy he espoused than because of the failure of his inspiration or artistic technique. To go further Čapek found he must transcend that philosophy of relativism. In 1922 he had written of a "group of themes I should like to put behind me," and it seems likely that the reference here is to the whole series of dystopian works directed against the cult of absolutism. Still, it cannot be said that the results of this second period of creativity were entirely a failure. The compact, incisive symbol of the robot as expressive of modern man dehumanized by his civilization; the sparkling, satirical theatricality of *The World We Live In;* the imposing figure of Emilia Marty, a woman who has gazed beyond life and who does not fear death—these are the distillations of his work during this period.

NEWSPAPER WRITING AND ESSAYS

Čapek had been active as a journalist since 1917, most of his literary works having first appeared in the newspaper *Lidové noviny,* a moderate organ published in Brno by Čapek's friend, the writer Eduard Bass. From 1924 to 1929, there was a hiatus in Čapek's literary production while his journalistic publication intensified, and Čapek's enemies were quick to conclude that his literary inspiration had deserted him. He himself explained that his silence was due to the necessity to "help educate the nation." This remark, though it may appear condescending, was a genuine attempt to express the writer's ethical obligation to his people. In retrospect it is clear that the charge of loss of inspiration was premature, for the 1930's brought a new period of creativity, Čapek's greatest.

Čapek's newspaper writing was in the genre of the feuilleton, a form that had served Czech literature in lieu of an essay. Čapek, following the Czech writer Jan Neruda (1834–1891), brought the genre to an almost essaylike perfection. Besides Neruda (and through him Heinrich Heine), influences on Čapek's feuilletons came from writers as diverse as Voltaire, Ralph Waldo Emerson, Henry David Thoreau, Walt Whitman, and G. K. Chesterton; philosophically they show the influence of Bergson and the American pragmatists. The predominance of American influence is striking, especially when we note that "American" for Čapek also implied a faceless, cultureless mass and the rule of monopolistic capitalism.

Čapek's feuilletons utilize the rhetorical and grammatical forms of a chat between writer and reader, with the reader's interjectory responses suggested by the use of colloquial forms on the part of the writer. Although rough, this form was perfected into a most expressive instrument in which style and subject both represent a unique mixture of aestheticism and "folksiness": Čapek writes about such matters as the varied world of a country boy, frost flowers on glass, the coming of spring, bird-watching, barrel organs, the magic power of names, the cult of the miniature, Prague in the snow. For an avowed philosophical writer such essays may seem to employ little philosophy other than the homespun kind. But if his views are at times a bit sentimental, they are rarely banal or obvious.

As early as 1925 Čapek had published a volume of collected feuilletons that aspired to be essays: *O nejbližších věcech* (*Intimate Things*). This title suggests that the correct word to characterize these essays and the subjects they treat is neither "homespun" nor "aestheticist," but "intimate." Obviously it is the small and the close that attracted him, just as the great, the titanic, the Nietzschean repelled him; here he was a true follower of Thomas Masaryk and his philosophy.

Čapek's critics reproached him for his apparent lack of concern for social and political matters. Indeed, *Intimate Things* does neglect these subjects. But one of Čapek's first newspaper pieces had been a savage portrayal of life in a Prague slum, and in 1932 he carved out of his newspaper writings a second collected volume: *O věcech obedných čili Zóon politikon* (On Political Matters, or Zoon Politikon), a volume that unfortunately has never been translated into English. The most celebrated article from this collection is "Proč nejsem kominista" (Why I Am Not a Communist), in which Čapek takes great pains to define his antipathy to the left. (Much of the Czech literary world at this time consisted of fellow travelers [persons who sympathize with communism but are not communists], and even Čapek's brother, Josef, had leftist sympathies.) Perhaps the most interesting and original articles, however, are those such as "Betlém" (Bethlehem) and "Malé po-

měry" (On a Small Scale), in which he finds fault with those of his countrymen who apologize for all Czech shortcomings by pointing to the small scale of Czech life. (In his later *Obrázky z Holandska* [*Letters from Holland*, 1932] Čapek is delighted to find that the Dutch have been taking his advice for centuries and have capitalized on their smallness.)

The three volumes of Čapek's interviews with Masaryk, *President Masaryk Tells His Story*, are the culmination of his journalistic writing. In them Čapek employed both his philosophic subtlety and his journalistic skill to create a memorable portrait of the philosopher–president of Czechoslovakia. But he viewed his task as one of passive expression, and there is very little of Čapek himself in these volumes. On Masaryk's death in 1935 he wrote a moving epilogue, "Mlčení s T. G. M." (Silence with T. G. M.).

Čapek's newspaper writing has survived and still has value; much of it has been collected in published volumes in Czech (though not always in English, with the exception of his popular travel sketches and his essays on gardening and on dogs and cats). In a larger sense, his newspaper writing must also be looked at as preparation for his fiction and plays of the 1930's, with their greater stylistic fluidity and greater use of colloquial speech.

PROSE FICTION: 1929–1937

Čapek broke his literary silence in 1929 when he published two volumes of stories: *Povídky z jedné kapsy* (Tales from One Pocket) and *Povídky z druhé kapsy* (Tales from the Other Pocket). Paul Selver, one of Čapek's English translators, made a one-volume English selection from both volumes, retitling them *Tales from Two Pockets* (1932). Thus the translator skimmed off the cream of the two volumes and made forever unlikely the translation of the remaining stories.

For the most part the two volumes are composed of detective and police tales, though a few elude these categories. Čapek had created models for these forms in the earlier "Wayside Crosses" and *Money and Other Stories,* and in the later *Tales from Two Pockets,* the influence of Chesterton's Father Brown tales and their pious, meditative amateur detective is again evident. In the earlier stories, as in *The Macropulos Secret* and *Krakatit* (both of which contain elements of a detective narrative), the detective story form serves to help unravel a metaphysical theme; this, too, is Chestertonian. In *Tales from Two Pockets,* however, the author is less pretentious; the narratives seem to exist chiefly for the pleasure they give. Indeed, evidence suggests that the writing of these tales served to fill the author's leisure time as well as his readers'.

Still, a few of the stories do have metaphysical or epistemological themes, though these are treated playfully. The quest for absolute truth that dominated "Wayside Crosses" here yields to a quest for relative truth, since this is all man can know. Man may confuse relative truth for truth concerning the Absolute, or again—and this is perhaps the central theme of the two volumes—one man's relative truth cannot serve another. In "Pád rodu Votických" ("The Fall of the House of Votický") an historian begs a police detective to help him solve a family mystery of the fifteenth century. The detective obliges him and advances the only hypothesis that can fit all the facts. But when the historian publishes his treatise, he still characterizes the mystery as unsolved, for as an historian he cannot use the kinds of evidence the detective had supplied.

In "Tajemstuí písma" ("The Secrets of Handwriting") a man believes a graphologist's unflattering analysis of his wife's character, ignoring the contrary evidence of their many years together. In "Experiment profesora Rousse" ("Professor Rouss's Experiment") a psychologist demonstrates the guilt of a criminal by administering a word-association test. The method, so convincing in this case, fails ludicrously when Professor Rouss examines a newspaperman from the audience, who responds with a string of journalistic clichés. In "Moudrá chrysantéma" ("The Blue Chrysanthemums") an idiot girl brings in the flowers of a new kind of chrysanthemum that no one can locate; it turns out that she picks them near a railroad track where no one goes because there is a No Trespassing sign there, a sign she cannot read.

Only a few of these tales conform to the rule of fair play in detective fiction; most do not give the reader all the clues necessary to arrive at the solution in an orderly fashion. Obviously detection is not Čapek's central purpose. Rather, the tales are witty epistemological improvisations; today's critics might well turn to them to discover an emphasis on codes, semiotic composition, and even intertextuality, since they contain elements borrowed from Chesterton and O. Henry.

If the first volume of the two emphasizes epistemology, the second volume is more concerned with ethics, a shift that became significant for Čapek's writing of the 1930's. "Závrat" ("Vertigo") focuses on the narrow borderline separating psychology and ethics. A psychoanalyst cures a patient of vertigo, which the man had acquired as a symptom of guilt when he had pushed his wife over a cliff. But the analyst cannot deal with the man's guilt itself, and when he leaves the analyst's office, ostensibly cured, the man hurls himself to his death from a staircase. The theme of guilt is almost omnipresent in this volume: "Balado o Juraji Čupovi" ("The Epic Exploit of Juraj Čup") is the story of a Ruthenian peasant who makes an impossible march through a snowstorm to give himself up to the police; he has murdered his sister at God's command, and now God commands him to surrender to the police..

"Soud pana Havleny" ("Mr. Havlena's Verdict") is an amusing story that seems to derive from the life of Čapek's fellow writer Jaroslav Hašek, a journalist who sometimes published fictitious stories as news. The story concerns a law student who never graduated and who makes his living inventing fictitious court cases and selling them to the newspapers. One of his "cases" concerns a man sentenced to pay a fine because he had trained a parrot to squawk abusive language at an old woman next door. The Ministry of Justice challenges the legality of the verdict and asks which court pronounced it. Havlena refuses to admit that he could have been mistaken in his account; he buys a parrot, teaches it to insult a neighbor lady, and even bribes her to take the case to court. But in spite of all his pleas, the court pronounces him innocent.

The transformations Čapek made in the detective story presumably proceeded from an urge to humanize it. The detective story in its classic form is on the periphery of literature; like science fiction, it is a special genre that shares only secondarily the customary ethical and human concerns of literature. Hence the mysteries in Čapek's tales are often quite simple and trite, and there is little obligation to follow the rule of fair play. Criminal motives are the simplest—usually greed or jealousy—and crime has little mystique; to the contrary, it is a sordid and banal business when it is not merely comical.

Čapek always had difficulty in the creation of complex human characters, and these tales show little, if any, advance in this respect. He did become more adept in these stories at creating the illusion of living character through the use of a colloquial conversational tone new in his fiction, and also by emphasizing eccentric features of personality. However, the characters he creates are hardly complex.

From early 1933 to late 1934, Čapek published the three novels that, taken together as a trilogy, represent the apex of his career. These are *Hordubal, Meteor,* and *An Ordinary Life.* In these works for the first time he created a firm balance between philosophic and literary expression.

Evidence suggests that Čapek had been working on these novels since the late 1920's: bits and pieces of them appear in the *Tales from Two Pockets.* Yet it remains uncertain at what point he decided to link the three together as a trilogy. They are diverse in characters, set-tings, and even, to an extent, in theme. Only at the very end of *An Ordinary Life* does Čapek supply an epilogue that serves to tie all three firmly together.

No doubt the three novels have connections with Čapek's earlier writing. *Hordubal* expresses his by-now familiar relativism, but it is a relativism that has become strangely pessimistic; Čapek at last grasped that relativism of truth must isolate human beings since in a completely relativist universe, each individual would know only his own truth, not the truth of others.

Hordubal is based on a true story, which Čapek could have come upon in *Lidové noviny.* In this newspaper's account, a Ruthenian peasant, Juraj Hardubej, returned home after eight years in America to find that his wife, Polana, had been unfaithful to him with the hired man, Vasil Maňák. To conceal her guilt she had betrothed their eleven-year-old daughter to Maňák. Hardubej broke off the engagement and threw Maňák out. In revenge, Maňák killed Hardubej by driving a basket-weaver's needle through his heart. Maňák subsequently confessed his guilt and was sentenced to life imprisonment. Polana was sentenced to twelve years, although her guilt was never proven.

The subject is obviously related to the crime stories of the *Two Pockets,* and the Ruthenian background to "The Epic Exploit of Juraj Čup," a story in the second volume of those tales. But the author changed many details of the real-life story. In the novel Hordubal never loses his love for Polana, and it is he who affiances their daughter to the hired man in order to protect his wife's good name as well as to shame her and bring her to her senses. The ruse does not work, however, and in the end the lovers kill him.

In *Hordubal,* Čapek endows his characters with rich pathos and symbolic imagery. The Slav Hordubal is linked with the mountains in which he lives and with the breeding of cattle; the Magyar Manya is linked with the plains and with horse culture. This imagery subtly associates the settled farmer Hordubal with stolid affection and a deep knowledge of inner pain, while Manya appears as a nomad aggressor and plunderer. From the mountaintop Hordubal twice views the clandestine meetings of the lovers, the second time to plot his murder, and as in "Wayside Crosses," the mountaintop provides absolute insight rather than relative truth.

The final part of the novel concerns the police investigation of the crime and the court trial. Although they can approximate the truth of the murder, the police and the court never arrive at an understanding of Hordubal or his deep love for Polana. His heart, pierced by the basket needle, is sent off for medical investigation since there is a possibility that he was already dead with fever when he was stabbed. As the novel's final sentence tells us, "The heart of Juraj Hordubal was lost somewhere and never buried." Thus, in metaphorical form, the reader learns that the truth about Hordubal can never be known. Yet paradoxically, it *is* known: through literary creation Čapek communicates it to his readers.

The second novel, *Meteor,* also grew thematically out of Čapek's relativism. By this time he had evidently become acquainted with the Spanish philosopher Ortega y Gasset's theory of epistemological perspectivism, in which disparate relativist view points can be joined together to form a single and coherent view of reality. Čapek's *Meteor* is composed of a group of fictional narratives told by a number of persons who join in an effort to reconstruct the life of an unknown man, a stranger who has been fatally injured in a plane crash. There is very little objective evidence for his identity, but what little evidence there is suggests that he has been to colonies in close proximity to each other, such as the West Indies. At the end of the novel this suggestion is corroborated: the stranger did in fact come from Cuba.

Three people in the hospital where the unknown man is dying attempt to solve his mystery. The first, a Sister of Mercy who watches by his bedside, dreams of him on successive nights. In her narrative he appears as a callow youth who flees his home because he lacks the courage to accept real love; when he has comprehended its nature and accepts it, he can go home again. The second narrator, a clairvoyant, supposes that the stranger is a chemist who has discovered a series of chemical formulas for new compounds but lacks the patience to demonstrate them experimentally. When by chance he comes upon a scholarly article partly confirming his views, he hastens home to claim the discovery as his own. The third narrator is a writer. In his version the stranger is a victim of amnesia who falls in love with a rich Cuban girl but cannot marry her until he recovers his identity and his past. Only when he has experienced the extreme of pain and suffering does he find his memory and fly home to reclaim his rightful position.

In outline these three accounts seem crude, but they are developed with great skill into finished narratives, and the writer's story contains many fresh observations on authorship and literature. To the objection that the forms of cognition Čapek has chosen (dreams, clairvoyance, fiction) are inadequate for real knowledge, it must be countered that these forms are only suggestive and symbolic. In any case, knowledge for the philosopher is more complex and less obvious than it is for the lay person.

Although the three accounts differ, they have enough in common to suggest the possibility of a cooperative search for the truth of both the individual's life and of life in general. Thus *Meteor* counters *Hordubal* as antithesis to thesis: all knowledge is relative and fragmentary, but relative, fragmentary knowledge can be assembled to provide us with an image of the truth.

The last novel of the trilogy, *An Ordinary Life,* pursues the quest for self-identity. A retired railway official decides to write the story of his life, partly because it is only an "ordinary life," in no way notable. As he proceeds with his task, however, he discovers that his compulsive belief in "ordinariness" is only partly justified. A few isolated memories invade the harmony of his concept: an erotic incident from his childhood, a period of wild, orgiastic life at the university, an episode in which he came very close to murdering his wife. He supposes that these were merely temporary interruptions, after which the pattern of ordinariness reasserted itself more strongly. But as his analysis proceeds he discovers more and more diverse beings within himself, some actualized, others only potential: an ambitious and ruthless person, a hypochondriac, a poet and dreamer, a hero who worked for the Czech resistance during World War I, a beggar who loves grime and poverty, a perverted sensualist. All these live within him, and by perceiving them he can understand and come to terms with the plurality of beings around him.

Thus *An Ordinary Life* brings a synthesis to resolve the thesis–antithesis of the first two novels: all human beings are relative and unknowable, but relative knowledge can adumbrate the truth, and by assembling pieces of relative knowledge we can apprehend a complex truth. Finally, in the synthesis, truth is pluralistic and forms a bridge that links the individual to society. Čapek therefore provides a definition of human society in his fiction, and implicitly he creates a metaphysical basis for that society as democratic: if the individual is linked to society by its plurality within himself, then individuals must in some sense be equal within that society.

In *An Ordinary Life* the use of self-analysis and the postulation of an unconscious mind is noteworthy. Čapek was well aware of Freud's theories but distrusted many of them, and thus the novel presents an unusual example of a non-Freudian psychology that accepts the existence of the unconscious and the utility of the psychoanalytic method as a road to truth.

The novel is original in that the serene narrative of recollection and self-analysis, a traditional novelistic form, breaks up into a hectic dialogue in rough, clipped speech among the multiplicity of persons within the "ordinary man." There can be little question that while the trilogy is Čapek's masterpiece, *An Ordinary Life* is his masterpiece within the trilogy. Indeed, the work has a very substantial claim to be regarded as the greatest Czech novel.

Čapek's final creative period comes after the trilogy. He seems to have regarded the statement of ideas embodied there as definitive, for he never returned to them. Indeed, the reiterative pattern of his earlier work does not reappear in this final period, with the exception of *The War with the Newts,* which reiterates the dystopian and science-fiction trends of his earlier writing. Each of the final works represents a new departure, ideological and formal, in his creation. This is perhaps part of the reason Čapek's last works failed to recapture the success of the trilogy or of *The War with the Newts.* It must be admitted that some are failures and one explanation for this may be that world events had interrupted the tranquillity in which Čapek had worked earlier; the idyllic suburban and garden existence of the 1920's was gone forever. The rise of Nazi Germany brought new ideological problems and new responsibilities, and at least three of Čapek's last works are ideological counterweights to the Nazi threat.

The first of these is a novel about heroism, *První parta (The First Rescue Party,* 1937), in which the need for solidarity in the face of a common danger is the lesson to be learned if the Nazi threat is to be opposed. In the novel eight members of a work gang unite to rescue three miners trapped by an explosion. Although completely free from the metaphysical concerns of the trilogy, the novel is a kind of epilogue to it: once the basis for a common democratic society is laid, that society must function to defend itself in time of need. Unfortunately, *The First Rescue Party* is an artistic failure, perhaps because its ideology is oversimplified, perhaps because its narrator (a boy training to become a miner) also undermines the theme with his naïveté.

THE FINAL YEARS: 1937–1938

In this period Čapek unexpectedly returned to the theater and wrote two more plays, perhaps because he considered the stage a more demonstrative and effective means to express his new ideology of resistance to Germany. The model of Bertolt Brecht's theater looms large in these plays.

The first of these works, *Bílá nemoc* (*Power and Glory*, 1937), is allegorical. A plague something like leprosy eats away human flesh, attacking only persons over forty—an intentional irony since men over forty do not fight wars. A physician, Dr. Galén (the choice of name is significant; Galen was a second-century Greek physician), discovers a cure, but he refuses to reveal its secret unless the state, intent on a war of conquest, will guarantee peace. The dictator, the marshal, rejects Galén's proposal because he is concerned with the manifest destiny he believes rightfully belongs to his people. However, when he contracts the plague, he yields to the doctor's proposal. On his way to treat the marshal, Galén is killed by a frenzied mob in the grip of war hysteria.

In its original conception the play was more openly anti-Nazi; protests from the German embassy in Prague forced Čapek to tone down certain details and to internationalize names to cloak the theme of German–Czech antagonism.

The drama suffers from many problems. The symbol of the plague, though eloquent and expressive of the irrational character of war and war psychology, is hardly as appropriate as the robot or newt had been. It fails insofar as it implies that the human race can combat war as it does disease. Furthermore, Čapek was unable to incorporate his central symbol of plague into an essentially realistic play. Galén has no power to impose peace on the warring nations; he can only obtain promises that any country is free to break. Only in the play's denouement does the author belatedly recognize the impotence of Galén's scheme; the ending of the play, in which Galén is destroyed by irra-tional human forces, does express something of the irrationality of war.

Čapek's final play is *Matka* (*The Mother*, 1938). Bothered apparently by the too realistic, insufficiently expressionistic character of *Power and Glory,* he wrote a purely expressionistic second antiwar play. In this, as well as in his choice of subject, he was influenced by Brecht. The play was inspired by the Spanish civil war, but following his common practice, Čapek internationalized the names of his characters. The mother, the play's only woman, has no name. She represents the eternal feminine, opposed to the men of the play who are dominated by masculine ideals: ambition, heroism, creativity, honor. For the author these traits represent the essence of what it is to be a man, and these the mother can never comprehend. She understands only the fact of life itself and the necessity to preserve it, and she suffers because her men lose their lives so casually in the name of those very ideals she cannot comprehend. One by one her men die, until she is left alone with her youngest son. She hides him, refusing to sacrifice him to the war that has broken out in her land. But at the end when she learns that the invading army is killing mothers and sons, she gives her son a rifle and bids him to go off to war.

Thus Čapek signals his abandonment of pacifism. But he also suggests (as he does in his other anti-Nazi works) the discovery of a moral absolute: whereas the views, ideologies, and career goals of the play's men are founded on a relativistic morality, in which one thing is not necessarily better than another but is simply different, the need to protect life is absolute. Curiously, this play achieved a certain spurious notoriety when it was set to music as a quarter-tone opera by the Czech composer Alois Hába.

Čapek's final work is *Život a dílo skladatele Foltýna* (*The Cheat,* 1939), a novel left unfinished because of the author's death. The novel is not a series of fragments, however, and Čapek's widow was able to supply an epilogue suggesting how it was to end.

The Cheat was begun after the Munich settlement of September 1938. The new Czech fascist government had introduced censorship, and Čapek could no longer continue his theme of resistance to aggression. Hence he found it necessary to choose a "neutral" subject, one that has its roots in his earlier work but that finds a new and fresh treatment. Associating the novel with *The First Rescue Party* and *The Mother* is the continuation of the search for absolutes. The novel is presented as a series of accounts told by those who have known Foltýn, the protagonist, but unlike *Meteor,* which uses the same technique, these accounts add up to a single and wholly coherent view of the truth about him. Another theme is that of art, which Čapek had touched on earlier (particularly in his essays), but which he had never before dealt with at such length in fiction.

The hero, Foltýn, is a shy young man who has a great proficiency in music and a perfect musical memory but no very evident musical vocation. From boyhood he loves to improvise at the piano. He calls his improvising "composition," but he is actually incapable of composing anything original. Possessed by compulsive ambition, however, he needs desperately to win recognition. A wealthy marriage allows him to assume the role of a musical patron, and soon he purchases bits and pieces of an opera, *Judith,* from young composers and poets. He justifies his actions by appealing to his frustrated career and to a weakness of musical training and argues that at least the conception of the heroine is his own. But in fact it is not, as one of the narrators explains. Finally Foltýn's opera is staged as a joke by his enemies, and the failure of his talent is exposed. He becomes aware of his complete artistic bankruptcy and is taken away to an asylum, where he dies a few days later.

In the concluding section of the novel, Čapek begins a long disquisition on art in which he opposes Foltýn's view of art as subjective self-expression. Foltýn supposes that the artist is possessed by passion, by frenzy sent upon him by an erotic deity, and that this passion and frenzy are to be expressed as art. For Čapek, on the other hand, art is creation: the imitation of God's creativity by human beings, the imparting of form to formless matter. The opposed views are both romantic, although Čapek doubtless intends a more neoclassicist view of the concepts "form" and "creation." For him art is labor, discipline, technique, observation. In spite of the lapse of many years, the aesthetic speculations of *The Cheat* continue and round out those of Čapek's early doctoral dissertation and his first fiction.

MISCELLANEOUS GENRES

Čapek cultivated many literary genres, largely in connection with his newspaper work. He seems to have been obsessed by a need for broader, more varied literary expression. Already mentioned in this essay is the 1920 collection of writings on language and style, *Kritika slov,* that ended his first literary period. But it is the mid-1920's and early 1930's, Čapek's postdystopian and final periods, that produced the richest and most varied types of writing. True, much of this work is both minor and second-rate, but it is impossible to form a complete view of Čapek as a writer without considering it.

Best known, probably, are Čapek's travel sketches, of which he published five volumes: *Italské listy (Letters from Italy,* 1923), *Anglické listy (Letters from England,* 1924), *Výlet do Španěl (Letters from Spain,* 1930), *Obrázky z Holandska (Letters from Holland,* 1932), and *Cesta na sever (Travels in the North*—that is, Scandinavia—1936). These were illustrated by Čapek since his brother, who customarily illustrated his books, did not follow him on these travels. The best is probably *Letters from England;* certainly it is the most popular in the English-speaking world. But paradoxically, the book demonstrates Čapek's essential remoteness from the British, even though he had the reputation (both in his own country and in Britain) of being an Anglophile. In fact it is his close observation and subtle critical irony that give this book both its charm and its intellectual substance.

Čapek's avocation as a gardener produced a humorous collection of sketches, *Zahradníkův rok* (*The Gardener's Year,* 1929), in which he repeatedly finds homespun analogies to the behavior of his plant favorites in the world of human beings. The collection was illustrated by Josef Čapek.

Marsyas čili na okraj literatury (*In Praise of Newspapers,* 1931) is a volume of essays on literature and aesthetics in which Čapek, like his brother, celebrates the minor arts. The lead article praises newspaper writing, while much of the volume is devoted to the folk and popular arts and to anonymity in art. There are entertaining essays on pornography and on romances written for servant girls, which Čapek considers to be the final lowest stage in the age-old development of the heroic epos.

Apokryfy (*Apocryphal Stories,* 1932) are in a sense a genre Čapek created (though earlier examples can be found in the work of Anatole France, Jules Lemaître, and Maurice Baring). These brief tales are a kind of marginal comment on characters and situations taken from the Bible, antique literature, and the classics; the "apocryphal" treatment consists in developing these characters and situations beyond the context of the original, or in looking at them from a fresh, at times anachronistic, point of view. In spite of the freshness of the literary form, the stories are fairly predictable; thus "Pilate's Credo" is a by-now thoroughly familiar preachment of philosophical relativism, with the author defending Pilate for his question "What is truth?"

Devatero pohádek (*Fairy Tales,* 1932) demonstrates Čapek's interest in the fairy tale genre and in marginal literature in general. But these tales, though charming, fail in comparison with true examples of the genre; for one thing, they emphasize action at the expense of imagery and symbolic ideas.

Dašenka čili Život štěněte (*Dashenka, or The Life of a Puppy,* 1933) is the first of a series of writings about Čapek's experiences with dogs and cats. These are continued in the posthumous volume *Měl jsem psa a kočku* (*I Had a Dog and a Cat,* 1939). Čapek employs animals to emphasize distinctions in a relativist world: human beings, dogs, and cats are all different, and the variety in their perceptions of the world is presented comically.

A number of volumes of Čapek's miscellaneous works, fictional and nonfictional, appeared posthumously. In some cases the author himself had designated material for these collections; in others they are simply a product of a wish on the part of the editors and publishers to collect and republish earlier newspaper articles in book form.

The best of these numerous volumes is *Bajky a podpovídky* (Fables and Would-be Tales, 1946). The fables, usually single sentences mouthed by a personified object, are masterpieces of concentrated insight: "*A match:* See I am the eternal flame!" or "*A mirror:* I've got it at last. The world is nothing but my idea. Outside me there is nothing." Some are "apocryphal tales" in miniature: "*Attila:* We too have come to save the world." The "would-be tales" also are related to the previously published *Apocryphal Stories.* The best is "Hamlet, princ dánský" (Hamlet, Prince of Denmark), in which Shakespeare's play is described by a spectator who is a partisan of Polonius and who is interested only in those parts of the play that relate to that personage. (Conceivably Tom Stoppard's play *Rosencranz and Guildenstern* found its inspiration here, since Stoppard, of Czech origin, may have been familiar with Čapek's story.)

CONCLUSION: ČAPEK'S PLACE IN MODERN LITERATURE

The passage of time has scarcely helped to define Čapek's place in world and in modern literature. Judging by the lack of current critical interest in or republication of his works, he is under something of a cloud at the moment, but it is obviously too soon to dismiss him entirely. The younger writers of his homeland speak of him as a living and vital influence, artistic and spiritual. Among these writers are the two outstanding Czech authors of prose fiction today, Milan Kundera and Ludvík Vaculík.

It is true that the development of Čapek's literary reputation has not been entirely normal in his homeland: after the turn to communism in 1948 Čapek, the friend of Thomas Masaryk, was consigned to oblivion by the official party line; but subsequently, following a switch of critical views in the Soviet Union, he was partly rehabilitated because of the anti-Nazi stance of his last works. Yet there is a certain contradiction here: Masaryk himself was never rehabilitated, although unquestionably Čapek's tie with that leader helped to preserve Čapek's memory for such younger writers as Kundera and Vaculík. It was also his anticommunism, for Czech readers never forgot (although of course their official critics did not remind them) that Čapek had written the political essay "Why I Am Not a Communist."

Outside Czechoslovakia the problem is different, and perhaps even more complicated. Čapek's plays, frequently anthologized and eminently stageable (whatever their dramatic faults), continue to enjoy a certain reputation and respect as avant-garde, expressionist works that can be compared with the plays of Brecht and others. Meanwhile, Čapek's fiction has fallen into almost total neglect. If *The War with the Newts* has survived as a classic of science fiction, and the peripheral genres (fairy tales, sketches of dogs and cats, essays on gardening) because of specialized literary demand, Čapek's major prose fiction achievements—the trilogy and his *Tales from Two Pockets*—are almost completely forgotten. There is a certain paradox in this, no doubt, for without question Čapek's expressionist plays are dated, while the detective tales and above all the philosophical trilogy read as well today as ever.

One tentative explanation for this paradox

may be that Čapek's major achievements in prose were shadowed by the events of the times: the rise of Hitler, World War II, and the 1948 communization of Czechoslovakia, which inspired a new and healthy growth of reputation for Čapek in the East European Communist world but tended to obscure his fame elsewhere.

The question of Čapek's reputation is in a sense part of a larger question of the reputation of his contemporaries, for whom Čapek appeared as a major literary phenomenon. Romain Rolland, Shaw, and Thomas Mann all praised Čapek's work, but many writers of the interwar period have fallen under a cloud today, and even Shaw and Mann have undergone a certain diminution of luster.

One outstanding characteristic of the writing of the interwar period is a tendency to regard literature as philosophical, as a vehicle for the expression of complex ideas. In the work of Proust and Joyce this tendency coexists with other pronounced literary qualities, such as highly cultivated imagery and style, but in other writers, such as Shaw, Wells, Chesterton, Aldous Huxley, perhaps André Gide or Brecht, we may regard the balance as top-heavy. Čapek undoubtedly belongs to this group of writers, and his future fate may well be linked to theirs.

Čapek's ideas are not always able to sustain his literary works, and it was only after he had transcended the relativism of his youth that he could create his masterpiece, the trilogy. The great mass and variety of his work also tend to work against him: the intellectual rigor and weight of such works as "Wayside Crosses" or the trilogy sharply contrast with the popular, homespun philosophy of many of his essays and newspaper feuilletons. Even Čapek's brother, Josef, with whom he was always very close, is reported to have been shocked by the shoddiness and banality of certain of Karel's ideas.

Undoubtedly Čapek was endowed with very great literary gifts. He was a fluent writer who worked quickly. He suffered from no shortage of literary ideas; on the contrary, perhaps he had too many of them. Although not an imagist, his finest work contains many eloquent and apt images. His one marked deficiency as a writer is a chronic inability to invent expressive characters; the figures in his work tend to a certain gray banality. There are notable exceptions of course, but the lack of brightness of characters combined with philosophic expression gives his work a certain heaviness and abstractness.

No writer survives in all his writing; time makes a selection. Although it may be premature to guess what the results of that selection will be, perhaps Čapek's works that have the best chance of survival are "Wayside Crosses," *The Macropulos Secret, The War with the Newts,* and the trilogy. All these have in common the philosophic trait of transcendence of relativism and the presence of an Absolute; most often this is fear of death. All are ultimately pessimistic; in spite of Čapek's efforts to mark his work and ideas with a certain pragmatist and relativist optimism, the lasting part of his work is that in which a sense of death's omnipresence and finality is felt.

No other modern writer expresses himself so democratically as Čapek, and none so celebrates the little man. In this cult of ordinary people Čapek doubtless embodies something typical of the Czech nation, and in this we might rank him next to his countryman Hašek, the author of *The Good Soldier Schweik.* But Čapek did not come without struggle or pain to his faith in the ordinary man. By inclination he was an individualist, even an anarchist. In art he was an aesthete (though with a certain plebeian strain). Lastly, he deserves credit as one of the few writers of our time to have turned decisively away from the romantic and symbolist cult of titanism and the superman.

Selected Bibliography

EDITIONS

INDIVIDUAL WORKS
Zářivé hlubiny (with Josef Čapek). Prague, 1916.

Boží muka. Prague, 1917.
Pragmatismus čili Filosofie praktického života. Prague, 1918.
Krakonošova zahrada (with Josef Čapek). Prague, 1918.
Francouzská poezie nové doby. Prague, 1920. Translations of modern French poetry.
Loupežník. Prague, 1920.
R.U.R. Prague, 1920.
Kritika slov. Prague, 1920.
Trapné povídky. Prague, 1921.
Ze života hmyzu (with Josef Čapek). Prague, 1921.
Lásky hra osudná. Prague, 1922.
Továrna na Absolutno. Prague, 1922.
Věc Makropulos. Prague, 1922.
Italské listy. Prague, 1923.
Krakatit. Prague, 1924.
Anglické listy. Prague, 1924.
O nejbližších věcech. Prague, 1925.
Adam Stvořitel (with Josef Čapek). Prague, 1927.
Hovory s T. G. Masarykem. Prague, 1928–1935.
Povídky z jedné kapsy. Prague, 1929.
Povídky z druhé kapsy. Prague, 1929.
Zahradníkův rok. Prague, 1929.
Výlet do Španěl. Prague, 1930.
Marsyas čili na okraj literatury. Prague, 1931.
Apokryfy. Prague, 1932.
Devatero pohádek. Prague, 1932.
O věcech obecných čili Zoon politikon. Prague, 1932.
Obrázky z Holandska. Prague, 1932.
Dašenka čili Život štěněte. Prague, 1933.
Hordubal. Prague, 1933.
Povětroň. Prague, 1934.
Obyčejný život. Prague, 1934.
Válka s mloky. Prague, 1936.
Cesta na sever. Prague, 1936.
Bílá nemoc. Prague, 1937.
První parta. Prague, 1937.
Matka. Prague, 1938.
Život a dílo skladatele Foltýna. Prague, 1939.
Bajky a podpovídky. Prague, 1946.
Měl jsem psa a kočku. Prague, 1939.

COLLECTED WORKS
Spisy bratří Čapků. Prague, 1929–1947.
Dílo bratří Čapků. Prague, 1955–1960.
Spisy. Prague, 1981–

TRANSLATIONS

The Absolute at Large. New York and London, 1927.

KAREL ČAPEK

Adam the Creator. Translated by Dora Round. London, 1929.

And So Ad Infinitum. Translated by Paul Selver. New York, 1923.

Apocryphal Stories. Translated by Dora Round. New York and London, 1939.

The Cheat. Translated by M. and R. Weatherall. London, 1941.

Dashenka, or The Life of a Puppy. Translated by M. and R. Weatherall. London, 1933.

Fairy Tales. Translated by M. and R. Weatherall. London, 1934.

The First Rescue Party. Translated by M. and R. Weatherall. London, 1939.

The Gardener's Year. Translated by M. and R. Weatherall. London, 1931.

"Help!" In *Czech Prose: An Anthology.* Edited and translated by William E. Harkins. Ann Arbor, Mich., 1983.

I Had a Dog and a Cat. Translated by M. and R. Weatherall. New York, 1941.

"*The Imprint.*" Translated by *The Best Continental Short Stories, 1923-24.* Edited by Richard Eaton. Boston, 1924.

In Praise of Newspapers. Translated by M. and R. Weatherall. London, 1950; New York, 1951.

Intimate Things. Translated by Dora Round. New York, 1931.

Krakatit. Translated by Lawrence Hyde. New York and London, 1925.

Letters from England. Translated by Paul Selver. London, 1925.

Letters from Holland. Translated by Paul Selver. London, 1933.

Letters from Italy. Translated by F. P. Marchant. London, 1929.

Letters from Spain. Translated by Paul Selver. London, 1931.

The Macropulos Secret. Translated by Paul Selver. Boston, 1925.

The Mother. Translated by Paul Selver. London, 1938.

Money and Other Stories. Translated by F. P. Marchant. London, 1929.

Power and Glory. Translated by Paul Selver. London, 1938.

President Masaryk Tells His Story. Translated by Dora Round. London, 1934.

R.U.R. (Rossum's Universal Robots). Translated by Claudia Novack-Jones. In *Toward the Radical Center: A Karel Čapek Reader,* edited by Peter Kussi. Highland Park, N. J., 1990. (Includes six previously untranslated stories.)

Tales from Two Pockets. Translated by Paul Selver. London, 1932. An abridged edition of *Povídky z jedné kapsky* and *Povídky z druhé kapsky.*

Three Novels: Hordubal, Meteor, An Ordinary Life. Translated by M. and R. Weatherall. New York and London, 1948.

Travels in the North. Translated by M. and R. Weatherall. London, 1939.

The War with the Newts. Translated by M. and R. Weatherall. New York and London, 1937.

The World We Live In. Translated by Paul Selver. London, 1923.

BIOGRAPHICAL AND CRITICAL STUDIES

Buriánek, František. *Karel Čapek.* Prague, 1978.

Burke, Kenneth. *Counter-Statement.* New York, 1931.

Černý, Václav. *Karel Čapek.* Prague, 1936.

Doležel, Lubomir. "Karel Čapek and Vladislav Vančura." In *Narrative Modes in Czech Literature.* Toronto, 1973. Pp. 91–111.

Harkins, William E. "Imagery in Karel Čapek's *Hordubal.*" PMLA 75: 616–620 (1960).

———. *Karel Čapek.* New York, 1962.

———. "Karel Čapek and the Ordinary Life." *Books Abroad* 36: 273–276 (1962).

———. "Pragmatism and the Czech 'Pragmatist Generation.'" In *American Contributions to the Fourth International Congress of Slavists.* The Hague, 1958. Pp. 107–126.

Klíma, Ivan. *Karel Čapek.* Prague, 1962.

Králík, Oldřich. *První řada v díle Karla Čapka.* Prague, 1972.

Matuška, Alexander. *Človek proti skaze: Pokus o Karla Čapka.* Bratislava, 1963. Published in English as *Karel Čapek, an Essay.* Prague, 1964.

Mukařovský, Jan. "Karel Čapek," In *Kapitoly z české poetiky,* vol. 2. Prague, 1948. Pp. 325–400.

Scheinpflugová, Olga. *Český román.* Prague, 1947.

Wellek, René. "Karel Čapek." *Essays on Czech Literature.* The Hague, 1963. Pp. 46–61.

WILLIAM E. HARKINS

BORIS PASTERNAK
(1890–1960)

PARADOXICAL AND MULTIFACETED, Boris Pasternak's personality eludes facile characterization. Who was the *true* Pasternak? The worshiper of Alexander Scriabin converted to Kant? The philosopher-turned-artist, the musician-turned-poet, the poet stammering with emotion and captivating his audience with his "scattered" speech as he recited his already famous verse? The generous and ardent friend and lover? The gentle maverick who unaccountably enjoyed Stalin's tolerance, if not admiration, and who mysteriously survived the purges of the 1930's? The self-effacing translator secluded in his dacha yet acclaimed for his *Hamlet* (1940) by countless Soviet playgoers? The middle-aged poet become the "grand old man" of Russian poetry, transfixing capacity crowds in postwar Moscow? The tragic victim of the "Pasternak affair" raging around his *Doctor Zhivago* (1957)?

LIFE

Problematic is the task of the writer endeavoring to recreate Pasternak's life. For any such endeavor seems to contravene the feelings of the poet who on the one hand strove to "immerse himself in obscurity / and hide his footsteps in it" and on the other hand intimated that he had conveyed in his autobiographical writings everything that there was to say about his life.

Boris Leonidovich Pasternak, the first child of pianist Rosa Isidorovna Kaufman and painter Leonid Osipovich Pasternak, was born in Moscow on 10 February 1890 (new style; 29 January, old style). While primarily and authentically Russian, Pasternak's parents were also refined cosmopolitans for whom communion with the mainsprings of western European culture was essential. Because of Leonid Osipovich's position at the Moscow School of Painting, Sculpture, and Architecture, as well as his conspicuous success as one of the city's most prominent portrait painters, he and his family could develop contacts with some of the most exclusive artistic and social circles of the day.

The person who probably played the most important role in bringing Pasternak, child of an assimilated Jewish family, to Christianity was his aged nanny, Akulina Gavrilovna. She frequently took him to Orthodox services and talked to him about God. Although he found inspiration in Christian thought as a child and adolescent, for many decades circumstances did not permit him to attend church regularly or to participate openly in the life of the Orthodox church. But the church's sensuous pageantry, orchestrated with elaborate choirs, incense, and rich costumes, had left its imprint on the sensitive youth. The religious awareness fostered by Pasternak's more sober parents was attuned to Leo Tolstoy's moralistic, nondenominational faith.

Another vivid imprint was left on him by the

Moscow circus, where he witnessed the parading of horsewomen. From this spectacle he derived his first physical sense of women: "I became the slave of forms earlier than I should have done because, in these women, I had seen too early the form of slaves." Such was probably the beginning of the shattering effect of women on the poet-to-be, who later viewed women as especially frail, vulnerable beings, particularly worthy of sympathy—a feeling that reverberates in many of his works, from *Povest'* (A Tale, 1934, translated as *The Last Summer*) through *Doctor Zhivago* to the poem "Zhenshchiny v detstve" ("Women in [My] Childhood," 1958).

In 1900 Pasternak met the young Austrian writer Rainer Maria Rilke. For Pasternak this encounter was the beginning of a spiritual dialogue that would be decisive for his creative life. More than any other single influence, the poems of Rilke provided a lasting stimulus throughout Pasternak's career. He recalled being arrested by "the urgency of what [the poems] had to say, the absoluteness, the gravity, the direct purposefulness of their language."

The years of Pasternak's studious adolescence coincided with the beginnings of the Russian symbolist movement, to which he began paying attention while he was still a schoolboy. Despite the differences in medium and emphasis, the symbolists were united in their attacks on social preachment and realism and in their individualistic and romantic reevaluation of time-honored artistic concepts. The intellectual effervescence of those times engaged and excited the precocious adolescent, who soon realized that the society in which he lived was doomed to undergo radical upheavals.

In the summer of 1903, Pasternak took long walks with his father and Alexander Scriabin. He listened to their discussions "about life, about art, about good and evil"; Leonid Osipovich strongly disagreed with Scriabin's anti-Tolstoyan stance and Nietzschean advocacy of the Superman's amorality. Pasternak's adoration for Scriabin soon stimulated in the boy a passion for musical improvisation and composition that dominated his life for the next six years.

While Pasternak's infatuation with Scriabin's creative genius followed its course in 1903 and 1904, literature and politics continued to develop their own spirited forms. The Russian symbolist movement began shifting away from an interest in stylistic innovation and impressionism toward mysticism and religion and even social concerns. The diversity and potential conflicts among literary styles and views were parallelled by tensions within the political arena. By 1904 the political movement toward "liberation" was commonly accepted. The revolution of 1905 was a landmark in the history of Russia, and its events deeply influenced Pasternak and his generation. He watched the student demonstrations and later recalled these episodes in his poem "Deviat'sot piatyi god" (The Year 1905, 1927) written in the 1920's.

After finishing his secondary education, Pasternak began to make contacts with literary circles. One of these groups was Serdarda, a band of about ten young poets, painters, and musicians, which Pasternak joined. Originally the Serdarda members viewed Pasternak as a musician rather than as a *littérateur*. However, in 1909 Pasternak made the radical decision to give up music. Although his peers and family were convinced of his musical vocation, and although he had already gained considerable success in composition, Pasternak felt that he lacked the necessary technical facility. It was at this point that he began writing verse.

Pasternak's literary interests gradually became more varied and intense, although they generally remained within the scope of symbolism. For Pasternak, Alexander Blok's poetry was a model of "melodic authenticity"; he was drawn to the great symbolist's poetry for its exquisite naturalness, its true-to-life quality. Decades later, a visitor to Pasternak's dacha came away with the impression that Pasternak still professed membership in a veritable cult of Blok. Indeed, the critic Henry Gifford has called Pasternak "the true successor to Blok in Russian poetry."

If for Pasternak's generation the discovery of Blok meant the opening of a window on the future, the death of Tolstoy in 1910 marked the end of an era. The impact on Pasternak of Tolstoy's death was considerable, in spite of the seeming irreconcilability between Tolstoy's worldview and other philosophies, such as Scriabin's quasi-Nietzschean lore, that held sway over the young man.

From 1909 to 1912, Pasternak's involvement with literature remained an avocation, while he immersed himself in philosophy at the University of Moscow. In the summer of 1912 Pasternak went to study under Professor Hermann Cohen at the University of Marburg. Although he did not absorb all of Cohen's theories, Pasternak was influenced by the philosopher's monotheism and high ethical standards and retained the marks of the dichotomies pervading the Kantian philosophical system. Of all the experiences that had an impact on Pasternak in Marburg, however, the most powerful was that of rejected love. A passage of the famous poem "Marburg" (1912) shows that the involvement with Ida Vysotskaia was a learning experience, an existential exercise in knowledge, and as such eliminated and replaced philosophy. The experience in Marburg fostered in him ceaseless devotion to his new poetic vocation. From July 1912, during his last weeks in Marburg, he was "completely taken up" with poetry, which he wrote "day and night, at every opportunity." Pasternak then returned to Moscow, where he finished his studies and in 1913 wrote his first collection of verse, *Bliznets v tuchakh* (Twin in the Clouds, 1914).

During the following years Pasternak participated in many literary groups, notably the new futurist group Centrifuge. Springing from the declining symbolist movement, Russian futurism opposed it, yet essentially continued the revolution of poetic form begun by the symbolists. Its tenets that all words may freely intermingle and that all subjects, even colloquialisms, may become "poetic" became central to Pasternak's aesthetic. At a meeting of two hostile futuristic groups in 1914, Pasternak met Vladimir Mayakovsky for the first time. The friendship that grew between the two poets was at once stormy, emotional, and strangely distant.

These artistic pursuits were disrupted by World War I. Pasternak was declared exempt from military duties because of a leg injury suffered in childhood. From 1915 to 1917 Pasternak managed a draft board in the Urals. There he met a young woman who at the time meant a great deal to him and who very possibly inspired several of his female characters, adolescents anguished by the discovery of their femininity: Zhenia Liuvers, of "Detstvo Liuvers" (The Childhood of Lyuvers, 1918, translated as "Zhenia's Childhood"), Zhenia Istomina, of "Uezd v tylu" ("A District Behind the Lines," 1938), and Lara, of *Doctor Zhivago.*

After the revolution of 1917 many intellectuals worked in public administration. In 1918, Pasternak was employed at Narkompros, or the People's Commissariat for Education, as a press screener. This job afforded him an excellent opportunity to become acquainted with literary life in the West at a time when regular access to the foreign press was almost impossible for Russian intellectuals. Here he first became acquainted with the work of Marcel Proust and Erich Maria Remarque.

Except for a very few poems, the composition of *Sestra moia-zhizn'* (*My Sister, Life,* 1922) and *Temy i variatsii* (*Themes and Variations,* 1923) had been completed by 1918. For the next few years he devoted most of his time to writing prose. Pasternak's first essays in prose date back to at least 1915. His desire to try his hand at a major fictional work probably also developed early and had in any case crystallized by the spring of 1918, when he told the poet Marina Tsvetaeva: "I want to write a big novel:

with love, with a heroine—like Balzac." His first volume of prose pieces, *Rasskazy* (Stories), appeared in 1925.

Of all the writers with whom Pasternak developed a dialogue during this period, Tsvetaeva became the most significant presence on his intellectual and spiritual horizon. Although their acquaintance began in 1918, the true friendship began four years later when Pasternak bought a copy of Tsvetaeva's *Versty* and at the same time an ecstatic Tsvetaeva discovered Pasternak's *My Sister, Life.* Pasternak wrote to her about his enthusiasm for her art, initiating an intense correspondence. Their dialogue was mainly on the plane of creative endeavor. They exchanged manuscripts and critical comments and dedicated many poems to each other. Their friendship is reflected in Pasternak's novel in verse, *Spektorskii* (1931), in a similar intercourse between two characters, the émigré poet Mariia Il'ina and the poet-protagonist, both artists who are out of tune with their environment, much like Pasternak and Tsvetaeva by the end of the 1920's.

In the fall of 1921 he met a fellow artist from Petrograd, the painter Evgeniia Vladimirovna Lourié, fell in love with her, and married her in the spring of 1922. Pasternak and his wife soon sailed for Germany, where he wished to introduce his wife to his family—all of whom except his brother, Aleksandr, had moved to Berlin the year before—and where he sought the literary and intellectual sophistication that the German capital promised.

Like many Russian intellectuals in Berlin, Pasternak had to make a decision: to return to the Soviet Union or to stay permanently in the West. Feeling that a writer could exist only in his own linguistic surroundings, he returned to Moscow with his wife in 1923. In September their son, Evgenii, was born.

Pasternak was adapting to the changing literary scene when he wrote *Vysokaia bolezn'* (*The Sublime Malady,* 1924). His later volume *Deviat'sot piatyi god* did not bring Pasternak any closer to "left-wing" literary groups. His

relationship with the neofuturist LEF (Levyi Front Isskustva, or "left front of the arts"), created in 1922, was sharply deteriorating. LEF's program emphasized "purposeful" (that is, "agitation") art and poetry conceived as a "useful craft" and opposed any return to conservative realism. It championed such activities as the "building of life" and the "production of things." Aspects of this platform grew increasingly distasteful to Pasternak, though he maintained ties with the movement solely out of friendship for Mayakovsky. The polemics that LEF conducted in 1927 triggered Pasternak's decision to part with the movement. His departure, which did wound Mayakovsky, was a significant step in the deterioration of the relationship between the two poets. Pasternak was never again connected with any literary group or school. From then on he worked as an independent, if often isolated, artist in pursuit of aims he defined for himself.

Mayakovsky committed suicide in 1930. The recent lukewarm and sometimes even hostile reaction of Soviet proletarian audiences to his poetry readings had convinced Mayakovsky that his work was a failure. Although a traumatic event for Pasternak, Mayakovsky's death also had a liberating effect—as depicted in *Okhrannaia gramota* (*A Safe-Conduct,* 1929–1931)—that made it possible for Pasternak to write *Vtoroe rozhdenie* (*Second Birth,* 1932).

Another factor that had a direct impact on Pasternak, impelling him to write *Second Birth,* was the upheaval taking place in his domestic life. In 1931 Pasternak and Evgeniia Vladimirovna decided to separate. As his estrangement from his wife grew, Pasternak drew closer to his friend Zinaida Nikolaevna Neigauz, the wife of the pianist Genrikh Neigauz. Late in 1931, Pasternak left with Zinaida Nikolaevna for the Georgian poet Paolo Iashvili's house in the Caucasus. Since the days of Alexander Pushkin and Mikhail Lermontov, Georgia had fascinated Russian writers. For Pasternak, Georgia was a symbol of the synthesis of opposites: man and the elements, the present and the past, the revolutionary upheaval that art constitutes and the continuity needed for artistic creation.

Back in Moscow, Pasternak soon divorced Evgeniia Vladimirovna, leaving with her their son. In 1934 he married Zinaida Nikolaevna. They had one son, Leonid.

During the 1930's, when writers were burdened with heavy Soviet censure, Pasternak made a courageous choice: to practice what Isaac Babel, at the 1934 Writers' Congress, called "the genre of silence." With the exception of his translations and two slim collections of wartime poetry, *Na rannikh poezdakh* (*Early Trains,* 1943) and *Zemnoi prostor* (The Breadth of the Earth, 1954, translated as *The Vast Earth*), no new book by Pasternak was published between *The Last Summer* and the appearance outside of the Soviet Union of *Doctor Zhivago.*

Although Pasternak had almost ceased writing poetry in the mid-1930's, he was not yet in any disfavor, and many editions of his poetry were published and reissued until 1936. His significance as a poet was both recognized abroad—by 1935 he had been translated into five foreign languages—and still frequently acknowledged at home.

Pasternak's translation activities were disrupted by necessary participation in a number of professional meetings: the First Congress of the Union of Soviet Writers of 1934 (organized because Stalin felt that writers were insufficiently enthusiastic in proclaiming socialism) and the International Congress for the Defense of Culture of 1935. In 1936, at a meeting in Minsk, Pasternak's address was characterized by an independence of thought that was rarely heard at such conferences. Alluding to "our socialist realism," the poet implied that with goodwill he was sharing the aesthetic platform of most of his fellow writers. However, he protested that poetry could not be written to order and would not take shape merely with conscientious labor. He outlined his own aesthetic desiderata: great boldness (*smelost'*)

of the imagination in the exercise of creative freedom, something that he claimed no "directives" from the board of the Writers' Union could provide. The conference exacerbated Pasternak's long-standing distaste for what he had termed the "rostrum-orientedness" (*estradnost'*) of most writers and for the publicity surrounding writers-turned-officials of the new Soviet society.

In the latter part of the 1930's most Soviet writers were traumatized by the episode in Soviet history known as the Great Purge or the Great Terror—a wave of state repression and killings that was triggered by the assassination of Sergei Kirov, a member of the Politburo, in December 1934. As Stalin's dictatorial rule prevailed, there emerged an atmosphere of heightened insincerity and fictitiousness that Pasternak denounced as "the reign of the lie" in the epilogue to *Doctor Zhivago.*

Pasternak's dauntless courage and independence of mind in defending some of those under fire and in refusing to conform made his existence precarious—as he promptly fell into disgrace—and made his own survival almost a paradox. Among the most signal of his courageous actions within this context are the promptness with which he flew to the defense of the poet Osip Mandelshtam and stood by his side at various times between 1934 and 1938; his unequivocal refusal to sign certain documents that most of the leading Soviet writers endorsed, such as a letter approving the arrest and condemnation of Marshal Mikhail Tukhachevskii and another condemning André Gide's book on the Soviet Union, *Retour de l'U.R.S.S.* (*Return from the U.S.S.R.,* 1937); his unflinching moral and material support of the Georgian poets Titsian Tabidze and Paolo Iashvili and their families; and his willingness to intercede for various friends and acquaintances, such as Anna Akhmatova's husband, Nikolai Punin (on whose behalf he successfully pleaded directly to Stalin). As a punitive measure, the establishment stopped printing Pasternak's works. Thus at the close of the decade a time of material difficulties set in for the family of the writer.

Germany's invasion of the Soviet Union on 22 June 1941 marked the end of Pasternak's period of disgrace. The declaration of war provided a welcome relaxation of the tense atmosphere for Russia's literati, and the consequent softening of formal restraints allowed them a greater freedom to write. As the advance of the German armies became an immediate threat to Moscow, Pasternak helped his family move to the Urals. The materially and spiritually insecure new existence Pasternak viewed as a privileged chance for writers to acquire "inner independence." In an enthusiastic effort to contribute to Russia's war effort, he enlisted in the Civil Defense Unit in Moscow, and in 1943 he and other Soviet writers chronicled the fighting at the front.

Pasternak's greatest loss of the war years was the suicide in 1941 of Tsvetaeva, who had returned from Paris to Russia in 1939. During the years of their friendship Pasternak became aware that Tsvetaeva was hiding from the everyday world behind a creativity he later called genius. By finding and helping her daughter, Ariadna, he attempted to ease the guilt he felt. Pasternak proved his reverence for Tsvetaeva's memory when, in his *Avtobiograficheskii ocherk* (*I Remember: Sketch for an Autobiography*, 1958), he made readers both in the Soviet Union and abroad aware of her art.

With wartime impressions fresh in his mind and postwar Russia struggling around him, Pasternak's ideas and perceptions were crystallizing into philosophical and literary material. He began composing sections of *Doctor Zhivago*. In 1946 his life took a dramatic turn. His encounter with Ol'ga Vsevolodovna Ivinskaia opened a new chapter in both his emotional and spiritual development; Ivinskaia became the poet's closest friend, adviser, assistant, lover, and muse.

Pasternak's career as a Soviet poet still appeared precarious at this time. From March 1947 on, he was abusively mentioned at literary gatherings and in the Soviet press. The attacks were part of the general witch-hunt instigated by Andrei Zhdanov, secretary of the Central Committee, against all persons designated by him as "anti-Soviet." Pasternak was harassed economically as well as critically. From 1947 until 1954 none of his original writings were published in the Soviet Union; only his translations were printed. Nevertheless, the poet continued to enjoy popular support: enthusiastic and often large audiences welcomed readings of Pasternak's poetry.

In 1949, the blissful relationship between Pasternak and Ivinskaia was interrupted when security police arrested Ivinskaia. She was sentenced to five years in a hard-labor camp "for close contact with persons suspected of espionage" but was released soon after Stalin's death in 1953. Pasternak's person remained inviolate, either because of a general recognition that arresting a writer of his stature would have unfavorable repercussions at home and abroad or because of instructions issued by Stalin. The security forces knew where Pasternak would be most vulnerable, however, and took reprisals against the person closest to him. The deeper concern of the authorities was whether Pasternak's novel would be the expression of the literary opposition.

During the winter of 1955–1956 Pasternak completed the manuscript of *Doctor Zhivago*. While he sent copies to several Moscow publishers, an emissary of the Italian Communist party, Sergio d'Angelo, persuaded Pasternak to publish the novel abroad, to the dismay of the Writers' Union. Soviet officials were concerned that should an expurgated version of *Doctor Zhivago* be agreed to by a Soviet journal while the Italians published the full text, a politically embarrassing situation might ensue.

In 1957, with Nikita Khrushchev firmly in power, the outward liberalism in art and literature that had prevailed for two or three years disappeared. Pasternak could no longer hope for a Soviet edition of his novel. On 22 November 1956 the first edition of the novel appeared in Italy under the title *Il Dottor Živago*. The first printing of six thousand immediately sold out.

Although there was no official comment in the months following the novel's publication, party authorities were attentive to both the foreign response to the novel and the preparation of various translations. Despite efforts of Soviet literary commissars to restrict the circulation of Pasternak's works, interest in him among connoisseurs of Russian literature was growing.

In 1958 the Royal Swedish Academy voted to award Boris Pasternak the Nobel Prize for literature in recognition of his lyrical poetry, his translations of Shakespeare, and especially *Doctor Zhivago*. Pasternak said of the award: "For me this is more than just a joy; it is a moral support; say as well that my joy is solitary." The appearance in the world press over the next few days of a number of statements by prominent Western political figures, interpreting the award in a political rather than a literary light, angered Soviet authorities, who believed that the novel was being exploited for political purposes and that a large-scale anti-Soviet campaign was under way. After a verbal onslaught by the Soviet press, the Writers' Union voted to expel Pasternak. The often base public assaults to which he and his novel were subjected hurt him deeply and aged him rapidly.

Under the pressure of the attacks leveled against him, Pasternak decided to pursue a course that he believed would foil the authorities: he renounced the prize. Pasternak's move was a great surprise to the Soviet hierarchy, and the campaign against the writer continued gathering momentum.

In order to remain in the Soviet Union, Pasternak had to sign a letter expressing his remorse for having been misled in assessing as "a literary distinction" a prize that turned out to be a political gesture with dire consequences. Pasternak wrote this letter of submission both because he found it difficult to endure further harassment and because he felt it his duty to consider all those dependent on him. After the publication of Pasternak's letter in *Pravda,* the direct attacks on him seemed to come to an end.

Until almost the very end of his life, Pasternak maintained an extraordinarily youthful appearance. He viewed daily writing as a vital intellectual duty. An important break in his routine was the long walk he took every day in Peredelkino or the surrounding countryside. Gardening was also an essential activity. At times it seemed to him that this work was something visible and real, as opposed to "all the rest," which looked like "something insubstantial, vague, and confused."

Yet the last few months of Pasternak's life were a time of agonizing mental strain. Pressures, worry, and illness had so debilitated him that he had great difficulty working. Pasternak's final illness was signaled by a series of blackouts early in May 1960. His problem was diagnosed as a heart condition, and it was discovered that he also had cancer of the lungs. He died on 30 May 1960.

Despite official efforts to downplay Pasternak's death, his funeral ceremony was fraught with meaning for both the many Russians and the foreigners who attended. The funeral appears to have been the first significant political demonstration of the new—post-thaw—Soviet intelligentsia, a group bolder and more conscious of the values it stood for. It was also the occasion for a spontaneous outpouring of thousands of ordinary Russians, including workers and peasants as well as students. A small team of KGB informers, clicking away unabashedly with their cameras, was also present. Thus the shadow of the police state, whose political pressure many see as the catalyst that brought on the poet's illness and death, fell across his funeral as well.

EARLY POETRY

During the whole of the summer of 1913, on an eighteenth-century estate in Molodi, Pasternak devoted all of his attention to poetry. He had brought with him a volume of Fedor Tiutchev's verse, and for the first time in his life he wrote poetry, "not as a rare exception, but often and continuously, as one paints or composes music." From this summer emerged his first collection of verse, *Bliznets v tuchakh* (Twin in the Clouds), which was published in 1914 and includes two poems describing his Western European experience of 1912, "Venetsiia" ("Venice") and "Vokzal" ("The Railway Station"). The poet Nikolai Aseev declared Pasternak to be an "original lyricist of modern Russian poetry" and his work a worthy heir to the great symbolist "armada" ("Fleet"). Pasternak later said that the title of his volume betrayed "quite stupid pretentiousness" in that it echoed the "cosmological ingenuities which were characteristic of the book titles of the symbolists."

From 1914 until early 1916, Pasternak successfully imitated the futurist poet Mayakovsky; some of the resulting poems appeared in *Poverkh bar'erov* (*Above the Barriers*, 1917). By mid- or late 1916 the imitative period was over, and Pasternak was experimenting with a new approach in longer narrative poems. Moreover, Pasternak ascribes the "nonromantic" elements in *Above the Barriers* to a conscious effort to renounce Mayakovsky's influence as he suppressed in himself elements he shared with his fellow poet, such as the "heroic tone" and the "desire for effects." (In a letter to Anna Akhmatova in 1940, Pasternak acknowledged her influence on his poetry in *Above the Barriers*.)

Themes and Variations

In 1923 Pasternak brought back from Berlin his book of poetry *Temy i variatsii* (*Themes and Variations*), which was written in 1915 and had been issued in a lilac cover during his stay there. The volume is composed of six cycles of poems, the most striking of which are "Themes and Variations," which revolves around allusions to Pushkin and his poetry, stressing the motif of the unity between the

creative artistic force and stormy natural elements and illustrating the extent to which a poetic piece can be influenced by music, in terms of both structure and devices; "Illness," which associates the poet (the sick man) with the Revolution, personified through natural phenomena; and "The Break," an evocation of the poet's final quarrel with his mistress, which is particularly masterful in its emotional tension and rhythmical force and which elicited superlative praise from Russian critics as diverse as Aseev, Dmitrii Sviatopolk-Mirskii, and Tsvetaeva. *Themes and Variations* solidified Pasternak's reputation as a great poet, which was established with the publication of *My Sister, Life*; Sviatopolk-Mirskii felt that *Themes and Variations*, "though not always on the same level" as *My Sister, Life*, nonetheless at times achieved "even greater things." Tsvetaeva viewed such a striking achievement as a signal that Pasternak should now write "a big thing."

My Sister, Life

The obvious literary influence of Mayakovsky, present in certain poems of *Over the Barriers*, had been overcome through Pasternak's own qualitative growth, demonstrated in the full maturity and originality of *My Sister, Life*. Pasternak felt that this volume was "immensely bigger" than both he himself and the poetic conceptions surrounding him.

Written in 1917 and 1918, *My Sister, Life* embodies Pasternak's vision of the revolutionary events, particularly of "that remarkable summer of 1917" in the interval between the two revolutionary episodes of February and October: "Together with people—roads, trees, and stars held meetings and made eloquent speeches." It was his sincere endeavor to apprehend the era's political turmoil, albeit in a peculiar mode of cosmic awareness. Thus it is not at the level of chronicle writing that Pasternak most intensely revives the events of 1917 but in poetry of a paradoxically intimate and delicate turn. Pasternak lived his political experience so intensely that he expressed external events as he felt them, eager to gather their meaning through the framework of his own dialectic, whence the transposition of these events onto the palette of his lyric emotion. From this perspective the importance of historic events seems to be reduced to that of natural events. As the critic Sir Maurice Bowra observes in "Boris Pasternak, 1917–23" (*The Creative Experiment,* pp. 150, 153), "This is precisely the importance that [Pasternak] finds in them. They are indeed natural events and therefore full of majesty and mystery. They are a special manifestation of the strange powers that can be observed in physical nature." Commenting on "Summer," a poem in the collection, Bowra emphasizes that the political events, forming part of the harmonious rustic scene, "are also its climax and its culmination." Pasternak is convinced, as Bowra says, "that such an eruption of natural forces must in the end be right and prevail, he finds in them a source of vitality and energy. What matters for him is this release of nature's powers which bring man closer to itself." To the very extent that he considers political events from afar, as though they were a faraway realm, Pasternak can say that in *My Sister, Life* he has succeeded in creating "expressions not in the least contemporary as regards poetry."

Pasternak shares this conception of life as an enchanting force, one that is yet as familiar as a close relative, with Saint Francis of Assisi. Indeed, the title *My Sister, Life* has obvious Franciscan connotations. It seems most probable that Pasternak derived some inspiration from *I Fioretti,* a Russian translation of which, *Tsvetochki,* had been published in 1913 by the futurist group Centrifuge. If anything, Pasternak's enthusiasm is even more breathless than that of the bard of Assisi. Pasternak later owned to Nadezhda Mandelshtam that the writing of *My Sister, Life* was the only instance in his life when "the miracle of a book in the making" had occurred. The miraculous nature of this process had undoubtedly to do with the poet's endeavor to bring his writing "as near as

possible to extemporization." He tells us, "In 1917 and 1918 I wrote down only what by the character of the language or by the turn of the phrase seemed to escape me entirely of its own accord, involuntary and indivisible, unexpectedly beyond dispute."

The results of such a method were utterly striking in their freshness. While the fifty poems in this cycle were composed under a single lyrical impulse, they unfold a diversity of topics. The setting ranges from the restriction and intimacy of a Mallarméan garden (with the expectable grass, lilacs, gardenias, dripping leaves and branches, siskin, goldfinch, swing) to the wide, empty spaces of the Russian steppe, made more immediate through the evocation of its peculiar vegetation in such localities as Saratov, Balashov, and Romanovka. Here the stock-in-trade of Russian lyric poetry has undergone an explosive renovation; the poems are invaded by such prosaic items as silkworms, corks, aprons, mignonettes, calico, nitrogen, and sunflower seeds. Cultural and literary references are frequent: the narrator mentions Lord Byron, Edgar Allan Poe, Mikhail Lermontov, and Rudyard Kipling as familiar interlocutors or references. The unifying focuses are the love story that unfolds during that one summer and the constant upsurge of a life force present primarily in the form of water images—vivifying downpours, spoutings, and drippings. The landscape and its objects metonymically describe the narrator, who is strangely absent as agent from most of these poems.

My Sister, Life established Pasternak as one of the masters of contemporary verse. The credo for life and art that he affirmed in the volume was not altered later. The book was met with wild enthusiasm by the more sophisticated of the younger poetry lovers. Nadezhda Mandelshtam viewed it as "a book of knowledge about the world, of thanksgiving and joy." Tsvetaeva claimed that the book was a high point of her stay in Berlin in 1922, saying that for ten days she "lived by this book—as on the high crest of a wave." Osip Mandelshtam saw in the poems "a collection of marvelous breathing exercises: each time the powerful breathing apparatus is adjusted differently." He also proclaimed that not since the Romantic Konstantin Batiushkov had "such a new and mature harmony sounded in Russian poetry," and he hailed Pasternak as the "founder of a new mode, a new system of Russian poetry." With this achievement, as the émigré critic Sviatopolk-Mirskii put it, Pasternak "gradually became the universal master and exemplar, . . . and very few poets escaped his influence."

EARLY PROSE

Although Pasternak's earliest prose went unnoticed, "Bezliub'e" ("Without Love"), published in 1918, stands out as a precursor of *Doctor Zhivago*. Sharing themes, events, characterizations, and names with the later novel, "Without Love" also foreshadows its central conception in the contrasting attitudes held toward the revolution and its supporters by the story characters Kovalevskii and Gol'tsev. The latter, indeed, is a prototype of Yurii Zhivago. Furthermore, the short story hints at a role that, when developed in *Doctor Zhivago,* becomes Lara. This early fragment mentions three names that are included in the novel—Gimazetdin, Galliul, and Mekhanoshin—and also depicts Chistopol in the Ural Mountains (an area familiar to Pasternak from 1915). As the critic Max Hayward has pointed out in "Introduction to Boris Pasternak's 'Without Love' " (*Partisan Review* 3–4:363 [1961]), the tramcar accident in "Without Love" foreshadows "three important events in the novel: the death of the hero's father, the interruption of a concert because of an accident to one of the performers, and the death of Zhivago himself." "Without Love" thus makes it clear that the revolutionary events had a significant artistic impact on Pasternak.

Already acclaimed as a poet, Pasternak received wide recognition as a prose writer in 1925 when his volume *Rasskazy* (Stories) appeared. The book comprises four stories, written and published individually between 1915 and 1924. Like "Without Love" they represent Pasternak's response to the revolutionary events and the post-revolutionary scene. The Tuscan atmosphere of "Apellesova cherta" ("The Apelles Mark") reminds us of Pasternak's visit to Pisa three years earlier; it is a lively mixture of anecdote and allegory, although the author is not fully successful in conveying what appears to be his deeper meaning: a statement on the signature of the artist and artistic reality. The narrator of "Pis'ma iz Tuly" ("Letters from Tula") is a young poet, tormented by his awareness of art as an exacting vocation, who writes from Tula (which he views as "the realm of conscience" insofar as it stands for the principles of Tolstoy, who lived nearby), suggesting that authenticity in art is over and above mere faithfulness to realistic method. In "Vozdushnye puti" ("Aerial Ways") we have the first depiction by Pasternak of communism and its atmosphere ("the sky of the Third International"), specifically of the iron-hearted morality of the high official Polivanov, an interesting precursor of *Doctor Zhivago*'s Strelnikov, who places an ideological cause above pity or other human concerns.

The most remarkable of these four stories, "Zhenia's Childhood," is concerned with fourteen-year-old Zhenia Liuvers, her adolescent encounter with the outside world, her discovery of womanhood. (Zhenia shares with the later Lara of *Doctor Zhivago* her radiant goodness and femininity.) As the Soviet critic A. Lezhnev notes ("Boris Pasternak," in Davie and Livingstone, *Pasternak: Modern Judgments*, p. 43), these experiences are told through the unfolding of a fine web of "sensations existing on the frontier between elementary, 'purely physiological' sensations and more complex 'mental' motions—sensations from things, rooms, trees, light and smell, sensations of the atmosphere of a house, a street, a spring corridor." Shortly after its appearance the poet Mikhail

Kuzmin commented on "Zhenia's Childhood" as "the freshest Russian prose of the past three or four years" and said that it reminded him of the novels of Goethe and the early Tolstoy. Maxim Gorky urged Pasternak to write more prose. Ilya Ehrenburg considered it one of the ten most important prose works written in the Soviet Union and went on to explain: "It was Pasternak who laid the true foundation of Soviet art." These and similar commentaries on the *Rasskazy* were the first evidence of serious critical attention to Pasternak's prose.

POLITICAL THEMES

In the mid-1920's Pasternak was faced with a changing literary scene, upon which political events and processes had their impact. Although Pasternak always "lacked the talent to be insincere," he tried to respond to the demands that the era, with a greater or lesser degree of direct pressure, was making on writers to adjust in terms of topic, style, and tone. Thus, when Lenin died in January 1924, Pasternak published a long poem, *Vysokaia bolezn'* (*The Sublime Malady*), which concludes with a description of Lenin's speech at the Ninth Congress of the Soviets in 1921. The focus in *The Sublime Malady* is the poet's place in a changing society, against the background of historical events. The Revolution is depicted as an elemental fury sweeping aside and leaving behind

> The idealist-intellectual
> Who printed and wrote placards
> About the joy of his decline.

In earlier days, Pasternak felt, the intelligentsia had worked for the Revolution; since then, however, they had lost contact with the masses and had become alienated from them to the point that they could do nothing but "step down from the stage." Conveying Pasternak's personal experience, the narrator relates how,

endeavoring to dispel his doubts and hesitations, he goes to the Congress of Soviets, where the impressive appearance of Lenin succeeds in restoring some of his faith. (Although Mayakovsky had reservations about some passages in the poem, which he thought were too obscure and inaccessible, he nonetheless loved other passages so much that he learned them by heart and would sometimes recite them.)

The time being ripe for literary treatments of revolutionary and patriotic themes, the appearance in 1927 of Pasternak's volume of poetry *Deviat'sot piatyi god* (The Year 1905) was a significant step in his artistic career. The book went through four editions and remains the part of Pasternak's achievement that is most often mentioned and praised by Soviet critics and anthologized in the Soviet Union. In this volume Pasternak for the first time deals squarely with the convergence of poetry and history, giving evidence that he shared with Tsvetaeva a notion of "the paradoxical phenomenon of the timelessness of art and its irrevocable connection with its time."

Pasternak dedicated the first poem, "Deviat'sot piatyi god," to the abortive revolution of 1905, which had sustained the hopes of Pasternak and his generation for socialism. The poem is composed of six episodes, which present us with a number of vivid scenes, amounting—somewhat impressionistically—to a poetic chronicle of the events of that year. The following vignettes successively unfold the distant background of 1905 (the deeds of the late-nineteenth-century intelligentsia), the Moscow scene drawn from the author's childhood recollections, and various groups in their roles in revolutionary events: peasants and workers confronting the Cossacks, *Potemkin* sailors mutinying, students rebelling in Moscow. As Benjamin Goriely rightly noted, the events of 1905, contemporary with Pasternak's youth, are described in the exalted tone of youth, well suited to the psychology of Russia of the time. An accelerated five-foot anapestic meter sometimes suggests the excitement and tension of the times. The poet sees in the riot the unleashing and explosion of a profound, uncontrollable force, symbolized by fire, "the inferno . . . flooding and swelling" in the last pages of the poem.

As opposed to the first poem in the volume, the somewhat less successful "Lieutenant Schmidt" deals with only one episode of the Revolution—the mutiny of the Black Sea fleet under Lieutenant P. P. Schmidt. Many aspects of the poem are memorable: the conflict between Schmidt's love for his mistress and his sense of mission, which provides psychological texture; his protest against the whole cycle of rebellion and repression (not just within the tsarist regime) and against the state as idol; his act of self-sacrifice.

This work constitutes both a rupture with Pasternak's previous poetry and an attempt at conciliation with the regime. It won the poet wide acclaim. In a lecture on "How to Write Poetry," Mayakovsky dwelled at some length on Pasternak's achievement and in particular on his treatment of the *Potemkin* episode. The critic A. Lezhnev welcomed the new social orientation of Pasternak's poetry. The émigré poet Nikolai Otsup pointed out that, while Pasternak had become "clearer" and more accessible in these poems, the results are more "ordinary" than the unique achievements of his previous three volumes; he concluded by paradoxically suggesting that Pasternak *not* try to get rid of the "shortcomings" in *My Sister, Life.*

A SAFE-CONDUCT

The poet's first autobiography, and a breviary for Pasternak connoisseurs, *A Safe-Conduct* was first published serially during the period 1929–1931. When it appeared in book form in 1931, the edition of ten thousand copies was immediately sold out. Simultaneously the volume was attacked: it was labeled "idealist" and considered so subversive that it was soon banned.

Appearing at this stage in Pasternak's life, *A Safe-Conduct* served a vital function for its author. Drained emotionally and creatively, Pasternak felt a need for self-definition; through an assessment of his past, he might somehow clarify or justify his future as a poet. In his autobiography Pasternak depicts the genesis of poetry in his life: it was born from the intertwining in his memory of the various orders of experience he describes in the book.

Written in a strikingly metaphoric and metonymic style, *A Safe-Conduct* is a selective autobiography. We learn little of Pasternak's family life, and there are gaps in time between some of the incidents described. But the people and events he does describe are those that had a major impact on the direction of his life. Indeed, Pasternak's emphasis is not on himself but on whatever it was that made him who he was.

The poet begins by recounting his meeting, at age ten, with Rilke. The appearance of Rilke at the opening of his autobiography is a foreshadowing of Pasternak's eventual decision to become a poet. Rilke was for many years Pasternak's chief source of inspiration, and his poetry served as the main prototype for the Russian poet's work. Even the organization of the book stresses Rilke's significance; as Pasternak goes from idol to idol in search of a true hero, Rilke's name recurs. After describing his meeting with Scriabin, Pasternak discusses the composer as the first major influence in his life. There follows the dramatic story of his love affair with music. Soon after his break with that art, Pasternak recounts, he discovered a volume of Rilke's poetry in his father's bookcase. This discovery signals, both realistically and symbolically, that poetry will eventually capture the young man. But for the time, Pasternak tells us, he suppressed his interest in poetry and turned instead to philosophy, which he expected would help him achieve cultural and intellectual wholeness.

Pasternak devotes about one-third of *A Safe-Conduct* to Marburg. This section of the autobiography is perhaps the most important, for here the reader discerns the impulses that ultimately drove the author toward poetry. Pasternak goes deeply into the intellectual motivation, from both past and present, of his interest in Marburg.

Pasternak's description of Marburg is detailed and highly figurative. He describes the streets, which "clung to the steep slopes like Gothic dwarfs," and the roofs of the houses, which "resembled a flock of doves, bewitched in midair as they swooped." These unexpected, mystical images, coupled with the legend of Elizabeth of Hungary, lend a supernatural feeling to the text. Indeed, Pasternak seems to have placed particular importance on signs and their interpretations. One feels that he was undertaking an elated, frenzied search—guided by signs—to realize transcendant values. Pasternak's realization—coinciding with the failure of his first courtship—that his interest in philosophy was misguided led him to abandon that pursuit and devote himself wholeheartedly to the writing of poetry.

Futurism was the next stage in Pasternak's quest, when Mayakovsky became the object of his worship. Pasternak was so overwhelmed with admiration for Mayakovsky's achievement that he contemplated abandoning literature—a testimony to his desire to do only that in which he could be original. Mayakovsky's death provided the catalyst that enabled Pasternak to review his own creative life. Meditating on the death of Mayakovsky, Pasternak speaks of the latter's confrontation with a new, incomprehensible, and unsympathetic city, in which Mayakovsky lost his former security, experiencing "the vulnerability of this new birth." In this context Pasternak contrasts "second birth" with "death" as mutually exclusive options. The implication seems to have been that with Mayakovsky's death the responsibility for carrying on the deeper purpose of Russian poetry had shifted to his own shoulders. Pasternak thus inherited from Mayakovsky the confrontation with the alternative—second birth or

death. To continue, renewed, Pasternak finally abandoned his quest for a hero and concentrated on realizing himself through his own creativity and originality.

Pasternak wrote that *A Safe-Conduct* had been conceived as "something midway between an article and artistic prose, dealing with the way in which, in [the poet's] life, life was transformed into art, and why." Like Mandelshtam the poet was developing his craft in a crucible of prose, melting earlier poetic ideas into new, reexamined images. In *A Safe-Conduct* we encounter Pasternak's fundamental insistence, characteristic of his postfuturist period, on actual experience as the origin of all art. To him art must grasp everyday reality—innate reality, human reality:

> We cease to recognize reality. It presents itself in some new category. This category seems to us to be its, not our, condition. Except for this condition everything in the world has been named. It alone is unnamed and new. We try to name it. The result is art.

Poetry is born from experience, "from the conflicting currents of these trends, from the difference in their flux, from the falling behind of the more tardy, and from their accumulation behind, on the deep horizon of remembrance." For Pasternak art must be an authentic transposition of that same dynamic process, reality.

Pasternak claims that if there is representation in art it is subject to transposition; it should aim not at representing the cold axles of reality but at changing them to hot ones. Art "is concerned not with the man but with the image of man. The image of man, as becomes apparent, is greater than man." The goal of art, then, is to convey that "disproportionate" image.

This image of man can come into being only in the act of transition:

> Focused on a reality that has been displaced by feeling, art is a record of this displacement. It copies it from nature. How then does nature become displaced? Details gain in sharpness, each

losing its independent meaning. Each one of them could be replaced by another. . . . When the signs of this condition are transferred onto paper, the characteristics of life become the characteristics of creation. The latter stand out more sharply than the former.

(p. 72)

This Pasternakian process of creation essentially takes its origin from a displacement, from movement. Thus, in *A Safe-Conduct,* Pasternak not only traces the genesis of poetry in his life but also sets forth the framework of his aesthetics. (It should be noted that as early as 1921 in "Neskol'ko polozhenii" ["Some Tenets"] Pasternak reflects on the organic nature of the work of art, insisting that the various components of the work as a whole should be a matter of indifference to the artist, provided that the whole is authentic.)

It has been rightly asserted that sections of *A Safe-Conduct*—notably the passages about the narrator's childhood and love for Ida Vysotskaia and about Scriabin, Rilke, and Mayakovsky—compare with the best of Russian prose. Pasternak depicts the genesis of poetry in his life: it was born from the intertwining in his memory of the various orders of experience he describes in *A Safe-Conduct*. In this book Pasternak gives us a forceful assessment of the origins of his poetic creativity, as well as a justification for its continuation.

SECOND BIRTH

Vtoroe rozhdenie (Second Birth) appeared in 1932, at a time when most Soviet writers were being forced to confront the problem of fundamentally altering their worldview and their style if they wished to survive as artists. *Second Birth* marks Pasternak's most significant effort since *Deviat'sot piatyi god* to follow the strategy of ideological adaptation, while conveying the rebirth in his personal life. More indisputably than any of the poet's previous works *Second Birth* and *A Safe-Conduct* reflect

his personal experience—the exhilarating and harrowing moments of his recent rebirth, with its emotional and political dimensions. The self-renewal described in *Second Birth* was the direct outcome of emotional upheavals during the years 1930 through 1932—his separation from his first wife, Evgeniia Vladimirovna; his love for Zinaida Nikolaevna; Mayakovsky's suicide. (Pasternak later depicted this pattern of creative self-renewal directly induced by a stormy passion in *Doctor Zhivago:* an outburst of creativity takes hold of Zhivago as a result of the separation from Lara.) As Kornelii Zelinskii, a leading Soviet critic, was quick to notice, Pasternak's poetry in *Second Birth* is "full of the hieroglyphs of his biography" and attains a special quality of "inner wholeness, bought at the price of biography."

Both Zelinskii and the émigré A. Bem (the founder of a "Pasternak circle" that met in the late 1920's and 1930's) concurred in their appraisal that Pasternak's new book of poetry was a major achievement. Bem acknowledged its author "a major poet, indisputably the most significant poet now alive." While Zelinskii remarked that *Second Birth* was "above all a book marked by simplicity," Bem listed some of the characteristics of the poet's new economy of material and directness of expression: simplification of his earlier complex syntax, more compact and intelligible lines, less reliance on formal, technical display. Both agreed that in much of this poetry a revival of certain strains of Russian romantic verse is evident, most obviously in the nature poetry, whether in the passages on the luxuriant, exotic wildlife and vegetation in the Caucasus or in those on the quietly picturesque charm of Irpen'. Akhmatova, however, criticized the volume for being "an effort at being comprehensible," indicating that she felt that the story "Zhenia's Childhood" and *A Safe-Conduct* were more credible.

Along with nature, two other themes are present in *Second Birth*: love and the poet's concern with civic consciousness. The collection contains some of Pasternak's most memorable love poems; even Zelinskii, prone to point out the volume's ideological shortcomings, could not but concede that certain of the poems would "always remain in Russian poetry . . . as masterpieces of intimate lyric poetry." Although at least one of the love poems, "Ne volnuisia, ne plach', ne trudi . . . " ("Don't fret, don't cry, don't pine . . . ") is addressed to Evgeniia Vladimirovna, most are to Zinaida Nikolaevna, and certain lines reflect the poet's concerns for femininity and the oppression of women.

Pasternak's new perception of his vocation is expressed most memorably in the short poem "O, znal by ia, chto tak byvaet . . . " ("Oh, had I known that it happens so . . . "), in which he looks back on his youthful indulgence in poetic virtuosity, comparing it with his present awareness of the craft's tragic obligations. The poet is now the vehicle not just of art and vitality but also of history and fate. The gush of liquid that recurs throughout his work is now not the waterspout of spring showers but blood—the poet is required no longer merely to turn on a tap but to stake his life. This new interpretation of the poet's role no doubt owes much to the tragic fates of Mayakovsky (the subject of a separate poem, "Death of a Poet") and Sergei Esenin. In this collection the poet is invited to sense the reality of the new ideology, of that "faraway [realm] of socialism," which is somehow presented as "close at hand" and yet assured of victory only in a dim future. This theme is presented in a major key in the introductory philosophical poem, "Waves." In that famous piece (whose appearance is recalled by one memoirist as an event almost as significant as that of Yury Olesha's *Zavist'* [*Envy*]), the poet states his intention of including "everything"—his past experiences, his present ideals and aspirations, his place as a poet in Soviet Russia. Such an all-embracing, secure, and near-triumphant vision is a new element in Pasternak's poetry.

In the long run, Pasternak's exercise in ideological tightrope walking in this collection—an attempt to balance his ideals with the more

noble of the aspirations professed by the regime—displeased readers in diverse camps. On the one hand, the Marxist Zelinskii, scrutinizing the "civic poetry" in the volume, found undue stress on "intimism." He criticized the poet's "social egocentrism"—an attitude fostered, he thought, by an elitist bourgeois upbringing—and was indignant at the poet's excusing of abuses of the Soviet era by means of a comparison with excesses committed under Peter the Great. On the other hand, for many readers in Eastern Europe, *Second Birth* created the impression that, reconciling himself to socialism, Pasternak was placing his moral credit behind the regime's ideology; that action they later interpreted as a deceit of sorts. Czesław Miłosz spoke of his own tendency to accuse Pasternak of "programmatic helplessness in the face of the world, of a carefully cultivated irrational attitude." It is probably unfair to reproach the author of *Second Birth* for making a courageous effort to establish a point of convergence for his aspirations and the new society's principles. While it is true that the effort does not amount to a unified ideological system, could it be expected of any poet of that period that he or she should forthwith achieve a unified vision of such a complex reality?

THE LAST SUMMER

During the period 1933–1938—the time when the purges were beginning—the atmosphere became stifling for poets and writers. Pasternak chose to remain silent. The last fictional volume to appear before his long silence was *The Last Summer*. This text breaks with the autobiographical mode of Pasternak's earlier works sufficiently to enter the realm of fiction. To be sure, he still includes a number of autobiographical details: the initial setting, a small town in the Urals; a flashback to the torrid summer of 1914; and the protagonist, Sergei (Serezha) Spektorskii, who spends that summer as a tutor in a well-to-do family, has an inconclusive love affair with the young Danish woman staying with the family, and is driven into the arms of another, the young prostitute Sashka, out of both sensuousness and compassion (Serezha connects this attraction with a generalized pity for the fate of women, which echoes the feeling that Pasternak had had since adolescence). The properly fictional structure adds complexity to this framework. The title has a double meaning: it refers both to Pasternak's text and to the story within the story—the "tale" that Serezha, an aspiring writer, is endeavoring to compose. The hero of this inner composition, a writer christened Y3, is consumed by the dream that also haunts Serezha—and Pasternak himself: the rescue of women from the humiliation and misery with which they are afflicted. This the artist (Y3/ Serezha) proposes to do through the redemptive value of his art and his life. Y3 is distinguished by an art that is "born of the richest, bottomlessly sincere, terrestrial poverty." Animated by the highest spiritual motives, he puts himself up for auction to achieve authenticity, choosing exterior, physical servitude because he has discovered within himself that he has "no current value in that large issue in which man has been printed. That he must make himself a commodity of exchange, and they must help him in this." Again, Pasternak resembles his fictional character: like Y3, Pasternak aspired to achieve some *podvig* (spiritual prowess), according to the Russian ascetic tradition.

Certain details in *The Last Summer* prefigure *Doctor Zhivago.* Serezha's sister is married to an official, Pasha (Pavel), and they live in a small town in the Urals; the complex structure of the hero's dual relationship to Anna and Sashka suggests Zhivago's dual allegiance to Tonia and Lara; Y3 is "a very Christ of passivity," a trait consonant with Zhivago. This and other evidence suggests that, like other prose fragments written by Pasternak from 1937 to 1939, *The Last Summer* was a sketch for the long novel that he had begun, renewing his endeavor of over a decade earlier. Investigating the relation between *Spektorski* and *The Last Summer* (a relation hinted at by the author himself), critic Michel Aucouturier argues convincingly that those two works, taken together, still remain incomplete because they represent only the "beginnings of Pasternak the novelist," a novelist still unsure of himself.

THE GENRE OF SILENCE

In spite of his decision to remain silent in the 1930's, Pasternak continued to be intensely active intellectually, and inasmuch as the circumstances of the decade clearly discouraged the expression of personal thought, he turned to translation. In addition, he soon came to appreciate translation as a means of earning a living when he found himself in political disfavor. By the end of his life Pasternak had published well over two thousand pages of poetic translations—approximately one-half of his entire literary output.

When, in 1933, Pasternak started working with Georgian poetry, he laid the foundation for a dedicated and fruitful career as a translator. He undertook his translation of Georgian poetry after hearing it interpreted for him during his first visit to Tbilisi in 1931. In the modern Georgian literary idiom Pasternak most appreciated the fiery strain, the natural and authentic rhetorical vein, the fantasy, the stylistic reflections of a quaint past and its beliefs, and the subtle formulas inherited from proverbs. Pasternak brought to life in a fresh and creative Russian idiom Georgian masterpieces that until then, in dull and inadequate translations, had gone unnoticed by the Russian public. Over the years Pasternak translated lyrics by such contemporary poets as Tabidze, Iashvili, and Georgii Nikolaevich Leonidze, as well as works by the prerevolutionary Vazha-Pshavela (pseudonym of Luka Razikashvili) and the Romantic Nikoloz Baratashvili.

Pasternak also devoted himself to English poetry (Ben Jonson, Keats, Byron, and Shelley); German poetry (both parts of Goethe's *Faust,* Schiller's *Maria Stuart,* Kleist, and Rilke); such

Romantics as the Pole Juliusz Słowacki, the Hungarian Sándor Petőfi, and the Ukrainian Taras Shevchenko; the French symbolist Paul Verlaine; and contemporaries such as the Czech surrealist Vitězslav Nezval.

For Pasternak the art of the translator is to turn "from the translation of words and metaphors to the translation of thoughts and scenes." Whereas in the Bryusov-Lozinskii tradition of *khudozhestvennyi perevod* (literary translation) the essential is extreme "objectivity," maximum care for historical accuracy, local color, and stylistic characteristics of the period—all concerns that magnify the *distance* between the text and the contemporary Russian reader—Pasternak believed in attempting an imaginative act of sympathetic and creative reconstitution that would make the author of the original appear as a contemporary. At times Pasternak's translations are so free that one may wonder whether his achievement belongs to the genre of translation proper or to that of a free and original poetic creation inspired by the primary work; the latter interpretation has been upheld by certain Soviet critics.

The crowning success of Pasternak's method of poetic translation was his ability to make William Shakespeare speak a markedly colloquial twentieth-century Russian. This, to be sure, he achieved through resolutely jettisoning many of the original's euphuisms, conventional turns, or occasional declamatory strains in order forcefully to bring out individual characterizations. Pasternak's translations of Shakespeare's plays and sonnets have come to be recognized in their own right as works of original genius. His tendency to present Shakespeare as a contemporary no doubt did much to change the Soviet attitude toward the ideological characterization of Shakespeare as an aristocrat.

The appearance of Pasternak's *Hamlet* in 1941 was enthusiastically received. (Much to Pasternak's chagrin, however, his *Hamlet* was not produced by the Moscow Art Theater, because Stalin was not pleased with certain themes—such as the abuse of princely power

—and stressed that the play was "a pessimistic and reactionary one.") The critic Nikolai Vil'iam-Vil'mont wrote: "No Russian translator has been able to convey the tragic language of *Hamlet* with as much force and with such accurate coincidence with the original as Boris Pasternak." The critic also raised a query about the extent to which "a true fusion of two authorial personalities" had been achieved in Pasternak's creation: "Instead, what there is is one authorial personality [Shakespeare], being submitted to another [Pasternak]." In so doing Pasternak was using the favorite method of the early-nineteenth-century poet-translator Vasilii Zhukovskii, whose approach was thereafter discarded by most Russian translators.

M. Morozov, the eminent Shakespearean scholar, noted that Pasternak stresses in *Hamlet* the psychological and that his language creates emotion. Morozov concluded by saying that through Pasternak's translation the reader clearly "believes that not merely a great play had ended but a strong, enchanting, promising, and energetic human being has perished in that cruel dark world in which it was determined that Hamlet should live." Thus Pasternak's version of a Hamlet who attempts to maintain integrity in an atmosphere of corruption and decay may be likened to the poet's own uncompromising stance.

Such intensive and prolonged interpretation of rich poetic voices other than his own had a far-reaching effect on Pasternak. It provided him with a spiritual refuge and kept him in touch with great masters at a time when Soviet intellectuals were being starved aesthetically. Shakespeare, whom Pasternak viewed as a "prophet" of a new age (our own), was especially important to him. He confided to a friend that in the Elizabethan he found an "inner freedom" inconceivable to his contemporaries. The discipline of translation, according to Henry Gifford, took Pasternak "further away from modernism and impelled him to examine again the problems of communication in poetry." It also brought him closer to the directness and simplicity necessary for communication with a large audience. Furthermore, the poet in many ways tried to do in translation, as the critic Vladimir Markov has observed, what he could not do in his original poems—"tell the truth about his own life, discuss problems of his generation, engage in polemics with the authorities" ("An Unnoticed Aspect of Pasternak's Translations," *Slavic Review,* October 1961, p. 508).

POETRY, 1943–1945

The publication of *Na rannikh poyezdakh* (*Early Trains*) in the summer of 1943 ended Pasternak's nine-year "creative silence." (Earlier, in December 1942, Pasternak had presented *Early Trains* at a poetry evening at the Writers' Club, attended by all of literary Moscow.) Reflecting on his anguish at becoming the prisoner of a profession that left too little scope for his creative talent, he remarked: "For six years I've been translating. I must at last write something." The appearance of *Early Trains* marks Pasternak's return to original work, the beginning of efforts that culminated in the completion of *Doctor Zhivago.*

Early Trains is a collection of poetry in four cycles, two written in 1936 ("The Artist" and "Summer Notes"), two in 1941 and 1942 ("Peredelkino" and "The War Months"). The poems, varied in content, are unified not so much by a common theme as by an ineluctable unity of spirit, by the same deep reverence for nature, for friendship, for the people, for the dignity of the artist. The poem "On Early Trains" is included in the cycle "Peredelkino" and shares many features with the other poems. In sheer simplicity (it tells a story in almost conversational quatrains) it is perhaps unsurpassed in Pasternak's poetry and as such is representative of the poetic manner he tried to attain after 1940. It speaks of nature at the time of awakening, early morning, bearing the idea of nature as eternally fresh and new, of nature as wonder and marvel. The narrator as a totally passive

recipient of impressions is another notable feature. Finally, the poem is pervaded by deep humanitarian respect and admiration for the simple people of Russia.

The poem "The Old Park" in the "Peredelkino" cycle reflects Pasternak's interest in the effects of war on the intelligentsia. This poem describes the ancestral Samarin estate as Pasternak had seen it before the war and in its present decimated condition, when a member of the Samarin family returns, injured, from battle. (Pasternak was clearly struck by this incident and by the death of another member of the Samarin family, Yurii, who died of typhus after his return to Moscow in the late 1920's; the sad end of either or both of the Samarins appears to have suggested to him Zhivago's later life.)

The cycle "The War Months" is also of interest in that it clarifies Pasternak's feelings about the war. It is a series of five poems, filled with unmasked hatred for the invader, deep sympathy for the victims of war, and praise for the heroic efforts of the Russian people. The poem "To the Memory of Marina Tsvetaeva" is attached to the end of this cycle. In it Pasternak conducts an internal monologue, trying to come to terms with the death of his old friend.

Pasternak's achievement in *Early Trains* represents in his own perception a landmark in his progression toward new aesthetic values. Throughout the 1940's and 1950's he expressed personal dissatisfaction with the earlier innovative works that had won him fame. In the 1940's he told Aleksandr Gladkov, his friend and confidant: "For decades, I've lived on my credit, and so far have achieved nothing. . . . My future collected works have not yet been written" (Gladkov, 1977). Since the 1930's Pasternak had experienced a sense of inadequacy, a lack of validity in his existence as a literary man. Writing in *Znamia* (The Banner) in 1943 about the "perfection of form" and the "purity of lines" of *Early Trains*, Pasternak's friend and fellow poet Pavel Antokol'skii also had a word to say about the relationship of the poet's earlier achievement to that of his recent and future tasks. Antokol'skii came to the conclusion that, impressive as it was, Pasternak's earlier work was the pledge of writing to be done "in a new notebook," in which the writer would convey an essential message about his time.

Pasternak's most important original work emerging from the war years is *Zemnoi prostor* (*The Vast Earth*). It is a short collection of poems written in 1943 and 1944 and presented in published form in 1945. Besides new poems, it contains some from the collection *Early Trains.* All the new poems in this collection directly or indirectly deal with war; in fact, they form something of a victory march that leads from the darkest days of the war to the sense of imminent triumph. Most of the poems, in quatrains of rhymed iambic tetrameters, recount wartime events, usually in terms of individual fates. The poems in the collection that do not deal directly with war are like hymns of praise and glory—one to past military heroes, one to southern Russia, one to victorious Leningrad, one to spring.

The Vast Earth continued Pasternak's effort to attain *neslykhannaia prostota* (an "unheard-of simplicity") in poetic manner. Here the forms are conservative, the images concrete, the meter regular, the thoughts direct and unadorned. Yet the poems are surcharged with genuine feeling, gained through the treatment of common but intense experiences of war.

Pasternak's war poetry did much to renovate his image as a poet close to the everyday concerns of the Soviet people and therefore make his work more ideologically acceptable. Even his severest critic from the 1930's, Surkov, conceded that there was a significant broadening of themes in Pasternak's poetry and that he was becoming more closely associated with the concerns of the nation. Later, A. Abramov, in his *Lyric and Epic Poetry of the Great Patriotic War* (1972), discussing Pasternak's wartime poem "Truth," stressed that the poet's craft underwent an ideological "rearmament" in terms of both thematics and vocabulary.

DOCTOR ZHIVAGO

That *Doctor Zhivago* was forty years in the making is attested to by the similarities in theme, structure, and content between the novel and some published as well as unpublished extant prose pieces of the 1920's and 1930's. It is not inconceivable that one of the stimuli prompting Pasternak to resume his lifelong project of writing a novel was the suggestion made in 1932 by an admirer of his work: "Compose a novel about our epoch; freshen it with our great reality."

To that end Pasternak devoted much time on and off, between 1934 and 1939, progressing toward what became *Doctor Zhivago.* During part of that time Pasternak used "Zapiski Zhivulta" (The Diary of Zhivult) as a working title for his text ("Zhivult" soon turned into "Zhivago"). These fragments cover the period of 1902 to 1905 and, taken together, represent an early draft of the first few chapters of *Doctor Zhivago.* In this "Ur"-Zhivago we witness the early life of the hero; Zhivult (who had been temporarily renamed Patrikii), a ten-year-old orphan from Kazan who comes to live with Aleksandr Aleksandrovich Gromeko, a professor of natural history, his wife, Anna Gubertovna, and their daughter, Antonina (Tonia). Patrikii grows up, plays, and studies with Tonia, and many episodes in the Gromeko household resemble those in *Doctor Zhivago.* In another excerpt the hero lives with his wife, Tonia, and son, Shura, in the wartime atmosphere of the town of Yuriatin in the Urals and visits Evgeniia Istomina, née Liuvers, the daughter of a foreign-born bankrupt lawyer from Perm and wife of the physics and mathematics teacher of the Yuriyatin secondary school. Dispersed among separate passages of the narrative are obvious autobiographical traits, such as the hero Patrikii's suffering from a prolonged, year-long chronic insomnia (as Pasternak himself did in 1934 and 1935).

Underlying this major venture into prose was Pasternak's intention to compose an important fresco depicting chapters of Russia's history and his generation's contribution to it. Thus he told the Mandelshtams—"every time" he met them—that he was writing a prose work "about [them] all." By 1937, Pasternak said that he had not yet made a final decision about the title but described the book as a three-part novel, with the first part dealing with the childhood of the protagonists. In a letter to his father Pasternak discussed the aesthetic and ideological conversion that he claimed motivated him to write the work:

> Well, though late, I too have at last seen the light. Nothing I have written so far is of any significance. That world has ceased and I have nothing to show to this new one. . . . But luckily I am alive, my eyes are open, and hurriedly I am trying to transform myself into a writer of a Dickensian kind, and later—if I have enough strength to do it—into a poet in the manner of Pushkin. Do not imagine that I dream of comparing myself with them! I am naming them simply to give you an idea of my inner change.
>
> ("Introduction," in Boris Pasternak, *Fifty Poems*, Lydia Pasternak Slater, trans., London, 1963, p. 16)

In a later communication to his parents he continued to discuss the novel, further elaborating on his new style, which he felt was close to that of Chekhov and Tolstoy.

But the purges of the 1930's brought Pasternak to an aesthetic stalemate and a standstill on his work. He wrote at this time: "some kind of period in general literary life and in my own personally has come to an end. Mine came to an end even earlier; I could not cope with my prose. I felt sick mentally, I did translations." Pasternak's involvement in the translation of *Hamlet* had an important side effect; it provided the poet with a vision of the Danish prince as the man born to set the times right, deriving inspiration from a great cause, and

ready to stand apart from society in order to serve the people from which he had removed himself. This vision would evolve in *Doctor Zhivago*, where the poem "Hamlet" presents a unique blending of Hamlet and Christ in the protagonist. The translation of *Faust* also helped Pasternak in the writing of *Doctor Zhivago*: *Faust* "helped me become bolder, freer, break up new paths not only in the sense of political or moral prejudices but also from the viewpoint of form. I freed myself from the impulse to be an original writer." Translating *Faust* had a definite impact on his search for a straightforward, "nonoriginal" style, which he brought to a successful completion in the final draft of *Doctor Zhivago*.

After the war, in 1945, Pasternak began composing sections of *Doctor Zhivago*, and, although he was tormented with doubts and uncertainties, he later said:

> I wrote it with great ease. The circumstances were so definite, so fabulously terrible. All that I had to do was listen to their prompting with my whole soul and follow obediently their suggestions. The epoch contributed the main element to the novel—that element which constitutes the greatest difficulty given a freedom of choice: the delimitation of its content.
>
> (Boris Pasternak letter to F. A. Stepun, June 1958; in F. A. Stepun, "B. L. Pasternak," *Novyi Zhurnal* 56 [1959]

As Pasternak conceived the main framework of *Doctor Zhivago* in 1945 and 1946 (when most of the "Poems of Yurii Zhivago" were written), it was to be an imaginative resolution of the crisis in Russia and of the effect of that crisis on the writer himself. The poem "Hamlet," written in 1946, reveals the profundity of that crisis, with its stark presentation of the spiritual anguish of a dramatis persona whose hopes for the establishment of justice in the state are dashed, with no chance for him to undertake any action that would further his ideals. The optimism that colors his proposed resolution is apparent in the epilogue to *Doctor Zhivago*, in a conversation between Gordon and Dudo-rov. Gordon reflects that the war came "as a breath of fresh air, a purifying storm, a breath of deliverance" and adds:

> The war had its special character as a link in the chain of revolutionary decades. The forces directly unleashed by the revolution no longer operated. The indirect effects of the revolution, the fruit of its fruit, the consequences of the consequences, began to manifest themselves. Misfortune and ordeals had tempered characters, prepared them for great, desperate, heroic exploits. These fabulous, astounding qualities characterize the moral elite of this generation.
>
> (*Doctor Zhivago,* p. 508)

The striking optimism in such passages as this, the expectations for and belief in the future, are the spirit of Pasternak's life and work.

In September 1946 a manuscript of the completed first part of *Doctor Zhivago* was circulating in Moscow. Being with Olga Ivinskaia and working with her on the manuscript had provided Pasternak with the support he needed to complete it. Ivinskaia, in fact, played a decisive part in shaping *Doctor Zhivago:* it has been correctly asserted that, belonging as she did to a generation younger than Pasternak's (and to that extent more sensitive to purely Soviet phenomena), she helped give the novel a more contemporary (and to that extent, more "Soviet") flavor.

The significance of Ivinskaia as an inspiration for Pasternak is reflected in *Doctor Zhivago.* When speaking to certain visitors, the novelist simply equated Lara with Ivinskaia. The truth, however, is more complex: Lara is in fact a composite portrait, combining elements of both Zinaida Nikolaevna and Olga Ivinskaia. Pasternak remarked that his wife aided the development of Lara in that she was an "eternal, authentically Russian, enduring element." (At the same time, certain traits of Zinaida Nikolaevna—such as her passionate love of domestic work and her nest-building instinct—were embodied in the character of Tonia, Zhivago's wife.) Although Ivinskaia

herself acknowledged this, she believed that she was the main inspiration for Lara. Indeed, such poems as "Separation" and "Bacchanalia" refer specifically to Ivinskaia. Pasternak's poem "August" concerns her alone, as homage to her courage and testimony of the poet's feelings for her.

In writing *Doctor Zhivago,* Pasternak was always concerned with "color and poetry." He believed that "thought draped itself in color and transformed itself in a vision of reality," a poetic image. Therefore, he conceived of the novel as "a long narrative poem, submitting to poetic intuition, which . . . is capable, more deeply than anything else, of expressing the atmosphere of life" (Yurii Krotkov, "Pasternak" [part 1], *Grani* 60:44–45 [1960]). This is a notion strongly reminiscent of Blok's conception in *Vozmezdie* (*Retribution,* 1911). The over-all poetic intuition as embodied in the "total conception" of the novel, he later stated, was far more important to him than any specific significance or symbolism of particular details.

After eight years of enforced creative silence, Pasternak published ten poems from *Doctor Zhivago* in the April 1954 issue of *Znamia.* The poems are prefaced by the following note from the poet:

> The novel will probably be completed in the course of the summer. It covers the period from 1903 to 1929, with an epilogue relating to World War II. The hero, Iu. A. Zhivago, a physician, a thinking man in search of [truth], with a creative and artistic bent, dies in 1929. Among his papers written in younger days, a number of poems are found, which will be attached to the book as a final chapter. Some of them are reproduced here.
>
> (*Znamia,* April 1954, p. 192)

Official reaction to the poems was at best lukewarm, yet Pasternak continued to nurture hopes for the publication of his novel. At last, during the winter of 1955–1956 Pasternak completed the manuscript of *Doctor Zhivago.* Unable to have it published in the Soviet Union, Pasternak gave the Milan publisher Giangiacomo Feltrinelli the rights to the Italian-language publication of *Doctor Zhivago*. The first edition of the novel appeared in Italy in 1957.

In a letter to Eugene Kayden, an American translator of his poetry, Pasternak stressed how necessary it was for critics and readers to acknowledge the crucial place he felt the novel occupied in his literary achievement:

> You say I am "first and last a poet, a lyric poet." Is it really so? And should I feel proud of being just that? . . . It hurts me to feel that I have not had the ability to express in greater fullness the whole of poetry and life in their complete unity. . . . What am I without the novel, and what have you to write about me without drawing upon that work, its terms and revelations?

For Pasternak *Doctor Zhivago* was also a "settlement" of sorts—and even an attempt to make amends for the "wrongs" suffered by some of those closest to him. In a letter of November 1948 he specifically mentions the ludicrously inadequate rewards and cruel trials that an "outrageously dark and unjust life" had meted out to such great artists as his father, Tsvetaeva, Yashvili, and Tabidze; he further remarks that in writing the novel he felt like an "avenger" of the wrongs they had suffered, attempting to "get even for *them.*"

Doctor Zhivago may be most concisely characterized as Pasternak's spiritual history of the Russian revolution, presented in the form of the life story of a representative fictional hero, Yurii Zhivago. The author claimed that Zhivago was conceived as someone intermediate between himself and Blok, Esenin, and Mayakovsky. This scion of the Russian intelligentsia is, successively, a doctor, a poet, a citizen in sympathy with the outbreak of revolution, a family man struggling to survive the material hardships of the early Soviet years, an involuntary member of the Red partisan army during the long civil war, a disgraced member of the former bourgeoisie, an internal refugee obliged by political dangers to part from the woman he loves, the common-law husband of the daughter of a former family servant and—through all this—a man whose external life goes to seed while in his writings he keeps alive a full measure of spiritual and creative integrity.

The novel's emotional drama turns on Zhivago's fated, ideal love for Lara Guichard, a woman of a social class a step beneath his, whom Pasternak presents as variously emblematic of female wholeness, of Russia's suffering humanity in need of social justice, and of Yurii's passion for visionary integrity. The differing social origin of Zhivago's three "wives"; his displacements from Moscow to the Urals, back to Moscow, away to Siberia, and finally back to Moscow again; his experiences as citizen, doctor, and family man; the increasing hardships he sees and endures; and the varieties of people whose fates converge with his—all these embrace the experience of Russians-at-large during a half century of tumultuous change.

Through Zhivago's experiences and reflections Pasternak develops an evaluation of the revolution and its spiritual consequences that, without denying the historical inevitability of the upheaval, defends the enduring values of individual integrity, humanity, art, and responsiveness to the wholeness of the natural world. Dwelling on the consequences of political change, Pasternak questions the ultimate validity and efficacy of such approaches to the complexities of existence. Thus, while the novel is clearly a depiction of a particular social moment, its style and values make it a work that is at least as lyrical and spiritual as it is historical and political.

In *Doctor Zhivago* Pasternak refers implicitly and explicitly to nature and history in communicating to us his vision of man. Ever since Kant, fundamental dichotomies similar to the Kantian opposition of nature and freedom have attracted thinkers. Nature and history appeared to Pasternak as the two obvious and convenient poles for the definition and evaluation of reality.

Like Pasternak's poetry *Doctor Zhivago* is

essentially a hymn to life, a song to celebrate "my sister, Life." It is a rapt meditation, but it is also a desperate claim in favor of that mysterious original force by one who is alarmed by the menace directed against life and its manifestations.

The world of nature is not, however, the last word for Pasternak, for whom history is "a second universe," a world of values in which man is called upon to live. Pasternak himself enumerates those values that constitute the diverse dimensions of the world of history: the idea of the free personality, love of one's neighbor, the idea of life as sacrifice.

Finally, for Pasternak art is the higher sphere where the values of the "universe of history" find their fulfillment. While being the culmination of the universe of history, art—through its communication of authentic emotion and experience—also holds the potential of maximum faithfulness to natural reality, to the pole of nature. Thus is a reconciliation of the two worlds achieved. To illustrate this synthesis of nature and history within the aesthetic function Pasternak wrote *Doctor Zhivago.*

SKETCH FOR AN AUTOBIOGRAPHY

Composed at the instigation of his editor Bannikov and completed in May and June 1956 under the title "In Lieu of a Foreword," *Sketch for an Autobiography* was originally intended to serve as a preface to the collection of earlier and more recent poems that Pasternak hoped to publish simultaneously with *Doctor Zhivago.* In 1958—the publication of the volume in the Soviet Union having become impossible because of the appearance abroad of *Doctor Zhivago*—Pasternak changed his plans and authorized publication of the more recent poetry as a separate volume (which appeared as *Kogda razguliaetsia* [*When the Skies Clear,* 1960]) while the introduction also appeared separately as *Essai d'autobiographie,* published by Gallimard in the summer of 1958.

Toward the end of the year Feltrinelli published the two texts together in Italy as *Avtobiografia e nuovi versi.* Unlike *Doctor Zhivago, Sketch for an Autobiography* was published in the Soviet Union several years after the author's death (an attempt to print it in the third volume of the almanac *Literaturnaia Moskva* [Literary Moscow] in 1957 failed, but it was published with a few abridgments in the journal *Novyi mir* in January 1967).

Although thirty years separate *Sketch for an Autobiography* from *A Safe-Conduct,* the second autobiography covers the same period of the author's life, updated only with one section on the Georgian poets Iashvili and Tabidze. *Sketch for an Autobiography* neither repeats nor continues *A Safe-Conduct;* as Gladkov notes, "It represents as it were a musical variation on it." Whereas the earlier volume mingles a description of the origins of Pasternak's poetry with broader aesthetic and cultural considerations, the later text is almost exclusively a discussion and reevaluation of those artists who influenced Pasternak. The *Sketch* reads like an intimate, intent (albeit impressionistic) conversation about people and places. Pasternak omitted much of what could not but shape him as an artist—his experiences in Moscow and Chistopol during World War II and his translations of Shakespeare—as if, Gladkov suggests, "selecting and retaining only that which, in his life, led him to compose *Doctor Zhivago.*"

Beginning with a criticism of what he calls the "unnecessary mannerisms" marring the earlier volume, Pasternak penned his second autobiography in lucid prose (this later denunciation by Pasternak is to be understood within the context of his shift in the 1940's toward an aesthetic of greater simplicity). *Sketch for an Autobiography* is divided into five sections. The first ("Infancy") is filled with Pasternak's early impressions, ranging from nannies and domestic scenes to his father's artistic activities. Here the author mentions Tolstoy twice, as a portent of his eventual devotion to literature and as a very real indication of the inspiration, moral as well as aesthetic, that Tolstoy provided. In "Scriabin" Pasternak lovingly describes the famous composer's music and personality (both were fresh and original), as well as Scriabin's hold on his imagination. But—perhaps more important—he says that Scriabin proved to him that, with the means that were at the disposal of his predecessors, a great artist can renew an art form "from its very foundations."

"The Nineteen Hundreds" opens with a description of events of the 1905 revolution, the political turmoil of the period being an appropriate introduction to the literary turmoil that began then. There is a tension in this section, produced by the repeated alternation of the old and the new. Characteristic of the older generations are Tolstoy—whose death, a symbol of the passing of a generation, is described—as well as Andrey Bely, to whom Pasternak ascribes "all the marks of genius," and Blok, whom he views as exemplary and endowed with the earmarks of a great poet. Within the context of his discoveries as a young poet, Pasternak also analyzes Rilke's poetry, which struck and amazed him in the same way that his first encounter with Blok's poems did—through "the urgency of what they had to say, the absoluteness, the gravity, the direct purposefulness of their language." The significance for Pasternak of Rilke's poetic diction was such that, to prove his point, he translated two examples of the latter's poems, quoting them in this text. In contrast to the uniqueness of these talents, Pasternak underscores the helplessness and inarticulateness—at that particular time—of the "new" Russian poets, a censure from which he absolves the early production of both Tsvetaeva and, surprisingly, the mediocre N. N. Aseev.

Pasternak then gives a single-page account of his summer at the University of Marburg (compared with forty-odd pages in *A Safe-Conduct*). The major emphasis in this section ("Before the First World War") is on Mayakovsky, whose *early* lyrical poetry the author views as "beautifully modelled, majestic, de-

monic, and, at the same time, infinitely doomed, perishing, almost calling for help." Pasternak was alienated by Mayakovsky's later poetry, however, and states over and over that his connections with him have been exaggerated. In *A Safe-Conduct* Pasternak's account of his friendship with Mayakovsky is long and detailed, warm, and filled with a sense of great loss; in *Sketch for an Autobiography*, however, Pasternak's attitude toward his fellow poet is marked by an intentional dryness of tone and a definite toughness. (Someone who had been a close friend of both Mayakovsky and Pasternak found the latter statement "unkind, cold, and . . . inaccurate." To that friend Pasternak seemed embarrassed and guilty for having spoken "badly" of Mayakovsky in his new autobiography.) Perhaps the most important part of this section is a short disquisition on suicide, which reveals Pasternak's belief in the vital importance of the continuity of inner existence; for him memories create this continuity, which is so necessary for survival—those who abandon their past, their memories, abandon their reason for existence. This is a deeply personal passage; Pasternak is contrasting his ability to survive with the suicides of his fellow poets Mayakovsky and Esenin.

The "Three Shadows" discussed in the conclusion are Tsvetaeva, Iashvili, and Tabidze. Pasternak writes: "The fate of these two men, and that of Marina Tsvetaeva, was to become my greatest sorrow." As had been noted, however, Pasternak "does not dwell on their deaths . . . but on the richness of life they gave him" (Sherman Paul, "An Art of Life: Pasternak's Autobiographies," *Salmagundi* 14:31 [1970]). Pasternak discusses the poetry of all three (Tsvetaeva's in the most depth) and relates memories of his friendship with each. Strengthened by his memories of these friends and others from his past, Pasternak seems in calm possession of himself and ready for what fate has in store for him. *Sketch for an Autobiography* "memorializes the dead," but more important, by calling off the names of the dead, Pasternak both illustrates (as he does in *A*

Safe-Conduct) his belief in the continuity of art in history and traces his own artistic genealogy.

LAST WORKS

A major achievement of the 1950's was the poetry grouped under the title *When the Skies Clear*. In its fullest edition this collection comprises forty-four poems in fuguelike sequences. Here the main interlocutors in the poet's dialogue are woman, nature, death, and God. The feminine element is present in many guises—the women in the poet's childhood, his apprenticeship in passion, women's Eve-like role in his life—but passion is portrayed here in a far more subdued vein than in *My Sister, Life*. Nature, even more pervasive, occupies about half the space in the collection—the usual proportion in Pasternak. All the seasons are represented in an order reflecting careful structural concern rather than the calendar. The landscapes depicted are mostly Pasternak's natural paradise of Peredelkino—Lake Izmalkovo, the River Setun, the mushrooms in the nearby forest, haystacks in the field. In a striking cultural insight wheat fields are seen as a page of man's writing. The natural experience is far from being merely picturesque and pleasurable, however; foul weather, disease, and death are part of it, and Jacqueline de Proyart's careful reconstruction of the cycle's composition has shown how these elements reflect Pasternak's experience of the years 1956 through 1959.

At a deeper level, nature is viewed as a long religious service that the poet-worshiper has attended. The abundant and heartwarming response of thousands of his readers reveals to Pasternak another aspect of "God's world." "V bol'nitse" ("In Hospital") provides a full acknowledgment of divine providence. Cosmic gratitude for natural and supernatural experiences pervades the collection in a devotional note that often borders on ecstasy; thus a meditation on Poland and Georgia evokes a vision of ultimate harmony between man and the elements.

It has been pointed out that the "child's freshness, the wonder, the strong joy of acclamation of a world just created" so characteristic of Pasternak's earlier poetry are absent from *When the Skies Clear* (Angela Livingstone, "Pasternak's Last Poetry," *Meanjin Quarterly* 22:388, 395 [1963]). It is true that here we see far less buoyancy than before and, as Angela Livingstone remarks, less of an active desire to "transform the given world into something new and intense and extraordinary." Yet the poet still seeks, in a more mature and refined way, to identify and understand the constant flow of changes affecting the world and to radiate this understanding. While the narrator reveals an awareness of the aging process, in *When the Skies Clear* he is not resigning from his former mission, only seeking to accomplish it from a different vantage point. He endeavors to communicate to his readers his mature vision of the values that inform an infinite universe. In essence the deeper message of the collection is similar to that of *Doctor Zhivago*: from death arises a new life of greater awareness. The poet feels a responsibility to enhance others' awareness of this rebirth. In this connection, the artist's vocation is shown as having its moral imperative: fame "is not a pretty sight," while the artist's only fulfillment lies in eschewing appearance for the sake of true being, which is achieved by the most rigorous and honest work. Authenticity is attained only if the artist pursues the aim of creation, which is "gift of self." The ultimate transfiguration of nature and self through art conceived as a superior, demanding mission fraught with renunciation is the culmination of the book's message.

To repay the recognition and affection that had come to him from all over the world with the appearance of *Doctor Zhivago*, Pasternak felt duty-bound to write the dramatic trilogy *Slepaia krasavitsa* (*The Blind Beauty*, 1969). Despite failing health, during the last year of his life he often sat at his desk until two or three in the morning to further this task. (The idea of writing a play had first occurred to the writer at the beginning of World War II, when he had devoted much time and energy to composing a play about the war.) *The Blind Beauty* was still unfinished at his death in 1960. There are only fragments of the first play in a projected trilogy—a two-scene prologue, an incomplete first act, and notes on how the rest of the drama was to be developed. Aesthetically, the fragments are certainly not on a par with Pasternak's best work, though it is difficult to say what the tone and structure of the completed trilogy would have been.

The Blind Beauty is a historical drama concerned with serfdom and the serf theater; it is set in nineteenth-century Russia but suggests a parallel with the contemporary scene. In its completed form it was to be Pasternak's statement on freedom and Russia's cultural tradition. Pasternak was fascinated by the institution of serfdom in Russia as it approached emancipation and the effect the time of transition must have had upon the artist. The play's characters talk much about freedom—especially social freedom—but after the emancipation soon realize that real freedom can be found only in art. An impassioned love story was to have been included in the drama, along with the reenactment of actual historical events of the period.

In the trilogy Pasternak was also apparently going to parallel between two radically different spheres of existence: art and history. In the play we see history in flux as Russia moves toward emancipation—a sort of social redemption. Its parallel in the twentieth century is the movement of art toward freedom from repression and censorship. Yet, for the poet, art is not on a parallel plane with history, but on a higher one. We see this through the allegorical figure Lusha, a young, pregnant serf who is blinded when an objet d'art shatters. The other "blind beauty" is Russia, which, as Pasternak said to a visitor, has been "oblivious for so long of its own beauty, of its own destinies." In the play Agafonov, an actor, is responsible for curing Lusha of her blindness, as art will cure Russia

of her blindness. From these fragments it is clear that Pasternak saw art as a thing of permanence and value in a constantly changing society.

Selected Bibliography

EDITIONS

Sochineniia. 3 vols. Edited by Gleb Struve and Boris Filippov. Ann Arbor, Mich., 1961.
Stikhotvoreniia i poemy. Edited by L. A. Ozerov. Moscow and Leningrad, 1965.
Doktor Zhivago. Milan, 1957.

TRANSLATIONS

The Blind Beauty. Translated by Manya Harari and Max Hayward. New York, 1969.
Boris Pasternak: Poems. Translated by Eugene M. Kayden. 2d ed., revised and enlarged. Yellow Springs, Ohio, 1964.
Doctor Zhivago. Translated by Max Hayward and Manya Harari. Includes "The Poems of Yurii Zhivago." Translated by Bernard Gilbert Guerney. New York, 1958.
I Remember: Sketch for an Autobiography. Translated and edited by David Magarshak. Includes "Translating Shakespeare," by Manya Harari. New York, 1959.
The Last Summer. Translated by George Reavey, with an introduction by Lydia Slater. London, 1960. Revised translation.
Letters to Georgian Friends. Translated and edited by David Magarshak. New York, 1968.
My Sister—My Life and A Sublime Malady. Translated by Mark Rudman with Bohden Boychuk, Ann Arbor, Mich., 1983.
Pasternak on Art and Creativity. Translated and edited by Angela Livingstone. New York, 1985.
Poems of Boris Pasternak. Translated by Lydia Pasternak Slater. Boston, 1984.
The Poems of Doctor Zhivago. Edited and translated by Donald Davie. New York, 1965.
A Safe-Conduct. Translated by Angela Livingstone. In *The Collected Prose Works of Boris Pasternak.* Edited by Christopher Barnes. New York, 1977.
Selected Poems. Translated by John Stallworthy and Peter France. New York, 1983.

Zhenia's Childhood and Other Stories. London and New York, 1982.

OTHER WORKS (not included above)

"Anketa sektsii poetov" and "Avtobiografiia." Edited by Milan Djurčinov. "Dva prilog za B. L. Pasternak." *Godishen zbornik na filozofskiot fakultet na univerzitetot vo Skopje* 26: 359–365 (1974).

"Boris Pasternak About Himself and His Readers." Translated by Gleb Struve. *Slavic Review* 23: 125–128 (1964).

"Dramatic Fragments." Translated and edited by Christopher Barnes. *Encounter* 15–21 (1970).

Fragmenty romana. Edited by Christopher Barnes and Nicholas J. Anning. London, 1973.

"Novogodnee pozhelanie." *Literaturnaia Rossiia* (1 January 1965) p. 9.

Perepiska s Ol'goi Freidenberg. Edited by Elliott Mossman. New York, 1981.

"Pervye opyty Borisa Pasternaka." Edited by E. V. Pasternak. *Trudy po znakovym sistemam* 4. Uchenye zapiski Tartuskogo gosudarstvennogo universiteta, no. 236. Tartu, 1969.

"O predmete i metode psikhologii." Edited and with a commentary by S. G. Gellershtein. *Slavica Hierosolymitana* 4: 274–285 (1979).

"Simvolizm i bessmertie: Tezisy." In L. Fleishman, *Stat'i o Pasternake.* Bremen, 1977.

"Slovo o poezii." In *Sbornik statei, posviashchennykh tvorchestvu B. L. Pasternaka.* Edited by Gleb Struve. Munich, 1962.

"Stikhi i proza." *Novyi Mir* (January 1965) pp. 163–184

BIOGRAPHICAL AND CRITICAL STUDIES

Aucouturier, Michel. *Pasternak par lui-même.* 1963.

———, ed. *Boris Pasternak, 1890–1960: Colloque de Cerisy-la-Salle (11–14 septembre 1975).* Paris, 1979.

Berger, Yves. *Boris Pasternak.* Paris, 1958.

Birnbaum, Henrik. *Doktor Faustus und Doktor Schiwago.* Lisse, 1976.

Bodin, Per Arne. *Nine Poems from Doktor Živago: A Study of Christian Motifs in Boris Pasternak's Poetry.* Stockholm, 1976.

Bowra, C. M. *The Creative Experiment.* London, 1949.

Conquest, Robert. *Courage of Genius: The Pasternak Affair.* London, 1961.

———, Donald Davie, and Angela Livingstone, eds.

Pasternak: Modern Judgments. Introduction by Donald Davie. London, 1969.

De Michelis, Cesare G. *Pasternak.* Florence, 1968.

Döring, Johanna Renate. *Die Lyrik Pasternaks in den Jahren 1928–1934.* Munich, 1973.

Dyck, J. W. *Boris Pasternak.* Boston, 1972.

Erlich, Victor, ed. *Pasternak: A Collection of Critical Essays.* Englewood Cliffs, N.J., 1978.

Fleishman, Lazar. *Boris Pasternak v dvadtsatye gody.* Munich, 1980.

———. *Stat'i o Pasternake.* Bremen, 1977.

France, Anna Kay. *Boris Pasternak's Translations of Shakespeare.* Berkeley, Calif., 1978.

Gifford, Henry. *Boris Pasternak: A Critical Study.* New York, 1977.

Gladkov, Alexander. *Meetings with Pasternak: A Memoir.* Translated and edited by Max Hayward. New York, 1977.

Hayward, Max. "Introduction to Boris Pasternak's 'Without Love.'" *Partisan Review* 3–4 (1961).

Hingley, Ronald. *Pasternak: A Biography.* London, 1983.

Hughes, Olga R. *The Poetic World of Boris Pasternak.* Princeton, N.J., 1974.

Ivinskaya, Olga. *A Captive of Time.* Translated by Max Hayward. New York, 1978.

Nilsson, Nils Åke, ed. *Boris Pasternak: Essays.* Stockholm, 1976.

Pasternak, Boris, and Thomas Merton. *Six Letters.* Lexington, Ky., 1973.

Plank, Dale L. *Pasternak's Lyric: A Study of Sound and Imagery.* The Hague, 1966.

Pomorska, Krystyna. *Themes and Variations in Pasternak's Poetics.* Lisse, 1975.

de Proyart, Jacqueline. *Pasternak.* Paris, 1964.

Rowland, Mary F., and Paul Rowland. *Pasternak's Doctor Zhivago.* Preface by Harry T. Moore. Carbondale, Ill., 1967.

Ruge, Gerd. *Pasternak: A Pictorial Biography.* London, 1958.

Ruoff, Z. F. *"Doktor Zhivago" kak zavershenie poetiki Borisa Pasternaka.* Moscow, 1961–1962.

———. *Pasternak i Rilke.* Moscow, 1968–1969.

Schewe, Heinz. *Pasternak privat.* Hamburg, 1974.

Schweitzer, Renate. *Freundschaft mit Pasternak.* Vienna, 1963.

Struve, G. P., ed. *Sbornik statei, posviashchennykh tvorchestvu Borisa Leonidovicha Pasternaka.* Munich, 1962.

GUY DE MALLAC

OSIP MANDELSHTAM

(1891–1938)

A CAMBRIDGE DON, one of the protagonists of Vladimir Nabokov's novel *Podvig* (*Glory,* 1932), maintains that with the advent of the Bolshevist rule Russia was concluded and unrepeatable, and, like a splendid Greek urn, it could be embraced and put behind glass. Indeed, the brief magnificent flowering of Russia's European culture, known as the St. Petersburg period, which produced such giants as Alexander Pushkin, Nikolay Gogol, Leo Tolstoy, and scores of other superb poets and prose writers, came to an end with the revolution of 1917, having lasted less than two centuries.

The greatest of Russian religious philosophers, Vladimir Soloviev, and an entire generation of symbolist poets spoke of the imminent downfall in an "accursed language of prophecy" as they pondered the famous equestrian statue of Peter the Great trampling a snake and the moral dilemma bequeathed to them by Pushkin in his poem *Mednyi Vsadnik* (*The Bronze Horseman,* 1833): Would the cosmos created by the imperial founder finally succumb to the "vindictive chaos" kept at bay but never completely vanquished by his and his spiritual heirs' superhuman will?

The poets and thinkers of the enormously rich last crop of Russian culture, named the Silver Age by the poet and critic Nikolay Otsup and, more perceptively, the Platinum Age by Professor Oleg Maslennikov, were divided in their attitude toward the expected cataclysm.

Some believed that it would be a just punishment for the hubris of Petrine Russia, which, like the Byzantium of yore, had renounced Christ's testament of love for the sake of the new Rome's temporal grandeur, a grandeur founded on intolerable social injustice and political oppression. In 1894 Soloviev prophesied in his poem "Panmongolism":

> O Rus! Forget your former glory;
> The two-headed eagle has been smashed,
> And to yellow children, for amusement,
> Are given the shreds of your banners.
>
> He will be humbled in trembling and fear
> Who dared forget the testament of love,
> And the Third Rome is lying in the dust,
> And surely there will be no fourth one.

The father of Russian postsymbolism, Innokentiy Annensky, a poet of supreme moral sensitivity, was even more pessimistic as he meditated on the spirit of rebellion worshiped by generations of radical intelligentsia:

> The sorcerer [Peter] gave us only stone,
> And the river of muddy yellow color,
> And the deserts of mute city squares
> Where people were executed before dawn;
>
> And what we have had on earth,
> What has made our two-headed eagle soar,
> The dark-laureled giant on the rock
> Will tomorrow become an amusement for children.

Though he was awe-inspiring and brave,
Yet his furious charger betrayed him;
The czar failed to crush the snake,
And, pinned down, it became our idol.

("Petersburg")

Others, notably such religious and historical thinkers as Dmitry Merezhkovsky, refused to see in St. Petersburg "an accursed error" and persisted in their paradoxical and dialectic affirmation of Peter's achievement: "Peter's cause is Christ's cause." Even the declining West remained for the Russian intelligentsia "the land of holy miracles," in the words of the great Slavophile Aleksey Khomyakov.

The most prominent poet of his age, Alexander Blok, in his unfinished narrative poem *Vozmezdie* (*Retribution,* 1910–1921), described the end of the nineteenth century in Russia as the years of sickly desolation and looked with sincere admiration toward Europe, in spite of its philistinism, as the place

where work proceeds without a hitch,
While here the dejected sunset
Stares, as before, into the swamp.

However, when Petrine Russia collapsed even Blok blamed Europe for the wave of hatred and bestiality that seemed to drown the world and Russia and saw the European war as an ultimate "betrayal of the spirit of music." Torn between Christianity and the ideas of new barbarism, he predicted, in "Skify" (The Scythians, 1918), the coming of the

ferocious Hun
[Who] will search the pockets of the dead,
Burn cities and drive his horses into the church,
And roast the flesh of his white brethren.

There were others who welcomed the great downfall as a fulfillment of their millenarian expectations: the leading symbolists Andrey Bely and Valery Bryusov and the peasant poets Sergey Esenin and Nikolay Klyuev. Russian futurists such as Vladimir Mayakovsky, of course, greeted it as the realization of the avant-garde dream of the old culture razed to the ground and the triumph of the new art serving the victors and expressing the futurist ideals of strength, speed, efficiency, and aggression. All of them, parochial peasant poets and cosmopolitan futurists alike, looked at the West with violent hostility or, at best, as Boris Pasternak, the most European of the Russian avant-garde, did, with the emotion of wistful dismissal:

Its farewell tears not yet dry,
Having wept all the evening long,
One's soul is leaving the West:
It has nothing to do there.

("Vesenneiu poroiu l'da"
[Springtime of Ice], 1931)

In retrospect it appears oddly significant that Osip Mandelshtam, the poet who had never repudiated Europe and yet, like his two closest poetic associates Nikolay Gumilev and Anna Akhmatova, refused to leave Russia, was born in Warsaw, which Blok described in *Retribution* as "the slummy Polish backyard of Russia," "inflated with vindictive fancy" and enlivened only by "the rail track to Europe glistening in the moist mist with its trustworthy steel." His lot was to express most potently the heritage of his age and to create a paradigm for its eventual rebirth in the spiritual memory of future generations: an immensely compact time capsule of enigmatically terse poetry and prose cast into the raging sea of blood and destruction and retrieved only a quarter of a century after his martyr's death to become a supreme challenge to that true culture that always perceives certain values and is itself perceived, to quote Mandelshtam's definition of classical poetry, as "what must be rather than what has been."

He was a Jew, a scion of an obscure Kurland branch of the well-known Mandelshtam rabbinical family, which, since the age of Jewish enlightenment, has produced famous physicians and physicists, Zionists and assimilationists, translators of the Bible and experts on Gogol. The poet's father, Emil Veniaminovich Mandelshtam, was a leather merchant, an observant Jew who taught himself Russian and German, and read Friedrich von Schiller, Johann Wolfgang von Goethe, and the German Romantics, a pathetic and endearing representative of an inarticulate transitional generation whose attempts at self-expression and self-realization were described in the memoirs of the first Jewish university student in Russia, another Mandelshtam (Arye-Leib), as "a martyred ghost of spirit devoid of body." The poet's mother, Flora Osipovna, née Verblovsky, was born and educated in Vilna. She stemmed from an enlightened and assimilated Jewish stock related to the family of the outstanding historian of Russian literature, S. A. Vengerov. A piano teacher, a woman whose artistic tastes were deeply rooted in the traditions of the Russian intelligentsia, she passed on to her son her love of music and of Russian literature.

Osip is a Russian colloquial, rustic, and plebeian form of Iosif (Joseph). Today it is widely used by Russian Jews, but a century ago it was a mark of deliberate russianization. Characteristically, Osip Emil'evich's distant relative and namesake, the Gogol scholar who taught at the University of Helsingfors, was Iosif Emelyanovich—with an assimilated Russian patronymic. A biographer must bear in mind the challenging words of the penultimate essay in Mandelshtam's book of historical and autobiographical reminiscences and reflections *Shum vremeni* (*The Noise of Time,* 1925):

> I could never understand the Tolstoys and the Aksakovs [a prominent family of Slavophiles], all those Bagrov-the-grandsons [a reference to the protagonists of K. S. Aksakov's childhood memoirs], cherishing their familial archives with the epic home memories. A *raznochinets* [this Russian term denotes those educated people who were not of inherited or personal nobility but no longer belonged to the civil estate from which they originated] has no use for memory; it is sufficient for him to tell about the books that he has read, and his biography is ready.

Even the date of his birth, 3 January 1891, Julian calendar (January 15, according to the Gregorian calendar introduced after the revolution), was significant for him because of its evocative literary association. In 1937, in "Stikhi o neizvestnom soldate" ("Verses About the Unknown Soldier"), Mandelshtam wrote emphatically

> I was born on the night of the second and third
> Of January, in the unreliable year
> Ninety-one-or-another . . .

This is the night of the first snow in chapter 5 of Pushkin's *Eugene Onegin* (1825–1831), full of ominous forebodings and portents auguring the violent death of one of its personages, the youthful and idealistic poet Lensky, in which readers have retrospectively perceived a premonition of Pushkin's own death, later described by Mandelshtam as "the source and the teleological reason" of the great artist's creative life.

A profound sensation of the uniqueness of the gift of life ("For the quiet joy of breathing and of living, / Tell me, whom should I thank") was blended in Mandelshtam's poetry with an obscure foretaste of eventual death as the token of the ultimate reality of life ("Can it be that I am real / And death will come indeed?"). Subsequently this vague premonition turned into a consciously tragic expectation and manly readiness acquired through, among other things, contemplation of the deaths and the last poems of great Russian poets, to which Mandelshtam frequently alludes in his verse. He wrote in his essay on Pushkin and Scriabin (1916) about "the fabulous posthumous growth of the artist in the eyes of the masses" in response to "the excess of the void" left by his redemptive death: "Our ally is only that which is redundant; / Not a drop but a depth sounding is ahead" ("The Unknown Soldier").

Every poet seems to have what the late Roman Jakobson has called "a personal myth." Like a genuine myth, it strives to create causal and purposeful models of existence, a frame that alone endows life with universal significance and value and without which being is but a meaningless and fearful episode; as Mandelshtam wrote in his essay on Dante Alighieri (1933), "totally out of touch with the future and the past, the present is conjugated as pure fear, as danger." Pascal's and Tyntchev's thinking and singing reed's birth out of chaos and its death into cosmos in order to fulfill—in the words of Apollon Grigoriev, one of Mandelshtam's favorite poets—"through struggle and trial the aim of purification and the aim of self-creation" are the alpha and omega of Mandelshtam's poetic myth of self:

From an evil and viscous pool
I grew, rustling with a reed;
Passionately, languidly, tenderly
Breathing forbidden life. [1910]

Oh, how much I would like,
Unsensed by anyone,
To fly in the wake of a ray
Where I do not exist. [1937]

I shall say this in a tentative whisper
Because it is not yet time:
With sweat and experience
The unaccountable sky's game is achieved.

And under the provisional sky of purgatory
We often forget that
The happy celestial storehouse
Is an expandable home leased for life. [1937]

And when I die, having done my service,
The lifelong friend of everyone alive,
Let the sky reverberate broader and higher
To fill all of my chest. [1937]

The main facts of Mandelshtam's life are now considerably better known in the West— owing to the celebrated memoirs of his widow and the efforts of his conscientious biographers—than is his astounding poetry. This is understandable: the fascination of truly great poetry tends to be lost both in faithful translation and in "creative adaptation." Yet, because so much of Mandelshtam's poetry is addressed to western culture, it would be a tremendous loss if its message never reached its "providential reader." Mandelshtam's biography is, of course, more relevant to his work than he claimed in *The Noise of Time*. Iurii I. Levin, a Moscow scholar, wrote (in *Slavica Hierosolymitana* 3, 1978):

> Mandelshtam, in the unity of his art and his destiny, is a phenomenon of high paradigmatic significance; an example of a destiny's full realization in art and at the same time of art's fulfillment in destiny. Mandelshtam is a call for unity of life and culture, for such profound and serious (not in the academic sense, of course) attitude toward culture of which our age apparently is not yet capable. . . .
>
> Precisely because of his having lived under the everyday conditions of Soviet life, because of his extreme incompatibility made, however, compatible with, and even somehow rooted in, this life, Mandelshtam is a link, a portent, a formula of transition from our contemporary age to something that not yet exists, but "ought to be." Mandelshtam must "change something in the structure and makeup" [this is a quotation from his letter to the critic Yurii Tynyanov] not only of "Russian poetry" but of world culture as well.

At times, the story of Mandelshtam's persecution and death seems to obscure the stature of his poetry, and one great writer and admirer of the poet has even suggested that today, through the prism of a tragic fate, his poetry seems greater than it actually is (Vladimir Nabokov, in his 1967 interview in *Paris Review*). However, the significance of Mandelshtam's life as a feat of spiritual endurance that makes his art glow with a halo of martyrdom cannot be derived from the mere historical fact of his "compatible incompatibility" with his surroundings; the unique excellence of his poetry was merely brought to universal attention, not magnified, by the poignant story of his sufferings. In his poetry Mandelshtam overcame the common lot of his generation and his own destiny and created not just a historical portent or a link but a promise of everlasting, joyful surprise for anyone who would follow its intricate pattern to retrieve its message. In one of his last poems, written in May 1937, Mandelshtam proclaims the independence of this promise from the frail, melting, mortal image of its bearer:

Today, an angel; tomorrow, a grave worm;
And after tomorrow merely a contour.
What was—the tread—would be beyond the
    trodden range.
Flowers are deathless. Heaven is a wholeness.
And what will be is but a promise.

A year or two earlier he wrote in an unfinished draft fragment an indictment of literature concerned with life's evil as such:

When a writer considers himself duty-bound at all costs to "hold forth tragically about life" whereas his palette lacks deep contrasting colors and, above all, if he is insensitive to the law according to which the tragic, no matter how narrow the range of its manifestation is, inevitably makes up *a general picture of the world,* he gives a "semimanufactured product" of horror or dullness, their raw material, which evokes in us a feeling of revulsion and is better known among the benevolent critics under the affectionate nickname: "description of everyday life."

His own aim as an artist was to make pain itself "festively flower like the royal staff in the prophets' tabernacle."

How, then, did Mandelshtam vanquish the "horror and dullness" implicit in the unredeemed suffering of man used as "building material" ("slaves, to be silent; and stones, to build with") and resolve what he called in his essay on the nineteenth-century Russian Catholic philosopher Petr Chaadaev (1915, reprinted in 1928) "the hoary antinomy of the inert boulder and the organizing idea"?

His childhood was marked by the twin presence of the imperial cosmos of St. Petersburg, to which Mandelshtam's family moved when he was still an infant, and the "Judaic chaos" of his immediate background. In his poetry Man-

delshtam later identified both with the same combination of "deep contrasting colors," black and yellow, the tallith and the emperor's standard:

Only where the firmament is bright
The black-yellow tatter is angry
As if the bile of the two-headed eagle
Were streaming in the air.
    ("The Palace Square," 1915)

Behold the black-yellow light, the joy of Judea.
    ("Among the priests, a
        young Levite . . . ," 1917)

Suddenly my grandfather produced from a chest of drawers a black and yellow silk kerchief, cloaked my shoulders with it, and made me repeat after him words composed of unfamiliar noises, but, displeased with my gibberish, grew angry.

(*The Noise of Time,* 1925)

The passage quoted last comes from *The Noise of Time,* called by the great literary historian Prince Dmitri Svyatopolk-Mirsky in a review published in Paris in 1925 "one of the three or four most significant books of our time." It is indeed a lasting monument to the fateful years of the empire and of its Jewish subjects, when in search of cultural emancipation and unity the Russian creative elite rejected the utilitarian positivist tradition of the 1860's and turned to the heritage of the eighteenth century and the age of Pushkin, whereas an entire generation of the Jews made a supreme spiritual effort "to graft alien blood," in Mandelshtam's words, to its ancient interpretative preoccupation with the sacred text: the Talmudic tradition of the ghetto, which had subliminally affected the poet's own attitude to the word and to the entire body of world poetry.

Mandelshtam called his family—as well as an entire generation of his Russian contemporaries born during the age of cultural stagnation, "the desolate eighties"—tongue-tied: "We learned not to speak but to gibber, and only as we listened to the surging noise of the age and were whitewashed by the foam of its crest we gained a tongue." Svyatopolk-Mirsky, in his review of *The Noise of Time,* alluded to "the sublime tongue-tied uniquely combined with sublime verbal art" in much of Mandelshtam's poetry and prose. It was an astute reference to Mandelshtam's friend Gumilev's lines:

> It is a symbol of celestial greatness
> That, as some covenant of grace,
> The sublime tongue-tie
> Is bestowed upon the poet.

Kosnoyazychie (tongue-tied) is the word in the Russian version of the Bible that is rendered in the King James version as "slow tongue": the speech defect of Moses.

In a poem written when he was nineteen, Mandelshtam contemplated this terrible inability to express a revelation:

> I became afraid of living my life to the end,
> And of springing away like a leaf from its tree,
> And of not falling in love with anything,
> And of sinking as a nameless stone;
>
> And in the void, as if upon a cross,
> Crucifying a living soul,
> Like Moses on the height,
> I am afraid of disappearing in the cloud of Sinai.
>
> And so I trace the threads that tie
> Myself to everything alive;
> And collate the ornamental smoke of being
> Upon the marble slab;
>
> And grasp through the nets
> The tremor of warm birds;
> And from decaying pages
> I draw the dust of centuries.

Mandelshtam reverted to an act of sympathetic magic, as it were, by evoking in this poem, beside all the scriptural allusions, the somber lines of Pushkin, who, eighty years earlier, compared the "dead trace" left by his own name on a keepsake page to "the ornamental pattern of a gravestone inscription in an incomprehensible tongue." The evidence of the poet's being, "collated" with the ineradicable trace left by his great predecessor, was now passed on by Mandelshtam to the next "providential interlocutor," the distant "reader in the future." It was not fame or emulation that Mandelshtam was concerned with, but rather the ontology of the poetic word. A few years later, in his manifesto of acmeism he proclaimed: "They *that are* participate as accomplices in the plot against the void and nonbeing. Love the existence of a thing more than the thing itself, and your own being more than yourself: this is the highest commandment of acmeism" ("Utro akmeizma" ["The Morning of Acmeism"], 1919). By that time the "nameless" stone, a simile for the oblivion to which unrevealed destinies are consigned, is itself turned into a name: *Kamen'* (*Stone*) was the title of Mandelshtam's first book of verse, published in 1913.

A carrier of the undying commandments on the eve of the age that denied being as spiritual manifestation, the poet strove to become his own Aaron bearing testimony of the word's and individual's struggle against oblivion, distortion, and the Egyptian bondage of the ideological commonplace. The reference to the almond tree, the rod of Aaron and of Jeremiah's dream, in his surname (*Mandelstamm* means "stem of almond") was for him a secret pledge of "acquiring a tongue."

He began to write poetry as a schoolboy at the Tenishev School, one of the best, most advanced and liberal private institutions in Russia, devoted to the ideas of political freedom and high-minded civic responsibility. Some of its graduates, among them Nabokov and the outstanding philologist Victor Zhirmunsky, recollected with certain exasperation their teachers efforts at "saving the civic souls" of the boys. Yet the famous Tenishev alumni do seem to share a lasting youthful spirit of inner freedom, loyalty, moral courage, and passionate rebelliousness against the monstrously oppressive delusions that have assumed such a murderous sway over millions of human souls in the twentieth century.

Mandelshtam, unlike Nabokov ten years later, could not resist the temptation of radical involvement. His earliest poems, written apparently during the first Russian revolution of 1905, have not survived, but his mood and the atmosphere of the school in the days of the Japanese war and the ensuing civil strife were vividly evoked in a poem that he wrote a quarter of a century later. Its central image is the stack of logs, "the mountain of firewood," a landmark of the Tenishev schoolyard, the refuge of the aloof little chess genius in Nabokov's novel *Zashchita Luzhina* (*The Defence*, 1930), and, in Mandelshtam's days, apparently the rostrum of the schoolboys' political gatherings:

> When to remote Korea
> The Russian gold piece rolled,
> I would run away to the greenhouse
> Holding a toffee in my cheek.
>
> It was the time of laughter's bubble
> And of the thyroid gland.
> It was the time of Taras Bulba
> And of the approaching thunderstorm.
>
> Arbitrariness, willfulness,
> The Trojan horse on the move,
> And above the pile of logs, an embassy
> Of ether, of the sun and fire.
>
> The air was fat with logs
> As a caterpillar in the yard,
> And the "Petropavlovsk" and Tsushima
> Were cheered on the mountain of firewood.
>
> "To the young czarevich Chlorus!"
> And—God bless us—how we went
> For chloroform up the mountain
> In our high-topped boots.
>
> I have survived that adolescent,
> And my path is broad:
> There are other dreams, other nests,
> But one cannot keep out of mischief.
>
> (1932)

The spirit of Taras Bulba, the rebellious Cossack chieftain in Gogol's story, presided over the little dissenters as they cheered the Japanese victories over the imperial Russian navy. Only a short time ago, in a fit of "infantile imperialism," little Mandelshtam admired the launching of the ironclad *Oslyabya* sliding down into the water "like a monstrous sea caterpillar." This symbol of Russia's might keeled over in the battle of Tsushima and went down with all hands. Yet the boys were jubilant. The Trojan horse was indeed on the move. Arbitrary power provoked willful response. Every Russian schoolboy before the Revolution knew Catherine the Great's allegoric fairy tale written for the edification of her grandson and the poet Gavrül Derzhavin's odic sequel to it: Prince Chlorus, with the help of Princess Felicity, ascends the high mountain to find the rose without thorns growing there, the ideal of virtue and justice. The utopian dream turned out to be chloroform for the young generation. Developing the pun on the name Chlorus originally invented by the insomniac poet Prince Petr Vyazemsky, Mandelshtam punningly contrasts it with ether, Plato's fifth celestial essence, the peaceful, divine "air of mountainous regions," as it is referred to in "Zverinets" ("The Menagerie," 1916), his "ode to peace at the time of war." A descendant of Catherine the Great, poor Czarevich Alexis was born in 1904, as the golden star of the empire was setting in "distant Korea." When he was shot in 1918 together with his parents, sisters, attendants, and a pet spaniel, he was a few months older than Mandelshtam had been in 1904. Mandelshtam considered that regicide the last act of the "Bloody Mystery Play of January Ninth"—commemorated by Mandelshtam in the essay "Krovavaia misteriia 9-go ianvaria" in 1922—the day in 1905 when a peaceful procession of St. Petersburg workers, carrying icons and praying, attempted to bring their grievances directly to their emperor and was dispersed with wanton cruelty, which claimed many victims among women and children. Mandelshtam believed that the blood of those innocents had sealed the fate of the last czar. And yet the line "I have survived that adolescent" seems to refer not only to schoolboy Mandelshtam but also to the unfortunate hemophiliac child guilty only of belonging to the dynasty of Chlorus, who has failed to find the rose.

Mandelshtam's path of "mischief" began early and ended only with his death. On 2 March 1907 the ceiling collapsed in the meeting hall of the Second Duma, the Russian legislative assembly recently elected by an imperial decree. The event was interpreted by the radicals as an attempt against the life of the deputies, and Mandelshtam, a sixteen-year-old schoolboy, made an inflammatory speech about it before the workers of his district. One wonders whether the poet's later preoccupation with the theme of the keystone, the vaulted ceiling, the inviolable dome, masonry, and roofmaking, developed into a maze of religious, freemasonic, historical, sociopolitical, cultural, and purely aesthetic associations, was not originally prompted by that event: the portentous fall of the young Russian parliamentarism's unstable firmament.

He obtained his high-school certificate on 15 May 1907. In September 1907, in Finland, he volunteered for the Socialist-Revolutionary Fighting Organization, which specialized in spectacular acts of individual terror, but was rejected as too young. His parents, very wisely, sent him out of harm's way to Paris, where the young historian Mikhail Karpovich (later a professor at Harvard) saw him at a Socialist-Revolutionary meeting where he was listening ecstatically to the celebrated terrorist and writer Boris Savinkov.

It was in Paris that a strong and prolonged bout of verse writing—the first one to leave lasting results—cured him of this youthful longing for the glory of revolutionary self-sacrifice. Yet the temperament of Russia's heroic, sometimes almost saintly, terrorists, the heirs of the populist People's Freedom party, who carried out political "executions" of the government officials condemned to death by the Socialist-Revolutionary Central Committee to avenge social injustice and political oppression and bravely mounted the scaffold themselves, persisted in Mandelshtam the poet even after he had repudiated terror of any kind. (In 1918, when Leonid Kanegisser, a Socialist-Revolutionary and a poet, killed Uritsky, the chief of the Soviet political police, Mandelshtam's comment was, according to his widow's memoirs, "Who appointed him [Kanegisser] to be the judge?")

In Paris Mandelshtam lived in the Latin Quarter (12, rue de la Sorbonne), vaguely attending some lectures at the university, working on his French, reading a great deal of French poetry, and feeling homesick for Finland rather than for Russia. He met Gumilev, five years his senior and already an author of a strikingly fresh book of verse, *Put' konkvistadozov* (The Path of the Conquistadors, 1905), dreaming of glory and exotic adventure, an admirer of Théophile Gautier and of the young "romanic" school of poetry founded by Jean Moréas to combat the mood of symbolist dejection. They formed a lasting friendship, and it was Gumilev who eventually "ordained" Mandelshtam as a Russian poet. "Nobody understood poetry better than Gumilev," Mandelshtam said in his later years. Gumilev's critical advice contributed a great deal to Mandelshtam's creative growth, although their tastes often clashed: Gumilev valued above all Gautier's pure precision of style and tended to dismiss Paul Verlaine as too "frivolous," as Mandelshtam pointed out in his unpublished sonnet about Gumilev, whereas Mandelshtam sought to overcome the spirit of gravity that weighed over Russian symbolism by turning precisely to Verlaine's "chanson grise," in which "the Vague is joined to the Precise."

A poem written apparently in 1908 as a result of these arguments is a clear statement of what became a lifelong ambition of Mandelshtam's poetics:

> In an unconstrained creative exchange,
> Who could skillfully combine, tell me,

The sternness of Tyutchev with the childishness of
  Verlaine
And add one's own imprint to this union?
Whereas grandeur is so appropriate to Russian
  verse,
In which there's vernal kiss and twitter of the birds.

The image of "stern" Fedor Tyutchev, the greatest Russian metaphysical poet, as the sublime source of "cosmic joy" and at the same time of "icy indifference" is represented in Mandelshtam's later poetry and prose through references to the melting of the eternal Alpine ice as a result of which "Tyutchev descends to our homes" in the valley. A short poem by Tyutchev that Mandelshtam often used to quote reads:

> Bright snow sparkled in the valley:
> The snow has melted and is gone;
> Vernal plant glitters in the valley:
> The plant will wilt and will be gone.
>
> But what century shines white
> There, upon the snowy heights?
> Yet the dawn even now is scattering
> Fresh roses upon them.
>
>   (1836)

Young Mandelshtam inherited the antimony of the eternal and the transient from the Romantics and the symbolists precisely at the time when Annensky and Mikhail Kuzmin, the fifth column of skeptical objectivity within Russian symbolism, were about to give up eternity for the sake of the power of things. An echo of this renunciation can be discerned in Mandelshtam's poem of 1909:

> Do not speak to me of eternity:
> I cannot contain it.
> But how can my love and my carelessness
> Fail to forgive eternity?
>
> I hear how it grows
> And rolls as a midnight billow;
> But he will pay too dearly
> Who approaches it too closely.
>
> And sometimes I rejoice from afar
> In the quiet reverberations
> Of its foamy bulk's noise,
> Thinking of what is sweet and insignificant.

Soon he solved the traditional antinomy in his own unique way, which has become an unmistakable and invariant motif of his art. Alexander Zholkovsky has described this motif as "the mastering, by an 'intimate and warm' subject, of 'alien' and great eternal objects through purely human, 'childish' means: inhaling, eating, drinking." Indeed, in a characteristic genre-picture-like poem written by Mandelshtam in 1914, the eternal ice of Tyutchev's Alps is transformed into the "itinerant icebox" of an ice-cream vendor:

> And into the world of chocolate with pink-glowing
>   dawn,
> Into the dairy Alps the reverie flies . . .
> And with avid attention an urchin is peering
> Into the chest full of miraculous cold.
>
> And the gods know not what he might take:
> Some diamondlike cream or a wafer with filling?
> But the divine ice will soon disappear
> Under a thin wooden strip, glittering in the sun.
>
>   ("Ice Cream!")

The Eucharist "lasts like an eternal noon" in Mandelshtam's poetry, but "the taste of whipped cream and the smell of orange rind," likewise, "are eternal."

Much has been said about Mandelshtam's religiousness, and, just as seven cities argued about the right of being called Homer's birthplace, so at least three denominations of devout critics claimed the Russian-Jewish poet's soul. An astute American scholar, Robert Alter, objects to these pious exaggerations: "Osip Mandelshtam did not believe either in Judaism or Christianity: he believed in poetry." This is correct in the sense that Mandelshtam the man visited churches rather than went to church and did not follow, as far as we know, the precepts of any organized religion, and Mandelshtam the poet used religion as material for poetry rather than the other way round. He did, however, turn quite sincerely to a succession of various religions and quasi-religious philosophical systems in his search for the "integral worldview" and the "internal sense of rightness" without which he found writing poetry unthinkable. With amazing facility and persuasive conviction he penetrated the most intimate emotional core of religious worship and used the most profound intellectual achievements of religious thought as the sources of vivid analogies in his approach to the mystery of the poetic word in its relation to history and society.

In his essay "A. Blok" (1922) he wrote about the "need for cult as a purposeful discharge of poetic energy," but in his own case "cult" was not a purpose but a cause of poetry, "which demanded nothing" in return for its spiritual advice and, in the Christian dispensation, it bestowed upon the poet the gift of ultimate creative freedom: "Jammes [Francis Jammes, the French Catholic poet] sings like a lark / Because a Catholic priest offers him advice" ("The Abbot," 1915).

The relationship between culture and cult was ambivalent for Mandelshtam, not only because of the historicism of his approach to the shifting frames of ideological reference, which allowed him to insist alternately on the hieratic and the lay nature of the Russian poetic language, but also because his thought transposed and blended cause and purpose, etiology and teleology. This is particularly evident in the inspired slips of his pen, which are stumbling blocks for those of his interpreters who do not bother to trace the significance of his "errors of fact" back to Grigoriev's famous observation that a great artist's "technical slips" are unconscious anticipations of, and hints at, some totally unexpected, new, and uniquely "lifelike" solutions of the most vital questions. In his mature prose work *Puteshestvie v Armeniiu* (*The Journey to Armenia*, 1933) Mandelshtam discussed the Latin gerundive—"the future imperative participle in the passive voice"—as the "prototype of our entire culture, and not only 'that which ought to

be,' but 'that which ought to be praised'—*laudatura est."* As Mandelshtam substituted the future active participle *laudatura* (prompted, of course, by the suffix it has in common with *cultura*), which means "that which intends to praise," for the technically correct gerundive *laudanda,* he laid bare the fruitfully ambivalent reciprocity of the perennial bond and conflict between poetry and worship, culture and cult.

Two letters written by Mandelshtam before he turned nineteen described that quest for varieties of religious experience that he had identified in an early poem with "the homeless sail of the spirit, ready to try out all winds." He wrote to Vladimir Gippius, the headmaster of Tenishev School and an excellent poet, in April of 1908 from Paris:

> I always saw in you a representative of a certain precious and, at the same time, inimical principle, the double effect of which formed even its fascination. Now it is clear to me that this principle is nothing else than religious culture, I don't know whether it is Christian, but in any case religious. . . . Long since I have striven toward religion hopelessly and platonically—but ever more consciously. My initial religious experiences belong to the period of my childish infatuation with Marxist dogma and are inseparable from that infatuation. But the link between religion and social involvement was broken for me when I was still a child. At fifteen I passed through the purifying fire of Ibsen, and although I did not retain the "religion of the will" [the reference is to Ibsen's *Brand,* 1866], I took, once and for all, a stand on the ground of religious individualism and opposition to social involvement. . . . My religious consciousness never rose above Knut Hamsun and the worship of "Pan," that is, a god of which one is not aware, which remains to this day my "religion." (Oh, rest assured, this is not "meonism" and, in general, with Minsky I have nothing in common.)
>
> (*Sobranie sochinenii,* vol. 2, 2d ed., 1971, p. 484)

The repudiation of meonism is symptomatic: Nikolay Minsky, a philosopher and poet popular then in the less demanding intellectual circles, was considered to be in bad taste. According to his system, the primeval absolute unity (God) sacrificed itself in an act of creative ecstasy in order to grant the joy of being to the multitude, which would experience religious ecstasy from realizing the opposition between its being and the unity's nonbeing. The idea derived from the ancient Gnostic tradition preserved by the Rosicrucians. In its original form it did influence Mandelshtam's and especially Gumilev's philosophy of artistic creativity: the latter's formula "to be annihilated as unity and to blossom out as plurality" and the former's description of the Gothic spire "stabbing the sky to reproach it for being empty" are obvious specimens of this influence.

The other letter stating Mandelshtam's attitude to faith was dated August 1909. In the interval he wrote and traveled hectically: his personal character of "a vagabond in the sublime sense of the word," as his friend Akhmatova described him, unable to stay in one place for more than a few months, was already in full evidence. In the summer of 1908 he went from Paris to Switzerland and Italy, visiting Genoa, the features of which he later recognized in its Crimean outpost, Theodosia. In the fall he returned to Petersburg and made attempts to enter its literary life. He visited Annensky, the self-effacing genius whose poetics eventually became the inspiration of Russian postsymbolism, and attended the meetings of the Religious-Philosophical Society, the focus of Russia's spiritual revival. On 16 May 1909, he took part in a poetry reading under the auspices of the Academy of Verse, a workshop established for young poets by Vyacheslav Ivanov, the magnificently learned mentor of Russian symbolists, who advocated a synthesis of culture and religion, of the individual and the universal, in a new, nationwide, and ecumenical Dionysiac art.

It was to Ivanov that Mandelshtam wrote from Montreux, Switzerland, where he went for his health: "Does a man when he steps under the vaults of Notre Dame reflect on the truth of Catholicism rather than become a Catholic simply by virtue of his standing under these vaults?" Over a century earlier, the early Romantics Wilhelm Wackenroder and Ludwig Tieck considered the same problem in reference to another Catholic cathedral, St. Peter's in Rome: "Can one truly understand a sublime painting and piously contemplate it without believing that minute in what it depicts?" For them, however, art was the path, while for Mandelshtam it was the aim. Already then, as a young apprentice of symbolist masters, he refused to accept the dualism of meaning and form, or any external, "utilitarian," mystical or social, purpose of the poetic word. The plummet, a masonic emblem of rightness that he adopted in his poetry, blended the biblical notion of testing moral rectitude and the platonic testing of manmade beauty. It expressed for Mandelshtam the undifferentiated aesthetic and ethical principle, as in the poem "Notre Dame" (1912), included in *Stone:*

An elemental maze, unfathomable forest,
The Gothic soul's judicious chasm,
Egyptian might and Christian meekness,
Beside a reed—an oak, and everywhere plummet is
  king.

Yet, the more closely I studied
Your monstrous ribs, stronghold of Notre Dame,
The more often I thought: out of unkind heaviness,
Some day I too will create the beautiful.

It would be wrong to identify "the sermon of the plummet," to which Mandelshtam refers again in "Grifel'naia oda" ("The Slate Ode," 1923), with the position of a self-righteous moral preacher. In several essays and poems written at the same time as "Notre Dame" he suggests, cautiously but firmly, that the stable, the upright, and the monumental in the Catholic Gothic art, or in any art nurtured by an authoritative worldview, must also have a complementary vigorous and dynamic aspect. which, in his essay on François Villon (1913), he finds in Villon's immoralism, attributing to it a special function, namely the capacity for being "eternally contemporary": "The present instant can bear the pressure of centuries and preserve its wholeness, remaining the same 'now.' One must only know how to pluck it out of the soil of time without damaging its roots—otherwise it will wither. Villon knew how to do it." In another essay of the same year, "Osobesednike" ("About an Interlocutor"), Mandelshtam continues: "The poet is linked only to his providential interlocutor. It is not necessary for him to be above his epoch or better than his society. The same François Villon stands far below the average moral and intellectual level of fifteenth-century culture."

The best Russian biographer of Mandelshtam, Alexander Morozov, wrote about "those sides of his nature [the erratic social behavior and total carelessness in mundane matters, reported by many of his friends] that he was to reveal in the painful course of his entry into the new state of time, devoid of history and dispossessed of spirit." In retrospect, the notorious defiant "irresponsibility" of the poet appears to be but a Villonian aspect of his ultimate moral freedom: the freedom "to play hide-and-seek with the spirit," as he wrote in the most complete statement of his religious ideas, the essay on Pushkin and Scriabin written in 1916, of which only some draft fragments have survived. In the total context of his poetry the religious themes do not outweigh the rest of his interests. The gods he contemplated were no different from his domestic deities, the poets of the past, who "allowed themselves" to be purposefully incorporated in his own verse by means of his unique method of transforming quotations into a purely poetic device, comparable to a distant rhyme. In a poem dated 1909 he wrote:

> There are chaste charms,—
> High harmony, deep peace;
> Far from the ethereal lyres
> Are the lares set up by me. . . .
>
> Some gods there is no need to praise:
> They are your equals, as it were,

> And, with a careful hand,
> It is permitted to replace them.

In churches, the spiritual essence of which he identified with their architecture, as in poetry and history, he valued the organic principle of "creative exchange" leading to eternal return and renewal of "joyful recognition." Notre Dame in his poem grew from the soil on which "the Roman judge sat in judgment over an alien people," while in its companion piece, "Hagia Sophia" (1912), also in *Stone*, "Justinian is an example for all ages" because "Ephesian Diana permitted then her one hundred seven green marble pillars to be stolen for the sake of the alien gods" and placed in the church of Divine Wisdom. Divine wisdom, God's memory as the master builder, was one of the very few concepts that young Mandelshtam inherited from Judaism, but only seven of its house's pillars came from *The Proverbs* of Solomon. The remaining one hundred were a gift of alien gods: the poet received the sophiological doctrine from Russian religious philosophers, Soloviev and especially Father Pavel Florenskii, whose *Stolp i utverzhdenie istiny* (Pillar and Ground of Truth, 1914) became Mandelshtam's favorite reading. Judaism inspired in young Mandelshtam fear and a sense of oppression. Only much later, in the 1920's, did he learn to "love and respect fear" as the source of spiritual guidance. Then he wrote to his wife: "I love only you and the Jews."

There is a parallel between Mandelshtam's quest for university education and his religious search. Both were formally desultory and creatively fruitful. Both made him experience his Judaism as a shameful burden: Russian imperial universities had a restrictive Jewish quota to protect the native population from unfair competition, and the otherwise liberal members of the Religious-Philosophical Society generally referred to Mandelshtam as "the little jew boy." Like many other Russian Jews, he decided to study in Germany and spent two terms at Heidelberg studying Old French, art history (especially Venetian painting), and philosophy. Here he wrote some excellent verse, including a piece in which he read the omens of the future war in "the indescribable flight performed by every soul in sacred fear: a swallow before the storm." Then apparently his health began to decline again, and he was forced to return to Russia. His affliction seemed to be cardiac asthma, angina pectoris or, perhaps, pulmonary sclerosis, and a number of nervous complaints.

He spent the spring of 1910 at a Finnish spa, where he befriended Sergey Kablukov, the kindly and refined secretary of the Religious-Philosophical Society, and one of the earliest unreserved admirers of his poetry, whose diary is an invaluable—and so far the only—documentary source on Mandelshtam's early years. In July Mandelshtam undertook what turned out to be his last trip to Europe: he went to a sanatorium near Berlin, then to Switzerland and Italy. In October he returned to Russia—penniless and resembling, according to a vicious later memoirist, Georgii Ivanov, Dostoevsky's Idiot under similar circumstances. However, while he was abroad, his poems were published for the first time, in the August issue of *Apollon*, a trend-setting and elegant journal of art and letters established a year earlier. The same memoirist could not help recording the pang of envy he had experienced reading those five poems. They were the high point of the abstract, somewhat decadent idealism that was associated in Russian symbolist poetry with Ivan Konevskoy and Fedor Sologub; they contained the traditional images of the world as a metaphysical prison, the artist as the creator of artificial worlds, and so on, but they also conveyed, in their shimmering, unsteady (and, of course, untranslatable) rhythm, a totally new intonation of intimate "teleological" warmth:

> I have a body—what shall I do with it,
> So single and so mine?
> For the quiet joy of breathing and of living,
> Whom shall I thank, tell me?

> I am the gardener and I am the flower;
> In the world's prison I am not alone.
>
> (1909)

During the ensuing period of twenty-three years when Mandelshtam was a published author in Russia and then in the USSR he was treated with unreserved admiration by some and utter contempt by others and was more often mocked than praised in print. Still, his presence in Russian poetry remains an indelible pattern ("mandelstamp," as it was called by Ilya Selvinsky, a Soviet author of constructivist doggerel verse), just as he predicted in his first publication:

> Eternity's glass has now been clouded
> With my breath, with my warmth.
> A pattern will be fixed upon it,
> Unrecognizable of late.
> Let the moment's mist trickle down:
> The loveable pattern cannot be crossed out.

The initial success with *Apollon*'s snobbish publisher, which Mandelshtam probably owed to Gumilev, who eventually became *Apollon*'s literary editor, was short-lived. Subsequently, that journal published Mandelshtam once or twice a year, and only as a result of much pressure from him and his friends. Liberal magazines would not print him because of his "antisocial" stance, conservative ones, because he was a Jew. Valery Bryusov, the anti-Semitic former dean of Russian decadence, who was institutionalized as the poetry editor of the sedate and well-paying monthly *Russkaia Myrl'* (Russian Thought), rejected all of his poems offhand. (After 1917, as a Communist censor, Bryusov continued to attack Mandelshtam in print and in his confidential reports.) Meanwhile the fortunes of Mandelshtam's family had changed for the worse. To go back to Heidelberg was out of the question. In May 1911 Mandelshtam formally converted in a Methodist Episcopal church in Finland and received, without much ado, from a sympathetic clergyman, the paper that Heinrich Heine had labeled, with bitter wit, "a Jew's entry ticket to European culture": the certificate of baptism. In the fall of 1911 he enrolled in the Romance department of the Historical-Philological Faculty of St. Petersburg University, the next best place to Europe that he never saw again. He promised his mother to persist and to get his degree, but his mother died, the revolution began, and in May 1917 he left the university having completed six full terms (in as many years) and without taking his final examinations. His magnificent essays on Danka, Villon, André Chénier, Henri-Auguste Barbier (1923), and the firm ground of philology that supports and motivates even the most whimsical and enigmatic of his poems are the final justification of his university years.

Two events that determined Mandelshtam's literary future and his poetic identity took place in March 1911. On 14 March, at Ivanov's "tower" apartment, he met Akhmatova. A few days later Gumilev, her husband and Mandelshtam's Parisian acquaintance, returned to Petersburg from his expedition to Ethiopia. (He loved Africa and exotic adventure, predilections that earned him in the simple-minded Soviet critical idiom the title of "a singer of Russian imperialism" and "a follower of Kipling"; he was neither.) The three met frequently at various poetry readings. At first, there were some frictions between them; Gumilev was dictatorial, Mandelshtam touchy, Akhmatova willful. Today their names are inseparable: they are acmeism, the most mysterious, challenging, and inspiring of the Russian postsymbolist currents, and the only one whose name remains a vivid evocation of the martyred Platinum Age rather than a mendacious term in a musty college survey. When it was coined, inimical contemporaries described it as a "meaningless catchword," an uninspired and unhallowed exercise in futility.

The movement began at first as a loose association formed when a number of poets left Ivanov's poetic academy to protest his violent attack upon Gumilev's latest long poem, "Bludnyi syu" ("The Prodigal Son," 1911).

Named Tsekh Poetov (The Guild of Poets), the new union stressed, first and foremost, craftsmanship. It is fascinating to compare the pieces of various members of the guild written at the same time and on the same subjects—which were apparently set in advance and included the building of the admiralty, Edgar Allan Poe, an American bar, and the eve of a market day in a medieval town—in order to reconstruct the guild's guidelines. The secret mentor of the guild was Mikhail Lozinsky, a poet and a translator of outstanding learning and taste, who published the guild's little magazine *Giperborei* (The Hyperborean). By the spring of 1912 there developed within the guild, originally so broad as to include even Blok, the inner circle of six or seven poets who proclaimed the new literary current. Its two manifestos published in *Apollon* in January 1913 were by Gumilev and Sergey Gorodetsky, the neopagan author of the poems that formed the libretto of Igor Stravinsky's *Le sacre du printemps* (*The Rite of Spring*, 1913). (Gorodetsky preferred to call the movement "Adamism.") Gumilev demanded a "more stable balance of forces" in poetic texts (for example, less irrational music and more intelligible meaning), a "more accurate definition of the subject-object relationship" than the mystically inclined Russian symbolists could provide, a "loyalty to this earth" in the spirit of Friedrich Nietzsche's Zarathustra, and less involvement with the "Beautiful Lady Theology."

Acmeism had been wrongly termed a conservative neoclassical revival movement by many critics. In fact, the acmeists, similar to their teacher Annensky, derived the very word "classical" from Latin *classicum,* which means the call of the military bugle, and Mandelshtam, who identified the classical not with what has been but with what ought to be, contrasted the inexhaustible newness of "Catullus' silver trumpet" with the "futuristic riddles" that so soon grow obsolete.

Mandelshtam attended the meetings of the guild regularly, and in 1912 his first book of poetry was announced under the title "Rakovina" (Seashell) on the back page of one of the guild's editions. That book never materialized. Mandelshtam's manifesto, "The Morning of Acmeism," prepared for publication together with the other two in *Apollon,* was likewise mysteriously supressed by the "syndics" of the guild; it was printed, in an apparently updated form, in 1919 by Mandelshtam's friend and fellow acmeist Vladimir Narbut in his Voronezh almanac *Sirena* (Siren).

Mandelshtam added to the program of acmeism the requirement that "the conscious meaning of the word, Logos," be redefined in formal aesthetic terms and granted "equal rights" with such constructive elements of poetry as rhythm and sound texture. "Word as Such," the slogan of Russian futurism, was accepted by Mandelshtam, but not, as the futurists would have it, as the word "liberated" from its conscious "vocabulary meaning" and therefore capable of becoming an artistic "thing." On the contrary, his manifesto affirmed the reality of meaning as poetic "building material." The essays "Slovo i Kul'tura" ("The Word and Culture," 1921) and "Oprirode slova" ("On the Nature of the Word," 1922) added to it a declaration, directed against both the futurists and the neorealists, of the "Word-Psyche's" spiritual independence from the "material thing" it denoted and of the "systemic" nature of the nexus between the meaningful sound and the audible meaning. These statements reflected Mandelshtam's careful reading of the linguistic passage in Florenskii's *Stolp i utverzhdenie istiny:*

> The "external form of the word," its "phoneme" and its "morpheme," exist for the sake of its soul,—the sememe—and outside it [the sememe], is not the word but merely the physical process; the sememe merely takes into account, to a certain point, the external form, but is not at all its slave.

(p. 786)

These abstract considerations were of utmost importance for Mandelshtam. The new poetics demanded total conviction; but whenever it became too normative, Mandelshtam

would repudiate it and proclaim a single valid criterion for a definition of poetics: taste and breadth of scope. In 1923 he wrote to an overzealous camp follower: "Acmeism wanted to be only the 'conscience' of poetry. It is a judgment over poetry, and not poetry itself." These words reflect a profound understanding of style as a code of reception, based on the criteria of rightness and value. Only superficially they appear to contradict the defiant definition of acmeism he gave ten years later to a hissing audience of Soviet vulgarians: "Acmeism was a longing for world culture."

More than any other twentieth-century style acmeism defied exact definition because it was a typical "final" style, literally "the last word of modernism," as Boris Eikhenbaum, the formalist scholar and critic, described it. Crowning as it did the antithetic succession of realism and symbolism, it overcame, in the Hegelian sense, both and evolved into a truly synthetic style. It upheld the banner of medieval nominalism in identifying essences with words and perceiving in the word the supreme miracle endowing human history with unity, durability, and purpose. The word of the acmeists did not have to provide an escape from the "blue prison" of the real world to the "more real"; the world was one, a God-granted palace; the products of human consciousness were as real as the objects of the external world, and much more durable, while the verbal art—the word as such in poetry—was the "monstrously condensed reality" of the phenomena. The aesthetics of acmeism presupposed a memory of the poetic texts of the past and their recognition in quotations, often transformed and cryptic, as a distanced poetic reiteration. At the same time it posited the ideal reader in the future and aimed at an effect of unexpectedness. Although constructed with unfailing logic, the message of an acmeist text is as unpredictable as a solution to a riddle. The dominant trope of acmeism's figurative language, too, is a riddle-like hybrid of metaphor and metonymy, which serves to build a complex system of intellectual analogies juxtaposing the similar in the most distant and at the same time bringing to light the occult similarity between parts and wholes. When young Mandelshtam called fate a gypsy woman the trope was motivated in a double way: fate is as inconstant as a gypsy, and gypsies tell fortunes. The third justification of the trope can be found outside Mandelshtam's poem: in Pushkin's tale "Tsygany" ("Gypsies," 1823–1824), which ends with the words "And from the fates there is no defense." This concealed reference is a sample of Mandelshtam's favorite poetic and semantic device. In his poetry, even more consistently than in the poetry of his friends, the semantic and poetic potentialities with which the word is endowed through the history of its use in other poetic contexts are activated by means of such elliptic riddlelike quotations, which force the reader to turn to their sources in order to find a frame of reference, the so-called subtext in terms of which his text has to be deciphered.

The essential features of this method were in full evidence already in *Stone,* Mandelshtam's first book of twenty-three short lyric poems (less than one-tenth of what he had ready), which finally appeared in 1913 at the author's expense with the mark of a nonexistent publishing house AKME on its moss-green cover, which was embellished with a baroque heraldic design: a cupid with a lyre riding a decrepit lion. Tyutchev, the poet of senile love, inspired one of the poems that Mandelshtam sent to Ivanov from Heidelberg. It was about a sad, childish Eros placed on a rock and surprised that there are such things in the world as old age and green moss over a wet stone. Typically for Mandelshtam, the poem did not enter the collection.

The first part of *Stone* is a culmination of the metaphysical tendency in symbolism and an ultimate confrontation of Verlaine's "musique avant toute chose" and Tyutchev's denial of the possibility of genuine communication ("a thought uttered is a lie") in an image of "primeval muteness," the unborn pure sound that preserves the precosmic unity of being:

> Remain foam, Aphrodite;
> And, word, revert to music;
> And, heart, shy away from another heart,
> Fused with the first principle of life.
> ("Silentium," 1910)

The second half of the book, as Gumilev notes in his excellent review of *Stone,* is acmeistic. Mandelshtam transforms symbols into analogies and mysteries into intellectual problems. A key to his new technique is the title of the collection, which, besides being an etymologically motivated anagram of ACME (*kamen* < Indo-European *akmen-,* same root as *akme,* originally, "sharp stone"), contains yet another reference to Tyutchev, evoking his poem "Problème" (1833), which is about the stone that "rolled down from the mountain to the valley, torn loose by itself, or cast by a thinking hand." The association became clear when Mandelshtam included in the 1916 edition of the book (three times the size of the first edition, but retaining its original composition) a sonnet that restates Tyutchev's "problem": "Who casts stones at us from on high? / And does the stone deny the bondage of earthly dust?" In "The Morning of Acmeism," Mandelshtam wrote:

> Tyutchev's stone . . . is the word. The voice of the matter sounds in this unexpected fall like articulate speech. [In a story published by Gumilev in 1907 the first word uttered by the first man was an imitation of the rumble of a falling stone.] This challenge can only be answered with architecture. The acmeists piously pick up the mysterious Tyutchevian stone and lay it in the foundation of their building.

Tyutchev was referring in his enigmatic quatrain to the "stone cut out without hands" in Daniel's vision, and, in view of the traditional messianic interpretation of this biblical passage, Mandelshtam identified this stone with Christ-Logos, "the Word made flesh" and "the stone which the builders rejected" that "is become the head of the corner." The kenotic myth of the suffering and redeeming word that shares the path of flesh and offers it life eternal, because of its tremendous explanatory metapoetic value, became the central analogy of poetic communication in the acmeist nominalism. From this starting point one can surmise a further system of more esoteric analogies that the masters of the Guild of Poets had borrowed from Freemasonry, which are expressed in such terms of masonic origin as "the Lost and Retrieved Word" and "the Occult Stone."

The title *Stone* replaced the original "Seashell" but did not eliminate its main theme, preserved in the title poem of the unrealized collection, which was included in all the editions of *Stone.* Together, "Seashell" and "Stone" represented two aspects of Mandelshtam's defense of poetry against the reproach of Nietzsche, who had so profoundly affected the insights and the outlooks of all twentieth-century trends in Russian poetry. Of all Russian poets, Mandelshtam alone took issue with the chapter "Von den Dichtern" (*Thus Spake Zarathustra,* 1883–1891), conveniently disregarded by Nietzsche's symbolist disciples, which reads in part:

> "But poets lie too much!" [Here Nietzsche quotes Plato, whom Mandelshtam addressed in another of his early defenses of poetry, "Deception is, I know, impossible in vision."] Ah, I have often cast my nets into your sea hoping to catch good fish, but I would always draw from it an old god's head. So the sea would give a stone to the hungry.

In Nietzsche's calling the gift of poetry a stone Mandelshtam could not fail to recognize Pushkin's famous anti-utilitarian argument: "You set the price upon the idol of Belvedere by its weight. You see no use for it. This marble is a god! So what? You still prefer your own cooking pot" ("The Rabble," 1828). Ten years later, in starving Petrograd, Mandelshtam found an image to reconcile the ancient feud of the mob crying for food and the poet craving for beauty:

the hellenistic earthenware utensil preserving the sacred warmth of human fireplace.

Zarathustra's attack does not end with that reproach. He further compares poets to hard sea creatures: "Of course, one finds pearls in them, but the more similar they are to shellfish. And instead of a soul I have often found in them salty slime." Mandelshtam took up polemically Nietzsche's image of the empty seashell and made it address Zarathustra's creative night in a poem that anagrammatized the very name of Nietzsche in the Russian verb *tsenish* (value):

Perhaps you have no use for me,
Night; out of the universal abyss,
Like a seashell without pearls,
I have been cast upon your shore.

You foam the waves indifferently
And sing uncompromisingly,
But you shall love and you shall value [*otsenish'*]
The falsehood of the needless shell. . . .

And the walls of the fragile seashell,
Like an uninhabited heart's home,
You shall fill with the whispers of foam,
With mist, wind, and rain.

A supremely sensitive receptacle, Mandelshtam's seashell was soon alerted to the growing rumble of a different swell. Early in 1914 he suddenly became interested again in civic poetry. On 30 March he gave a talk about it to the Society of Poets. Then he composed a short poem about the ambiguous bond between the sovereign and the poet in Russia: the name of the victim in that poem, Alexander, can be taken to refer either to Pushkin, or to the emperor, or to both. Although not a Wagnerite, he wrote, using the rhythm of Heinrich Heine's *Knittelvers,* a piece about the performance of Richard Wagner's *Der Ring des Nibelungen* (1853–1874), with an ominous image of the final curtain:

The Valkyries are flying; the bows are singing;
The cumbersome opera is coming to an end.

OSIP MANDELSHTAM

With heavy fur coats the flunkeys are waiting
On the marble staircases for their masters.

The curtain is ready now to fall for good.
The fool is still clapping at the gods.
The coachmen stomp their feet by the fires outside.
"The carriage of So-and-so!" Exit. The end.

During the summer he composed several poems about Rome ("There are entrails of sacrifice to foretell the war"), an ominous piece about the ripening fruit inspired by Amos' vision, and a magnificently anagrammatic evocation of the European map changing its mysterious borders for the first time since a hundred years earlier "Metternich had pointed his quill at Bonaparte."

Paradoxically, to Mandelshtam and most of his friends and literary contemporaries, the war came as a revelation of Russian, European, and universal unity: a communion of sacrificial blood. For the last time in history Europe still shared certain basic common principles, and the German ambassador could shed tears of grief on the shoulder of the Russian foreign minister after delivering the declaration of war. Of the guild poets, only Mikhail Lozinsky immediately realized, in his poem "To byl poslednii god" ("The Last Year," 1914), that the offering would be rejected and the miracle of communion would not take place. Mandelshtam, on the other hand, evoked the spirit of July 1914 a year later in the most remarkable of his poems of ecumenic devotion:

Now the monstrance, like a golden sun,
Is suspended in the air—a magnificent moment.
Here only the Greek language must resound:
Hands hold the whole world like an ordinary apple.

The solemn zenith of the divine service,
Light in the rotund edifice, under the dome, in July,
To make our brimming breast heave with a timeless
 sigh
For the meadow where time does not run.

And the Eucharist lasts like an eternal noon—
All take communion, play and sing;

And, in full view of all, the divine vessel
Streams inexhaustible gladness.

Gumilev and some other friends of Mandelshtam's volunteered. At the end of 1914 Mandelshtam himself went to Warsaw to try to enlist as a medical orderly (as Nietzsche had done in 1870). He did not succeed, and his experience there allegedly led to a suicide attempt. In January 1915 he returned to the capital. During the rest of the war he worked for the Union of Lands and Cities, an auxiliary war relief organization of the liberal circles. Soon the spirit of warlike elation abandoned him. He now affirmed that not the city of Rome but the place of man in the universe lives in ages:

Kings try to gain possession of it;
Priests justify wars;
And without it houses and altars
Are as contemptible as trash.

In 1915 he became passionately involved with the poet Marina Tsvetaeva, who was of an outspoken pro-German orientation. Under her influence he wrote his "Zverinets" ("Menagerie," 1916), a heraldic ode to peace with the famous words about the "Slavic and Germanic flax in the proto-Aryan cradle," and an anti-English poem calling upon Europe, "the New Hellas" (1916), to reject the gifts of Albion, "whose freedom will ruin Europe." Tsvetaeva was a Muscovite, and he received from her as a love gift the city he had always dreaded as "the obscene capital of Eurasia." He responded with a charming poem about the fifteenth-century cathedrals in the Kremlin, the work of Aristotele Fioraventi ("Tender Assumption Church—Florence in Moscow"). The allusion is especially elegant because the root of the name *Tsvetaeva* means "flower."

Mandelshtam's religious friend Kablukov may have been naive in trying to exorcise, as is evident from his diary, Tsvetaeva's powerful erotic influence, but there is something to his assertion that the Tsvetaeva cycle was "a betrayal of the best traditions of *Stone.*"

Fortunately, the infatuation did not last long. Tsvetaeva was a remarkable poet but a rather depraved woman with a propensity for mythomania and romantic play-acting. Her attitude toward Mandelshtam, judging by her poems, memoirs, and letters, ranged between tenderness and cruelty. Mandelshtam eventually condemned the pseudo-historicity and fake Muscovite folksiness of Tsvetaeva's poems about Russia, some of which were dedicated to him, whereas she, in exile, literally tore to pieces copies of his book *The Noise of Time* as a betrayal of the white cause. Her sister Anastasiia, on the other hand, left the earliest and most lovingly drawn portrait of Mandelshtam, with the texts of some of his then-unpublished poems, in her book *Dym, dym, dym* (*Smoke, Smoke, Smoke,* 1916).

The best of Mandelshtam's love poems written at that time, such as "Solomiulea" (The Straw, 1916) were dedicated to Princess Salomeya Andronnikova, a famous Petersburg beauty. A result of his immersion in Poe, they recapture the mood of "Ligeia" (1838) and "The Raven" (1845) and contain some remarkable bilingual homonyms and transpositions of Poe's sound patterns into Russian.

In the summer of 1916, while Mandelshtam was in the Crimea and still in love with Tsvetaeva, his mother died of a heart attack—after discovering that Mandelshtam's father had a mistress. The poem that Mandelshtam wrote on the occasion of his mother's death is one of the thematic and emotional keys to his second book of verse. It expresses the overlapping presence of two eras, emblematized by two suns, the old one, which refuses to relinquish its light and die, and the new one, the essence of which is the anticipation of the end of the world:

> This night is irreparable,
> While at your place there is still light.
> At the gates of Jerusalem
> The black sun has risen.
>
> The yellow sun is more terrible —
> Lullaby, lullaby—

> In a bright temple the Jews
> Were burying my mother.
>
> Having no grace
> And deprived of priesthood,
> In a bright temple the Jews
> Were chanting prayers over a woman's
>   remains.
>
> And over Mother were ringing
> The voices of the Israelites.
> I woke in my cradle
> In the aura of the black sun.

The tribal law of the family and sexual procreation is the yellow sun that shines over the old era of Judaism and its temple. The eschatological image of the black sun in this particular poem derives from *Temnyilik* (*The Dark Visage,* 1911), a book by Vasilii Rozanov, the heretical Russian philosopher and brilliant writer who was preoccupied with the reciprocal relationships among Judaism, Christianity, sex, and human sacrifice. The ascetic trend in the Orthodox church, he wrote, was "the black halo around the Black Sun. This Black Sun, the great universal *Death,* the metaphysics of Death, is worshiped by the black-robed monks." Yet Mandelshtam found the yellow sun of his kinfolk more terrible. At the time he saw in Judaism an attempt to stop the setting sun of history.

Mandelshtam spent New Year's Eve 1917 with Kablukov. According to the latter's diary, the poet was so depressed by his "erotic madness" that he contemplated conversion to Russian Orthodoxy "because sex was particularly dangerous to those who have left Judaism." He did not convert, but in his poetry written during the first year of the Revolution contemplated the destiny of the Russian church. The democratic republic proclaimed in March freed it from government control and reestablished the office of the patriarch, abolished under Peter I. But it was too late for the church to influence the course of the events. As Alexander Kartashov, a member of the Religious-

Philosophical Society appointed by the Provisional Government to take charge of religious affairs, had pointed out a year earlier, "the dynamic spirit of prophecy had left the church." Mandelshtam dedicated to Kartashov his remarkable poem about the young levite among the priests, who prophesies, while "the destroyed temple is being gloomily rebuilt," a new exile, "the night of Jerusalem and the fume of nonbeing." (Kartashov died in exile in 1960.)

The poems of 1917 speak of the path of oblivion and darkness that the revolution had taken. Only the recollections of Pushkin's "Vol'nost" (Ode to Freedom), written exactly a century earlier, and the images of Mandelshtam's friends, the heroic democrats crucified or torn to pieces by the ignorant mob, shine as torches of memory in that bestial night. There is no grudge, only infinite sadness, in Mandelshtam's evaluation of the common people's role in the Bolshevist takeover. He wrote in "To Cassandra" (1917), a poem addressed to Anna Akhmatova:

> In December of 1917,
> We lost everything through love:
> One was robbed by the will of the people;
> The other [the people] robbed itself.

In December, the Communists abolished the freedom of the press. Lenin appears in Mandelshtam's poems as the "October favorite, preparing for us the yoke of violence and malice," along with the other protagonists of the "disgusting Scythian festivity," the murderous armored car, the bristling machinegunner, and the chorus: "the applauding evil rabble." The concluding piece of the thematic cycle dealing with the revolution, "Sumerlei svobody" ("The Twilight of Freedom"), blends the images of the church and the state in a single traditional symbol of the ship, and the historical characters of Tychon, "the belated patriarch," and Alexander Kerensky, "Peter's cub," the last ruler of free Russia, in one unforgettable portrait of the people's leader tearfully assuming the "fatal burden of authority." The last words of the poem answer Kartashov's speech on the church reform and fulfillment, in which he pointed out that, while the early church lived in anticipation of the kingdom of God, the later church, sailing its ship in the "twilight of history," has become oblivious of its final aim. Now Mandelshtam, echoing St. Paul, encouraged "men and brethren" on the sinking ship of time to take heart at the end of freedom's "crepuscular year," bear whatever "the vast, clumsy, squeaking turn of the rudder" might bring, and "remember even in the Lethean cold that earth was worth ten heavens to us." Written for the first anniversary of the March revolution, the poem, one of Mandelshtam's most difficult, was misunderstood by most of its readers—and published by the Soviets.

Meanwhile, the poet's path of reluctant accommodation had begun. His main motive was astutely pinpointed in the memoirs of his widow: "The decisive part in the subjugation of the intelligentsia was played not by terror and bribery (though, God knows, there was enough of both), but by the word 'Revolution,' which none of them could bear to give up." Mandelshtam's attempts at finding a place for himself in the new Soviet Russia of ruthless class struggle and increasing ideological control of every sphere of intellectual endeavor followed a uniform pattern from the very outset until the bitter end. He would first persuade himself that his work in the People's Commissariat of Enlightenment (his first Soviet job, which lasted until the summer of 1918) or as a literary editor in a particularly obnoxious Young Communist League newspaper (in Moscow in 1929) was honest service to the working class. However, as the poet Vladislav Khodasevich, Mandelshtam's greatest contemporary, who likewise worked in Soviet institutions for several years, observed, "the revolution demanded from everybody not honest service but slavery and flattery." Revolted, Mandelshtam would leave his job, usually with a tremendous row, and rely on his protectors to sort things out. (In those early years he was protected by Larisa

Reysner, a young writer and influential Bolshevik.) Having left his government job, Mandelshtam went to the Crimea. During the rest of the Civil War he kept moving back and forth between the south, held by the Germans or the White Army, and the north, held by the Reds. The German revolution and withdrawal apparently found him in the south; one of his poems contains an obscure reference to the suicide of the Austrian military governor of Odessa.

In spring 1919 he emerged in the Red-occupied Kiev, where he met his future wife Nadezhda Khazina. From there he returned to the Crimea held by the White forces of General Peter Wrangel. In Koktebel and Theodosia he wrote a great deal of poetry inspired by the Mediterranean-Hellenic associations of the place; the Black Sea had always been for him the gateway to the classical world. In the summer of 1920 he was arrested for a reason that remains unclear. The times were violent, the White counterintelligence vindictive, and Mandelshtam Jewish. According to one version, the poet from whom Mandelshtam had borrowed a beautiful French edition of Dante asked the Theodosia port authority to prevent Mandelshtam from leaving the Crimea with his book. There may also have been other reasons: Mandelshtam had read his prosocialist poem "Akter i Rabochii" ("The Actor and the Workman," 1920) in public. However it may have been, he was very soon freed through the intervention of a friendly White colonel and sailed for Georgia, then an independent republic. Promptly jailed by its Menshevik government as a "double agent" (Moscow's and Wrangel's), he was eventually suffered to leave; he returned to Soviet Russia in the company of his old acquaintance Ilya Ehrenburg, who described their grotesque trip in his memoirs.

In October 1920 he arrived in Petersburg and was feted as the victim of Wrangel's White terror—and even more as the author of new and marvelous poems. After one of his public readings even Blok, who hated acmeism and loathed the Jews, confided to his diary: "Mandelshtam has grown a great deal. Gradually one gets used to the kike and sees the artist. His poems grow out of dreams—very original ones, lying entirely in the realm of art." A stern critic, although a personal friend, Gumilev too acclaimed Mandelshtam as "the creator of eternal values."

In March 1921, "sensing the coming executions," as he wrote in a poem ten years later, he "escaped from the roar of the mutinous events [it was the time of the Kronstadt uprising against the Bolsheviks] to the Nereids of the Black Sea." On his way south he went to Kiev and found Nadezhda Khazina. Together they traveled to the now Red Crimea and the still nominally independent Georgia. The news of Gumilev's execution by the Petersburg Cheka on trumped-up charges of "monarchist conspiracy" reached Mandelshtam in Tiflis. Ten years earlier the young members of the Guild of Poets lamented the make-believe, toylike lot of the poet in the modern world. Now that destiny turned out to be real and terrifying. Courage, manliness, loyalty, and long memory were the acmeist virtues, and the heroic death of Gumilev became the new cornerstone of the acmeist temple-legend. The poem that Mandelshtam wrote after the event opened a new period in his poetry. It spoke about the star beam shining like salt upon the blade of the ax and melting in the black barrel: the salt of the covenant that purifies the sacrifice and makes "the earth truer and more fearsome."

In 1922 Mandelshtam and Khazina went to live in Moscow. In spite of the political drive beginning against acmeism, which at the time had many young followers, he and Akhmatova stubbornly refused to emigrate when many of their friends left. Mandelshtam's reason was both personal and philosophical. He believed, with Horace and Pushkin, that one's fate is the same everywhere. He also believed in what he had written in his essay about the Russian Catholic philosopher Chaadaev (1915): the moral freedom of choice, "the most precious gift of the Russian land to Europe," implies being able to return from "the immortal spring of Rome" to "stuffy Moscow."

While he was traveling, a little volume of his poetry appeared in Berlin early in 1922. Kuzmin was responsible for its composition and title, for which he used the heading of one of the poems, "Tristia," a reference to the elegies written by Ovid in his Black Sea exile. Soon Mandelshtam prepared and published in Moscow his own version of his new poems, *Vtoraia kniga* (The Second Book, 1923). Its unifying theme is the reiterated image of the final periods in political, national, religious, and cultural history: the end of the Pelopids, Troy before its fall, postexilic Judea, the declining Moscow of the time of troubles, Venice in the eighteenth century, the dying St. Petersburg of 1918, the "wolf's tracks of misfortune" upon the steps of St. Isaac's Cathedral closed by the Bolsheviks (in the last of Mandelshtam's ecclesiastic poems), man's place in the world growing cold after his death. This was the time of Oswald Spengler's *Der Untergang des Abend landes* (*The Decline of the West*, 1918–1922), but Mandelshtam's historical attitude was quite different. It was rather a justification of Goethe's message "Stirb und Werde" (Die and Become) and of the thoughts expressed by Mandelshtam's favorite Konstantin Leontíev on the margin of the French edition of Eduard von Hartmann's *Die Religion der Zukunft* (*The Religion of the Future*, 1876): "The good, the best, the higher philosophy always emerges only before the end of cultural and political periods, and some principles of this deathbed philosophy nourish the roots of the possible future politico-religious growths." Mandelshtam now accepted the necessity of "social adaption" and of grafting the old, humanist, and humane traditions to the wild new growth. The government newspaper *Izvestiia* published a poem out of *Vtoraia kniga* in which Mandelshtam expressed a hope of finding his useful place and compared himself to "the drying make-weight of the loaves baked earlier, the stale stepson of the ages."

The ebb and tide of the spirit of grace ("the dove in the ark") visiting the dying cultures constitutes the emotional rhythm of the book, the title of which etymologically expresses in Russian (*vtoraia*, meaning "second"; *povtoriat'*, meaning "to repeat") the idea of return and repetition, the fulcrum of Mandelshtam's pan-poetic worldview. In the poem "Tristia" Mandelshtam recollects and reinterprets Nietzsche's doctrine of the eternal return, quoting almost verbatim the words of Zarathustra, "I have taken many a leave; I know the heartbreaking last hours," against the thematic background of Ovid's last night in Rome before his exile:

> I have learned the art of parting
> In the bareheaded night laments.
> Oxen chew, and expectation lingers:
> This is the last hour of the city vigils.

The endlessly repeated parting in flesh and the eternal reunion in spirit are for Mandelshtam the sources of purely poetic joy:

> Everything was before: everything will be repeated anew;
> And we find sweet only the instant of recognition.

The most personal poems of the *Vtoraia kniga* are the so-called Lethean Lines, which give the fullest expression, in quasi-mythological form, to the acmeist preoccupation with historical, cultural, verbal, and personal memory. Here the reality, soul, word, and name appear as protagonists in four interrelated texts that describe the act of recollection in terms of the Orphic or Eleusinian descent to the kingdom of the dead: "To die means to remember!"

The final, third and greatly enlarged, edition of *Stone* followed the *Vtoraia kniga* in 1923, and it was brought out by the State Publishing House. Both collections contain some of Mandelshtam's latest and rather different poems, eventually separated out into a distinct sequence "1921–1925." These became the artistic and intellectual focal point of his life's work. Their complexity, depth, and tragic power remain unsurpassed in modern poetry. The sequence in its final published form commenced with "Kontsert na vokzale" ("Concert at the Railroad Station"), which completed—and reversed—the main theme of *Vtoraia kniga.* The poem is a dirge for the dead nineteenth century, the much-reviled iron age of the railroads—and, at the same time, the golden age of music. At the Pavlovsk *vauxhall* near Petersburg, by the side of the first railroad station in Russia (hence the word *vokzal* has come to mean in Russian a station building), where concerts used to be given every summer, "music sounds for the last time at the funeral feast of the beloved shadow" before fulfilling Gogol's old prophecy and leaving mankind forever. There is no intimation of its return: universal harmony enchants for the last time the fearful, trembling, suffocating "iron world" of the station under a sky seething with worms. A tremendous range of images of the dying century emerges from other poems of the cycle: the beautiful, pitiful, and cruel beast whose back is broken and whose vertebrae can only be mended with sacrificial blood; the agonizing saturnine idol of Daniel's vision sharing its illness and its earthenware fragility with the son of the age keeping vigil over his sovereign's deathbed; the resonant, responsive, hollow golden apple that suddenly vanishes although its vibrations still ring.

When Mandelshtam worked on *Vtoraia kniga* the imminence of the world's end seemed to be in the air as in the days of early Christianity. The end did not come then, but the historical fabric of Russian life had disintegrated, and the brotherhood of culture in Russia, no longer "of this world," began to live like the suffering church, in a permanent state of emergency. In 1922, Pasternak proclaimed a "moratorium on Doomsdays." He later wrote to Mandelshtam that the "final nature" of the epoch had lost its validity: "Only that ends that is allowed to end."

Mandelshtam vacillated. In 1921 he welcomed the end of history and compared it in his essay "The Word and Culture" to Leconte de Lisle's ultimate "virgin forest" of a "new nature"

without man, "nature-Psyche, wherein every tree will be a dryad, and every phenomenon will bespeak of its metamorphosis." He began to search for a protective talisman to prevent the end of history. In his poem about "the language of Parisian cobblestones," "Iazyk bulyzhnika" (1923), the lion cub—Barbier's allegorical figure of the betrayed revolutionary people—pitifully displays the thorn in its paw, but there is no Androcles to help him and therefore no mercy for its future victims to expect. In the elegy "1 ianvarie 1924" ("January 1, 1924," 1924) the bureaucratic thorn in the flesh of the workers' state assumes the form of "the pike's bone" of old injustice, a stuck key of the Underwood typewriter on which Moscow attempts to perform its "simple sonatina"—a pale "shadow of the powerful sonatas" of nineteenth century liberal Russian political philosophy. This fishbone, once removed from the choking typewriter, would become a talisman against the hunger of the Leviathan, the murderous and deceitful modern political state that craves adulation.

The most abstract and cryptic of the "talismanic" poems of that period is "The Slate Ode," which conveys by means of its incantatory intonations, multidimensional semantics, and quasimagical composition pattern Mandelshtam's model of the poetic word's ontology in its ambivalent relation to the greatest predator of all: the hungry time ready to "swallow all the works of men." In the passage of "The Word and Culture" inspired by Florenskii's parable about the name of the Creator imprinted in every building brick of the creation, Mandelshtam writes:

> Cultural values color the state, endowing it with tint, form, even gender. Inscriptions on state buildings, tombs, and gates insure the state against being destroyed by time. . . . Time wants to devour the state. . . . Compassion for the state that denies the word is the modern poet's path of social involvement and his selfless feat.

The image of the obliterated slate-board draft of Derzhavin's last poem, "Reka vremen" ("The

River of Time," 1816), based on the introductory lines of Anna Comnena's twelfth-century Byzantine chronicle *The Alexiad*), is blended in "The Slate Ode" with the scenery of one of Mikhail Lermontov's last poems, "Vykhozhu odin ia na dorogu" ("I set out alone on the road," 1841): the lonely "flinty path" glittering through the mist under festive stars that "talk to each other." The manly hardness of Lermontov's "flint" is forced in the ode to succumb to the authority of time the teacher: "Blessed is he who called the flint / A disciple of the flowing water." The creative union of water and stone is protected by two talismans: the sacred ring of the predestined return and the lowly horseshoe of earthly historical rhythm.

The latter image is explored further in "Nashedshii podkovu" ("He Who Finds a Horseshoe," 1923), written the same year as "The Slate Ode." This long piece in unrhymed free verse is subtitled "A Pindaric Fragment." The bard of good fortune, of victory, and of divine luck granted by the gods, Pindar taught that the most durable of blessings was the name glorified in songs. From Pindar, Mandelshtam learned to unravel the significance of new events by tracing not only their genealogy but also their mythological and historical analogies in the past. All of Pindar's similes and definitions were reversible for Mandelshtam: not only the song protects the name, but a name can protect the song:

> Thrice blest is he who introduces a name in his
>   song:
> A song adorned with a name
> Lives longer among her peers.

The name that Mandelshtam introduces in his poem is "Neaera": "Neaera's humid black earth, turned up anew every night." This Neaera, also known in classical mythology as Metaneira, mother of Triptolemus of the Eleusinian mysteries of fertility, who was the first man taught by Demeter to plow, converges in the fragment with several other bearers of this name (in the poetry of Albius Tibullus, Chénier, and Lermontov), while preserving its etymological meaning of "newness." Thus Mandelshtam found a name for the goddess of innovation newly invented by him and placed Mnemosyne beside her in his poetic pantheon to illustrate, as it were, his critical pronouncement: "Invention and recollection go hand in hand in poetry; to remember means also to invent; a rememberer is but another kind of inventor" ("Literaturnaía Moskva" [Literary Moscow], 1922).

The thematic center of the "Pindaric Fragment" is an assortment of images of the Russian state and culture, its original ingredients and surviving remains: the timber of the ship "built not by the peaceful Bethlehem carpenter but by the other one"—Peter the Great—used to be, like the Pelion-grown timber of the Argo celebrated by Pindar and Catullus, a forest that had wished "to barter its noble burden for a pinch of salt"; the racehorse lying in the dust still remembers its run, and the horseshoe, all that remains of Peter's steed, preserves the immortal rhythm of Russia's glorious course, just as Russian poetry does. A token of good fortune, it will protect the threshold of its finder and preserver, "and it will never have to strike sparks from the flint again."

Mandelshtam's poems were, to quote Lord Byron, "a talisman to all save him who bore." The intrigues of his fellow writers drove him out of Moscow. He moved to Leningrad in 1924 and was promptly silenced by some secret party ukase directed against the survivors of "former acmeism." The last two poems he had succeeded in publishing in 1925, "Segodnia nochivu . . . " (To-night . . .) and "Ia budu skitat'sia . . . " (I shall roam . . .), were written for his great love, the beautiful and unfortunate Olga Vaksel.

These were still the years of the New Economic Policy, and, although the state-owned periodicals and publishing houses would accept his translations, a small private firm directed by the excellent literary scholar Georgii

Blok, the poet's cousin, brought out Mandelshtam's collection of autobiographical essays, *The Noise of Time,* a landmark in the history of modern Russian prose style, in 1925. Their brilliant wit made at least one learned contemporary critic recall Heine, but their warmly intimate informality devoid of any bitterness continued the unique confessional trend of Rozanov's prose.

In 1928, Mandelshtam's guardian angel in the higher communist circles, Nikolai Bukharin, the most civilized and decent of Lenin's Old Guard, helped him to publish his collected poetry, *Stikhotvoreniia* (*Poems*), which includes the poems of 1921–1925 and a volume of selected critical essays, *O poèzii* (*On Poetry*). Both editions, however, were mutilated by the heavy hand of the censors. The 1922 article "Konets romana" ("The End of the Novel") suffered especially badly, losing the most pertinent passages on "social adaptation" and "survival" as the mainsprings of the new novel, the personages of which had had their biographies and their sense of personal worth expropriated by "real forces."

As if to make up for the loss of his critical argument, Mandelshtam wrote his only work of fiction, a novella entitled *Egipetskaia marka* (*The Egyptian Stamp*), which appeared in the May 1928 issue of the Leningrad monthly *Zvezda* (The Star). It is a maze of dazzling digressions held together by an ostensibly conventional Russian "human interest" story about the ordeal of a little man. Against the background of the disappearing way of life and civilization, "the dear Egypt of things," melting like the water-soluble design on a tamper-proof Egyptian postage stamp, a timid and poor Jewish intellectual, "his head grown bald at Skryabin concerts," attempts to stop, in the summer of 1917, the lynching of a pickpocket by a dutiful mob of revolutionary burghers. A masterpiece of vivid and vigorous intellectual prose, the tale picks up the classical theme of Pushkin's and Gogol's St. Petersburg and develops it as an unexpected and wise rejoinder

to the moral and artistic concerns of the fashionable current literature: Yury Olesha's *Envy,* Yurii Tynianov's *Smert' Vazir-Mukhtara* (*Death of the Minister Plenipotentiary*), and the stories of Mikhail Zoshchenko and Isaak Babel.

Mandelshtam's own ordeal also began in 1928. The publication of his books resulted in a concerted effort on the part of Soviet hack writers to stifle him again. He was accused in the press of having plagiarized somebody else's translation. The incident developed into a long and vicious campaign, in the course of which he lost his Leningrad apartment, had to move to Moscow, and eventually resigned his membership in the writers' professional union. The affair had inaugurated a series of hostile and even violent conflicts between Mandelshtam and Soviet writers, which all followed the same basic pattern. The lynch mob enjoyed baiting him. He and his wife were subjected to humiliating insults or even attacked physically; there was no way of defending their honor except through litigation. The predictably inconclusive or demeaning judgments of various kangaroo "comrades' courts" provoked increasingly furious reactions on his part. Knowing his outspokenness and his temper, Mandelshtam's enemies correctly counted on his eventually saying or doing something that under Soviet conditions would be tantamount to suicide.

Mandelshtam's endless suit against his torturers produced one immortal result. In 1929 he began writing his *Chetvertaia proza* (*Fourth Prose*), an incomparably witty and devastating indictment of "the blood-stained Soviet land" and its "socialism soiled with filthy paws." He renounced "writerdom" as harlotry: "It is incompatible with the honorable title of Jew, of which I am proud. My blood, burdened with the inheritance of sheep breeders, patriarchs, and kings, rebels against the thieving gypsyishness of the writing tribe." The prodigal son was returning to what he had once called the "incestuous bosom" of Jewish identity. *Fourth Prose* was published in the Soviet Union only in 1988, but it became, less one particularly anti-Soviet chapter missing even in the Western editions, an underground samizdat bestseller in the 1960's.

To earn a living, Mandelshtam worked for a Moscow newspaper of the Young Communist League. In the spring of 1930 Bukharin rescued him again by arranging his trip to Armenia, which turned out to be Mandelshtam's last joyful encounter with his beloved south. Subsequently, Bukharin also obtained for him a retirement (at the age of thirty-nine) with a so-called personal pension and, at the end, even a small but separate co-op apartment in a writers' house in Moscow. Bukharin's supporting statement showed as much good will as a man of his declining influence could muster in the face of the ugly mood of the writers' organizations; it acknowledged Mandelshtam's past contributions to Russian (not Soviet) literature and the total impossibility of "putting him to any use under the present circumstances."

He was not allowed to settle down in the Caucasus. Yet even a short sojourn in "the Sabbath land of Armenia" had provided an impetus for the new flowering of his poetic genius. After his "forced return to the Buddhist Moscow where blood squirts from kitchen sinks and women's fingers smell of kerosene," he resumed writing poetry. In a way the urgent, immediate, lyrically unconstrained and passionately outspoken poems of the early 1930's, in which Mandelshtam conveys the poignant mood of the Siberian convicts' traditional songs, are an antithesis of the 1921–1925 poems. Mandelshtam no longer felt it necessary to adapt now that the revolutionary state had begun to massacre its erstwhile ally, the peasantry. He became, like his friend the outstanding peasant poet Klyuev, a spokesman for the millions of victims of Stalin's collectivization: "the terrible shadows of the Ukraine and the Kuban', the hungry peasants." The old populist Socialist-Revolutionary leaven in his blood began to ferment again, and he regained his "sense of rightness."

Owing to the government's treacherous policy of enlisting the support of the traditional, "nonparty" intelligentsia in its struggle against the so-called Trotskyites, Mandelshtam, along with a number of other former "ideological representatives of the class enemy," was suddenly allowed to publish and even to have public readings of his poetry. He did not, however, live up to the government's expectations. His poetry frightened even his friends. He wrote defiantly about the voices of the dead coming from the Leningrad telephones. He repudiated the imperial world but admitted that Petersburg still "ruled sovereign over his thought and emotions" because in a children's book he had seen Lady Godiva with a rippled red mane. This reference to Alfred, Lord Tennyson's "Godiva," 1842 ("Not only we that prate of rights and wrongs have loved the people well") in Ivan Bunin's popular Russian translation seems in retrospect to be an odd and grim prophecy: both Mandelshtam's Petersburg and Tennyson's Coventry were deliberately sacrificed during World War II. In "Za gremuchuiu doblest . . . " (For the resonant valor, 1931)—eventually translated into English by Nabokov—he predicts his own exile to Siberia, physical death, and poetic invulnerability. He does not want to die, but wistfully yet firmly he rejects the alternative path of richly rewarded compromise:

> You and I are so much afraid,
> My big-mouthed mate!
> Oh, how our tobacco crumbles,
> My friend, you nutcracker, you fool!
> Yet one might have whistled
> Through one's life like a starling
> And had a nut cake for dessert. . . .
> But it seems there is no way of doing it.

There are several poems written between 1931 and 1934 in which he addresses the languages he loved best. He begged the Russian language to

Preserve his speech forever for its tang of misfortune and smoke,

For its tar of all-round patience, for the scrupulous
   pitch of work,
Just as the water in the Novgorod wells must be
   black and sweet
To reflect at Christmas the seven-finned star.

In another poem, "Ne iskushai chuzhikh nare-
chii" ("Do not attempt foreign tongues . . . "
1933), he discusses the phonetic temptations
of the Italian language. At the time he was
reading Ariosto and Tasso in the original,
translating Petrarch, and writing a profound
essay on poetics entitled *Razgovor o Dante*
(*Conversation About Dante*, first published in
the United States, in 1966), in which he had
recapitulated by analogy also his own mature
style.

"Knemetskoi rechi," the last poem he ever
published (it appeared in *Literaturnaia gazeta*
on 23 November 1932), was addressed to the
German speech. He invoked in it the enigmatically untraditional "God Nachtigall," a reference to the suffering nightingale, the redeemer
of the forest birds, in Heine's poem "Im Anfang
war die Nachtigall" (In the beginning was the
Nightingale, 1840); the substitution of this
phrase for St. John's "In the beginning was the
Word" is especially effective in the implied
Russian subtext because of the phonic similarity between *slovo* (word) and *solovey* (nightingale). Blending, in accordance with his favorite
technique, this newly created god of German
poetry with the historical image of Ewald
Christian von Kleist, the bilingual German-
Italian poet killed by the Russians during the
Seven Years' War, Mandelshtam affirmed
again the eternal spiritual bond between Russian and German poetry, sealed by the nightingale's sacrificial blood, and repudiated the future "new plague." (It seems that at the time he
was translating the prophetic "Pir vo vremia
chumy" ["Feast During the Plague," 1839] by
Pushkin into the German.)

In May 1933 Mandelshtam's fascinating
travelogue *The Journey to Armenia* appeared
on the pages of *Zvezda*. On 30 August he was
severely taken to task by the official party
newspaper *Pravda* for "slandering Soviet Armenia." The brave editor of *Zvezda* was fired.
Since then Mandelshtam had not published a
single line. On 13 May 1934 the secret police
arrived at his apartment in Moscow when
Akhmatova was visiting from Leningrad. After
a house search he was taken away.

Mandelshtam's impulsive recklessness had
always been as proverbial as his caustic wit.
Decorous old-fashioned critics, hoodlums of
the Young Communist League, genteel old ladies of both sexes, and the Byzantine Soviet
officialdom all agreed that his manners were
insufferable. He borrowed money and composed funny epigrams about his creditors. In
1918 he had snatched a list of hostages to be
executed by the Cheka from the hands of Yakov
Blyumkin, the future killer of the German ambassador Count Wilhelm von Mirbach-Harff,
tore it up, and denounced Blyumkin's arbitrariness to the all-powerful chief of the Bolshevik
political police, Felix Dzerzhinsky. Through
the open window of his room in the writers'
house in Moscow he mocked and challenged
his fellow tenants. He shared a cab with a poet-
ess of Sapphic tastes and made her pay the
fare. During a dignified literary party given by
the Pasternaks for their influential Georgian
friends he made critical remarks about his
host's poetry and attempted to recite some of
his own verse. His frankness seemed to be suicidal—or a deliberate act of provocation. Even
Bely, the greatest of the survivors of symbolism
and certainly not a communist, apparently felt
it advisable to report on the "tiresome anti-So-
viet-allusions" of Mandelshtam and his wife in
his letter to Fedor Gladkov, a pillar of the Soviet literary establishment. In one of Mandelshtam's last outbursts he called the court
set up by the writers' union to discuss his
grievances a "monkey trial" and publicly
slapped the face of the court's president, "the
red count" Alexey Tolstoy. Finally, in November 1933, he wrote an indignant satire about
Stalin, calling him a Kremlin mountain tribes-
man and a fat-fingered peasant-slayer. He read
it to everybody who was willing to listen, at a

time when Joseph Stalin was officially referred to as "the greatest genius of mankind."

In jail Mandelshtam was deprived of sleep and water. The investigator knew all of Mandelshtam's acquaintances and forced him to confirm the tentative list of those who had listened to the poem. Emma Gershtein, one of those whose name Mandelshtam had allegedly listed, used this instance in her memoirs as an example of Mandelshtam's unconcern for the fate of his friends. However, the facility with which Mandelshtam spread the dangerous poem and then talked about it should rather be explained in terms of the poem's purpose, which was to break the conspiracy of silence vividly evoked in its first lines: "We live without feeling the land underneath our feet; / What we say can't be heard at ten paces." What he had said was heard. People were shot for much less than what he had done. Fortunately, at the time Mandelshtam's friends still had some influence. Stalin's orders at the end of Mandelshtam's interrogation were "to isolate but to spare." Mandelshtam was sent to the distant northern town of Cherdyn'. His wife accompanied him. In Cherdyn' he attempted to commit suicide while suffering from hallucinations and other symptoms of posttraumatic mental disorder. His friends intervened again. Bukharin, for the last time, personally interceded. He wrote to Stalin: "Poets are always right; history is on their side." Jurgis Baltrušaijtis, the prominent Russian-Lithuanian poet and the ambassador of independent Lithuania in Moscow, too, was very active on Mandelshtam's behalf. Finally, Stalin telephoned Pasternak and asked him a few questions about Mandelshtam. There are many versions of that talk, and its final effect on Mandelshtam's fate remains unclear. For the time being, the dictator obviously decided, for a number of important political reasons, to show magnanimity. Mandelshtam was transferred from Cherdyn' to a far less severe place of exile, Voronezh.

The years of exile are chronicled in detail in his widow's memoirs. His suffering and humiliation defy description. He bravely fought his anxiety: "Fear and the Muse took turns of duty in his room," Akhmatova wrote in a poem entitled "Voronezh" (1936) about her visit to Mandelshtam. Almost immediately upon his arrival to Voronezh he began composing poetry. One of the first verse cycles he wrote in exile consisted of the so-called "Poems About Iron" ("Zhelezo"). Here he repudiated the Lermontovian temptation of answering the iron compulsion of the era with "an iron verse steeped in bitterness and malice." The vicious circle of "iron battling iron" (as Velimir Khlebnikov had described Lermontov's conflict with his society) had to be broken. Mandelshtam did so in the three batches of the *Voronezhskie tetradi* (Voronezh Notebooks, 1980), the incomparable collection of poetry, animated by a truly unique spirit of humble defiance, that he composed between 1935 and 1937. The meek long-suffering Russian land seemed to have found a tongue in these poems. Fresh layers of richly colloquial dialectal Russian entered Mandelshtam's linguistic consciousness. He now reveled in the nonfinal, raw, open-ended freedom of draft variants, producing numerous versions of the same poetic task, depending on his addressee or current preoccupation. All of the *Voronezhskie tetradi* are masterpieces, but the towering achievement among them is the long oratorio of "Verses on the Unknown Soldier" (1937), a celebration of the air and of space (in the spirit of Charles Babbage and of Poe's "Power of the Words" [1845], as well as Camille Flammarion's *Lumen* [1872]) as the eternal and faithful witness of all human acts, a repository of millions and billions of "wholesale" unknown dead whose names are immortal in the roll call of light.

Throughout his exile in Voronezh Mandelshtam continued to dream about Europe: the hills of Tuscany, the winding mountain path still resounding with Goethe's whistling, the vertical ocean ripple of the French cathedrals. His vision now expanded; Marian Anderson's gospel singing, which he heard on the radio, made him visualize again the primeval cradle of the world's first-born:

I am submerged in the lion's den and dungeon,
And sinking lower, lower, lower
To the tune of this yeasty downpour,
Stronger than the lion, more potent than the
  Pentateuch.

How close, how close your summons comes
—Childbirth and firstlings which preceded the
  Commandments—
A string of Oceania's pearls
And the meek baskets of Tahiti women.

Continent of punishing singing,
Let loom the lower reaches of your deep voice!
The savage-sweet looks of our rich daughters
Are not worthy of your ancestral little finger.

My own time is still unlimited,
And I have accompanied the universal rapture
As muted organ-playing
Accompanies a woman's voice.

In May 1937 the term of his exile in Voronezh was over. He spent an additional year in and out of Moscow, trying to get permission to settle there. He went to various magazines peddling his poetry. The editors were afraid even to talk to him. He panhandled. Viktor Shklovsky, Valentin Stenich, Ehrenburg, Pasternak, Valentin Kataev, and some other old friends and kindly acquaintances helped him as they could. Before sunrise, on 2 May 1938 he was arrested again, with the technical assistance of the Union of Soviet Writers. Sentenced automatically to five years' hard labor, he was deported to East Siberia. Horace did not accompany Regulus to the Carthaginian rack, nor shall we follow the most sensitive of Russian poets to the heap of refuse upon which he died, according to one of the unverifiable accounts of his end, in the Vtoraia Rechka transit camp near Vladivostok. The date of his death officially given to his widow is 27 December 1938.

A major part of Mandelshtam's unpublished work was saved by the heroic efforts of his widow and a few courageous friends. The fabulous resurrection of his poetry, the memory of which was obliterated and concealed from the younger readers in the USSR, began in the United States in the 1950's. Gleb Struve of the University of California at Berkeley, in collaboration with Boris Filippov, published several editions of his collected works; Clarence Brown of Princeton wrote his biography and translated much of his prose and poetry into English; Kiril Taranovsky of Harvard established a reliable scholarly method of Mandelshtam research and interpretation. A great deal of critical and scholarly interest in Mandelshtam has also been in evidence since the early 1960's in the USSR, where some of his poetry and prose has been published in limited and often heavily expurgated editions.

The language barrier has somewhat distorted the image of Mandelshtam's poetry in the perception of the Anglo-Saxon reader. The best and most faithful translations of his work are into German by Paul Celan. Those who read Russian invariably experience the purely sensual fascination of Mandelshtam's verbal harmony. It is only recently, however, that interpreters have begun to unravel the profound message of his art, rooted deeply in the entire tradition of Western poetry, music, and culture, and reaching out to the "sympathetic understanding" of the unimaginable "reader in the future."

Selected Bibliography

EDITIONS

INDIVIDUAL WORKS

POETRY
Kamen'. St. Petersburg, 1913. 2d ed. Petrograd, 1916. 3d ed. Moscow-Petrograd, 1923.
Tristia. Petersburg-Berlin, 1922.
Vtoraia kniga. Moscow-Petrograd, 1923.
Stikhotvoreniia. Moscow-Leningrad, 1928.

PROSE
Shum vremeni. Leningrad, 1925.
Egipetskaia marka. Leningrad, 1928.
O poèzii. Leningrad, 1928.

OSIP MANDELSHTAM

COLLECTED WORKS

Sobranie sochinenii. Edited by Gleb Struve and Boris Filippov. New York, 1955.

Sobranie sochinenii. 3 vols. Edited by Gleb Struve and Boris Filippov. New York, 1964–1971. Supplement vol. 4. Edited by Gleb Struve, Nikita Struve, and Boris Filippov. Paris, 1981. There are revised and expanded second editions of vols. 1 and 2.

Stikhotvoreniia. Edited by Nikolai Khardzhiev. Leningrad, 1973.

Slovo i kul'tura. O poèzii. Razgovor o Dante. Stat'i. Retsenzii. Edited by Pavel Nerler. Moscow, 1987.

INDIVIDUAL POSTHUMOUS WORKS

Razgovor o Dante. Edited by Aleksandr Morozov and Leonid Pinskii. Moscow, 1967.

Voronezhskie tetradi. Edited by Victoria Shveitser. Ann Arbor, Mich., 1980.

Chetvertaia proza. Edited by B. Sokolov. In *Raduga*, no. 3, Tallinn, Estonia, 1988.

TRANSLATIONS

The Complete Critical Prose and Letters. Edited by Jane Gary Harris. Translated by Jane Gary Harris and Constance Link. Ann Arbor, Mich., 1979.

Complete Poetry of Osip Mandelstam. Translated by Burton Raffel and Alla Burago. Introduction and notes by Sidney Monas. Albany, N.Y., 1973.

Fifty Poems. Translated by Bernard Meares. Introductory essay by Joseph Brodsky. New York, 1977.

Journey to Armenia. Translated by Sidney Monas. San Francisco, 1979. Includes *Mandelstam and the "Journey"* by Henry Gifford.

Osip Mandelstam's "Stone." Translated and introduced by Robert Tracy. Princeton, N.J., 1981.

Poems. Edited and translated by James Greene. Forewords by Nadezhda Mandelstam and Donald Davie. Boulder, Colo., 1978. 2d ed., revised and enlarged, London, 1980.

The Prose of Osip Mandelstam. Translated, with a critical essay, by Clarence Brown. Princeton, N.J., 1965. Includes *The Noise of Time* and *The Egyptian Stamp.*

Selected Essays. Translated by Sidney Monas. Austin, Tex., 1977.

Selected Poems. Translated and introduced by Peter Russel. London, 1958.

Selected Poems. Translated by Clarence Brown and W. S. Merwin. London, 1973.

Selected Poems. Translated by David McDuff. Cambridge, England, 1973.

BIOGRAPHICAL, CRITICAL, AND PHILOLOGICAL STUDIES

Alter, Robert. "Osip Mandelstam: The Poet as Witness." *Defenses of Imagination.* Philadelphia, 1977.

Baines, Jennifer. *Mandelstam: The Later Poetry.* London, 1976.

Brown, Clarence. *Mandelstam.* Cambridge, England, 1973.

Broyde, Steven. *Osip Mandel'štam and His Age.* Cambridge, Mass., 1975.

Cohen, Arthur A. *Osip Emilievich Mandelstam: An Essay in Antiphon.* Ann Arbor, Mich., 1974.

Freidin, Gregory. *A Coat of Many Colors. Osip Mandelstam and His Mythologies of Self-Presentation.* Berkeley, Calif., 1987.

Harris, Jane Gary. *Osip Mandelstam.* Boston, Mass., 1988.

Isenberg, Charles. *Substantial Proofs of Being: Osip Mandelstam's Literary Prose.* Columbus, Ohio, 1987.

Koubourlis, Demetrius J. *A Concordance to the Poems of Osip Mandelstam.* Ithaca, N.Y., 1974.

Mandelstam, Nadezhda. *Hope Against Hope.* Translated by Max Hayward. New York, 1970.

———. *Hope Abandoned.* Translated by Max Hayward. New York, 1974.

Nilsson, Nils Åke. *Osip Mandel'štam: Five Poems.* Stockholm, 1974.

Przybylski, Ryszard. *An Essay on the Poetry of Osip Mandelstam: God's Grateful Guest.* Translated by Madeline G. Levine. Ann Arbor, Mich., 1988.

Ronen, Omry. *An Approach to Mandel'štam.* Jerusalem, 1983.

Taranovsky, Kiril. *Essays on Mandel'štam.* Cambridge, Mass., 1976.

OTHER REFERENCES

Bayer, Thomas. "Osip Mandel'shtam i Geidel'bergskii Universitet." *Minuvshee* 5:222–227 (1988).

Eikhenbaum, Boris. *Anna Akhmatova. Opyt analiza.* Petersburg, 1923.

Florenskii, Pavel. *Stolp i utverzhdenie istiny.* Moscow, 1914.

Gershtein, Èmma. *Novoe o Mandel'shtame.* Paris, 1986.

Levin, Iurii. "Zametki o poèzii O. Mandel'shtama tridtsatykh godov, I." *Slavica Hierosolymitana* 3:110–173 (1978).

Maslennikov, Oleg. *Lyrics from the Russian: Symbolists and Others.* Berkeley, Calif., 1972.

Morozov, Aleksandr. "Mandel'shtam v zapisiakh dnevnika S. P. Kablukova." *Vestnik Russkogo Khristianskogo Dvizheniia* 129:131–155 (1979).

———. "Pis'ma O. E. Mandel'shtama k V. I. Ivanovu." Publikatsiia A. A. Morozova. *Zapiski Otdela rukopisei* 34:258–274 (1973).

Nabokov, Vladimir. *Strong Opinions.* London, 1974.

Otsup, Nikolai. "Serebrianyi vek." *Chisla* 7–8:174–178 (1933).

———. *Sovremenniki.* Paris, 1961. Pp. 127–140.

Ronen, Omry. "Mandelshtam, Osip." *Encyclopaedia Judaica Year Book 1973.* Jerusalem, 1973. Pp. 294–296.

Tsvetaeva, Anastasiia. *Dym, dym, dym.* Moscow, 1916.

Zholkovskii, Aleksandr. "Invarianty i struktura teksta. II. Mandel'shtam: 'Ia p'iu za voennye astry . . . '." *Slavica Hierosolymitana* 4:159–184 (1979).

OMRY RONEN

PAVLO TYCHYNA

(1891–1967)

THE MEASURE OF Pavlo Tychyna's preeminence in the history of twentieth-century Ukrainian literature is perhaps best conveyed by the fact that he is considered the outstanding poet of his time, and arguably of this century, by both Soviet and non-Soviet readers and critics. Apart from this point of convergence, however, the understanding and reception of Tychyna and his poetry is marked by profound oppositions and often virulent dispute. Capping the ideological polarization surrounding Tychyna is a widely held belief in the radical discontinuity of his poetry, in the nearly total disjunction, indeed antithesis, between the early and late Tychyna, summarized in the irreconcilable images of the spontaneous Orphic poet who expressed the very spirit of a newborn nation and the official and canonized bard of the Soviet Ukraine. In one sense this general impression is valid: the contrasts between his early and late work in theme and diction, in emotional and psychological complexity, and in the very definition of the poetic self can be as stark as the difference between the unchained, elemental aspirations of the Ukraine during the time of the Revolution and the official, reductive doctrine of socialist realism. Yet both extremes served organically as the material for Tychyna's poetry.

Tychyna's decisive impact on the course of Ukrainian poetry has been profound—and, what is no less important, manifest from the publication in 1918 of his first collection of poetry, *Soniachni klarnety* (Clarinets of the Sun). It was not only the broad readership, but the writers, and especially the poets, who felt that in Tychyna they were witnessing a sea change, a revolution in Ukrainian poetry. For Mykola Bazhan, another eminent contemporary Ukrainian poet, his first reading of *Soniachni klarnety* was a heady rediscovery of the beauty of the Ukrainian word and "a plunge into a deeper understanding of the authority and the secrets of Ukrainian poetry." For the prose writer Yurii Smolych, Tychyna stood directly in line after the great nineteenth-century triad of Taras Shevchenko, Ivan Franko, and Lesia Ukrainka, and the present age was indeed the "epoch of Tychyna."

To be sure, the genre of memoirs and officially sanctioned (and posthumous) recollections, from which the above comments are taken, naturally tends to plaudits and platitudes, while the phenomenon of Tychyna, including his meteoric rise and, for some, his precipitous decline, requires a distanced, nonmetaphoric approach, precisely because his poetry is so difficult to extricate from its emotional and subliminal resonance. For while much still remains to be examined and tested (all the more so as only now a more or less complete canon of his work is becoming available), one thing is fairly certain: the dominant paradigms of the vast majority of Tychyna critics to date have been more evaluative than analytical; even where the argument has refrained

1651

from blatantly ideological praise or blame, the very reliance on such metaphoric constructs as "bard of the Ukrainian Revolution," or "elemental voice (or conscience) of the nation," or the "agricultural Orpheus," or, alternatively, the borrowing of his own image to describe his early poetry as "clarinetism" have tended only to obscure the object of inquiry.

While Tychyna has come to exemplify the energy and reach of the new, full-fledged Ukrainian literature of the twentieth century—especially its drive for innovation and experimentation—he is also a writer who in manifold ways, varying from the deliberate to the intuitive and unconscious, draws on the rich repertoire of Ukrainian poetic traditions. This ear for the various devices, genres, and cadences of folklore is only the most obvious recourse to such traditions. Underlying discrete moments of textual use—be it modeling on a genre like the folktale or riddle, echoes of folk beliefs, or simply the introduction of folk sayings or epithets—is the basic structure of identification with the folk, the *narod,* its experience and its values. This clearly is a central issue, but also one that can easily be distorted into a quasi-metaphysical notion (so apparent in much of Soviet criticism) that a great poet must necessarily be a "faithful son of the people (the *narod*)," and, conversely, that poetic greatness is contingent precisely on such a bond. Yet though a normative application of such a perceived bond is to be resisted, there is little doubt that Tychyna's poetics and his worldview are profoundly influenced by this paradigm. In this Tychyna recapitulates much of Ukrainian nineteenth-century literature with its implicit, but also often programmatic, populism. A specifically literary articulation of the imperative to speak *to* and *for* the *narod*—one that also clearly draws on Romantic premises that were particularly prominent in various Slavic literatures—is the belief that the poet should be tribune and bard, spokesman for the *narod* and indeed its acknowledged leader. It is precisely this stance that animates much of the poetry of the outstanding Ukrainian nine-

teenth-century figure Taras Shevchenko. As witnessed by various texts, the specifically Shevchenkian legacy, the general bardic and tribunicial stance, and above all the readiness to blur the boundary between poet and *narod,* self and collective, emerge as the central ethical and poetic choice in Tychyna. Compared to the psychological and cultural resonance of this felt and desired bond, it is almost superfluous to note that the concrete historical and political circumstances also continued to justify it: in Tychyna's as in Shevchenko's time, literature, and in the Ukrainian case poetry in particular, served as a surrogate for political discourse. With all political power concentrated in the hands of the state, literature—poetry—seemed to many to be the only vehicle for expressing dissenting opinions or simply even commenting on the political sphere. When, in addition, the prerevolutionary Ukrainian context was marked not just by the political repression that characterized the entire Russian empire, but also by a specific and relentless oppression of national aspirations, of cultural self-expression, it is hardly surprising that being a Ukrainian writer was also inevitably a political statement.

By the turn of the century, however, there was an ever-growing willingness on the part of various Ukrainian writers to question the identification of literature with the cause of national and social emancipation. While the rejection of this equation was never total or militant and never approached anything like an art-for-art's sake argument, and while even its timid formulations met with harsh attacks from the older, populist-oriented establishment, such as the poet and eminent literary figure Ivan Franko or the literary historian Serhij Iefremov, the movement toward modernism, as it came to be known, was not to be stopped. It was, after all, an organic development reflecting the differentiation and growing sophistication of the Ukrainian reading public. In this early and hardly developed phase of Ukrainian modernism two poets, Oleksandr Oles' and Mykola Voronyi, can be seen as precursors of, or at least a bridge to, Tychyna. Oles', by far the most popular poet of the pre-revolutionary period, introduced a new, intensely emotional lyrical poetry that treated the self, society, patriotism, even the revolution of 1905 as pure feeling unmediated by history or even reason. Voronyj, a talented but highly eclectic poet (and one who dedicated more effort to underground political activity than to literature), brought into Ukrainian poetry—from the contemporary Western European, Polish, and Russian literatures—a wealth of new themes, subgenres, and forms of verification; thanks to him such topics as the cult of pure beauty (with the poet as high priest), or contemplations of the ethereal "music of the spheres," such modalities as lighthearted erotic poetry or bohemian mock-spleen and most significantly perhaps an impressive range of often recherché stanzaic and metrical forms found their way into the expanding repertoire of early twentieth-century Ukrainian poetry. Apart from these two, there is also the possible influence on Tychyna of two minor poets, Hryhorii Chuprynka, whose brief poetic career and small output was oriented toward somewhat jejune sound experimentation, and the interesting but little known presymbolist Mykola Filianskyi. All of them—even if points of continuity or influence can be demonstrated—are hardly of the caliber of Tychyna and are precursors only in the strictly historical sense.

LIFE AND CAREER

Pavlo Tychyna was born on 27 January (15 January old style) 1891, in the village Pisky in the Chernihiv *gubernia* (region) of north-central Ukraine, as one of nine children of a destitute village cantor. After attending the local school for two years Tychyna was enrolled first in the choir and boarding school of the Ielets monastery in Chernihiv and then, one year later, in the choir and school of the Troitsk monastery in the same town. In 1906, the year in which Tychyna is known to have written his first poem, his father died, and when in the following year Pavlo entered the Chernihiv seminary it was as an "impoverished orphan" with a government stipend; to support himself Tychyna also worked as choir conductor. In later autobiographical references Tychyna would invariably (in large measure no doubt to be in harmony with the obligatory, official interpretation of such things) depict the seminary as stifling, slovenly, and gratuitously cruel; however, this is also the picture of the seminary that he paints in three short prose pieces, "Theology," "On the Rivers of Babylon," and "Temptation," which he published in 1913. For all that, the seminary did leave its mark on Tychyna, not only by way of the prominent religious imagery and motifs in his early poetry or in the genre models that the liturgy provided, but more deeply, perhaps, in the significant presence of a spiritual dimension that clearly set the early Tychyna apart from his contemporaries. And whatever his later efforts at repudiating this influence and replacing it with a fervently professed (and of course obligatory) materialism, a certain quality of spiritual sensitivity, of openness to a higher order of existence came to characterize Tychyna's poetry—and not only the early period.

A major event in Tychyna's life as a seminary student, and one that he particularly highlighted in later autobiographical writings and his poetry, was his friendship beginning in 1910 with the outstanding Ukrainian master of impressionist prose, Mykhailo Kotsiubynskii. In effect, Kotsiubynskii was the first to "discover" Tychyna, singling him out on the basis of his early poetic efforts from the group of talented young students he would invite to his house each Saturday for a literary salon. Kotsiubynskii was instrumental in helping Tychyna publish, in 1912, his first poem in the prestigious *Literaturno-naukovyi visnyk* (Literary-Scholarly Herald). Although the relationship was short-lived due to the older writer's early death, it apparently had a lasting impact on Tychyna. The influence of Kotsiubynskii's impressionist technique—which is quite evident in Tychyna's early collections—is only the lesser consequence. The more important effect was undoubtedly the sense of validation and even mission that this warm recognition by the foremost Ukrainian writer of the time gave to the young poet.

In 1913, Tychyna finished the seminary and enrolled in the Commercial Institute in Kiev. To support himself he took the job of technical secretary for a minor Ukrainian educational journal. When with the outbreak of World War I the czarist authorities closed down this journal along with virtually every other Ukrainian periodical, Tychyna found work in a government statistical office in Chernihiv and later as assistant choir director in a Kiev theater. And even though now no Ukrainian journal existed where he could publish, Tychyna wrote poetry. He also engaged in what was to be a lifelong passion—the collecting of folk songs.

Tychyna's first published collection of poetry, *Soniachni klarnety* appeared sometime in November or December of 1918. The "war to end all wars" had finally ended in the West, but in the East, in what had been the Russian Empire, bloodshed and chaos continued unabated. The events of the Russian revolution of 1917 were answered in the Ukraine by the creation of a new government, the Ukrainian National Rada (Council), which first proclaimed autonomy and then full independence from Russia. The general feeling of euphoria and hope at the rebirth of a nation was articulated more powerfully by Tychyna than by any other contemporary; some of his poems of this period, however, poems marked precisely by an elemental national consciousness that was quite distant from the criteria of class consciousness and proletarian internationalism, were fated never to be republished in the Soviet Union. In 1917 and 1918 the Ukraine had seen three Ukrainian governments and a Russian-dominated Soviet one. In the course of the next three years the civil war in the Ukraine involved fighting between the Ukrainian national forces, the Bolsheviks, the Russian White Army, various anarchist formations, Western

interventionist forces, and the Poles. In this turbulent period Tychyna was remarkably productive, publishing in 1920 the collections *Pluh* (The Plow) and *Zamist' sonetiv i oktav* (Instead of Sonnets and Octaves). With the establishment of Soviet rule and the resumption and then rapid expansion of cultural and literary activities, Tychyna's involvement in them was also marked. Already in 1918 he had participated in the largely symbolist *Literary-Critical Almanac.* In 1919 he was prominently involved in the programmatically symbolist and aesthetically discriminating almanac *Muzahet;* it is in the latter that Tychyna published "Pluh," the lead poem for the collection by the same name, in which he welcomed the revolution—significantly, however, not with any ideological-political commitment, but, precisely as in the case of various Russian symbolists, with an apocalyptic sensibility and with the hope for an elemental purgation. Dithyrambs to the Revolution appeared in yet another symbolist journal of 1919, *Mystetstvo* (Art), and here, too, Tychyna was a prominent participant.

Music also continued to be a prime interest in Tychyna's life. In the fall of 1920, with the civil war still very much active, he traveled, as a kind of chronicler, with the kapelle of the Ukrainian composer Kyrylo Stetsenko on a tour of the Right-bank Ukraine, from Kiev to Odessa. It was on this tour that he met another, more famous Ukrainian composer, Mykola Leontovych. The next year, in Kiev, Tychyna became director of a choir and musical studio named after Leontovych. In 1922, with another composer, Hryhorii Veriovka, Tychyna helped to found the Ukrainian School of Music.

Beginning in 1923 Tychyna turned to literary activity with a new intensity. He moved to Kharkiv, then the capital of the newly formed Soviet Ukrainian Republic, assumed the post of literary editor of one of the two major Ukrainian literary journals, *The Red Path,* and joined *Hart,* a newly formed union of proletarian writers.

The proliferation of literary organizations,

and the involvement in them of the great majority of writers—many of whom were politically quite unengaged—is one of the most salient features of this period. Underlying it were several important sociocultural developments. The first and historically the most momentous was that now, for the first time in the modern period, Ukrainian literature had the support of a state; rather than being suppressed (as it had been by the czarist authorities in roughly the last third of the nineteenth century) or merely neglected, it could count on a whole range of governmental functions, programs, and subsidies designed to further the growth and authority of literature. After all, the writer, according to Trotsky's dictum, was to be the engineer of human souls. At the same time, the government's prime cultural policy from the early to late 1920's was one of "Ukrainization." Designed to defuse political opposition, and reflecting the power of the Ukrainian component in the Communist Party, it was a policy of furthering the spread of the Ukrainian language into the various areas of social and cultural and political life that had up to then been served only by Russian; the effects were most pronounced in education and the mass media, and the cutting edge, again, was literature. Finally, by a somewhat reluctant decision, but one which, like Lenin's New Economic Policy, reflected the Party's awareness of its own weaknesses, and hence its tactical moderation, no single literary organization was given the mandate to speak for the regime, and a certain pluralism was tacitly allowed.

In the Soviet Ukraine the second half of the 1920's witnessed a broadly based and at times ferocious debate over the paths to be taken by the new Soviet Ukrainian literature. Apart from such intrinsically literary and, in this context, relatively innocuous issues as those of artistic style and direction (where, for example, both the futurists and the "revolutionary romantics" laid claim to representing true proletarian art), some of the issues raised were far-reaching and politically dangerous. They devolved on the following choices: Should Ukrainian litera-ture be populist and literary organizations reflect the broadest—and lowest—common denominator, or should aesthetic quality be given primacy? Should native, frequently ethnographic and provincial, traditions suffice, or should Ukrainian literature look to the European avant-garde? Should Russian literature continue to serve as an "older brother," to be the perennial model for and conduit to high literature and art, or should Ukrainian literature perform this function for itself, and indeed go to the sources without any intervening interpretation? A most passionate answer to these questions was given by Mykola Khvyl'ovyi, a prose writer and polemicist and the single most dynamic force on the Ukrainian scene of that time. His theses of aesthetic quality and creative elitism, of openness to the West and to the avant-garde and of "away from Moscow" and "to the sources," adumbrated further by a romantic vitalism and a somewhat mystical belief that the Ukraine, as the quintessential newly awakened nation, was fated to lead an "Asian Renaissance," constituted the agenda and the clearest platform in the ongoing "literary discussion." The implications of this discussion, it goes without saying, went far beyond literature.

In 1925, Khvyl'ovyi, having attained a leading role in *Hart,* proceeded to reconstitute this organization into a new entity. While still proletarian in name, this group, VAPLITE (an acronym for Free Academy of Proletarian Literature), came to embody Khvyl'ovyi's ambitious vision. Most propitiously it attracted into its ranks the best talents, the "Olympians" (as Khvyl'ovyi wryly called them) of Ukrainian writers—prose writers, dramatists, and poets, Tychyna among them. Tychyna was also a contributor to this group's publications, first *Vaplite* and then *The Literary Marketplace.* And even as the Party turned, ever more harshly, against what it saw as the "nationalist deviation" of VAPLITE, Tychyna remained a member until its dissolution in the late 1920's.

In 1921 Tychyna published a short cycle of ten poems entitled *V kosmichnomu orkestri* (In the Cosmic Orchestra) and in 1924 a major collection of poetry, *Viter z Ukrainy* (Wind from the Ukraine). For the rest of the decade, just as he did not play an active role in the swirling debates and conflicts, Tychyna did not come out with new collections. He was hardly inactive, however. Apart from writing his own poetry, which he published in various journals, he now began translating, particularly from Armenian. In time this activity became a major passion and achievement and grew to include translations from various cultures and nationalities of the Soviet Union—Georgian, Tatar, Bashkir, Yiddish, as well as Russian and Byelorussian.

Throughout the 1920's and into the 1930's, Tychyna worked on what he envisioned as his summa—a long poem, subtitled "A Symphony," on the life and meaning of the eighteenth-century Ukrainian wandering mystic philosopher and poet Hryhorii Skovoroda. *Skovoroda* was never completed; parts of it were read to close friends and colleagues, and some parts published in 1941; as a book, reconstructed from a mass of variants, drafts, notes, plans, and even Tychyna's appended dictionary of arcane Ukrainian words, it appeared only posthumously, in 1971.

By the 1920's Tychyna's reputation as the leading Ukrainian poet was firmly established. His poetry was translated into Russian and not infrequently quoted by such figures as Vladimir Mayakovsky; the Polish poet Jarosław Iwaszkiewicz, writing in 1922 in the leading Polish literary journal, *Skamander,* saw Tychyna's poetry, building as it did on the native Ukrainian tradition and the achievements of French and Russian symbolism, as something "exceptionally powerful and fresh." The year 1927 saw the first Czech translation of Tychyna's poetry. With increasing frequency Tychyna was chosen to participate in various official delegations, whether to meet with workers in the Ukrainian industrial heartland of the Donbas, to formally visit the soviet Republics of Byelorussia, Armenia, and, of

course, Russia, or indeed to represent Ukrainian literature abroad, for example to Czechoslovakia (1925) or Turkey (1928). In 1929, as if capping the official recognition Tychyna had received in this decade, he was elected a full member of the Academy of Sciences of the Ukrainian SSR.

But Tychyna's renown did not fully shield him from criticism or attack: in 1927 he was accused by Ulas Chubar, then chairman of the Council of People's Commissars for the Ukraine, of "insinuating a nationalist opiate under the banner of proletarian literature." The offending work, actually an untitled fragment of a longer poem that begins with the words "Mother was peeling potatoes . . . ," appeared in the almanac *Vaplite* (in 1926); it depicted with an eerie mix of naturalist detail and a metaphysical sense of impending doom a typical village scene in the midst of the horror of the Civil War. In a letter to the editor published in the newspaper *Komunist* (where the attack initially appeared), Tychyna denied the charge and noted that the fact of depicting famine, wretched poverty, or the peasants' belief that Lenin was the anti-Christ could hardly be construed as their acceptance; indeed his sympathy—as is evident from his poem—is with the son in the family, the Communist, symbol and creator of the new order.

Chernihiv (1931), a slim collection of eight poems that thematically constituted a kind of reportage about the city on the eve of the new Five-Year Plan, did not please the critics, who were now acutely conscious of the demands of the newly promulgated socialist realism. The volume's overtly orthodox and timely thematics (industrialization, Stalin's latest directives, anti-Western invectives) did apparently compensate for its complex and disorienting poetics. Still, the book was criticized and with time largely excised from the canon of Tychyna's poetry.

The following year saw the beginnings, in full earnest, of Stalin's great terror. In the Ukraine, during 1932 and 1933, a manmade famine was engineered to break the back of a recalcitrant peasantry and cow the nationally conscious intelligentsia as well as the Party cadres that opposed Stalin's policies. Some seven million died of starvation. In the course of the 1930's, hundreds of intellectuals, writers, and cultural figures were arrested as class enemies and either summarily executed (the first wave of such executions came in 1934) or allowed to perish in Siberian labor camps. Tychyna, a man who by all accounts was generally timid and self-effacing, was in this period subject to extreme stress as each day brought news of new arrests of friends and colleagues. In May 1933, Khvyl'ovyi, the national-communist whose vision of a reborn Ukrainian culture had inspired many, who had been a friend and colleague and to whom Tychyna had dedicated the title poem of *Viter z Ukrainy*, committed suicide. In July, Mykola Skrypnyk, the old-guard Bolshevik and colleague of Lenin who as People's Commissar had implemented the policy of Ukrainization and who had long tried to reconcile his loyalty to the Party with a belief that the Ukrainian Soviet Republic was a real entity with real rights, also committed suicide. Later that month, the chairman of the Ukrainian Organizing Committee, preparing for the formation of the Union of Soviet Writers, in response to the demoralization among Ukrainian writers following the suicide of Khvyl'ovyi, publicly appealed to his Russian counterparts to send Russian cadres to help stabilize the situation in the Ukraine; the Stalinist policy of total centralization and Russian hegemony was now being ruthlessly applied to Ukrainian literature. In October 1933 the Berezil' theater of Kharkiv, the most avant-garde and sophisticated of Ukrainian theaters, one with strong roots in the expressionist and experimental stage, was disbanded, and its highly talented director, the producer Les' Kurbas, was removed, later to be arrested and exiled.

That same month Tychyna wrote a poem entitled "Partiia vede" ("The Party Leads"). On 21 November 1933 the lead editorial in *Pravda*, the central Party newspaper, was likewise entitled "The Party Leads," and dealt with the successes of the grain harvest and of collectivization in the Ukraine; this same issue included Tychyna's poem—in the original Ukrainian, and with the same title—as a kind of poetic elaboration or illustration of that central verity. For all it was more than clear that Tychyna, *the* national poet, had unconditionally accepted— for many, unconditionally capitulated to—the new power and reality. But while this judgment was quite accurate with respect to the rest of Tychyna's life and career, in effect, as that of the *official* Soviet Ukrainian poet, the poetry itself was ambiguous. The title aside, it was ambiguous and in retrospect perhaps even parodic by virtue of being a song, or chant, implicitly emanating from the collective mouths of the Young Communist League (Komsomol), and reflecting the kind of fervor and simplicity of perspective that only children or adolescents can muster.

For the remainder of his years Tychyna's life was one of ever greater official duties, honors, and rewards, punctuated every few years by a new collection of poetry. Thus 1934, the year when the collection entitled *Partiia vede* (and subtitled, significantly, "Pisni, peany, himny" ["Songs, Paeans, Hymns"]) was published, was also the year he was given the degree of Doctor of Philology. In 1938, when he published the collection *Chuttia iedynoi rodyny* (A Feeling of One Family), Tychyna was also elected deputy to the Supreme Council of the Ukrainian SSR (The title of the collection became the official phrase for conveying the "brotherhood" of the various Soviet nationalities; in time it became the name of a major annual literary prize given in commemoration of Tychyna.) In 1941, Tychyna published *Stal' i nizhnist'* (Steel and Tenderness). (One could hardly help noticing that in the elision of normal speech the title immediately gives "Stalin.") That same year Tychyna was awarded two major government prizes—the first of many. For the term 1936–1939 he was appointed director of the Institute of Literature of the Academy of Sciences, an institute that had been decimated and virtually silenced by the still on-going purges.

During the war, after the Germans had occupied both Kiev and Kharkiv, Tychyna was evacuated to Ufa, beyond the Urals; he continued in his official duties—from 1941 to 1943 he was director of the combined Institute of Language and Literature of the Ukrainian Academy of Sciences—and he did write poetry. While much of it was unabashedly agitational, the intensity of his horror at the atrocities of the Nazis and the suffering of his countrymen led him at times to recapture, most strikingly in the long poem *Pokhoron druha* (A Friend's Funeral, 1943), a subtle and tragic sense of history and of human existence.

In the following years Tychyna's official status continued to rise: still during the war he was named National Commissar of Education for the Ukrainian SSR (Somewhat anticlimactically, he became a member of the Communist party only in the following year.) In the next two decades, apart from periodically receiving awards, officiating at opening ceremonies, and indeed publishing several more collections of poetry, Tychyna was repeatedly elected to various government bodies: in 1953, for example, he was elected chairman of the Supreme Council of the Ukrainian SSR, and in 1952, 1956, 1960, and 1966—a year before his death—he was elected a member of the Central Committee of the Communist Party of the Ukraine. At the end he appeared the complete official poet: bemedaled, orthodox, still alive but already cast in bronze.

For many, Tychyna's death on 16 September 1967 was a technicality: the poet in him was believed to have died much earlier. For most emigrés and nationalists it was at the moment, signaled as early as in the 1924 collection *Viter z Ukrainy*, when he enthusiastically accepted the Bolshevik Revolution and the Soviet state; for others it was with *Partiia vede* and the apparently unqualified acceptance of socialist realism and with it an unresisting subordination of the creative self to the collectivist diktat. But the very opposition of physical death/poetic death obliges one—in fairness to the poet—to look at his reputation after 1967. Ironically, this approach is also favored in official Soviet biographies of Tychyna, but here it is done with an eye not so much for the poetry as for the propaedeutic value of the cult of the poet.

In fact, thanks to various Soviet Ukrainian scholars and critics, the last two decades have seen a steady and by now substantial rehabilitation of Tychyna the poet. The process has been multitracked and involved, at the outset, publishing much of the still unpublished oeuvre and rolling back the accreted layers of censorship. (It is a monument to the Stalinist system that by far the larger measure of that censorship had been self-imposed, by Tychyna himself—to anticipate and forestall censure.) At the end it meant reconstituting, through criticism and scholarship, the very stature and dimensions of the poet.

The first step in this process, beginning almost immediately after Tychyna's death and continuing to this day, was the publication first in literary journals, and soon in separate publications, of Tychyna's concealed poetic legacy, particularly of the early period; the major stages here were a small volume of Tychyna's "unpublished and largely forgotten" poetry, *V sertsi u moim* (In My Heart, 1970), and the "symphony" *Skovoroda* (1971); the collected editions of his works that appeared also tended to be "revisionist" by the very fact of progressively restoring more and more of the poetry excised from the multivolume collected editions of 1946, 1957, and 1961.

Moreover, in the twenty years since his death, writing about Tychyna has constituted a kind of growth industry in Soviet Ukrainian letters and criticism. It would seem that the poet who said "Za vsikh skazhu, za vsikh pereboliiu" (I will say it for all, I will ache for all) has had the favor returned by a fair portion, if not the entirety, of the literary community.

What is most important is that such endemic Soviet failings as hidebound orthodoxy and sheer pedantry notwithstanding, Tychyna criticism has seen a real improvement in quality and subtlety and has to some extent even served as a vehicle for rehabilitating the period of the 1920's from Stalinist distortions and censorship.

The culmination of this manifold process of restoring Tychyna—not only from censorship but from self-censorship as well—has been the ongoing publication in twelve volumes (of which eleven have already appeared) of his entire oeuvre, poetry, essays, diaries and memoirs, and so on. While not an academic edition—there are a few individual poems that are still considered too sensitive to be made available to the broad readership—*Zibrannia tvoriv v dvanadtsiaty tomakh* (1983–) is remarkably complete and objective, and greatly facilitates our understanding of the poet.

EARLY POETRY

By the "early poetry" one usually means Tychyna's first four or five collections, that is, *Soniachni klarnety, Pluh, Zamist' sonetiv i oktav, V kosmichnomu orkestri,* and most probably (although those who were ideologically offended might dispute this) the 1924 collection *Viter z Ukrainy.* As recent editions of Tychyna's "unpublished and forgotten" poetry have shown, however, a substantial body of additional poetry (larger in bulk than any one or even two of these early collections) was written before 1918. This poetry, in turn, can be divided into Tychyna's earliest poetic efforts, from 1906 to 1914, and then poetry written at the same time as those poems that entered the first collection, but not included there.

The earliest poetry is now for the most part of merely historical interest. It is often derivative, drawing on such models as Shevchenko and Oles', and circumscribed by conventional themes and stances. Here Tychyna tends to patriotic sentiment, to a morbid preoccupation with his own death (not all that strange for young poets), to rapturous but vague and ultimately rhetorical contemplation of nature, to misty and at times jejune love poems, and to a religious but again diffuse meditation on man's mortality that shades off into generalized melancholy. And yet, despite all these weaknesses, the poetry clearly shows talent and in retrospect can be found to reveal in embryo whole phrases, images, moods, and poetic devices that will soon bloom forth in *Soniachni klarnety.* The few poems that Tychyna actually published in this period are invariably superior to the others, and as good or better than most of the Ukrainian poetry of that time. This is all the more true of the second subgroup, that is, poems written between 1914 and 1918 but not included in *Soniachni klarnety.* With few exceptions they are excellent poetry; their exclusion only reflects the high demands Tychyna placed on this collection.

Above all, *Soniachni klarnety* is a complex and dynamic unity. It is held together not so much by its thematics, which at most can be said to provide clusters of themes, or by narrative continuity, but by a strikingly new poetics, and beyond that by an intense and powerful lyrical voice. As was noted before, for the first time since Shevchenko in the mid-nineteenth century, this voice and personality transfixed its audience, average readers and literati alike. Indeed *Soniachni klarnety* could perhaps best be described as a celebration of the self: the poetic self, first of all, the self as subject and object of love, the self as witness to nature and then history. The apotheosis of the self—in what may seem a paradox but really signals a higher stage of awareness and existence—is its absorption by the cosmos. This will become a paradigm for Tychyna's understanding of himself as a poet.

Tychyna's poetry has not been translated into English, and given its play with sound, with conscious and unconscious (frequently folkloric) associations, and in its readiness to draw on neologisms and a nonstandard Ukrainian syntax, coupled with a diction that is apparently all simplicity and immediacy, it would seem to epitomize the "untranslatable." In fact, even translations of his works into such close languages as Polish and Russian seldom yield more than pale approximations. Literal translations (which the following will be) invariably reduce and flatten out the manifold codes of the text. For all that, in some works, such as the untitled opening poem of *Soniachni klarnety*, which is as close to a poetic manifesto as Tychyna was to come, the semantic core and emotional tenor are unmistakable:

Neither Zeus, nor Pan, nor the Spirit-Dove—
But Clarinets of the Sun.
I am in dance, the rhythmic motion
In eternity, with all the planets.

I was—not I. Only a vision, a dream.
Around me—tolling sounds
And the chiton of creative darkness
And announcing hands.

I awoke—and I was You:
Beneath me, above me
Worlds flame, worlds run
In a musical river.

And I watched, and I was Spring:
Planets coalesced into chords.
For all time I knew that you are not Wrath—
But Clarinets of the Sun.

(1:37)[1]

The cosmic expansiveness of this poetic act, or more precisely, self-generation, could not be more obvious; it is the thematic and narrative given. But it is effected as something utterly natural and the very opposite of rhetorical or *willed* self-assertion. The crux, it appears, is in the two-step transition signaled by the first lines of the two "inner" stanzas: "I was—not I" and "I awoke—and I was You." It is a transformation, a transition into a oneness with the

[1]All quotations, unless otherwise indicated, are taken from the edition of collected works *Zibrannia tvoriv v dvanadtsiaty tomakh* (Kiev, 1983–).

cosmos, which, as in a mystical experience or a Buddhist attainment of "final liberation," is achieved passively, so to say, through being, through awakening, through awareness, and not through doing or acting. The movement of the self, its crystallization (one can observe the increments of the pronoun "I" in the course of the four stanzas), is actualized only in the product, however, in the poetry.

It is the poetry that is apotheosized. It is—as the opening and concluding lines assert—the new religion, contrasted to and elevated above the Greek deities (Zeus, Pan) and the God of the Old and New Testament (Wrath and the Spirit-Dove). The poet produces it, of course, and the metathematic point that the poetry produced in this cosmic genesis—"Clarinets of the Sun"—is also the poetry to which Tychyna is now introducing the reader is dramatically highlighted in the conclusion. (This metathematic point will become a favorite device for Tychyna, and in several of his subsequent collections, especially *Pluh* and *Zamist' sonetiv i oktav*, the introductory poem will identify the newly offered concrete collection of poetry with a new vision and indeed a new apotheosis of poetry as such.) But the poet himself stands behind it, so to speak. He is, to expand his own allusion to the Annunciation ("announcing hands"; in the original, *blahovisni ruky*), like the Virgin imbued with the knowledge that she is pregnant with the God-child. The poetry that was to come, in this collection itself and in the volumes that were still to be written, would dispel any notion that Tychyna (as some did indeed argue at first) was merely a passive tympanum, a cosmic ear that catches and then conveys, virtually impersonally, all that it perceives. The manifest subtlety of his art, the psychological depth and the social and cultural perspicacity of his work must dispel any notion that his was a kind of automatic reconstituting of reality. And yet the tension between self and nonself ("I was—not I"), between the individual and the collective, is never easily resolved, and itself becomes a source of energy and anxiety for the poet. It is hardly surprising that the last stanza of one of the last poems Tychyna is known to have written, *V sertsi u moim,* turns precisely to this self-definition through, not self-effacement, but self-projection onto the collective:

> For I am not in myself, but entirely—in the people,
> Because all of that is mine, whether it is close or far.
> And hence the earth boils like the heart in the breast,
> And the heart moans like the entire earth.
>
> (3:305)

In *Soniachni klarnety* nature becomes the most resonant model for self-definition. To put it differently, it serves as the ultimate correlative for the gamut of feelings, from the euphoric to the melancholy, that swell in the poet's heart. The poem "Tsvit v moiemu sertsi" ("A Blossom in My Heart") gives in its second stanza what amounts to a compact grammar of the themes and stances animating this collection:

> I listen to the melodies
> of the clouds, the lakes and the wind.
> I resonate like the strings
> Of the steppe, the clouds and the wind.
> We all ring with one heart
> We dream with red wine—
> Of the sun, the clouds and the wind.
>
> (1:42)

Nature provides an ever-changing and yet ever-abiding matrix for the experience of romantic love, which in its ebb and flow, successes and failures, is the dominant concern for something like the first half of the collection. Paradigmatically, in a poem entitled "Des' nadkhodyla vesna" ("Somewhere Spring Was Approaching"), a stormy love affair is depicted through the change of seasons. In each of the four stanzas the planes of nature and of the human relationship are linked, and the narrative of the changing seasons and the changeable love affair interwoven. Thus in the opening stanza he describes and addresses both nature and his beloved:

> Somewhere spring was approaching.—
> I said to her: you are spring!
> In the corners of her mouth
> Something in her fluttered up with smiles
> And sank in my soul . . .
>
> (1:41)

The emotional tonality of the love poems, and generally the first half of the collection, is one of harmony with life, and despite moments of melancholy and sorrow the world exists as in a joyous forcefield. This sense and tonality is conveyed above all by a voice and diction that is extraordinarily intimate and almost childlike in its directness. To achieve this, Tychyna, among other resources, draws on a wide range of folk elements—diminutives, traditional expressions and images, echoes of folk songs or folk beliefs—that subtly and powerfully reinforce the sense of simplicity and naturalness. At the same time, these traditional, native elements are paired with and resonate against a no less varied range of sophisticated poetic devices that, in this collection in particular, seem to echo impressionist and symbolist techniques.

Tychyna's impressionism can be found both in individual moments and images that coexist with other elements in a larger narrative construct, and in the very principle by which a poem is organized. As the former it is ubiquitous, and virtually every poem contains images designed to capture the fleeting moment, the shimmering play of sensory perception that—implicitly—is precisely the essence of the phenomenon, and the truest way of communing with it. We see it in such striking images as "the day dims, losing petals like a poppy . . ." (in the poem that begins "Tam topoli . . ." [The poplars, there . . .]); we see it as the dominant modality of images in a poem like "Ishche ptashky . . ." ("The Birds are Still . . ."), a poem that, though it is early (1914–1916), already anticipates the apocalyptic tone of the next few years (the punctuation, here and throughout, adheres to Tychyna's idiosyncratic but motivated usage):

The birds are still bathing the blue day in ringing
    songs,
the robe of wheat is still turning yellow in waves of
    gold in the sun
(the winds are lying low, the winds are playing
    harps);—
But in the heavens someone is already quarreling.
A black-grey curtain silently covers half of the sky.
The earth puts on shadow . . . Man hides like a
    beast.
—The Lord is coming—the wormwood thinks
Rain begins to weep . . . . . and stops.
The mountain is silent. The valley is silent.
—The Lord's shadow,—the wormwood whispered.

And suddenly—the curtain splits in two!—Silence.
    Dead . . .
Fire surges: blooms, falls apart—until the waters
    boil!
And the song burst forth, the sacrifice was made.
The roads smoke, running, running . . .
Whirlwinds tear, like veins, the thin roots of old
    willows that pray in tears.
And the grasses—they do not even dare to weep.
Powerful forces are on the move! Darkness.
    Terror . . .
    . . . And they are ringing in the village.
And already the silver doves are trembling
Already they are sowing peace in the heavens.

                                (1:52)

The impressionist technique is even more pronounced when it is used as the organizing principle, the modality, as it were, of the given poem. Throughout Tychyna's early poetry, and indeed into the poetry of the 1930's, this is reflected in his predilection for the vignette. A scene, a fleeting moment, is what Tychyna's vision is most frequently drawn to; it may, of course, come in clusters—either explicitly, by appearing in a cycle, or through an implicit patterning of images—but the narrative connections are not spelled out. The immediately given perception-impression is the meaning,

and any "explanation" by the poet would be superfluous. Thus, in the cycle of four short poems called "Enharmoniine" (Enharmonic), "Mist," "Sun," "Wind," and "Rain" are depicted as four virtually identical "notes" that happen to be played on different "instruments." The depiction is pure association and impression; for example, "Rain":

And on the water in someone's hand
Snakes are climbing . . . Dream. To the very Bottom.
He gusted, breathed, scattered seeds
Run!—Something whispered to the river banks
Lie down . . . —it rocked the flowers.
A cloud let fall on the meadows
her embroidered hems.

                                (1:57)

In general, the impressionist technique is a major component of Tychyna's poetry. It may determine a poem or a cycle—not only the "light," purely sensual "Enharmonic" or the very similar "Pasteli" ("Pastels"), but also the much more substantial, philosophically and historically probing *Zamist' sonetiv i oktav*; it may appear, in the later poetry only as an isolated image, as a moment of pure feeling in a surrounding mass of standardized sentiments. Whatever the path of Tychyna's style, however, it remains an irreducible, identifying trait.

The question of Tychyna's symbolism, on the other hand, is rather more difficult to answer, in large measure because Tychyna (in contrast to, say, the major French or Russian symbolists) never expanded on its role in his poetry and his sense of himself as a poet, or even very much acknowledged its presence. In an undated questionnaire, attributed by the editor of *Iz shchodennykovykh zapysiv* (Excerpts from Diaries, 1981) to sometime in 1921, Tychyna is quite offhand about such matters: "The literary figure who influenced me with all his personality was Mykhailo Kotsiubynskii. I cannot include myself in any given school. I show some symbolism, and impressionism, and even futurism and to some degree imagism" (p. 43). Another reason may be that

Ukrainian symbolism as such was a rather tenuous phenomenon, with none of the theoretical or organizational features of its Russian counterparts. But the issue is not only valid, it is central. For one, the impressionist elements themselves speak for an imagination that is in many of its forms of perception clearly associated with the symbolist one; the prominent role synesthesia plays in both is a case in point. The primacy of the immediately given perception-as-feeling is not, however, so absolute in Tychyna as to obviate the presence of meaning.

Already in *Soniachni klarnety*, even its early parts, but especially in the next two collections, a very clear sense is given of levels of meaning and correspondences between them. While Tychyna's symbols may not be programmatically highlighted in his poetry (and while he does not discuss them in his other writings), they become apparent nonetheless. The natural elements—wind, storm, sun, and so on— are more than the phenomena themselves; they appear as players on a cosmic stage, and later project, symbolize, human historical forces as well. Their role as symbols is greatly facilitated by their prominence, frequently in anthropomorphic form, in Ukrainian folklore. Religious, Christian motifs and images—at times with their own tie to folklore through apocrypha—also serve as powerful symbols, be it in the personal context, adumbrating the birth of the poet (that is to say, the Annunciation, Genesis itself), or, with a darkening vision, the trials of his native land during the revolution and civil war.

It is as a technique, however, that Tychyna's symbolism is most apparent, and, in the context of Ukrainian poetry, most innovative. The language is pushed to what would seem the limit of its musicality and allusiveness, and syntax is consistently dislocated— through inversions or interruptions of the normal sequence, through deletions of purportedly essential elements, and even through a convention of punctuation that is at the very least idiosyncratic, and at times (purposefully) disorienting. Thus, a sentence or even a whole stanza may interrupt a phrase; the subject may be omitted, but is, therefore, probably even more stressed, as in the conclusion to the poem "Terror" from *Zamist' sonetiv i oktav:*

> The University, museums, libraries cannot give
>> What can be given by
> dark,
> gray,
> blue . . . (1:132)

("Eyes," the missing term, may or may not be the entirely apparent closure in English; in Ukrainian, however, the last three qualifiers— *kari, siri, blakytni*—can only refer to eyes.) Narrative, as in various poems of *Soniachni klarnety* or most evidently in *Zamist' sonetiv i oktav*, where it is the determining structure, may be antiphonal, with two (or more) distinct voices carrying the message.

Throughout, music and musicality is the very lifeblood of this poetry. It appears in a dazzling plenitude of guises and levels: as the mellifluousness of the language, with its inexhaustible rhythms, as ranges of images and allusions to music, and most effectively and subtly perhaps, as the utilization of musical tropes, leitmotifs, phrasing, and later whole genres and modalities (the movement, the cantata, the symphony) as a model for poetic expression. Ultimately, music becomes the key, the grand cognitive metaphor for understanding the complex polyphony of history, life, one's role in them, and one's own soul.

An intersection of the symbolist and impressionist techniques, and at the same time the formal correlative of the nexus of an internal and external music, is the already mentioned device of synesthesia. The fusing of different sensory planes, here of the visual and the auditory, is programmatically signaled by the very title "Clarinets of the Sun." In the course of the collection, such fusion, such melding (not necessarily only of these senses, but of various other combinations) becomes not only a recurrent motif, an evocative sensory shorthand, but something very close to a philosophical statement about the poet's calling. Any given instance may be powerful and moving in its own right. Thus, an early untitled poem begins:

> I stand on a cliff—
> Beyond the river, bells:
> I await your sails—
>
> (1:47)

The last line, literally, says: "Shadows are melting there, shadows in the distance," but in the original—"Tin' tam tone, Tin' tam des' . . ."—it is palpably clear that even more than the play of light on clouds and landscape there is the echo here of the distant bells. (Here, too, we see a characteristic distortion of the logical narrative, for the third line should follow the first, and the fourth line the second.) Such moments are many, each with its own poignant or dramatic message, but it is their totality that can reveal a profound truth: the autonomy, the chosen status of the poet. For one who is so attuned to nature, to the cosmic melody that is the universe, must surely have a special role to play in the affairs of men. And this premise, which is basically only implicit in the early, lyrical, romantic and self-centered parts of the first collection, becomes, in its second half, and then with great intensity in the following two collections, a conscious (though still hardly ideological), moral involvement in the historical experience of his nation.

A sense of historical context, more pointedly of an ongoing, bloody cataclysm—World War I—begins in the early parts of *Soniachni klarnety* only with solitary images and allusions. In the poem that begins "Tam topoli u poli na voli" (The poplars, there, free in the field), the very second line is the parenthetical, in effect, antiphonal, "Khtos' na zakhodi zhertvu prynis" (In the West someone made sacrifice)—which, of course, refers both to the carnage of battles and the red sunset that is emblematic of it. (It is another monument to the obtuseness of Soviet censorship that in the several collected editions of Tychyna that have appeared between 1957 and 1983, the line has been bowdlerized to remove the reference to "sacrifice"—with its unwelcome religious coloration.) In the poem that opens with the line "Na strimchastykh skeliakh" ("On steep cliffs"), the second stanza gives the following image:

> From the valley to the sky
> Hands were outstretched:
> O, lend us storms,
> A downpour of blueness!—
> Suddenly
> Down
> Fell drops of blood!
> Fell drops of blood . . .
>
> (1:67)

and concludes with the repeated words "Death rustles with a scythe."

In these and several similar instances the sense of that historical, ominous external reality is given impressionistically—as if purposefully not connecting that perception with any integrated and rational understanding of the world and the poetic self in it. In the poem beginning with the line "Odchyniaite dveri—" ("Open the doors") a transition to that understanding is now provided:

> Open the doors—
> The bride is coming!
> Open the doors—
> Azure blueness!
> Eyes, heart and chorals
> Stopped,
> Waiting . . .
>
> The doors opened—
> Night of tempest and deluge!
> The doors opened—
> All the roads in blood!
> With unweepable tears
> Darkness
> Rain . . .
>
> (1:69)

The very next cycle, "Skorbna Maty" (The Sorrowing Mother, or Mater Dolorosa), dedicated to the memory of the poet's own mother, takes one of many apocryphal stories of the Virgin Mary walking the earth and interceding for man, and locates the story in the Ukraine, in the period of its extreme tribulation. The Sorrowing Mother, now a composite symbol of the poet's mother, the Mother of God, the idealized, ever-grieving and victimized Ukraine of popular tradition (which icon rests, above all, on the poetry of Shevchenko) comes to serve as an ideal antipode to and clearest perspective on the destruction visited on this land; in this Ukraine she again witnesses the crucifixion, and herself dies of grief, forgotten—like this land—by the very angels in heaven.

"Zolotyi homin" ("The Golden Resonance"), the long poem that concludes the collection, addresses the historical context in an entirely different light: in its overt message, its imagery, and its emotional tonality it is a hymn of joy and hope celebrating the rebirth of a nation. Its rhapsodic tone resonates with elevated, religious (certainly more mystical than orthodox) imagery and an ideal, transcending historiography (the present rebirth of the Ukrainian nation is cast as a recapitulation of that distant—and apocryphal—event fixed in the Primary Chronicle of Kievan Rus' when Saint Andrew the Apostle was believed to have traveled up the Dnieper and blessed from the hill that is now the center of Kiev the surrounding territories). The poet is hardly unaware of the fratricidal strife that continues to exist; indeed his major dramatic opposition is between the overwhelming sense of joyful brotherhood and optimism that imbues him as it does so many of his countrymen, and the class rancor and hatred of others; his depiction of the latter in terms of "A black bird, with eyes that are claws! A black bird from the rotting crevices of the soul" or of cripples who "scuttle and whine and curse the sun, / the Sun and Christ" and who "nurture the beast within" makes his stance entirely unambiguous. The poem concludes with a crescendo of optimism and with the voice of the poet merged with the voice of the Ukrainian nation:

I have listened intently to your golden resonance—
And I have heard.
I have looked into your eyes
And I have seen.
The mountain of stones that they had piled up on
    my breast
I have thrown off as easily—
As down . . .
I am the unquenchable Beautiful Flame,
Eternal Spirit
Greet us then with the sun, with doves.
I am a strong nation!—with the Sun, with doves.
Greet us with our native songs!
I am young!
Young!

(1:86)

In no other poem of Tychyna's, or indeed of any other Ukrainian poet's, was this moment of rebirth ever conveyed with greater intensity or clarity of vision. But as a poem animated by a transcendent and religious—not to speak of national—sensibility, it was fated to be suppressed and bowdlerized; it remains bowdlerized even in the most recent relatively complete and honest Soviet edition.

In his next collection, *Pluh* (1920), Tychyna confronts the Revolution directly, in a concerted attempt to perceive its many facets and its higher meaning, and with an enormously expanded sense of confidence in his role and mission as poet. The opening, title poem immediately establishes the new parameters:

Wind.
Not wind—storm!
Crushing, breaking, tearing up from the earth . . .
Behind black clouds
(with flashes! with blows!)
behind black clouds a million million muscular
    arms . . .
Rolling. Cutting into the earth
(be it city, road, or meadow)
a plow into the earth.
And on the earth—men, beasts and orchards,
and on the earth gods and temples:
o pass, pass over us,
judge us!
And there were those that fled.

Into caves and lakes and forests.
—What power art thou?—
they asked.
And none of them rejoiced, none sang.
(The wind sped a fiery horse—
a fiery horse—
in the night—)
And only their dead staring eyes
 reflected all the beauty of the new day!
Eyes.

(1:89)

Tychyna, of course, accepts the Revolution, but, as was mentioned earlier, a Revolution that is conceived—specifically here, in the prologue, as it were, to this collection—not ideologically, nor even logically, but elementally, symbolically—and ambiguously. The dominant metaphor is that of apocalypse, and even though the end result of plowing is the prospect of a new beginning, of new life, its action in the here and now for the denizens of the sod, the earth men dwell on, is one of death and destruction. In the quintessentially impressionist, and symbolist, fabric of this poem this is precisely the cutting edge of the share: dead staring eyes. And the fact that it is *only* these eyes that reflect the beauty of the new day, the Revolution's promise, constitutes a very ambivalent endorsement. As much of the poetry of this collection, and especially of the next one, *Zamist' sonetiv i oktav,* will show, it is an endorsement that comes from the will, from the increasingly insistent imperative to be consonant with the age, and not from the whole self, certainly not from its reservoir of human empathy. (That, however, will soon also be given full voice.)

What lends resonance and power to this act of will is that it involves not only the real world, the Revolution that is turning upside down the Russian Empire, but the metaworld, that of Tychyna's poetry. For the plow (like the clarinets of the sun) refers through Tychyna's characteristic metathematic device to the poetry now unfolding before the reader. And the development from the one world to the other entails not only

a shift of metaphors, but of worldviews and self-perceptions: the dominance of a unifying, harmonious, and at heart beneficent vision now gives way to a vision of separation and judgment and authority. Its major expression is the crystallization of the role of the poet as tribune and moral legislator. The very next poem, "Siite . . ." ("Sow"), continues the grand metaphor of the Revolution as an agricultural cycle: after the plowing, the sowing. The poet's role (and voice) is now that of an enthusiastic taskmaker, as literally each sentence of the poem is in the imperative mood; to take but the first lines of each stanza:

Sow into the fertile black earth.
. . . .
Work—the beehive is awake.
. . . .
Be possessed—not cold.
. . . .
Strike the brass, dispel the clouds!

(1:90)

The poem is a far cry from mere exhortation or sloganeering: it is replete with neologisms, and its striking, futurist-influenced imagery overpowers the ideological content of the message. Thus, the last stanza:

Strike the brass, dispel the clouds!
Believe (don't lyricize!), go,
shout out with fanfares in the night:
put sharps, sharps in your keys!

(1:90)

The enthusiasm that is already so apparent here leads Tychyna in a few poems to reach for a new genre—the poetical equivalent of the ubiquitous exhortatory poster, where everything is simple and exaggerated and hard-hitting, where the new titans of labor, as he envisions in "Perezoriuiut' zori" ("They Will Outshine the Stars"), for example, will inherit a new, industrialized paradise:

With songs, with hammers!—
(the motif is the locomotive!)—

Rushing to meet them—factories
oceans, fields of grain . . .

(1:94)

This does not at all become the dominant theme or mood of *Pluh,* however. In fact, to use a Tychynian image, the ringing chord that this collection is clearly intended to be breaks apart into several distinct and hardly consonant notes. This does not detract from its aesthetic achievement: *Pluh* remains at the very apex of Tychyna's art. But the Revolution— which is no longer just that, but an extended and brutal civil war—can no longer be reduced to a single elemental force, or an unequivocal value. The poet's openness and sensitivity to experience, and sense of duty toward what he perceives as his calling, quite simply militate against this.

Several different stances emerge here. The poet continues the role of spokesman for the nation, exhorting it to accept the emerging new order as part of the cosmic plan (e.g., the cycle "Sotvorinnja svitu" [The Creation of the World], or the cycle "Psalom zalizu" [Psalm to Steel]). And he even couches this, as in "Palit' universaly" ("Burn the Decrees") in the perfervid language of a political orator—with an anarchist bent ("Curse the laws and bureaucratic fury— / Freedom!—let that be your only order"). At the same time, Tychyna turns to his fellow poets, castigating them for their gamut of weaknesses (false aestheticism, eroticism, hunger for love, simple shallowness) and enjoining them to realize their true potential in the moment of national trial.

The moralizing and didacticism surging here are kept in check and are ultimately defused by Tychyna's own agonizing reappraisal of himself as a poet. We see it in two poems (actually a diptych and triptych) on the theme of Shevchenko (with the second depicting a private pilgrimage, in times of war, to his grave on the banks of the Dnieper) and a triptych entitled "Lysty do poeta" (Letters to the Poet). The latter becomes the first of many exercises in self-criticism with the authors, simple village people, telling the poet that they don't quite understand him, that his poetry is not really close to life, and boldly asking him "who needs those rachitic sonnets and songs!" The criticism is deflected by the fact that the last accusatory letter ends with "You are a power / and you will still be a communist," and by the more basic fact of poetically identifying, naming, and thus purging the anxiety about one's reception "among the people." As history shows, the issue, however, will not be laid to rest.

Perhaps the most powerful notes in *Pluh* are those that reflect Tychyna's anguish at the destruction befalling his land. In the poem "I Bielyi i Blok i Iesenin i Kliuiev" (And Bely and Blok and Esenin and Kluiev), this is again connected with the imperative of speaking for and serving one's nation. The four Russian poets mentioned in the title have provided a voice for Russia, and Russia has its messiah—Lenin. But who will lead the Ukraine from its bondage, who will be its Moses? The answer, of course, is the Poet. And yet the answer is undercut by the concluding lines, addressed to the Poet by himself, and implicitly by the land itself: "to love one's land is no crime / if it is for all." The assertion would seem self-evident, even naively so, only in "normal" circumstances. The bleak fact is that Ukrainian patriotism must always guard against the charge of chauvinism, and that in its relation with Russia—for it is this that the poem examines, if obliquely—any native sentiment can be a political crime, to be called "separatism" by the czarist regime, or "bourgeois nationalism" by the Soviet one.

Still, virtually all the poems that turn to the theme of death and destruction are not programmatic, not tribunicial, but intensely personal and laconic; at times they rise to a luminous, almost mystical sense of man's tragic fate. The poem beginning "Na maidani kolo tserkvy" ("On the green by the church"), one of the most anthologized of Tychyna's poems, depicts with ever more somber colors a group of men choosing a leader and going off to fight for the Revolution and freedom—and to die. The highly symbolist and difficult "Mizhplanetni intervaly" ("Interplanetary Intervals") attempts to visualize the void where the spirits of the fallen revolutionary heroes are trapped, unable to join the classical deities (Jupiter, Mars, Venus) or to be apotheosized by them into constellations (as the Greek heroes were), because they no longer share that belief. "Zrazuzh za selom" ("Directly Beyond the Village"), arguably the most moving of these poems, depicts the aftermath of a massacre—by whom, of whom, is not given and not important. They were simply people; cold, implacable, and ever-present death has settled upon the land, and the very people searching at night among the corpses for relatives are themselves shadows of death.

With its gamut of different themes and stances, *Pluh* does appear heterogeneous; if it attains unity—and it does—it is through its overriding sense of purposefulness and need to break new ground. *Zamist' sonetiv i oktav,* also published in 1920 and consisting of an introductory short poem and a cycle of eleven poems, each with an antistrophe, is quite openly a collage, or a montage, of scenes, impressions, recollections, and ruminations, all dealing with the Revolution and the ongoing civil war. And yet this is a remarkably coherent and unified, even tightly knit collection. This is achieved by several converging factors: above all, by the poet's stance of high moral seriousness, which leads him to probe and question the values and verities of society and of ideology, his own values, and his own character. This moral or, loosely speaking, philosophical inquiry is compounded with an introspectiveness that is entirely open and honest, as a consequence of which the impressionistic poetic technique becomes a form of meditation; at times it is very much like a stream of consciousness, one, however, that is not naturally aimless but is channeled by the twin banks of ethical and aesthetic concerns. Finally, the form also establishes coherence and unity: it is poetic prose, with no apparent conventional metrical or rhyming or strophic pattern, but with a clear rhythm of images, tropes, and moods that seems eminently appropriate to the implicit goal of attaining openness, full clarity of perception, and honesty of judgment. For this, Tychyna is implying, a sonnet or octave would be a dissonance.

The title of the collection is again woven into the opening poem. An impressionistically captured moment—mixing images of the coming dawn, the sound of distant trumpets and cannon, an insistently recurring line from the poetry of Skovoroda and a memory of the poet's dead mother—culminates with a cry of despair: "A curse on all, a curse on all those who have become beasts!" (*Zamist' sonetiv i oktav* [1:127]). The poems that follow are hardly curses, but they are an excoriation, and hopefully an exorcism, of the beast in man. And curiously, this is done on two seemingly incompatible levels: on the one hand by direct didactic and aphoristic statements, moral prescriptions for an age that scoffs at them, and on the other by a subtle interweaving, sometimes through the barest of hints and allusions, of the mythic story of Orpheus, the archetypal poet and musician, the reputed son of Apollo, who with his lyre could move even the savage beasts to forget their ferocity, who was the first of several poets to descend to hell in search of his muse and to return, and who was fated to be torn to pieces by the wild followers of Bacchus. The fate of the poet, a tragic, grim fate, is the symbolically coded, unquestionably autobiographical, deep structure of this cycle.

"Terror," the second poem of the cycle, shows both levels at work:

Again we take the Gospels, the philosophers, the poets. The person who said: to kill is a sin!—is found in the morning with his head shot through. And the dogs fight over his body on the trash heap.

Lie still, my mother, do not wake!

A great idea requires sacrifices. But is it a sacrifice, when beast eats beast?

—do not wake, mother . . .

Cruel aestheticism!—when will you stop
delighting in a slit throat?

Beast eats beast.

(1:131)

The injunctions, the pleas for humanness are
evident, and they are repeated in various regis-
ters, for example "Indeed: no number of can-
nons will suffice to establish a socialism without music" (the antistrophe to "The Highest
Power"), or "Join that party where they look on
the person as a treasure belonging to the whole
world, and where all, to the last man, are
against the penalty of death" (antistrophe to
"Evoe") or "Everything can be excused by a sublime goal—except for the soul's emptiness"
(antistrophe to "Porozhnecha" ["Emptiness"]).
The Orpheic story in "Terror" is alluded to in
the image of the person preaching nonviolence
(by contiguity, one with the evangelists, philosophers, and poets) who is found killed in
the morning. (The first such reference occurs
in the very first poem, "Osin'" ["Autumn"], in
the image of the head—in the Orpheic myth the
decapitated head is explicitly described—that
has been planted, but will not stay upright
and will not speak.) Indeed these references,
precisely like Orpheus' body, are scattered
throughout the cycle, seemingly randomly.
And this in turn points to the organizing principle of the whole: as any individual poem, the
collection itself is given synchronically, it is all
simultaneously present, and no summation
can replace the total effect of experiencing the
whole. (It is very revealing, for example, that
several poems depict the fleeting moment between sleep and awakening when disparate
threads of thought, mental images, and precon-
scious sensations converge into a profound insight.) One can, however, single out the poem
that is the most autobiographical; it is the last
one, the antistrophe to "Kukil'" ("Tare"):

To have the prison guards play Scriabin—that
is not yet Revolution.

The Eagle, the Trident, the Hammer and
Sickle . . . and each claims to be native . . .

That which is native to us was killed by the
rifle. That which is native lies at the
bottom of the soul.

Will I, too, kiss the Pope's slipper?
(*Zolotyi homin. Poezii,* p. 100)

For some emigré Ukrainian critics this was
Tychyna's anguished prophecy of imminent
capitulation. As one writer dramatized it: "The
red slipper that he kissed concealed in its fabric a poison that entered him like a spiritual
paralysis and killed the Orpheic strings of the
heart." For Soviet critics, to the small extent
that they can comment on this highly heterodox
text, the competition of the symbols (of the imperial eagle, the nationalist trident, and the
Bolshevik hammer and sickle) is illusory, for
Tychyna was already clearly siding with the
latter; the ritual of subjugation in the kissing of
the slipper is simply dismissed. But the answer is surely in neither of these reductive extremes but in the totality of Tychyna's canon,
and to the extent that it is still expanding any
answer must still be qualified. One should
note, however, that ever since its first publication, *Zamist' soneti i oktav* has been in greater
or lesser degree banned from the Soviet editions of Tychyna: its humanism and questioning of ideologically sanctioned ruthlessness
made it simply too heretical. Even now, when
the collection has been basically rehabilitated, the last, above-cited antistrophe is still
missing.

THE MIDDLE PERIOD

There is no consensus as to the periodiza-
tion of Tychyna's poetry; on this issue as on so
many others relating to Tychyna there is rather
ideological polarization. But the case for a distinct period that lies between the one just discussed and the last period of his creativity,
which is diametrically different, is a persua-

1669

sive one. In effect, the 1920's and even the early 1930's together constitute a separate phase of Tychyna's work and achievement, a phase that we can preliminarily describe as one where features of his early poetry and of his late poetry coexist in an artistically effective, often remarkably innovative new modality. Furthermore, even if the poetry produced in this period is far from being uniform in style or even quality, the chronological points of demarcation are clear. The difference between *Zamist' soneti i oktav,* and even *Pluh,* on the one hand, and *V kosmichnomu orkestri* on the other is significant and demonstrable; the one between *Partiia vede* and *Chuttia iedynoi rodyny* is much less so, especially for the general reader. Still, the changes that are occurring here on a deeper poetic level are important, and generally a positing of a transitional period does not hinge on an unequivocal upper limit.

V kosmichnomu orkestri is a cycle of ten poems and as such the shortest of Tychyna's published collections; individual poems were often reprinted in various anthologies and school textbooks; in various subsequent collected editions most of the cycle was included as part of the next large collection, *Viter z Ukrainy.* Yet the cycle is *sui generis.* It reflects a then highly topical fascination with cosmic imagery (particularly evident in various futurist and constructivist publications) and a conjoining of that imagery with an assertive and hyperbolic celebration of the new Soviet state. In many respects this poetry picks up and continues earlier themes and already familiar cognitive and emotional attitudes, and most concretely some already established symbols and images. It does so with a new energy and a palpable sense of liberation—from fear, grief, despair, and doubt. As he has done before and as he will do again, Tychyna is showing how closely his psyche resonates with the life of the collective. The assertiveness, the confidence in the new, bright world is different from that in *Pluh,* however: it is not willed, it is without any tinge of the declamatory. At the same time, it echoes the inspired and expansive cosmic consciousness of *Soniachni klarnety,* as when he speaks, in the second poem ("Ia dukh, dukh vichnosti"), in the name of a cosmic force that extends from the infinite to the mundane:

> I am spirit, the spirit of eternity, of
>   matter, I am the primal muscles.
> I am the spirit of time, the spirit of
>   measure and space, the spirit of numbers.
> Aerolithic rivers flow
> from just one of my oars . . .
>
> I am the spirit-mover, the machine-measure,
>   choruses of automobiles
> My yard-garage surges with motors
> And effortlessly, like children to the beach
> I lead titans into space.
>
> (1:155)

The poet's all-encompassing, Whitmanesque consciousness allows him to see the universe's master plan, to overcome and reconcile all oppositions, for "What are our tears and moans and shouts? / What are all the earthly dramas in the face of the tragedy of the cosmos?" From this ultimate perspective, even the moral qualms and anguish of his preceding collection recede in significance, as in "Nedokrovna planeta kruh sontsia sokhla":

> Be like an airplane my soul, like an airplane,
> Don't lower your flight, don't fall
> Are you the only one outraged by the man-beast,
>   by cruelty and lies?
> Are not the hearts of all pierced by bullets?
> And thousands buried alive in the earth—is it
>   not they who each night crucify the soul
>   with cries of:
> Revenge, revenge. Blood for blood.
> Whom shall we punish? The sun that pours
>   handfuls of fire into the earth's arteries?
> The earth that cannot give birth without dying?
> Christ was not the first, Robespierre not the
>   last, but blood was always there, in
>   different measure, and each battle is
>   akin to its age.
>
> (1:162)

Viter z Ukrainy continues in various ways the unparalleled energy of *V kosmichnomu ork-*

estri, but again the aerolithic river of Tychyna's poetry begins to turn in unexpected directions, unexpected, that is, from the ground-zero perspective of his contemporaries. More than his previous collections it is diverse in theme and tone, and spans a gamut from the already encountered elevated celebration of the new age, of socialist construction, and of high rhetorical excoriations of ideological enemies, specifically the emigré's, to purely personal, lyrical depictions of everyday things, of a May Day parade in Kharkiv, of leaves swirled by an autumn wind—depictions that are formal masterpieces of a new futurist-inspired, but still inimitably Tychynian poetics. This new poetic idiom—nervous, quick, seemingly a direct copy of the rough, jerky speech and tempo of the new life—is most striking when wedded to his reworkings of folk genres. It is here that Tychyna's ever more pronounced drive to reach the greatest possible audience, to be *the* poet of the new masses, finds its most innovative medium. In such poems as "Try Syny" ("Three Sons") or "Kozhumiaka" ("The Tanner") or "Plach Iaroslavny" ("Iaroslavna's Lament") he takes either a motif already existing in the folk repertoire (a story about three brothers, or a tanner who slew the dragon) or in high literature, which in the case of the latter is a famous passage from *The Igor Tale,* a medieval masterpiece, and reworks it into a contemporary "folktale" or "folk poem" that blends traditional folkloric tropes and devices with his new idiom and expresses in a highly militant, almost brutal manner the class consciousness, the power and will of the triumphant proletariat. In effect, the poet becomes the *vox populi*—in form (which is highly stylized and sophisticated) and content (which is increasingly adhering to the dominant ideology). And if one accepts the Latin saying "Vox populi vox dei" (The voice of the people is the voice of God), then in this voice Tychyna has again found that all-powerful, animating source of energy. Before, his voice resonated with the music of the spheres; now it is with the "inevitability of history"; either way, the imperative of consonance

is met. As Tychyna put it in a line from the "Symphony" *Skovoroda*: "How can one not roar / if the age, the age is roaring."

Tychyna's attempt to fully merge his poetic role and voice with the tempo, concerns, and emotions of the current day is exemplified in *Chernihiv,* a small collection of eight poems that was published in 1931 and almost immediately encountered resistance and criticism from average readers and critics alike. As Tychyna himself spoke about it, *Chernihiv* was conceived as a "poetic sketch," or as others put it, a reportage, of a trip through the city of his youth to witness the changes wrought by the Revolution, and the first Five-Year Plan, and to capture its new pulsing rhythms. To do so the poet's persona must be entirely suspended, bracketed out of the picture (all that is left of it are brief descriptive titles to the poems, for example, "My Friend the Worker Leads Me Around the City and Boasts" or "We Buy a Newspaper"); the poetry itself is a purportedly pure recording of the voices of the people, the sounds and voices of the age. Here, in short, Tychyna presents the new society speaking for itself, unabashedly revealing its monochromatic ideology, its incessant repetition of slogans, its din and its shouting. To capture it, Tychyna uses the most elemental forms—chanted slogans, the simplified language and cant of newspaper articles, the argot of popular songs. The language becomes refracted and distorted, words and lines crowd into each other and collide, punctuation disappears. Again, without any fanfare or programmatic commentary, Tychyna is introducing a new poetics, this time of constructivism. Its theoretical premises (as elaborated by the Russian critic Kornelii Zelinskii) of "loading down" the word, of maximizing the expressiveness of the smallest units, of replacing the voice of the author with that of his characters, of total fidelity to local color and finally formal and acoustic experimentation, are all amply illustrated in this collection.

Every poem in *Chernihiv,* without exception, presents or makes specific reference to boasts, threats, vows, curses, or shouts. This explosion of noise (one of the lines of the concluding poem speaks of "exploding with a negation of the past") is countered, however, by the theme of deafness, which occurs in several places, and which on the one hand reflects the inability to perceive the new reality (indeed echoing poems from *Pluh*) and on the other, a very natural and human desire to shut one's ears against this acoustic rape of the psyche. In keeping with a subtle note of introspection that is present in this poetry, and in true dialectical fashion, we are shown that assertiveness is inevitably accompanied by doubt.

In fact *Chernihiv* can be said to have a false bottom: at various moments it seems quite parodic. The poem entitled "A chy ne iest' tse sami nakhvalky abo zh zapomorochennia vid uspikhov" ("But Is This Not Simply Bragging or Dizziness from Success"), which pointedly echoes a speech by Stalin ("Dizziness from Success," published in *Pravda,* 2 March 1930), has this for a third stanza:

> Let Europe croak on
> our thought's but one
> only one perturbation
> tradition's decapitation
> collectivization
>
> (1:229)

The last poem, "Stara Ukraina Zminytys' musyt' " (Old Ukraine Must Change), presents a kind of final mise-en-scène where all the players encountered in the cycle—marchers in a demonstration, workers, Komsomol youth, and so on—gather for what would seem a final chorus, one that pushes everything to its utter limit. As the first (and last) stanza shows, slogans, hyperbole, and snippets of Marxist-Leninist doctrine are mixed in a brew that seems part sonorous chant and part gibberish:

> Transmigrating satiating
> quantitatively qualitatively oversloshing
> mutually interpenetrating contradictions
> exploding with a negation of the past

following the law of dialectics we are headed for a boundless future

> (1:235)

In a word, Tychyna seems to be hoisting "the age" by its own petard. "The crying contradiction between content and form," as one critic lamented, seems to be intentional.

Between the poetry of *Viter z Ukrainy* and *Chernihiv,* Tychyna did write other works that diverged significantly from the dominant tone of these collections. These are the personal and introspective poems from the so-called Crimean cycle, the three parts of the dramatic poem that begins "Chystyla maty kartopliu" (Mother was peeling potatoes), and the "Symphony" *Skovoroda.* Tychyna was to work on the latter throughout the 1920's and 1930's, but he never did complete it. From the beginning, the eighteenth-century Ukrainian mystic philosopher and poet Skovoroda was a kind of model for Tychyna, and it is to him that he devoted his *Zamist' sonetiv i oktav,* but not entirely surprisingly, the poem from its inception had an autobiographical cast, with Skovoroda serving as a kind of ideal alter-ego for Tychyna. The various redactions and drafts of the poem show how with the years Tychyna attempted to make the historical Skovoroda fit more and more the obligatory Marxist-Leninist and socialist realist interpretation of Ukrainian culture and history, which here meant making Skovoroda—in contradiction to all the available evidence, both historical and of his own texts—into an engaged social revolutionary, a supporter of peasant rebels. It is more than likely that Tychyna found the discrepancy untenable, not only for historical reasons, but for the violence done to Skovoroda's spiritual and mystical core.

In sum, none of these works, finished or not, published or not, broke the overall pattern: by the early 1930's, Tychyna had become a bard and for all practical purposes only a bard. The sense of autonomy, indeed of the sovereignty that one normally associates with great poetry, and which at various crucial moments had imbued Tychyna's work, had disappeared. The collection that was generally seen (and particularly stressed by zealous critics) as finalizing Tychyna's transition into officially sanctioned poetry, and officialdom, was *Partiia vede.* Here, too, however, there is more—and less—than meets the eye. For one, to at least the same degree as and probably more than in *Chernihiv,* the poet, as persona, as voice, simply as a human presence, is absent. The collection is subtitled "Pisni, peany, himny" ("Songs, Paeans, Hymns"), which accurately reflects the impersonal, collective tonality of the whole and of its constituent pieces. The poems here, beginning with the title poem, then "Pisnia Chervonoi Armii" (Red Army Song), "Pisnia komsomol'tsiv" (Komsomol Song), two installments of "Pisnia traktorystky" (Song of the Woman Tractor Driver), "Pisnia pro Kirova" (Song about Kirov), and all the rest, are like the texts of *Chernihiv:* seemingly overheard by the poet in the street, not created by him. There is still, to be sure, evidence of Tychyna's excellent ear for the rhythm of the period and the tenor, the "feel" of the collective, but the other determining qualities—the searching and the moral intensity, the free play of the imagination, even the formal complexity that still animated *Chernihiv*—all these are removed. The poetry is now for the most part regular, unambiguous, and accessible to the dullest reader and the most watchful Party critic. And yet a careful reading shows that even in these songs, paeans, and hymns there remains a subtle formal consciousness that only becomes apparent when viewed retrospectively, from a temporal and psychological distance.

THE LATE POETRY

The sight of a poet consciously and effectively remaking himself in his later years is quite rare, but not entirely unprecedented in world literature. The remarkable achievement of William Butler Yeats rests on the work of the last third, the last twenty-five years of his life,

and stems from a deliberate decision to slough off his pre-Raphaelite beginnings. The not uncommon decline of a great poet in older age may be epitomized by the fate of William Wordsworth, who at the end, as a critic noted, was a shrunken giant "carried off the stage on the double shield of religious orthodoxy and political conservatism." With Tychyna we have the cheerless instance of a compounding of these two scenarios: to all appearances a deliberate, continuous, and willingly self-inflicted restructuring for the worse.

In terms of quantity, the poetry Tychyna wrote after *Partiia vede* and before his death in 1967 is roughly equal to his earlier work—if one includes *Skovoroda* in the latter. Aesthetically, qualitatively speaking, this later poetry is undoubtedly inferior. It is not entirely devoid of poetic achievement, however, and it does provide an invaluable mirror to the age and the man.

On the most immediate level, the later poetry tends to the prosaic (speaking both literally and metaphysically). Here, the early poetry's dominant impressionism, the focus on the detail that is lit from within by a corresponding idea and emotion, is supplemented by large, theoretical, and ultimately abstract formulations. The later poetry is also entirely normative and orthodox, and it achieves this state by avoiding at all cost any ambiguity or polysemy. All the *i*'s are dotted—almost literally, for in the later editions of his earlier work punctuation is standardized and all the formal experiments, the truncated or enjambed words of *Chernihiv,* for example (not to speak of the religious or even cosmic imagery of the earlier poetry), are forgotten. Furthermore, the poetry becomes relentlessly official: Tychyna not only adheres to the Party line (which many writers did) but proceeds to invoke it enthusiastically in contexts that hardly require it. In poems written in the 1960's, for example, he seemingly cannot complete a lyrical poem, or a reminiscence of childhood, without decrying the American involvement in Vietnam or, say, the junta of colonels in Greece. In this connection it is important to note that whereas in the 1930's—as we have now learned—Tychyna often wrote fine lyrical poems for his private use, so to speak, with no intention of publishing them, in the postwar period this is rarely if ever the case. Indeed, World War II seems to be the final watershed, with the poetry that follows it being in the main the most stunted.

In terms of genre, the last period shows a predilection for the large form (long narrative and dramatic works) as well as for occasional poetry (the déclassé descendant of the high ode of earlier times). Here, too, some works may be entirely successful, as for example the heroic epic poem *Shablia Kotovs'koho* (Sword of Kotovs'kyi, 1938), which depicts the Soviet-Polish war of 1920. The dramatic poem *Shevchenko i Chernyshevs'kyi* (1941), on the other hand, is an obvious failure, again because it is written entirely *à thèse*—to illustrate the official line as to what Shevchenko's relations with the Russians should have been.

It is precisely in the matter of genre, however, that a central structure in Tychyna's poetry begins to emerge, a structure, moreover, that once more obliges us to rethink the criteria by which Tychyna is described and evaluated. Stated most succinctly, this is the process of blurring the line between adult and children's poetry. Youth and youthfulness is a virtual constant in Tychyna's poetry. As a theme, as an ideal, youth is already highlighted in the first collection, but in the early poetry youthfulness or childhood does not determine the level and modality of the poetic discourse. By all appearances, in the later poetry, especially of the last two decades, it does. Many poems (particularly the long narrative ones) not only deal thematically with children, kindergartens, grade schools and schoolmarms, and, of course, Tychyna's own childhood, but as if by a natural extension adjust their arguments and tonality to a childlike and childish level. To be sure, this is not uniform and universal: there are several significant works, such as the powerful war poem *Pokhoron druha,* and various lyrical or meditative poems that show a high moral

and intellectual level of discourse—but they are the exception. The great majority of Tychyna's late poetry, with its simplistic ideology, its didacticism and catechetic elaboration of selected (or simply current) points of doctrine, its sentimental and reductive understanding of human motivation and history, implies a reader entirely different from what one would normally assume—in effect an adolescent or child, not an adult. Not only the addressee, but the implied speaker, the voice, seems to come from the ranks of adolescents or children, as seen most crucially in the poem "The Party Leads." With this factor in the equation, the whole question of Tychyna's purported unconditional capitulation assumes a different cast. (How do the "articles of surrender" couched in the militant doggerel of fourteen-year-olds obligate the forty-three-year-old poet?)

Two moments need to be addressed here. One is the hard fact that to write in this way, totally simplifying the surrounding (and basically ignoring the internal) reality and accepting as unalloyed truth all that is handed down by the "adults," the all-wise Father Stalin (later: Father Lenin) and the nurturing Mother Party (the images are Tychyna's, and generally topical) was the safe course. (It is instructive, perhaps, that in the mid-1930's, specifically 1934-1938, the time when hundreds of Ukrainian writers and scholars, thousands of intellectuals, and indeed, with but a handful of exceptions, the entire Ukrainian party and government apparatus was being purged and liquidated, the only works that Tychyna published, and repeatedly republished, were *Partiia vede* and a small book of explicitly children's poems entitled *Ku-ku!* (Coo-Coo!, 1934) It was the way of survival, and many writers fell back on something akin to it. The second, no less concrete fact is that it was eminently accurate and psychologically realistic. Even today the dominant value in Soviet society is control and authority, and in the period prior to the post-Stalinist thaw (and Tychyna, sadly, never allowed himself to thaw), it was all the more oppressively evident. No paradigm, one may submit, does more to capture the sense of total powerlessness and the mind set—and social value and reality—of total control than the image of a kindergarten with children being gently but firmly indoctrinated by a Tychynian schoolmarm. The eminent twentieth-century Polish writer Witold Gombrowicz described society's relentless attempts at controlling, molding, "infantilizing" the individual through a comic and analytic perspective—and from without. Tychyna, drawing on the harrowing reality around him, on trauma, and on the need to survive, illuminates and illustrates this reality from within.

The option of not writing, of falling silent or turning to translating (as was done by the Russian poet Boris Pasternak) was apparently not available to and not really contemplated by Tychyna. He was, by his own doing and choice, the official bard. He continued writing. Tragically, at the end, in the last phase, his ideal reader was the censor, and not even the real censor, but the censor within. For though he may have been National Commissar of Education and even chairman of the Supreme Council of the Ukrainian SSR, the party critics never allowed Tychyna to forget that he had "vacillated" in his early poetry, that he had "deviated" into VAPLITE, or that he had repeatedly slipped into "formalism." Probably the most poignant fact of all is that in the 1960's, when Ukrainian poetry was undergoing a genuine revival, with honesty and openness and artistic daring becoming the coin rather than the exception, Tychyna, counseling caution and ideological orthodoxy, was loath to join or much support this youthful revolt. The notion that the poet must teach and preach, that no poetry without politics is possible, had become a part of Tychyna; it, too, was now in Tychyna's heart.

In the larger historical perspective, however, these and similar failings have already begun and will continue to recede in significance. Not because history is forgiving—it never is—but because Tychyna's true achievement tran-scends them. His parameters are provided not by his life and career, nor by the complex and cruel times he lived in, but by the poetry he created.

Selected Bibliography

FIRST EDITIONS

INDIVIDUAL WORKS

POETRY

Soniachni klarnety. Kiev, 1918.
Pluh. Kiev, 1920.
Zamist' sonetiv i oktav. Kiev, 1920.
V kosmichnomu orkestri. Kharkiv, 1921.
Viter z Ukrainy. Kharkiv, 1924.
Chernihiv. Kharkiv, 1931.
Partiia vede. Kharkiv, 1934.
Chuttia iedynoi rodyny. Kiev, 1938.
Shablia Kotovs'koho. 1938.
My idemo na bii. Kiev-Kharkiv, 1941.
Stal' i nizhnist'. Kiev, 1941.
Volia neprelozhna. Kiev, 1941.
Peremahat' i zhyt'. Ufa, 1942.
Tebe my znyshchym—chort z toboiu! Ufa, 1942.
Den' nastane. Ufa, 1943.
Poezii (1941–1944). Kharkiv, 1945.
I rosty i diiaty. Kiev, 1949.
Mohutnist' nam dana. Kiev, 1953.
My svidomist' liudstva. Kiev, 1957.
Zrostai, prechudovnyi svite. Kiev, 1960.
Komunizmu dali vydni. Kiev, 1961.
Sribnoi nochi. Kiev, 1964.

CHILDREN'S POETRY AND STORIES

Ivasyk-Telesyk. kazka. Kharkiv, 1924.
Ku-ku! Kiev-Kharkiv, 1934.
Lidka. Kiev, 1940.
Syritka. Kiev-Kharkiv, 1944.
Svity nashe sonce! Kiev, 1947.
Sad zelenyi. Kiev, 1949.
Dudaryk. Kazka. Kiev, 1950.
Slava Bat'kivshchyni. Kiev, 1951.
A ia u hai khodyla. Kiev, 1952.
Muzychnyi ranok v konservatorii. Kiev, 1955.
Khor lisovykh dzvinochkiv. Kiev, 1956.
Slukhaiem pro Lenina. Kiev, 1956.
Do molodi mii chystyi holos. Kiev, 1959.

Sad sadyv nam Lenin. Kiev, 1961.
Hai Shumliat. Kiev, 1967.

MODERN EDITIONS OF INDIVIDUAL WORKS

Podorozh do Ikhtimana. Kiev, 1969.
V sertsi u moim. Kiev, 1970.
Skovoroda. Symfonia. Kiev, 1971.
Z mynuloho v maibutnie. Kiev, 1973.
Chytaiu, dumaiu, notuiu. Kiev, 1974.
Iz shchodennykovykh zapysiv. Kiev, 1981.
Podorozh z kapeloiu K. H. Stetsenka. Kiev, 1982.

COLLECTED WORKS

Zolotyi homin. Poezii. L'viv-Kiev, 1922. Reprint, State College, Pa., 1967. Includes the first three collections of poetry.
Poezii. Kharkiv, 1929.
Poezii. Kharkiv, 1932.
Vybrani tvory. Kiev, 1939.
Vybrani tvory v tr'okh tomakh. Kiev, 1946–1947.
Vybrani tvory v tr'okh tomakh. Kiev, 1957.
Vybrani tvory v shesty tomakh. Kiev, 1961.
Zibrannia tvoriv v dvanadtsiaty tomakh. Kiev, 1983–. The most complete Soviet collected edition; some poetry from various periods still not included.

BIOGRAPHICAL AND CRITICAL STUDIES

Biletskyi, Oleksandr. Introduction to *Pavlo Tychyna, tvory v shesty tomakh.* Kiev, 1961.
Grabowicz, George G. "The Poetry of Reconstitution: Pavlo Tyčyna's *V sertsi u mojim.*" *Recenzija* 2:3–29 (1972).
———. "Tyčyna's *Černihiv.*" *Harvard Ukrainian Studies* 1:79-113 (1977).
———. "Continuity and Discontinuity in the Poetry of Pavlo Tychyna." In E. Bristol, ed., *East European Literature. Selected Papers from the Second World Congress for Soviet and East European Studies.* Berkeley, Calif., 1982.
Nieuważny, Florian. Introduction to *Pawło Tyczyna. Poezje.* Warsaw, 1969.
Novychenko, Leonid. *Poeziia i revolutsiia.* Kiev, 1959.
———. Introduction to *Pavlo Tychyna, V sertsi u moim.* Kiev, 1970.
Tel'niuk, Stanislav. *Chervonykh sonts protuberantsi.* Kiev, 1968.
———. *Pavlo Tychina.* Moscow, 1974.

GEORGE G. GRABOWICZ

PÄR LAGERKVIST

(1891–1974)

A T THE TIME of his death at age 83 in 1974, Pär Lagerkvist's position in Swedish literature was undisputed. Behind him lay a long writing career that began in the first decade of this century. His production includes works in all the literary genres—poetry, drama, prose fiction (novels as well as short stories), essays, and aesthetic and philosophical manifestos. Outside of Sweden, where Lagerkvist is probably best known as the author of the novels *Dvärgen* (*The Dwarf,* 1944) and *Barabbas* (1950), his works have been translated into thirty-six languages. There is a happy play on words in the author's last name, which in Swedish means "laurel twig," and in the course of his career Lagerkvist received many distinctions traditionally associated with Apollo's sacred tree: in 1928 he was given a prestigious literary prize by Samfundet De Nio (a Swedish society of writers and literary critics); in 1940 he was elected one of the "Eighteen Immortals" of the Swedish Academy of Literature; in 1941 he received an honorary doctorate from the University of Gothenburg; and in 1951 he was awarded the Nobel Prize for literature.

Despite international attention Pär Lagerkvist remained an extremely private person who shunned publicity and was unwilling to discuss his own life or comment on his work. It is therefore not surprising that he has presented a challenge to readers and scholars who have tried to evaluate and to interpret the man and his work.

THE ETERNAL QUESTIONS

There is an aura of sage or prophet around the aged Lagerkvist, the man who had looked deep into the mystery of existence and whose whole life as a writer was a pilgrimage through the strange regions of the soul in search of a distant holy land. The novel *Sibyllan* (*The Sibyl,* 1956) is a disguised autobiography, and the final pages of this work suggest the nature of Lagerkvist's vision. The restless wanderer Ahasuerus has sought out the old Pythia in her mountain cave high above Delphi. As he leaves in the morning, the old woman stays behind, "watching him go and looking out over the ancient valley, with its city and its temple and all the things she knew so well." Her dark face seems ravaged by fire, and with her inscrutable eyes that have seen God she watches the crowds far below. "The morning sun poured down upon the crowd as it moved forward—down over the whole valley and the mountains around it—down on all that mighty landscape." And the novel ends: "She sat looking out over it all with her old eyes." To the wanderer's questions she has been able to offer no answers:

> You want me to look into the future. I can't do that. But I know enough of the life of mankind and can glimpse enough of the road that lies before him to know that he can never escape the curse and the blessing that comes to him from god.
>
> (pp. 219–220)

As readers of Lagerkvist's work, we too want answers to the eternal questions concerning life and death, man and God he spent a lifetime probing. With singleminded persistence this self-proclaimed "religious atheist" wrestled with the fundamental riddles of life, the infinite desolation of space, the silence of the galaxies, and the existence or the absence of God, stating his themes in stark contrasts between good and evil, light and darkness, faith and doubt and expressing them in a deliberately simple form. It is this formal aspect of his work that has earned him the epithet "deceptively simple," a label that has become a cliché in Lagerkvist criticism. Like most clichés, however, it contains a basic truth: Lagerkvist's "simplicity" *is* deceptive. His stark juxtapositions of contrasts yield ambiguities and complexities that blur distinctions, break down opposites, and reveal disquieting dualities, to the point where the seemingly "simple" is viewed as "obscure"—another recurring epithet in Lagerkvist criticism. This is why a figure like Barabbas has been claimed with enthusiasm by Christians, atheists, and existentialists alike.

It is tempting to view Lagerkvist's search as fruitless and ultimately futile; we may find the questions embarrassingly "obvious"; we may experience a certain impatience with his characters who forget to "live" in their obsessive quest for the meaning of life; we may even register a sense of frustration with the author for raising again and again the eternal questions to which we suspect or know that no answers will be found. Isn't there a certain presumption in this pounding at the closed doors? Couldn't it be seen as a lack of true development, this refusal to accept the human condition as given? For all the artistic mastery in the presentation, couldn't Lagerkvist's search be viewed as a case of arrested growth, an inability to break out of an adolescent deadlock with existence?

Such objections become self-indictments, for only the most complacently materialistic or self-deludingly myopic can go through life un-

affected by its mystery. Refuting Lagerkvist's search is denying our own humanity. His questions, posed more nakedly and brutally than most, continue an infinite inquiry from the earliest manifestations of the human spirit, from Plato and Job and Christ, to Friedrich Nietzsche, Franz Kafka, Rainer Maria Rilke, Carl Jung, and T. S. Eliot. They are as ancient as the Rig Veda and as modern as Samuel Beckett's *Waiting for Godot.*

Lagerkvist's private notes, which became available to the public after his death, show us a man tormented by the unanswered questions and by his compulsion to keep searching. In one of his last work notes, while he is wrestling with material for an unfinished book, he writes, "I don't *want* to write this book. But that's the way it has always been. I don't *want* to write the book I'm writing. I don't want to write again about God." But his notes also testify to the joy and ecstasy experienced in the act of creation, when like the Sibyl he is "possessed by the divine." "To art I say what many cry to the Lord: without Thee I would be nothing but an empty shell." Many of his notes offer explanations and justifications for his unending search. Thus in an early note, he says, "Whoever seeks only that which *can* be found will find nothing." The search itself, man's unsatisfied longing, is the essence of religion and that which makes man fully human. In a note written in the 1930's with direct reference to the political situation of the day, he writes, "Religion in the true sense cannot be dispensed with. If the religious need is not satisfied in a natural way, it will seek satisfaction in an unnatural way as demonstrated by our time's worship of the state and of man." He is ever concerned with "man, his destiny, despair and want—his longing for the unattainable, which is ultimately the most essential reality of his world." And in another note he explains that "although we may not believe in God, we still have to acknowledge life's importance and inscrutability and recognize the immense, unknown forces within ourselves and around us which we call God and which we will surely have to call divine. Whatever name we choose, the meaning still remains the same." And again he says, "What is man but an escape to something else—to the holy land—to something 'outside' himself (to something that exists inside him in the form of longing)?"

Lagerkvist's emphasis on words such as "void," "lack," "longing"—the negatives against which the human spirit pits itself—is striking. This concept of "want," "poverty," or "absence" is familiar from the Sermon on the Mount, but it is also found in Nietzsche's philosophy and in Rilke's poetry. In the Swedish tradition the idea figures prominently in the writings of the nineteenth-century writer Carl Jonas Love Almqvist (1793–1866) as well as the essays of Vilhelm Ekelund (1880–1949) and Lagerkvist's contemporary Gunnar Ekelöf (1907–1968). Ekelund, whom Lagerkvist revered as a master, points in one of his aphorisms to the Greek term *Pénia* (want, poverty) in Plato's *The Symposium,* where Diotima asserts that Eros is the son of *Pénia.* To Ekelund, want/poverty is the necessary source of Eros, of art and poetry: "What is productive comes from want. . . . from the ingenious capacity for *always* feeling want, for having hell entire in one's breast and the joyous anxiety of creating rather than wanting to be happy." The words could serve as a motto for Lagerkvist's restless search and creativity.[1]

Lagerkvist's search is ultimately predicated on the belief in the existence of a reality beyond the one immediately apprehended by our senses. The often noted Platonic element in his metaphysics is clearly stated in some of his personal notes:

> There are other worlds beyond reality, or rather the totality must be more complex than the surface phenomena we call reality. Maybe it is at the same time simpler than we are able to perceive, the way a mathematical problem seems (hopelessly) intricate before we have found the formula, the solution, and have been able to set up the equation. Man's thoughts and feelings and longings must ever deal with these other worlds, for he belongs to them, is part of them (for this, too, he carries within himself).

What we call "reality" is only a world of symbols (created by man) of poetry, religion, science, and the past—a world of human culture built upon a reality whose innermost essence is inaccessible. Most remarkable of all these human creations are, according to Lagerkvist, the religions, the myths, the spiritual worlds that were once inhabited and subsequently abandoned like ruins. Religions, however, are not things of the past; they are a vital concern of the future.

Lagerkvist is religious in the deepest sense of the word, but not "Christian" in the narrow sense. Regarding this ambivalence the Lagerkvist scholar Ingrid Schöier writes:

> Lagerkvist feels that Christianity will have to be overcome just as, in its own time, it conquered contemporary religions—it must be replaced by a higher religious form, for with its elements of cruelty and crudeness, the sacrifice of the god (the son), etc., it retains too many features from the old religions. Thus it is evident that Lagerkvist's relation to the divine is a kind of love/hatred, where the seeming contradictions will one day be canceled and reconciled in a faith capable of embracing both "life on earth and god."

(p. 251)

Lagerkvist possessed in ample measure what Ekelund calls "the ingenious capacity for *always* feeling want." Along with a highly developed artistic awareness there is also an ingenuous quality about him, the true naïveté of the genius, as if he belonged to that particular species of men referred to by August Strindberg in *The Ghost Sonata* as "Sunday children" who see reality more directly with a sense of wonder or more nakedly with a sense of terror that is largely lost to the rest of us. This is undoubtedly at the root of such people's feeling of alienation, of being strangers, or in Lagerkvist's words, "guests of reality."

---

[1] I owe the insights of this particular discussion to Dr. Erik Thygesen and his forthcoming annotated translations of Gunnar Ekelöf's essays, entitled *Modus Vivendi.*

CHILDHOOD AND YOUTH

Lagerkvist very early experienced this sense of being an outsider, an observer rather than a participant. In his basically autobiographical novel *Gäst hos verkligheten* (*Guest of Reality*, 1925) he describes his childhood attitude as that of someone listening through a door. His background marked him for life despite youthful attempts to rebel against it.

Pär Lagerkvist was born on 23 May 1891 in the town of Växjö in the southern province of Småland. His father was a foreman at the railway station and the large family (Pär was the youngest of seven children) lived in a two-room apartment above the railway restaurant. Both parents were first-generation town dwellers with their roots still in the farming community a few miles from Växjö. The county of which Växjö is the administrative center was traditionally a poor and sparsely populated region, sometimes referred to as "darkest Småland." Despite its limited size the county has contributed more than its share of famous people. The botanist Carolus Linnaeus (1707–1778), the opera singer Christina Nilsson (1843–1921), and the author Vilhelm Moberg (1898–1973) had their modest beginnings in the rural areas of small homesteads and deep forests around Växjö. In his tetralogy *The Emigrants* Moberg raises a monument to the mass exodus to North America that took place from this region in the nineteenth century. Växjö is also closely associated with Esaias Tegnér (1782–1846), the Goethean national poet of Sweden, who was bishop in Växjö from 1824 until his death.

During Lagerkvist's childhood Växjö had about eight thousand inhabitants. It was a town marked by political conservatism and religious orthodoxy, a stern Lutheranism with pietistic elements, which had existed unchanged for centuries. The tension between this old order and the new times of industrialism, socialism, and radical ideas was acutely felt by young Lagerkvist. His parents were impervious to the new and viewed it with disapproval as upsetting a God-ordained order of hierarchies. To them obedient submission to the Lord and to worldly authorities was seen as a duty and a virtue.

In *Guest of Reality* Lagerkvist describes this world through the eyes of his young protagonist Anders. There are his parents reading the Bible in the evening and the mother going about her everyday tasks, patiently cleaning the windows of soot deposited by the trains passing through this stagnant world. And there are the grandparents out on their little farm a few miles from the town, the old grandfather raising his head from his Bible to comment on the frightening thunderstorm: "It's good to hear the thunder, for then you know that God is in charge." This is a gentle but stern world, where voices are rarely raised or feelings shown, where love is expressed in simple actions rather than words, and death is accepted as submissively and naturally as life itself by everybody—except the youngest boy. To him it all seems strange, at times oppressive, and he is filled with inarticulate terrors, his terror of death bordering on hysteria as he tries to conjure it away in feverish prayers by his own secret "prayer stone" in the woods.

The figures of the mother and grandmother are drawn with great tenderness. Their quiet stillness is suffused with an inner light. The type appears throughout Lagerkvist's works. Among his best loved poems are the ones about his mother in the collection *Den lyckliges väg* (The Way of the Happy Man, 1921). In one poem he tells about receiving a letter from his old mother, written in her big and shaky hand, a letter about "currant bushes and cherry trees"; in another poem he evokes the scene of his mother turning a page in her Bible. By the side of the tormented shoemaker Daniel in the play *Han som fick leva om sitt liv* (*The Man Who Lived His Life Over*, 1928) is his wife Anna, another symbol of light and peace, just like the woman who shares the life of the title figure in *Bödeln* (*The Hangman*, 1933). In the prose sketch "Morgonen" (The Morning, 1920) Lagerkvist is reminded of his grandmother when he sees an old woman in an Italian town

1680

weaving a basket; both lend a quiet dignity, even greatness, to their humble tasks; both have an ability to make reality truly real. In *The Sibyl* the old Pythia remembers her simple pious parents, who are Lagerkvist's own Småland parents and grandparents transposed to ancient Greece without any sense of anachronism or contradiction.

Outside this world of quiet acceptance the young boy senses another world, another reality—brutal, chaotic, and devoid of meaning. An early realization of the immensity of space and of the impersonal coldness of the stars must have been a traumatic experience. Much of Lagerkvist's search is played out against a cosmic backdrop. Like Albert Camus, he is early aware of man's loneliness and absurd situation under "the eternal silence of infinite space." In his last collection of poetry, *Aftonland* (*Evening Land,* 1953), there is a poem describing how a little boy is sent down in the evening to fetch wood for the kitchen stove. On his way back he stops and looks up into the starlit night, transfixed and annihilated by the vertigo of the void:

I stood completely still. And everything vanished for
  me,
all that had existed before, all that had been mine,
my little horse with three legs, my rubber ball,
my joy at waking up in the morning,
the sunshine, my marbles and the big one made of
  glass,
all my toys.
When I came back to Mother again and laid down
  the wood by the kitchen stove,
no one saw anything special about me, I'm sure of
  that.
But when I walked over and sat down on my stool far
  away from the others,
I was no longer a child.

(p. 49)

At the root of his existential insecurity is the knowledge that he is alone, delivered to an engulfing desolation, against which his parents' world can offer no protection. In a famous story, "Far och jag" (Father and I) from *Onda sagor* (Evil Tales, 1924), Lagerkvist describes a Sunday walk into the forest along the railway tracks. It is a bright and sunny spring day, the birds are feverishly busy, the air is fragrant, and the railway ties are sweating in the sun. The little boy walks along with his father in an ecstasy of well-being. Father knows all the answers, and the boy swells with pride when the engineer of a passing train salutes them. On their way back it is getting dark and the previous idyll is changed into ominous and fearful strangeness. Suddenly a train is heard and rushes past them; all the car windows are darkened, and they catch a glimpse of the engineer staring straight ahead of him, his impassive face lit up by the burning fire. The father is puzzled by this unscheduled train, and the boy trembles in every limb. To him the ghostlike train conveys a special message: it represents all the anguish awaiting him, the unknown world against which the world of his father will not be able to shield him. "It was no real world, no real life. It just came crashing, burning, into all that darkness that had no end."

Lagerkvist attended secondary school in his hometown. He was sure about his future as a writer very early in life and as a member of a literary group he wrote conventionally patriotic poems, some of which were accepted by newspapers. He read playbills outside the town's theater and probably also attended occasional performances by touring theater groups offering plays by Shakespeare, Henrik Ibsen, August Strindberg, Maurice Maeterlinck, Oscar Wilde, and George Bernard Shaw. A couple of years before his matriculation a science teacher introduced his class to the evolutionary theories of Charles Darwin, what Lagerkvist refers to in *Guest of Reality* as "the new doctrine that swept away God and all hope, laying life open and raw in all its nakedness, in all its systematic meaninglessness." Lagerkvist then was openly rebelling against the confining atmosphere of his home. As a member of a small discussion group he flaunted a broadbrimmed hat and a red neckerchief to demonstrate his anarchism and radicalism, which was probably more metaphysical than political: the members met to discuss (and ultimately unanimously to deny) the existence of God rather than to denounce the injustices of society.

It is evident that Lagerkvist's early experience of "the two worlds"—the secure world of religious acceptance of his parents and the other world of blind forces and cosmic infinitude as taught by the natural sciences—is at the root of Lagerkvist's lifelong attempt to reconcile these opposites.

At the time of his graduation from Växjö *gymnasium* in 1910, he already viewed himself as a poet, some of his revolutionary poems having begun to appear in socialist journals. He was penniless and rebellious but had a sense of newly won freedom when he left his parents and his hometown, a sense of relief tinged with guilt for the pain he caused them by alienating himself from them and their simple faith. His parents were quiet and humble people, unremarkable in their insignificance, hardworking and pious, who could only grieve over his restless hungers, never comprehend them; who could follow him out into the world with their prayers only, never with their imagination. In his writing Lagerkvist created some of his most unforgettable portraits of individuals like them.

THE AESTHETIC PROGRAM

It was through school and his outside reading that Lagerkvist was able to orient himself toward the new tendencies in art and letters. The only literature in his home consisted of the Bible and collections of sermons. His mother had read a novel once and considered it a sinful indulgence. What his parents were unable to give their youngest son by way of encouragement and understanding was compensated for by his only brother, Gunnar, who was a schoolteacher, one of history's unsung brothers, who, like a Theo van Gogh, offered self-sacrificing support and loyalty to the struggling genius of the family. After his graduation the fledgling poet moved in with this brother, his eyes set on

studies at the University of Uppsala. He attended lectures in literature and art history, but found academic life confining and soon abandoned his formal studies. His association with young modernist artists in the circle around Isaak Grünewald was far more stimulating than academic studies.

In 1913 Lagerkvist was able to travel to Paris thanks to the financial assistance of Gunnar and his sisters. He had then published his first book, the novella *Människor* (People, 1912), and submitted a second, *Två sagor om livet* (The Tales About Life, 1913). The few months Lagerkvist spent in Paris were of crucial importance to him. There he discovered Paul Cézanne and Vincent van Gogh and was confronted with the latest trends in the arts, in the cubist works of Pablo Picasso and Georges Braque, in the paintings of the fauvists and the naivist Henri Rousseau. He had an opportunity to view some of these works in Gertrude Stein's collections. With particular eagerness he studied Guillaume Apollinaire's *The Cubist Painters* (1913). These were powerful and electrifying impulses for the novice writer, who was burning to make use of the new tenets and formal experimentations in his own writing. The radicalism, which in his school years expressed itself in metaphysical anarchism and later in politically revolutionary rhetoric, was now predominantly aesthetic. The editors of the socialist journals were disappointingly uncomprehending, even hostile, unwilling to sacrifice the conventional form and traditional idiom of the poems they accepted for publication. But Lagerkvist was able to channel his enthusiasm for the new in critical articles and newspaper reviews.

Back in Sweden again and filled with impressions, the twenty-two-year-old Lagerkvist, not unduly burdened by modesty, published his literary manifesto *Ordkonst och bildkonst* (Word Art and Pictorial Art, 1913) with the subtitles "On the Decadence of Modern Literature" and "On the Vitality of Modern Art." The pamphlet, with a cover vignette by his friend Isaak Grünewald, was written in Lagerkvist's youthfully radical new spelling, simplified along phonetic lines (a spelling reform he would later abandon for lack of followers). As a program the manifesto was to find only one follower—Lagerkvist himself, but its publication placed him in the vanguard of Swedish modernism.

In *Ordkonst och bildkonst* Lagerkvist blames contemporary literature for failing to capture the spirit of the times and the innermost essence of man. According to him the prose fiction of the day is formless, catering to the public's demands to be entertained. By subscribing to an ideal of verisimilitude, it tries to act as a mirror to reality, excelling in descriptions of external life and in psychological probings into the obscure depths of the human soul, thus entering domains that should be reserved for nonfictional documentation. The decadence of contemporary literature, Lagerkvist continues, lies in its betrayal of what is quintessentially artistic and in its inability to reflect the times. These times he sees as virile, unsentimental, even brutal.

The writer, Lagerkvist claims, should learn from the latest movements in the pictorial arts, most particularly from cubism. He treads his way assuredly through the various schools of art as he encountered them in Paris. Symbolism is full of atmosphere, a feminine sensitivity to music, mirage, and dreamy meditation, but it fails to render the pulse beat of the times. Futurism is seen as an interesting but rather isolated phenomenon with as yet very few proponents in the pictorial arts and only a handful of rather mediocre poets singing ecstatic hymns to the century of the airplane, the engineer, and electricity. Expressionism, with which Lagerkvist was later to be intimately linked, was helpful in destroying the old without, however, offering any constructive alternative. Its appeal is primarily to our emotions.

Lagerkvist reserves his unqualified praise for cubism, an art that appeals to the intellect. Its form is rigidly disciplined, structured, and architectural. It turns its back on naturalism and strives for simple lines toward the stylized, the decorative, the monumental, away from the individualized toward the general and the universal. The writer could learn from cubism to extract from reality its artistic essence, revealing and interpreting sides of life and objects that, if it were not for him, would remain unexplained. Lagerkvist is anxious to point out that the artistic representations of a Picasso are based on minute observations of reality. The same intimate contact with reality can be found among primitive peoples; in their art the same stylization away from naturalistic representation can be observed. Thus in a sense, cubism is not "modern" at all; it draws its inspiration from ancient sources, in particular from the art of primitive peoples and the cultures of Egypt and the East.

Similarly, the modern writer should turn to the nameless authors of the distant past, to the beauty and monumental simplicity of such works as the Bible, the Avesta, and the Koran. In the Scandinavian tradition Lagerkvist points to the ballads, the medieval provincial laws, and the old Icelandic literature, in particular the poems of the Edda. In all of these models the structural elements are strong. The carefully selected naturalistic detail, which is often found in the general stylization of these works, has a powerful impact. Rather than indulge in realistic descriptions and psychological reconstructions, the writer should concentrate on "simple thoughts, basic feelings before life's eternal powers, sorrow and joy, reverence, love and hatred, expressions of the universally human, which rises above the narrowly individual" (pp. 46–47).

Lagerkvist's early implementations of his rigorous program were not entirely successful. His collection of prose poems in the manner of Charles Baudelaire, *Motiv* (Motives, 1914), creates jarring and brutal effects in lyrical outbursts, aesthetically effective but basically unconvincing. But in the collection of short stories, *Järn och människor* (Iron and Men, 1915), with themes taken from the war raging in Europe, he shows greater maturity in handling his literary cubism. In subsequent works this cubism was to become modified, although certain elements from his early manifesto remain constant throughout his production: the simplicity of expression and a predilection for stark contrasts and universal themes, which for all their general character always reflect a contemporary reality. There is great deliberation behind Lagerkvist's formal experimentations. His seemingly artless form is highly artistic in its cultivation of extreme simplicity and in aesthetic risk-taking, through which the religious may be expressed in the banal, the profound in the colloquial, the transcendental in the naive, or the grotesque in the idyllic, in ever new and daring combinations.

The violent emotional oscillations in Lagerkvist's works from the war years reflect the world situation but also have their counterpart in his private life. Very little has been known about this period in Lagerkvist's life when he moved from Sweden to live in Denmark, but the scanty information can now be complemented with the personal notes, diaries, and letters that were donated to the Royal Library in Stockholm after the author's death in 1974. These papers have stimulated a considerable amount of recent scholarship. The years in Denmark were marked by desperate financial difficulties, temporarily relieved by support from his brother Gunnar and by advances from his publisher. In 1916 he met and fell in love with the Dane Karen Sörensen. They were married in 1918 and had one daughter, Elin. Like his admired countryman Strindberg, Lagerkvist was leading a peripatetic life without a home of his own, and like Strindberg's, his first marriage was a stormy one marked by passionate love and bitter quarrels. The diary entries speak of deep conflicts: "For some time on the streets, often without food. A horrible time. And poor Karen. We have been standing in the rain torturing, torturing each other. Then we have made up because of our terror of the future, the same for both of us. I have left her, she me, only to run back again, desperate, crying, until we've found each other in the crowds." Among Lagerkvist's papers is also the com-

pleted manuscript of a novel, *Den langa resan* (The Long Journey), which is a continuation of his autobiographical *Guest of Reality* and covers the events of his first marriage. Lagerkvist consented to having it published after his death, and it appeared in the late summer of 1985.

With the collection of poetry *Ångest* (Anguish, 1916), Lagerkvist finds his own voice. The title poem makes a defiant break with the poetry of the preceding era by evoking distorted echoes, easily recognizable to Swedish readers, of well-known poems of the national romanticism of the 1890's. The euphonious rhythms and the highflown patriotism of those poems are replaced by a human consciousness that screams its agony in raw and lacerating impotence in a metaphysical waste land of no nationality. This landscape is a projection of the soul, hard, sterile, and frozen, where the red of blood is the only contrast to the blacks and grays that predominate throughout the collection. In *Ordkonst och bildkonst* Lagerkvist dismisses expressionism as being non-constructive, but here it is the perfect vehicle for his vision. Although World War I is never mentioned, it forms the emotional background to this collection, in which the crisis and the response of a whole generation are translated into powerful metaphors, all centered on a single experience of anguish and despair. Lagerkvist's expressionistic period is informed by the same spirit of violent but powerless protest against a life devoid of meaning. In *Kaos* (Chaos, 1919), a volume containing works in different genres, there are tentative gropings toward more positive values in the form of human love and hope for the future embodied in the child.

In 1918 Lagerkvist published his second literary manifesto, *Modern teater (Modern Theater)*, the result of intensive drama studies in Copenhagen. Lagerkvist pleads for a dramatic art that utilizes the unique opportunities offered by the theater to express and condense contemporary reality into effectively stylized images. Lagerkvist finds traditional naturalism hopelessly unequal to the task: the main thrust of his criticism is directed at the Ibsen drama and its "soundless treading on carpets through five endless acts amidst words, words, words." Against these misguided attempts at dramatic realism, Lagerkvist holds up the revolutionary and liberating techniques of the late Strindberg in *A Dream Play* and the Chamber Plays. As in his earlier programmatic essay, Lagerkvist points to older models, in particular to the moralities and mystery plays of the Middle Ages.

Lagerkvist, who made considerable contributions to Swedish drama, remained basically faithful to his early program. With few exceptions his plays discard recognizably realistic settings. The year before he published *Modern Theater*, Lagerkvist made his dramatic debut with the play *Sista mänskan* (The Last Man, 1917). The apocalyptic vision of this play is perhaps a more ominous possibility today than at the time of its publication. It depicts a world that has been laid waste and is about to die under an extinguishing sun, while the last surviving members of the human race give expression to their anguish and, human to the very end, also to hatred and pettiness. Despite the cosmic grandeur in its conception, the play is more lyrical than dramatic in its concentration on a single mood, so typical of Lagerkvist's expressionism. It remains the only dramatic work of Lagerkvist's that has never been performed.

Together with his essay *Modern Theater* Lagerkvist published three one-act plays under the common title *Teater. Den svåra stunden* (The Difficult Hour, 1918). Their action takes place in a dark and disorienting region where the protagonist of each play arrives immediately following his death, a Dante's limbo from which a unique perspective is given on life on earth. The same bold generalization is demonstrated in the play *Himlens hemlighet* (The Secret of Heaven, 1919), which was included in the volume *Kaos*. The naked stage is dominated by a curving outline suggesting the surface of the globe, on which a handful of

bizarre characters are scattered: an old woman picking her toes, a demented girl plucking the strings of a guitar, a strutting dwarf, and an old man on crutches. Prominent among these characters is the figure of Death, a strong man in flesh-colored tights who is busy twisting the heads off an endless supply of human dolls. In the background an old man keeps sawing wood, Lagerkvist's highly original representation of God as an indifferent, yet sustaining presence. The dramatic action of the play is provided by the young man who enters this scene in search of the meaning of it all and the possibility of redeeming happiness. The girl rejects his love in favor of the dwarf, and in the end the young man throws himself over the edge into the darkness, followed by the cynically trivial and indifferent comments of the others.

In *Himlens hemlighet* we find an early example of Lagerkvist's use of human deformity. His works abound in characters who are hunchbacked, blind, harelipped, mutilated, and crippled in varying degrees. The symbolic function of such deformities is not one-sidedly positive or negative; they may express thwarted spirituality but also human victory over the condition of existence. Ultimately they express Lagerkvist's view of man as unfinished and lacking in wholeness through an integration of the opposites, spirit and nature.

A DIALOGUE WITH LIFE

During the 1920's Lagerkvist traveled extensively in France and Italy as well as North Africa, residing for long periods of time in southern Europe. His first marriage ended in divorce, and in 1925 he married Elaine Sandels, née Hallberg. At the beginning of the next decade the couple settled in Lidingö in the immediate vicinity of Stockholm. This became the permanent residence of the couple and their three children, except for frequent sojourns on the island of Tjörn in the western province of Bohuslän and continued travels in Europe and the Near East.

The end of the war and Lagerkvist's encounter with the more affirmative spirit of the Mediterranean south resulted in works that attempt to arrive at an acceptance of life and a reconciliation of the dualities inherent in existence, away from the paralyzing stalemate of his earlier position. The works of the 1920's take the form of a continuous (and often literal) dialogue with life, documented in prose, poetry, and drama. At the end Lagerkvist is able to formulate a tenuous alternative to the spirit of impotent protest of the preceding period.

The new spirit of acceptance is expressed in the prose work *Det eviga leendet* (*The Eternal Smile,* 1920) and summed up in the confession, "I acknowledge you, life, as the only thing conceivable before all that which is inconceivable." The simple declaration is made after a long pilgrimage that takes place in eternity. The story opens with a group of dead people gathered in a vast darkness, who are reminiscing about their earthly existence in order to "while away eternity." As in *The Decameron* or *The Canterbury Tales* each member of the group tells a story, each offering a different view on life, here literally presented *sub specie aeternitatis* (from the aspect of eternity). Lagerkvist demonstrates his mature mastery in these tales. One is about the young man's love for Giuditta, about the warm, pulsing blood of life itself, about fragrant spring and summer, and about untimely death; another story is a magnificent Rabelaisian fabulation of another young man and his adventures with the insatiable miller's wife. Or there is the story of the insignificant little man who found meaning in his humble calling in life as the attendant of an underground lavatory. After listening to each other's tales and vainly trying to grasp the meaning of life, an enterprising shoemaker among them suggests they all go in search of God to demand an answer of Him. It is an endless journey, and they wander for centuries, their ranks swelling as more and more people join the pilgrimage. Finally they discern the light of a weak lantern in the distance, and as they come closer, they see God, again an old man sawing wood. He seems very helpless and humble, and to their angry questions regarding why he created them and what he intended with their lives, he answers quietly that he has never asked anything for himself but always kept working. As for them, he never intended anything special, he only meant that they should not have to be content with nothing. The answer may seem highly unsatisfactory, but it stills the anger of the masses. Some children are brought to the old man, whose eyes fill with tears. With them, he claims, he had meant nothing; then he had simply been happy.

In proportion as God is brought down to a human level, benevolent and ineffectual, man himself becomes more central and human life the only reality. This new spirit is expressed in the 1921 collection of poetry *Den lyckliges väg*, in which the extreme subjectivity, even egocentricity, that marks Lagerkvist's earlier position with its violent outbursts from a stagnant present, here yields to a tenuous social and ethical awareness:

> I live among people,
> a man among you

A sense of temporality is established; symptomatically he now returns to his past with the already mentioned poems about his mother, while the child provides an extension into the future beyond his own mortality, and love—or the memory of love—suffuses the present with transfiguring light. This light assumes cosmic dimensions as it dispels chaotic darkness and spreads into "blond eternities."

The harmony expressed in *Den lyckliges väg* is, however, transitory and the reconciliation with life a temporary truce. The reality of death and the existence of evil make the cosmic idyll untenable. In the play *Den osynlige* (The Invisible One, 1923) Lagerkvist attempts to resolve the conflict. In form *Den osynlige* is close to a medieval mystery play with its allegorical figures such as Death and depersonalized characters representing humanity, the Man, the Woman, the Girl, the Hero, and so forth. There is also an obvious dependence on *A Dream Play:* as in Strindberg's drama, an extra-terrestrial being, here the Invisible One, descends to earth in order to learn about the human condition. Like Indra's daughter, he meets suffering and strife (and very Strindbergian quarrels between husband and wife). The elements of Indian philosophy in *A Dream Play* are also evident in Lagerkvist's play, which shows influence from Rabindranath Tagore.

The Invisible One finds mankind cursing the earth as people toil under the whip of the Caretaker, also referred to as the Ravager. The curse is extended to life itself, whose only aim seems to be to devour and annihilate them, leading them on to certain death. The Hero, a figure combining features of Christ and Prometheus, has gone out into the world to alleviate the lot of mankind, only to discover on his return that during his absence his own parents have been worked to death under the relentless Caretaker. When the Hero confronts the Caretaker, the Invisible One comes to the Hero's aid and strikes down his adversary. But evil continues in spite of the defeat of the Caretaker and in spite of moments of happiness experienced in the love of the Hero and the Girl. In the end Death appears and makes everyone bow to his power. Only the Invisible One remains defiant and triumphant in the midst of Death's devastation, as he declares himself to be the human spirit.

Den osynlige was performed with some success at the Dramatic Theater in Stockholm in the year of its publication. It is an interesting footnote to theater history that one of the extras in this first performance was a fledgling actress, Greta Gustavsson, later considerably better known as Greta Garbo.

For all its flaws *Den osynlige* is important in Lagerkvist's production in that it marks the beginning of a new phase in the author's development. In it he formulates his new idealism and introduces for the first time the principle of the indestructible human spirit as opposed to "life." There is also a deepened insight into the ambiguous nature of such concepts as good and evil. The Hero and the Caretaker are not simply opposites—the Invisible One acknowledges both as his instruments, seeing both as vicarious sufferers. The concept of evil as a negative Christ and scapegoat, playing an obscure role in a larger design, will find mature artistic formulation in the title figures of *The Hangman* and *The Dwarf.*

In the 1924 collection of short stories *Onda sagor* there is one common denominator in Lagerkvist's exposure of life as unredeemed by any kind providence. The already mentioned "Far och jag," which could be seen as a preliminary study of the autobiographical *Guest of Reality* of the following year, describes the little boy's violent realization of the blind and brutal contingency of life as symbolized by the ominous train crashing through the darkness. In "En hjältes död" ("A Hero's Death") Lagerkvist satirizes the shallowness of contemporary society, its sensationalism and callous disregard for human values in the description of the man who consents to perform a much publicized stunt of falling to his death from the top of the church spire in return for five hundred thousand crowns. His satire is Swiftian in its corrosive acidity. In "Frälsar-Johan" ("Saviour John") a demented inmate of a workhouse believes he is Christ. When the workhouse burns down in a fire, he rushes in to rescue the others who, as it turns out, have already been safely evacuated. "Experimentvärlden" ("The Experimental World") is a satire of the gospel of progress and uncritical belief in science and technology and can be seen as a blueprint for *Brave New World* eight years before Aldous Huxley. "Hissen som gick ner i helvete" ("The Lift That Went Down into Hell") is a nightmarish story of an adultery, where the protagonists' mundane banality and vacuity make them experience an existentially terrifying situation as a piquant and titillating adventure. In "Källarvåningen" ("The Basement") the severely crippled Lindgren rises above the adversities of his life and finds contentment in his neat and orderly basement apartment and takes pride in the landlord's pronouncement that it is necessary to have good and reliable people down in the basement of his house.

The cripple Lindgren could be seen as an illustration of what Lagerkvist refers to in *The Eternal Smile* as the possibility "to experience the greatest within narrow confines." He is one more in a long line of insignificant characters, who in a quiet and unquestioning acceptance seem to realize the divine in the most humble circumstances and who serve as illustrations of the Sermon on the Mount, "Blessed are the poor in spirit: for theirs is the Kingdom of Heaven." Lindgren is a brother of the attendant in the underground lavatory, both of them ironic contrasts to Feodor Dostoevsky's Underground Man. Already in *Ångest* there is a poem, "Pa frälsningsarmén" ("At the Salvation Army"), describing a young woman in a threadbare coat rising in ecstasy and hovering like a figure in a Marc Chagall painting in her meeting with God. The harelipped woman in *Barabbas* as well as the humble temple servant in *The Sibyl* also belong among the chosen. They all stand in sharpest contrast to Lagerkvist's own metaphysical rebellion and restless seeking.

The cripple Lindgren, who finds contentment in the midst of his wretched existence, is also an example of Lagerkvist's ongoing struggle to come to terms with the conflicting elements in life as presented in the play *Den osynlige,* in which the human spirit stands victorious in the end. In this struggle Lagerkvist draws an ever sharper dividing line between "life" on the one hand and the human spirit on the other, summarizing his position most pointedly in the line "I revere man, despise life" from one of the poems in his collection of poems *Hjärtats sånger* (*Songs of the Heart,* 1926).

In the prose book *Det besegrade livet* (The Conquered Life, 1927) Lagerkvist professes his new faith, expressing his views in aphoristic form. It becomes evident that his definition of "life" as opposed to the human spirit owes little to the Christian dichotomy of spirit versus the world. Life to Lagerkvist is an indifferent force, neither good nor evil, an animalistic, blind process sustaining itself on death like the flowers on a meadow "cannibalistically" draw nourishment from the rotting remnants of previous organisms. "If only life were evil, the way Christianity teaches, then, after all, it would be a clean and glorious battle." Only in an outward sense does man fight *for* life in order to be able to exist; in his innermost being he fights *against* it in order to conquer and to be free. The human spirit is like an eagle imprisoned in life's cage. "Only in us is there a spark of something higher, an antithesis of you, life, wallowing around us. We are in your power, but not as slaves; we are free men whom you have enslaved. To you we owe our fetters, our slave mark, otherwise nothing." Against a materialistic worldview Lagerkvist thus attempts to establish a transcendental humanism without God. Instead of belief in God, he proclaims his belief in the divine in man. It becomes our holy duty as humans to recognize the divine in others, to give support and aid in the uneven battle against the animal elements in them. "To fight against life is to fight for humanity," is Lagerkvist's paradoxical conclusion. It may come as a surprise that he assigns very low priority to human intellect in this fight. Indeed, man's search for truth and his scientific investigations are rather viewed as obstacles in the search for "that in man which is greater than life." Lagerkvist turns with particular vehemence against the psychoanalytical probings into the hidden recesses of the mind and people "who think they are seekers, questioners, and promoters of spiritual interests, because they occupy themselves with gossip on the murky backstairs of the human soul, gathered in confidentiality with slop pails and chamber pots in their hands." This antirationalist stance was reversed in the 1930's when Lagerkvist openly defended analytical psychology against the Nazi condemnations of such inquiries.

In the two works following *Det besegrade livet* Lagerkvist demonstrates the struggle of the human spirit to reach beyond the limitations of life. In the 1928 play *The Man Who Lived His Life Over* he turns his searchlight on the dangerously irrational impulses inside man. The setting is completely realistic, the modest shoemaker shop of Daniel, the man who had murdered his beloved and is now given a chance to start with a clean slate. He restricts himself to a life of duty and carefully guarded impulses in order not to repeat his earlier crime, only to drive his son to suicide through his rigid demands.

The collection of short stories *Kämpande ande* (Struggling Spirit, 1930) contains the story "Bröllopsfesten" (The Marriage Feast), which marks a high point in Lagerkvist's realistic prose fiction. The story of the love between the old maid Frida, who owns a little notions store, and the good-natured and slow-witted Jonas balances precariously on the narrow line that separates the ridiculous from the sublime. Frida's relatives and neighbors view the match with disapproval and criticize her wedding preparations and her insistence on dressing up in white like a young bride. During the wedding they make coarse jokes and end up getting drunk. By contrast the couple are filled with awe and wonder before the miracle of their love and the solemnity of the ceremony, ignoring the fact that the minister is performing it with perfunctory disapproval. The bridegroom's awkward officiousness as a host and the bride's anxious glances to the practical details are moving and highly comical at the same time. When the couple finally retire from the wedding guests and their union is consummated, Frida, at the height of their excitement, accidentally bites her lover with her false teeth. The grotesque and the lyrical blend in this story, and the ending seems perfectly appropriate as it opens up a cosmic perspective:

She crept down beside him and she, too, fell asleep with his hand clasped hard in hers. They lay together in the darkness, close together, with hot cheeks and their mouths half-open for kisses. And like a heavenly song of praise, like a hosanna of light around the only thing that existed, the stars arose in mighty hosts surrounding their resting place, in ever greater numbers the darker it got.

(p. 33)

FIGHTING HUMANISM

Earlier than most writers of his generation, Lagerkvist was alert to the true significance of the gathering storm clouds over Europe in the 1930's. During his travels he had gained firsthand knowledge of the nature of Mussolini's fascism and Hitler's Nazism, and from the very beginning he took an unequivocal stand against these threats to human freedom and dignity. The collection of poetry *Vid lägereld* (Beside the Watch-Fire, 1932) reflects a new spirit of vigilance. The same year also saw the publication of the play *Konungen* (The King, 1932), in which fundamental political issues are discussed.

Konungen is a complex and very impressive work by a mature dramatist. Set in an ancient Eastern court, its fable follows a mythic pattern as described in James Frazer's *The Golden Bough,* according to which the sovereign once every eight years is driven from his throne to become a despised beggar for three days, while a convict is elevated to take his place and then be sacrificed at the end of his short reign. But the convict, Iream-Azu, who replaces King Amar-Azu, brings about a bloody revolution of the oppressed people and secures the throne for himself. On this political level the drama carries on a discussion about violence, the ends and means of revolution, and the nature of democracy with obvious points of reference in the twentieth-century world. There are also echoes of Plato's *Republic*: the idealistic Amar-

Azu could be seen as an illustration of the failure of a Platonic "philosopher king." On the mythical level the play reenacts a ritual of purification through debasement. On a more personal level Lagerkvist projects in the figure of Amar-Azu his own search and tests his own idealism. The King's descent deprives him of all his former ideals, including the ideal of love, and he rejects them as beautiful illusions when he is confronted with man's basest nature, his bloodthirsty and destructive side. Lagerkvist's positions are never easily won, and in *Konungen* he continues the polemic, begun with *The Man Who Lived His Life Over,* against his own idealistic views expressed in *Det besegrade livet.* His descent into doubt and disillusionment is necessary in order to rebuild his faith on a more realistic foundation.

With the novella *The Hangman,* Lagerkvist openly attacks the totalitarian ideologies of the day. The dramatized version of the following year was a major success throughout Scandinavia, even though some whistles and boos were mixed with the applause, which was usually preceded by shocked silence after the curtain came down. Some critics saw the work as an unnecessary provocation of a "friendly neighbor nation," while others, lacking Lagerkvist's prophetic foresight, found it excessive in its violent pathos.

The Hangman is divided in two parts, the first set in a tavern in the Middle Ages, the second in a contemporary dance restaurant. Common to both parts is the title figure, a broodingly silent presence, conspicuous in his red clothes. In the first part he is a figure inspiring fear and awe, the object of superstitious speculation of whose mysterious power many drastic examples are given. He is an outcast whose unclean and gruesome occupation surrounds him with a powerful taboo.

In the second part the figure of the hangman, still aloof and inaccessible, is surrounded by a mundane nightclub crowd and dancing couples in an erotically overcharged atmosphere. Some uniformed people in the crowd as well as exchanges of greetings with a "Heil" and up-lifted arm point unmistakably to Hitler's Germany. The snatches of conversation among the guests express the fascist ideology with deadly accuracy. In this company the hangman is viewed as an honored guest, hailed as a hero, courted as a celebrity, and ogled by the women. But he remains impervious to any advances. With an impassive face he watches the hectic merrymaking around him and the sudden outbreak of racial violence when the black jazz musicians get lynched and, bleeding from their wounds or dying, are brutally driven back to resume their playing in an ever harder tempo. In the midst of this frenzy, a man leaps up on a table and, wildly swinging his gun, proclaims a new era of discipline and order; turning to the hangman, he harangues him as the representative of everything they value most in life. But the hangman only looks at him in silence, and the man seems at a loss what to do next: " 'Heil!' he shouted again, a little hesitantly with his arm in the air, and all around him did the same." Finally the hangman rises to his feet, big and terrible. There is a sudden silence, and he speaks for the first time, delivering a long and impassioned monologue. He reveals himself as mankind's constant servant since the dawn of time, condemned to take upon himself the blood of millennia. It is a burden from which he wants to be delivered. He remembers how he crucified the man who called himself Messiah. "I long for my sacrificial death—as my poor helpless brother did. To be nailed to a cross and to give up the ghost in the large, merciful darkness. But that hour will never come. I must go on and on as long as you exist." Echoing Nietzsche, he proclaims that God is dead, disintegrating like a leper on his throne, his dust being spread by the wind of eternity through the desolation of Heaven.

It is a magnificent speech, filled with dark and sinister emotions, which defies rational interpretation. Lagerkvist's alleged "obscurity" has its roots in inspirations and intuitive insights that his particular genius is able to express in artistic symbols. We are again reminded of the Sibyl, whose divinely inspired utterances it was left for others to interpret. The difficulties of interpretation become almost insurmountable as Lagerkvist probes ever deeper into the problem of good and evil, revealing their ambiguities, inherent contradictions, and symbiotic relationships.

It is a mistake to view the hangman as the incarnation of evil, a one-dimensional symbol of death and violence. Clearly the hangman is an instrument of these forces, condemned to do their work. The redeeming, human features about him, which lend him tragic stature and inspire compassion, do not redeem the ideology of violence and inhumanity that employs him for its bloody ends. It is also a mistake to equate the two time periods in which the hangman dominates the scene. Critics have wanted to see the medieval part as an illustration of the barbarity of the "dark ages" reappearing in our twentieth century. Lagerkvist undoubtedly intends a contrast rather than a parallel—and in the process he shows the contemporary world to be the more barbaric. People of the Middle Ages had a clear notion of God and the Devil and their respective places in the metaphysical hierarchy; for all their primitive superstitions, their instincts were sound when they feared and shunned the dark powers with which they associated the hangman.

Throughout the 1930's Lagerkvist continued his battle against encroaching barbarism. It was a fight under the banner of humanism, and he used all the weapons in his arsenal—poetry, drama, satire, and nonfiction. Of these genres, poetry seems the least effective and the collections *Genius* (Genius, 1937), *Sang och strid* (Song and Battle, 1940), and *Hemmet och stjärnan* (The Home and the Star, 1942), with the exception of isolated poems, do not count among the author's best efforts. His plays of this period, *Mannen utan själ* (*The Man Without a Soul,* 1936) and *Seger i mörker* (Victory in the Dark, 1939) both unfold in a recognizable contemporary world and reflect the political unrest of the time. On another level they carry on Lagerkvist's exploration of the nature of evil and his attempts to solve the conflict of con-

structive spiritual values versus explosive, subliminal instincts in man.

In the spring of 1933, the year of Hitler's seizure of power in Germany, Lagerkvist traveled to Palestine and Greece, driven by a need to seek out the two cultural spheres that he felt had contributed more than any others to the shaping of western civilization. The most precious values of that civilization were now being threatened with destruction. His travels resulted in his humanistic manifesto *Den knutna näven* (The Clenched Fist, 1934). The book is an inventory of the spiritual resources of our culture, whose origin Lagerkvist traces to the fruitful meeting of East and West. The resulting dualistic tensions between spirit and nature, light and darkness, good and evil, life and death account for the vitality of our culture. In the title chapter Lagerkvist stands in awe before the Acropolis and sees it as a symbol of the light and the freedom that characterize the spirit of Hellas and from which the West has developed its particular concepts of individualism, freedom of thought, and scientific inquiry as well as its ideal of internationalism as opposed to "barbaric nationalism." Lagerkvist "drinks light and health" in the bracing air around the Acropolis: "The temples stand open to the light and in their naked purity they themselves give out light. They are no prisons for gods and captive souls." But the sky beyond the Acropolis is not clear: "To the north a cloud bank is lying over Europe. I know what it means." In the evening he returns to the foot of the Acropolis. His mind is filled with the blood stench of the newspaper reports. The temples are not visible in the dark, but the rough cliff rises with violent thrust toward the sky, threatening and defiant. With its ancient fortifications it stands like a clenched fist against the night sky, summoning the faithful to combat, to a fighting humanism.

In the next chapter Lagerkvist moves from the Acropolis, "the holy mountain of the West," to Mount Olive in Palestine. This, too, becomes a pregnant symbol. To one side it faces the flowering valley of Kidron, where Christ preached his message of love among people, and to the other side the sterile mountainous desert descending to the Dead Sea. This Lagerkvist sees as the birthplace of man's transcendental strivings, where man, who is the only being to rebel against death, symbolically became capable of raising his spirit and thought against the world of nothingness. It is the greatness of the human spirit never to find rest, always striving to reach beyond itself. As a bleeding outpost it lies on its Mount Olive at the border of the great unknown, facing the Dead Sea.

It is in this Palestine chapter that Lagerkvist most clearly marks his own paradoxical religious position: "I'm a believer without belief, a religious atheist. I understand Gethsemane, but not the jubilation of victory." He can identify with Christ's anguish before death, but he cannot accept Christ's victory over death. His encounters with the various Christian sects in Jerusalem fill him with nausea and revulsion, and he describes them as "religion suffering from intestinal obstruction." In words directly addressed to Christ he claims, "In my innermost being I have never experienced you in any mystical way and will never do so. But the love of mankind for which you made yourself a spokesman gives resonance in the very foundation of my being."

The chapter "Undret i Delphi" (The Miracle at Delphi) is of special interest as an account of Lagerkvist's mature synthesis of earlier unresolved conflicts between good and evil, spirit and nature. In a further development of the Nietzschean dichotomy of the Apollonian and the Dionysian, Lagerkvist locates the "miracle" at Delphi, where subterranean and chaotic forces of destruction were domesticated and made subservient to light and creative powers. The human tree has roots that strive downward to life's and nature's secret depths in search of nourishment. The two principles nature and spirit are both necessary to ensure the health of life and culture. But they must be kept in fruitful balance: repressing or denying the hidden forces is just as fatal as unleashing them in the manner of the contemporary dictatorships.

The collection of short stories *I den tiden* (In That Time, 1935) contains some of Lagerkvist's best satires. "Det lilla fälttåget" ("The Children's Campaign") matches Swift's "A Modest Proposal" in angry virulence, all the more effective for being presented in a naively uncritical tone of heroicizing praise. The narrator is full of admiration for the patriotism and courage of the army of children aged ten to fourteen that invades a relatively harmless neighbor nation to avenge an insult to their own great nation. The fierce warriors, "armed to their milk teeth," are sent off by proud and teary mothers. When the greatly decimated army returns, the little invalids hobbling on bloody stumps or being carried on stretchers, a whole grateful nation cheers and honors its heroes.

"Det märkvärdiga landet" ("The Strange Country"), which like the previous story is set in a dystopian future, describes a small nation that has been left intact as a preservation of an ancient culture in the midst of a totalitarian world. Groups of well-disciplined tourists and scientists arrive to watch and study the strange customs of this primitive land and its hopelessly civilian ways with its inhabitants' ridiculous individualism and tolerance of people who look different and think differently. Their scientists keep questioning the correctness of their observations, their newspapers often express conflicting opinions, and their authors are allowed to write whatever they please. In matters of race hygiene and marriage they are highly irrational and degenerate. No wonder that the tourists are relieved to return to their own world of law and order!

On the eve of the outbreak of World War II, Lagerkvist wrote his philosophical essay *Den befriade människan* (The Liberated Man, 1939), which he intended to be his testament "if anything should happen to me." This little book is a summary of the author's convictions as a fighting humanist and his belief in the indestructability of the human spirit. As if anticipating his own probable fate in case Sweden were to be occupied, Lagerkvist projects himself into the situation of those who are in prisons and concentration camps for their resistance to the terror. Yet the book breathes confidence, even optimism. The present is placed in a very long time perspective and reduced to an episode in a continuous creative process of transformations and renewals. His new vision allows him again to affirm life and refute the stand from *Det besegrade livet* by proclaiming that life is no prison but that which unites us with the living and the dead of all times. He is even able to see the negative forces as instrumental in the victory of the eternal values: when man is violated and mutilated, his essential greatness becomes all the more visible; thus the very destructive forces will unwittingly assist at the deliverance of the immortal.

Lagerkvist's most significant work from the war years is the novel *The Dwarf,* which will be dealt with separately below. In the 1940's he also wrote three dramas, *Midsommardröm i fattighuset* (*Midsummer Dream in the Workhouse,* 1941), *De vises sten* (The Philosopher's Stone, 1947), and *Låt människan leva* (*Let Man Live,* 1949). In the first of these plays, a blind inmate of the workhouse makes an eloquent plea for the power of love, poetry, and dreams to transform reality. The second act of this three-act play is a fairy-tale representation of the blind man's vision of goodness and beauty, which is in sharp contrast to the gray poverty of the other two acts.

De vises sten is a Faustian drama, published in the same year as Thomas Mann's *Doktor Faustus.* The alchemist Albertus is a scientist obsessed with his search for truth, for which he sacrifices all human values and sells his daughter to the cynical Prince and drives her into whoredom. His dialectical counterpart is the Rabbi Simonides, whose religious fanaticism is equally destructive to human values. The love between Albertus's daughter and Simonides's son becomes the ultimate victim of

the two fathers' inflexible stands. The symbolic fable of the drama is a clear warning against rigid dogmatism and irresponsible pursuit of scientific truth, since the future of mankind is at stake. In the post-Hiroshima version of his play *Life of Galileo* Bertolt Brecht raises the same issue: the modern scientist's readiness to prostitute himself and sell his findings to any "prince" in order to satisfy his passionate search for the philosopher's stone.

Maybe it is this threat to mankind's survival that makes Lagerkvist entitle his last play *Let Man Live.* Because of its lack of dramatic plot it could more accurately be called a stage oratorio. Against the darkness of a barren stage people are lined up in a semicircle. They are all martyrs through the ages, from Socrates and Jesus to a black lynch victim and a young resistance fighter. One by one they introduce themselves and tell of their martyrdom—a Christian martyr, Giordano Bruno, Jeanne d'Arc, an Inca chief, Dante's Paolo and Francesca, a contessa from the French Revolution—their voices raised in what Robert Spector terms "a kind of antiphonal poetry." The viewer or the reader listens in vain for the voice of Anne Frank or any of the other victims of our century's systematic genocide. We may assume that Lagerkvist intended this silence to be most eloquent of all.

THE DWARF

With the novel *Dvärgen* (*The Dwarf,* 1944) Lagerkvist created a masterpiece in which the different levels—the realistic, the historical, the psychological, and the symbolic—all combine and reinforce one another to produce a consummate work of art. It has secured a place for itself in world literature. As in all his works with a historical setting, Lagerkvist did painstaking research for this novel. The Renaissance Italy he evokes is the Italy of the Medicis, the Sforzas, and the Borgias, of Leonardo da Vinci and Machiavelli. This was a time when the "vertical," metaphysical orientation of the Middle Ages had given way to a "horizontal," humanistic orientation with an unprecedented expansion of the human spirit and an awakening of scientific interests. It was also a time of plagues and warfare between rivaling states, of mercenaries, of power struggles and intrigues with nefarious deeds of poisoning and swift stabbings in the dark.

In *The Dwarf* several threads of action, associated with the main characters at the princely court, are woven into this Renaissance tapestry. There is the story of the Prince, his humanistic interests and his love affairs, but also his war preparations and the campaign against his neighbor, Il Toro, the siege of his castle, the retreat, the concluding of peace, and the great "reconciliation banquet" at which Il Toro and his men are treacherously poisoned. There is also the story of the da Vinci figure Messer Bernardo, who is a guest at the court, his discussions with the Prince, his metaphysical speculations, his art, and his insatiable scientific curiosity, but also his designing of war machines. Another thread follows the licentious and adulterous Princess through her conversion and eventual transformation into a saint. Finally there is the Romeo and Juliet story of the young couple, Angelica and Il Toro's son Giovanni.

At the center of this world is the figure of the dwarf; it is through his eyes that events are viewed and it is his journal we are reading. The perspective he provides is a chilling one. On a purely psychological level, the vain, pompous and thoroughly malignant narrator is a perfectly convincing study in overcompensated inferiority, of personal lovelessness turned into destructive lust and hatred of mankind. Lagerkvist's continued explorations into the nature of evil find a compelling symbol in the twisted, stunted, and sterile mind of the dwarf.

The dwarf is incapable of dissimulation—indeed, there is an uncompromising authenticity about him in the existentialist sense of the word. He remains entirely true to himself and takes pride in this consistency, which he con-

trasts with the complexity and the contradictions he finds in the people around him. The possibility of harboring opposing views or of combining contradictions in a single vision is foreign to him. Hence he is totally devoid of humor, irony, or even satire, all of which are predicated on a "double vision." For the same reason he is unable to experience remorse or guilt. The only duality he understands is duplicity, and then entirely for practical ends. He notes with approval that the Prince is "false."

The most significant feature of the dwarf is his one-dimensionality, his complete "thereness." He notes with pride that he is never afraid, since he recognizes everything within himself and nothing there is shrouded in mystery. The incoherent and the unknown, which frighten people, do not exist for him: "There's no 'otherness' in me." By the same token there are no impulses to get beyond the narrow confines of the moment. Symptomatically, he is baffled by little Angelica's play or the play of adults, which he views as meaningless pretense and an insult to his concept of "authenticity." He is filled with wonder and contempt over Messer Bernardo, who is captivated by the study of the stars, by a dissected human body, or an ordinary pebble. Such inquiries are simply further examples of people trying to satisfy their childish desires. It is also very presumptuous, for they think everything is made for their well-being and happiness, to make life great and wonderful for them. If they really could look into the heart of nature, he muses, it would fill them with terror.

The dwarf sees himself as belonging to a more ancient race than ordinary humans. He is incapable of transcending his own confinement and this is what constitutes his unhumanity. He understands religion only in its most formalistic, utilitarian sense. He listens to the discussions between the Prince and Messer Bernardo and he cannot grasp their enthusiasm for the greatness of the human spirit nor their despair over its inability to stretch its wings further. Least of all can he understand how they are able to hold both views at the same time: "I who am always the same, who am quite inalterable, find it utterly incomprehensible." And with impatience and his own grim logic he adds, "Well, what is it then?"

Transcendence through human love is equally incomprehensible to the dwarf. All physical aspects of man fill him with revulsion. He speculates about the artists and poets who "abuse the Prince's hospitality." Above all they seem to sing the praises of love, and this is quite as it should be, thinks the dwarf, for nothing stands in greater need of being transformed into something different. He himself is sterile; dwarfs have no need to procreate since they let themselves be born by ordinary humans. The licentiousness of the Princess, the erotic adventures of the Prince, the sexual orgies during the campaign, all fill him with puritanical outrage. But the most vehement reactions are reserved for Angelica's and Giovanni's young love, which he becomes instrumental in bringing to a tragic end.

The Dwarf is a study in negation and evil. Relentlessly Lagerkvist penetrates the starless universe of the dwarf, down to its heart of darkness and unredeemed suffering, where the dwarf celebrates his somber communion in a mockery of Christ's last supper, offering his own poisoned blood and bilious flesh. At the "reconciliation" banquet, which marks the climax of the novel, the dwarf is at the height of his power; here he officiates at a mass communion, passing around the poisoned wine to the guests, a dispenser of death. In the description of this scene Lagerkvist's prose is unmatched in dark intensity as he makes the dwarf recite his litany of nihilism.

Lagerkvist shows that there is a dwarf in all of us, the stunted survivor of an ancient race, impotent before man's transcendental aspirations, but ever ready to serve his prince at his bidding. The novel describes what happens when the dwarf is invited to participate. He holds the key that unlocks the forbidden doors and unleashes the destruction and the chaos with which he is in league. War, bloodshed, and pestilence sweep over the principality when the bastions erected by the human spirit are left undefended.

At the end of the novel the dwarf is imprisoned, chained to the wall of a dungeon in the castle. But he is in good cheer. He knows that his lord will not be able to do without his dwarf for long, and he waits for the day when they will loosen his chains because the Prince has sent for him again. At the time of the novel's publication no reader could fail to realize that the dwarf had been summoned back.

BARABBAS

The novel *Barabbas* (*Barabbas,* 1950) is Lagerkvist's most widely translated work and the one that decisively tipped the scales in favor of his receiving the Nobel Prize in 1951. Although there is remarkable unity in the midst of great diversity in Lagerkvist's authorship, it is possible to see *Barabbas* as the beginning of a new phase, in which there is a narrowed focus on man's relationship with the divine, his search for or escape from God.

In the figure of Barabbas, Lagerkvist portrays a man who is both searching and escaping. Barabbas, of whom the New Testament only tells us that he was the criminal released instead of Jesus, witnesses the crucifixion of the man who literally died in his place. The symbolism is obvious and the irony only one of many in this novel, which depicts Barabbas both as an individual in a unique situation and as a representative of man in general. What could be more general or anonymous than *bar Abbas,* "son of the father," a name which in turn associates with "son of man" and "son of God"?

Barabbas is the leader of a band of robbers in the mountains, a man of action in a negative sense—brutish, sullen, and inarticulate. Lagerkvist's particular narrative technique, a mixture of omniscience and third-person accounts of characters' thoughts, makes us follow very closely what stirs inside Barabbas's mind: his primitive reactions to what he observes, his contempt and resentments, his skepticism and doubt, but also his bewilderment and utter loneliness and despair.

After witnessing the events on Golgotha and experiencing the inexplicable darkness following Christ's death, Barabbas lingers on in Jerusalem. He stays with the Fat Woman, who finds him listless and restless and without his usual zest. He is bothered by the recent events and only wishes to put them behind him once and for all. Before sunrise on Sunday morning he goes to the tomb and waits there to be able to refute the rumors of Christ's resurrection. At a distance from him a woman is kneeling with her face also turned to the tomb. It is the girl with the harelip, who once sheltered him in the mountains and later gave birth to their stillborn child. The tomb lies in darkness and as the sun rises, Barabbas is blinded by the light, and then he notices that the tomb is empty and he concludes that the disciples must have removed the body during the night. But the young woman's face is transfigured in ecstasy. During his stay in Jerusalem, Barabbas comes across several followers of "the crucified one," and he even attends one of their secret meetings, but they turn away from him when they discover that he is "the acquitted one." Through the sniveling speech of the woman with the harelip he hears the strange message of the crucified Rabbi: "Love one another!" Later he watches the stoning of the woman and in a fit of silent rage he expertly stabs the Pharisee who threw the first stone. In the evening he returns; he picks up her mutilated body, carries it out into the barren wilderness, and buries it next to their child. He rejoins the robbers, but his changed behavior and gloominess make his presence uncomfortable for them. One day he disappears.

Years later we again encounter Barabbas, now a slave in the Cyprian copper mines, where he is chained to the Christian slave Sahak, who has Christ's name engraved on the back of his slave disk. Barabbas lets Sahak scratch the name on his own disk too. Through a sympathetic overseer who shows great interest in Sahak's god, Sahak is released from the dark inferno of the mine and allowed to work above ground, but he refuses to go without Barabbas and points to Christ's name on his disk. Thus Christ saves Barabbas for the second time. When the Roman governor hears rumors about Sahak's god, the two slaves are summoned to him. Sahak radiantly confesses that his god is more important to him than the Roman emperor, and he is sentenced to be crucified. Barabbas admits that he would like to believe in Sahak's god but is unable to do so. The governor praises him for his good sense and with a knife he crosses over the name on the disk. Sahak is crucified on a brilliantly sunny day. At a distance Barabbas watches his agony, kneeling in mute impotence.

In the final section of the book Barabbas has been allowed to come with the governor's household to Rome. There are Christians among the slaves, and driven by his unrest, he wants to attend their meeting in the catacombs. He loses his way in the dark labyrinths, and panicking like a trapped animal, he finally finds his way out. Fires are burning in Rome and he hears cries that the Christians are responsible. In a frenzy of activity Barabbas rises to the occasion and begins to throw firebrands into houses, at last showing that he is worthy of the man to whom he owes his life, that he is not going to fail him this time. He is captured and put in prison with a number of Christians, among them Peter, whom he had met in Jerusalem on the day after his acquittal. They are all crucified. Barabbas is the last to die.

This story of Barabbas' life is told with great simplicity in a style whittled down to stark monumentality, which is reminiscent of woodblock prints. Individual figures are drawn with a few masterly strokes. There is a glimpse of Christ's mother at the foot of the cross, a stern and reproachful peasant woman wiping her nose with the back of her hand, a *mater dolorosa* not to be found in traditional

Christian iconography. And there is her opposite, the fat harlot, voluptuous, maternal, sentimental, and solicitous, as well as the pathetic figure of the woman with the harelip, who feels inadequate in her role as a witness for Christ. The powerless figure of Jesus, his thin and spindly body hanging on the cross, fills Barabbas with fascinated revulsion. The fisherman Peter is a big and simple man with ingenuous blue eyes and a broad dialect, who could have his roots in Lagerkvist's Småland rather than Galilee.

The episodes in the novel are described with the same bold sureness, through which the realistic and the symbolic, the natural and the stylized merge into compelling visions. The narrative approaches the sublime in the description of the woman with the harelip as she dreams of the new kingdom of Christ under the brilliant stars, oblivious of the stench and squalor among the lepers and outcasts by the Dung Gate. Or there is the sheer existential terror in the scene describing Barabbas' frantic search out of the darkness of the catacombs, out of his own insulating selfhood, as he chases treacherous glimmers of light.

His whole life, from the moment he was "condemned to freedom," is a search for that elusive light. But his true element is darkness, and his home is the realm of living death. In this he is the antithesis of Christ, who is associated with life and light. It is symptomatic that Barabbas can believe in the darkness on Golgotha, but not in the light at the tomb. The only light he understands is destructive fire. He is excluded from or unable to share in the fellowship and love among the believers—the only communion he partakes of is the salt and bread ("tasting of corpse") offered him by Lazarus, who had experienced the nothingness of death and to whom nothing else is anything after that. As opposed to Jesus, the son of a loving father, conceived by the Holy Spirit, and blessed in the womb, Barabbas is the unwitting murderer of his father, conceived through rape, and cursed at birth by his dying mother.

We are reminded of the Palestine chapter in Lagerkvist's *Den knutna näven*. Mount Olive was seen as standing on the dividing line between the flowering valley of Kidron, a metaphor of Christ's message of love, and the sterile mountain deserts descending to the Dead Sea. Lagerkvist saw this as the birthplace of man's metaphysical strivings, a place where man was able to raise his spirit and thoughts against nothingness. Barabbas is a denizen of the desert, his face is turned to the Dead Sea, and the landscape around him is the landscape of his soul. It is his curse that he is incapable of "turning around," of converting. Like the dwarf, he possesses a negative authenticity, and he is uncompromising in his honesty, a rationalist who can only believe what he sees with his eyes. He can only see the great nothingness, but his spirit cannot rise against it.

Most English editions of *Barabbas* have a foreword by André Gide, in which he comments on the ambiguity in the last words of the novel: "When he felt death approaching, that which he had always been so afraid of, he said out into the darkness, as though he were speaking to it: 'To thee I deliver my soul.' "

The ambiguity is Lagerkvist's own. The atheist part of this "religious atheist" was always turned toward the darkness and the great nothingness. It forms the very real background of the little boy's terrors and of the outbursts of violent despair in *Ångest;* it is the powerful opponent against which Lagerkvist later raises his own and mankind's spirit in a defiant *quand même.* It is worth noting that Lagerkvist's own religious position is much closer to that of Barabbas than to that of the woman with the harelip or Sahak.

THE PILGRIMAGE

After *Barabbas,* Lagerkvist wrote six more books, the collection of poetry *Evening Land* (1953), *The Sibyl* (1956), *Ahasverus död* (*The Death of Ahasuerus,* 1960), *Pilgrim på havet* (*Pilgrim at Sea,* 1962), *Det heliga landet* (*The Holy Land,* 1964), and *Mariamne* (*Herod and*

Mariamne, 1967). *Evening Land,* perhaps Lagerkvist's greatest poetic achievement, is a summation of familiar themes and preoccupations from his earlier writings, including childhood memories that are here viewed in a transfigured perspective; it is also a poetic prefiguring of themes and concepts that are developed in the subsequent prose works. These prose works form a complex unity, which allows for a number of groupings and regroupings according to thematic similarities and dialectical parallels and opposites.

Lagerkvist's private notes from the later part of his life reflect a spirit that is still restless, still questioning. He writes of "this troubled time in life called old age that I thought was serene, peaceful, wise, but is the most troubled of all." But he is no longer seeking peace. In a poem from *Evening Land* he prays

That my heart's unrest never cease.
That I never find peace.
That I never be reconciled with life, nor with death.
That my road be infinite, its destination unknown.

His poems deal more and more with man's relationship with God. Always a master at finding expressive images for the most elusive concepts and intuitive insights, Lagerkvist now finds simple and poetic metaphors for man's experience of God in dictions that could have been borrowed from St. John of the Cross. God is the Stranger with his head averted; like man himself, he is a Wanderer who passes by our tents, maybe on his way somewhere else:

His shadow is not he,
but it filled the tents with light.

Man is the unsuspecting target of God's spearpoint, hurled through the darkness. Or God is an absence, the God who does not exist, yet holds a paradoxical power over man:

Who are you who fill my heart with your absence?
Who fill the whole world with your absence?

In Lagerkvist's "humanistic period" God is synonymous with the human spirit, man's own creation. By focusing on the divine in himself and others, man was spiritually perfectible and might in time become worthy of his God. Beginning with *Barabbas,* God is described as an outside force, a stranger, a spear-caster, or, as in *The Sibyl,* a rapist, a force against which the human individual is defenseless.

In *The Sibyl,* Ahasuerus and the old Pythia each offer a variation on man's relationship with God. Ahasuerus is the man who refused Christ permission to lean his head against his house on his way to Golgotha and was punished to perpetual unrest as the Wandering Jew. The Sibyl is the woman who as a young girl was taken from her pious parents and consecrated to service in the temple of Apollo. Here she experiences the both ecstatic and terrifying presence of God in violent possessions down in the dark pit below the radiant temple above. (We are reminded that Apollo's temple was built on the site of an ancient cult that was dedicated to the earth goddess Gaia, the daughter of Chaos, which suggests that religious possessions as well as poetic inspirations metaphorically speaking have "subterranean" roots.) The price she pays for her raptures is loneliness and exclusion from human fellowship. On a visit to her home village she meets the one-armed man, who doesn't know that she is the Pythia. With him she experiences the fullness and the beauty of human love. On her return to the temple her jealous god takes a terrible revenge by raping her in the shape of a goat and killing her lover. When it becomes apparent that she is pregnant, she is chased out of the temple and nearly stoned. A humble little temple servant, who has always shown her kindness and compassion, helps her escape safely. She seeks refuge up in the mountain cave, where she gives birth to an idiot child. This son, now a graying man with a perpetual, meaningless smile on his face, silently disappears while the Sibyl is telling her story. Together with Ahasuerus she follows his footsteps up the mountain and in the snow, until the tracks suddenly and mysteriously disappear. The Sibyl realizes that it was the son of her god whom she had borne.

The Sibyl is a beautiful and terrifying book. The old Pythia has experienced God as total "otherness"—as *Mysterium tremendum et fascinosum*—but also as a deep violation of her humanity. Through Lagerkvist's personal work notes it is possible to follow his wrestling with the subject, and his fascination with the figure of the old Sibyl, who has seen through everything and has seen nothingness in everything: "The Sibyl—the old poet's disillusion—his outrage over having been exploited—of what use and to what end?" In the finished version of the book the nihilism expressed in the work notes is sacrificed for greater complexity. To the Sibyl, God is alien, repulsive, evil, fatal, and sometimes madness. But she suggests that he may be both good and evil, both meaningless and possessing a meaning that she cannot perceive. She is ultimately grateful for having experienced something beyond her own self. Looking back on *The Sibyl*, Lagerkvist writes in his notes, "How will I be able to write anything after *The Sibyl*, in which I gave myself so mercilessly and completely? I have often felt as if I were cursed by God for having written *The Sibyl*. That's how Ahasuerus feels for having offended God (God's son)."

In *The Death of Ahasuerus* the Wandering Jew reappears in the Middle Ages among a group of pilgrims on their way to the Holy Land. Like Barabbas, he is persecuted by God and like Barabbas, who was condemned to a life which turned out to be living death, Ahasuerus is cursed with perpetual life. But whereas Barabbas can respond with his primitive and negative instincts only, Ahasuerus continues to question and to challenge his persecutor. He becomes a rebel, a Prometheus figure. In a long monologue at the end of the book he formulates his creed, through which Lagerkvist makes a clean sweep of the human distortions of true religion, of all "the sacred rubbish" that obscures the holiness, ineffable and inaccessible, that exists beyond it. It is God that separates us from the divine. Ahasuerus addresses Christ, accusing him of being vindictive, of thinking that he is unique in his suffering; it is man himself who lies abandoned on his bed of suffering in a desolate world, sacrificed and deserted. And he reminds Christ of how the one who called him his son had sacrificed and deserted him. Ahasuerus now blames this god who demands sacrifices and crucifixions and begins to realize that it is he, not Christ, who is vindictive and has cursed him. Christ is his brother, himself unhappy and cursed. The realization is at the same time a revelation to Ahasuerus, who feels that he has lifted the curse off his own shoulders by unmasking God. He can finally feel the approach of that merciful death that had been denied him before.

Ahasuerus' monologue is Lagerkvist's most explicit criticism of the Christian religion, but it does not mark a new position in his religious thinking. In *Den knutna näven* he addresses Christ, proclaiming "I have never experienced you in any mystical way and will never do so." As early as 1920, in *The Eternal Smile*, Jesus is only one among the innumerable dead who are "whiling away eternity." In *The Hangman* the title figure refers to him as "my poor helpless brother," and in *Let Man Live* Jesus accuses God of having deserted him.

Ahasuerus is Prometheus in that he takes the part of humanity against the gods. He is an ironic variation on the Invisible One who represents the human spirit against which Death is powerless.

We find Ahasuerus on his deathbed in a monastery, tended by a barefooted lay brother, whose wrinkled face is always lit up by a kind smile. Ahasuerus has a strange feeling that he recognizes him, but he cannot remember when and where he met him: "It was probably just his imagination." We may venture a guess that he is the kind and charitable temple servant in the Sibyl's story so many centuries ago. His simple and cheerful services may have contributed to the great peace that radiates from Ahasuerus' face when he at last finds death.

Ahasuerus' recognition that it is God that separates man from the divine and that the holy land is located beyond "all the sacred rubbish" makes us wonder whether the pilgrims, whom Ahasuerus has joined in this book, will ever reach their destination. One of the more unlikely travelers is Tobias, the "involuntary pilgrim," whose story Ahasuerus listens to and whom he recognizes as yet another brother. The erstwhile student-turned-soldier and then bandit is a man who takes life as it comes to him. But he, too, cannot escape the summons to the beyond. Maybe it is symptomatic that the name *Tobias* means "God's goodness" and that he is given a number of pushes in the right direction—from a dead stigmatized woman and her dog, from a woman he once loved and called Diana, who sacrifices her life for him, and from Ahasuerus, who throughout the story ushers him along. The theme of human fellowship and sacrifice runs strong through this book. The recognition that man is responsible for his brothers contributes to Ahasuerus' victory over his curse.

In *Pilgrim at Sea,* Tobias is again in bad company. In the previous book he is last seen desperately negotiating with the suspect crew members of a not very seaworthy ship after having just missed the last pilgrim ship of the season. He hands over all his ill-gotten money, is allowed onboard, and the ship disappears into the night. In this new novel, he is not taken to the promised land. Indeed, he has ended up on a bandit ship of scoundrels. Among the men is Giovanni, a defrocked priest, who once saved Tobias' life. This creates a bond between the two, which is further strengthened when Giovanni tells his story. These stories that link the fates of the characters together are like cogs that grip onto a larger wheel in this pilgrims' progress toward the holy land. Giovanni is the apostate who has learned to deliver himself to the sea, to take insecurity and uncertainty as the only certain things. He shows Tobias a

locket that he always carries in a chain around his neck. It once belonged to a married woman, whose confession he had received and for whom he conceived an ardent passion. As a result of this affair Giovanni was excommunicated. The woman claimed that the locket contained the picture of her greatest love. On their last night together Giovanni took it away from her and when he opened it, he found that it was empty.

The theme of human love runs through all of Lagerkvist's works as the greatest redeeming factor in life, whether it is shared by Paolo and Francesca or Frida and Jonas. The symbolism of the empty locket places love alongside religious yearning as a mysterious force behind man's search for transcendence. The emptiness may indicate that it is all an illusion, but it is an emptiness man has always filled with dreams and longing.

The Holy Land is the last volume in Lagerkvist's "Pilgrim Trilogy" and also the most baffling and the most difficult to interpret. The symbolism is in part of a very private nature. In his work notes Lagerkvist writes, "This book will be personal, my own, written for my own sake. My own evening book. Others need not understand it."

After an unspecified number of years Tobias and Giovanni, who is now blind, have been set ashore on the desolate coast of a barren country, inhabited only by old shepherds without women and children. They are also without god or religion, although there are ruins of ancient temples. In this hauntingly desolate world a series of enigmatic events take place. In a hut at the foot of the mountain live a man and his baby child, whose mother had died at its birth. The child is the object of the primitive shepherds' reverence. Above this windswept landscape vultures are suddenly appearing and the sheep are dying. A bald man kills one of the birds and performs an augurlike ritual, sacrificing a lamb. Tobias digs up a stone face from the ground, a face with a meaningless smile. A mysterious woman comes walking down from the mountain carrying a snake in a basket, with the aid of which she kills the little child. She releases Giovanni from life by removing the locket from his neck and places it around Tobias' neck. It is a strange holy land, sketchy, unfinished with its ruins and fragments and aborted beginnings, an apocalyptic world where myths have become powerless—unless they are just about to be formed. Tobias sets off into the mountains, where there seems to be permanent twilight, comes to a hill with three crosses that he recognizes as equally important, sees a stranger by a river, but only encounters his own aged reflection in the water, and extinguishes his thirst in an absolutely clear spring (whose water has no taste at all); he finally rests under a wooden sculpture of the madonna. The sculpture brings back a long-repressed memory of a young woman he had once wronged, when he made her abort their child. The sculpture comes alive and assumes the features of the young woman. She offers him her forgiveness and then lifts the chain with the empty locket and places it around her own neck. Tobias dies, "and his face seemed to be filled with a great peace."

Lagerkvist's last work, *Herod and Mariamne,* is the story of the cruel and ruthless King Herod, like Barabbas a man of negative action and a man of the desert. We are told that his relationship with the divine is nonexistent, yet he builds a magnificent temple. He is powerful in everything except in his love for his queen Mariamne, whose cool and fragile beauty, whose inability to love him fully in return, and whose compassion make her inaccessible and only increase his suspiciousness and his jealousy. Mariamne is loved by the people, she manages to soften some of Herod's worst cruelties, and she transforms parts of the desolate palace into a home. But Herod cannot be transformed by his love. After Mariamne's death both his evil deeds and his loneliness increase. When he is struck by an incurable illness, his servants desert him, and he is alone in the palace. As he is dying, he drags himself through the palace, again and again crying her name: Mariamne! Mariamne! The empty halls return the hollow echo of his beloved's name.

Herod and Mariamne was written in the year of the death of Lagerkvist's wife. In his private notes we find the following: "When [Herod] calls for her in the empty palace, then it's like me."

Herod's cry is one of longing. The object is unreachable. But the longing is very real. In essence, this is what Lagerkvist's writing is all about.

Selected Bibliography

EDITIONS

FIRST EDITIONS

Människor. Stockholm, 1912.
Ordkonst och bildkonst. Stockholm, 1913.
Två sagor om livet. Stockholm, 1913.
Motiv. Stockholm, 1914.
Järn och människor. Stockholm, 1915.
Ångest. Stockholm, 1916.
Sista mänskan. Stockholm, 1917.
Teater. Den svåra stunden. Stockholm, 1918.
Kaos. Stockholm, 1919.
Det eviga leendet. Stockholm, 1920.
Den lyckliges väg. Stockholm, 1921.
Den osynlige. Stockholm, 1923.
Onda sagor. Stockholm, 1924.
Gäst hos verkligheten. Stockholm, 1925.
Hjärtats sånger. Stockholm, 1926.
Det besegrade livet. Stockholm, 1927.
Han som fick leva om sitt liv. Stockholm, 1928.
Kämpande ande. Stockholm, 1930.
Konungen. Stockholm, 1932.
Vid lägereld. Stockholm, 1932.
Bödeln. Stockholm, 1933.
Den knutna näven. Stockholm, 1934.
I den tiden. Stockholm, 1935.
Mannen utan själ. Stockholm, 1936.
Genius. Stockholm, 1937.
Den befriade människan. Stockholm, 1939.
Seger i mörker. Stockholm, 1939.
Sang och strid. Stockholm, 1940.
Midsommardröm i fattighuset. Stockholm, 1941.
Hemmet och stjärnan. Stockholm, 1942.
Dvärgen. Stockholm, 1944.
De vises sten. Stockholm, 1947.
Låt människan leva. Stockholm, 1949.

Barabbas. Stockholm, 1950.
Aftonland. Stockholm, 1953.
Sibyllan. Stockholm, 1956.
Ahasverus död. Stockholm, 1960.
Pilgrim på havet. Stockholm, 1962.
Det heliga landet. Stockholm, 1964.
Mariamne. Stockholm, 1967.
Antecknat. Edited by Elin Lagerkvist. Stockholm, 1977.
Den långa resan. Stockholm, 1985.

COLLECTED WORKS

Dramatik. 3 vols. Stockholm, 1956.
Prosa. 5 vols. Stockholm, 1956.
Dikter. Stockholm, 1965.

BIBLIOGRAPHIES

Ryberg, Anders. *Pär Lagerkvist in Translation. A Bibliography.* Stockholm, 1964.
White, Ray Lewis. *Pär Lagerkvist in America.* Stockholm and Atlantic Highlands, N.J., 1979.
Willers, Uno. *Pär Lagerkvists bibliografi på sextioårsdagen, 23 maj 1951.* Stockholm, 1951.
Yrlid, Rolf. *Pär Lagerkvists kritiker: En recensionsbibliografi.* Lund, 1970.

TRANSLATIONS

Barabbas. Translated by Alan Blair. New York, 1951.
The Death of Ahasuerus. Translated by Naomi Walford. New York, 1960.
The Dwarf. Translated by Alexandra Dick. New York, 1945.
The Eternal Smile and Other Stories. Translated by Alan Blair, Erik Mesterton, Denys W. Harding, Carl Eric Lindin. New York, 1954.
The Eternal Smile: Three Stories. Translated by Erik Mesterton, Denys W. Harding, and David O'Gorman. New York, 1971. Includes *The Hangman, Guest of Reality,* and *The Eternal Smile.*
Evening Land. Translated by Wystan H. Auden and Leif Sjöberg. New York, 1974.
Herod and Mariamne. Translated by Naomi Walford. New York, 1968.
The Holy Land. Translated by Naomi Walford. New York, 1966.
Let Man Live. Translated by Henry Alexander and Llewellyn Jones. *Scandinavian Plays of the Twentieth Century.* Third Series. Princeton, 1951.

The Man Who Lived His Life Over. Translated by Walter Gustafson. *Five Modern Scandinavian Plays.* New York, 1971.
The Man Without a Soul. Translated by Helge Kökeritz. *Scandinavian Plays of the Twentieth Century.* First Series. Princeton, 1944.
Midsummer Dream in the Workhouse. Translated by Alan Blair. London, 1953.
Pär Lagerkvist: Modern Theater: Seven Plays and an Essay. Translated by Thomas Buckman. Lincoln, Nebr., 1966.
Pilgrim at Sea. Translated by Naomi Walford. New York, 1964.
Seven Swedish Poets. Edited by Frederic Fleisher. Malmö and Lund, 1963.
The Sibyl. Translated by Naomi Walford. New York, 1958.
Twentieth-Century Scandinavian Poetry. Edited by Martin S. Allwood. Stockholm, 1950.

BIOGRAPHICAL AND CRITICAL STUDIES

Buckman, Thomas. "Pär Lagerkvist and the Swedish Theater." *Tulane Drama Review* 6:3–89 (1961).
Ellestad, Everett M. "Pär Lagerkvist and Cubism. A Study of His Theory and Practice." *Scandinavian Studies* 45:37–52 (1973).
Fearnley, Ragnhild. *Pär Lagerkvist.* Oslo, 1950.
Gustafson, Alrik. *A History of Swedish Literature.* Minneapolis, 1961.
Henmark, Kai. *Främlingen Lagerkvist.* Stockholm, 1966.
Johannesson, Eric O. "Pär Lagerkvist and the Art of Rebellion." *Scandinavian Studies* 30:19–29 (1958).
Linnér, Sven. "Pär Lagerkvists barndomsmiljö." *Samlaren* 58:53–90 (1947).
Malmström, Gunnel. *Menneskehjertets verden. Hovedmotiv i Pär Lagerkvists diktning.* Oslo, 1970.
Mjöberg, Jöran. *Livsproblemet hos Lagerkvist.* Stockholm, 1951.
Schöier, Ingrid. *Som i Aftonland.* Stockholm, 1981.
Sjöberg, Leif. *Pär Lagerkvist.* New York, 1976.
Spector, Robert D. *Pär Lagerkvist.* New York, 1973.
Tideström, Gunnar, ed. *Synpunkter på Pär Lagerkvist.* Stockholm, 1966.
Vowles, Richard B. "The Fiction of Pär Lagerkvist." *Western Humanities Review* 8:111–119 (1954).
Weathers, Winston. *Pär Lagerkvist. A Critical Essay.* Grand Rapids, Mich., 1968.

LARS G. WARME